ENCYCLOPEDIA OF WAR CRIMES AND GENOCIDE

Leslie Alan Horvitz and Christopher Catherwood

Facts On File
An imprint of Infobase Publishing

Facts On File, Inc.
An imprint of Infobase Publishing
132 West 31st Street
New York NY 10001

Library of Congress Cataloging-in-Publication Data

Horvitz, Leslie Alan.
Encyclopedia of war crimes and genocide / Leslie Alan Horvitz
and Christopher Catherwood.
p. cm.
Includes bibliographical references and index.
ISBN 0-8160-6001-0 (hardcover : alk. paper)
1. Genocide—Encyclopedias. 2. War crimes—Encyclopedias. 3. Human rights—
Encyclopedias. 4. Racism—Encyclopedias. 5. Geopolitics—Encyclopedias.
I. Catherwood, Christopher. II. Title.
HV6322.7.H67 2006
364.1'1'38'03—dc222005014961

Facts On File books are available at special discounts when purchased in bulk
quantities for businesses, associations, institutions, or sales promotions. Please call our
Special Sales Department in New York at (212) 967-8800 or (800) 322-8755.

You can find Facts On File on the World Wide Web at http://www.factsonfile.com

Text design by Joan M. McEvoy

Cover design by Cathy Rincon

Printed in the United States of America

VB Hermitage 10 9 8 7 6 5 4 3 2 1

This book is printed on acid-free paper.

Contents

LIST OF ENTRIES
iv

INTRODUCTION
viii

ENTRIES A TO Z
1

LIST OF APPENDICES
489

PRIMARY DOCUMENTS
490

RESOURCES
544

SELECTED BIBLIOGRAPHY
551

INDEX
563

List of Entries

Aboriginals (Australia), mistreatment of
Aceh, war crimes in
Acosta, Jorge Eduardo
act of war
Additional Protocols to the Geneva Conventions
Afghanistan, human rights violations in
aggression
Albania, human rights violations in
Algeria, human rights violations in
Alien Tort Claims Act
American Convention on Human Rights
Amherst, Jeffrey Amherst, first baron
Amin, Idi
amnesty
Amnesty International
Angola, war crimes in
Anti-Terrorism, Crime and Security Act
apartheid
Arbour, Louise
Argentina, human rights violations in
Argentine Anticommunist Alliance
Arkan
Armenia, human rights violations in
Armenian genocide

arms, trafficking in and control mechanisms
Article 3 Common to the Geneva Conventions
asylum, political
Aung San Suu Kyi
Australia, human rights violations in
Azerbaijan, human rights violations in
Babi Yar
Bahrain, human rights violations in
Bangladesh, human rights violations in
Barbie, Klaus
Bashir, Abu Bakar
Basson, Wouter
Belarus, human rights violations in
Belgian war crimes tribunal
belligerent status
Benenson, Peter
Berbers, human rights abuses of
Bhutan, human rights violations in
Biafra, war crimes in
biological weapons
Bokassa, Jean-Bédel
Bolivia, human rights violations in
Bormann, Martin
Bosnia and Herzegovina, human rights violations in

Bousquet, René
Brandt, Karl
Brazil, human rights violations in
Brunner, Alois
Bulgaria, human rights violations in
Bunche, Ralph
Burkina Faso, human rights violations in
Burundi, war crimes in
Cambodia, human rights violations in
Cambodia, war crimes in
Cambodian Genocide Program
Cameroon, human rights violations in
carpet bombing
Carter Center, The
Cavallo, Ricardo Miguel
Ceauşescu, Nicolae
Chad, human rights violations in
Chechnya, war crimes in
chemical weapons
children's rights
Chile, human rights violations in
China, human rights violations in
Choeun, Chhit (Ta Mok)
CIA war crimes archives
civilian immunity
Clark, Ramsey
Clauberg, Carl

collateral damage
collective punishment
Colombia, human rights violations in
combatants, rights of
comfort women
Committee to Protect Journalists
Comoros, human rights violations in
concentration camps
conflict diamonds
Congo (Brazzaville), human rights violations in
Congo, Democratic Republic of the, war crimes in
Contreras, Manuel
Convention against Torture
Convention on Prohibitions or Restrictions on the Use of Certain Conventional Weapons . . .
Convention on the Prohibition of the Use, Stockpiling, Production and Transfer of Anti-Personnel Mines and on Their Destruction
Convention on the Rights of the Child
Convention Relating to the Status of Refugees
crimes against humanity
Crimes of War Project

Croatia, human rights violations in
Cuba, human rights violations in
cultural property, protection of
customary law
Cyprus, human rights violations in
dams and dikes, protection of
Darfur, war crimes in
D'Aubuisson, Roberto
Dayton accords
de Kock, Eugene
Del Ponte, Carla
deportations
dirty war
disappearances
displaced person camps
Doctors' Trial
Doctors Without Borders
Doihara, Kenji
Dominican Republic, human rights violations in
Dönitz, Karl
due process
Dunant, Jean-Henri
Duvalier, François ("Papa Doc")
Duvalier, Jean-Claude ("Baby Doc")
East Timor, war crimes in
ECOWAS Monitoring Groups (ECOMOG)
Ecuador, human rights violations in
Egypt, human rights violations in
Eichmann, Adolf
Einsatzgruppen
Eizenstat, Stuart
El Mozote, massacre in
El Salvador, war crimes in
Equatorial Guinea, human rights violations in
Eritrea, human rights violations in
Ethiopia, human rights violations in
ethnic cleansing

European Community Humanitarian Office (ECHO)
European Convention for the Protection of Human Rights
euthanasia program (Nazi)
extrajudicial killings
extraordinary rendition
Final Solution
Finta, Imre
forced labor
forensic medicine and human rights
Frank, Hans
Freedom House
free-fire zones
Frick, Wilhelm
Fritzsche, Hans
Fujimori, Alberto
Funk, Walther
Garzón, Balthasar
Geneva Conventions
genocide
Genocide Convention
Genocide Watch
Georgia (Republic of), human rights violations in
germ warfare
Gestapo
ghost prisoners
Global Rights
Global Witness
Goebbels, Joseph
Goldstone, Richard J.
Göring, Hermann
Gotovina, Ante
Grotius, Hugo
Guantánamo detainees
Guatemala, human rights violations in
Guinea, human rights violations in
Gujarat, massacres in
gulags
Guyana, human rights violations in
Guzmán, Juan
Habré, Hissene
Hague Conventions
Haiti, human rights violations in

Haitian human rights violators
Halabajah (Iraqi Kurdistan)
Hama, massacre in
Hamdi, Yaser Esam
Hazara, persecution of
Helsinki accords
Hernández Martínez, Maximiliano
Hess, Rudolf
Heydrich, Reinhard
high-value detainees
Himmler, Heinrich
Hitler, Adolf
Hmong, persecution of
Honduras, human rights violations in
hors de combat
hostages
humanitarian aid, barring of
humanitarian intervention
Human Rights Convention
human rights reports (U.S. State Department)
Human Rights Watch
human shields
Hussein, Saddam al-Tikriti
Ibrahim, Ashraf
identification of combatants
Ieng Sary
illegal acts
immunity from attack
imprisonment of civilians
incitement to genocide
India, human rights violations in
indiscriminate attacks
Indonesia, human rights violations in
Inter-American Court of Human Rights
Internal Displacement Project
internally displaced persons
International Action Network on Small Arms (IANSA)
International Commission on Missing Persons
International Committee of the Red Cross (ICRC)
International Court of Justice (ICJ)

International Covenant on Civil and Political Rights
International Criminal Court
International Criminal Tribunal for Rwanda
International Criminal Tribunal for the Former Yugoslavia (ICTY)
International Humanitarian Fact-Finding Commission (IHFFC)
international humanitarian law (IHL)
International Labor Organization (ILO)
International Monitor Institute
Iran, human rights violations in
Iraq, human rights violations in post-Saddam
irregulars
Ivory Coast, human rights violations in
Izieu, children of
Jackson, Robert
Jamaica, human rights violations in
Jedwabne, massacre in
Jemaah Islamiyah
Jiang Yanyong (Chiang Yen-yung)
Jodl, Alfred
Jordan, human rights violations in
journalists, protection of
just and unjust wars
Kaltenbrunner, Ernst
Karadžić, Radovan
Kashmir and Jammu, human rights violations in
Katyn Forest, massacre in
Kazakhstan, human rights violations in
Keitel, Wilhelm
Kenya, human rights violations in
Khieu Samphan
Kiang Kek Iev (Deuch)
Kim Il Sung
Kim Jong Il

Klarsfeld, Serge
Koch, Erich
Kony, Joseph
Kosovo, war crimes in
Kramer, Josef
Krupp, Gustav
Kurdistan (Iraq),
    suppression of
Kyrgyzstan, human rights
    violations in
Laos, human rights
    violations in
Lawyers Without Borders
League of Nations
legitimate military targets
Lemkin, Raphael
Leopold II
levée en masse
Ley, Robert
Liberia, human rights
    violations in
Libya, human rights
    violations in
Lidice, massacre in
Lieber Code (Instruction
    for the Government of
    Armies of the United
    States in the Field)
limited war
López Rega, José
MacBride, Sean
Macedonia, human rights
    violations in
Majid, Ali Hassan al-
Malaysia, human rights
    violations in
Manchuria, Japanese war
    crimes in
Martens Clause
mass graves
Matsui Iwane
Matsuoka Yosuke
Mau Mau uprising
Mauritania, human rights
    violations in
medical experiments
medical personnel,
    protection of
Memorial
Mengele, Josef
Mengistu Haile Mariam
mercenaries

Meron, Theodor
Mexico, human rights
    violations in
military necessity
Milošević, Slobodan
Mladić, Ratko
Mobutu Sese Seko
Montesinos, Vladimiro Ilyich
Morocco, human rights
    violations in
Mothers of the Plaza de
    Mayo
Mullah Omar
Müller, Heinrich
Myanmar, human rights
    violations in
My Lai massacre
Nanjing (Nanking),
    massacre in
National Intelligence
    Directorate
Nazar, Miguel Haro
Nazi Party, Leadership
    Corps of
Nepal, human rights
    violations in
Neuvrath, Konstantin von
Ngugi Wa Thiong'o
Nigeria, human rights
    violations in
No Gun Ri (Korea),
    massacre in
Nokmin
nondefended localities
Noriega, Manuel
North Korea, human rights
    violations in
nuclear arms and
    international law
Nuon Chea
Nuremberg Charter
Nuremberg Laws
Nuremberg Trials
Nzapali, Sebastian
Oberheuser, Herta
Obote, Milton
occupying power
Office of Special
    Investigations
Okawa, Shumei
Olivera Castillo, Jorge
Operation Condor

Oradour, massacre in
Organization for Security
    and Cooperation in
    Europe
Organization of American
    States
Oxfam
Padilla, José
Pakistan, human rights
    violations in
Palestine, human rights
    violations in
Papen, Franz von
Papon, Maurice
Pavelić, Ante
Philippines, human rights
    violations in
Phoenix program
Physicians for Human
    Rights
pillage
Pinochet, Augusto
pogrom
Pohl, Oswald
Pol Pot
Priebke, Erich
prisoners of conscience
prisoners of war
protected persons
Protocol on Prohibitions or
    Restrictions on the Use
    of Mines, Booby-Traps
    and Other Devices
Protocol to the Hague
    Convention of 1954 for
    the Protection of
    Cultural Property in the
    Event of Armed Conflict,
    Second
public property, protection
    of
Qaeda, al-
Raeder, Erich
rape as a tactic of war
refoulement
refugees
Refugees International
religious persecution
reparations
Ribbentrep, Joachim von
reprisal
Ríos Montt, José Efraín

Rom (Roma, Rroma,
    Romany, Gypsies),
    persecution of
Rome Statute of the
    International Criminal
    Court
Rosenberg, Alfred
Russia, human rights
    violations in
Rwanda, genocide in
Rwandan human rights
    violators
Sabra and Shatilla,
    massacres in
safe havens
Sakai, Takashi
sanctions
Sankoh, Foday
Sant'Anna di Stazzema,
    massacre in
Sarajevo, siege of
Saravia, Álvaro
Sauckel, Fritz
Saudi Arabia, human rights
    violations in
Sawoniuk, Anthony
Schacht, Hjalmar Horace
    Greeley
Schellenberg, Walter
Schirach, Baldur von
scorched earth
Serbia, human rights
    violations in
Seselj, Vojislav
Seyss-Inquart, Arthur
Shattuck, John
Shimada, Shigetaro
Shining Path
siege
Sierra Leone, human rights
    violations in
slavery
Slovenia, human rights
    violations in
Solzhenitsyn, Aleksandr
    Isayevich
Somalia, human rights
    violations in
Somoza Debayle,
    Anastasio
Somoza García, Anastasio
Souaidia, Habib

Soyinka, Wole (Akínwande Oluwole Soyinka)
Special Court for Sierra Leone
Speer, Albert
Srebrenica, massacre in
Sri Lanka, human rights violations in
SS (Schutzstaffel)
Stalin, Joseph
starvation as a tactic of war
Stockholm Declaration on Genocide Prevention
Streicher, Julius
Strössner, Alfredo
Stuckart, Wilhelm
Sudan, human rights violations in
Suharto Thojib, N. J.
Sullivan Principles
Syria, human rights violations in
Taliban
Taylor, Charles Ghankay
Taylor, Telford
terrorism and international humanitarian law
Thailand, human rights violations in
Tiger Force
Tigers, Tamil

Togo, human rights violations in
Tojo, Hideki
Tokyo Trials (International Military Tribunal for the Far East)
torture
total war
Touvier, Paul
trafficking in persons
Trafficking Protocol
transfer of civilians
Trujillo, Rafael Molino
Truth and Reconciliation Commission
Tudjman, Franjo
Tunisia, human rights violations in
Turkey, human rights violations in
Turkmenistan, human rights violations in
Tutu, Desmond
Uganda, human rights violations in
Ukraine, human rights violations in
United Nations and the Geneva Conventions
United Nations Guiding Principles on Internal Displacement

United Nations High Commissioner for Human Rights
United Nations High Commissioner for Refugees
United Nations Human Rights Commission
United Nations Resolution 1368
United Nations Working Group on Enforced and Involuntary Disappearances
Universal Declaration of Human Rights
universal jurisdiction
unlawful imprisonment
Uruguay, human rights violations in
Ustache
Uzbekistan, human rights violations in
Velpke Baby Farm
Vergès, Jacques
victims, rights of
Victims Trust Fund
Vieira de Mello, Sérgio
Vienna Convention on Diplomatic Relations
Vietnam, human rights violations in

voluntary codes of conduct
Waldheim, Kurt
Walleyn, Luc
Wannsee Conference
War Child Project
war crimes, categorization of
war criminals of Japan
war criminals of the former Yugoslavia
war dead, treatment of
weapons in the conduct of war
weapons of mass destruction
Wei Jingsheng (Wei Ching-sheng)
Wernich, Christian von
White Brigades
Wiesenthal, Simon
willful killing
Wiranto, General
women's rights, violations of
Yad Vashem
Yamashita, Tokoyuki
Yugoslavia, war crimes in
Zimbabwe, human rights violations in

°Asian names are not inverted; surnames precede given names.

Introduction

The title *Encyclopedia of War Crimes and Genocide* was chosen for the sake of simplicity and compression, because the book's scope extends to such topics as crimes against humanity, crimes against peace, and human rights violations. Many of the individuals profiled here—a veritable "rogues' gallery"—were never formally indicted for war crimes; indeed, they committed their crimes during periods when their countries were not at war. Nonetheless, their excesses and abuses of human rights warrant their inclusion. Some of them, such as Pol Pot, Idi Amin, and Joseph Stalin, none of whom have ever had to answer for their crimes in a court of law, are well known. Other men profiled here—and they are nearly all men—while hardly household names, nonetheless stand out, whether because their cases shed light on an important issue (the destruction of public or cultural property, for example) or because they establish a crucial legal precedent. Although these pages are crowded with dictators, mass murderers, and torturers, we would have been remiss if we had not given space to prominent human rights organizations and activists who have done so much to redress grievous wrongs often at great risk to their lives.

War crimes, crimes against humanity, crimes against peace, and genocide all have a legal definition. Therefore, a great many entries are concerned with what is known as international humanitarian law, or IHL, dealing with the rules and conduct of war, the distinction between international and internal conflicts, types of weapons that can and cannot legally be used in conflicts, and the treatment of prisoners of war and civilians under occupation. You will find lengthy discussions about the principal treaties that constitute IHL, including, but by no means limited to, the Geneva Conventions of 1949, the Additional Protocols to the Geneva Conventions of 1977, the Conventions against Genocide and Torture, and the London Charter that established the rules under which the Nuremberg Trials of Nazi war criminals would be conducted. In addition, you will find a discussion of how IHL applies to terrorism and whether suspected terrorists should be treated as prisoners of war. If it is not enforced, of course, the law enshrined in all these treaties, protocols, and conventions means very little. So several entries are devoted to institutions and mechanisms that have emerged in the postwar era to resolve international and regional disputes and investigate and prosecute human rights abuses. For instance, several entries focus on each of the three special ad hoc courts that have been set up by the

United Nations in order to try individuals implicated in war crimes committed in the former Yugoslavia, Rwanda, and Sierra Leone.

It would be gratifying if this encyclopedia were mostly historical in nature, a chronicle of past atrocities in Nazi Germany, Cambodia under the Khmer Rouge, or Rwanda during the genocide of 1994. Unfortunately, human rights violations are still going on. As this book was being written in 2004–5, for instance, Arab militias in the western Sudan region of Darfur were engaged in an ethnic-cleansing campaign against black African farmers that defied efforts of the international community to put a halt to the bloodshed. The authors do not pretend to know the future, and several entries about developments in such troubled places as Iraq, Somalia, the Democratic Republic of the Congo, Palestine, and Haiti, just to name a sampling, are likely to be overshadowed by developments that cannot be foreseen. Nonetheless, we hope that the entries will provide readers with a context—a historical perspective, if you will—that will allow them to understand and assess events in these countries in light of what came before.

Abe Koso *See* WAR CRIMINALS OF JAPAN.

Aboriginals (Australia), mistreatment of

The history of the relations between the white Australian majority and the Aboriginals has been tainted by persecution and discrimination. It is only in the 20th century that the Australian government and justice system began to acknowledge Aboriginal rights and make some efforts to redress their grievances. Nonetheless, the Aboriginals (also called Aborigines) for the most part remain at the bottom of the socioeconomic ladder. According to the government's own statistics, while the Aboriginal adult population represented just 1.6 percent of the adult population of Australia as a whole, Aboriginals made up approximately 20 percent of the total prison population. The Aborigines were mistreated by the new emigrants almost from the outset. When the British began to settle Australia in the 19th century, the original Tasmanian Aboriginal population was estimated at 8,000. The settlers proceeded to uproot the Aboriginals and forcibly relocate them to remote islands where their conditions were abominable. They might as well have been in prison since they were forbidden to leave. Disease brought to Australia by the Europeans also helped to decimate the population, which by 1847 had been reduced to a handful. It is believed that Aboriginals may have numbered as many as 1 million in 1788, but by 1901 their population had dwindled to about 93,000. Today, according to the Australian census, Aboriginals number about 427,000 in a country of over 20 million.

Those Aborigines who survived (some of mixed blood) were subjected to a number of restrictive Protection Acts enacted in the late 19th and early 20th century that sharply curtailed their human rights. (They were dubbed "protection acts" because they purported to protect Aboriginals from abuse and exploitation.) These laws prohibited Aboriginals from owning property, restricted their ability to work at certain jobs, and, in the worst abuse, allowed the government to take their children. Most of these laws were repealed by the time World War II broke out, although one province, Queensland, did not get rid of all of its restrictions until the 1970s. These laws also defined who could be considered an Aboriginal, but in such a way as to indicate that the indigenous people were biologically inferior. A person with two Aboriginal parents was a "full blood," for instance, while a person with one Aboriginal and a Caucasian parent was a "half-caste." In some instances, though, it was impossible to be classified as a "full blood." This was the case with Tasmanian Aborigines since disease and European depredation killed the last Tasmanian Aborigines in 1873. Historians only got around to revising their definition in the 1970s to include several thousand Australians who had at least some Tasmanian Aboriginal blood. And it was only in a 1967 referendum that Australians voted to allow Aboriginals to be counted as native Australians in the national census.

Aboriginal rights are now officially acknowledged by the government, which has established bodies to review and adjudicate cases of racial discrimination. Nonetheless, problems persist, as the prison statistics show. In March 1999, after a fact-finding mission to Australia, AMNESTY INTERNATIONAL reported that "a pattern of ill treatment and arbitrary arrest occurs against a backdrop of systematic discrimination against Aborigines." An Aboriginal child is three to five times more likely to die in infancy than other Australian children. Mortality rates for adult Aboriginals are similarly dismal; most will die in their 50s, in contrast to white Australian adults, who live, on average, into their 70s. Aboriginal men are also 25 times more likely to serve prison time than white men.

In April 2004 the conservative government of John Howard abolished the Aboriginal and Torres Strait Islander Commission, an elected council, which was established in the 1980s as a means of self-determination for indigenous people. Although the elected council was considered corrupt, many Aboriginals and social activists saw the move as marginalizing the issue of indigenous people. "Aborigines are effectively off the white agenda," said Hugh Mackay, a social researcher in a story carried by the *New York Times.* The national newspaper, the *Australian,* said the decision would "take Aboriginal governance back 30 years." Howard's action was seen as a repudiation of policies instituted by previous governments during the 1970s and 1980s to redress injustices done to the Aboriginals.

See also AUSTRALIA, HUMAN RIGHTS VIOLATIONS IN.

Further Reading:
Broome, Richard. *Aboriginal Australians.* London: Allen & Unwin, 2002.

Abu Ghraib *See* IRAQ, HUMAN RIGHTS VIOLATIONS IN POST-SADDAM.

Aceh, war crimes in

For the last several years the Indonesian province of Aceh has been mired in a war between separatists and the Indonesian army. Although both sides have committed atrocities, 90 percent of the civilian murders in the region have been carried out by Indonesia's armed forces and paramilitary police. In May 2003 the central government in Jakarta imposed a state of emergency that barred almost all outsiders from entering the province, including humanitarian groups and international observers. Over the next 18 months some 2,000 people were killed. The island's abundant timber resources account in large part for the Indonesian army's eagerness to retain control over it.

Aceh, a specially designated province of Indonesia, has been mired in a long-running war that has resulted in atrocities, abuses by the military, and the internal displacement of thousands. Located on the northwestern tip of the island of Sumatra, Aceh occupies about 3 percent of Indonesia's land mass and has a population of more than 4,200,000. Like the vast majority of Indonesia's people, the inhabitants of Aceh are Muslim, but they have ethnic and cultural differences that set them apart. In 1959 Aceh gained a certain degree of autonomy as a result of an agreement with the central authority in Jakarta. However, since 1969 the Indonesian government has settled significant numbers of people from outside the territory, many of them military personnel and civil servants. The industrial development promoted by Jakarta, while improving the local economy, has aroused resentment on the part of the indigenous population, who feel that Aceh isn't benefiting from the newly created wealth. The Acehnese—the dominant ethnic group—also came to believe that the central government was not showing sufficient sensitivity to their culture and form of devout Islamic worship. This led to the emergence

in the mid-1970s of a militant group known as the Free Aceh Movement (Gerakan Aceh Merdeka, or GAM), which advocated an independent Islamic state. In 1977 the Indonesian army responded with a crackdown that accounted for scores of deaths and imprisonments. In 1990 Aceh was designated a military operational area, which gave the military a free hand. Aceh did gain some relief from the army's crackdown when Indonesia's strongman, Suharto, was forced from power in May 1998, which led to a pullout of large numbers of troops from the province.

In the wake of Suharto's fall, there was a surge of complaints about human rights violations during the period of occupation. Although GAM was the army's target, it was the civilian population that suffered most, even after the militants had been defeated. According to a report by AMNESTY INTERNATIONAL, thousands of civilians were tortured, disappeared, or were killed in extrajudicial slayings carried out by military forces or their allies. Although formal military occupation was lifted, the situation did not perceptibly improve for most Acehnese. Violence erupted again, and the central government blamed a revival of GAM, but many observers contended that the threat of a rebellion was a pretext to justify further military excesses. In early January 1999 several massacres took place; these were blamed on government forces and claimed the lives of scores of civilians. Many others were illegally detained and tortured. The army conducted a scorched-earth policy in which hundreds of schools were torched. In the worst atrocity, at least 70 people were killed at a Muslim religious school. By this point GAM had reemerged as a real force, and militants retaliated by attacking dozens of government buildings. In the ensuing chaos tens of thousands of villagers fled from their homes and took refuge in makeshift camps. The army decided to adopt a new strategy called Operasi Sadar Rencong II, in which mass killings were eschewed in favor of a campaign of attrition. This campaign was marked by the killings of civilians under mysterious circumstances so that it became more difficult to assign guilt. Not surprisingly, the intensified military activity had the effect of mobilizing grassroots support for GAM. Human rights groups acknowledge that the rebels have committed some serious human rights abuses but maintain that the military is responsible for the worst violations. In August 1999 Aceh was paralyzed by a three-day general strike, which was followed by a rally in November that brought out over a million people—almost a fourth of the province's population—demanding a referendum to advance prospects of a cease-fire. Efforts to bring the two sides together, however, have been unsuccessful.

In yet another change in strategy, the army initiated Operasi Sadar Rencong III at the end of 1999, which officially was meant to hunt down 800 members and supporters of GAM. But the operation also was directed at humanitarian workers and human rights advocates, partly in an effort to keep the outside world from finding out what was happening. The death toll continued to rise: According to reports collected by local humanitarian workers, 215 civilians were slain during the first three months of 2000 alone. Then on August 9, 2001, in one of the worst single massacres of the war, dozens of armed men in camouflage uniforms invaded a housing area on a rubber and palm oil plantation in east Aceh, where they proceeded to gun down 30 men as well as a two-year-old child. Almost immediately a dispute broke out as to who was responsible; the Indonesian government blamed GAM, and GAM accused the government. Subsequent investigations failed to identify the perpetrators, but some evidence indicates that they were linked to the military and security forces.

In December 2002 hopes were raised by a "Cessation of Hostilities Agreement," which provided the framework for a fragile cease-fire, but by the following spring the cease-fire crumbled amid renewed hostilities. Then on May 19, 2003, the government of President Megawati Sukarnoputri announced a decree imposing a state of emergency on Aceh and authorizing military operations for a six-month period that could be extended. The state of emergency, human rights organizations warned, would only lead to further human rights violations and atrocities. The situation in Aceh remains unsettled, and by early 2004 no party in the conflict was willing to predict when or if peace would come to the province.

The political dynamic changed again after the devastating tsunami on December 26, 2004, which caused nearly 200,000 deaths and widespread destruction on the island. For the first time in nearly two years, the Indonesian government opened Aceh to outsiders, allowing in relief workers (including the U.S. military). Although some clashes between separatists and the army continued, in the wake of the catastrophe there was a renewed impetus for negotiations. A few weeks after the tsunami, representatives of the government and the insurgents met for exploratory talks in Helsinki. In August 2005 the Indonesian government and GAM signed a peace deal that allowed greater autonomy, though not independence, for the province. "This peace process has required a leap of faith from GAM," said the head of the GAM delegation. "It is a leap of faith we have taken to give the people of Aceh the opportunity to build a brighter future." The rebels also agreed to disarm. At the same time the Indonesian government promised to release political prisoners and provide farmland to ex-combatants in hope of reintegrating them into civilian life. Given the tortured history of Aceh, it was impossible to predict whether a lasting settlement was realistic.

See also INDONESIA, HUMAN RIGHTS VIOLATIONS IN.

Further Reading:

Aspinall, Edward. *The Aceh Peace Process: Why It Failed.* Washington, D.C.: East-West Center, 2003.

Schulze, Kirsten E. *The Free Aceh Movement (GAM): Anatomy of a Separatist Organization.* Washington, D.C.: East-West Center, 2004.

Siegel, James T. *The Rope of God.* Ann Arbor: University of Michigan Press, 2000.

Sjamsuddin, Nazaruddin. *The Republican Revolt: A Study of the Acehnese Rebellion.* Singapore: Institute of Southeast Asian Studies, 1988.

Sukma, Rizal. *Security Operations in Aceh: Goals, Consequences, and Lessons.* Washington, D.C.: East-West Center, 2004.

Acosta, Jorge Eduardo (1942–) *Argentine military officer*

Jorge Eduardo Acosta, a former navy captain, presided over the notorious Argentine Intelligence Task Force (better known by its acronym ESMA) Navy unit GT-332 based at the Navy Mechanics School during the dirty war of the 1970s. In this capacity he was allegedly responsible for about 5,000 DISAPPEARANCES, TORTURE, and murders. Many of the victims were drugged, bundled into planes, and dropped into the Atlantic Ocean. Among those who perished on Acosta's orders was a Swedish teenage girl; the French nuns of the Church of Santa Cruz; and the founder of the Mothers of Plaza de Mayo, a group that carried out daily protests in the heart of Buenos Aires, demanding information about the whereabouts of family members who had disappeared. In 1986, in testimony before a civilian court, Acosta denied knowing that any prisoners were held at the Mechanics School at all. On another occasion he said, "There were no detentions as such. It was like someone goes to a police commission and they're asked, 'Is this what you did?' If he said he did nothing . . . he could leave." In 1998 Acosta, who had been indicted for GENOCIDE by a Spanish court, surrendered to Argentine authorities investigating cases in which children of prisoners were abducted by security officers.

See also ARGENTINA, HUMAN RIGHTS VIOLATIONS IN.

act of war

What constitutes an act of war has undergone a dramatic change in the years since the end of World War II. Until 1945, determining an act of war did not seem to pose many problems. If a state was attacked by an adversary, then the international law in effect during peacetime was suspended, and a state of war was entered into. Often the nation being threatened would announce that if its adversary had committed certain acts—moving forces close to its border, for instance, or blockading its ports—then these actions constituted an act of war. By the same token, a third country could be considered to commit an act of war if it violated its neutrality by coming to the assistance of a state that was already engaged in a war.

The proclamation of official declarations of war came to a halt with the adoption of the United Nations Charter in 1945, banning the first use of force. Article 2 of the charter states: "All members shall refrain in their international relations from the threat or use of force against the territorial integrity or political independence of any State." In fact, no country has formally declared war since World War II. (The last declaration of war was made by the Soviet Union against Japan in 1945.) The Korean War, for instance, was defined as a "police action." The reluctance of countries to admit what is patently obvious can reach absurd extremes. In 1956 Great Britain adamantly denied that it was at war with Egypt when its forces invaded the Sinai Peninsula, which was (and is) Egyptian territory, and briefly seized the Suez Canal. Similarly, Britain insisted that it was not at war with Argentina during the Falkland Islands War in 1982, even though it continued to adhere to the laws of armed conflict governed by the GENEVA CONVENTIONS.

If the term *act of war* is used at all, it is mainly as a rhetorical conceit, according to David Turns, a British expert on international law. In 1997, he observed, "the People's Republic of China asserted that any attempt by the Republic of China (Taiwan) to declare independence would be regarded as an act of war." In August 1998 Madeleine Albright, then the U.S. secretary of state, attributed the bombings of U.S. embassies in Nairobi and Dar Es Salaam to Osama Bin Laden, saying that because he had struck first he had "declared war on the United States." For all practical purposes as a term that has any legal significance, *act of aggression* has supplanted the expression *act of war*. The earlier term, however, continues to be employed in certain specific applications. The term *act of war* might have slipped into complete obsolescence were it not for the September 11, 2001, attacks on the World Trade Center and the Pentagon. The declaration by President George W. Bush that the United States is conducting a war on terrorism has, to some degree, breathed new life into the term.

In an essay for the online magazine *Logo*, Christopher Morris, a philosophy professor, considers whether the September 11 strikes constituted an act of war or a crime. "Commentators have disagreed," he writes. "Presumably, if it is a crime then the appropriate response is to apprehend the guilty and to try them in a court of law, constrained by the standards of evidence and the rules of procedural justice of the criminal law." Some commentators, he notes, contend that the attacks were not, legally speaking, an act of war because only states can enter into a war. Morris disdainfully dismisses such an argument, observing that wars were fought long before states existed. If, on the other hand, the attacks were an act of war, he states, "then we may retaliate against the enemy with military means and

need not be burdened with the criminal law's demanding standards of proof." Indeed, this is exactly what the United States did in Afghanistan. Morris concludes that the question as to whether the attacks were an act of war or a crime was not important since a reasonable case could be made that they were both. "But this question is not the important one to settle," he writes. "Rather we should ask what it is that we aim to achieve by our response to this act?"

See also AFGHANISTAN, HUMAN RIGHTS VIOLATIONS IN.

Additional Protocols to the Geneva Conventions

The United Nations' Additional Protocols, agreed to by UN member states in June 1977, are intended to supplement and strengthen laws embodied in the four GENEVA CONVENTIONS of 1949 covering the conduct of belligerents in wartime, especially in relation to the protection and treatment of civilian populations. These two protocols basically reaffirm the principle that belligerents are limited in terms of the ways in which they wage war. Generally, the use of any means of war must be necessary to achieve military objectives. If a belligerent power targets civilians, mistreats prisoners of war, or destroys cultural or vital nonmilitary installations (dams, electrical power plants, etc.), it is in violation of international law. Similarly, behavior on the part of a belligerent must be governed by the principle of proportionality. A state or an OCCUPYING POWER, for instance, is obliged by the protocols (and the earlier Conventions) to apply force only to the degree that it is necessary to accomplish military objectives. These principles were universally agreed upon—at least in theory—in the aftermath of the Nazi atrocities that occurred during World War II in countries occupied by the German army. The principles were used by the Allies as their basis for conducting the NUREMBERG TRIALS of Nazi war criminals.

The first 1977 protocol strengthens the protection of civilians in wars between states called for in the fourth Geneva Convention. The second 1977 protocol builds on protections of civilians who are at risk in cases that do not involve international combat. The second protocol was considered necessary because of the human rights abuses of civilians that occurred in anticolonial wars and the civil conflicts in many emerging states. The second Protocol is an addition to the protection afforded by Common Article 3 to the Geneva Conventions.

The two protocols also take into account the need to protect the environment and the cultural paternity of a country at war. Article 53 of Protocol 1, for instance, prohibits "any acts of hostility directed against the historic monuments works of art or places of worship which constitute the cultural or spiritual heritage of peoples." Article 53 also prohibits the use of cultural property "in support of the military effort," which means that a church or a mosque, for instance, cannot be used as a command center. The protocol does acknowledge, however, that in certain instances destruction of a cultural site might be unavoidable. The provision governing cultural properties was intended to reinforce guidelines found in the 1954 Convention for the Protection of Cultural Property. Similarly, Article 56 of Protocol I prohibits attacks on "works or installations containing dangerous forces, namely dams, dikes, and nuclear electrical generating stations, shall not be made the object of attack, even when these objects are military objectives, if such attack may cause the release of dangerous forces and consequent severe losses among the civilian population."

Among some of the protocols' most important points in addition to the above:

"In cases not covered by this Protocol or by other international agreements, civilians and combatants remain under the protection and authority of the principles of international law derived from established custom, from the principles of humanity and from the dictates of public conscience."

" 'Wounded' and 'sick' mean persons, whether military or civilian, who, because of trauma, disease or other physical or mental disorder or disability, are in need of medical assistance or care and who refrain from any act of hostility."

"The physical or mental health and integrity of persons who are in the power of the adverse Party or who are interned, detained or otherwise deprived of liberty . . . shall not be endangered by any unjustified act or omission."

"The civilian population shall respect the wounded, sick and shipwrecked, even if they belong to the adverse Party, and shall commit no act of violence against them. The civilian population and aid societies, such as national Red Cross (Red Crescent, Red Lion and Sun) Societies, shall be permitted, even on their own initiative, to collect and care for the wounded, sick and shipwrecked, even in invaded or occupied areas. No one shall be harmed, prosecuted, convicted or punished for such humanitarian acts."

"A person who is recognized or who, in the circumstances, should be recognized to be hors de combat shall not be made the object of attack."

"A person who takes part in hostilities and falls into the power of an adverse Party shall be presumed to be a prisoner of war, and therefore shall be protected by the Third Convention, if he claims the status of prisoner of war."

"In order to ensure respect for and protection of the civilian population and civilian objects, the Parties to the conflict shall at all times distinguish between the civilian population and combatants and between civilian objects and military objectives and accordingly shall direct their operations only against military objectives."

"The civilian population and individual civilians shall enjoy general protection against dangers arising from military operations."

"Attacks shall be limited strictly to military objectives. In so far as objects are concerned, military objectives are limited to those objects which by their nature, location, purpose or use make an effective contribution to military action and whose total or partial destruction, capture or neutralization, in the circumstances ruling at the time, offers a definite military of advantage."

"Care shall be taken in warfare to protect the natural environment against widespread, long-term and severe damage."

See also ARTICLE 3 COMMON TO THE GENEVA CONVENTIONS; CARPET BOMBING; CIVILIAN IMMUNITY; CULTURAL PROPERTY, PROTECTION OF; HUMANITARIAN AID; BARRING OF; INDISCRIMINATE ATTACKS; INTERNATIONAL HUMANITARIAN FACT-FINDING COMMISSION; LEGITIMATE MILITARY TARGETS; MASS GRAVES; MERCENARIES; PRISONERS OF WAR; PROTECTED PERSONS; PUBLIC PROPERTY, PROTECTION OF; REPRISAL, SIEGE; SLAVERY, STARVATION AS A TACTIC OF WAR; TERRORISM AND INTERNATIONAL HUMANITARIAN LAW; TRANSFER OF CIVILIANS; UNLAWFUL IMPRISONMENT; VICTIMS, RIGHTS OF; WAR CRIMES, CATEGORIZATION OF; WILLFUL KILLING.

Further Reading:

Aryeh, Neier. *War Crimes: Brutality, Genocide, Terror, and the Struggle for Justice.* New York: Crown, 1998.

Ball, Howard. *Prosecuting War Crimes and Genocide: The Twentieth-Century Experience.* Lawrence: University Press of Kansas, 1999.

Bass, Gary Jonathan. *Stay the Hand of Vengeance: The Politics of War Crimes Tribunals.* Princeton, N.J.: Princeton University Press, 2001.

Bassiouni, M. Cherif. *Crimes against Humanity in International Criminal Law.* Boston: Martinus Nijhoff, 1999.

Beigbeder, Yves, and Theo van Boven. *Judging War Criminals: The Politics of International Justice.* Sydney, Australia: Palgrave Macmillan, 1999.

Jinks, Derek. *The Rules of War: The Geneva Conventions in the Age of Terror.* Oxford: Oxford University Press, 2005.

Pilloud, Claude. *Commentary on the Additional Protocols of 8 June 1977 to the Geneva Conventions of 12 August 1949.* Boston: Brill Academic Publishers, 1987.

Roberts, Adam, and Richard Guelff. *Documents on the Laws of War.* Oxford: Oxford University Press, 2000.

Afghanistan, human rights violations in

The fall of the TALIBAN regime in 2001, while bringing a degree of democracy to the country, did not put an end to human rights violations, ethnic tensions, or continued instability in large parts of the country outside the capital of

Kabul. However, the newly installed government of Hamid Karzai has been credited with trying to establish the rule of law and an independent judiciary, though these efforts have been hampered by a scarcity of funds and resources. Perpetrators of human rights abuses largely escape punishment. Practically no attempt has been made to bring to justice those responsible for the worst injustices, including captured officials of the Taliban and the warlords who opposed them. People are often subjected to arbitrary detentions and held in atrocious conditions without prompt recourse to the courts. Torture is common, and security is unreliable at best (and often absent entirely) beyond Kabul. Members of the Taliban and al-QAEDA continue to harass, kidnap, and kill foreign aid workers and terrorize villages, especially in the north and along the border with Pakistan. In spite of the relaxation of harsh restrictions on women imposed by the fundamentalist Islamic Taliban regime, persecution of women and girls remains a persistent problem. Warlords who dominate many of the provinces with their own private armies are increasingly seen as posing one of the greatest dangers to the authority of the central government and are responsible for some of the worst human rights violations. Ethnic violence also persists among the larger ethnic groups in the country: Pashtuns, Uzbeks, Tadjiks, and Hazaris. The U.S. military, which by early 2004 had deployed 13,000 troops in the country, has also come under fire from human rights organizations for carrying out bombing strikes that have inadvertently targeted civilians and for mistreatment of Taliban prisoners. In 2004 news began to emerge indicating that U.S. troops and intelligence officers were implicated in the torture of detainees. As if all these problems are not enough, Afghanistan also must cope with a growing refugee crisis, worsened by the return of thousands of Afghanis who had sought sanctuary in neighboring Iran and Pakistan during the bloody conflicts that raged throughout the 1980s and 1990s.

Security Situation

Lawless conditions prevail in large areas of the country (particularly in the north) that are either controlled by warlords or threatened by Taliban and al-Qaeda guerrillas. The International Security Assistance Force (ISAF), the United Nations peacekeeping operation, to which NATO (North Atlantic Treaty Organization) forces contribute, is largely confined to the capital. There have been widespread calls on the part of members of Congress, UN members, and human rights organizations to bolster the force and extend it to other parts of the country. In many villages the local people live in a chronic state of terror; various groups regularly break into homes at night, stealing money and valuables, sometimes killing the residents. Rapes of women, girls, and boys are frequent, and young men are often kidnapped and held for ransom. Young men are also regularly

abducted and forced to join the ranks of one armed group or another. Reconstruction and humanitarian relief programs have been undermined by suspected members of the Taliban. Foreign workers have been killed and kidnapped, nongovernmental organization (NGO) offices robbed, and vehicles fired upon. In one particularly gruesome incident, an international staff worker was gang-raped. This intimidation campaign is intended to undermine the Karzai government, demoralize large segments of the population, and halt the reconstruction of Afghanistan. In many instances, this campaign of terror has succeeded in causing the temporary withdrawal of UN and NGO relief organizations from vulnerable parts of the country. In 2004 the terror campaign escalated in an effort to hamper the registration of millions of Afghanis in advance of the presidential and parliamentary elections scheduled for fall of 2004 and fall of 2005, respectively. Attacks by Taliban guerrillas on election officials, candidates, and civilians intensified in the summer of 2005. To some extent the attacks had an impact. Turnout for the parliamentary elections was slightly less than 50 percent, significantly down from the number of people who voted in the presidential election. In some villages women did not vote at all because of intimidation. There were also fears that discredited warlords who were running for office might succeed in reestablishing power as a result of the democratic experiment.

Treatment of Women and Girls

Repression of women and girls has continued in spite of newly introduced laws guaranteeing them civil rights and a right to education denied them under the Taliban regime. Entrenched cultural and religious prejudice against women continues to manifest itself in sexual violence by armed factions and public harassment. This violence can take the form of rape, forced marriage, or kidnappings. Women seldom have the opportunity to seek legal redress, and the judicial system is barely functional in any case. The only practical system of justice in much of Afghanistan is the tribal authority, which more often than not discriminates against women. Women have made some gains in Kabul, where they can hold jobs, are free to walk about without the body-shrouding burqas, and have even opened their own businesses. In other cities like Herat and in the countryside, however, women are routinely subjected to onerous restrictions. Because of this intimidation, women in rural areas seldom venture out of their homes, effectively disenfranchising themselves. Access to education remains difficult. The United Nations estimates that only 32 percent of the total school population is made up of girls. That statistic is deceptive; in some provinces the number of girls attending schools is as low as 3 percent. Fear, rather than cultural prejudice, seems to be the major factor in keeping girls out of the classroom. The fears are hardly baseless. Pamphlets often appear mysteriously, warning families against sending their daughters to school. In 2002, for instance, girls' schools in at least five different provinces were set on fire or destroyed by rocket attacks, according to HUMAN RIGHTS WATCH. In many cases, local police and security forces impose the same restrictions on locales that were imposed by the Taliban, forcing women to wear burqas and banning music and television. In 2003 a justice on the Afghan supreme court publicly repudiated the broadcast of a female singer on the state-run television station, even though the tape was over 10 years old and the singer a beloved figure for millions of Afghans.

Warlords

Afghanistan has a long tradition of warlords, and since the collapse of the Taliban regime they have reasserted their power. For practical purposes, the U.S. military has had to put up with them, if not openly support them, simply because in the absence of central authority, they hold power in many provinces. In some instances, however, the United States has mediated, diplomatically or with military force, to impose cease-fires between forces under rival warlords. Without the cooperation of forces led by some of these warlords, it would have proven vastly more difficult for the U.S. military to push the Taliban and al-Qaeda terrorists out of the country. With their own militias, often subsidized by money from the sale of opium— Afghanistan's most profitable, if illegal, export—many warlords have been responsible for some of the most egregious human rights violations recorded since the Taliban ouster. Evidence of their atrocities continues to turn up. One of the more notorious warlords, General Abdul Rashid Dostum, has been blamed for the deaths of hundreds of Taliban prisoners who suffocated to death while being transported in sealed containers to a prison near Mazar-e Sharif in 2001; their mass grave only recently came to light. Some witnesses who came forward to name Dostum were subsequently harassed, arrested, tortured, and killed.

In February 2003 Afghanistan agreed to become a party to the UN INTERNATIONAL CRIMINAL COURT (ICC) Treaty, which took effect the following May. The ICC now has the authority to investigate and prosecute serious war crimes, genocide, and crimes against humanity committed on Afghan soil. Human rights organizations hailed the accord, noting that the ICC is likely to have a larger role in Afghanistan than in many other countries because the law enforcement and judiciary systems are so fragile that they have only limited ability to bring perpetrators to justice. In fact, under the treaty, the ICC can only take action if Afghanistan is unable or unwilling to act on its own. So far the Afghan government has shown little will or ability to prosecute war criminals. The only attempt—a case involving Abdullah Shah, a militia commander accused of grave human rights violations—did not inspire much confidence on the part of human rights organizations, since the accused was never represented by a defense lawyer and given no right to examine the evidence against him. Nonetheless, he was sentenced to death. It is hoped that the potential of the ICC to intervene will result in more prosecutions conducted under an equitable legal regime. "Afghanistan's warlords now know that the game has changed," said Human Rights Watch spokesman John Sifton at the time. "After May 1, if they resort to systematic torture, rape or murder, they can be called to The Hague." Past abuses were not, however, subject to the provisions of the treaty. Only three Afghans have been put on trial for war crimes committed in Afghanistan, and those trials were held abroad. In July 2005 a former Taliban commander was convicted in Britain of torture and hostage-taking during the years the Taliban were in power and sentenced to 20 years in prison. A few months later, two senior officials of the previous communist regime went on trial in The Hague, Netherlands, on charges of torture and war crimes. Witnesses testifying at the trial of the two men, both former officials of the dreaded Khad secret police, stated that they'd been beaten, starved, deprived of sleep for days, and administered electric shocks. "These are the only trials to date dealing with Afghan human rights crimes," said Patricia Gossman of the Afghanistan Justice Project, a Kabul-based human rights group. "But they are critical because this is the first sign people see here that there is no complete immunity for the past. The Afghan judiciary is not capable of handling any such sensitive cases." The trial of the secret police officials was held under both Dutch and international law, relying on the concept of UNIVERSAL JURISDICTION, which allows courts in any country that adheres to the norms of justice to try suspects implicated in human rights abuses, regardless of their nationality or the country where the crime occurred. Specifically, the Afghans are charged under Dutch laws derived from the Geneva Conventions and from the United Nations CONVENTION AGAINST TORTURE of 1984. At the time of their arrests, the two men had been living in the Netherlands in hope of obtaining political asylum.

It is possible that more Afghans in positions of power might face similar tribunals as new evidence of past crimes comes to light. In September 2005, for instance, mass graves containing as many as 550 bodies were found in Afghanistan that were linked to two former warlords who had sought election to Parliament earlier that month. Afghan authorities said that the bodies were those of communist troops who had surrendered to mujahideen— Islamic militias—in 1989 after the Soviets had withdrawn from Afghanistan and the communist regime in Kabul had crumbled. This wasn't the first time that a mass grave had been uncovered in the country; a similar grave was revealed in 2002 containing bodies of hundreds of Taliban fighters captured by the former communist warlord Abdul Rashid Dostum, who switched alliances and has since joined the administration of Hamid Karzai.

Ethnic Tensions

There are several ethnic groups in Afghanistan, the largest of which is the Pashtuns, who are believed to constitute about two-fifths of the population (estimated at about 27 million). During the Taliban regime (1996–2001), members of the Hazara were persecuted, but more recently ethnic Pashtuns have suffered from violent attacks, forcing thousands from their villages. These attacks, which have taken the form of murders, beatings, sexual violence, abductions, looting, and extortion, are blamed on armed factions drawn largely from the Uzbek, Tajik, and Hazara ethnic groups. The animosity of these other ethnic groups is thought to originate in resentment for the Pashtun affiliation with the Taliban. However, such ethnic clashes must be seen in the context of political dominance, particularly in the north. Incidents against the Pashtun population reached a peak in 2002 and have subsided since then.

Refugees

Nearly 2 million Afghans have returned from exile in Pakistan (1.6 million) and Iran (300,000) following the ouster of the Taliban, saddling the country with a humanitarian crisis for which it has neither the resources nor the political will to adequately address it. Many of these refugees have been repatriated under a special program organized under the auspices of the UNITED NATIONS HIGH COMMISSIONER FOR REFUGEES (UNHCR). Some other countries, which do not share borders with Afghanistan, have seized the opportunity to get rid of their own Afghan refugees including asylum seekers in Australia, the United Kingdom, and France. In some cases, Afghan refugees are offered cash incentives to return voluntarily. (A significant number of Afghans are reluctant to return until security is firmly reestablished.) But conditions for the refugees within Afghanistan are inadequate to meet the demand: The lack of infrastructure, functioning health and education systems, and systematic human rights violations as well as chronic drought have impeded the successful absorption of these peoples into society.

U.S. Military Involvement and Treatment of Prisoners

In its campaign to root out armed Taliban insurgents and members of al-Qaeda, the United States continues to carry out bombing raids on suspected terrorist targets. However, flawed intelligence has resulted in an unknown number of air strikes that have injured and killed civilians. (In some cases it appears that rival warlords are attempting to use the American military to destroy rivals by falsely accusing them of harboring al-Qaeda or Taliban elements.) It is impossible to estimate civilian casualties that have resulted from these raids owing to an absence of independent investigators and the remoteness of some of the sites that were attacked. But one incident did draw considerable public attention: On July 1, 2003, an estimated 48 civilians died and more than 100 were injured when U.S. warplanes bombed a wedding party in the village of Kakarak, in the Dehrawad district of Uruzgan province. At first the U.S. Department of Defense blamed a bomb that had gone astray, but officials later offered a revised account, saying that the warplanes had responded because they had come under fire. Witnesses on the ground said it was celebratory gunfire for a wedding. The American authorities have acknowledged that civilians were killed and ordered an investigation.

Human rights organizations have also expressed concern over the treatment of the estimated 1,000 Afghans and foreigners who are held by U.S. military authorities. In a report issued in March 2004, Human Rights Watch contended that the conditions of their detention at the U.S. base in Bagram and other facilities in Afghanistan violated international human rights law. The advocacy group specifically cited the death of three Afghans in American custody in 2002 and 2003. Initial military medical investigators declared two of the deaths homicides. There have also been allegations that the United States has practiced interrogation techniques that it condemns as torture in countries like North Korea and Iran, including shackling prisoners, stripping them naked, or depriving them of sleep. The American military has refused to release information about the number of detainees it is holding, their nationalities, or their names. Detainees in Afghanistan were "in a legal limbo," said Human Rights Watch, since they could be held in indefinite secret detention without being formally charged and prevented from seeing lawyers and journalists. (Only the INTERNATIONAL COMMITTEE OF THE RED CROSS has been permitted access to the prisoners.) "They are held at the apparent whim of U.S. authorities, in some cases for more than a year," the report said. "The general lack of due process with the U.S. detention system violates both international humanitarian law and basic standards of human rights law." To human rights groups it is unconscionable for detainees to be treated as "unlawful combatants," as the Bush administration has labeled them, denying them the rights and protections afforded by the Geneva Conventions that would be in effect if they were formally designated prisoners of war. The U.S. military authorities objected to the report's conclusions, saying that prisoners were being treated properly and that because of the nature of the conflict in Afghanistan, using law enforcement measures applicable in peacetime were not appropriate in time of war. Subsequent revelations of torture and other abuses by American military and intelligence personnel have, however, led to the opening of several investigations and pledges to rectify the problems.

Throughout 2004 members of the CIA and the U.S. military as well as contract workers working for the American government were accused of mistreating, injuring, and killing detainees. The United States Army launched a criminal investigation that implicated 28 active-duty and reserve soldiers in the deaths of two Afghan men detained at the American air base at Bagram in December 2002. The men were charged with several possible offenses, including involuntary manslaughter, assault, and conspiracy. In another case, a CIA contract employee was charged in a North Carolina court with abusing al-Qaeda prisoners, also in 2002. Although only a relatively few cases had gone to trial, it was expected that there were more allegations—and indictments—to come. In March 2005 the Pentagon announced that 26 detainees had suffered from mistreatment and died as a result of criminal homicide in U.S. military detention centers in Afghanistan and Iraq, a far greater number than previously suspected. Although the U.S. Army's Criminal Investigation Division recommended that 28 U.S. soldiers be charged in connection with the beating to death of two prisoners at Bagram in December 2002, only one soldier had been charged a year later—with assault, maltreatment, and dereliction of duty. The army was also investigating a report that U.S. Special Forces beat and tortured eight Afghan soldiers over a two-week period in March 2003 at a base near Gardez, resulting in one fatality.

See also Hazara, persecution of; Iraq, human rights violations in.

Further Reading:

Coll, Steve. *Ghost Wars: The Secret History of the CIA, Afghanistan, and Bin Laden, from the Soviet Invasion to September 10, 2001.* New York: Penguin, 2004.

Ewans, Martin. *Afghanistan: A Short History of Its People and Politics.* New York: Perennial, 2002.

Micheletti, Eric. *Special Forces in Afghanistan 2001–2003: War against Terrorism.* Paris: Historie & Collections, 2003.

Tanner, Stephen. *Afghanistan: A Military History from Alexander the Great to the Fall of the Taliban.* New York: Perseus Books Group, 2003.

aggression

International law defines aggression as the use of force by one state against another that cannot be justified by self-defense or other exceptions that are legally recognized. The illegality of aggression is considered one of the most fundamental norms of modern international law. The United Nations, like the League of Nations before it, owes its creation to an international consensus that aggressive activity by states needs to be restrained by law. In both the Nuremberg Trials and Tokyo Trials set up after World War II to prosecute Nazi and Japanese war criminals, the tribunals considered aggression a crime against peace.

Although aggression might not seem like a difficult concept to define, the UN General Assembly took 20 years to do so. The definition, agreed upon in 1974, states that the "first use of armed force by a State in contravention of the [UN] Charter" constitutes prima facie evidence of aggression. The official definition encompasses invasion, attack, or occupation of whatever duration; bombardment; blockade; attack on another state's armed forces; allowing territory to be used for aggression; and using proxy forces to carry out aggression. In the event that a state initiates an act of aggression, the United Nations recognizes two types of lawful response: (1) individual or collective self-defense by the state undergoing attack or (2) the creation of a force to oppose the aggression by the United Nations itself; this was the case in 1991, when a coalition force was assembled to oust the Iraqi forces from Kuwait under Chapter VII of the UN Charter. Of course, this definition leaves open many questions. Is it possible to conform to the UN Charter and still be the first to use force? That is a matter of context. For instance, because it was authorized by the UN Security Council, the deployment of U.S. forces in Somalia in 1992 would not be considered "aggression," although it represented a first use of force. Similarly, a nation isn't thought to be committing aggression if it takes action to protect citizens facing danger in another country, especially if a foreign government is unable or unwilling to do so on its own. In that sense, the Israeli raid to free Israeli hostages held in Entebbe by Ugandan authorities in 1976 would not be considered aggression and indeed might be thought of as self-defense. Because of the broadness of the General Assembly definition, some scholars and human rights activists have called for it to be expanded to support humanitarian intervention even if it is not approved by the United Nations. Whatever definition is reached, however, it is undisputable that aggressive acts by states and groups like al-Qaeda that operate beyond any state authority occur with alarming regularity.

See also Uganda, human rights violations in.

Further Reading:

Dormann, Knut, and Louise Doswald-Beck. *Elements of War Crimes under the Rome Statute of the International Criminal Court: Sources and Commentary.* Cambridge: Cambridge University Press, 2003.

Falk, Richard A. *Crimes of War: A Legal, Political-Documentary, and Psychological Inquiry into the Responsibility of Leaders, Citizens, and Soldiers for Criminal Acts in Wars.* New York: Random House, 1971.

Akayesu, Jean-Paul   *See* RWANDAN HUMAN RIGHTS VIOLATORS.

Albania, human rights violations in

In general, the human rights situation has improved considerably in Albania since the end of the war in neighboring Kosovo, the breakaway Yugoslav province predominantly populated by Albanians. During the war—which ended in 1999 only after NATO intervention against Yugoslavia—more than 450,000 Kosovo refugees sought a safe haven in northern Albania. The repatriation of these refugees allowed Albania to focus on much-needed political and economic reforms. During the 1990s Albania agreed to a number of important international human rights treaties, including the European Convention for the Prevention of Torture and Inhuman or Degrading Treatment in 1996, and adopted a new constitution in 1998. In another significant development, the Albanian parliament elected the country's first national ombudsman (people's advocate), giving him the power to investigate complaints by citizens against state authorities. In spite of these steps, human rights organizations continue to raise several important human rights concerns: persistent corruption; the use of TORTURE and excessive force by police, usually during arrests and in the initial period of detention; and reports of children being tortured and mistreated after being arrested for alleged criminal offenses. In addition, police singled out members and supporters of the Democratic Party (the main opposition party) for arrest. Thanks to the newly created post of ombudsman, though, several of the worst offenders among the police have been dismissed and prosecuted. Improved training and recruitment practices were expected to curb the abuses of suspects in the future.

Unfortunately, violations of WOMEN'S RIGHTS do not appear to have abated. Like thousands of other women in the former Soviet Union and Eastern Europe, Albanian women are prey to traffickers who lure them into virtual slavery and sell them for about $1000 each. Women have been abducted and forced into prostitution in brothels in Italy and other European Union countries. Human rights organizations continue to pressure the government to relax its restrictions on the media. Journalists are often placed under surveillance by security services and bribed to write stories that will embarrass opposition parties. Drug trafficking was blamed for much of the corruption in the country, and several senior police officers with high-level political connections were suspected of involvement in the illegal trade. In 1997, for instance, Interpol reported that 14 percent of those arrested on drug-trafficking charges in Europe were Albanian speakers; those

taken into custody had an average of 120 grams in their possession. (Some of the Albanian smugglers have come from neighboring Kosovo.) Bowing to pressure from the European Union, the Albanians have vowed to intensify efforts to address the problem. "The situation in Albania, which has remained an important country for the traffic of narcotics, is worrisome," stated a EU report, which added that Tirana should adopt an "efficient strategy" in its fight against drug trafficking.

See also KOSOVO, WAR CRIMES IN.

Algeria, human rights violations in

Algeria has been beset by violence for decades, beginning with a wrenching rebellion against French colonial rule that took an estimated million lives before independence was achieved in 1962. The country was once again plunged into war in 1992 in a bloody struggle with an Islamic insurgency that cost about 100,000 lives over the next decade. The immediate cause of the civil war was the cancellation of the first round of the 1991 general election, which was won by Islamic parties. Rather than accept the result, the military assumed control over the country, setting the stage for a declaration of a state of emergency and civil war. Egregious human rights violations were committed by both sides in the conflict, which was marked by DISAPPEARANCES, TORTURE, massacres, and summary executions. Pinning blame for many of the massacres—often carried out in villages far from the capital of Algiers—is difficult. Although Muslim militants are undoubtedly responsible for a number of them, the army has also been implicated. Eyewitnesses, including survivors and journalists, have reported the presence of men in military uniforms and former members of the security force when these atrocities have taken place. At one point some 200 people were being killed every month in the conflict, among them many women and children. In 1993 a more militant insurgency emerged, spearheaded by the Armed Islamic Group (Groupe Islamique Armé, or GIA), which launched a new wave of terror that took the form of planting bombs in public places, killing the entire population of unprotected villages, kidnapping, rape, and assassinating journalists and political enemies.

In 1999 AMNESTY INTERNATIONAL issued a report, asserting that the military and police, together with so-called self-defense groups, had participated in the assassinations of hundreds of innocent people caught up in antiterrorist operations. Most of these abuses have gone unpunished. The government not only has failed to conduct investigations of past abuses but has had a tendency to throw roadblocks in the way of nongovernmental organizations that do try to uncover the truth. This was in keeping with the government's efforts to censor news about the conflict, concealing, for instance, the true casualty rate of victims. For years in various international forums, Algerian officials insisted that "there was no crisis of human rights in Algeria" but rather "a terrorist phenomenon which violated human rights." The distinction was lost on the UNITED NATIONS HUMAN RIGHTS COMMISSION, which in blunt language characterized the Algerian situation in 1998 as a "widespread human rights crisis." Then in 1999 the government announced a change in policy and asserted that it would take steps to investigate unresolved cases of EXTRAJUDICIAL KILLINGS that extended back to 1994, when the army was given a free hand to detain anyone without permission of the police or courts. Even so, it is unclear as to whether any significant progress has been made. And while reports of human rights violations have diminished in recent years, Amnesty International and other human rights groups charge that the government is still carrying out extrajudicial killings of suspects linked to the militants, even as the war has largely wound down.

Of particular concern to human rights organizations is the fate of the disappeared. It is estimated that some 7,000 people have been disappeared by security forces and Islamic militants, most of which still remain unaccounted for. The disappeared are made up of men and women of all ages, drawn from every level of society, with diverse political allegiances and beliefs. Many of them are suspected members of Islamic groups or their sympathizers. International pressure forced the Algerian government to acknowledge that these disappearances represented a serious problem, and in 1998 it promised an investigation. While disappearances have fallen off markedly, there are still reports of police abuses of prisoners. Provisions that a suspect's arrest must be reported and his detention regulated are often ignored by security agents. Families and friends who publicly protest these disappearances are frequently subject to harassment by police. As late as 2003—four years after the war effectively came to an end—the UN and human rights organizations were still being stonewalled by Algiers in their efforts to obtain information about the cases.

Responding to the outcry, Algerian president Abdelaziz Bouteflika announced a new body in September 2003 to investigate the thousands of cases of persons who were disappeared and remain unaccounted for. Even so, the new body was given little power to conduct serious investigations and was limited in the type of information that it could obtain. Nonetheless, the president, who was elected in 1999 on a promise to restore peace and harmony, has taken some measures that have been applauded by the international community. He has released thousands of Muslim militants from prison and held out an offer of amnesty to rebels, some—but not all—of whom have agreed to lay down their arms. In 2001 Bouteflika also moved to quell another growing threat, this one from the minority Berber community, by agreeing to a series of demands that included official recognition of the Berber language. In spite of all the unrest and continued human rights problems, Algeria has fitfully begun to emerge from its isolation after a decade of strife. In late summer of 2005 President Abdelaziz Bouteflika promoted a plan to reconcile the country called the Charter for Peace and National Reconciliation, which he put before the voters in a nationwide referendum. The document calls for amnesty for Islamist insurgents unless their crimes were especially severe, exoneration for military and security forces, and compensation for families of victims and the disappeared. "Reconciliation, in my view, must protect us from experiencing once again the two evil phenomena of terrorist violence and extremism, which brought us misfortune and destruction," the president said. Human rights organizations expressed skepticism, pointing out that the charter had no provision for investigating human rights abuses or calling anyone to account for his crimes. The charter also confers immunity on the government for the disappearances, stating specifically: "The sovereign Algerian people reject any allegation aimed at holding the state responsible for the phenomena of the disappeared."

See also BERBERS, HUMAN RIGHTS ABUSES OF; SOUAIDIA, HABIB.

Further Reading:
McNamara, Ronald J. *Democracy and Human Rights in the Mediterranean Partner States of the Osce: Algeria, Egypt, Israel, Jordan, Morocco, and Tunisia: Briefing of the Committee on Security and Cooperation in Europe.* Chicago: Diane Pub. Co., 2004.
Sammakia, Nejla. *Algeria, Elections in the Shadow of Violence and Repression.* New York: Human Rights Watch / Middle East, 1997.
Waltz, Susan Eileen. *Human Rights and Reform: Changing the Face of North African Politics.* Berkeley: University of California Press, 1995.
Whitley, Andrew. *Human Rights Abuses in Algeria: No One Is Spared.* New York: Human Rights Watch, 1994.

Alien Tort Claims Act

The Alien Tort Claims Act (ATCA) is a centuries-old U.S. law dusted off to prosecute war criminals in the 21st century. First enacted in 1789, the act grants jurisdiction to federal courts over "any civil action by an alien for a tort only, committed in violation of the law of nations or a treaty of the United States." The statute has been interpreted to mean that U.S. courts have jurisdiction over abuses that occur anywhere in the world—that is, UNIVERSAL JURISDICTION—as long as the alleged wrong is in violation of international law. ATCA cannot be used in criminal prosecutions but only in civil cases. However, civil cases can—and frequently are—used in cases where criminal proceedings have also been undertaken. (Although O. J. Simpson was acquitted on criminal charges in the murders of his wife and another victim, he lost a civil case brought by the victims' families based on essentially the same charges.) In civil cases the judgment can only involve monetary damages; a court cannot impose a prison sentence on a convicted defendant.

ATCA was virtually forgotten for two centuries and was seldom invoked until 1978. That was when a Paraguayan national named Dr. Joel Filartiga, a New York resident, learned that the police officer responsible for torturing his teenage son to death in Paraguay was also living in the United States. Until this time, foreigners residing in the United States who had human rights complaints had little recourse in seeking legal redress. But in this case the Center for Constitutional Rights, an advocacy group providing legal advice to Filartiga, revived the use of the 200-year-old statute. Using ATCA's provisions Filartiga filed suit against the accused torturer in New York District Court. Although the alleged crime had taken place in another country and involved only Paraguayan citizens, the U.S. Court of Appeals for the Second Circuit allowed the suit to proceed, noting that torturers were "enemies of all mankind." Filartiga was eventually awarded $10 million but never collected because American immigration officials had deported the Paraguayan officer. Nonetheless, the precedent was established. Encouraged by the Filartiga ruling, several more plaintiffs came forward to file claims. Filipinos, for instance, have sued the family of the late dictator Ferdinand Marcos for torture carried out while he was in power. An Ethiopian sued his torturer and won a large judgment, and several Guatemalan peasants successfully sued the country's former defense minister, who was implicated in acts of TORTURE and EXTRAJUDICIAL KILLINGS. In 2000, when world leaders gathered in New York for the Millennium Summit of the United Nations, several were stunned to receive summons (which they ignored) involving allegations of crimes committed in their homelands. One suit was brought against Li Peng, the former Chinese premier, and another against Robert Mugabe, president of Zimbabwe. Since then plaintiffs from East Timor have tried to sue the former chief of the Indonesian armed forces in federal court for human rights violations. Although defendants seldom have the resources to pursue any judgment, plaintiffs at least have the satisfaction of a symbolic victory.

For human rights advocates, ATCA was seen as a powerful new tool in bringing human rights violators to account for abuses that might otherwise go unacknowledged and unpunished in their native lands. One advocate called the statute "a beacon to the world." But many critics contend that it is being used in ways for which it was never intended. They maintain that it raises significant constitutional concerns, that it has the potential of undermining the U.S. war on terrorism and imperils the ability of American corporations to conduct business abroad. Many U.S. companies are already fielding suits being brought by foreign nationals in countries where they operate, sometimes because they are alleged to have caused serious environmental damage or because they are accused of collaborating with repressive governments. "The litigation is often high stakes," stated John Niblock, a Washington lawyer who specializes in defending corporations named in ATCA cases. "It usually involves inflammatory allegations of human rights violations seeking damages in the millions or billions of dollars." Human rights organizations disagree. "We only go after the corporation where the company directly participated in human rights abuses," said Jennifer Green of the New York–based Center for Constitutional Rights, adding that these suits are brought only when compelling evidence exists of corporate complicity.

Other critics of a broad interpretation of the statute observe that the ability of the U.S. government to effectively apprehend terrorists could be thrown in jeopardy by plaintiffs suing under ATCA. Foreign individuals, for instance, who provide assistance in the detention and interrogation of al-QAEDA suspects might be eventually liable to prosecution by individuals who claim to have been tortured by military or security officers. Other legal authorities believe that, on the contrary, ATCA can help the authorities. "Independent lawsuits by victims of terrorist acts can be extremely helpful to the government in its effort to track down terrorists and their sources of funding," says a friend-of-the-court brief filed on behalf of people who lost relatives in the attacks on the World Trade Center and Pentagon on September 11, 2001. After all, the brief notes, 209 foreign nationals were killed on September 11, and under ATCA they may one day have the right to seek redress in U.S. courts against individuals responsible for ordering the attacks.

In April 2004 the U.S. Supreme Court heard arguments in a landmark case that is likely to have significant implications for how broadly courts interpret ATCA in the future. The case—*Sosa v. Alvarez-Machain*—involved a lawsuit filed by a Mexican doctor abducted and brought to the United States in 1990 at the behest of the Drug Enforcement Administration (DEA). The DEA had sought the doctor, Humberto Alvarez-Machain, because he was believed to have participated in the torture death of a DEA agent investigating a drug cartel in Mexico. The agency had taken no steps to extradite the doctor but instead had relied on Mexicans to undertake the kidnapping so he could be tried by a U.S. court. The judge, however, threw the case out on the grounds of insufficient evidence. Once back in Mexico, Alvarez-Machain filed suit in the United States under ATCA, stating that his abduction by Mexicans acting at the direction of the DEA violated international human rights. He was awarded $25,000, a judgment upheld by the Ninth U.S. Circuit Court of Appeals. The Supreme Court was not asked to rule on whether federal judges can hear lawsuits brought by foreign nationals who were harmed by violations of international law; that was never in question since the right to sue was clearly specified by the statute. What was at issue was whether there were any limits on what *kinds* of violations were applicable. Lawyers for José Sosa, one of the Mexicans involved in the kidnapping, contended that the statute never established jurisdiction for such cases. "They have opened U.S. courts to suits that interfere with political branch management of foreign affairs, that undermine executive branch efforts to protect the nation's security, and that force courts to usurp the constitutional power of the political branches to decide which norms of international law should be binding and enforceable," declared Carter Phillips, an attorney for Sosa in his brief. Plaintiff attorney Paul Hoffman countered in his brief that "Dr. Alvarez relies on the plain words of the ATCA and the overwhelming historical evidence that the first Congress intended the federal courts to hear and decide claims of 'torts committed in violation of the law of nations.' " The Bush administration sided with the defendants, basically arguing that the statute should have very limited specific application.

In June 2004 the Supreme Court upheld ATCA while dismissing Alvarez-Machain's claim on the grounds that it did not constitute a violation of the act. In its ruling the Court stated, "A single illegal detention of less than a day, followed by the transfer of custody to lawful authorities and a prompt arraignment, violates no norm of customary international law." Writing for the majority, Justice David H. Souter observed that this was not the type of egregious human rights violation that the Alien Tort Statute was intended to cover. But the larger issue under consideration was the scope of the act, and in its ruling the Supreme Court determined that it was fairly broad—a position at odds with the argument presented by the Bush administration. Although Souter agreed that the law should be applied with "judicial caution," his majority opinion supported the plaintiff's contention that the act was intended to cover international rights violations by the First Congress. "It would take some explaining to say now that federal courts must avert their gaze entirely from any international norm intended to protect individuals," he said. At the time of the First Congress, he noted, there were three principal violations of international law: violation of a promise to give "safe conduct," piracy, and "infringement of the rights of ambassadors." The high court's decision held that these violations had a contemporary equivalent in international norms with "definite content and acceptance among civilized nations." In his dissent Justice Anthony Scalia wrote, "American law—the law made by the people's democratically elected representatives—does not recognize a category of activity that is so universally disapproved by other nations that it is automatically unlawful here, and automatically gives rise to a private action for money damages in federal court."

While human rights advocates hailed the decision in *Sosa v. Alvarez-Machain,* corporate representatives were disappointed because they believed that the Supreme Court's ruling might encourage more suits against U.S. companies accused of committing human rights abuses abroad. A lawyer with the U.S. Chamber of Commerce said the Supreme Court's decision "leaves far too much discretion to courts" and created "an ever-expanding universe of judge-made law."

Further Reading:
Hufbauer, Gary Clyde, and Nicholas K. Mitrokostas. *Awakening Monster: The Alien Tort Statute of 1789 (Policy Analyses in International Economics).* Washington, D.C.: Institute for International Economics, 2003.
Steinhardt, Ralph G., and Anthony A. D'Amato, eds. *The Alien Tort Claims Act: An Analytical Anthology.* Ardsley, N.Y.: Transnational Publishers, 1999.

al-Majid, Ali Hassan   *See* MAJID, ALI HASSAN AL-.

al-Qaeda   *See* QAEDA, AL-.

American Convention on Human Rights (Pact of San Jose, Costa Rica)

Concern over widespread human rights abuses in Latin America during the 1970s impelled the ORGANIZATION OF AMERICAN STATES (OAS) to create an agreement guaranteeing certain inalienable human rights that all member states would agree to uphold. In 1978 the organization sponsored the American Convention on Human Rights, which resulted in a treaty that entered into force July 18, 1978; it is also known as the Pact of San Jose, Costa Rica. The treaty states in its preamble that "States Parties to this Convention undertake to respect the rights and freedoms recognized herein and to ensure to all persons subject to their jurisdiction the free and full exercise of those rights and freedoms, without any discrimination for reasons of race, color, sex, language, religion, political or other opinion, national or social origin, economic status, birth, or any other social condition." In ringing tones it reaffirms the basic principles of human rights: "Every person has the right to have his life respected. This right shall be protected by law and, in general, from the moment of conception. No one shall be arbitrarily deprived of his life."

The treaty also recognizes that some member states might still impose the death penalty, especially the United States, which had only just resumed executions in 1977 after a four-year hiatus. Nonetheless, the pact calls for capital punishment to be used "only for the most serious crimes and pursuant to a final judgment rendered by a competent court and in accordance with a law establishing such punishment, enacted prior to the commission of the crime." While the treaty also acknowledges that in time of war or threat to "the independence or security of a State Party," certain emergency measures might be needed, it also specifies that under no circumstances can a member state suspend fundamental rights such as the right to life, right to humane treatment, freedom from slavery, freedom from ex post facto laws, freedom of conscience and religion, and judicial guarantees. To ensure that the rights guaranteed by the treaty were enforced, the Convention established two organs: the Inter-American Commission on Human Rights and the INTER-AMERICAN COURT OF HUMAN RIGHTS. The court was defined as "an autonomous judicial institution whose purpose is the application and interpretation of the American Convention on Human Rights."

Ten years later the OAS adopted the Additional Protocol to the American Convention on Human Rights in the Area of Economic, Social and Cultural Rights, also known as the Protocol of San Salvador. The Additional Protocol, which was signed on November 17, 1988, was meant to reaffirm and amplify the rights and commitments agreed on in the San Jose treaty. Its preamble states: "Recognizing that the essential rights of man are not derived from one's being a national of a certain State, but are based upon attributes of the human person, for which reason they merit international protection in the form of a convention reinforcing or complementing the protection provided by the domestic law of the American States." Among its guarantees: the right to work; the right of workers to unionize; the right to social security for protection "from the consequences of old age and of disability which prevents him, physically or mentally, from securing the means for a dignified and decent existence"; the right to health; the right to adequate nutrition; the right to education; and the right "to take part in the cultural and artistic life of the community." The Protocol also stated that everyone has the right to form a family and guaranteed the protection of children, the elderly, and the handicapped.

Further Reading:

Fawcett, Louise L'Estrange, Andrew Hurrell, and Louise Fawcett. *Regionalism in World Politics: Regional Organization and International Order.* Oxford: Oxford University Press, 1996.
Guillermopriet, Alma. *Looking for History: Dispatches from Latin America.* New York: Vintage, 2002.
Skidmore, Thomas F., and Peter H. Smith. *Modern Latin America.* Oxford: Oxford University Press, 2000.
Williamson, Edwin. *The Penguin History of Latin America.* New York: Penguin Books, 1993.

Amherst, Jeffrey Amherst, first baron (1717–1797)
British general

Although Jeffrey Amherst enjoys a deserved reputation as a military strategist in the French and Indian War (1754–63), he is better known to history for conducting (or at least contemplating) an early form of biological warfare. The allegation, however, has been disputed. Amherst was born in Kent, England, and began his military career as an ensign in the foot guards in 1731. A veteran of the War of Austrian Succession and the Seven Years' War in Europe, he was promoted to major general and dispatched to North America to lead British forces in the French and Indian War (an extension of the Seven Years' War in another theater). In July 1768 he led a successful campaign against the French that resulted in the capture of a strategic fort on Cape Breton Island, giving the British forces access to the St. Lawrence River. Under his command the British scored a series of triumphs over the French in what became known as the "Year of Victories."

Amherst's reputation has been tarnished by allegations that he was responsible for germ warfare against American Indian tribes allied with the French during the Pontiac Uprising of 1763. In letters to a subordinate, Henry Bouquet, Amherst proposed spreading smallpox to the Indians by making gifts out of infected blankets. A year previously such a method had been tried by the commander of Fort Pitt, who had given infected blankets to the Delaware tribe. Historians are divided as to whether Amherst's plan was ever realized, but it is known that tribes in western Pennsylvania involved in the uprising suffered from a devastating epidemic of smallpox at the time. Nonetheless, Amherst continued to enjoy prestigious promotions: He was appointed governor of Virginia in 1763, and in 1778 he became commander in chief of the British army in North America. In 1776 he was made Baron Amherst. Amherst College in Massachusetts is named for him.

See also BIOLOGICAL WEAPONS.

Amin, Idi (Idi Amin Dada) (c. 1925–2003) *Ugandan dictator*

Idi Amin, the former president of Uganda, gained worldwide fame as one of Africa's most brutal—and colorful—

despots. In his nine years in power (1971–1979), Amin, who was also known as Idi Amin Dada, was responsible for the deaths of hundreds of thousands of civilians and the forced expulsion of the Asian Ugandan population. His public grandstanding earned him a reputation as a buffoon, but anyone who failed to take him with the utmost seriousness did so at his peril.

Many of the facts regarding Amin's early years are in dispute, including the year of his birth, though it is believed he was born around 1925. His father was a policeman who deserted his family shortly after his son's birth. Amin's mother was reputed to be a witch doctor. Her attachment to a clerk in a colonial British army unit, the King's African Rifles (KAR), might have inspired the young Amin to contemplate a military career. When he was old enough he joined the KAR as a cook; whether he actually fought in Burma in World War II, as he later claimed, is not clear. Physically imposing and athletic, Amin impressed his superiors by becoming heavyweight boxing champion of Uganda in 1951; he held the title for the next decade. He continued to move up the ranks. One former commander remembers Amin "as a splendid and reliable soldier and a cheerful and energetic man." Another former commander described him as "an incredible person who certainly isn't mad—very shrewd."

In 1962 Amin was ordered to disarm a number of cattle raiders in northeastern Uganda and nearby Turkana, Kenya. In an incident that demonstrated his willingness to perpetrate indiscriminate violence, Amin's forces tortured and beat the thieves to death, in some cases even burning them alive. The British conducted an investigation of what became known as the Turkana Massacre, but since they were soon to declare Uganda's independence and pull out of the country, they decided against a court-martial. Instead the authorities simply rebuked Amin for his "overzealous" methods. The new prime minister, Milton OBOTE, also declined to prosecute and promoted him to captain. By 1964 Amin was deputy commander of the Ugandan army. To further his military education, he was sent to Israel to attend a paratrooper course. The Israelis took to him and made him a conduit to supply arms and ammunition to Israeli-backed rebels locked in a bitter civil war in Sudan; they would later learn to regret this alliance. At the same time Amin was building up his personal power base by recruiting troops from his own Kakwa tribe. He also used his position to embezzle millions of dollars in military funds.

Obote finally became increasingly wary of his onetime protégé and relieved him of his command. When Amin discovered that Obote meant to arrest him, he seized power himself, staging his coup when Obote was out of the country attending a British Commonwealth conference in Singapore. Obote went into exile, calling Amin "the greatest

Former dictator of Uganda Idi Amin *(Landov)*

brute an African mother has ever brought to life." Initially the coup was applauded by most Ugandans, as Amin promised a return to democracy after Obote's repressive rule. But rather than abolish the secret police, as he had vowed to do, he only tightened his own grip on the country, failing to hold the elections that he had announced when he moved into the presidential palace. He insisted that he was really a modest man deep down. "I am not an ambitious man, personally," he said after taking power, "I am just a soldier with a concern for my country and its people." Almost at once, though, Amin began to hunt down his enemies, ordering the mass executions of officers and troops he believed to be loyal to Obote. In one gruesome incident, 32 army officers were blown up by dynamite while they were still held in their prison cell. It is thought that some 6,000 soldiers—out of a total of 9,000 constituting the army—were executed in Amin's first year in power alone.

At first Amin was regarded as pro-Western, but in 1972 he decided that he would transform Uganda into "a black man's country." He proceeded to expel the country's 40,000–80,000 Indians and Pakistanis (many of whom were entrepreneurs and critical to the economy), claiming that he had received a message from God in a dream instructing him to do this. "I am going to ask Britain to take responsibility for all Asians in Uganda who are holding British passports, because they are sabotaging the economy of the country," he declared at the time. He gave them 90 days to leave a country that the Asian community had called home for generations. "If they do not leave they will find themselves sitting on the fire," he warned.

As Britain and Israel began to turn away from their former ally, Amin curried favor with the Palestinians and sought a new alliance with Libya's erratic leader Muammar al-Gadhafi. In defiance of the former colonial power, he instigated a campaign to appropriate British property and threatened to expel British citizens just as he had the Indians and Pakistanis. In 1975, as a publicity stunt covered in the international media, he forced the white residents of Kampala, Uganda's capital, to carry him on a throne and then kneel before him and recite an oath of loyalty. To drive home his threat against the British, he had a British subject named Denis Hills arrested and sentenced to death for having described Amin as "a village tyrant." Hills was saved only by the intervention of the British foreign secretary. After being freed, he offered an assessment of the Ugandan leader that conveyed grudging admiration: "[Amin] has the successful tribal chief's compensatory qualities for his lack of formal education: cunning, a talent for survival, personal strength and courage, an ability to measure his opponents weaknesses and his subject's wishes." Hills cautioned against dismissing Amin simply "as a buffoon or murderer," saying that he "is an African reality. He has realized an African dream. The creation of a truly black state. He has called into being a new crude, but vigorous, middle class of technicians and businessmen."

The more power Amin exercised, the more insecure he became. He orchestrated the assassinations of members of his own government, including cabinet ministers, the chief justice, supreme court judges, and diplomats. He did not stop there: Academics, educators, Roman Catholic and Anglican clergymen, physicians, bankers, tribal leaders, journalists, and even the "vigorous" technicians and businessmen went to their deaths on his orders. To carry out these murders, he relied on three squads of security forces called the Public Safety Unit, which at its height consisted of 18,000 men, and even used his own Presidential Guard to moonlight as a death squad. He undertook campaigns against rival tribes and any suspected Obote supporters who might have survived his earlier depredations. In the process entire villages were wiped out. Estimates of the dead range from 300,000 to 500,000. So many corpses piled up in the Nile that it was all workers could do to pluck them out fast enough to keep the ducts from becoming clogged. Even with all this carnage, one case in particular stands out. In 1974 Amin divorced his second wife, Kay Amin, and two of his other wives. In August that year he had Kay arrested on the grounds that she had stolen a pistol from him. The judge let her off with a warning and released her, but only a few days later her dismembered body was found in the trunk of a car belonging to a doctor—who was not available for questioning because he had "committed suicide" earlier in the day. When the minister of health reported this to Amin "he simply ordered me to have the dismembered parts sown back on to the torso and then arrange for him to view the

body with the deceased's children after which it was flown to Arua for burial! There was no grieving."

By the mid-1970s all pretense of civilian rule in Uganda had vanished, and for all intents and purposes the military controlled the country. Funds intended for civilian use were diverted to the military, accelerating the collapse of the national economy, which was already in dire straits after the expulsion of the Asian community. (The United States cut off all economic assistance. President Jimmy Carter observed that Amin's policies "disgusted the entire civilized world.") Amin, however, thought that he deserved to be applauded for his misdeeds, and in 1975 he promoted himself to field marshal and also awarded himself the Victoria Cross. The following year he declared himself president for life.

In 1976 Amin had the chance to monopolize media attention once more when Palestinian hijackers seized an Air France passenger jet carrying 105 Israelis and Jews from other nations, forcing it to land at Entebbe Airport near Kampala. Amin took charge of the hostage negotiations but made little secret where his sympathies lay. The Israelis mounted a surprise raid on Entebbe on July 4, freeing all but three of the hostages. (Two were killed in the raid and one, Dora Bloch, a British-Israeli grandmother who had been taken off the plane after falling ill, was presumably killed in a Kampala hospital.) It was a devastating blow to Amin's not inconsiderable ego. In revenge he launched a new vendetta, executing 200 senior officers and government officials and ordering the expulsion of all foreigners. When the British broke off diplomatic relations, he proclaimed that he had beaten them and assumed the title of Conqueror of the British Empire. A year later he accused the Anglican archbishop of Uganda of conspiring against him; the next day, the archbishop and two cabinet ministers were murdered.

The collapse of the price of coffee, Uganda's major export, caused a further decline in the economy. Armed rebellions began to spring up in the southwest of the country, and Amin lived in constant fear of coup attempts. Even his onetime allies, the Libyans, began to shun him. As a desperate diversionary tactic, he launched an attack on neighboring Tanzania. It was a grave mistake. The Tanzanians, aided by Ugandan exile forces, quickly beat back the Ugandan forces and were occupying Kampala by the middle of April 1979. Obote was returned to power, and Amin went into exile in Libya, taking with him his four wives, several of his 30 mistresses, and about 20 of his children. Libya refused to play host for long, however, and Amin and his entourage then moved on to Iraq before finally settling in Jeddah, Saudi Arabia, where he was provided with a monthly stipend of about $1,400, domestic servants, cooks, drivers, and cars. He never gave up his dream of returning to power, though, and in 1989 he actually made an attempt to do so. But he was spotted in Kinshasa, Zaire (now Democratic Republic of the Congo), and forced to return to Saudi Arabia.

In 1999, in an interview with a Ugandan reporter, Amin talked about his life in exile, saying that he kept himself occupied playing the accordion, fishing, swimming, and reading. He claimed that he also recited verses from the Koran and read. He expressed no remorse for any of the abuses or atrocities he had committed. "I'm very happy now," he said, "much happier now then when I was president." In July 2003 Amin was admitted to the King Faisal Specialist Hospital in Jeddah with high blood pressure. He soon fell into a coma and was put on life support, dying of multiple organ failure on August 16. He was buried in Jeddah's Ruwais cemetery. According to reports, the funeral ceremony held just hours after his death was a small family affair.

See also UGANDA, HUMAN RIGHTS VIOLATIONS IN.

Further Reading:

Allen, John. *Idi Amin.* History's Villains. San Diego: Blackbirch Press, 2003.

Allen, Peter A. P. *Interesting Times: Life in Uganda Under Idi Amin.* London: Book Guild, Limited, 2000.

Mutibwa, Phares. *Uganda since Independence: A Story of Unfulfilled Hopes.* London: Africa World Press, 1992.

amnesty

The word *amnesty* comes from the Greek stem *amnestia,* which means to forget. An amnesty is a legal mechanism that effectively eradicates a past deed, at the same time lifting the possibility of punishment for the person responsible for the deed. By definition an amnesty is retroactive; individuals are not given an amnesty for acts that they might commit in the future. Amnesties cover a limited time period, apply to only a select group of individuals, and can either erase a sentence that has already been imposed or else prevent any future trials or convictions from taking place. An amnesty can also close down an ongoing investigation into cases that it is designed to cover.

Acts of amnesty are one-time-only events, frequently enacted after the change of a regime. For instance, after majority rule came to South Africa, a form of amnesty was introduced for those who had committed human rights violations during the apartheid era. That amnesty, which was contingent on a public acknowledgment by the offender of his culpability, was intended to usher in a period of reconciliation. It was felt that putting the accused on trial would only open old wounds and retard the process of uniting the white and black populations. The South African model stands in sharp contrast to the amnesty conferred upon Argentine military officers who conducted a "DIRTY WAR"

in the 1970s and early 1980s that resulted in serious human rights abuses and atrocities. That amnesty, later rescinded, was seen less as an act of reconciliation (which was how it was initially presented by the government) than as a kind of cover-up, allowing war criminals to go unpunished and preventing the full truth of the violations from becoming known. Something similar happened in Chile in April 1978, when the dictator Augusto PINOCHET introduced an amnesty law covering any crimes that might have occurred since he took power in a coup in 1973. Once he lost power, however, and was on foreign soil—in Britain seeking medical treatment—attempts were made to prosecute him for his crimes.

An amnesty does not, however, cover victims or their families and so cannot "silence" them or prevent them from seeking redress, although their legal options may be limited because of the amnesty. In Uruguay an amnesty law covering abuses committed by the army and police during the dictatorship there (1973–75) was actually put to a vote, but 60 percent of those who went to the polls preferred to let bygones be bygones.

Amnesties continue to be controversial, and some international initiatives have sought to limit their applicability. In December 1992 the United Nations General Assembly adopted a declaration that prohibits any amnesty that would confer impunity on those responsible for disappearances. The INTERNATIONAL COURT OF JUSTICE in The Hague (more popularly known as the World Court) has also declared that an amnesty cannot have the effect of forgiving severe war crimes or crimes against humanity, since such an amnesty would itself be viewed as a human rights violation. In other words, an amnesty cannot be directed against the victims of human rights crimes, nor can it be in contravention of the legal obligations of states that have signed the Geneva Conventions and other relevant accords. According to the draft Principles for the Protection and Promotion of Human Rights through Action to Combat Impunity of the UNITED NATIONS HUMAN RIGHTS COMMISSION: "Impunity arises from a failure by States to meet their obligations to investigate violations, to take appropriate measures in respect of the perpetrators, particularly in the area of justice, by ensuring that they are prosecuted, tried and duly punished, to provide victims with effective remedies and reparation for the injuries suffered, and to take steps to prevent any recurrence of such violations." The Vienna Declaration and Program of Action, adopted during the World Conference on Human Rights of 1993, echoes this principle: "States should abrogate legislation leading to impunity for those responsible for grave violations of human rights such as torture and prosecute such violations, thereby providing a firm basis for the rule of law."

Some legal precedent, however, seems to contradict these lofty principles. For instance, in 1968 a Paris court ruled that a former commander of a French prisoner-of-war camp in Vietnam could not be prosecuted for crimes committed against prisoners under an amnesty law enacted two years previously. In 2001 another court in Paris ruled that French colonial authorities or military officers could not be prosecuted for crimes committed in Algeria under an amnesty during an uprising there and that, further, no appeal of its decision was possible. There is an exception for war crimes committed during World War II, however, which allows the prosecution of those like Klaus BARBIE.

See also CHILE, HUMAN RIGHTS VIOLATIONS IN; TRUTH AND RECONCILIATION COMMISSION; URUGUAY, HUMAN RIGHTS VIOLATIONS IN.

Amnesty International

Amnesty International (AI) is an international human rights organization made up of volunteers who undertake campaigns for the release of prisoners of conscience, fair trials, and an end to TORTURE, DISAPPEARANCES, EXTRAJUDICIAL KILLINGS, and the death penalty. Based in London, where the organization was founded in 1961, AI often works in tandem with other nongovernmental organizations (NGOs), the United Nations, and regional intergovernmental organizations. Its founder, Peter BENENSON, was a leading British barrister (lawyer), a former military intelligence officer in World War II, and an unsuccessful Labor candidate for Parliament. He outlined his idea for what would become AI in an article for the *Observer:* "Open your newspaper any day of the week and you will find a report from somewhere in the world of someone being imprisoned, tortured or executed because his opinions or religion are unacceptable to his government," he wrote. Inevitably, the response of the reader would be "a sickening sense of impotence." But, Benenson said, the reader could make a difference, after all: "Yet if these feelings of disgust all over the world could be united into common action, something effective could be done." He proposed establishing an office in London to "collect information about names, numbers and conditions of what we have decided to call Prisoners of Conscience." These PRISONERS OF CONSCIENCE, he said, would be considered any "person who is physically restrained (by imprisonment or otherwise) from expressing (in any form of words or symbols) an opinion which he honestly holds and which does not advocate or condone personal violence."

Within a year after Benenson's article, AI had become a full-fledged organization with dues-paying members. At first its principal focus was securing the freedom of people who had been unjustly imprisoned. It conducted fact-finding missions led by individuals who could command respect, such as the Irish human rights advocate Sean MACBRIDE, who was later elected chairman. The influence of the organization was amplified by letter-writing campaigns. Its first full Urgent Action, as these campaigns were called, was launched on behalf of Professor Luiz Basilio Rossi, a Brazilian arrested for political reasons. After being freed, Rossi credited his release to the attention AI brought to his case: "I knew that my case had become public, I knew they could no longer kill me. Then the pressure on me decreased and conditions improved."

Amnesty has mounted campaigns on behalf of high-profile figures such as Václav Havel, the Czech dissident who later became president of his country; AUNG SAN SUU KYI, the Burmese opposition leader; and Kim Dae-jung, who would later assume the presidency of South Korea. But most of the prisoners of conscience are unknown to the world. Between 1970 and 1977, when it won the Nobel Peace Prize, AI adopted 15,000 political prisoners and helped free about half of them. In bestowing the coveted award, the Nobel committee cited AI for "having contributed to securing the ground for freedom, for justice, and thereby also for peace in the world." Over time, however, Amnesty has begun to turn its focus from helping individuals to tackling regional and global issues such as human rights abuses in Saudi Arabia, the trade in CONFLICT DIAMONDS, and the rights of women and children. Possibly Amnesty's most important work to date has been to lobby for the creation of the INTERNATIONAL CRIMINAL COURT and push for the abolition of the death penalty throughout the world.

Amnesty International USA has some 330,000 members with about 1.5 million dues-paying members and donors in more than 140 countries. It operates on an annual budget of about $40 million. AI has also established several specialized "networks" that focus on different issues or the rights of certain groups: the International Lawyer's Network; the Military Security and Police Network, which among other things campaigns for better police training and laws on arms trading; the Business and Economic Relation Network, which works to strengthen corporate accountability; the Health Professionals Network, which has conducted campaigns to improve conditions in mental health institutions in Bulgaria and raise awareness of torture; the Children's Network; the Women's Network; and the Lesbian, Gay, Bisexual and Transgender Network. AI also knows how to attract money and members. To launch a campaign called Conspiracy of Hope in 1986, the organization sponsored a rock concert tour with U2, Sting, Peter Gabriel, Bryan Adams, Lou Reed, and the Neville Brothers. In 1988, to mark the 40th anniversary of the UNIVERSAL DECLARATION OF HUMAN RIGHTS, AI sponsored the Human Rights Now! concert tour featuring Sting and Bruce Springsteen, which was performed in 19 cities in 15 countries. Not surprisingly, these events brought in new members and a substantial increase in donations.

For all its influence, AI's campaigns have little effect in countries where the government has minimal control over its own territory, as was the case when the TALIBAN were in power in Afghanistan. It is unlikely that the leadership of al-QAEDA, for instance, would be swayed by a letter-writing campaign.

Further Reading:

Andreopoulous, Claude, and Richard Pierre. *Human Rights Education for the Twenty-first Century.* Pennsylvania Studies in Human Rights. Philadelphia: University of Pennsylvania Press, 1997.

Claude, Richard Pierre, and Burns H. Weston. *Human Rights in the World Community: Issues and Action.* Philadelphia: University of Pennsylvania Press, 1992.

Falk, Richard A. *Human Rights Horizons: The Pursuit of Justice in a Globalizing World.* London: Routledge, 2000.

Forsythe, David P. *Human Rights in International Relations, Themes in International Relations.* Cambridge: Cambridge University Press, 2000.

Winner, David. *Peter Benenson: Taking a Stand against Injustice—Amnesty International.* Milwaukee: Goreth Stevens Pub., 1992.

Angola, war crimes in

Angola, a former Portuguese colony on the southwestern coast of Africa, is slowly recovering from decades of civil war that left over half a million dead and displaced at least 3.5 million people. The UN-brokered effort to disarm the combatants and return the refugees to their homes, while making some progress, has nonetheless been marred by a number of human rights violations. Although Angola stands to reap billions of dollars from its considerable oil reserves, international watchdogs are concerned that the revenues will not be adequately accounted for or distributed equitably.

The origins of Angola's current problems can be traced back to the struggle for independence against Portugal waged by three guerrilla factions: the National Front for the Liberation of Angola (Frente Nacional de Libertação de Angola, or FNLA), the Popular Movement for the Liberation of Angola (Movimento Popular de Libertação de Angola, or MPLA), and the National Union for the Total Independence of Angola (União Nacional para a Independência Total de Angola, or UNITA). Once the country was granted its independence in 1975, civil war broke out as the rival groups competed for power. The MPLA formed one government based in the capital of Luanda under Agostinho Neto, and the other two groups established a second government in Huambo under the command of Joseph Savimbi. The two regimes sought allies outside its borders, with the Soviets aiding Neto and the United States support-ing Savimbi. In effect, Angola became the setting for a proxy hot war in the context of a global cold war. South Africa, then under white rule, also intervened in the war on the side of UNITA. During the 1970s Cuban troops were dispatched by Fidel Castro to bolster MPLA forces. Even though Washington continued its support of Savimbi, it also sought a diplomatic solution, and in 1992, when a cease-fire was reached and elections agreed upon, the U.S. officials thought they had found one. But after the MPLA candidate, Jose dos Santos, won the presidency (Neto had died in 1979), Savimbi experienced a change of heart and resumed fighting.

Efforts to restore peace over the next eight years repeatedly failed until Savimbi was slain in 2000. Within weeks of his death, UNITA at last agreed to lay down its arms, which finally allowed the painful process of reconciliation to begin. Since UNITA could put tens of thousands of troops in the field, the task was not going to be easy. However, human rights organizations monitoring the process have raised concerns about the way in which the government is going about demobilizing combatants and returning REFUGEES to their homes. According to HUMAN RIGHTS WATCH, authorities have used violence or intimidation to evict refugees from settlements or drive them out of the capital, which had become home to over 100,000 people fleeing war in the interior. The human rights organization also reported incidents of rape and other forms of sexual violence in connection with the relocation of refugees. Millions of internally displaced people and ex-combatants either remain in exile or are still in refugee camps. Moreover, the government also appears to be giving priority to the resettlement of ex-combatants at the expense of women and children, failing, for instance, to provide them with identity documents that would help them obtain humanitarian assistance. In some cases, though, children and ex-combatants are one and the same. UNITA was known for abducting children and pressing them into service on the front lines; there may be as many as 11,000 such child soldiers who were involved in fighting in the last years of the war. The INTERNATIONAL COMMITTEE OF THE RED CROSS has instituted a program to reunite these children with their families, but most of such child soldiers were boys. There is ample evidence that a far larger number of girls were abducted—some estimates put the figure at close to 30,000—many of whom were then forced to serve as cooks, domestics, and porters or as "wives" of UNITA fighters, in effect, sex slaves. Human rights organizations are especially concerned about the reception that these girls will get once they return to their home villages.

See also CONFLICT DIAMONDS.

Further Reading:

Guimaraes, Fernando Andresen. *The Origins of the Angolan Civil War: Foreign Intervention and Domestic*

Political Conflict. Sydney, Australia: Palgrave Macmillan, 2001.

Hodges, Tony. *Angola from Afro-Stalinism to Petro-Diamond Capitalism.* Bloomington: Indiana University Press, 2001.

Anti-Terrorism, Crime and Security Act (2001)

The Anti-Terrorism, Crime and Security Act was enacted in Great Britain in 2001 after the September 11 terrorist attacks. To pass the act, set to expire in 2006, the government of Prime Minister Tony Blair opted out of its obligations under the European Union's Human Rights Convention, to which the United Kingdom is a party, based on an article that allows exemptions under emergency circumstances. (No other member of the EU had taken such a step.) The legislation, which is roughly the equivalent of the U.S. Patriot Act of 2001, allows the government to detain foreigners suspected of terrorist activities if they cannot return to their home countries out of fear of persecution. The law does give these suspects the right to choose to return home voluntarily or go to any other country that will accept them. In December 2004, however, Britain's highest court—a panel of nine judges drawn from the House of Lords—ruled that the law was illegal and that suspects cannot be detained indefinitely because it violated the Human Rights Convention, which requires all persons to have a fair trial if they are charged with a crime. Moreover, the Lords ruled that the law was discriminatory because it applied only to foreigners and not to British nationals. The Lords pointed out that a British national could be just as culpable of subversive activities as a foreigner.

At the time of the ruling, the government had been holding 11 suspects, all Muslim, for three years. Most of them were held in Belmarsh prison in London, which human rights groups call "Britain's Guantánamo" (referring to the GUANTÁNAMO DETAINEES who are being held at the U.S. naval base in Cuba because they are suspected terrorists). "The real threat to the life of the nation, in the sense of a people living in accordance with its traditional laws and political values, comes not from terrorism but from laws such as these," wrote Leonard Hoffmann, one of the eight justices in the majority. The Lords further stated that Britain had no right to opt out of the Convention, which they said could only be done in times of war or public emergency, neither of which was the case at the time the law was passed.

Public support of more vigorous antiterrorist measures increased dramatically after the July 2005 subway and bus bombings by Islamic radicals that killed 52. Prime Minister Tony Blair announced tougher laws to combat terrorism, which included the deportation of imams (Muslim clerics) who publicly called for violence. At the same time the British government lent support to police proposals to hold terror suspects for three months without charge instead of the current 14 days. Whether the Blair government would be able to push the antiterrorist legislation through Parliament in the face of criticism by human rights advocates was still unclear three months after the attacks on London's transportation network.

apartheid

Apartheid was the name of the policy imposed by the white minority government of South Africa with the intention of restricting the fundamental human rights and civil liberties of the black majority. The word *apartheid,* which is derived from Afrikaans and Dutch and literally means "aparthood," or separation, refers to the enforced segregation of the races. It was used first in a 1917 speech by the future prime minister of South Africa, Jan Smits. Although the British had given South Africa its independence in 1910, only the whites—British or Boers (descendants of the 17th-century Dutch colonists)—were permitted to wield any political power. As a policy, apartheid had a precedent in the 1913 Natives Land Act, which segregated ownership of land by race. There were also workplace color bars denying blacks the right of employment in certain businesses. Nonetheless, the laws on the books pertaining to race were not systematically enforced until after World War II, when the opposition National Party, taking issue with the more liberal policies of the government of Jan Smits, advocated an even stricter approach to segregation of the races. In their view, segregation should be extended to virtually all spheres of life. Thus was born the concept of apartheid.

When the 1948 elections brought the National Party to power, it immediately set about implementing laws to make apartheid a reality. The Population Laws were instituted to classify people as Bantu (black Africans), colored (people of mixed race such as Indians), and white (the descendants of the Dutch and the British). Other laws dictated where members of each race could live and work or own land. Under the Pass Laws, nonwhites were obliged to show a pass if they wished to travel to or work in a white area. Additional legislation was enacted that barred sexual and social mixing of the races and restricted the type of employment that nonwhites could obtain. Segregation was imposed throughout the entire educational system. Apartheid conferred the most advantage to whites, but those of mixed race enjoyed greater privileges and rights than blacks. Under the pretext that black Africans were being permitted the right of self-determination, the apartheid regime established Bantustans—small so-called nations within the country's borders set aside for blacks—and then made them citizens of these entities regardless of where they lived. In fact, the Bantustans were "nations" in name only, since they were unable to sustain themselves economically and were recognized only by the white South African government. In any case, whites were given control over more than 80 percent of South Africa's land even though they made up only 10 percent of the population.

In 1976 violent resistance against apartheid broke out in the black township of Soweto. Revulsion at the apartheid regime led to South Africa's becoming a virtual pariah state, subject to political and economic sanctions. In the early 1990s Prime Minister F. W. de Klerk opened negotiations with Nelson Mandela, the imprisoned leader of the principal black opposition party, the African National Congress (ANC). These talks led to the dismantling of the white-dominated government and the end of apartheid. South Africa held its first free elections in 1994.

See also TRUTH AND RECONCILIATION COMMISSION.

Further Reading:

Mathabane, Mark. *Kaffir Boy: The True Story of a Black Youth's Coming of Age in Apartheid South Africa.* New York: Free Press, 1998.

Waldmeir, Patti. *Anatomy of a Miracle: The End of Apartheid and the Birth of the New South Africa.* New York: W. W. Norton, 1997.

Arbour, Louise (1947–) *United Nations prosecutor*
As chief UN prosecutor trying war crimes committed in the Balkan wars in the 1990s, Canadian judge Louise Arbour was responsible for indicting former Yugoslav president Slobodan MILOŠEVIĆ and other suspects for war crimes. Arbour, who was born in 1947, had previously served as a member of the Court of Appeal for Ontario and as trial judge for the High Court of Justice for the Supreme Court of Ontario. In 1996 she was appointed to the INTERNATIONAL CRIMINAL TRIBUNAL FOR THE FORMER YUGOSLAVIA, based in The Hague. In May 1999 she announced the indictment of Milošević as well as Milan Milutinović, president of the Republic of Serbia; Nikola Sainović, deputy prime minister of Yugoslavia; Dragoljub Ojdanić, chief of the general staff of the Yugoslav armed forces; and Vlajko Stojiljković, minister of internal affairs of the Republic of Serbia. "I believe that it is an extraordinary achievement, by any law enforcement standard, for us to have brought to successful confirmation, an indictment against the five accused, for crimes of this magnitude committed since the beginning of this year," Arbour announced in a press statement at the time. She pointed out that the evidence to support the indictment had been collected in less than five months—an astonishingly short period of time. Declaring her conviction that "the product of our work will make a major contribution to a lasting peace" in the Balkans, which was only beginning to recover from

three wars instigated by Milošević, she commented, "The refusal to bring war criminals to account would be an affront to those who obey the law, and a betrayal of those who rely on it for their life and security."

Arbour's work on the court has won plaudits from human rights organizations. "This is someone who has shown by indicting Milošević that she can stand up to bullies," said Reed Brody, special counsel to HUMAN RIGHTS WATCH. "But she has also shown she has the diplomatic skills to make democratic governments do the right thing, the way she did when she persuaded NATO to arrest war criminals in the former Yugoslavia." His comments are echoed by Irene Kahn, secretary general of AMNESTY INTERNATIONAL: "Louise Arbour's broad human rights background, distinguished legal career and service as UN prosecutor give her the experience to be both bold and creative in promoting and protecting human rights."

Arbour stepped down from the court at the end of her four-year term. In February 2004 she was appointed by UN secretary-general Kofi Annan to the position of UNITED NATIONS HIGH COMMISSIONER FOR HUMAN RIGHTS, succeeding Sergio Vieira de Mello of Brazil, who was killed in a bomb blast during an attack on the UN headquarters in Baghdad on August 19, 2003.

Further Reading:

Hagan, John. *Justice in the Balkans: Prosecuting War Crimes in the Hague Tribunal.* Chicago Series in Law and Society. Chicago: University of Chicago Press, 2003.

Hazan, Pierre, and James Thomas Snyder. *Justice in a Time of War: The True Story behind the International Criminal Tribunal for the Former Yugoslavia.* Eugenia and Hugh M. Stewart Series on Eastern Europe. Austin: Texas A&M University Press, 2004.

Ardeatine caves massacre   *See* PRIEBKE, ERICH.

Argentina, human rights violations in
Argentina is still trying to shake off the bitter legacy of the "DIRTY WAR" of the 1970s, when the country was under the grip of a succession of military juntas. Since 2003, with a change of government, military officers who had previously managed to escape prosecution under AMNESTY laws enacted in the 1980s have been called to account for their crimes.

The dirty war in Argentina began in 1975 at a time when unrest and insurgency had spread throughout much of Latin America. Terrorist activity, carried out by both militant right and left-wing groups, had led to the killings of more than 700 people. A wave of strikes and demonstrations added to an increasing sense of instability. Soaring inflation was also robbing the Argentines of their wealth on a daily basis. In 1976 a military junta led by Lieutenant General Jorge Rafael Videla seized power in a coup and proclaimed martial law. The new rulers then instigated a program called "Process of National Reorganization," which was, in effect, a declaration of what became known as the dirty war: a campaign of terror launched against suspected leftists, political dissidents, intellectuals, and civilians suspected of sympathizing with the leftist insurgents. For the Argentine military *golpistas*—the leaders—this campaign was nothing less than the initial stage of a third world war against a global communist threat. The junta believed that because of its hardline anticommunist stance, it would have the complete support of Washington and Western European governments. By the time it was over, the dirty war had claimed the lives of about 30,000 people, of which about 15,000 were simply *desaparecidos* (Spanish for "disappeared ones") who vanished into secret prisons, underwent TORTURE, and were later executed. In many cases, the young children of these disappeared were abducted by the authorities and given up for adoption.

As the economy continued to falter, the military had an increasingly difficult time clinging to power. In 1981 General Roberto Viola replaced Videla, but he proved unable to cope with a resurgence of political and labor opposition and renewed leftist activity. Viola gave way to General Leopoldo Galtieri. In a futile attempt to divert Argentina from its internal troubles, Galtieri tried to retake the Falkland Islands (known in Argentina as Islas Malvinas), which Great Britain had taken from Argentina in 1833. In June 1983, after less than a month of fighting, the Argentines conceded defeat. Galtieri resigned and a new military official came to power, announcing that elections would be held. The junta hoped that these elections would bring to power a pliable leader who would make no attempt to prosecute officers for their crimes committed between 1976 and 1983. To their dismay, however, the people voted in the Radical Party under Raúl Alfonsín, which gained its first absolute majority in the National Congress since 1928.

The new democracy was still fragile and its judicial and legal institutions quite weak. Nonetheless, in 1984 Videla, the first military leader, was tried and convicted on charges of murder and torture along with the naval commander Admiral Emilio Massera. Both were sentenced to life terms. Three other junta leaders also received long prison sentences. Then the courts turned their attention to lower-ranking officers. The military reacted angrily and demanded that Alfonsín put a halt to the investigations and prosecutions. Too weak to confront the military and fearful of a coup, Alfonsín agreed in December 1986 to a Full Stop Law, which was intended to end the trials. When the trials went on anyway, a second law, called the Due Obedience

Law, was passed with the justification that the legislation would protect democracy and public order. Most of the trials ground to a halt. Alfonsín's successor, Carlos Menem, went even further, issuing pardons to many of the officers found guilty, and 10 senior officers convicted by the courts went free.

But there was widespread revulsion at the blanket amnesty that the laws offered the worst offenders, both within Argentina and without. Relatives of the disappeared were especially outraged. Not only were the perpetrators evading all punishment for their crimes, but bereaved families were denied any accounting of what had become of their loved ones. In March 1999 the National Congress responded to pressure by repealing the Full Stop and Due Obedience Laws. The revocation of these laws, however, still failed to address the problem.

Menem's government had little interest in renewing the prosecutions, and some members of the judiciary preferred to interpret the repeal of the laws as having no retroactive application. In other words, any officer who had been pardoned or whose trial had been cut short was not liable to prosecution. In the face of inaction on the part of the Argentinian judiciary, families of the victims looked abroad for legal redress. Some Spanish courts proved particularly aggressive in trying to extradite war criminals, arguing that they had the legal authority to do so because many Spanish civilians were also among the victims of the dirty war. Menem, however, refused to cooperate with the foreign courts, turning down extradition requests from Italy and France for naval intelligence officer Alfredo Astiz, wanted for the disappearance of French and Italian citizens who were caught up in Argentina's dirty war. In November 2001 Buenos Aires turned down requests from Spain and Germany for the extradition of 19 former officers wanted for murder and torture.

However, in November 2001 the Argentine high court suddenly showed unexpected independence by nullifying the Full Stop and Due Obedience amnesty laws on the grounds that they were unconstitutional and violated the country's human rights obligations under international law. The court also allowed the first trial of an officer since 1987 to go forward, opening the way to future prosecutions. Events began to move quickly. In July 2002 Leopoldo Galtieri was arrested for human rights abuses. Thirty other military officers were charged by an Argentine court in connection with the disappearance of a dozen members of a leftist insurgent group known as the Monteneros. These insurgents included Horacio Campiglia and Susana Binstock, who were part of a special Montenero unit called the TEI (Special Infantry Troops) and whose abduction had been carried out in cooperation with Brazilian agents. Arrest warrants were also issued for two other top-level officers in the junta. A federal judge ruled that the three shared responsibility for the disappearances of 18 members of the Monteneros in 1979 and 1980.

The Monteneros were a militant Peronist youth group that emerged in Argentina in the late 1960s and early 1970s. (Peronists took their name from former president Juan Perón.) The clandestine war that began in 1975 embroiled elements of the security forces, the ARGENTINE ANTICOMMUNIST ALLIANCE (Alianza Anticomunista Argentina), and the leftist People's Revolutionary Army (Ejército Revolucionario del Pueblo, or ERP) as well as the Monteneros. The Monteneros carried out a number of terrorist operations; in 1970 they were responsible for kidnapping and murdering General Pedro Aramburu, former head of the military government from 1955 to 1958 as well as a political party leader. They also kidnapped and then killed the U.S. honorary consul, John Patrick Egan; they left his body wrapped in a banner reading "Perón or death." In 1976, as soon as the military had fully consolidated its power, it targeted the Monteneros and suspected supporters, rounding up and sometimes "disappearing" thousands of unionists, students, professionals, teachers, journalists, academics, nuns, and priests, as well as ordinary citizens.

In August 2003 the Argentine Senate followed the lower house by voting to annul the country's amnesty laws, which human rights organizations called a major victory for justice. The election of Nestor Kirchner, a former state governor, to the presidency in 2003 also made the country more welcoming to human rights advocates. Soon after taking office, Kirchner repealed a decree that prevented the extradition of Argentines from standing trial abroad for human rights crimes. But Balthasar Guzmán, the Spanish judge who had initially pressed for the extraditions, expressed his willingness to allow Argentine courts to take over now that the political climate had changed so dramatically. Indeed, several trials of military officers have recently been reopened. One of the most important of these trials will investigate crimes committed in the Navy Mechanics School, a notorious torture and secret detention center known by its acronym ESMA. One of the accused who is expected to be tried is Alfredo Astiz, the former naval intelligence agent whom the Menem government had refused to extradite to France.

See also ACOSTA, JORGE EDUARDO; LÓPEZ REGA, JOSÉ; OPERATION CONDOR; WERNICH, CHRISTIÁN VON.

Further Reading:
Arditti, Rita. *Searching for Life: The Grandmothers of the Plaza de Mayo and the Disappeared Children of Argentina.* Berkeley: University of California Press, 1999.

Davis, William Columbus. *Warnings from the Far South: Democracy versus Dictatorship in Uruguay, Argentina, and Chile.* New York: Praeger Publishers, 1995.

Goni, Uki. *The Real Odessa: How Peron Brought the Nazi War Criminals to Argentina.* London: Granta Books, 2003.

Guest, Iain. *Behind the Disappearances: Argentina's Dirty War against Human Rights and the United Nations.* Pennsylvania Studies in Human Rights. Philadelphia: University of Pennsylvania Press, 2000.

Lewis, Paul H. *Guerrillas and Generals: The Dirty War in Argentina.* New York: Praeger, 2001.

Moyano, Maria. *Argentina's Lost Patrol: Armed Struggle, 1969–1979.* New Haven, Conn.: Yale University Press, 1995.

Rombero, Luis Alberto. *A History of Argentina in the Twentieth Century.* University Park: Pennsylvania State University Press, 2002.

Argentine Anticommunist Alliance

The Argentine Anticommunist Alliance (Alianza Anticomunista Argentina) was a right-wing death squad active in the "dirty war" against leftist guerrillas in Argentina during the 1970s. The Triple A, as it was known, was organized by Jose Lopez Rega, a Nazi ideologue and adviser to the former Argentine dictator, President Juan Perón. The Triple A carried out mass arrests, torture, and summary executions. Victims were often flung from helicopters into the Atlantic or left in the streets at night as a warning to supporters of the leftist insurgents. Although the Triple A was formally dissolved in the mid-1970s, its members were incorporated into other death squads. The dirty war, which claimed as many as 30,000 lives, continued until 1983, ending with the collapse of the military junta that had ruled the country for nearly a decade.

See also ARGENTINA, HUMAN RIGHTS VIOLATIONS IN.

Further Reading:
Lewis, Paul H. *Guerrillas and Generals: The Dirty War in Argentina.* New York: Praeger, 2001.

Aristide, Jean-Bertrand   *See* HAITI, HUMAN RIGHTS VIOLATIONS IN.

Arkan (Željko Raznatović) (1952–2000) *Serbian warlord and mobster*

Željko Raznatović, better known by his nom de guerre, Arkan, was one of the most notorious paramilitary leaders during the Bosnian War of the early 1990s. His private army, the Serb Volunteer Guard (SDG/SSJ)—the "Tigers"—was blamed for several atrocities during those conflicts. Before the outbreak of war, Arkan had already acquired infamy as a gangster and bank robber wanted by several police forces in Europe; he had reportedly escaped prison on a number of occasions. A number of members of the Tigers, like Arkan, had criminal backgrounds. There is significant evidence indicating that his forces had close ties with regular Serbian forces and ruling circles in Belgrade that relied on the Tigers to carry out assassinations and other crimes.

Arkan was responsible for committing massacres in 1991 in Eastern Slavonia (Croatia) and for launching a campaign of "ethnic cleansing" in eastern Bosnia against Bosnian Muslims. In April 1992 his forces, together with other paramilitary units, killed some 1,400 Bosnian Muslims in Foca and burned all Muslim villages and parts of largely Muslim cities to the ground. Arkan subsequently withdrew his forces from Foca, deploying them in western Bosnia, where they remained until April 1996. After the end of the war in 1995, his former allies broke with him, and the Serbian State Security Service undertook to eliminate those of his criminal confederates who might inconveniently decide to come clean about their shady alliance with Serb forces. Many of Arkan's associates were killed—very professionally—within a short period of time.

In spite of Arkan's notoriety, the INTERNATIONAL CRIMINAL TRIBUNAL FOR THE FORMER YUGOSLAVIA (ICTY) sitting in The Hague did not include his name on its initial list of 75 war crime indictments. However, a CNN report on Arkan in 1997 sparked renewed interest in bringing him to justice. Interpol issued an international arrest warrant for him—there had been seven earlier warrants—charging him with genocide. Shortly afterward the ICTY indicted him in connection with incidents that occurred in Bosnia and the Eastern Slavonia region of Croatia between 1991 and 1995. In spite of the mounting pressure for his arrest, Arkan continued to enjoy a lavish lifestyle, living openly in Yugoslavia. He had enriched himself from war profiteering and owned a casino, a transport company, and a radio station. He basked in the attention and enjoyed posing for magazine photographers in the company of his glamorous wife, the folk singer Ceca. In 1998 he won reelection as chairman of the nationalist Party of Serbian Unity (SSJ) by unanimous vote. In national elections he was chosen by Kosovo Serbs as their representative to Parliament. There were rumors—denied by Arkan—that he was also involved in fighting in Kosovo when war broke out in the province in 1998 between Serb forces and Kosovar Albanian insurgents.

On January 15, 2000, Arkan was assassinated in a Belgrade hotel, felled by at least 38 bullets fired at close range. When police apprehended suspects a week later, they announced that Arkan was killed because of a gangland feud. Nonetheless, suspicion persisted that he was killed by then-President Slobodan MILOŠEVIĆ's security services because he knew too much about the involvement of top Serbian officials in his crimes. At the time the British foreign secretary, Robin Cook, said that he regretted Arkan's death "because it prevents us doing justice to the victims of his atrocities by seeing him in the dock at the Hague tribunal." Former U.S. secretary of state Madeleine Albright echoed his words, saying, "We take no satisfaction in Arkan's murder and would have wanted him to stand trial in The Hague for his crimes."

See also KOSOVO, WAR CRIMES IN.

Further Reading:
Bassiouni, M. Cherif. *Sexual Violence: An Invisible Weapon of War in the Former Yugoslavia.* Chicago: International Human Rights Law Institute, DePaul University, 1996.
Harris, Nathaniel. *The War in Former Yugoslavia.* New Perspectives. London: Hodder & Stoughton, 1997.

Armenia, human rights violations in

Armenia has only recently begun to recover from a bitter war with neighboring Azerbaijan over the region of Nagorno-Karabakh. The conflict began in the 1980s before the Soviet Union collapsed, and with the independence of the two former Soviet republics, the strife only intensified. Although the disputed region was initially a part of Muslim Azerbaijan, its population was predominantly Armenian Christian. Although Armenian forces achieved success on the battlefield, the region's fate is still to be resolved. In spite of the fact that Armenia is nominally democratic, its leader, President Robert Kocharian, has used his sweeping constitutional authority to consolidate power and neutralize his political opponents. The system of checks and balances enshrined in the constitution is honored more in the breach than in the observance. The president chooses the prime minister, and the parliament is subservient. Elections to both the presidency and Parliament in 2003 were widely considered flawed by international observers. The judiciary displays little independence and is subject to political pressure; HUMAN RIGHTS WATCH has charged that "the willingness of judges to admit coerced evidence abetted the routine police practice of extracting confessions through beatings and other forms of torture." Security forces have come under fire from the U.S. State Department for having committed extrajudicial killings, routinely beating detainees during arrest and interrogation, and making arrests without warrants. Impunity was also a problem, the State Department said, noting that few of those who are responsible for the abuses of suspects are ever brought to justice.

Political opponents are intimidated and often arbitrarily detained by police. Freedom of association is restricted; a group who tried to demonstrate against the government prior to presidential elections but failed to get a license from the state have been rounded up and held for several days by the police under provisions of the Soviet-era Administrative Code. There is some freedom of the press, but journalists have been intimidated—a prominent reporter was wounded in a mysterious grenade attack in 2002 without arrests being made—and self-censorship is routinely practiced. Television stations are also tightly controlled by the state, which can deny broadcast licenses to independent outlets.

Further Reading:

De Waal, Thomas. *Black Garden: Armenia and Azerbaijan through Peace and War.* New York: New York University Press, 2004.

Sunny, Ronald Grigor. *Looking toward Ararat: Armenia in Modern History.* Bloomington: Indiana University Press, 1993.

Armenian genocide

The Armenian massacres of 1915 have been described as "the murder of a nation." The campaign to exterminate the Armenian population and expel them from the Ottoman Empire (which was superseded by Turkey) was so organized and systematic that it became a model for the prosecution of even more devastating genocidal programs later in the 20th century. Adolf HITLER famously cited the annihilation of the Armenians when he made plans to carry out genocidal warfare against the Jews. Nonetheless, successive Turkish governments continue to deny or downplay the Ottomans' culpability for the massacres.

The roots of the conflict can be traced back to the late 18th century. Armenians, who are Apostolic Catholics, and Turks, who are predominantly Muslims, had lived in relative peace for some 2,500 years, but in the last years of the 18th century, inspired by the French Revolution, Armenian nationalists began to agitate for greater autonomy. In the process a religious minority became more politicized. Increasingly concerned by demonstrations and uprisings by Armenian nationalists, the Ottoman authorities and their Kurdish allies retaliated against the Armenian population. A series of massacres ensued from 1894 to 1896, which directly or indirectly resulted in some 200,000 Armenian deaths; these are now referred to as the Sultan Abdul al-Hamid–era Armenian Massacres. (Al-Hamid was then the Ottoman ruler.) But these massacres were only a prelude to a genocidal program that would be carried out on a much broader scale.

The reign of the sultans barely survived the arrival of the new century: An uprising by a core group of officers and civilian sympathizers known as the Young Turks led to the deposition of Abdul Hamid and the restoration of Par-

liament. But the Young Turks' reformist instincts didn't extend to their treatment of the Armenians. Within a few years of assuming power, they began to respond to political and ethnic dissidence with terror and intimidation. They proceeded to stumble into two disastrous wars in the Balkans in 1912 and 1913. In response to the losses in those conflicts, a more radical wing of the Young Turks gained added leverage. The national crisis may to some degree account for the resistance by the Ottomans to moderate their harsh treatment of the Armenians in response to international pressure. If anything, because of their vulnerability the Armenians were seen as a convenient target. As the last major non-Muslim minority in the empire, they were also viewed as a subversive force—a danger to the empire's security—with suspected ties to its rival Russia. In 1909 another massacre took place in the town of Adana, resulting in the deaths of 23,000 Armenians. The Ottomans took encouragement from the fact that the executions had proceeded smoothly, without any intervention.

The outbreak of World War I gave the Ottomans the pretext needed to denounce the Armenians as treasonous and intensify their genocidal campaign, which took place in four stages. The first stage targeted all able-bodied Armenian men aged 20–45 who were recruited into the army not to fight but to serve as laborers; many of them were later executed. In the next stage, which began in April 1915, prominent figures in the community, including political leaders, intellectuals, and priests, were rounded up, deported to central Iran, or executed. Then, in May, the Ottomans deported the remaining Armenian population, claiming that they were being resettled in the deserts of Mesopotamia. Thousands perished from starvation and exposure during these deportations, but about 200,000–300,000 survived. In the fourth stage, additional massacres were ordered to eliminate the remnant of the uprooted population. Three methods of murder were employed: beating with clubs, mass drowning, and burning. Young Turk functionaries fanned out to supervise the operation. Local party leaders and hardened criminals were conscripted to help with the executions.

The massacres did not entirely escape international attention. News reports from the time vividly illustrate the concerns raised by governments and relief agencies in response to the atrocities. On April 27, 1915, for instance, the *New York Times,* in a story headlined "Appeal to Turkey to Stop Massacres," reported that the secretary of state had instructed the U.S. ambassador to Turkey to "make representations to the Turkish authorities asking that steps be taken for the protection of imperiled Armenians and to prevent the recurrence of religious outbreaks." The diplomatic effort was in vain. On July 29 the British Foreign Office reported that the killings of Armenians "had recently increased both in number and in degree of atrocity." On

August 18 the *New York Times* carried the headline "Turks Accused of Plan to Exterminate Whole Population—People of Karahissar Massacred." Quoting a letter from Constantinople a month previously to a British member of Parliament, the story recounted the forced deportations:

> We now know with certainty from a reliable source that the Armenians have been deported in a body from all the towns and villages in Cilicia to the desert regions south of Aleppo. The refugees will have to traverse on foot a distance, requiring marches of from one to two or even more months.
>
> We learned, besides, that the roads and the Euphrates are strewn with corpses of exiles, and those who survive are doomed to certain death, since they will find neither house, work, nor food in the desert. It is a plan to exterminate the whole Armenian people. . . . Many have fallen from blows from clubs.

In early September the American Armenian Relief Fund Committee quoted letters from witnesses on the scene: "These [Armenian] people are being removed without any of their goods and chattels, and to places where the climate is totally unsuited to them. They are left without shelter, without food, and without clothing, depending only upon the morsels of bread which the Government will throw before them, a Government which is unable even to feed its own troops." A second letter, written on July 12, observes: "A population of 1,500,000 are marching today, the stick of forced pilgrimage in hand, toward the Mesopotamian wilderness, to live among Arabian and Kurdish savage tribes. Very few of them will be able to reach the spots designated for their exile, and those who do will perish from starvation, if no immediate relief reaches them."

Estimates of the total number of Armenians who died as a result of the massacres and deportations vary, ranging up to 1.5 million out of a prewar Armenian population estimated at 1.8 million. An Ottoman interior minister has acknowledged that 800,000 were killed outright. Several thousand, however, managed to escape—250,000 to the Caucuses, either to present-day Armenia, then under Russian influence, or Georgia. It is believed that about 100,000 Armenian women were forced to convert to Islam. Thousands of other survivors went to Europe or America. In spite of the atrocities, approximately 60,000 Armenians currently live in Turkey, mainly in Istanbul.

Although the Allies had promised to investigate and prosecute the crimes committed against the Armenians, they did nothing to fulfill their pledge once World War I had ended, leaving the imposition of justice in the hands of the new Turkish government, which had supplanted the Ottomans. The Turkish military authorities conducted a series of courts-martial from 1919 to 1921 that convicted a number of officials, including cabinet ministers, but many of the guiltiest fled the country to escape arrest. With the ascension to power of Turkish wartime hero and revolutionary Mustafa Kemal (better known as Atatürk), the Republic of Turkey was created, and practically all arrests and prosecutions came to an abrupt halt.

The motivation for the massacres is still a matter of vigorous dispute among historians. One debate has focused on the issue of "contingency"—in essence a chicken-or-egg question. Did the Young Turks embark on a program of genocide as a response to specific circumstances of the First World War, or did the war simply give a convenient cover to pursue a ruthless policy that had been planned all along? A second debate focuses on the political ambitions of the Young Turks. Historian Bernard Lewis has characterized the events of 1915 as "a desperate struggle between two nations for the possession of a single homeland," a view that is sharply disputed by Ronald Grigor Suny, professor of political science at the University of Chicago. Lewis's argument, Suny contends, is the equivalent of pretending that the Turks and Armenians were on an equal footing, engaged in a civil war. In other words, in Suny's opinion, the Young Turks didn't see the Armenians as a threat to their expansionist designs; rather, their campaign was a deliberate effort to exterminate a minority population. Thus, the second wave of atrocities is to be distinguished from the earlier Sultan Abdul al-Hamid Massacres; the former, Suny believes, were intended to suppress dissent but not destroy an entire people, which was the objective of the second wave. The GENOCIDE required "a major strategic decision by elites in power." Jolted by humiliating reverses in the first year of World War I, Suny says, the Young Turks convinced themselves of "an imminent Armenian danger."

Selim Deringil, a professor of history at Bogazici University in Istanbul, takes issue with Suny's position that the massacres of the 1890s and the events of 1915 differed in intent: "Sultan Abdülhamid's restraint in the matter of selecting the target population and the duration of the organized mass murder appear as signs of exigency and expediency rather than of moderation and mercifulness." The massacres of the 1890s, he maintains, paved the way for 1915 by providing the Young Turks with "a predictable impunity." In Deringil's reading, the success of the earlier atrocities, which were at least genocidal in nature, inspired the second. There was nothing "spontaneous" about the 1915 genocide, he says: It was not a violent response to the circumstances of war, so it cannot be considered a "crime of passion." On the contrary, the war was an "engineered opportunity" that the Young Turks seized to put their program into effect.

Whatever the motivation of its perpetrators, the Armenian massacres were very much on Hitler's mind when in 1931—before he came to power—he discussed the need for a resettlement policy for non-German minorities: "We intend to introduce a resettlement policy. Think of the biblical deportations and the massacres of the Middle Ages . . . and remember the extermination of the Armenians. One eventually reaches the conclusion that the masses of man are mere biological plasticine." In 1939 Hitler echoed these words in the context of the treatment of the Polish population: "I have placed my death-head formations in readiness—for the present only in the East—with orders to them to send to death mercilessly and without compassion, men, women, and children of Polish derivation and language. Only thus shall we gain the living space [*Lebensraum*] which we need. Who, after all, speaks today of the annihilation of the Armenians?"

In spite of Hitler's prediction, people today still speak of the Armenian genocide. The failure of the Turkish government to acknowledge the extent of the massacres has been a source of continuing controversy. Turkey claims instead that Armenians were killed in the civil unrest that accompanied the collapse of the Ottoman Empire. Both Great Britain and France have declared the massacres to be genocide, but the United States has refrained from doing so. Successive administrations in Washington have been reluctant to press Ankara on the matter because of Turkey's strategic importance to the United States. (Turkey is a member of NATO and is seeking admission to the European Union.) In January 2004 descendants of some of the Armenians who were killed nearly a century before won a $20 million settlement of a lawsuit for unpaid life insurance benefits. According to the state insurance commissioner, the settlement with New York Life Insurance Co. was intended to help bring justice to survivors of those killed during "a deliberate, systematic and government-controlled genocide that began in April 1915." The attorney who represented the plaintiffs expressed his hope that the settlement would represent a useful step toward gaining U.S. recognition of the Armenian genocide.

See also TURKEY, HUMAN RIGHTS VIOLATIONS IN.

Further Reading:
AkCam, Taner. *From Empire to Republic: Turkish Nationalism and the Armenian Genocide.* London: Zed Books, 2004.
Balakian, Peter. *The Burning Tigris: The Armenian Genocide and America's Response.* New York: Harper-Collins, 2003.
Miller, Donald E., and Lorna Touryan Miller. *Survivors: An Oral History of the Armenian Genocide.* Berkeley: University of California Press, 1999.
Peterson, Merrill D. *Starving Armenians: America and the Armenian Genocide, 1915–1930 and After.* Charlottesville: University Press of Virginia, 2004.

arms, trafficking in and control mechanisms

Practically all of the bloodiest conflicts of recent years could not have taken place without a flourishing and generally uncontrolled trade in small arms. While the world's attention is understandably riveted by the threat of nuclear, biological, or CHEMICAL WEAPONS—the WEAPONS OF MASS DESTRUCTION—it is the traffic in small arms that constitutes the gravest threat to civilian populations caught up in civil unrest and ethnic and regional wars. In the hands of despotic regimes and insurgent or terrorist groups, small arms have become one of the principal instruments of repression.

Small arms and light weapons are broadly defined as weapons that can be handled by one or two people; these can include (for example) pistols, rifles, carbines, machine guns, mortars, and rocket launchers. International law regards an arms sale or transfer "legal" if these transactions comply with national law. But that does not necessarily mean that a weapon sold with the approval of a particular government will not end up being used in a conflict to kill civilians. There is no question of the illegality of sales and transfers of arms on the black market, but there is a much murkier "gray" market where it is often difficult to pin down whether a sale is legal or not. A government of one country, for example, may approve the transfer of weapons to an insurgent group in another country against the express wishes of that government. What makes the trade even harder to regulate is the fact that so many countries have fragile and ineffective regimes or laws governing the production and trade of weapons. By some estimates 80 percent of the trade in arms is illegal. Arms used in conflict areas such as Rwanda and Colombia, for instance, come from a variety of sources: Some have been transferred legally through government-to-government sales and gifts, while others were sold by private firms and still others obtained on the black market.

What is beyond dispute is the carnage that these weapons cause. It is estimated that nearly 1,000 deaths occur daily because of small arms and that the vast majority of the victims are women and children, with an average annual fatality rate of 300,000. Put in another light, the INTERNATIONAL COMMITTEE OF THE RED CROSS reported in 1999 that an estimated one out of every two people killed in war during the 1990s was a civilian. According to a 2001 survey of small arms, civilians represent between 30 and 90 percent of all conflict-related deaths. Both governments and rebel groups are blamed for the slaughter.

The example of Rwanda offers a particularly vivid case history of how the trade in small arms was used to exacerbate a genocidal conflict. In October 1990, when the war began, the country's army was made up of 5,000 soldiers, equipped with a modest number of small arms. By the time the war ended less than a year later, the army had expanded to include 30,000 soldiers who were now equipped with a wide range of small arms, including grenade launchers, antipersonnel land mines, and mid- and long-range artillery. In addition, the army had armed and trained a number of civilian militias that carried out some of the worst incidents of genocide. It is believed that some 85 tons of weapons were distributed to various groups before the massacres of Tutsis and moderate Hutus began. These arms originated in more than a dozen countries including Zaire (now Democratic Republic of the Congo), Bulgaria, France, South Africa (then under white rule), and Egypt. Without the importation of small arms, the Hutu militias responsible for most of the slayings would have been mainly limited to machetes, which would have restricted their ability to kill in such large numbers. (More than 800,000 people, mostly civilians, were killed in the war.) The infusion of arms into the country was probably responsible for tipping the balance in the Hutus' favor in spite of a UN arms embargo imposed on Rwanda in May 1994.

Control Mechanisms

Efforts to establish a legal framework to control the trade of arms—legal and illegal—have accelerated in recent years, but enforcement remains a serious problem. In July 2001 the United Nations hosted a world conference on small arms and light weapons. Delegates agreed to "work towards a consensus on a comprehensive strategy to eradicate" these weapons, but the results of the two-week conference were decidedly mixed. Although some delegations said they were prepared to begin negotiations on developing legal methods to regulate arms traffic, others were concerned about any protocol that would supersede national authority. The United States delegation, expressing the viewpoint of the Bush administration, opposed any international effort to control the sale of legal firearms. "The vast majority of arms transfers in the world are routine and not problematic," Deputy Secretary of State John Bolton told the General Assembly. "Each member state of the United Nations has the right to manufacture and export arms for purposes of national defense." This position was widely decried at the time by many delegations and nongovernmental organizations (NGOs) eager to see more restrictions on arms trading. They charged the Bush administration with being beholden to the National Rifle Association, a powerful American lobbying group. The United States was by no means alone in having misgivings about sweeping restrictions on arms production and trade. Other nations, including China, Russia, and Egypt, objected to any attempt to regulate what they consider to be legitimate arms sales. Some countries were wary of the financial loss from any diminishment of the arms trade as well. Many types of arms brokering were not considered at all because states do not enforce the laws on their books.

(By contrast, the United States has very strict laws governing the licensing of conventional weapons and their sale abroad by private brokers.)

Even if the conference had achieved a more comprehensive protocol than the one that finally emerged, it is likely that very little would have been done to enforce its provisions. With the terrorist attacks of September 11, 2001, the problem of small-arms trade was effectively placed on the back burner. Nonetheless, in 2001 the United Nations adopted the Firearms Protocol as a supplement to its Convention against Transnational Organized Crime, intended to establish "comprehensive procedures for weapons (excluding state-to-state transfers) import, export and in transit movement (of firearms, their parts, components and ammunition) and a reciprocal system of state authorization to ensure high levels of transparency." The protocol includes provisions for record keeping, exchange of information, and marking of newly manufactured and imported weapons.

The United Nations has made increasing use of one of the few mechanisms at its disposal to restrict the flow of small weapons and light arms into countries embroiled in conflict and rife with human rights violations. Under Article 41 of the United Nations Charter, all states are obligated to abide by arms embargoes enacted by the Security Council. In recent years the UN Security Council has imposed such embargoes on several countries including Angola, Rwanda, Haiti, South Africa, Libya, Liberia, Sierra Leone, Somalia, Sudan, Iraq (then under Saddam HUSSEIN), Afghanistan (then under TALIBAN control), and the former Yugoslavia. However, many of these embargoes have not proved very successful because enforcement is often inadequate and violators go unpunished.

Some concrete steps have also been taken—at least on paper—to put a rein on illegal traffic in small arms and light weapons on a regional level. The European Union, the ORGANIZATION FOR SECURITY AND COOPERATION IN EUROPE (OSCE), the Organization of African Unity (OAU), and the Economic Community of West African States have all adopted codes of conduct or statements in support of controlling small arms trade. None of them, however, are legally binding. The European Union Code of Conduct on Arms Exports, for example, establishes criteria that must be taken into account before licensing exports of all types of conventional arms; among the factors to be taken into account is the human rights record of the country seeking to import the arms. But critics say these provisions are too vague and point out that that even in cases where humanitarian law is violated, the code does not obligate a state to refuse to sell or donate arms. It is merely one of many factors that needed to be considered. Nevertheless, supporters of the code believe that it represents an important model and an improvement in standards from what was in place before. On the other side of the Atlantic, every member of the ORGANIZATION OF AMERICAN STATES (OAS), which includes the United States, has signed the Inter-American Convention against Illicit Manufacturing and Trafficking in Firearms, Ammunition, Explosives and Other Related Materials. This convention is aimed at reducing the flow of small arms into the region, and several Latin American states have revised their laws to take its provisions into account. In Africa, where many of the most horrific conflicts have occurred in the last decade, there is still little evidence that regional efforts to curb arms trade have had much effect. There is, however, one heartening exception in Mali. In the early 1990s Mali was wracked by violence fueled to a large extent by a proliferation in small arms. After a peace accord was reached, UN peacekeepers helped collect 3,000 weapons, which were then set ablaze in a great bonfire in Timbuktu in what UN secretary-general Kofi Annan called "a vivid display that the conflict had come to an end . . . the symbolism of that event burns still."

See also BIOLOGICAL WEAPONS; INTERNATIONAL ACTION NETWORK ON SMALL ARMS; NUCLEAR ARMS AND INTERNATIONAL LAW; RWANDA, GENOCIDE IN.

Further Reading:

Barnaby, Frank. *How to Build a Nuclear Bomb: And Other Weapons of Mass Destruction*. New York: Nation Books, 2004.

Cornish, Paul. *Anti-personnel Mines: Controlling the Plague of "Butterflies."* London: Royal Institute of International Affairs, 1994.

Harpviken, Kristian Berg, ed. *The Future of Humanitarian Mine Action Third Worlds*. Sydney, Australia: Palgrave Macmillan, 2004.

Prokosch, Eric. *The Technology of Killing: A Military and Political History of Anti-personnel Weapons*. London: Zed Books, 1995.

U.S. Congressional Budget Office. *Convention on Prohibitions or Restrictions on the Use of Certain Conventional Weapons*. Report to Accompany Treaty Doc. 103-25. Washington, D.C.: U.S. Government Printing Office, 1995.

Winslow, Philip C. *Sowing the Dragon's Teeth: Land Mines and the Global Legacy of War*. Boston: Beacon Press, 1998.

Article 3 Common to the Geneva Conventions

Article 3, agreed to in 1949 by signatory states to the GENEVA CONVENTIONS, is intended to offer minimal protections to victims of noninternational (or internal) conflicts. Article 3 is unique because the text is repeated in all four Geneva Conventions and is the only part of the conventions that applies explicitly to internal armed conflicts. Because it represents an effort to apply the same codes of conduct intended for war crimes to CRIMES AGAINST HUMANITY, it has been called a "treaty in miniature."

The article prescribes the minimum protections and standards of conduct to be followed by both the state and its adversaries within its borders. In effect it sets out provisions for internal conflict that are also intended to apply to conflicts between states. One provision declares that people who are not combatants—including any opponents who have laid down their arms or have been rendered unable to fight because of illness—must be treated humanely and without discrimination based on sex, race, color, religion, or faith. Wounded opponents are to receive proper medical care. According to the article, rebels who are taken prisoner have the right to be seen by representatives of the INTERNATIONAL COMMITTEE OF THE RED CROSS (ICRC) or other international humanitarian organizations, just as other PRISONERS OF WAR do. Certain acts are also specifically prohibited by Article 3: "(a) violence to life and person, in particular murder of all kinds, mutilation, cruel treatment and TORTURE; (b) taking of HOSTAGES; (c) outrages upon personal dignity, in particular humiliating and degrading treatment; (d) the passing of sentences and the carrying out of executions without previous judgment pronounced by a regularly constituted court, affording all the judicial guarantees which are recognized as indispensable by civilized peoples."

The lofty principles of Article 3 are not always so easily put into practice. To some degree this is a result of the ambiguity inherent in the article itself. For one thing, with so many civil conflicts, insurrections, and undeclared wars, it is often difficult for international jurists to determine when exactly humanitarian law applies to a particular situation. How can "armed conflict" be described in a way that satisfies all parties to it? The ambiguity of the article was probably necessary to enlist the support of the signatories. If it were written too specifically or too restrictively, several nations might not have agreed to its inclusion.

Implementing Article 3 raises some thorny questions. In many respects, implementation is voluntary. At present there is only so much that international tribunals can do, especially if they do not receive the cooperation of the countries where conflicts have taken place. Some national legislatures enact their own humanitarian laws using Article 3 as a model, which would mean that violators could be prosecuted for breaching laws of the individual states. In the United States an amendment to the War Crimes Act of 1996 extends the jurisdiction of national courts to violations of Article 3. Similarly, Ethiopia, the former Yugoslavia, Bosnia and Herzegovina, and Slovenia have also criminalized certain types of war crimes without regard to the intensity of a conflict. In addition, military forces in many parts of the world receive training in humanitarian practices in an effort to stop crimes against humanity in an internal conflict before they can occur.

Although it is indisputably helpful to enshrine humanitarian law in national legal codes or military manuals, the problem of determining when that law should be applied, and under what circumstances, remains. Sometimes the only useful criterion is the level of the violence. In some cases, even those involving GENOCIDE, national courts have ruled that the crimes fall outside the scope of Article 3. At other times the state simply decides that the law doesn't apply to *any* internal conflict whatsoever. Even the provision calling on states to accept supervision from impartial humanitarian bodies, such as the ICRC, may or may not be accepted. When the offer is accepted, the state may orchestrate the visit in such a way that it gives the appearance of compliance without really honoring either the letter or the spirit of the article.

When states take action against violent disturbances—street riots, for example—or engage in putting out guerrilla uprisings, they often prefer to keep Article 3 out of the picture entirely. For example, an armed rebellion by Maoist insurgents has been going on in the Himalayan state of Nepal for many years. In January 2004 the Nepalese Supreme Court rejected a writ petition filed against the government for alleged violation of the Geneva Conventions of 1949 in connection with government efforts to suppress the insurrection. The court dismissed the petition out of hand, contending that the conventions pertain only to conflicts between states. The ruling did not necessarily mean that Maoist rebels should be denied the rights afforded by Article 3, especially when it comes to the prosecution of civilians who might have given aid or comfort to the rebels. If these people are taken into custody or are wounded, they cannot be tortured or summarily executed, actions forbidden by Article 3. Even though the implementation of Article 3 may be erratic and inconsistent and its applicability a source of exhaustive debate, its moral and legal influence cannot be doubted even when nations only give lip service to it.

See also HORS DE COMBAT; NEPAL, HUMAN RIGHTS VIOLATIONS IN; UNLAWFUL IMPRISONMENT; WAR CRIMES, CATEGORIZATION OF.

Further Reading:

Bassiouni, M. Cherif. *Crimes against Humanity in International Criminal Law.* Boston: Martinus Nijhoff, 1999.

May, Larry, and Gerald Postema. *Crimes against Humanity: A Normative Account.* Cambridge Studies in Philosophy and Law. Cambridge: Cambridge University Press, 2004.

Robertson, Geoffrey. *Crimes against Humanity: The Struggle for Global Justice.* New York: New Press, 2003.

asylum, political

Asylum is a guaranteed right under international humanitarian war. Under the 1967 Declaration on Territorial Asylum, enacted by the United Nations General Assembly, a person fleeing persecution in his or her native country has the right to take sanctuary in another country without fear of repatriation. The document states: "Everyone has the right to leave any country, including his own, and to return to his country." Individuals who receive sanctuary are also entitled to return to their homes when the situation improves. There are some provisos, however: An individual cannot invoke the right of asylum if he or she is fleeing from prosecution (assuming that the legal proceedings are fair), and once granted asylum, he or she cannot conduct any activities that violate "the purposes or principles of the United Nations."

U.S. asylum policy (as well as procedures for refugee admission) is governed by the Refugee Act of 1980, which is consistent with the 1967 United Nations Protocol on Refugees. Asylum seekers are exempt from quotas imposed on immigrants based on countries of origin. No limits are set on the number of individuals who may be granted asylum in the United States, but an asylum seeker must reside in the country for one year once his or her eligibility is approved.

U.S. law requires three criteria for asylum: "[T]he alien must prove: (1) that he or she has a well-founded fear of persecution or has suffered past persecution; (2) that such persecution is on account of race, religion, nationality, membership in a particular social group or political opinion; and (3) that asylum should be granted in the exercise of discretion." The U.S. Supreme Court has held that the term *well-founded fear of persecution* means a "reasonable" fear of persecution. The applicant must prove, however, that he or she experienced persecution in the past or has a reasonable expectation of undergoing persecution in the future if forced to return home. Several American courts have defined persecution in broad terms so that the term can encompass murder, torture, prolonged detention, slavery, and cumulative mistreatment. Persecution can be economic as well, but only in exceptional and extreme cases. More recently individuals have been granted asylum because of sexual persecution (including rape, assault, female genital mutilation, and mistreatment because of stigma based on homosexuality or being infected with sexually transmitted diseases). There have also been moves on the part of policymakers to grant political asylum to women fleeing countries that condone severe domestic abuse. However, refusal to be drafted in the country's armed forces does not constitute persecution.

Practically, though, it is becoming more difficult to receive asylum almost anywhere. Since the terrorist attacks of September 11, 2001, refugee admissions to the United

States have fallen sharply; in 2002 and 2003 they only reached about 40 percent of the annual goal of 70,000. Rates of asylum also differed sharply by national groups between 2000 and 2004: More than 80 percent of Cubans and more than 60 percent of Iraqis were given a permanent right to stay, but that right was granted to only about 10 percent of Haitian asylum seekers and fewer than 5 percent of those from El Salvador. Detainees represented by lawyers were up to 30 times more likely to gain asylum, but in some places only 50 percent of the asylum seekers had lawyers.

In the United Kingdom the number of immigrants claiming political asylum dropped by more than 40 percent in 2003, which the government attributes to tougher border controls and other restrictions. That translates to 61,050 asylum seekers and their dependents, compared to 103,080 the year before. In the final three months of 2003, there were 52 percent fewer applicants for asylum than during the same period in 2002. Australia has clamped down even harder: Instead of taking in asylum seekers from Afghanistan and Iraq, the government has tried to repatriate them on the grounds that conditions in their homelands are now safe and stable. On a per capita basis, though, Australia still takes in five times as many REFUGEES as the United States.

In a report issued in 2005 by the U.S. Commission on International Religious Freedom, asylum seekers to the United States are frequently treated like criminals while their claims are being evaluated. Many are strip-searched, shackled, and held in solitary confinement in local jails and federal detention facilities. Asylum seekers may receive better or worse treatment depending on where they enter the country, according to the bipartisan commission. It was found, for instance, that only 3.8 percent of asylum seekers were freed from the detention center in Elizabeth, New Jersey, compared with 94 percent who were freed in San Antonio.

Some countries are reluctant to take in more refugees because of national security concerns or because of fears that increasing numbers of immigrants will take away jobs from natives or pose a threat to political or social stability. It is also difficult to separate political from economic refugees since the majority of asylum seekers will claim a well-founded fear of persecution if they are threatened with repatriation. In response, refugees—political and economic alike—are resorting to ever more desperate stratagems to reach asylum. Hundreds die annually in the attempt.

The toll on asylum seekers—psychological as well as physical—can be considerable. The Department of Homeland Security, which is in charge of processing asylum seekers, follows the practice of imprisoning them while their cases are reviewed by the courts. A report by PHYSICIANS FOR HUMAN RIGHTS found that the mental health of asylum seekers detained in the New York City metropolitan area "was extremely poor and worsened the longer the individuals were in detention." In interviews with 70 asylum seekers from Africa, Eastern Europe, and elsewhere, the human rights group observed that "high levels of anxiety, depression and Post Traumatic Stress Disorder (PTSD)" could be attributed to the length of detention time and limited access to mental health services. Even those who ultimately received asylum spent an average of 10 months in prison before they were admitted.

The asylum seekers complained of encountering problems when they arrived at U.S. airports, saying they were verbally abused by officials and in some instances weren't informed of their right to asylum. Some reported being mistreated during detention as well. "Asylum seekers typically suffered tremendous indignities—torture, rape—at the hands of their own government," said Dr. Allen Keller, one of the authors of the study and an expert on torture. "We should be offering protection rather than making worse their already fragile state of health by indiscriminately detaining asylum seekers."

Further Reading:

Feller, Erika, Volker Turk, and Frances Nicholson, eds. *Refugee Protection in International Law: UNHCR's Global Consultations on International Protection.* Cambridge: Cambridge University Press, 2003.

Fritz, Mark. *Lost on Earth: Nomads of the New World.* New York: Routledge, 2000.

Groenewold, Julia, and Doctors Without Borders. *World in Crisis: The Politics of Survival at the End of the Twentieth Century.* London: Routledge, 1996.

Helton, Arthur C. *The Price of Indifference: Refugees and Humanitarian Action in the New Century.* A Council on Foreign Relations Book. Oxford: Oxford University Press, 2002.

Hyndman, Jennifer. *Managing Displacement: Refugees and the Politics of Humanitarianism.* Minneapolis: University of Minnesota Press, 2000.

Ingleby, David, ed. *Forced Migration and Mental Health: Rethinking the Care of Refugees and Displaced Persons.* International and Cultural Psychology: Topics, Issues, and Directions. New York: Plenum US, 2004.

Lischer, Sarah Kenyon. *Dangerous Sanctuaries: Refugee Camps, Civil War, and the Dilemmas of Humanitarian Aid.* Cornell Studies in Security Affairs. Ithaca, N.Y.: Cornell University Press, 2005.

Aung San Suu Kyi (1945–   ) *Burmese democratic activist*

Likened to Nelson Mandela and Mahatma Gandhi, Aung San Suu Kyi is the leader of the democratic opposition in

Burma (known today as Myanmar), which for decades has been under the thumb of military dictatorship. She has spent much of her adult life under house arrest or in prison. Even as the military authorities have blown hot and cold in their treatment of her—at one point negotiating with her, at another locking her up and keeping her incommunicado—Suu Kyi continues to adhere to a vision of democracy for her country.

Politics is in Suu Kyi's blood. She was born Aung San (pronounced Awng Sahn) in Rangoon (now Yangon), the capital, on July 19, 1945. Her father was the heroic independence leader General Daw Aung San, but she had no chance to get to know him: He was assassinated two years later, only six months before the country won independence from Great Britain. She dedicated her life to his legacy, even adding his name to hers. "I always felt close to my father," she said in an interview with *Vanity Fair* in 1995. "It never left my mind that he would wish me to do something for my country . . . A life of politics held no attraction for me. But the people of my country were demanding for democracy and as my father's daughter I felt I had a duty to get involved."

Many years were to pass, however, before Suu Kyi actually entered the political fray. At the age of 15 she left for India with her mother, who had been appointed ambassador to Delhi. Four years later she went to Oxford University to study; while there she met her future husband, Michael Aris, a British scholar. During the next several years she lived in Japan, Bhutan, and England. By the late 1970s she seemed to have settled down to a life as the wife of an English don and the mother of two children. This period of tranquil domesticity came to an end in 1988 when she traveled back to Burma to tend to her ailing mother. Shortly after her arrival, protests broke out against the totalitarian regime of the military ruler General Ne Win. Thousands of students, office workers, and Buddhist monks took to the streets to demand democratic reform. The 8-8-88 mass uprising, as it was called, soon spread beyond Rangoon until millions throughout the country were mobilizing against the regime.

"I could not, as my father's daughter, remain indifferent to all that was going on," Suu Kyi said in a speech in Rangoon in August 1988. The protests, she believed, were Burma's second struggle for independence. Assuming the leadership of the opposition, she traveled around the country, organizing rallies and calling for the restoration of democracy. On August 26 she gave a speech in Rangoon that drew as many as half a million people. But in September 1988 hard-liners in the military seized power in a coup and imposed a brutal regime—known as the State Law and Order Restoration Council (SLORC)—which basically remains in effect today, albeit under another name. Thousands perished in the resulting crackdown. Nonetheless,

the beleaguered democratic movement formed an opposition party, the National League for Democracy (NLD), and named Suu Kyi as its general secretary. In July 1989 the military placed her under house arrest without either lodging charges or trying her. She was kept under house arrest for the next three years during which time AMNESTY INTERNATIONAL adopted her as a prisoner of conscience. Then the military government decided to risk holding elections in 1990. For the government the results were a humiliating defeat. The NLD won a commanding majority in Parliament, taking 82 percent of the seats, even though Suu Kyi herself was forbidden from running. The junta, however, simply refused to acknowledge the results. As international pressure mounted to secure her freedom, SLORC said it would release her but only on the condition that she leave the country to join her family in England. She refused.

In 1991 Suu Kyi was awarded the Nobel Peace Prize. As she was unable to attend the award ceremony in Oslo, her two sons accepted it on her behalf. In his presentation, the chairman of the Nobel Peace Prize Committee, Francis Sejested, called her "an outstanding example of the power of the powerless." Suu Kyi gave instructions for the $1.3 million prize money to be used to establish a health and education trust for the Burmese people. Over the next several years the military regime continued to extend her detention under one pretense or another. During her confinement she told reporters that she meditated, studied French and Japanese, exercised, and relaxed by playing Bach on the piano. The whole time, though, she has continued to hold out the possibility of negotiating with her captors. In a 1995 interview with *Time*, she said, "I have always felt I could work with the army. It was they who felt they could not work with me. I have not changed in any way at all about this matter. I always thought we could talk things over and work together for the good of the nation."

In 1994 two generals actually took her up on her offer and met with her on two occasions. In July 1995 the government released her from house arrest. But any promise of political relaxation soon proved illusory. The military took a dim view of her political activities and began to restrict her freedom of movement around the country. In 1999, when her husband was dying from cancer, the authorities declared that she could leave the country to see him, but with the stipulation that she could not return. Although she had not seen him for three years, she felt she had no choice but to refuse. In September 2000, in defiance of travel restrictions, she traveled to rally supporters in the northern city of Mandalay. The military once again placed her under house arrest. Nonetheless, she remained in contact with leaders of the NLD and was permitted to receive diplomats. Two years later, in May 2002, the authorities engaged in secret negotiations with Suu Kyi. In what was now a familiar pattern, she was released and immediately returned to campaigning.

In May 2003, while traveling with members of the NLD, Suu Kyi came under attack by government thugs. Four supporters were killed—some accounts say many more—and several others injured in the incident, which HUMAN RIGHTS WATCH characterized as having the appearance of "a deliberate attempt by the government to provoke violence to justify a crackdown." Suu Kyi was detained and held incommunicado for several weeks, ostensibly for her own "protection," and subsequently underwent surgery for a gynecological problem. In fall 2003 she went back home once again under house arrest. In early 2004 the military-led government indicated that they intended to free her and reopen negotiations, but by fall of 2005 she still remained under detention.

See also MYANMAR, HUMAN RIGHTS VIOLATIONS IN; PRISONERS OF CONSCIENCE.

Australia, human rights violations in

In general Australia receives high marks from monitoring organizations for its human rights record. There are two areas, however, in which the country has been faulted. One involves the indigenous Aboriginals, whose rights have been fully recognized by the government and judicial institutions only in the last few decades. More recently Canberra has drawn fire from human rights advocates for its restrictive immigration policy. Under Prime Minister John Howard, the government has imposed added barriers to ASYLUM seekers from Afghanistan, Iraq, and other troubled regions. Officially, Australia's policy is relatively welcoming, especially compared to other Western countries. The country grants temporary status to REFUGEES who are designated as asylum seekers because they are "genuinely in need of protection for 1951 Refugee Convention reasons."

According to Australian law, refugees enjoy full and permanent protection after they have undergone the refugee determination process. But internal political considerations have impelled Canberra to toughen the criteria necessary to obtain temporary status. Many Australians fear that a surge of refugees would threaten the country's economic and social stability. The Canberra Refugee Action Committee, an advocacy group, has sharply criticized the government for interning refugees in detention for weeks or months while their applications for asylum are being processed and for failing to inform refugees of their rights. In many cases the government has argued that some refugees, especially those from Iraq and Afghanistan, should be repatriated because conditions in their homelands are now safe. Human rights organizations have taken issue with this position, contending that on the contrary the situation in both war-torn nations are still extremely unstable, and refugees could not possibly hope to find safer conditions than those they had left behind. Nonetheless an effort is being made to persuade them to leave, even though the refugees may not be aware of what awaits them at home. Information provided to Afghan refugees by Australia's Immigration Department, for instance, makes no mention of any human rights abuses in their country. Iraqi refugees—numbering over 4,100 in 2004—face similar pressure to return.

In 2002 AMNESTY INTERNATIONAL released a report entitled "By Invitation Only: Australian Asylum Policy," which claimed that the government's policy was in "breach of the country's international obligations to protect refugees." HUMAN RIGHTS WATCH contended that these refugees "have been failed by the system at every stage," adding, "They should not be treated differently from the refugees Australia invites to resettle from refugee camps overseas."

Hundreds of asylum seekers have tried to reach Australian shores in unsafe vessels. In response the Australian Defense Forces have moved to head them off. Human Rights Watch charged that in October 2001 the Australian naval personnel violated the rights of asylum seekers by boarding boats full of refugees, detaining single men "under inhumane conditions, beat[ing] several of them with batons and [using] other unnecessary force against vulnerable refugee families." These assertions, based on interviews with the refugees themselves, flew in the face of a report released by the Australian Senate that praised "the humanitarian conduct of the naval operations."

Refugees who are denied permission to land in Australia are frequently sent to Christmas Island, an Australian territory, or to the Pacific island nations of Nauru and Papua New Guinea. Human rights organizations maintain that the resettled refugees have been arbitrarily detained, denied access to legal assistance, forcibly separated from their families, and not allowed to appeal their cases to an independent body. Other asylum seekers have been warehoused in camps in Indonesia. What is called Australia's "Pacific Solution" seems only to have placed the refugees in a kind of legal limbo. Some refugees on Nauru have gone on a hunger strike to protest their continued detention and their uncertain legal status.

It is possible that the negative publicity is having some effect. In March 2004 the Australian minister for immigration announced that in 2004–5 Australia would increase its offshore refugee intake by 50 percent from its previous level of 4,000 places to 6,000. Amnesty International commended Australia as "one of only a handful of countries that makes a serious commitment to providing resettlement to refugees beyond its obligations as a signatory to the 1951 Refugee Convention."

See also ABORIGINALS (AUSTRALIA), MISTREATMENT OF.

Azerbaijan, human rights violations in

The regional dispute with Armenia over the region of Nagorno-Karabakh overshadows Azerbaijan's political landscape. Sporadic fighting still takes place in spite of a cease-fire in effect since 1994, and Armenian forces continue to occupy about 16 percent of Azerbaijan's territory. The sustained tensions with its neighbor have hampered Azerbaijan's ability to strengthen its democratic institutions. Possibly the most important recent political development was the death in late 2003 of the longtime president Heydar Aliyev. In failing health for several months, Aliyev had taken the precaution of preserving his family's dominance over the country by grooming his son, Ilham Aliyev, to take his place. Manipulating elections was hardly unprecedented for the elder Aliyev; in 1998 he was reelected in an election that was decried as flawed by international observers. In October 2003, shortly before his father's death, Ilham was declared the winner of the presidential election by an overwhelming majority. Election observers with the ORGANIZATION FOR SECURITY AND COOPERATION IN EUROPE called the vote fraudulent, and violent protests against the results broke out in the capital of Baku.

By most accounts the government's human rights record remains poor. According to the 2002 Country Report by the U.S. State Department, torture and arbitrary detentions were common, and there were reports of prisoners who had died in custody due to mistreatment by police. In 1999 a prison uprising ended in a bloody massacre in which 11 prisoners were shot. The authorities claimed the revolt had been led by two political prisoners and called it a coup attempt. An AMNESTY in 1998 was said to have freed 4,000 prisoners, but opposition groups said that few political prisoners were among them. According to accounts by HUMAN RIGHTS WATCH, some family members of prisoners are also targeted for harassment by police. International humanitarian groups have been allowed to visit some but not all detainees to observe the conditions under which they are being held. In most cases, the government has failed to punish those responsible for the abuses.

The judiciary demonstrates little independence and is influenced by outside political pressures. Nongovernmental organizations (NGOs) estimate that 200–300 political prisoners are held in custody, although some organizations put the number much higher. Freedom of speech and the press are restricted, and journalists are often harassed. Some have been arrested for criticizing the government, and their newspapers have been shut down. The state also uses libel suits to bankrupt offending newspapers. In one case a criminal libel case was instituted against a journalist for writing an article in a Baku newspaper alleging that Heydar Aliyev's brother was involved in illegal gasoline distribution. In 1998 a journalist was sentenced to 18 months in prison for an *unpublished* article that prosecutors alleged had called for a coup. Radio and television, the principal media through which the majority of the population of 8 million gets its news, are kept under tight state control. However, the government has shown some sign of relaxing its grip and has taken steps to grant licenses to private television stations.

The political opposition is checked by a variety of restrictions. Demonstrations are frequently suppressed by police, and some opposition parties have been evicted from their offices, their members harassed by police. In some cases, opposition parties are not allowed to register at all and thus are effectively banned. In the same manner, human rights organizations are prevented from working in the country because they are denied registration licenses. Practitioners of so-called nontraditional religions, such as Jehovah's Witnesses, have also faced official persecution. Although the government is officially committed to developing a market economy, corruption and patronage are rife, and there is little evidence of any effort to bring about needed economic reforms. The only economic bright spot is the oil and gas sector, which brings in 90 percent of the country's revenues.

Further Reading:

De Waal, Thomas. *Black Garden: Armenia and Azerbaijan through Peace and War.* New York: New York University Press, 2004.
Goltz, Thomas. *Azerbaijan Diary: A Rogue Reporter's Adventures in an Oil-Rich, War-Torn, Post-Soviet Republic.* Armonk, N.Y.: M. E. Sharpe, 1999.

Babi Yar

Babi Yar, a ravine, is the site of the brutal extermination of thousands of Jews by Nazi mobile killing units known as EINSATZGRUPPEN near Kiev in the Ukraine. At the time of the killings, Kiev had a Jewish population of 175,000. In mid-September 1941 the German army captured Kiev. Within a period of two weeks the Nazis had rounded up some 34,000 Jews—men, women, and children—living in the city's ghetto. They were stripped and taken to a wooded area near the Jewish cemetery where, on September 29 and 30, they were systematically killed by machine guns. The bodies of one group of victims would be covered by a thin layer of dirt and the next group would be forced to lie on top of them. A small number managed to survive and escape after the executions had ended. Subsequently, the site was turned into a permanent extermination center known as the Syrets camp, where thousands of other victims from elsewhere in the Ukraine met their deaths. Babi Yar might have faded into obscurity were it not for the publication in 1961 of the poem "Babi Yar" by the celebrated Russian poet Yevgeny Yevtushenko. The poem served to remind the world of the horror of the Nazi atrocities while at the same time delivering a scathing attack against anti-Semitism prevalent in Soviet society of the time.

Further Reading:

Dawidowicz, Lucy. *A Holocaust Reader.* Library of Jewish Studies. Chicago: Behrman House Publishing, 1976.

Dwork, Deborah, and Robert Jan Van Pelt. *Holocaust: A History.* New York: W. W. Norton & Company, 2003.

Gilbert, Martin. *The Holocaust: A History of the Jews of Europe During the Second World War.* New York: Owl Books, 1987.

Bahrain, human rights situation in

The Persian Gulf state of Bahrain has been credited with making significant strides in upholding human rights. In 2001 Bahrainis backed proposals put forward by the emir—now the king—to make Bahrain a constitutional monarchy with an elected parliament and an independent judiciary. The last parliament, known as the National Assembly, was dissolved in 1975. Elections were held the following year for a new parliament. Throughout the 1980s and mid-1990s there were periodic bursts of violence sparked by militant Shia—the Shia constitute about 70 percent of the country's population, though the ruling elite is predominantly Sunni—inspired by the 1979 revolution in neighboring Iran that brought the Ayatollah Khomeini to power. By 2001 all political prisoners and detainees were released, and a series of security laws enacted in 1974—as well as a special State Security Court—were abolished. There are fewer cases of arbitrary arrest or reports of TORTURE and ill-treatment. These reforms stand in marked contrast to the situation less than a decade ago when arbitrary arrests were common and even women and children were held without charge or trial. At the time the use of torture by police was frequent and at least 10 people died in custody, possibly victims of EXTRAJUDICIAL KILLINGS.

Bangladesh, human rights violations in

Bangladesh, an impoverished, densely populated East Asian nation, continues to experience spasms of violence three decades after achieving independence from Pakistan. The government's human rights record remains poor, and it has been blamed for numerous serious human rights abuses. According to the U.S. State Department's 2003 *Country Report,* security forces committed a number of EXTRAJUDICIAL KILLINGS, while deaths in custody more than doubled in 2002 over the previous year. Bangladesh is a parliamentary democracy where political competition is "vigorous" in the words of the report—possibly too vigorous. Both major political parties—the Bangladesh National Party (BNP) and the Awami League—frequently resort to violence; indeed violence has become a regular aspect of election campaigns. Clashes occur not only between competing parties but between factions within each party. According to human rights organizations, more than 420 persons were killed and nearly 8,741 others were injured in politically motivated violence in 2002. More recently there have been troubling signs of a third political force coming to the fore: Islamic militancy. In 2004, two avowedly Islamic parties were represented in the coalition government. The Taskforce against Torture, a Bangladeshi human rights organization, has recorded more than 500 cases of people being intimidated and tortured by Islamic militant groups. Islamists have attacked not only communists and members of religious minorities—Hindus, Christians, and Buddhists—but also moderate Muslims who do not follow its fundamentalist doctrine. In recent years, Muslims who belong to the Ahmadiyya, a sect of some 100,000 Muslims who do not believe that Muhammad was the last prophet, have been assaulted and their mosques burned.

Although the Bangladeshi constitution prohibits torture and "cruel, inhuman, or degrading punishment," police routinely engage in physical and psychological torture ranging from threats and beatings to the use of electric shock. Arbitrary detentions are common under special laws that allow for arrests without warrant and preventive detentions. Very few of the abusers are ever punished. According to one human rights organization, 83 people were killed by the police and other security forces in 2003, 15 of whom died in an anticrime drive spearheaded by the army known as "Operation Clean Heart," which began in October 2002. An additional 36 suspects swept up in the operation died in custody. Initially the government ascribed their deaths to heart attacks or said that they had drowned while trying to escape. Then the government changed its story and asserted that no one had died in custody at all. In conducting the operation, the army has been given instructions to "shoot on sight," a policy that HUMAN RIGHTS WATCH and other humanitarian groups have deplored. "A crime wave does not justify law enforcement that does not observe basic standards of due process," said a Human Rights Watch representative. The government, however, credited the operation with reducing robberies, muggings, and extortions by criminal gangs. Nonetheless, stung by the charges of extrajudicial deaths, the government shut down the operation in 2003 and troops were withdrawn.

Even though the higher levels of the judiciary demonstrate "a significant degree of independence," the lower levels are riddled with corruption and usually give into political pressure from the government. The media is hamstrung from reporting abuses by a climate of intimidation that has impelled journalists to practice self-censorship. Those journalists who do criticize the government are liable to be imprisoned. In 2003, three were killed while reporting on corruption and the growing power of militant Islam. Nongovernmental organizations (NGOs) are generally allowed to conduct their activities without interference from the government, though some NGOs have been placed under surveillance.

The State Department also observes that both violence and discrimination against women and abuse of children were pervasive and serious problems. The persecution of women—which includes trafficking and forced prostitution—has stoked what Human Rights Watch calls "an emerging AIDS epidemic." Intravenous (IV) drug use, unprotected sex, and rapes are all contributing factors. The police also compound the problem by abusing sex workers, who face the prospect of abduction by both the police and powerful criminals known as *mastans*. There are even instances of abuse against AIDS outreach workers. "Bangladesh is brutalizing exactly the people it most needs as allies if it is to avoid a severe AIDS epidemic," said a researcher with Human Rights Watch. "Violence against at-risk people traumatizes them and drives them out of reach of HIV prevention services, which can increase their risk of infection."

Another area of concern for human rights organizations is the Chittagong Hill Tracts, a hilly, forested area in southeastern Bangladesh which for many hundreds of years has been home to people from 13 indigenous tribes. Tribal resentment of settlers from other parts of the country led to an armed rebellion that began in the mid-1970s. Although a peace accord in 1997 ended the armed conflict, human rights violations against the tribal people persist, albeit on a smaller scale than at the peak of fighting. According to AMNESTY INTERNATIONAL, the peace accord was flawed insofar as it failed to provide for punishing perpetrators of past injustices in the conflict. This failure, says Amnesty, "reinforced the climate of impunity within which attacks by Bengali settlers against tribal people with reported army connivance continue to occur." Eyewitnesses report assaults on tribal women, the killing of a man in front of his family, and the strangling of a nine-month-old baby. Hundreds of houses have been burned down and dozens looted. There is little likelihood that the guilty will be brought to justice any time soon. In February 2004, Bangladesh's President Iajuddin Ahmed signed a controversial bill granting troops immunity from civilian court prosecution for deaths of suspects while in custody and other abuses connected to the operation. Soldiers can, however, still be tried under military law.

Barbie, Klaus (Nikolaus Barbie, The Butcher of Lyon)

(1913–1991) *Nazi SS commander in France*

Called "The Butcher of Lyon," Klaus Barbie was ultimately convicted of war crimes committed in Nazi-occupied

France but not before having enjoyed a life on the run, facilitated with some degree of U.S. connivance. Born in Bad Godesberg, a quiet town on the Rhine, on October 25, 1913, Nikolaus "Klaus" Barbie was the son of two schoolteachers. Barbie did poorly in school except for his fluency in languages, a skill that would later serve him well during the war and later in exile. He apparently developed a hatred for the French after his father died of complications from a bullet wound he had sustained while fighting the French in the Battle of Verdun in the First World War. After earning his degree and finding himself broke and without prospects, Barbie began to respond to the message of the Nazi party, which was just coming to power in Germany. He joined the Hitler Youth and became so enthralled by the party's ideology that he even volunteered for six months of hard labor at the party's work camp of Schleswig-Holstein. In 1934 he volunteered again, this time to fight with the German resistance movement waging an insurgency against the French authorities in the occupied Rhineland. (The French presence in the Rhineland was provided for by the Versailles treaty.)

In 1935, after establishing his racial and medical purity, necessary to advance in the Nazi party, Barbie joined the SS (Schutzstaffel). He was soon elevated to the elite SD (Sicherheitsdienst) security service. His first assignment for the SD came in 1937 when he was sent to work as an undercover investigator and interrogator in Berlin. Specifically, he was charged with helping the "cleansing" of the capital. He specialized in infiltrating brothels and homosexual nightclubs, an experience that reportedly turned him into a rabid misogynist and homophobe. In 1940, in recognition of his service to the party, he was promoted to SS *Untersturmführer* (second lieutenant).

Barbie's next assignment was to travel to The Hague to research the Jewish "situation" in that city, which had fallen to the Germans only months before. He continued his work in Amsterdam, where he was given responsibility for rounding up and deporting that city's Jewish population. He acquired a reputation for brutality considered excessive even by the standards of the Gestapo. He earned his first Iron Cross for executing an "enemy of the Reich"; this was actually a bludgeoning death of a German-Jewish ice cream peddler in public view. The peddler had made the mistake of failing to salute him properly.

But it was in the south-central French city of Lyon that Barbie achieved the notoriety and the sobriquet that would follow him until the end of his life. The city was a hotbed of French Resistance activity, and Barbie was given the job of cleansing the city of political opponents as thoroughly as he had Amsterdam. But it was not only members of the Resistance and their supporters who were targeted. Barbie's Section IV (Gestapo) was responsible for deporting thousands of Jews to the death camps. Barbie was known for singling

out his victims on a whim and ordering them brought back to his headquarters, located at the aptly named Hotel Terminus, so he could torture them. He also took charge of one of occupied France's most horrifying crimes: rounding up 44 Jewish children hiding out in the village of Izieu and sending them off to their deaths in Auschwitz.

In June 1943 Barbie's efforts to hunt down top members of the Resistance were rewarded with the capture of René Hardy, who had carried out several successful acts of sabotage against the Germans. From Hardy, Barbie obtained enough information to arrest Jean Moulin, the highest-ranking Resistance fighter ever to fall into Nazi hands, and two other Resistance leaders, Pierre Brossolette and Charles Delestraint. Moulin and Brossolette died while they were undergoing torture; Delestraint was put to death at Dachau. Barbie received the First Class Iron Cross with Swords from Hitler himself for killing Moulin. In September 1944, as it became clear that the Allies were rapidly approaching Lyon, Barbie removed or destroyed the Gestapo records. (According to some accounts, he stole some dossiers that had high intelligence value, assuming

Klaus Barbie, head of the German Gestapo in Lyon, France, leaving his trial for the murder of more than 4,000 people. *(Landov)*

that he could use them as a bargaining chip.) To cover his tracks, he took the added precaution of killing anyone in a position to give firsthand testimony about his torture sessions at the Hotel Terminus. Among his victims were 20 double agents whom he had relied on for intelligence about Resistance activities. He then fled to Germany, where he hid out—but only for a time. His presence was soon discovered by the Americans, who, however, considered him not a war criminal but an important asset in the fight against communism. Barbie was also highly regarded for his "police skills." As a result, from 1945 until 1951 he enjoyed the protection of the U.S. Counterintelligence Corps (CIC).

Barbie had also apparently learned a good deal about U.S. intelligence targets and methods, even though he had not had any occasion to put his knowledge to use. One American intelligence analyst described his importance in blunt terms: "To have exposed Barbie to interrogation and public trial would not have been in consonance with accepted clandestine intelligence operational doctrine. . . . [H]e was knowledgeable of high level operations and operational procedures, which would have been compromised."

In 1951, as his situation became increasingly precarious, Barbie and his wife and children escaped to Latin America, eventually finding a congenial haven in Bolivia, where he obtained citizenship in 1957. Taking the alias Klaus Altmann, Barbie found a new use for his skills, contracting his services out to dictators and drug dealers and working as an interrogator and torturer, primarily in Peru and Bolivia. During his exile he made only half-hearted attempts to conceal his true identity. He and his family regularly took long vacations, including one to Paris in the 1960s. In 1971, Beatte and Serge KLARSFELD, the husband-and-wife team of Nazi hunters, identified Barbie. But the rightist Bolivian government rebuffed efforts by France to extradite Barbie on the grounds that he was technically a Bolivian citizen. The French did not press the case very hard, and in 1977, confident that he would never have to face justice, Barbie went so far as to grant an interview to a Bolivian journalist. Asked about the war, he voiced no regrets. "Of course I am proud of what I did during the war," he said. "If it hadn't been for me, France would be a Soviet Socialist Republic by now."

In 1980 Barbie helped aid a coup backed by drug dealers that brought Luis García Meza to power in Bolivia. Once again he found that there was a need for his particular talents. Under his supervision, critics of the regime and political dissidents were rounded up and made to disappear. The "narcocracy" in La Paz was swept away within a few years, and the moderate leftist-oriented government that replaced it proved far less hospitable to Barbie. Moreover, a Socialist government had come to power in France that was more interested in seeing Barbie tried for war crimes. In 1983 he was extradited, although there is some

evidence that France had to pay dearly for him; three days later a French cargo plane bearing arms and cash landed in La Paz. The timing did not appear to be a coincidence.

Barbie, who had already been tried and convicted in absentia by a French court, faced a sweeping indictment that included charges of murder, torture, unlawful arrest, summary execution, and the deportation of dozens of Jewish children from the Izieu orphanage. He was blamed for some 26,000 killings. Barbie's lawyer, Jacques VERGÈS, instructed his client not to attend the trial, which was his right under French law. Barbie took the advice. In his statement to the court, he fell back on the old claim of Bolivian citizenship: "Mister Prosecutor, I would like to say that I am a Bolivian citizen and that if I am present here it is because I have been deported illegally. . . . And I ask of you, your honor, the President to take me back to the Saint Joseph's Prison. I place it fully in the hands of my lawyer to defend my honor in front of justice, despite the climate of vengeance [and] the lynching campaign set forth by the French media."

In spite of Barbie's profession of outraged innocence, Vergès was hard pressed to deny his guilt, especially when it came to the charges stemming from the deportation of Jewish children from Izieu. Prosecutors presented as evidence a note written in Barbie's hand to drive home their case:

> This morning, the Jewish children's home, Children's Colony, at Izieu has been removed. 41 children in all, aged 3 to 13, have been captured. Beyond that, the arrest of all the Jewish personnel has taken place, namely 10 individuals, among them 5 women. It was not possible to secure any money or other valuables. Transportation to Drancy will take place on 4/7/44.

The note was signed Klaus Barbie.

After a protracted trial, Barbie was convicted and sentenced to life in prison. He died there of cancer four years later, in 1991. Nonetheless, he had done much better than the majority of his victims; all told, he had spent only eight years in captivity after the war, compared to the 38 years he had enjoyed as a free man.

Further Reading:

Bower, Tom. *Klaus Barbie, the Butcher of Lyons.* New York: Pantheon Books, 1984.

Dabringhaus, Erhard. *Klaus Barbie: The Shocking Story of How the U.S. Used This Nazi War Criminal as an Intelligence Agent.* New York: Acropolis Books, 1984.

Bashir, Abu Bakar (Abu Bakar Ba'asyir) (1939–   )
Indonesian Islamic leader

Abu Bakar Bashir (also spelled Ba'asyir), a firebrand Islamic cleric, is accused of masterminding terrorist plots in

Indonesia and Singapore. He was born in 1938 in east Java and spent decades in relative obscurity, teaching Islam in Solo, central Java. Even after being charged with masterminding terrorist acts, he maintained that he was only a simple preacher, according to a BBC report. Bashir has never made any secret of his desire for Indonesia to become an Islamic state. He was jailed by the SUHARTO regime for subversion in the late 1970s; after being freed, he sought refuge in Malaysia for 13 years to avoid being jailed again. He returned only after Suharto was driven from power in 1998.

Bashir sat on the executive of the Mujahideen Council, which was formed in 2000 as an umbrella group for advocates of an Islamic state that would follow strict Sharia law, such as practiced in Saudi Arabia. The Indonesian cleric, who is in his mid-60s, is considered the spiritual leader of JEMAAH ISLAMIYAH, a militant Islamic group that is reportedly linked to al-QAEDA. Some observers believe that his true objective is to form a radical Islamic state on the Indonesian archipelago and that he orchestrated a campaign from 1993 to 2001 to topple the Jakarta government. Yet Bashir continues to insist that the Jemaah Islamiyah doesn't even exist and is simply an invention of the West. In September 2003 he was convicted by an Indonesian court after being found guilty of immigration and forgery offenses; he was given a three-year sentence. Prosecutors had also charged that he had approved the bombings of churches in several Indonesian cities on Christmas Eve 2000 in an effort to undermine the government.

In March 2004, however, Bashir's sentence was virtually halved. According to Western intelligence officials, Omar al-Faruq, a captured al-Qaeda operative, stated that Bashir had been behind a plot by members of Jemaah Islamiyah to blow up the U.S., Australian, and Israeli embassies in Singapore. The conspirators were arrested before they could carry out their plans. The terrorist group is also believed to be responsible for the October 2002 nightclub bombings on the island of Bali that killed more than 200 people, most of them young Australians. The court trying Bashir found no evidence that he was the head of the outlawed Jemaah Islamyiah. Bashir himself vigorously denies any involvement in terrorism and has even said that as the head of a Muslim boys' boarding school, he has sympathy for those young Westerners who were killed on Bali in "sinful nightclubs." (One former student of his was later convicted of importing 21 tons of ammonium nitrate into the Philippines, 10 times the amount used in the 1995 Oklahoma City bombing.) He has also asserted that the Western intelligence agents were responsible for the bombings, not Islamic radicals. "I think the bomb was done by foreign intelligence, especially U.S. intelligence. The indications are Americans and Jews did it to justify the claims that have been made so far that Indonesia is a terrorist haven.

What they mean by terrorists is Muslims. So to prove their theory they created the incident in Bali." Asked whether he had any advice to give to the grieving families in Australia, he said, "My message to the families is please convert to Islam as soon as possible." That way, he implied, they could avoid the same fate as their loved ones, all of whom were non-Muslims whom he believed were condemned to hell.

Bashir's hard-line attitude is in marked contrast to the more moderate form of Islam practiced by the majority of Indonesia's population. In March 2005 he was convicted of conspiracy in connection with the Jemaah Islamiyah but acquitted on charges that he was involved in either the Bali nightclub bombing or a subsequent bombing of the Marriott Hotel in Jakarta. His sentence of 30 months was more lenient than prosecutors had demanded. A few months later, Indonesia's Supreme Court upheld the guilty verdict but made no change in the cleric's two-and-a-half-year sentence. The United States and Australia protested the sentence, contending that it was too short for the crimes he was implicated in. Supporters denounced the verdict for just the opposite reason, maintaining that he should have been found innocent of any charges and released.

See also INDONESIA, HUMAN RIGHTS VIOLATIONS IN.

Basson, Wouter (1951–) *South African physician*
Dr. Wouter Basson, a South African cardiologist and military surgeon, has been implicated in participating in a secret germ-warfare program on behalf of the former APARTHEID regime. His notoriety won him the sobriquet Dr. Death. In 1997 he was indicted for complicity in plans to murder top leaders of the African National Congress (ANC), which led the new democratic government. He was subsequently indicted on 27 charges of murder and conspiracy to commit murder in Mozambique, Swaziland, and Namibia, where the white-minority South African government carried out anti-insurgency operations. (These charges were dropped because of jurisdictional issues.) Basson was also charged with having taken part in the killing of 200 Marxist guerrillas and concocting poisons intended for ANC leaders (to be concealed in umbrellas or impregnated in the victims' underwear). In addition, Basson was charged with having invented a particularly lethal type of beer that would kill blacks but not whites and of trying to derive a genetic additive that if put into the water supply was supposed to sterilize blacks. "Basson is a genocidal killer. He must be put away for life because we are dealing here with an animal that shows no remorse" asserted an ANC representative.

At his trial, one of Basson's subordinates, Johan Theron, testified that the doctor had ordered him to chain three black ANC activists to some trees and cover their bodies with a toxic chemical jelly "to see if it would kill them."

When the jelly failed, Basson allegedly directed Theron and another soldier to inject the three men with a muscle relaxant that eventually caused the men to suffocate. An associate of Basson testified that Basson had discussed the idea of killing Nelson Mandela, the future South African president, by giving him cancer. His plots scandalized even supporters of apartheid. "This is horrible. It is a poor reflection," a former South African police intelligence officer in an interview. "A small group of bad apples has helped destroy the Christian reputation of the Akrikaners."

Basson's trial lasted for two and half years, but because the judge excluded certain evidence and other legal technicalities, he was acquitted on all charges in 2002. However, in September 2005 the Constitutional Court of South Africa ruled that his case could be heard again on charges of crimes against humanity.

See also BIOLOGICAL WEAPONS; CHEMICAL WEAPONS.

Beara, Ljubisa   *See* WAR CRIMINALS OF THE FORMER YUGOSLAVIA.

Belarus, human rights violations in

A decade after the collapse of the Soviet Union, Belarus remains under the grip of one-man rule. Although Belarus is nominally a republic, in fact its leader, President Alexander Lukashenko, has never allowed free elections. When he was reelected to a second term in 2001, monitors from the ORGANIZATION FOR SECURITY AND COOPERATION IN EUROPE (OSCE) described the process as neither free nor fair. Lukashenko, who rules in the style of an old-style Soviet boss, retains complete control over the security apparatus. In a 1998 report on the country, HUMAN RIGHTS WATCH asserted that Lukashenko was "steering Belarus back toward Soviet era repression by leading a government that is engaged in violations of a broad spectrum of basic civil and political rights." According to the 2003 *Country Report* issued by the U.S. State Department, the regime's human rights record not only remained very poor but had actually deteriorated in several areas over the previous year. Political opposition is severely curtailed, and there are continuing accounts of police abuse and occasional TORTURE. Police also carry out arbitrary arrests; many of those who are targeted appear to be singled out for their political beliefs. The security forces closely monitor the activities of opposition politicians, human rights activists, and other segments of the population. "Lukashenko's main partner is fear," says a political opponent.

Opposition groups seeking to hold political demonstrations have to go through a cumbersome process and cut through a great deal of red tape. Penalties for violating these procedures can be serious; although most demonstrators arrested are usually released within hours, there have been cases where they are held far longer. In one case, in February 1998, a solitary demonstrator with a placard was imprisoned for 15 days. In another, political activists were locked up, including two who circulated a leaflet in which they noted that Lukashenko had taken ski vacations in Austria and was "having a good time at your expense." They received two years in prison. Lawyers representing imprisoned dissidents have been stripped of their license to practice law. The rules pertaining to peaceful assembly allow the authorities to change the time, location, and even the number of participants of a given demonstration at whim. The government even regulates the type of symbols that demonstrators can use. Allegations of even greater violations of human rights have been given credence in a Council of Europe report that implicated senior government officials in the disappearances of Belarusan opposition leaders and a journalist in 1999 and 2000. The report indicated that the government had blocked any attempt to investigate the cases.

Similarly, free association is limited, and a series of new decrees have forced several newspapers to shut down. In a two-month period in 2004, Lukashenko closed no fewer than nine newspapers. A number of journalists have been locked up on libel charges. There is, effectively, no independent media—print or broadcast—that is allowed to freely criticize the president or government policy. Religious freedom of various groups has also been curbed in favor of the Russian Orthodox Church.

At the same time, efforts to organize workers or secure collective bargaining rights have also been hampered by the government. Trafficking in women and children continues to be a significant problem, although the government has taken some steps to deal with it. In spite of the increasing restrictions, the U.S. State Department has reported no incidents of political killings or forced DISAPPEARANCES, though the government has shown little inclination to investigate cases of disappearances of political figures in the past.

The government has taken steps to limit academic freedom as well, which Human Rights Watch says has "given rise to a climate of fear and suspicion on Belarusian campuses." Faculty members and students who dare to participate in political demonstrations on and off campus are subject to warnings, reprimands, and expulsions. Teachers can be fired for speaking out. Ironically, in 1998 the government introduced human rights and ethics as part of a compulsory curriculum.

The authorities react to the charges that they are restricting political freedoms with defiance, either by repudiating reports of human rights advocates or denying that instances of abuse occur at all. Some officials say that progress is being made and that Belarus does indeed wish to comply with its international rights obligations, but that outside observers should show more patience. Officials also point out that Belarus, in contrast to many other former Soviet republics, remains free of the ethnic unrest and conflict that has undermined political and economic development elsewhere.

To keep himself in power, Lukashenko held a referendum in late 2004 that would change the constitution to permit him to extend his term in office. The president won in balloting that was widely seen as flawed. Antigovernment protests held in Minsk and elsewhere were put down and opposition leaders arrested; several were later fined or received jail sentences for participating.

Belgian war crimes tribunal

In 1993, in one of the most far-reaching efforts to establish UNIVERSAL JURISDICTION, the Belgian government adopted a law giving the country jurisdiction to try war crimes, GENOCIDE, and other CRIMES AGAINST HUMANITY wherever they were committed. Perhaps the most notable success achieved by the law was the trial in the spring of 2001 of two Rwandan nuns for their role in the country's genocide in 1994. The two were sentenced to 12 and 15 years in prison. The Belgian government had earlier filed charges against Congolese foreign minister Yerodia Ndombasi for his role in the 1998 killings of ethnic Tutsis in the Democratic Republic of the Congo. It soon became clear, though, that the Belgian law had overreached; in February 2002 the INTERNATIONAL COURT OF JUSTICE in The Hague ruled that Belgium was constrained from prosecuting a foreign government minister for war crimes because representatives of foreign governments are entitled to diplomatic immunity. If Belgium had continued to confine its prosecutions to low-level officials and fugitives from justice, it might have avoided a firestorm. Instead, the government allowed complaints to be brought against high-profile military officers and heads. They soon discovered that one person's war criminal was another person's political hero. At one point Belgium was prepared to bring charges against Israeli prime minister Ariel Sharon on the grounds that he was responsible for the killings of hundreds of civilians at the Palestinian refugee camps in Lebanon by a Lebanese Christian militia allied with Israel in 1982. At the time Sharon was Israel's defense minister. The case was ultimately dropped. Another case had been filed against Palestinian leader Yasser Arafat for war crimes but nothing came of this effort, either.

The U.S. government, which has vigorously expressed its opposition even to the UN-sponsored INTERNATIONAL CRIMINAL COURT warned Belgium, a NATO member, of retaliatory action if it persisted in conducting such international trials. In 2003 Secretary of Defense Donald Rumsfeld warned Belgium to scrap the war crimes law entirely or face a U.S. cutoff of financial support for the construction of a new NATO headquarters in Brussels. Rumsfeld railed against the law for creating a climate of what he termed "divisive politicized lawsuits." He was not speaking simply in the abstract. In May 2003, shortly after the formal end of the war in Iraq, a group of 10 Iraqi citizens were prepared to file a complaint in Brussels against General Tommy Franks, the head of the U.S.-led coalition forces in the Iraqi invasion, alleging that he had failed to prevent looting and that in some cases, U.S. soldiers under his command actually encouraged Iraqi looters. The complaint further charged Franks for the indiscriminate killing of Iraqi civilians, for the bombing of a marketplace in Baghdad, and for U.S. troops' firing on an ambulance. In theory, if the legal process had been allowed to continue, an arrest warrant could have been issued by Belgian courts but Brussels quickly backed down in the face of U.S. diplomatic pressure.

See also CONGO, DEMOCRATIC REPUBLIC OF THE, WAR CRIMES IN; WALLEYN, LUC; WAR CRIMES, CATEGORIZATION OF.

belligerent status

Belligerent status is a term that has more historical interest than it does current applicability to international law. In the past, rebel movements that sought secession might claim belligerent status, which would confer legal standing on them and in effect create a more equal playing field in terms of international law. To claim this status, however, the rebel group would have to meet several criteria: Its objective was secession, its forces were well organized, it had initiated hostilities against the government, and the government recognized it as a belligerent. But in recent times there are few instances when a government has extended such recognition, because it means acknowledging that it no longer maintains effective control over its territory. The last time that any such status was awarded to a belligerent party was during the Boer War in 1902. Even during the Civil War in the United States, belligerency status was never officially conferred on the Confederacy. "In practice the traditional international law on recognition of insurgency and belligerency is more theoretical than real," observes Heather A. Wilson in *International Law and the Use of Force by National Liberation Movements*. "Since World War I the recognition of belligerency has scarcely ever occurred and not at all since World War II. Even in the Spanish Civil War (1936–39) the insurgents were never recognized as belligerents."

However, failure to invoke belligerent status is not in itself an excuse for governments to avoid compliance with its humanitarian obligations under international law. Belligerent status is implied in the event of certain circumstances even in the absence of a formal designation. First of all, a confrontation must be deemed to be an internal armed conflict. This can occur when fighting reaches a certain level of intensity, the insurgency is organized, and the conflict is protracted rather than a brief spasm of unrest. Moreover, the conflict cannot involve any outside powers. When these conditions are met, parties are expected to conform to a distinct body of humanitarian law crystallized most notably in ARTICLE 3 COMMON TO THE GENEVA CONVENTIONS of 1949 and in Additional Protocol II of 1979. This is stated explicitly in Common Article 3: "The application of the preceding provisions (minimum humanitarian rules in internal armed conflicts) shall not affect the legal status of the parties to the conflict." In other words, application of humanitarian rules in an internal conflict does not depend on the legal status of a rebel group that has taken up arms. Nor does it affect the rights of a people to self-determination; international law provides for the right of people to freely determine their political status and pursue economic, social, and cultural development. Self-determination can take many forms, after all; it does not only imply secession. On the contrary, the goal of self-determination of a particular group may be better advanced by greater integration into society, not separation from it.

Further Reading:

Jackson, Nyamuya Maogoto. *War Crimes and Realpolitik: International Justice from World War I to the 21st Century.* Boulder, Colo.: Lynne Rienner Publishers, 2004.

Jokie, Aleksander. *War Crimes and Collective Wrongdoing: A Reader.* London: Blackwell Publishers, 2001.

Jones, Adam, ed. *Genocide, War Crimes and the West: History and Complicity.* London: Zed Books, 2004.

Meron, Theodor. *War Crimes Law Comes of Age: Essays.* Oxford: Oxford University Press, 1999.

Benenson, Peter (1921–2005) *founder of Amnesty International*

Peter Benenson is one of the world's best-known human rights advocates; his principal achievement was the creation of AMNESTY INTERNATIONAL. When he founded Amnesty International in 1961, inspired by a news account of two Portuguese students who were jailed for toasting liberty, his initiative was dismissed by the British press. One newspaper called it "one of the larger lunacies" of the day. Benenson, who was born to a British Jewish family on July 31, 1921, went on to study at Eton, the famous British public school (actually an elite private school). While studying at Eton, he raised $24,000 to rescue two young Jews from Nazi Germany. Faculty members cited him for his "revolutionary tendencies." He continued his education at Oxford University and later enlisted in the British army during World War II.

After the war, Benenson embarked on a career in law, specializing in labor law. He soon gained an international reputation as a tireless labor and human rights advocate in countries where the rights to organize, assemble, and speak one's mind were severely curtailed. "I became aware that lawyers themselves were not able sufficiently to influence the course of justice in undemocratic countries," he said. "It was necessary to think of a larger group which harnessed the enthusiasm of people all over the world who were anxious to see a wider respect for human rights."

Amnesty International was conceived in a front-page appeal Benenson wrote in the *Observer* titled "The Forgotten Prisoners." As its symbol, Amnesty adopted a candle surrounded by barbed wire. In 1966, however, Benenson distanced himself from the organization, contending that it was being infiltrated by British intelligence and urged it to move its headquarters to a neutral country. His charges were rejected by an independent investigation. After retiring from Amnesty, Benenson dedicated himself to writing and religion. (He had become a convert to Catholicism.) Nonetheless, he never abandoned his advocacy of human rights; in the 1980s he became the chair of the newly created Association of Christians against Torture. He also returned to Amnesty International, albeit in a less official capacity, and continued to speak and campaign on its behalf during the final years of his life.

Further Reading:

Benenson, Peter. *Persecution.* London: Penguin Books, 1961.

Winner, David, and Peter Benenson. *Taking a Stand against Injustice: Amnesty International (People Who Have Helped the World).* Milwaukee: Gareth Stevens Pub., 1992.

Berbers, human rights abuses of

Berbers are a non-Arabic people who have lived for centuries in North Africa. They are ethnically mixed, and while most are Muslim, some are Christian. Berbers, who number approximately 22 million, are found in Morocco (where they make up about 40 percent of the population), Algeria (about 30 percent of the population), and Tunisia (1 percent). They are mainly united by their language, Tamazight (also known as Amazigh). In spite of their numbers, Berbers still face discrimination in Algeria and Morocco. One of the primary grievances is a lack of official recognition for the Berber language and culture; traditionally, Arabic is the only language that can be taught in either country. In April 2002, Berbers staged mass protests in the Kabylie region of Algeria, where they are a majority. The demonstrations were triggered by the death of a Berber high-school student who was shot while he was held in a gendarme (police) barracks. The Berber community refused to believe official claims that the shooting was accidental, especially in light of earlier incidents of harassment of Berber youths by the gendarmes. Although many of the protests were peaceful, several turned violent. Protesters threw stones and Molotov cocktails, destroying public property and commercial buildings. The gendarmes turned on the protesters, opening fire without warning. According to local nongovernmental organizations, more than 90 people were killed, mostly by security forces. The government claimed that only 50 were killed and another 218 wounded. The protests continued sporadically for months and spread to other regions.

Tensions between the Berbers and the Algerian government had been building for years even while the military was waging a bloody war with Islamic militants. The 2002 protests were by no means the first expressions of Berber discontent nor were they the most violent. The first major demonstrations took place in 1980—known as the "Tamazight Spring" uprising—and hundreds of Berbers were subsequently killed in the "Black October" riots of 1988. Riots broke out again in 1998 when the government announced a decree making Arabic the official language.

Hoping to quell further unrest after the 2002 protests, Algerian president Bouteflika announced the creation of a commission to investigate the events. In its report, issued three months later, the commission found that the gendarmes had "kept the pot boiling by shooting live ammunition, ransacking, plundering, provocations of every sort, obscene language, and beatings." Self-defense, the commission agreed, could not justify the gendarmes' actions. The report appears to have had some impact; gendarmes have shown more restraint in their use of live ammunition, and many of the troops involved in the worst abuses of demonstrators have been redeployed, though not necessarily punished.

In spite of the government's moves to defuse tensions, more protests broke out in May and June 2002 in the city of Tizi-Ouzou and in the capital of Algiers, where about half a million Berber demonstrators turned out. Amid the looting and clashes with police that ensued in Algiers, more than 300 were injured, and four were killed. This time the government reacted forcefully. President Bouteflika banned all demonstrations in Algiers "until further notice," and police were deployed on roads leading from Kabylie to prevent demonstrators from reaching Algiers.

In October 2002, in a gesture of reconciliation, the prime minister met with Berber representatives. He announced that the constitution would be amended to make Berber a national language; in addition, he promised that victims of police abuse during the demonstrations would be compensated and the guilty gendarmes punished.

In Morocco, too, Berbers confront similar problems, even though they constitute an even larger proportion of the country's population. About three-quarters of the population is of Berber descent, but most Moroccans—particularly in the cities—speak Arabic. Because so many Berbers and Arabs have intermarried, it is often difficult to distinguish who is a Berber and who is not. Berbers are "people in their own country who don't exist," observed a political leader. Even in Berber areas, classes are taught in Arabic, not Tamazight. All legal documents must be translated into Arabic; Tamazight cannot be used in any legal proceedings. Berbers in Morocco, however, have not reacted as violently to the government's discriminatory practices as their cousins have in Algeria. Under the country's monarch, King Mohamed VI, who ascended to the throne in 1999, there is greater freedom for public discussions of Berber rights. Nonetheless, the government has still imposed restrictions on the Berbers, banning demonstrations and curbing the ability of Berber rights groups to meet. In a gesture to the Berber community King Mohamed has announced the creation of the Royal Institute for Amazigh Culture "to strengthen the pillars of our ancestral identity" and "to give a new impulse to our Amazigh culture, which is a national treasure." The new institute, said the king, would undertake to integrate Amazigh into the educational system. While Berber advocates welcomed the announcement, they remained skeptical, recalling that the Moroccan parliament had approved the formation of a similar national institute for Berber studies in 1978, but nothing came of it. In April 2004, in a show of displeasure at the government's halting progress in securing their rights, Berbers boycotted the presidential elections.

See also ALGERIA, HUMAN RIGHTS VIOLATIONS IN; MOROCCO, HUMAN RIGHTS VIOLATIONS IN.

Bhutan, human rights violations in

The tiny Himalayan country of Bhutan has been governed by a monarchal system without a constitution, although some quasi-democratic institutions do exist, including a National Assembly, a cabinet, and a council of ministers. (A draft constitution has been debated by the National Assembly.) According to the 2004 U.S. State Department *Country Report*, Bhutan's human rights record remained poor. It did note some improvements; there were no cases of arbitrary arrests or detentions, for instance, reported in 2003. Most of the power still resided in King Jigme Singye Wangchuck, and no political parties were permitted to function. Nongovernmental organizations and human rights groups are banned. Fundamental civil freedoms—of speech, press, assembly, and association—are restricted. The government also imposes restrictions on freedom of religion; most of Bhutan's population is Buddhist, and those who do not subscribe to Buddhism face discrimination. For instance, the government requires that all citizens, including minorities, wear traditional Buddhist attire in public places, including government offices and schools. The police have been accused of frequently conducting house-to-house searches for suspected dissidents without legal justification. The media cannot be relied upon to monitor human rights compliance by the monarchy. The country has only one regular publication—a weekly newspaper called *Kuensel,* with a circulation of 15,000 (which also has a daily online edition)—but some human rights groups outside the country say that government ministries review editorial material and suppress or change its content.

Probably Bhutan's most serious human rights issue is a refugee crisis, sparked by tensions between the majority Buddhist population and minority ethnic Nepalese, who make up about a quarter of the population and who are largely Hindu. (Nepal adjoins Bhutan's border.) In the late 1980s and 1990s, approximately 100,000 Nepalese either fled the country or were forced out because of harsh government policies. These refugees have temporarily settled in seven camps in Nepal and another 15,000 have found sanctuary in the Indian states of Assam and West Bengal. Their fate has been the subject of intense negotiations between the two nations ever since. The prospect of their eventual repatriation is in some doubt because of the position taken by Bhutan. The government has contended that many of the refugees were never citizens to begin with and therefore had no right to return, and that some Nepalese had "voluntarily emigrated" and in so doing had forfeited their citizenship.

See also NEPAL, HUMAN RIGHTS VIOLATIONS IN.

Biafra, war crimes in

In 1967 Biafra, an eastern region of Nigeria, declared its independence from Nigeria, setting the stage for a bitter civil war. By the time it ended in 1970, the conflict had claimed an estimated 2 million lives, many of them women and children, and uprooted 3 million people from their homes. As an independent state, Biafra existed only from May 30, 1967, to January 15, 1970. The civil war was the first major test of the integrity of national borders in Africa established by the colonial powers.

Nigeria had been independent for only seven years when simmering ethnic tensions between the majority Yoruba people and the minority Igbo, found largely in Biafra, exploded in violence. War was precipitated by a pair of coups; the first occurred in January 1966 when the commander of the army, Major General Johnson Aguiyi-Ironsi, an Igbo, took power. The favoritism that he exhibited to the Igbos in the east stirred resentment among the northerners, provoking a second coup in July 1967 by army officers, most of whom were Muslim. Ironsi was assassinated and replaced by Lieutenant Colonel Yakubu "Jack" Gowon, a

Christian. In the ensuing chaos, several thousand Igbo were massacred in northern cities. Panicked survivors fled their homes and took refuge in the east. The Muslim officers named 31-year-old Lieutenant Colonel (later Major General) Yakubu Gowon, a Christian from a small ethnic group who wasn't a participant in the coup, as their commander. A new governing body was set up called the Federal Military Government (FMG).

In May 1967 the Biafrans, feeling pushed to the margins by the new regime, declared independence and named Lieutenant Colonel Odemegwu Ojukwu to head the fledgling nation. For the next several months the central government in Lagos tried to find a political solution, but violence intensified and Muslims renewed attacks on Igbo living in the north. The massacres, which claimed 8,000–30,000 lives, accelerated the exodus of Igbos to the eastern region. Ultimately more than 1 million Igbo refugees sought sanctuary in Biafra. At the same time, Igbos in the east carried out massacres of northerners, which impelled survivors to flee in the other direction. (It should be noted that not all the supporters of the Biafran secessionist were Igbos.) The federal government imposed an economic embargo on the secessionist state, which only compounded Biafra's woes. The eastern region had few resources of its own; it was a net importer of food and had little industry, and its economy was largely based on its oil reserves, most of which it would ultimately lose in the war.

At first, though, Biafran troops enjoyed some successes on the battlefield, in spite of the fact that its forces were outgunned and outnumbered. Biafrans also mounted surprise commando attacks, which had the effect of pinning down larger concentration of Nigerian forces. The FMG responded with massive force by air, land, and sea. In September 1968 federal troops captured Owerri, and Gowon announced the "final offensive," but he was being overly optimistic. The Biafrans succeeded in recapturing Owerri and threatened major Nigerian cities.

The Biafrans weren't only waging war on the ground; they were also conducting a surprisingly effective diplomatic campaign for support abroad. Several African countries recognized Biafra's independence, including Tanzania, Zambia, Gabon, and the Ivory Coast, but recognition by the APARTHEID regime of South Africa and colonialist Southern Rhodesia (now Zimbabwe) wasn't quite so welcome. While not formally conferring diplomatic recognition, the Soviet Union became an important backer of Biafra supplying military aid, as did France. Otherwise, Biafra had to buy arms on the open market. On the other side, Britain, the former colonial power, lent its support to the federal government. (The United States, while recognizing the Lagos government, refused to sell arms to either side as long as the fighting continued.)

As the military noose tightened around Biafra, international relief organizations and religious groups conducted a campaign to raise funds for humanitarian assistance. The humanitarian crisis deepened as the war went on; it is thought that about a million civilians died as a result of malnutrition. Starvation was rampant. In October 1969 Ojukwu made a desperate appeal for United Nations mediation, but the federal government refused to accept anything less than unconditional surrender. "Rebel leaders had made it clear that this is a fight to the finish and that no concession will ever satisfy them," Gowon declared. Biafran resistance collapsed, and Ojukwu fled to the Ivory Coast. On January 12 Biafra announced an unconditional cease-fire. How many people actually perished in the war from the fighting, disease, and starvation is unknown, but estimates range from 1 to 3 million. More than 3 million refugees found themselves crowded into a 2,500-square-kilometer (1,000-sq. mi.) enclave. The economy was in shambles and the infrastructure devastated. A massive humanitarian relief aid effort was mounted to tackle the crisis.

In spite of the ferocity of the civil war, the federal government moved swiftly to bring reconciliation to the country, supplying funds to the eastern region to rebuild. Biafran soldiers were reintegrated into the Nigerian army; no trials were held, and few officials in the secessionist regime were imprisoned, though some were dismissed from their posts. The only person whom the government made any attempt to blame was the former Biafran leader Ojukwu, who remained in exile; all efforts to have him extradited failed. Remarkably, within a three-year period, the Biafran state government was able to repair much of the damage sustained in the war, rehabilitating 70 percent of its industrial base.

See also NIGERIA, HUMAN RIGHTS VIOLATIONS IN.

Further Reading:

Ekwe-Ekwe, Herbert. *The Biafra War: Nigeria and the Aftermath.* African Studies, vol. 17. Philadelphia: Edwin Mellen Press, 1990.

Njoku, H. *Tragedy Without Heroes: The Nigeria-Biafra War.* Chicago: Fourth Dimension Publications Ltd., 1987.

Thompson, Joseph E. *American Policy and African Famine: The Nigeria-Biafra War, 1966–1970.* Contributions in Afro-American and African Studies. Westport, Conn.: Greenwood Press, 1990.

Biamby, Philippe   *See* HAITIAN HUMAN RIGHTS VIOLATORS.

Bin Laden, Osama   *See* QAEDA, AL-.

biological weapons

Efforts to rein in the use of biological agents as an instrument of war have a long history that parallels the history of their use. In the 14th century, there are accounts of plague-infected corpses being flung into enemy encampments by catapult, and during the French and Indian War (1754–63) the British colonial army used blankets contaminated with smallpox to infect Indians. In general, however, armies have shied away from the use of biological weapons because of moral, cultural, religious, or military reasons. It was only in the 20th century, however, that serious attempts were made to codify prohibitions against biological weapons. Although most nations ban the production and development of biological organisms for military purposes, the relevant international accords still have many loopholes—enforcement mechanisms are flawed, for instance—and there is growing concern that terrorist groups, such as al-QAEDA, are actively seeking to acquire these weapons. The 2001 anthrax attacks in the United States, which killed five people and severely sickened several more, offers ample evidence that there is still much to be done to control the proliferation of these pathogens. According to U.S. Defense Department estimates, at least 13 countries are currently pursuing biological weapons.

In the immediate aftermath of World War I, chemical and biological weapons were associated with each other in the public mind. Understandably, CHEMICAL WEAPONS dominated the agenda when it came to banning unconventional weapons; the extensive use of poison gas in the war had caused more than 100,000 deaths and over a million injuries. The result was the 1925 Geneva Protocol to the Hague Convention, which prohibited the use of both poison gas and bacteriological agents in warfare. It soon became apparent that the protocol was inadequate, as biological and chemical weapons were still being stockpiled. Attempts at the 1932–37 Disarmament Conference to come to an agreement to halt the production and stockpiling of biological and chemical weapons failed to get anywhere. After World War II broke out, researchers scrambled to develop new and ever more toxic nerve gases and derive deadly biological weapons. "Use of such weapons has been outlawed by the general opinion of civilized mankind," President Franklin Roosevelt declared in a warning to the Axis powers. "This country has not used them and I hope we never will be compelled to use them. I state categorically that we shall under no circumstances resort to the use of such weapons unless they are first used by our enemies." In fact, biological and chemical weapons were not used during World War II, even though experimental work continued on both sides.

Serious efforts to negotiate new accords to cover unconventional weapons (which now included nuclear weapons) began in the early 1960s during meetings of the Eighteen-Nation Disarmament Committee (ENDC). During these sessions, plans were floated to eliminate chemical and biological weapons. Much of the debate centered on whether biological and chemical weapons should be treated separately. Unlike biological weapons, chemical weapons had actually been used in warfare, and many countries had accumulated large stocks of them and were not eager to give them up without ironclad guarantees that other states wouldn't develop or produce them. On the other hand, since biological weapons programs had not advanced nearly as far, it offered neogtiators a more tractable issue to address. The United States argued that there was little sense in delaying a ban on biological weapons while negotiations continued on a ban on chemical weapons. Indeed, it was the United States that took the first significant action to enforce a ban on both types of weapons. In 1969 President Richard Nixon declared that the United States unilaterally renounced first use of lethal or incapacitating chemical agents and weapons while unconditionally repudiating *all* methods of biological warfare. (His decision did not, however, affect research on biological agents that might have a bearing on defense.) The Department of Defense was ordered to draw up a plan for the disposal of existing stocks of biological agents and weapons. On February 14, 1970, the ban was extended to include toxins—those substances that, while acting like chemicals, are ordinarily produced by biological or microbiological processes. Canada, Sweden, and the United Kingdom quickly followed suit and declared that they neither possessed biological weapons nor had any intention of producing any.

But these unilateral initiatives, as welcome as they were, could not substitute for a binding international commitment. After considerable wrangling, in 1972 negotiators reached a new agreement that built on the 1925 Geneva Protocol. Called the Biological Weapons Convention (BWC), the agreement (which was approved by the U.S. Senate two years later) obliges the signatories not to develop, produce, stockpile, or acquire biological agents or toxins "of types and in quantities that have no justification for prophylactic, protective peaceful purposes." It also included all weapons and means of delivery of these weapons. Complaints of a breach of obligations were to be taken up by the UN Security Council. Significantly, the BWC did not only cover the use of biological weapons between states but their use "for hostile purposes or in armed conflict," meaning that the accord applied equally to internal conflicts or terrorism. However, it pointedly did not impose any ban on biological research, even on lethal pathogens. The same technology that could be employed for military objectives could, after all, also be used for medical or biological research.

The accord still had several problems. For one, the BWC is difficult to verify. It allows research and development to take place for "justifiable" reasons, but fails to clarify what "justifiable" actually means. The dual-use nature of biological agents makes it difficult for investigators to detect whether a country is developing a lethal capacity or is pursuing legitimate medical or academic research. Biological agents also pose another danger in that they are usually self-replicating, which means that even the production of a minute amount can quickly generate sufficient quantities for weapon production. In 1992, for example, Russian president Boris Yeltsin admitted that the former Soviet Union had aggressively pursued a biological weapons program. Not long afterward, a special UN commission found evidence of a biological weapons program in Iraq. Negotiations then resumed to strengthen the BWC. Another problem stemmed from the development of other programs that made use of pathogens—coca eradication, for example. The Pentagon has called for using microbes that can destroy certain materials, like oil-consuming microbes.

Moreover, scientists are concerned that scientific advances that have been made since the treaty was signed are outstripping its provisions, citing the mapping of the human genome, new gene therapies and drug delivery systems, and genetic engineering experiments, all of which might have hostile uses. In one alarming incident, Australian scientists accidentally created a lethal organism when they added a gene they believed to be "harmless" to a mousepox virus during an experiment.

See also AMHERST, JEFFREY AMHERST, FIRST BARON; HAGUE CONVENTIONS.

Further Reading:

Alibek, Ken, and Stephen Handelman. *Biohazard: The Chilling True Story of the Largest Covert Biological Weapons Program in the World—Told from Inside by the Man Who Ran It.* New York: Delta, 2000.

Barnaby, Frank. *How to Build a Nuclear Bomb: And Other Weapons of Mass Destruction.* New York: Nation Books, 2004.

Guillemin, Jeanette. *Biological Weapons.* Columbia Contemporary Issues in National Security Policy. New York: Columbia University Press, 2005.

Langford, R. Everett. *Introduction to Weapons of Mass Destruction: Radiological, Chemical, and Biological.* New York: Wiley-Interscience, 2004.

Lederberg, Joshua, ed. *Biological Weapons: Limiting the Threat.* BCSIA Studies in International Security. Cambridge, Mass.: MIT Press, 1999.

Mangold, Tom, and Jeff Goldberg. *Plague Wars: The Terrifying Reality of Biological Warfare.* New York: St. Martin's Press, 2001.

Blagojević, Vidoje   *See* WAR CRIMINALS OF THE FORMER YUGOSLAVIA.

Blaškić, Tihomir   *See* WAR CRIMINALS OF THE FORMER YUGOSLAVIA.

Bokassa, Jean-Bédel (1921–1996) *emperor of the Central African Republic*

A megalomaniac despot and alleged cannibal, Jean-Bédel Bokassa presided over the impoverished Central African Republic (which he renamed Central African Empire) from 1966 to 1979 before being driven into exile. Born in 1921, he was orphaned at age six after his father, a village chief, was murdered and his mother killed herself. He was subsequently raised by missionaries in what was then a French colony. Like thousands of African and North African Arabs, he joined the Free French forces in 1939 and in 1944 took part in the invasion of Provence, France, which was then under Vichy control. After the war he distinguished himself in combat missions in Indochina and Algeria, earning both the Légion d'Honneur and the Croix de Guerre. He left the French army with the rank of captain in 1961, a year after the country achieved independence. He then assumed command of the new army, a position he used to advance his own ambitions.

In 1966, promising "the abolition of the bourgeoisie," Bokassa instigated a coup against his cousin, President David Dacko, and assumed power. In 1972 he declared himself president for life. Still not satisfied, he crowned himself emperor, emulating the example of Napoléon, and renamed his country the Central African Empire. He could have been dismissed as a buffoon if it were not for the atrocities he committed to maintain his power. In the most heinous incident, 100 schoolchildren were massacred in prison in May 1979. They had been locked up for the "crime" of protesting against the increased costs of school uniforms. In the aftermath of the massacre, rumors spread that Bokassa had taken part in the slaughter and had even eaten some of the victims, whose body parts he stored in a refrigerator at his palace. Bokassa professed his innocence, contending that as a devout Christian (in spite of a brief flirtation with Islam) and as the father of a large family himself, he could never have harmed children. He was not exaggerating about having a large family; he is said to have had 55 children by no fewer than 17 wives.

Nonetheless, he could hardly dispute the fact that the schoolchildren had been killed. Worldwide outrage spurred the former colonial power to action. Later that year, in a coup backed by French paratroopers, the former president Dacko ousted Bokassa (then on a visit to Libya) and returned to power. Bokassa tried to seek exile in France,

but he was denied permission. Nonetheless, he indirectly ended up influencing the election for the French presidency. In the run-up to elections, a scandal erupted that centered on a gift of diamonds that Bokassa had presented to then-president Valéry Giscard d'Estaing, who was seeking a second term. The resulting furor contributed to Giscard d'Estaing's defeat in 1981 by his Socialist rival, François Mitterrand. (Ironically, Giscard d'Estaing had supported the coup that removed Bokassa from power.)

Bokassa remained in the Ivory Coast for four years before the French finally relented and permitted him to settle at a home he owned outside of Paris. In 1986 he unexpectedly returned to the Central African Republic (which had reverted to its original name), even though he had been sentenced to death in absentia. He was immediately arrested on charges of torture, murder, and cannibalism—crimes that he was accused of carrying out during the 14 years he held power. His sentence of death was later commuted to life imprisonment and then reduced to 20 years in prison. In 1993, however, he was granted amnesty and freed. He retired to a villa in the capital, Bangui, where he died of a heart attack three years later at the age of 75. One of his 55 sons reported that he had been "lucid" until the end. In spite of his crimes, the government held a state funeral for him.

Bolivia, human rights violations in

Bolivia is a landlocked, impoverished South American country whose political fate has long been inextricably bound up with cocoa production. Since gaining independence from the Spanish in 1825, the country has rarely experienced a prolonged period of stability; its history has been characterized by revolutions, coups, civil wars, and wars with its neighbors. Even though the current government of Carlos Mesa is credited with making some progress in guaranteeing human rights, serious abuses on the part of security forces persist.

In October 2003 President Sánchez de Lozada was forced out of office by violent protests triggered by his decision to build a controversial natural-gas pipeline. The gas was to be shipped from Bolivia to a Chilean port and sold to the United States and Mexico. The majority of Bolivians believed that the pipeline would enrich a small elite. In September 2003 thousands took to the streets, and in two months of violent protests, several people were killed; estimates of fatalities range from 59 to more than 80. In one day alone—October 12—26 civilians were killed in El Alto, a poor industrial city outside of the capital, La Paz. Another 14 protesters were shot and killed in La Paz by security forces. (In a subsequent referendum, conducted in 2004, a majority of Bolivian voters supported the pipeline.)

Although efforts have been made in the Bolivian congress to conduct a "trial of responsibilities" to hold accountable the perpetrators of the violence, the military has shown little sign of cooperating with investigators. In a letter to President Carlos Mesa (who assumed power after Lozada stepped down), HUMAN RIGHTS WATCH expressed its concern that the military courts might intervene. Military courts in Bolivia have a reputation for acquitting their own in similar cases involving civilian deaths. The military intervention has resulted in "a perception of impunity," Human Rights Watch said. Various government bodies, including the Ombudsman's office and the Ministry of Justice, as well as nongovernmental organizations continued to press the government to take action in the cases. Nonetheless, the precedent is not reassuring. Many other incidents—the killing of 31 people in February 2002 during and after a riot in La Paz, for instance—has never been thoroughly investigated, and there is little likelihood that this will happen in the future since military courts have assumed jurisdiction.

As in the case of natural gas, disputes over another natural resource—coca—have also provoked violence. Since 1995, Washington has pushed the Bolivian government to pursue an aggressive coca eradication effort. Predictably, coca growers have resisted the threat to their livelihood. Over several years the principal coca-growing region of Chapare has been the scene of sporadic violence. In response, the government has cracked down on the farmers, accounting for serious human rights abuses, including the excessive use of force, arbitrary detention, and suppression of peaceful demonstrations. Most of the abuse in Chapare has been attributed to the Mobile Rural Patrol Unit, the rural antinarcotics police. The government maintains that it is only trying to enforce the law, but some human rights groups have blamed the eradication program for the abuses. In January 2003 events came to a head when thousands of demonstrators broke into the offices of the General Coca Directorate and swept into the main market, setting cars ablaze and damaging other property. The police responded with tear gas, rubber bullets, and live ammunition. Over the following days the violence continued to escalate, resulting in the killing of five security troops. At the same time police and security forces reportedly tortured some of the demonstrators taken into custody.

In spite of recent moves by the government to institute reform, the judicial system remains largely dysfunctional and riddled with corruption and inefficiency; arbitrary arrests and protracted detentions are common, prison conditions are harsh, and violence inside the prisons is endemic, accounting for several deaths annually. With the exception of one maximum security prison, the security forces have for all practical purposes abandoned authority over the prison system, guarding only the outer walls. Inside the walls, though, prison officials and prisoners vie for control. Child labor is a major problem in this poor country, and workers are subjected to brutal conditions in the mining industry. Bolivia was thrown into turmoil in January 2005 when protests erupted against privatization of the public water system. The unrest, which began in the city of El Alto, precipitated a new political crisis. President Carlos Mesa was forced to quit in June after weeks of mass demonstrations against his government and blockades that paralyzed the country. Interim President Eduardo Rodriguez promised to hand over power to an elected president before the year was out. The presidential campaign was joined by representatives of two diametrically opposed ideologies: a U.S.-educated industrial engineer, Jorge "Tuto" Quiroga, who had the backing of business, and an Aymara Indian, Evo Morales, whose main support came from Indian coca growers. In December 2005 Morales was elected president.

See also OPERATION CONDOR.

Further Reading:

Grindle, Merilee S., and Pilar Domingo. *Proclaiming Revolution: Bolivia in Comparative Perspective.* David Rockefeller Center Series on Latin American Studies. Cambridge, Mass.: Harvard University Press, 2003.

Gutierrez, Alberto Ostria. *The Tragedy of Bolivia: A People Crucified.* Westport, Conn.: Greenwood Press, 1981.

Lopez Levy, Marcela. *Bolivia.* Oxfam Country Profiles. London: Oxfam, 2001.

bombardment, bombing   *See* CARPET BOMBING.

Bormann, Martin (1900–1945?) *German chancellor*
The head of the Nazi Party Chancellery, private secretary and confidant of Adolf HITLER, Martin Bormann is known to history as the "shadow man" because he exercised power behind the scenes and became, in effect, Hitler's shadow. He was such a masterful intriguer that by the end of World War II he was second in importance only to Hitler in the Nazi hierarchy. Bormann was born in the town of Halberstadt on June 17, 1900. After World War I, in which he had served briefly in an artillery regiment, he gravitated to right-wing organizations. He was arrested in connection with the slaying of his former elementary school teacher, who had betrayed a right-wing extremist figure to French occupation authorities in the Ruhr.

Incarceration did nothing to temper Bormann's extremist political tendencies. After his release in 1928, he joined the elite Sturm Abteilung (SA) Supreme Command of the Nazi Party, and in 1933, the year the Nazis came to power in Germany, he was promoted to Reichsleiter. In the same year he was appointed as the chief of cabinet in the office of the deputy führer, Rudolf HESS, acting as his personal secretary and right-hand man. Bormann knew how to play the part of the model secretary, an obscure bureaucrat; he was unremarkable in appearance, being both short and squat. But his diligence, competence, and adaptability caused other Nazi officials to underestimate him. As he outmaneuvered rivals, he also ingratiated himself with Hitler. A superb fund-raiser, he took charge of the Adolf Hitler Endowment Fund to which German business heads were obliged to contribute. In 1941 his superior Rudolf Hess absconded to Britain for reasons that are still not quite clear. His departure, however, allowed Bormann to take his place, putting even greater power in his hands.

In his new capacity, Bormann was responsible for appointments and promotions. He dealt with questions of security and assumed the role of guardian of Nazi orthodoxy. No one in the party was more anticlerical than Bormann. In his view, the Christian churches represented a threat to the Nazi hold on power that, he said, "must absolutely and finally be broken." He initiated the *Kirchenkampf*—the "war between the churches." He also loathed the Slavs, whom he referred to as a "Sovietized mass" of subhumans. As more and more Russians fell under German control, he determined that there was only one thing to be done with them. In August 1942 he wrote a memo in which he declared: "The Slavs are to work for us. In so far as we do not need them, they may die. Slav fertility is not desirable."

But it was the Jews whom Bormann reviled most of all. At first he ordered the deportation of European Jews under the pretext that they were needed to supply labor. By 1942, though, he saw no reason to disguise the truth about the fate that lay in store for the millions of Jews in the countries Germany occupied. On October 9, 1942, he signed a decree in which he proclaimed that "the permanent elimination of the Jews from the territories of Greater Germany can no longer be carried out by emigration but by the use of ruthless force in the special camps of the East." On July 1, 1943, he signed another decree giving Adolf EICHMANN and the GESTAPO complete power over Jewish affairs. Hitler came to depend more and more on Bormann, who simplified things for the German leader and relieved him from paperwork. He set up Hitler's appointment calendar and decided whom the führer would or would not see. Calling him "my most loyal Party comrade," Hitler had even served as a witness at Bormann's 1929 wedding to Gerda Buch, a rabid Nazi in her own right, and later became godfather to Bormann's son, Martin Junior. (For Christmas 1939 Hitler had given his godson a box of toy soldiers and a model antiaircraft gun.) In 1945, when the Red Army was already in the streets of Berlin, Bormann reciprocated by serving as witness at Hitler's marriage to Eva Braun, the day before the newlyweds committed joint suicide. Hitler did not demand that Bormann follow his example; instead he urged his deputy "to put the interests of the nation before his own feelings" and to save himself.

On April 30, 1945, Bormann left Hitler's bunker. What happened to him after that is still disputed. According to Hitler's chauffeur, Bormann was killed by a shell as he was trying to cross Soviet lines. Hitler youth leader Artur Axmann claimed that Bormann had committed suicide and said he'd seen Bormann's body on May 2. In 1946, however, several witnesses asserted that they had seen him in a northern Italian monastery. Then rumors began to circulate that he had escaped to South America and had settled in Argentina, although there were also sightings of him in Brazil, Paraguay, and Chile.

On October 29, 1945, Bormann was indicted in absentia by the International Military Tribunal at Nuremberg, better known as the NUREMBERG TRIALS. He was sentenced to death—also in absentia—on October 1, 1946. A West German court officially declared him dead in April 1973. His wife had died of cancer in 1946, but his 10 children all survived the war. The eldest, Martin Junior, Hitler's godson, recalled his father fondly, calling him a "strict but loving" man.

Further Reading:

Russell of Liverpool, Edward Frederick, Langley, Baron. *The Scourge of the Swastika: A Short History of Nazi War Crimes.* London: Greenhill Books/Lionel Leventhal, 2002.

Bosnia and Herzegovina, human rights violations in

The Federation of Bosnia and Herzegovina and the Republika Srpska (RS) is a creation of the 1995 General Framework Agreement for Peace in Bosnia and Herzegovina established by the DAYTON ACCORDS, which ended the 1991–95 war in the Balkans. Until the war the Federation had been one of the constituent republics of the former Yugoslavia. The two entities were created to take into account the region's bitter ethnic division; the Federation has a postwar Bosnian Muslim (Bosniak) and Croat majority, while the RS is dominated by a postwar Bosnian Serb majority. In 2003 a new government took power based on the results of elections held the previous November. The coalition is made up of nationalist parties from all three groups, none of which, according to a report by the Helsinki Committee, a human rights–monitoring group, showed much inclination to undertake major reforms to ameliorate ethnic and political divisions or take steps necessary to improve the economy. Peace has been maintained by a force of 31,000 NATO peacekeepers called the Stabilization Force, or SFOR, which at the end of 2004 was replaced by a contingent of troops from the European Union.

The three parties have exploited nationalist and ethnic passions to consolidate their power, fueling restiveness and

A Muslim family in Bosnia stands in front of their destroyed home. *(United Nations)*

occasional acts of violence. The Helsinki Committee charges that extremists are under the impression that they will not be punished for flouting the law. In many cases, religious leaders from all three communities have exacerbated tensions by encouraging xenophobia. In spite of the presence of SFOR, violent incidents continue to occur between members of different ethnic groups or political parties. Although the law allows for the creation of an ombudsman of Bosnia and Herzegovina who would be charged with alleviating ethnic tensions, the government has failed to follow up in any serious way. In light of this failure, it is not surprising that severe discrimination exists against ethnic minorities especially in areas dominated by Serb and Croat ethnic groups.

The government's human rights record remained poor, although some gains have been noted in recent years. The degree of respect for human rights continues to vary among the Bosnian Muslim, Bosnian Croat, and Bosnian Serb populations. In spite of constitutional prohibitions against torture and mistreatment, abuses of suspects and detainees

by police persists although the incidence of cases of arbitrary arrest and detention has diminished. Of the 193 incidents of police misconduct reported during the period from April 1 to June 30, 2001, 113 involved officers from the Federation, 78 from the RS. Such cases included assault, beatings while in custody, excessive use of force, harassment, police inaction, illegal detention, restriction of movement, improper seizures, abductions, sexual assaults, negligence, corruption, and abuse of power.

At the same time, cases of abuse by police are infrequently investigated. Those officers who were successfully prosecuted usually received mild punishments. Moreover, victims of police abuse are often reluctant to report the abuse out of fear of reprisal. The RS has retained the old communist practice of holding suspects for up to six months without bringing formal charges but the Federation has cut the pre-arraignment time to three days.

Authorities and dominant political parties in all three communities continue to maintain influence over the media and restrict freedom of speech and the press, although the degree of restriction varies. Some limits are still placed on freedom of assembly.

According to the Helsinki Committee, the Federation has made progress in restoring property to REFUGEES and people displaced by the war. About 90 percent of property appropriated or abandoned during the war (representing 224,000 claims) was returned to its prewar owners by the end of 2003. (The overall numbers are somewhat deceptive since some regions have proven slow to return property. Some municipalities, for instance, have only returned 7 percent of the property to its prewar owners.) The pace of restoration quickened dramatically in 2003 after years of obstruction and discrimination. However, the pace of return by refugees and displaced persons has lagged behind the rate at which property is being returned. Under provisions of the Peace Agreement, 55,687 persons returned in 2003 to their prewar homes (down from 85,189 the previous year), of which 28,470 to the Federation and 24,928 to the Republika Srpska. (Another 2,289 returned to a separate enclave called Brčko District.)

To a great extent, the future of the Federation and Republika Srpska is predicated on the willingness of its governments and their peoples to come to terms with the past. It is impossible to escape the legacy of the wars. During the 1992–95 conflicts an estimated 1 million land mines were planted in the country, many of which remain in place. Since 1995, land mines have killed 318 persons, 34 during 2002 alone. Information on thousands of people missing during the war is still difficult to come by.

Since the establishment of the INTERNATIONAL CRIMINAL TRIBUNAL FOR THE FORMER YUGOSLAVIA (ICTY) in 1993, several attempts have been made to bring to account perpetrators of crimes committed in Bosnia and Herzegovina in those wars. According to the Helsinki Committee, individuals are still wanted on charges related to their responsibility for up to 8,000 killed by the Bosnian Serb army after the fall of Srebrenica, in addition to those responsible for up to 13,000 other people still missing and presumed killed as a result of "ethnic cleansing" in Bosnia. Two of the most notorious criminals—Radovan KARADŽIĆ and Ratko MLADIĆ—are still at large. Until Karadžić, who was the head of the Bosnian Serb paramilitaries, and Mladić, former commander of Serb forces, are brought to justice, normalization of relations both within the country and with the international community cannot take place. Although the RS parliament passed a law on cooperation with the ICTY, the Bosnian Serb government has failed to turn over any suspects to the court, which is based in The Hague. Some war criminals have been arrested and tried in the Bosnian courts, however. There has also been an increasing willingness on the part of Serb, Croat, and Bosniak (Bosnian Muslim) suspects in war crimes to surrender voluntarily. Certainly the most signal success to date

has been the arrest of former Yugoslav president Slobodan MILOŠEVIĆ, who is accused of being principally responsible for the war in Bosnia and Herzegovina.

See also RELIGIOUS PERSECUTION; SARAJEVO, SIEGE OF; TUDJMAN, FRANJO; YUGOSLAVIA, WAR CRIMES IN.

Further Reading:
Glenny, Misha. *The Fall of Yugoslavia: The Third Balkan War*. New York: Penguin Books, 1996.
Hagan, John. *Justice in the Balkans: Prosecuting War Crimes in the Hague Tribunal*. Chicago Series in Law and Society. Chicago: University of Chicago Press, 2003.
Harris, Nathaniel. *The War in Former Yugoslavia*. New Perspectives. London: Hodder & Stoughton, 1997.
Mertus, Julie. *Former Yugoslavia: War Crimes Trials in the Former Yugoslavia*. Helsinki: Human Rights Watch/Helsinki, 1995.
Rossanet, Bertrand de. *War and Peace in the Former Yugoslavia*. Boston: Martinus Nijhoff, 1997.

Bousquet, René (1909–1998) *French war collaborator*
A promising young government official, René Bousquet was named secretary-general of police in April 1941 by Pierre Laval, who headed the collaborationist French state of Vichy (the collaborationist government formed after Nazi Germany invaded France). In his new position Bousquet, who was 41, helped the Germans round up and deport Jews, but later he fell out with the Nazis and was forced to leave his post at the end of 1943. He had the good fortune of being arrested by the GESTAPO in 1944, just before the Normandy invasion in 1944, which allowed him a convenient alibi. He was arrested by the Allies and tried for collaboration but only received a five-year suspended sentence. In 1949, a so-called purge court, which was charged with rooting out former collaborators, determined that Bousquet, far from being a traitor, had "rendered important services to the Resistance." At the time, Bousquet insisted that as a police official he had had nothing to do with Jews.

Bousquet went on to become a successful businessman. But his victims and their families had not forgotten him. An association of Jewish children, deported during World War II, filed a complaint against him, alleging that he was guilty of crimes against humanity. The lawyer representing the group—the Association of Sons and Daughters of Jews Deported from France—was the renowned Nazi hunter, Serge KLARSFELD. He accused Bousquet, then 80, of culpability for the deaths of 194 Jewish children. Although twice indicted (in 1976 and 1988), Bosquet had never been tried before. "What we are seeking through this trial," Klarsfeld stated at a press conference, "is the condemnation of the

Vichy regime in its most odious aspect: the deportation of children." Klarsfeld explained his move by saying that it was necessary after the French judicial system had failed to act. (Under French law, the victims of the Nazis are entitled to bring complaints alleging war crimes; it is up to magistrates to determine whether the charges should be pursued.) As evidence of Bousquet's guilt, Klarsfeld cited hitherto undiscovered documents indicating that Bousquet had telegrammed local police chiefs, ordering them to lift an exemption against the deportation of Jewish children under age 18. In another telegram he wrote: "The head of the government wants you to personally supervise the control of the measures decided against the foreign Jews. You should not hesitate to break any resistance encountered within the population and report the officers who by their passivity, ill will or indiscretion have complicated your task."

There was considerable resistance toward reopening the case against Bousquet. François Mitterrand, then the French president, said that the case could "prove harmful to the civil peace," indicating a reluctance to confront the crimes of Vichy France (with which Mitterrand himself had been associated). Even leading figures in the French Jewish community called for an end to prosecutions, saying that it was preferable to educate future generations to avoid a repetition of the Holocaust. The Paris Court of Appeals nonetheless indicted Bousquet for crimes against humanity. In 1998 Bousquet's life came to a violent end when he was assassinated by a French writer named Christian Didier.

Brandt, Karl (1904–1948) *German physician*

Karl Brandt, who had served as Adolf HITLER's personal physician, was one of the doctors convicted in the DOCTORS' TRIAL in the NUREMBERG TRIALS for criminal MEDICAL EXPERIMENTS conducted on concentration camp inmates. Born in Alsace (then in Germany), Brandt became a medical doctor in 1928. In 1932 he joined the NSDAP (the Nazi Party), becoming a member of the SA (Sturm Abteilung) a year later and a member of the SS (Schutzstaffel) in 1934. In summer 1934 he was appointed Hitler's "escort physician," and he went on to secure ever more prestigious positions in the SS. By January 1943 he was a major general.

In August 1944 Brandt was appointed as the Reich's commissioner for sanitation and health, which put him in charge of the medical organizations of the government as well as the health services of the party and the armed forces. He was also responsible for carrying out the Nazi EUTHANASIA PROGRAM that had begun in 1939. The euthanasia program is of special importance in German history because it represents the first step in what was to become a systematic genocidal program to eliminate entire groups of people, including Jews and Romanies. Brandt

took action even though no legal basis existed for the program at the time. The first case in 1938 involved a child known as "Baby Knauer." The child's father had appealed to Hitler to put his son to death because the child was blind, retarded, and missing an arm and a leg. Hitler turned the case over to Brandt, who decided to comply with the father's wishes. A committee was then established to examine how other such children could be administered "mercy deaths." Disabled children were placed in a hospital at Eglfing Haar and starved until they died of "natural causes." Soon other institutions were also used for the same purpose. Medical personnel who expressed misgivings were reassured that by withholding treatment, they were only "letting nature take its course."

In 1939 Hitler officially sanctioned the euthanasia program in a letter that stated: "Reichleader Bouhler and Dr. Med. Brandt are responsibly commissioned to extend the authority of physicians to be designated by name so that a mercy death may be granted to patients who, according to human judgment, are incurably ill according to the most critical evaluation of the state of their disease." The program was extended from retarded, disabled, or incurably ill children to the elderly and the mentally ill, all of whom were classified as "useless eaters" and a burden to society.

Before the end of the war, Brandt fell out of favor with the Nazi regime, and in April he was placed under arrest by the GESTAPO and condemned to death by a Berlin court. Admiral Karl DÖNITZ, who had taken over the dying Reich after Hitler's suicide, ordered the release of Brandt but he had little time to enjoy his freedom. On May 23, 1945, he was arrested again, this time by the British. He went on trial in October 1946 at the Palace of Justice in Nuremberg with 23 other Nazi physicians and scientists. Although known to history as the Doctors' Trial, the case was officially designated *United States of America v. Karl Brandt et al.* He was accused of having "special responsibility for, and participation in, Freezing, Malaria, Lost Gas, Sulfanilamide, Bone, Muscle and Nerve Regeneration and Bone Transplantation, Sea-Water, Epidemic Jaundice, Sterilization, and Typhus Experiments . . . [also] in connection with the planning and carrying out of the Nazi's T-4 Euthanasia Program of the German Reich . . . [and] with membership in the SS." In his defense he declared: "The underlying motive was the desire to help individuals who could not help themselves and were thus prolonging their lives in torment. . . . I never intended anything more than or believed I was doing anything but abbreviating the tortured existence of such unhappy creatures." He said that he only regretted that he may have caused pain to the families of the dead. Even so, he asserted, "I am convinced that today they have overcome their distress and personally believe that the dead members of their families were given a happy release from their sufferings."

Brandt's justification failed to sway the judges. On August 19, 1947, he and six other defendants were sentenced to death by hanging. The sentences were carried out in Landsberg Prison on June 2, 1948.

Further Reading:
Buscher, Frank. M. *The U.S. War Crimes Trial Program in Germany, 1946–1955.* Contributions in Military Studies. Westport, Conn.: Greenwood Press, 1989.
Russell of Liverpool, Edward Frederick Langley, Baron. *The Scourge of the Swastika: A Short History of Nazi War Crimes.* London: Greenhill Books/Lionel Leventhal, 2002.
Weindling, Paul Julian. *Nazi Medicine and the Nuremberg Trials: From Medical War Crimes to Informed Consent.* Sydney, Australia: Palgrave Macmillan, 2005.

Brazil, human rights violations in

Brazil is a functioning democracy and one of the world's largest, most populous countries. In 2002 Luiz Inácio Lula da Silva (known as Lulu) was elected president, the first leader of the left-leaning Workers' Party, which had never before achieved national power. Lulu's victory was widely seen by millions of his supporters as ushering in a new era of human rights and economic justice, but practical concerns and the need to reassure international financial institutions have hampered his ability to introduce reforms as quickly as many Brazilians had hoped. There are also some detractors who express skepticism as to whether he will ever fulfill the progressive program he espoused during his campaign for office.

Although the federal government generally respects the human rights of its citizens, serious abuses continue to occur with disturbing frequency. The U.S. State Department's 2003 *Country Report* notes a pattern of extrajudicial killings, torture, beatings of suspects, and arbitrary arrests on the part of many state police forces (both civil and military). The police were also implicated in a variety of criminal activities; some officers have been known to moonlight as hired killers who undertake kidnappings for ransom, participate in death squads, and engage in illegal drug trafficking. There is little evidence that the federal police take action to investigate reports of abuses by renegade state police forces.

EXTRAJUDICIAL KILLINGS by both civil and military state police do not only involve suspected criminals. Civilians, including children, have also been victims. Land reform activists, environmentalists, and indigenous peoples in rural areas are at particular risk for summary executions carried out by police or by gunmen hired by local landowners. In 2002 the police ombudsman of São Paulo (with a population of about 10 million) reported that 825 people had been killed by police under suspicious circumstances. The spate of police homicides has become so embarrassing that in 2000 the Rio de Janeiro state government simply stopped releasing the statistics altogether. Even in cases where data are released, such as São Paulo, nongovernmental organizations suspect that the numbers are deliberately falsified to make them seem lower. Research conducted by the Institute for Religious Studies (ISER) in the mid-1990s, for instance, cited 40 cases in Rio de Janeiro alone which suggested that police first immobilized the victims and then shot them at point-blank range—usually in the back.

In the *Report on Extra-Judicial and Summary Execution* released in 2004, based on a survey of eight states, the United Nations special rapporteur stated that the "use of deadly police violence against civilians is rife" in Brazil. Among the victims were two witnesses who had been interviewed by the special rapporteur. The report cited the lack of independent oversight, failure to provide for independent forensic research, and a failure on the part of the public prosecutor's office to investigate abuses.

Even when investigations of human rights abuses by police do occur, they are limited to internal police reviews and are not referred to the Office of the Public Prosecutor. This "climate of impunity," as the U.S. State Department calls it, flourishes especially in the military police tribunals, which function outside the civilian judicial system and where abuses are seldom investigated. Prison conditions, the report observes, "ranged from poor to extremely harsh." The prisons are overcrowded and filthy. "The use of torture and ill-treatment remained widespread and systematic throughout the criminal justice system at point of arrest, in police stations and prisons as well as in juvenile detention centers," stated AMNESTY INTERNATIONAL in its 2002 report on Brazil. (In 2002 there were approximately 10,000 juveniles in detention in the country.) Large-scale riots have broken out in prisons, often with considerable loss of life among the prisoners. Inmates are frequently beaten and tortured, and prisoners are often held for unconscionable lengths of time without their cases coming to trial. In certain regions of the country, people who face criminal charges have little chance of getting a fair trial even when their cases are heard. Local judges are often subject to pressure from powerful economic interests. To address some of these problems, the Workers' Party government has established a National Human Rights Program, which is intended to focus on social, cultural, and economic rights. Further, in an effort to curb abuses by state police, the Brazilian congress enacted into law a presidential decree giving federal police authority to intervene at the state level in certain human rights cases and in politically motivated kidnappings. Nevertheless, there was scant evidence that the federal police actually exercised their new powers.

Discrimination against a number of groups also remains a difficult problem, especially in a country of such diversity. (Brazil is made up of a mixture of people of European and African ancestry and indigenous Amerindians.) Federal and state governments have come under criticism by human rights groups for failing to protect women, children, Afro-Brazilians, and homosexuals. But perhaps no segment of the population has faced more discrimination and human rights abuses than Brazil's indigenous population, whose lands have been appropriated by outsiders. Human rights activists who have tried to mobilize the Indians into demanding their rights have been harassed and killed.

Like many of its Latin neighbors, including Chile, Uruguay, and Argentina, Brazil endured a military dictatorship during the 1970s that was responsible for widespread extrajudicial killings, torture, and DISAPPEARANCES. The officials responsible for the worst excesses, however, have not been called to account because of immunity laws. In 1968 hard-line military officers seized power in a coup, ostensibly to combat a violent leftist insurgency, and then instituted a crackdown on political opponents. Thousands were tortured, and several hundred are thought to have been killed. The military took control over labor unions and purged universities of ideologically suspect faculty members. The repressive regime caused many of the country's best-known intellectuals and artists to flee into exile. A more moderate military regime under General Ernesto Geisel came to power in 1973 in response to mounting pressure for a restoration of democracy. In 1979, under the presidency of General João Baptista Figueiredo, the government significantly relaxed its grip; a general amnesty was declared for all political crimes committed since 1964, the last political prisoners were freed, and the media were allowed to function without censorship. But the amnesty was double-edged; while it applied to former leftist guerrillas and allowed exiles to return to Brazil without fear of retribution, it also conferred immunity on the military and police officers guilty of torture, disappearances, extrajudicial slayings, and other crimes.

Atrocities committed under military rule continue to come to light, threatening to reopen old wounds. In 2004 several bodies were exhumed in a remote part of the southwest region of the Amazon, a grisly legacy of a clandestine war by government forces against communist guerrillas between 1970 and 1974. In what became known as the Araguaia guerrilla war, Brazilian forces pursued Maoist insurgents through the jungles in carrying out what has been described as a deliberate policy of extermination. Civilians caught in the middle of the fighting were also killed, and hundreds more were uprooted from their homes. Most of those they captured were subsequently executed, some by beheading. According to a book on the case published in Brazil, the government had decided on a policy of killing all the rebels rather than taking them prisoner. "This business of killing people is a barbarity, but I think it has to be done," General Geisel said early in 1974. "We can't let go of this war."

In July 2003 a federal judge ordered the military to provide relatives of the deceased with information related to the circumstances of their slayings and the location of their graves. To the distress of supporters of the Workers' Party, the government moved to block the release of the information. Some observers believe that it was an attempt by the new government to solidify relations with the military. An announcement by the government that it would set up a commission to investigate the guerrillas' deaths failed to appease critics who pointed out that there was no enforcement mechanism to bring perpetrators of the killings to justice. "The creation of this commission serves to protect those who apprehended, killed and disappeared opponents of the dictatorship," said the head of the human rights group Torture Never Again, who went on to charge the government with "strengthening impunity in our country."

Nonetheless, da Silva's government, following the example of its predecessors over the last three decades, continues to resist a full accounting of the episode. In 2005 yet more new documents came to light that revealed more about Brazil's dictatorship. One crate opened by the former director of the government's Special Commission on the Death and Disappearance of Political Prisoners revealed not only papers but almost a complete skeleton of a guerrilla killed by security forces 30 years previously in the Amazon. The documents, long concealed and thought destroyed, represented only a part of a cover-up that also involved the vandalization of cemeteries, the destruction of bodies of victims slain in extrajudicial killings, and the coercion of witnesses. Whether these documents should be made public was a subject of intense debate. Da Silva's national security chief, General Jorge Armando Félix, warned that "some dossiers worry us, because they deal with people in extremely embarrassing situations" and added that "nobody should know about this except with the authorization of the person involved." Human rights advocates, by contrast, call for the "complete, unrestricted and immediate" opening of all files and the establishment of museums and other institutions where all citizens can have access to documents and other material relating to a shameful episode in the country's history.

See also OPERATION CONDOR.

Further Reading:

Levine, Robert M. *The History of Brazil.* Greenwood Histories of the Modern Nations. Sydney, Australia: Palgrave Macmillan, 2003.

Veloso, Caetano. *Tropical Truth: A Story of Music and Revolution in Brazil.* New York: Knopf, 2002.

Brunner, Alois (1912–?) *Nazi mass murderer*

During World War II, SS Hauptsturmführer Alois Brunner acted as second in command to Adolf EICHMANN, who carried out the systematic execution of millions of European Jews in the FINAL SOLUTION. Brunner functioned as something of a troubleshooter in occupied areas, especially in France, and was charged with expediting the killings. Personally, Brunner has been implicated in the deportation of 128,500 Jews from Nazi-occupied Europe to their deaths in concentration camps. Born in Austria in 1912, he joined the Austrian Nazi Party in 1931 at the age of 19. He was such a rabid anti-Semite that he was put in charge of the Nazis' Jewish affairs office (officially known as the Central Office for Jewish Emigration) in prewar Vienna and later became Eichmann's private secretary; he was so loyal that he was called Eichmann's right-hand man.

At the beginning of World War II, Brunner supervised the deportation of 47,000 Austrian Jews to the concentration camps. He was then relocated to Berlin to organize mass roundups there and subsequently transferred to Greece, where he was responsible for deporting all 43,000 Jews in the city of Salonika in just two months. His next assignment, in June 1943, took him to France, where he was given the command of the Drancy transit camp near Paris, a position he was to hold for 14 months. In France he organized the deportation of some 25,000 men, women, and children to their deaths. He was also responsible for sending the Jewish children of IZIEU to their deaths in Auschwitz.

After the end of the war, Brunner secured employment with the CIA thanks to Reinhard Gehlen, former head of the German anti-Soviet intelligence network who offered Brunner's services to the Allies. (Gehlen was chief of West Germany's Federal Intelligence Service from 1956 to 1968.) Brunner subsequently took refuge in Syria, where he reportedly became a government adviser. Using the name of his cousin, Georg Fischer, he was believed to have lived either in an apartment on Haddad Street or in a room at the Meridian Hotel in Damascus under police protection. Attempts by Israeli agents to assassinate him failed twice—in 1961 and in 1980—but he sustained the loss of an eye and several fingers of his left hand from letter bombs as a result. Interviewed in Damascus by an Austrian journalist, Brunner declared that he did not suffer from a bad conscience for "getting rid of that garbage" and only regretted that he had not managed to kill more Jews. In a telephone interview with the *Chicago Sun-Times* in 1987, he reiterated his belief that the Jews deserved to die. Yet he has also professed innocence, saying in another interview, "I first heard about gas chambers after the end of the war."

Brunner was sentenced to death in absentia in France in 1953 and 1954. Since then Germany, Austria, Slovakia, France, and Poland have all sought his extradition, but the Syrians have rebuffed their requests. There were uncon-firmed reports that he died in 1997 and was buried in a Damascus cemetery. In 2000, though, there were rumors that Poland was renewing its effort to extradite him, suggesting that he was still alive. In 2001 he was found guilty in absentia by a French court for crimes against humanity.

Bulgaria, human rights violations in

Bulgaria, a former Communist country, is credited with a fairly good record on human rights, but problems persist. Police officers frequently beat suspects and prison inmates and harass minorities. In 2000 a survey by the Bulgarian Helsinki Committee (BHC) found that 49 percent of prisoners interviewed by its investigators reported that police officers used physical force against them during arrest. Romany street children were particularly at risk for abuse by police. In its 2004 *Country Report,* the U.S. State Department cited cases of arbitrary arrest and detention, most of which go unpunished because of problems of accountability and serious corruption in the judiciary. With the adoption of an antidiscrimination law and the introduction of new rules for the Interior Ministry, some improvements have taken place and police violence has diminished. Nonetheless, according to the Helsinki Committee, a human rights group, one-third of those held in police custody in 2003 had suffered mistreatment at the hands of the police. Freedom of the press is still restricted by the government, although almost 15 years have passed since Bulgaria was under Soviet influence. The government has taken television broadcasts off the air, and some journalists have been jailed for violating libel or slander laws. Freedom of assembly is also limited. Harassment of people who practice a faith other than the dominant Eastern Orthodox has declined in recent years, however. The State Department also points to problems facing women: discrimination and trafficking for the purpose of prostitution.

Bunche, Ralph Johnson (1904–1971) *human rights advocate*

At home in the United States, Ralph Johnson Bunche distinguished himself as a courageous crusader for civil rights; abroad, he achieved recognition as a peacemaker for the United Nations, which brought him a Nobel laureate. He was born in Detroit to a barber who worked in a shop catering exclusively to whites; his mother was an amateur musician. His grandmother, who lived with his family, had been born into slavery. At a young age, Bunche was already demonstrating the brilliance and ambition that would characterize his life. He obtained his undergraduate degree from UCLA in 1928 and earned his master's from Howard University and a doctorate from Harvard. He was also an outstanding athlete, equally adept at football, basketball, baseball, and track. In 1932 he secured a fellowship that allowed him to conduct research in Africa for a dissertation on French colonial rule in Togoland and Dahomey.

Bunche was never a radical—although some of his fellow students at Howard thought of him as one—but he was an ardent advocate of civil rights. In 1936 he wrote *A World View of Race* and participated in the Carnegie Corporation's well-known survey of the African Americans in the United States, under the direction of the Swedish sociologist Gunnar Myrdal (published under the title *An American Dilemma* in 1944). During World War II both the U.S. Department of State and the Pentagon called on him as a consultant on African colonial regions of strategic military importance.

Near the end of the war, Bunche became a member of what became known as the Black Cabinet—an unofficial group of prominent African Americans who acted as consultants on minority problems for the Roosevelt administration. President Harry S. Truman offered him a position as assistant secretary of state, but he refused because of the segregated housing conditions that existed in Washington, D.C., at the time. During the 1960s Bunche helped Martin Luther King, Jr., organize the famous civil-rights march in Montgomery, Alabama, in 1965. He was also active in the National Association for the Advancement of Colored People (NAACP) and the Urban League.

But Bunche's fame rests mainly on the work he undertook on behalf of the United Nations. He had assumed a variety of diplomatic responsibilities for the U.S. State Department that brought him to the attention of UN secretary-general Trygve Lie. At Lie's request, Bunche was loaned to the United Nations and placed in charge of the Department of Trusteeship, dealing with countries still under colonial rule. His most important assignment took him to Palestine (then under British mandate) in June 1947; he remained in the region until August 1949. As assistant to the UN Special Committee on Palestine, and then as principal secretary of the UN Palestine Commission, Bunche was given a nearly impossible task: carrying out the partition approved by the UN General Assembly, which created the state of Israel. The partition plan was torpedoed, however, when war broke out between Arabs and Jews. The United Nations then dispatched Count Folke Bernadotte as principal mediator and named Ralph Bunche as his chief aide. Four months later, on September 17, 1948, Count Bernadotte was assassinated in Cairo by Jewish extremists, and Bunche assumed the role of mediator in his place. It took another 11 months of difficult negotiations, but finally Bunche was able to arrange an armistice between Israel and the Arab states.

When he returned home, Bunche was greeted as a hero; New York gave him a ticker-tape parade up Broadway, and Los Angeles declared a Ralph Bunche Day. But for all the honors that he would receive for his work, none was greater than the Nobel Peace Prize that was awarded to him in 1950. He began his Nobel acceptance address by noting that "it is not easy to speak of peace with either conviction or reassurance." While statesmen paid "homage to peace and freedom in a perpetual torrent of eloquent phrases," he said, they "also speak darkly of the lurking threat of war; and the preparations for war ever intensify, while strife flares or threatens in many localities." As a result, their words no longer had "a common meaning." He noted, "Freedom, democracy, human rights, international morality, peace itself, mean different things to different men." Instead, he said, words were used as propaganda "to confuse, mislead, and debase the common man." Democracy, he observed, "is prostituted to dignify enslavement; freedom and equality are held good for some men but withheld from others." He went on to quote Voltaire: "War is the greatest of all crimes; and yet there is no aggressor who does not color his crime with the pretext of justice."

Until his retirement in 1971, Bunche continued to serve the United Nations in a number of capacities: as undersecretary for special political affairs and as undersecretary-general. The United Nations called on him to take on several peacekeeping assignments that took him to the Congo, Cyprus, Kashmir, and Yemen. In the last years of his life he was also given responsibility for the UN program on peaceful uses of atomic energy.

Further Reading:
Fasulo, Linda. *An Insider's Guide to the UN.* New Haven, Conn.: Yale University Press, 2003.
Meisler, Stanley. *United Nations: The First Fifty Years.* New York: Atlantic Monthly Press, 1997.

Burkina Faso, human rights violations in

The West African nation of Burkina Faso (formerly Upper Volta) has a poor human rights record. Security forces have committed EXTRAJUDICIAL KILLINGS, and few of the perpetrators have been called to account. Although the government has received some credit for democratic reforms—recent legislative elections saw gains by opposition parties—power largely rests in the hands of President Blaise Compaore and his ruling party, and freedom of assembly is often restricted. Arbitrary arrest and detention and lack of due process have raised the misgivings of human rights organizations. Suspects are often subject to beatings and threats to extract confessions. Prisons are overcrowded and unsanitary, and prisoners are inadequately fed. The judicial system has also been faulted for bowing to political pressure.

Freedom of the press has been called into question. In its *Country Report* of 2002, the U.S. State Department cited the death of an internationally respected journalist, Norbert Zongo, who died along with his brother and two other men in a suspicious car fire in 1998; the deaths have never been thoroughly investigated. The State Department also listed several other areas of concern, such as violence and discrimination against women, including female genital mutilation, child labor, and child trafficking. However, the government has made efforts to halt genital mutilation and trafficking in persons.

According to the Burkinabe Human and Peoples' Rights Movement (MBDHP), the country's largest human rights organization, as many as 106 suspected extrajudicial killings, mostly of criminals, within a three-month period in 2002 had gone uninvestigated. According to MBDHP, the unburied dead bodies were found handcuffed, bullet-ridden, and "thrown to the dogs and vultures." Although the numbers and names of victims could not be independently verified, these reports are considered credible. Indeed, the minister of security acknowledged that the police had been involved in these killings, but he adamantly denied that they were summary executions: "What may have happened is that in the face of the menace that bandits constitute, security forces were compelled to use rigorous methods to overpower armed gangs."

Burma   *See* MYANMAR, HUMAN RIGHTS VIOLATIONS IN.

Burundi, war crimes in

Burundi has been consumed by civil war for more than a decade, resulting in a massive humanitarian crisis that only recently has begun to be resolved. The East African country, which has a population of 6.7 million, was poor before the war began in 1993; approximately 90 percent of the population is dependent on subsistence agriculture. But the war has plunged Burundi into near destitution. Its cost in blood and money is staggering: The conflict has taken the lives of between 200,000 and 300,000 people and turned several hundred thousand more into refugees whose survival depends on outside humanitarian aid. In one measure of the devastation, the country's gross domestic product dropped from $4.1 billion in 1998 to $695.3 million in 2002.

By the end of 2003, more than 280,000 people were living in refugee camps inside Rwanda, although the number of people who were internally displaced by the war may add up to another 100,000. Several thousand are classified simply as "dispersed," without any access to humanitarian assistance. Another 500,000 Burundians have taken refuge in neighboring Tanzania. Several thousand more are in detention, many without being charged or put on trial for years.

The conflict stems from tensions between the two principal ethnic groups in the country: the Tutsis, who long dominated the government, and the Hutus. In 1994 tensions between these two ethnic groups in neighboring Rwanda exploded into a genocidal campaign against Tutsis and moderate Hutus that claimed at least 800,000 lives in a matter of months. The Burundi civil war had already begun in 1993 with the assassination of the first democratically elected president only four months after he had taken office.

It took nine years before the warring parties even consented to sit down to try to work out a peace agreement. In November 2001, after intense negotiations, a new transitional government was formed as a first step toward holding national elections in three years. In 2002 the Tutsi-dominated government signed a cease-fire agreement with three of Burundi's four Hutu rebel groups, but none of the parties honored it, and within months fighting had resumed.

In the several years of civil war, none of the parties to the conflict has demonstrated much respect for civilian lives or property, nor has there been any significant move to bring violators of human rights to justice. In April 2003, for example, one of the rebel groups called Forces for the Defense of Democracy (FDD) shelled residential neighborhoods in the capital of Bujumbura, even though there were no military targets anywhere in the city. Similar incidents occurred in other locales. When asked why the FDD had launched these attacks, a spokesman said that they were meant to prod the government back to the negotiating table. The government behaved no better. In the same month, government troops were reported to have massacred some 20 civilians just outside of Bujumbura in apparent reprisal for a rebel attack on a local military outpost. The violence continued to escalate over the next several months. Both sides carried out massacres, raped women, looted civilian property, and abducted civilians (including human rights activists), who were used as slave labor. All sides are accused of kidnapping children and pressing them into service as combatants. Tens of thousands of civilians fled from their homes in terror. "Civilians still have no faith that they won't become the targets of unpredictable violence, either from the government or from the rebels," observed a representative of HUMAN RIGHTS WATCH at the time. His words were echoed by one victim who said, "We are victims every day. We are truly the forgotten ones."

In October 2003 the government and the FDD once again agreed to a peace accord called the Pretoria Protocols. (South Africa has been intensively involved in brokering a deal.) Under the terms of the agreement, the FDD would join the Tutsi party as a part of a coalition government. As part of the agreement, 2,800 peacekeepers from neighboring countries were deployed in Burundi. The African Mission in Burundi, as it is called, is charged only with overseeing implementation of the accords, not the protection of civilians. The most controversial provision was one that conferred "provisional immunity" on rebels for crimes committed during the war. This was not the first attempt to shield human rights violators from justice. In the previous August the Transitional National Assembly had passed a similar immunity law meant to protect a limited number of Hutu leaders from immediate prosecution, effectively nullifying an earlier law intended to punish acts of GENOCIDE. The law included no time limit to this protection. A force of 10,000 UN peacekeepers was deployed to maintain the accord and prevent the country from backsliding into war.

The agreement was by no means universally acclaimed, mainly because of the immunity protections. There was, for one thing, a question of what exactly "provisional immunity" meant since it was not a term that was defined by international law. But it seemed to indicate that those responsible for massacres, rapes, abductions, and pillaging in the previous months and years would never have to face prosecution. Supporters of the peace deal, which included the South African government and UN secretary-general Kofi Annan, contended that without the immunity guarantees, the warring parties might never have come to the negotiating table at all. Human rights organizations point out, though, that agreements that are based on immunity seldom work out, citing the abortive 1999 Lomé Accord that was supposed to end the civil war in Sierra Leone. In practice, though, very few soldiers had ever been prosecuted by military tribunals for war crimes.

Human rights advocates might have had a point. The fragility of the accord was underscored by continued insurgencies on the part of factions that had refused to take part in negotiations. While government and FDD forces generally observed the cease-fire, a second rebel group, the Forces for National Liberation (FNL), staged several attacks, clashing with both government troops and the rival FDD.

Human rights in Burundi have been one of the principal casualties of the war even in areas where government control is largely uncontested by rebels. The government has detained opposition political leaders and cracked down on journalists who defied its edicts not to broadcast or paraphrase statements by rebel leaders, although the law guarantees freedom of the press. Security forces have carried out numerous EXTRAJUDICIAL KILLINGS of civilians suspected of supporting insurgents in reprisal strikes. According to the U.S. State Department's 2003 *Country Report*, there are credible reports of DISAPPEARANCES, TORTURE, beatings, and rape perpetrated by security forces. Most of

these crimes went unpunished, and human rights organizations were prevented from investigating them. There are a few heartening exceptions, though; for instance, senior police officials were arrested in 2002 and charged with the murder of a local representative of the World Health Organization a year before.

Women are especially vulnerable and are frequently victims of violence and discrimination. Both sides have used rape as a strategic and tactical weapon of war, putting women and girls at increased threat of contracting sexually transmitted infections and HIV/AIDS. Women widowed by the war face heightened risks because they have no one to protect them, and there are widespread incidents of rape at refugee camps.

The first months of 2004 brought some measure of hope to the war-torn country, although there has been a marked increase in lawlessness and instability. Improved respect for human rights remains more of a dream than a reality. Analysts note that while political leaders have called for a restoration of justice, they are unlikely to ever be called to account for the crimes they have committed.

In August 2004 a massacre of more than 160 Congolese refugees—mainly Tutsis—by a Burundian Hutu rebel group, the National Liberation Forces, put added pressure on the fragile peace accord. The Hutu group claimed that it was targeting Congolese Tutsi militia men known as Banyamulenge, who had fled fighting in their country, but UN observers report that most of the dead were women and children. In early 2005 thousands of Burundians went to the polls to elect a new parliament, a demonstration of democracy that was notably free of violence. The election brought a former Hutu rebel leader Pierre Nkurunziza to power. On taking office he pledged to honor the peace accord. While one of the Hutu rebel groups, the Forces for National Liberation (Forces Nationales de Libération, or FNL), refused to sign the accord and continued to mount attacks, elections for the National Assembly in July took place without major incident.

See also RAPE AS A TACTIC OF WAR; RWANDA, GENOCIDE IN.

Further Reading:

Lemarchand, Reni, and Lee H. Hamilton. *Burundi: Ethnic Conflict and Genocide.* Cambridge: Cambridge University Press, 1996.

Southall, Roger, and Kristina Bentley. *African Peace Process: Mandela, South Africa, and Burundi.* Pretoria, South Africa: Human Sciences Research Council, 2005.

C

Cambodia, human rights violations in

It was only in 1998 that war came to an end in Cambodia after three decades of fighting. Human rights violations, however, continue to bedevil its recovery. Political opposition to the Hun Sen government is often stifled and harassed. Politically motivated murders remain unsolved. TORTURE of prisoners in custody is commonplace, the judiciary is seen as corrupt by citizens and police alike, and reports regularly surface of security forces carrying out EXTRAJUDICIAL KILLINGS. Abuses by the authorities go unpunished. Trafficking in humans is flourishing, and some 20 percent of the population is denied many of the rights granted to the majority because they are not ethnic Cambodians.

All that said, it cannot be overemphasized that the situation in Cambodia has improved in recent years and that people are considerably better off than they were during the war, especially during the five years that the radical Khmer Rouge controlled the country. However, 25 years after the fall of the Khmer Rouge in 1979, not a single one of its leaders has ever been compelled to answer for his crimes. While levels of political violence have decreased in recent years, according to HUMAN RIGHTS WATCH, this did not necessarily indicate that the government was demonstrating any greater respect for basic civil and political rights. Violence that used to mar elections appears to have been supplanted by threats and intimidation by local officials loyal to Hun Sen's Cambodian People's Party (CPP). In the run-up to national elections in July 2003, Human Rights Watch reported a pattern of intimidation, harassment, and denial of noncompliant villagers with access to community resources. For activists and dissidents who criticize the government, the punishment can be even direr. Thirteen opposition activists were killed before the elections, which followed a killing of a senior adviser to Prince Norodom Ranariddh, the royalist leader and a judge and court clerk. The killings did not stop after the election. In October a radio journalist and a popular singer, both affiliated with FUNCINPEC, the opposition royalist party, were slain, and in January 2004 a labor activist Chea Vichea was assassinated. He had been an outspoken supporter of the political opposition leader Sam Rainsy.

Such killings have characterized Cambodian political life in the last several years. Research by human rights organizations found that within a 22-month period (1997–99), the police and military, along with local officials, might have killed 263 people or more. Many of them appeared to be deliberate executions, according to Human Rights Watch. In addition, the Cambodia Office of the High Commissioner for Human Rights documented an estimated 130 crimes, including assassinations and DISAPPEARANCES, that might have been linked to politics. None of the perpetrators have been arrested. Even if the security forces made a concerted effort to find the killers, it is doubtful whether they would receive a fair trial. The judiciary is not independent, nor does it enjoy a reputation for integrity or professionalism. Important institutions such as the Supreme Council of Magistracy and the Constitutional Council have been mainly inactive and in any case lack credibility.

The government has made some effort to collect weapons from an excessively armed population but even this well-publicized campaign has had problems, not least of which was the discovery that many of the confiscated weapons later ended up being sold on the black market. Another campaign to dispose of the millions of antipersonnel land mines has also run into trouble. The country's national de-mining agency, the Cambodian Mine Action Center (CMAC), has been accused of corruption and mismanagement. Freedom of the press does exist, and though the government controls most of the radio and television stations, there has been a marked decline in attacks on journalists, and the royalist party was permitted to purchase a radio station.

Further Reading:
Chandler, David. *A History of Cambodia.* Philadelphia: Westview Press, 2000.

59

———. *The Tragedy of Cambodian History: Politics, War, and Revolution since 1945.* New Haven, Conn.: Yale University Press, 1993.

Coates, Karen J. *Cambodia Now: Life in the Wake of War.* Jefferson, N.C.: McFarland & Company, 2005.

Gottesman, Evan. *Cambodia after the Khmer Rouge: Inside the Politics of Nation Building.* New Haven, Conn.: Yale University Press, 2004.

Romano, Cesare, Andre Nollkaemper, and Jann K. Kleffner, eds. *Internationalized Criminal Courts and Tribunals: Sierra Leone, East Timor, Kosovo, and Cambodia.* International Courts and Tribunals Series. Oxford: Oxford University Press, 2004.

Cambodia, war crimes in

The Cambodian GENOCIDE of 1975–79—in which possibly as many as 1.7 million people (21 percent of the country's population of about 10 million) were killed or died from starvation and exposure—represents one of the great tragedies of the 20th century. (Although some historians put the fatality rate as low as 750,000 most analysts agree that the higher estimates are closer to the truth.) In its five years in power, a fanatical Maoist movement known as the Khmer Rouge orchestrated a ruthless campaign that was to re-create society from the ground up. Three million people were expelled from the cities and resettled in rural areas, while all those labeled as capitalists or intellectuals—even eyeglasses could be incriminating—were to be assassinated. Markets were destroyed, schools were closed, private property was banned, and the use of money was outlawed. It was one of the most sweeping and radical social experiments ever to be tried in history—and it proved to be a gigantic failure.

Although a quarter of a century has passed since the Khmer Rouge was ousted from power, its surviving leaders have yet to be called to account for their crimes. The Khmer Rouge is an offshoot of the Communist Party of Kampuchea (CPK), which was founded in 1951 but later tried to dissociate itself from its roots because of the party's alliance with its Vietnamese counterpart. Vietnam's Communist Party came to be seen by the Khmer Rouge leadership as an overbearing older brother. Many of the future Khmer Rouge leaders including KHIEU SAMPHAN, Hu Nim, and Hou Youn received their doctorates in either law or economics from the prestigious Sorbonne University in Paris. There they fell under the influence of the French Communist Party. However, these Western-educated men would later serve the Khmer Rouge mainly as figureheads; real power in the movement was wielded by Cambodians who disdained intellectualism. The core of the Khmer Rouge consisted of Saloth Sar (known by his nom de guerre as POL POT), Son Sen, NUON CHEA, Ke Pauk, TA MOK, and Ieng Thirith.

Skulls of the victims of the Khmer Rouge in Cambodia *(Landov)*

By 1960 Pol Pot, known as "Brother Number One," was named to the CPK's central committee and later became chairman. He then moved to consolidate power by launching a purge aimed at eliminating thousands of party members—even some of his old friends—whom he believed were closely allied with the Vietnamese communists. Pol Pot resented all outside help and espoused a philosophy of self-reliance. But self-reliance would have to wait for a while; the Khmer Rouge still needed the help of its neighbor, North Vietnam. For its part Hanoi was willing to overlook the purges and continued to back the Khmer Rouge viewing the insurgent group as a valuable ally in its war against the United States and its South Vietnamese allies. With North Vietnamese support, the Khmer Rouge launched an insurgency to take over Cambodia. By 1970 the Khmer Rouge and Vietcong guerrillas had taken control of almost two-thirds of the country. Its ranks had swelled to 30,000 by 1973—10 times the number of fighters it had managed to mobilize just three years earlier. Their success at recruitment allowed most of the North Vietnamese and Vietcong allies to withdraw.

The Vietnam War next door soon spilled over into Cambodia. In 1970 a military coup d'état sent King Norodom Sihanouk into exile and replaced what had been a constitutional monarchy with a regime run by a pro-American officer, Lon Nol. Sihanouk found a needed ally in China and formed a coalition called the National United Front for Kampuchea (FUNK) based on an uneasy alliance of communists and royalists. Henceforth Cambodia, Vietnam, and Laos were to be a "single battlefield" where the communists could wage war against U.S. imperialism. To close off supply routes to the Vietcong on the Cambodian side of the border, the United States launched a series of bombing attacks on Cambodia. Between 1970 and 1973, U.S. forces dropped three times the quantity of explosives on Cambodia that it had dropped on Japan during World War II.

By 1975 the turmoil had left the Cambodian people exhausted and war-weary. The economy was in shambles; hyperinflation, brought about by speculation and a large infusion of U.S. aid, had made the currency practically worthless. The war had even made rice, the national staple, hard to come by. In February and March 1975, the Khmer Rouge came steadily closer to the capital of Phnom Penh, which was subjected to constant shelling. The new lunar year began in April, but for the Khmer Rouge it was the beginning of a new era: Year Zero, the reincarnation of Cambodia into Democratic Kampuchea. "Two thousand years of Cambodian history have virtually ended," declared Phnom Penh Radio.

In mid-April, amid increasing chaos, the Lon Nol government collapsed, and on April 17, 1975, the Khmer Rouge entered the capital in triumph. Thousands of the city's residents came out into the streets to greet them in the belief that with their victory the civil war was finally at an end and they could return to some form of normal life. They did not know how wrong they were.

Year Zero was the beginning of the end: From then on, all structures that constituted the foundations of civilization—the family, markets, health care, education, books, holidays, art, and music—were prohibited. As one writer put it, all that was left was "only work and death." No sooner had the Khmer Rouge occupied Phnom Penh than they began to empty it. Within hours hundreds of thousands of people were ordered to leave the city—the elderly, children, and the infirm as well as healthy adults—on the pretext that their evacuation was necessary because the Americans were about to attack. No attack materialized or was ever contemplated. The Khmer Rouge had long viewed cities as capitalist redoubts—they reviled Phnom Penh as "the great prostitute of the Mekong"—and therefore if a model peasant-oriented society was to be created, its populace had to be dispersed. City dwellers were known as the "new people" (or "April 17 people") and were thus suspect, regardless of whether they were doctors, teachers, tailors, carpenters, or artisans. Ideology or political views were irrelevant; simply to have practiced a profession, acquired fluency in French (the former colonial language), or been born into a family of merchants was sufficient to implicate an individual. The practice of religion was banned in defiance of history; Cambodia had always been a traditional Buddhist culture. Money and private ownership were banned; communications with the outside world became illegal, and families were dismantled as a threat to the power of the state. Consorting with a relative without government permission was an offense.

But who was in charge? The new regime was so secretive that it refused to identify any of its leadership to the Cambodians; for that matter the new rulers even refused to acknowledge that they belonged to the CPK. They chose to hide behind the facade of the Angka—"The Organization." For the first two years most people had no idea who was running the country. A four-year plan was instituted "to build socialism in the fields." The newly resettled Cambodians were ordered to produce an average national yield of 1.4 tons of grain per acre. It was an impossible demand. Even in peacetime the average national yield was considerably less. Workers were forced to work in the fields 12 hours a day without adequate rest or food. Those who couldn't keep up were severely punished—frequently with death—but only after being compelled to dig their own graves. Foraging for food was a capital offense. Hundreds of thousands were killed or starved to death on the "killing fields." Workers were expendable. "Keeping new people is no benefit" declared a Khmer Rouge slogan; "Losing them is no loss." People were encouraged to inform on one another. The Khmer Rouge taught children to betray their parents as enemies of the state if, for instance, they were trying to conceal their backgrounds by pretending to be peasants. In exchange, children would receive extra privileges. So many adolescents were put in charge of work camps and farms that they ended up holding more power than the adults, most of whom had been executed.

"Materially, we had to denounce those who had more than the people," a survivor named Ong Thong Hoeung recounted to David Chandler, author of *The Tragedy of Cambodian History*. "In terms of thought, each of us had to keep an eye on everyone else, to disclose any attitude that didn't conform to the line of the party. Everything was interpreted: words, gestures, attitudes. Sadness was a sign of spiritual confusion, joy a sign of individualism, [while] an indecisive point of view indicated a petty bourgeois intellectualism."

But for all the threats, denunciations, and executions, the collectivization effort was running into difficulty. Rice quotas for 1977 and 1978 were not being met, even though the Angka was demanding higher production levels. A malnourished workforce was simply incapable of farming successfully. Making matters worse, farming had to be done all by hand since technology was banned. Most of what rice was produced was intended for the Khmer Rouge cadre; everyone else was left to fight over scraps.

The Khmer Rouge reserved a different fate for political prisoners and their families, who were confined to special detention centers. The most notorious center, S-21, was located in the abandoned suburban high school of Tuol Sleng—"hill of the poison tree," a chillingly apt description. Neighbors called it *konlaenh choul min dael chenh*—"the place where people go in but never come out." This was no exaggeration; about 20,000 people are known to have entered Tuol Sleng; only six are known to have emerged. Most of those executed in S-21—"pests buried within" as they were called—had been members of the Khmer Rouge. But as the regime became increasingly paranoid, the number of "traitors" increased. Conspirators were everywhere: By some estimates these alleged traitors made up 1–5 percent of the population.

Executions, however, were not performed before a confession could be extracted from the prisoners. The torturers were under orders to "investigate their personal biographies clearly," ostensibly to gain a better understanding of what had caused them to become traitors in the first place (notwithstanding the fact that many of these interred had committed no crimes.) A grim legacy of these interrogations survives in the form of thousands of confessions and several thousand photos of the victims. To extract confessions, torturers used electric shocks, hot metal prods, and knives, as well as a converted wood structure in the prison courtyard that had once been used by students for gymnastic practice.

Throughout the years that the Khmer Rouge was in power, tensions increased between Cambodia and Vietnam, exacerbated by ethnic conflict between the two nations. The Khmer Rouge began to covet land in the south of Vietnam mainly populated by ethnic Cambodians. In 1977 Pol Pot flew to Beijing to forge an alliance that would bolster the Khmer Rouge's position against Vietnam. While pledging support, China recommended that Cambodia refrain from going to war. At the end of 1977, Vietnam launched a preemptive strike, sending forces 20 miles into Cambodian territory and seizing some villages. A month later, the Vietnamese pulled back, but their withdrawal did not put a stop to the strife, and sporadic skirmishes went on throughout the following spring. On the diplomatic front, the Vietnamese signed a friendship treaty with the Soviet Union as a counterweight to the Khmer Rouge's fledgling alliance with China.

On Christmas Day, 1978, 100,000 Vietnamese troops invaded Cambodia with the objective of creating a buffer zone. The campaign went so smoothly that the Vietnamese kept going, reaching Phnom Penh on January 7, 1979, less than two weeks after they had begun their attack. The Khmer Rouge fled back into the countryside from which they had emerged five years earlier. The Cambodian people then confronted a dilemma: On the one hand, they were grateful to be freed from the Khmer Rouge; on the other hand, they owed their liberation to a foreign invader and an ethnic rival. What was once called "National Liberation Day"—January 7—was subsequently renamed "End of Genocide Day." (Younger Cambodians born after the Khmer Rouge horrors have adopted a more strident nationalist tone, denouncing January 7 as "Vietnam Invasion Day.") The Vietnamese proceeded to establish a new government known as the People's Republic of Kampuchea (PRK) and installed as its new prime minister Hun Sen, a former Khmer Rouge member who had defected to Vietnam the previous year.

With the Khmer Rouge gone from the capital and other cities, hundreds of thousands of displaced Cambodians began the trek back home—only to find that in many cases no homes remained. The Khmer Rouge did not disappear, though; on the contrary, they remained the legal government of Cambodia and for several years afterwards occupied Cambodia's seat in the UN General Assembly. In spite of the atrocities the group had committed while in power, the Khmer Rouge even had the official support of the U.S. government, which still viewed Vietnam with hostility and regarded its invasion of Cambodia as a violation of international law. The Khmer Rouge became in effect a cold war pawn. At the same time the United States was eager to nurture its budding relationship with the People's Republic of China. Zbigniew Brzezinski, President Jimmy Carter's national security advisor, admitted that the relationship with the radicals was purely pragmatic. "I encouraged the Chinese to support Pol Pot" he said. "The question was how to help the Cambodian people. Pol Pot was an abomination. We could never support him, but China could." Nor could the Khmer Rouge be considered a spent force; it retained an army of some 10,000 troops, which operated from bases near the Thai border. However, in 1982, seeking a measure of political legitimacy, the Khmer Rouge named Khieu Samphan, a man Prince Norodom Sihanouk dismissed as a "bit player," its leader and formed a coalition with Sihanouk and a noncommunist leader Son Sann. Sihanouk only agreed to form this uneasy alliance with the Khmer Rouge because of pressure from China, which played host to the monarch in exile. (Sihanouk had no love for the Khmer Rouge, which had killed five of his children and might have assassinated him if the North Vietnamese had not invaded.) The coalition received millions of dollars in support from the United States under both the Carter and Reagan administrations, neither of which took action to censure the Khmer Rouge or acknowledge its responsibility for genocide. At the same time, the United States maintained an embargo against the Vietnamese-backed Cambodian regime. Nonetheless, it was generally thought that Pol Pot continued to pull the strings. In 1991 the Khmer Rouge agreed to a treaty calling for UN-supervised elections and the disarmament of most of its forces. Then Prince Sihanouk, always the opportunist, broke with the Khmer Rouge and lent his support to the Vietnamese-backed Hun Sen government instead. The reversal jolted the Khmer Rouge and led to their boycotting the elections in 1993. From that point on, although the Khmer Rouge remained a destabilizing force, it never again posed a serious threat. The movement began to implode, and mass defections sapped its strength. By 1996 it was reduced to about 3,000–4,000 fighters. Factional fighting broke out in which Ta Mok and other leaders mutinied against Pol Pot and placed him under house arrest. Pol Pot died in April 1998. Within a year most of the top-ranking Khmer Rouge figures had defected, surrendered, or been captured. But not all of them were imprisoned; some actually seemed to enjoy a comfortable retirement.

The Hun Sen government has repeatedly balked at setting up a mechanism to bring the surviving Khmer Rouge leaders to justice. Hun Sen has, on the one hand, rejected the United Nations' involvement in holding trials, insisting that Cambodian courts were competent to do so. According to many human rights organizations, Hun Sen's reluctance has more to do with fear of government figures (including Hun Sen himself) being implicated in Khmer Rouge crimes. "The tribunal is the issue that refuses to die," said Youk Chhang, director of the Documentation Center of Cambodia, an organization dedicated to recording Khmer Rouge atrocities. "Those who survived refuse to be killed again."

On March 17, 2003, after five years of difficult negotiations, the United Nations reached a draft agreement with the Cambodian government to establish an international criminal tribunal to try former Khmer Rouge leaders. The cost of the tribunal was estimated at $50 million, and it was expected to be in operation for three years. Under terms of the agreement, the judges were to be Cambodian, a stipulation that angered human rights groups that maintained that the judges would be subjected to pressure by the government. However, by March 2004 the United Nations was confident that an arrangement could be worked out in which at least one-third of those involved in the tribunal would be drawn from outside Cambodia.

Not unexpectedly, internal politics have hamstrung diplomatic efforts to conduct the war trials of former Khmer Rouge officials. If Hun Sen is reluctant to try them because of fears they may implicate him or others now in power, the political opposition is concerned that a tribunal, sure to be widely covered by international media, might burnish the prime minister's image. In spite of the obstacles, the Cambodian parliament finally approved a law to establish a war crimes tribunal for surviving members of Cambodia's Khmer Rouge regime in October 2004. It remains unclear how many of the top leaders will actually face prosecution. But it is likely that most of those who fought for the Khmer Rouge will never be called to account. According to the British newspaper *Guardian*, as many as 50,000 former Khmer Rouge fighters are now serving in government positions; five of them have been cabinet ministers. Several of the highest-ranking Khmer Rouge leaders—including Pol Pot's brother-in-law, Nuon Chea, and former foreign minister IENG SARY—have been effectively pardoned.

Further Reading:

Chandler, David. *A History of Cambodia.* Philadelphia: Westview Press. 2000.

Coates, Karen J. *Cambodia Now: Life in the Wake of War.* Jefferson, Mo.: McFarland & Company, 2005.

Gottesman, Evan. *Cambodia after the Khmer Rouge: Inside the Politics of Nation Building.* New Haven, Conn.: Yale University Press, 2004.

Hinton, Alexander Laban, and Robert Jay Lifton. *Why Did They Kill?: Cambodia in the Shadow of Genocide.* California Series in Public Anthropology, vol. 11. Berkeley: University of California Press, 2004.

Kiernan, Ben. *How Pol Pot Came to Power: Colonialism, Nationalism, and Communism in Cambodia, 1930–1975.* New Haven, Conn.: Yale University Press, 2004.

———. *The Pol Pot Regime: Race, Power, and Genocide in Cambodia under the Khmer Rouge, 1975–79.* New Haven, Conn.: Yale University Press, 2002.

Pran, Dith, comp. *Children of Cambodia's Killing Fields: Memoirs by Survivors.* Edited by Kim DePaul. New Haven, Conn.: Yale University Press, 1999.

Short, Philip. *Pol Pot: Anatomy of a Nightmare.* New York: Holt Rinehart, 2005.

Ung, Loung. *First They Killed My Father: A Daughter of Cambodia Remembers.* New York: Perennial, 2001.

Cambodian Genocide Program

The Cambodian Genocide Program (CGP), a project of the Genocide Studies Program at the Yale Center for International and Area Studies, was established in 1994. The objective of the CGP is "to learn as much as possible about the tragedy, and to help determine who was responsible for the crimes of the POL POT regime." The CGP has acquired access to the 100,000-page archive of the Santebal, the Khmer Rouge security police; it is now on microfilm at Yale University's Sterling Library and is available to scholars worldwide. In addition, the CGP has compiled and published 22,000 biographic and bibliographic records and more than 6,000 photographs, documents, translations, and maps as well as books and research papers on GENOCIDE in Cambodia. In 1995 the CPG established the Documentation Center of Cambodia in Phnom Penh to document the genocide under the Khmer Rouge while they held power between 1975 and 1979. The program has since expanded to document and research the Holocaust and genocides that have occurred in countries such as Bosnia, Rwanda, East Timor, Guatemala, and Sudan.

According to its director, Ben Kiernan, the Yale project has received cooperation from both the Cambodian and U.S. governments. In 1995, when the CGP was still new, the Khmer Rouge, then in its last days, denounced Kiernan as an "arch war criminal" and "an accessory executioner of the U.S. imperialists." One of the CGP's major efforts is directed toward the preservation of documents and other evidence and make it available to any court or tribunal that might eventually try the perpetrators of the mass killings. "A mass of probative evidence is now available to the international and Cambodian co-prosecutors and judges," Kiernan has said. "We can only hope that a fair trial of perpetrators of the genocide and other CRIMES AGAINST HUMANITY will help entrench the rule of law in Cambodia and deter criminals in other countries from contemplating such outrages against human rights in the future."

See also CAMBODIA, WAR CRIMES IN.

Further Reading:

Hinton, Alexander Laban, and Robert Jay Lifton. *Why Did They Kill?: Cambodia in the Shadow of Genocide.* California Series in Public Anthropology, vol. 11. Berkeley: University of California Press, 2004.

Kiernan, Ben. *How Pol Pot Came to Power: Colonialism, Nationalism, and Communism in Cambodia, 1930–1975.* New Haven, Conn.: Yale University Press, 2004.

———. *The Pol Pot Regime: Race, Power, and Genocide in Cambodia under the Khmer Rouge, 1975–79.* New Haven, Conn.: Yale University Press, 2002.

Pran, Dith, comp. *Children of Cambodia's Killing Fields: Memoirs by Survivors.* Edited by Kim DePaul. New Haven, Conn.: Yale University Press, 1999.

Short, Philip. *Pol Pot: Anatomy of a Nightmare.* New York: Holt Rinehart, 2005.

Ung, Loung. *First They Killed My Father: A Daughter of Cambodia Remembers.* New York: Perennial, 2001.

Cameroon, human rights violations in

The West African state of Cameroon has a poor human rights record. In 2003 the U.S. State Department released a report sharply critical of conditions in the country's prisons and also citing unlawful killings by security forces. The government under President Paul Biya has also restricted the activities of the political opposition, making meaningful elections difficult, if not impossible.

Prisons are staggeringly overcrowded; prisoners are not fed properly and lack basic medical care. One prison, for instance, originally intended for 1,500, now houses 7,000 inmates; another that can comfortably accommodate 2,000 is crammed with nearly 10,000. There are reports of TORTURE by the gendarmerie, who are rarely held accountable, although one case known as the "Douala 9" drew so much attention that a special tribunal was established. Eight gendarmes went on trial for their suspected role in the disappearance of nine teenagers in Douala, the economic "capital" of the country, in 2001. The boys had been arrested on suspicion of stealing a cooking-gas bottle and held in a facility maintained by Commandement Opérationnel, a special anticrime unit; it is believed that they were then killed by police. In July 2002 a military tribunal convicted two gendarmes of "abuse of authority" and "complicity in the abuse of authority" and sentenced them to short prison terms. The other six gendarmes were acquitted. The outcome effectively meant that no one would be punished for the teenagers' deaths.

Members of the opposition Southern Cameroons National Council are frequently arrested and detained without trial for weeks, even though by law they should be charged within 72 hours. Critics of the government are subject to random searches, and passports have been confiscated to prevent them from traveling abroad to participate in international meetings. Human rights activists and independent publishers and journalists also suffer from harassment and intimidation by the security forces and are often detained for weeks without charges being brought. According to AMNESTY INTERNATIONAL, abuses by security forces have become worse in recent years.

carpet bombing

The history of aerial bombardment began on November 1, 1911, when an Italian pilot dropped four small bombs on Libyan Arabs in the hope of terrorizing them. Carpet bombing is distinguished from military bombing because it is not aimed at a particular military objective but targets an entire city. Carpet bombing is justified for a number of reasons: to destroy an enemy's industrial base, to demoralize an enemy population, or simply as retaliation. The blitzkrieg—Germany's fierce bombardment of British cities during World War II—is an example of carpet bombing, as is the destruction of Rotterdam by German bombardment. Allied aircraft regularly carried out carpet bombing of German cities; in February 1945, in the course of a single night, American and British aircraft rained down enough bombs to kill 135,000 people and devastate 80 percent of Dresden. The use of atomic bombs on Hiroshima and Nagasaki can also be classified as carpet bombings.

There was little discussion of carpet bombing during the NUREMBERG TRIALS. However, human rights advocates maintain that the practice is a flagrant violation of the Fourth Geneva Convention of 1949, which provides for the protection of civilians in combat. Nonetheless, carpet bombing continued throughout the cold war, especially during the war in Vietnam when U.S. B-52s regularly carried out carpet bombing of North Vietnamese cities. In an attempt to demonstrate American air superiority and reassure its South Vietnamese allies, the United States launched the so-called Christmas bombing of 1972 against Hanoi and Haiphong, which critics contend constituted illegal acts under international law.

It was only in 1977 that international law was modified to specifically prohibit carpet bombing, also referred to as area bombardment. Additional Protocol I to the Geneva Convention bans any indiscriminate attack from the air against cities, towns, villages, or other areas where a civilian population might be concentrated. The targeting of any location where it is known in advance that bombing will cause civilian casualties or damage vital nonmilitary installations (such as dams) is considered a serious violation of the law. The prohibition does not affect military targets, which can still be legally bombed in a conflict. Although the United States is not a party to Protocol I, it has accepted this principle as international binding CUSTOMARY LAW.

As defined by the Additional Protocol, indiscriminate attacks are considered:

a. an attack by bombardment by any methods or means which treats as a single military objective a number of clearly separated and distinct military objectives located in a city, town, village or other area containing a similar concentration of civilians or civilian objects; and

b. an attack which may be expected to cause incidental loss of civilian life, injury to civilians, damage to civilian objects, or a combination thereof, which would be excessive in relation to the concrete and direct military advantage anticipated.

Problems arose during negotiations over the reference in the text to the precise meaning of "clearly separated." Just how far away does a military target have to be from an area populated by civilians? While precision-guided missiles—widely used prior to the ground invasion of Iraq by U.S. forces—have made targeting a more exact science, aerial bombardment is notoriously unreliable. Civilian casualties or damage to civilian installations might result even if the bombing were directed against a military objective. Experts in international law believe that if it can be shown that the principal target was military in nature and that if efforts were made to avoid civilian areas, then the party would not be in breach of the protocol. During the Gulf War, allied forces claimed to have adhered to the standards established in Protocol I in strikes against Iraqi military targets, although they had no legal obligation to do so. The issue is further complicated by the practice of the parties that are coming under attack to place civilians in locations close to military targets, either to deter air strikes or to use the resulting civilian losses to stir international outrage against the party responsible for the bombing.

See also ADDITIONAL PROTOCOLS TO THE GENEVA CONVENTIONS; GENEVA CONVENTIONS.

Further Reading:
Gutman, Roy, ed. *Crimes of War: What the Public Should Know.* New York: W. W. Norton & Company, 1999.
Jackson, Nyamuya Maogoto. *War Crimes and Realpolitik: International Justice from World War I to the 21st Century.* Boulder, Colo.: Lynne Rienner Publishers, 2004.
Robertson, Geoffrey. *Crimes against Humanity: The Struggle for Global Justice.* New York: New Press, 2003.

Carter Center, The

The Carter Center is a nongovernmental human rights organization that seeks to strengthen democracies in 65 countries in Africa, Asia, and Latin America, alleviate suffering, and promote economic development. The Atlanta-based foundation was founded in 1982 by former President Jimmy Carter and his wife, Rosalynn, in partnership with Emory University. A nonpartisan body, the center has taken a leading role in conflict disputes in countries such as Sudan and Liberia. The center is perhaps best known for deploying monitors to ensure that elections are conducted fairly, especially in countries with fragile democratic institutions.

In its two decades of operations, the Carter Center has earned a reputation for integrity and authority. In 2004, for instance, representatives of the center, including Jimmy Carter, monitored a recall referendum in Venezuela to determine whether President Hugo Chavez would remain in office. Even though the opposition claimed fraud when preliminary results showed Chavez retaining power, advocates of the recall effort said that they would wait for Carter's assessment before taking any action. A recall vote was held in August 2004 with nearly 4 million voting no and 3.5 million voting yes, ensuring that the controversial Venezuelan leader would continue his hold on power. The Carter Center is also involved with other activities aimed at improving conditions in the developing world, including increasing grain production in 15 African countries, eradicating Guinea worm disease, and diminishing the stigma of mental illness. The Carter Center is supported financially by charitable foundations and individual donations.

Further Reading:
Carter, Jimmy. *The Personal Beliefs of Jimmy Carter: Winner of the 2002 Nobel Peace Prize.* New York: Three Rivers Press, 2002.

Castro, Fidel   *See* Cuba, human rights violations in.

Cavallo, Ricardo Miguel (1952–   ) *Argentine naval captain*

A former captain of the naval forces in Argentina, Ricardo Miguel Cavallo became a test case of the principle of UNIVERSAL JURISDICTION in international law, when in June 2003, the Mexican high court ruled that he could be extradited to Spain to answer an indictment that charged him with GENOCIDE and terrorism. Cavallo was accused of committing human rights abuses during the military dictatorship that had ruled Argentina from 1976 to 1983. He later sought refuge in Mexico, where he was apprehended in August 2002. The issue before the Mexican court was whether an individual alleged to be responsible for human rights violations in one country, who was residing in a second country, could be extradited to face charges stemming from those violations in a third country. The ruling by the Mexican Supreme Court was considered by human rights advocates to represent a ringing affirmation of the principle of universal jurisdiction. This principle is based on the presumption that human rights atrocities committed in one country can be subject to criminal prosecution by courts in

another country, making it more difficult, although by no means impossible, for human rights abusers to find sanctuary in any part of the world. "This case represents a real victory for international justice," said José Miguel Vivanco, executive director of the Americas Division of HUMAN RIGHTS WATCH when the ruling was announced. "Mexico will become the first Latin American country to extradite someone for gross human rights violations under the principle of universal jurisdiction."

According to a November 1999 indictment issued by Spanish Judge Balthasar GARZÓN, Cavallo was affiliated with the notorious Navy Mechanics School, a detention center known as Escuela de Mecánica de la Armada (ESMA) in Buenos Aires during the military regime. Between January 1977 and October 1978, the indictment states, Cavallo was an active participant in Working Group 332, which carried out kidnappings and TORTURE of suspected leftists viewed as a threat to the ruling junta. The so-called school was only one of the 340 such detention centers where torture was conducted by the military.

It is estimated that at least 9,000 Argentines "disappeared" during the seven years the military held power; almost all of them were presumably killed after being tortured. Some were drugged and flung out of planes into the Atlantic Ocean. Cavallo (also known variously as Serpico, Marcelo, and Ricardo) had taken part in the torture of suspects. He is specifically accused of the abduction, torture, and murder of at least 227 people, the torture of 110 others, and the kidnapping of 16 babies whose parents were killed while they were in military custody. Although five witnesses have come forth to claim that they were tortured by Cavallo, the former naval captain denies any complicity in these acts. The Spanish indictment accused Cavallo of having been involved in "a massive extermination of citizens . . . kidnapping, the forced disappearance of people and torture inflicted by 'scientific' methods."

While living as a refugee in Mexico, Cavallo lived under the name Ricardo Angel Cavallo for several years, managing a company established by the Mexican government to compile a national registry of motor vehicles. Despite questions about his background, it is possible that he was given the job as a special favor by the government of President Ernesto Zedillo. In August 2000, while on vacation in Cancun, Cavallo was arrested for illegally importing secondhand cars from Central America. He fought subsequent efforts to extradite him to Spain, and a lower court ruled that he could not be extradited, saying that under Mexican law, the statute of limitations for prosecuting torture had expired. In addition, the Argentine government had adopted amnesty laws in 1986 and 1987 that would appear to have granted immunity to alleged human rights abusers like Cavallo. Assuming that the defendant would have no trouble getting off once he was back home, Cavallo's lawyers urged the court to return him to Argentina. Nonetheless, on January 12, 2001, the Mexican Supreme Court ruled that he could be extradited to Spain to answer charges of GENOCIDE and terrorism. The court based its decision on the fact that both Mexico and Spain ratified the United Nations Convention against torture and other forms of degrading or cruel punishment, which meant that anyone responsible for torture in one country could be forced to stand trial in the other. In 2003 Cavallo was extradited to Spain—to be tried.

See also ARGENTINA, HUMAN RIGHTS VIOLATIONS IN; TERRORISM AND INTERNATIONAL HUMANITARIAN LAW.

Ceauşescu, Nicolae (1918–1989) *Romanian dictator*

The communist dictator Nicolae Ceauşescu ruled Romania from 1965 until 1989, when he and his wife were executed in the midst of a bloody uprising. Born the son of a peasant in 1918, the young Ceauşescu moved to the capital, Bucharest, to become a shoemaker's apprentice. In the early 1930s he joined the illegal Communist Party and was arrested for labor agitation in 1933 and 1934. Two years later he was captured a third time and sent to prison for antifascist activities. In 1939, after he was released, he met Elena Petrescu, who would become his wife and his political collaborator. (They married in 1946). His freedom did not last long; he was thrown into prison again in 1940.

In 1943 Ceauşescu was transferred to Targu Jiu concentration camp, where he shared a cell with another communist, Gheorghe Gheorghiu-Dej, who was to become the future leader of postwar Romania. The two cellmates formed a close association, and Ceauşescu became Gheorghiu-Dej's protégé. In 1945, newly liberated, Ceauşescu became secretary of the Union of Communist Youth, and in 1947 the Communists took power in Romania. Few people benefited more from the new political order than Ceauşescu, who quickly rose in the ranks. In 1952, with his old friend Gheorghiu-Dej now in power, he was appointed deputy minister of the armed forces. He also became a member of the Politburo, composed of top Communist officials. (In communist bloc countries like Romania, the Communist Party and the government were parallel institutions, but it was the Communists who exercised real authority.) In time Ceauşescu became number two in the party hierarchy.

With Gheorghiu-Dej's death in March 1965, Ceauşescu was quick to assume leadership of the Communist Party, and in 1974 he was named president of Romania as well. Unlike other communist dictators in neighboring Eastern European states, Ceauşescu had no intention of toadying to the party bosses in Moscow but resolved instead to steer his own course. He pulled out of the Warsaw Pact, the Soviet-dominated military alliance that was designed as a counterweight to NATO. He also declared that henceforth the country would be known as the Socialist Republic of Romania, rather than the People's Republic, as most Eastern bloc countries were called. Ceauşescu condemned the Soviet invasions of Czechoslovakia (1968) and Afghanistan (1979) and sent a Romanian team to participate in the 1984 Summer Olympics organized by the United States—the only communist nation to do so. (The U.S. team had boycotted the 1980 Olympics in Moscow to protest the Soviet invasion of Afghanistan, prompting the Soviets to retaliate with a boycott of their own four years later.) Ceauşescu also initiated a trade agreement with the European Union, another unprecedented step for a communist country. He further aggravated Moscow by courting the Chinese Communist regime at a time of heightened tensions between the Soviet Union and China.

If there was one country that Ceauşescu seemed to admire above all, it was North Korea, the isolated communist nation. Both China and North Korea had instituted sweeping programs intended to transform their countries in order to realize a communist utopian vision without regard to the cost in capital or human life. Ceauşescu was particularly struck by the philosophy of *juche,* or self-reliance, promulgated by the North Korean dictator, KIM IL SUNG. After state visits to Beijing and Pyongyang in the early 1970s, Ceauşescu returned home with the intention of remaking Romania in similar fashion. In 1972 he promoted a program called systematization, though which he claimed the country could build a "multilaterally developed socialist society." This program was to advance urbanization and industrialization. To fulfill Ceauşescu's ambitious plans, though, whole towns and villages had to be razed and their inhabitants resettled in apartment blocs in the cities. He embarked on a misguided campaign to remodel Bucharest, ordering the demolition of one-fifth of the central part of the city, destroying churches and historical buildings in the process, so that he could refashion the capital in a style more to his liking.

At the same time Ceauşescu instituted a bizarre social program meant to keep Romania's population from declining. Abortion was prohibited, and contraception was made difficult to obtain. Mothers of at least five children were rewarded with benefits, while those of at least 10 children were declared "heroic mothers" who would be entitled to a gold medal, a free car, and an all-expenses-paid resort vacation once a year. All this might have sounded enticing on paper, but in fact no mother ever acquired heroic status. The program produced more children as intended, but because their parents were unable to feed them, thousands of "decree babies," as they were called, ended up in squalid state-run orphanages where many died of mistreatment and deprivation. Ceauşescu refused to allow for any testing of AIDS, a policy that led to the spread of the illness through shared needles and untested blood supplies. Countless numbers of decree babies contracted AIDS as well.

To ensure that he would meet no resistance from any disaffected citizens Ceauşescu relied on his dreaded secret police, the Secuirtate. Free speech and political dissent were squelched. To pay off foreign debt, he preferred to bankrupt the nation, selling food and industrial goods abroad and leaving almost nothing for his own citizens to consume. (Ironically, the debt was paid off by 1989, shortly before Ceauşescu was overthrown.) Ordinary Romanians were driven to the brink of destitution, barely able to feed themselves. Heating, gas, and electric shortages were common. Ceauşescu's inner circle, however, did not have to suffer any deprivation. He rewarded his family with high positions, privileges, and lavish gifts. He even made plans to build a palace for himself that was nearly equal in size to the Pentagon, calling it Casa Poporului (People's House). By this time his wife, Elena, had become a powerful political figure in her own right; if anything, she was even more ruthless than her husband.

Like his model, Kim Il Sung, Ceauşescu created a cult of personality, giving himself honorifics—Conducător (Leader) and Geniul din Carpaţi (Genius of the Carpathians)—and having a scepter made. Although Romania was Europe's fourth-biggest exporter of weapons, he harbored hope of winning the Nobel Peace Prize. He assumed the role of mediator between the PLO and Israel, with which Romania, unlike other communist states, retained diplomatic relations after the 1967 Middle East war. He held rallies for peace and even went so far as to write a poem about peace that was included in a literature book that every schoolchild had to read:

> Let us make from cannons tractors
> From atom lights and sources
> From nuclear missiles
> Plows to labour fields.

Ceauşescu's regime finally collapsed. A dispute over the expulsion of a popular Hungarian minister sparked anticommunist demonstrations in the city of Timişoara on December 17, 1989. The protests gathered force and spread to other cities, eventually reaching Bucharest. Meanwhile dissidents within the Securitate exploited the political crisis to stage a coup while Ceauşescu was delivering a speech in Bucharest. In the ensuing chaos Ceauşescu and Elena fled the capital by helicopter and took refuge in the countryside, but they were tracked down by police and turned over to the army. On Christmas Day the military tried them in a kangaroo court that charged them with genocide among other crimes; then soldiers took the couple into a courtyard and shot them.

Further Reading:

Kirk, Roger, and Mircea Racenu. *Romania versus the United States: Diplomacy of the Absurd, 1985–1989.* New York: St. Martin's Press, 1994.
Siani-Davies, Peter. *The Romanian Revolution of December 1989.* Ithaca, N.Y.: Cornell University Press, 2005.

Cédras, Raoul   *See* HAITIAN HUMAN RIGHTS VIOLATORS.

Cesić, Rajko   *See* WAR CRIMINALS OF THE FORMER YUGOSLAVIA.

Chad, human rights violations in

Chad, an impoverished West African nation, has the potential to reap unimagined prosperity due to its oil riches; yet the question remains whether a country with a history of despotism, rebellion, widespread human rights abuses, and corrupt government can ever manage the expected windfall for the benefit of its people. By 2004 the country was relatively calm after the signing of a peace treaty between the government and the rebel Movement for Democracy and Justice in Chad (MDJT), led by Youssof Togoimi, a former defense minister. The rebels still maintained some control over parts of northwestern Chad, and fighting flares up periodically. In retaliation for rebel attacks in northern and eastern Chad, government troops have carried out acts of reprisal against the local population, burning villages and killing livestock.

Since 1990 Chad has been under the rule of its strongman president Idriss Déby, leader of the Patriotic Salvation Movement (MPS), who seized power in a coup. Although he won reelection in May 2001, the voting was marred by fraud. To consolidate power, Déby has sought to co-opt rivals and use patronage as well as intimidation to maintain a stable coalition government. Most senior positions in the government are held by members of Déby's ethnic group. Nonetheless, Déby has brought to Chad more openness and freedom than his predecessor, Hissène Habré, who ruled the former French colony from 1982 until he was deposed by Déby. In his effort to crush all opposition to his regime, Habré had conducted several military operations in the north directed against ethnic groups regarded as threats to his regime, wiping out entire communities in the process. It is believed that his forces—notably his political police known as the Documentation and Security Directorate (DDS)—tortured and murdered tens of thousands.

Even though Déby's regime represents a considerable improvement over Habré's, it is hardly a model of democracy. Chad's human rights record is still rated poor by recent *Country Reports* issued yearly by the U.S. State Department. Chad's citizens have only limited ability to influence or change their government. The ruling party holds all but a handful of seats in the parliament. Political opposition figures are often arrested and detained, and in spite of constitutional guarantees of freedom of assembly, the government bans demonstrations by the opposition.

Abuses on the part of security forces are by no means limited to political opponents. They have been implicated in EXTRAJUDICIAL KILLINGS, abductions, TORTURE, and rape of civilians. Perpetrators of such crimes rarely face prosecution, and the judiciary is known to buckle under political pressure from the executive branch. Security forces also carry out illegal searches and wiretaps.

Freedom of the press does exist—private newspapers that are highly critical of the government freely circulate in the capital—and in contrast to Habré's regime, journalists do not have to fear being detained for what they write. But they are at risk of legal action if they turn out articles on the rebellion in the northern part of the country or write about corruption among senior government officials.

In July 2003 the Chad-Cameroon oil pipeline became operational. Even based on conservative estimates, Chad is likely to double its oil revenues in 2004. In an agreement with the World Bank, Chad pledged to dedicate part of its new wealth to reducing poverty and improving social services and the education and health-care systems. How the agreement will be implemented in practice, however, remains to be seen.

In 2004 Chad found itself in the news because it had suddenly become home to hundreds of thousands of REFUGEES from the Darfur region of Sudan who had been driven out of their homeland by Arab militias. International relief agencies were furiously trying to get aid to the destitute population while policymakers scrambled to find a solution to the crisis, with which Chad was ill-equipped to cope.

See also DARFUR, WAR CRIMES IN; SUDAN, HUMAN RIGHTS VIOLATIONS IN.

Chamblain, Louis Jodel   *See* HAITIAN HUMAN RIGHTS VIOLATORS.

Chechnya, war crimes in

Since 1991, with only occasional interludes of peace, the Russian republic of Chechnya has been embroiled in a bloody war of independence. Located in southwestern Russia, Chechnya has a long history of resistance to Russian rule that extends back several centuries. The population is Muslim, in contrast to Russia, where the vast majority belong to the Russian Orthodox Church. There have been two wars since Chechnya declared its independence from Russia in 1991, a move that Moscow refused to recognize. The first conflict began in December 1994 when Russian troops invaded the republic and lasted until August 1996, resulting in some 40,000 deaths and the displacement of hundreds of thousands of people. After three years of uneasy peace, hostilities resumed in 1999 and have continued ever since.

By all accounts the two wars have created a humanitarian disaster: Human rights organizations estimate that at least 15 percent of the entire population has been eliminated. Before the war, Chechnya's population was about 1 million; it is now closer to 700,000. Russian losses have also been high: As many as 10,000 Russian soldiers have died in the second campaign, double the Russian losses in the 1994–96 war. In addition, tens of thousands of people have been uprooted from their homes. Human rights violations have been widespread and rampant; abuses include TORTURE, EXTRAJUDICIAL KILLINGS, PILLAGE, UNLAWFUL IMPRISONMENT, kidnappings, rapes, and DISAPPEARANCES. Few of the perpetrators have been prosecuted; all sides in the conflict are to blame.

The current fighting can be traced back to August 22, 1991, when thousands of jubilant Chechens poured into the main square of the capital, Grozny, to celebrate what turned out to be an abortive coup against the Soviet leader, Mikhail Gorbachev. Chechens regarded this as their independence day, but Moscow rejected Chechnya's bid for secession. By the time the secessionist leader Dzhokhar Dudayev took the oath of office on November 9, 1991, Russian President Boris Yeltsin had already declared a state of emergency in the Chechen-Ingush Republic. Acting under the mistaken assumption that the rebellion could be easily put down, Yeltsin sent a battalion of troops into the republic to restore order. Russian jets bombed Grozny's airport, and Yeltsin issued an ultimatum demanding that Chechens lay down their arms in 48 hours. The Chechens refused. After several days of wavering, Yeltsin, pressured by Kremlin hard-liners, imposed a land-and-air blockade on Chechnya; then the Russians invaded. The Russian defense minister, Pavel Grachev, boasted that resistance would crumble in a few hours, a view that many Russian generals did not share. Ironically, the Russian bombardment of Grozny ended up killing more Russian civilians than Chechens. But Chechen civilians didn't escape the violence, and up to 40,000 were killed in the two years of fighting in the first Chechen war. In a desperate attempt to reach a settlement, the Russian government offered the Chechens almost complete autonomy within the Russian Federation but stopped short of granting the republic the independence it sought. Chechens were divided; some

Russian soldiers patrolling the streets of Grozny, Chechnya *(Landov)*

were prepared to accept the offer but the rebels fought on, determined to obtain independence. In August 1996, Chechen rebels retook the capital, dealing the Russian troops a humiliating blow. A renewed push for a peace agreement led to an accord that essentially put off dealing with the issue of independence, postponing any decision on Chechnya's final status until 2001. By December 1996 all Russian troops had withdrawn from the republic. Moscow persisted in the fiction that Chechnya remained an integral part of the Russian Federation, and the Chechen rebels clung to the fiction that they had effectively secured their independence. The false peace, as it proved to be, would not last for long.

If Russians elsewhere in the country felt safely removed from the Chechen conflict, they were soon to be disabused of their comforting illusion. In 1999 Moscow and other cities in Russia were rocked by a series of bombings that leveled apartment buildings and killed more than 300 people. The unprecedented terrorist attacks shocked the country, and the Kremlin was quick to blame the blasts on Chechen separatists. The identity of the actual perpetrators has never been established to the satisfaction of neutral observers, but there is no question that the Chechen rebels had decided on a more aggressive strategy. Chechen rebels launched raids into the neighboring republic of Dagestan, sparking fears that an Islamic uprising would soon engulf Russia's southern borders. Russian prime minister Vladimir Putin, who was shortly to replace the ailing Yeltsin as president, promised to suppress the Chechen insurrection once and for all. Once again Russian troops moved into Chechnya and reestablished control of Grozny. The Russian military began to experience some success in pushing the rebels out of the capital and into the mountainous countryside but was incapable of consolidating their gains. Even their hold over Grozny remained fragile. Although the majority of Russians supported Putin's uncompromising stance—and for the most part the media toed the Kremlin's line—the war ground on, seemingly without end.

The September 11, 2001, attacks on the United States offered Putin a pretext to declare that the conflict in Chechnya was only another battle in the overall war on terrorism. By making common cause with Washington, Putin was trying to immunize Russia from criticism for its human rights violations in Chechnya, a strategy that has proven largely successful. But Putin was not being entirely disingenuous: Chechen rebels were in fact becoming more radicalized; many rebels found haven in Afghanistan, then under the TALIBAN's rule, where they joined the ranks of al-QAEDA. During a meeting with Secretary of State Colin L. Powell, Putin described bombings in Saudi Arabia and Chechnya as "links in the same chain of acts by international terrorists."

Meanwhile, nearly anarchic conditions prevailed in the republic. In 2002, 1,132 civilians were killed by Russian soldiers or rebels—a rate five to eight times the murder rate for Russia, and between 10 and 15 times the murder rate for Moscow. In the first two months of 2003 alone, there were 70 murders, 126 abductions, and 25 cases in which human corpses were found. Security forces were implicated in 185 of the crimes reported.

Russian troops in Chechnya have committed hundreds of forced disappearances, extrajudicial executions, and widespread acts of torture and ill-treatment. Few officers or soldiers have been called to account for these crimes. In 2003, even after fighting had tapered off to some extent, the Russian human rights group MEMORIAL documented 478 disappearances. The true number, Memorial said, was probably much higher, citing the reluctance of witnesses to come forward because of the possibility of retaliation. In 50 of these cases, the disappeared were later found dead; another 155 were either freed or ransomed by families, and the remaining 273 were still unaccounted for. HUMAN RIGHTS WATCH estimated that disappearances were only accelerating—at roughly three people per week, the highest rate Human Rights Watch had documented since the beginning of the conflict. The organization also saw no diminishment of cases of extrajudicial execution, torture and ill-treatment, and arbitrary detention. Nor did the Russian government show any more inclination to investigate these abuses than in the past. For their part, Chechen rebels are believed to be responsible for a continuing pattern of assassinations of village administrators and other civil servants working for the pro-Moscow government in Grozny.

Officially, Moscow maintains that it is committed to seeing justice done. In February 2003 President Putin declared that the Chechen judiciary and legal system was up and running, adding that "we will not cover those who committed crimes in the Chechen Republic, including servicemen of the Russian Army." Some officers have been prosecuted on charges of atrocities, and officials offer statistics meant to indicate that several criminal cases have been opened against soldiers and police officers for crimes against Chechen citizens. But human rights organizations dismiss the significance of these figures, pointing out that without any context—how many criminal cases have been brought, how many investigated, and so on—there is no way to establish whether the violators of human rights are being punished. Evidence compiled by human rights organizations suggests that the authorities have taken few concerted measures to curb the crimes committed by security forces.

In March 2003 a new constitution was introduced in Chechnya that reaffirmed its status as a republic within the Russian Federation. In October 2003 an election was held for president of the republic; the winner, handpicked by the Kremlin, was Akmad Kadyrov, a former rebel leader. International observers considered the election fraudulent. Nevertheless, once again Moscow declared that the war was over and that order had been restored, but inevitably events proved such assertions wrong. Chechens have taken the war to Moscow and other major cities in Russia. In one of the most spectacular attacks, rebels seized a theater in the center of Moscow in October 2002, holding hundreds of theatergoers, including many children, hostage. The siege was brought to an end by force; the rebels were all killed, and scores of hostages died, mostly from the effects of the gas security forces used to immobilize the assailants.

Chechen rebels have now adopted a new terrorist tactic already popularized elsewhere: suicide bombings. In July 2003 at least 16 persons were killed when two women blew themselves up at an outdoor rock concert in Moscow. An explosion on the Moscow subway on February 6, 2004, killed at least 39 persons. Although the identity of the attackers was not known, most Russians inevitably saw it as the work of Chechen separatists.

For the most part, the media's acquiescence to the government—most broadcast networks, through which most people get their information, are under state control—meant that relatively few Russians were aware of the humanitarian disaster unfolding in Chechnya. Moreover, the Russian government has made it difficult for outsiders to find out what is happening. The Kremlin has refused to renew the mandate of the ORGANIZATION FOR SECURITY AND COOPERATION IN EUROPE (OSCE) Assistance Group to Chechnya; it has also barred visits to the region by several UN special missions and regularly prevents Human Rights Watch and other humanitarian groups access to Chechnya since the outbreak of the conflict in 1999. Chechen human rights advocates are especially at risk for harassment by the authorities, and at least one of them disappeared after being taken into custody.

The war—and human rights abuses connected to the conflict—has not been limited to Chechnya. Declaring that the situation in Chechnya had "normalized," Russian authorities began to pressure internally displaced persons in refugee camps in the neighboring republic of Ingushetia to return home in 2002. Among other things, Moscow did not want to suffer the embarrassment of REFUGEES being sheltered on Russian soil. The government used a combination of various inducements—compensation for the refugees' lost homes, for instance—as well as threats of arrest on trumped-up charges. To underscore their message, the Russians cut off gas, electricity, and water to many of the camps. The names of thousands of refugees were struck off the official aid lists, depriving them of the food rations they depended on. When that was not sufficient to remove the refugees, Russian forces based in Chechnya moved into Ingushetia, where they committed many of the same abuses as they had in Chechnya, including arbitrary arrests and detention, the mistreatment of civilians, and looting. These operations were intended to compel the tens of thousands of internally displaced people to return to Chechnya, although Ingushetia was a much safer environment for them than their homeland. By spring 2003 practically all of these refugee camps in Ingushetia had been shut down, although more than 40,000 Chechen refugees remained in the republic outside the camps, living in abandoned factories and Soviet-era collective farms.

According to a Memorial representative, "through the liquidation of refugee camps the Russian leadership is trying to remove the evidence that the situation in Chechnya is far from normal." The human rights group said the forced repatriation was reminiscent of the mass DEPORTATIONS that went on during the Stalin era.

By spring 2004, four years after Putin had sent in troops to pacify Chechnya, intensive fighting has fallen off, but rebels continue to stage devastating raids, and much of the republic remains beyond the control of the Russian military. The war has also fostered lawless conditions in which ordinary gangland crimes flourish and robberies, kidnappings for ransom, and murders are widespread. Putin had hoped that the president elected in October 2003, Akmad Kadyrov, would somehow be able to create at least a facade of legitimacy. Although initially derided by most Chechens, Kadyrov began to acquire some credibility with his open criticism of Russia. However, in May 2004 he was assassinated in a bomb attack that killed several other officials, dealing a severe blow to Putin's plans to resolve the Chechen crisis. In June 2004, in a show of unexpected strength, Chechen rebels launched a devastating stealth attack against towns inside Ingushetia, taking the Russians by surprise and resulting in about 100 deaths. If anything, the threat of a widening war was growing as Chechen rebels began to make good on their promises to bring the war to the Russian people.

The Chechnyan crisis turned even deadlier in the summer of 2004, beginning with the downing of two commercial jetliners, apparently by two Chechen female suicide bombers who smuggled themselves on board the aircraft, and culminating in the attack on a school in Beslan, North Ossetia, in September 2004 that left 344 people dead. (North Ossetsia in the central Caucuses is part of the Russian Federation.) The hostage taking began on the morning of September 1, the opening of the school year, as 32 heavily armed terrorists took over School Number One in Beslan, North Ossetia, a region near Chechnya. More than 1,200 people—students, teachers, and parents—were in Middle School Number 1 when terrorists broke in, taking them hostage and planting bombs. Security forces quickly surrounded the building. After a SIEGE lasting three days, a bomb in the gymnasium detonated, whether by intention or accident, setting off a fire. Security forces attacked. In the ensuing mayhem, 344 students and teachers (of which 172 were children) were slain as well as all the terrorists. The Russian government was widely criticized for taking actions that put the lives of children and teachers in danger, and allegations surfaced in January 2005 that some law-enforcement officials had abetted the terrorist attack, prompting calls in Moscow for an investigation. Although an official probe of the Beslan tragedy was initiated and a surviving Chechen terrorist was put on trial, practically no one in Russia was satisfied with the way the Kremlin had carried out the inquiry. A year after the massacre grief-stricken families in Beslan remained convinced that the government was ducking responsibility for botching the rescue of the victims trapped in the school. In August 2005 the Russian government refused to renew the accreditation of a journalist working for ABC News because the network had run an interview with Chechen rebel leader Shamil Basayev, who claimed to have orchestrated the seizure of the school. Meanwhile, the war in neighboring Chechnya ground on, undermining the Kremlin's attempts to claim the conflict was largely over.

See also RUSSIA, HUMAN RIGHTS VIOLATIONS IN.

Further Reading:

Meier, Andrew. *Chechnya: To the Heart of a Conflict.* New York: W. W. Norton & Company, 2004.

Orr, Michael. *Russia's Wars with Chechnya 1994–2003.* Essential Histories. London: Osprey Publishing, 2005.

Politkovskaya, Anna. *A Small Corner of Hell: Dispatches from Chechnya.* Chicago: University of Chicago Press, 2003.

Tishkov, Valery, and Mikhail Gorbachev. *Chechnya: Life in a War-Torn Society.* California Series in Public Anthropology. Berkeley: University of California Press, 2004.

Chemical Ali *See* Majid, Ali Hassan al-.

chemical weapons

Chemical weapons were first used on a massive scale during the First World War, resulting in 100,000 deaths and several hundred thousand additional injuries. More recently, Iraq employed chemical weapons against Iranians during the Iran-Iraq war (1980–88). It is thought that as many as 45,000 Iranians died as a result of attacks using these weapons. In August 1988 Iraq mounted an assault using chemical weapons on Kurdish villages in northern Iraq. Observers from the Physicians for Human Rights (PHR) concluded that the Iraqis probably used mustard gas and a lethal nerve agent. Estimates of fatalities in the attack against Kurds range from 3,000 to 5,000. The horror that the use of such weapons provokes galvanized the international community to take steps to ban them. During the cold war, both the United States and the Soviet Union found it in their interest to control the production, stockpiling, and proliferation of chemical-warfare agents.

There are two basic types of chemical weapons: agents that target the surface of the body and the lungs and agents that affect the nervous system. Surface agents include phosgene gas, chlorine gas, and hydrogen cyanide, as well as mustard gas, which was employed in trench warfare during World War I. Agents in the first category act in a variety of ways; phosgene, for example, causes the lungs to fill with water, chlorine destroys the cells lining the respiratory tract, and mustard gas is a blistering agent that damages any surface it comes into contact with, including the skin, eyes, and lungs. Nerve agents such as sarin, soman, tabun, and VX can either be inhaled, like chlorine or phosgene, or absorbed through the skin. Even a single drop of such an agent can immobilize the nervous system. The most powerful of this category of agents is VX, which can kill within minutes after exposure. In addition, herbicides such as Agent Orange, used to defoliate jungle terrain in the Vietnam War, have also been linked to serious health problems.

The widespread revulsion caused by these weapons has spurred an international effort to outlaw their use and destroy existing stockpiles. The most important treaty banning chemical weapons is the 1993 Convention on the Prohibition of the Development, Production, Stockpiling and Use of Chemical Weapons and on Their Destruction (otherwise known as the Chemical Weapons Convention, or CWC), which entered into force on April 29, 1997, after its ratification by the U.S. Senate. The treaty established the Organization for the Prohibition of Chemical Weapons (OPCW) in The Hague to implement its provisions. The treaty bans the production, acquisition, stockpiling, transfer, and use of chemical weapons. Imports of chemicals that could be used in making such weapons were also curtailed;

there are also specific prohibitions against the transfer of controlled chemicals to states that are not party to the treaty. It is now estimated that the United States will not complete the process of destroying its chemical weapons stockpile until 2012. Signatories of the CWC that possess chemical weapons are required to destroy their stockpiles by April 2007.

The CWC is arguably the most ambitious treaty in the history of arms control. It differs from other arms control treaties in that, rather than limiting a particular type of weapon, it requires their elimination outright. Approximately 170 states have ratified or acceded to the CWC or have signed the treaty but not yet ratified it. By May 2000 the OPCW had conducted 739 inspections of 352 sites in 35 countries that had signed the treaty. Even though many states had not adhered to all of the CWC's timetables, they submitted their initial declarations to the OPCW stating how they intended to go about destroying their stockpiles.

The CWC is distinct from other arms control treaties in another way, since it is the first such treaty to have a significant impact on the private sector. Chemicals, like microorganisms, are a perfect example of dual-use agents since they can be used for both peaceful and lethal purposes. Even though the United States no longer manufactures chemical weapons, many of the chemicals that are routinely used in industrial production and manufacture can be turned into chemical weapons. A solvent commonly used in ballpoint-pen ink, for instance, can be easily converted into mustard gas, and chemicals widely used to produce fire retardants and pesticides can also be used to make nerve agents. That is why, if it is to be effective, the treaty requires that commercial facilities producing, processing, or consuming dual-use chemicals be monitored as well.

American soldiers in full anti-chemical gear *(United States Department of Defense)*

However, the CWC does not prevent research or the maintenance of defensive programs intended to protect countries from chemical warfare. Nor does it prevent states from taking retaliatory action against a chemical attack with the important stipulation that the means of retaliation not include chemical weapons. In Senate testimony about the 1992 Gulf War, John Shalikashvili, former chairman of the Joint Chiefs of Staff, stated that "the U.S. military's ability to deter chemical weapons in a post-CW [cold war] world will be predicated upon both a robust chemical weapons defense capability, and the ability to rapidly bring to bear superior and overwhelming military force in retaliation against a chemical attack." The implication was clear: Effective conventional military force was adequate to deter or retaliate against a chemical strike by an adversary.

The CWC penalizes countries that do not join the treaty by barring them from obtaining certain chemicals controlled by the treaty. Because of their dual-use nature, some of these chemicals have industrial and commercial value. Thus, failure to sign or accede to the treaty may mean paying a heavy economic price. There is also a political stigma attached to being a holdout, which Iraq discovered after the Gulf War in 1991.

According to official U.S. estimates, some 20 countries are suspected of possessing or developing chemical weapons. There is little doubt on the part of intelligence agencies that terrorist groups are eager to get their hands on chemical weapons. These weapons are attractive to countries or groups that hope to obtain a mass-destruction capability: They are relatively cheap to produce, they do not require a great deal of technical knowledge or infrastructure (unlike nuclear weapons) to produce, and in most cases they are easily transported.

Some violations of the CWC have occurred since the treaty went into effect. In 1995 the Japanese religious cult Aum Shinrikyo staged a sarin-gas attack on a Tokyo subway that killed 12 people, underscoring the danger of such chemicals falling into the possession of terrorist groups. In 2002, human rights advocates charged the Laotian and Vietnamese governments, both under Communist rule, with using chemical (as well as biological) weapons against Hmong tribesmen, reportedly killing 250 and injuring another 274 in Xieng Khouang Province, Laos.

See also HAGUE CONVENTIONS; HALABAJAH; HMONG, PERSECUTION OF; IRAQ, HUMAN RIGHTS VIOLATIONS IN; KURDISTAN (IRAQ), SUPPRESSION OF; LAOS, HUMAN RIGHTS VIOLATIONS IN.

Further Reading:
Barnaby, Frank. *How to Build a Nuclear Bomb: And Other Weapons of Mass Destruction.* New York: Nation Books, 2004.
Langford, R. Everett. *Introduction to Weapons of Mass Destruction: Radiological, Chemical, and Biological.* New York: Wiley-Interscience, 2004.
Price, Richard M. *The Chemical Weapons Taboo.* Ithaca, N.Y.: Cornell University Press, 1997.
Tucker, Jonathan B., ed. *Toxic Terror: Assessing Terrorist Use of Chemical and Biological Weapons.* BCSIA Studies in International Security. Cambridge, Mass.: The MIT Press, 2000.

children's rights

As the most vulnerable population, children are at particular risk of suffering from human rights abuses. In many parts of the world, children are exploited for labor and as sexual slaves. In conflict zones, children are abducted and forced to take part in combat. Street children are frequently singled out by police and brutalized or imprisoned with adults in inhumane conditions. AIDS has created millions of orphans without families to care for them or are placed in institutions where they are mistreated. Without power or voice, they have, in the words of HUMAN RIGHTS WATCH, "fallen through the cracks in the international human rights arena."

Most human rights campaigns focus on the rights of adults, especially political dissidents. To redress the gap, the United Nations General Assembly adopted the CONVENTION ON THE RIGHTS OF THE CHILD in November 1989; it went into force in 1990. The preamble states that children "should grow up in a family environment, in an atmosphere of happiness, love and understanding." Children should be "protected against all forms of discrimination or punishment on the basis of the status, activities, expressed opinions, or beliefs of the child's parents, legal guardians, or family members." Children are promised the same rights as guaranteed by other UN conventions to adults: the right to life, liberty, education, and health care. The convention makes it illegal to use children in armed conflict and protects them from discrimination; TORTURE; cruel, inhuman, or degrading treatment; and sexual and economic exploitation. Most states ratified the convention, yet in spite of its lofty principles, hideous abuses and violations of the rights of children take place throughout the world.

Children in Conflict
Conflict exacts a fearsome toll on children in two different ways: as victims and as conscripts. Because of their inherent vulnerability they often suffer the most when violence breaks out. UNICEF estimates that within a recent 10-year period, 2 million children died as a direct result of armed conflict, and an additional 6 million were injured or disabled. About 1 million children have been orphaned or separated from their families by conflict in the 1990s.

Sierra Leone offers a vivid illustration of the catastrophic effects war can have on children. In the decade-long war in Sierra Leone, children were murdered, mutilated, tortured, beaten, raped, and enslaved for sexual purposes. The brutalizing of children by rebels is almost unimaginable: Infants and children were burned alive, the hands of two-year-old toddlers were lopped off with machetes, and girls as young as eight were sexually abused. One Sierra Leone hospital reported that in just a three-month period in 1998, approximately one-quarter of 265 casualties admitted were children. In a nine-day period in February 1998, 111 children were killed in one area of the countryside.

But children are victims in another way: In many conflicts they are conscripted into serving as fighters or turned into slave labor providing support for combatants. Girls and young women are often abducted and forced to become sex slaves (also known as "wives" and camp followers) of the fighters. But according to a study carried out by Rights and Democracy, a Canadian human rights group, girls have been recruited as fighters in 34 countries. During the war in Mozambique that erupted after the country gained independence, girls served both the government and rebel forces as fighters, intelligence officers, spies, porters, medics, and slave labor. Some were recruited, some joined of their own free will, and others were abducted. In many instances, human rights organizations ignored the problem. Mozambique is by no means an exception. Human Rights Watch has documented the recruitment of children as soldiers in armed conflicts in Myanmar (Burma), Colombia, the Democratic Republic of the Congo, Lebanon, and Uganda, among other countries. Children are given the same arms to use as adults and are forced to undertake dangerous assignments such as laying explosives or serving as human mine detectors. They are further brutalized by being forced to participate in suicide missions and commit atrocities.

In the northern Ugandan countryside, families send their children to makeshift shelters in nearby towns and cities every night to avoid abduction by the rebel Lord's Resistance Army (LRA), which has a practice of targeting children ranging in age from eight or nine to 16, although they are said to prefer older children. Children who fail to keep up with the workload or who try to escape are generally put to death. And these deaths are not quick; in cases where children attempt to escape, other children are forced to kill the miscreant; in the event that one child refuses, he or she may be killed as well.

In the Democratic Republic of the Congo, too, thousands of children have been recruited by government forces, progovernment militias, and rebel forces. In Myanmar the army has forcibly recruited thousands of children who are used as porters, guards, and combatants. All of

A child soldier in the Democratic Republic of the Congo (Jean-Patrick DiSilvestro/ICRC)

them are subjected to degrading treatment, and there is some evidence that many are executed. Children who commit infractions—falling asleep at their posts, for example—are likely to be severely beaten. According to two teenage recruits who were interviewed by Human Rights Watch, military training was characterized by beatings, sleep deprivation, and starvation. Boys with only one year of training are sent to the front line.

If anything, the situation in Colombia is worse; in the bloody conflict between the government and various insurgent movements, thousands of children have been recruited as fighters on all sides, and thousands have perished. The paramilitaries, which constitute a third force in the conflict, have recruited children as young as eight years old. According to some estimates, up to 50 percent of some paramilitary units are made up of children. After one clash with rebels, the Colombian army announced that 20 of the rebels killed were children, and 32 of those captured turned out to be 17 or younger, including several who were under 14; a third of them were females. Children who try to escape from their rebel abductors are considered deserters and are summarily executed. Children who give information to the army are put to death as well. Even children who are captured and placed in detention centers are at risk of being killed by other imprisoned guerrilla children. Between 1994 and 1996, the Public Advocate's Office reported that 13 percent of the children convicted of belonging to guerrilla groups and then imprisoned were killed while in custody.

When a conflict comes to an end, new problems arise when children are released from their captors. For countries such as Sierra Leone that are recovering from a decade of civil war, it is a staggeringly difficult task to reintegrate these former child soldiers into society and provide them with schooling and job training. Many humanitarian programs actually exclude children since their focus is on adults. In Mozambique, for example, some girl soldiers end up remaining with the same men who captured them. Others drift into cities where they have sometimes formed a community with other girls with similar experiences. Moreover, females who have been recruited as sex slaves are at greater risk of HIV infection.

Wars such as those in West Africa and Colombia also inflict devastation on children in a myriad of ways. When children are forced to flee from their homes to escape the brunt of war, they face other dangers. Refugee camps are notoriously unsafe in many parts of the world, and children suffer from physical abuse, sexual violence, and exploitation. Families will often send their children back to their ravaged homelands to search for food, which places them at heightened risk of being captured, injured, or killed by forces that have overrun the territory from which they have fled. In times of chaos, children find themselves lost, abandoned, or orphaned. Unaccompanied children constitute an estimated 2–5 percent of the refugee population in the world, according to UNICEF.

In an investigation of refugee camps in Guinea, for example, Human Rights Watch found that children who had been separated from their families suffered from physical abuse by the families who had taken them in. According to some accounts, they were mistreated because they were accused of wasting time or making a mistake in work. Female refugees live in fear of rape, assault, and other forms of sexual violence. Burundian girls in Tanzanian refugee camps were often attacked even when they carried out such routine tasks as gathering firewood or collecting vegetables.

Child Labor

According to the INTERNATIONAL LABOR ORGANIZATION (ILO), some 250 million children between the ages of

five and 14 work in developing countries—at least 120 million on a full-time basis; 61 percent were in Asia, 32 percent in Africa, and 7 percent in Latin America. In rural areas children work in agriculture; in urban areas most children work in trade and services. Work conditions vary widely, ranging from virtual SLAVERY—four-year-olds who are tied to rug looms to keep them from running away—to 17-year-olds who help out on the family farm. The principal forms of childhood abuse occur in forced and bonded labor or under dangerous and unhealthy conditions where children are at risk of sustaining physical and psychological harm. Children who work at looms, for example, may suffer from eye damage, lung disease, stunted growth, and a susceptibility to arthritis as they grow older. Human rights organizations are particularly concerned about labor conditions where children are confined and beaten, deprived of both their freedom and a right to an education.

A child laborer cutting sugarcane in Brazil (J. Etchart/Exile Images)

Bonded labor is otherwise known as debt bondage or peonage. It is outlawed by the 1956 UN Supplementary Convention on the Abolition of SLAVERY, the Slave Trade, and Institutions and Practices Similar to Slavery. Bonded labor involves a business transaction whereby an advance payment is made to a (usually destitute) family, who in exchange hands over their child to an employer. The amount paid may be as little as $15 depending on the type of work and the age and skill of the child. In theory the child can work off his debt, but in practice this almost never occurs; the child is unable to work off the debt, and the family is seldom able to buy the child back. Unscrupulous employers debit a variety of "expenses" or deduct "interest" from their paychecks, effectively keeping them in debt indefinitely. In some cases, bonded labor agreements are multigenerational, meaning that each generation in a family is obliged by the contract to turn over a child to an employer, often for no payment at all. As the child gets older, he or she may be freed but only on condition that another younger child from the family is offered as a replacement.

Millions of children work as bonded child laborers in countries around the world—15 million in India alone, where the practice has a long tradition. (If all forms of child labor in the country are taken into account, as many as 60–115 million children may be employed, the largest number of working children in the world.) These children, some as young as four or five, are put to work in fields, stone quarries, and mills or sent out into the streets to pick rags. Some work as indentured domestic servants. Their fates are grim: old age by 40, death by 50.

Trafficking and Sexual Exploitation of Children

Trafficking in children is a growing problem. As many as 1.2 million children may be trafficked every year. According to the International Organization for Migration, there is scarcely a part of the world where trafficking does not take place, including western Europe and the United States. The U.S. State Department estimates that 50,000–100,000 women and children are trafficked into the United States each year and forced to work as bonded laborers in sweatshops or in domestic servitude. Nearly 90 percent of children trafficked in West and central Africa who work as domestic workers are girls. Approximately 1,000–1,500 Guatemalan babies and children are trafficked each year for adoption by couples in North America and Europe. Trafficking of children in Asia, Latin America, and Africa is even more epidemic. In addition to debt bondage, traffickers resort to deception, fraud, intimidation, isolation, threats, and physical force to obtain their victims. Families often willingly turn over their children to traffickers in exchange for cash. However, they often do so because they are deceived into believing that they are providing their children with a better life than they could offer themselves.

Thousands of children are recruited into the sex industry. According to UNICEF, 30–35 percent of all sex workers in the Mekong region of Southeast Asia are between 12 and 17 years of age. And in Lithuania, 20–50 percent of prostitutes are believed to be minors, some as young as 11. Children have even been recruited from children's homes—some 10–12 years old—for use in pornographic films. In Mexico, more than 16,000 children are engaged in prostitution; many of them work in popular resorts catering to tourists. Girls are also available as mail-order brides—some as young as 13—for affluent Westerners who prefer to stay at home and find a girl on the Internet. Because child trafficking is linked to criminal activity and corruption, it can be difficult to detect. In some instances trafficked children are even arrested and detained as illegal aliens.

Violence

At its extreme, violence directed against children can lead to death or injury, but it can also impair children's health, undermine their self-confidence, and create a heightened risk of depression and suicide in later life. As many as 40 million children in the world below the age of 15 suffer from abuse and neglect, according to the World Health Organization (WHO). In South Africa, 21,000 cases of child rape or assault are documented by police each year; in one horrifying instance, one of the rape victims was nine months old. But the number of rapes and assaults of children is undoubtedly much higher, since police say that only an estimated 1 in 36 cases of rape are reported. According to a 1996 survey in Egypt as many as 37 percent of children report that they have been beaten or tied up by their parents, and 26 percent say that they had sustained injuries such as fractures or loss of consciousness or suffered some form of permanent disability. According to a report by *China Daily* in 2005, 60 percent of Chinese children suffer corporal punishments. In 2005, 23 states in the United States to one degree or another allowed corporal punishment. Five percent of American parents admit that they have hit, kicked, or beat their children or threatened them with a knife or gun.

Discrimination

Children are subject to widespread discrimination. The most egregious types of discrimination are directed at females who are derided as inferior in many parts of the world. Demographers believe that there are 60–100 million fewer females in the world than there should be. One possible explanation is that they have been killed off by families who do not want them by means of infanticide, abortion, malnutrition, and neglect. The practice of aborting female fetuses was a special problem in China, where the government promulgated a one-family, one-child policy to curb the rise in population. Because they would be fined if they had more than one child, many mothers in rural areas would have abortions if they were carrying a girl.

Disabled children in particular suffer from discrimination. UNICEF estimates that between 120 and 150 million of the world's children and young people are disabled. Whether because of their disabilities or because they are stigmatized, very few of them attend school—less than 2 percent. In many parts of the former Soviet Union and central and eastern Europe, disabled children make up 20 percent of the child population confined in institutions.

Children can also receive a bad hand simply by being born if they are of the wrong race, ethnicity, or caste. In India, the majority of the 15 million bonded child workers are from the lowest castes. In Japan, the law entitles illegitimate children to inherit half of what children born in wedlock receive. If they do not have any parents at all, they may face even more difficult circumstances. Orphans are more at risk of being victims of violence, exploitation, trafficking, malnutrition, and physical and psychosocial trauma. In central and eastern Europe alone, almost 1.5 million children are raised in public institutions. In Russia, the situation is getting worse: The annual number of children without parental care has more than doubled over the last 10 years, despite birthrates that have fallen dramatically in recent years. According to UNICEF, an estimated 106 million children under age 15 are projected to lose one or both parents by 2010, with the number of children orphaned by HIV/AIDS expected to jump to more than 25 million. In 12 African countries, projections show that orphans will comprise at least 15 percent of all children under 15 years of age by 2010.

See also COLUMBIA, HUMAN RIGHTS VIOLATIONS IN; CONGO, DEMOCRATIC REPUBLIC OF THE, WAR CRIMES IN; MYANMAR, HUMAN RIGHTS VIOLATIONS IN; SIERRA LEONE, HUMAN RIGHTS VIOLATIONS IN; SRI LANKA, HUMAN RIGHTS VIOLATIONS IN; TRAFFICKING IN PERSONS; UGANDA, HUMAN RIGHTS VIOLATIONS IN; WAR CHILD PROJECT.

Further Reading:

Apfel, Roberta, and Bennett Simon, eds. *Minefields in Their Hearts: The Mental Health of Children in War and Communal Violence.* New Haven, Conn.: Yale University Press, 1996.

Dodge, Cole P., and Magne Raundelen. *Reaching Children in War: Sudan, Uganda and Mozambique.* London: Taylor & Francis, 1992.

Pran, Dith, comp. *Children of Cambodia's Killing Fields: Memoirs by Survivors.* Edited by Kim DePaul. New Haven, Conn.: Yale University Press, 1999.

Raymond, Alan. *Children in War.* New York: TV Books Inc, 2000.

Singer, P. W. *Children at War.* New York: Pantheon, 2005.

Chile, human rights violations in

On September 11, 1973, Chilean General Augusto PINOCHET ousted the leftist government of Salvador Allende in the bloodiest coup South America experienced in the 20th century. Until he relinquished power in 1990, Pinochet presided over an authoritarian regime responsible for serious human rights violations, including TORTURE, DISAPPEARANCES, EXTRAJUDICIAL KILLINGS, and suppression of political dissent. More than 3,000 people were killed during Pinochet's 17-year rule—2,095 verifiable deaths and 1,102 others who were disappeared and are presumed dead. In addition, thousands of others were tortured. Nearly a million people were forced to flee the country. The Pinochet era was also characterized by chronic instability as a result of sporadic rioting, violent attacks, and assassination attempts. In recent years various attempts have been made in Chile and Europe to prosecute Pinochet and other high-ranking officials in his regime for CRIMES AGAINST HUMANITY, with mixed results.

Until the coup, Chile was known as a free and democratic nation, in sharp contrast to the forms of government prevailing in much of South America. In 1970 Chileans elected Allende to the presidency. Washington viewed the ascent of an avowed leftist with alarm, and President Richard Nixon authorized the CIA to destabilize the regime. While it does not appear that the United States played a direct role in fomenting the coup, declassified documents—released in 2000 under the title "CIA Activities in Chile"—indicate that the CIA supported the military junta's attempts to undermine Allende's Popular Unity (UP) government, although many CIA officers had misgivings about the initiative. In 1971 Allende began to nationalize the copper mines, industries, banks, and large rural estates. Management in many factories was turned over to the workers; wages were allowed to rise, while prices were controlled. The socialization program, while initially popular, caused a severe downturn of the economy, and opposition to Allende began to intensify. The government tried to spend its way out of the crisis, but the result was an annual inflation rate of 500 percent. The government was paralyzed and riven by dissent, and the country was plunged into a state of chaos marked by strikes, lockouts, and daily demonstrations by both the left and the right. A strike of dockworkers in the port of San Antonio threatened to deprive the capital of Santiago of enough flour to make bread.

To ensure the army's loyalty, Allende turned to a respected officer he thought he could trust and, on August 23, 1973, appointed him commander in chief. That man was Augusto Pinochet. Weeks later Pinochet mounted a violent coup d'état that ended with Allende's death, apparently by his own hand. Several of his top aides were arrested and taken to a military base, where they were executed and buried. On September 12 the four commanding generals of the armed forces and the police officially established a military junta and appointed General Pinochet president. Then the junta set about eliminating all opposition—a formidable task in light of the fact that Allende's party had garnered more than 40 percent of the vote in the presidential election. An additional 30 percent had supported the opposition Christian Democratic Party. The military determined that the most effective means to stamp out dissent was through the use of terror. The junta declared a state of siege, imposed martial law, shut down the parliament, suspended the constitution, and purged the universities of supporters of the UP. Political parties were outlawed, union activities were banned, the media were either shut down or censored, and books judged seditious were burned.

Labor leaders who tried to mount strikes in defiance of the regime were executed. Bodies began to wash up on beaches; some were identified as people injured after the coup who had been dragged out of their hospital beds. A special military expedition called the Caravan of Death traveled through the provinces, hunting for political opponents and executing 79 of them. During the first few months of Pinochet's rule, as many as 250,000 people were taken into custody and held for short periods in stadiums, military bases, and naval vessels. To accommodate the burgeoning population of political prisoners on a more permanent basis, the junta opened several new prison camps. In some cases prisoners were kept in large shipping crates or in shacks. Officially, however, prison camps did not exist. No prisoner lists were made public, and the authorities rebuffed efforts by families to locate the detainees and disappeared.

Within a short time, Santiago had taken on the appearance of a city under occupation. In exchange for the populace's quiescence, the new government held out the promise of economic reform, introducing free-market principles. Nationalized industries and businesses were returned to their former owners, and trade barriers were cut. Pinochet declared that he intended "to make Chile not a nation of proletarians, but a nation of entrepreneurs." A new team of economists was brought in, and the new measures did succeed in bringing inflation to heel.

In November the terror campaign became institutionalized in the form of the National Prisoners Service (Servicio Nacional de Detenidos, or SENDET), which was given responsibility for the network of prison camps. The same decree also called for the creation of a Department of National Intelligence (Departamento de Inteligencia Nacional, or DINA), whose mission was "to determine the degree of dangerousness of the prisoners and to maintain permanent co-ordination with the Intelligence services of the Armed Forces, Carabineros, and Investigaciones."

DINA—the NATIONAL INTELLIGENCE DIRECTORATE—was actually a secret police force under the direct command of Manuel CONTRERAS, a Pinochet loyalist. DINA mounted operations typified by disappearances in which men without uniforms made arrests after curfew and drove off with their victims in pickup trucks without any license plates. The campaign of terror began to have its desired effect, and in September 1974 Pinochet proclaimed that Chile had become "an island of tranquility" in a violent world.

Thousands of people sought to escape Chile, many of whom faced prison terms or death if they remained. Mexico opened its doors to several leaders of the UP, including Allende's widow, Hortensia Bussi, and her daughter Isabel (who later became a popular novelist). Prominent Christian Democrats went into exile as well, and opposition centers sprung up in Mexico City, Buenos Aires, and Rome. To counter the threat from outside the country, DINA initiated clandestine missions abroad, targeting exiled opposition leaders for death. In 1976 DINA struck again in the heart of Washington, D.C., blowing up the former Chilean ambassador to the United States, Orlando Letelier, and an aide. Two years later, DINA agents working in collaboration with agents of the Argentine military junta carried out the assassination of General Carlos Prats, Pinochet's predecessor as commander in chief of the army and an outspoken opponent of the junta in Santiago. In 1988, in a move to bolster his legitimacy, Pinochet organized a plebiscite to allow voters to decide whether he deserved a new eight-year term as president. The vote went against Pinochet, surprising him and opening the way for free elections the following year, under the terms of a constitution the military junta had introduced in 1980. Pinochet voluntarily stepped down as president on March 11, 1990, but insisted on maintaining his post as commander in chief of the army (which he retained for another eight years). In addition, he became a senator for life—a position guaranteed all ex-presidents thanks to the constitution he had drafted—which had the added advantage of conferring immunity on him.

In 1998, however, while on a private visit to London to seek medical treatment, Pinochet was arrested on the basis of a Spanish warrant accusing the general of human rights crimes. His house arrest was hailed by human rights activists, but in Chile the response was more muted. The government of Eduardo Frei, a Christian Democrat, stated that only Chilean courts should try Pinochet. Democracy was still fragile, and Frei was anxious not to offend the military, where the former dictator still commanded considerable support. After several tumultuous weeks of debate, the British government decided to release Pinochet. He returned to Chile, but while some supporters gave him a hero's welcome, he no longer had an aura of invincibility. "We finally felt free to discuss and say things that were considered taboo even after years of civilian rule," observed one human rights advocate. "It was as if an oppressive shroud had been lifted from the country." Polls showed that 70 percent of the population wanted to see Pinochet put on trial.

In 2000 the Chilean Supreme Court ruled that Pinochet could be stripped of his immunity and made to stand trial. The charges previously lifted against him in Chile were reinstated in January 2001, and he was once more placed under house arrest, this time in his homeland. Prosecutors hoped to try him first for the deaths in 1973 of 19 supporters and officials of the ousted Allende regime. Meanwhile, Argentina was prepared to request his extradition to face charges related to the assassination of General Prats. But in 2002 the Chilean Supreme Court dealt a blow to human rights advocates, ruling that the former dictator was too ill to stand trial. Subsequent rulings by the high court, though, have left open the possibility that the former dictator might still be tried.

With a few notable exceptions—former DINA chief Manuel Contreras and his deputy, Pedro Espinosa—no high-ranking official of the junta has been tried for his crimes. Chile's Supreme Court barred many cases from proceeding on the grounds of the 1978 amnesty law immunizing any member of the armed forces from prosecution for crimes committed between 1973 and 1978. Other cases were transferred to military courts where the accused were certain to receive lenient treatment. In the late 1990s the pace picked up, but only slightly, with the conviction of the assassins of former Chilean ambassador Letelier and his aide in 1976. Another 20 members of the security forces have been convicted for human rights violations between 1978 and the end of military rule in March 1990, but 16 of them were implicated in the same crime.

Nonetheless, prosecutors are still hopeful of bringing high officials in the junta to account in spite of the AMNESTY because of specific cases involving the "disappeared." Because the courts have determined that these are continuing crimes—in other words, the victims are not officially dead and could still, theoretically, be alive—they can still be prosecuted since the crimes would not be subject to the amnesty. Some legal experts have disputed this interpretation. In addition to the amnesty, prosecutors are also hampered by a lack of evidence relating to the victims, in large part because the military has failed to turn it over or produced material that is too cryptic to be of value. There is no way to determine when victims were killed, how they were killed, and how their bodies were disposed of. The armed forces have, however, released a report detailing the fate of 200 victims; the report disclosed that more than 150 corpses of prisoners were dumped into the ocean or in rivers and lakes.

As one indication of the dramatic change that has occurred in Chile, a socialist government was voted into power in 2000. Moreover, the new president, Ricardo Lagos Escobar, appointed as his defense minister Michelle Bachelet, the daughter of an air force general who worked with President Allende and died at the hands of Pinochet's torturers in prison. A socialist with presidential aspirations of her own, Bachelet has actually earned the grudging respect of the armed forces. "There was a group of Pinochet supporters who thought when the wives of the disappeared died off the problem will die with it," she has been quoted as saying. "But their children and grandchildren have taken up the flag."

In an unprecedented move announced in fall 2004, the Chilean army finally acknowledged institutional responsibility for human rights abuses during the Pinochet dictatorship. For decades the army had denied overall culpability, holding that only individual officers should be blamed. At the same time, the government released a report, based on testimony from more than 30,000 people, that some 3,190 people were killed during the dictatorship in addition to the thousands who were illegally imprisoned and tortured or forced into exile. Human rights advocates, while welcoming the military's disclosures, appealed for more information regarding the fate of 1,000 people who were disappeared by the Pinochet regime and are presumably dead.

See also OPERATION CONDOR.

Further Reading:
Constable, Pamela. *A Nation of Enemies: Chile under Pinochet.* New York: W. W. Norton & Company, 1993.

Davis, William Columbus. *Warnings from the Far South: Democracy versus Dictatorship in Uruguay, Argentina, and Chile.* New York: Praeger Publishers, 1995.

Dinges, John. *The Condor Years: How Pinochet and His Allies Brought Terrorism to Three Continents.* New York: New Press, 2004.

Dorfman, Ariel. *Exorcising Terror: The Incredible Unending Trial of Augusto Pinochet.* New York: Seven Stories Press, 2002.

Kornbluh, Peter. *The Pinochet File: A Declassified Dossier on Atrocity and Accountability.* A National Security Archive Book. New York: New Press, 2003.

Politzer, Patricia, and Diane Wachtel. *Fear in Chile: Lives under Pinochet.* New York: New Press, 2001.

China, human rights violations in

Human rights violations in the People's Republic of China remain a grave problem even as the country continues to enjoy unprecedented economic growth. Political opponents and adherents of certain religious faiths are subjected to arbitrary detentions and imprisonment. The government takes a dim view of any attempt to question the legitimacy of the Communist Party's rule or publicly raise such sensitive issues as the violent crackdown of student protest in Tiananmen Square in June 1989 in which hundreds might have been slain.

TORTURE and mistreatment of detainees are widespread. The government restricts freedom of assembly and rights of laborers to organize and form independent unions. The economic boom has also brought with it increasing corruption and crime. In response, in 2003 the authorities launched what it called a "strike hard" campaign, which was expanded to include political dissidents, ethnic separatists, and those individuals the regime labels "terrorists" and "religious extremists." Suspects arrested in the crackdown seldom receive fair trials if they are not simply held for long periods without any charges being brought at all. In many of these cases, the accused are convicted after a brief hearing and executed. In 2002, according to AMNESTY INTERNATIONAL, the authorities carried out 1,060 executions. Suppression of dissent was particularly harsh in the Xinjiang Uighur Autonomous Region (XUAR) in western China and in Tibet, where freedom of expression and religion continued to be severely restricted. Further, in 2004 Beijing made it clear that it was unwilling to meet Hong Kong citizens' demands for greater democracy, declaring that it had no intention of permitting universal suffrage for many years to come.

Political Repression

In spite of various changes in the laws on the books—in 1997 the Criminal Procedure Law revisions strengthened the rights of defendants in theory—defendants are not entitled to the presumption of innocence. Legal rights of defendants are routinely compromised or ignored by police officials, prosecutors, and judges. Counsels are seldom provided, and even if they are, they cannot gather evidence in their clients' defense. Many defendants are sent to reeducation-through-labor camps without any judicial review. Officially, some 310,000 people were reported to be in these camps as of 2002, although human rights groups estimate that the actual number is far higher.

Stability has always been regarded as one of the most important national priorities in a country that has been repeatedly fractured by rebellion and civil war throughout its history. Suppression of political, religious, and ethnic dissent has all been justified on this basis. The "strike hard" campaign against crime of 2003, for instance, has led to even more egregious violations of legal protections for defendants, resulting in harsher prison sentences without DUE PROCESS. To wrest confessions from suspects, the police have used such methods of torture as kicking, beating, electric shocks, suspension by the arms, shackling in painful positions, and sleep and food deprivation. But polit-

ical dissenters are not the only victims of human rights abuses: Bystanders at protests, homeless children, migrant workers, vagrants, and suspected prostitutes have all been rounded up and held without charge under a system of administrative detention known as "custody and repatriation"—approximately a million people in total, according to Amnesty International.

The death penalty is being imposed with greater frequency, too, occasioned by the enactment of "antiterrorist" amendments to the Criminal Law in December 2001. The definition of *terrorist* was so vague that it raised concerns that the classification could be applied to many individuals and organizations that tried to exercise their legitimate rights. They are right to be concerned: Political activists, human rights defenders, and even Internet users have been arrested when they have attempted to freely associate or express their views. Many of those arrested have been accused of being "subversives" or passing "state secrets" to foreigners (whether directly or over the Internet), a charge that can result in the death penalty. Political and religious dissenters are not the only ones who are condemned to death. Drug dealers and violent criminals face the death penalty, as do tax cheats and pimps. Executions—by shooting or lethal injections—often are carried out within hours of the sentencing. In June 2002, to commemorate the United Nations' International Anti-Drugs Day on June 26, the government executed at least 150 drug offenders.

The government has acknowledged some of these abuses. A senior official in the Public Security Ministry admitted that police had used torture to extract confessions and called for greater police discipline and more investigations of abuses. Some moves were actually made to put the official's words into effect; death sentences were lifted for five members of an unregistered Christian organization who alleged that they had been tortured into confessing their guilt in a rape case. Instead, they received a retrial because of "insufficient evidence and unclear facts," which resulted in long prison sentences. Nonetheless, according to Amnesty International, widespread human rights abuses continue because of the "combined effects of repressive and vaguely worded criminal legislation, the use of administrative detention, a weak judiciary and impunity for officials who abuse their power."

However, in early 2005 the Chinese government signaled a possible relaxation in its policy regarding political prisoners, whom it had never previously acknowledged. The government provided U.S. officials with a list of 51 political prisoners whose sentences it said been reduced or who were being considered for early release. Most of the prisoners on the list were charged with "endangering state security" or "counterrevolution," crimes defined vaguely in Chinese law and routinely used against dissidents. The gesture, while welcome by Washington, was also driven by Chinese eagerness to stave off a resolution critical of its human rights policies under consideration by the United Nations Security Council. The Chinese had already agreed to resume formal talks with the United States about human rights that had broken off earlier. Some U.S. officials, however, believed that the list might mark a real change in policy, noting that some of the names on it were previously unknown outside China. Moreover, in the past, Beijing would respond to inquiries by the United Nations and foreign governments only if a name was provided, while refusing to comment about others it was holding. It was unclear whether China would also break with policy and permit visits of prisoners by inspectors from the INTERNATIONAL COMMITTEE OF THE RED CROSS, who have generally been barred except under controlled conditions. The ICRC is not the only NGO that the government has restricted. Other NGOs involved with the environment, legal aid, health, and education have been forced to find government sponsors or shut down. Fearful of U.S. disruptive influence, which China blames for the fall of hard-line governments in Ukraine, Georgia, and Kyrgyzstan, Beijing has also pressured many NGOs to stop accepting money from the United States and other foreign countries.

Freedom of Association and Labor Rights

Although China's constitution and the International Covenant on Economic, Social, and Cultural Rights (which China has ratified) guarantee the right to freedom of association, independent trade unions are banned. Nonetheless, laborers are insisting on greater rights in response to low wages, unjustified layoffs, oppressive management, and dangerous conditions in the workplace. Protests by workers have been met by excessive force, and several labor organizers have been sentenced to prison terms ranging from four to seven years after trials considered "problematic" by human rights organizations. Labor conditions are especially difficult in the rural provinces where the majority of China's 1.2 billion people live.

Unrest has been spreading in the countryside, as peasants, who still make up the vast majority of China's population, find themselves left farther and farther behind by the new economy. Angered by a growing disparity in wealth, rising health costs, and corruption, millions of impoverished peasants have resorted to protests. Many of these demonstrations, while initially peaceful, have been brutally suppressed by police and have escalated into violence. Some protest leaders have gone underground to escape arrest. Even the government has been compelled to acknowledge the increasing number of "incidents." According to the minister in charge of the public security bureau, the number of disturbances reported in 2004 rose to 74,000 from 58,000 in 2003 and involved 3.6 million people.

Religious and Ethnic Groups

The government targets religious and spiritual groups that are seen to pose a threat to stability, including some unregistered Christian groups that conduct services in underground churches and especially the Falun Gong movement, which Beijing has labeled a "heretical organization." Tens of thousands of Falun Gong followers have been arrested and tortured for their beliefs; many are placed in "reeducation through labor" centers or psychiatric institutions. Similarly, members of banned Christian groups have been mistreated and tortured while in custody.

Forced Eviction

Because economic development is given priority, other considerations—environmental factors or human rights—often go ignored. The government has proceeded with forced evictions of both rural and urban populations in its drive to build dams or raze certain city districts to make way for skyscrapers. By law these evictions can proceed even while the people being affected are trying to fight them. In any case, courts often refuse to hear the cases. In recent years protests against the evictions have become more frequent—including suicide protests—but they are often suppressed and the participants jailed.

Restrictions on the Internet and the Press

The Internet in China, while accessible in the cities, is closely monitored, and individuals have been convicted on charges of subversion for expressing views critical of the government in chat rooms or posting "reactionary articles and essays." Many foreign sites are blocked altogether, especially those that carry news or opinions objectionable to the government. There are reports that China is training "cyber police" who will monitor the use of the Internet by activists. In November 2002 the Ministry of Culture introduced new regulations to restrict access to the Internet and the operations of Internet cafés. Under the leadership of President Hu Jintao the government has continued a crackdown on the media, firing editors at publications that defied orders from the party's Propaganda Department even as the country's more diversified media has been flexing its muscles, investigating scandals and mismanagement it would never have dared to in the past. Observers note that the campaign to discipline the media since Hu took over in 2002 has actually intensified.

Repatriation of North Korean Asylum Seekers

Driven by poverty and political oppression, thousands of REFUGEES from North Korea have illegally taken refuge in China. China has responded by forcibly repatriating hundreds, perhaps thousands, of these refugees without reviewing their claims for asylum, even though it is a party to the 1951 Refugee Convention and its 1967 Protocol, which prohibit such repatriation. China has not permitted the UNITED NATIONS HIGH COMMISSIONER FOR REFUGEES to establish a presence on the China–North Korean border. Nonetheless, the conditions in North Korea are so dire that many refugees continue to risk arrest and repatriation. (Those who are returned are liable to be sent to harsh labor camps for the crime of leaving the country illegally.) In desperation, several North Koreans have slipped into foreign embassies—often the South Korean embassy—in an effort to obtain asylum in other countries.

Xinjiang-Uighur Autonomous Region

Xinjiang-Uighur is a region in western China with a large Muslim population. (Most of the rest of the country is Han.) A separatist Muslim movement known as the East Turkestan Islamic Movement has emerged in this area, which is largely desert; the central government has responded by declaring a "war on terror" of its own. But human rights organizations report that the Chinese have made little or no distinction between violent and peaceful protest and that its crackdown on the Muslim Uighur population has resulted in summary trials, torture, and excessive use of the death penalty. Muslim religious expression has been severely curbed; mosques have been razed, traditional gatherings outlawed, religious classes raided, publishing houses closed for printing "unauthorized" religious literature, and religious leaders forced to undergo "patriotic reeducation" campaigns. The security forces have increased their surveillance of Muslim weddings and funerals and other religious ceremonies.

Tibet

Tibet has long been considered a political problem for Beijing, and the government has tried to eliminate any expression of support for an independent Tibet or for the exiled spiritual and political leader, the Dalai Lama. The government has ruthlessly cracked down on dissent and sentenced prominent lamas and their supporters, who are viewed as disloyal. Buddhist monasteries have been closed and monks and nuns expelled. In 2002 about 180 people, mostly monks and nuns, were illegally held in prison. Arbitrary arrests and torture are frequent, people are held incommunicado for months, and death sentences have been imposed on individuals on trumped-up charges such as "inciting separatism" and "causing explosions."

Hong Kong

Although the Basic Law guaranteed Hong Kong a degree of autonomy, Beijing has begun to clamp down on the freedoms that its residents expected after Britain handed the territory back to China in 1997, dashing hopes that universal suffrage would be introduced. In April 2004 Beijing announced that the citizens of Hong Kong would not be allowed to directly elect their own leaders in elections set for 2007 and 2008. Most power is now retained by the chief executive of the territory, who is chosen by the central government, and a parliament, half of whose members are appointed, not elected. Human rights groups express fears that an antiterrorist ordinance passed by Beijing in 2002 could be used to restrict human rights. Some activists who have taken part in large demonstrations for greater democracy have been arrested and charged with organizing unlawful assembly under a revised Public Order Ordinance that had never been applied before. In July 2004 an estimated 500,000 people gathered peacefully in Hong Kong to protest Beijing's decision to restrict the right to directly elect representatives to the municipal government. Fears that the mainland might impose further restrictions were heightened after three popular radio hosts known for being outspoken resigned or were forced from their jobs. Police in Hong Kong have also targeted Falun Gong members who participate in demonstrations in spite of the fact that Falun Gong is a legally registered society in the territory.

HIV/AIDS Epidemic

For many years China refused to acknowledge the gathering threat of AIDS/HIV. Public health officials fear that the epidemic of the disease in China might become the worst in the world. Until recently, the government denied that there was a problem at all and even went so far as to harass and detain officials and physicians who tried to raise the issue in public. Some people with the illness were denied treatment by hospitals and those at high risk for contracting AIDS, such as drug users, were detained without trial in forced detoxification centers. In many respects the state is at fault for the explosion of the disease in the first place: In the 1990s many impoverished peasants sold their blood to state-run blood collection centers, which in turn sold the blood without testing it for HIV. So far the government has done little to investigate these centers. While China has recently taken steps to officially acknowledge the extent of the problem and try to curb the spread of the disease, little progress has been seen in protecting the rights of those who actually have the illness. The failure of the government's health system to deal with the threat of an epidemic was underscored in 2003 when it failed to respond promptly to the outbreak of SARS (Severe Acute Respiratory Syndrome), which proved difficult to contain because of its dangerously infectious nature.

The Tormented Legacy of World War II

Sixty years after the end of the war and more than three decades after Japan and China reestablished diplomatic ties, bitterness still persists between the two countries.

Unlike Germany, Japan has never entirely come to terms with its past or explicitly acknowledged its culpability for crimes committed during the war, much less for abuses committed during Japanese colonial rule over Korea. Even though Japanese prime minister Junichiro Koizumi has made measured apologies, as some of his predecessors have, he has failed to assuage the Chinese, Koreans, and other Asians whose countries suffered at the hands of the Japanese. Koizumi has further stirred the waters by making annual pilgrimages to a famous Shinto shrine where several Class A war criminals are interred. These former government officials and military officers had been convicted by the International Military Tribunal for the Far East at the TOKYO TRIALS on several charges, including war crimes, crimes against peace, and CRIMES AGAINST HUMANITY. Nonetheless, many Japanese still believe that their memories should be honored because of their patriotism and courage.

In April 2005 mass demonstrations against Japan took place in several major Chinese cities, orchestrated by the Communist government. There were several precipitating factors that included the granting of a concession to gas fields by Japan in waters claimed by China and the publication of a Japanese textbook that downplayed atrocities perpetrated by Japan during its occupation of Manchuria and other Chinese territory. However, the dispute between the two nations transcends lingering rancor over the past; Japan and China are both vying for political and economic domination of Asia, and with its annual growth rate of about 9 percent, China would appear to be winning.

China is also causing alarm in Tokyo by flexing its military muscles, enacting a law, for instance, threatening to invade Taiwan if the breakaway province is even seen as taking steps toward a declaration of independence. The rivalry between Beijing and Tokyo is reflected in a massive public-relations campaign by China to prevent Japan from gaining permanent membership on the United Nations Security Council. All the same, Beijing appears unwilling to allow a crisis to undo relations entirely, as this might jeopardize current and future Japanese investments in the country.

In late April 2005, as protests against Japan turned violent, the Chinese authorities cracked down, declaring a moratorium on further demonstrations and closing anti-Japanese Internet sites. The government was also acting in its own self-interest. Several times in modern Chinese history, demonstrations that had begun in protest of a foreign power had gotten out of hand and led to uprisings against the central government. The Communist regime had no wish to see history repeated.

See also JIANG YANYONG; MANCHURIA, JAPANESE WAR CRIMES IN; NORTH KOREA, HUMAN RIGHTS VIOLATIONS IN; RELIGIOUS PERSECUTION; WEI JINSHENG.

Further Reading:

Foot, Rosemary. *Rights beyond Borders: The Global Community and the Struggle over Human Rights in China.* Oxford: Oxford University Press, 2001.

Kent, Ann. *Between Freedom and Subsistence: China and Human Rights.* Oxford: Oxford University Press, 1995.

Munro, R. *Punishment Season: Human Rights in China after Martial Law.* Asia Watch Report. New York: Human Rights Watch, 1990.

Santoro, Michael A. *Profits and Principles: Global Capitalism and Human Rights in China.* Ithaca, N.Y.: Cornell University Press, 2000.

Weatherley, Robert. *The Discourse of Human Rights in China: Historical and Ideological Perspectives.* Sydney, Australia: Palgrave Macmillan, 1999.

Choeun, Chhit   *See* TA MOK.

CIA war crimes archive

Under a 1998 law, the Central Intelligence Agency (CIA) was ordered to disclose millions of pages of classified documents relating to the relationship U.S. intelligence agencies had with Nazi war criminals after World War II. A special group, the Nazi War Crimes and Japanese Imperial Government Records Interagency Working Group (IWG), was set up and tasked with the responsibility of examining these papers. It was hardly a secret that to counter a growing Soviet threat in Europe, the United States had made use of suspected war criminals in intelligence operations. For example, the Americans recruited the spy network of General Reinhard Gehlen, a top-ranking intelligence officer under Adolf HITLER. (His network later developed into the BND, the West German spy agency.) While Gehlen was never accused of committing any war crimes himself, it was known to the Americans that he employed former Nazis, including war criminals. According to the CIA history *Forging an Intelligence Partnership: CIA and the Origins of the BND, 1945–49*, the alliance was a "double-edged sword" because the Soviet Communists were able to exploit the relationship for propaganda purposes.

The CIA has refused to declassify many of the documents, defining the law narrowly; the agency says that it has already released some 1.2 million pages of documents (most of them from the Office of Strategic Services, the CIA's predecessor). These documents revealed a much closer relationship between U.S. intelligence and Nazi war criminals or Nazi collaborators than previously suspected. However, the CIA refused to declassify other archives until Congress complained, admitting that it had held onto material "that does not relate to war crimes per se." This admission suggested that the documents might deal with the

CIA's association with individuals who had committed the crimes. In January 2005, after a prominent senator and members of the working group aired their grievances against the agency in public, the CIA relented, pledging for the first time in an e-mail sent to Senator Mike DeWine of Ohio that it would "acknowledge any relationship" between the CIA and SS members, regardless of whether there was any information specifically tying them to war crimes. In the message, the CIA also agreed that documents "concerning acts performed by Nazi war criminals, to include members of the SS, on behalf of C.I.A." were relevant—a change from its previous position—and should be disclosed under the law.

civilian immunity

The concept of immunity is based on the belief that certain people should have protection in wartime. Historians can trace the concept back as far as 1582, when a Spanish judge declared that "intentional killing of innocent persons, for example, women and children, is not allowable in war." Under this principle, military forces are constrained from directly targeting civilian populations for attack. These prohibitions include INDISCRIMINATE ATTACKS such as CARPET BOMBING intended to terrorize civilian populations. By aiming Scud missiles at Israeli cities during the Gulf War in 1992, for instance, Iraq was waging indiscriminate warfare. No military objective was involved; the intention was to bring terror to a civilian population. However, as Heike Spieker observes in an essay on civilian immunity written for the CRIMES OF WAR PROJECT, a case can be made that a similar strike directed at Kurdish towns in northern Iraq "could not easily have been characterized as unlawful indiscriminate attacks, provided Iraq had claimed to direct them against insurgents."

In addition, civilian immunity is taken to mean that certain groups of people shall not be attacked: the elderly, the infirm, pregnant women, children under fifteen, the elderly, and mothers of children under seven. There are also some noncivilian groups that are entitled to immunity, including combatants who are injured in battle or prisoners of war. The GENEVA CONVENTIONS of 1949 codified civilian immunity, which was extended as well to civilian "objects" such as hospitals and religious institutions. For the purpose of protection, hospitals are broadly defined; they can be both fixed and mobile, taking the form of hospital ships, medical aircraft, and even ambulances. Moreover, the medical staff that works in the hospital—whether civilian or military—is also entitled to protection from hostile fire under the Geneva Conventions. The medical staff includes not only doctors, nurses, and orderlies but the drivers, cleaners, cooks, and crews of hospital ships. Some aid workers—Red Cross volunteers, for example—as well

as military chaplains who treat the wounded on the battlefield are also covered. The convention does, however, stipulate that a medical facility be clearly marked with a red cross, red crescent, or red diamond. (The introduction of the red diamond in 2005 resolved a dispute about conferring recognition on the Jewish Star of David.) The facility cannot be used as camouflage for military activities or located near a military objective, thus making it into a "shield." Other buildings and sites are guaranteed protections by the 1954 Convention on Cultural Property: places of worship, historic monuments, civic institutions, cultural treasures, libraries, and schools that are not related to military purposes.

In conflicts that involve urban areas, however, it is difficult to distinguish between military and civilian targets where buildings of many different kinds can be closely situated. Of course, in many instances, strikes on urban areas fall under the category of indiscriminate attacks—such as the Serbian siege of Sarajevo (1992–96) during the Bosnian war—and therefore are considered war crimes.

In terms of international law, the most specific stipulations pertaining to civilian immunity are found in the 1977 ADDITIONAL PROTOCOLS TO THE GENEVA CONVENTIONS, which state: "The civilian population and individual civilians shall enjoy general protection against the dangers arising from military operations." Common Article 3 of the Geneva Conventions, however, applies to civilian immunity in "all cases of declared war or of any other armed conflict which may arise between two or more of the High Contracting parties, even if the state of war is not recognized by one of them." The convention does not refer to civilian protections in internal conflicts, however. What is meant by "civilian" and "civilian population" had to wait until Protocol I, which defined the terms in Article 50:

1. The civilian population comprises all who are civilians.
2. The presence within the civilian population of individuals who do not come within the definition of civilians does not deprive the population of its civilian character.

Article 51 of Protocol I spells out the protections civilians are entitled to:

1. The civilian population and individual civilians shall enjoy general protection against dangers arising from military operations. To give effect to this protection, the following rules, which are additional to other applicable rules of international law, shall be observed in all circumstances.
2. The civilian population as such, as well as individual civilians, shall not be the object of attack. Acts or threats of violence the primary purpose of which is to spread terror among the civilian population are prohibited.

3. Civilians shall enjoy the protection afforded by this Section, unless and for such time as they take a direct part in hostilities.
4. Indiscriminate attacks are prohibited. . . .

Under Protocol I, belligerents have the obligation to discriminate between combatants and civilians (or "noncombatants") in wartime. (A noncombatant can be defined as a person who does *not* take part in hostilities *and* who does not have a legal right to do so under the law of armed conflict.)

Additional Protocol II to the Geneva Conventions attempts to address the lack of codified protections for civilians in noninternational or internal conflicts (those conflicts that do not involve wars between states). Article 1 of Protocol II states:

1. This Protocol . . . shall apply to all armed conflicts which are not covered by Article 1 of . . . (Protocol I) and which take place in the territory of a High Contracting Party between its armed forces and dissident armed forces or other organized armed groups which, under responsible command, exercise such control over a party of its territory as to enable them to carry out sustained and concerted military operations and to implement this Protocol.

It should be noted, however, that Protocol II, which is exclusively concerned with noninternational armed conflict, does not explicitly distinguish between civilians and combatants. And although it prohibits targeting civilians for an attack or spreading terror among the civilian population, it does not specifically codify a prohibition against indiscriminate attacks as such.

These treaties do not make it illegal to cause harm to civilians or protected objects in all cases. If an attack is proportional to the military objective and civilian deaths ensue as a result, no violation of international law has occurred. By the same token, otherwise-protected civilian facilities—a school or library, for example—can be struck if there is a legitimate military purpose, e.g., enemy forces have taken up position in the building. Hospitals pose a more complicated issue since innocent patients are at risk even in the event that armed forces are using it for military purposes. If a belligerent force comes under fire from a hospital, international law allows it to retaliate but only after first asking its adversary to cease using the hospital and permitting a reasonable time for compliance.

See also ARTICLE 3 COMMON TO THE GENEVA CONVENTIONS; COLLATERAL DAMAGE; CULTURAL PROPERTY, PROTECTION OF; HOSTAGES; IMMUNITY FROM ATTACK; LEGITIMATE MILITARY TARGETS; LIEBER CODE; MEDICAL PERSONNEL, PROTECTION OF; MILITARY NECESSITY; PRO-TECTED PERSONS; PUBLIC PROPERTY, PROTECTION OF; SAFE HAVENS.

Further Reading:

Jinks, Derek. *The Rules Of War: The Geneva Conventions in the Age of Terror.* Oxford: Oxford University Press, 2005.
Gutman, Roy, ed. *Crimes of War: What the Public Should Know.* New York: W. W. Norton & Company, 1999.
Pilloud, Claude. *Commentary on the Additional Protocols of 8 June 1977 to the Geneva Conventions of 12 August 1949.* Boston: Brill Academic Publishers, 1987.
Roberts, Adam, and Richard Guelff. *Documents on the Laws of War.* Oxford: Oxford University Press, 2000.
Trombly, Maria. *Journalist's Guide to the Geneva Conventions.* Indianapolis: Society of Professional Journalists, 2000.

Clark, Ramsey (1927–) *American political radical activist*

The former U.S. attorney general in the Lyndon Johnson administration, Ramsey Clark has ignited a storm of controversy in recent years by providing legal counsel for such clients as Sheik Omar Abd El-Rahman, accused of masterminding the 1993 World Trade Center bombing; Radovan KARADŽIĆ, the indicted Bosnian Serbian war criminal; and a Rwandan pastor who stood trial for genocide. He has also sought to put NATO commanders on trial for the alliance's bombing strikes on Belgrade, which were to force the withdrawal of Yugoslav troops from Kosovo in 1995. In 2005 he agreed to represent Saddam Hussein at his war crimes trial in Baghdad, Iraq.

Clark comes from a distinguished Southern pedigree. His father, Tom Clark, was an attorney general before him and later served on the Supreme Court before resigning in 1967 to prevent any conflict of interest when Lyndon Johnson appointed his son attorney general. While attorney general, Ramsey Clark was responsible for prosecuting Dr. Benjamin Spock, the noted authority on child rearing, for conspiracy to encourage draft dodging during the Vietnam War. In 1976 he ran unsuccessfully for the U.S. Senate from New York. It was only later, when he went into private practice, that he began to shift his political views to the left. Since then he has become an ardent critic of U.S. foreign and military policy around the world. He has called American government officials "international outlaws" who are "killing innocent people because we don't like their leader."

In 1998 Clark attended a human rights conference in Baghdad, Iraq—then under the control of Saddam HUSSEIN—where he declared that "the governments of the rich nations, primarily the United States, England and France," dominated the wording of the UNIVERSAL DECLARATION OF HUMAN RIGHTS, which showed "little concern for economic, social and cultural rights." He founded an antiwar movement called the International Action Center and has made well-publicized visits to countries such as Iraq, Serbia, and Vietnam to investigate the effects of American bombing and economic sanctions in those countries. But his current notoriety mainly derives from the clients he has chosen to represent, who are almost invariably unpopular. He has represented the antiwar activist Father Philip Berrigan; the Native American political activist Leonard Peltier; the far-right extremist political figure Lyndon LaRouche; and the Branch Davidians, the religious movement whose compound in Waco, Texas, was destroyed with considerable loss of life during a confrontation with government agents in 1993.

He defended the indicted Karadžić in a civil suit in New York in 1997 and flew to Belgrade in 1999 to show his support for President Slobodan Milošević while NATO was carrying out its air campaign against the former Yugoslavia. He advised Milošević to file a suit against NATO for GENOCIDE at the INTERNATIONAL COURT OF JUSTICE, ignoring the fact that the court had already initiated legal action against Yugoslavia to stop committing genocide against the Bosnians. (Milošević later went on trial in The Hague for war crimes in 2003.) Clark took on the case of another indicted war criminal, Pastor Elizaphan Ntakirutimana, who, during the Rwandan genocide in 1994, handed over Tutsi members of his congregation to Hutu militias, who murdered them. Clark lost the case, and Ntakirutimana was turned over to the UN tribunal prosecuting war crimes in Rwanda.

In other controversial cases, Clark has defended Bernard Coard, who assassinated Prime Minister Maurice Bishop of Grenada. He defended Charles TAYLOR in 1988 in the Liberian leader's attempt to avoid being extradited to Liberia from the United States to face embezzlement charges. Taylor, who later returned to Liberia on his own terms, was subsequently indicted for war crimes committed after he had taken power. Clark also undertook the defense of the Palestinian Liberation Organization (PLO) against a lawsuit brought by the family of Leon Klinghoffer, the disabled American Jew who was killed during the 1985 hijacking of a cruise ship by PLO guerrillas. Asked why he has taken on such unsympathetic—and often reviled—clients, he said, "Are they human beings? Do they need help? Is that your calling? You can't do it all, but you do what you can." His detractors nonetheless wonder why he has chosen the clients he has. In addition to his work for the International Action Center, Clark is also affiliated with the Workers' World Party and the antiwar group ANSWER (Act Now to Stop War and End Racism).

Clauberg, Carl (1898–1957) *Nazi physician*

Professor Carl Clauberg was a Nazi physician at the Auschwitz extermination camp. He was tried by a Soviet court after World War II for conducting lethal MEDICAL EXPERIMENTS on inmates in which he injected chemical substances into the wombs of thousands of Jewish and gypsy women. The victims were sterilized and suffered from intense pain, inflamed ovaries, bursting spasms in the stomach, and bleeding. Clauberg tortured both men and women by repeatedly exposing them to X-ray machines; when their radiation burns made them no longer suitable for further experimentation, they were sent to the gas chambers. He also organized a program in which men's testicles were removed, supposedly in order to subject them to pathological examination.

Clauberg was convicted and sentenced to 25 years in prison. However, seven years later, he was pardoned under an agreement between Bonn and Moscow and returned to West Germany. As soon as he arrived, he held a press conference in which he boasted of his scientific work at Auschwitz. Outrage at his bravado caused the government to move to arrest him in 1955, but he died in August 1957 before he could be tried.

Further Reading:

Weindling, Paul Julian. *Nazi Medicine and the Nuremberg Trials: From Medical War Crimes to Informed Consent.* Sydney, Australia: Palgrave Macmillan, 2005.

collateral damage

Ever since the Vietnam War, *collateral damage* has become a familiar term; it has even served as the title of an Arnold Schwartznegger movie. It is generally taken to refer to civilian casualties or damage to property that occurs inadvertently as a result of attacks on a military objective. Collateral damage is more likely when the military objectives being targeted are situated within or close to concentrations of civilians. The *United States Air Force Intelligence Targeting Guide* of February 1998 defines collateral damage as "unintentional damage or incidental damage affecting facilities, equipment or personnel occurring as a result of military actions directed against targeted enemy forces or facilities. Such damage can occur to friendly, neutral, and even enemy forces." The targeting guide cites the example of the Operation Linebacker air strikes against North Vietnam, noting that "some incidental damage occurred from bombs falling outside target areas. Consequently, there was an effort to minimize such collateral damage to civilian facilities in populated regions." The guide states that determination of collateral damage constraints is a command responsibility.

International law does not prohibit collateral damage per se; it is difficult to enact laws forbidding accidents, after all. However, international laws related to armed conflict do restrict INDISCRIMINATE ATTACKS that can inflict harm on civilian populations and property. Article 57 of the 1977

Additional Protocol I to the 1949 GENEVA CONVENTIONS states that, in an international conflict, "constant care shall be taken to spare the civilian population, civilians, and civilian objects." Article 51 prohibits attacks using weapons that cannot be properly controlled—CARPET BOMBING, for instance. The protocols also stress that the use of force must be proportionate to the objective. If these standards are likely to be violated, then it is incumbent on military commanders to refrain from instigating an attack or to suspend an operation if it is seen as being disproportionate to secure the military advantage.

Collateral damage was widespread during World War II, which was characterized by indiscriminate bombing of cities such as London, Dresden, Rotterdam, Tokyo, Leningrad, Hiroshima, and Nagasaki, causing massive civilian casualties and devastating damage to property. Most of these attacks had little or no effect on an adversary's military capacity; they were intended instead to terrorize and demoralize civilian populations, though there is little evidence that the attacks succeeded in doing so. Even when military commanders take great pains to minimize civilian casualties and unintended damage to property, collateral damage is almost impossible to avoid. In the bombing of Baghdad that preceded the U.S.-led invasion of Iraq in 2003, the use of precision-guided missiles did indeed result in many fewer casualties than in previous conflicts, although some errant missiles did result in several deaths. But once the war begins in earnest on the ground—especially in countries like Iraq, where much of the fighting takes place in or near cities—collateral damage almost invariably increases.

Collateral damage is a loaded term. In the view of one party to a conflict, it may be perceived as an unavoidable consequence of a proportional strike on a legitimate military target, while the defender may label the attack indiscriminate. Neutral observers may also have their own opinion. NATO rejected charges that any civilian casualties resulting from its 1995 air strikes on Bosnian Serb military targets in the Bosnian war were disproportionate. The same case was more difficult to argue in NATO bombing strikes on Belgrade during the war in Kosovo, which killed three employees in the Chinese embassy. Many civilians also died in the Gulf War because by bombing power plants, coalition aircraft cut off electricity to hospitals. There is no question that these deaths were the result of collateral damage—hospitals were not being bombed and their patients were not being targeted—but whether these casualties can be justified as proportional is a matter of debate. It is worth noting that preceding the invasion of Iraq in 2003, U.S. bombers did not target power plants. Thus, besides having legal implications, the term is often used to win political support for a specific method of warfare or to counter allegations of violations of humanitarian law.

Trying to assess collateral damage poses several problems. Even leaving aside measuring long-term effects, calculating casualties from an attack is a problematic exercise. The military might prefer to lump civilian and military casualties together to avoid negative publicity or to boost the body count of enemy dead, a notorious and discredited practice used for many years by the Pentagon during the Vietnam War. More recently, human rights organizations and journalists have encountered considerable difficulty learning how many Iraqi civilians have been killed or injured as a result of collateral damage during the U.S.-led invasion or in the subsequent occupation.

To define collateral damage as applying only to casualties and damage inadvertently caused as a result of an attack on a military objective is too limited. These are *direct* effects of combat. Collateral damage also refers to the *indirect* effects of combat—long-term physical or mental trauma, for instance, or illness resulting from exposure to toxic substances in a conflict zone. In this sense, American veterans who have suffered from the use of Agent Orange, a herbicide, while they were serving in Vietnam or from Gulf War Syndrome in the First Gulf War in 1991 could be said to be victims of collateral damage. In fact, conflict zones can be fairly accurately looked at as environmental disasters. Thousands of civilians are maimed or killed on almost a daily basis in countries such as Cambodia and Afghanistan that have been seeded with millions of mines over decades of war. These injuries and deaths can justifiably be considered collateral damage as well, even though they may occur years after the conflict has come to an end. In Iraq, civilians as well as combatants have been exposed to a variety of toxic substances that are likely to have critical long-term consequences. In addition to land mines, environmental contaminants also include explosive remnants of war (ERWs), defined as live munitions left after conflict, and depleted uranium (DU), which is used in antitank ammunition and produces a chemically toxic (though weakly radioactive) dust upon detonation.

International law is not as specific about prohibitions to collateral damage when it comes to internal conflict. According to Additional Protocol II, civilian populations are guaranteed "general protection against the dangers arising from military operations" and "shall not be the object of attack," so long as they do not take part in hostilities. Protocol II also outlaws acts or threats of violence meant "to spread terror among the civilian population."

See also ADDITIONAL PROTOCOLS TO THE GENEVA CONVENTIONS; CIVILIAN IMMUNITY; MILITARY NECESSITY; PUBLIC PROPERTY, PROTECTION OF.

Further Reading:
Cornish, Paul. *Anti-personnel Mines: Controlling the Plague of "Butterflies."* London: Royal Institute of International Affairs, 1994.

Gutman, Roy, ed. *Crimes of War: What the Public Should Know.* New York: W. W. Norton & Company, 1999.

Jinks, Derek. *The Rules of War: The Geneva Conventions in the Age of Terror.* Oxford: Oxford University Press, 2005.

Pilloud, Claude. *Commentary on the Additional Protocols of 8 June 1977 to the Geneva Conventions of 12 August 1949.* Boston: Brill Academic Publishers, 1987.

Roberts, Adam, and Richard Guelff. *Documents on the Laws of War.* Oxford: Oxford University Press, 2000.

Trombly, Maria. *Journalist's Guide to the Geneva Conventions.* Indianapolis: Society of Professional Journalists, 2000.

collective punishment

Collective punishment is a form of reprisal that seeks to inflict pain on a particular group or population for crimes supposedly carried out by one or more of its members. Because it means imposing punishment on many innocent people for the actions of a few, collective punishment is outlawed by international law. In practice, however, it is still widely used by various armies and security forces in conflict situations around the world. Article 50 of the 1907 Geneva Convention specifically bans collective punishment: "No general penalty, pecuniary or otherwise, shall be inflicted upon the population on account of the acts of individuals for which they cannot be regarded as jointly and severally responsible." That provision, however, failed to deter German forces from executing Belgian villagers in retribution for resistance activity during the First World War less than a decade later. During World War II the Nazis used collective punishment as a principal tool to intimidate and demoralize civilian populations in occupied Europe. In one of the most widely known cases of collective punishment, the Germans executed 173 male residents of Lidice, Czechoslovakia, in retaliation for the assassination of a top Nazi official, Reinhard HEYDRICH, by men believed to have come from the village. The women and children were deported to CONCENTRATION CAMPS, and the village was razed to the ground.

The harsh lessons of World War II were not lost on delegates from around the world meeting in Geneva to develop and strengthen international laws pertaining to human rights in conflict situations. The INTERNATIONAL COMMITTEE OF THE RED CROSS (ICRC) observed that while parties to a conflict often resorted to "intimidatory measures to terrorize the population," these practices were illegal because they were directed at "guilty and innocent alike" and thus were "opposed to all principles based on humanity and justice."

The Fourth Geneva Convention, Relative to the Protection of Civilian Persons in Time of War (August 12, 1949), refers to collective punishment in two different places. Article 33 states: "No protected person may be punished for an offence he or she has not personally committed. Collective penalties and likewise all measures of intimidation or of terrorism are prohibited." It outlaws two specific types of such punishment: PILLAGE and reprisals "against protected persons and their property." Article 53 discusses collective punishment in the context of occupation: "Any destruction by the OCCUPYING POWER of real or personal property belonging individually or collectively to private persons, or to the State, or to other public authorities, or to social or cooperative organizations, is prohibited, except where such destruction is rendered absolutely necessary by military operations."

Additional Protocol II of 1977 also bans collective punishment. These prohibitions apply equally to wars between states and to internal conflicts. Armies and security forces, however, continue to impose collective punishment on a depressingly regular basis, especially in areas where the loyalty of the local population is in doubt. To shore up white rule in Rhodesia (now Zimbabwe) during the early 1970s, the government of Ian Smith enacted a law that specifically permitted the use of collective punishment on villages thought to support the insurgents. During the civil war in Algeria, both sides resorted to collective punishment; guerrillas would kill and abduct Europeans as well as Muslims who failed to show support for their cause (even though they were not actively opposing them), and in response French forces would conduct raids of villages and urban areas, massacring, bombing, or relocating people who were suspected of supporting the insurgents.

Israel has come under scathing criticism for applying what amounts to collective punishment against Palestinian populations in Gaza and the West Bank, territories it seized in the Six-Day War in June 1967. With the exception of Jericho, most Palestinian cities and towns as well as many villages have been placed under curfew for up to 24 hours a day ever since Israel reoccupied most of the West Bank in 2002. The Israeli Information Center for Human Rights in the Occupied Territories observed that because of closures and Israeli checkpoints, freedom of movement is severely curbed. Palestinians require Israeli permits to travel from one area to another. The Israeli Defense Force (IDF) has also been charged with demolishing homes and orchards without military purpose, sometimes causing injuries and the loss of life of civilians. In the Nablus area, for instance, two houses belonging to families of men wanted for organizing attacks on Israelis were destroyed as collective punishment in July 2002, but the blasts used to destroy the homes also damaged neighboring houses as well. The Israelis used British mandate law, in effect before independence, as a legal basis for these actions. According to B'Tselem, an Israeli human rights organization, the 1945

Regulation 119 of the Defense (Emergency) Regulations allows the military commander to demolish or seal a house or to confiscate the land on which the house is built, "thus prohibiting the residents of the house from rebuilding or constructing a new house where their home had been sealed. As a result, thousands of Palestinians, among them hundreds of children, are left homeless."

Israel contends that the Fourth Geneva Convention or the Additional Protocols apply to the West Bank de jure (in law) but at the same time argues that it is abiding by humanitarian provisions—without, however, being specific. Further, the IDF maintains that actions such as closures, curfews, and demolishing homes do not constitute collective punishment at all. The IDF insists instead that the purpose of such acts "is not to punish the Palestinian populations, but rather to provide a solution for a specific and defined security need."

There is no question that security concerns do play a part in the army's response. In some instances, destruction of property occurred immediately after Palestinian militants attacked Israeli civilians or security forces. In other cases, the IDF destroyed property in the area where the attack took place. The Israeli Information Center for Human Rights in the Occupied Territories asserts that by targeting property because it was the site of an attack, these actions raise "the concern that the objective . . . was to punish the Palestinians for the attack and to deter others from committing similar acts." (In 2005 Israel's defense minister ordered a halt to the demolitions.)

Pakistan has also resorted to the use of collective punishment in the pursuit of al-QAEDA fighters in the northwest provinces bordering Afghanistan. According to AMNESTY INTERNATIONAL, Pakistani security forces have not only "failed to provide adequate protection to people in the tribal areas who are unconnected with such political violence" but that they have held whole tribes "responsible for allegedly sheltering 'terrorists' and punished." In January 2004 the army destroyed several houses to punish tribes suspected of hiding "terrorists" and refusing to cooperate with the army's efforts to root them out. The army has also adopted British colonial-era tactics of collective punishment against Waziri tribesmen, who are told that they must hand over TALIBAN and al-Qaeda suspects or their houses will be blown up. The army has threatened to take hostages if the suspects are not surrendered.

U.S. forces in occupied Iraq have also received widespread criticism for employing tactics that impose collective punishment. In one incident, recorded in October 2003, the U.S. military was accused of bulldozing ancient groves of date palms and citrus trees in central Iraq because villagers in the area had refused to disclose information about insurgent activity. In a report carried by the British newspaper *Independent*, the incident took place near Dhu-

luaya, a small town 50 miles north of Baghdad. Farmers reported that they were told by U.S. troops "over a loudspeaker in Arabic, that the fruit groves were being bulldozed to punish the farmers for not informing on the resistance which is very active in this Sunni Muslim district." In April 2004, in conducting an operation against Sunni insurgents inside Fallujah, a Sunni stronghold, the American military sealed off the city of 200,000 for several days even though it meant trapping thousands of civilians in the fighting, depriving them of food and emergency medical aid. The U.S. command defended the move as necessary to restore order and flush out insurgents who can easily melt into the population after carrying out their attacks. But the siege of Fullujah only underscores the difficulty of distinguishing between actions taken because of legitimate security concerns and actions that inflict pain and suffering on innocent civilians who happen to find themselves in the wrong place at the wrong time.

See also ADDITIONAL PROTOCOLS TO THE GENEVA CONVENTIONS; GENEVA CONVENTIONS; IRAQ, HUMAN RIGHTS VIOLATIONS IN; POST-SADDAM; LIDICE, MASSACRE IN; PAKISTAN, HUMAN RIGHTS VIOLATIONS IN; PALESTINE, HUMAN RIGHTS VIOLATIONS IN; SANCTIONS.

Colombia, human rights violations in

Colombia is one of the most violent places on earth. South America's oldest democracy, Colombia has been ripped apart by a civil war that has created a staggering humanitarian crisis. Rampant crime and entrenched corruption, fueled by drug money, have undermined the country's social foundations. A new government that came to power in 2002 has pledged to bring peace to the shattered land and redress past injustices, but analysts and human rights advocates express doubts whether the government is sincere, much less whether a democratic Colombia is even possible. Because Colombia is one of the largest foreign recipients of U.S. financial aid and military assistance, Washington has an enormous stake in the outcome.

By most estimates the central government has control over only about 60 percent of the country; the rest is considered either "demilitarized" or under the control of the leftist insurgents. There are two rebel groups: FARC (Revolutionary Armed Forces of Colombia), which can muster between 15,000 and 20,000 troops, and ELN (National Liberation Army), which has about 5,000 fighters. Because the government's ability to protect much of the countryside is so limited, or even nonexistent, many wealthy ranchers and small farmers have formed private armies—known as paramilitary forces—with several thousand troops of their own. These groups have terrorized villages and, like the guerrillas, rely on extortion and collaboration with narcotraffickers to subsidize their operations. The paramilitaries have been responsible for many of the war crimes and human rights abuses in recent years, and there is evidence that in some cases they have committed atrocities with the backing, and even the active collaboration, of government security forces. The Brookings Institute, a Washington, D.C.–based think tank, estimates that over 1 million Colombians have been made refugees in their own homes as a result of the conflict, many of them women and children under the age of five.

Political violence reaches to the highest levels. In a period of 15 years (1985–2000), four presidential candidates have been assassinated in addition to 200 judges, investigators, and 1,200 police officers. Human rights defenders, community leaders, government investigators, trade unionists, and journalists faced threats, attacks, and death. During the first 10 months of 2000, four human rights defenders were killed and three "disappeared." In 2002, one presidential candidate was kidnapped by guerrillas, and both the current president and his predecessor have escaped attempts on their lives. It is also unsafe to document the conflict or human rights violations: In that same 15-year period, 151 journalists were killed as well.

According to Colombian law, cases involving allegations of crimes against humanity (*lesa humanidad*) and crimes of unusual gravity (*una gravedad inusitada*) fall under the jurisdiction of the civilian courts. These crimes include TORTURE, GENOCIDE, and forced DISAPPEARANCES, as well as other gross violations of human rights such as EXTRAJUDICIAL KILLINGS and the aiding and abetting of paramilitary groups. In theory, if there is a jurisdictional conflict between civilian and military courts, the law should favor the former. But in fact, the Colombian government continues to violate its own laws and has failed to enforce the ruling of the Constitutional Court. The armed forces will not relinquish their authority to try cases involving allegations of serious human rights violations by officers and soldiers, which human rights organizations believe will only perpetuate "a virtually unbroken record of impunity."

Humanitarian Crisis

"Violations of international humanitarian law—the laws of war—are not abstract concepts in Colombia, but the grim material of everyday life." This depressing assessment by HUMAN RIGHTS WATCH is hardly an exaggeration. One of the principal reasons that the crisis is so widespread is that in this war there is no battlefield as such nor any safe havens. Every village, every farm, and every city are equally at risk. Civilians are as liable to be caught up in the violence as the combatants, perhaps more so. In theory, ARTICLE 3 COMMON TO THE GENEVA CONVENTIONS of 1949—which pertains to armed conflict between well-organized groups within a sovereign state—should apply to Colombia. And all parties to the conflict do claim to adhere to human rights norms codified by Article 3 and other conventions and protocols, but in practice they demonstrate scant respect for human rights governing the protection of civilians in such internal conflicts.

The paramilitaries consist of several groups—at least seven—that have formed an alliance under the name AUC (United Defense Units of Colombia). AUC units operate both together with and independent of the state security forces. It maintains its own command structure and boasts its own source of weapons and supplies. Although the former AUC leader, Carlos Castaño, had repeatedly stated that his forces were willing to comply with international law, he also said that the nature of Colombia's war, where it is difficult to distinguish combatants from civilians, makes it difficult to apply. Some human rights advocates believe that the paramilitaries may be responsible for carrying out up to 80 percent of the massacres that take place each year.

The army has been implicated in the killings of noncombatants, especially in the east of the country, where the paramilitaries have relatively little presence; rebel fighters who have surrendered or been taken prisoner have been killed and tortured in direct violation of the GENEVA CONVENTIONS that confer certain protections on PRISONERS OF WAR. In other parts of the country, the army and paramilitary groups have both participated in human rights abuses. According to Human Rights Watch, the National Police is more respectful of human rights and is more willing to investigate reports of abuses. But EXTRAJUDICIAL KILLINGS by police still occur, and in some regions police work with paramilitaries and even help prepare death lists. These lists are supposedly meant to target rebels or their supporters, but there are many cases where the police have labeled entire communities as consisting of guerrilla fighters or their sympathizers and have been known to withdraw from these marked communities so that paramilitary death squads can move in and massacre the inhabitants, essentially condemning them to death. In addition to the private armies that form the so called paramilitaries, many villages are patrolled by "self-defense" units known as *convivirs*, which are made up of civilians—effectively, vigilante groups licensed by the government. Many of these groups have also collaborated with army, police, and paramilitaries in operations against the guerrillas. They are often armed with government-supplied weapons and have been implicated in human rights violations as well. Because these *convivirs* are composed of civilians, human rights groups are concerned that their existence blurs the distinction between combatants and noncombatants, which puts all civilians at risk. Abuses by these groups have gone uninvestigated and unpunished.

Like their adversaries, FARC, the largest rebel group, has shown only contempt for international law in conducting operations unless it can score points with the international community. FARC is implicated in massacres and targeted killings of civilians; it has killed prisoners of war, taken hostages engaged in looting and torture, and attacked medical aid workers. FARC is the largest and most powerful insurgent movement operating in the beleaguered South American nation. It began in 1964 as the military wing of the Communist Party and drew most of its support from landless and impoverished peasants. In the intervening years it has grown into a formidable military—and political—force. The strength of the guerrilla organization is put at 9,000–12,000 armed combatants and several thousand supporters, mostly in rural areas. FARC has carried out bombings, murders, mortar attacks, kidnappings, extortion, and hijackings. In parts of the country they have created a climate of terror, threatening, kidnapping, or attacking so many mayors that civic institutions can no longer function effectively, if at all. In addition to targeting the administrative branch, politicians, and the military, FARC has also struck at industrial and agricultural facilities, blowing up petroleum pipelines and taking over banana plantations. Like their enemies on the right—the paramilitaries who are equally, if not more, ruthless—FARC also sustains itself on profits from illegal drugs and now control much of the production, distribution, and taxation of the lucrative cocaine trade. Large parts of the country have fallen under the control of FARC, which has ruled as a state within a state, extorting "taxes" from municipalities to subsidize operations. Although it initially operated in rural areas, FARC guerrillas have now established bases in urban centers as well. Support for the guerrillas peaked during the 1980s but has since diminished as the war shows no signs of letting up. In 1998 the then-president, Andres Pastrana, initiated a peace process that he hoped would bring about a settlement with FARC and a smaller leftist guerrilla group, ELN, but the talks eventually collapsed. In a sign of displeasure with the new administration, FARC carried out a surprise mortar attack in the heart of Bogotá just as the incoming head of state, President Alvaro Uribe, was being inaugurated.

Even as President Uribe was trying to negotiate with paramilitaries, FARC seized the initiative and began to reassert its control over territory the paramilitaries had relinquished. In one incident FARC guerrillas massacred 34 coca farmers. ELN, the smaller rebel group, has given lip service to international law and called for negotiations aimed at "humanizing" the conflict, but in the field it has also been responsible for its share of atrocities. It has a record of targeted killings of civilians, killing enemy combatants who have surrendered, executing patients in hospitals, and indiscriminate attacks on houses and buses. ELN has also bombed oil pipelines in order to extort money from oil companies.

Both guerrilla groups and the paramilitaries have violated international law by recruiting children as combatants—more than 11,000 children altogether, one of the highest totals in the world. Only Burma (Myanmar) and the Democratic Republic of Congo are believed to have significantly larger numbers of child combatants. The use of child combatants is prohibited by Article 4 of Additional Protocol II, which outlaws the recruitment of children under the age of 15 or allowing them to take part in hostilities. Use of children as soldiers also contravenes both domestic law and the CONVENTION ON THE RIGHTS OF THE CHILD, which Colombia has ratified.

Eighty percent of the children bearing arms belong to the guerrilla groups. At least one of every four irregular combatants in Colombia is under 18 years of age, thousands of whom are under 15. (UNICEF reports that some are as young as eight.) Not all of these children are pressed into service by force; many join up to survive—they are desperate for food and shelter—or because they are induced by promise of money; a number are street children. Of course, many join out of coercion or fear. Children as young as 13 are trained to use assault rifles, grenades, and mortars.

The Plague of Crime

The lethal cocktail of war and drugs has turned Colombia into a treacherous environment for even the ordinary citizen. The U.S. State Department notes that the risk of being kidnapped is greater than anywhere else in the world; more than half of the world's kidnappings take place in Colombia. According to a Colombian police report, 1,833 persons were kidnapped in 1997 and 2,609 in 1998. A civilian also runs a higher risk of being murdered: 77.5 killings per 100,000—eight times greater than in the United States. From 1985 to 2000, 300,000 Colombian civilians became victims of homicide. An estimated 75 percent of the killings were attributed by the government to ordinary criminals. In that same period, 200 bombs went off in Colombian cities, some powerful enough to destroy entire buildings. Drugs have clearly contributed to the crime problem: Several thousand youths have carried out killings for pay on behalf of rival drug traffickers. Street crime, highway robberies, bank robberies, and extortion are commonplace. According to the United Nations, Colombia's drug wars have created the largest crisis for civilians in the Americas, displacing as many as 2 million people from their homes and threatening Indian tribes with extinction. Only Sudan and the Democratic Republic of the Congo have more internally displaced people.

Background

It is fair to ask how Colombia got into this parlous state. According to Laura Garces, a political scientist and the author of *The Globalization of the Monroe Doctrine*, geography has had a significant—and adverse—influence on the nation's political development. The Andes and dense forests have divided the country and fostered the growth of isolated communities that had little contact with the rest of the country, threatening the domination of the capital, Bogotá, with countervailing political forces exerted by mid-sized cities elsewhere in the country. At the same time, Garces points out, the country's proximity to the Pacific in the west and to the Caribbean in the north made it a paradise for smugglers.

In the 19th century, two rival elites formed, one calling itself Conservatives, the other Liberals. In spite of their names, they were less interested in promulgating a particular ideology than in vying for power. Most of the population remained agrarian, impoverished, and illiterate. With no external enemies to unite Colombia, most people shunned nationalism in favor of loyalty to political parties and local bosses who wielded power in their name. Instead of suppressing political dissent, the parties simply co-opted the dissenters. The uneasy balance between the two parties collapsed in 1946, and civil war—known as *La Violencia*—broke out. It is thought that as many as 300,000 people were killed before a power-sharing accord was agreed upon in the mid-1960s. (This power-sharing arrangement, which relied on coalition governments and a presidency that rotated between parties, remains in effect to this day.)

Persistent unrest, however, resulted in government crackdowns—states of SIEGE—but at the same time central authority continued to erode. As a result, people living in other parts of the country began to form defense forces of their own. The privatization of military force gradually evolved into the various factions involved in the fighting today. Initially, when the leftist insurgencies began, they relied on backing from communist countries, especially Cuba, but with the end of the cold war, they were compelled to search for new sources of revenue, a problem they solved by resorting to kidnapping for ransom. Wealthy landowners and businessmen who were particularly vulnerable to kidnapping responded to the threat by organizing armed militias for protection—the present-day paramilitaries. Then in the late 1970s a new threat arose: drug lords.

Drugs forever altered the political landscape. The seduction of drugs was so powerful that FARC effectively abandoned land reform—one of the linchpins of its program—and joined forces with drug traffickers, offering them protection and security for their vast estates. The narco-traffickers became a state within a state. Violence increased, although now it was driven less by politics than by criminal activity related to drugs.

Peace negotiations, begun between the government and the leftists in the early 1980s, made little progress. In 1998 the Conservative presidential candidate, Andres Pastrana, ran on a platform of reaching a settlement with the guerrillas and the paramilitaries, and his election was seen as a plebiscite for peace. He even went so far as to offer FARC a demilitarized zone in the south of the country, which effectively allowed them a free hand to run a state within a state. But the peace efforts, which had garnered wide international support, foundered. If anything, the violence intensified with the average number of victims of political violence and deaths in combat reaching 14 per day in 2000, more than in the previous year. The same year, more than 228,000 people were displaced, 93,000 between July and September alone, the result of a record 53 massacres, most committed by paramilitary groups, often in collaboration with security forces. Pastrana's credibility suffered as well because of allegations that he had taken money from drug traffickers in his run for president. Efforts at accommodation with the insurgents having failed, Colombia turned in 2002 to a man who pledged to use force, if necessary, to bring the strife to an end.

The Uribe Administration

According to the Colombian Human Rights Network, Álvaro Uribe Vélez was elected in 2002 because a hard core of 5.8 million voters out of about 44 million eligible believed his promise that he would eradicate the guerrillas. In a show of defiance, FARC guerrillas shelled the presidential palace on the day Uribe was sworn into office. Although he was unharmed, 19 residents of a poor Bogotá district lost their lives when a shell went astray.

Since assuming office, Uribe claims that his policies have lowered the level of violence, citing a diminished number of massacres, killings, kidnappings, and attacks on towns. Human rights advocates contend that the diminishment of violence is not necessarily due entirely to the actions Uribe's government has taken. Instead, they say that by instituting a reign of terror in areas under their control, the paramilitaries have brought about a temporary halt to violent outbreaks by guerrillas, but at an unconscionable price. Moreover, it is unclear whether FARC's power has been significantly diminished by Uribe's pacification policies. In late 2004 and early 2005, for instance, rebels launched a new wave of attacks in which 45 soldiers were killed in nine days, possibly signaling a new round of fighting after a period during which FARC had been in retreat. Approximately 1,000 soldiers had already died in a year-long campaign to rout the rebel force. There was widespread suspicion that Uribe had trumpeted his success against FARC in an effort to win a constitutional amendment allowing him to run for a second term.

Plan Colombia and Its Implications

Currently Colombia receives the third-largest amount of U.S. military aid after Israel and Egypt and was due to receive more than $700 million in 2004. The Bush administration sees in Uribe a critical ally in implementing what is known as Plan Colombia, which includes $1.3 billion in annual U.S. aid funds mainly dedicated to the eradication of coca crops. Since Plan Colombia began in 2000, the United States has granted Colombia $3.15 billion. It is estimated that at least 80 percent, or $2.52 billion, is directed to the military and police, or about a seventh of Colombia's security budget. The eradication program, however, must be seen in a larger context since the production and sale of coca have been a principal source of revenue for the insurgents. So Plan Colombia has become a counterinsurgency effort as well, putting American military advisors and security personnel hired by the U.S. government at risk. In fact, a number of contract workers have been kidnapped by FARC guerrillas. One CIA report, released to the National Security Archive through the Freedom of Information Act, concluded that "officials in Lima (Peru) and Bogotá, if given anti-drug aid for counterinsurgency purposes, would turn it to pure antiguerrilla operations with little payoff against trafficking."

Nongovernmental organizations (NGOs) and human rights organizations have protested Plan Colombia on several grounds. For one thing, they contend that too much money goes to the military and police and not enough to social initiatives and the defense of human rights. Moreover, some scientists and environmentalists argue that spraying herbicides to eradicate the coca will cause long-term damage to the farmland. In addition, given the profitability of coca, they also express doubts that farmers will agree to substitute alternative crops. There is some evidence that the eradication program may not succeed even under the best of circumstances; analysts point out that since spraying began in 1992 (before Plan Colombia), the acreage devoted to coca has actually tripled.

Human rights organizations have viewed with alarm the increasing U.S. involvement in Colombia's conflict. They expressed outrage at the decision by Secretary of State Colin Powell to certify Colombia in 2004—for the eighth year in a row—as being in compliance with human rights standards, which released $34 million in aid to the Colombian Armed Forces. "The U.S. certification suggests that the Bush administration sees the defense of human rights as a matter of paperwork, not concrete actions," said José Miguel Vivanco, executive director of Human Rights Watch's Americas Division. "It also demonstrates how readily the administration sacrifices human rights concerns to other interests." Of special concern was the failure of the Colombian government to bring the paramilitaries to heel, which would mean severing their connection with the military and security forces and bringing to justice those responsible for committing war crimes.

The Uribe administration maintains that it is moving to deal with the problem of the paramilitaries. In 2003 Uribe opened negotiations with Carlos Castaño, the paramilitary leader whom the *New York Times* dubbed "Colombia's most infamous warlord" in an effort to demobilize his fighters. In exchange, though, Castaño refused to accept a deal without guarantees that he would not be extradited to the United States to face cocaine-trafficking charges. Some paramilitaries have in fact laid down their arms—though with mixed results. In November 2003, one paramilitary group, Bloque Cacique Nutibara (BCN), demobilized 850 members (though they only turned in 112 weapons) in a nationally televised event. But the sincerity of the demonstration was put in doubt when only a month later the BCN assassinated a municipal politician. (In April 2004 Castaño disappeared and was assumed to have been assassinated possibly by a rival, Diego Fernando Murillo, who is linked with the cocaine trade, throwing into doubt the success of the talks between the government and paramilitaries. Extradition requests for paramilitary leaders on drug charges by the United States have also cast a shadow on the negotiations.)

In September 2003 Uribe presented a bill to the Colombian congress that would allow paramilitary members who have committed atrocities to avoid a prison term for a fee. Some doubt exists as to whether the congress was interested in seeing justice done, either. After Uribe's election, one of the paramilitary leaders boasted that his organization controlled 30 per cent of the legislature. Uribe's decision to invite paramilitary leaders to participate in peace talks in Bogotá and allow them to sit in a session of congress in 2004 drew widespread condemnation from human rights activists.

Critics of legislation designed to ensure the demobilizing of the paramilitaries contend that the government allows the worst offenders to escape punishment and that Uribe's plan fails to guarantee that the paramilitaries will truly disband or reveal the truth about their activities, including involvement in atrocities and drug trafficking. Under one bill, paramilitary leaders would not be required to disclose anything about their organizational structure or even have to guarantee that their members would disarm. Even those found guilty of war crimes might be liable to prison sentences of no longer than five years, and there was an added provision that might allow them to serve out their sentence on their own farms.

There is little evidence that the government has made a serious effort to prosecute members of its own military for atrocities. One case involves an army officer, Colonel Víctor Matamoros, who, the State Department reported, had been detained for alleged paramilitary ties in 2001. Accused of collaborating with a paramilitary leader in orchestrating a number of massacres in 1999, he was later released on technical grounds. In March 2004 the attorney general announced that he would not file charges against a cashiered army officer, General Rito Alejo del Río, who had been under investigation for alleged links to paramilitaries between 1995 and 1997. Del Río was accused of providing support for paramilitaries that had attacked villages, executed local civic leaders, and displaced thousands of civilians. According to one witness, del Río had ordered his troops to conceal evidence of paramilitary responsibility for the massacres. It is doubtful whether Colombia can come to terms with its past, let alone resolve its ongoing human rights crisis, without bringing the perpetrators of atrocities, like del Río, to justice. The Justice and Peace Law, a plan announced by President Uribe at the end of 2004 to demobilize the paramilitaries, has been greeted by heated criticism in Colombia and among members of the U.S. Congress, which has appropriated billions of dollars in aid to the nation. Because so many of the former paramilitaries are implicated in perpetrating egregious human rights abuses and engaging in illegal drug trafficking, critics of the plan fear that the paramilitary officials might escape any punishment for their crimes. Some of the newly legitimized paramilitaries have even announced their intention to run for political office. A run for office may not even be necessary, though, to gain political influence. An official affiliated with the United Self-Defense Forces of Colombia (known as AUC, from its Spanish initials) claimed that AUC already exercised a good deal of control over Colombia's Congress. "I think that we can affirm that we have more than 35 percent of Congress as friends," he said. "And for the next elections, we're going to increase that percentage of friends." Although the majority of paramilitary leaders would be pardoned, some of those found guilty of crimes against humanity including kidnapping and murder would be prohibited from seeking public office.

See also ADDITIONAL PROTOCOLS TO THE GENEVA CONVENTIONS; ARMS, TRAFFICKING IN AND CONTROL MECHANISMS; CHILDREN'S RIGHTS.

Further Reading:
Bergquist, Charles, Ricardo Penaranda, and Gonzalo Sanchez, eds. *Violence in Colombia 1990–2000: Waging War and Negotiating Peace.* Latin American Silhouettes. Wilmington, Del.: Scholarly Resources Inc., 2001.
Pearce, Jenny. *Inside Colombia: Drugs, Democracy, and War.* New Brunswick, N.J.: Rutgers University Press, 2004.
Rabasa, Angel, and Peter Chalk. *Colombian Labyrinth: The Synergy of Drugs and Insurgency and Its Implications for Regional Stability.* Santa Monica, Calif.: Rand Corporation (NBN), 2001.

combatant identification   *See* IDENTIFICATION OF COMBATANTS.

combatants, rights of

The rights of combatants have received renewed attention as a result of U.S. military actions taken in the aftermath of the September 11, 2001, terrorist attacks on New York City and Washington, D.C. The Bush administration has taken the position that "enemy combatants" taken in the war in Afghanistan that ousted the TALIBAN regime in 2001 should not be classified as PRISONERS OF WAR under the provisions of international law. These detainees, most of whom are being held in Guantánamo, Cuba, are considered terrorists by the United States even if they were captured on the battlefield, and therefore they can remain in custody indefinitely, without having their cases heard by any tribunal, military or civilian. Nonetheless, Washington insisted that all prisoners were being treated humanely and has allowed inspections by the INTERNATIONAL COMMITTEE OF THE RED CROSS. In 2004 the U.S. Supreme Court ruled that the GUANTÁNAMO DETAINEES and enemy combatants held elsewhere by American authorities were entitled to legal representation and that their cases should be subject to some degree of legal scrutiny.

The protection of the rights of combatants in international law extends back to the first Geneva Convention in 1864, when delegates of 16 European nations adopted the Convention for the Amelioration of the Condition of the Wounded in Armies in the Field. The St. Petersburg Declaration of 1868 called on states not to use arms that cause unnecessary suffering and prohibited the use of explosive bullets. Successive conventions at The Hague in 1899 and 1907 built upon these codes, prohibiting the use of poisonous gases and soft-nosed bullets during combat.

In 1929 a convention was adopted in Geneva relating to the treatment of prisoners of war (a subject with which negotiators at the earlier Geneva and Hague conventions were also concerned). A prisoner of war is defined as any combatant who falls into the hands of the adversary. However, spies and mercenaries (defined by Additional Protocol 1) do not fall into the category of combatants entitled to the protections of international law. The Third Geneva Convention of 1929 describes prisoners of war as "privileged belligerents." Essentially, the rules for prisoners of war required that a prisoner must not be treated as a criminal and must receive adequate nourishment clothing and shelter. A prisoner was not obliged to supply any information aside from name, rank, and serial number. These provisions were strengthened in the Geneva Convention of 1949, while the Additional Protocols of 1979 contain provisions pertaining to combatants who are no longer able to take part in hostilities. These persons cannot be murdered, tortured, mutilated, or subjected to corporal punishment. The same protections also apply to the sick, wounded, and shipwrecked.

In addition to these treaties, the United Nations General Assembly also passed a series of resolutions, beginning in 1970, that extended the rights of combatants to "participants in resistance movements and freedom fighters." This meant that if insurgents of an organized rebel army fell into enemy hands, they were entitled to the same protection as prisoners of war who fought for conventional armies. The legal status of irregular combatants in such internal wars as revolutions and civil war was defined by the General Assembly in 1973 as long as the struggle was "legitimate"— that is, it was directed "against colonial and racist régimes" that were considered "incompatible with the UN Charter, the UNIVERSAL DECLARATION OF HUMAN RIGHTS and the Declaration on the Granting of Independence to Colonial Countries and Peoples and in full accord with the principles of international law."

See also ADDITIONAL PROTOCOLS TO THE GENEVA CONVENTIONS; GENEVA CONVENTIONS.

Further Reading:

Berry, Nicholas O. *War and the Red Cross: The Unspoken Mission.* New York: St. Martin's Press, 1997.

Gutman, Roy, ed. *Crimes of War: What the Public Should Know.* New York: W. W. Norton & Company, 1999.

Jinks, Derek. *The Rules of War: The Geneva Conventions in the Age of Terror.* Oxford: Oxford University Press, 2005.

Moorehead, Caroline. *Dunant's Dream: War, Switzerland and the History of the Red Cross.* New York: Carroll & Graf Publishers, 1999.

Pilloud, Claude. *Commentary on the Additional Protocols of 8 June 1977 to the Geneva Conventions of 12 August 1949.* Boston: Brill Academic Publishers, 1987.

Shelton, Dinah. *Remedies in International Human Rights Law.* Oxford: Oxford University Press, 2001.

comfort women

Comfort women is the term used to describe women who were forcibly recruited as sexual slaves for Japanese occupation forces in the Asian Pacific region before and during World War II. It is derived from the Japanese euphemism *jugun ianfu*, which translates as "military comfort women." The women were originally called *teishintai*, which means "voluntary corps." According to Yun Chungok, the founder of the Korean Council for the Women Drafted for Sexual Military Slavery by Japan, the term was intended to imbue the concept of "drafting of women for sexual service to Japanese troops" within the concept of performing a patriotic duty. Korean women, the Japanese authorities believed, would feel more obligated to assume the role of comfort women because of the influence of the Confucian tradition of self-sacrifice embodied in the term *teishintai*. In reality, the system was institutionalized rape. A Japanese military doctor, Aso Tetsuo, has said that Korean women were treated like "female ammunition" and often referred to as "sanitary public toilets."

While precise numbers are impossible to come by, historians believe that between 80,000 and 200,000 women were involved throughout the period of Japanese colonial rule, about 80 percent of whom were Korean. (The Japanese occupied Korea from 1910 until 1945). Comfort women also came from Japan and other occupied territories, including Taiwan, the Philippines, Indonesia, Burma, and the Pacific islands. According to the Korean-based Comfort Women Project, which investigates the history of comfort women, the Japanese rationale for such sanctioned prostitution was "to enhance the morale of the military by providing amenities for recreational sex." The military believed that the use of comfort women would curb rape and other types of sexual violence that had caused problems during earlier actions in which Japanese troops had gotten out of control. Moreover, the Japanese believed that this system would allow them to maintain hygiene and limit the spread of sexually transmitted diseases. Scant attention was given to the abuses of these women by the Allies after the war came to an end. Only one military tribunal was set up to investigate the sexual abuse of comfort women in Batavia (Jakarta), the Indonesian capital. The tribunal, which convened in 1948, convicted several Japanese military officers in cases involving 35 Dutch women. However, the tribunal neglected to prosecute cases of abuses involving Indonesians or women of any other ethnic group.

Until the late 1980s, it seemed that the world had forgotten all about the existence of comfort women, and human rights advocates began to despair that the survivors would ever receive justice. But in 1991 several Koreans, including three former comfort women, brought a class-action suit against the Japanese government, demanding compensation for the violation of human rights under the colonial occupation. In addition, they demanded a thorough investigation of their cases, the revision of Japanese school textbooks to take into account the existence of comfort women under colonial rule, and the building of a memorial museum.

The suit brought renewed worldwide attention to the ordeal of the comfort women, but it did not bring the response the Koreans were hoping for. Initially the Japanese officials denied that the former Japanese government had ever condoned such a system or taken a part in recruiting comfort women, and because there was no evidence of government involvement, no apology was necessary. Moreover, Japan insisted that all claims of compensation for war crimes had already been settled by a treaty between Japan and South Korea in 1965. The Japanese representatives noted, however, that textbooks would "continue" to reflect Japan's regret for aggression against the rest of Asia. The Koreans refused to accept

Tokyo's denials, and a group called the Korean Council for the Women Drafted for Military Sexual Slavery by Japan was formed to pursue the issue. In August 1991, for the first time, the Korean Council heard public testimony by a comfort woman, which only gave further impetus to Korean demands for acknowledgement of responsibility and compensation from Japan. But the silence regarding the crimes of the Japanese Imperial Army half a century before had finally been broken.

As international pressure mounted, the Japanese government began to backpedal, and in August 1993 it finally admitted that there had been official involvement in the system and that deception and coercion had been used to recruit the comfort women. Nonetheless, the issue is far from resolved, and nationalist conservatives in Japan continue to insist that no evidence exists to show that either the state or the military coerced women into prostitution. The debate in Japan also continues to hamper efforts to resolve the related issue of compensation for the survivors.

Commission on Human Rights   *See* UNITED NATIONS HUMAN RIGHTS COMMISSION; UNITED NATIONS HIGH COMMISSIONER FOR HUMAN RIGHTS.

Committee to Protect Journalists

The Committee to Protect Journalists (CPJ) is an independent, nonprofit organization founded in 1981 with the objective of promoting press freedom "by defending the right of journalists to report the news without fear of reprisal." The organization was begun by a group of U.S. foreign correspondents alarmed by the treatment of journalists in many countries under repressive regimes. Based in New York City, CPJ has a full-time staff of 22 and works in more than 120 countries. It takes on cases of journalists who are imprisoned or threatened and defends news media against censorship and government intimidation. If necessary, the CPJ organizes "vigorous protest at all levels—ranging from local governments to the United Nations—and, when necessary, works behind the scenes through other diplomatic channels to effect change." As one measure of the degree of threats to press freedom around the world, the CPJ says that its research staff documents over 600 attacks on the press annually.

Comoros, human rights violations in

The Indian island nation of the Comoros—officially known as the Union of Comoros—has only recently begun to enjoy a measure of stability after years of coups and unrest. The current head of the government, President Azali Assoumani, took power in a coup in April 1999. In 2002, however, he won an election for the presidency that was judged free and fair by international observers. The country, which has a population of more than 800,000, consists of three islands (Grande Comore, Anjouan, and Moheli) and claims a fourth, Mayotte, which is governed by France. For many years the country's human rights record remained poor. Political opponents were often subject to arrest and held in detention without trials. In the early 1970s four former ministers disappeared. Until 1990 the government routinely restricted freedom of speech, press, and association and curtailed the rights of workers and women. Coup attempts, some successful, recurred with astonishing frequency, sometimes on the order of one every two or three years. These coups and coup attempts were often followed by arbitrary arrests, political killings, and TORTURE. In the 1990s the Comorian Human Rights Association reported that the government had carried out EXTRAJUDICIAL KILLINGS of political opponents. By 2002, however, most of these abuses had ended, and there were no reports by human rights organizations of instances of arbitrary arrest, torture, or DISAPPEARANCES. Prison conditions, however, were still considered deplorable.

concentration camps

Concentration camps are defined as places intended for the confinement of select groups of people of both sexes and all ages, based on their religion, ethnicity, political views, or country of origin. Concentration camps are also called corrective labor camps, relocation centers, and reception centers. Whatever name they are known by, though, these camps are typically characterized by inhumane conditions. Inmates are housed in barracks, huts, or tents, which are heavily guarded and surrounded by barbed wire, high walls, or watchtowers. Inmates are confined for indefinite periods of time without any recourse to legal redress. Camp authorities generally exercise complete and arbitrary control over the inmates.

There are two basic types of concentration camps: labor camps, where inmates are exploited for slave labor, and death (or extermination) camps, where all inmates are condemned to death. Most of the world learned about the horrors of concentration camps only after World War II when reports began to emerge from the survivors and their liberators. More than 6 million Jews and others perished in German concentration camps during the war, but these camps actually have a history that goes back at least a century.

The term *concentration camp* first came into use to describe camps operated by the British in South Africa in the Boer War (1899–1902), which pitted British forces against Dutch settlers. (A case can be made that prisoner-of-war camps in the American Civil War such as Andersonville, where Confederate prisoners were confined, were, in

Cremation ovens inside the Buchenwald concentration camp, Germany *(Library of Congress)*

effect, concentration camps as well.) Boers and black labor-ers from their farms died in these British camps from star-vation, thirst, and appalling sanitation conditions. The use of the word *concentration* is taken from the concentration of the imprisoned population in one easily controlled loca-tion. But it was only during the 20th century, in the Soviet Union and in Nazi Germany, that concentration camps were used as an unsurpassed instrument of state terror.

In the early years of the Soviet Union—after the Bol-sheviks came to power in 1917—the new communist regime set to work corralling "class enemies" as well as ordinary criminals, confining them in the Northern Special Purpose Camps in isolated regions. A vast network of camps known as GULAGS sprang up, consisting of five major camp systems. (*Gulag* is an acronym of the Chief Adminis-

tration of Corrective Labor Camps.) Millions of prisoners were put to work on major industrial and infrastructure projects such as the White Sea–Baltic Canal, at the cost of thousands of lives. Other prisoners were forced to work on coal mines and oil wells near Vorkuta and the gold mines on the Kolyma River in the Arctic region. Throughout the 1930s and 1940s, Joseph STALIN sent millions of people to the gulags: small farmers (known as kulaks), political pris-oners, civilian populations deported from annexed Polish and Baltic countries, and various ethnic groups such as the Volga (Germans whose loyalty to the state was judged sus-pect). In World War II the camp population swelled with PRISONERS OF WAR and people whose countries had fallen under control of the Red Army. Countless millions of peo-ple died in the gulags from killings, maltreatment, starvation, and exposure to the brutal Siberian cold, and it was only in the late 1950s, after Stalin's death, that most of the camps began to empty.

In Germany the Nazis moved quickly to establish concentration camps soon after taking power in January 1933. They issued a decree that removed legal protections from arbitrary arrest, which allowed police to arrest anyone they chose and confine the detainee to a prison camp for an indefinite period. The political police—the GESTAPO— took a variety of political opponents into what was called "protective custody," including communists, socialists, religious dissenters, Jehovah's Witnesses, and Jews. The first group of prisoners confined in Dachau in 1933 consisted mainly of communists. Even then the camps had already acquired a reputation for their harsh regimes. For their part, the Kripo (criminal police) used what they called "preventive arrest" to take into custody professional criminals and other groups deemed asocials such as the Rom (Gypsies), homosexuals, and prostitutes. (Under Paragraph 175 of the German legal code, male homosexuality was punished by imprisonment, but not lesbianism.) The camps themselves were run by the SS (Schutzstaffel, or protective units), who discharged their mandate with brutal efficiency. (The elite Death's Head of Unit of the SS at Dachau, was originally set up to guard political prisoners.) By 1939, six major camps had been established, including three of the most notorious: Dachau, Buchenwald (which opened in 1937 for political prisoners), and Mauthausen. These camps held about 25,000 prisoners, who were soon joined by millions of new inmates. To accommodate them, several additional camps were constructed in Germany and in the occupied countries, finally reaching a total of 22 camps.

In August 1940 Hans FRANK, the Nazi governor of occupied Poland (which had fallen to the Nazis in 1939), announced that he would move to make the city of Kraków free of Jews. "The Jews must vanish from the face of the earth," he declared. In Alsace, France, also under German occupation, the Nazis set up a labor camp, Natzweiler-Struthof, where primarily German prisoners worked in factories producing V-2 rockets that would later be launched against British cities. The use of slave labor by the Nazis extended beyond concentration camps to industrial plants such as I. G. Farben, which were essential to maintain the German economy. Natzweiler-Struthof later took in Jews, Rom, and captured Resistance fighters from France, Belgium, and the Netherlands, many of whom were put to death.

Even today historians still dispute when the decision was made to exterminate all Jews, but by 1942 the machinery of death was being geared up to kill large numbers of people simultaneously, primarily by gassing. Crematoria were installed in many camps to dispose of the bodies. There were two main extermination centers operating in concentration camps, Auschwitz-Birkenau and Lublin-Majdanek, both under the authority of the SS Central Office for Economy and Administration (Wirtschafts-Verwaltungshauptamt, or WVHA), which had taken over the camps in 1942. Other major death camps established by regional SS and police leaders included Betżec, Sobibór, and Treblinka in eastern Poland; Kulmhof (Chelmno) in western Poland; and Semlin outside Belgrade, Yugoslavia. In addition to the central camps, the WVHA also operated hundreds of subsidiary camps, while local offices of the security police in the occupied territories maintained their own forced labor camps where slave laborers were worked to death.

In July 1944 soldiers of the advancing Red Army stumbled on the abandoned Majdanek extermination camp near Lublin, in Poland. When American reporters visited the site two months later, they found 800,000 shoes that had once belonged to the victims. The same month Free French forces took over Natzweiler, the first major Nazi concentration camp to be uncovered in the West. In a description of the French camp, *New York Times* correspondent Milton Bracker wrote, "It might have been a Civilian Conservation Corps camp, from the winding road to the bald hilltop, the sturdy green barrack buildings looked exactly like those that housed forestry trainees in the United States during the early New Deal." But unlike forestry dormitories, the camp contained a small, dark room with S-shaped hooks where prisoners were hanged before they were killed by Zyklon-B gas. There was also an incinerator where bodies were burned. It is believed that about 4,000 prisoners were killed out of a total of 16,000 imprisoned in the camp between 1941 and 1944.

Even eyewitnesses had trouble absorbing the horrifying sights that greeted them as, one by one, these camps were liberated. In April 1945, just before the war ended, U.S. forces came on their first camp—Ohrdruf—where they discovered prisoners still alive among piles of corpses. One soldier, who had participated in the liberation of Nordhausen, recalled that his fellow GIs "thought that any stories they had read in the paper, or that I had told them out of first-hand experience, were either not true or at least exaggerated." "We are constantly finding German camps in which they have placed political prisoners where unspeakable conditions exist," observed General Dwight D. Eisenhower, the commander of the Allied forces in Europe, "From my own personal observation, I can state unequivocally that all written statements up to now do not paint the full horrors."

It is estimated that approximately 6 million people were killed in the German concentration camps, the majority of them Jews. Millions were also killed elsewhere in Nazi-occupied countries, for an approximate total of 11 million. The Allies quickly moved to arrest and prosecute the officials in the Nazi regime who were responsible for ordering and carrying out the atrocities. At the NUREMBERG TRIALS of Nazi war criminals, a new crime (indeed, a new word) was introduced into their indictments: GENOCIDE.

Concentration camps continued to be opened in various parts of the world even after World War II, in spite of several human rights treaties banning them. In Communist countries in Asia, such as Vietnam, large numbers of political prisoners were confined to so-called reeducation camps after the end of the Vietnam War. In the late 1960s the Indonesian government established island camps for political opponents. Even the British established emergency detention camps in colonial Kenya at a time when they were combating an insurgency. As late as the 1970s, political opponents and suspected leftist sympathizers were tortured and executed in secret detention camps in Argentina. Today North Korea maintains a network of concentration camps where conditions are reportedly even more brutal than the Stalinist gulags.

See also FINAL SOLUTION; MEDICAL EXPERIMENTS; POHL, OSWALD; ROM (ROMANY, GYPSIES), PERSECUTION OF; WANSEE CONFERENCE.

Further Reading:

Bloxham, Donald. *Genocide on Trial: War Crimes Trials and the Formation of Holocaust History and Memory.* Oxford: Oxford University Press, 2003.

Dawidowicz, Lucy. *A Holocaust Reader.* Library of Jewish Studies. Chicago: Behrman House Publishing, 1976.

Dwork, Deborah, and Robert Jan Van Pelt. *Holocaust: A History.* New York: W. W. Norton & Company, 2003.

Gilbert, Martin. *The Holocaust: A History of the Jews of Europe during the Second World War.* New York: Owl Books, 1987.

Lagnado, Lucette Matalon, and Sheila Cohn Dekel. *Children of the Flames: Dr. Josef Mengele and the Untold Story of the Twins of Auschwitz.* New York: Penguin Books, 1992.

Overbey, Fern. *The Dachau Defendants: Life Stories from Testimony and Documents of the War Crimes Prosecutions.* Jefferson, N.C.: McFarland & Company, 2004.

Roseman, Mark. *The Wannsee Conference and the Final Solution: A Reconsideration.* New York: Metropolitan Books, 2002.

Wistrich, Robert S. *Hitler and the Holocaust.* Modern Library Chronicles. New York: Modern Library, 2001.

Conference on Security and Cooperation in Europe   *See* HELSINKI ACCORDS; ORGANIZATION FOR SECURITY AND COOPERATION IN EUROPE.

conflict diamonds (blood diamonds)

Diamonds, as the advertising slogan goes, may be a girl's best friend, but they also seem to be the best friend of many insurgent groups that have relied on them to fund several wars and commit atrocities. *Conflict diamonds* are officially defined as diamonds that originate from areas controlled by forces or factions opposed to legitimate and internationally recognized governments. It is estimated that 4 percent of the gems on the world market are conflict diamonds. They have largely subsidized insurgencies in Angola, the Democratic Republic of the Congo, Sierra Leone, and Liberia. Investigators have even uncovered substantial evidence that conflict diamonds (or, more colorfully, blood diamonds) have provided al-QAEDA and Hezbollah, a militant Shiite group in Lebanon, with significant sources of revenue. Diamonds are favored by guerrilla and terrorists because they are portable, small, quickly sold, and virtually untraceable.

In Angola, the rebel group National Union for the Total Independence of Angola (UNITA) relied on conflict diamonds to sustain over a decade of guerrilla warfare. When UNITA defied the United Nations and refused to disarm and implement a peace accord (the Lusaka Protocol), the Security Council adopted two resolutions in 1998, prohibiting direct or indirect import of diamonds from Angola unless they were sanctioned by the government. An insurgency launched in the early 1990s by Charles TAYLOR—intended to topple the Liberian government—could not have been sustained without millions of dollars of diamonds appropriated from Sierra Leone. To stake his claim in the diamond-rich eastern district of Sierra Leone, Taylor sponsored an insurgency in that country led by Foday SANKOH. Sankoh's ragtag group, the Revolutionary United Front (RUF), carried out a campaign of terror that was unusual both in its brutality and in its methods. Its signature atrocity was dismemberment—the amputation of the limbs of civilians, even children. Initially indifferent to these horrors, the international diamond dealers based in Europe continued to buy about $125 million worth of conflict diamonds every year, according to UN estimates. The RUF used the profits to establish bank accounts for its leaders and to subsidize a network of middlemen and weapons smugglers. In July 2000 the United Nations imposed a ban on the import of rough diamonds from Sierra Leone unless the diamonds were approved by the government. The RUF, however, managed to evade these sanctions by smuggling the diamonds to other countries where they were then sold to diamond markets abroad. Much of this smuggling was facilitated by the Liberian government then under the control of Charles Taylor, who had assumed power as a result of a peace accord. By 2003, diamond-fueled conflicts in both Liberia and Sierra Leone were settled through international mediation, and Charles Taylor was forced into exile.

As a result of these diamond-fueled wars, more than half a million people have died or sustained serious injuries in Sierra Leone, and 1.5 million people—nearly half the population—were made homeless in Liberia. Three million people have lost their lives in the civil war in the Democratic Republic of Congo, which has also been partly subsidized by conflict diamonds.

al-Qaeda Involvement

The RUF is also believed to have sold its gems to terrorist organizations. FBI sources believe that members of al-Qaeda purchased diamonds from the RUF in 1998, the year that the U.S. embassies in Kenya and Tanzania were blown up by al-Qaeda terrorists. According to GLOBAL WITNESS, a human rights organization, al-Qaeda laundered as much as $20 million through purchases of diamonds; payments were made either in the form of cash or weapons. According to a report in the *Washington Post,* two al-Qaeda operatives implicated in the embassy blasts had been in Sierra Leone in 2001, supervising diamond production. When the United States and other Western governments froze the assets of banks and groups associated with al-Qaeda after the September 11, 2001, attacks, the terrorist organization drew on its cache of diamonds to make up for the deficit.

Hezbollah, too, has tapped a network of Lebanese businessmen operating in Western and Central Africa. The Shiite group, largely operating out of southern Lebanon, has reportedly used conflict diamonds to purchase weapons used in its ongoing low-key war against Israel.

Kimberly Process

Concerted pressure by human rights organizations and the media to end the trade in conflict diamonds gradually began to have an impact. Two human rights organizations, Global Exchange and AMNESTY INTERNATIONAL, threatened to launch an anti-diamond ad campaign, proposing to replace the image of a diamond bracelet on a woman's wrist with a diamond bracelet on the stump of a child amputee's arm. A diamond executive reportedly had a nightmare in which the tagline of a televised diamond commercial read: "Amputation Is Forever."

In July 2000 the World Diamond Congress, representing international diamond dealers, met in Antwerp, Belgium, and adopted a resolution intended to block conflict diamonds from reaching world markets. In December 2000 the UN General Assembly unanimously adopted a resolution that barred the illicit transaction of rough diamonds. The collaborative effort on the part of the diamond industry, nongovernmental organizations (NGOs), the United Nations, and individual governments, is known as the Kimberely Process (after the diamond-producing area of South Africa). Under this arrangement, introduced in January 2003 and subsequently ratified by over 50 countries, diamonds can be traded on the world market only if each gem is placed in a tamper-proof container and accompanied by a nonforgeable certificate attesting that its provenance is legitimate. Participating countries also agreed they would trade diamonds only with other signatories to the agreement.

However, the Kimberly Process still lacks teeth, and critics contend that its regulations cannot be enforced. No paper trail, they say, is foolproof so that it is impossible, even with a certificate, to be certain that a diamond has not originated in territory held by rebels or terrorist groups. Moreover, once a conflict diamond reaches Europe, it becomes difficult to interdict, given the ease with which people can travel across unmanned borders within the European Union. The Kimberly Process is widely viewed as a positive and necessary step forward, but only if it marks the start of a serious attempt to restrict the trade of illegal diamonds rather than embraced as its culmination. That much remains to be done can be seen in a revelation in 2004 that the Republic of Congo (Brazzaville) was selling far more diamonds on the world markets than it was producing. In spite of the government's denials, international watchdogs believe that the Congo was laundering the diamonds for insurgents, possibly based in Angola.

See also ANGOLA, WAR CRIMES IN; CONGO, DEMOCRATIC REPUBLIC OF THE, WAR CRIMES IN; LIBERIA, HUMAN RIGHTS VIOLATIONS IN; SIERRA LEONE, HUMAN RIGHTS VIOLATIONS IN.

Further Reading:

Campbell, Greg. *Blood Diamonds: Tracing the Deadly Path of the World's Most Precious Stones.* New York: Perseus Books Group, 2002.

Saracin, Philip. *Blood Diamonds.* Victoria, Canada: Book-Surge Publishing, 2002.

Tamm, Ingrid J. *Diamonds in Peace and War: Severing the Conflict Diamond Connection.* WPF Report #30. Cambridge, Mass.: World Peace Foundation, 2002.

Congo (Brazzaville), human rights violations in

The Congo (Brazzaville) is a former French colony that gained its freedom in 1960. (The Congo is not to be confused with the Democratic Republic of the Congo, the former Belgian colony, which it borders.) Human rights violations continue to be a grave problem, based on findings by the United Nations and human rights organizations. According to the UN Commission on Human Rights, these violations include "summary or extrajudicial executions; arbitrary arrest and detention; TORTURE and rape; forced or involuntary DISAPPEARANCES; and violations of the freedom of expression, opinion and assembly." These abuses have taken place in a context of unrest and civil war, sparked by ethnic strife and rivalries within the political elite.

From 1964 to 1991, the Congo was a one-party state dominated by a Marxist ideology. An experiment with democracy in the early 1990s went badly awry when losing parties in legislative elections contested their legality. A civil war broke out in 1993 in which militias with colorful names like the Cobras, Ninjas, and Cocoyes vied for power. The war ended within a year, but by then some 2,000 people had been killed and tens of thousands displaced. Provisions in the peace agreement calling for the disarmament of the militias were not rigorously enforced, and violence continued. Far from disbanding, the Ninja militia forces loyal to former Congolese prime minister Bernard Kolelas are responsible for abductions, torture, and EXTRAJUDICIAL KILLINGS. (Kolelas has been sentenced to death in absentia by a court in the Congo.) According to AMNESTY INTERNATIONAL, "From June 1997, *Ninja* and *Cocoye* combatants reportedly killed hundreds and possibly thousands of unarmed civilians at roadblocks in their Bacongo and Makélékélé strongholds." The two militia groups took advantage of a July 1997 cease-fire to carry out executions of members of the security forces and civil servants, as well as many other civilians who had the bad luck of trying to pass through their roadblocks. Several other attacks on civilians by these militias have taken place since then.

The government, however, has also been sharply criticized for human rights abuses. "Hundreds of unarmed civilians and captured combatants were extrajudicially executed by government forces and allied militia," Amnesty International stated in a 2003 report. It maintained that government forces, "together with allied Angolan and Chadian government forces, reportedly killed hundreds more civilians during an offensive against the 'Ninja' armed opposition group in the Pool region. Despite widespread reports of violence, including the burning of hundreds of homes, the authorities failed to investigate the killings or take any action against the perpetrators."

Moreover, Amnesty International has established that several hundred Congolese citizens who had fled the capital of Brazzaville at the end of 1998 to escape the violence were "disappeared" by members of the security forces in mid-1999. The organization also gathered evidence indicating that 353 refugees returning to Brazzaville from temporary refuge in the Democratic Republic of the Congo in May 1999 were extrajudicially executed and their bodies secretly disposed of. According to testimony from a survivor of these killings, the security forces first detained and tortured these individuals on the grounds that they had Ninja connections. They were taken to a room, said the survivor, where there were about 200 bodies. The detainees were ordered to make piles out of these bodies, which were then incinerated.

Tens of thousands of people have been displaced by the turmoil, and tens of thousands more have been denied humanitarian assistance. The violence shows no sign of abating. In early 2003 more than 170 people, including unarmed civilians, were killed in Brazzaville alone by security forces. Perpetrators of these abuses have largely eluded prosecution or punishment for their acts. Successive Congolese governments have been too preoccupied by the need to secure their power to investigate abuses, especially those committed by its own forces.

The culture of impunity is certainly in no danger from the country's judiciary, which the U.S. State Department has described as "overburdened, underfinanced, and subject to corruption and political influence." The State Department also cited serious abuses by security forces, which included "summary executions, disappearances, rapes, beatings and physical abuse of detainees and the civilian population, arbitrary arrests and detentions, and arbitrary searches and widespread looting of private homes."

Congo, Democratic Republic of the, war crimes in

The Democratic Republic of the Congo (DCR) occupies a strategic position in central Africa and is abundantly endowed with natural resources, including cobalt, copper, uranium, gold, and diamonds. With a land mass the size of western Europe, it has the most extensive tropical forests on the continent, covering 60 percent of its territory. But its considerable natural resources have made it vulnerable to exploitation, and what ought to have been a blessing for its 55 million people has turned out to be its curse. Beginning in 1998, the country was engulfed by what has been called Africa's first "world war," which embroiled nine of its neighbors. Although, it was formally ended in 2003, the multinational war has left the Congo devastated and created a catastrophic humanitarian crisis. It has cost more lives than any conflict since World War II: By the end of 2004, it was estimated at least 3.8 million people, most of them civilians, had died as a result of the civil war, either directly or indirectly by famine or disease. About half the victims are children. OXFAM, the British relief agency, says that 1 million people were killed in the last two years of the conflict alone, and deaths continue from both the war and related causes at a staggering rate of about a thousand people every day. An additional 2 million or more people have been internally displaced, most of them in the eastern DRC. The United Nations Office for Coordination of Humanitarian Affairs (UNOCHA) estimates that about 33 percent of the population is now at risk of hunger, disease (especially HIV/AIDS), and death. Government spending on health and education, never generous in the best of times, has diminished to less than 1 percent of all government expenditure, with the result that nearly a third of

The Red Cross distributing the basic necessities to families in the Democratic Republic of the Congo *(François de Sury/ICRC)*

the country's children are malnourished—10 percent at risk of starvation.

Although a peace accord, reached in July 2003, has led to a subsidence of hostilities, various guerrilla and paramilitary groups continue to carry out atrocities, especially in eastern Congo, creating conditions of continued instability and leading to more casualties. Much of the country remains beyond any effective control by the central government in Kinshasa led by President Joseph Kabila. The continuing violence has been marked by massacres, ethnic cleansing, systematic rape, abductions, summary executions, the forced recruitment of child soldiers, and even incidences of cannibalism.

Background

Within months of gaining freedom from Belgium in 1961, the Congo was plunged into a secessionist war with the mineral-rich province of Katanga that led to UN intervention. Even in its earliest years of freedom, foreign forces were already intervening in the country, which turned into

a cold war proxy conflict between forces allied with the Soviet Union and those supported by the United States. In 1965 the Cuban insurgent leader Che Guevara led a small volunteer force in an abortive effort to liberate the eastern part of the country. Meanwhile the APARTHEID South African government sent mercenaries in what their leader Mike Hoare, called "the adventure of their lives" to prop up the pro-Western government.

In 1966 General MOBUTU SESE SEKO emerged as the country's strongman. For the next 32 years, Mobutu dominated the Congo (which he renamed Zaire) with such ruthlessness and avariciousness that his despotic regime can rightly be called a kleptocracy. Nonetheless, he retained the steadfast support of the West for most of his reign because he was regarded a valuable cold war ally who could stave off Soviet influence. The uprising that led to Mobutu's ouster began along the border with Rwanda and Burundi, when a small minority of Zairian Tutsis known as the Banyamulenge were harassed by Zairian troops and other ethnic minorities. The Tutsis, who had lived in the area for 200 years, called upon the support of the Tutsi government in neighboring Rwanda, which had taken power in the aftermath of the GENOCIDE there in 1994. Rwanda lent its support to an insurgent organization, the Alliance of Democratic Forces for the Liberation of Congo (AFDL), led by a longtime guerrilla fighter, Laurent-Désiré Kabila (father of the current president).

Kabila eventually won the backing of four other neighboring countries: Uganda, Burundi, Angola, and Zambia, all of which had longstanding grievances against Mobutu because of his support for rebel groups in their countries. The ensuing conflict in the Congo was inextricably linked with events in Rwanda next door because of the presence of thousands of Hutu refugees who had fled into the Congo after Tutsis had reclaimed control of the country. Rwandan troops and AFDL forces struck at Hutu militias known as the Interahamwe, which operated out of refugee camps (and had taken part in the genocide in 1994). The AFDL forced hundreds of thousands of civilians to seek safety deeper into inhospitable jungles, creating a catastrophic humanitarian crisis. In 1997 Kabila's forces took the Congolese capital of Kinshasa. Mobutu, weakened by prostate cancer, went into exile. (He would die within a short time.) Kabila changed the country's name from Zaire back to the Democratic Republic of the Congo.

Instead of repaying their loyalty, Kabila turned against his former allies and tried to expel the Tutsis from the country, spurring a rebellion by Tutsi ethnic groups who formed a new insurgent movement called the Congolese Rally for Democracy (RCD). The RCD had the support of Uganda and Burundi in addition to Rwanda. They were opposed by a loose coalition of armed groups called the Alliance of Democratic Forces (ADF) made up of the Interahamwe Hutu militias and other rebel factions in the east of the country. Angola, Chad, Namibia, and Zimbabwe entered the fray on the side of Kabila's government: While each of these countries had its own motives, all of them sought access to the Congo's vast mineral and timber resources. (In April 2001 a UN panel of experts accused Rwanda, Uganda, and Zimbabwe of illegally appropriating diamonds, cobalt, gold, and other lucrative resources from the DRC and recommended that the Security Council impose sanctions.)

Various attempts by the United Nations to arrange a cease-fire and hammer out a peace accord among the warring parties ended in failure, unsurprising in light of the many competing interests and governments represented at the bargaining table. By 1998 there were no fewer than 13 governments and rebel factions engaged in the conflict. In spite of the continued hostilities, the UN Security Council agreed to deploy a small contingent in 1999 to support a cease-fire agreement reached in Lusaka, Zambia. The force was expanded in 2000, although by that time the agreement

had broken down. That same year Laurent Kabila was assassinated, and power passed to his son Joseph, who took significant steps to bring about a settlement and pave the way for national reconciliation. In April 2003 the warring parties finally agreed to share power and signed the All Inclusive Agreement on the Transitional Government. The treaty calls for the disarmament and demobilization of the armed groups and the integration of rebel factions into the army. The agreement also envisioned the creation of political parties, which had been long banned, to take part in free elections. A few months later, a Government of National Unity (GNU) was sworn in.

Nonetheless, political stability remains fragile, and the conflict still continues in parts of the country, especially in eastern Congo, where an estimated 15,000–20,000 Hutu militias still operate. In addition, heightened tensions between two tribal groups in the region—the Hema and Lendu—has resulted in horrific massacres by both sides. Hundreds of thousands of people have been uprooted as a result of the continued violence, and the Congo is for all practical purposes divided into two countries: the western half, largely under the control of the central government in Kinshasa, and the eastern half, which is still contested by several rebel groups and forces deployed by neighboring countries. As of 2004 there was still no firm commitment by any party to the conflict, including Kinshasa, to uphold the terms of the treaty establishing the transitional government. To maintain the peace, the UN contingent was increased from 5,700 to 8,700, but that number is considered by human rights organizations to be too low to enforce the peace accord. Human rights organizations charge all sides with war crimes, CRIMES AGAINST HUMANITY, and other violations of INTERNATIONAL HUMANITARIAN LAW. Even in 2003, after the treaty went into effect, outside observers reported violations of basic human rights, particularly in the Ituri region in the east, which included sexual assault; extortion; arbitrary detention and execution; kidnapping; TORTURE; repression; looting; and attacks on and massacres of civilians, some of which have involved cannibalism. Violence against women has increased. International aid organizations have estimated that as many as 10,000 women and girls may have been raped by combatants. Children are also among those most victimized by the war; thousands were forcibly recruited by all the armed groups either as combatants or forced labor. Child recruitment is believed to have continued in spite of the formal end of hostilities.

Recent Developments

Although the provisional constitution contains an AMNESTY for "facts of war, infractions of policy and of opinion," it excludes war crimes, GENOCIDE, and crimes against humanity. But the transitional government has taken few steps to actually investigate, let alone prosecute, these humanitarian violations. Proposals have been advanced to establish a Truth and Reconciliation Commission, presumably based on the South African model, but with the DRC's judicial system in such disarray, it is difficult to imagine how such a commission would even be able to operate. Several years will be required before it will be possible to institute an independent judiciary capable of being impartial and fair. Currently, most of the courts are not functional; magistrates and other staff have gone unpaid for years, and they are so corrupt that the population has virtually no confidence in them. In fact, a court dispute is believed to have contributed to the bitter ethnic conflict between the Hema and Lendu in Ituri. With little expertise available and a lack of will to carry out investigations of war crimes by the Congolese themselves, the role has largely fallen to the United Nations. Luis Moreno Ocampo, chief prosecutor of the INTERNATIONAL CRIMINAL COURT (ICC), has already taken the initiative regarding the ongoing strife in Ituri, declaring his hope that the DRC would refer alleged war crimes in the eastern region to his office. He indicated that he expected to broaden his inquiry over time. Over 5,000 potentially indictable offenses, including murders, DISAPPEARANCES, acts of torture and mutilation, rapes, and the forced enlisting of child soldiers have been recorded in the region since July 1, 2002.

There is some question as to which body—the United Nations or the Congolese government—would have jurisdiction over such crimes. If Ocampo determines that the DRC lacks the judicial capacity and political will to try perpetrators, he must prevail on the International Criminal Court to assume the prosecutions instead. To do this he must have sufficient evidence that a crime has been committed, which is difficult to do in such a chaotic environment. Moreover, Ocampo has also announced that he is prepared to pursue political and military officials and their financial backers if they are found complicit in these crimes. This is a far more ambitious objective than simply settling for a prosecution of the soldier who wielded the machete or fired the AK-47. Ocampo cited in particular the illegal diamond trade, which, according to the Diamond High Council in Antwerp, amounts to close to $1 billion a year in the Congo. Ocampo has stated that there are "links between the activities of some African, European and Middle Eastern companies and the atrocities taking place in the Democratic Republic of Congo." In addition to the exploitation of natural resources, many of these companies are also involved in arms trafficking while relying on the international banking system to keep their illicit commerce flowing. In the case of Ituri, Ocampo also pointed to activities of organized criminal groups from Eastern Europe, which, he said, "allegedly include gold mining, the illegal exploitation of oil, and the arms trade." To make such cases in court, though, he will need extensive cooperation from judicial and financial authorities in several nations.

In spite of the presence of UN peacekeepers, violence in the volatile eastern Ituri region has persisted into 2005. At least 30,000 armed militiamen and youths continued to carry on a campaign of terror, looting villages and driving as many as 70,000 civilians from their homes, adding to a total of 2.5 million people who have been displaced by the war. None of the militias were parties to the peace accord and show no interest in participating in the political process. In a brazen attack, militias struck UN troops in February 2005, killing nine. In response, UN forces launched a counterattack, slaying 50 militiamen.

See also ARMS, TRAFFICKING IN AND CONTROL MECHANISMS; CHILDREN'S RIGHTS; CONFLICT DIAMONDS; NZAPALI, SEBASTIAN; RWANDA, GENOCIDE IN.

Further Reading:

Edgerton, Robert. *The Troubled Heart of Africa: A History of the Congo.* New York: St. Martin's Press, 2002.

Hochschild, Adam. *King Leopold's Ghost.* Boston: Mariner Books, 1999.

Wrong, Michela. *In the Footsteps of Mr. Kurtz: Living on the Brink of Disaster in Mobutu's Congo.* New York: HarperCollins Publishers, 2001.

Congolese Rally for Democracy   *See* CONGO, DEMOCRATIC REPUBLIC OF THE, WAR CRIMES IN.

Constant, Emmanuel "Toto"   *See* HAITIAN HUMAN RIGHTS VIOLATORS.

Conte, Lansana   *See* GUINEA, HUMAN RIGHTS VIOLATIONS IN.

Contreras, Manuel (Juan Manuel Contreras Sepúlveda) (1930–) *Chilean spymaster*

Retired General Juan Manuel Contreras Sepúlveda was the head of DINA, Chile's feared secret police under the dictatorship of Augusto PINOCHET. As the head of DINA (the Spanish acronym for the NATIONAL INTELLIGENCE DIRECTORATE), Contreras was one of the most influential and powerful officials during the first several years of General Pinochet's military rule over Chile. Between 1973 and 1978, he presided over a clandestine network of detention centers where thousands of people were imprisoned, tortured, and executed. He also orchestrated operations by death squads that hunted down political opponents in Latin America, Europe, and the United States. Contreras has been imprisoned for his role in planning the September 1976 car-bomb assassination of exiled Chilean diplomat Orlando Letelier and his aide on Washington's Embassy Row. More recently he has faced legal action for other crimes he committed in his capacity as spymaster.

Contreras was born into a middle-class military family and studied at the Chilean military academy, where one of his professors was Pinochet, who later adopted him as a protégé. He also developed important contacts in the United States while spending two years, 1967–69, at the Army Career Officers School in Fort Belvoir, Virginia. After Pinochet overthrew the Socialist government of Salvador Allende in 1971, Contreras supervised interrogations of Allende supporters that were described as "methodical and productive." The TORTURE sessions—conducted in a music room—yielded a trove of information about the resistance movement to military rule.

With Pinochet's backing, Contreras began to acquire more power and responsibilities. He was appointed military governor of Port San Antonio (his base of his operations) and took over the management of a gigantic fisheries complex, which proved a lucrative source of revenue. In 1974 he was given control of the newly created secret police. At the age of 44, Contreras became one of the youngest colonels in the Chilean army; he subsequently one of its youngest generals.

When he took over DINA, Contreras had two objectives: instilling terror and gathering political intelligence. In the process, he succeeded in making DINA into a state within a state. "At the beginning of 1974 [Contreras] had a full set of plans, and six months later he had built an empire," a former DINA agent said. Contreras not only relied on traditional methods of suppressing dissent, such as arrest, torture, and EXTRAJUDICIAL KILLINGS, but he added a new innovation: DISAPPEARANCES. Suspects would be taken away without any warrant by men in civilian clothes, never to be seen again. Soon about 50 people were being disappeared every month.

The terror campaign had its effect—in September 1974 Pinochet called Chile "an island of tranquility" in a world of violence—but it was not enough to stifle political opposition in Chile. The search for enemies spread farther afield; alliances were forged with military and security forces in Argentina and Uruguay to assassinate leftist sympathizers, including prominent Chilean exiles. In 1976 Contreras arranged for the assassination of former Chilean ambassador Orlando Letelier, an outspoken critic of Pinochet. In an unprecedented car bombing carried out in Washington, D.C., Letelier and his aide, Ronni Moffitt, were both killed.

Contreras retired in 1978, but with Pinochet firmly in control, he had little reason to believe that he would ever face prosecution for his crimes. His confidence turned out to be misplaced. A year later a suspect in the Letelier assassination named Michael Townley implicated Contreras and two of his aides. The United States demanded the extradition of the three men, but the Chilean Supreme Court refused. Contreras remained free until Pinochet stepped down in 1990; DINA was disbanded that year. In September 1991 the Chilean government arrested Contreras and his aide, Brigadier General Pedro Espinoza, on charges of manslaughter and the use of false passports in connection with murder. In 1993 Contreras and Espinoza were tried in Chile and convicted for the Letelier assassination and sentenced to prison for seven and six years, respectively. In 2003 Contreras was indicted along with Espinoza and three other Chilean secret agents for the assassination of former army commander General Carlos Prats and his wife, Sofía Cuthbert, in Buenos Aires on September 30, 1974. He was subsequently convicted and sentenced to prison. In a court document, Contreras accused his former boss Pinochet of being responsible for the abuses perpetrated by police under his command. He asserted that he was writing his confession in order to counter "the permanent, ominous silence maintained by my superior," referring to Pinochet. He also disclosed that some 500 dissidents were killed, and in many cases their bodies thrown into the sea.

See also CHILE, HUMAN RIGHTS VIOLATIONS IN.

Further Reading:

Constable, Pamela. *A Nation of Enemies: Chile under Pinochet.* New York: W. W. Norton & Company, 1993.
Davis, William Columbus. *Warnings from the Far South: Democracy versus Dictatorship in Uruguay, Argentina, and Chile.* New York: Praeger Publishers, 1995.
Dinges, John. *The Condor Years: How Pinochet and His Allies Brought Terrorism to Three Continents.* New York: New Press, 2004.
Dorfman, Airel. *Exorcising Terror: The Incredible Unending Trial of Augusto Pinochet.* New York: Seven Stories Press, 2002.
Kornbluh, Peter. *The Pinochet File: A Declassified Dossier on Atrocity and Accountability.* A National Security Archive Book. New York: New Press, 2003.
Politzer, Patricia, and Diane Wachtel. *Fear in Chile: Lives under Pinochet.* New York: New Press, 2001.

Convention against Torture (United Nations Convention against Torture and Other Cruel, Inhuman or Degrading Treatment or Punishment)

The Convention against Torture (CAT) was adopted by the United Nations General Assembly in 1984 and opened for ratification in February 1985. Under this convention, TORTURE is banned under all circumstances, and countries are required to take legal and other actions to prevent the practice. Other types of cruel or degrading treatment, which do not meet the definition of torture, are also forbidden. The treaty defines *torture* as "any act by which severe pain or suffering, whether physical or mental, is intentionally inflicted on a person . . . by or at the instigation of or with the consent or acquiescence of a public official or other person acting in an official capacity." This definition does not, however, include "pain or suffering arising only from, inherent in or incidental to lawful sanctions." According to the U.S. State Department's interpretation, this distinction reflects the belief by the drafters of CAT that torture must be "severe," whereas "rough treatment," such as police brutality, "while deplorable," does not amount to "torture" for purposes of the convention. By this definition, torture requires "a specific intent to cause severe pain and suffering" as opposed to an act that results in "unanticipated and unintended severity of pain and suffering," which is not classified as torture for purposes of the convention.

Under no circumstances—including a state of emergency, external threats, or orders from superiors—can torture be justified. The drafters of CAT viewed such an explicit prohibition to be necessary if the treaty was to have any effect at all, since state emergencies are commonly invoked as a source of extraordinary powers or as a justification for restricting fundamental rights and freedoms. The treaty also forbids states from returning REFUGEES to their country of origin if they have a legitimate fear that they will be tortured on their return. The state where the refugee has taken refuge is therefore obliged to consider the human rights record of the country of origin. The convention also provides for appropriate punishment for torturers and obliges countries to investigate and prosecute cases of torture and to extradite suspects to face trial before another competent court. States are also required to cooperate with any civil proceedings against accused torturers and to ensure that military and law-enforcement officials receive proper training in interrogation methods and agree to promptly investigate allegations of torture by officials. If a complaint proves to be justified, the victim is entitled to compensation and medical care; compensation is also to be paid to families in the event that the victim dies as a result of torture. To monitor how countries are meeting their obligations under the treaty, the convention also established the Committee against Torture and set out the rules on its membership and activities.

After its adoption in 1985, the CAT was signed by 25 member states; another 65 have ratified it since then, and 16 more have signed but have not yet ratified it. How the United States intends to meet the provisions of the treaty in light of the war on terrorism can be found in its *Report to Congress* issued by the *Congressional Research Service.* In general, the report states, "under U.S. law the removal or extradition of all aliens from the United States must be consistent with U.S. obligations under CAT." This means that an alien cannot be deported to a country "where he is more likely than not to be tortured," but at the same time the United States has greater latitude when it comes to refusing admission to an individual on "security or related grounds such as terrorism." That is to say, an alien who is already domiciled in the United States enjoys greater protections under the treaty, according to this interpretation, than an individual who is prevented from entering the country because of the threat he or she poses to national security. But this exception raises difficult questions. What happens if an alien suspected of terrorism is sent to a country that is known to practice torture? In 2004 Maher Arar, a dual citizen of Canada and Syria, filed suit against U.S. officials whom he claimed seized him when he tried to enter the United States and sent him to Syria, where he was allegedly tortured and interrogated for suspected terrorist involvement, which he denied. The affair caused a scandal in Canada, and he has since been released.

Further Reading:

Goldstone, Richard. *For Humanity: Reflections of a War Crimes Investigator.* Castle Lectures Series. New Haven, Conn.: Yale University Press, 2000.

Gutman, Roy, ed. *Crimes of War: What the Public Should Know.* New York: W. W. Norton & Company, 1999.

Jackson, Nyamuya Maogoto. *War Crimes and Realpolitik: International Justice from World War I to the 21st Century.* Boulder, Colo.: Lynne Rienner Publishers, 2004.

Convention for the Protection of Human Rights and Fundamental Freedoms   *See* HUMAN RIGHTS CONVENTION.

Convention on Prohibitions or Restrictions on the Use of Certain Conventional Weapons . . .

In April 1981 the United Nations adopted the Convention on Prohibitions or Restrictions on the Use of Certain Conventional Weapons Which May be Deemed to be Excessively Injurious or to Have Indiscriminate Effects, commonly known as the CCW. The CCW is an umbrella treaty under which specific agreements have been concluded in the form of protocols. Four protocols are attached to the agreement:

- Protocol I on nondetectable fragments
- Protocol II on land mines and booby traps
- Protocol III on incendiary devices
- Protocol IV on blinding laser weapons

Protocol I refers to the use of any weapon that causes injury by fragments that can escape detection by X-rays.

Intentional use of mines against civilians is banned entirely by Protocol II; remotely delivered mines are allowed only if their location is accurately recorded. Reliable records of the location of mines must be maintained and efforts undertaken to clear the mines as soon as hostilities end. In May 1996 a Review Conference of the Convention adopted the Amended Protocol II (AP II), officially titled the PROTOCOL ON PROHIBITIONS OR RESTRICTIONS ON THE USE OF MINES, BOOBY-TRAPS AND OTHER DEVICES, which applies to the use of mines, booby traps, and other devices on land, beaches, or river crossings, but not to antiship mines at sea or in inland waterways. Protocol III prohibits the targeting of a civilian population, individual civilians or civilian facilities, using any weapon designed to cause burn injury by flame, heat, or chemical reaction of inflammable substances. Protocol IV prohibits the use of laser weapons specifically designed for combat to cause permanent blindness.

Further Reading:

U.S. Congressional Budget Office. *Convention on Prohibitions or Restrictions on the Use of Certain Conventional Weapons.* Report to Accompany Treaty Doc. 103-25. Washington, D.C.: U.S. Government Printing Office, 1995.

Winslow, Philip C. *Sowing the Dragon's Teeth: Land Mines and the Global Legacy of War.* Boston: Beacon Press, 1998.

Convention on the Prevention and Punishment of the Crime of Genocide   *See* GENOCIDE CONVENTION.

Convention on the Prohibition of the Development, Production, Stockpiling and Use of Chemical Weapons and on Their Destruction   *See* CHEMICAL WEAPONS.

Convention on the Prohibition of the Use, Stockpiling, Production and Transfer of Anti-Personnel Mines and their Destruction

The Convention on the Prohibition of the Use, Stockpiling, Production and Transfer of Anti-Personnel Mines and on Their Destruction was agreed to according to the provisions of the earlier Anti-Personnel (AP) Mine Ban Convention in December 1997—also known as the Ottawa Conference—and entered into force on March 1, 1999. The Ottawa treaty was initially signed by more than 125 countries, not including the United States, Russia, China, India, and Pakistan. For the treaty's purposes, a mine is defined as "a munition placed under, on or near the ground or other surface area and designed to be exploded by the presence, proximity or contact of a person or vehicle." It is classified as being among those munitions that are "primarily designed to be exploded by the presence, proximity or contact of a person and that will incapacitate, injure or kill one or more persons."

The convention is the first attempt to impose a universal ban on antipersonnel mines (APMs). In contrast to many other conventional arms agreements, this convention is unusual in that it was largely motivated by exclusively humanitarian concerns. Other accords are based on security concerns and confidence building among states, whereas this convention is concerned with the individual since it is aimed at preventing the killing and maiming of civilians, especially children, by APMs. The convention supports the complete ban on their use.

The AP Mine Ban Convention is equally applicable to both internal and international conflicts. Parties to the convention are obliged to render "technical and material assistance" where the mines they have laid are now under the control of another party in order to clear the mines. They have agreed to destroy all stockpiles of APMs within four years after the treaty entered into force and destroy all APMs that they have deployed in the ground within 10 years after the treaty entered into force, although in the event that a signatory cannot meet this deadline, it can seek an extension for up to 10 additional years. Parties "in a position to do so" are also encouraged to provide assistance to victims of mines and to work with other state parties to destroy stockpiles and mines already deployed. In addition, the convention provides for maintaining careful records of the location of mines and booby traps and other devices and for relaying this information to the relevant parties as well as to the United Nations regarding the progress each state party is making toward meeting its obligations under the convention. Critics point out, though, that the convention does not apply to nonstate actors such as insurgents or rebel groups, nor does it include antitank mines.

See also PROTOCOL ON PROHIBITIONS OR RESTRICTIONS ON THE USE OF MINES, BOOBY-TRAPS, AND OTHER DEVICES.

Further Reading:

Cornish, Paul. *Anti-personnel Mines: Controlling the Plague of "Butterflies."* London: Royal Institute of International Affairs, 1994.

Harpviken, Kristian Berg, ed. *The Future of Humanitarian Mine Action.* Third Worlds. Sydney, Australia: Palgrave Macmillan, 2004.

Prokosch, Eric. *The Technology of Killing: A Military and Political History of Anti-personnel Weapons.* London: Zed Books, 1995.

U.S. Congressional Budget Office. *Convention on Prohibitions or Restrictions on the Use of Certain Conventional Weapons.* Report to Accompany Treaty Doc. 103-25. Washington, D.C.: U.S. Government Printing Office, 1995.

Winslow, Philip C. *Sowing the Dragon's Teeth: Land Mines and the Global Legacy of War.* Boston: Beacon Press, 1998.

Convention on the Rights of the Child

The Convention on the Rights of the Child, which was adopted by the United Nations General Assembly on December 12, 1989, bans discrimination against children and provides for special protection and rights for minors. The convention, which defines *children* as anyone under age 18, emphasizes the primary importance of families—and parents in particular—in protecting CHILDREN'S RIGHTS. It does not usurp the authority of the family in favor of the government, as some detractors have charged. Rather, governments of signatory states are required to fulfill certain obligations to help protect and assist families in discharging their responsibilities toward their children while ensuring children's rights. In this context, Article 5 of the convention rejects the concept that parents "own" their children and have absolute rights over them. Parents have an obligation to promote and protect their children's rights. The convention also recognizes the changing balance between children and their families as children mature and assume more responsibilities for their own care and protection. The convention states that children have "the right to survival; to develop to the fullest; to protection from harmful influences, abuse and exploitation; and to participate fully in family, cultural and social life."

The convention establishes standards for children in health care; education; and legal, civil, and social services. These standards are benchmarks against which progress can be measured. States that are party to the convention are obliged to develop and undertake all actions and policies in the light of the best interests of the child. A special body called the Committee on the Rights of the Child is charged with monitoring how the states are meeting their commitments under the treaty. (A monitoring system is common to all UN human rights treaties.) States must report to the committee at regular intervals on their progress. The committee also obtains information from other sources, including sister UN agencies, nongovernmental organizations, academic institutions, and the media to assess the situation in each state, which it then uses in issuing its reports and recommendations, referred to as "concluding observations." By the end of 2005, 192 member states of the United Nations had ratified the convention, making it the most widely and quickly ratified human rights treaty in history.

See also SLAVERY.

Further Reading:
Dodge, Cole P., and Magne Raundelen. *Reaching Children in War: Sudan, Uganda and Mozambique.* London: Taylor & Francis, 1992.

Convention Relating to the Status of Refugees

In July 1951 the United Nations General Assembly adopted the Convention Relating to the Status of Refugees, which is based on the principle embodied in both the United Nations and the UNIVERSAL DECLARATION OF HUMAN RIGHTS "that human beings shall enjoy fundamental rights and freedoms without discrimination." The plight of REFUGEES was especially acute in the immediate aftermath of World War II, and it was clear to member states of the United Nations that the law needed to be codified for the protection of their rights. The convention and a subsequent protocol are considered the most comprehensive instruments applying to the legal rights of refugees. These instruments spell out the minimum humanitarian standards for the treatment of refugees and detail procedures pertaining to the granting of asylum.

According to the convention, a *refugee* is defined as a person who is outside one's country of origin (or customary residence in the case of stateless persons) and who is either unwilling or unable to return to that country because of a well-founded fear of persecution on account of his or her race, religion, nationality, membership in a particular social group, or political opinion. The convention excludes from refugee status persons who have committed war crimes, CRIMES AGAINST HUMANITY, and serious nonpolitical crimes committed outside the country of refuge. The convention stipulates that refugees cannot be returned to territory where their life or rights would be threatened or penalized for having sought asylum. Only in exceptional circumstances can a state expel a refugee, and then only to protect national security and public order. By the same token, refugees are obliged to obey the laws and regulations of the state where they have taken asylum. The convention also establishes standards that apply to the economic and social rights of refugees and bans discrimination against refugees because of their race, religion, or country of origin. Signatories of the convention pledge to cooperate with the Office of the UNITED NATIONS HIGH COMMISSIONER FOR REFUGEES (UNHCR) to ensure adherence to the provisions of the Convention.

See also ASYLUM, POLITICAL.

Further Reading:
Feller, Erika, Volker Turk, and Frances Nicholson, eds. *Refugee Protection in International Law: UNHCR's Global Consultations on International Protection.* Cambridge: Cambridge University Press, 2003.

Fritz, Mark. *Lost on Earth: Nomads of the New World.* New York: Routledge, 2000.

Groenewold, Julia, and Doctors Without Borders. *World in Crisis: The Politics of Survival at the End of the Twentieth Century.* London: Routledge, 1996.

Helton, Arthur C. *The Price of Indifference: Refugees and Humanitarian Action in the New Century.* A Council on Foreign Relations Book. Oxford: Oxford University Press, 2002

Hyndman, Jennifer. *Managing Displacement: Refugees and the Politics of Humanitarianism.* Minneapolis: University of Minnesota Press, 2000.

Ingleby, David, ed. *Forced Migration and Mental Health: Rethinking the Care of Refugees and Displaced Persons.* New York: Plenum US, 2004.

Lischer, Sarah Kenyon. *Dangerous Sanctuaries: Refugee Camps, Civil War, and the Dilemmas of Humanitarian Aid.* Cornell Studies in Security Affairs. Ithaca, N.Y.: Cornell University Press, 2005.

Moorehead, Caroline. *Human Cargo: A Journey among Refugees.* New York: Henry Holt and Co., 2005.

Ogata, Sadako, and Kofi Annan. *The Turbulent Decade: Confronting the Refugee Crises of the 1990s.* New York: W. W. Norton & Company, 2005.

Country Reports on Human Rights Practices
See HUMAN RIGHTS REPORTS.

crimes against humanity

When used in the context of international law, the term *crimes against humanity* refers to any crime committed against a civilian population whether before or during war. Such crimes can include murder, enslavement, the destruction of cultural property, and deportations. The term also applies to a state-sponsored program of persecution directed against individuals or groups based on their race, ethnicity, religion, or political beliefs. In an essay written for the CRIMES OF WAR PROJECT, Cherif Bassiouni of DePaul University in Chicago distinguishes between crimes against humanity and the crime of GENOCIDE. Genocide requires a legal finding of intent—for example, a state (or organization) has determined to exterminate a group of people based on their race, ethnicity, religion, or political beliefs. The legal equivalent would be premeditation. (Premeditated murder is considered a graver crime than murder committed in the heat of the moment; intent is present in the former case, absent in the latter.) By contrast, crimes against humanity, Bassiouni writes, differ from genocide "in that they do not require an intent to 'destroy in whole or in part' . . . but only target a given group and carry out a policy of 'widespread or systematic' violations." Bassiouni also

points out that crimes against humanity are distinguishable from war crimes "in that they not only apply in the context of war—they apply in times of war and peace."

The earliest use of the term is found in the Hague Convention of 1907, although it is based in CUSTOMARY LAW during armed conflict. That is to say, the codified law pertaining to crimes against humanity evolved from principles and values that have gained almost universal acceptance throughout history. Even though most international agreements in the early years of the 20th century covered the conduct of armed parties to a conflict, there were exceptions, notably the forced deportations and massacres of Armenians by Ottoman Turks in 1915, which involved the use of military force against an unarmed civilian population. A commission established in 1919 found that Turkish officers had in fact been culpable of "crimes against the laws of humanity" for their treatment of the Armenians, yet both the United States and Japan opposed the criminalizing of these acts because they were violations of moral law but not of existing positive or codified law. In other words, the two nations espoused a view that since a law was not on the books, its violation could not be considered a crime that could be prosecuted in a court of law.

In the aftermath of World War II, however, no government was about to resort to such legal technicalities. In 1945 the victorious Allies developed the framework for an international military tribunal to try Nazi war criminals at Nuremberg. Under the NUREMBERG CHARTER (or London Charter), as this framework was known, the defendants would be charged with three basic types of crimes: (1) crimes against peace, which were defined as the planning, initiating, and waging of aggressive war; (2) war crimes, which were defined as violations of the laws and customs of war as agreed upon in the HAGUE CONVENTIONS of 1899 and 1904; and (3) crimes against humanity, which were defined as the persecution and extermination of civilian populations based on their race, ethnicity, and religious faiths. The London Agreement and the subsequent Nuremberg Charter represent the first time that crimes against humanity were incorporated into positive international law—that is to say, these crimes could now be prosecuted and punished under an enforceable body of codified law.

Crimes of humanity are characterized by systematic persecution of a group based on its characteristics: their guilt is collective. Henceforth civilians were to be protected from certain acts of violence regardless of their nationality, citizenship, domicile, or country of origin. There have been no fewer than 11 different international agreements since the Nuremberg Charter that refer to crimes against humanity, although there has been no international convention to address the issue. Since Nuremberg the definition of crimes against humanity has been expanded through a series of accords to include rape and torture. These legal instruments also make it clear that all states have jurisdiction over these crimes. In other words, if a nation is unable or unwilling to prosecute a crime against humanity committed within its territory or extradite a suspect wanted by another nation, jurisdiction can be assumed by any signatory state or by an international body. No perpetrator is allowed to maintain a defense based on the excuse that he or she was "only following orders." Similarly, no official or political figure, regardless of his or her position, can claim immunity from statutes governing the prosecution of these crimes. Thus, a former leader of state, former President Slobodon MILOŠEVIĆ of the former Yugoslavia, could be made to stand trial for war crimes in the Balkan wars of the 1990s.

Arguably, the most important international accords relating to humanitarian law are the two ADDITIONAL PROTOCOLS TO THE GENEVA CONVENTIONS adopted in 1977, which grant protections to victims of international armed conflict (Protocol I) and to noncombatants caught up in civil wars and anticolonial uprisings (Protocol II). These protocols strengthen protections guaranteed to victims of war in ARTICLE 3 COMMON TO THE GENEVA CONVENTIONS. Additional Protocol II took into account the increasing problem of distinguishing between noncombatants and soldiers in internal conflicts.

In spite of these laws, some significant difficulties remain in ensuring that these protections are enforced. For one thing, the 1977 protocols have not been ratified by all member states of the United Nations. Moreover, the protocols are intended to apply to legitimate states, not to insurgent or terrorist groups who do not feel constrained by international law even as they are becoming more responsible for conflicts raging in the world today. Until recently there has been no effective international authority to ensure that these laws are followed and violators punished.

See also ARMENIAN GENOCIDE; CULTURAL PROPERTY, PROTECTION OF; NUREMBERG TRIALS.

Further Reading:

Bassiouni, M. Cherif. *Crimes against Humanity in International Criminal Law.* Boston: Martinus Nijhoff, 1999.

Dormann, Knut, and Louise Doswald-Beck. *Elements of War Crimes under the Rome Statute of the International Criminal Court: Sources and Commentary.* Cambridge: Cambridge University Press, 2003.

Falk, Richard A. *Crimes of War: A legal, political-documentary, and psychological inquiry into the responsibility of leaders, citizens, and soldiers for criminal acts in wars.* New York: Random House, 1971.

Goldstone, Richard. *For Humanity: Reflections of a War Crimes Investigator.* Castle Lectures Series. New Haven, Conn.: Yale University Press, 2000.

Gutman, Roy, ed. *Crimes of War: What the Public Should Know.* New York: W. W. Norton & Company, 1999.

Jackson, Nyamuya Maogoto. *War Crimes and Realpolitik: International Justice from World War I to the 21st Century.* Boulder, Colo.: Lynne Rienner Publishers, 2004.

Jokie, Aleksander. *War Crimes and Collective Wrongdoing: A Reader.* London: Blackwell Publishers, 2001.

Jones, Adam, ed. *Genocide, War Crimes and the West: History and Complicity.* London: Zed Books, 2004.

May, Larry, and Gerald Postema. *Crimes against Humanity: A Normative Account.* Cambridge Studies in Philosophy and Law. Cambridge: Cambridge University Press, 2004.

Meron, Theodor. *War Crimes Law Comes of Age: Essays.* Oxford: Oxford University Press, 1999.

Robertson, Geoffrey. *Crimes against Humanity: The Struggle for Global Justice.* New York: New Press, 2003.

Crimes of War Project

The Crimes of War Project (CWP) is a collaboration of journalists, lawyers, and scholars who have made it their mission to raise public awareness of the laws of war and their application to conflicts. The CWP seeks to broaden an understanding of INTERNATIONAL HUMANITARIAN LAW (IHL) in conflicts, whether internal or international, in the hope of putting pressure on policymakers, representatives of the media, and the public that might help prevent future conflicts and lead to the punishment of perpetrators of past abuses. The CWP offers several educational resources, including *Crimes of War: What the Public Should Know*, a compilation of essays by scholars and journalists on such subjects as the GENEVA CONVENTIONS, military necessity, and humanitarian intervention; and a magazine that covers pertinent topics of current interest. Both the book and the magazine are available online. In addition, the CWP holds seminars and educational programs.

The creators of CWP recognize that international humanitarian law can seem "an arcane and specialized field of study" and that it may not ordinarily be viewed as a "tool for fighting human suffering." The CWP seeks to correct that impression by encouraging "wider appreciation of international law as a framework for understanding and responding to conflicts around the world" and promoting increased compliance with international humanitarian law by bringing together journalists, legal experts, and humanitarian agencies. The CWP notes that IHL has undergone significant changes since the 1949 Geneva Conventions brought about new and more effective enforcement mechanisms. The CWP tries to clarify this body of law and keep the general public aware of the latest developments and debates that surround them. A private, nonprofit corporation, CWP was established in 1999 and receives its funding from philanthropic organizations and individual donations.

Further Reading:
Gutman, Roy, ed. *Crimes of War: What the Public Should Know.* New York: W. W. Norton & Company, 1999.

Croatia, human rights violations in

Croatia emerged as an independent republic after the violent breakup of the former Yugoslavia. The country has made significant progress in human rights since the death in 1999 of Franjo TUDJMAN, the strongman who led Croatia during its war against Serb-dominated Yugoslavia, and generally receives good marks from the U.S. State Department. Serious problems remain, however, especially in its treatment of the Serb minority. There have been instances of arbitrary arrest and lengthy pretrial detention. In spite of attempts at reform, courts still convict suspects in mass trials and in absentia. Courts also are subject to political influence and are hobbled by bureaucratic inefficiency, insufficient funding, and a severe backlog of cases. In contrast to the Tudjman regime, the government has generally kept its hands off the media, although there is still political pressure on journalists, which often takes the form of filing libel lawsuits against them.

The government of President Stepjan Mesić has stepped up the arrests and prosecutions of individuals for war crimes committed during the 1991–95 conflicts in Bosnia and Croatia and has opened or reopened cases against Croatian officers alleged to have taken part in these crimes. At the same time, his government has emphasized that the arrests of suspects was not being carried out at the behest of the UN-sponsored INTERNATIONAL CRIMINAL TRIBUNAL FOR THE FORMER YUGOSLAVIA (ICTY) but, in the words of Prime Minister Ivica Racan, were being undertaken because it was "a matter of justice." Nonetheless, Mesić's government has shown more willingness to send indicted war criminals to stand trial in The Hague. The government's cooperation with The Hague set off a political firestorm, although it easily survived a vote of confidence. Even so, one of the most-sought suspects, Ante Gotovina, captured in 2005, had received clandestine help from elements in the military. Carla DEL PONTE, the ICTY prosecutor, blames the Croatian government for failing to apprehend the general. International observers express skepticism about whether Croatian courts can bring suspected war criminals to justice, especially ethnic Serbs who are more likely to be prosecuted than Croatians, often on minor charges from which Croats are generally immune. Nonetheless, arrests of ethnic Serbs for war crimes have fallen in recent years.

All the same, there are still doubts in the international community about whether Croatian courts have the ability to conduct fair and transparent trials, especially in emotionally charged cases. There are reports of chronic intimidation of witnesses and resistance on the part of the public to the prosecution of officers for crimes committed against their former enemy. In December 2001, for instance, four Croatian police officers were acquitted of war-crime charges for killing six PRISONERS OF WAR in 1991 after a key prosecution witness changed his testimony at the trial, possibly as a result of pressure put on him to change it. When the same four officers went on trial in another case involving TORTURE, three were found guilty but only received a sentence of one year in prison. Similar cases involving officers accused of torture or murder of ethnic Serbs have led to acquittals.

Under the terms of the 1995 DAYTON ACCORDS that brought an end to the Bosnian war, refugees were given the right to return to their homes. It is believed that between 300,000 and 350,000 Serbs were uprooted from their homes in Croatia during the 1991–95 war. Resettlement of these REFUGEES has proceeded slowly, and human rights organizations contend that the government has been unwilling and unable to solve this problem for the vast majority of displaced Serbs. In spite of the AMNESTY law, ethnic Serbs still fear arbitrary arrest on trumped-up war-crime charges and still face discrimination in employment and pension benefits if they do return. In many cases, local courts refuse to evict Croatians who have illegally appropriated property belonging to ethnic Serb refugees. The UNITED NATIONS HIGH COMMISSIONER FOR REFUGEES (UNHCR) estimated that over 100,000 Croatian Serbs had returned by June 2001. In many cases, though, refugees finding an inhospitable reception will leave again for sanctuary in Serbia, Montenegro, or the Serb republic in the Federation of Bosnia and Herzegovina. Most of those who do stay are elderly. HUMAN RIGHTS WATCH estimates that within two decades the Serb population in most parts of Croatia will have all but disappeared. In 1991, before the war, Serbs made up 12.1 percent of Croatia's population; the 2001 census showed their number had fallen to a mere 4.5 percent.

In addition to problems involving the resettlement of refugees who had fled during the war, Croatia also still has to grapple with the need to account for those who died as a result of the war. By 2001 more than 3,350 victims missing from the 1991–95 war were exhumed from mass and individual graves. Another 1,317 persons (mostly ethnic Croats) remained missing in unresolved cases stemming from the conflict. The government has been credited with cooperating with the international community in conducting exhumations of the bodies and in trying to identify the remains.

See also USTACHE; YUGOSLAVIA, WAR CRIMES IN.

Further Reading:
Glenny, Misha. *The Fall of Yugoslavia: The Third Balkan War.* New York: Penguin Books, 1996.

Hagan, John. *Justice in the Balkans: Prosecuting War Crimes in the Hague Tribunal.* Chicago Series in Law and Society. Chicago: University of Chicago Press, 2003.

Harris, Nathaniel. *The War in Former Yugoslavia.* London: Hodder & Stoughton, 1997.

Mertus, Julie. *Former Yugoslavia: War Crimes Trials in the Former Yugoslavia.* Helsinki, Finland: Human Rights Watch/Helsinki, 1995.

Rossanet, Bertrand de. *War and Peace in the Former Yugoslavia.* Boston: Martinus Nijhoff, 1997.

Cuba, human rights violations in

Since 1959, when Fidel Castro took power in a revolution, Cuba has been a one-party nation. The government continues to crack down on political dissent, and critics are frequently intimidated, placed under house arrest, or taken into custody. Even if they are allowed to remain at liberty, political opponents are kept under surveillance and harassed. Police monitor the activities of people who, while not found guilty of any illegal acts, are viewed with suspicion and classified as dangerous—*estado peligroso.* In a report on the island nation, HUMAN RIGHTS WATCH observed that "Cuba's legal and institutional structures were at the root of rights violations." The law restricts such basic rights as freedom of expression, association, assembly, and movement. Laws forbidding the dissemination of "unauthorized news" or the defamation of patriotic symbols have been used to curb freedom of speech. Journalists still send reports abroad, but only at the risk of being questioned by police or being detained for short periods. There is only one government-authorized labor union; no other labor organizing is allowed. Defendants are frequently denied the right to a defense at their trial or DUE PROCESS. All prisoners are compelled to take part in politically oriented "reeducation" sessions or face punishment. Human rights organizations have no legal standing, and in many cases international human rights groups are barred from attending court proceedings.

In spite of these limits and periodic crackdowns, the government has failed to stamp out political dissent. In a challenge to the regime, the prominent dissident Oswaldo Paya spearheaded a petition drive called the Varela Project in 2002, relying on a constitutional protection guaranteeing the right to petition. The petition demanded such civil and political rights as competitive elections, freedom of the press, and an AMNESTY for political prisoners. The petition has collected more than 25,000 signatures. Similar initiatives, such as the Assembly to Promote Civil Society, followed suit. Not to be outdone, the government instituted a signature drive of its own to support the socialist system; it claimed that it managed to gather more than 8 million signatures in two days. The National Assembly then approved an official proposal calling the socialist system "irrevocable." The government seemed content to let the democracy advocates continue their activities, but as events would soon prove, its patience was about to run out.

In March 2003 the security forces suddenly rounded up almost 90 peaceful dissidents, including independent journalists, human rights defenders, economists, independent labor union activists, librarians, doctors, and teachers. Some had been active in the political opposition for a decade or more. They were accused of a variety of offenses: subversion, spying for the United States, and spreading false reports to the foreign press about the state of the Cuban economy. Within three weeks, 75 of them were tried, convicted, and given prison sentences ranging from six to 28 years. Human rights organizations criticized the trials for their lack of fairness; defense lawyers had no time to prepare an adequate defense and in most cases had no opportunity to speak to their clients until an hour before the trial began. Those convicted are being held in prisons in deplorable conditions hundreds of miles from their homes, making family visits difficult. Some of the incarcerated men are in deteriorating health and have not received adequate medical care.

In spring 2003 the government tried three young Cuban men on the charges of hijacking a boat in a futile effort to escape to the United States. Leaving Cuba without permission is a crime under Cuban law. Even though they had harmed no one in the course of the hijacking, they were condemned to death and executed seven days later. The executions, too, were a departure from previous policy; since April 2000 Cuba had adhered to a de facto moratorium on putting people to death.

The crackdowns surprised—and discouraged—many observers because in the last several years Cuba had actually been liberalizing its policies. With some exceptions, the number of political dissidents in prison had been declining steadily. As AMNESTY INTERNATIONAL (AI) noted: "The Cuban authorities had seemed to be moving away from the blanket imposition of lengthy prison sentences as a means of stifling dissent, and towards a more low-level approach of harassment, designed more to discourage than to punish critics." It appeared that Cuba was taking "an alarming step backwards in terms of respect for human rights" as AI put it.

The government permits more freedom of religion than in the past—spiritual leaders and religious institutions enjoy more autonomy than other institutions—but there are still some official limitations; new church construction is restricted, for instance, and church schools must confine their curricula only to religion.

Since 1962, at the height of the cold war, the United States has imposed a financial and trade embargo against

Cuba. Although the embargo has failed to bring down the Castro regime, it has caused considerable hardship for the Cuban people, and it is opposed by many nations including members of the European Union and nongovernmental organizations such as Amnesty International, which maintain that the embargo has actually undermined the exercise of civil and political rights "by fuelling a climate in which such fundamental rights as freedom of association, expression and assembly are routinely denied." AI contends that, in addition, the embargo gives the Cuban government a pretext to perpetuate its repressive policies and generates sympathy for Cuba in other developing countries. The embargo has also come under fire from many lawmakers on both sides of the aisle in the U.S. Congress. But as long as the Cuban exile community in Florida retains its political influence in American politics, it is unlikely that the embargo will be lifted before Fidel Castro fades from the scene.

Further Reading:
Chomsky, Aviva, Barry Carr, and Pamela Maria Smorkaloff, eds. *The Cuba Reader: History, Culture, Politics.* Latin America Readers. Durham, N.C.: Duke University Press, 2004.
Hatchwell, Emily. *In Focus Cuba: A Guide to the People, Politics, and Culture.* New York: Interlink Publishing Group, 1999.

cultural property, protection of

The idea that the destruction and theft of cultural property was a war crime took root during the American Civil War. The first modern legal guidelines protecting cultural property—the LIEBER CODE—was introduced in 1863. Although the code applied only to American troops, it influenced the codification of cultural protection embodied in a succession of international treaties that have emerged in the aftermath of World War II. The NUREMBERG TRIALS of Nazi war criminals represent the first time that individuals were held to account for cultural war crimes. Field Marshal Hermann GÖRING—second in power only to Adolf HITLER in the ranks of the Nazi party—was one of the worst offenders: during the war he orchestrated the systematic looting of museums and private collections throughout Europe. The looting of the national museum and the torching of the national library in Baghdad following the U.S. occupation of Baghdad in 2003 brought renewed attention to the vulnerability of cultural institutions in wartime.

In May 1954 the United Nations General Assembly adopted the Convention for the Protection of Cultural Property in the Event of Armed Conflict. This was the first comprehensive international agreement to focus exclusively on the protection of cultural heritage. According to the convention, the definition of *cultural property* is broad enough to include architectural monuments; archaeological sites; works of art; manuscripts of artistic or historical significance; books; and other objects of artistic, historical, or archaeological interest, as well as scientific collections of all kinds. It also covers buildings "whose main and effective purpose is to preserve or exhibit the movable cultural property . . . such as museums, large libraries and depositories of archives." However, the convention does allow the protection for cultural property to be lifted, but "only in cases where military necessity imperatively requires such a waiver." Although the phrase *military necessity* is not defined, it is reasonable to assume that an exceptional case might arise where a church or museum is damaged as a result of a stray missile that was aimed at a nearby munitions factory, which is referred to as COLLATERAL DAMAGE. It would also seem to apply in cases where a cultural institution was used for military purposes by an adversary, which is outlawed by the Additional Protocol II to the GENEVA CONVENTIONS (see below).

As of March 2003, 105 member states had signed the treaty. The states that are party to the convention have agreed to take measures to safeguard and respect cultural property in peacetime as well as in armed conflict. The convention's provisions apply equally as well to internal conflicts as well as to conflicts between nations. To ensure that there will be no ambiguity about what constitutes a cultural property, the convention established a special documentation mechanism known as the International Register of Cultural Property under Special Protection. Under this system, certain important buildings and monuments were to be designated by a special protective emblem. The convention also required signatories to create special military units that would be responsible for the protection of cultural property.

The convention was strengthened by the Additional Protocol II of 1977. Article 53 of this protocol prohibits "any acts of hostility directed against the historic monuments, works of art or places of worship which constitute the cultural or spiritual heritage of peoples." The protocol also forbids the export of cultural property from occupied territory, requires states to return any confiscated property to its rightful owner, and outlaws the appropriation of cultural property as war reparation. Further, Article 53 prohibits the use of cultural property "in support of the military effort," by using a church or museum as a command center, for instance. In that event, the destruction of or damage to the property during an attack would not be classified as a war crime.

In spite of the safeguards codified in the convention, cultural property still sustained destruction in wars of the 1980s and in the early 1990s in the Balkans. The INTERNATIONAL CRIMINAL TRIBUNAL FOR THE FORMER YUGOSLAVIA in The Hague was given the right to prosecute individuals responsible for the "seizure of, destruction or willful damage done to institutions dedicated to religion, charity and education, the arts and sciences, historic monuments and works of art and science." Successive violations of the safeguards in the convention vividly underscored a glaring loophole in both the convention and the additional protocol: No punishment or enforcement mechanism was provided for. In 1991 state parties to the convention realized that they needed to strengthen the convention even further, leading to the adoption of the Second Protocol to the Hague Convention in March 1999. This protocol provides greater protections on cultural property than set forward in the convention and Additional Protocol II: It creates a new category of protection for cultural heritage judged important for humanity, imposes sanctions for serious violations of cultural property, and spells out the conditions when criminal charges could be brought. In addition, it established an intergovernmental committee to ensure that the provisions of both the convention and the Second Protocol were implemented.

There is another international accord on cultural property that should also be cited: the 1970 UNESCO Convention on the Means of Prohibiting and Preventing the Illicit Import, Export and Transfer of Ownership of Cultural Property, which covers cases in which a cultural patrimony of a member state is threatened by PILLAGE, theft, or destruction. Under such circumstances, other member states are required to make an effort to control the exports and trade of any cultural objects that have been illegally acquired. For instance, countries where antiquities looted from Iraqi historical sites in the aftermath of the 2003 war in Iraq are obliged to seize and repatriate those objects.

See also ADDITIONAL PROTOCOLS TO THE GENEVA CONVENTIONS; PROTOCOL TO THE HAGUE CONVENTION OF 1954 FOR THE PROTECTION OF CULTURAL PROPERTY IN THE EVENT OF ARMED CONFLICT, SECOND.

Further Reading:
Gutman, Roy, ed. *Crimes of War: What the Public Should Know.* New York: W. W. Norton & Company, 1999.
May, Larry, and Gerald Postema. *Crimes against Humanity: A Normative Account.* Cambridge Studies in Philosophy and Law. Cambridge: Cambridge University Press, 2004.
Meron, Theodor. *War Crimes Law Comes of Age: Essays.* Oxford: Oxford University Press, 1999.

customary law

There are two types of humanitarian law: treaty law and customary law. Treaty law consists of codified agreements, such as the GENEVA CONVENTIONS. Customary law, by contrast, is not written but based on certain norms or principles of behavior that are acknowledged by all states. Unlike treaty law, which binds only those states that have signed the agreement, customary law is considered binding on all states. A rule is considered customary when it reflects practices by states that are seen by the international community as morally sound. In areas that are not specifically dealt with by treaties, customary law can be drawn upon to fill the void.

In his book *The Enterprise of Law: Justice without the State,* Bruce Benson points out that law can be made in two basic ways. It can, for instance, be imposed from above by some authority—whether a king, a legislature, or a court—which has the power to enforce the law. Alternatively, a law can evolve from the bottom up, as it were. If this body of law gains wide acceptance, it becomes customary law. It is reasonable to suppose that this was the kind of law that kept societies intact before the introduction of written language. Customary law, writes Benson, "must correspond to the practices on which the everyday conduct of the members of the group was based." These practices or customs "give rise to expectations that guide people's actions, and what will be regarded as binding."

In other words, customary law has force not because it is imposed or enforced by some authority or institution but "because each individual recognizes the benefits of behaving in accordance with other individuals' expectations." Individuals generally expect that in the course of their everyday lives, they will not be robbed or killed. Although robbery and murder are, of course, outlawed in every country, the expectations that arise within a society that people should be safe from robbery and murder make the codified law far more effective than it would otherwise be. There are many other laws on the books—for instance, against forms of gambling, speeding, or other types of behavior—that do not enjoy such wide acceptance (because these laws did not develop from the bottom up), and so it is not surprising to find that the written laws in these cases are more often flouted. Customary law is based on reciprocities, according to Benson—"That is, individuals must 'exchange' recognition of certain behavioral rules for their mutual benefit."

Customary law has important implications in terms of INTERNATIONAL HUMANITARIAN LAW. To an extent, customary law provided the foundation of the earliest conventions dealing with war crimes: the HAGUE CONVENTIONS of 1899 and 1907. The preamble of the 1899 convention provides for a minimum threshold of humanitarian law in the treatment of combatants even in the absence of specific language in a treaty. What is known as the Martens clause (after Feodor de Martens, a Russian Foreign Ministry adviser) states: "Until a more complete code of the laws of war is issued, the High Contracting Parties think it right to declare that in cases not included in the Regulations adopted by them, populations and belligerents remain under the protection and the empire of the principles of international law, as they result from the usages established between civilized nations, from the laws of humanity, and the requirements of the public conscience." Similarly, a good case can be made that customary law underlies the four Geneva Conventions of 1949 and many of the provisions, principles, and rules contained in the ADDITIONAL PROTOCOLS TO THE GENEVA CONVENTIONS. (Treaties outlawing the use of CHEMICAL WEAPONS and BIOLOGICAL WEAPONS also reflect customary law.)

Allied prosecutors at the NUREMBERG TRIALS of Nazi war criminals relied on customary law. To some degree, customary law has also guided the deliberations of the INTERNATIONAL CRIMINAL TRIBUNAL FOR THE FORMER YUGOSLAVIA (ICTY). That is not to say that customary law can supplant or is even necessarily more significant than written law. Rather, customary law imbues legal codes with moral status. Theodor MERON, a judge on the ICTY, has written about the relevance of customary law: "Both scholarly and judicial sources have shown reluctance to reject as customary norms—because of contrary practice—rules whose content merits customary law status perhaps because of the recognition that humanitarian principles express basic community values and are essential for the preservation of public order."

See also REPRISAL.

Further Reading:

Benson, Bruce. *The Enterprise of Law: Justice without the State.* San Francisco: Pacific Research Institute for Public Policy, 1990.

Goldstone, Richard. *For Humanity: Reflections of a War Crimes Investigator.* Castle Lectures Series. New Haven, Conn.: Yale University Press, 2000.

Gutman, Roy, ed. *Crimes of War: What the Public Should Know.* New York: W. W. Norton & Company, 1999.

Jackson, Nyamuya Maogoto. *War Crimes and Realpolitik: International Justice from World War I to the 21st Century.* Boulder, Colo.: Lynne Rienner Publishers, 2004.

Meron, Theodor. *War Crimes Law Comes of Age: Essays.* Oxford: Oxford University Press, 1999.

Cyprus, human rights violations in

Cyprus has long been an international problem that still remained unresolved as of 2004 in spite of determined efforts by the United Nations (UN) and the European Union (EU). The island has been divided ever since Turkey invaded it in 1974. Tensions between the two peoples had simmered since Cyprus won independence from Great Britain in 1960. The Turkish intervention was justified as necessary to protect the smaller Turkish community (Turks make up 18 percent of the total population), and an independent Turkish Cypriot state was declared in 1975. As a result, about 200,000 Greek Cypriots (about 40 percent of the total Cypriot Greek population) living in the largely Turkish north fled to the southern Greek part of the island. The Turkish enclave, which constitutes about 37 percent of the island, is only recognized by Turkey; the Greek area is far more prosperous. A UN peacekeeping force has kept hostilities at bay for the last three decades. A last-ditch peace plan put forward by UN secretary-general Kofi Annan was rejected in an April 2004 referendum that required the approval of the majority in both communities to pass. (Greeks overwhelmingly voted against it, while the Turkish population voted for it.) Had the peace plan gone forward, it would have paved the way for Cyprus to join the European Union, a move expected to yield considerable economic benefits. As it stands now, only the Greek part of the island will be able to join the EU. Observers believe that the tensions between the two groups accounted for the failure of the peace plan. One of the most vexing problems is the right of REFUGEES to reclaim property lost when they were forced to abandon their homes in 1974.

In sharp contrast to the violence and forced evictions that followed in the wake of the Turkish invasion, Cyprus remains relatively free of serious human rights abuses, according to the U.S. State Department's 2004 *Country Report.* The Greek government generally respected the island's human rights, although there were problems in some areas, including incidence of police brutality against detainees, violence against women, and the imposition of some restrictions on persons traveling to the Turkish enclave in the north. (A relaxation of border controls in April 2003 has allowed a freer flow of travel from one part of the nation to the other than was permitted in the past.) The police also interfered with some demonstrations. Journalists have come under some pressure from the authorities for their reporting, and criminal charges have been brought against some. The State Department reported more problems in the Turkish enclave, where authorities restricted freedom of movement to government-controlled areas and prohibited most contacts between Turkish Cypriots and Greek Cypriots. Cooperation between Turkish Cypriot authorities and the UNITED NATIONS HIGH COMMISSIONER FOR REFUGEES (UNHCR) was uneven.

One outstanding problem is the continuing attempt by both Greek and Turkish Cypriot authorities to resolve the fate of people who have disappeared as a result of clashes extending as far back as 1963. Little progress was made by the joint Committee on Missing Persons in Cyprus (CMP) in 2003. The Greek Cypriot government, however, has been exhuming sites believed to contain the remains of people missing since 1974. As of 2001, a total of 127 remains had been identified, all of them Turks. (No Greeks were identified through DNA testing in the same year.) According to the Greek Cypriot government, 1,493 Greek Cypriots remained missing.

D

dams and dikes, protection of

From ancient times, water resources and facilities have been viewed as strategic assets whose destruction can inflict grievous harm on an enemy. As far back as 596 B.C. the Babylonian monarch Nebuchadnezzar breached an aqueduct supplying the city of Tyre to end a long SIEGE. During the warring-states period of ancient China (c. third century B.C.), water was used as a weapon; dams were destroyed to flood an enemy's territory or else constructed to prevent an enemy state from obtaining access to water at all. The tradition persisted into the 20th century: In 1938 Generalissimo Chiang Kai-shek ordered the destruction of dikes on a section of China's Yellow River in order to flood areas threatened by the Japanese army. His action succeeded in deterring the Japanese invaders, but it also had the effect of killing thousands of Chinese living nearby. During World War II, both the Allies and the Axis powers showed no compunction about bombing hydroelectric dams. In the Vietnam War, U.S. aircraft carried out systematic bombing of dikes in North Vietnam, causing great loss of life and dislocation among civilian populations as well as environmental devastation. In the 1999 war in the breakaway Yugoslav province of Kosovo, Serbs contaminated water supplies and wells used by the Albanian civilians.

It is civilians who are likely to suffer most of all when dams and other water resources are targeted militarily. In general, INTERNATIONAL HUMANITARIAN LAW does allow for the targeting of dams and dikes if the destruction of these installations is required for a military objective—to stop an enemy's advance, for example—but with the added qualification that the destruction involved is proportionate to securing that objective. According to Article 56 of Additional Protocol I to the GENEVA CONVENTIONS, destruction of dams and dikes is allowed when the installation is used for "other than its normal function and in regular, significant and direct support of military operations and if such attack is the only feasible way to terminate such sup-

port." Article 54 of Protocol I specifically prohibits "attacking, destroying, removing of 'objects indispensable to the survival' of civilian population, such as 'drinking water installations and supplies and irrigation works.' " Article 56 expands the list to prohibit attacks against "works and installations containing dangerous forces, namely dams, dykes and nuclear electrical generating stations." Even if these installations are legitimate military objectives, Additional Protocol I still prohibits an attack if the destruction of the installation causes "the release of dangerous forces and consequent severe losses among the civilian population"—emphasizing the concept of proportionality in the application of force. This stipulation places a special obligation on the defending force as well, since the defender is constrained from placing the installation—and the civilian population dependent on the installation—at serious risk. This same principle also applies to other civilian facilities and cultural properties that are entitled to protections under international law as long as they are not used for military purposes.

In addition, international law provides for protections for civilians and civilian "objects" that are also applicable to the deliberate destruction of water resources and installations by a belligerent. This law has been repeatedly confirmed by international treaties including the Hague Convention of 1907 and the Geneva Conventions of 1949. The Hague Convention has two specific prohibitions that are, at least indirectly, related to the protection of water resources. One forbids the use of poison or poisoned weapons, and the other forbids the destruction and seizure of an enemy's property unless it is "demanded by the necessities of war."

In November 2002 access to safe and secure drinking water was declared a human right with the adoption of the General Comment on the Right to Water, adopted by the Covenant on Economic and Cultural Rights (CESCR), which has been ratified by 145 countries. However, this accord only applies in times of peace, not during conflict.

In spite of these laws, some significant difficulties remain in ensuring that these protections are enforced. For one thing, the 1977 protocols have not been ratified by all member states of the United Nations. Moreover, the protocols are intended to apply to legitimate states, not to insurgent or terrorist groups that do not feel constrained by international law even as they are becoming more responsible for conflicts raging in the world today. Until recently there has been no effective international authority to ensure that these laws are followed and violators punished.

See also ADDITIONAL PROTOCOLS TO THE GENEVA CONVENTIONS; HAGUE CONVENTIONS.

Darfur, war crimes in

Until 2003, Darfur, a region in western Sudan, was largely unknown to the outside world. Tensions in Darfur were overshadowed by a 20-year civil war between the mainly Muslim north against a Christian and animist south. Significant progress was being made in resolving that conflict when the crisis in Darfur escalated to such an extent that U.S. secretary of state Colin Powell characterized the situation as GENOCIDE, an unprecedented declaration on the part of a top American official.

Although most of Darfur's inhabitants are Muslim, they are divided along ethnic lines between Africans, most of them farmers, and Arabs, most of them herders; however, because of intermarriage it is often difficult to distinguish the two groups. The Africans have complained of being deprived of political power in favor of the Arab minority. Tensions between the African farmers and Arab herders erupted in violence in the 1980s. Increasing desertification and droughts set the stage for the most recent conflict as grazing land became scarce, compelling farmers and herders to compete for territory. An uprising by two African insurgent groups—the Sudan Liberation Army and the Justice and Equality Movement—provided the pretext for a violent government crackdown. The government in Khartoum relied on proxy forces: Arab militiamen known as the Janjaweed, backed by government soldiers and helicopter gun ships. The Janjaweed were given license to raid and destroy villages and rape and kill as they pleased. Within a matter of months, close to a million people had either been internally displaced or pushed over the border into neighboring Chad. By fall 2004 an estimated 70,000 Africans had been killed. (Some experts put the number of dead as much higher—up to 300,000 as of the beginning of 2005.) Hundreds of villages were burned to the ground, farmland was destroyed, and animals were killed, making large parts of the region uninhabitable. Women have been particularly singled out for abuse in Darfur, and substantial evidence points to the use of RAPE AS A TACTIC OF WAR by the Arab militias.

Women have been the victims of beatings, robberies, and harassment as well. They are particularly at risk when they wander away from refugee camps in search of firewood, making them more vulnerable to attack.

What was unclear, as of late 2004, was the extent of the abuses and whether they fell under the legal definition of war crimes. A special panel of experts was formed by the United Nations to resolve the issue. "Depending on the magnitude of it, it can constitute a crime against humanity," said Louise ARBOUR, the UNITED NATIONS HIGH COMMISSIONER FOR HUMAN RIGHTS. Throughout the conflict the Sudanese government vehemently denied that it was collaborating with the Janjaweed or that it condoned ethnic cleansing, even in the face of overwhelming evidence. Hundreds of REFUGEES have reported that they had heard racial epithets as they were attacked, while three-quarters of them said that they had seen government insignia on the uniforms of their attackers.

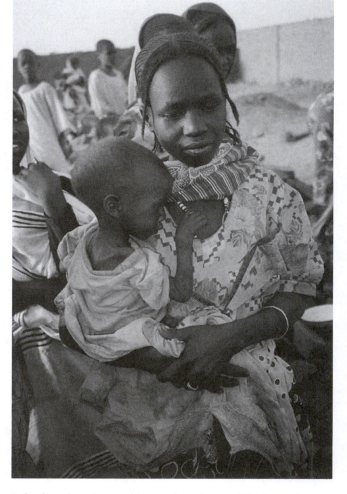

A displaced mother and her malnourished child in north Darfur, Sudan *(USAID)*

The humanitarian crisis provoked a fierce outcry by human rights groups. UN secretary-general Kofi Annan and Colin Powell visited Darfur to meet with the refugees and Sudanese officials, and the African Union dispatched a small contingent of monitors. Debate raged in the halls of the United Nations and in the European Union as to how to resolve the crisis. Khartoum's responses ranged from defiance to offers of cooperation. Sanctions against Sudan were considered, but even Western nations were divided as to whether they would prove effective or simply stiffen Sudanese resistance. Powell declared that the massacres carried out by the Janjaweed and Sudanese regular forces constituted genocide, the first such declaration since the adoption of the UN GENOCIDE CONVENTION in 1948. There is no question that U.S. and UN administration officials were mindful of the mass killings in Rwanda in 1994, during which 800,000 Tutsis and moderate Hutus were slaughtered within 100 days. At no time during that crisis did any official use the word *genocide*. Repeated assertions by the Sudanese authorities that they are intent on restoring order have been cast into doubt by reports that the Janjaweed who carried out rapes and massacres have been given police uniforms and are now charged with protecting the same Africans whom they had previously targeted.

In January 2005 the United Nations commission investigating the situation in the Darfur region of Sudan issued a report in which it said that while it had found a pattern of mass killings and forced displacement of civilians, genocide had not taken place. The commission cautioned that failure to make a finding of genocide "should not be taken in any way as detracting from the gravity of the crimes perpetrated in that region." It further stated that "international offenses such as the CRIMES AGAINST HUMANITY and war crimes that have been committed in Darfur may be no less serious and heinous than genocide." The commission recommended that perpetrators of these crimes should be sent to the INTERNATIONAL CRIMINAL COURT (ICC) for prosecution. Among the crimes cited by the commission were "the killing of civilians, TORTURE, enforced DISAPPEARANCES, destruction of villages, rape and other forms of sexual violence, pillaging and displacement." However, the United States, while calling for the crimes in Darfur to be vigorously punished, objected to the use of the ICC as the place in which to do it. The Bush administration has opposed the ICC since its inception on the grounds that it could be used to bring politically motivated prosecutions against American political officials or military officers for actions committed on foreign soil. Washington took the position that the crimes in Darfur should be prosecuted in a special court, similar to those prosecuting war crimes committed in Rwanda or the former Yugoslavia. Most governments, however, prefer the ICC, both because it has the support of most nations and because it would be more expeditious and less costly than establishing a new ad hoc court.

By 2005 human rights groups estimated that some 2 million civilians had been displaced by the conflict. Efforts to stop attacks on civilians have been halting at best. The African Union (AU) has deployed some troops in the region—with NATO contributing planes to airlift them in—but their numbers were still insufficient to defend the at-risk population. Even as peace talks got under way in Abuja, Nigeria, between the Sudanese government and insurgent groups, the violence showed little sign of abating.

See also SUDAN, HUMAN RIGHTS VIOLATIONS IN.

Further Reading:
De Waal, Alexander. *Famine That Kills: Darfur, Sudan.* Oxford Studies in African Affairs. Oxford: Oxford University Press, 2004.

Gutman, Roy, ed. *Crimes of War: What the Public Should Know.* New York: W. W. Norton & Company, 1999.

May, Larry, and Gerald Postema. *Crimes against Humanity: A Normative Account.* Cambridge Studies in Philosophy and Law. Cambridge: Cambridge University Press, 2004.

Meron, Theodor. *War Crimes Law Comes of Age: Essays.* Oxford: Oxford University Press, 1999.

Peterson, Donald. *Inside Sudan: Political Islam, Conflict, and Catastrophe.* Philadelphia: Westview Press, 1999.

Power, Samantha. *A Problem from Hell.* New York: Perennial, 2003.

D'Aubuisson, Roberto (1943–1992) *Salvadorian death squad leader*

Roberto D'Aubuisson was once one of the most powerful—and feared—figures in El Salvador's political history. He was known as "Blowtorch Bob" for what was reportedly his favorite method of TORTURE; former U.S. Ambassador Robert White called him "a pathological killer." An admirer of Adolf HITLER, D'Aubuisson was quoted as saying, "You Germans were very intelligent. You realized Jews were responsible for the spread of Communism and you began to kill them."

Born in 1943, D'Aubuisson studied intelligence in the United States, and on his return to El Salvador, he joined ANSESAL, the Salvadoran intelligence agency, eventually becoming third in command. Before leaving the agency in 1979, he made sure to take dossiers on leftist sympathizers. A coup that same year brought to power a military junta that attempted to institute reforms, even going so far as to invite leftists and moderates into the government. D'Aubuisson, however, was part of a faction opposed to the new junta, which he accused of being "infiltrated by Marxist officers." Convinced that the country was seriously threatened by a communist insurrection, he formed death squads to eliminate political opponents on the left. He was able to rely for support on wealthy landowners and businessmen inside and outside El Salvador who offered him the use of their estates, homes, vehicles, and bodyguards. He also had the secret support of the security and intelligence services, using the information he acquired from them for what was called "direct action," meaning assassinations, abductions, theft, and sabotage. One of his victims was Archbishop Oscar Romero, a human rights advocate and outspoken critic of the government, who was gunned down while he celebrated Mass in 1980.

In 1981 D'Aubuisson founded the Nationalist Republican Alliance, known by its acronym ARENA, which became the principal rightist party. A charismatic leader, he was able to exercise power under a cover of political legitimacy. As a measure of his growing influence, he became president of the new Constituent Assembly, which was charged with drafting the national constitution. But when he tried to run for president in 1984, he was defeated by José Napoléon Duarte, a moderate backed by the United States.

By 1986 D'Aubuisson had become such a controversial figure that even his former allies began to distance themselves from him. But while he gave up the presidency of ARENA, he continued to wield power behind the scenes. His protégé, Alfredo Cristiani, succeeded him as ARENA's head and was later elected president. On February 20, 1992, shortly after the signing of a peace accord ending the civil war between the government and leftist insurgents, D'Aubuisson succumbed to cancer of the throat at the age of 48. As he lay dying in the hospital his sister, Maria Luisa D'Aubuisson de Martinez, implored him to ask forgiveness for his crimes. A committed follower of Archbishop Romero, whom her brother had ordered killed, she recalled the incident in an interview. "I took him by the hand," she said. "Roberto, you have to die in peace. I beg you, deliver yourself up to Romero. Ask him for forgiveness from the innermost part of your heart. This will give you peace, Roberto." She recalled that he had opened his eyes, drew her close, and then burst into tears, but because of the cancer he was barely able to speak. Eight years later, as she helped prepare for the commemoration of the 20th anniversary of Romero's death, she admitted that she could not be certain whether her brother had ever had any regrets for the crimes he had committed.

See also EL SALVADOR, WAR CRIMES IN; SARAVIA, ALVARO.

Further Reading:

Armstrong, Robert. *El Salvador: The Face of Revolution.* Boston: South End Press, 1982.

Danner, Mark. *The Massacre at El Mozote.* New York: Vintage, 1994.

Wood, Elisabeth Jean, Peter Lange, et al., eds. *Insurgent Collective Action and Civil War in El Salvador.* Cambridge Studies in Comparative Politics. Cambridge: Cambridge University Press, 2003.

Dayton accords (General Framework Agreement for Peace)

The Dayton accords of 1995 represent the culmination of a diplomatic effort by the United States to bring peace to the former Yugoslavia after four years of war. The war was essentially a three-way conflict between the rump state of Yugoslavia (consisting of Serbia and Montenegro), Croatia, and Bosnia and Herzegovina. By the time the three leaders of the warring parties met in Dayton, Ohio, some 300,000 people had been killed, and an estimated 1 million people internally displaced. There were widespread accusations of GENOCIDE and other atrocities from all sides. Several previous efforts had been made to bring the conflict to an end—the United Nations Security Council had passed 61 resolutions calling for a cessation of hostilities—and 36,000 UN peacekeepers were already deployed in Croatia and Bosnia. Nonetheless, the violence continued unabated.

International pressure mounted to settle the conflict, especially after reports began to filter out of the region regarding ethnic cleansing—primarily massacres of Bosnian Muslim men and boys carried out by Serb forces and irregulars. The United States mounted a furious last-ditch effort to reach a peace agreement reinforced by the threat of NATO military force. The U.S. negotiating team was lead by former UN ambassador Richard Holbrooke, who worked in coordination with the United Nations to bring the leaders of the three countries together: Serbian president Slobodan MILOŠEVIĆ, CROATIAN PRESIDENT FRANJO Tudjman, and Bosnian president Alija Izetbegović. Wright-Patterson Air Base in Dayton, Ohio, was chosen as the negotiating site, not least because it was isolated and would allow the diplomats to work without distraction. The negotiations began on November 1, 1995, and stretched on for three weeks. They were conducted as "proximity peace talks"—meaning that the three adversaries relied on Holbrooke and other U.S. diplomats to convey their positions to one another instead of conferring face-to-face. A formal agreement was signed in Paris on December 14, 1995, providing for the General Framework Agreement for Peace (GFAP), which was signed a month later.

The accords provided for a new, multiethnic Bosnian state. The accords also established a new peacekeeping mission known as the International Stabilization Force (IFOR), which includes a contingent of U.S. troops, to deploy a military presence in Bosnia and Herzegovina with a mandate to preserve the peace and stability. A year later, in December 1996, as the NATO mandate was coming to an end, the United Nations Security Council authorized its continuation. The military force was henceforth called Stabilization Force, or SFOR. In spite of continuing ethnic tensions in the region the peacekeeping mission has largely proven effective in maintaining stability. At the end of 2004, SFOR transferred authority for security to forces drawn from the European Union. The three leaders who signed the accords have since disappeared from the scene: Tudjman and Izebegović have died, and Milošević was arrested and forced to stand trial for war crimes in The Hague. As of 2004, though, the peace agreement reached at Dayton remains in effect.

See also BOSNIA AND HERZEGOVINA, HUMAN RIGHTS VIOLATIONS IN; CROATIA, HUMAN RIGHTS VIOLATIONS IN; SERBIA, HUMAN RIGHTS VIOLATIONS IN; YUGOSLAVIA, WAR CRIMES IN.

Further Reading:
Glenny, Misha. *The Fall of Yugoslavia: The Third Balkan War.* New York: Penguin Books, 1996.
Harris, Nathaniel. *The War in Former Yugoslavia.* London: Hodder & Stoughton, 1997.
Kim, Julie. *War in the Former Yugoslavia: Chronology of Events August 16, 1992–May 30, 1993.* CRS report for Congress. Washington, D.C.: Foreign Affairs and National Defense Division, Congressional Research Service, Library of Congress, 1993.
Mertus, Julie. *Former Yugoslavia: War Crimes Trials in the Former Yugoslavia.* Helsinki, Finland: Human Rights Watch/Helsinki, 1995.
Rossanet, Bertrand de. *War and Peace in the Former Yugoslavia.* Boston: Martinus Nijhoff, 1997.

Death's Head Units   *See* CONCENTRATION CAMPS; POHL, OSWALD.

Déby, Idriss   *See* CHAD, HUMAN RIGHTS VIOLATIONS IN.

de Kock, Eugene (1951–   ) *South African special forces operator*
Eugene de Kock, a former South African special forces operative, earned the sobriquet Prime Evil for atrocities he committed in the service of the former APARTHEID regime. The product of a conservative Afrikaner family, he proved his capacity to wage "dirty wars" in his position as head of the army's counterinsurgency unit, Koevoet, in Namibia (formerly Southwest Africa), then under South African rule. During the 1980s, de Kock supervised a center in South Africa called Vlakplaas, where security forces were trained in such lethal techniques as producing letter bombs and booby-trapped headphones and vehicles. De Kock specialized in planting bombs to assassinate members of the African National Congress, the underground opposition group led by Nelson Mandela. He was also involved in fomenting divisions between South African blacks to sustain white rule. "Bad he was, but mad he wasn't, not at all," observed his biographer Gobodo-Madikizela. "He was looked up to by the entire country as a fixer, he was the kingpin in the machinery of destruction."

In 1995 de Kock went on trial. After being sentenced to 262 years in prison on 89 charges, including six murders, he went before became the highest-ranking security official of the apartheid regime to testify before the TRUTH AND RECONCILIATION COMMISSION, which had been established to investigate crimes committed during the apartheid era. Under the terms of the commission, any person convicted of crimes committed on behalf of the white government could be granted AMNESTY if he acknowledged his culpability and also demonstrated that the crime was politically motivated. De Kock's candor impressed even his former enemies, who lauded his willingness to identify the men who had given him his orders. At the same time he denied that he was a psychopath or had ever taken pleasure in committing violence. The commission granted de Kock amnesty for some but not all of his crimes in exchange for his testimony, meaning that he would still have to spend the rest of his life in prison.

Del Ponte, Carla (1947–   ) *UN tribunal prosecutor*
Carla Del Ponte became the first chief prosecutor of the INTERNATIONAL CRIMINAL TRIBUNAL FOR THE FORMER YUGOSLAVIA (ICTY). She is considered highly competent, driven, and strong-willed—too strong willed in the eyes of her detractors, who have called her, among other things, "the new Gestapo," "the whore," "the unguided missile," and "the personification of stubbornness." She shrugs off the insults, asserting that such labels only show that she is doing her job.

Born in 1947 in Lugano, Switzerland, Del Ponte studied law in Great Britain, Bern, and Geneva. She began her legal career in 1972 in a private law firm in Lugano. In 1981 she became a public prosecutor in the office of the Lugano district attorney. Her first major high-profile case was the so-called "pizza connection" investigation that focused on the Sicilian Mafia. She narrowly avoided an assassination attempt when half a ton of explosives were discovered in the foundation of her home in Palermo. In 1994, after being appointed Switzerland's federal attorney general, Del Ponte began to tackle money laundering. Her aggressive efforts to investigate notoriously secretive Swiss banks were derided by the subjects of her inquiries. Nonetheless, her investigations resulted in the freezing of bank accounts of former Pakistani prime minister Benazir Bhutto and the confiscation of $100 million from accounts belonging to Raul Salinas, brother of former Mexican president Carlos Salinas.

But it is in her role as prosecutor for the criminal tribunal for the former Yugoslavia that Del Porte has achieved her greatest fame. She was appointed to the tribunal on September 15, 1999, and from the outset she made clear her intention to bring then-president Slobodan MILOŠEVIĆ of Yugoslavia to justice for war crimes. It took 18 months and a change of government in Belgrade, but Del Ponte succeeded in securing Milošević's extradition. It was the first time that a former head of government had been arrested and put on trial for crimes he allegedly committed in office. In 2004 the trial was still in progress with the former president undertaking his own defense.

Del Ponte has also prosecuted other high officials from Serbia, Bosnia, Croatia, and Kosovo for human rights violations and war crimes in the Balkan wars of the 1990s. Yugoslavian officials have accused her of trying to destabilize the country and asserted that their courts are perfectly able to dispense justice without outside intervention. Authorities in Bosnia and Croatia have also opposed her attempts to extradite indicted officials from their own countries. She sparked Washington's ire when she announced a preliminary inquiry about whether NATO was implicated in war crimes during its 11-week bombing campaign against Yugoslavia during the Kosovo War in 1999. She also antagonized the United States when she derided its "zero-risk" policy for peacekeeping troops in the Balkans, referring to the Bush administration's efforts to immunize its troops from jurisdiction by the INTERNATIONAL CRIMINAL COURT.

Until 2004, Del Ponte also served as chief prosecutor at the INTERNATIONAL CRIMINAL TRIBUNAL FOR RWANDA, which sits in Arusha, Tanzania. The Rwandan court was set up to prosecute the instigators of the GENOCIDE that had racked the country in 1994. (Both tribunals are under United Nations auspices and adhere to the norms of INTERNATIONAL HUMANITARIAN LAW.). By all accounts she managed to acquit herself in both capacities quite well. However, critics accused her of being too distracted to pay adequate attention to the Rwandan tribunal and blamed her for the slow pace of prosecutions. UN secretary-general Kofi Annan agreed that trying to preside over two monumental prosecutions was too much for any one individual, and he replaced her.

Asked about her motivation, Del Ponte has said: "Not to forget the victims, that's the important thing. In these trials we focus so much on the people who have been charged. I want to be a voice for the victims, so they can see justice being done."

Further Reading:

Hagan, John. *Justice in the Balkans: Prosecuting War Crimes in the Hague Tribunal.* Chicago Series in Law and Society. Chicago: University of Chicago Press, 2003.

Hazan, Pierre, and James Thomas Snyder. *Justice in a Time of War: The True Story behind the International Criminal Tribunal for the Former Yugoslavia.* Eugenia and Hugh M. Stewart Series on Eastern Europe. Austin: Texas A&M University Press, 2004.

Mertus, Julie. *Former Yugoslavia: War Crimes Trials in the Former Yugoslavia.* Helsinki, Finland: Human Rights Watch/Helsinki, 1995.

United Nations War Crimes Commission. *Law Reports of Trials of War Criminals: Four Genocide Trials.* Boulder, Colo.: Lynne Rienner Publishers, 1992.

deportations

Individual or mass deportations are considered violations of INTERNATIONAL HUMANITARIAN LAW. Deportations were first defined as war crimes and CRIMES AGAINST HUMANITY during the NUREMBERG TRIALS of Nazi war criminals after World War II. They are also classified as war crimes under the Fourth Geneva Convention of 1949, which stated: "Individual or mass forcible transfers, as well as deportations of protected persons from occupied territory to the territory of the OCCUPYING POWER or to that of any other country, occupied or not, are prohibited, regardless of their motive." The Convention does, however, allow for the "total or partial evacuation" of any area if it is required for "the security of the population or imperative military reasons" and "when for material reasons it is impossible to avoid such displacement." But even in these circumstances, the evacuated population must be returned to their homes "as soon as hostilities in the area have ceased."

Deportations are also outlawed by the 1950 European Convention on Human Rights. Under the convention, no one can be deported to a country where he or she faces a risk of TORTURE or inhuman or degrading treatment. The convention also emphasizes that respect for the family should not be interfered with because it is essential for a "democratic society," which is taken to mean that families should not be split apart by the deportation of one or more of its members. However, a state is within its rights to split a family by deporting a member if that person has been found criminally culpable or for other reasons, such as posing a security risk.

Deportations can also lead to a finding of GENOCIDE under international law if they result in a large loss of life while they are being carried out. Certain conditions, however, must be met to characterize deportations as genocidal—namely, that the responsible authority intended to inflict harm on the group of people being deported and that the group is being targeted because of its national, ethnic, racial, religious, or political complexion. A case can be made that the deportations of black Africans from the Darfur region of Sudan constitutes genocide because the Arab militias have singled out their victims on the basis of their race. Before World War II, there was no specific prohibition against deportation in international law primarily because it was already considered a violation of CUSTOMARY LAW. The Hague Convention of 1907, for instance, pointedly omitted any prohibition against mass expulsions because they fell below "the minimum standard of civilization and, therefore, not requiring express prohibition."

Under the Nazi regime, deportations were used to displace entire populations. It is estimated that the Germans deported up to 12 million people who fell under their rule in occupied Europe, including a million Poles from western Poland who were sent to slave labor camps in the east. The forcible relocation of these peoples was examined during the Nuremberg Trials, which condemned the "Germanizing" of conquered territories by uprooting the indigenous population and replacing it with Germans. The Fourth Geneva Convention specifically forbids this practice.

Under Joseph STALIN, the Soviet Union also engaged in some of the most dramatic mass deportations in history. It is believed that more than 1.5 million people, mostly Muslims, were resettled during and after World War II with a huge loss of life. The USSR also undertook the systematic deportation of Volga Germans, Crimean Tatars, Kalmyks, Chechens, Ingush, Balkars, Karachai, and Meskhetians and uprooted Bulgarians, Greeks, and Armenian minorities from the Black Sea coastal region. In many of these instances, the Soviet Union contended that it was resettling these populations because they were collaborating with German forces that had occupied large parts of the country during World War II. Historians estimate that close to two-fifths of the deported populations perished. In defiance of the Fourth Geneva Convention, the Soviet Union also expelled some 15 million ethnic Germans from Poland, Czechoslovakia, Hungary, Romania, Yugoslavia, and East Germany, which fell under its control after World War II. An estimated 2–3 million died as a result.

In 1948 several hundred thousand Palestinians were uprooted by the Israeli War for Independence. Thousands fled at the urging of Arab governments, which promised that Israel would soon be crushed and they could return to their homes. But thousands more were expelled by Israeli forces on the grounds that they constituted a threat to the Jewish population. More recent upheavals and internal wars have resulted in large-scale deportations. During its occupation of Kuwait in 1992, Iraq deported a large number of Kuwaitis into Iraq and resettled Iraqis in their place, a violation of international law condemned by the UN Security Council. In the 1990s Serbs engaged in the ethnic cleansing of Muslims in Bosnia, which was carried out by mass expulsions and killings.

See also GENEVA CONVENTIONS; HAGUE CONVENTIONS; WAR CRIMES, CATEGORIZATION OF.

Further Reading:
Feller, Erika, Volker Turk, and Frances Nicholson, eds. *Refugee Protection in International Law: UNHCR's Global Consultations on International Protection.* Cambridge: Cambridge University Press, 2003.
Fritz, Mark. *Lost on Earth: Nomads of the New World.* New York: Routledge, 2000.
Groenewold, Julia, and Doctors Without Borders. *World in Crisis: The Politics of Survival at the End of the Twentieth Century.* London: Routledge, 1996.
Helton, Arthur C. *The Price of Indifference: Refugees and Humanitarian Action in the New Century.* A Council on Foreign Relations Book. Oxford: Oxford University Press, 2002.
Hyndman, Jennifer. *Managing Displacement: Refugees and the Politics of Humanitarianism.* Minneapolis: University of Minnesota Press, 2000.
Ingleby, David, ed. *Forced Migration and Mental Health: Rethinking the Care of Refugees and Displaced Persons.* New York: Plenum US, 2004.
Lischer, Sarah Kenyon. *Dangerous Sanctuaries: Refugee Camps, Civil War, and the Dilemmas of Humanitarian Aid.* Cornell Studies in Security Affairs. Ithaca, N.Y.: Cornell University Press, 2005.

Deronjić, Miroslav   *See* WAR CRIMINALS OF THE FORMER YUGOSLAVIA.

detainees   *See* GUANTÁNAMO DETAINEES; HIGH-VALUE DETAINEES.

Deuch   *See* KIANG KEK IEV.

DINA   *See* NATIONAL INTELLIGENCE DIRECTORATE.

dirty war
The term dirty war (*guerra sucia* in Spanish) is often used to refer to the clandestine conflict in Argentina between 1976 and 1983, but it has also been applied to similar conflicts during the 1970s and 1980s throughout Latin America, including Chile, Brazil, Uruguay, Bolivia, Honduras, El Salvador, Guatemala, and Mexico. (Pundits and writers have used the term more widely, applying it to conflicts in countries ranging from Ireland to Myanmar.) Almost without exception, these conflicts pitted authoritarian regimes or military juntas

against leftist insurgents and political dissidents. Dirty wars were characterized by state terrorism intended to suppress all political opposition by the use of torture, disappearances, illegal detention and imprisonment, and extrajudicial killings. Families of suspected dissidents were often targeted as well. Intellectuals, labor leaders, human rights workers, priests and nuns, and reporters were also frequently at risk. In Argentina it is estimated that anywhere from 10,000 to 30,000 people were executed without trial. Typically, the police and security services would deny any knowledge of the whereabouts of suspects taken into custody. Crackdowns by the authorities precipitated ever more violent responses from insurgents, in some cases triggering a civil war. In Argentina the military regime collapsed in the aftermath of the disastrous Falklands War against England. Changing political and economic conditions—a withdrawal of American support for some of the most egregious regimes, for instance—brought a halt to most dirty wars by the end of the 1980s. However, many officials responsible for the abuses passed amnesty laws, conferring immunity on themselves for their crimes, before agreeing to cede power, making it more difficult to bring them to account. It took until June 2005, for instance, for the Argentine Supreme Court to overturn these amnesty laws, allowing prosecutions of members of the discredited juntas to move forward.

See also ARGENTINA, HUMAN RIGHTS VIOLATIONS IN; HONDURAS, HUMAN RIGHTS VIOLATIONS IN; MEXICO, HUMAN RIGHTS VIOLATIONS IN.

Further Reading:

Guest, Iain. *Behind the Disappearances: Argentina's Dirty War against Human Rights and the United Nations.* Pennsylvania Studies in Human Rights. Philadelphia: University of Pennsylvania Press, 2000.

Lewis, Paul H. *Guerrillas and Generals: The Dirty War in Argentina.* New York: Praeger, 2001.

disappearances

When used as a transitive verb, *disappear* means arresting a person in secret with the intention of subjecting him or her to TORTURE and/or extrajudicial execution. The world first became aware of the practice of disappearing individuals during the "dirty wars" of Latin America during the 1970s and 1980s, when military regimes were trying to suppress leftist insurgencies. However, the phenomenon has become widespread in countries ranging from Kuwait to Chechnya and Algeria to El Salvador. The practice affords governments responsible for these abuses the ability to deny that they know what became of the disappeared individuals. In an essay for the CRIMES OF WAR PROJECT, Corinne Dufka points out that when it comes to INTERNATIONAL HUMANITARIAN LAW, the question of disappearances becomes complicated because it

Bosnian girl holding a photograph of a family member who disappeared during the war *(Paolo Pellegrino/ICRC)*

entails several separate war crimes "including unlawful confinement, failure to allow DUE PROCESS, and failure to allow communication between the arrested person and the outside world." In addition, disappearances often involve torture, degrading treatment, and often murder.

Typically, a disappearance takes place in three stages: capture, detention, and execution. In the first stage, security forces place the person in custody, violating international laws against arbitrary arrest. According to the Declaration on the Protection of All Persons from Enforced Disappearance, proclaimed by the UN General Assembly in December 1992, an enforced disappearance occurs when "persons are arrested, detained or abducted against their will or otherwise deprived of their liberty by officials of different branches or levels of Government, or by organized groups, or private individuals acting on behalf of, or with the support, direct or indirect, consent or acquiescence of the Government, followed by a refusal to disclose the fate or whereabouts of the persons concerned or a refusal to acknowledge the deprivation of their liberty, which places such persons outside the protection of the law."

In disappearances, the arrest takes place without a warrant or any due process whatsoever. In the second stage, the person detained has no recourse to any of the protections conferred by Additional Protocol II to the GENEVA CONVENTIONS, which states that once in custody, a person is entitled to humane treatment, including the presumption of innocence, the right to communicate with family members, and the right to obtain legal consul. Moreover, torture is expressly prohibited, a provision that is almost invariably violated in cases of disappearances. In the final stage, the disappearance is made permanent by murder. The victim receives no trial or appeal—just a death sentence.

When disappearances take place during insurgencies or police actions, they are covered by ARTICLE 3 COMMON to the Geneva Conventions. The Rome Statute of the International Criminal Court (ICC) makes "enforced disappearances . . . by or with the authorization, support or acquiescence of a State or a political organization" a crime against humanity.

The practice of enforced disappearances infringes upon an entire range of human rights embodied in the Universal Declaration of Human Rights and established in the International Covenants on Human Rights as well as in other major international human rights instruments. Disappearances may also be violations of the Standard Minimum Rules for the Treatment of Prisoners, approved by the United Nations Economic and Social Council, as well as in the Code of Conduct for Law Enforcement Officials and the Body of Principals for the Protection of All Persons under Any Form of Detention or Imprisonment.

Of course, the disappearance is not only directed at the victim; it also imposes severe hardship and psychological trauma to the victim's families and friends. A disappearance creates an atmosphere of dread for survivors who are left in doubt as to whether they also will be arrested in secret and disappear. By trying to discover the truth, they may be placing themselves in greater danger. They live in constant expectation of news of their loved one that may never arrive. The family and friends of the victim are put through a form of agonizing mental torture that may persist indefinitely. There are economic repercussions as well, especially if the disappeared person had been the family's main provider. Even obtaining a certificate of death may be a major obstacle for families—for example, a widow who wishes to remarry. Amnesty laws immunizing the guilty parties from prosecution may prevent the truth from emerging even years later. Even if the disappeared person does survive, he or she may be so physically or psychologically damaged that readjusting to society is difficult or impossible. In spite of the difficulties and dangers, family members have persisted in trying to account for the fates of their loved ones. There is no more notable example than the Mothers of the Plaza de Mayo (also known as Grandmothers) who gathered daily in the center of Buenos Aires to protest the government's failure to take responsibility for the disappearances of family members during the dirty wars of the 1970s.

Children are also victims of disappearances. In a number of cases, many of them documented in Argentina, infants and young children have been illegally put up for adoption by security forces after their parents have been disappeared and put to death. These children may grow up without having any idea of their origins. The disappearance of a child is a clear violation of several provisions of the Convention on the Rights of the Child, including the right to a personal identity.

See also Additional Protocols to the Geneva Conventions; children's rights; crimes against humanity; United Nations Working Group on Enforced or Involuntary Disappearances.

Further Reading:

Arditti, Rita. *Searching for Life: The Grandmothers of the Plaza de Mayo and the Disappeared Children of Argentina.* Berkeley: University of California Press, 1999.
Davis, William Columbus. *Warnings from the Far South: Democracy versus Dictatorship in Uruguay, Argentina, and Chile.* New York: Praeger Publishers, 1995.
Guest, Iain. *Behind the Disappearances: Argentina's Dirty War against Human Rights and the United Nations.* Pennsylvania Studies in Human Rights. Philadelphia: University of Pennsylvania Press, 2000.
Gutman, Roy, ed. *Crimes of War: What the Public Should Know.* New York: W. W. Norton & Company, 1999.
Kornbluh, Peter. *The Pinochet File: A Declassified Dossier on Atrocity and Accountability.* A National Security Archive Book. New York: New Press, 2003.
Politzer, Patricia, and Diane Wachtel. *Fear in Chile: Lives under Pinochet.* New York: New Press, 2001.

displaced person camps

Displaced person (DP) camps were established after the end of World War II in Germany, Poland, France, Italy, and Belgium for refugees, many of them Jews, who had survived the worst depredations of the conflict. In some cases the DP camps were set up on the sites of labor or concentration camps such as Bergen-Belsen. At first the Allied Forces and the United Nations Rehabilitation and Relief Administration (UNRRA) took charge of the DP camps, providing basic necessities and medical assistance, but later most of their functions were assumed by Jewish welfare organizations. By 1947 the camps had developed into self-sustaining communities; there were over 70 newspapers in Yiddish and other European languages published in the camps. The refugees were eager to resettle in other countries, with many eager to go to Palestine. However, the British, then the occupying power, opposed Jewish emigration because of opposition from the Arab population. That situation changed when Israel gained its independence in 1948 and extended a welcome to all Jews. Other DPs, after sometimes waiting in camps for years, migrated to the United States, Canada, and Australia or found new homes elsewhere in Europe. By 1951 practically all DP camps had closed.

Doctors' Trial (Nuremberg Medical Trial)

Also known as the Nuremberg Medical Trial, the Doctors' Trial revealed to the world the horrors perpetrated by Nazi physicians on concentration camp inmates under the pretext of legitimate medical experimentation. Twenty-four physicians and scientists (all but one of them men) were tried in proceedings that lasted from October 1946 to August 1947. They were charged with conducting unethical and sometimes lethal MEDICAL EXPERIMENTS on camp inmates between 1933—shortly after the Nazis came to power in Germany—until 1945. Some of them had actually achieved positions of prominence before the war, raising questions how physicians dedicated to alleviating suffering could have betrayed their highest principles. The most notorious physician, Josef MENGELE, however, had fled and was not among the defendants. In one case Mengele eliminated an infestation of lice among a block of female inmates by gassing all the 750 women assigned to it. The defendants who were present, however, had been responsible for any number of atrocities in their own right. Though the exact number of victims of these experiments is unknown, it is thought to be in the hundreds of thousands; only a relatively few managed to survive.

Officially, the trial was designated *United States of America v. Karl Brandt et al.* (Dr. Karl BRANDT was one of the leading defendants.) The trial was heard by four judges; the chief prosecutor was Telford TAYLOR. The court heard 85 witnesses and examined nearly 1,500 documents. The experiments that were at the heart of the trial were as varied as they were barbaric.

1. High altitude experiments: Victims were placed in low-pressure chambers to simulate conditions at high altitude; the pressure was elevated until the subject either died or was seriously injured.
2. Incendiary bomb experiments: Victims were exposed to phosphorous material derived from bombs.
3. Freezing experiments: Victims were forced to remain in a tank of freezing water for up to three hours. Those victims who survived were then exposed to heat to thaw them out.
4. Sea-water experiments: Victims, deprived of all food and drink, were given only chemically processed sea water to consume in an experiment meant to find out whether airmen downed at sea could survive on seawater.
5. Malaria experiments: Victims were infected with malaria and then administered drugs to determine whether they had any beneficial effects.
6. Mustard gas experiments: Victims were deliberately exposed to mustard gas, whose use had been outlawed by international law, as a way of determining the most effective treatments for injuries.
7. Sulfanilamide experiments: Prior to the introduction of penicillin, sulfa drugs were the most effective treatment for infections. In these experiments, victims were infected with streptococcus, gas gangrene, and tetanus and other bacterial agents to determine the efficacy of the drugs. To ensure that the infection would take hold, blood circulation in the affected area was tied off at both ends of the wound.
8. Poison experiments: Victims were fed poison in their food without being aware of it to determine their efficacy. Others were shot with poison bullets.
9. Typhus experiments: Victims were infected with the typhus (spotted fever) virus and then treated with various vaccines, costing the lives of 90 percent of those forced to endure the regimen.

The defendants were also charged with experiments involving bone transplantation, sterilization, and skeleton collection. Of the 24 defendants, 16 were found guilty, and eight were acquitted. Of those convicted, seven were sentenced to death by hanging, and nine were given prison terms. Karl Brandt was among those who were hanged for their crimes.

See also CONCENTRATION CAMPS; NUREMBERG TRIALS; OBERHEUSER, HERTA.

Further Reading:

Bloxham, Donald. *Genocide on Trial: War Crimes Trials and the Formation of Holocaust History and Memory.* Oxford: Oxford University Press, 2003.
Cooper, Belinda and Richard Goldstone. *War Crimes: The Legacy of Nuremberg.* New York: TV Books Inc., 1999.
Weindling, Paul Julian. *Nazi Medicine and the Nuremberg Trials: From Medical War Crimes to Informed Consent.* Sydney, Australia: Palgrave Macmillan, 2005.

Doctors Without Borders (Médecins Sans Frontières [MSF])

Doctors Without Borders, or *Médecins Sans Frontières* (MSF), is an international organization dedicated to delivering emergency aid to victims of armed conflict, epidemics, and natural and human-made disasters, as well as to any others who are in desperate need of health care because of geographical, political, or economic circumstances. MSF is an international network with sections in 18 countries, but its reach is worldwide. Each year more than 2,500 volunteer doctors, nurses, paramedics, and other medical professionals, as well as logistics experts, administrators, and water and sanitation engineers, join 15,000 locally hired staff to provide medical aid in more than 80 countries. MSF claims to be the largest independent medical aid agency in the world. Based in Paris, the organization operates on an annual budget of about $235 million, of which roughly 56 percent comes from private contributions, including corporations and individuals, with the other 44 percent coming from governments (including the United States) and international and regional bodies.

MSF was founded in 1971 by a small group of activist French doctors, many of whom were radicalized by the antiwar and antiestablishment movements of the 1960s. They were convinced that the way in which emergency medical care was being delivered was inadequate and encumbered by excessive red tape. The founders of MSF were especially disenchanted with the INTERNATIONAL COMMITTEE OF THE RED CROSS (ICRC) which, as a matter of policy, strives to maintain a position of neutrality in any theater of operations. Like many other humanitarian organizations, the Red Cross contends that to take sides in a conflict would jeopardize its ability to deliver aid to all in need and would also put the lives and safety of its own personnel at risk.

The founders of MSF, however, believed that in cases where human and civil rights were being violated, it was impossible to adhere to a position of strict neutrality. In their view, to act as if both sides were on an equal moral footing when, for example, one party to a conflict was systematically murdering civilians was an abdication of responsibility. Its mandate declared that "all people have the right to medical care regardless of race, religion, creed or political affiliation, and that the needs of these people supersede respect for national borders." MSF avowed that it had two missions: One was to provide emergency medical assistance, and the other was to bear witness to the plight of the populations they served. "We are by nature an organization that is unable to tolerate indifference. We hope that by arousing awareness and a desire to understand, we will also stir up indignation and stimulate action," declared Dr. Rony Brauman, a former president of the organization. True to their mandate, MSF volunteers have acted as a voice for the voiceless, speaking out about atrocities they have witnessed in places like Chechnya, Angola, Kosovo, Sri Lanka, and Cambodia.

Given the dangers and deprivations they face, candidates for MSF must undergo rigorous testing and be prepared to make sacrifices. They might end up fighting malaria in East Africa, famine in Somalia, floods in the Philippines, or AIDS in South Africa, or they may find themselves negotiating with hostile Russian forces in Chechnya. They certainly do not do it for the money: Most new hires earn about $700 monthly, depending on the assignment. The majority of the recruits work in the field only for about six months.

From the outset, MSF acquired as much of a reputation for attracting publicity as it did for providing aid. In 1972 it spearheaded the mobilization of medical teams to save victims of floods in East Pakistan and a major earthquake in Nicaragua. But the organization had its detractors who dubbed the young, radical-left French doctors and nurses "medical hippies" and "cowboy docs."

By publicizing the humanitarian abuses taking place in regions of the world that often escape media attention

MSF hopes to mobilize the public and prod policymakers into action. In 1999, in recognition of its efforts on both of these fronts, MSF was awarded the Nobel Peace Prize. In his acceptance speech on behalf of the organization, Dr. James Orbinski, an outspoken Canadian physician, left no doubt in the minds of his listeners why MSF has acquired a reputation for bluntness in its public statements—and why, too, it has a habit of unsettling the powerful. In his address, Orbinski called on the Russians to stop bombing defenseless civilians in Chechnya. He then went on to say that, unlike many previous Peace Prize laureates, his organization was not intended to act as a tool to end war nor to create peace, but was rather "a citizens' response to political failure."

Further Reading:

Bortolotti, Dan. *Hope in Hell: Inside the World of Doctors Without Borders*. Richmond Hill, Ontario, Canada: Firefly Books Ltd., 2004.

Leyton, Elliot. *Touched by Fire: Doctors Without Borders in a Third World Crisis*. Toronto: McClelland & Stewart, 1998.

Weissman, Fabrice. *In the Shadow of "Just Wars": Violence, Politics, and Humanitarian Action*. Ithaca, N.Y.: Cornell University Press, 2004.

Doe, Samuel   *See* LIBERIA, HUMAN RIGHTS VIOLATIONS IN; TAYLOR, CHARLES.

Doihara Kenji (1883–1948) *Japanese spy and saboteur*

Doihara Kenji spent much of his career operating in the shadows as a spy and saboteur to advance Japan's aggressive designs on China before and during World War II. He even orchestrated the incident that provided Japan with the pretext to invade Manchuria in September 1931. Doihara espoused the principle of "Asia for the Asiatics," although by *Asiatics* he meant the Japanese. He was convicted for war crimes at the TOKYO TRIALS after the war and sentenced to death.

Born in 1883, Doihara longed for a military career, but his family's low social status stood in the way. He therefore contrived to recruit his attractive sister as a concubine for a prince, who, in exchange, rewarded him with a military rank and a posting to the Japanese embassy in Beijing, China. This incident established a pattern in Doihara's life. He showed no compunction about resorting to blackmail, bribery, extortion, rape, assassination, and mass murder if it would serve his purpose. Over the next decade, he organized a network of Japanese spies, plucking his recruits from brothels and opium dens. Disguised as a peddler, teacher, or missionary, he traveled through China, seeking out local political figures and warlords who could be bribed or manipulated to help an eventual Japanese conquest. His cause was abetted by the tendency of warlords to wage war against one another.

From these excursions through the countryside, Doihara hit upon the strategy of targeting the northeast province of Manchuria, which had the advantage of having a small population. Doihara persuaded his superiors in Tokyo that Manchuria could serve as an optimal staging area for Japanese occupation of the whole country. By the 1920s, his spy network had expanded to 80,000 recruits, many of them disaffected Chinese and White Russian criminals who had sought refuge in China after being driven out of Russia when the Soviets took control. These spies carried out assassinations and acts of sabotage and, when required, instigated riots as well. But in order to make it appear as if the Chinese were responsible for war, not the Japanese, Doihara staged a provocation known in history as the Mukden Incident. In September 1931 his agents set off explosives on the Japanese South Manchurian Railway, detonating them in such a way as to cause no significant damage. Using this as their pretext, the Japanese blamed the Chinese and launched an invasion. The ruse fooled no one. Rather than acquiesce to demands from the international community to withdraw from Manchuria, Japan instead withdrew from the LEAGUE OF NATIONS instead and proceeded to advance into Mongolia.

As a reward for his service, Doihara was given the right to install a puppet leader in Manchuria. He soon achieved one of his great ambitions and won an appointment as major general in the Japanese air force. In addition, he was permitted to join the elite war council of Prime Minister Hideki TOJO, and on November 4, 1941, he cast his vote to approve the attack on Pearl Harbor. Throughout the rest of the war, he divided his time between the air force and his intelligence operations. After the war he was tried by the Tokyo Tribunal for war crimes along with Tojo and other Japanese military officials. He was found guilty and sentenced to be hanged. He was 65 when the sentence was carried out on December 23, 1948.

See also MANCHURIA, JAPANESE WAR CRIMES IN.

Dominican Republic, human rights violations in

The Dominican Republic's human record remains mixed; although the government has taken significant steps in curbing abuses by police and military forces, there are still reports of EXTRAJUDICIAL KILLINGS, TORTURE, and arbitrary arrest. Detainees and prisoners are frequently beaten. Although the U.S. State Department in its 2003 *Country Report* found that there were no reports of political killings, security forces were responsible for 126 unlawful killings during the previous year. Some of the killings might have been unintentional—civilians shot in exchanges of gunfire with police, for instance—but others were what the State Department called "encounter" killings, which were staged by police. The exact number of extrajudicial deaths is not known because of inadequate documentation.

Similarly, the use of deadly force against criminal suspects by police has diminished in recent years—credit is given to replacing the head of the National Police—but the use of unwarranted force has continued. Criminals who refuse to pay bribes to the police to overlook their illegal activities are sometimes beaten or shot in a leg or arm. The police force itself is in need of reform; there is, for instance, no overall policy governing the use of deadly force, and unlawful killings are seldom investigated. Programs have been instituted, however, to improve training and respect for human rights among police. Nonetheless, according to the State Department, abuses of detainees remain a persistent problem, especially among lower-ranking officers who conduct various forms of torture, beatings, and sexual abuse. Police and prison authorities have used asphyxiation with plastic bags to elicit confessions, as well as a method called "roasting the chicken" in which the victim is placed over hot coals and turned. Another form of torture is called "the toaster," whereby shackled prisoners are laid on a bed of hot asphalt for an entire day and beaten if they scream. Prison conditions can be harsh, and some prisoners have died from neglect while in custody. Police still conduct illegal searches and hold suspects without DUE PROCESS, and though the judiciary has made strides in consolidating its independence, lengthy pretrial detentions and long delays still bedevil the legal system.

Another area of concern is the treatment of Haitians and those who are considered "Haitian-looking." Haiti shares the island of Hispaniola with the Dominican Republic, but the relations of the two neighbors have not always been cordial. Suspects who are believed to be undocumented Haitians are often taken into custody and deported to Haiti without any legal means to contest their expulsion. In many cases they are separated from their families. Dominico-Haitians have considerable difficulty proving that they have the legal right to remain in their own country, which has led generations of ethnic Haitians to be denied recognition as citizens, placing them into what the Inter-American Commission on Human Rights has called a state of "permanent illegality." The denial of citizenship to people of Haitian descent also means that their children are barred from schools, particularly at the primary level. However, the government of President Hipólito Mejía has been credited with making progress in bringing the treatment of Haitians and Dominico-Haitians into compliance with international human rights standards.

See also TRUJILLO, RAFAEL MOLINO.

Dönitz, Karl (1891–1980) *German naval commander, successor to Adolf Hitler*

Admiral Karl Dönitz is best remembered for orchestrating German U-boat operations against Allied shipping and warships during World War II. He also earned a footnote in history for briefly assuming power over the Third Reich in its last days of existence after Adolf HITLER's suicide. He was convicted of crimes against peace at the NUREMBERG TRIALS, though he was not found culpable of committing any war crimes.

Born in September 1891 in Berlin-Grenau, Dönitz was 19 years old when he went to sea as a naval cadet. Commissioned as an officer in 1913, he spent the First World War on a cruiser and later on submarines in the Mediterranean until he was captured in 1918. After the war he stayed on in the German navy, and in 1935 he was put in charge of the development of a new generation of U-boats to replace the smaller 750-ton Type VII U-boats. It was Dönitz who derived the strategy of using "wolf-packs"—squadrons of U-boats—against American and British ships in World War II. To neutralize the threat, the Allies began to rely on convoys guarded by destroyers and aircraft patrols. By May 1943, so many U-boats were being destroyed by depth charges that Dönitz withdrew them from the Atlantic. Undeterred, he urged accelerated U-boat construction and introduced technological innovations that made them the most advanced submarines in the world. In 1944 some 42 all-electric boats were being produced a month, but by then it was too late, as the Germans were losing the war.

In 1944 Hitler appointed Dönitz commander in chief of the navy, succeeding Erich RAEDER. The Nazi leader subsequently decreed that Dönitz be made head of state after he had taken his own life. Dönitz had only five days in his new role. He was left with one task: negotiating surrender to the Allies, which took place on May 8, 1945. A loyal and unrepentant Nazi, he went on trial in 1946 before the International Military Tribunal at Nuremberg. Unlike many high officials in the Nazi Party, Dönitz, who had become a party member only in 1944, was not charged with CRIMES AGAINST HUMANITY. Historians believe that he had no knowledge of the Holocaust or other atrocities committed by the Nazis. However, he was charged with waging aggressive war, conspiracy to wage aggressive war, and crimes against the laws of war, including waging unrestricted submarine warfare. On one occasion, the indictment read, he also gave orders not to rescue survivors of ships sunk by his U-boats in violation of international laws governing conduct at sea. In his defense, he contended that the United States had also used unrestricted warfare in the Pacific and that while he was responsible for pushing the U-boat program, he was not involved in the planning of the war at sea in which they were used.

The Nuremberg judges decided that Dönitz was aware of the purpose for which the U-boats were being built even before the start of hostilities and, further, that he had coordinated the U-boat strategy with other arms of the military, which made him culpable of seeking to wage an aggressive war. Found guilty of crimes against peace, he was sentenced to 10 years in prison, although the Soviet judge voted for acquittal. After serving his sentence, Dönitz was freed from prison in 1956. Two years later he published his memoirs, entitled *Ten Years and Twenty Days*. By the end of his life he had refurbished his image enough so that following his death on December 24, 1980, scores of his former servicemen and foreign naval officers turned out to pay their respects at his funeral.

due process

Due process refers to a set of established legal principles and procedures to ensure that individual rights are protected. The concept of due process has a venerable history, extending back to the Magna Carta of 1215. In the U.S. Constitution the term *due process* first appears in the Fifth Amendment in the Bill of Rights, but the amendment refers only to actions by the federal government and not the states. (This omission was rectified by the 14th Amendment, which was ratified in 1868.) The amendment declares: "No State shall make or enforce any law which shall abridge the privileges or immunities of citizens of the United States; nor shall any State deprive any person of life, liberty, or property, without due process of law; nor deny to any person within its jurisdiction the equal protection of the laws." The principle, although not always the practice, of due process is almost universally accepted and codified in international law.

It should be noted that some legal experts believe that there are two kinds of due process: procedural and substantive. *Procedural due process* refers to the legal procedures that must be followed by the particular government in detaining, trying, convicting, and sentencing a defendant. It also refers to how a government can lawfully deprive a person of his freedom, life, and property when the law gives it the right to do so. By contrast, *substantive due process* confers upon the individual rights that the government cannot take away without adequate justification. These are general rights that are reserved to the individual to possess or to do certain things regardless of the government's wishes, including such rights as freedom of speech and religion. Substantive due process has been developed by the U.S. Supreme Court in a series of decisions that have, for instance, prevented the U.S. government from interfering with the private behavior of American citizens, even though in many states the law on the books specifically prohibited certain types of behavior.

International law gives high priority to due process, in the absence of which all other legal mechanisms are merely a sham. The Fourth Geneva Convention of 1949, as well as the INTERNATIONAL COVENANT ON CIVIL AND POLITICAL RIGHTS, set out the legal standards for trials of enemy civilians, including the right to be informed of charges, to be tried without undue delay to prepare and mount a defense, to have the assistance of counsel, and to be presumed innocent until proven guilty. Defendants also have the right not to be forced to confess, which reinforce stipulations against the use of torture. Due process also figures in ARTICLE 3 COMMON TO THE GENEVA CONVENTIONS of 1949, which applies to internal armed conflict and forbids "the passing of sentences and the carrying out of executions without previous judgment pronounced by a regularly constituted court, affording all the judicial guarantees which are recognized as indispensable by civilized peoples."

Thus, any attempt to prevent detainees and their lawyers from knowing the charges against them is forbidden under international law. Defendants should be permitted to know what witnesses are testifying against them and be aware of the evidence being presented to the court. The basic rights of due process are guaranteed by international law even under emergency situations. If a nation uses what is known as administrative detention to lock up suspects for protracted periods of time as an alternative to legal proceedings, it is in violation of international law, specifically Article 14 of the Covenant on Civil and Political Rights, which sets minimum standards for a trial. Administrative detention is, however, permitted by the Fourth Geneva Convention only for vital security needs.

Both the Third and Fourth GENEVA CONVENTIONS of 1949 establish the requirements that constitute due process: A defendant must be informed about the charges in language that is clear and comprehensible. A defendant is innocent until proven guilty and is entitled to be tried without undue delay. The trial must be conducted by an impartial legal body. The defendant has the right to prepare and present a defense and depose witnesses, and he or she cannot be forced to confess or testify against himself or herself. A sentence must be proportionate to the offense the defendant is convicted of, and the defendant should have the ability to appeal.

The INTERNATIONAL CRIMINAL TRIBUNAL FOR THE FORMER YUGOSLAVIA has adopted such standards in conducting trials of suspects in the Balkan wars of the 1990s. In general, the tribunal is guided by the provisions relating to due process found in the Bill of Rights and the 14th Amendment to the U.S. Constitution, with the notable exception that verdicts are rendered by a panel of judges and not by a jury. The tribunal, which is based in The Hague, limits its jurisdiction to "grave breaches of the 1949 Geneva Conventions," "violations of the laws or customs of war," "GENOCIDE," and "CRIMES AGAINST HUMANITY." The classification of these crimes is based on killing, inflicting injury, and causing destruction in acts that were not warranted by military necessity. Before a defendant can be made to stand trial, a judge must first issue an arrest warrant or summons based upon an indictment. No indictment can be handed up, however, without a preparatory process in which an investigation is conducted, and the indictment is subject to an independent judicial review. A defendant has a right to choose his own legal counsel; if the defendant does not choose a counsel or is too poor to afford one, the tribunal will appoint one. (Former Yugoslav president Slobodan MILOŠEVIĆ is an exception; he chose to shun any counsel and undertake his own defense.)

The defendant must be notified of the charges against him and, in addition, must be informed by the prosecution of any exculpatory evidence, which is also the case under U.S. law. Defendants are entitled to the presumption of innocence. Trials are open to the public and the media, although in extreme cases—for example, to protect the identity of a witness—the tribunal can decide to close its proceedings. A defendant can only be convicted when the judges agree that the prosecution has proven its case "beyond reasonable doubt," which also follows established U.S. law in criminal proceedings. Finally, a defendant has the right to appeal to a separate appellate chamber if there is a claim that the verdict was tarnished by errors of fact or law in the original trial.

Further Reading:
Gutman, Roy, ed. *Crimes of War: What the Public Should Know.* New York: W. W. Norton & Company, 1999.

Dunant, Jean-Henri (1828–1910) *founder of the Red Cross*

Jean-Henri Dunant is a pioneering humanitarian who founded the INTERNATIONAL COMMITTEE OF THE RED CROSS (ICRC) and won the Nobel Peace Prize. He was born into a middle-class Geneva family that has been described as religious, humanitarian, and civic-minded. After a period as a representative of the Young Men's Christian Association, Dunant turned to business at the age of 26. He traveled to North Africa and Sicily on behalf of his company and published *An Account of the Regency in Tunis*, based on his experiences. This book would not be worth noting were it not for one chapter entitled "Slavery among the Mohammedans and in the United States of America," an early sign of his humanitarian concerns.

In June 1859, while on a business trip, Dunant found himself in the northern Italian town of Solferino. By chance he ended up witnessing one of the bloodiest battles in the 19th century between French and Italian forces on one side and Austrians on the other (part of the Franco-Austrian War). The event made such a searing impression on him that he wrote a book about the experience entitled *A Memory of Solferino* (1862). In it he described the appalling conditions he witnessed on the battlefield and detailed the effort to care for the wounded. In the last part of the book, Dunant called for the formation of relief societies around the world to provide care for those wounded in wartime. In his vision, these societies would be governed by leading political figures and rely on volunteers with special medical training. The book proved very influential, and on February 7, 1863, one part of Dumont's proposal was realized when the Société Genevoise d'Utilité Publique (Geneva Society for Public Welfare) appointed a committee of five, including Dunant, to examine the practicality of such a relief society. This committee essentially formed the basis of the Red Cross.

One of the committee's first actions was to call for an international conference. Dumont was tireless in his efforts on the committee's behalf, contributing money and traveling through Europe to obtain the cooperation of governments. The conference took place from October 26 to 29, 1863, with 39 delegates representing 16 nations. The following year, on August 22, 1864, 12 nations signed an international treaty, commonly known as the First Geneva Convention, in which they agreed to guarantee neutrality to medical aid personnel and to ensure that they were provided with the supplies they needed to do their work. At the same time they adopted an emblem which has become known the world over: the red cross on a field of white. Dunant encouraged efforts to expand the mandate of the Red Cross so that it would also encompass naval personnel in wartime, just as it did soldiers on the ground. The Red Cross also expanded its peacetime role to cover people injured or uprooted by natural catastrophes. In 1872 Dunant convened a gathering to take up the possibility of holding an international convention to deal with the treatment of PRISONERS OF WAR and the use of arbitration to resolve international disputes, an alternative he considered far preferable to the use of force.

Throughout this period, Dunant had become so distracted by his humanitarian pursuits that his business ventures collapsed, leaving him in bankruptcy by 1875. High-placed friends in Geneva society shunned him because of his reverses, and within a few years he was reduced to destitution. Dunant said that there were times when he was forced to sleep on the streets with only a crust of bread to eat. For the next 20 years he lived as a recluse, wandering from place to place, until he eventually settled in a small Swiss village called Heiden in 1890. A local teacher realized who he was and announced the news to the world, which had by this time lost track of him. Two years later, in declining health, Dunant moved into a village hospice, where he spent the last 18 years of his life. But now that he was rediscovered, the world was eager to bestow honors and awards on him. In 1901 he shared the first Nobel Peace Prize with the French statesman Frédéric Passy, the founder of the first French peace society. The Nobel Peace Prize was awarded at a meeting of the Norwegian parliament, which opened at 10:00 on the morning of December 10, 1901. In his opening address the Parliament's president, Carl Christian Bremer, acknowledged Dunant's achievement: "Today when this Peace Prize is to be awarded for the first time, our thoughts turn back in respectful recognition to the man of noble sentiments who, perceiving things to come, knew how to give priority to the great problems of civilization, putting in first place among them work for peace and fraternity among nations. We hope that what he has done in the interest of this great cause will achieve results which will live up to his noble intentions."

The Nobel Prize did not change Dunant's life; he continued to live in Room 12 of the Heiden hospice. Instead of spending any of the prize money, he bequeathed much of it to the people who cared for him and to the village. He also endowed a free bed in the village hospital that was to be put at the disposal of any poor person who fell ill. When he died there was no funeral ceremony and no mourners, and according to his wishes he was simply carried to his grave "like a dog."

See also GENEVA CONVENTIONS.

Duvalier, François "Papa Doc" (1907–1971)
Haitian dictator

François Duvalier, known as Papa Doc, ruled Haiti with an iron fist throughout the 1960s. Born in Port-au-Prince, Haiti's capital, in 1907, François Duvalier was one of the few Haitian youngsters to receive an advanced education. He attended medical school and participated in a U.S.-funded public health campaign to eliminate the scourge of yaws, a crippling bacterial disease, which had infected thousands. Duvalier came of age at a time of violent turmoil; in 1915 U.S. Marines invaded Haiti and installed a puppet regime. The American intervention spurred the growth of a nationalist and ethnic movement known as negritude, championed by the Haitian author Dr. Jean Price-Mars. Duvalier became increasingly involved in the movement, which tapped into the resentment of the country's impoverished black majority. He also conducted an ethnological study of voodoo, Haiti's indigenous religion. Duvalier understood that negritude and voodoo could make a potent political combination.

The withdrawal of the marines in 1934 was followed by a rapid turnover of regimes—presidents held power on the average of two years—alternating between authoritarian military figures and populist rabble-rousers. Duvalier preferred to bide his time and work behind the scenes while maintaining the facade of the "quiet country doctor." He made sure that he was not forgotten, though, by spreading exaggerated stories about his heroic role in the eradication of yaws from the island. His chance to take the reins of power came in elections in 1957, which he manipulated to ensure his victory. But he could only have achieved—and held on to—the presidency with the army's backing. "The peasants love their doctor, and I am their Papa Doc," he declared. As Papa Doc, he fostered a bizarre cult of personality in which he identified himself with Jesus Christ and God. Posters were distributed that depicted Jesus with his right hand draped over Papa Doc's shoulder and bore the legend: "I Have Chosen Him." But he also assumed another, more sinister guise as Baron Samedi—a *vodou loa* (spirit) of the dead. He strengthened the image of Baron Samedi in the minds of superstitious peasants by adopting the *loa*'s traditional costume of top hat and tails.

To keep dissidents in place, Duvalier organized a secret police force known as the Tontons Macoutes, which derived their name from a mythical Haitian boogeyman that snatches people and makes them the disappear forever. They proceeded to round up Duvalier's enemies—among them politicians, journalists, and radio station owners—who were confined in the notorious prison of Fort Dimanche, where they were often tortured to death. From

time to time Duvalier's political opponents would attempt to invade Haiti, using the Dominican Republic (which shares the island of Hispaniola with Haiti) as their staging ground. Surprisingly, the invasion force that came closest to toppling him consisted of only eight men, half of them Haitians, half of them sheriff's deputies from Dade County, Florida.

To neutralize threats from abroad, Duvalier reached deals with Dominican dictator Rafael TRUJILLO Molinas and the Cuban dictator Fulgencio Batista, who provided him with a $4 million loan (which Duvalier pocketed) in exchange for a medal of honor. When Fidel Castro came to power in Cuba, Duvalier masterfully played on Washington's fear of the communist dictator to gain financial assistance and political support for Haiti. Duvalier's regime could properly be called a kleptocracy. Not content with shaking down foreign governments, he extorted Haitians and foreign businessmen alike for a half-baked utopian scheme called "Duvalierville," a city that would never be built because all the money ended up in his own coffers. Proclaiming himself "President for Life," Duvalier had the constitution rewritten to pass the presidency to his only son, Jean-Claude "Baby Doc" DUVALIER, after his death.

Duvalier died in 1971 after 15 years as Haiti's strongman. He left the economy in even worse condition than he had found it: The GDP had plummeted, malnutrition and famine were rife, thousands of peasants had been forced from their land, and the slums of Port-au-Prince had swollen with destitute peasants from the countryside. Human rights advocates estimate that under the reign of the two Duvaliers (1957–86), 40,000–60,000 people were killed. Thousands more had gone into exile, many professionals among them, resulting in a serious brain drain.

See also HAITI, HUMAN RIGHTS VIOLATIONS IN.

Further Reading:
Arthur, Charles. *Haiti: A Guide to the People, Politics, and Culture.* Northampton, N.Y.: Interlink Publishing Group, 2002.
Farmer, Paul. *The Uses of Haiti.* 2d ed. Monroe, Me.: Common Courage Press, 2003.
Heinl, Nancy Gordon, and Robert Debs Jr. *Written in Blood: The Story of the Haitian People, 1492–1995.* Lanham, Md.: University Press of America, 1996.

Duvalier, Jean-Claude "Baby Doc" (1952–   )
Haitian dictator

In 1971, at the age of 19, Jean-Claude Duvalier assumed the presidency of Haiti as his father François "Papa Doc" DUVALIER lay dying. The elder Duvalier, who had tyrannized Haiti for nearly 15 years, had rewritten the constitution to allow his son to inherit the office, although

Notorious former president-for-life of Haiti, François "Papa Doc" Duvalier *(Associated Press)*

Jean-Claude—known as "Baby Doc"—had shown no competence for such a responsibility. On the contrary, the younger Duvalier was considered an overweight playboy of little intelligence. Nonetheless, upon taking power, he proceeded to make a show of introducing some political reforms, softening the brutal image of Papa Doc's regime abroad even though his rule was only slightly less brutal. Haitian exile groups accuse him of participating in some 60,000 assassinations carried out under his 15-year rule and his father's 14-year rule. Baby Doc was alleged to have tortured and executed opponents in the basement of his presidential palace. Some of the exiles have called for him to be charged for crimes against humanity.

The inexperienced Baby Doc kept most of his father's closest advisers in their positions, but his mother, Simone Duvalier, and his young wife, Michele Bennet, whom he married in 1980, probably exerted the greatest influence over him.

Poverty and dictatorship drove thousands of Haitians to flee and seek refuge in the United States. The massive exodus focused worldwide attention on Baby Doc's regime. In 1986 unrest inside Haiti prompted Duvalier to abandon power and seek sanctuary in France. For several years he enjoyed an extravagant lifestyle on the French Riviera thanks to the millions of dollars he had looted from his country. In addition to his villa above Cannes, he and his wife also owned a château outside Paris and two apartments in the city. (Haitian and American officials believe that he embezzled at least $500 million during his last decade of rule.) But Duvalier managed to run through his stolen fortune, and there are reports that after their divorce in 1993, Michele took the remaining money for herself.

Baby Doc has never abandoned the notion of regaining power. "The whole time I've been here [France], my heart and my spirit have been in Haiti," he has said. Although human rights organizations contend that 40,000–60,000 people were killed during the nearly 20 years the two Duvaliers were in power, Duvalier denies that he ever jailed or killed an opponent. "If I were dictator, I would have done everything in my power to stay in power," he told a *Wall Street Journal* reporter. At the same time, he denied stealing. "I laugh when I hear the amounts: $400 million, $800 million. It's a lot of blah, blah, blah . . . People said I always paid for others' meals at restaurants. But many times it was friends who invited us out and they paid the bill."

See also HAITI, HUMAN RIGHTS VIOLATIONS IN.

Further Reading:

Arthur, Charles. *Haiti: A Guide to the People, Politics, and Culture.* New York: Interlink Publishing Group, 2002.

Farmer, Paul. 2d ed. *The Uses of Haiti.* Monroe, Me.: Common Courage Press, 2003.

Heinl, Robert Debs, Jr., and Nancy Gordon Heinl. *Written in Blood.: The Story of the Haitian People, 1492–1995.* Lanham, Md.: University Press of America, 1996.

E

East Timor, human rights violations in

After a wrenching separation from Indonesia that was marred by violence and countless human rights abuses, East Timor finally became a fully independent republic on May 20, 2002. (West Timor remained part of Indonesia. The country with a population of about 860,000 gained its freedom following a 1999 referendum conducted under the auspices of the United Nations. A special peacekeeping mission—the UN Transitional Administration in East Timor (UNTAET)—guided the state in the intervening years. East Timor represents one of the rare unqualified UN success stories; it has a functioning parliament, and elections to the assembly have been free and fair. Violence has significantly diminished since the withdrawal of Indonesian forces in 1999, although there have been sporadic incursions by Indonesian militias based in West Timor, which is still an integral part of Indonesia. These militias have been responsible for robberies and occasional murders of local villagers and peacekeepers.

Indonesia—the world's fourth-largest nation—did not give up East Timor without a struggle. Its claim on the country extended back to 1975, when Portugal, the former colonial power, abandoned it. Almost at once the Indonesian occupying force confronted an insurgency spearheaded by an independence movement called Fretilin. In response, the Indonesian military resettled hundreds of thousands of villagers in hamlets in the hope that the move would dry up support for the guerrillas. But by uprooting peasants from their land, the Indonesians also cut them off from their sources of sustenance, causing widespread famine that, combined with the civil war, may have resulted in as many as 100,000 deaths between 1975 and 1979.

In 1983 the Fretilin leadership engaged in talks with the Indonesian government to negotiate a settlement leading to East Timorese independence. The talks broke down amid a renewal of violence, and a state of emergency was imposed, intensifying resistance. Indonesia now embarked on a campaign intended to remove tens of thousands of the province's indigenous people and replace them with Indonesians, most of whom settled in the western regions of Timor. Up until this time, though, the tumult in East Timor had largely escaped the world's attention. Then in November 1991 Indonesian troops fired on a pro-independence demonstration in the capital of Dili, killing 100–180 people and arresting hundreds more. About 100 of those taken into custody were subsequently executed without trial, because as witnesses to the massacre, they might have implicated the Indonesian troops in the commission of war crimes.

The atrocities in Dili stirred worldwide outrage and for the first time put East Timor in the international spotlight. Even after the arrest of Fretilin's leader, José Alexandre Gusmão, in 1992, two activists urging nonviolent resistance—Bishop Carlos Filipe Ximenes Belo and José Ramos-Horta—continued to seek a peaceful resolution. (In 1996 the two men were awarded the Nobel Peace Prize for their efforts.) However, it required political change in Jakarta, the capital of Indonesia, to create the conditions that would lead to independence. In 1997 President SUHARTO, who had dominated Indonesia for a generation, was forced to step down. His successor, Bucharuddin Jusuf Habibie, was determined to resolve the East Timor crisis and announced a referendum in which the population would vote either to remain an autonomous part of Indonesia or become independent. Many of the members of the militias and their supporters, who had relied on Indonesian largesse for their power and livelihood, were adamantly opposed to independence. The months leading to the referendum were overshadowed by an upsurge in violence as pro-Indonesian militias clashed with pro-independence forces. One militia leader declared that if East Timor were to become independent, he would turn it into a "sea of fire." Though precise figures are unknown, it is thought that in the year before the vote, militias killed a total of 1,000 civilians. In the worst single incident, 57 people were shot and hacked to death in a churchyard west of Dili in April 2000.

The first day of school in East Timor after the end of the war with Indonesia *(United Nations/DPI)*

Nonetheless, the vote went ahead in August 1999 under UN supervision. The outcome was never in doubt; by an overwhelming majority—approximately 80 percent—the East Timorese chose independence. What was in question was the willingness of Indonesia to abide by the vote and pull its troops out. In October the Indonesian government announced that it was revoking the 1978 parliamentary decree that had annexed East Timor, setting the stage for the establishment of the UN Transitional Administration. But if Jakarta was officially prepared to relinquish East Timor, it soon became apparent that the military and as many as 13 allied militia groups had no intention of allowing the people to celebrate their liberation. Before an international peacekeeping force could arrive in Dili, militias went on a rampage, killing hundreds of civilians, driving thousands from their homes, razing the city, and destroying the territory's entire infrastructure. Most of the capital's buildings were destroyed. It is estimated that 250,000 people—out of a population of 800,000—were forced into mili-

tia-controlled camps in West Timor. Others fled to the mountains above Dili. It began to look as if the East Timorese stood to inherit an empty shell. It was only with the arrival of peacekeepers—including a large Australian contingent—that the violence came to an end and conditions were safe enough for the uprooted East Timorese to return to their homes—what remained of them.

The process of bringing people to justice for the most serious crimes in East Timor has been halting at best. In December 2000, UNTAET filed indictments against 141 Indonesians suspected of committing war crimes and related atrocities in 1999. At the time, 84 of the accused were thought to be in Indonesia. The Transitional Administration established a Serious Crimes Investigation Unit to address the most recent and serious cases. For its part, Indonesia set up the Commission for Investigation of Violations of Human Rights in East Timor (KPP-HAM), which recommended an investigation of more than 30 persons, including General WIRANTO, who had commanded the security forces, as well as other high-ranking officials of the military and police. At the same time, the Indonesian attorney general announced that his office would prosecute major cases involving the massacres of civilians, the assassinations of independence activists, and the slayings of three priests and at least 50 civilians. Indonesian courts have tried various suspects in the 1999 violence, including one of the most notorious militia leaders, Eurico Guterres, who received a 10-year sentence after being found guilty of "murder and persecution." A former governor was sentenced to three years, and an officer who commanded the Dili military district was sentenced to five years for his crimes.

The U.S. State Department expressed misgivings over the way these cases were conducted, stating: "The Indonesian government prosecutors in these cases did not fully use the resources and evidence available to them from the United Nations and elsewhere." Indeed, human rights organizations have raised doubts about whether Jakarta was really interested in prosecuting these cases with the vigor that the gravity of the crimes warranted. HUMAN RIGHTS WATCH observed that in the case of one massacre, the judges were poorly trained, the prosecutors demonstrated "no interest in accountability," and the suspects had not even been detained before the trial. Nonetheless, prosecutions have continued. In 2001 a three-judge panel established by UNTAET sentenced a militia leader to 12 years in prison for having murdered a village chief in a police station where he had taken refuge. (Some 40 people were later massacred in the same police station.) However, even this success was a mixed one. The militia leader was convicted for ordinary murder, not for having committed a crime against humanity, because the investigators could not establish that the 1999 mayhem was part of a larger policy on the part of the Indonesian government and military to attack civilians and destroy their homes. Evidence that would have allowed them to prove that the crimes of the militia leader—and others still at large—resides in Jakarta, inaccessible to the authorities in East Timor. And there are other problems, as Human Rights Watch pointed out: "It has been a source of great frustration inside East Timor that justice has proceeded so slowly. The courts had to be created from scratch last year, and the investigation process has been plagued by inadequate training of investigators, changes in administrative structure, and lack of resources and personnel."

In March 2005 the governments of East Timor and Indonesia reached an agreement that would establish a Commission of Truth and Friendship. According to East Timor's foreign minister, José Ramos-Horta, the commission would "resolve once and for all the events of 1999" and "finally close this chapter." But closing the chapter apparently means conferring immunity on the Indonesian offi-

cers responsible for human rights abuses. The provisions of the agreement do not exclude the possibility of an international tribunal, modeled on those for Sierra Leone or Rwanda, but observers believe that is very unlikely. The commission, which will be composed of five representatives from each nation, is considered weaker than similar bodies, such as South Africa's TRUTH AND RECONCILIATION COMMISSION, and in some ways it is an acknowledgement that many of the most-wanted Indonesian suspects will never be brought to justice. (An East Timorese court, set up with the help of the United Nations, had already indicted 400 Indonesian officers, but because 300 of them were in Indonesia, only a relative handful—mostly members of homegrown East Timorese militias—have come to trial or been sentenced to prison.) Many human rights advocates are not convinced that the commission represents a satisfying resolution. "Crimes committed against humanity are a matter of concern for the entire international community," declared the Judicial System Monitoring Program, an independent East Timorese legal organization, "They cannot be ignored or disposed of as a matter of bilateral political concern."

See also INDONESIA, HUMAN RIGHTS VIOLATIONS IN; RELIGIOUS PERSECUTION.

Further Reading:

Dunn, James, and Xanana Gusmão. *East Timor: A Rough Passage to Independence.* Seattle: University of Washington Press, 2004.

Jardine, Matthew. *East Timor: Genocide in Paradise. The Real Story Series.* Monroe, Me.: Odonian Press, 1999.

Pinto, Constancio, and Matthew Jardine. *East Timor's Unfinished Struggle: Inside the Timorese Resistance.* Boston: South End Press, 1996.

Romano, Cesare, Andre Nollkaemper, and Jann K. Kleffner, eds. *Internationalized Criminal Courts and Tribunals: Sierra Leone, East Timor, Kosovo, and Cambodia.* International Courts and Tribunals Series. Oxford: Oxford University Press, 2004.

ECHO   See EUROPEAN COMMUNITY HUMANITARIAN ORGANIZATION.

ECOWAS Monitoring Group (ECOMOG)

ECOMOG is the acronym for the Economic Community of West African States (ECOWAS) Monitoring Group, which has dispatched peacekeeping troops to several troubled countries in the region, including Liberia, Guinea-Bissou, Sierra Leone, and the Ivory Coast. ECOWAS is a group of 16 West African states founded in 1975 to promote economic stability and closer relations among its members. In 1977 the group agreed to a formal defense treaty, which obliged signatories to uphold democracy and the rule of law. The monitoring group was initially established on an ad hoc basis as a multinational peacekeeping force, made up of troops drawn from member states. As the largest country in ECOWAS, Nigeria has inevitably contributed the largest share of troops, and its officers have taken charge of many operations.

ECOMOG was principally responsible for the restoration of peace in Liberia in 1997 and later extended its involvement to other nations torn by conflict. These missions have not come without considerable cost: In 2001 the Nigerian government stated that it had spent $13 billion on them over the previous 12 years. Several hundred Nigerian soldiers have also been killed, primarily in Liberia and Sierra Leone. At the same time, ECOMOG missions have come under harsh criticism because of the group's own role in committing grave human rights abuses. "The history of ECOWAS peacekeeping operations in the subregion has been mixed," HUMAN RIGHTS WATCH said in a statement issued in 2003. "Important successes have been offset by serious human rights abuses and a lack of accountability." Human Rights Watch credits ECOMOG with helping to restore security in Liberia but also charges that its troops became "complicit in serious abuses through its alliance with abusive warring factions." ECOMOG soldiers engaged in extensive looting, harassment, and arbitrary detention of civilians, and its forces violated international humanitarian law by conducting indiscriminate air strikes against civilians and civilian property. Its record in Sierra Leone is somewhat better, but even there ECOMOG troops carried out summary executions of suspected rebels, conducted indiscriminate bombing strikes against civilians, and made use of child soldiers. In one incident on January 11, 1999, soldiers stormed a hospital and dragged wounded rebels from their beds, executing them on hospital grounds. ECOMOG soldiers also sexually exploited women and solicited child prostitutes.

Although ECOWAS pledged to conduct an investigation into abuses by ECOMOG in Sierra Leone at its April 1999 summit, there is no indication that such an investigation has actually been initiated as of 2005.

See also IVORY COAST, HUMAN RIGHTS VIOLATIONS IN; LIBERIA, HUMAN RIGHTS VIOLATIONS IN; SIERRA LEONE, HUMAN RIGHTS VIOLATIONS IN.

Further Reading:
Adekeye, Adelbajo. *Liberia's Civil War: Nigeria, ECOMOG, and Regional Security in West Africa.* Boulder, Colo.: Lynne Rienner Publishers, 2002.
———. *Building Peace in West Africa: Liberia, Sierra Leone, and Guinea-Bissau.* International Peace Academy Occasional Paper Series. Boulder, Colo.: Lynne Rienner Publishers, 2002.
Ellils, Stephen. *The Mask of Anarchy: The Destruction of Liberia and the Religious Dimension of an African Civil War.* New York: New York University Press, 2001.
Kulah, Arthur F. *Liberia Will Rise Again: Reflections on the Liberian Civil Crisis.* Nashville, Tenn.: Abingdon Press, 1999.
Sirleaf, Amos Mohammed. *The Role of the Economic Community of the West African States: Ecowas—Conflict Management In Liberia.* Bloomington, Ind.: AuthorHouse, 2000.

Ecuador, human rights violations in

In a troubling sign of the Ecuadorian government's priorities, none of the candidates in the 2002 presidential campaign would declare that they would commit themselves to protecting human rights if they won. Indeed, the outgoing president was known to criticize the activities of human rights defenders, and activists were harassed, intimidated, and arbitrarily detained. In one case the offices of a national human rights organization, INREDH (Regional Foundation for Human Rights Assistance), were broken into by men apparently looking for confidential information. According to an AMNESTY INTERNATIONAL report issued in 2003, violations of human rights by security forces are seldom punished, and those prosecutions that are undertaken of abusers are tried by police courts, not civilian courts, which are considered "neither impartial nor independent." Because legal proceedings take so long, some suspects end up walking free since the law calls for release after a year if no trial is held. Victims of abuse or their families as well as witnesses to crimes committed by security forces are frequently intimidated and threatened after lodging a complaint. Amnesty also found that TORTURE and ill-treatment of detainees and prisoners are common; violations occur during the arrest or in police stations, prisons, and detention centers. Some prisoners have died because of abuse while in police custody. Prisoners without the financial resources to expedite the legal process are kept in abominable conditions for months. In one detention center in Guayaquil, 350 prisoners were kept in cells intended to accommodate about 100.

Ecuador, the world's largest banana exporter, has failed to enforce its own labor laws on banana plantations. According to a report by HUMAN RIGHTS WATCH, children as young as eight are forced to work on these plantations under hazardous conditions. Adult workers who attempt to organize are in danger of being fired for exercising their rights.

Further Reading:
Gerlach, Allen. *Indians, Oil, and Politics: A Recent History of Ecuador.* Latin American Silhouettes. Wilmington, Del.: Scholarly Resources, 2003.

Roos, Wilma, and Omer Van Renterghem. *Ecuador in Focus: A Guide to the People, Politics and Culture.* 2d ed. London: Latin America Bureau, 2000.

Egypt, human rights violations in

Egypt has placed a higher priority on security than on protecting human rights. Under the Emergency Law, in effect since 1981, many basic rights are restricted, and its provisions have allowed authorities to detain thousands of people without charge on suspicion of illegal terrorist or political activity. According to the U.S. State Department, the security forces have committed numerous human rights abuses in its continuing campaign against Islamic terrorism, mistreating and torturing prisoners, arbitrarily arresting and detaining suspects, and holding detainees in prolonged pretrial detention. The use of excessive force by local police has resulted in EXTRAJUDICIAL KILLINGS, TORTURE, and criminal abuses of suspects. There are credible reports of torture and mistreatment at police stations as well as at State Security Intelligence (SSI) headquarters in Lazoghly Square in Cairo. AMNESTY INTERNATIONAL has found evidence that several people have probably died as a result of their mistreatment in these stations. In 2002 the U.S. State Department reported that 14 people had died while in police custody. Suspects were subjected to electric shocks, beatings, and suspension by their wrists or ankles, which were the most common methods of torture. "Torture is generalized and systematic, from Alexandria to Aswan," stated Dr Magda Adly, director of the Al Nadim Center for the Rehabilitation of Victims of Torture. Although the government has prosecuted some offenders, the punishments are seldom proportionate to the gravity of the crimes. Many cases are tried by Security Emergency Courts and military courts rather than civilian courts, in spite of the right of a defendant to be tried before an independent judiciary, as guaranteed by the country's constitution. Amnesty International has condemned these military trials as "grossly unfair." Moreover, some serious cases are never investigated at all.

The use of the Emergency Law has also allowed the government to infringe on civil liberties. While individuals generally have the right to speak freely, the press is more limited in what it can say. Furthermore, the government has restricted freedom of assembly and association. In one of the most famous cases, a State Security Court convicted Dr. Saad Eddin Ibrahim and four codefendants of defaming the state and illegally accepting foreign funds. Dr. Ibrahim, an internationally renowned sociologist and advocate of democracy and human rights, is the director of the Ibn Khaldun Center for Developmental Studies, a nongovernmental research organization that advocates the development of democracy and human rights. Because he is such a well-known political figure, the verdict against him caused an international furor. The case was seen as a bellwether of Egypt's commitment to freedom of expression and human rights. The U.S. State Department weighed in with a condemnation of the verdict. (Egypt is the second-largest beneficiary of U.S. foreign aid after Israel.)

The international pressure had a positive impact: In March 2003, Egypt's Court of Cassation overturned the verdict and acquitted Ibrahim and the other codefendants. This decision was seen by Ibrahim's supporters as well as human rights organizations as an important victory for the rule of law and protection of human rights in Egypt. Indeed, numerous local nongovernmental human rights organizations have sprung up recently, and the government for the most part has allowed them to function unhampered. Human rights advocates in particular see the establishment of the National Commission for Human Rights as "a new phase on the long road to guaranteeing the protection of men and women from abuses and violations of fundamental freedoms."

However, the government has not been inclined to extend human rights protections to those suspected of being homosexuals. Police have launched a crackdown against suspected homosexuals in recent years that has met with fierce criticism from other governments and nongovernmental organizations alike. Hundreds of men have been rounded up, placed in detention, and tortured—suspended in painful positions, burned with cigarettes, submerged in ice-cold water, and subjected to electroshock—because of their sexual inclinations. HUMAN RIGHTS WATCH alleges that the head of the vice squad has personally taken part in such treatments. Doctors are recruited in the torture sessions, ostensibly to find "evidence" of homosexual behavior. In 2001, 52 men were put on trial on charges of the "habitual practice of debauchery"—the legal charge used to criminalize homosexual conduct.

In March 2005 Egyptian president Hosni Mubarak, responding to pressure from the United States and other governments, announced that Egypt would hold freely contested presidential elections. In September 2005 elections took place with several candidates competing (but none from the largest opposition party, the banned Muslim Brotherhood). As expected, Mubarak won easily amid allegations of vote rigging and intimidation. The vote, hailed by the United States as a first, if tentative, step toward true democracy, was derided by many Egyptians and human rights organizations as a charade. However, the campaign was notable for an antigovernment demonstration in the heart of Cairo that was allowed to proceed without interference from police.

Further Reading:
Dalacoura, Katerina. *Engagement or Coercion?: Weighing Western Human Rights Policies towards Turkey, Iran,*

and Egypt. London: Royal Institute of International Affairs, 2004.

Hicks, Neil. *Escalating Attacks on Human Rights Protection in Egypt: A Report of the Lawyers Committee for Human Rights (North Africa / Lawyers Committee for Human Rights).* New York: Lawyers Committee for Human Rights, 1995.

McNamara, Ronald J. *Democracy and Human Rights in the Mediterranean Partner States of the Osce: Algeria, Egypt, Israel, Jordan, Morocco and Tunisia: Briefing of the Committee on Security and Cooperation in Europe.* Chicago: Diane Pub. Co, 2004.

Eichmann, Adolf (1906–1962) *Nazi mass murderer*
Karl Adolf Eichmann, chief of the Jewish Office of the GESTAPO Department IV for Jewish Affairs, is widely considered to be the architect of the FINAL SOLUTION—the Nazi program to exterminate the Jewish population from Europe and the Soviet Union. He was abducted by Israeli agents from Argentina, where he had sought refuge after World War II, and stood trial in Jerusalem in 1961 for war crimes. Convicted and sentenced to death, he remained unrepentant to the end.

Eichmann was born into a middle-class Protestant family in Solingen, Germany, on March 19, 1906. As a boy he was nicknamed "the little Jew" by classmates because of his appearance and dark complexion. He was an unexceptional student, and instead of completing his studies he went to work first as a laborer for his father's small mining company and later as traveling salesman for the Vacuum Oil Company. However, it was only when he joined the Austrian Nazi Party in 1932 that he found his true calling. In September 1934 he entered the Security Service (SD) under Heinrich HIMMLER, who assigned him to the Jewish section in the SD's Berlin head office. He immersed himself in Jewish culture, studying Zionism and learning Hebrew; he was even able to speak a bit of Yiddish. As a self-proclaimed "Jewish specialist," he soon won appointment to the newly created SD Scientific Museum of Jewish Affairs, where he was charged with researching possible "solutions to the Jewish question"—essentially, devising ways of ridding Europe of the Jews.

In 1937 Eichmann paid a visit to Palestine (then under British mandate) to explore the possibility of resettling Jews there. The following year he was placed in charge of the "Office for Jewish Emigration" in Vienna, which had been established by the SS (Schutzstaffel) and assumed the responsibility for evacuating Jews from Austria. Within the first 18 months as head of the office, he oversaw the "forced emigration" of approximately 150,000 Jews from Austria; their confiscated possessions became the property of Eichmann's office. This was only a prelude; he would soon take control of DEPORTATIONS of Jews from Czechoslovakia and Poland when those countries fell to the Germans as well.

In 1939 Eichmann was appointed the head of Gestapo Section IV B4 (*SS-Obersturmbannfuehrer*) of the new Reich Main Security Office (RSHA), a position that gave him responsibility for the disposition of the Jewish population in Germany and—eventually—all 16 occupied European territories. But no country held more Jews than Poland—3.35 million. As a first step to their elimination, Eichmann ordered them into ghettoes, which were strategically located near railway junctions, preparatory to their eventual deportation. Meanwhile another policy was being pursued in the regions of the Soviet Union that had fallen to German forces. Special military units known as EINSATZGRUPPEN followed the army into the conquered areas and rounded up and executed Jews and other "undesirables." In the first year of the German occupation, some 300,000 Jews were killed, mostly by machine-gun fire.

To view the Einsatzgruppen in action, Eichmann went to Lvov, where he witnessed an execution. He would later

Former Nazi Adolf Eichmann on trial in Jerusalem *(Library of Congress)*

recall a fresh mass grave with blood gushing out of the ground "like a geyser" from the pressure of gases released by the bodies. Himmler, who was more squeamish and nearly fainted, advocated a "more humane method"—gassing. Initially, mobile vans were used for this purpose, but in July 1941 Hermann GÖRING—second in command only to Hitler—gave the order to prepare "a general plan of the administrative material and financial measures necessary for carrying out the desired Final Solution of the Jewish question." To meet this objective, Eichmann organized a conference in January 1942 in the Berlin suburb of Wannsee. Eichmann described this meeting in blunt terms: "The discussion covered killing, elimination, and annihilation." The conference marked the official beginning of a concerted program to exterminate European Jewry. Essentially, 15 high-ranking Nazi officials made the decision to issue a death warrant for six million men, women, and children.

To implement the Final Solution, newer and larger death camps were constructed and equipped with gas chambers and crematoria, and preparations were made to fill them as quickly as possible. "Europe would be combed of Jews from east to west," declared Reinhard HEYDRICH, Himmler's deputy. Although Eichmann avowed that he was not an anti-Semite and had nothing "personally" against Jews, he was a ruthlessly efficient bureaucrat. He had to deal with staggeringly complex logistical problems: registering, assembling, and deporting millions of people to CONCENTRATION CAMPS such as Sobibór, Chelmno, Treblinka, Auschwitz-Birkenau, and other camps. In 1941, as an SS lieutenant colonel, he had toured Auschwitz and other death camps to analyze their efficiency. He had taken a personal interest in the location of the gas chambers and the Zyclon B gas that would be employed in them. "Corpses, corpses, corpses. Shot, gassed, decaying corpses," he later recalled of his visit. "They seemed to pop out of the ground when a grave was opened. It was a delirium of blood. It was an inferno, a hell, and I felt I was going insane."

But instead of going insane, Eichmann complained constantly about logjams in the machinery of death that caused concentration camps to fall short of their quota of corpses. He returned to Auschwitz a number of times. In his posthumously published memoirs, Eichmann described his role this way: "The area of my section's authority was those Jewish matters within the competence of the Gestapo. Originally this centered on the problems of finding out whether a person was a Gentile or a Jew. If he turned out to be a Jew, we were the administrative authority which deprived him of his German citizenship and confiscated his property. Ultimately we declared him an enemy of the state. . . . We supervised Gestapo seizures of German Jews and the trains that took them to their final destination. . . . For all this, of course, I will answer. I was not asleep during the war years." Even as late as 1944, Eichmann was still coordinating the deportation of 725,000 Hungarian Jews, the largest remaining Jewish population in Europe. In August 1944 he reported to Himmler that some 4 million Jews had perished in the concentration camps in addition to the approximately 2 million who had been killed by mobile extermination units. At the end of 1944, Himmler ordered him to halt all deportations, but Eichmann proceeded to round up another 50,000 Hungarian Jews and forced them to undertake a death march to Austria.

In spite of his leading role in carrying out the Final Solution, Eichmann's name was little known outside the Nazi hierarchy. In May 1945, days after the fall of the German Reich, he was captured by the Americans and briefly confined. The Americans, though, had no idea of his importance, and he succeeded in escaping. In 1950 he reached Argentina, his escape facilitated by allies in the SS underground. Once in Buenos Aires, he assumed the identity of Ricardo Klement. In 1960, however, agents of the Mossad (the Israeli spy agency) tracked him down. After keeping him under surveillance for several weeks, they seized him on May 2, 1960. Surprisingly, Eichmann cooperated with his captors. "Gone was the SS officer who once had hundreds of men to carry out his commands," recalled one of the Mossad agents. "Now he was frightened and nervous, at times pathetically eager to help." A week later, using a ruse, the Israelis spirited him out of the country.

The Argentine government reacted with outrage when it learned of the abduction and demanded Eichmann's return. Israel refused and proceeded to put the former Nazi on trial in Jerusalem on April 11, 1961. Eichmann was charged with war crimes, CRIMES AGAINST HUMANITY, and crimes against the Jewish people. During the four months of the trial, which was televised and broadcast throughout the world, more than 100 witnesses testified against him. In his defense, Eichmann contended that he was only a functionary—"a small cog in the machinery," as he put it—a man who was only following orders of his superiors. "Obeying an order was the most important thing to me," he said. "It could be that is in the nature of the German." He ascribed this tendency to his upbringing: "From my childhood, obedience was something I could not get out of my system. When I entered the armed services at the age of 27, I found being obedient not a bit more difficult than it had been during my life to that point. It was unthinkable that I would not follow orders." At one point he seemed bemused by the fact that he had been singled out for prosecution: "Why me?" he asked. "Why not the local policemen, thousands of them? They would have been shot if they had refused to round up the Jews for the death camps. Why not hang them for not wanting to be shot? Why me? Everybody killed the Jews." The philosopher and writer Hannah Arendt, who was covering the proceedings, was struck by how a man capable of such monstrosity could seem so ordinary, and she coined the famous phrase *banality of evil* to describe the incongruity.

On December 2, 1961, Eichmann was found guilty on all counts and sentenced to death. He was hanged on May 31, 1962, in Ramleh prison. His last words were reputed to be: "Long live Germany. Long live Austria. Long live Argentina. These are the countries with which I have been most closely associated and I shall not forget them. I had to obey the rules of war and my flag. I am ready." His body was cremated and his ashes scattered in the Mediterranean—well beyond the territorial waters of Israel.

See also WANNSEE CONFERENCE.

Further Reading:

Dawidowicz, Lucy. *A Holocaust Reader.* Library of Jewish Studies. Chicago: Behrman House Publishing, 1976.

Dwork, Deborah, and Robert Jan Van Pelt. *Holocaust: A History.* New York: W. W. Norton & Company, 2003.

Gilbert, Martin. *The Holocaust: A History of the Jews of Europe during the Second World War.* New York: Owl Books, 1987.

Goni, Uki. *The Real Odessa: How Peron Brought the Nazi War Criminals to Argentina.* London: Granta Books, 2003.

Overbey, Fern. *The Dachau Defendants: Life Stories from Testimony and Documents of the War Crimes Prosecutions.* Jefferson, N.C.: McFarland & Company, 2004.

Roseman, Mark. *The Wannsee Conference and the Final Solution: A Reconsideration.* New York: Metropolitan Books, 2002.

Einsatzgruppen

The Einsatzgruppen—the "action groups"—were Nazi mobile killing squads, composed primarily of SS and police personnel, that were set up to kill political opponents. Later these squads broadened the scale of their operations to include the killings of Jews and other "undesirables" in parts of Eastern Europe occupied by German forces. Initially, their purpose was more political in nature, and their weapons of choice consisted mainly of the gun and the knife. By 1941, however, with the advent of Operation Barbarossa—the code name for the German invasion of the Soviet Union—the objectives and function of the Einsatzgruppen changed. Its four principal divisions—known simply as Groups A, B, C, and D—were given responsibility for a vast swath of Eastern Europe that stretched from the Baltic in the north to the Black Sea in the south. Operating behind advancing German troops, they were given the mission of rounding up and eliminating Jews, Rom (Gypsies),

communists, Polish government officials, and political dissidents in cities, towns, and village.

In one of the most infamous massacres, carried out in the course of just two days in late September 1941, the Einsatzgruppen killed 34,000 Jewish men, women, and children at a ravine in the Ukraine known as BABI YAR. The mobile units were responsible for the murders of as many as 1.2 million Jews (out of a total of 6 million killed by the Nazis in carrying out their FINAL SOLUTION) and tens of thousands of Soviet and Polish political officials, partisans, and Rom.

To carry out executions on such a vast scale, the Einsatzgruppen needed the help of other units including the Order Police battalions, Waffen SS units, the Higher SS, and Police Leaders (Nazi officials who commanded large groups of SS) as well as auxiliary police and local collaborators. Because these units acted with such speed, initiating operations within days of the capture of a locality, most of their victims were caught unaware and had no chance to escape. The killings took place in five stages. In the first stage, Jews and other people deemed enemies would be rounded up. In the second stage, they would be marched or transported to the outskirts of the city, where they were shot (the third stage). In the fourth stage, their bodies were buried under loose layers of dirt. Finally, the next group of victims would be executed on top of the bodies of the preceding group.

During the NUREMBERG TRIALS, conducted by the victorious Allies, several former SS officials were tried for war crimes they had carried out on behalf of the Einsatzgruppen. Known as Case No. 9, the "Einsatzgruppen" Trial took a year and a half, from September 27, 1947, to April 9, 1948. Twenty-four of the defendants were convicted; 14 were sentenced to be executed, but 12 of these later had their sentences commuted. One committed suicide during the trial, and the rest were sentenced to various terms of imprisonment.

Further Reading:

Bloxham, Donald. *Genocide on Trial: War Crimes Trials and the Formation of Holocaust History and Memory.* Oxford: Oxford University Press, 2003.

Dawidowicz, Lucy. *A Holocaust Reader.* Library of Jewish Studies. Chicago: Behrman House Publishing, 1976.

Russell of Liverpool, Edward Frederick Langley Russell, Baron. *The Scourge of the Swastika: A Short History of Nazi War Crimes.* London: Greenhill Books/Lionel Leventhal, 2002.

Gilbert, Martin. *The Holocaust: A History of the Jews of Europe during the Second World War.* New York: Owl Books, 1987.

Roseman, Mark. *The Wannsee Conference and the Final Solution: A Reconsideration.* New York: Metropolitan Books, 2002.

Eizenstat, Stuart (1943–) *American diplomat*

Stuart Eizenstat has served in several capacities in the U.S. government—ambassador to the European Union, undersecretary of commerce, undersecretary of state, and deputy secretary of the Treasury—but he may be best remembered for having negotiated a settlement that provided for REPARATIONS for surviving victims of Nazi Germany. From 1995 to 2001, while simultaneously serving as ambassador to the European Union on behalf of the Clinton administration, he played a significant role in negotiating an agreement with the governments of Austria, Germany, and France as well as Swiss banks and several private corporations worth $8 billion. The negotiations were especially complex because of the effort needed to track down millions of dollars of assets and property stolen from forced laborers, Jews, and other victims of the Nazis during World War II and then obtain restitution from the governments, banks, and companies still holding the assets.

There are a number of reasons why no major effort was mounted to secure restitution until the mid-1990s, according to Eizenstat. For one thing, when the war ended, resettlement of REFUGEES displaced by war took precedence over recovering lost assets. For another, many of the documents that would support survivors' compensation claims did not become available until after the Berlin Wall fell and the archives of Eastern European states and Russia were opened to investigators. Eizenstat also had a personal stake in the outcome, having discovered that some of his relatives had perished in the Holocaust. The settlement, he admitted, was necessarily incomplete. "I call the work that we did 'imperfect justice,'" he said, "and if that seems a contradiction, it is not one here," he remarked. "There can be no final accounting, even for those who did recover something. And yet, there was still an accountability, a sense that justice has been done."

El Mozote, massacre in

The village of El Mozote in El Salvador came under attack by forces of the government on December 11, 1981, resulting in the massacre of some 900 civilians, an incident that is believed to represent the worst atrocity in modern Latin American history. The massacre came as part of an antileftist insurgency operation in the midst of a civil war that had its origins in the late 1970s, and it is regarded as the turning point that eventually led to a peace accord.

Washington backed the Salvadoran government in a conflict that it viewed through the prism of the cold war. The attack was staged by the army's elite Atlacal Battalion, which had received training from the U.S. military. In what was dubbed Operation Rescue, the battalion reached the remote village on December 10, 1981, seeking to root out leftist rebels of the Farabundo Martí National Liberation Front [FMLN]. The soldiers ordered the inhabitants of the village out of their homes and into the square so that they could search and interrogate them about possible connections to the rebels. When that was done, the villagers were told to return to their homes and stay there through the night. In the morning the soldiers again ordered the villagers to assemble in the main square, where they separated the men from the women and children before locking them inside a church, a convent, and several houses. Finally, after subjecting several people to further interrogation, the soldiers began to execute the entire population, beginning with the men and then moving onto the women and children. Once they had finished their work, they set the village ablaze. The victims were left unburied. The following day the battalion moved into another village, Los Toriles, less than two miles away, and killed any inhabitants there who had not managed to escape before their arrival.

Although the guerrilla radio station began to broadcast accounts of the massacre within days, the U.S. embassy in the capital of San Salvador played down the reports and cited safety concerns to explain why it would not send envoys to examine the site for themselves. But FMLN representatives arranged for reporters from the *New York Times* and *Washington Post* to visit the site about a month later. The *Times* correspondent, Raymond Bonner, reported that he had seen "the charred skulls and bones of dozens of bodies buried under burned-out roofs, beams, and shattered tiles." The *Post* correspondent, Alma Guillermoprieto, who visited the village separately a few days later, observed "dozens of decomposing bodies still seen beneath the rubble and lying in nearby fields, despite the month that has passed since the incident." The reporters also spoke to witnesses who had succeeded in eluding the soldiers. One woman recounted how her husband, five-year-old son, and three daughters—ages five, three, and eight months—had all been gunned down.

The firestorm that news of the massacre set off caused the governments of both El Salvador and the United States to scramble for political cover. The Reagan administration denounced the reports of a massacre as "gross exaggerations," while El Salvadoran authorities denied that it had occurred at all. Thomas Enders, then assistant secretary of state for inter-American affairs, went before a congressional subcommittee to repudiate the *Post* and *Times* reports, insisting that while there had been a firefight between guerrillas and the army in the area, "no evidence could be found to confirm that government forces systematically massacred civilians." Elliot Abrams, the assistant secretary of state for human rights and humanitarian affairs at the time, said that reports of the killings "were not credible" and that "it appears to be an incident that is at least being significantly misused, at the very best, by the guerrillas." The *Wall Street Journal* denounced Bonner for being "overly credulous," while *Time* magazine carried a report asserting that women and children, too, could be active guerrillas. Some conservative organizations even went so far as to accuse Bonner of being a communist, and eventually pressure on the reporter mounted to such an extent that Bonner left the *Times*. Guillermoprieto, too, quit her job after she was reassigned to a beat covering suburban Washington.

Although Bonner wrote a book on the event, *Weakness and Deceit: U.S. Policy and El Salvador*, the story seemed to die. In the interim, the Atlacatal Battalion continued to commit atrocities, although the army as a whole had begun to reassess its previous hard-line strategies to avoid further accusations of human rights abuses. Then, in October 1990, a survivor of the massacre filed a criminal complaint against the battalion, contending that soldiers had killed his family and neighbors. Five witnesses came forward to corroborate the complainant's account, and a judge ordered the remains exhumed. Two years later, in 1992, representatives of the government and FMLN signed a peace agreement—the Chapultepec Peace Accords—which were to be carried out under supervision of the United Nations. A UN-sanctioned Truth Committee was established to investigate human rights abuses, including the killings at El Mozote. In November 1992 forensic experts who were part of a UN team exhumed remains from the site, but even then the Salvadoran minister of defense and the chief of the armed forces joint staff claimed that there was no way to identify any officers who might have participated in the slayings because records from the period were lost. Nonetheless, the Truth Commission was able to conclude: "There is full proof that on 11 December 1981, in the village of El Mozote, units of the Atlacatl Battalion deliberately and systematically killed a group of more than 200 men, women and children, constituting the entire civilian population that they had found there the previous day and had since been holding prisoner."

In 1993 a special panel commissioned by the U.S. State Department found that American diplomats had failed to fulfill their obligations when allegations of the massacre were raised, determining that "mistakes were certainly made . . . particularly in the failure to get the truth about the December 1981 massacre at El Mozote."

See also EL SALVADOR, WAR CRIMES IN.

Further Reading:
Armstrong, Robert. *El Salvador: The Face of Revolution.* Boston: South End Press, 1982.
Bonner, Raymond. *Weakness and Deceit: U.S. Policy and El Salvador.* New York: Crown, 1984.
Danner, Mark. *The Massacre at El Mozote.* New York: Vintage, 1994.
Wood, Elisabeth Jean, Lange Peter (Series Editor), et al. *Insurgent Collective Action and Civil War in El Salvador.* Cambridge Studies in Comparative Politics. Cambridge: Cambridge University Press, 2003.

El Salvador, war crimes in

El Salvador is slowly recovering from a wrenching civil war that convulsed the country throughout the 1980s. The conflict had its roots in the gross disparity between the wealthy elite who controlled political and economic power and the overwhelming majority of the Salvadorian people eking out a subsistence living. It is estimated that 70,000 people were killed in the war, with economic losses totaling $2 billion. The dislocation and economic devastation wrought by the conflict has been compounded by entrenched poverty and natural disasters. In spite of reforms and free elections, El Salvador remains among the most violent and crime-ridden countries in the Americas.

El Salvador fell under military rule in 1972, and the regime began to use increasingly repressive tactics to curb dissent. This spurred the creation of leftist insurgencies, which merged into the Farabundo Martí National Liberation Front (FMLN). At the same time, rightist paramilitary death squads began an indiscriminate campaign of terror. Members of the FMLN were not the only ones targeted: Scores of activists, priests, and human rights workers were disappeared and presumably executed. In 1979 a new military junta tried to bring about political reconciliation, even inviting some moderates and leftists into the government. The most notorious death squad known as ORDEN was ordered to disband, but other death squads rushed to fill the void, and assassinations, TORTURE, and DISAPPEARANCES continued. The leftists walked out of the government, which was now firmly controlled by the right-wing Nationalist Republican Alliance (ARENA) that had been formed by Major Roberto D'AUBUISSON. In spite of ARENA's well-documented atrocities, it still retained the support of Washington, which was alarmed by the threat of leftists coming to power in its own backyard and therefore willing to overlook the links between ARENA and the death squads.

The civil war, which went on for 12 years, was marked by human rights violations by both the government security forces and left-wing guerrillas. In its war against the government, the FMLN carried out assassinations, kidnappings, bombings, and sabotage. In regions they controlled, the guerrillas extorted money from landholders and business owners. Even as the insurgents were making gains in the countryside, security forces and death squads were terrorizing the cities, conducting arbitrary arrests, torture, and EXTRAJUDICIAL killings. The army, trained and equipped by the United States, is believed to have kidnapped and disappeared more than 30,000 people and carried out large-scale massacres of thousands of peasants, including the elderly, women, and children.

Human rights activists were especially at risk for exposing the government's complicity in human rights violations. Several members of the Commission on Human Rights of El Salvador (CDHES), founded in 1978 to promote and protect human rights, were murdered or disappeared as a result of their work. In 1980 Archbishop Oscar Arnulfo Romero, who had helped to form CDHES, was assassinated as he celebrated mass. His slaying came shortly after he had appealed to President Jimmy Carter to withhold military assistance from El Salvador. No one has ever been brought to justice for his murder, although Alvaro SARAVIA, a Salvadorian national residing in the United States, has been named as a conspirator in the assassination. The rapes and killings of three U.S. Catholic nuns and a church worker, however, stirred such outrage that the government felt compelled to take action, and five members of the Salvadoran National Guard were later convicted for the crimes, although the officers suspected of giving the orders were never prosecuted.

In 1984 an election brought a moderate civilian to power, the Christian Democrat José Napoleón Duarte. Although he was regarded as an alternative to the leftists and ARENA and also had Washington's backing, he was ill with cancer and unable to bring an end to the war. Furthermore, his party was accused of corruption. A devastating earthquake in 1986 brought further misery to the country and played havoc with the economy. In 1989 ARENA won parliamentary elections—and the presidency—with the support of small farmers and businessmen. D'Aubuisson was appointed as head of the Salvadoran Constitutional Convention, which drafted a new constitution. That same year the FMLN launched a successful offensive in which guerrillas gained large parts of the countryside; even though they later withdrew, their show of strength demonstrated that neither side was capable of achieving a military victory. The year also saw the beginning of peace talks, which culminated in a UN-mediated agreement known as the Chapultepec Accord in January 1992. (The negotiations were conducted in Chapultepec, Mexico.) Under the terms of the agreement, most of the FMLN forces and the government army were to be disbanded, and the security forces, National Police, National Guard, and Treasury Police were to be eliminated altogether. In their place a new civilian police force was to be created that would include former officers of the National Police and FMLN insurgents. A UN commission was charged with assisting the Salvadorans in implementing the agreement.

Before the reconciliation process could get underway, however, El Salvador was struck again by a series of natural disasters including Hurricane Mitch in 1998 and several earthquakes in 2001, accounting for at least 1,200 deaths (200 in Hurricane Mitch alone) and leaving a million people homeless. A severe drought, also in 2001, destroyed 80 percent of the country's crops, leading to famine in the countryside. Nonetheless, El Salvador was able to make progress in putting the agreement into effect. Subsequently the constitution was amended to prohibit the military from assuming an internal security role except under extraordinary circumstances. Several security services were abolished, as called for by the accord, and by 1993, nine months ahead of schedule, the military force had been reduced to 32,000 troops from a wartime high of 63,000.

The agreement also established a Truth Commission under UN auspices to investigate the most serious cases of crimes committed during the civil war. In 1993, in one of its first acts, the commission recommended purging all officials accused of corruption and human rights violations from the government and the military. Most international observers agree that the military is now composed of a more professional force than in the past and adheres to a doctrine that requires it to refrain from meddling in politics. Several officers have since been convicted in the murders of Jesuits in 1989, while former FMLN guerrillas have been arrested for the 1991 murders of two U.S. servicemen. In addition, the Truth Commission recommended changes to bolster the judiciary system, which involved replacing inept judges and strengthening the offices of the attorney generals and public defenders. In its 1993 report, the commission also reexamined the unsolved Romero assassination and found sufficient evidence to conclude that former major Roberto D'Aubuisson gave the order to kill the archbishop. They could not bring d'Aubuisson to trial, however, as he had died the year before of cancer.

Although conditions have improved considerably since the end of the civil war, human rights defenders are still in danger of being attacked, though at a diminished level. In spite of its tarnished reputation, ARENA has managed to gain the presidency in every election since the peace agreement was signed. On March 2, 2004, the conservative party's candidate, Antonio Saca, won the presidential election. A former radio and TV sports presenter, Saca pledged to work with other parties in the government. During his campaign he promised to crack down on criminal gangs and create a transparent government. When, however, he touched on the more combustible issue of the death squads previously connected to ARENA he grew more circumspect. His victory, Saca said, was "a moment to forget all the past."

See also EL MOZOTE, MASSACRE IN.

Further Reading:
Armstrong, Robert. *El Salvador: The Face of Revolution.* Boston: South End Press, 1982.

Danner, Mark. *The Massacre at El Mozote.* New York: Vintage, 1994.

Wood, Elisabeth Jean, Peter Lange, et al., eds. *Insurgent Collective Action and Civil War in El Salvador.* Cambridge Studies in Comparative Politics. Cambridge: Cambridge University Press, 2003.

Equatorial Guinea, human rights violations in

The former Spanish colony of Equatorial Guinea might have remained a destitute West African backwater were it not for the discovery of oil in the 1990s. Only three other sub-Saharan countries have benefited from as much American investment since 1996 (after South Africa, Nigeria, and Angola) for a total of about $5 billion, mostly dedicated to the energy sector. Some 350,000 barrels of oil are pumped out of Equatorial Guinea a day, accounting for 90 percent of the country's exports. However, the new wealth has not helped most of Equatorial Guinea's people—estimates of the population vary from half a million to a little more than a million—and much of the money has been misappropriated by the government.

While ostensibly a multiparty state, Equatorial Guinea is in actuality run by one man through his family and subclan of the majority Fang tribe. The country has been dominated by President Teodoro Obiang Nguema since he seized power in a military coup in 1979, making him one of the continent's most enduring dictators. Elections are held, but they are considered fraudulent by outside observers, an assertion supported by tallies showing Obiang winning 98 percent of the vote. Obiang's brother is director general of national security, and as the head of the police and security forces, he has been responsible for numerous human rights abuses. According to a 1999 U.S. State Department report, he is a torturer whose subordinates have urinated on their victims, sliced off their ears, and rubbed oil on their bodies to attract stinging ants. Obiang's relatives hold the most important positions in the military. One of Obiang's sons is in charge of the ministry of natural resources, and a brother-in-law serves as ambassador to the United States.

Obiang's regime has not gone unchallenged. Coups are a constant feature of the political landscape—five since 1996—though they have all failed so far. In 2004 a bizarre coup attempt, involving foreign mercenaries, was spectacularly foiled when the invaders were intercepted in Zimbabwe before they could reach Equatorial Guinea.

The government's human rights record is poor. Freedom of assembly and association is restricted. The government has also limited freedom of religion and movement. Although freedom of the press is limited, there has been some improvement in the ability of people to say what they think without fear of reprisal. Security forces are responsible for arbitrary arrests and hold prisoners incommunicado.

While in custody, suspects are subject to TORTURE and beatings to extract confessions, with the result that some have died. There are credible reports that the police have carried out EXTRAJUDICIAL KILLINGS. Members of opposition parties are particularly at risk. There is no indication that abusers in the security forces have been brought to justice for their crimes. Nor can victims seek redress from the justice system, which has no independence to speak of.

Eritrea, human rights violations in

The East African state of Eritrea finally won its independence from Ethiopia in 1993 after 30 years of struggle. With a population of about 4.5 million, Eritrea had in fact thrown off Ethiopian rule two years previously, after the fall of Ethiopian dictator MENGISTU Haile Mariam. The new government in Addis Ababa, the capital of Ethiopia, quickly recognized Eritrea, but tensions soon developed between the two countries over political and economic issues. In 1998 Eritrea and Ethiopia began a war that would last for two years; the immediate cause of the conflict was a border dispute. Tens of thousands of fighters on both sides were killed or injured in clashes that reminded some observers of the trench warfare in World War I. Ethiopian minorities in Eritrea and Eritrean minorities in Ethiopia were subjected to harsh treatment, and large numbers of people were forcibly expelled in contravention of international humanitarian law. The Eritrean government interned some 7,500 people and deported thousands, some of whom reported being tortured and raped by Eritrean officials.

Although the war was ended through international mediation, relations between the two states remain tense. The December 2000 peace agreement called for the establishment of a boundary commission and a claims commission and provided for release of PRISONERS OF WAR. However, the accord did not address the plight of the thousands of civilians who had been mistreated and deported from both countries. The Horn of Africa has not only suffered from war but has been among the regions hardest hit by natural disasters, including successive famines and drought that affected half of Eritrea's population in 2002–3. These calamities have impeded the country's economic growth and jeopardized political stability.

Eritrea's human rights record is considered poor. Eritrea is a one-party state, and as of 2004 national elections had not been held since independence. Elections that were scheduled have been canceled on various pretexts. With the threat of insurgency from an armed opposition group called the Eritrean National Alliance (ENA), based in Ethiopia and Sudan, the government has become more repressive. (For its part, Eritrea supports insurgencies against Addis Ababa.) The government withholds basic freedoms that its people voted for in a 1997 referendum.

Eritrean refugees returning from Sudan in July 2001   *(United Nations)*

There is an absence of freedom of expression and a suppression of peaceful political dissent. Security forces arbitrarily detain and TORTURE suspects, and the judiciary is manipulated for political purposes. Hundreds of suspected political opponents as well as publishers, editors, and journalists have been incarcerated for years without being brought to trial, and others have been disappeared and presumed killed on the grounds that they belong to political dissident groups in exile. President Issayas Afwerki has denounced these detainees as "traitors" and "spies," but even under pressure from human rights organizations, he has refused to file charges as required by the constitution.

The government has also cracked down on ordinary civilians and arrested REFUGEES attempting to flee the country, holding them incommunicado. Religious minorities, too, including members of Pentecostal Christian churches and Jehovah's Witnesses, face arrest for practicing their faith. Security forces have arrested so many people, in fact, that they have run out of prison space and have held some prisoners in empty cargo containers. Attempts by the INTERNATIONAL COMMITTEE OF THE RED CROSS to visit the prisoners have been rebuffed.

See also ETHIOPIA, HUMAN RIGHTS VIOLATIONS IN.

Further Reading:

Jacquin-Berdal, Dominique. *Unfinished Business: Ethiopia and Eritrea at War.* London: Red Sea Press, 2004.

Marcus, Harold G. *A History of Ethiopia: Updated Edition.* Berkeley: University of California Press, 2002.

Pausewang, Siegfried, Kjetil Tronvoll, and Lovise Aaeln, eds. *Ethiopia since the Derg: A Decade of Democratic Pretension and Performance.* London: Zed Books, 2003.

ESMA   *See* ARGENTINA, HUMAN RIGHTS VIOLATIONS IN.

Ethiopia, human rights violations in

Ethiopia's human rights record is generally poor, although some improvements have taken place in recent years. There is no question that Ethiopia has made considerable progress since the overthrow of the brutal regime of MENGISTU Haile Mariam in 1991. While political parties are allowed to compete in elections, they are hobbled by poor organization and a lack of funds and have little opportunity to make substantial gains against the dominant

Ethiopian Peoples' Revolutionary Democratic Front (EPRDF). Freedom of assembly and association is limited, and the police have used excessive force to disperse demonstrators. In 2004 as many as 350 students were arrested after staging a peaceful protest at the University of Addis Ababa. The students were taken to prison, forced to run and crawl—barefooted and bare-kneed—across sharp gravel for several hours and then released without charges. This kind of abuse is part of a larger pattern, human rights advocates charge, placing Ethiopia in violation of the International CONVENTION AGAINST TORTURE, to which Ethiopia has been a party since 1994.

The country's political landscape is still overshadowed by a two-year border war with Eritrea (which was once a part of Ethiopia) that ended in 2000. The plight of some 75,000 ethnic Ethiopian refugees of Eritrean nationality, forced by the war from their homes in Ethiopia, has yet to be resolved. These refugees, now resettled in Eritrea, had their Ethiopian citizenship revoked and their identity documents confiscated or marked "Expelled—never to return." In violation of INTERNATIONAL HUMANITARIAN LAW, many of these people were separated from their families and stripped of their property. Other ethnic Eritreans who did remain in the country faced TORTURE or internment under harsh conditions.

Although the peace agreement brokered by the United Nations has restored an uneasy calm to the region, tensions remain and insurgents continue to operate in both countries. Guerrilla groups based in neighboring Sudan, Somalia, and northern Kenya frequently carry out incursions in Ethiopia. Many suspects taken into custody by security forces have been charged with membership in these groups, especially the Oromo Liberation Front (OLF). In 2002, for example, some 142 teachers were detained and accused of being OLF sympathizers. Security forces have been implicated in arbitrary arrests, torture, beatings, DISAPPEARANCES, and mistreatment of detainees as well as EXTRAJUDICIAL KILLINGS. In 2002, according to the U.S. State Department, the security forces unlawfully killed at least 1,000 and perhaps as many as 1,500 people. Thousands remain incarcerated without being charged, although the government has taken steps to release and repatriate Eritrean PRISONERS OF WAR and civilians detained during the war with Eritrea. The judiciary is considered weak, DUE PROCESS is often violated, and suspects are arrested without warrants. To date the government has demonstrated little inclination to bring abusers to justice. No disciplinary action, for instance, was taken against members of the security forces responsible for several extrajudicial killings in 2001 during riots between Christians and Muslims in Harar or in the slayings of at least 31 students during a violent demonstration at Addis Ababa University. Several killings by security forces in the previous year also went uninvestigated.

More recently, ethnic clashes have broken out in western Ethiopia involving the Anuak and darker-skinned Gambellas, known as highlanders. The former are farmers and fishermen, the latter are shopkeepers. Anuak are newcomers, while the highlanders are relative newcomers, having settled in the area only in the early 1990s. Because the highlanders have enjoyed government support, the army has intervened on their behalf. Hundreds of Anuak have reportedly been killed. Political figures in Addis Ababa, including Prime Minister Meles Zenawi, have denied that the army has been involved in any killings, however. "Is this a tragedy? Yes," said the Ethiopian minister responsible for the Gambella region. "Is this something that's grave? Yes. But why is it necessary to inflate it?"

See also ERITREA, HUMAN RIGHTS VIOLATIONS IN.

Further Reading:
Jacquin-Berdal, Dominique. *Unfinished Business: Ethiopia and Eritrea at War.* London: Red Sea Press, 2004.
Marcus, Harold G. *A History of Ethiopia: Updated Edition.* Berkeley: University of California Press, 2002.
Pausewang, Siegfried, Kjetil Tronvoll, and Lovise Aaeln, eds. *Ethiopia since the Derg: A Decade of Democratic Pretension and Performance.* London: Zed Books, 2003.

ethnic cleansing

The forcible removal of a civilian population from their homeland is a tactic that while outlawed by international law has been widely employed in conflicts throughout history. If anything, the practice has become even more systematic and pervasive in the last half century. As a term, ethnic cleansing first gained popular currency during the war in Bosnia and Herzegovina in the early 1990s when Serb armed forces and militias uprooted thousands of Bosnian Muslims from their homes in order to carve out a greater Serbia. (The original Serbo-Croatian term is *etničko čišćenje*). Some etymologists have traced the usage of the term to Viktor Gutić, a Croatian fascist leader who declared in a speech given in 1941: "Every Croat who today solicits for our enemies not only is not a good Croat, but also an opponent and disrupter of the prearranged, well-calculated plan for cleansing [*čišćenje*] our Croatia of unwanted elements . . ." Serbs again implemented a policy of ethnic cleansing in 1999 in the breakaway province of Kosovo in an attempt to evict Albanian Kosovars who made up the majority of the population. Ethnic cleansing has a long and notorious history. European colonizers of Africa and the Americas beginning in the 15th century massacred and deported large numbers of indigenous people. American Indians, for instance, were killed and uprooted from their homes and survivors confined to reservations. In Australia British settlers massacred and removed the Aborigines from their traditional territories starting in 1788. During the 19th century, millions of Congolese were deported or massacred by their Belgian colonizers. The most infamous program of ethnic cleansing, however, was organized by the Nazis in territories seized by German forces during World War II; millions of Jews, Poles, ROM (Gypsies), and other indigenous populations were deported from their homelands, forced to work as slave laborers, or exterminated in CONCENTRATION CAMPS. (Areas from which all Jews had been eliminated were known as *judenrein*—freed of Jews). Ethnic cleansing was carried out in an especially horrifying way in 1994 in Rwanda when members of the Hutu ethnic group, which constituted the majority, went on a rampage, massacring 800,000 ethnic Tutsis and moderate Hutus in an attempt to eliminate the country of all Tutsis. More recently, the world has witnessed a similar phenomenon in Darfur in western Sudan, where Arab militias known as the Janjaweed have carried out a deliberate policy of driving black African farmers from their homes, while simultaneously conducting a SCORCHED EARTH policy, burning crops and villages and stealing livestock in order to make the land uninhabitable. The term *ethnic cleansing* has entered the official vocabulary of the United Nations and other international organizations, although it has yet to be clearly defined under international law. Generally, ethnic cleansing is characterized by robbery, terrorization, intimidation, and discrimination. At first a regime may try to make life so unbearable for the targeted minority that they are willing to leave of their own accord. As a result, ethnic cleansing may take various forms especially in its earlier stages: elected authorities of a particular ethnic group are removed from office, members of a minority ethnic group are subject to intensified surveillance, harassment, and frequent identity checks and denied access to public or commercial facilities and services and barred from holding certain types of jobs. Media campaigns are instituted by the government to inflame passions of the majority population against the minority. In its later stages, ethnic cleansing typically takes the form of arrests and illegal detentions of the minority group, confinement to concentration camps, the seizure and destruction of property and businesses belonging to members of the minority, and confiscation or desecration of their cultural and religious institutions. At its most extreme, though, ethnic cleansing has many of the characteristics of genocide, in which people are forcibly deported and murdered. Very often the perpetrators accuse the victims of responsibility for their plight. The Nazis made Jews the scapegoats for Germany's ills, for example, and the Sudanese government has charged that violent secessionists are to blame for the crisis in Darfur.

See also AUSTRALIA, HUMAN RIGHTS VIOLATIONS IN; DARFUR, GENOCIDE IN; SUDAN, WAR CRIMES IN; YUGOSLAVIA, WAR CRIMES IN.

Further Reading:
Bell-Fialkoff, Andrew. *Ethnic Cleansing.* Sydney, Australia: Palgrave Macmillan, 1999.

Naimark, Norman M. *Fires of Hatred: Ethnic Cleansing in Twentieth-Century Europe.* Cambridge, Mass.: Harvard University Press, 2002.

Power, Samantha. *"A Problem from Hell": America and the Age of Genocide.* New York: Harper Perennial, 2003.

Prunier, Gerard. *Darfur: The Ambiguous Genocide.* Ithaca, N.Y.: Cornell University Press, 2005.

European Community Humanitarian Organization (ECHO)

ECHO, as the European Community Humanitarian Organization is known, is an agency of the European Union (EU), established in 1992 to deliver humanitarian assistance where needed on an emergency or long-term basis. ECHO states that it helps some 18 million people annually in 85 mostly undeveloped countries in cooperation with 200 partners, including the United Nations, nongovernmental organizations (NGOs), and the INTERNATIONAL COMMITTEE OF THE RED CROSS. ECHO's Humanitarian Aid Office spends more than €500 million (about $600 million) a year on financing humanitarian projects. These projects range from relief from natural disasters to providing emergency assistance to victims of armed conflicts outside the EU. In Burundi, for instance, ECHO has funded projects intended to reduce mortality and morbidity, particularly among REFUGEES, internally displaced people, women, and children. In Haiti, ECHO responded to the political crisis of March 2004 by directing about $2 million in emergency humanitarian aid to benefit 3 million people living in the cities most affected by the turmoil, including emergency health care and protection to help victims of the violence.

Further Reading:
Aall, Pamela R., Daniel Miltenberger, and George Weiss. *IGOs, NGOs, and the Military in Peace and Relief Operations.* Washington, D.C.: United States Institute of Peace Press, 2000.

Byman, Daniel, Ian Lesser, Bruce Pirnie, Cheryl Benard, and Matthew Waxman. *Strengthening the Partnership: Improving Military Coordination with Relief Agencies and Allies in Humanitarian Operations.* Santa Monica, Calif.: Rand Corporation (NBN), 2000.

Erskins, Toni. *Can Institutions Have Responsibilities: Collective Moral Agency and International Relations.*

Global Issues Series. Sydney, Australia: Palgrave Macmillan, 2004.

European Convention for the Protection of Human Rights

The European Convention for the Protection of Human Rights, which came into force on September 3, 1953, is based on the principles enshrined in the 1948 UNIVERSAL DECLARATION OF HUMAN RIGHTS. Parties to the convention, which had expanded to 44 by 2000, pledged to recognize the fundamental rights and freedoms of individuals in their jurisdiction. The convention guaranteed such basic freedoms as the right to enjoy liberty, a fair trial, the presumption of innocence, the right to DUE PROCESS, and no unlawful imprisonment. Three institutions were established to enforce the rights put forward in the convention: the European Court of Human Rights, the European Convention on Human Rights, and the Committee of Ministers of the Council of Europe (composed of foreign ministers of member states). Complaints can be submitted to the court by both legal entities and individuals residing in member states. That individuals are also allowed to appeal to the court represents a significant development in international law since other regional courts usually accept complaints only from member states or institutions. There is an important caveat, however: The European Court of Human Rights has jurisdiction over a case only if the defending state agrees. If, after an investigation, a complaint is found admissible, the court can seek a settlement between the alleged victim and the defending state. If a settlement cannot be achieved, the court can render a final judgment in compliance with guidelines set by the Committee of Ministers. Since the fall of the Berlin Wall in 1989, the court's caseload has increased enormously, with some 30,000 applications submitted annually.

Further Reading:
Fawcett, Louise L'Estrange, Andrew Hurrell, and Louise Fawcett. *Regionalism in World Politics: Regional Organization and International Order.* Oxford: Oxford University Press, 1996.

euthanasia program (Nazi)

Years before the mass exterminations of Jews, Rom (Gypsies), and other peoples labeled "subhuman" by the Nazis, Germany had already instituted a euthanasia program that in some way can be seen as a prelude to the atrocities that would follow. The Nazi mythology espoused an ideal of racial purity that had no room for people suffering from mental retardation, psychiatric illness, or genetic abnormalities. Under the slogan "National Socialism is the polit-

ical expression of our biological knowledge," the Nazi euthanasia program was responsible for putting to death some 500,000 people between 1933 and 1945. Rudolf HESS, Adolf HITLER's powerful deputy, stated that the foundation of Nazism rested on "applied biology."

Trying to "apply biology" by culling individuals with mental or genetic afflictions from a society did not originate with the Nazis. The eugenic movement had been gathering steam since the late 19th century; in England and elsewhere in Europe, eugenics was used as a justification for imperialist ambitions insofar as white Europeans, by virtue of their supposed intellectual and physical superiority, had the right—indeed, the obligation—to dominate "inferior" races of Africa and Asia. Eugenics enjoyed popularity even among leading biologists and other scientists in the United States. In the late 1920s, for example, some 16,000 sterilizations of people took place in two dozen states for the purpose of ensuring that people judged genetically unfit could not pass their genetic abnormalities to another generation. But no country had carried out the eugenics movement to its logical and murderous extreme until the Nazis initiated their policy shortly after coming to power in 1933.

The Nazis encouraged the study of racial difference as a legitimate subject for anthropological study. The belief took hold that an examination of skulls or physiognomy could reveal racial and ethnic characteristics; one German anthropologist even went so far as to steal 220 Jewish skeletons from a Viennese cemetery so he could analyze them. As Hitler was writing his memoir, *Mein Kampf,* he consulted a treatise that advanced this racial theory, entitled "Foundations of Human Genetics and Racial Hygiene." By 1942, 10 million Germans had taken part in a formal registry that sought to trace their genetic lineage.

The Nazis put several laws on the books calling for the application of a radical eugenics policy to create a so-called healthy people. One was called Law for the Prevention of Genetically Diseased Offspring. The Nazis took these laws seriously. What was called the T-4 Program was established by Hitler and operated under authority of Chief of the State Chancellery Philip Bouhler and Dr. KARL BRANDT. (The name came from the address of the Berlin office, Tiergartenstrasse 4.) It was designed to kill any German citizen who did not meet standards of racial purity, including the physically deformed, the handicapped, and the mentally disabled. Some 400,000 people were forcibly sterilized—a number representing 1 percent of the entire German population of reproductive age. More horrifyingly, pediatricians used drugs to kill 5,000 children who were considered "undesirable" because of their mental, physical, or genetic abnormalities. Six facilities in Germany and Austria were designated for "mercy deaths"; carbon monoxide gas was used to kill over 70,000 adults with various mental and physical disorders.

Initially an effort was made to apply the euthanasia program to Jews in an attempt to purge them from society. A public relations campaign was conducted to promote the sterilization of Jews, but when this method proved too cumbersome, the Nazis instituted the FINAL SOLUTION, the mass extermination of European Jewry in the CONCENTRATION CAMPS. Not all of these policies were carried out in the open, especially where non-Jewish Germans were involved. One secret program was code-named T-4, but efforts to keep it under wraps did not always succeed. In one instance, some 2,000 people were reported to have died of "natural causes" at one asylum in 40 days, even though the facility only had 100 beds. For many Germans, these macabre genetic experiments were so repellant that the Nazis were compelled to curtail their use on non-Jewish Germans.

See also MENGELE, JOSEF.

Further Reading:

Lagnado, Lucette Matalon, and Sheila Cohn Dekel. *Children of the Flames: Dr. Josef Mengele and the Untold Story of the Twins of Auschwitz*. New York: Penguin Books, 1992.

Roseman, Mark. *The Wannsee Conference and the Final Solution: A Reconsideration*. New York: Metropolitan Books, 2002.

Weindling, Paul Julian. *Nazi Medicine and the Nuremberg Trials: From Medical War Crimes to Informed Consent*. Sydney, Australia: Palgrave Macmillan, 2005.

extrajudicial killings

Extrajudicial killings are executions by police or security forces that take place without any legal authority. National and international law forbids the execution of individuals without a fair trial and the right to appeal a conviction. Humanitarian law, which covers crimes committed during armed conflict, outlaws "willful killing without judicial process." Under the Third Geneva Convention of 1929, combatants are prohibited from killing enemy PRISONERS OF WAR or others affiliated with an adversary, including civilian suppliers, contract workers, chaplains, and accompanying journalists. The Fourth Geneva Convention of 1949 prohibits the executions of enemy civilians as well.

Both enemy military personnel and civilians are entitled to DUE PROCESS: They have the right to mount a defense, the right to secure an attorney, the right against self-incrimination, and the right to appeal. By the same token, no ex post facto law can be enacted to criminalize an action that was not an offense at the time it was committed. Similar rights are enshrined in international law governing situations in which no armed conflict is taking place. In November 1998 the INTERNATIONAL CRIMINAL TRIBUNAL FOR THE FORMER YUGOSLAVIA issue a statement saying: "As it is prohibited to kill protected persons during an international armed conflict, so it is prohibited to kill those taking no active part in hostilities which constitute an internal armed conflict." In spite of these laws, extrajudicial killings continue to occur, especially in regional conflicts and in countries where central authority has broken down or is nonexistent.

As a form of state terror, extrajudicial execution has often been carried out by paramilitaries or death squads with ties to the government or the army. In many cases, the membership of the death squads overlaps with that of the armed forces. However, by outsourcing the killings and disappearances (which often precede the killings), governments have managed to avoid responsibility for the deaths and whereabouts of the bodies. For instance, death squads operated freely in Latin America during the 1970s in the DIRTY WARS, hunting down those deemed subversive, a loose classification that can include political dissidents, clerics, labor organizers, student activists, academics, and members of religious or ethnic minorities. Bodies of victims may be buried in mass graves or, as in the case in Argentina, flung into the sea. Extrajudicial killings still take place in many countries including Chechnya, Colombia, Haiti, Iran, Iraq, the Philippines, Sudan, and Thailand.

See also GENEVA CONVENTIONS; MASS GRAVES.

Further Reading:

Ball, Howard. *Prosecuting War Crimes and Genocide: The Twentieth-Century Experience*. Lawrence: University Press of Kansas, 1999.

Falk, Richard A. *Crimes of War: A legal, political-documentary, and psychological inquiry into the responsibility of leaders, citizens, and soldiers for criminal acts in wars*. New York: Random House, 1971.

Lewis, Paul H. *Guerrillas and Generals: The Dirty War in Argentina*. New York: Praeger, 2001.

Moyano, Maria. *Argentina's Lost Patrol: Armed Struggle, 1969–1979*. New Haven, Conn.: Yale University Press, 1995.

extraordinary rendition

Rendition usually refers to the extrajudicial transfer of wanted suspects from a foreign country to the United States for the purpose of answering criminal charges. Drug dealers, for instance, who have been abducted in Mexico and brought to the United States to face charges of smuggling drugs into the country are said to have been "rendered" to justice. Extraordinary rendition, on the other hand, is a transfer of terrorist suspects by U.S. intelligence agencies to other countries extrajudicially (without legal authority). According to former CIA director George Tenant, there were about 70 cases of rendition in which suspects were handed over to other nations for detention and interrogation from the mid-1990s until 2001. After the terrorist attacks of 9/11, however, the United States has relied on the practice even more and, as of early 2005, has turned over as many as 150 suspected terrorists to Egypt, Jordan, Saudi Arabia, and Syria, where they can be interrogated using methods outlawed under U.S. law and which are banned by the GENEVA CONVENTIONS and the United Nations CONVENTION AGAINST TORTURE. Human rights campaigners say this "is a system of TORTURE by proxy."

The authority to carry out renditions originates in a presidential directive first issued under the Clinton administration and renewed by the Bush administration. According to a U.S. Justice Department memo, rendition also allows the United States the ability to plausibly deny that any abused prisoner was ever in the custody of American authorities. International law forbids transferring a detainee to another country if there is a likelihood that that person will be subject to torture or other forms of mistreatment. According to former intelligence officials cited in a report in the *New York Times*, the CIA was holding about three dozen terrorist suspects in detention in various places around the world as of 2005 and had handed over "scores" of others extrajudicially to other countries. The practice drew so much attention in the media, however, that there were increasing calls for a congressional investigation. In February 2005 the Senate Intelligence Committee announced that it would conduct a formal inquiry. Meanwhile the CIA was beginning to rethink its role in taking custody of the terrorist suspects whom it was holding in secret sites around the world. The agency was concerned that the legal authority giving it the right to detain and transfer suspects was eroding. Nor was there any provision for the CIA to deal with a small number of aging detainees who no longer had any significant intelligence value. "No one has a plan for what to do with these guys," a former senior intelligence official said, "and the CIA has been left holding the bag."

Further Reading:
Danner, Mark. *Torture and Truth: America, Abu Ghraib, and the War on Terror.* New York: New York Review Books, 2004.
Hersh, Seymour M. *Chain of Command: The Road from 9/11 to Abu Ghraib.* New York: HarperCollins, 2004.

F

FARC *See* COLUMBIA, HUMAN RIGHTS VIOLATIONS IN.

Final Solution (Holocaust)

The Final Solution (*Entlösung* in German) refers to the Nazi policy of eliminating all Jews from Europe. The "solution" was seen as a way of resolving what was called the *Jewish Question,* a term that dates back to 19th-century Germany. At first the Nazi leadership had contemplated forced emigration of Jews from Europe to Palestine (then under British rule) or even to Madagascar. But early in World War II a decision was reached to physically annihilate all Jews living in the German Reich and all the territories it conquered as well as England. The policy called for the systematic slaughter of 11 million people altogether. If the war had not ended in 1945, the Nazis might have succeeded in reaching their goal; as it was, they managed to kill 6 million Jews in a matter of seven years—what history knows as the Holocaust.

Anti-Semitism was hardly unknown in Germany (or in other European nations for that matter). Jews had long been stigmatized as Christ-killers and devil worshippers, but never had hatred of the Jews manifested itself in such a lethal form prior to Adolf HITLER's ascent to power in 1933. Historians offer several explanations for why the Nazis were so obsessed with the idea of the eradication of Jews. To some degree, the source of the hatred lies in a belief that history can be seen as a struggle between races. In this scheme the Jews have long sought world domination, infiltrating the media and the banking system, and so they must be destroyed if the superior race—the Aryans—is to achieve its destiny. Jews were considered criminal and incorrigible, incapable of rehabilitation. Moreover, Hitler believed that Germany had lost the First World War because it had been betrayed and that Jews were responsible. The Jews became a scapegoat for all the problems that beset Germany after its defeat.

Historians divide into two basic camps—"intentionalists" and "functionalists"—to account for how the Final Solution came about. To the intentionalists, the extermination of the Jews had always been Hitler's intention even before his rise to power. In this view, even the invasion of the Soviet Union was integral to the success of the policy since it would allow the Germans to exterminate the millions of Jews there as well. Certainly some evidence can be adduced for this theory. In a letter written in 1919, Hitler declared that the Jewish problem would be solved by methodically depriving Jews of their privileges and rights and classifying them as foreigners. He concluded: "The final goal, however, must steadfastly remain the removal of the Jews altogether." In 1923 Hitler publicly repudiated the Jews in his book *Mein Kampf* (*My Struggle,* written in 1923); he compared Jews to "bacilli," calling them "our greatest evil," and warned the Jews that they would be destroyed if war did break out. Moves to isolate Jews from the commercial and political life of the German Reich had been underway for some time, and in November 1938 Jewish-owned businesses and synagogues were looted and Jews beaten in a pogrom (massacre) directed by the Nazis.

These actions, however, do not necessarily indicate that the annihilation of the Jews was an official policy prior to the beginning of the war. The functionalists contend that the GENOCIDE (a word coined in 1944 by a Jewish refugee) only became an approved policy when other solutions—such as DEPORTATIONS, for one—no longer appeared practical. In this view, the Final Solution was dictated in large part by logistical considerations. What is not disputed is that—whether it was planned all along or emerged out of particular circumstances—the Final Solution was the culmination of almost a decade of policies perpetrated by the Nazis to deprive Jews of their rights, privileges, and livelihoods, just as Hitler had advocated in the early 1920s.

It may never be possible to determine which side is correct, because little documentation exists to establish when the extermination of the Jews was adopted as official policy of the German Reich. Although an unprecedented effort and a mobilization of extraordinary resources would be required to carry out the murder of so many millions, the enterprise was still shrouded in secrecy. Hitler was still conscious of world opinion, and the Germans were remarkably successful at concealing the truth about the atrocities until nearly the end of the war. The extent of the atrocities was so unimaginable that even the accounts of survivors of the death camps were met with incredulity.

It should be noted that the Jews were by no means the only people who were targeted by the Nazis. Millions of people regarded as inferior or "undesirable," including Rom (Gypsies), Slavs, homosexuals, and the mentally and physically disabled, were subject to abominable treatment and killed in large numbers. (As many as 1.5 million Poles, 3.5 million Soviet PRISONERS OF WAR, and 200,000 Rom are believed to have been killed by the Nazis, either outright or by exposure and starvation.) Upon the conquest of the Soviet Union, for instance, the Nazis planned to treat the captive Slav population as serfs or, worse, as slave labor for the Reich. Those Slavs considered of superior stock would be removed to Germany to be raised as Aryans. The Jews, however, were the only group singled out for systematic annihilation. Other enemies of the state or the socially or political "undesirables" might be sent to CONCENTRATION CAMPS, but their families did not invariably share their fate. That was not the case with Jews: Infants and children were marked for death along with adults.

The first major step in implementing the Final Solution was an attempt to force Jews to emigrate out of Germany. The elimination of Jews from the German Reich would achieve two of Hitler's objectives: It would ensure the "racial purity" of the state, and it would create *Lebensraum* (living space) for German nationals of Aryan blood. To bring about the emigration of Jews, Hitler's regime passed legislation—the NUREMBERG LAWS of 1935—to strip away the rights of citizenship from Jews. Before this could occur, though, a system of classification of Jews had to be devised. A Jew was officially defined as any person with three Jewish grandparents; or a person with two Jewish grandparents who belonged to the Jewish community on September 15, 1935, or joined thereafter; or who was married to a Jew or Jewess on September 15, 1935, or married one thereafter; or who was the child of a marriage or extramarital liaison with a Jew on or after September 15, 1935. Individuals who were not classified as Jews but who had some Jewish blood were categorized as *mischlinge* (hybrids).

On the nights of November 9 and 10, 1938, a pogrom was launched against the Jews called Kristallnacht, or the Night of Broken Glass. The day after the pogrom—for which the victims were blamed by the press—Hermann GÖRING, second only to Hitler in the Nazi hierarchy, declared, "The Jewish question is to be summed up and coordinated once and for all and solved one way or another. . . . If the German Reich should in the future become involved in conflict abroad then it is obvious that we in Germany will first of all make sure of settling accounts with the Jews." Kristallnacht, in which 2,000 to 2,500 Jews lost their lives, marked the beginning of a systematic program to segregate German Jews by depriving them of their civil rights and access to many professions and educational institutions.

In a famous speech given to his generals before the German invasion of Poland (September 1, 1939), Hitler proclaimed, "Genghis Khan had millions of women and men killed by his own will and with a gay heart. History sees in him only a great state builder. . . . I have sent to the east . . . my 'Death's Head Units,' with the order to kill without mercy men, women and children of the Polish race or language. Only in such a way will we win the 'Lebensraum' that we need. Who, after all, talks nowadays of the extermination of the Armenians [ARMENIAN GENOCIDE]?"

Early conquests by the Germans brought ever-greater numbers of Jews under Nazi control, over 3 million in Poland alone. Initially a special agency was established within the GESTAPO to organize the Jewish populations in the occupied territories headed by Adolf EICHMANN. Jews were deprived of their rights and property and corralled into ghettos, but these steps were considered a temporary, not a permanent, solution to the Jewish Question. Although it is unclear whether genocide was official policy, massacres of Jews began shortly after Poland and large swaths of the Soviet Union fell to German forces. These executions were carried out by special mobile death squads known as EINSATZGRUPPEN, which relied on shooting and mobile gas vans to kill Jews and others rounded up in newly occupied areas. In a September 1939 memorandum to the Einsatzgruppen, Reinhard HEYDRICH, head of the German security service (SD), observed that a distinction must be made between "the final aim (which will require extended periods of time) and the stages leading to the fulfillment of this final aim (which will be carried out in short periods)." Within a period of 18 months, the Einsatzgruppen killed 1,300,000 Jews in occupied Poland and the Soviet Union, which was home to 2.1 million Jews.

These massacres still represented only another stage leading to "the final aim." There were many millions of Jews still remaining, including heavy concentrations in Lithuania, Latvia, and Estonia to the north and Hungary, Yugoslavia, Romania, Greece, and Bulgaria to the south. There were also significant Jewish populations in France, Norway, Denmark, Belgium, Luxembourg, and the Netherlands, all of which came under German domination. (Altogether 16 European territories were occupied by the Germans.) Poland, because it contained the largest population of Jews in Europe, presented a special problem. Using machine guns or mobile gas vans was not considered efficient enough to exterminate such a large number of people with the rapidity demanded by Berlin. Moreover, the executioners were becoming demoralized by shooting women and children at such close range. Mobile gas vans suffered from leaks and could not kill people at the desired rate. It was a problem that would only be solved by a greater reliance on—and a greater number of—concentration camps. These were not a new phenomenon. Dachau, the oldest concentration camp, had been in operation in Germany since 1933. But for the most part these camps were used to hold criminals, homosexuals, mental patients, forced laborers, war prisoners, journalists, uncooperative industrialists, and political prisoners (mostly Communists and Social Democrats). It was only much later that these camps were specially constructed to gas and dispose of the remains of tens of thousands of people.

If there is any event that can be cited as the "official" initiation of the Final Solution, it occurred in January 1942 when 15 SS officials met in a Berlin suburb called Wannsee to determine how the Jewish Question would be settled once and for all. New gassing facilities were built in three concentration camps in Poland: Bełzec Sobibór, and Treblinka. In a period of five months—March through July 1942—750,000–950,000 Jews were killed at Treblinka, 500,000–600,000 at Bełzec, and about 200,000 at Sobibór. Two additional camps were built near Auschwitz (Oświęcim in Polish): Auschwitz I (the smaller of the two) and Auschwitz II (otherwise known as Birkenau.) Nearly 1 million Jews perished at Birkenau of gassing, starvation, or disease.

Within a short time, Jews from all over Europe were being sent to the death camps. As planned, the killings could proceed with far more efficiency. In Birkenau, for instance, 2,000 people at a time could be killed in the gas chambers, in contrast to the 30 who could be exterminated using mobile gas vans. The true horror and magnitude of the genocide—subsequently called the Holocaust—only became known to the world after the camps were liberated in 1945 by the Allies and Soviet forces. That millions of people could be deliberately targeted and their extermination carefully planned and systematically carried out on such a scale caused worldwide revulsion and demands for justice. One of the most important legacies of the Holocaust was the Nuremberg Tribunal, established to try the perpetrators of the genocide for their crimes. In addition, there was a growing recognition that INTERNATIONAL HUMANITARIAN LAW would need to be revised and its protections strengthened so that similar atrocities could be avoided. The Fourth Geneva Convention of 1949 was an outgrowth of this sentiment. However, as the genocidal campaigns in such countries as Cambodia, Bosnia, and Rwanda have shown, the Holocaust was not the aberration it had seemed at the time.

See also BABI YAR; CAMBODIA, WAR CRIMES IN; GENEVA CONVENTIONS; NUREMBERG TRIALS; RWANDA, GENOCIDE IN; WANNSEE CONFERENCE; WIESENTHAL, SIMON.

Further Reading:

Bloxham, Donald. *Genocide on Trial: War Crimes Trials and the Formation of Holocaust History and Memory.* Oxford: Oxford University Press, 2003.

Dawidowicz, Lucy. *A Holocaust Reader.* Library of Jewish Studies. Chicago: Behrman House Publishing, 1976.

Dwork, Deborah, and Robert Jan Van Pelt. *Holocaust: A History.* New York: W. W. Norton & Company, 2003.

Gilbert, Martin. *The Holocaust: A History of the Jews of Europe during the Second World War.* New York: Owl Books, 1987.

Lagnado, Lucette Matalon, and Sheila Cohn Dekel. *Children of the Flames: Dr. Josef Mengele and the Untold Story of the Twins of Auschwitz.* New York: Penguin Books, 1992.

Overbey, Fern. *The Dachau Defendants: Life Stories from Testimony and Documents of the War Crimes Prosecutions.* Jefferson, N.C.: McFarland & Company, 2004.

Roseman, Mark. *The Wannsee Conference and the Final Solution: A Reconsideration.* New York: Metropolitan Books, 2002.

Wistrich, Robert S. *Hitler and the Holocaust.* Modern Library Chronicles. New York: Modern Library, 2001.

Finta, Imre (1907–1997) *Hungarian fascist leader*

Imre Finta would have remained an obscure figure if it were not for a 1994 Canadian Supreme Court decision on war crime charges based on his actions during World War II. As a commander of the Hungarian Gendarmerie (which collaborated with the German occupiers), Finta was charged with four counts: robbery, unlawful confinement, kidnapping, and manslaughter in connection with the forced DEPORTATIONS of 8,617 Hungarian Jews from the provincial town of Szeged. Most of the Jews were loaded onto sealed trains and sent to Auschwitz; many died en route. In 1948 Finta was convicted in absentia of "crimes against the people" by a Hungarian court, but he succeeded in emigrating to Canada three years later. He became a Canadian citizen in 1956, and for many years he operated a Hungarian restaurant in Toronto, a short distance from a local Jewish Community Center.

After a trial in 1994 lasting nine months the jury acquitted Finta of all charges. The Crown appealed, but on March 24, 1994, in a 4-3 decision, the Supreme Court of Canada upheld the acquittal. In its ruling the court stated that an accused must not only be shown to have the requisite mens rea (criminal intent) to commit a criminal act, such as murder or kidnapping, but must also realize the act is part of a war crime. The court seemed to be suggesting that he was able to escape responsibility because he was only following orders, a rationale specifically rejected by the NUREMBERG TRIALS. Many legal scholars, though, were critical of the Supreme Court's ruling, saying that it had set the bar so high that it would make it practically impossible to prosecute other Nazi war criminals who had taken up residence in Canada. Leo Adler, director of national affairs for the Simon Wiesenthal Centre, predicted that the court's decision in the Finta case would in effect put an end to war crimes prosecutions in Canada altogether. Finta died in 1997 at the age of 90.

forced labor

Forced labor is similar to SLAVERY in that it entails the loss of freedom, but it is different in that there is no claim of ownership in forced labor. To those people who are compelled to work without pay or have no ability to escape, the distinction is irrelevant. Although INTERNATIONAL HUMANITARIAN LAW limits the use of forced labor by states—it is a punishment employed in prisons—it does not ban the practice completely. However, its use by individuals or organizations not under state authority is outlawed completely. Forced labor is often used in internal wars where belligerents frequently conscript civilians—very often children and teenagers—to work as laborers, prostitutes, or combatants. In some cases, these conscripts are forced to march ahead of the main force, turning them into cannon fodder.

Perhaps in no other country was the practice of forced labor so pervasive and regulated as in the former Soviet Union, where an elaborate system of forced-labor camps was established within a few years of the Communists coming to power. Forced labor under brutal conditions was used by the government, especially during Joseph STALIN's rule, to build massive engineering projects, including dams and canals. Hundreds of thousands of people perished from abuse, malnutrition, and exposure. As the Soviet empire expanded, so did the number of labor camps, until by 1952 the International League for the Rights of Man determined that there were over 400 forced-labor camps in communist countries in central and eastern Europe.

Forced labor was also widely used by the Nazis before and during the Second World War. Jews were singled out in particular for forced-labor camps in Poland. While work conditions in the labor camps were abominable, forced labor was a far preferable alternative to being deported to CONCENTRATION CAMPS to be put to death. At least forced labor offered the prospect, however dim, of survival. Forced labor was crucial to keeping the German wartime economy going, and as Germany suffered ever more serious reverses on the battlefield, the industrial machine relied increasingly on prisoners to run industrial plants. Auschwitz in Poland and Buchenwald in Germany were turned into the centers of vast networks of forced-labor camps. Private companies such as Messerschmidt, Junkers, Siemens, and I.G. Farben contracted with the Nazis to use forced laborers. For example, Auschwitz III, otherwise known as Monowitz, supplied prisoners to I.G. Farben to work in a synthetic rubber plant until they expired from exhaustion.

More recently, forced labor was used by all the belligerents taking part in the wars in the former Yugoslavia of 1993–96. Bosnian Muslim men who came under the control of Serbian military forces were forced to work in factories and mines or dispatched to the front lines. The use of forced labor continues today in Myanmar (Burma), where the practice is prevalent in the strife-ridden eastern part of the country.

Since World War II there has been a concerted effort to curb forced labor. ARTICLE 3 COMMON TO THE GENEVA CONVENTIONS, which covers internal conflicts, obliges states to treat civilians not involved in combat in a humane manner, which many analysts believe limits the use of forced labor by implication. The Fourth Geneva Convention of 1949 prohibits the use of conscripted labor by an OCCUPYING POWER, nor can individuals be made to do certain types of war-related work—manufacture of munitions, for instance—and forbids the use of child laborers altogether, defined as younger than 18. The Fourth Convention also bans enforced prostitution. Similar prohibitions against the use of PRISONERS OF WAR in forced labor are found in the Third Geneva Convention of 1929, which stipulates, among other things, that prisoners must be paid a wage (with the exception of routine maintenance work on the facility where they are detained) and cannot be made to work in conditions that are unhealthy or degrading. If civilians fall under military occupation as a result of either wars between nations or internal conflicts, they cannot be compelled to work longer hours or under inhumane conditions. There is an exception in wartime, when it is permissible to employ civilian internees who are ordinarily employed in the health field, administration, food delivery, or civil defense, or other work that benefits other internees.

According to Convention 29 of the INTERNATIONAL LABOR ORGANIZATION (ILO), a UN body, forced labor, if practiced, is limited to able-bodied males 18–45 years old and to those whose work will not adversely affect their family or community. ILO Convention 105 bans the use of forced labor as a punishment for political expression. This prohibition is reaffirmed in the UN INTERNATIONAL COVENANT ON CIVIL AND POLITICAL RIGHTS. According to John Ryle in an essay written for the CRIMES OF WAR PROJECT, there are limits on the applicability of these conventions; forced labor can, for instance, be used in emergencies, which includes war. Even so, he writes, these conventions have proven effective because they draw attention to the use of forced labor in countries such as Myanmar (Burma). Signatories are obliged to regularly submit reports about labor conditions in their countries, and if they are found to be in violation, they may face embargos on exports produced by a conscripted labor force.

See also GENEVA CONVENTIONS; MYANMAR, HUMAN RIGHTS VIOLATIONS IN; YUGOSLAVIA, WAR CRIMES IN.

Further Reading:

Gutman, Roy, ed. *Crimes of War: What the Public Should Know.* New York: W. W. Norton & Company, 1999.
Solzhenitsyn, Aleksandr. *The Gulag Archipelago.* New York: HarperCollins, 1978.

forensic medicine and human rights

Forensic medicine has become a vital tool in the detection and recording of gross abuses of human rights, especially GENOCIDE, murder, forced DISAPPEARANCES, and TORTURE. Before it is possible to prosecute a crime, it is first necessary to ascertain that a crime has been committed. In conflicts where the victims have been disappeared, such as the "dirty wars" of Latin America in the 1970s, or who have been killed and interred in unmarked or mass graves, evidence of crime is often difficult to come by. It is the job of pathologists and forensic anthropologists to recover and identify the remains of people and to determine the cause of death if possible. (Forensic anthropology is also concerned with people who die as a result of natural and human-made disasters, not just political violence.)

Over the last 30 years, governmental and nongovernmental organizations (NGOs) have become actively involved in carrying out forensic investigations, relying on the assistance of forensic pathologists, physicians, police, lawyers, and other experts. The use of forensic anthropology in human rights investigations can be traced back to the DOCTORS' TRIAL at Nuremberg in which the defendants—Nazi doctors in the SS—were found guilty of conducting horrific human experiments on concentration-camp inmates. A British army pathologist, Professor Keith Mant, was responsible for obtaining much of the forensic evidence used in the trial. But the application of forensic medicine to human rights cases didn't come into its own until the early 1980s, when the American Association for the Advancement of Science organized a team of forensic pathologists, forensic anthropologists, and others in 1984–85 to assist with the exhumation and identification of people who had disappeared under the military junta in Argentina between 1976 and 1983.

Beginning in 1984, Argentina became one of the first countries to initiate investigations that would lead to exhuming the remains of large numbers of disappeared people, identifying them and establishing the cause of death. Similar expeditions, many under the auspices of the U.S.-based PHYSICIANS FOR HUMAN RIGHTS, were carried out in many other parts of the world where atrocities had occurred and been covered up. Argentina's example was followed by Chile, El Salvador, Guatemala, Ethiopia, Rwanda, South Africa, and later Croatia, Bosnia and Kosovo, where forensic investigations were still continuing in 2004. Forensic expertise is now in great demand to provide evidence in cases being heard before the INTERNATIONAL CRIMINAL TRIBUNAL FOR THE FORMER YUGOSLAVIA and the INTERNATIONAL CRIMINAL TRIBUNAL FOR RWANDA.

What makes such forensic investigations so difficult in many instances is that when a person has died as a result of a disaster—a plane crash, for instance—it is the governing authority that takes responsibility for finding the remains and ascertaining the cause of death. But in instances of political violence, the government itself is often responsible for the murders and thus will have no interest in having the bodies of the victims exhumed and its role in the deaths exposed. In a high proportion of cases, the bodies of the disappeared are either hidden or destroyed. Many investigations have proceeded only after regimes have changed, as happened in Latin America and in the former Yugoslavia. Pressure from families of the victims who insist on an accounting have also moved these investigations forward. The United Nations has also undertaken investigations in connection with peace accords negotiated between governments and insurgent movements involved in internal conflicts.

Whether it is preferable to use the results of these investigations to open cases against the perpetrators or to simply resolve the uncertainty of families usually depends on the circumstances. Nor can answers as to questions of identity or causes of death always be determined definitively. These problems are compounded when the victims are poor, as they most often are. Dental records, for instance, are frequently used to identify remains, but impoverished peasants are rarely seen by dentists. And while it is indisputable that the use of DNA evidence has revolutionized the legal system, it is difficult to extract DNA from remains that consist mostly of bones. Additionally, there are few laboratories with the capacity to process large quantities of samples, and there are costs involved that many countries cannot afford. These limitations lead to situations in which unidentified bodies are exhumed and then stored indefinitely because the resources are unavailable to conduct further investigation.

See also ARGENTINA, HUMAN RIGHTS VIOLATIONS IN.

Further Reading:

Cox, Margaret, and Jon Sterenberg. *Forensic Archaeology, Anthropology and the Investigation of Mass Graves.* London: CRC Press, 2006.

Ferllini, Timms, Roxana. *Silent Witness: How Forensic Anthropology Is Used to Solve the World's Toughest Crimes.* Buffalo, N.Y.: Firefly Books Ltd, 2002.

Frank, Hans (1900–1946) *Nazi governor-general of occupied Poland*

As the Nazi-appointed governor-general of occupied Poland, Hans Frank was responsible for the execution of Poland's elite, intellectuals, and clergy as well as the enslavement of hundreds of thousands of Polish workers. Under his rule, Poland became for all practical purposes a slave state. He also took charge of the DEPORTATIONS of most of the 3.5 million Jews then living in Poland, sending them to certain death in CONCENTRATION CAMPS. After the war he was found guilty of war crimes at the NUREMBERG TRIALS and executed.

Born in 1900, Frank started out studying economics but would later turn to law. A veteran of World War I, which had inflicted a disastrous defeat on Germany, Frank joined the German Workers' Party, or NSDAP (the precursor of the Nazi Party), in 1921 and took part in Adolf HITLER's famous Beer Hall Putsch of November 1923, in which he attempted unsuccessfully to seize power in the state of Bavaria. He quickly rose in the party ranks, assuming the role of chief legal counsel and becoming Hitler's personal lawyer. In 1933, after becoming chancellor, Hitler appointed Frank as minister of justice in Bavaria. Once Poland fell to German forces in 1939, Frank was sent to Warsaw to take control of the country's civil administration. He would remain governor-general of Poland until the end of the war.

In his new position, Frank proved himself a loyal Nazi ideologue, ordering the execution of hundreds of thousands of Poles and the confiscation of their property. Although he was in charge of rounding up and deporting Jews to the death camps, he claimed not to know the fate that awaited them since the camps were under the authority of Heinrich HIMMLER, who headed the SS. Frank would later contend that he had raised the issue of the Holocaust with Himmler in 1944, close to the end of the war, but that Himmler had claimed not to know about it, either. (However, Frank's assertions of ignorance, which he later made to the judges sitting on the Nuremberg Tribunal, fall flat when weighed against his own statements. In a speech he gave on December 16, 1941, for instance, he spoke about the Polish Jews who had come under his authority in emphatic terms. "We cannot shoot these 3.5 million Jews," he said, "we cannot poison them, but we will take measures that will somehow lead to successful destruction; and this in connection with large-scale procedures which are to be discussed in the Reich, the Government-General must become as free of Jews as the Reich. . . . We must destroy the Jews wherever we find them and wherever it is at all possible, in order to maintain the whole structure of the Reich . . ." In another statement, he put it even more bluntly: "We must destroy the Jews wherever we find them . . ."

Frank was captured by U.S. Army troops on May 4, 1945. A year later he was indicted for trial before the International Military Tribunal at Nuremberg on charges of war crimes and CRIMES AGAINST HUMANITY. Unlike many of the other high-ranking Nazi officials who stood trial, he seemed genuinely remorseful, perhaps because he had become a recent convert to Catholicism. "I myself have never installed an extermination camp for Jews, or promoted the existence of such camps," he testified, "but if Adolf Hitler personally has laid that dreadful responsibility on his people, then it is mine too, for we have fought against Jewry for years; and we have indulged in the most horrible utterances." At his trial he also made a famous prediction: "A thousand years will pass and the guilt of Germany will not be erased." His show of repentance did not win him a mitigation of his sentence. He was found guilty and sentenced to death. He was hanged on October 1, 1946. According to witnesses, Frank was the only Nazi war criminal condemned to death who entered the execution chamber with a smile on his face. When asked if he had any last words, he said in a near whisper: "I ask God to accept me with mercy."

Further Reading:

Bloxham, Donald. *Genocide on Trial: War Crimes Trials and the Formation of Holocaust History and Memory.* Oxford: Oxford University Press, 2003.

Dawidowicz, Lucy. *A Holocaust Reader.* Library of Jewish Studies. Chicago: Behrman House Publishing, 1976.

Dwork, Deborah, and Robert Jan Van Pelt. *Holocaust: A History.* New York: W. W. Norton & Company, 2003.

Gilbert, Martin. *The Holocaust: A History of the Jews of Europe during the Second World War.* New York: Owl Books, 1987.

FRAPH   *See* HAITI, HUMAN RIGHTS VIOLATIONS IN.

Freedom House

Freedom House was established in 1941 by Eleanor Roosevelt, Wendell Willkie, and other prominent Americans to promote democratic values and expose human rights abuses by dictatorships around the world. A nonprofit and nonpartisan institution, Freedom House has taken an active part in various campaigns on behalf of the Vietnam boat people in the 1970s, Poland's Solidarity movement, and the Filipino democratic opposition in the 1980s, among other causes. At the same time, Freedom House has mounted vigorous protest campaigns against despotism in the Americas, the former APARTHEID regime in South Africa, the Soviet invasions of Czechoslovakia in 1968 and Afghanistan in 1979, GENOCIDE in Bosnia and Rwanda, and human rights abuses in such countries as Cuba, Myanmar (Burma), China, and Iraq. In its mission statement, Freedom House declares that it is "a leading advocate of the world's young democracies, which are coping with the debilitating legacy of statism, dictatorship and political repression."

free-fire zones

A free-fire zone, according to the *American Heritage Dictionary*, is defined as a "battle area or combat zone in which no restrictions are placed on the use of arms or explosives." The world first became aware of free-fire zones in the Vietnam War when they were established in certain areas heavily infiltrated by Vietcong guerrillas. However, many hamlets and villages fell within these zones, where Vietcong sought to camouflage themselves among the local populace. U.S. forces were at an added disadvantage in that they frequently had difficulty distinguishing between innocent villagers and enemy combatants. Both guerrillas and civilians wore the same black pajama-like clothes.

The institution of free-fire zones, however, contravenes INTERNATIONAL HUMANITARIAN LAW, which limits belligerents to targeting enemy military forces and installations. Civilians are never to be attacked under any circumstances, although there is an exception if civilians are injured or killed because they happen to be close to a military target when an attack takes place. The U.S. Department of Defense tried to get around this requirement by putting out a warning to civilians in advance, advising them to evacuate before a strike; otherwise they would face the consequences. According to Lewis M. Simons, a former war correspondent, the stipulation against an attack on civilians is absolute and cannot be modified by simply issuing a warning. "The rule prohibiting direct attacks on civilians provides no basis for a party to a conflict to shift the burden by declaring a whole zone to be 'civilian free,'" he wrote in an essay for the CRIMES OF WAR PROJECT. Moreover, he says, establishing a free-fire zone—with or without warnings to civilians—is a violation of laws forbidding an indiscriminate attack against civilians. That prohibition applies even though enemy combatants might be hiding among the civilian population. According to the GENEVA CONVENTIONS, civilians lose their immunity only if they take "a direct part in hostilities."

The existence of free-fire zones in Vietnam drew so much international opprobrium that the Pentagon began to add new restrictions—for instance, only after civilians had been removed from a known communist village could the village be declared a free-fire zone and attacked. Many of these rules, however, were either ignored by the U.S. military or else the warnings they sent were ineffective because illiterate peasants were unable to comprehend leaflets dropped from the air warning them that they were about to be bombed or shelled. By the end of the 1960s, the term *free-fire zone* had vanished from the U.S. military lexicon, indicating that the Pentagon recognized how difficult it was to justify the necessity for using such tactics in future conflicts.

See also CIVILIAN IMMUNITY; VIETNAM, HUMAN RIGHTS VIOLATIONS IN.

Further Reading:
Gutman, Roy, ed. *Crimes of War: What the Public Should Know.* New York: W. W. Norton & Company, 1999.

Frick, Wilhelm (1877–1946) *Nazi administrator*

Wilhelm Frick has been described as "the administrative brain" of the Nazi Party both because of his organizational skills and because of his role in preparing Germany to undertake aggressive war. Born in Germany in 1877, he served as a police officer in Munich before gravitating to the National Socialist German Workers' Party (NSDAP), the precursor of the Nazi Party. He was one of the participants in the Beer Hall Putsch led by Adolf HITLER in November 1923, on abortive coup to take power in Bavaria, for which he was sentenced to a year in prison. In 1924, as a free man, he won a seat in the Reichstag, the national parliament, and subsequently was appointed as minister of the interior in the state of Thuringia, becoming the first Nazi Party official to reach high office.

Upon assuming power as chancellor in 1933, Hitler tapped Frick as his government's minister of the interior. Within a short time, Frick signed no fewer than 235 laws and decrees, including laws that abolished all opposition parties as well as the infamous NUREMBERG LAWS, which restricted the freedom and rights of German Jews. A rabid anti-Semitic, Frick was instrumental in establishing the legal basis to exclude Jews from the political and economic life of the country; it was he who made the decision requiring Jews to wear a yellow star. Jews were prohibited from practicing various professions such as law and medicine, and they were obliged to forfeit their property to the Reich. In 1943 he signed a decree placing Jews "outside the law" and assigned responsibility for them to the GESTAPO. These laws were intended to advance the objectives of the FINAL SOLUTION in annexed and several occupied territories.

Frick is credited with creating the German Reich's first uniformed police system and appointed the Gestapo chief, Heinrich HIMMLER, to run the police as well. He signed the law that annexed Austria to the Reich, and later signed the laws incorporating other areas into the Reich, including the Sudetenland, Memel, Danzig, the Eastern territories (West Prussia and Posen), Eupen, Malmedy, and Moresnot. Once the territories were annexed, Frick took responsibility for conferring German citizenship and applying Nazi laws in them as well.

As minister of the interior, Frick held authority over the CONCENTRATION CAMPS and tended to such bureaucratic tasks as ensuring the legal acquisition of the land that would be used for Auschwitz. He also exercised control over asylums, nursing homes, and medical institutions where thousands of Germans and foreign laborers were subject to TORTURE and forced sterilizations. Euthanasia was systematically employed on the mentally ill, sick, and elderly, who were derided as "useless eaters." It is estimated that some 275,000 people were killed in institutions under Frick's jurisdiction. As the war went on, though, he became involved in a power struggle with Himmler and in the process lost his position as interior minister. As compensation, Hitler made him the "protector" of Bohemia and Moravia, a position he held until the end of the war. In his new position, he oversaw the transfer of thousands of Jews from the Terezin ghetto in Czechoslovakia to Auschwitz, where they were put to death.

After the war, Frick was indicted for war crimes, crimes against peace, and CRIMES AGAINST HUMANITY at the NUREMBERG TRIALS. The indictment against Frick stated that he was largely responsible for the legislation suppressing the trade unions, the church, and the Jews, tasks that he performed with "ruthless efficiency." From testimony provided by witnesses, the tribunal determined that Frick was aware of the atrocities that were going on in the concentration camps as well as in the occupied territories. "Frick knew full well what the Nazi policies of occupation were in Europe, particularly with respect to Jews, at that time," the tribunal said, "and by accepting the office of Reich Protector he assumed responsibility for carrying out those policies in Bohemia and Moravia." During his trial, Frick contended that he had never meant for the Nuremberg Laws to be used as an instrument of mass murder, though in fact they were. Found guilty on three of four counts against him, Frick was sentenced to hang. He was executed on October 1, 1946.

See also EUTHANASIA PROGRAM.

Further Reading:
Bloxham, Donald. *Genocide on Trial: War Crimes Trials and the Formation of Holocaust History and Memory.* Oxford: Oxford University Press, 2003.
Buscher, Frank M. *The U.S. War Crimes Trial Program in Germany, 1946–1955.* Contributions in Military Studies. Westport, Conn.: Greenwood Press, 1989.
Dawidowicz, Lucy. *A Holocaust Reader.* Library of Jewish Studies. Chicago: Behrman House Publishing, 1976.
Dwork, Deborah, and Robert Jan Van Pelt. *Holocaust: A History.* New York: W. W. Norton & Company, 2003.
Russell of Liverpool, Edward Frederick Langley Russell, Baron. *The Scourge of the Swastika: A Short History of Nazi War Crimes.* London: Greenhill Books/Lionel Leventhal, 2002.

Fritzsche, Hans (1900–1953) *Nazi propagandist*
Hans Fritzsche was head of the Wireless News Service (Drahtloser Dienst), an agency of the Reich government, which was subsequently incorporated into the Reich Ministry for People's Enlightenment and Propaganda under Joseph GOEBBELS. He was born in Bochum in the industrial Ruhr valley and served in the German army at the end of World War I. After a brief foray into academia, he turned to journalism, becoming a correspondent for the *Hamburg Press.* He found a more promising opportunity in a new medium—radio—and went on to become head of the Drahtloser Dienst. (The use of this relatively new medium for propaganda purposes was only beginning to come into its own.) In May 1933 he joined the staff of the Reich Ministry for People's Enlightenment and Propaganda, serving first as chief of the Home Press Division and later as the head of the radio division, until the Nazi collapse in spring 1945.

Fritzsche was captured by the Red Army within days of its taking Berlin. At the NUREMBERG TRIALS he was charged with conspiracy to commit crimes against peace, war crimes, and CRIMES AGAINST HUMANITY, but the judges found that the accusations were not supported by the evidence. Fritzsche was one of only three defendants who stood trial before the Nuremberg Tribunal to be acquitted. However, he did not escape prison. Rearrested almost immediately upon his release, he was tried by the West German government for a variety of crimes, found guilty, and sentenced to nine years of hard labor. His sentence was reduced, and he was freed in 1950, but he had only a brief time to enjoy his freedom: He died of cancer three years later.

Fujimori, Alberto (1938–) *president of Peru*
Alberto Fujimori was an obscure agronomist when he became president of Peru in 1990. Initially hailed for resuscitating the country's economy and stamping out terrorism, he was later driven into exile, charged with corruption and numerous human rights violations.

Born in Lima, Peru's capital, in 1938, Fujimori was the son of Japanese immigrants. There was little about his background to indicate a future in politics. He was a dean of the faculty of sciences at the Agrarian National University and host of a popular TV show called *Getting Together.* He was able to translate his media success to politics, founding a political party, Cambio 90, which he promoted with the slogan "honesty, technology and work." That same year, 1990, he scored a surprising electoral victory by winning the presidency and defeating a much better-known opponent, the distinguished novelist Mario Vargas Llosa.

Fujimori came into office as Peru teetered on the brink of economic collapse. In addition, the country was bedeviled by corruption, mismanagement, narcotics trafficking, and two guerrilla insurgencies: Sendero Luminoso (SHINING PATH) and Tupac Amaru. Fujimori went to work on the economy, implementing free-market reforms that included privatizing state-owned companies and ending state subsidies—shock therapy to a nation long accustomed to a semisocialist economy. His reforms produced results almost at once: Within a year, he had succeeded in reducing the annual inflation rate from a whooping 7,650 percent to a more tolerable 139 percent. (By the time he left office in 2000, the annual inflation rate had fallen to a mere 3.7 percent.)

Fujimori then turned his attention to the two radical guerrilla groups terrorizing much of the countryside. Of the two, the Shining Path was by far the more dangerous and insidious. For years its mysterious founder, Abimael Guzmán, had managed to elude capture. In 1992, as the security situation deteriorated further, Fujimori engineered a coup: Since he lacked a majority in Congress, he simply dissolved the legislative body and suspended the constitution, justifying his actions as necessary to fight corruption, rein in the drug traffickers, and crush terrorism. As an added precaution, he fired 13 of 23 Supreme Court justices as well as several judges in lower courts. At first it appeared as if his gamble had paid off. In a surprise raid on a Lima hideout, police finally caught up with the elusive terrorist leader.

Guzmán's arrest dealt a blow to the Shining Path from which the movement would never recover, but the government's victory had come at a steep price. The justice system had become deformed, human rights violations had become more egregious and more frequent, and abusers went largely unpunished. There was little protest from the press, since the media knuckled under to government pressure. Nonetheless, Fujimori was more popular than ever; his strong-arm tactics seemed to be having their desired effect, after all. An abortive coup only succeeded in strengthening his hand and gave his party enough of a boost to win a majority in Congress.

Now Fujimori had a compliant legislature to pass the laws he wanted as he take the credit for reopening

Congress. In 1995 he ran for and won the presidency by an overwhelming majority. In a bizarre twist, Fujimori's estranged wife Susan had been prepared to oppose him but was prevented from doing so when her husband had the constitution rewritten so that she was not permitted to run. Voters said they were willing to overlook his authoritarian proclivities (and his marital problems) because of the success he had achieved in putting an end to the threat of guerrillas and the scourge of hyperinflation.

But the guerrilla threat had not been eliminated entirely. On December 17, 1996, 14 members of the Tupac Amaru movement staged a spectacular raid on the official residence of the Japanese ambassador, who was giving a party in honor of the emperor's birthday at the time. The guerrillas seized the residence and took 452 guests hostage, including Fujimori's brother, the foreign minister, the agriculture minister, and the Japanese ambassador. Fujimori adamantly rebuffed demands to free Tupac Amaru prisoners in exchange for the release of the hostages. After months of negotiations, he ordered his security forces to retake the residence. Of the 72 hostages still being held, all but one survived the raid, while all the guerrillas were killed. Predictably, Fujimori's poll ratings soared in response. He decided to run for an unprecedented third term based on his novel reinterpretation of the constitution, which limited the presidency to two terms. This prompted a surge of protests, and when the constitutional court begged to differ, Fujimori replaced three judges with ones who would rule in his favor. Fujimori's support began to wane, and in the weeks before the voting it looked as if his opponent, Alejandro Toledo, a former World Bank economist, would win. Nonetheless, Fujimori came out ahead amid claims of fraud and sharp criticism from Washington and the ORGANIZATION OF AMERICAN STATES (OAS). Officially, though, the president had not received 50 percent of the vote, meaning that a second vote would have to be held two months later. But Toledo, convinced that the election was rigged, dropped out, ensuring Fujimori's victory.

Throughout Fujimori's tenure, the National Intelligence Service, known by its chilling acronym SIN (Servicio de Inteligencia Nacional), was increasing its power, becoming in effect a clandestine government under Fujimori's security adviser, Vladimiro MONTESINOS. A Rasputin-like figure, Montesinos was a cashiered army captain who operated a spy network and engaged in money laundering while trafficking in arms and drugs on the side. There are credible reports that he also had ties to a notorious death squad. In September 2000 a video, obtained under mysterious circumstances, was broadcast that showed Montesinos handing a bribe to a congressman to influence his vote. The public reacted with outrage as it soon became apparent that Montesinos had made 1,000 such compromising tapes. In a desperate effort to distance himself from his spy chief, Fujimori announced that he was dissolving SIN, but this was not enough to placate the public. Soon more unsavory revelations began to pour out about money laundering, secret Swiss bank accounts, and deals with drug barons. Fujimori ordered Montesinos's arrest. Montesinos went into hiding but was finally caught in Venezuela in 2001 and extradited to stand trial in Peru.

However, by this time Fujimori himself had become engulfed in the scandal. Previously allegations had surfaced that the notorious Colombian cocaine trafficker Pablo Escobar had contributed a million dollars to Fujimori's first election campaign in exchange for allowing drug shipments to pass unimpeded through Peru. In November 2000 Fujimori arrived unexpectedly in Japan after attending an economic conference. He then tendered his resignation to the Peruvian Congress—by fax—but the legislators decided to sack him rather than accept it. Congress then filed criminal charges against him for abandoning office and dereliction of duty. At the same time, prosecutors investigating Montesinos began to look into allegations that Fujimori, too, was implicated in money laundering. Old cases were reopened—one of them an incident that had been seen at the time as among Fujimori's greatest triumphs. In 2002 a Peruvian judge ordered the arrest of 12 army officers involved in lifting the siege at the Japanese ambassador's residence in 1997 on the grounds that they had summarily executed the hostage takers. Peruvian authorities also decided to charge Fujimori with treason in connection with the sale of obsolete fighter planes to Ecuador in 1996, only a year after the two countries had gone to war over a border dispute.

In March 2003 Interpol issued an international arrest warrant for Fujimori, but there was little likelihood that he would ever be returned to Peru to stand trial. Because his parents were both Japanese, Fujimori was entitled to Japanese citizenship, and Japan had no extradition treaty with Peru. In an interview, his daughter placed the blame for her father's fate on Montesinos, who is now serving an eight-year sentence in a Peruvian prison. Fujimori's greatest error, she said, "was not realizing the magnitude of the problem caused by Dr. Montesinos' presence." Fujimori continues to insist on his innocence and claims that he had made "a small fortune" not from money laundering but from a Christmas tree farm he owned and the money he receives for giving lectures. He has told the press that he can return to Peru and revive its ailing economy just as he did while he was president. "I want to go back to Peru and put it back on the right path," he has said. "There's nothing to stop me legally, politically or ethically from becoming president again." In a survey taken in March 2003, a survey showed that in spite of all the allegations swirling around Fujimori, the public gave his administration a 41 percent approval rating—nearly four times that of his successor, President Alejandro Toledo.

Further Reading:

Gorriti Ellenbogen, Gustavo. *The Shining Path: A History of the Millenarian War in Peru.* Translated by Robin Kirk. Latin America in Translation. Chapel Hill: University of North Carolina Press, 1999.

Kenney, Charles D. *Fujimori's Coup and the Breakdown of Democracy in Latin America.* Notre Dame, Ind.: University of Notre Dame Press, 2004.

Kimura, Rei. *Alberto Fujimori of Peru: The President Who Dared to Dream.* Woodstock, N.Y.: Beekman Books Inc., 1998.

Palmer, David Scott, ed. *The Shining Path of Peru.* Sidney, Australia: Palgrave Macmillan, 1991.

Vargas Llosa, Alvaro. *The Madness of Things Peruvian: Democracy under Siege.* New Brunswick, N.J.: Transaction Publishers, 1994.

Funk, Walther (1890–1960) *Nazi financier*

Walther Funk, the Nazi minister of economic affairs from 1937 to 1945, was found guilty of war crimes and CRIMES AGAINST HUMANITY at the NUREMBERG TRIALS. Born in 1890, he was a financial journalist and editor before he joined the Nazi Party (The National Social Workers' Party, or NSDAP) in 1931, becoming Adolf HITLER's personal economic adviser. He also had valuable contacts with some of Germany's major industrialists, bankers, and corporate directors, who thought of him as a "Liberal Nazi," a potential moderating influence. Believing it was in their best interest to curry favor with the Nazis, Funk's business connections helped subsidize the Nazi Party with generous contributions. For his part, Funk tried his best to steer Hitler into leaving socialism behind—in spite of the party's name—in favor of a program emphasizing private enterprise.

In 1938 Funk was appointed Reich minister of economics. The following year he assumed the presidency of the Reichsbank. In this position he was responsible for the financial planning for war—carried out in secret—which entailed converting all of Germany's foreign reserves into gold and increasing exports to earn the revenues needed to gear up the arms industry. He also took an active role in ensuring that the inevitable labor shortage could be compensated by the use of PRISONERS OF WAR and slave labor. Funk participated in the economic planning for the attack on and occupation of the Soviet Union. Shortly after the invasion of the USSR, he gave a speech describing the plans he had made for the economic exploitation of the "vast territories of the Soviet Union," which could then be used as a source of raw material for Nazi-occupied Europe.

To replenish Germany's treasury, he contrived to loot the national banks of occupied Yugoslavia and Czechoslovakia of their gold reserves.

Although Funk later contended that he was shocked by anti-Jewish pogroms carried out by Nazi-inspired mobs on the night of November 9, 1938—known as Kristallnacht (the Night of Broken Glass)—he nonetheless gave a speech in which he said that the violence was understandable in light of "the disgust of the German People, because of a criminal Jewish attack against the German People." He lent his support to the official Nazi program of eliminating Jews from the economic life of the country. In 1942 he entered into a secret agreement with Heinrich HIMMLER, the head of the SS, regarding the disposition of gold, jewels, currency, and other valuables taken from Jews, which were to be deposited in a special account of the Reichsbank credited to the SS. Himmler warned him not to ask too many questions about the details of these transactions. It was later learned that some of the gold that ended up in the vaults of the Reichsbanks originated from eyeglasses, gold teeth, and fillings belonging to Jewish victims of the CONCENTRATION CAMPS. (The Nuremberg Tribunal determined that Funk was aware of how the gold had been obtained but was "deliberately closing his eyes to what was being done.")

As the war continued, Funk began to lose some of his influence, and after 1943 he no longer initiated any eco-nomic programs of his own. At the war's end he was captured by the Allied troops and subsequently stood trial before the Nuremberg Tribunal. Funk insisted on his innocence, claiming that he had only been an official implementing the plans conceived by the top Nazi leadership. But the tribunal established that even if he had not been the architect of war planning, he was deeply involved in carrying it out. Funk was found guilty of three of the four counts in the indictment, including war crimes and crimes against humanity. He received a sentence of life in prison but was released for reasons of health in May 1957. He died three years later on May 31, 1960.

Further Reading:

Bosch, William J. *Judgment on Nuremberg: American Attitudes toward the Major German War-Crime Trials.* Durham: University of North Carolina Press, 1970.

Buscher, Frank M. *The U.S. War Crimes Trial Program in Germany, 1946–1955.* Contributions in Military Studies. Westport, Conn.: Greenwood Press, 1989.

Russell of Liverpool, Edward Frederick Langley Russell, Baron. *The Scourge of the Swastika: A Short History of Nazi War Crimes.* London: Greenhill Books/Lionel Leventhal, 2002.

Persico, Joseph. *Nuremberg: Infamy on Trial.* New York: Penguin Books, 1995.

G

Gacumbitsi, Sylvestre *See* RWANDAN HUMAN RIGHTS VIOLATORS.

Gadhafi, Muammar al- *See* LIBYA, HUMAN RIGHTS VIOLATIONS IN.

Galić, Stanislav *See* WAR CRIMINALS OF THE FORMER YUGOSLAVIA.

Garzón, Balthasar (1955–) *Spanish judge*

The Spanish judge Balthasar Garzón gained worldwide attention by indicting former Chilean dictator Augusto PINOCHET in 1997 for CRIMES AGAINST HUMANITY committed while in power. The judge's aggressive stance in tracking down and bringing to justice alleged war criminals has prompted admirers to refer to him as a "super judge." Other commentators call him a "star judge," but they do not mean it as a compliment. They accuse him of exercising judicial overreach and too apt to grab headlines.

Raised in the Andalucia region of southern Spain, Garzón was schooled in Catholic doctrine and seemed destined for the priesthood. Temperamentally, though, he did not seem cut out for the life of a priest. A fan of bullfights, rock concerts, and flamenco music, he was expelled from school for serenading a female student who would later become his wife. He decided to become a lawyer, and at 32 he was appointed as an investigating judge on the Audiencia Nacional, the highest court for criminal cases, where he earned a reputation for toughness and fairness. Never one to shy away from the spotlight, Garzón orchestrated the arrest of 54 drug dealers in a widely covered event, only to see most of the suspects get off with little or no jail time. After a brief flirtation with politics, he returned to the judiciary and began probes into national security cases. In the process he found evidence that Spanish police had tortured Basque separatists in custody, and he secured convictions against the former interior minister and 11 other officials. By prosecuting such high-profile cases, Garzón caused a scandal that inflicted serious political damage to his one-time ally, Socialist prime minister Felipe González. But in another demonstration of his evenhandedness, the judge also closed down a Basque newspaper that was accused of fostering terrorism. His determination to prosecute such sensitive cases has put his life in jeopardy. He never goes anywhere without bodyguards and frequently changes his schedule to thwart potential assassins.

In September 1996 Garzón took the unprecedented action of extending his jurisdiction to another country by opening an investigation into 320 murders of Spanish citizens who were slain in the "dirty war" in Argentina from 1976 to 1983. Garzón contended that the crimes were little different from the war crimes committed by the Nazis in World War II. His investigation came at a time when former political and military officials involved in TORTURE, EXTRAJUDICIAL KILLINGS, and DISAPPEARANCES enjoyed immunity from prosecution in their own country because of AMNESTY laws. Garzón was undeterred. "According to the law, these crimes must be investigated and hundreds of assassinations cannot remain unpunished," he told the *New York Times*. "We have a moral debt with the relatives of hundreds of victims." Although few expected the former military dictators of Argentina to be arrested or extradited to Spain, Garzón's indictment renewed scrutiny of abuses that had been systematically carried out during the conflict. He did achieve one modest success when a former Argentine officer, Adolfo Scilingo, was arrested while on a visit to Spain. Scilingo became the first Argentine officer to publicly acknowledge his complicity in the mass execution of political dissidents who were shackled together and then dropped from a plane to their deaths in the Atlantic. But no case that Garzón had prosecuted was as charged as his effort to put Augusto Pinochet in the dock.

In October 1997, while on a private visit to England for medical treatment, Pinochet was placed under arrest by Scotland Yard officers who were acting on an arrest warrant issued by Garzón. The former Chilean strongman was immune from prosecution in his homeland as a result of amnesty laws enacted while he was still in power. Eventually Garzón lodged 81 complaints against Pinochet. In bringing the case, he was not acting on his own initiative; he had an important ally on the judiciary, Manuel García-Castellon. Pinochet was held under house arrest while the British courts considered the Spanish extradition request. Garzón's was not the only legal move against Pinochet: Following his indictment, France, Belgium, and Switzerland filed their own charges. Nonetheless, it was Garzón's action that set off a firestorm. Even the Spanish prime minister denounced his attempt to try Pinochet. But the prime minister's views evidently did not reflect those of most Spanish people. According to polls in two major Spanish newspapers, *El Mundo* and *El País,* 70–80 percent of the people were in favor of putting Pinochet on trial in their country.

The ex-dictator did not lack for supporters in the United States and Britain. Former British prime minister Margaret Thatcher came to his defense, calling Pinochet "a friend of England during the Falklands War" between Britain and Argentina in 1982. Pinochet's arrest, lamented conservative columnist Charles Krauthammer, was "a blow for the most ideologically selective justice, and for the rankest hypocrisy" by leftists. The conservative writer and publisher William F. Buckley denounced the charges as "an act of ideological malice" against a military leader who had ousted "a president [Salvador Allende] who was defiling the Chilean constitution and waving proudly the banner of his friend and idol, Fidel Castro."

Eventually the British courts ruled against the extradition request, and Pinochet was freed and allowed to return home. But Garzón was hardly discouraged from pursuing other well-known high officials. He even tried to bring former U.S. secretary of state Henry Kissinger to Spain for "questioning" in connection with American policy toward Latin America during the late 1960s and early 1970s when several countries were embroiled in dirty wars, pitting military governments against leftist insurgents. Not surprisingly, Kissinger refused to comply. Garzón enjoyed more success in 2003 when he obtained the extradition from Mexico of a former Argentine naval officer, Ricardo Miguel CAVALLO, who was implicated in the TORTURE and killings of political dissidents held at a notorious Buenos Aires detention center.

Garzón has broadened the scope of his investigations to al-QAEDA as well. In June 2004, after an eight-year probe into Islamic extremist activity in Spain, he issued a report expected to lead to formal charges and trials for 15 suspected militants accused of helping the September 11, 2001, terrorist attacks on the World Trade Center and the Pentagon. Garzón contends that Spain has jurisdiction in the case because much of the planning for the attacks is believed to have taken place in Spain.

General Framework Agreement for Peace
See DAYTON ACCORDS.

Geneva Conventions

The Geneva Conventions constitute the international legal framework that obliges signatories to uphold human rights in conflict and in peacetime. All the conventions share one common element: They establish minimum rules to be observed in internal armed conflicts.

The first Geneva Convention dates back to the mid-19th century, and there have been several Geneva Conventions since then. Generally, though, contemporary usage of the term refers to the Fourth Geneva Convention of 1949.

- Convention I (1864): For the Amelioration of the Condition of the Wounded and Sick in Armed Forces in the Field
    This establishes safeguards for members of the armed forces who become wounded or ill.
- Convention II (1906): For the Amelioration of the Condition of Wounded, Sick and Shipwrecked Members of Armed Forces at Sea
    This applies the protections in Convention I to wounded, sick, and shipwrecked members of naval forces.
- Convention III (1929): Relative to the Treatment of Prisoners of War
    This specifies the obligations of belligerents toward PRISONERS OF WAR.
- Convention IV (1949): Relative to the Protection of Civilian Persons in Time of War
    This provides for the protection of civilian populations during conflict situations.

The earlier conventions were designed to codify behavior of combatants on the battlefield and the treatment of war victims, while the later conventions dealt with the obligations of states toward civilians, property, and cultural landmarks. Together, these conventions and protocols are known as "The Law of Geneva" so as to distinguish them from "The Law of The Hague," referring to international agreements signed in the capital of the Netherlands in 1899 and 1907. While the former applies primarily to the treatment of combatants and civilians in war and peace, the latter deals principally with the permissible means and methods of war and mechanisms to ensure that human rights are respected in armed conflicts. The evolution of the Law of Geneva is in many ways inextricably linked to a particular form of conflict. Just as World War I gave rise to the Third Geneva Convention in 1929, so did World War II provide the impetus for the Fourth Convention in 1949.

Similarly, the insurgencies and civil wars of the 1960s and 1970s in much of the developing world spurred the adoption of the two ADDITIONAL PROTOCOLS TO THE GENEVA CONVENTIONS in 1977.

In addition, several other instruments have been adopted to strengthen protections of human rights, including the UNIVERSAL DECLARATION OF HUMAN RIGHTS (1948), the EUROPEAN CONVENTION FOR THE Protection of HUMAN RIGHTS (1953), the GENOCIDE CONVENTION (1951), and the CONVENTION AGAINST TORTURE (1986).

The restrictions in the Geneva Conventions are not necessarily absolute; some, but not all, human rights obligations may be waived under emergency situations or in wartime. But certain protections of human rights can never be violated—TORTURE is forbidden even in an emergency, for instance. To emphasize the priority given to human rights, negotiators added an article that is common to all four conventions. Article 3 states that in times of conflict, persons safeguarded by the conventions should "in all circumstances be treated humanely, without any adverse distinction founded on race, color, religion or faith, sex, birth or wealth, or any other similar criteria."

The First Geneva Convention was largely the work of one man, Jean-Henri DUNANT, a businessman who, appalled by the carnage he witnessed at the Battle of Solferino in 1859 between French and Austrian armies, proposed the creation of international societies to tend to the wounded and dead on the battlefield. What was unique about Dunant's proposal was that the societies would be made up of neutral doctors and nurses who would treat all combatants equally, regardless of their allegiance, nationality, or religion. His vision was realized in the establishment of the INTERNATIONAL COMMITTEE OF THE RED CROSS (ICRC). In 1864 the delegates of 12 European nations met in Geneva and adopted the Convention for the Amelioration of the Condition of the Wounded and Sick in Armies in the Field. (The United States signed this treaty in 1882.) This was the First Geneva Convention, and it provided for the protection of all medical facilities, all medical personnel, and any civilians tending to the wounded. At the same time the Convention recognized the ICRC as an official neutral group to facilitate carrying out the provisions set forth in the accord. But the importance of the first convention transcends the specific safeguards and codifies the principles of universality and tolerance: All people are to be treated the same regardless of race, nationality, religion, or political affiliation. The first convention also laid the groundwork upon which a body of INTERNATIONAL HUMANITARIAN LAW would be constructed. Following up on the First Geneva Convention, in 1868 negotiators signed the St. Petersburg Declaration, which called on states to refrain from employing arms which cause unnecessary suffering, including the prohibition of explosive bullets.

The Second Geneva Convention of 1906 extended the protection of the first convention to wounded combatants at sea and shipwrecked sailors. The devastation and enormous human cost of World War I, however, offered compelling evidence that the protections of the two conventions were still inadequate. In 1925 the Geneva Gas Protocol was signed, which prohibited the use of poison gas and bacteriological warfare. The Third Geneva Convention in 1929 set forth specific protections for prisoners of war and reinforced existing provisions for the treatment of the sick and wounded. Yet after the unspeakable loss of life and devastation wrought by the Spanish civil war (1936–39) and the Second World War (1939–45), it was obvious that new laws were urgently needed to protect civilians who were increasingly victims of conflict in the 20th century.

The Fourth Geneva Convention was negotiated at an international diplomatic conference held from April to August 1949. Signed on August 12, it basically reaffirmed the principles and laws of the first three conventions and provided additional protections for civilians during wartime. Over the next 40 years, the increasing number of internal conflicts spurred a new international initiative, culminating in the Diplomatic Conference on the Reaffirmation and Development of International Humanitarian Law, which met in Geneva from 1974 to 1977. The result was the adoption of the Additional Protocols to the 1949 Conventions, signed on June 8, 1977. Protocol I provides for the protection of victims of wars against racist regimes, wars of self-determination, and oppression by outside forces. Protocol II deals with the protection of victims of internal armed conflicts and broadens the application of the law so that it refers not only to armed conflicts between states but also to rebel forces or other organized groups that control part of a territory within a state. Protocol II does not, however, apply to riots or sporadic episodes of violence, nor does it pertain to terrorist groups such as al-QAEDA.

It is important to keep in mind that the Geneva Conventions and the Additional Protocols distinguish between combatants and civilians, who are to be treated in different ways under the law. Ironically, in some respects, a combatant may benefit from the legal distinction; if, for example, a soldier shoots an enemy and is then taken captive, he or she is considered a prisoner of war and is entitled to certain protections afforded by the conventions. He or she cannot be punished for shooting the soldier. If, on the other hand, a civilian shoots an enemy soldier and is captured, he or she may be held liable for murder. To ensure that this distinction is maintained, combatants are obliged to wear clearly identifiable uniforms and carry weapons openly. (Thus, the conventions do not apply to spies and mercenaries defined as soldiers who are not nationals involved in the conflict.) Not all persons in uniform are necessarily combatants; the laws exempt medical and religious personnel from being classified as combatants. Medical personnel are entitled to carry small arms and use them in self-defense.

Combatants are entitled to the following protections:

- Prisoners of war must be treated humanely. They cannot be tortured, intimidated, threatened, or subjected to degrading treatment, including their public display.
- Prisoners of war are required only to give their names, ranks, birth dates, and serial numbers.
- Prisoners of war must be removed from the battlefield as soon as possible, must not be exposed to danger unnecessarily, and cannot be used as human shields.
- Prisoners of war cannot be punished for acts committed during combat unless those acts violate international law.

Combatants who deliberately use civilians and noncombatants in military operations are in violation of the law and thus lose their protections under the Geneva Conventions.

Civilians are afforded basic protections under the Fourth Geneva Convention and the two Additional Protocols:

- Civilians cannot be attacked, and any area populated by civilians cannot be targeted by a belligerent.
- Property cannot be attacked unless justified by military necessity.
- Civilians cannot be deported unless for their own safety or because of military necessity.
- Civilians must not be used as hostages.
- Civilians must be treated with respect and not subject to demeaning treatment.
- Civilians must not be tortured, raped, or enslaved.
- Civilians must not be subject to collective punishment and reprisals.
- Civilians must not be discriminated against, threatened, intimidated, or punished because of their race, religion, nationality, or political allegiance.
- Children must not be recruited to participate in warfare or for labor on behalf of an armed force.

See also ARTICLE 3 COMMON TO THE GENEVA CONVENTIONS; CIVILIAN IMMUNITY; COLLECTIVE PUNISHMENT; GENOCIDE; HAGUE CONVENTIONS; NONDEFENDED LOCALITIES; OCCUPYING POWER; PRISONERS OF WAR; PROTECTED PERSONS; REPRISAL; SAFE HAVENS; SIEGE; STARVATION AS A TACTIC OF WAR; TERRORISM AND INTERNATIONAL HUMANITARIAN LAW; UNITED NATIONS AND THE GENEVA CONVENTIONS; UNIVERSAL JURISDICTION; UNLAWFUL IMPRISONMENT; WAR CRIMES; CATEGORIZATION OF; WAR DEAD, TREATMENT OF; WILLFUL KILLING.

Further Reading:

Gutman, Roy, ed. *Crimes of War: What the Public Should Know.* New York: W. W. Norton & Company, 1999.

Jackson, Nyamuya Maogoto. *War Crimes and Realpolitik: International Justice from World War I to the 21st Century.* Boulder, Colo.: Lynne Rienner Publishers, 2004.

Jinks, Derek. *The Rules of War: The Geneva Conventions in the Age of Terror.* Oxford: Oxford University Press, 2005.

Pilloud, Claude. *Commentary on the Additional Protocols of 8 June 1977 to the Geneva Conventions of 12 August 1949.* Boston: Brill Academic Publishers, 1987.

Roberts, Adam, and Richard Guelff. *Documents on the Laws of War.* Oxford: Oxford University Press, 2000.

Trombly, Maria. *Journalist's Guide to the Geneva Conventions.* Indianapolis: Society of Professional Journalists, 2000.

genocide

The word *genocide* owes its origin to a Polish Jew named Raphael Lemkin, who coined it in 1944. (Winston Churchill had earlier called the practice of genocide "a crime without a name.") It is derived from *genos* (Greek for family, tribe, or race) and *-cide* (Latin for killing). Although the term is relatively recent, genocide has been practiced for millennia. In the fifth century, forces of the Atilla the Hun rampaged through Europe and the Middle East, carrying out indiscriminate killings, and Genghis Khan and his Mongul hordes slaughtered thousands as they pushed westward. But it is only in the 20th century that genocide became so systematic and was carried out with such brutal efficiency, beginning with the deportation of Armenians from Ottoman territory, which may have taken the lives of as many as 1.8 million people in 1915. Nazi Germany engaged in mass extermination on a scale never seen before: By the end of World War II, the Nazis and their allies had killed about 6 million Jews, or about two out of every three Jews living in Europe prior to the war. (In addition, the Germans were responsible for the deaths of about 500,000 Rom [Gypsies], half of all captured Soviet PRISONERS OF WAR, and an estimated 10–20 percent of peoples in Eastern European countries occupied by German forces. Croatian forces, then allied with Germany, carried out a bloodbath in which as many as 340,000 Serbs perished. But these killings, however appalling, do not constitute genocide under the provisions of the 1948 Convention on Genocide, because the German intent in these cases was not to eradicate an entire people, which was the case with the Jews.)

Since World War II, several international treaties have been ratified outlawing genocide. Even a partial list of genocidal episodes since the end of World War II offers considerable evidence that these treaties do not have adequate enforcement mechanisms: Cambodia between 1975 and 1979 (1.7 million killed); East Timor in 1975 (200,000 killed); Guatemala between 1960 and 1996 (200,00 killed); Bosnia in 1992–98 (200,000 killed); Rwanda in 1994 (800,000 killed); and Darfur, beginning in 2003 (approximately 200,000 killed in three years). The principal treaty dealing with genocide is the Fourth Geneva Convention of 1949, which defines *genocide* in Article II as "any of the following acts committed with intent to destroy, in whole or in part, a national, ethnical, racial or religious group, as such:

(a) Killing members of the group;
(b) Causing serious bodily or mental harm to members of the group;
(c) Deliberately inflicting on the group conditions of life calculated to bring about its physical destruction in whole or in part;
(d) Imposing measures intended to prevent births within the group;
(e) Forcibly transferring children of the group to another group."

Students of genocide have identified different stages of genocide that are characteristic of many outbreaks of violence directed against a particular group. In an essay written for the U.S. State Department, Gregory Stanton broke down the commission of genocide into eight separate stages:

1. Classification: Practically all societies are divided, whether by ethnicity, religion, political views, or country of national origin. For genocide to occur, people must view their societies in terms of "us and them." Societies that are most at risk for genocide are those that Stanton calls "bipolar"—consisting of two principal groups, one of which holds more political and economic power and the other which tends to feel disenfranchised. Rwanda and Burundi, both of which have been torn apart by clashes between Hutus and Tutsis, are examples of such bipolar societies.
2. Symbolization: People regarded as "different" must be separated from the rest of the population by name or dress or by special insignias, such as the yellow Stars of David used by the Nazis to identify—and stigmatize—Jews who might otherwise be indistinguishable. Classification and symbolization alone do not necessarily lead to genocide, but these stages generally must take place for genocide to occur.
3. Dehumanization: The group targeted for destruction must be made to seem less than human, uncivilized, mentally or physically unfit, or even animal-like. This step is necessary so as to overcome the instinctive revulsion against killing innocent people, especially the elderly, women, and children.
4. Organization: Genocide is distinguished from ordinary outbursts of violence in that it is not impulsive. Genocide is always organized, and although the state is often responsible, terrorist and insurgent groups have increasingly been involved in planning and carrying out genocidal attacks.
5. Polarization: Once the environment is favorable for genocide to take place, people must be stirred up against the targeted group. Members of the group are harassed and intimidated. Special laws are frequently enacted to codify discrimination against the group, such as forbidding intermarriage or the right to operate a business. The first defendants to be convicted of war crimes for the genocide in Rwanda were responsible not for killing but for inciting the killers by inflammatory radio broadcasts.
6. Preparation: Members of the group are segregated in detention camps or in ghettos so they can be more easily eliminated. It is at this stage that death lists are drawn up.
7. Extermination: Mass killing is accorded legal sanction and, if it is being carried out by the state, may entail the use of both regular army and militias. It is no coincidence that a word more commonly applied to disposing of pests is used to describe this stage, since the victims are considered less than human by the killers.
8. Denial: The perpetrators of the genocide almost invariably try to hide evidence of their crimes. Mass graves are concealed; blame for the crimes is attributed to others, including the victims themselves; investigations are impeded and amnesties passed to confer impunity on the guilty. In many cases, the state will claim that any attempt to bring the guilty to account will jeopardize national reconciliation or "reopen old wounds."

Another type of genocide should be noted: Retributive genocide is a preemptive strike intended to eliminate a real or potential threat. Retributive genocide tends to take place when one group fears that its power will be undermined by another group unless it takes action. This was the case in Rwanda in 1994 when radical Hutus launched a genocidal campaign against Tutsis (and moderate Hutus) out of fear that the Tutsis were prepared to seize power themselves.

See also Armenian genocide; Bosnia and Herzegovina, human rights violations in; Burundi, war crimes in; Cambodia, war crimes in; Cambodian genocide program; Darfur, war crimes in; East timor, war crimes in; Final Soultion; Geneva Conventions; Guatemala, human rights violations in; incitement to genocide; Rom (Romany, Gypsies), persecution of; Rwanda, genocide in.

Further Reading:
AkCam, Taner. *From Empire to Republic: Turkish Nationalism and the Armenian Genocide.* London: Zed Books, 2004.

Balakian, Peter. *The Burning Tigris: The Armenian Genocide and America's Response.* New York: Harper-Collins, 2003.

Bloxham, Donald. *Genocide on Trial: War Crimes Trials and the Formation of Holocaust History and Memory.* Oxford, U.K.: Oxford University Press, 2003.

Gutman, Roy, ed. *Crimes of War: What the Public Should Know.* New York: W. W. Norton & Company, 1999.

Jones, Adam, ed. *Genocide, War Crimes and the West: History and Complicity.* London: Zed Books, 2004.

Miller, Donald E., and Lorna Touryan Miller. *Survivors: An Oral History of the Armenian Genocide.* Berkeley: University of California Press, 1999.

Peterson, Merrill D. *Starving Armenians: America and the Armenian Genocide, 1915–1930 and After.* Charlottesville: University Press of Virginia, 2004.

Genocide Convention (International Convention on the Prevention and Punishment of the Crime of Genocide)

The Genocide Convention was created in 1948 in response to the slaughter of millions of Jews and other religious and ethnic groups by the Nazis during World War II. The convention specifies various acts which, even if they do not involve killing or indirectly causing death, are still considered genocidal under the law. Thus, incitement to commit GENOCIDE, deporting children for political purposes, or curbing the ability of a people to have children are all criminal activities. In fact, any act that seeks to destroy a group of people based on ethnicity, religion, political views, or nationality falls into the category of genocide according to the treaty.

The Genocide Convention was adopted by the United Nations General Assembly on December 9, 1948, and entered into force on January 12, 1951. As of September 2005 the number of parties to the convention had grown to 137; more than 70 nations have made provisions for the punishment of genocide in domestic criminal law. Article II of the Genocide Convention making, the commission of genocide a crime, has been incorporated in the 1998 ROME STATUTE OF THE INTERNATIONAL CRIMINAL COURT.

The Convention on the Prevention and Punishment of the Crime of Genocide, as it is officially known, was the first legal instrument to formally define genocide. According to the convention, genocidal acts are not limited to murder but pertain to any attempt to cause serious bodily or mental harm to members of a group, or "deliberately inflicting on the group conditions of life calculated to bring about its physical destruction in whole or in part." Genocide is not only a crime against a particular group of people but also a crime whose intent is the obliteration of their history, their culture, and their future existence as well. The

Fourth Geneva Convention employed a similar definition in Article II, which describes genocide as "any of the following acts committed with intent to destroy, in whole or in part, a national, ethnical, racial or religious group, as such:

(a) Killing members of the group;
(b) Causing serious bodily or mental harm to members of the group;
(c) Deliberately inflicting on the group conditions of life calculated to bring about its physical destruction in whole or in part;
(d) Imposing measures intended to prevent births within the group;
(e) Forcibly transferring children of the group to another group."

These acts are banned under international law regardless of whether they are committed in war or in peacetime. All signatories are obliged to prevent and punish any acts of genocide that take place under their jurisdiction. Signatories agree to enact appropriate legislation to make these acts illegal under national law and provide appropriate penalties for violators. The convention also declares it illegal to conspire to commit genocide, incite others to commit genocide, attempt to commit genocide, or become complicit in the commission of genocide. Individuals who carry out such outlawed acts are culpable whether they are acting in an official or private capacity. The convention provides for tribunals for those who are suspected of acts of genocide; trials can take place in the country where the genocide occurred or in an international venue whose jurisdiction is recognized by the state or states involved. States are bound to extradite suspects for trial "in accordance with national laws and treaties." Any state party to the convention also has the right to call upon the United Nations to prevent or punish acts of genocide. The final part of the convention deals with procedures for resolving disputes between nations about whether specific acts constitute genocide and details the procedures for ratifying the accord.

The convention's definition of genocide may appear relatively inclusive and straightforward, but several outstanding issues remain unresolved even 50 years later. One of these issues touches on intent, another on responsibility. There can be no doubt that the FINAL SOLUTION of the Nazis represented a systematic effort to exterminate the Jews. The Rom (Gypsies), too, were singled out for extermination in a genocidal campaign that was deliberately planned and documented. So in this case intent is not in question. In most Western countries, criminal law extrapolates intent from the act; in other words, if a person commits homicide, then the law presumes that he intended to kill his victim. The accused must establish that he did not have the *intent* to kill the victim; he might, for instance, have acted out of passion without realizing the consequences of his action at the time. Showing intent is important since the law treats premeditated acts as much-graver offenses than an act that occurred as a result of a particular set of circumstances. Someone who gives an overdose to a terminally ill family member may be found guilty of murder, but surely his or her intent differs quite a bit from a person who breaks into a home and murders the occupant so as to eliminate a witness to his crime.

How, then, is it possible to determine whether a state or a group has acted with the intent to commit genocide? In some instances, regimes do follow the Nazi example and announce beforehand that they are determined to conduct a campaign of extermination. This occurred in Rwanda in 1990 when Hutu militants took to the airwaves and used the radio to direct partisans to sites where their victims could be found and massacred. However, most governments are more sophisticated and try not to leave such incriminating evidence for future prosecutors to find. The drafters of the convention were aware of this potential loophole. In other words, a government could assert that even if actions by its forces had contributed to the deaths of thousands of members of a particular group, that did not mean that genocide had been committed. All the government had to do was to demonstrate that it had never desired or planned the deaths of this group. The Turkish government for decades has argued that the deaths of up to 1.5 million Armenians in 1915 was not genocide but rather came about because of civil unrest that broke out during the First World War.

There is an additional problem related to the issue of intent. The Convention on Genocide omits whole categories of people who, in many countries, are victims of atrocities. In a 2002 article for the *Yale Human Rights and Development Law Journal,* Joy Gordon argues that "Under the Genocide Convention, there is nothing that prohibits the extermination of any groups other than those named. The mass killing of political opposition, for example, does not violate the Genocide Convention. More importantly, it does not prohibit the extermination of racial, ethnic, or religious groups, so long as it is done for some other reason." Put another way, if a government marks a religious group for persecution and death because of economic, political, or military purposes rather than because they hold a certain belief, then, technically speaking, the crime of killing them may not fall under the classification of genocide. Gordon points out that while GENEVA CONVENTIONS on the conduct of war specify that COLLATERAL DAMAGE must be proportional—that is, an army is obliged to inflict only so much damage as necessary to achieve a military objective; it cannot wreak more destruction simply to demoralize a population—this is not the case in the Convention on Genocide, which "has nothing to say about whole categories of atrocities, including some that are

deliberate and planned and where the actor knowingly inflicts massive, indiscriminate human damage." She goes on to say that "the nature of the intent requirement is such that it not only exculpates certain categories of actors who have committed acts of massive human destruction but also serves to remove the acts altogether from the most important domains of moral and legal judgment. . . ."

Another source of debate is the issue of accountability. Does international law hold states accountable or individuals? Is it possible, some analysts wonder, to "de-couple" the state and its representatives when, say, atrocities are committed in an internal conflict? After all, a state is an abstraction; the actual crimes are carried out by representatives acting in its name. If individuals can escape culpability for actions that they are carrying out on behalf of the state and if only the state is penalized (by an embargo, for example), then they will have little or no incentive to comply with international law. From that perspective, then, if a Slobodan MILOŠEVIĆ or a Saddam HUSSEIN knew in advance that he would have to pay a personal price for his crimes, he might have been less inclined to order them carried out.

Enforcement has always been seen by human rights advocates as the weakest part of the Genocide Convention. "For a time, it was the forgotten convention, drafted in the aftermath of the Holocaust," writes William Schabas in an article entitled "The Genocide Convention at Fifty." But then, he notes, the treaty was "relegated to obscurity as the human rights movement focused on more 'modern' atrocities: APARTHEID, TORTURE, DISAPPEARANCES." The atrocities in the wars of the 1990s in the former Yugoslavia and the genocide in Rwanda in 1995 brought the treaty renewed attention. Interest in the treaty was also stirred by the attempt in 1998 by Spanish judge Balthasar GARZÓN to extradite former Chilean president Augusto PINOCHET to stand trial for war crimes committed under his rule. As Schabas observes, many difficult questions have been raised in the half-century since the Genocide Convention was adopted that have yet to be resolved. What groups are protected by the convention? Could an attack on a particular political or social group fall under the provisions of the convention in the same way as an attack directed against an ethnic or religious group? What are the obligations of states when a person suspected of genocide is found on their territory? When Garzón issued his warrant for Pinochet, for instance, the Chilean dictator was visiting Britain. Ultimately the British court refused the extradition request and allowed him to return home.

Another question that the convention fails to address definitively is whether, if genocide is committed, a state has an obligation under the treaty to intervene to stop it, even if this calls for military action. This very question still weighs on the world's conscience after the failure of any state or the United Nations to take action to prevent the genocide in Rwanda. "What the convention means by preventing genocide remains enigmatic," Schabas writes, "but defining it is an urgent priority, given the recent failure to stop genocide in Rwanda."

The Convention on Genocide is by no means the only legal instrument created by international law to deal with genocide. Since the establishment of the NUREMBERG TRIALS and TOKYO TRIALS after World War II, several international courts have been formed to prosecute genocidal crimes, notably the INTERNATIONAL CRIMINAL TRIBUNAL FOR THE FORMER YUGOSLAVIA, the INTERNATIONAL CRIMINAL TRIBUNAL FOR RWANDA, the SPECIAL COURT FOR SIERRA LEONE, and the permanent INTERNATIONAL CRIMINAL COURT. Each judgment rendered by these courts adds to a growing body of precedent that supplements and elaborates upon the principles embodied in the 1948 convention.

The Rome Statute of the International Criminal Court (ICC) of 2002 is essentially a complementary treaty to the convention insofar as both share a common definition of genocide and both are concerned with the punishment of genocide. The principal distinction is that the convention addresses the issue of preventing genocide; the Rome Statute is only concerned with the prosecution and punishment of those responsible for genocide. The Rome Statute has been signed and ratified by more than 90 states, and another 48 have signed but have not yet ratified it. (This represents about two-thirds of the member states of the United Nations, which is a relatively low figure compared with the number that have ratified other major human rights treaties. African states have been notably slow to sign the treaty, and even the United States signed the convention only in 1988 after decades of debates.) There are, in addition, 18 nations that have not become parties to the Genocide Convention of 1948 but have nonetheless become parties to the Rome Statute. Nevertheless, by 1951 it had been ratified by more than one-third of the United Nations membership, enough for it to enter into force.

All these legal instruments and institutions have another crucial role: deterring genocide. As worthy a goal as that is, much work remains to be done. Several outstanding issues remain to be resolved: should the definition of genocide be broadened, and if so, to whom should it apply? Who should be enforcing the prohibitions against genocide, how is guilt to be decided, and what penalties are adequate to punish the crime and prevent others from repeating it in the future?

See also ARMENIAN GENOCIDE; INCITEMENT TO GENOCIDE; RWANDA, GENOCIDE IN.

Further Reading:

Bass, Gary Jonathan. *Stay the Hand of Vengeance: The Politics of War Crimes Tribunals.* Princeton, N.J.: Princeton University Press, 2001.
Beigbeder, Yves, and Theo van Boven. *Judging War Criminals: The Politics of International Justice.* Sidney, Australia: Palgrave Macmillan, 1999.
Bloxham, Donald. *Genocide on Trial: War Crimes Trials and the Formation of Holocaust History and Memory.* Oxford: Oxford University Press, 2003.
Cooper, Belinda, and Richard Goldstone. *War Crimes: The Legacy of Nuremberg.* New York: TV Books Inc., 1999.
Dormann, Knut, and Louise Doswald-Beck. *Elements of War Crimes under the Rome Statute of the International Criminal Court: Sources and Commentary.* Cambridge: Cambridge University Press, 2003.
Falk, Richard A. *Crimes of War: A Legal, Political-Documentary, and Psychological Inquiry into the Responsibility of Leaders, Citizens, and Soldiers for Criminal Acts in Wars.* New York: Random House, 1971.
Gutman, Roy, ed. *Crimes of War: What the Public Should Know.* New York: W. W. Norton & Company, 1999.

Genocide Watch

Genocide Watch is a nongovernmental organization (NGO), founded in The Hague, Netherlands, in 1999. It was established to "predict, prevent, stop, and punish genocide and other forms of mass murder." The organization accepts the definition of GENOCIDE employed by the GENOCIDE CONVENTION as "the intentional destruction, in whole or in part, of a national, ethnic, racial or religious group, as such." Genocide Watch serves as the coordinating organization of the International Campaign to End Genocide (ICEG), an international coalition of organizations whose goal is to raise public awareness about genocide and issue warnings when a potential for genocide exists. It supports the creation of a Genocide Early Warning Center in the Secretariat of the United Nations and lobbies for effective punishment for perpetrators of genocide and justice for victims and survivors.

Georgia (Republic of), human rights violations in

Georgia, a former Soviet republic, occupies a strategic position, squeezed between Russia in the north and Turkey and Iran to the south. In recent years the country has acquired additional importance because of an oil pipeline, which will carry oil from the Caspian Sea through Georgia to ports on the Turkish Mediterranean coast. Since becoming independent in 1991, Georgia has been racked by insurrection, civil war, ethnic conflict, and violent separatism that has fractured the country. A peaceful uprising in 2004, however—known as the Rose Revolution—led to the formation of a new government with wide popular support. Whether the promise of greater democracy and prosperity held out by the leaders of the Rose Revolution will be fulfilled remains to be seen. Since becoming independent, Georgia has been led—or misled—by two presidents: Zviad Gamsakhurdia, who was deposed in 1992, and Eduard Shevardnadze, the former Soviet foreign minister. Under Shevardnadze's tenure, Georgia was plagued by corruption, increasing poverty, and sporadic energy shortages. Furthermore, with three regions declaring their independence, Georgia could not even lay claim to sovereignty over all its territory.

Ironically, Georgia was once so prosperous that it had a reputation as the Soviet Union's "fruit basket" for its bountiful harvests of citrus fruit as well as tea and tobacco. But years of war, corruption, and misrule have succeeded in draining the country of its wealth. At the time of Schevardnadze's fall, unemployment stood at 20 percent and the majority of the population lived below the poverty line. Most people scraped by on $5–$8 a month, and pensioners were forced to live on as little as $6 a month. Conditions have deteriorated to such a degree that almost a third of Georgia's 3.5 million people are in exile.

The rampant poverty has fueled much of the conflict and violence and led to grave human rights abuses. At the end of Schevardnadze's rule, about 100 political prisoners languished in prison. AMNESTY INTERNATIONAL has documented "numerous reports of TORTURE and ill-treatment in detention" by police. Some improvements have been noted, however; witnesses to crimes are now given the right to legal representation, a welcome change from an earlier policy that permitted police to call people as witnesses and hold them in detention without access to a lawyer. Courts were known to convict suspects based on confessions forcibly extracted under torture, and defendants were barred by law from obtaining or presenting forensic evidence of torture.

Young women in some rural areas are at particular risk of bride kidnapping and rape, crimes that prosecutors usually decline to investigate or punish. At the same time legislators have done very little to criminalize trafficking of women, and employment and travel agencies continue to operate as fronts to lure women into prostitution or sell them abroad unimpeded.

The country has seen a surge in religious violence in recent years. Authorities have sanctioned the formation of vigilante gangs that have threatened and terrorized religious groups that do not belong to the Russian Orthodox faith, targeting Jehovah's Witnesses, Pentecostals, and Baptists. Assailants have broken up religious services, looted property, and burned religious tracts. The Jehovah's Witnesses reported more than 40 attacks on their followers in the first half of 2001 alone. Police were accused of allowing these attacks to take place without doing anything to stop them. In some instances police have actually participated in the assaults.

In 2003, faced with Georgians' increasing restiveness, Shevardnadze agreed to hold parliamentary elections, which took place in November. The results, which gave parties loyal to the president a majority, were at odds with opinion polls showing an overwhelming majority prepared to vote against the regime. Public skepticism was heightened when the government refused to release the vote count for weeks. The disputed elections (later nullified by the country's high court) brought thousands of protesters into the streets of the capital Tbilisi. After three weeks of demonstrations, Shevardnadze grudgingly but peacefully gave up power.

In January 2004 the leading opposition figure, Mikhail Saakashvili, a 36-year-old U.S.-trained lawyer, won a landslide victory—96 percent of the vote—in new elections and took office as president. International observers, however, caution against unrealistic expectations, given the country's entrenched poverty and violent history. Whether Saakashvili and his team of young technocrats will take significant steps in resolving many of the outstanding human rights problems is still unclear. However, the new president has made some progress in resolving one of the three separatist crises that have bedeviled the country almost from its inception. Three different regions—Abkhazia in the northwest; South Ossetia, which has strong ethnic and cultural ties with Russian North Ossetia; and Ajaria in the southwest—have all declared their independence from Tbilisi. In one of his first acts in office, Saakashvili confronted Abkhazia's strongman, Aslan Abashidze. After a show of defiance, Abashidze capitulated and fled to Moscow without a shot being fired.

The other two breakaway regions are likely to prove more difficult to return to the fold. There are concerns that some of these regional conflicts are being encouraged by Russia, with instances of cross-border crossings on the part of Russian troops against Georgia witnessed by observers of the ORGANIZATION FOR SECURITY AND COOPERATION IN EUROPE. In summer 2004 there were reports of clashes between Georgian and South Ossetian forces. Several thousand refugees from Chechnya have been living in Georgia—in a volatile region known as the Pankisi Gorge—as a result of ongoing strife in their homeland since 1999. A number of kidnapped businessmen and other Georgian citizens are believed to be held for ransom by terrorists and criminal gangs in the gorge, where the rule of law is virtually unknown and which also happens to be the center of Georgia's illegal drug trade. Russians have used the presence of Chechens in Pankisi Gorge to justify incursions and have threatened direct intervention, threatening Georgia's stability.

Given its investment in the projected oil pipeline and Georgia's strategic location, the United States has become increasingly involved in the troubled nation, providing subsidies and military training to Georgian troops to counter

Russian influence. As a demonstration of U.S. support for the new government, Secretary of State Colin Powell attended the Saakashvili's inauguration as president in January 2004. In mid-2004 tensions intensified between Georgia and Russia over Abkhazia, which borders the Black Sea. In an effort to curb Abkhazia's separatism, Saakashvili tried to impose a naval blockade of tourist boats filled with Russian tourists who spent their summer vacations on Abkhazia's beaches. Russia responded with accusations that Georgia was condoning piracy, and there were reports of shooting between Georgian and separatist forces. Some observers believe that Russia is trying to retain as much influence as it can in Abkhazia to counter the growing U.S. support for Georgia's military.

Gerike, Heinrich   *See* VELPKE BABY FARM.

German High Command Trials   *See* NUREMBERG TRIALS.

germ warfare

Germ warfare, also known as biological warfare, is the use of pathogens (disease-causing agents) to terrorize a civilian population or obtain military advantage. The use of BIOLOGICAL WEAPONS is banned under international law. (Pathogenic agents are classified as unconventional weapons, a designation that also includes chemical and nuclear weapons). It has long been observed that plagues can wreak immense havoc among civilian populations and destroy morale; approximately one-quarter of Europe's medieval population (25 million people) perished in the Black Death (bubonic plague) between 1347 and 1351, for instance, and as many as 50 million died in the Spanish influenza pandemic of 1918–19. The Spanish Flu, which took more lives in four months than World War I did in four years, struck down so many German troops that some historians believe that it caused Kaiser Wilhelm to declare an end to the conflict earlier than he would have done otherwise. Germ warfare, however, has so far proven a rare phenomenon, not necessarily because of moral or legal constraints, but because of logistical difficulties. Pathogens, after all, make no distinction between friend and foe, and their effectiveness is limited by environmental factors; a shift in the direction of the wind, for instance. Nonetheless, many nations have pursued research programs into germ warfare. During World War II, the Japanese in occupied Manchria conducted a clandestine operation in which Chinese civilians were exposed to biological agents, often with lethal results. At the height of the cold war, the United States and the Soviet Union embarked upon intensive bio-

logical research programs. In 1979 an experiment on anthrax (a deadly bacterial agent) at a Soviet biological weapons facility located in Sverdlovsk (now Ekaterinberg, Russia) went horribly awry, causing the deaths of at least 68 people. In 2001, 22 people in the United States were exposed to anthrax spores sent through the mails; five people died. (Five years later the perpetrator was still at large.) Possibly no pathogen arouses more concern than smallpox, which was finally eliminated after a concerted public health campaign. Officially, only two samples of the smallpox virus remain—one in a lab in Moscow, the other at the Centers for Disease Control in Atlanta, Georgia. Since most people have never been vaccinated against the disease, a smallpox pandemic could have a catastrophic impact. Fears that rogue nations or terrorists could gain possession of a virus such as smallpox or stockpile a sufficient quantity of anthrax to infect tens of thousands of people have only increased in the aftermath of the 9/11 terrorist attacks on the United States. In recent years scientific advances have brought a new threat to the fore; it is now possible to add human, animal, insect, or plant genes to any microbe to create disease-causing organisms—dubbed superbugs—to which humans have no immunity whatsoever.

See also BIOLOGICAL WEAPONS.

Further Reading:
Miller, Judith, Broad, William, Engelberg, Stephen. *Germs: Biological Weapons and America's Secret War.* New York: Simon & Schuster; Touchstone edition, 2002.

Null, Gary, Feast, James. *Germs, Biological Warfare, Vaccinations: What You Need to Know.* New York: Seven Stories Press; 1st edition (February 2003).

Regis, Ed. *The Biology of Doom: America's Secret Germ Warfare Project.* New York: Owl Books, 2000.

Gestapo

The Gestapo, an abbreviation of Geheime Staatspolizei, or Secret State Police, served the Nazis as an instrument of terror from 1933 to 1945. Founded by Hermann GÖRING, one of Adolf HITLER's chief deputies, the Gestapo grew out of the political section of the Weimer police. So that it could fulfill its purpose—suppressing all political opponents (including Nazis who had fallen out of favor)—the organization was freed from any legal or constitutional constraints. The Gestapo worked in tandem with the SD (Sicherheitsdienst, or Security Service), which carried out the intelligence-gathering function for the Gestapo. It was up to the Gestapo to determine whether a suspect was tried or released if acquitted; many detainees simply ended up in a concentration camp without any legal formalities.

The first head of the Gestapo was Rudolf Diels, who had impressed Göring for his work as head of Department

1A of the Prussian State Police. Heinrich HIMMLER, chief of the rival Schutzstaffel, or Defense Squads (SS), wrested control of the Gestapo from Göring in April 1934. Two years later Himmler appointed Reinhard HEYDRICH head of the Gestapo, with Heinrich MÜLLER as the chief of operations. After Heydrich's assassination in 1942, Müller became effective head of the Gestapo, a post he held until the end of World War II in 1945.

At its peak, the Gestapo had 45,000 full-time members and possibly as many as 160,000 agents and informants. Whenever the German army occupied a new territory, they were accompanied by the Gestapo, who were responsible for identifying and arresting communists, partisans, and Jews. Although the Gestapo was nominally in charge of the CONCENTRATION CAMPS and death camps, they were actually managed by the SS. Rivalries between different branches of the security systems persisted throughout the war even though, in principle, they were all answerable to a central staff, the RSHA (Reichssicherheitshauptamt, or State Security Head Office). The RSHA had been set up in September 1939 with the mandate of eliminating all opponents and "undesirables"—Jews and Rom (Gypsies) in particular—in territories that would fall under German control.

At the NUREMBERG TRIALS held by the victorious Allies after the war, the Gestapo was one of several Nazi entities declared a criminal organization and indicted for CRIMES AGAINST HUMANITY. By the time the trial was underway, however, most of the Gestapo leaders were either dead or else, like Müller, had managed to escape.

Further Reading:
Browder, George C. *Hitler's Enforcers: The Gestapo and the SS Security Service in the Nazi Revolution.* Oxford: Oxford University Press, 1996.
Butler, Rupert. *The Gestapo: A History of Hitler's Secret Police 1933–45.* Havertown, Pa.: Casemate Publishers and Book Distributors, 2004.
Douglas, Gregory. *Gestapo Chief: The 1948 Interrogation of Heinrich Muller, Volume 3.* San Jose, Calif.: R. James Bender Pub., 1998.
Hohne, Heinz Zollen. *The Order of the Death's Head: The Story of Hitler's SS.* Classic Military History. New York: Penguin, 2001.

ghost prisoners
In conducting secret intelligence operations since the September 11, 2001, terrorist attacks on the United States, the CIA has seized several terrorist suspects in various parts of the globe and then concealed their whereabouts. This practice is in violation of the GENEVA CONVENTIONS, signed by the United States, which oblige governments to permit international aid organizations such as the INTERNATIONAL COMMITTEE OF THE RED CROSS (ICRC) access to PRISONERS OF WAR and other detainees. Some of these so-called ghost prisoners might have been placed in detention centers in Afghanistan and Iraq as well as at the U.S. naval base on Guantánamo Bay, Cuba; others were reportedly consigned to the custody of U.S. allies. According to a report in the *Los Angeles Times* on September 10, 2004, the CIA was still holding as many as 100 detainees without revealing their identities or locations. At the time even the Defense Department admitted that it was unaware of the exact number because CIA officials had denied the information to Pentagon investigators. Earlier the CIA had only acknowledged between a dozen and three dozen unregistered prisoners, all of whom who were being held at Abu Ghraib prison near Baghdad.

See also GUANTÁNAMO DETAINEES; IRAQ, HUMAN RIGHTS VIOLATIONS IN POST-SADDAM.

Further Reading:
Danner, Mark. *Torture and Truth: America, Abu Ghraib, and the War on Terror.* New York: New York Review Books, 2004.
Hersh, Seymour M. *Chain of Command: The Road from 9/11 to Abu Ghraib.* New York: HarperCollins, 2004.

Global IDP Project   *See* INTERNAL DISPLACEMENT PROJECT.

Global Rights
A human rights advocacy group founded in 1978, Global Rights works with local partners in various countries around the world to address issues of human rights abuses, promote racial and gender equality, and foster legal and policy reform. It also supports an information gathering role, documenting and publicizing incidents of human rights violations. The Washington-based group believes that human rights can only be advanced from the ground up and views its primary purpose as that of a facilitator, offering partners "support, protection, guidance and training to strengthen the impact and visibility of their work." It specializes in several areas: racial discrimination, women's human rights, human trafficking, human rights legal training, and international criminal law.

In 2003 Global Rights worked successfully for the acquittal of Amina Lawal, a young mother in Nigeria whose case had stirred worldwide outrage after she was sentenced to death for adultery by a Sharia (Islamic law) court. In Afghanistan the group organized and trained Afghan women to participate in the first Loya Jirga, a groundbreaking political convention that chose the president. One of the women in the program actually ran for president, a remarkable event in a country that, under TALIBAN rule, had brutally suppressed women. In the Democratic Republic of the Congo, Global Rights assisted a group of Congolese human rights advocates in their efforts to establish a Human Rights Observatory and helped incorporate provisions for a Truth and Reconciliation Commission in the Congolese peace agreement. The advocacy group has worked in the United States as well, helping domestic and migrant workers to fight discrimination, lobbying for affirmative action, and supporting rights of detainees taken into custody after the terrorist attacks of September 11, 2001.

Further Reading:

Aall, Pamela R., Daniel Miltenberger, and George Weiss. *IGOs, NGOs, and the Military in Peace and Relief Operations.* Washington, D.C.: United States Institute of Peace Press, 2000.

Erskins, Toni. *Can Institutions Have Responsibilities: Collective Moral Agency and International Relations.* Global Issues Series. Sydney, Australia: Palgrave Macmillan, 2004.

Global Witness

Global Witness is an advocacy group that seeks to link human rights abuses and environmental exploitation. The group collects evidence to document abuses and works to bring about long-term reforms. Global Witness focuses on the illicit trade in natural resources because it engenders corruption, deprives a country of its assets, and hampers the efforts of developing countries to make economic and social progress, threatening stability. Moreover, such trade has the potential to fund—and fuel—conflict, as the trade in CONFLICT DIAMONDS has done in Liberia, Sierra Leone, and Angola. To bring about needed changes Global Witness works with governments, nongovernmental organizations (NGOs), international donors, development organizations, the media, and the general public.

Global Witness was founded in 1993 and is based in London, with project offices in Africa and Asia. If circumstances warrant, the group will use what it terms "covert" as well as conventional investigative methods to identify and document the mechanisms through which natural resources are exploited and removed from countries such as Angola, Cambodia, Liberia, and the Democratic Republic of the Congo. Once the exploitation is uncovered, the group then produces reports about the situation that are presented to policy makers to prod them into action. One of the most shocking examples of this kind of exploitation was seen in Cambodia. In what Global Witness calls the "Million Meter Deal," the Cambodian government and the Khmer Rouge, enemies on the battlefield, came together

for business and agreed to illegally export 1 million cubic meters of tropical timber, which would have netted the Maoist-inspired insurgents some $90 million. Global Witness managed to thwart the deal before it could go through.

Global Witness is especially concerned with developing countries, which, while rich in resources, fail to distribute wealth equitably, leading to what the group calls "the paradox of plenty." Global Witness cites the Kimberly Process—an international accord to outlaw the trade in conflict diamonds—as a model for future frameworks that can bring governments, international corporations, and consumers together to prevent natural exploitation and the corruption and human rights violations that come about as a result.

See also CAMBODIA, HUMAN RIGHTS VIOLATIONS IN.

Further Reading:

Aall, Pamela R., Miltenberger, Daniel, Weiss, George. *IGOs, NGOs, and the Military in Peace and Relief Operations.* Washington, D.C.: United States Institute of Peace Press, 2000.

Erskins, Toni. *Can Institutions Have Responsibilities: Collective Moral Agency and International Relations (Global Issues Series).* Sydney, Australia: Palgrave Macmillan, 2004.

Goebbels, Joseph (1897–1945) *Nazi propagandist*

Described as "a nightmare and goblin of history," Joseph Goebbels was chief propagandist of the Nazi regime, a position that allowed him to consolidate control over Germany's cultural life for 12 years. The child of a strict Catholic, working-class family from the Rhineland, Goebbels was born on October 29, 1897. A childhood bout with polio had left him partially crippled, and for the rest of his life he suffered from a sense of physical inadequacy. But he had a penetrating intelligence and a sharp tongue. Rejected for military service during World War I because of his disability, he threw himself into his studies and obtained a doctorate from the University of Heidelberg. However, far from exulting in his academic accomplishments, he was terrified of being labeled a "bourgeois intellectual," and he overcompensated by embracing the image of a robust, blond Aryan promoted as the ideal Germanic type espoused by the National Socialist German Workers' Party (NSDAP), precursor of the Nazi Party, which he joined in 1922. His association with the Nazis helped jump-start a career as journalist—he had failed as a poet—and he found work as editor of two Nazi Party magazines: *Völkische Freiheit* (National freedom) and, later, *Nationalsozialistischen Briefe* (NS letters).

In 1926 Adolf HITLER made Goebbels the gauleiter (district leader) for Berlin, putting him in charge of the party's operations in the capital. This was a difficult challenge given the proleftist sentiment that prevailed in the city, but Goebbels proved to be a skillful organizer, printing posters, staging parades, and sending groups of thugs into the streets and taverns to battle communists. He also earned a reputation as an effective orator. In 1927 he launched his own newspaper, *Der Angriff* (The attack). His efforts on behalf of the Nazis in Berlin appeared to pay off. "Dr. Goebbels was gifted with the two things without which the situation in Berlin could not have been mastered: verbal facility and intellect," Hitler said. "For Dr. Goebbels, who had not found much in the way of a political organization when he started, had won Berlin in the truest sense of the word." Hitler was sufficiently impressed to appoint Goebbels reich propaganda leader of the NSDAP in 1929. When the Nazis came to power in 1933, he was further rewarded with a new position: Reich minister for public enlightenment and propaganda.

In his new capacity Goebbels, then only 35, was in charge of all media: the press, publishing, radio, film, and the arts. He presided over a propaganda and publishing empire that included 120 daily or weekly newspapers regularly read by about a million people across the country. With the same efficiency he had demonstrated in Berlin, he undertook the "cleansing" of the arts, imposing censorship and removing Jews and political dissidents from influential positions in the media. A vehement anti-Semite, he exploited the stereotype of the Jewish banker as the embodiment to the excesses of Western capitalism on the one hand and the "Jew-Bolsheviks" in the Soviet Union on the other. In May 1933 he orchestrated the public burning of books written by Jews, Marxists, and others considered seditious. Five years later, in November 1938, he instigated a two-day pogrom known as Kristallnacht (Night of the Broken Glass), which resulted in large-scale destruction of Jewish property. Later Goebbels became one of the principal planners of the FINAL SOLUTION, which led to the mass deportations of Jews from Germany and the occupied territories. Jews and Gypsies (Rom), he asserted, were "unconditionally exterminable."

During World War II, while Goebbels actively sought the annihilation of Jewry, he made sure that the media he controlled avoided any mention of the CONCENTRATION CAMPS or the fate that the Nazis planned for their victims. Hitler relied more and more on him as the war went on. To shore up morale, the propaganda minister gave a famous speech in February 1943 in the Berlin Sportpalast and via radio broadcast declared that Germany was certain to triumph, as it was fabricating "secret weapons" and mountain fortresses that would allow their forces to withstand the Allied assault. The German historian Helmut Heiber observed that Goebbels "was able, until the very last minute, to encourage and exploit a blind trust in Hitler and his genius. It is indeed one of the macabre phenomena of

the Third Reich that even in their country's agony the mass of the German people remained docile and faithful to Hitler's banner . . . In spite of everything they had experienced, they kept the faith."

Goebbels continued to turn out a series of readable, highly polished articles for his newspapers with lofty titles such as "On the Meaning of War," "The Essential Nature of the Crisis," "On the Work of the Spirit," "On Speaking and Being Silent," "The Indispensability of Freedom," and "About National Duty in War." Decisive action on Goebbels's part after an abortive attempt on Hitler's life by disaffected army officers on July 20, 1944, is credited with saving the Nazi regime. A major in the Guards Battalion, Otto Remer, was dispatched by the conspirators with orders to arrest Goebbels, the only leading Nazi in Berlin at the time. But Goebbels convinced Remer, a loyal Nazi, that he was mistaken to think that Hitler was dead. He then put Remer in direct contact with Hitler, who charged the major—whom he promptly promoted to colonel—with rounding up his would-be assassins. That same month he won appointment as general plenipotentiary for total war, a position which put him in charge of the civilian population and the country's material resources, even though there was no real power left for him to exercise. Nonetheless, he continued to fill the columns of his newspapers with words intended to fortify his readers against the bitterness of certain defeat. "We have become a people on the defensive," Goebbels wrote in *Das Reich* on February 11, 1945, just 11 weeks before the end. "We work and we fight, we wander, we leave our homes, we suffer and endure, and we do all this with a silent dignity which, in the end, will arouse the admiration of the entire world. Europe may well

Hermann Göring (right) and Joseph Goebbels *(Library of Congress)*

be happy that it still possesses such a people. Today this people is the salvation of Europe. Tomorrow, therefore, it will be Europe's pride."

As Soviet forces approached the outskirts of Berlin, Goebbels took refuge in the Führerbunker under the Chancellery, where he and Hitler and their families spent their last days. Convinced that the fall of Berlin would bring about the apocalypse and that no redemption was possible for the Nazi leadership, Goebbels declared, "We shall go down in history as the greatest statesmen of all time, or as the greatest criminals." Although Hitler, who committed suicide, had designated him as a successor in his last testament, Goebbels was head of the Reich for only a few hours. On May 1, 1945, determined to follow Hitler's example, he ordered an SS doctor to administer a lethal injection to his six children. He then shot himself, allowing an SS orderly to kill his wife, Magda.

Although he was denounced by the Allies as a master of the Big Lie, Goebbels was cleverer than that. He preferred to twist the truth to suit his ends, averring that it was preferable to being caught out in a lie. "Everybody must know what the situation is," he claimed. Whether Goebbels himself ever understood the situation, however, is doubtful.

Further Reading:

Read, Anthony. *The Devil's Disciples: Hitler's Inner Circle.* New York: W. W. Norton & Company, 2004.

Reuth, Rolf Georg. *Goebbels.* New York: Harvest Books, 1994.

Roberts, Jeremy. *Joseph Goebbels: Nazi Propaganda Minister.* Holocaust Biographies. New York: Rosen Publishing Group, 2000.

Goldstone, Richard J. (1938–)

Richard J. Goldstone became known to the world for his role as one of the judges sitting on South Africa's TRUTH AND RECONCILIATION COMMISSION, which was established to expose the crimes of the APARTHEID era and smooth the transition to democracy. He has also served as chief prosecutor for the United Nations international criminal tribunals for the former Yugoslavia and Rwanda. More recently, he became chairperson of the International Independent Inquiry on Kosovo established in 1999 to investigate crimes carried out in the war in the separatist Yugoslav province. In December 2001 he was appointed as the chairperson of the International Task Force on Terrorism established by the International Bar Association. He has also served on an international panel charged with investigating Nazi activity in Argentina since 1938.

Goldstone was born in South Africa on October 26, 1938, and began practicing law in 1962. In 1980 he was made a judge of the Transvaal Supreme Court; nine years

International Justice Richard Goldstone *(Landov)*

later he was appointed judge of the Appellate Division of the Supreme Court. Between 1991 and 1994, he served as chairperson of the Commission of Inquiry regarding Public Violence and Intimidation, which came to be known as the Goldstone Commission. He became justice of the Constitutional Court of South Africa in 1994, shortly after the end of white rule. As a justice, he had the responsibility of interpreting the country's new constitution. Goldstone also holds several other positions, including chancellor of the University of the Witwatersrand, Johannesburg, and membership on the board of its School of Law; governor of the Hebrew University, Jerusalem; and president of World ORT (an international technical and technology training organization). He has been a recipient of several awards, including the International Human Rights Award of the American Bar Association (1994), and holds honorary doctorates of law from the universities of Cape Town and Witwatersrand, Natal; Hebrew University, Jerusalem; Notre Dame; Maryland University College; Wilfred Laurier in Ontario; the University of Glasgow; the Catholic University of Brabant in Tilburg, the Netherlands; the University of Calgary; and Emory University.

In assessing the success of the South African Truth and Reconciliation Commission, chaired by Archbishop Desmond TUTU, Goldstone observed that a difficult trade-off had to be made. According to the commission's mandate, if an individual freely came forward and confessed to committing a crime during the apartheid era, he was entitled to AMNESTY; full disclosure was obligatory, however. "There have been thousands of applications for indemnity," Goldstone said in an interview. As a result, a great deal of information emerged, including the identities of the people who had killed antiapartheid activists. But, he added, there was a cost. "The cost of the Truth Commission is denying justice to some people who are demanding it. And that's difficult." Victims or their families frequently demand that the perpetrators be prosecuted—"They want them (the murderers) imprisoned"—but once the commission grants them amnesty, the guilty individuals are allowed to go free. "So there is a cost to victims," said Goldstone. Yet, paradoxically, without the commission the families would probably never know the individuals responsible for the murders in the first place—"So it's not a choice between prosecution and truth. It's a compromise between truth and nothing."

See also INTERNATIONAL CRIMINAL TRIBUNAL FOR THE FORMER YUGOSLAVIA; INTERNATIONAL CRIMINAL TRIBUNAL FOR RWANDA; KOSOVO, WAR CRIMES IN.

Further Reading:
Cooper, Belinda, and Richard Goldstone. *War Crimes: The Legacy of Nuremberg.* New York: TV Books Inc., 1999.
Goldstone, Richard. *For Humanity: Reflections of a War Crimes Investigator.* Castle Lectures Series. New Haven, Conn.: Yale University Press, 2000.

Göring, Hermann (1893–1946) *Nazi official and Luftwaffe chief*

Hermann Wilhelm Göring, commander in chief of the Luftwaffe and president of the Reichstag (or parliament), was second only to Adolf HITLER in the Nazi hierarchy, the designated successor of the führer. The son of a judge, Hermann Göring (also spelled Goering) was born in Rosenheim, Bavaria, on January 12, 1893. In 1914, at the start of the First World War, he joined the army but was later transferred to the air force, in which he served as a combat pilot. He was so proficient that he is credited with shooting down 22 Allied planes. But he also displayed no compunction about striking civilian targets, angering his superior, the legendary fighter pilot Baron von Richtofen. After von Richtofen's death, Göring replaced him as squadron leader, and he emerged from the war a decorated war hero. In 1921 he met Hitler, and within a year he had become one of the leaders of the newly formed National Socialist (Nazi) Party. Hitler appointed him commander of the SA, a paramilitary unit better known as the Brown Shirts. For Göring, Nazism offered the adventure and comradeship that he had experienced in the war, and it had the additional advantage of giving him an opportunity to satisfy his hunger for power.

In 1923 Göring took part in the abortive Munich beer hall putsch (coup) along with Hitler. Gravely wounded in the incident, he resorted to morphine to ease the pain, which led to a lifelong addiction to the drug. Forced into exile, he spent the next four years in Austria, Denmark, Italy, and Sweden, occasionally performing in air shows. In Sweden he was briefly hospitalized in an asylum for patients considered dangerous. In 1927 he returned to Germany under a general amnesty and, a year later, made a successful run for the Reichstag. He was instrumental in expediting Hitler's rise to power, using his influence with business interests and military officers to overcome their misgivings about the Nazi leader.

In July 1932 the Nazis secured power at the ballot box, and Göring became president of the Reichstag the same year. Soon after being appointed as chancellor on January 30, 1933, Hitler conferred several appointments on Göring, making him Prussian minister of the interior, commander in chief of the Prussian police and GESTAPO, and commissioner for aviation. As the head of the Gestapo, the Nazi secret police, Göring together with Heinrich HIMMLER and Reinhold HEYDRICH, was responsible for establishing some of the first CONCENTRATION CAMPS to detain political prisoners. Göring then proceeded to suppress all opposition, carrying out purges of officers and police officers whose loyalty to the Nazis was questionable, replacing them with members of the SA (Sturm Abteilung) and the SS (Schutzstaffel). On February 27, 1933, the Reichstag, the seat of the government, was set ablaze, and a mentally ill Dutch bricklayer and communist sympathizer, found at the scene, was arrested for the crime. The fire, possibly set at Göring's instigation, was used as a pretext for the Nazis to crack down on political opposition and to impose a series of emergency decrees to suppress civil liberties. Communists and socialists were rounded up and jailed; the leftist press was shut down. Göring did not neglect rivals in the Nazi Party, either, eliminating his principal rivals in the SA in the Bloody Purge of 1934.

In March 1935 Hitler made Göring commander in chief of the air force. In large measure, Göring created the Luftwaffe, pushing for increased aircraft production and training of pilots. He was so effective that Hitler named him plenipotentiary for the implementation of the Four-Year Plan, which effectively put Göring in charge of the German economy. In 1937 he established the Hermann Göring Works, a gigantic, state-owned industrial enterprise that employed 700,000 workers and made him a fortune. No one in the Nazi regime was as openly avaricious as Göring. He enjoyed a life of ostentatious luxury, residing in a palace in Berlin and holding feasts at his hunting lodge, where he also displayed his collection of stolen art. He changed his uniforms and suits five times a day, sported medieval peasant hats, and carried boar spears. He considered himself "the last Renaissance man," but in spite of his extravagance, debauchery, and corruption, he remained popular with the German public, who considered him an embodiment of German manhood.

After Kristallnacht (Night of the Broken Glass)—the November 1938 pogrom against the Jews—Göring fined the Jewish community a billion marks and ordered the

"Aryanization" of their property. He warned of a "final reckoning with the Jews" and put in motion preparations to expel Jews from Germany and the territories that Germany would soon occupy. Göring was intimately involved in the plans for war, but he preferred to use diplomacy if it would achieve his purposes. Indeed, both Austria (enthusiastically) and Czechoslovakia (reluctantly) acquiesced to German rule without a shot being fired.

Göring proved to be equally effective when Germany went to war in September 1939. As head of the Luftwaffe, he coordinated operations between the air force and forces on the ground, which allowed German forces to overrun Poland, Norway, Denmark, the Netherlands, Belgium, and France in two years. Göring also instituted a campaign of terror bombing against civilian populations, but after these initial successes, the Luftwaffe's performance began to flag. The resistance of the Royal Air Force (RAF) was so effective that it put an end to Hitler's dream of conquering England, and the air war against the USSR encountered serious drawbacks as well. And in spite of Göring's pledge to keep Berlin safe, the RAF managed to penetrate German defenses and bomb the capital.

Göring's star was fading: Hitler despised him and blamed him for German losses, and his rivals in the party began to gain power at his expense. Increasingly isolated, he sank into lethargy and despair, although he found some solace in hunting and in expanding his collection of looted art. Close to the end of the war, Göring misinterpreted a declaration by Hitler to mean that the führer had abdicated. In a last-ditch attempt to regain power, he requested that he be put in charge of the dying Reich so that he could personally negotiate Germany's surrender. Hitler was outraged and ordered Göring sacked from his posts, expelled from the party that he had helped found, and arrested. Just days later he was taken prisoner again, this time by advancing American troops. Following the war, went on trial before the Nuremberg Tribunal established by the Allies to prosecute Nazi war criminals. He was indicted on four counts: conspiracy to wage war, crimes against peace, war crimes, and CRIMES AGAINST HUMANITY.

Göring mounted a vigorous defense and dominated many of the proceedings, convinced that he would be immortalized by future generations as a German war hero. The judges were not impressed and found him guilty on all counts. "There is nothing to be said in mitigation," they observed in their judgment. "For Göring was often, indeed almost always, the moving force, second only to his leader. He was the leading war aggressor, both as political and as military leader; he was the director of the slave labor program and the creator of the oppressive program against the Jews and other races, at home and abroad. All of these crimes he has frankly admitted. . . . His guilt is unique in its enormity. The record discloses no excuses for this man."

Göring was sentenced to death by hanging, but two hours before his execution the "last Renaissance man" committed suicide, taking a cyanide capsule he had managed to smuggle into his cell. How he acquired the capsule is a matter of dispute. One theory holds that a sympathetic U.S. army captain who had access to his cell was responsible. Over the months in captivity, the two had developed a close friendship, and according to some accounts, Göring had managed to charm the captain with stories about his life. He even left the captain some of his possessions, including a watch he had once worn.

See also FINAL SOLUTION; NUREMBERG TRIALS.

Further Reading:
Mosley, Leonard, *The Reich Marshal: A Biography of Hermann Göring.* London: Weidenfeld and Nicolson, 1974.
Paul, Wolfgang. *Hermann Göring: Hitler Paladin or Puppet?* Translated by Helmet Bogler. New York: Arms & Armour, 1998.
Swearingen, Ben. *Mystery of Hermann Göring's Suicide.* New York: Harcourt, 1985.

Gotovina, Ante (1955–) *Croatian military officer*
Ante Gotovina is a Croatian officer charged by the INTERNATIONAL CRIMINAL TRIBUNAL FOR THE FORMER YUGOSLAVIA (ICTY) for CRIMES AGAINST HUMANITY, committing violations of the laws and customs of war during the Balkan wars of the early 1990s. A professional soldier and former member of the French foreign legion, Gotovina took over as commanding officer of the Split military district in 1995 and thereafter became involved in the military operation that resulted in his indictment.

According to the court, Gotovina was in charge of Croatian forces carrying out atrocities against Serbs living in a region of Croatia known as Krajina. At the time of Operation Oluja (Storm), as it was called, war had broken out between Serbia, Croatia, and Bosnia, all of which previously had formed Yugoslavia. (Yugoslavia now consists only of Serbia and Montenegro.) Serb minorities in Croatia were at particular risk, as were Croatian and Bosnian minorities in parts of the former Yugoslavia with large Serb populations. In August 1995 Croatia launched a military offensive intended to retake the Krajina region from Serb forces. Prosecutors allege that Gotovina planned and carried out several crimes for the duration of the operation, which lasted until November. Although thousands of Serbs fled to Bosnia and Herzegovina and to Serbia, others were stranded in the beleaguered region because of sickness, infirmity, or age. The indictment charges that troops under Gotovina's command "systematically harassed, and/or unlawfully killed" many of these Serbs and plundered or destroyed their property. Gotovina was held responsible for the killings of at least 150 Serbs and the DISAPPEARANCES of hundreds of others.

In 2000 Gotovina was relieved of his command, and he was indicted by the ICTY a year later. He is not without his defenders in Croatia who contend that Gotovina is a war hero who defended his country and has been unjustly accused of crimes committed by troops and Croatian civilians returning to Krajina over whom he had little or no control. In June 2001, the day before he was to be served with the indictment, he disappeared. In 2005 he was arrested in Spain and extradited to the Netherlands for trial by the ICTY. His importance is underscored by the fact that the European Union (EU) insisted on his arrest and extradition before it would permit Croatia to join the EU.

See also BOSNIA AND HERZEGOVINA, HUMAN RIGHTS VIOLATIONS IN; CROATIA, HUMAN RIGHTS VIOLATIONS IN; SERBIA, HUMAN RIGHTS VIOLATIONS IN.

Further Reading:
Glenny, Misha. *The Fall of Yugoslavia: The Third Balkan War.* New York: Penguin Books, 1996.
Hagan, John. *Justice in the Balkans: Prosecuting War Crimes in the Hague Tribunal.* Chicago Series in Law and Society. Chicago: University of Chicago Press, 2003.
Harris, Nathaniel. *The War in Former Yugoslavia.* New Perspectives. London: Hodder & Stoughton, 1997.
Hazan, Pierre, and James Thomas Snyder. *Justice in a Time of War: The True Story Behind the International Criminal Tribunal for the Former Yugoslavia.* Eugenia and Hugh M. Stewart Series on Eastern Europe. Austin: Texas A&M University Press, 2004.

Grotius, Hugo (Hugo de Groot) (1583–1645) *Dutch philosopher of war conduct*
Hugo de Groot, better known by his Latin eponym Grotius, has been called the "father of the law of nations." A Dutch jurist, humanist, and statesman, he wrote two famous treatises on international law. The first was *Mare Liberum* (*The Free Sea*, 1609), which contended that the seas belonged to all nations and that no state could claim exclusive rights over any part of it. He found the basis of his assertions in higher moral laws, which he called natural law and the basic law of humanity. These laws, he said, governed relations between states and individuals. He appealed to what he termed a "society of mankind," which transcended the laws of individual states.

Grotius employed the same moral approach to international law in his next major work, *De Jure Belli ac Pacis* (*On the Law of War and Peace*, 1625). In this treatise he maintains that war violates natural law, which applies to the conduct of nations and of individuals. War is permissible only in cases where there is a moral imperative for it and when attempts at conciliation have failed. Even then, there are limitations on the way that a war can be fought. For instance, Grotius concludes that a "universal law" can be adduced from Christian and Muslim traditions forbidding the enslavement of enemies captured in war. This presaged the provisions of the GENEVA CONVENTIONS covering treatment of PRISONERS OF WAR.

In a similar vein, Grotius asserted that a belligerent could not seize territory in "possession of long standing" held by another country because it was "contrary to the common sense of nations." It was his conviction that there was a benefit to the development of larger and more powerful states—a trend that was already in progress in Europe at the time he was writing—because larger states would have a greater interest in promoting rational policies that would in turn improve chances for peace. But in spite of his optimism, Grotius had to acknowledge that powerful states could wreak tremendous destruction if they did go to war, whether impelled by nationalism or religion.

See also JUST AND UNJUST WARS.

Further Reading:
Onuma, Yasuaki, and James Crawford, eds. *A Normative Approach to War: Peace, War, and Justice in Hugo Grotius.* Oxford: Oxford University Press, 1993.
Tuck, Richard. *The Rights of War and Peace: Political Thought and the International Order from Grotius to Kant.* Oxford: Oxford University Press, 2001.

Guantánamo detainees
Since late 2001 the United States naval base on Guantánamo Bay, Cuba, has served as a high-security prison for detainees arrested in Afghanistan and elsewhere in the U.S.-led war against terrorism. Several foreign fighters captured in clashes in Iraq since the American-led invasion of that country have also been imprisoned in Guantánamo. The status of the detainees—of whom there were approximately 550 in early 2005—has been a source of rancorous dispute. The Bush administration has taken the position that as "unlawful" or "enemy combatants," the detainees are not entitled to the same rights and protections guaranteed by the GENEVA CONVENTIONS that ordinarily apply to PRISONERS OF WAR taken in international or internal conflicts. Moreover, the U.S. Justice Department has argued that because these detainees are not being held on American territory—the base is rented from Cuba under the terms of a 1903 treaty that the Cuban government has repudiated—the U.S. courts have no jurisdiction over their fate.

Under the policies put forth by the Bush administration, detainees can be held indefinitely without charges or

A detainee at Guantánamo Bay (GITMO) prison in Cuba
(David P. Coleman/U.S. Department of Defense)

any access to legal counsel. Washington has justified these measures as necessary to protect the security of the United States. For instance, detainees may be able to shed light on terrorist plans and operations; were they given prisoners-of-war status, they would have no obligation to tell interrogators anything other than their name, rank, and serial number. The Justice Department also contends that putting a detainee on trial carries several risks. For one, a trial might reveal interrogation practices that intelligence officers use to extract information. For another, it might force prosecutors to drop a case rather than reveal evidence against a defendant that might jeopardize national security. Even if the detainee were no longer of any intelligence value, U.S. officials maintain that there is good reason to keep him in custody anyway. "You're basically keeping them off the battlefield, and unfortunately in the war on terrorism the battlefield is everywhere," a senior administration official said.

Human rights groups, the United Nations, and such international bodies as the INTERNATIONAL COMMITTEE OF THE RED CROSS (ICRC) have, however, insisted that the prisoners are entitled to the protections conferred by the Geneva Conventions as prisoners of war. Critics of the

Bush administration have also pointed out that many of the prisoners may not be members of al-QAEDA or other terrorist groups but simply had the misfortune of being in the wrong place at the wrong time during a military sweep by U.S. forces. The CIA itself expressed concerns about some of the individuals being taken into custody. In September 2002 a secret CIA study raised questions about the significance of the Guantánamo detainees and apparently suggested that many of them might be low-level recruits or innocent of any wrongdoing.

Generally speaking, U.S. courts, while recognizing broad discretion on the part of the executive branch to conduct military operations in times of war, have nonetheless asserted jurisdictional authority over Guantánamo, contending that for all practical purposes, the base falls under U.S. sovereignty. Nor have federal courts been inclined to accept the government's argument that the detainees have no right to legal counsel whatsoever. In June 2004 the U.S. Supreme Court ruled that detainees at Guantánamo had the right to challenge their imprisonment but left it to lower courts to handle individual appeals. In response, the American military established Combatant Status Review Tribunals, which were intended solely to determine whether detainees were properly held as "enemy combatants." The tribunals could determine whether a detainee could be released depending on whether he was deemed to represent a security threat or whether he had any significant intelligence value. Before being disbanded, these tribunals had ordered three individuals freed and another 25 to remain in custody. (All hearings were conducted in secret.) Several other detainees—mostly nationals of U.S. allies such as the United Kingdom and Australia—have been repatriated, often under pressure from their governments. In January 2005, however, U.S. District Court judge Joyce Hens Green of the District of Columbia ruled that the tribunals were unconstitutional because detainees were not allowed lawyers or allowed to hear classified information against them. "Although this nation unquestionably must take strong action under the leadership of the commander in chief to protect itself against enormous and unprecedented threats," Green wrote in her opinion, "that necessity cannot negate the existence of the most basic and fundamental threats for which the people of this country have fought and died for well over 200 years." Her decision, however, was exactly the opposite of one issued only two weeks before by another judge in the same court, setting the stage for a new appeal to the Supreme Court in hope of obtaining clarification about the legal status of Guantánamo detainees and their right of redress.

The debate over the legal status of detainees has been intensified by allegations over their treatment. Although the Bush administration issued assurances that it intended to treat detainees "humanely and, to the extent appropriate and consistent with military necessity, in a manner consistent with the principles of Geneva," considerable evidence has emerged that the detainees have been mistreated and suffered serious abuse. Human rights groups have contended that the mistreatment amounted to TORTURE under the definition of the Geneva Conventions and the CONVENTION AGAINST TORTURE. These allegations set off a heated debate in Congress that carried over into hearings for the nominations of Alberto Gonzales as attorney general and Michael Chertoff as the head of Homeland Security. As Bush's legal counsel, the former had offered opinions that might under some interpretations condone abuse, while Chertoff, as deputy attorney general, had also been criticized for sanctioning impermissible treatment of detainees. (Both men were ultimately confirmed.)

Revelations about inhumane practices being used at Guantánamo as a means of extracting information from prisoners surfaced only months after the public learned of abuses by U.S. authorities at Abu Ghraib prison in Iraq and at American military bases in Afghanistan. Defense Department officials adamantly denied that torture went on at Guantánamo while offering assurances that any credible accounts of abuse would be fully investigated. "U.S. policy condemns and prohibits torture," a Pentagon spokesman declared. "U.S. personnel are required to follow this policy and applicable law. The U.S. policy requires that all detainees are treated humanely." The spokesman also pointed out that al-Qaeda training manuals call on captives to make false allegations of torture. Nonetheless, declassified reports by FBI agents appear to bear out some of the allegations. According to the *Washington Post,* the agents reported that detainees "were shackled to the floor in fetal positions for more than 24 hours at a time, left without food and water, and allowed to defecate on themselves." Dogs were used to intimidate detainees. In one case, a detainee was "wrapped in an Israeli flag and bombarded with loud music in an apparent attempt to soften his resistance to interrogation." The FBI agents cited in the report further said that military interrogators impersonated FBI agents, apparently as a way of avoiding legal responsibility for any abuse. In one case, Mamdouh Habib, an Australian arrested in Pakistan as an al-Qaeda supporter, claimed that he had suffered from physical abuse while in U.S. captivity that ranged from a kick "that nearly killed me" to electric shocks administered through a wired helmet. Although his account of torture—which he gave after being freed—was not confirmed, it was similar in many respects with other documented reports from other former detainees, human rights groups, and some government agents involved in the detention system. Other eyewitnesses have stated that female interrogators allegedly used seductive techniques and employed degrading practices on Muslim men to

soften them up—for instance, touching them suggestively, dressing provocatively, and smearing them with red dye meant to simulate menstrual blood. There have also been several incidents, termed "self-injurious," as well as a number of suicide attempts among detainees.

Whether the White House has ever sanctioned harsh methods of interrogation that could lead to such abuses is a matter of intense debate. In principle, the Bush administration has condemned torture, issuing a memo in January 2005 that repudiated an earlier memo which offered only a constricted definition of torture. The later memo did not, however, mention "cruel, inhuman or degrading treatment," which is also prohibited by the Convention against Torture, to which the United States is a signatory. In 2003, however, White House counsel Gonzales issued a legal opinion in which he asserted that non-Iraqis captured by U.S. forces in Iraq were not entitled to the protections of the Geneva Conventions, which he had earlier characterized as "quaint" and "obsolete." "There was a fear about creating a sanctuary for terrorists if we were to say that if you come and fight against America in the conflict with Iraq, that you would receive the protections of a prisoner of war," he testified during his Senate confirmation hearings for attorney general. Shortly after the terrorist attacks of September 11, 2001, John C. Yoo, then deputy assistant attorney general, wrote a memo in which he said that "the power of the president is at its zenith under the Constitution when the President is directing military operations of the armed forces," adding that he had the authority "to take whatever actions he deems appropriate to pre-empt or respond to terrorist threats from new quarters" whether or not such entities could be "demonstrably linked to the September 11 incidents."

According to Gonzales, the "new paradigm renders obsolete Geneva's strict limitations on questioning of enemy prisoners." Under this policy it appeared that the executive branch had the power to overrule congressional laws and INTERNATIONAL HUMANITARIAN LAW, allowing the president, in effect, to exempt the United States from its obligation to comply with the Geneva Conventions. Under such authority the president could, in theory, approve of torture or detain prisoners without a hearing. In another memo, Gonzales suggested that if the conventions were inapplicable, then U.S. officials could escape prosecution for war crimes in the future. Nonetheless, he did allow that such a determination would risk "widespread condemnation among our allies" and provide a pretext for other countries to try to avoid jurisdiction of the Geneva Conventions. There was an additional problem: If the United States repudiated the conventions at least in certain circumstances, U.S. soldiers might not be accorded POW protections in retaliation. President Bush nonetheless accepted his counsel's position when he signed an order classifying fighters seized in Afghanistan as "unlawful combatants," stating on February 7, 2002, "I accept the legal conclusion of the Department of Justice and determine that none of the provisions of Geneva apply to our conflict with al Qaeda in Afghanistan or elsewhere throughout the world." His words echoed remarks by Vice President Dick Cheney shortly after the strikes on the World Trade Center and Pentagon in which he said that the United States would have to work "sort of the dark side" and that "it's going to be vital for us to use any means at our disposal, basically, to achieve our objective." Secretary of Defense Donald H. Rumsfeld subsequently approved the use of special interrogation techniques for some terrorist suspects in Iraq that might have influenced interrogators at Guantánamo. In August 2002 Justice Department lawyers defined *torture* in a legal memorandum as "equivalent in intensity to the pain accompanying serious physical injury such as organ failure, impairment of bodily function or even death."

Then-Secretary of State Colin L. Powell took issue with others in the administration, contending that if POW status were withheld from every al-Qaeda and TALIBAN suspect, it would "reverse over a century of U.S. policy and practice," "undermine the protections of the law of war for our troops," have "a high cost in terms of negative international reaction," and "undermine public support among critical allies." But Powell's opinion was ignored. Instead, Justice and Defense Department officials tried to set new ground rules about what kind of interrogation methods could be acceptable while distinguishing between "torture" and "cruel, inhuman, or degrading treatment." Some 35 different interrogation techniques were described according to their "utility" and assessed as to whether they were in compliance with U.S. and international law. In many cases, *torture* was defined very narrowly. In an August 2002 memo, then-Assistant Attorney General Jay S. Bybee stated that torture would occur only if a victim experienced the sort of pain and suffering "associated with serious physical injury so severe that death, organ failure, or permanent damage resulting in a loss of significant body function will likely result." Officials debated "the lowest boundary of what constitutes torture," and conducted a "risk benefit analysis" of interrogation techniques. In another 2002 memo, Bybee wrote: "Certain justification defenses might be available that would potentially eliminate criminal liability. Standard criminal law defenses of necessity and self-defense could justify interrogation methods needed to elicit information to prevent a direct and imminent threat to the United States and its citizens." A Pentagon working group report on detainee interrogations in 2003 suggested that "lawfulness will depend in significant part on procedural protections that demonstrate a legitimate purpose and that there was no intent to inflict significant mental or physical pain."

Amid all the controversy, the CIA and the Pentagon were still moving ahead on plans to house the detainees permanently, including those who might fall into U.S. custody in future conflicts or counterterrorism operations. "We've been operating in the moment because that's what has been required," said a senior administration official. Acknowledging that the detention system in Guantánamo had strained relations between the United States and other countries, he added. "Now we can take a breath. We have the ability and need to look at long-term solutions."

Short-term solutions to resolving the problem of the detainees, however, have not come easily. The Pentagon has made attempts to comply with the Supreme Court's ruling by establishing some form of legal proceedings for the detainees. But federal courts and human rights advocates have questioned the proposed military tribunals that have classified nearly all detainees as enemy combatants—38 of 596 detainees, meaning that they were not entitled to protections of the Geneva Conventions. Under the Pentagon's proposal, the detainees are not allowed to have legal representation before the tribunals and are denied access to classified information that has been used to designate them as enemy combatants. The lower federal courts have disagreed about how these cases should be handled; for instance while U.S. district court judge Joyce Hens Green ruled that the tribunal hearings were unconstitutional, U.S. district court judge Richard Leon dismissed a lawsuit by some detainees on the grounds that any challenges should be submitted to the U.S. military, not to civilian courts. A year and a half after the Supreme Court's ruling, the Bush administration was still facing legal suits on behalf of detainees who had claimed that they had no opportunity to challenge their classification as enemy combatants. Many detainees, despairing of any legal redress, have staged hunger strikes. In late summer 2005, a lawyer for several Kuwaiti detainees reported that hundreds of prisoners had stopped eating to protest their conditions; for its part, the U.S. military maintained that while at one point 105 detainees were on a hunger strike, the number had dropped off, and, as of September 2005, only 36 were still on a hunger strike, 16 of whom were being fed intravenously. In February 2006 a UN report accused the United States of torturing detainees at the prison.

See also IRAQ, HUMAN RIGHTS VIOLATIONS IN POST-SADDAM.

Further Reading:
Burke, Jason. *Al-Qaeda: Casting a Shadow of Terror.* London: I. B. Tauris, 2004.
Danner, Mark. *Torture and Truth: America, Abu Ghraib, and the War on Terror.* New York: New York Review Books, 2004.

Gunaratna, Rohan. *Inside Al Qaeda: Global Network of Terror.* New York: Berkley Publishing Group, 2003.

Hersh, Seymour M. *Chain of Command: The Road from 9/11 to Abu Ghraib.* New York: HarperCollins, 2004.

Scheuer, Michael. *Imperial Hubris: Why the West Is Losing the War on Terror.* Washington, D.C.: Potomac Books, 2004.

Guatemala, human rights violations in

Guatemala is emerging painfully from decades of civil war, but grave human rights abuses persist, and the government has taken only halting steps to bring perpetrators of war crimes to justice. According to estimates by the United Nations, in the 35-year civil war (1961–96), approximately a million people were displaced and untold numbers mentally or physically traumatized. The war was marked by numerous atrocities. According to a 1999 report by the Historical Clarification Commission, which investigated human rights violations during the war, the army was responsible for 93 percent of all massacres, TORTURES, DISAPPEARANCES, and killings. Most of the victims were unarmed civilians. Left-wing guerrillas of the Guatemalan National Revolutionary Union accounted for 3 percent of all abuses. The commission also accused the CIA of directly and indirectly sponsoring illegal state operations during the armed conflict. Although a peace accord was reached in 1996, the country has yet to overcome the legacy of war. A truth commission established after the war has found evidence of tens of thousands of abuses. The justice system is weak, and most of the perpetrators of crimes during the war in Guatemala have yet to be brought before a court of law.

The war began in 1961 when communist-inspired insurgents launched a series of strikes in response to egregious human rights abuses by the army and government, who were backed by powerful business and landholding interests. The Mayan peasants who make up more than 50 percent of the population bore the brunt of the army's oppression. (The rest of the population consists of people of mixed Spanish and Indian descent, called Ladino.) The conflict was fueled to some degree by the failure of the government to make good on its promise of social, agrarian, and economic reforms. In an attempt to mollify the Indian peasants, the government did begin to take steps to improve their living conditions, but only at the cost of losing support from hard-line rightists who initiated terrorist attacks on the government as well.

In 1968 communist guerrillas expanded the conflict, first by killing two U.S. embassy military attachés in Guatemala City, the capital, in January and then by assassinating the U.S. ambassador the following August as he resisted a kidnap attempt. Two years later leftists kidnapped the West German ambassador. By this point the entire country was engulfed in terror and fear. During the 1970s, rightist death squads murdered an estimated 50,000 leftists and political opponents. Opposition politicians, judicial officials, trade unionists, academics, medical staff, priests, nuns, and human rights workers were all at risk of being targeted. In the early 1980s, violence spread to the countryside. The army considered all Mayan peasants to be guerrilla supporters and adopted a strategy known as *quitarle el agua del pez*—taking water away from fish, which in practical terms meant destroying all sources of food or support for the insurgents. Army troops proceeded to systematically destroy entire villages and communities, uprooting hundreds of thousands of Mayans from their homes. Many of them fled to the mountains or took refuge in Mexico, the United States, or Canada. The atrocities perpetrated against the Indians—called *la violencia,* a period from the late 1970s to the early 1980s—is considered to be genocidal in nature insofar as it was directed against a particular group. Many of the atrocities bore the signs of being planned at the highest reaches of government, according to

Mortar rounds being prepared for destruction with other ammunition in Guatemala *(United Nations/DPI)*

evidence compiled by human rights groups. To protect the abusers from prosecution, the legislature enacted laws that made it impossible to prosecute them.

In mid-1978, General Romeo Lucas García became Guatemala's president, and he immediately set about to kill political opponents, possibly ordering the deaths of up to 5,000 people. The excesses of his regime were too much for Washington to stomach, and the United States cut off all military assistance. (However, the U.S. government continued to provide significant financial and political support to Guatemala, viewing the country as an ally in the global struggle against communism. In 1998 President Bill Clinton issued a public apology in Guatemala for the United States' role in supporting a succession of brutal regimes.) President Lucas's support eroded, even among his closest supporters, and he was ousted by dissident army officers who staged two coups in 1983. Although civilian rule was restored two years later, it did not last for long. In 1993 President Jorge Serrano Elias was ousted by military, business, and political leaders when he attempted to dissolve Congress and suspend constitutional rights. On December 29, 1996, a peace agreement was signed by four top leftist rebel leaders representing the Unidad Revolucionaria Nacional Guatemalteca (URNG) and representatives of the government.

Since 1996 both the government and the former guerrillas have publicly apologized for their crimes. The military, however, has shown no indication to do likewise. In the years since the peace accord, local rights groups have had little success bringing human rights cases before the Guatemalan courts. One of these cases involves a massacre at Las Dos Erres, which occurred in 1982. In that incident soldiers killed more than 160 civilians in the village of Las Dos Erres, burying some alive in the village well, killing infants by slamming their heads against walls, and raping young women for three days straight. But this was only one of 400 massacres documented by human rights groups. Twenty-one indigenous communities have brought charges against former military commanders for CRIMES AGAINST HUMANITY, including GENOCIDE.

Only two major human rights cases have resulted in convictions of senior army officers. Even these came about only after a concerted campaign of intimidation and violence in which witnesses were assassinated and investigators, judges, and prosecutors were forced to flee the country. (Both convictions were subsequently overturned on dubious grounds and remain under review in the courts.) Although the prosecutor's office has opened other cases, there is little sign that they are being actively pursued. The government has, however, made settlements with some families of victims of state violence. Most of the investigations of the war crimes have been conducted by the Historical Clarification Commission, sponsored by the United Nations, and by the Catholic Church—a role that carries significant risks. In

1998 Bishop Juan Gerardi Conedera was beaten to death only a few days after he had presented a report issued by the commission entitled *Never Again in Guatemala,* which attributed the overwhelming number of human rights violations during the war to the army.

HUMAN RIGHTS WATCH maintains that the lack of accountability has contributed to what it calls "a general climate of insecurity" in the country which has led to corruption, drug trafficking, and organized crime. In fact, violent crime is a principal concern of most ordinary citizens. Much of the violence stems from poverty; Guatemala has the third most unequal distribution of income in the world.

The U.S. State Department in its 2003 *Country Report* notes a deterioration of human rights in certain areas in the previous year. Security forces have been accused of committing a number of EXTRAJUDICIAL KILLINGS. MINUGUA, the French acronym for the United Nations Human Rights Mission to Guatemala, reported that it had received 89 allegations of extrajudicial killings between July 2001 and June 2002 and had confirmed the validity of the claims in 13 cases and 25 attempted killings. Some of these cases were the result of accidental discharging of weapons, drunkenness, and "questionable crowd control techniques." Other cases appear to be politically motivated and might have involved municipal officials and mayors. Large landowners in rural districts have also been implicated in employing agents or local police to execute peasants occupying their property illegally. In the large majority of these murders, the criminals have not been charged, let alone convicted. The judiciary and prosecutors are unable to ensure fair trials and due process. The legal apparatus of the government is hamstrung by corruption, a lack of will, and a lack of resources. In the cities, police have carried out killings under the pretext of "social cleansing"—the executions of gang members, juvenile delinquents, street children, prostitutes, and homosexuals who are considered "socially undesirable." Security forces have also tortured and abused suspects and prisoners. Arbitrary arrests and prolonged detentions continue to be problems.

In 2003 the UN Special Rapporteur for Human Rights Defenders warned of a rising level of threats against judicial personnel, human rights workers, journalists, witnesses, labor organizers, church activists, and labor unionists. Local and international observers have been alarmed by attacks and threats directed against Guatemalans seeking justice for past abuses, especially those stemming from the war. According to Human Rights Watch, those human rights cases that are brought tend to languish without being investigated or heard because of the inefficiency of the judicial system. In its *Country Report,* the U.S. State Department took note of the phenomenon: "While some of these attacks may have been instances of common crime, the numbers and patterns of the attacks point to a deliberate, systematic effort to intimidate human rights workers." Those responsible for this campaign of terror, says Human Rights Watch, "are affiliated with private, secretive, illegally armed networks or organizations, commonly referred to in Guatemala as 'clandestine groups.' " The groups appear to be linked to both elements in the state security agencies and organized crime.

In 2003 retired General Efraín RIOS MONTT, one of the military leaders blamed for many of the worst abuses while in power, was allowed by the Guatemalan Supreme Court to run for the presidency. The ruling sparked fears of renewed oppression should he have won. According to Human Rights Watch, Rios Montt is implicated in the massacres of "tens of thousands of civilians," including the massacre of Las Dos Erres. The United States had once embraced Rios Montt; President Ronald Reagan called him "a man of great personal integrity" and stated that he had gotten a "bum rap" over allegations of atrocities. Human rights advocates were immensely relieved when Rios Montt was came in third in a field of three. Oscar Berger emerged as the winner, and one of his first acts was to sign an accord with the United Nations to create an international commission to investigate the clandestine groups that have been responsible for much of the recent political violence. The Commission of Investigation into Illegal Groups and Clandestine Security Apparatuses, as it is known, or CICI-ACS, is led by a UN-appointed commissioner and works with the Guatemalan attorney general's office. At the same time the commission is supposed to take steps to curb the attacks and threats against human rights defenders, justice officials, journalists, and other groups that have been victimized in the past. According to Human Rights Watch, the commission will be judged by how well it succeeds in gathering evidence for criminal prosecutions that will allow state institutions the ability to purge corrupt officials while "providing the general public with a clearer understanding of who these groups are and how they operate."

Nonetheless, it is not clear whether Guatemala is truly prepared to confront its violent legacy. In January 2005 the country's highest court closed down a crucial war crimes trial against 16 soldiers accused of killing hundreds of 226 civlians in the village of Don Erres in 1982 at the height of the civil war, ruling that they were exempt from prosecution.

Further Reading:

Archdiocese of Guatemala. *Guatemala: Never Again!* Maryknoll, N.Y.: Orbis Books, 1999.

O'Kane, Trish. *In Focus Guatemala: A Guide to the People, Politics and Culture.* London: Latin America Bureau, 1999.

Wilkinson, Daniel. *Silence on the Mountain: Stories of Terror, Betrayal, and Forgetting in Guatemala.* Boston: Houghton Mifflin, 2002.

Guinea, human rights violations in

One of the poorest countries in Africa, Guinea actually has mineral wealth that, properly exploited, could make it one of the richest. Its misfortunes are due to several factors, among them misrule and corruption. Moreover, it has the bad luck of being located next door to Liberia and Sierra Leone. It could be said that in the last decade Liberia's principal export to its neighbors has been war. The civil strife that began in Liberia in the early 1990s has had a devastating impact on both Sierra Leone and Guinea. The spread of war into these countries, which were not known for a pristine reputation for human rights to begin with, only made things worse for civilians caught up in the violence. Because of its geographical position, Guinea has ended up becoming a temporary home to one of the largest refugee populations on the continent, surpassed only by Tanzania, which is much larger. By 2000 Guinea was playing grudging host to up to half a million REFUGEES fleeing fighting in Sierra Leone and Liberia. Their presence strained an already beleaguered economy and heightened ethnic tensions. The border areas, where they initially took sanctuary, were targeted by Liberian forces, and more than 40,000 refugees were relocated into the interior for their protection. Nonetheless, Guinea has shown little regard for the refugees. According to reports by human rights organizations, security forces routinely harassed the refugees whether in camps or on the move. Refugees seeking safety in the interior were routinely stopped at military checkpoints where they were subjected to arbitrary strip searches, beatings, sexual assault, and extortion. According to HUMAN RIGHTS WATCH, some refugees were tortured or beaten to death in prison.

Guinea cannot be considered an innocent party in the conflict that engulfed its neighbors beginning in the 1990s, however. For several years the government backed a rebel group that was mounting an insurgency against the rule of President Charles TAYLOR in Liberia. The group known as Liberians United for Reconciliation and Democracy (LURD) operated for several months from bases in Guinea as well as Liberia. In 2003 Taylor sent forces into Guinea in retaliation. LUND has also been implicated in human rights violations, especially in the forcible conscription of children to fight on the front lines. (To be fair, LUND's human rights violations were less frequent or egregious than those committed by Liberian forces.) The conflict also closed off significant areas of Guinea to human rights organizations and aid agencies, making it impossible for outside observers to assess conditions among the refugee and indigenous civilian populations. A cease-fire, agreed to in Ghana on June 17, 2003, brought an end to the armed conflict, and a fragile peace has since taken hold of the region. Although thousands of refugees have returned home, there were still more than 100,000 refugees in Guinea in 2004.

Even in the absence of war, Guinea still suffers from despotism. The country is led by Lansana Conte, who has ruled the country since he seized power in a bloodless coup in 1984. Although he gives lip service to democracy, a referendum held in 2003, which returned him to power for a third term, was considered fraudulent and boycotted by the opposition in protest. Critics called the vote, which removed a previous limit of two terms, nothing less than "a constitutional coup." They suspect that Conte intends to become president for life. Any chance that the opposition will be allowed to express its views, however, is minimal; the state controls the newspapers, radio, and TV.

See also CHILDREN'S RIGHTS; LIBERIA, HUMAN RIGHTS VIOLATIONS IN; SIERRA LEONE, human rights violations in.

Gujarat, massacres in

Gujarat is one of India's most industrialized states, but in 2002 it became best known not for its thriving economy but for the massacres of thousands of Muslims by mobs of Hindu fanatics. Relations between the country's majority Hindu and minority Muslim population have a long and bloody history, extending back to the partition of the Indian subcontinent—then under British rule—in 1947. That act set in motion one of the most massive transfers of peoples ever witnessed, with millions of Hindus fleeing Pakistan and millions of Muslims going the other way to India. Up to 1 million people on both sides were killed in the chaos and bloodshed that followed the British departure. Even after partition, however, India still had one of the largest Muslim populations in the world—about 150 million. About 9 percent of Gujarat's population of over 50 million is Muslim.

Much of the slaughter that took place after partition occurred on trains transporting REFUGEES in either direction. What made the February 2002 Gujarat massacres particularly chilling was that the first spasm of violence also occurred on board a train. On February 27 fire broke out on a train carrying a group of Hindu pilgrims to the temple town of Ayodhya in central India. Hindus at the scene claimed that Muslims were responsible. The fire killed 58 people, most of them women and children. (A subsequent investigation by the Indian government in early 2005 ruled the fire an accident.) The chief minister of the state—a Hindu nationalist—called the conflagration a "terrorist attack." His words were construed as a signal for Hindu nationalists to take revenge on the Muslim community. Over the next several days, mobs rampaged through Muslim neighborhoods in the city of Ahmedabad and in other cities and villages across the state, destroying property and killing over 300 people. Women were raped, and mosques, houses, and businesses were looted and burned. In most cases police did little or nothing to halt the violence. There were some reports that police even seized fleeing Muslims and turned them over to the mobs. The central government in New Delhi, then dominated by the Hindu nationalist Bharatiya Janata Party (BJP), refused to send in the army. Over 35,000 Muslims were driven from their homes in Ahmedabad alone.

According to HUMAN RIGHTS WATCH, considerable evidence indicates that the attacks on Muslims was planned in advance and organized with the assistance of the police and cooperation of state officials. The human rights group lays much of the blame for the violence on the National Volunteer Corps (RSS), a militant Hindu organization with links to the BJP. (It was an RSS follower who murdered Mahatma Gandhi in 1948.) A plot to uproot the Muslim population from the state had been underway for some time; the RSS had circulated computerized lists of Muslim homes and businesses that were to be targeted by mobs in advance. The Godhra incident simply provided the militants with the pretext they needed to initiate the pogrom. A report by Human Rights Watch accuses the Gujurati government of "a massive cover-up of the sources of the killing." To back up this allegation, the group cites the pressure applied to police not to arrest instigators and participants in the violence who were identified by eyewitnesses, as well as the failure of prosecutors and courts to bring the guilty to justice. More than half the 4,252 cases filed after the riots were dismissed, while others resulted in acquittals. However, in 2004, after the Congress Party had taken power, the Supreme Court ordered new investigations of 2,472 cases relating to the violence in Gujarat.

See also INDIA, HUMAN RIGHTS VIOLATIONS IN.

gulag

The Soviet gulag, chronicled in the works of Nobel laureate Aleksandr SOLZENITSYN, was a system of labor camps to which millions were exiled during the years of Joseph STALIN's rule. The word is an acronym for Glavnoye Upravleniye Lagere (Chief Administration of Corrective Labor Camps). During the czarist era, political dissidents were frequently exiled to Siberia, but after the Russian Revolution of 1917, which brought the Communists to power, these camps were shut down. (Approximately 1.5 million people were exiled to Siberia during the 19th century and, several Bolshevik leaders, including Lenin, Trotsky, and Stalin, served time in these camps.) The camps were reopened several years later by Stalin.

About 50 million people perished in the gulag between 1930 and 1950, succumbing to starvation, exposure, execution, and mistreatment. The victims came from all strata of society. Any person whom Stalin considered a threat or potentially subversive was sent to Siberia. Artists and writers who failed to hew to the party line or did not adhere to the officially sanctioned style of socialist realism were liable to find themselves sentenced to the gulags for several years. Others were accused of "individualistic tendencies" or were arrested for having opposed the establishment of collective farms. People who had lived abroad or those with relatives abroad were frequently rounded up and deported as well. Membership in the Communist Party was no guarantee of immunity. Entire populations were targeted by Stalin's secret police, including Ukrainians, Kazakhs, Uzbeks, Kirghiz, Mordovians, and Caucasians. Thousands of Japanese and Chinese who lived on the western borders and represented a potential source of subversion were deported to the gulag before the outbreak of World War II. Followers of many faiths were also at risk of deportation to the camps, including Catholics, Baptists, and members of the Ukrainian Orthodox Church.

The numbers of prisoners in the camps swelled during World War II as people suspected of collaborating with the Nazis were rounded up and deported. Even Soviet soldiers who had been held as PRISONERS OF WAR by the Germans were thrown into the camps because their loyalty to the Soviet state was in question. Prisoners were put to work on massive industrial and hydroelectric projects such as the White Sea–Baltic Canal or toiled in coal mines and oil wells near Vorkuta and gold mines on the Kolyma River in the Arctic region. One of the worst camps was located at Kolyma in northeastern Siberia, where temperatures dropped as low as –90°F during the winter. About 30 percent of the inmates at Kolyma died every year. Most of the camps were closed in the years following Stalin's death in 1953, and the surviving prisoners were liberated.

Further Reading:
Solzhenitsyn, Aleksandr. *The Gulag Archipelago.* New York: Harpercollins 1978.

Guyana, human rights violations in

Located on the northern coast of South America, Guyana has a population almost equally divided between East Indians and blacks of African descent. Its human rights record remains mixed. EXTRAJUDICIAL KILLINGS and the abuse of detainees by police, however, has been a persistent problem, and there has been little progress in prosecuting the violators. There is some evidence that the problem might even be worsening. In 2002, for instance, the Guyana Human Rights Association (GHRA) reported that the police had killed 24 civilians, a sharp rise from 16 civilians slain by police in 2001. Most of the deaths occurred while the police were making arrests; almost no efforts were made to investigate these cases. In a 2000 case involving the death of a suspect in police custody, a coroner's jury

ruled that the police were responsible, but its verdict was overturned by the Supreme Court. Although TORTURE is prohibited by the constitution, the U.S. State Department cites credible evidence of continued police abuse of those considered "problem" prisoners. In 2004 a cattle farmer named George Bacchus went on television to accuse the government of forming a hit squad intended to hunt down criminals. Shortly after the government promised to open an inquiry, Bacchus was shot to death.

The judicial system is ineffective; delays in bringing cases and lengthy pretrial detentions are common. In principle the country is a democracy, but there have been disturbing signs that the government has clamped down on political opposition, charging political activists. In 2002 the government pushed four problematic laws through the National Assembly, ostensibly intended to curb a growing crime problem. AMNESTY INTERNATIONAL (AI) contends that two of these laws violate international human rights standards to which Guyana is a party. One law defined a "terrorist act" so broadly that it undermined the principle of legal certainty and presumption of innocence and "risks facilitating politically motivated prosecutions," according to AI. Moreover, the new law also drastically extended the scope of the death penalty to include crimes other than murder, to which it was previously limited. A second law criticized by AI would expand the categories of individuals who could be arrested on executive orders and held indefinitely in arbitrary detention.

Guzmán, Abimael   *See* SHINING PATH.

Guzmán, Juan (Juan Guzmán Tapia) (1939–)
Chilean judge
The Chilean judge Juan Guzmán Tapia achieved prominence by pursuing former dictator General Augusto PINOCHET for crimes committed while he ruled Chile. In December 2004 he indicted Pinochet on charges related to assassinations carried out by his regime in collaboration with other Latin American juntas in the 1970s known as OPERATION CONDOR. For several months it appeared that Pinochet would be assured of immunity because he was suffering from dementia, but Guzmán ordered additional tests which suggested that Pinochet was mentally fit to stand trial. Because of the judge's tough stand and his defiance of death threats, he earned the nickname "Fearless Juan."

What made Guzmán's move so surprising was that he is conservative himself and comes from an aristocratic military family, exactly the kind of credentials that would seem to argue against his taking a decisive stand against Pinochet. He was appointed to investigate the general, who seized power in a military coup in 1973, in the expectation that he would bury the case. Prior to Guzmán's involvement, Pinochet had been held for 17 months under house arrest in Britain, where he was on a personal visit, based on a warrant issued by Spanish magistrate Balthasar GARZÓN. However, after British courts refused to extradite Pinochet to Spain to stand trial, the general returned to Chile, apparently under the impression that he would never have to face charges in his native land.

Guzmán had originally supported Pinochet when he overthrew the Socialist president Salvador Allende in 1973. It was Guzmán's belief that the military would bring order to a country that was in a state of near total economic collapse. As a judge, however, he was troubled by the number of habeas corpus suits being brought by families of victims who had been disappeared by Pinochet's secret police. In 1990, the year that Pinochet stepped down from power, Guzmán served on a special panel that heard the case of an ex-intelligence officer accused of killing a union leader. He was one of the judges who voted to convict the officer and sentenced him to 10 years in prison—the first sign that his loyalty to Pinochet had its limits.

In an interview, Guzmán has attributed his willingness to handle the prosecution of Pinochet—which began in January 1998, shortly before his return from London—to his evolution as a judge. He has stated that "international opinion was something of a recognition, a moral support, that made us realize that we are in the era of human rights." Moreover, the evidence in the case was so overwhelming—more than eight volumes of material—that it could not be ignored. Even though the newly elected Socialist government of Ricardo Lagos urged caution, fearing a violent reaction from the military and Pinochet's supporters, Guzmán plunged ahead. He insisted on a mental examination for the ex-dictator, who had contended that he was too mentally ill to stand trial. "I am a very stubborn man," Guzmán said, decrying attempts by politicians "to try to influence a judge." He has also become a convert to the idea of the INTERNATIONAL CRIMINAL COURT playing a more active role in preventing abuses similar to those that happened in Chile between 1973 and 1990.

Further Reading:

Constable, Pamela. *A Nation of Enemies: Chile under Pinochet.* New York: W. W. Norton & Company, 1993.

Davis, William Columbus. *Warnings from the Far South: Democracy versus Dictatorship in Uruguay, Argentina, and Chile.* New York: Praeger Publishers, 1995.

Dinges, John. *The Condor Years: How Pinochet and His Allies Brought Terrorism to Three Continents.* New York: New Press, 2004.

Dorfman, Airel. *Exorcising Terror: The Incredible Unending Trial of Augusto Pinochet.* New York: Seven Stories Press, 2002.

Kornbluh, Peter. *The Pinochet File: A Declassified Dossier on Atrocity and Accountability.* A National Security Archive Book. New York: New Press, 2003.

H

Habré, Hissene (1942–) *ruler of Chad*

Hissene Habré, the dictator of Chad from 1982 to 1990, came to power in a coup and proceeded to rule his impoverished West African nation with brutality. He abolished the post of prime minister, established single-party rule, and executed political opponents, using a newly created police force, the Documentation and Security Directorate (DSD), to suppress any opposition. The DSD terrorized the population and routinely tortured suspected dissidents. One of the most commonly applied methods of torture was called the Arbatachar, in which the prisoner's four limbs were tied together behind his back, resulting in a loss of circulation and paralysis. The DSD was also responsible for carrying out a campaign Habré launched against ethnic groups opposed to his regime, killing and arresting their leaders and extended families, sometimes eliminating whole communities. A 1992 Truth Commission accused Habré's government of tens of thousands of political murders and systematic torture, but the exact number of victims is unknown. Habré's regime had the backing of both France (the former colonial power) and the United States because it was seen as a bulwark against Muammar Gadhafi of Libya, which in the 1980s was actively lending support to anti-Western elements. Libya invaded Chad in 1975 when Habré was prime minister and by 1980 had occupied all of northern Chad. But forces under Habré's command drove Libyan troops out of most of the country a year later. (The war did not formally end until 1988.) The United States set up a secret base in Chad to train captured Libyan forces in a bid to establish an anti-Gadhafi force. During this period the U.S. maintained close ties with the regime and provided assistance to the DSD. Habré was ousted in a 1990 coup by Idriss Déby and went into exile in Senegal. But attempts to bring him to justice continued over the next 15 years. In September 2005 Belgium issued an international warrant for his arrest, charging him with torture and murder committed while he was in power. To bring its case Belgium was relying on the doctrine of UNIVERSAL JURISDICTION, which allows a court in a country that complies with international norms of justice to try a suspect in human rights cases, regardless of his or her nationality or the country where the abuses took place. "This is a great day for Habré's thousands of victims and a milestone in the fight to hold the perpetrators of atrocities accountable for their crimes," said a Human Rights Watch representative when the warrant was announced. It was possible that the former Chadian tyrant could become the first president to be extradited to another country for trial for crimes against humanity. Although Belgium had diluted an earlier law allowing such trials under pressure from Washington, earlier cases were still allowed to go forward. In addition, three of the 21 witnesses against Habré are Belgian citizens. "The indictment of Habré shows how the Belgian law was supposed to work," said a lawyer for the plaintiffs. "Habré's crimes are serious and are well-documented."

An earlier attempt to extradite a national leader in 1998—Chilean dictator AUGUSTO PINOCHET to face trial in Spain for abuses committed while he was in power in Santiago—failed when a British court ruled that because of Pinochet's failing health he ought to be returned to Chile.

See also BELGIUM, WAR CRIMES TRIBUNAL; CHAD, HUMAN RIGHTS VIOLATIONS IN.

Hague Conventions

There are several Hague Conventions or international accords that cover such issues as sales of goods, child abduction, control of opium, and service of process. But two conventions merit special consideration: The Hague Conventions of 1899 and 1907. These two conventions, negotiated and signed in The Hague, the capital of the Netherlands, form the basis of laws governing the conduct of war along with the better-known GENEVA CONVENTIONS.

The first conference in The Hague was requested by Russia to consider rules to limit warfare and curtail the spread of arms. Representatives of the 26 countries in attendance approved several provisions, but their most notable accomplishment was the prohibition of the use of hollow-point bullets, certain types of BIOLOGICAL WEAPONS and CHEMICAL WEAPONS as well as aerial bombing. (Since planes had yet to be invented, the treaty was intended to apply to bombing from balloons.) The convention also created a Permanent Court of Arbitration. Signed at the First Peace Conference on July 29, 1899, and entered into force on September 4, 1900, the convention consisted of four main sections and three additional declarations.

I. Pacific Settlement of International Disputes
II. Laws and Customs of War on Land
III. Adaptation to Maritime Warfare of Principles of Geneva Convention of 1864
IV. Prohibiting Launching of Projectiles and Explosives from Balloons
Declaration I. On the Launching of Projectiles and Explosives from Balloons
Declaration II. On the Use of Projectiles the Object of Which Is the Diffusion of Asphyxiating or Deleterious Gases
Declaration III. On the Use of Bullets Which Expand or Flatten Easily in the Human Body

The Second Peace Conference in 1907 was intended to expand upon the original Hague Convention. Some provisions were modified, and new provisions were added. There was increased emphasis on arms control and rules governing naval warfare. The conference, called by President Theodore Roosevelt, was attended by representatives from 44 countries. The delegates agreed in principle to convene again in eight years. (The outbreak of world war, however, made that impossible.) The Second Hague Convention was signed on October 8, 1907, and 12 of its 13 sections were ratified and entered into force on January 26, 1910.

I. The Pacific Settlement of International Disputes
II. The Limitation of Employment of Force for Recovery of Contract Debts
III. The Opening of Hostilities
IV. The Laws and Customs of War on Land
V. The Rights and Duties of Neutral Powers and Persons in Case of War on Land
VI. The Status of Enemy Merchant Ships at the Outbreak of Hostilities
VII. The Conversion of Merchant Ships into War-Ships
VIII. The Laying of Automatic Submarine Contact Mines
IX. Bombardment by Naval Forces in Time of War
X. Adaptation to Maritime War of the Principles of the Geneva Convention
XI. Certain Restrictions with Regard to the Exercise of the Right of Capture in Naval War
XII. The Creation of an International Prize Court [Not Ratified]*
XIII. The Rights and Duties of Neutral Powers in Naval War

The Geneva Protocol to the Hague Convention, signed on June 17, 1925, was intended to strengthen provisions in the 1899 convention dealing with chemical and biological warfare. (Declaration 4 of the convention banning "asphyxiating gases" had not been renewed in the later convention.) Widespread condemnation of the use of mustard gas and other lethal agents in World War I served to mobilize negotiators to limit their use in future conflicts. The accord permanently banning these weapons is found in a section entitled Protocol for the Prohibition of the Use in War of Asphyxiating, Poisonous or Other Gases, and of Bacteriological Methods of Warfare. The protocol entered into force on February 8, 1928; it was subsequently augmented by the Biological Weapons Convention of 1972 and the Chemical Weapons Convention of 1993.

See also MARTENS CLAUSE; PILLAGE; PROTOCOL TO THE HAGUE CONVENTION OF 1954 FOR THE PROTECTION OF CULTURAL PROPERTY IN THE EVENT OF ARMED CONFLICT, SECOND, VICTIMS, RIGHTS OF.

Further Reading:
International Committee of the Red Cross. *International Law Concerning the Conduct of Hostilities: Collection of Hague Conventions and some Other Treaties.* Geneva, Switzerland: International Committee of the Red Cross, 1989.

Haiti, human rights violations in

Haiti has a human rights record that is possibly the worst in the Western Hemisphere. No discussion about human rights can ignore the parlous state of the economy or the deplorable living conditions that most Haitians suffer. Haiti is ranked as the fourth-poorest country in the world and the poorest in the Western Hemisphere. It is also the third-hungriest country in the world (after Somalia and Afghanistan); on the United Nations Human Development Index, which ranks quality of life, Haiti is 146 out of 173. Life expectancy is 52 for women and 48 for men; about 50 percent of the people are illiterate. Haiti has also been ravaged by disastrous hurricanes and floods that have killed hundreds of people and left thousands homeless. In addi-

---

* Section XII, which was not ratified, would have established an international court for the resolution of conflicting claims to captured shipping during wartime.

A small boy trying to get water from a dirty well in Haiti *(Exile Images)*

tion, the country has had to cope with a catastrophic AIDS/HIV outbreak that struck the island in the early 1980s, shortly after the disease was identified. One more telling statistic: Half the country's wealth is in the hands of 1 percent of the population. This disparity has been at the root of much of the political instability that has bedeviled the island since it achieved independence in 1804 as a result of a historic slave uprising against the French colonists.

Hopes for improvement in the economy have repeatedly been shattered by political developments. In 1990 Haiti held its first free elections in modern times. This democratic experiment came after the country had endured decades of autocratic rule under François "Papa Doc" DUVALIER and, briefly, his son, who was ousted in 1986. The election brought a former Roman Catholic priest, Jean-Bertrand Aristide, to power as president. Although he had wide support from Haiti's impoverished masses—he received 67 percent of the vote—he was viewed with deep misgivings by the elite, the business community, and the military. A year later he was toppled by a

military coup led by Lieutenant General Raoul Cédras, which brought to power a sinister paramilitary group known as the Revolutionary Front for Haitian Advancement and Progress (Front révolutionnaire pour l'avancement et le progrès haïtien), or FRAPH. Later renamed the Armed Revolutionary Front of the Haitian People, the acronym FRAPH carried a sinister connotation since it resembled both the French and Creole words for "to beat" or "to thrash." True to its name, FRAPH murdered and tortured political activists, journalists, and Aristide supporters; it was described by one U.S. diplomat as a group of "gun-carrying crazies."

Founded by Emmanuel "Toto" Constant, and under the command of Louis Jodel Chamblain, FRAPH was responsible for carrying out a campaign of terror directed against supporters of former president Jean-Bertrand Aristide that may have killed as many as 5,000 Haitian civilians. In 1994 FRAPH thugs gunned down about 20 people in the slum of Raboteau, which was considered an Aristide stronghold. (Aristide himself had gone into exile.) Later that same year, Aristide was returned to power with the help of U.S. armed intervention, but he proved a disappointment even to many of those who had hoped for his return. Members of his government were implicated in serious human rights abuses, EXTRAJUDICIAL KILLINGS, and the violent suppression of peaceful political demonstrations. Attacks on journalists and political opposition figures continued. Much of the violence was attributed to Popular Organizations—vigilante groups that supported Aristide—or by members of Aristide's own Lavalas Party. Haiti's poverty remained as deep as ever with corruption rampant and foreign aid suspended because of political disarray in the government of Prime Minister René Préval.

In winter 2004—Haiti's bicentennial year—amid a wave of increasingly violent protests against President Aristide, an insurgency took hold in the north and west of the island. Some of the same figures involved in the coup of 1991 resurfaced in the western port city of Gonaives, many of whom had been convicted of TORTURE and murder but had either escaped from prison or had gone into exile and escaped punishment altogether. (There did not appear to be any strong links between the rebels and the Democratic Convergence, the anti-Aristide alliance demonstrating in the capital. Instead, the paramilitaries seem to have exploited the upheaval for their own purposes.) The rebellion spread. The police put up little resistance—the army had been disbanded in 1994—and Aristide was once again forced to flee the country. Whether he went voluntarily or was pressured to leave by Washington, which had voiced sharp criticism of his administration, is a matter of some dispute. The rebels began to assume trappings of legitimacy, taking positions as mayors, police chiefs, and judges. Human rights abusers—who had killed police officers and burned down police stations during the coup—now became policemen themselves. The fear that the country might plunge into anarchy impelled the United States to dispatch marines to the island. In April 2004 the United Nations organized a force called the United Nations Stabilization Mission in Haiti (MINUSTAH), consisting mainly of Brazilian troops, to replace the U.S. contingent. A former foreign minister, Gérard Latortue, was named interim prime minister.

The presence of an international mission, however, did not prove sufficient to suppress the violence that is attributed to both Aristide partisans who have terrorized neighborhoods of the capital Port-au-Prince and paramilitary groups and police. In September 2004 the Inter-American Commission on Human Rights issued a statement expressing concern "over several key areas in which the basic rights and freedoms of Haitians remain weak and imperiled." Two weeks later, Latortue complained in a radio interview that human rights criticism was hampering his ability to work with donor nations. On the same day as Latortue's interview, police raided the offices of the Con-

federation of Haitian Workers (CTH), a labor union, and arrested nine union members without a warrant on the grounds that they were "close to the Lavalas authorities." Hours later, masked men broke into the office of Committee for the Protection of the Rights of the Haitian People (CDPH), a human rights group. On October 2 police arrested four Lavalas legislators, including former prime minister Yvon Neptune (who had succeeded René Préval) and imprisoned them after they had criticized the interim government in a radio broadcast.

The government has promised to prosecute former members of the Aristide regime for human rights violations—including Aristide himself—but justice officials have shown little indication that they will prosecute the rebel leaders and former members of FRAPH. The justice minister has even raised the possibility of pardoning the former FRAPH leader, Jean Tatoune (whose real name is Jean-Pierre Baptiste), who was convicted for his role in a 1994 Raboteau massacre. "The contrast between the Haitian government's eagerness to prosecute former Aristide officials and its indifference to the abusive record of certain rebel leaders could not be more stark," observed the deputy director of the Americas Division for HUMAN RIGHTS WATCH. Then-secretary of state Colin Powell expressed similar concerns, denouncing some of the rebel leaders as "murderers and thugs." Latortue did not appear to share his opinion, however, referring to the same men as "freedom fighters."

Further Reading:

Arthur, Charles. *Haiti: A Guide to the People, Politics, and Culture.* New York: Interlink Publishing Group, 2002.

Farmer, Paul. *The Uses of Haiti.* 2d ed. Monroe, Me: Common Courage Press, 2003.

Heinl, Robert Debs, Jr., and Nancy Gordon Heinl. *Written in Blood: The Story of the Haitian People, 1492–1995.* Lanham, Md.: University Press of America, 1996.

Haitian human rights violators

Since the end of the Duvalier dynasty (1957–86), during which Haiti was ruled by François "Papa Doc" DUVALIER and his son and successor, Jean-Claude "Baby Doc" DUVALIER, the impoverished island nation has been in a state of constant turmoil. The election in 1990 of a former Roman Catholic priest, Jean-Bertrand Aristide, as president was initially greeted by thousands of mostly poor Haitians as a sign of a new day, but within a year he was ousted in a military coup. In the next three years, Haiti was dominated by a thuggish clique of officers and members of a paramilitary force called the Revolutionary Front for Haitian Advancement and Progress (FRAPH), which carried out a campaign of terror and repression aimed at Aristide supporters. After Aristide was restored to power with U.S. military backing in 1994, most of the coup leaders managed to find sanctuary abroad, and even those few who were caught and imprisoned later managed to escape. In 2004 Aristide was forced out of office a second time after an uprising spread through the island and many of the same people implicated in atrocities a decade before resurfaced, brazenly claiming to represent the political will of the Haitian people.

Biamby, Philippe

As the Haitian army chief of staff, Philippe Biamby was one of the principal figures in the 1991 coup led by Lieutenant General Raoul Cédras that ousted Jean-Bertrand Aristide from the presidency. During the three years of repressive dictatorship that followed, it is believed that thousands were killed and tortured. In 1994 Cédras and Biamby agreed to relinquish power in the face of a U.S. invasion intended to restore Aristide to power. Under the terms of the agreement, Biamby and Cédras were allowed to go into exile in Panama. In fall 2000 Biamby and Cédras and several others suspected of atrocities were tried in absentia for their roles in an April 1994 massacre in a beachside slum called Raboteau. They were sentenced to life in prison, but Biamby and Cédras have little fear of ever serving their terms: There are reports that they are enjoying exile thanks to millions of dollars they looted from Haiti's treasury. In 2004 Aristade was forced from power a second time, and former allies of Biamby and Cédras once again threatened the stability of the country.

Cédras, Raoul

For three years, 1991–94, Lieutenant General Raoul Cédras ruled as dictator of Haiti. Although convicted of war crimes, he resides in comfortable exile in Panama, beyond the reach of justice. Backed by a wealthy and powerful élite, Cédras and his confederates seized power in a coup, ousting Jean-Bertrand Aristide, who had won the presidency in a democratic election in 1990. In demanding that Cédras relinquish power, President Bill Clinton and other U.S. officials used unusually harsh language to describe him, calling him among other things a "thug," "stooge," and "killer." These characterizations seem apt. Cédras is held responsible for murder, TORTURE, assassination, and looting the national treasury.

The Clinton administration took the position that as a democratically elected leader, Aristide should be restored to power. Yet Washington was reluctant to employ force to remove Cédras and made a last-ditch diplomatic push to secure his voluntary departure, relying on a trio of celebrated emissaries to make its case: former president Jimmy Carter, former senator Sam Nunn, and General Colin Powell. Powell is credited with being most responsible for pre-

vailing on the tyrant to leave office or face a U.S.-backed invasion. But the power of persuasion only went so far: Cédras demanded money—what some reports have described as a kind of golden parachute worth over a million dollars—and insisted that he be allowed to keep his two homes in Haiti and rent them out. He and his close ally, General Philippe Biamby, then went into exile in Panama. In September 1994, 20,000 U.S. troops arrived in the country to restore Aristide to power. Cédras and his family settled down in a beach villa in Panama. According to the *Economist* magazine, Washington kicked in the rent for the villa as part of the deal to get him to leave.

In 1998 Aristide's government tried to extradite Cédras and Biamby to stand trial, but Panama refused. "It would be a dangerous precedent to grant the right of asylum to resolve a political problem in a neighboring country and later deny the rights of those given asylum," the Panamanian foreign ministry said. So Haiti proceeded to try Cédras in absentia, charging him with conducting a massacre of Aristide supporters in the shantytown of Raboteau, in the port of Gonaïves. In that incident, soldiers and paramilitaries rounded up several residents, tortured them, and made them sprawl in open sewers. When some tried to flee, they were shot and killed; estimates of the dead range from eight to 20. Though Cédras was convicted, he continues to enjoy life in exile.

Chamblain, Louis Jodel

Louis Chamblain was in charge of Haitian army death squads that operated with impunity under the military rule of General Raoul Cédras, who seized power in 1991 after ousting the freely elected president Jean-Bertrand Aristide. The "Commandante," as Chamblain was known, spent a year as the head of the paramilitary wing of the notorious Front for Haitian Advancement and Progress (better known by its acronym FRAPH). During that time it is believed that FRAPH carried out the killings of possibly as many as 5,000 people, mostly civilian supporters of Aristide. After Cédras and his allies were forced to give up power in 1994 under a deal brokered by the United States, Chamblain went into exile. In 2004 resurfaced in Haiti, along with several others implicated in human rights abuses, during an uprising against Aristide. After a three-week conflict, in which Chamblain figured prominently, Aristide was forced from power and went into exile.

In April 2004, as a new Haitian government was still trying to establish its legitimacy, Chamblain turned himself into the authorities to face charges for crimes he is alleged to have committed during the Cédras era. He continues to claim that he has done nothing wrong. In August 2004, after a trial lasting only a few hours, Chamblain was acquitted of the murder of Antoine Izméry, an importer who bankrolled former President Jean-Bertrand Aristide's presidential bid in 1990. Human rights groups deplored the acquittal, pointing out that of the eight witnesses called by the prosecution, only one appeared, and he was able to say nothing about the incident. Nonetheless, Chamblain was not set free since he still faced charges on for ordering the killings of Aristide supporters in a shantytown in 1994.

Constant, Emmanuel "Toto"

Emmanuel "Toto" Constant was the founder and head of FRAPH, a paramilitary organization that was responsible for numerous murders and other human rights violations in Haiti in the mid-1990s. (FRAPH is an acronym for the Revolutionary Front for the Advancement and Progress of Haiti, later renamed Armed Revolutionary Front of the Haitian People.) In a blunt, undiplomatic assessment, a U.S. embassy cable referred to FRAPH as a group of "gun-carrying crazies," eager to "use violence against all who oppose it." Constant served as a close advisor to the military leaders of the country who came to power in a coup that ousted President Jean-Bertrand Aristide in September 1991. In 1992 and 1993, under Constant's supervision, FRAPH tortured and killed up to 5,000 Aristide supporters.

In October 1993, to thwart a U.S.-brokered peace accord, Constant organized a violent FRAPH demonstration to meet troops on board the USS *Harlan County* when it docked in Port-au-Prince, the capital. Wielding guns, sticks, and machetes, the demonstrators shouted, in English, "Kill foreigners! Kill foreigners!" Rather than risk a confrontation, the ship left Haiti. A year later, the United States tried a second time to implement a settlement that would restore Aristide to power and force the Haitian military dictators into exile. When U.S. troops returned, Constant urged each FRAPH man to "put down one American soldier." This time, though, Washington did not retreat under threats.

In spite of his defiant attitude toward the Americans, Constant nonetheless found refuge in the United States in 1994, legally entering the country on a six-month tourist visa to evade a subpoena issued by a Haitian court on behalf of a group called Anti-FRAPH. The Haitian government tried to have him extradited so he could stand trial. In September 1995, after a deportation proceeding by the U.S. Immigration and Naturalization Service, a judge ordered him returned to Haiti, saying that "his continued presence in the United States sends the message that the United States actively endorses his position and undermines the United States' [democratizing] mission in Haiti." The order, however, was never executed. Not long afterward, Constant went on the CBS show *60 Minutes* to say that while he was a leader of FRAPH, he had worked for the CIA. (Reportedly he had been paid $500 a month by the agency.)

The U.S. government refused to clarify why, instead of deporting Constant, the Immigration and Naturalization Service allowed him to go free under "supervised release."

Speaking on condition of anonymity, a State Department official said that returning him to Haiti might make him" a potential source of instability," acknowledging at the same time that "given FRAPH's and Constant's alleged responsibility for an enormous number of human rights violations during the de facto regime, he is clearly one of the most reviled figures in Haiti today."

In November 2000 a Haitian court convicted Constant of murder, in absentia, for his role in the Raboteau Massacre, in which several civilians were rounded up by elements of FRAPH, tortured, and killed. Nonetheless, Constant continued to walk freely about Queens, New York, where he made his home. In 2004 an uprising toppled the Aristide government for a second time and forced the president into exile. Many Haitian activists and human rights organizations feared that Constant and other former members of the military regime might take advantage of the unsettled environment to return to power. Constant's statements to the press in recent years have only fueled such fears. In August 1997 he told the *Village Voice*, "I am still the leader of FRAPH" and maintained that he was still coordinating activities with allies in Haiti. In another interview for the *Atlantic Monthly*, he expressed his ambitions for the future: "I've been prepared since young for a mission. . . . I'm either going to be President of Haiti or I'm going to be killed." In 2005 Constant was still alive and in exile in the U.S.

Tatoune, Jean

Jean Tatoune (Jean-Pierre Baptiste) is a Haitian paramilitary leader convicted of participating in a massacre of civilians during a military coup that brought military dictatorship to Haiti in 1991. After escaping from prison, he subsequently resurfaced in February 2004 as part of an insurgent group seeking to oust then-President Jean-Bertrand Aristide. Tatoune was a former police commissioner and leader of the paramilitary group FRAPH (Revolutionary Front for the Advancement and Progress of Haiti) who became the criminal strongman of Gonaïve, Haiti's third-largest city. The rebellion that ultimately led to Aristide's ouster—he was forced into exile—and the appointment of an interim government began in Gonaïve, where Tatoune organized insurgent units and supplied them with arms. In spite of his notorious reputation, he promoted himself a "freedom fighter." His men reportedly interdicted shipments of disaster-relief supplies to the Gonaïve region after it was hit by devastating floods in late 2004. Tatoune's political resurrection is all the more remarkable because of his earlier conviction for gross violations of human rights and murder; he was sentenced to life imprisonment for his part in the Raboteau massacre in 1994 but later managed to escape and plot his comeback.

Further Reading:

Arthur, Charles. *Haiti: A Guide to the People, Politics, and Culture.* New York: Interlink Publishing Group, 2002.

Farmer, Paul. *The Uses of Haiti.* 2d ed. Monroe, Me.: Common Courage Press, 2003.

Heinl, Robert Debs, Jr., and Nancy Gordon Heinl. *Written in Blood: The Story of the Haitian People, 1492–1995.* Lanham, Md.: University Press of America, 1996.

Halabajah (Iraqi Kurdistan)

Halabajah, a Kurdish village in Iraq close to the Iranian border, has become virtually synonymous with chemical warfare. In 1988, during the Iran-Iraq War, approximately 5,000 Kurds were killed in gas attacks by Iraqi warplanes. Although rumors that Iraq had relied on outlawed CHEMICAL WEAPONS had circulated previously, Halabajah was one of the first cases where their use was documented. The gassing of Kurds in Halabajah was frequently cited by the Bush administration as it made its case for a preemptive strike against Iraq in 2002 and 2003; if Saddam HUSSEIN's regime had shown no compunction about using these weapons in 1988 against civilians, Washington argued, then it was almost certain to use them again. That gas attack had been precipitated by the capture of Kurdish territory on March 15, 1988, by Iranian forces with the aid of Kurdish separatists. Iraq retaliated by dropping chemical bombs that are thought to have consisted of several toxic agents, including cyanide and mustard gas, whose use is prohibited under the Geneva Conventions. Although Iraq acknowledged their use, Baghdad claimed that Iran had used them first. Iran called for a UN investigation of the matter; the UN inspectors concluded that both sides were culpable in the use of chemical weapons. The official in charge of the Kurdish "pacification"—Ali Hassan al-MAJID—became known as Chemical Ali for ordering the chemical gas attack.

See also IRAQ, HUMAN RIGHTS VIOLATIONS IN; KURDISTAN (IRAQ), SUPPRESSION OF.

Further Reading:

Aburish, Said K. *Saddam Hussein.* London: Bloomsbury Publishing, 2001.

Bodansky, Yossef. *The Secret History of the Iraq War.* New York: Regan Books, 2004.

Cockburn, Andrew, and Patrick Cockburn. *Out of the Ashes: The Resurrection of Saddam Hussein.* New York: Perennial, 2000.

Cordesman, Anthony H. *The Iraq War: Strategy, Tactics, and Military Lessons.* Washington, D.C.: Center for Strategic and International Studies, 2003.

Coughlin, Con. *Saddam: King of Terror.* New York: Ecco, 2002.

Dodge, Toby. *Inventing Iraq: The Failure of Nation-Building and a History Denied.* New York: Columbia University Press, 2003.

Karsh, Efraim. *The Iran-Iraq War 1980–1988.* London: Osprey Publishing, 2002.

Hama, massacre in

Hama, a Syrian city of 200,000, was the site of a 1982 massacre carried out by Syrian troops against a militant Muslim group known as the Moslem Brotherhood. It is believed that as many as 20,000 people were killed and much of the city razed in the process. The Moslem Brotherhood began in the 1930s in Egypt and took root in Syria. It was alternately tolerated and banned by the government until the Baathist Party took power in Syria in 1963, at which time the organization was again driven underground. Nonetheless, the Moslem Brotherhood and its allies remained a powerful force. It held a special attraction for many doctors and lawyers and other professionals in the political opposition; religion, too, accounted for the Brotherhood's popularity; the group was 70 percent Sunni Muslim in contrast to the Baathist regime dominated by members of the minority Alawite Muslims.

The Moslem Brotherhood did not consider the Alawites to be true Muslims at all. When an Alawite, Hafiz al-Assad, took power in 1971 he made some overtures toward the group but was rebuffed. After a failed assassination attempt on his life on June 25, 1980, Assad decided to clamp down on the group once and for all. He forced Parliament to pass a law making membership in the Brotherhood a capital offense, and security forces executed 1,200 supporters of the Brotherhood in their prison cells. More massacres were carried out by the army and security forces in the city of Aleppo, setting the stage for the atrocities in Hama, Syria's third largest city. The army was sent into the city with orders to liquidate the loose coalition that had formed around the Brotherhood. In February 1982, as the troops moved through Hama, they not only killed thousands, including civilians, but also leveled vast sections of the city where insurgents had taken refuge, leveling mosques, businesses, and residential blocks. Most of the surviving militants fled to neighboring countries. Even though more than 20 years have passed, the Syrian government refuses to discuss the massacres, considering the Hama killings an "internal matter." It is almost as if the slaughter had not taken place at all.

See also SYRIA, HUMAN RIGHTS VIOLATIONS IN.

Hamdi, Yaser Esam (1980–) *American terrorist suspect*

Yaser Esam Hamdi was one of hundreds of suspected TALIBAN and al-QAEDA fighters captured in the American invasion of Afghanistan in autumn 2001. What distinguished him from his fellow detainees who were imprisoned by U.S. military authorities was that he was an American citizen. He was first held in the American base at Guantánamo Bay, Cuba, and later, after his nationality was uncovered, in Navy prisons in Virginia and South Carolina. Hamdi was deemed an "enemy combatant" and as such was denied access to legal counsel. No attempts were made to charge or try him. In a terse statement, a representative of the U.S. Defense Department contended that Hamdi had joined the Taliban forces fighting the United States and the Northern Alliance, an anti-Taliban coalition, and had been taken prisoner with a Kalashnikov assault rifle in his possession.

The scion of a wealthy Saudi family, Hamdi was born in Baton Rouge, Louisiana, in 1980 but was raised in Saudi Arabia. Without letting his family know his intentions, he abandoned his studies when he was 18 and traveled to Afghanistan. He denied that he had fought with the Taliban and maintained that in such a lawless country, nearly every adult male carried a gun. What was at issue in the case was not, however, Hamdi's innocence or guilt. Rather, it hinged on whether, even in the war against terrorism, the U.S. government could prevent an American citizen from obtaining legal representation or hold him indefinitely without adhering to the rules of DUE PROCESS. The case went to the U.S. Supreme Court, which ruled in June 2004 that Hamdi was entitled to his day in court. Rather than place him on trial, however, the Bush administration negotiated with Saudi authorities to repatriate him. Under the terms of his release, which came in October 2004, Hamdi was required to renounce his U.S. citizenship, which he says he did with no regret. In its only statement about the case, a Defense Department spokesperson commented, "Hamdi was no longer considered a threat to the United States and did not possess any further intelligence value."

See also GUANTÁNAMO DETAINEES.

Further Reading:
Danner, Mark. *Torture and Truth: America, Abu Ghraib, and the War on Terror.* New York: New York Review Books, 2004.
Hersh, Seymour M. *Chain of Command: The Road from 9/11 to Abu Ghraib.* New York: HarperCollins, 2004.

Haradinaj, Ramush   *See* WAR CRIMINALS OF THE FORMER YUGOSLAVIA.

Hazara, persecution of
The Hazara is an ethnic group found mainly in central Afghanistan in a mountainous region called Hazarajat.

They make up 20–30 percent of the country's population; large numbers of Hazaris also reside in Iran to the west and Pakistan to the east. Throughout their history, they have suffered from discrimination and persecution because they adhere to the Shia branch of Islam, while the majority of Afghans are Sunnis.

In 1997 Hazaris staged an uprising against the TALIBAN, who were then in control of the country. Initially the rebellion enjoyed success; the Taliban suffered a crushing defeat at Mazar-e Sharif in the north of the country in which more than 7,000 Taliban soldiers were reportedly killed. Victory was short-lived, however. The Taliban retook Mazar-e Sharif and in retaliation summarily executed some 10,000 Hazara civilians. Ethnic tensions involving Hazaris extended to Pakistan, where many Afghan refugees had taken refuge to escape the fundamentalist Islamic Taliban regime. In 1987 fighting broke out between armed members of the Hazari tribe and Sunnis in Quetta, Pakistan. (There are between 100,000 to 200,000 Hazaris still living in the country.) In spite of the conflicts with Sunni tribes, Hazaris made common cause with Uzbeks and Pashtuns, both Sunni tribes, to fight the Taliban. In 2001 the coalition of forces known as the Northern Alliance routed the Taliban once the United States entered the war after the attacks of September 11, 2001.

See also AFGHANISTAN, HUMAN RIGHTS VIOLATIONS IN; PAKISTAN, HUMAN RIGHTS VIOLATIONS IN.

Further Reading:
Ewans, Martin. *Afghanistan: A Short History of Its People and Politics.* New York: Perennial, 2002.

Helsinki accords
In 1975, while the cold war was at its height, representatives of 35 nations gathered in Helsinki, Finland, for a Conference on Security and Cooperation in Europe (CSCE). Participants included all the European states (with the exception of Albania), the United States, Canada, the Soviet Union, and Turkey. The conference, which opened on July 3, 1973, concluded on August 1, 1975. The Soviet Union had been pressing for such a conference since in the early 1950s in the hope of acquiring international recognition for the new borders of Europe established after World War II. It took decades before the Western states agreed that a conference would be in their interest as well. In May 1969 the Finnish government proposed that it play host to the delegates in its capital, Helsinki. The Final Act of the conference, known as the Helsinki accords, was not a treaty but a politically binding agreement adopted on the basis of consensus that sets forth a number of measures contained within three main sections, informally known as "baskets."

Basket I deals with questions of maintaining security in Europe and declares that the basis of the accord is to promote better relations among the participating states "ensuring conditions in which their people can live in true and lasting peace free from any threat to or attempt against their security." Participating states were also expected to respect the sovereignty of all other participants, "including in particular the right of every State to juridical equality, to territorial integrity and to freedom and political independence." Among these rights was the ability "freely to choose and develop its political, social, economic and cultural systems as well as its right to determine its laws and regulations." This provision was particularly important for the Soviet Union and its Eastern European satellites because it represented recognition by the West of the changed borders of both Germany and Poland after World War II. But Basket I also sets forth several provisions dealing with human rights that were routinely violated by the USSR and its communist allies. The most important of these provisions is Principle VII, which bears the title "Respect for human rights and fundamental freedoms, including the freedom of thought, conscience, religion or belief." It calls on states to "respect human rights and fundamental freedoms, including the freedom of thought, conscience, religion or belief, for all without distinction as to race, sex, language, or religion." Participants also agreed to "promote and encourage the effective exercise of civil, political, economic, social, cultural, and other rights and freedoms" and "recognize and respect the freedom of the individual to profess and practice, alone or in community with others, religion or belief acting in accordance with the dictates of his own conscience." Basket I also includes a section on confidence-building measures and curbing the spread of arms.

Basket II deals with economic, scientific, technological, and environmental cooperation, as well as migrant labor, vocational training, and the promotion of tourism. Basket III is devoted to cooperation in other areas of humanitarian concern, including freer movement of people, family reunification and visits, freedom of information, and cultural and educational exchanges. Because of their emphasis on humanitarian ideals, Principle VII and Basket III together have come to be known as "The Human Dimension."

Basket III proved to be the most contentious of the three sections in the context of the ideological rift between the West and the Soviet Union. Stung by accusations that they were abridging and violating the human rights of their citizens, the communist nations asserted that the West was interfering in their internal affairs. It was apparent that while the Soviets and their allies were willing to put their signatures to the Final Act, they had no intention of fulfilling the humanitarian ideals enumerated in it. Nonetheless, these ideals, embodied in Basket III and Principle VII,

inspired dissident movements in central and Eastern Europe to establish Helsinki Watch Committees to monitor their governments' compliance with the Final Act's provisions. Although these groups were usually small and had little impact at first, they ultimately played a vital role in bringing about the collapse of communism. For one thing, they acted as a national conscience, making the citizens of their respective countries aware of the rights that their governments had pledged to uphold. For another, these groups—such as Charter 77 in then Czechoslovakia (now the Czech Republic and Slovakia)—formed the core of a political opposition force to the communist regimes. In the late 1980s, as the communist empire was tottering, these groups often took a lead role in negotiating the peaceful transition from communism to democracy.

Although the cold war ended with the dissolution of the Soviet Union in 1991, Helsinki Watch Committees remain active, bringing attention to abuses of human rights in countries which, while freed from communism, still suffer from radical nationalism, poverty, and corruption. The Conference for Security and Cooperation in Europe remained as an important vehicle for the promotion of human rights, disarmament, and other issues in Europe. In 1994 the CSCE was renamed the ORGANIZATION FOR SECURITY AND COOPERATION IN EUROPE (OSCE). Since 1975 the number of countries signing the Helsinki accords has expanded to 55, reflecting changes such as the breakup of the Soviet Union, Czechoslovakia, and Yugoslavia.

Further Reading:

Kavass, Igor I., ed. *Human Rights, European Politics, and the Helsinki Accord: The Documentary Evolution of the Conference on Security and Co-operation in Europe 1973–1975*. Buffalo, N.Y.: William S. Hein & Co., 1981.

Korey, William. *Human Rights and the Helsinki Accord: Focus on U.S. Policy*. New York: Foreign Policy Assn., 1983.

Hernández Martínez, Maximiliano (1882–1966)
Salvadorian dictator

General Maximiliano Hernández Martínez established a dictatorship in El Salvador in 1931 and maintained power until 1944. He was thought to be responsible for massacres as part of an anticommunist purge that may have taken the lives of as many as 40,000 peasants and destroyed the indigenous Indian culture.

In 1931, six weeks after coming to power in a coup, Hernández Martínez was confronted with an uprising organized by El Salvador's Communist Party. In the ensuing crackdown, the dictator proved unsparingly brutal. Bodies littered the roads and filled drainage ditches. "Hotels were raided," wrote Raymond Bonner, a former *New York Times* correspondent, "individuals with blond hair were dragged out and killed as suspected Russians. Men were tied thumb to thumb, then executed, tumbling into mass graves they had first been forced to dig." The United States supported the general in his efforts to suppress the communists, even going so far as to station warships off the coast of El Salvador with the authority to send in the marines in case the general suffered setbacks.

Born in 1882, Hernández Martínez was an ardent admirer of fascism and reportedly dabbled in the occult. "It is a greater crime to kill an ant than a man," he once said, "for when a man dies he becomes reincarnated, while an ant dies forever." Hernández Martínez was overthrown and forced to go into exile in Honduras in 1944, but he wasn't forgotten even after his death in 1966. His name was memorialized by a right-wing death squad fighting another leftist uprising in the 1980s; it was called the Maximiliano Hernández Martínez Brigade and was responsible for the assassinations of several prominent Salvadoran leftists.

See also EL SALVADOR, WAR CRIMES IN.

Further Reading:

Armstrong, Robert. *El Salvador: The Face of Revolution.* Boston: South End Press, 1982.

Hess, Rudolf (1894–1987) *Nazi official*

Rudolf Hess was deputy führer in Nazi Germany, the third highest-ranking official in the hierarchy after Adolf HITLER and Hermann GÖRING. Hess is best known for his mysterious flight to Scotland on May 10, 1941, which he claimed to have made in order to negotiate peace with Britain. His true motivation for this improbable act is still not known.

Born in Alexandria, Egypt, on April 26, 1894, Hess was the son of a prosperous wholesaler and exporter; the family moved to Germany when he was 14. At the University of Munich, Hess was influenced by the Thule Society, a secret anti-Semitic political organization that espoused the idea of Aryan supremacy. He enlisted in the German army in 1914 to fight in World War I, during which he was wounded twice. He subsequently became an airplane pilot after the war and joined the Freikorps, a right-wing mercenary organization made up of army veterans who were hired to suppress communist uprisings in postwar Germany.

In 1920 Hess joined the newly created Nazi Party after hearing Adolf Hitler speak at a Munich beer hall; he was the party's 16th member. When he met Hitler, he said that he felt "as though overcome by a vision." Shy and insecure, he virtually worshipped Hitler and became fanatically devoted to him. To demonstrate his loyalty, Hess flung himself into Nazi Party activities, enthusiastically participating in brawls with communists who tried to break up Hitler's speeches. He was arrested in 1923 along with Hitler after the abortive Munich Beer Hall Putsch in which Hitler made an unsuccessful grab for power. While in prison, Hess ingratiated himself further with Hitler, taking dictation for Hitler's memoir and manifesto, *Mein Kampf (My Struggle)*, and even offering the occasional editorial suggestion.

Hess resumed his role as Hitler's secretary upon the two men's release in 1925. In 1932 Hitler rewarded him by appointing him chairman of the Central Political Commission of the Nazi Party and an SS general. He ascended higher still in April 1933, after the Nazis took power in Germany, becoming deputy führer. In spite of the elevated title, the position was largely ceremonial. In 1934 Hess gave a speech in which he described Hitler in almost religious terms: "With pride we see that one man remains beyond all criticism, that is the Führer. This is because everyone feels and knows: he is always right, and he will always be right. The National Socialism of all of us is anchored in uncritical loyalty. . . . We believe that the Führer is obeying a higher call to fashion German history. There can be no criticism of this belief."

For all his devotion Hess never enjoyed much influence in the inner circles of the Nazi upper echelon. His idolization of Hitler also blinded him to the intrigues of others around him, like Göring, Martin BORMANN, and Heinrich HIMMLER, whose jockeying for power succeeded in marginalizing him even further. On May 10, 1941, on the eve of the German invasion of the Soviet Union, in what was apparently an effort to grab the spotlight once again, Hess donned a Luftwaffe uniform and climbed into a Messerschmitt ME-110, a German fighter plane. He took off alone and headed toward Scotland on what he would later declare was a "peace" mission. He was under the impression that he could arrange a meeting with the duke of Hamilton, whom he had met briefly during the Berlin Olympics in 1936, and who he hoped would introduce him to King George VI. (The duke denied ever meeting him.) Six thousand feet over Scotland, Hess bailed out of the plane, parachuting safely into a rural area, having overshot the duke's home by 14 miles. Encountering a startled farmer, he said in English, "I have an important message for the Duke of Hamilton." Hess intended to tell the duke that the Germans had no interest in attacking Britain because they were both Aryan nations. Well aware of German designs on Russia, he was convinced that opening another front with Britain would be a grave mistake.

Hess was never allowed to see the duke. Instead he was taken into custody by the British army and interrogated. He attempted to persuade his captors that the British would be spared if they gave the German Reich free rein to do as it wished in the rest of Europe. German victory, he said, was inevitable, and if the British resisted they would be starved by a German blockade. The British government decided that Hess was mentally unbalanced and had not come as Hitler's personal representative as he claimed. Hitler was so embarrassed by the incident that he declared the deputy führer insane and repudiated him. A Nazi Party memorandum described Hess as suffering from "an illness that has been going on for years" and added that he demonstrated "traces of a mental breakdown." Prime Minister Winston Churchill decided to lock him up for the duration of the war and treated him like any other high-ranking prisoner of war. In prison, Hess became increasingly unbalanced and paranoid. "They put substances in my evening meal that robbed me of sleep," he wrote on one occasion. At another point he wrote, "Outside my garden moonstruck men wandered up and down with loaded guns—moonstruck men surrounded me in the house, and when I went for a walk moonstruck men went before and behind me."

Once the war was over, he was returned to Germany to stand trial before the International Military Tribunal at Nuremberg. He was often disoriented and confused, sometimes claiming to have amnesia. But in his lucid moments he was as consistent as ever, still avowing his fealty to Hitler. In his final speech to the court, he said, "It was granted me for many years to live and work under the greatest son whom my nation has brought forth in the thousand years of its history. Even if I could I would not expunge this period from my existence. I regret nothing. If I were standing once more at the beginning I should act once again as I did then, even if I knew that at the end I should be burnt at the stake. . . ."

Hess's mental condition was not considered a cause for mitigating his sentence in the eyes of the judges who sentenced him to life in prison. He was to spend the next 41 years as the only inmate at Spandau Prison. He occupied himself writing—without any remorse—about the Nazis, contending that they would be resurrected to assume a leading role in the "Fourth Reich" he envisioned. At first he would goose-step along the corridors of Spandau, giving the Nazi salute, but later he adapted to his new home. From time to time there were calls for the release of the aging prisoner, but the Soviets blocked any attempt to free him. On August 17, 1987, he committed suicide at the age of 92, putting an end to the life of the last defendant who had been prosecuted at the NUREMBERG TRIALS.

Further Reading:

Nesbit, Roy Conyers. *The Flight of Rudolf Hess: Myths and Reality.* New York: Sutton Publishing, 2003.

Padfield, Peter. *Hess: The Fuhrer's Disciple.* London: Cassell, 2001.

Heydrich, Reinhard Tristan (Butcher of Prague, Hangman) (1904–1942) *Nazi official*

Known as the "Hangman" and the "Butcher of Prague" for his brutality, Reinhard Heydrich served in various high-ranking positions in the Nazi regime. Even one of his protégés, Walter SCHELLENBERG, described him as a man with "a cruel, brave and cold intelligence" for whom "truth and goodness had no intrinsic meaning." Heydrich was born in 1904 in Halle, Germany; his father was a singer and composer, and his mother was an actress. He was steeped in a virulent strain of anti-Semitism from an early age, influenced by both his father and his classmates. Too young to serve in World War I, he instead joined the right-wing Maracker Freikorps, a paramilitary group that battled communist supporters in the streets of Halle. Subsequently he joined the Truzbund, a nationalist anti-Semitic organization. He spent the next several years in the German navy, but in April 1931, he was accused of having seduced the daughter of a prominent businessman and discharged.

Infuriated over the way he had been treated, Heydrich joined the National Socialist German Workers' Party (NSDAP)—the Nazi Party. He came to the attention of the head of the SS (Schutzstaffel), Heinrich HIMMLER, who invited him to join the elite Nazi paramilitary force. Heydrich later assumed responsibility as head of the SD (Sicherheitsdienst), the Nazi intelligence agency as well. In 1934 he took over the Prussian GESTAPO, the largest political police force in the Third Reich, also known as the Security Police, which he described as "the state's defensive force that could act against the legally identifiable enemy." The SS, on the other hand, was "the offensive force that could initiate the final battle against the Jews." Already the SD was gathering files on the Jews in Germany in anticipation of the day when they would be rounded up. In 1936 Heydrich took over as head of the Reichssicherheitshauptamt (RSHA, Department of Security), which linked the department of security (secret security police and criminal police) and the NSDAP, the department of security. The position effectively put him in charge of the security apparatus of the German reich.

When preparations were under way to launch a pogrom against the Jewish community in November 1938, Heydrich issued orders that struck a cautious note: "Whatever actions occurred should not endanger German lives or property; synagogues could be burned only if there was no danger to the surrounding buildings. Healthy, non-elderly adult Jewish males were to be seized first, and concentration camps notified." A few days after the pogrom took place, Heydrich declared that simply curbing the rights of Jews, whom he referred to as "the eternal subhumans," and limiting their participation in the civil and professional life of the reich were not going to be sufficient. They had to be eliminated entirely. The following January, Field Marshal Hermann GÖRING, the second-highest official in the regime after Adolf HITLER, ordered Heydrich to solve the "Jewish problem" by "emigration and evacuation."

On September 21, 1939, just three weeks after the German invasion of Poland, Heydrich hosted a conference in which he called for placing the Jews in "as few concentration centers as possible," so that it would be easier to fulfill what he called the "ultimate aim"—a euphemism for the extermination of the Jews. Killing of Jews and political enemies was already beginning. Mobile death squads known as EINSTATZGRUPPEN would follow German troops into conquered territories and execute Jews found living in those areas. Most of the officers in these squads were supplied by Heydrich's SD. As head of the secret police, Heydrich orchestrated the massacre of thousands of Jews, Polish leaders, communists, and clergymen. "We have had to be hard," he said. "We have had to shoot thousands of leading Poles to show how hard we can be."

Still, no official policy had been developed that called for the extermination of the Jews. Heydrich complained to the reich's foreign secretary, Joachim von RIBBENTROP, that as a policy, emigration was inadequate if they were to remove all the Jews from the Reich, stating, "A territorial FINAL SOLUTION has thus become necessary." In 1941 Heydrich assumed the responsibility for the deportation of Jews from occupied Europe to CONCENTRATION CAMPS in Poland, which were under SS authority. After the German Wehrmacht (army) invaded the Soviet Union on July 31, 1941, Göring gave Heydrich orders to prepare an "overall solution of the Jewish question in the German controlled European areas." On January 20, 1942, Heydrich chaired the WANSSEE CONFERENCE in which the "Final Solution" was adopted as official Nazi policy, setting the stage for the execution of 6 million Jews.

On September 24, 1941, Hitler appointed Heydrich Reichsprotektor (Reich protector) of Bohemia-Moravia (Czechoslovakia), a position that Heydrich used to crush Czech resistance—"Germanize the Czech vermin," as he put it—and to carry out the deportation of Czech Jews to Polish extermination camps. On May 27, 1942, two Czech agents—Jan Kubis and Josef Gabcik—were parachuted into Czechoslovakia from a British plane for the purpose of assassinating Heydrich. (This is the only instance in which the Allies actively participated in the assassination of a top Nazi leader during the war.) The two men ambushed Heydrich's Mercedes in Prague, throwing a grenade into the front seat. Heydrich was critically injured.

Retaliation was swift: Blaming the Jewish "terrorists" for the attack, the Nazis arrested 500 Jews in Berlin and warned Jewish leaders that "for every Jewish act of terrorism or sedition, one hundred or one hundred fifty of the Jews in our hands will be shot." A number of Jews already being held in the Sachsenhausen concentration camp were executed as well. In Prague, Nazi leaders declared a state of emergency and offered 10 million crowns for the capture of the assassins. Many Czechs were killed in a wave of reprisals as well, most notably in the town of Lidice. In Prague alone, 1,331 Czechs, including more than 200 women, were executed. The SS laid siege to the Karl Borromaeus Church, where the assassins and more than 100 members of the Czech resistance were hiding; all those inside were killed. The intensity of Nazi reprisals took the Czechs by surprise and caused an erosion in support for continued resistance. The attempt on Heydrich's life was so unpopular, in fact, that the Czech government-in-exile denied all responsibility for it.

On June 4, 1942, Heydrich succumbed to his wounds. At his funeral five days later, both Himmler and Hitler eulogized Heydrich for his contribution to Nazism. As a tribute to Heydrich's memory, SS officers gave the code name Operation Reinhard to the deportation of Polish Jews to the death camps of Betżec, Sobibór, and Treblinka.

Further Reading:

Dawidowicz, Lucy. *A Holocaust Reader.* Library of Jewish Studies. Chicago: Behrman House Publishing, 1976.

Dwork, Deborah, and Robert Jan Van Pelt. *Holocaust: A History.* New York: W. W. Norton & Company, 2003.

Gilbert, Martin. *The Holocaust: A History of the Jews of Europe during the Second World War.* New York: Owl Books, 1987.

MacDonald, C. A. *The Killing of Reinhard Heydrich: The SS "Butcher of Prague."* New York: Da Capo Press, 1998.

Roseman, Mark. *The Wannsee Conference and the Final Solution: A Reconsideration.* New York: Metropolitan Books, 2002.

Whiting, Charles. *Heydrich: Henchman of Death.* Barnsley, S. Yorkshire, U.K.: Leo Cooper, 1999.

high-value detainees

High-value detainees are a special category of detainees suspected of terrorist activities who are in the custody of an ally of the United States at the behest of Washington. There were estimated to be about two dozen such detainees held in prisons abroad at the end of 2004. In December 2004 a U.S. federal district court ruled that the practice was illegal and that the U.S. government cannot avoid legal responsibility for a detainee by the expedient of having the person held by the authorities of another country. The case involved an American citizen, Ahmed Abu Ali, of Falls Church, Virginia, who was imprisoned in Saudi Arabia as a terrorism suspect and whose family complained that he was being mistreated by the Saudis acting on the authority of U.S. officials. The Bush administration had sought to curtail the ability of the courts to extend their jurisdiction in such cases. The question considered by the court was whether the United States was in fact responsible for Ali based on credible allegations that it had sanctioned his arrest, detention, and interrogation. "The full contours of this position would permit the United States, at its discretion and without judicial review, to arrest a citizen of the United States and transfer her to the custody of allies overseas in order to avoid constitutional scrutiny," the judge wrote. If the administration's position was sustained, he said, it would allow the government "to deliver American citizens to foreign governments to obtain information through the use of TORTURE." That would confer on the government "unreviewable powers to separate an American citizen from the most fundamental of his constitutional rights merely by choosing where he will be detained or who will detain him." Some of the ruling applies to noncitizens as well as Americans. In addition, the CONVENTION AGAINST TORTURE, to which the United States is a signatory, forbids the transfer of detainees to any country where there is a likelihood that they will be tortured or otherwise abused.

See also GUANTÁNAMO DETAINEES.

Further Reading:

Danner, Mark. *Torture and Truth: America, Abu Ghraib, and the War on Terror.* New York: New York Review Books, 2004.

Hersh, Seymour M. *Chain of Command: The Road from 9/11 to Abu Ghraib.* New York: HarperCollins, 2004.

Himmler, Heinrich (1900–1945) *Gestapo chief*
As head of the GESTAPO and the Waffen-SS, Reichsführer Heinrich Himmler was one of the principal architects of the mass murder of Jews carried out by Nazi Germany. Dull, pedantic, and dogmatic, he was also shrewd and ambitious, rising to prominence as one of Adolf HITLER's closest and most servile associates.

Born in Munich on October 7, 1900, Himmler was the son of a Roman Catholic schoolmaster. After serving as a military cadet in 1918 just before the end of World War I, he attended a technical school with the intention of eventually becoming an agronomist. He briefly tried his hand as a chicken farmer and fertilizer salesman, but found his true calling in fascism and racism. He was fascinated by mysticism, mesmerism, and the occult and believed himself to be a reincarnation of the pre-Christian Saxon Henry the Fowler. He believed that, like Henry, he was destined to march on the east and conquer the Slavs. Before he could conquer the Slavs, however, he had to acquire some combat experience. He first joined the Freikorps, a paramilitary unit that engaged in street brawls with Marxist gangs, and shortly afterward enlisted in Hitler's newly formed National Socialist German Workers Party (NSDAP). In 1923 he participated in the Munich Beer Hall Putsch of November 8–9, 1923, when Hitler staged an unsuccessful attempt to seize power.

Hitler could have had no more devoted follower than Himmler, who believed his führer was the Messiah, destined to lead Germany to greatness. In 1929 Hitler appointed Himmler as leader of his personal bodyguard, the Schutzstaffel, better known as the Ss or the Black Shirts for their distinctive uniform that included a silver death's head badge and a black tie. (Later they wore all-black uniforms.) Himmler was charged with "safeguarding the . . . embodiment of the National Socialist idea" and ensuring that its racial ideology was put into practice by concerted action. Initially, the SS was a small force, made up of only 280 members. Himmler proceeded to expand the SS, recruiting only those men who exemplified the blonde, blue-eyed Nordic ideal espoused by the Nazis. By 1933, when the Nazis took power in Germany, the ranks of the SS had swelled to 52,000, and it had become a virtual state within a state. Himmler also organized the Security Service (SD), which began as the party's ideological intelligence service under Reinhard HEYDRICH. In March 1933 he was appointed Munich police president, and shortly afterward he became commander of the political police throughout Bavaria. Hitler then gave Himmler an additional job as head of the Gestapo, the German political police, except in Prussia, where it was under the control of Hermann GÖRING. By June 1936 Himmler was in charge of the entire police system—both political and criminal—in the Third Reich. He proved an efficient administrator and a Machiavellian one who was always interested in acquiring more power.

Himmler was obsessed by race, and to propagate the Aryan nation he arranged for the enactment of special marriage laws which would ensure that only those of "high value"—meaning that the couple were sufficiently Aryan in appearance—were allowed to marry. But marriage was not necessary for breeding, of course: In October 1939 he issued a directive to the entire SS that "it will be the sublime task of German women and girls of good blood acting not frivolously but from a profound moral seriousness to become mothers to children of soldiers setting off to battle." To carry out this mandate, he instituted a system of state human stud farms known as Lebensborn, where young girls selected for their perfect Nordic traits were mated with SS men. Himmler also demanded that war heroes should be allowed a second marriage as a reward for their service.

Himmler was deeply involved in establishing CONCEN-TRATION CAMPS; as early as 1933, the year the Nazis came to power, he set up the first camp in Dachau, Germany, and then found people to fill it, expanding the categories of those legally subject to internment. "There is no more living proof of hereditary and racial laws than in a concentration camp," Himmler declared in a 1937 speech. "You find there hydrocephalics, squinters, deformed individuals, semi-Jews: a considerable number of inferior people." The German people were obliged to conduct "the struggle for the extermination of any sub-humans, all over the world who are in league against Germany, which is the nucleus of the Nordic race; against Germany, nucleus of the German nation, against Germany the custodian of human culture: they mean the existence or non-existence of the white man; and we guide his destiny." His Death Head units, which guarded the concentration camps, were to carry out a campaign based on these genocidal and racist ideas, exterminating Jews and Slavs in the camps or killing them on the ground in German-occupied Poland and Russia. Meanwhile, the SS continued to grow larger: By the end of the war, it would have more than 800,000 members divided into three divisions—Hitler's Body Guard (200,000), Waffen (594,000), and Death Head units (24,000).

Himmler inculcated in his SS forces an unswerving conviction of their mission, freeing them from any guilt for their crimes. "One principle must be absolute for the SS man," he stated in an address he delivered in October 1943 to the SS Group Leaders in Poznan, Poland, "we must be honest, decent, loyal, and comradely to members of our own blood and to no one else. What happens to the Russians, what happens to the Czechs, is a matter of utter indifference to me. Such good blood of our own kind as there may be among the nations we shall acquire for ourselves, if necessary by taking away the children and bringing them up among us. Whether the other peoples live in comfort or perish of hunger interests me only in so far as we need them as slaves for our Kultur. . . . We Germans, who are the only people in the world who have a decent attitude to animals, will also adopt a decent attitude to these human animals, but it is a crime against our own blood to worry about them and to bring them ideals."

Himmler, however, was capable of maintaining a facade of a bland bureaucrat—"a man of quiet unemotional gestures, a man without nerves," as he was once described. He exhibited such "exquisite courtesy" that one English observer was moved to say that "nobody I met in Germany is more normal." But this "normal" man "without nerves" suffered from psychosomatic illness, severe headaches, and intestinal spasms. When his SS men staged the execution of 100 Jews on the Russian front for his benefit, he was so sickened that he ordered a "more humane means" of killing. His order led to installing gas chambers in concentration camps—disguised as shower rooms—which proved to be a more efficient method of executing large numbers of people, though not necessarily a more humane one.

In October 1939 Hitler appointed Himmler Reichskommissar für die Festigung des Deutschen Volkstums (Reich Commissar for the Strengthening of Germandom), which effectively gave him absolute control over the parts of Poland that were annexed to the Third Reich. (Poland had fallen to German forces in September.) Himmler initiated a massive operation to uproot the native Poles from their homeland in central Poland and replace them with more Nordic peoples (the Volksdeutsche) from the Baltics and various outlying parts of Poland. Within a year, more than a million Poles and 300,000 Jews had been removed and deported to the east. In spite of the apparent success of the policy, Himmler did not want anyone to underestimate its difficulty. In a speech to an SS regiment, he said that fighting on the battlefield was much easier "than to suppress an obstructive population of low cultural level, or to carry out executions or to haul away people or to evict crying and hysterical women."

In 1943 Hitler made Himmler interior minister and then, after an unsuccessful assassination attempt against the führer in July 1944, chief of the army's home organization. In his new position, Himmler was put in charge of the war effort on the western front, where he was expected to mount a defense against advancing American forces. In 1945, as the German army was near collapse, he was placed in charge of the defense against the Red Army on the eastern front. But he proved ineffectual in either capacity, alienating many of the SS leaders under his command and stirring alarm in the highest reaches of Nazi circles, especially Martin BORMANN, who had maneuvered himself into a position second to none in Hitler's confidence. Convinced that only a negotiated peace with Britain and the United States would spare Germany from utter defeat, Himmler initiated contacts with Allied forces. Hitler learned of his betrayal and late in April 1945 ordered his arrest. To avoid detection, Himmler disguised himself and tried to pass himself off with false papers, but he was caught by British troops in Bremen on May 22. Before he could be interrogated, however, he took a cyanide capsule and killed himself.

See also NAZI PARTY, LEADERSHIP CORPS OF.

Further Reading:

Browder, George C. *Hitler's Enforcers: The Gestapo and the SS Security Service in the Nazi Revolution.* Oxford: Oxford University Press, 1996.

Butler, Rupert. *The Gestapo: A History of Hitler's Secret Police 1933–45.* Havertown, Pa.: Casemate Publishers and Book Distributors, 2004.

Douglas, Gregory. *Gestapo Chief: The 1948 Interrogation of Heinrich Muller, Volume 3.* San Jose, Calif.: R. James Bender Pub., 1998.

Hohne, Heinz Zollen. *The Order of the Death's Head: The Story of Hitler's SS.* New York: Penguin, 2001.

Padfield, Peter. *Himmler: Reichs Fuhrer-SS.* London: Cassell, 2001.

Hitler, Adolf (Alois Schickelgruber) (1889–1945)
Nazi leader of Germany

Born Alois Schickelgruber in Braunau am Inn, Austria, on April 20, 1889, Adolf Hitler has come to be such an embodiment of evil that it is difficult to separate out the man and the myth. Hitler and a sister were the only children of Alois and Klara Schickelgruber to survive infancy. As a boy, he was said to be a resentful, moody child without much ambition. Psychologists have made much of the fact that he was raised by a strict, authoritarian father whom he strongly disliked and a mother whom he loved. Her death from cancer when he was 11 came as a terrible blow. He sustained a second major setback when he was rejected by the Viennese Academy of Fine Arts, dashing his hopes of becoming an artist and plunging him into misery. It was during this period that historians believe that he developed his abiding hostility toward Jews, Marxists, and liberals. While in Vienna, eking out a living at odd jobs, he fell under the sway of demagogues such as the defrocked monk Lanz von Liebenfels and the Austrian Pan-German leader Georg von Schoenerer, who promulgated anti-Semitism and crackpot theories of racial purity.

When World War I broke out in August 1914, Hitler joined the 16th Bavarian Infantry Regiment. He showed courage on the battlefield; wounded twice and temporarily blinded, he was decorated with the Iron Cross. Nothing could sway him from the conviction that Germany's defeat was the fault of Jews and others who had stabbed Germany in the back. In the summer of 1919, still on the army payroll and now a lance corporal, he was ordered to spy on political parties springing up in postwar Munich. One party held a particular fascination for him: the German Workers Party, which was soon to change its name to the National Socialist German Workers Party (NSDAP), or Nazis. Its right-wing ideology appealed to him, and by July 1921 he had managed to become its chairman, partly because he proved so gifted at oratory.

Within a few months the party had gathered some 3,000 members. Hitler organized goon squads to keep order at party meetings and disrupt opposition rallies: the storm troopers (SA) under Captain Ernst Rohm and Hitler's own black-shirted personal bodyguard, the Schutzstaffel (SS). As part of the party's program, Hitler called for the exclusion of Jews from the German (Volk) community, based on what he called "the anti-Semitism of reason," and advocated Aryan supremacy. This policy, he wrote, must lead "to the systematic combating and elimination of Jewish privileges," whose "implacable goal" was "total removal of the Jews."

In 1923, convinced that the Weimer Republic was on the verge of collapse, Hitler took the opportunity to launch the "Beer Hall Putsch," a coup intended to topple the Bavarian government. Accompanied by the World War I hero General Erich Ludendorff and trailed by 3,000 supporters, Hitler marched through Munich, only to run into police fire that left 16 dead. Hitler was arrested and tried; at his conviction he declared, "Pronounce us guilty a thou-

sand times over: the goddess of the eternal court of history will smile and tear to pieces the State Prosecutor's submission and the court's verdict for she acquits us." He was sentenced to five years in Landsberg fortress but was released after nine months—time enough for him to compose his memoirs *Mein Kampf* (*My Struggle*), which laid out his rabidly anti-Semitic views and his belief in lebensraum, a policy that called for emptying Europe of "inferior" peoples, such as Slavs, and replacing them with racially pure Germans. The book was an enormous success, selling millions of copies in 11 languages.

Prison had tempered Hitler insofar as he decided that if he were to seize power, he would have to take a more covert and political approach rather than resorting to outright confrontation. With the assistance of two party loyalists, Hermann GÖRING and Joseph GOEBBELS, he began to rebuild the Nazi Party, which had fallen into disarray following his arrest. In 1925 the ban on the Nazis was lifted, allowing Hitler license to move into the political mainstream. The party managed to win 12 seats in the 1928 elections, aided by growing disenchantment with the Weimar Republic because of a failing economy. Its success attracted the interest of military figures, conservative aristocrats and industrialists who would later dig into their pockets to support the party. In the 1930 elections the Nazis did even better, gaining

Adolf Hitler shaking hands with a member of the Nazi Party (*Library of Congress*)

6,409,000 votes, or 18.3 percent of the total, a dramatic success in view of the 810,000 votes it had won only two years previously.

The Nazis now had 107 seats in the Reichstag, or parliament. In 1932 Hitler challenged Paul von Hindenburg, who was running for reelection to the presidency. Although he lost, he made such a credible showing that leading conservative politicians led by the diplomat Franz von PAPEN prevailed on the victorious Hindenburg to appoint Hitler reich chancellor on January 30, 1933. Hitler quickly moved to consolidate power, abolishing free trade unions and suppressing communists and social democrats. True to his promise, he also undertook to marginalize Jews, removing them from the political, business, and cultural life of the country. He also established the first CONCENTRATION CAMPS to imprison his political opponents.

In February 1933 a fire in the Reichstag gave Hitler the pretext he needed to crush dissent and create the legal framework for a totalitarian state. (The fire, blamed on a communist, was most likely started by the Nazis.) In the last free German elections in March 1933, the Nazis captured 44 percent of the vote but managed to form a government with a coalition partner. When Hindenburg died in August 1934 Hitler merged the offices of president and chancellor, appointing himself leader (führer) of Germany and obliging every member of the armed services to take an oath of personal loyalty. The Third Reich was born, a new empire Hitler predicted would last 1000 years. *Third Reich* is derived from the German expression *Drittes Reich*—literally, *Third Empire*. It refers to the state, not the land or its inhabitants. The term was first used in 1922 as the title of a book by a conservative writer and was adopted by the Nazis, who considered themselves the inheritors of two previous empires—the Holy Roman Empire (254–1806) and the German Empire (1871–1918). Over the next several years he set out to abrogate Germany's obligations under the Versailles treaty that ended World War I on terms highly unfavorable to Germany. He also began to remilitarize the country.

In 1935 Hitler formally repudiated the Treaty of Versailles. In March 1936 German troops marched into the demilitarized Rhineland without a shot being fired. The incursion into the Rhineland was followed in 1938 by the Anschluss, which incorporated Austria into Germany, and then the "liberation" of the Sudeten Germans. Although the British and French governments had committed themselves to the defense of Czechoslovakia, they had no stomach to go to war over it. British prime minister Neville Chamberlain famously claimed after he had signed the Munich Agreement, ceding Czechoslovakia to Germany in 1938, that he had achieved "peace in our time." The words would soon come back to haunt him. In the meantime, the campaign to exclude Jews from society and corral them into ghettoes intensified with the racial NUREMBERG LAWS, which among other provisions required Jews to wear yellow stars. Then, in November 1938, coordinated attacks against Jewish businesses and synagogues—what became known as Kristallnacht (Night of the Broken Glass)—signaled the start of a new campaign of state-authorized terror against the Jewish population of Germany. Some 10,000 Jews were kidnapped and held for ransom; about 2,000 were killed. After Kristallnacht, the Jews were encouraged to leave Germany, but the freedom to migrate would end a year later with the invasion of Poland. In 1939 Hitler made a statement in which he again blamed the Jews for World War I, declaring that "if the international financial Jewry within and outside Europe should succeed once more in dragging the nations into a war, the result will be . . . the annihilation of the Jewish race in Europe."

As Germany edged closer to war, Hitler formed alliances with Italy and Japan—together with Germany they were called the Axis powers—and signed a nonaggression pact with the Soviet Union that secretly divided up Poland and other parts of Eastern Europe between them. Then, on September 1, 1939, Germany invaded Poland; it took only 19 days for Poland to fall. In a startlingly effective tactic known as the blitzkrieg, German troops swept across much of Europe, taking Denmark and Norway in two months and Holland, Belgium, Luxemburg, and France in six weeks. German aircraft bombed Warsaw, Rotterdam, and Belgrade, all undefended cities, to cow their populations. After France fell in June 1940—the country became divided between occupied France and a collaborationist regime in the south known as Vichy France—only Great Britain was left to conquer. However, the British Royal Air Force (RAF) managed to stave off the German Luftwaffe, forcing Hitler to forgo Britain and turn his attention to the Balkans.

Hitler believed that the war against the USSR was necessary to rid the world of communism and with it the potential for Jews to regain a footing in Europe. He was determined to liquidate the 3.3 million Jews living in Russia and the Ukraine. His decision to invade the USSR, however, was probably the most serious mistake he ever made. His obsession with uprooting the Jews from Europe took a more insidious turn after the WANNSEE CONFERENCE in January 1942. At this meeting, Nazi officials determined on a policy known as the FINAL SOLUTION, which called for the elimination of Europe's entire Jewish population, numbering about 12 million. Orders were given to Nazi officials in all regions occupied by German troops to kill Jews or deport them to the concentration and extermination camps located mainly in Poland and Germany. Other occupied peoples—especially Poles and Ukrainians—were deported from their homes and sent to work as slave labor in German factories. Special units—EINSATZGRUPPEN—

were established to follow soldiers and massacre Jews as part of liquidating the "biological roots of Bolshevism."

When Germany began to suffer reverses on the battlefield, Hitler purged his generals, and his behavior became increasingly erratic as his health declined. He appeared in public less and less, preferring the seclusion of his retreat in the Prussian forest known as the Wolf's Lair. The turning point of the war came in June 1943 at the Battle of Stalingrad. With the German Sixth Army cut off by the Red Army, General Friedrich von Paulus was forced to surrender, spelling doom for German hopes to conquer the Soviet Union. A year later the Allies were marching up the Italian peninsula and taking Rome, and on June 6, 1944, the Allies landed at Normandy. Fearing utter defeat, several German generals concluded that their only hope lay in opening negotiations with the Allies for peace on any terms, but given Hitler's intransigence, they realized that they would have to assassinate him. The plot—attempted on July 20, 1944—failed, and the conspirators were arrested, tortured, and executed.

Nonetheless, the end of the Third Reich was near. Attempts to mobilize the Germans to take a last stand enjoyed only limited success. There were few men left to fight, and by the time the Red Army was at the gates of Berlin, boys were being recruited to defend the beleaguered capital. Hitler withdrew into his Führerbunker in Berlin, still nurturing the illusion that a German victory was possible. In March 1945 he ordered the destruction of all German industry and communications and transport systems—orders that were never carried out. On April 29 he married his mistress, Eva Braun, and dictated his final political testament, declaring, "Above all I charge the leaders of the nation and those under them to scrupulous observance of the laws of race and to merciless opposition to the universal poisoner of all peoples, international Jewry." Then he appointed Admiral Karl DÖNITZ as the new führer and Goebbels as Germany's new chancellor. Hitler, who was 56, and Braun shot themselves in the head the following day. Rather than accept his new appointment, which was meaningless anyway, Goebbels committed suicide along with his wife, Magda, and their six children on May 1, 1945. Germany surrendered a week later, on May 8. Hitler's "Thousand Year Reich" had lasted a little over 12 years. Most historians agree that Hitler's aides, carrying out his instructions, burned his and Braun's bodies in the garden of the Reich Chancellery after their deaths. After discovering the remains, the Red Army buried them behind the East German counterintelligence headquarters in Magdeburg. Reportedly they were exhumed and destroyed in 1970.

Historians have searched in vain for any document containing a written order by Hitler authorizing the Holocaust. Their failure to find such evidence has led to disputes among Hitler scholars as to the extent of his responsibility for the 6 million Jews who died as a result of Nazi policies. For instance, David Irving, a British historian, has taken the position that the Final Solution was orchestrated by underlings without Hitler's sanction—a theory that has found few supporters in academia—while American scholars including Richard Breitman and Daniel J. Goldhagen have argued that Hitler decided on the Final Solution in 1941. Another view is championed by the distinguished German historian Hans Mommsen, who maintained that Hitler was a "weak dictator" and that the Holocaust proceeded on its own momentum. Still another German scholar, Christian Gerlach, contends that Hitler made a personal decision to kill all German Jews and Jews in occupied Europe on December 12, 1941, based on a document attributed to Heinrich HIMMLER, the SS chief, that turned up in Soviet archives. Gerlach also claims that Hitler decided to liquidate all of European and Soviet Jews only after the United States entered the war. Other historians have taken issue with Gerlach, contending that the decision was taken earlier than December 1941. Breitman, who teaches history at American University, allows, however, that the absence of any written order from Hitler was in keeping with his methodology. "Hitler's style seems to have been to do as much of the dirty work as possible through oral communications," Breitman said.

Nonetheless, when—or whether—Hitler ordered the extermination of European Jewry still raises the problem of why so many ordinary people participated in the atrocities, condoned them, or simply turned a blind eye to them. Anti-Semitism had existed in Germany for centuries before Hitler came to power. Moreover, anti-Semitism was common elsewhere in Europe, and yet, in spite of pogroms and discrimination, no European country had ever mounted a campaign against the Jews on the scale of the Final Solution. Some historians believe that Hitler did not merely exploit the anti-Semitism that was already present in German society but instead changed its nature. Until Hitler, anti-Semitism had been based on religion. Jews were often locked into ghettoes, forcibly converted to Christianity, or denied the right to practice certain professions. But the Nazis went further and used the pseudoscience of eugenics to classify Jews as inferior and subhuman. Hitler and his propagandists—Alfred ROSENBERG, Julius STREICHER, and Goebbels—promoted the idea that Jews were evil and should be held accountable for Germany's loss in World War I. Jews were denounced as a people intent on world domination who controlled the press and the banking system for sinister objectives. In spite of his hatred for the Jews, Hitler could not institute the Final Solution at once; instead he had to guide the German people, leading them step by step to his ultimate goal of annihilating all Jews— first by separating Jews from society, then by casting them in the role of pariahs, and finally by transforming them into pathogens that had to be extirpated from the earth for the greater good of the superior Aryan races.

Further Reading:

Dawidowicz, Lucy. *A Holocaust Reader.* Library of Jewish Studies. Chicago: Behrman House Publishing, 1976.

Dwork, Deborah, and Robert Jan Van Pelt. *Holocaust: A History.* New York: W. W. Norton & Company, 2003.

Giblin, James Cross. *The Life and Death of Adolf Hitler.* New York: Clarion Books, 2002.

Gilbert, Martin. *The Holocaust: A History of the Jews of Europe during the Second World War.* New York: Owl Books, 1987.

Hitler, Adolf. Manheim, Ralph, trans. *Mein Kampf.* New York: Mariner Books, 1998.

Roseman, Mark. *The Wannsee Conference and the Final Solution: A Reconsideration.* New York: Metropolitan Books, 2002.

Toland, John. *Adolf Hitler: The Definitive Biography.* New York: Anchor, 1992.

Wistrich, Robert S. *Hitler and the Holocaust.* New York: Modern Library, 2001.

Hmong, persecution of

The Hmong are a minority ethnic group scattered throughout Southeast Asia, where about 2 million Hmong live; another 10 million are found in China. The Hmong have experienced almost 30 years of persecution in Communist Laos for their role in assisting the United States during the Vietnam War. The CIA trained and armed Hmong hill tribes, which mainly eked out livings as slash-and-burn farmers, to fight a covert war in Laos against the North Vietnamese and Pathet Lao armies from 1962 to 1975. They were given two principal missions: to slow the advance of the North Vietnamese army along the Ho Chi Minh Trail and disrupt their supply lines through Laos. The Hmong saved downed American pilots and facilitated the ability of the CIA to set up radars, which allowed U.S. warplanes to carry out more accurate strikes against North Vietnamese targets. Approximately 70,000 North Vietnamese troops moved into Laos to crush the Hmong. Some experts credit the Hmong with actually extending the United States' ability to continue their prosecution of the war for years longer than it could have without their help. According to the Lawyer's Committee for Human Rights, as many as 30,000 Hmong were killed in the war, and possibly as many as 100,000 may have been killed by Laotian security forces over the next five years.

With the end of the war in 1975, the Hmong were placed at particular risk. Considered traitors by the Lao-tian Communist regime, the Hmong took refuge in mountainous jungles, where they remain. Before 1974, 350,000 Hmong were living in Laos, but their numbers have fallen drastically. According to the BBC, there are now only about 200,000 left, including 12,000 former CIA-trained soldiers and their families. (Some estimates of the pre-1975 Hmong population in Laos are as high as 500,000.) It is unlikely that the Hmong insurgents will ever pose much of a threat to the government since they are armed only with Ak-47s and U.S. rifles left over from the war. Ammunition is at a premium; a BBC report said that the rebels had only five bullets apiece.

In an attempt to aid its former allies, Washington orchestrated a resettlement program for thousands of Hmong. (The last major contingent of Hmong REFUGEES living in Thai refugee camps were resettled in the United States in 2004.) Approximately 127,000 Hmong now reside in the United States, where they are concentrated largely in Wisconsin, Minnesota, and California. Thousands of Hmong also fled to neighboring Thailand, where they were housed in refugee camps. In the early 1990s, however, when threatened with forced repatriation to Laos, an estimated 35,000 Hmong refugees escaped from the camps. International relief agencies have expressed alarm at the fate of these displaced peoples, many of whom no longer enjoy the protective status of refugees and lack the resources to meet their basic needs. Thousands of refugees who have been forced to return to Laos have been arrested in violation of international laws governing the treatment of refugees. Because of the country's isolation and the inaccessibility of the Hmong themselves, it is difficult to verify what is actually happening in the jungles. However, repeated reports of atrocities and human rights abuses by Laotian forces, which have included the use of assault helicopters, ground troops, and systematic shelling and spraying of CHEMICAL WEAPONS near Hmong settlements, appear to confirm that the Hmong are in grave danger. Some reports of massacres have been documented in a 1997 White Paper by Dr. Vang Pobzeb for the Laotian Human Rights Council, which estimated that some 25,000 Hmong have been arrested, imprisoned or killed in the preceding seven years. The White Paper cites informed sources who report that between "November 1994 and April 1995, the Communist Lao government sent many thousands of soldiers to massacre, torture, arrest, and kill about 5,000 Hmong men, women and children, including innocent civilians of the general public . . . in northern Laos." The same White Paper states that many of the Hmong (as well as dissident Laotians), including political prisoners, were killed through "medical injections" and "food poisoning."

See also LAOS, HUMAN RIGHTS VIOLATIONS IN; VIETNAM, HUMAN RIGHTS VIOLATIONS IN.

Further Reading:
Hamilton-Merritt, Jane. *Tragic Mountains: The Hmong, the Americans, and the Secret Wars for Laos, 1942–1992.* Bloomington: Indiana University Press, 1999.
Quincy, Keith. *Hmong.* Cheney: Eastern Washington University Press, 2003.

Holocaust   *See* FINAL SOLUTION; WANNSEE CONFERENCE; WIESENTHAL, SIMON; YAD VASHEM.

Honduras, human rights violations in

Honduras has become one of the poorest and least-developed countries in Central America as a result of years of military rule, corruption, crime, and natural disasters. (In 1998 Hurricane Mitch devastated the country, killing 5,000 people and destroying 70 percent of the country's crops, with an estimated loss of $3 billion, setting development back by decades.) The military has long dominated the government, and it is only in recent years that efforts have been made to return the country to civilian rule. Some progress has been seen in this area: Several military officers have been charged with human rights violations committed during operations against leftist insurgents and supporters in the 1980s. Approximately 20 active and former military and police officials have been charged with criminal charges on human rights abuses, most of them accused of illegal detention and murder. DISAPPEARANCES do not constitute a crime under Honduran law, although 184 people were disappeared during the 1980s, all of whom are presumably dead. That means that a body must be produced in order for the victim's family to bring a case of suspected human rights abuse to court. Human rights organizations are troubled by the slow pace of the search for clandestine graves that would lead to exhumations, which in turn would advance prosecutions.

Poverty, disease, and malnutrition continue to hamper the government's ability to maintain political stability and curb violent crime committed mainly by gangs of youths. Police, too, have been implicated in crime, forming death squads with former military and security officials and right-wing paramilitary groups. There is no question that violent crime is a grave threat to public security. In 2002 an average of 3–10 violent deaths occurred every day in Honduras. But the police have proven largely ineffective in restoring order. As the 2003 U.S. State Department *Country Report* puts it: "The police forces are underfunded, undertrained, and understaffed. . . ." Further, the judicial system is weak. Attempts to suppress crime by violent youths have led to summary killings of several of them; members of the security forces have been connected to direct involvement in approximately 24 of the estimated 1,250 extrajudicial, arbitrary, and summary killings of children and young men from 1998 to June. The majority of killings of children and youths, however, are believed to have been perpetrated by death squads. According to Casa Alianza, a nongovernmental organization (NGO), the average number of killings of children and youths through June 2002 (most of them members of street gangs) increased by 16 percent over the first six months of 2001, rising from 197 to 230 murders. In the large majority of cases (60–70 percent), no perpetrators were identified. According to Casa Alianza, 549 children and youths age 23 and under were killed during 2002.

The spate of killings of young people has caused the UN special rapporteur on extrajudicial, arbitrary, and summary executions to issue a report in 2002, based on her August 2001 visit. The report claimed that security forces and police were involved in covering up their involvement in some of the summary killings of youth and children. Many of the slayings, however, appear to be the work of private, often unlicensed, guard services and neighborhood watch groups called Citizen Security Councils (CSCs). In rural areas, security forces have also taken part in criminal activity, often in the service of large landowners eager to evict poor farmers and peasants squatting on their property. Several "murders for hire" have taken place in which landless farmers have been killed in land disputes. Indigenous Indians have been disproportionately victims in these types of crimes.

The Ministry of Public Security has taken some action to rein in the police and security services, firing or demoting police personnel, security agents, and judges for corruption and abusive behavior. The government has even gone so far as to acknowledge the involvement of some officials in crime. In September 2002 the director of internal affairs of the police force announced that high-level officials had been involved either directly or indirectly in at least 20 EXTRAJUDICIAL KILLINGS of youths suspected of being gang members. Some cases against the accused have been opened by state prosecutors.

Although an informed citizenry might also provide a much-needed corrective to abuses by government officials and security agents, the media is too restricted by the legal system to fulfill that role. Punitive defamation laws on the books and requirements that journalists must identify sources in certain cases have created an atmosphere of intimidation. Editors and journalists practice self-censorship to avoid offending powerful political and economic interests. There have also been instances where journalists have taken bribes to write stories favorable to the government.

Hong Kong   *See* CHINA, HUMAN RIGHTS VIOLATIONS IN.

hors de combat

Hors de combat is a French term meaning "out of combat." It refers to a category of combatants who are no longer able to fight and who are therefore entitled to protection under international human rights law. The most important provision covering hors de combat is found in ARTICLE 3 COMMON TO THE GENEVA CONVENTIONS of 1949, which covers internal conflict. Article 3 states: "Persons taking no active part in the hostilities, including members of armed forces who have laid down their arms and those placed *hors de combat* by sickness, wounds, detention, or any other cause, shall in all circumstances be treated humanely." Persons who fall into the category defined by Article 3 cannot be attacked. A party to the combat is prohibited from committing "violence to life and person, in particular murder, mutilation, cruel treatment and torture." The ban is absolute. As the INTERNATIONAL COMMITTEE OF THE RED CROSS Commentary to Common Article 3 makes clear: "No possible loophole is left; there can be no excuse, no attenuating circumstances." The execution of soldiers who are considered hors de combat is considered a war crime under international law.

See also GENEVA CONVENTIONS; PROTECTED PERSONS.

Further Reading:
Gutman, Roy, ed. *Crimes of War: What the Public Should Know.* New York: W. W. Norton, 1999.

hostages

Hostages are defined by the INTERNATIONAL COMMITTEE OF THE RED CROSS (ICRC) as "persons who find themselves, willingly or unwillingly, in the power of the enemy and who answer with their freedom or their life for compliance with the orders of the latter (the enemy) and for upholding the security of its armed forces." The seizure of civilians in times of war is prohibited under international law; the practice is banned by ARTICLE 3 COMMON TO THE GENEVA CONVENTIONS and by the Fourth Geneva Convention of 1949. Hostage taking is also banned by the 1977 ADDITIONAL PROTOCOLS TO THE GENEVA CONVENTIONS. In addition, the Geneva Conventions prohibit the use of either PRISONERS OF WAR or civilians from being "used to render certain points or areas immune from military operations." In other words, it is impermissible to use noncombatants or those who are no longer engaged in combat as HUMAN SHIELDS.

Hostage taking has traditionally been employed to intimidate or extort an occupied population. In World War II, the taking of civilians as hostages as a means of REPRISAL was often employed by the Nazis as a prelude to summarily executing them. That accounts for why hostage taking was specifically prohibited in the 1949 Geneva Convention, which grew out of the NUREMBERG TRIALS of Nazi war criminals. Under international law, a belligerent is permitted to retaliate for an illegal act by an adversary, but the reprisal should be proportionate to the act and not entail "excessive" force, and under no circumstances does international law permit an adversary from executing civilians or prisoners of war. Further elaboration of the laws against hostage taking is found in the International Convention Against the Taking of Hostages, a United Nations treaty signed in December 1979. It prohibits the use of hostages—whether by killing, injuring, or detention—"to force the hand of a state, an intergovernmental organization, a natural or juridical person, or a group of persons, to do or abstain from doing any act as an explicit or implicit condition for the release of the hostage commits the offence of taking of hostages." Signatories are obliged to secure the release of hostages held within their territories and ensure the hostage's return.

Determining when and to whom the relevant legal provisions apply in practice is a tricky exercise. As Sean Maguire points out in an essay written for the CRIMES OF WAR PROJECT, many problems arise because of the nature of modern warfare. For instance, he writes, the Geneva Conventions would not cover an airline hijacking because the conventions state that for hostage taking to occur it must involve "an authority"—a government or established military organization. Instead, a hijacking would fall under the 1979 International Convention Against the Taking of Hostages, which explicitly outlaws crimes that take place across borders. When Bosnian Serbs detained 400 UN peacekeepers in Bosnia in May 1995 during the war in the former Yugoslavia, the United Nations labeled them hostages. But the ICRC contended that, in fact, the peacekeepers were not neutrals at all but were a party to the conflict since the United Nations had ordered air strikes. Under that interpretation, according to the ICRC, the UN troops should be considered prisoners of war. But when Serb forces attempted to use the UN troops as human shields, the ICRC objected, asserting that they were being exploited as hostages in violation of international law. Nonetheless, the Serb officials responsible, Radovan KARADŽIĆ AND RATKO Mladić, have both been charged with hostage taking by the INTERNATIONAL CRIMINAL TRIBUNAL FOR THE FORMER YUGOSLAVIA in The Hague.

See also CIVILIAN IMMUNITY.

Further Reading:
Gutman, Roy, ed. *Crimes of War: What the Public Should Know.* New York: W. W. Norton & Company, 1999.
Robertson, Geoffrey. *Crimes against Humanity: The Struggle for Global Justice.* New York: New Press, 2003.

Taylor, Telford. *Nuremberg Trials: War Crimes and International Law (International Conciliation).* New York: Carnegie Endowment for International Peace, 1949.

Tutorow, Norman E. *War Crimes, War Criminals, and War Crimes Trials: An Annotated Bibliography and Source Book.* Westport, Conn.: Greenwood Publishing Group, 1986.

humanitarian aid, barring of

The barring of humanitarian aid is prohibited under international law. The Fourth Geneva Convention of 1949 obliges signatories to allow "the free passage of all consignments of medical and hospital stores" and of "all consignments of essential foodstuffs, clothing and tonics intended for children under fifteen, expectant mothers and maternity cases"; this provision applies even to belligerent forces. The 1977 ADDITIONAL PROTOCOLS TO THE GENEVA CONVENTIONS covers the obligations of belligerents toward civilians. OCCUPYING POWERS have the obligation to provide relief supplies to the population of its adversary "without any adverse distinction." Articles necessary for religious practice must also be allowed to reach a population under occupation. If a relief effort is "humanitarian and impartial in character," a belligerent is obligated to accept it.

These provisions, however, are not absolute. Article 23 of the Fourth Geneva Convention, for instance, states that a belligerent should have no "serious reasons" for thinking that the relief supplies will be diverted from the intended recipients or that the relief agency or nongovernmental organization (NGO) delivering the supplies will not control their distribution. In addition, the belligerent should be satisfied that the relief supplies are humanitarian in nature and will not bolster the military capacity of the enemy or boost its economy. Article 18 of Additional Protocol II reinforces the concept that relief efforts must be of an "exclusively humanitarian and impartial nature." In order to ensure that this is the case, a belligerent has the right to inspect relief convoys before permitting them access to the enemy.

Both the Fourth Geneva Convention and the Additional Protocols envision the application of these provisions to conventional warfare between armies of two states. But the situation is far more complicated when ethnic conflicts occur. In cases such as the Bosnian war of the 1990s or the Rwandan genocidal campaign of 1994, where the suppression or extermination of a particular group of people is the aim, humanitarian aid is routinely barred or relief supplies are seized before they can be delivered to the population for which they are intended. In such instances, feeding or providing shelter to a targeted population is inimical to the interests of the aggressor. In the Bosnian war, not only did Serb forces have no interest in allowing Muslims to obtain religious articles, as required by international law, but they frequently blew up mosques. In many internal conflicts throughout the world, the distinction between civilian and combatant is difficult, if not impossible to make, so that considerable confusion can arise as to when a relief effort is or is not "exclusively humanitarian and impartial in nature."

In many conflict zones, the barring of humanitarian aid for various periods is justified on the basis of security concerns. Israel has often been the subject of harsh criticism by international relief agencies for obstructing their operations in the occupied territories. Agencies such as Médécins Sans Frontières (DOCTORS WITHOUT BORDERS), Care International, and OXFAM have complained that curfews imposed on Palestinians, excessive delays at military checkpoints, and restrictions on movement of their staff have interfered with delivering vital services and supplies. The Israeli government has said that it wants aid to reach the Palestinians but that delays sometimes occur because of security needs or because of ongoing military operations. The Sudanese government has come under even more scathing attacks from humanitarian agencies for impeding the flow of food to several hundred thousand refugees forced from their homes by Arab militias and paramilitary forces in the Darfur area of western Sudan. The INTERNATIONAL COMMITTEE OF THE RED CROSS (ICRC) has said that it has been denied permits necessary to enter the region even though Khartoum claims that it will permit humanitarian aid to reach the people who are at risk of starvation.

Another humanitarian crisis has been brewing in the eastern region of the Democratic Republic of the Congo where violence erupted in spring 2004, sparked by suddenly restive rebel groups. The United Nations Emergency Fund Relief Coordinator warned that some 3.3 million civilians were at risk of starvation because humanitarian aid had been barred by armed factions operating in the area. Moreover, because of the changing nature of internal conflicts, international relief workers are increasingly likely to be targeted themselves. Rather than being seen as neutral or impartial, aid workers are often intimidated or killed to destabilize governments, attract media attention to a cause, or demoralize a population. Aid workers have frequently been marked for deaths in rural areas of Afghanistan and kidnapped in Chechnya, with the result that relief agencies have been forced to withdraw staff and curb the flow of relief supplies to vulnerable populations. In July 2004, for instance, Doctors Without Borders announced that it was pulling out of the country after over two decades of providing assistance because of the failure of the Afghani government to investigate the killing of five of its workers.

See also CONGO, DEMOCRATIC REPUBLIC OF THE, WAR CRIMES IN; DARFUR, WAR CRIMES IN; GENEVA CONVENTIONS; RWANDA, GENOCIDE IN.

Further Reading:

Aall, Pamela R., Daniel Miltenberger, and George Weiss. *IGOs, NGOs, and the Military in Peace and Relief Operations.* Washington, D.C.: United States Institute of Peace Press, 2000.

Byman, Daniel, Ian Lesser, Bruce Pirnie, Cheryl Benard, and Matthew Waxman. *Strengthening the Partnership: Improving Military Coordination with Relief Agencies and Allies in Humanitarian Operations.* Santa Monica, Calif.: Rand Corporation (NBN), 2000.

Erskins, Toni. *Can Institutions Have Responsibilities: Collective Moral Agency and International Relations.* Global Issues Series. Sydney, Australia: Palgrave Macmillan, 2004.

Gutman, Roy, ed. *Crimes of War: What the Public Should Know.* New York: W. W. Norton & Company, 1999.

Rieff, David. *A Bed for the Night: Humanitarianism in Crisis.* New York: Simon & Schuster, 2002.

Vaux, Anthony. *The Selfish Altruist: Relief Work in Famine and War.* London: Earthscan Publications, 2001.

Welch, Claude E., Jr. *Ngos and Human Rights: Promise and Performance.* Pennsylvania Studies in Human Rights. Philadelphia: University of Pennsylvania Press, 2000.

humanitarian intervention

Humanitarian intervention usually takes the form of a proactive action to address a serious humanitarian crisis. On one extreme, it can involve the delivery of relief aid; on the other, it can involve the use of military force. No formal legal definition of humanitarian intervention exists; however, in general a humanitarian intervention should be distinguished from a political intervention; the former is intended to protect people who are being victimized in a country even if the state (or nonstate actor) happens to be the perpetrator; in the latter, one state is trying to impose its will on another by force. Issues of sovereignty figure in both instances, which accounts for much of the controversy surrounding humanitarian intervention. Two basic questions have arisen: When does humanitarian intervention become necessary, and how should it be achieved? The goal of all humanitarian interventions is—at least in principle—to rescue a civilian population that is threatened with the deprivation of human rights protected under international law.

An inherent tension exists between ensuring respect for human rights and the universally recognized inviolability of territorial integrity and the right of self-determination. The United Nations Charter, for instance, establishes principles that apply to the maintenance of peace and international security but does not include provisions or mechanisms for the protection of human rights. Article 2 of the charter prohibits the United Nations from intervening "in the domestic jurisdiction of any state." It further states: "All Members shall refrain in their international relations from the threat or use of force against the territorial integrity or political independence of any state, or in any other manner inconsistent with the Purposes of the United Nations." A body of international law has reaffirmed this principle. There are two major exceptions. A state has the right to use force in self-defense, and a right of collective defense is also granted under Article 51 of the charter.

The rationale for humanitarian intervention is found in Article 39, which allows the use of force to counter a "threat to international peace and security," and in Article 42, which allows the use of force "to maintain or restore international peace and security." Over the years the Security Council has gradually expanded the definition of a "threat to international peace and security" to justify military intervention to deal with humanitarian crises, although many of these crises arise because of purely internal conflicts. What is left unstated is whether the UN Security Council has the *obligation* to act even in the face of a grave humanitarian crisis. Legal experts are divided. UN secretary-general Kofi Annan has taken the position that where CRIMES AGAINST HUMANITY are being committed "and peaceful attempts to halt them have been exhausted, the Security Council has a *moral* duty to act on behalf of the international community."

But morality aside, the Security Council has not acted consistently in these crises, often because of political or bureaucratic considerations. Obviously public opinion has a great deal of influence—nationally and internationally. Televised images of mass murder have aroused such indignation throughout the world that it becomes harder for the United Nations and member states to avoid humanitarian intervention. But it is often difficult to get the word out: Only in mid-2004 has the world become aware of a devastating human rights crisis in the Darfur region of western Sudan, where several hundred thousand black tribespeople have been killed and uprooted from their homes by Arab paramilitary groups supported by Khartoum. As of mid-2004, no serious effort had been taken by the United Nations or by any state to intervene with force, but the United States has threatened Sudan with sanctions if it fails to stop what increasingly appeared to be GENOCIDE (although the United Nations and U.S. State Department have not used that term to characterize events in Darfur). In many cases where the political will seems to be lacking, international relief organizations, human rights groups, and other nongovernmental organizations (NGOs) have frequently taken the initiative and campaigned for interventions.

There are, of course, some instances in which states act even in the absence of public support for action. In fact, a case could be made that humanitarian intervention provides states with a justification for action when no domestic support exists for it. By the same token, a humanitarian intervention can be used as a cover for what is really a political intervention. Perhaps the most egregious example of inaction on the part of the United Nations was its paralysis in the face of the genocide in Rwanda in 1994, which took the lives of some 800,000 people. The United States has come under sharp criticism for blocking the deployment of an effective intervention force while the genocide was going on. On the other hand, the French did intervene in Rwanda on humanitarian grounds—at least to a limited extent—in what was called Operation Turquoise. However, this action prompted some skepticism about its motives since France had long enjoyed cordial relations with the Hutu government. Thus, the French intervention was seen less as humanitarian in nature than as an effort to influence events in Rwanda with military force and to save a regime that it supported even as it carried out a genocidal campaign.

In 1992 the United Nations (spearheaded by the United States) undertook what was described as a humanitarian mission to Somalia to avert widespread starvation but later became entangled in a civil war between rival clan leaders. The result was a military and political disaster—the subject of the book and movie *Black Hawk Down*—that impelled the pullout of the UN force.

By way of contrast, the Security Council more recently has authorized the deployment of a small UN peacekeeping contingent in the eastern part of the Democratic Republic of the Congo, where more than 3 million people have been endangered by several military and insurgent groups involved in a civil war. (Though a peace treaty has formally ended the conflict, periodic flare-ups continue to occur.) However, many observers believe that the UN force, which is made up of only several hundred troops, is inadequate to fulfill its mandate. In 2004, when factional fighting resumed in the area, the United Nations was blamed by many Congolese for failing to keep the peace. One major factor is the political will for undertaking such interventions, especially at a time of proliferating internal conflicts. In addition, fewer nations are willing to commit troops because of lack of popular support or because their forces are already overextended.

The UN Security Council is further hobbled in responding to a humanitarian crisis by its own composition. The interests of the Permanent Five (The United States, the United Kingdom, Russia, China, and France) often impede the ability to agree on a unified policy to confront a humanitarian crisis. There is no chance, for instance, that any intervention will ever be authorized by the Security Council in Chechnya, in spite of years of human rights abuses, because of Russian opposition. As ethnic cleansing escalated in the Kosovo war in 1998 and 1999, Russia (an ally of Serbia) and China continued to veto any attempt to intervene on behalf of the beleaguered Kosovo Albanian population. Ultimately, humanitarian intervention did take place in the province (which was—and legally remains—part of the former Yugoslavia), but it was NATO, not the United Nations, which was responsible. Although the Kosovo debate in the Security Council highlighted a major gap in international law about humanitarian intervention, it did establish a precedent for states or alliances to act on their own. UN secretary-general Kofi Annan noted the problem at the time: "This year's conflict in Kosovo raised equally important questions about the consequences of action without international consensus and clear legal authority. . . . On the one hand, is it legitimate for a regional organization to use force without a UN mandate? On the other, is it permissible to let gross and systematic violations of human rights, with grave humanitarian consequences, continue unchecked?"

This question remains unresolved. Whether an intervention for humanitarian purposes should be the exclusive right of the UN Security Council or whether a state or group of states can assert the right to do so in the absence of UN action is the source of intense debate. While the invasion of Iraq by a U.S.-led coalition in 2003 was not justified as a humanitarian intervention but rather as a means to disarm Saddam HUSSEIN, Washington insisted that it was taking action to enforce resolutions on Iraq that the Security Council had adopted, in effect, putting forward the argument that the United States was acting on the behalf of the United Nations when it proved incapable of action itself. This type of ad hoc intervention is unilateral in contrast to collective intervention authorized by the Security Council. One of the arguments among legal scholars is whether individual human rights enjoy greater importance than the sovereign rights of states; if this is indeed the case, one group of legal experts contend, then states or alliances on their own initiative do have the right to intervene without obtaining the Security Council's approval, as in the case of Kosovo.

See also CONGO, DEMOCRATIC REPUBLIC OF THE, WAR CRIMES IN; DARFUR, WAR CRIMES IN; INTERNATIONAL HUMANITARIAN LAW; KOSOVO, WAR CRIMES IN; RWANDA, GENOCIDE IN; SOMALIA, HUMAN RIGHTS VIOLATIONS IN.

Further Reading:

Price, Monroe, and Mark Thompson, eds. *Forging Peace: Intervention, Human Rights, and the Management of Media Space.* Bloomington: Indiana University Press, 2002.

Shelton, Dinah. *Remedies in International Human Rights Law.* Oxford: Oxford University Press, 2001.

Steiner, Henry J., and Philip Alston. *International Human Rights in Context: Law, Politics, Morals.* Oxford: Oxford University Press, 2000.

Human Rights Convention (Convention for the Protection of Human Rights and Fundamental Freedoms)

The Convention for the Protection of Human Rights and Fundamental Freedoms—better known as the Human Rights Convention—was adopted in 1950 by the Council of Europe to enshrine protections of human rights. Most members of the Council have signed the convention, although it is not obligatory to do so. The convention established the European Court of Human Rights; any individual who believes that his or her rights have been violated by a state party to the accord has the right to take the case to the court. Decisions of the court are legally binding, and the court is entitled to exact monetary damages as punishment. Signatory states also have the right to take other state signatories to the court, but this power is rarely used.

As of 2002, 13 protocols had been added to the convention, some which involve the mechanics of the convention itself and some which provide for more human rights protections. The convention confers on every person a right to life and liberty, although there are exceptions—cases of lawful executions and deaths that result from "the use of force which is no more than absolutely necessary" in self-defense or to enforce the law. Protocol 6, however, subsequently enjoined signatories from imposing the death penalty except in times of war.

The convention prohibits TORTURE and "inhuman or degrading treatment or punishment" without exception. This provision also has been interpreted to mean that no signatory can send an individual to a country where torture or the death penalty is used. The convention similarly forbids SLAVERY and FORCED LABOR (although not from conscription or the use of prison labor). A person must be informed why he or she is being arrested and apprised of the charges; a suspect is to have prompt access to jurisdictional proceedings and is entitled to presumption of innocence and a fair trial. The convention also provides a right to respect for one's "private and family life, his home and his correspondence," subject to certain restrictions that are "in accordance with law" and "necessary in a democratic society." Furthermore, individuals are granted freedom of thought, conscience, and religion, and they are entitled to freedom of expression and freedom of assembly and association.

The convention includes a more surprising provision, guaranteeing those of marriageable age the right to marry. The European Court of Human Rights has not, however, agreed to interpret this provision to give legal standing to same-sex marriages. In addition, the convention prohibits discrimination on the basis of sex, race, color, language, religion, and several other criteria. Article 15 allows signatories to derogate or opt out of the convention in times of emergency, a provision that the United Kingdom invoked when it passed antiterrorism legislation allowing indefinite detention of those suspected of terrorism in 2001. The British high court found, however, that the British government had acted illegally.

In addition to the limits against the death penalty, the more significant protocols that have been opened for signature provide for the protection of private property; the right for parents to have children educated in accordance with their religion or other beliefs; the prohibition of the imprisonment of people because of their "inability to fulfil a contractual obligation"; the guarantee of the right of an individual to move about and leave his or her country; the prohibition of the collective expulsion of "lawfully resident aliens"; the right of appeal for defendants and the prohibition of double jeopardy; and the reinforcement of prohibitions against discrimination based on "sex, race, colour, language, religion, political or other opinion, national or social origin, association with a national minority, property, birth or other status."

human rights reports (U.S. State Department)

The *Country Reports on Human Rights Practices*, published annually by the U.S. State Department, are in effect a report card about the progress (or the lack of it) that countries around the world are making in the protection of their citizens' human rights. These country reports have been issued since 1977 and over the years have come to play a significant role in the formation of U.S. foreign policy. The reports are not intended to be a history or a recapitulation of the previous year's events; according to the State Department, "They are documents backed by the full weight of the U.S. people and Government. They speak for those who have no voice, bearing witness for those who have not had access to free trials, nor have enjoyed other fundamental human rights and protections."

The reports focus on several critical issues of importance to human rights such as freedom from TORTURE, cruel and inhuman punishment, freedom of the press, religious freedom, workers' and women's rights, and corporate responsibility. These reports are predicated on a belief in universal human rights that, according to the State Department, "aim to incorporate respect for human dignity into the processes of government and law. All persons have the inalienable right to change their government by peaceful means and to enjoy basic freedoms, such as freedom of expression, association, assembly, movement, and religion, without discrimination on the basis of race, religion, national origin, or sex." The reports offer an overview of global trends, noting advances in democracy and the inevitable setbacks in securing the freedoms and rights of people in countries where governments have committed serious abuses and violations of human rights. In this regard, the reports examine the transparency and fairness of elections and the freedom of the media to criticize the government, in addition to noting where breakdown of law and governance has occurred.

The impetus to issue these reports first came about in the mid-1970s during the cold war. During this turbulent period in U.S. history, the United States had been forced to withdraw from South Vietnam, which would soon fall to the Communists. Sensational revelations about CIA efforts to destabilize unfriendly regimes and assassinate political leaders in Chile, Cuba, and the former Belgian Congo had sent shockwaves through Washington. Because the fight against communism was such a preoccupying factor in setting policy, successive administrations, both Republican and Democratic, had often ignored international law and given short shrift to human rights concerns. Among the American public there was a growing unease about the government's practice of carrying out clandestine, extralegal activities, especially in the aftermath of the Watergate scandal that brought down the Nixon presidency. Moreover, the civil rights struggle and fight for racial equality at home had made Americans more aware of the suppression of individual, ethnic, and religious rights abroad.

Beginning in 1973, however, lawmakers in Congress began to attach amendments to foreign aid measures as a tool to raise the profile of human rights. Henceforth, if countries wanted to receive U.S. financial and military aid, they would have to meet certain human rights standards. These efforts led to an amendment to the Foreign Assistance Act in 1976 requiring annual reports on human rights. To gather the material for the reports, the State Department—then headed by Henry Kissinger—sent a cable to all overseas posts requesting information that would be helpful in formulating American aid programs. The promotion of human rights, the cable said, was "a principal goal of U.S. foreign policy." The embassy staffs were told that in preparing their reports they should bear in mind the "considerable public and media attention to human rights questions in U.S. foreign affairs."

The first formal *Human Rights Report* (relating to conditions in the previous year) published by the State Department appeared in 1977. At the same time, legislation authorized the creation of a new office of human rights and humanitarian affairs within the department, the administrator of which was known then as coordinator of human rights, a position later upgraded to assistant secretary. (In 1994 the Bureau of Human Rights and Humanitarian Affairs was reorganized and renamed as the Bureau of Democracy, Human Rights, and Labor to recognize the interrelationship of human rights, worker rights, and democracy.) The initial report covered only 82 countries and was focused primarily on nations with whom the United States had formal security assistance programs,

most of them long-standing allies. The first report needed a mere 143 pages to cover all the countries it elected to survey. By contrast, in 2001 the number of countries covered had grown to 195, and the size and scope of the reports had expanded significantly.

The new country reports began to reflect an important change in how human rights were being viewed. This was because hundreds of nongovernmental organizations (NGOs) were springing up, including HUMAN RIGHTS WATCH, AMNESTY INTERNATIONAL, and DOCTORS WITHOUT BORDERS. These NGOs were able to issue reports about what was happening on the ground—free of the filter of government censorship—and gain access to international media to raise issues about human rights abuses that otherwise might be ignored. Pointedly, the first country report relied on an NGO called FREEDOM HOUSE to rank each country under three categories: free, partly free, or not free.

In 1978 an additional 33 countries were added, all of which were recipients of U.S. economic aid, but that list would soon expand to take in nearly every country on the planet thanks to an amendment to the Foreign Assistance Act, which required an entry for every member of the United Nations. In addition to U.S. allies and friends, the reports would also look at conditions in adversaries such as Cuba, the Soviet Union, and the People's Republic of China. By this point the format of these reports had been fairly well established. The first section, for instance, was called "Respect for the Integrity of the Person," with subsections on torture; cruel, inhuman, or degrading treatment or punishment; arbitrary arrest or imprisonment; denial of fair public trial; and invasion of the home. The second section was entitled "Government Policies Relating to the Fulfillment of such Vital Needs as Food, Shelter, and Health Care." The third section was "Respect for Civil and Political Liberties," with subsections on freedom of speech, the press, religion, and assembly; freedom of movement within the country for travel and immigration; and freedom to participate in the political process. The fourth section was "Government Attitude and Record Regarding International and Nongovernmental Investigation of Alleged Violations of Human Rights." In 1981 a subsection was added to take into account DISAPPEARANCES—the abduction and disappearance of political or religious opposition figures, a pernicious practice that was widely used in the so-called dirty wars in Latin America during the 1970s and early 1980s.

Several other topics were subsequently added to the reports as events demanded—sections on fulfillment of vital needs, "Economic and Social Circumstances"; political and EXTRAJUDICIAL KILLINGS; and the right of citizens to change their government. Other sections on freedom of speech and the press, peaceful assembly, religion, movement, and the political process were expanded. In 1986 a new section entitled "Discrimination Based on Race, Sex, Religion, Language, or Social Status" was introduced, along with another section on the "Status of Labor" (which would later include the right to organize and bargain collectively, minimum age for employment of children, and acceptable conditions of labor). In 1989 a subsection was added on the use of excessive force and violations of human rights in internal conflicts. Four years later the section on discrimination was expanded to include specific discussions of the rights of women; children; indigenous people; people with disabilities; and national, racial, and ethnic minorities. (In 1994 Congress also created a position of senior adviser for women's rights as well.) In 1996 subsections were added on REFUGEES and the right to ASYLUM, and in 1998 a section was added to deal with the growing problem of the TRAFFICKING IN PERSONS. With all these changes and additions, the country reports now take up two volumes. The reports can also be found on the State Department Web site.

Preparation

To prepare these reports, U.S. embassies are required to collect information throughout the year from a variety of sources, including government officials, jurists, military sources, journalists, human rights monitors, academics, and labor activists. In many cases, investigating allegations of human rights abuses, flawed elections, and disappearances can prove risky, especially as governments have a vested interest (a possible cut-off in aid) in not having such violations of law brought to light. Once the initial draft of the report is prepared by the embassy, it is sent to Washington, where it is reviewed by the Bureau of Democracy, Human Rights, and Labor, in cooperation with other State Department offices. During the review process, State Department officers may incorporate information into the reports that they have acquired from their own sources, which might include reports issued by the United States, the United Nations, human rights groups, foreign government officials, academics, and the media. On specific issues—labor or women's or children's rights, for instance—officers also consult with experts in the relevant field. Once published, the reports are intended to serve as a resource for shaping policy, conducting diplomacy, and providing assistance.

Not surprisingly, the reports have drawn criticism. On the one hand, in some instances the reports are seen as jeopardizing relations with allies or countries with which the United States has a strategic stake. On the other hand, human rights advocates often question the objectivity of certain reports for downplaying human rights abuses in countries with which the United States desires good relations. They also cite a tendency to perceive in a government's symbolic gestures—an amnesty or the release of a well-known political figure from prison—real progress in ending human rights violations that is not necessarily supported by the evidence. Nonetheless, as report cards go, these annual documents do provide a useful measure with which to grade governments of nearly 200 nations as free, partly free, or not free at all.

Human Rights Watch

Human Rights Watch, based in New York, is the largest human rights organization in the United States. It began in 1978 as Helsinki Watch, to monitor the compliance of Soviet bloc countries with the human rights provisions of the HELSINKI ACCORDS. A sister advocacy group, Americas Watch, was set up in the 1980s. Other "Watch" committees were formed to cover human rights issues in different regions of the world, leading to the amalgamation of all the Watch committees in 1988 as Human Rights Watch.

Human Rights Watch relies on the expertise of more than 150 dedicated professionals, including lawyers, journalists, academics, and country experts of many nationalities. Its researchers conduct fact-finding investigations into human rights abuses throughout the world and then publish the results in print and on its Web site. By raising awareness of human rights abuses, the group seeks to influence policymakers, nongovernmental organizations (NGOs), and the public alike. In crisis situations, Human Rights Watch tries to provide the media with up-to-date information about what is taking place, bolstering their accounts with eyewitness testimony taken from REFUGEES and others with firsthand knowledge of the events. In addition to its auxiliary offices in Brussels, London, Moscow, Hong Kong, Los Angeles, San Francisco, and Washington, Human Rights Watch will also establish temporary offices in areas where it is conducting intensive investigations.

Human Rights Watch not only tracks events in over 70 countries but also specializes in such issues of global importance as women's rights, children's rights, and the flow of arms to forces responsible for human rights abuses. In the past the group has lobbied for the adoption of a treaty banning the use of child soldiers, providing for the minimum age of 18 for participation in combat. It also shared the Nobel Peace Prize with other NGOs in 1977 for its work in advancing the International Campaign to Ban Landmines, which led to the approval of an international treaty to ban the mines. Human Rights Watch was also among the first NGOs to urge the creation of an international war crimes tribunal for crimes committed in the former Yugoslavia. It was instrumental in pressing for the establishment of a similar court to prosecute those responsible for GENOCIDE in Rwanda in 1994. To fund its operations, Human Rights Watch relies on contributions from foundations and individuals.

Land-mine victims from Kenya and the Sudan *(B. Heger/ICRC)*

Further Reading:

Aall, Pamela R., Daniel Miltenberger, and George Weiss. *IGOs, NGOs, and the Military in Peace and Relief Operations.* Washington, D.C.: United States Institute of Peace Press, 2000.

Erskins, Toni. *Can Institutions Have Responsibilities: Collective Moral Agency and International Relations.* Global Issues Series. Sydney, Australia: Palgrave Macmillan, 2004.

Welch, Claude E., Jr. *Ngos and Human Rights: Promise and Performance.* Pennsylvania Studies in Human Rights. Philadelphia: University of Pennsylvania Press, 2000.

human shields

The term *human shields* refers to people who are put in the line of fire to prevent an attack. In most instances threat or force is required to place a person in jeopardy, but in some cases people will voluntarily become human shields. The four GENEVA CONVENTIONS prohibit the use of either civilians under the control of a belligerent or PRISONERS OF WAR from being used as human shields. Nonetheless, states have often flouted the ban. In 1990, after invading Kuwait, Saddam HUSSEIN's forces held more than 800 Western, Japanese, and Kuwaiti nationals who were used as human shields to protect strategic installations in Iraq and Kuwait from attack by the international coalition then being mobilized. At the same time, Saddam refused to allow thousands of other foreigners, whose countries had joined the coali-

tion to leave Iraq or Kuwait, declaring that he was prepared to use them as human shields as well. They were later released without harm before hostilities began. Again in 1997, during a crisis provoked by his expulsion of UN weapons inspectors, Saddam urged hundreds of Iraqi families to become "voluntary" human shields at palaces and strategic facilities to deter retaliatory bombing by U.S. and British aircraft.

In 1991, in a crackdown on insurgents in Kachin State, the government of Myanmar (Burma) moved thousands of ethnic Kachins into cities vulnerable to attack by rebels, in effect using them as human shields. More recently, the Israel Defense Force (IDF) has come under fire from Israeli human rights groups for using Palestinians as human shields in the occupied territories. Israeli soldiers have reportedly ordered Palestinian civilians to inspect buildings to check if they are booby-trapped, remove suspicious objects from roads used by the army, position themselves in buildings occupied by IDF troops to forestall an attack by Palestinian militants, or walk ahead of soldiers down dangerous streets. According to B'Tselem, an Israeli human rights group, the use of human shields was an established military policy and not the result of spontaneous decisions on the part of the soldiers. In 2002 HUMAN RIGHTS WATCH issued a report on this issue, and shortly thereafter seven human rights organizations petitioned the Israeli High Court of Justice to end the practice. Two days later the government informed the court that "the IDF has decided to issue immediately an unequivocal order to the forces in the field. The order states that forces in the field are absolutely forbidden to use any civilians as a means of 'living shield' against gunfire or attacks by the Palestinian side." However, the government contended that that ordering Palestinians to direct other Palestinians to leave their homes did not constitute using them as human shields, a policy known as "the neighbor procedure." B'Tselem argues, however, that the neighbor policy is simply the use of human shields by another name.

In October 2005 the Israeli Supreme Court handed down a definitive ruling, ordering the army to stop using Palestinian civilians as human shields in operations against militants, which in several cases have led to the injury or death of the civilians. The court ruled that the practice is illegal under international law, strengthening a temporary injunction issued in 2002. "The army has no right to use civilians as human shields. . . . It is cruel and barbaric," Supreme Court Justice Aharon Barak wrote in a 20-page judgment.

There have been occasions when people volunteer to become human shields, most famously in the run-up to the 2003 invasion of Iraq by U.S. and British forces. Volunteers from Europe, Canada, and the United States traveled to Iraq to become human shields in what turned out to be a futile effort to deter an attack by making it "politically untenable" since it would result in a significant loss of Western civilians. At one point the number of volunteer human shields from the West reached almost 700, of which only a small fraction—about 20—were Americans. While volunteers were prepared to place themselves at strategic installations liable to be bombed, including water plants, power plants, communications facilities, and oil refineries, Saddam ultimately decided not to make use of them, and most of the volunteers left the country before the invasion. Their actions were highly controversial; they were praised for their idealism, dismissed or derided as naive, or repudiated as traitors. A number of editorial columnists noted the irony of volunteering to be a human shield for Saddam's regime in 2004 when he had forced so many Westerners to become human shields during the Kuwait war in 1990. The U.S. government responded by threatening at least some of the American protesters with substantial fines for violating laws that prohibit "virtually all direct or indirect commercial, financial or trade transactions with Iraq."

See also CIVILIAN IMMUNITY; MYANMAR, HUMAN RIGHTS VIOLATIONS IN; PALESTINE, HUMAN RIGHTS VIOLATIONS IN.

Further Reading:
Gutman, Roy, ed. *Crimes of War: What the Public Should Know.* New York: W. W. Norton & Company, 1999.

Hussein, Saddam al-Tikriti (1937–) *Iraqi dictator*

Once one of the most feared despots in the world, Saddam Hussein will almost certainly end his days in prison if he is not sentenced to death by an Iraqi tribunal for war crimes and CRIMES AGAINST HUMANITY. "Saddam is a dictator who is ready to sacrifice his country, just so long as he can remain on his throne in Baghdad," an exiled Iraqi diplomat once said. The prediction was borne out by his years in power. As the president of Iraq for two decades, Saddam fostered a cult of personality, propagating images that depicted him as a defender of the Arab people against Western crusaders or as an eighth-century caliph who founded the capital of Baghdad. He even wrote two novels whose heroes bore a suspiciously close resemblance to their author. Hussein led Iraq into two disastrous wars—the first against Iran in 1980 and the second against Kuwait in 1991—and until his ouster by a U.S.-backed coalition in April 2003, he maintained a rule based on terror and intimidation. His regime is responsible for hundreds of thousands of deaths, although it is unlikely that the exact number will ever be known.

Hussein was born in April 1937 in a village outside of Tikrit in an area that has become famous as the Sunni Triangle. (Sunnis compose about 20 percent of the population, while Shiites constitute the majority.) His family made their living as sheepherders. His mother called him Saddam, which in Arabic means "one who confronts." Saddam lived up to his name. His mother had given birth to him after both his father and his older brother had died, leaving her so bereft that she attempted to abort Saddam and kill herself. She wanted nothing to do with him after his birth and sent him to live with the family of his maternal uncle. She took him back when he was three after she had remarried, but his stepfather was abusive and forced the young Saddam to steal for him. At the age of 10, Saddam ran away and went to live again with his uncle, who inculcated in him the idea that he should never back down from his enemies even if they were more powerful. It was a lesson that stuck.

After attending secondary school in Baghdad, Saddam fell under the sway of the revolutionary pan-Arab Baath Party, which he joined in 1957 at the age of 20. A year later the monarchy that had been installed by the British was overthrown by a group of army officers led by Abdel Karim Qassem. The Baathists opposed the military regime, and Saddam became involved in a plot to kill him. The assassination attempt failed, and Saddam fled to Syria and then to Egypt. Condemned to death in absentia, he remained in exile in Egypt, where he attended the University of Cairo law school. He returned to Iraq in 1963 after elements of the Baath Party came to power in a coup, but in the factional feuding that ensued, Saddam was arrested and thrown in prison. He escaped in 1967 and a year later participated in another coup attempt that returned the Baathists to power. This time Saddam had chosen the right side. He was named vice chairman of the Iraqi Revolutionary Command Council and vice president in the new regime headed by his relative Hassan al-Bakr, also a Tikriti.

Over the next decade, Saddam acquired more influence, effectively becoming the power behind al-Bakr. In 1976 he was appointed a general, and although three more years were to pass before he was undisputed leader of Iraq, he was already de facto ruler and the major architect of Iraq's foreign policy. Once he had secured authority for himself in 1979, Saddam embarked on a modernization program that was financed by revenues from oil. (He was instrumental in nationalizing the oil industry to obtain a monopoly for the state.) Although he now has a deserved reputation for tyranny, it should also be recalled that he introduced social services on a scale never before witnessed in the Arab world, instituting programs such as the National Campaign for the Eradication of Illiteracy and the campaign for Compulsory Free Education in Iraq. Iraqi students were entitled to free schooling, hospital care was guaranteed without charge, and subsidies were granted to farmers.

But modernization came at a price. To ensure his grip on power, Saddam relied on a repressive security apparatus that tortured, killed, and arbitrarily detained opponents with impunity. Once when an interviewer asked him whether accounts of TORTURE and EXTRAJUDICIAL KILLINGS were true, he replied, "Of course. What do you expect if they oppose the regime?" His image was ubiquitous—on portraits, posters, statues, and murals, even on the currency. He demonstrated a theatrical flair as well, appearing variously in Bedouin robes, traditional peasant outfits, military uniforms, and Western business suits. An avowedly secular leader, he could assume the role of a devout Muslim, especially after Ayatollah Khomeini came to power in neighboring Iran in 1979, spurring a resurgence of Islamic fundamentalism throughout the Middle East.

Saddam also sought to make Iraq a major player on the world stage, flirting first with the Soviet Union, which supplied him with arms until Saddam switched sides, executing Iraqi Communists, and finding new friends in the West. When Egypt reached a peace agreement with Israel in 1979, Saddam led the Arab opposition. In keeping with his grandiose vision, he began to push for a nuclear weapons program, relying on French technical assistance, but before the nuclear reactor of Osiraq was up and running, it was bombed and destroyed by Israeli war planes.

Ayatollah Ruholla Mussaui Khomeini's ascension to power in 1979 after the fall of the shah in Iran portended an end to peaceful relations between Iraq and Iran, and the two countries went to war in September 1980. Although the immediate cause was a dispute over the Shatt al-Arab waterway that divides Iraq from Iran, the conflict was rooted in the fears of a spreading Islamic revolution. Even though neither the United States nor the Soviet Union openly supported Iraq, it was no secret that both superpowers wanted to curb any export of Iran's brand of Islamic radicalism. The war, which went on for eight years, resembled nothing so much as trench warfare in World War I, with neither side able to achieve a decisive victory. Taking advantage of Baghdad's distraction, Kurds in northern Iraq staged an uprising. On March 16, 1988, Saddam launched the Al-Anfal Campaign to crush the Kurds. In the most notorious incident, Iraqi planes targeted the Kurdish town of HALABJAH, dropping bombs that are thought to have contained gas and nerve agents and killing as many as 5,000 people.

When the war with Iran finally ended, it had claimed about 1.8 million lives on both sides and left hundreds of thousands injured. Iraq now found itself saddled with a war debt of $75 billion, some of which was borrowed from the United States—about $40 billion—and other Arab states that feared Iran's growing influence. Some $10 billion was due to Kuwait. Saddam, believing that Kuwait should thank Iraq for sparing it from Iranian conquest, asked that country to forgive the debt. Kuwait refused and provoked Saddam further by rejecting Iraqi bids to cut its oil production

and keep the price of oil high, a strategy that would have increased revenues for Iraq's reconstruction and allow it to pay off its debt. Claiming that Kuwait had been part of Iraq historically and convinced that the United States would not intervene, Saddam ordered the invasion and annexation of Kuwait in August 1990. Iraq's conquest of Kuwait gave him control over 20 percent of the entire oil reserves of the Persian Gulf.

To force Iraq out of Kuwait, a UN coalition force was organized, spearheaded by President George H. W. Bush; this had the backing of several Arab states, including Syria and Saudi Arabia. In an attempt to break the unified front against him, Saddam offered to withdraw if Israel would give up its control over the West Bank and Gaza. The offer was rejected out of hand but did have the effect of gaining him some support among Arabs. When coalition forces attacked Iraqi troops to force their withdrawal, Saddam ordered Scud missile strikes against Israel; the missiles caused some damage but few casualties. The Iraqis were quickly routed, sustaining grave losses. According to data compiled by the United States, 20,000 Iraqi soldiers were killed. (Some estimates put the figure as high as 100,000.)

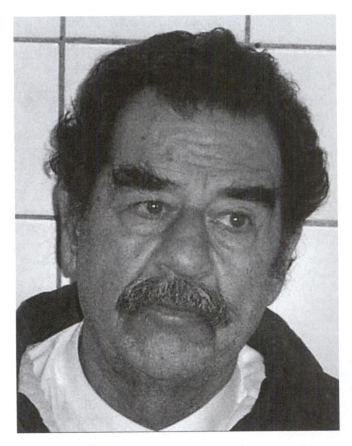

Iraqi dictator Saddam Hussein shortly after his capture in December 2003 *(Sgt. David Bennett/U.S. Army)*

As part of its cease-fire agreement, Iraq agreed to eliminate its poison gas reserves and germ weapons and allow UN inspectors to examine weapons production and stockpiles.

In the immediate aftermath of the Gulf War, Kurds in the north and Shiites in the south rose up against Saddam, inspired by the belief that he would soon fall and that they would receive assistance from the United States. Saddam ruthlessly crushed both rebellions with a large loss of life. Iraqi helicopter gunships strafed Shiite cities, and government troops uprooted thousands of Shiites known as Marsh Arabs from their homes. The Iraqi forces drained the marshes to deprive rebels of a hiding place, creating an environmental catastrophe and robbing the Arabs of their livelihood while virtually annihilating an ancient culture. According to HUMAN RIGHTS WATCH, systematic bombardment of villages, widespread arbitrary arrests, TORTURE, DISAPPEARANCES, summary executions, and forced displacement reduced the Marsh Arab population from more than 250,000 to as few as 40,000. About 100,000 were internally displaced, and another 40,000 fled across the border into Iran. The Kurds, however, fared better after the United States and Britain intervened to carve out a no-fly zone in Iraqi Kurdistan. From 1991 until the U.S.-backed invasion of Iraq in 2003, Kurdistan enjoyed an autonomous status, relatively free from interference by Baghdad.

Over the next several years, Saddam's regime became increasingly repressive and arbitrary. Saddam allowed his two sons, Uday Hussein and Qusay Hussein, free rein to torture and kill at whim. In 1988 Uday shot his father's valet, reportedly because the valet had incurred his displeasure by arranging trysts with Saddam's mistress. According to *Middle East Quarterly,* Uday was alleged to have murdered at least half a dozen women and tortured several others. In one case, Uday had a woman "stripped naked, covered in honey and killed by three starving Dobermans." He also headed the Iraqi National Olympic team, spreading terror among the athletes with good reason. "In sport you can win or you can lose," he once told a boxer who had lost a match in the Gulf Games. "I told you not to come home if you didn't win." The boxer was tortured and killed.

In spite of sanctions—Iraq was placed under a UN regime called the Oil for Food program—Saddam continued to prosper from kickbacks and oil smuggling, possibly reaping close to $1 billion, even as his own people suffered. (UNICEF and the World Health Organization have estimated that between 500,000 and 1.2 million people, mainly under the age of five, died of malnutrition and medical shortages between 1991 and 2000 because of the sanctions; other estimates put the number at closer to 350,000.) True to his uncle's admonition never to back down even in the face of insurmountable odds, Saddam provoked the international community by expelling UN weapons inspectors in

the late 1990s, a move that stirred fears he was once again pursuing an illegal weapons program. Bowing to pressure from the United States, Saddam permitted inspectors to return in 2002, but they were withdrawn before they could complete their mission. Until then they had found no evidence of biological, chemical, or nuclear programs intended to produce weapons of mass destruction. However, it appeared that the United States was determined to invade. It is unknown whether Saddam believed that President George W. Bush intended to fulfill his pledge to disarm Iraq by force. The invasion by the U.S.-backed coalition, launched in March 2003, succeeded in routing Iraqi troops and the elite Republican Guards. Baghdad fell a month later. After defiantly proclaiming that Iraq would repel the invader, Saddam disappeared from sight. His two sons, however, were located in July 2003 and killed in a firefight with U.S. troops. Saddam remained in hiding for several months until he was discovered by U.S. forces on December 14, 2003, in what was described as a rat hole. Bearded and shabbily dressed, Saddam was initially described as being "talkative and cooperative," although months later interrogators acknowledged that he was disclosing very little to them.

At his arraignment on July 1, 2004, Saddam chastised the judge, maintaining that he had no right to try him and asserting that he was still the legitimate leader of Iraq. He called the court a "play aimed at Bush's chances of winning the U.S. presidential elections." At the same time he rejected charges against him. "This is all theatre. The real criminal is Bush," he stated. When asked by the judge to identify himself in his first appearance before an Iraqi judge, he answered, "I am Saddam Hussein al-Majid, the President of the Republic of Iraq." He added, "I am still the president of the republic and the occupation cannot take that away." He defended the August 1990 invasion of Kuwait, referring to Kuwaiti rulers as "dogs," drawing an admonition from the judge. Saddam also refused to sign a legal document indicating that he understood the charges against him. Although no attorney represented him at the arraignment (or any of the other 11 top Iraqi officials who were arraigned at the same time), his wife Sajida Talfah said that she had hired a multinational legal team, consisting of 10 Iraqi and 25 foreign lawyers, to defend him.

Human rights groups estimate that Saddam Hussein's government was responsible for the murder of at least a quarter of a million Iraqis. Kurds suffered disproportionately; as many as 100,000 Kurdish men and boys are believed to have been machine-gunned to death during the 1988 Al Anfal campaign; another 30,000 Shiites and Kurds were killed after the 1991 uprising; other Shiites were killed during the 1980s because of their perceived sympathy for Iran. Iraqi leaders have stated that they had compiled "miles" of incriminating documents and that investigators will eventually find hundreds of mass graves. Throughout 2004 a team of 400 Iraqis working for the tribunal—supported by 50 mostly American lawyers and investigators who are part of a group known as the Regime Crimes Liaison Office—examined "tons" of seized documents, interviewed witnesses, and reviewed evidence gathered by forensic teams from at least 12 mass graves. For prosecutors, though, such documentation is insufficient to establish an evidential chain tying a leader to orders authorizing underlings to carry out extrajudicial killings and other crimes. This problem is exemplified by the trial of former Yugoslav strongman Slobodan MILOŠEVIĆ, who, while accused of atrocities in Bosnia and Kosovo, apparently never put his name to an order that would implicate him. Nonetheless, legal scholars believe that establishing that Saddam committed crimes against humanity, including systematic murder, enslavement, imprisonment, torture, rape, or other crimes directed against civilians, should not be difficult since so many atrocities have been well documented. It would not even have to be proven that Hussein was directly responsible for the crimes. According to Ruth Wedgwood, a law professor at Johns Hopkins University in Washington, he could still be found guilty if he knew or could have known that crimes were being committed by his subordinates: "You don't have to prove he ordered it. You only have to prove that he failed to adequately supervise." GENOCIDE would be a more difficult charge to prove. "You actually have to prove intent to destroy, in whole or in part, a group," observed Fiona McKay, director of the international justice program at Human Rights First.

How Saddam would be tried, however, was a more controversial issue. The Coalition Provisional Authority, in charge of the country until an interim government was put in place in July 2004, created the Iraqi Special Tribunal for Crimes against Humanity, with jurisdiction over war crimes, genocide, and crimes against humanity. The tribunal was to use both the common-law system as practiced in Britain and the United States and the civil-law system of France, Germany, and other Western European countries. In spite of calls to try Saddam in an international forum with a reputation for impartiality, such as the INTERNATIONAL CRIMINAL COURT (ICC) in The Hague, Washington adamantly opposed trying him outside of Iraq. Moreover, the United States has consistently rejected the authority of the ICC. Iraq has no history of an independent judiciary, and legal experts expressed fears that it would be incapable of holding a trial that was not seen as a show trial or as administering "victor's justice." Nor was there much likelihood that international legal experts wished to lend their services advising the new tribunal about how such a complex case was to be conducted without an improvement of the security situation in Iraq, which was still unsta-

ble throughout 2005. "You can't send judges and defense lawyers and all the rest of it to a situation where their lives are in imminent danger," said Richard J. Goldstone, chief prosecutor for the International Criminal Tribunals for the former Yugoslavia and Rwanda. In February 2005 Bakhtiar Amin, the human rights minister in the Iraqi interim government, said that 11 high officials of the Baathist regime would be first to go on trial so that prosecutors could establish "command responsibility" for the atrocities committed under Saddam's rule. Many observers expected that once Saddam was brought before the tribunal, his defense lawyers would argue that the court was illegal because it was set up by the American occupation authority before Iraq resumed formal sovereignty in elections in 2005.

In September 2005 Iraqi authorities surprised the world by announcing that Saddam Hussein would be put on trial within a month even though observers had widely anticipated that his would be the last trial after other top Baathist officials had been prosecuted so that their testimony could be used against him. The move sparked speculation that the authorities hoped to shore up its support by focusing attention on the tyrant's crimes and distracting the public from the deteriorating security situation. However, the Special Tribunal, which would conduct the trial, decided to charge him only with the 1982 massacre of more than 140 Shiites following an assassination attempt on Hussein's life, reasoning that that incident would be the easiest to tie directly to the dictator.

See also IRAQ, HUMAN RIGHTS VIOLATIONS IN POST-SADDAM; KURDISTAN (IRAQ), SUPPRESSION OF.

Further Reading:

Aburish, Said K. *Saddam Hussein.* London: Bloomsbury Publishing, 2001.

Bodansky, Yossef. *The Secret History of the Iraq War.* New York: Regan Books, 2004.

Cockburn, Andrew, and Patrick Cockburn. *Out of the Ashes: The Resurrection of Saddam Hussein.* New York: Perennial.

Cordesman, Anthony H. *The Iraq War: Strategy, Tactics, and Military Lessons.* Washington, D.C.: Center for Strategic and International Studies, 2003.

Coughlin, Con. *Saddam: King of Terror.* New York: Ecco, 2002.

Dodge, Toby. *Inventing Iraq: The Failure of Nation-Building and a History Denied.* New York: Columbia University Press, 2003.

Dormann, Knut, and Louise Doswald-Beck. *Elements of War Crimes under the Rome Statute of the International Criminal Court: Sources and Commentary.* Cambridge: Cambridge University Press, 2003.

Karsh, Efraim. *The Iran-Iraq War 1980–1988.* London: Osprey Publishing, 2002.

Karsh, Efraim, and Inari Rautsi. *Saddam Hussein: A Political Biography.* New York: Grove Press, 2003.

Keegan, John. *The Iraq War.* New York: Knopf, 2004.

MacKey, Sandra. *The Reckoning: Iraq and the Legacy of Saddam Hussein.* New York: W. W. Norton & Company, 2003.

Miller, John, and Aaron Kenedi. *Inside Iraq: The History, the People, and the Modern Conflicts of the World's Least Understood Land.* New York: Marlowe & Company, 2003.

HVO militia   See YUGOSLAVIA, WAR CRIMES IN.

I

Ibrahim, Ashraf (1968–) *Egyptian human rights*
  activist

Ashraf Ibrahim has become known throughout the world as a champion of political rights in Egypt. An engineer by profession, he was arrested by the government in April 2003 on charges that he headed an illegal revolutionary socialist organization and intended to distribute seditious information about Egypt abroad that harmed the reputation of the country. The state produced no evidence that Ibrahim was engaged in any violent activities. A member of numerous popular committees, including the committee for Solidarity with the Palestinian People, an antiglobalization group, and Egyptians against the War, he played a prominent role in arranging demonstrations against the U.S.-led invasion of Iraq in 2003. He faced a prison sentence of 15 years if he were found guilty. (Hundreds of others involved in these demonstrations were also detained and many later asserted that they had been tortured.) Ibrahim's defenders pointed out that the supposedly "false" information that he was accused of distributing actually documented human rights abuses by the state. In March 2004 he was acquitted of all charges by the State Supreme Court and freed from prison.

See also EGYPT, HUMAN RIGHTS VIOLATIONS IN.

identification of combatants

For military purposes, combatant identification (CID) is based on the capacity to differentiate potential targets as friend, foe, or neutral in a timely manner, with a high degree of confidence that the determination is correct. Where INTERNATIONAL HUMANITARIAN LAW is concerned, distinguishing combatants from civilians is important for other reasons: International law prohibits targeting civilians, and therefore it becomes imperative in times of conflict for belligerents to determine who is a combatant and who is a civilian. The distinction is usually much easier to make in conflicts between nations than in internal conflicts.

Although a military uniform offers some evidence that a person is a lawful combatant, it does not provide absolute proof. Status also matters; if a person is not authorized to take part in hostilities and does so anyway, he or she would not be entitled to be treated as a prisoner of war and might be liable to prosecution as an unlawful combatant. That is why it is so important for combatants to carry proper identification. Soldiers in most armies carry identity disks, known popularly as dog tags in the U.S. army. The disks often bear the soldier's name, identifying number, blood type, and religion and are used to identify soldiers who, because they are dead or critically injured, cannot identify themselves. These identity disks are specifically cited in the first Geneva Convention of 1949 in the context of identifying the wounded and the dead. The conventions do not require the use of any identification disks. However, Article 17 of the third Geneva Convention of 1949 does require that soldiers carry identity cards in case they become PRISONERS OF WAR. The card must include the soldier's name, rank, identifying number, and birth date, and it can also contain other information such as a signature, fingerprints, and a photograph. This card must be shown upon demand but cannot be confiscated. In the event that the card is lost, the belligerent detaining the soldier is obliged to provide one. If a representative of the INTERNATIONAL COMMITTEE OF THE RED CROSS (ICRC) or other outside observer entitled to visit prisoners of war discovers that a soldier is not in possession of an identification card, the representative may take this as evidence that the captor is in violation of international law. The rank listed on the card is also important in terms of prisoner of war status. According to international law, officers, for instance, are to be treated differently from ordinary soldiers. Under interrogation, a soldier is obligated only to provide the same information on the identification card. The prisoner of war is not required to give interrogators added information and cannot be punished or mistreated for failing to do so.

In internal conflicts it becomes much more difficult to distinguish between combatants and noncombatants. In many of these conflicts combatants are not members of an organized military force and as a result may not wear easily recognizable military uniforms or carry identity disks or identity cards with the information required by the Third Geneva Convention. Individuals in civilian clothes may also take part in hostilities. Although distinguishing between combatants and civilians is important in order to identify REFUGEES and confer protected status on the civilians and prisoners of war—meaning that they cannot be forced to participate in combat or be mistreated—it is more problematic in crisis situations. For instance, many Hutu militiamen involved in the slaughter of Tutsis and Hutu moderates in Rwanda in 1994 subsequently fled to neighboring Zaire (now the Democratic Republic of the Congo) where they assumed the identity of fleeing refugees to avoid reprisal.

See also CIVILIAN IMMUNITY; GENEVA CONVENTIONS.

Further Reading:
Gutman, Roy, ed. *Crimes of War: What the Public Should Know.* New York: W. W. Norton, 1999.

Ieng Sary (1930–   ) *Khmer Rouge leader*
Ieng Sary was "Brother Number Three" in the radical Khmer Rouge leadership that dominated Cambodia between 1975 and 1979. He was born Kim Trang in 1930 in southern Vietnam, the son of a Khmer landowner. In 1946 he showed a precocious aptitude for political activism, organizing a student group called Liberation of Cambodia from French Colonialism. He even led the first strike in the country's modern history. (France was the OCCUPYING POWER of Cambodia, Laos, and Vietnam.) A brilliant student, he earned a government scholarship to study in Paris, as did his fellow student nationalists POL POT and KHIEU SAMPHAN. While in Paris he fell under the spell of communism and became so close to Pol Pot, the future "Brother Number One," that they even double-dated. They eventually married two sisters, and on their return to Cambodia they set up house together in the capital, Phnom Penh, where Ieng Sary took up work as a schoolteacher.

The police began to take an interest in Ieng Sary's and Pol Pot's clandestine revolutionary activities and their involvement in the Communist Party of Kampuchea. When the government of Prince Norodom Sihanouk launched a crackdown against the communists in 1963, the two men fled to the jungles of eastern Cambodia. There they began to lay the foundation for the radical communist movement that would become the Khmer Rouge. In 1970 a military coup forced Sihanouk into exile in Beijing. By this point he had allied himself with the Khmer Rouge, and Ieng Sary's job was to go to the Chinese capital to keep watch on the prince. Sihanouk resented the attention and complained that he could not move without Ieng Sary spying on him.

In 1975, after a protracted guerrilla war, the Khmer Rouge seized power and marched into Phnom Penh. As deputy prime minister and foreign minister, Ieng Sary was one of the principal architects of a radical program to empty the cities and resettle millions in the countryside to toil in what became known to history as the killing fields. Nearly 2 million were killed or died from starvation in the five years the Khmer Rouge held power. When Vietnamese troops forced the Khmer Rouge from Phnom Penh in 1979, Ieng Sary took refuge on the Thai border and later flew to Beijing, where China's supreme leader, Deng Xiaoping, rebuked him for being responsible for a "somewhat excessive" pogrom.

For the next two years Ieng Sary kept his post as foreign minister. The Khmer Rouge was still recognized by the United Nations and the West as the legitimate government of Cambodia at this time, in spite of deep misgivings on the part of successive administrations in Washington. An American diplomat once inadvertently shook his hand, realizing who he was too late: "I looked up and saw it was Ieng Sary," the diplomat said. "I felt like washing my hands."

In 1982, Ieng Sary transferred formal responsibility for foreign affairs to Khieu Samphan after the creation of the Coalition Government of Democratic Kampuchea, which had formed an alliance with pro-Sihanouk forces against the Vietnamese and acted as an intermediary between the Khmer Rouge and China, which kept supplying it with arms. In 1991, however, Chinese aid had all but dried up, and the Khmer Rouge signed a peace agreement brokered by the United Nations intended to pave the way to elections. The Hun Sen government, installed by the Vietnamese, began to woo old enemies. Sihanouk, who had returned to Cambodia (only now as a figurehead), lifted the death sentence hanging over Ieng Sary's head, restored his property rights, and pardoned him for belonging to an outlawed group. In spite of these inducements, several years passed before Ieng Sary defected to the government in 1996. He was joined by scores of his fighters. When pressed by reporters about his role in the Khmer Rouge, he laid the blame for the mass killings on Pol Pot, who was ailing and soon to die. Ieng Sary denied, however, that he bore any responsibility. In an interview he told the *Bangkok Post* that the mass media had made a "gross mistake" by giving him the title of Brother Number Three and depicting him as "Pol Pot's right hand." It is unclear whether he will ever have to stand trial for his crimes.

See also CAMBODIA, WAR CRIMES IN.

Further Reading:
Chandler, David. *A History of Cambodia.* Philadelphia: Westview Press. 2000.

———. *The Tragedy of Cambodian History: Politics, War, and Revolution since 1945.* New Haven, Conn.: Yale University Press, 1993.

Hinton, Alexander Laban, and Robert Jay Lifton. *Why Did They Kill?: Cambodia in the Shadow of Genocide.* California Series in Public Anthropology, vol. 11. Berkeley: University of California Press, 2004.

Kiernan, Ben. *How Pol Pot Came to Power: Colonialism, Nationalism, and Communism in Cambodia, 1930–1975.* New Haven, Conn.: Yale University Press, 2004.

———. *The Pol Pot Regime: Race, Power, and Genocide in Cambodia under the Khmer Rouge, 1975–79.* New Haven, Conn.: Yale University Press, 2002.

Pran, Dith, comp. *Children of Cambodia's Killing Fields: Memoirs by Survivors.* Edited by Kim DePaul. New Haven, Conn.: Yale University Press, 1999.

illegal acts

Illegal acts in this book's context are those acts prohibited under international law. In general, these acts fall into two basic categories: prohibitions against the use of certain types of weapons or methods of war (Hague Law) and prohibitions against mistreatment of civilians, the wounded, and PRISONERS OF WAR and the destruction of vital civilian installations and public, religious, or cultural property (Geneva Law). The first set of prohibitions evolved out of the HAGUE CONVENTIONS of 1899 and 1907, which banned weapons capable of causing unnecessary suffering such as poison gas and biological agents. By the same token, these laws outlaw tactics that are intended to cause excessive harm to civilian populations or property unrelated to military objectives. The second body of law, governing the treatment of civilians and prisoners of war, is derived from the GENEVA CONVENTIONS, especially the four conventions of 1949 and the 1977 ADDITIONAL PROTOCOLS TO THE GENEVA CONVENTIONS.

International law also distinguishes between serious and grave breaches of the law. The former, while subject to prosecution, are not acts that fall under universal jurisdiction—that is, they are not crimes that can be punished by a national or international court regardless of where the criminal act took place. War crimes, for instance, are considered grave breaches of the law; if the state where the crime occurred will not or cannot prosecute the perpetrator, then the accused can be brought to trial in another state with the proviso that he or she is still assured of receiving a fair trial, a concept known as UNIVERSAL JURISDICTION. Prohibited acts codified in the Geneva Conventions and the Additional Protocols include GENOCIDE, the use of unlawful combatants, PILLAGE, barring humanitarian aid, destruction of civilian property, indiscriminate attacks on or bombing of civilian populations, and the carrying out of reprisals by an OCCUPYING POWER that is disproportionate to the offense.

Further Reading:
Gutman, Roy, ed. *Crimes of War: What the Public Should Know.* New York: W. W. Norton & Company, 1999.

immunity, civilian   *See* CIVILIAN IMMUNITY.

immunity from attack

Under INTERNATIONAL HUMANITARIAN LAW, certain people and places enjoy protected status. Even as far back as 1582, a Spanish judge ruled that the intentional killing of innocent persons was not allowable even in war. The GENEVA CONVENTIONS of 1949 confer immunity on civilians in wartime and under enemy occupation; immunity is also extended to physicians and medical staff and to schools, hospitals, hospital ships, ambulances, religious, cultural, and civic institutions. These principles are reinforced by the 1977 ADDITIONAL PROTOCOLS TO THE GENEVA CONVENTIONS, which state: "The civilian population and individual civilians shall enjoy general protection against the dangers arising from military operations."

International law forbids the targeting of civilians for military purposes and, in addition, gives priority to certain classifications of people, including women, children, elderly, the sick, and the wounded. Other individuals, such as PRISONERS OF WAR and those considered HORS DE COMBAT (out of combat) because they have sustained wounds in fighting, are also guaranteed immunity. There are exceptions, however. A belligerent is not in violation of international law if civilians are injured or killed because of COLLATERAL DAMAGE as a result of a strike on a legitimate military target. Moreover, the law provides no protection to an institution such as a church or hospital if it is being used for military purposes by a belligerent. In spite of these prohibitions, in practice it is difficult to distinguish between protected and legitimate military targets, especially when the combat is taking place in a city or in internal conflicts where the distinction between noncombatants and combatants is blurred. In some cases, there is no attempt to make the distinction at all; this occurred in the siege of Sarajevo (1992–95) when Serbs indiscriminately rained fire down on the city, killing over 10,000 civilians.

For policymakers and military officials, another problem arises where the use of air power is contemplated. Current U.S. military doctrine, which grew out of the 1991 Gulf War, calls on air power to be employed to destroy the enemy's "centers of gravity," which are defined as "capabilities, or localities from which a military force derives its freedom of action, physical strength, or will to fight." This concept is based on the idea, first propounded by Sun Tzu in *The Art of War,* that it is preferable to subdue the enemy by capturing forces than engaging in combat. But as Michael A. Carlino, an officer who has served in the 101st Airborne, writes in an essay for *Parameters Magazine,* "the nature of the modern battlefield inherently blurs the distinction between combatants and noncombatants; soldiers and civilians are now inextricably woven together in an amorphous battle space. . . ." Military leaders, he says, are faced with a dilemma as to how to balance CIVILIAN IMMUNITY and military objectives. "The obvious problem is which notion—force protection or noncombatant immunity—ought to have priority and to what extent." Moreover, a commander might be putting his soldiers at greater risk if he chooses to give priority to an enemy civilian population. The use of air power might kill more civilians, but it will also be likely to keep one's own soldiers out of harm's way. "When technology advances to the point that munitions have the same powers of discrimination as a soldier on the ground," Carlino says, "aerospace power may well be sufficient." Until then, however, he contends, "jointly packaged forces from all services must be employed (to protect civilians) even when it entails more risk and associated costs."

See also SARAJEVO, SIEGE OF.

Further Reading:

Gutman, Roy, ed. *Crimes of War: What the Public Should Know.* New York: W. W. Norton & Company, 1999.

Jackson, Nyamuya Maogoto. *War Crimes and Realpolitik: International Justice from World War I to the 21st Century.* Boulder, Colo.: Lynne Rienner Publishers, 2004.

Jokie, Aleksander. *War Crimes and Collective Wrongdoing: A Reader.* London: Blackwell Publishers, 2001.

Robertson, Geoffrey. *Crimes against Humanity: The Struggle for Global Justice.* New York: New Press, 2003.

imprisonment of civilians

Imprisonment of civilians in times of conflict has been outlawed by international law since the NUREMBERG TRIALS. Until that time, international law did not specifically cover crimes committed by a state against its own people. During World War II, Nazi Germany had deported millions of civilians to CONCENTRATION CAMPS, and the Allies who established the International Tribunal to try Nazi war criminals wanted to address the gap in the law to make such atrocities a prosecutable crime in the future. To that end they conceived a new crime—CRIMES AGAINST HUMANITY—which included "murder, extermination, enslavement, deportation, and other inhumane acts done against any civilian population, or persecutions on politi-

cal, racial, or religious grounds." Acts of imprisonment were specifically classified as a crime against humanity. Such crimes could take place either in times of war or in peacetime. The statute authorizing the creation of the INTERNATIONAL CRIMINAL COURT in The Hague reinforced the Nuremberg prohibitions against mistreatment of civilians by the state, declaring that "imprisonment or other severe deprivation of physical liberty in violation of fundamental rules of international law, if carried out as a widespread or systematic attack on any civilian population, is a crime against humanity." Two special United Nations tribunals set up in recent years—one to try crimes committed in Rwanda and the other to prosecute crimes committed in the former Yugoslavia—both have designated imprisonment of civilians as an indictable offense.

See also CIVILIAN IMMUNITY; INTERNATIONAL CRIMINAL TRIBUNAL FOR RWANDA; INTERNATIONAL CRIMINAL TRIBUNAL FOR THE FORMER YUGOSLAVIA.

Further Reading:

Dormann, Knut, and Louise Doswald-Beck. *Elements of War Crimes under the Rome Statute of the International Criminal Court: Sources and Commentary.* Cambridge: Cambridge University Press, 2003.

Gutman, Roy, ed. *Crimes of War: What the Public Should Know.* New York: W. W. Norton, 1999.

Jackson, Nyamuya Maogoto. *War Crimes and Realpolitik: International Justice from World War I to the 21st Century.* Boulder, Colo.: Lynne Rienner Publishers, 2004.

Romano, Cesare, Andre Nollkaemper, and Jann K. Kleffner, eds. *Internationalized Criminal Courts and Tribunals: Sierra Leone, East Timor, Kosovo, and Cambodia.* International Courts and Tribunals Series. Oxford: Oxford University Press, 2004.

incitement to genocide

Incitement to GENOCIDE is a prosecutable offense under international law based on two basic documents: ARTICLE 3 COMMON TO THE GENEVA CONVENTIONS of 1949 and the GENOCIDE CONVENTION of 1948. Article 3 states that civilians "shall in all circumstances be treated humanely without any adverse distinction founded on race, color, religion, sex, birth, or wealth." Article 3 further states that "direct and public incitement to commit genocide" is punishable. The Genocide Convention of 1948 defines the crime of genocide as "acts committed with intent to destroy, in whole or in part, a national, ethnical, racial or religious group as such." Genocide can encompass acts that do not specifically involve killing per se but are intended to bring about the destruction of a people. For instance, forbidding a people to have children or forcibly uprooting an entire people from their homeland would be considered genocidal acts.

The first person to be convicted of incitement to genocide was Julius STREICHER, editor of the virulently anti-Semitic magazine *Der Sturmer* in Nazi Germany. Although he had not personally killed anyone, he was judged at the NUREMBERG TRIALS to be just as responsible for the atrocities he encouraged as he would have been had he pulled the trigger. The magazine, the Nuremberg Tribunal found, was a poison "injected into the minds of thousands of Germans which caused them to follow the National Socialists' Party policy of Jewish persecution and extermination."

No one was charged with a similar crime until three Rwandan Hutu journalists, Ferdinand Nahimana, Hassan Ngeze, and Jean-Bosco Barayagwiza, stood trial before the United Nations INTERNATIONAL CRIMINAL TRIBUNAL FOR RWANDA (ICTR), sitting in Arusha, Tanzania. Article 5 of the statute establishing the court in 1998 listed genocide first among the crimes over which the court had jurisdiction. Nahimana and Barayagwiza had founded a talk radio station called Radio Television des Milles Collines, or RTMC, and Ngeze was the owner of a popular newspaper called *Kangura*. The three were accused of inflaming public opinion against Tutsis in the months leading up to the 1994 genocide in Rwanda, which took the lives of 800,000 people, mostly Tutsi and moderate Hutus. The radio broadcast songs whose lyrics urged the slaughter of Tutsis. Announcers also read articles drawn from the pages of *Kangura*, including an article called the "Hutu Ten Commandments," which extolled Hutu supremacy and called on Hutus to kill the minority Tutsis. The Tribunal charged that the three men were actively involved in plotting and abetting genocide long before it actually erupted in April 1994. During the 101 days that the massacres raged, RTMC announcers directed Hutus to locations where Tutsis had taken refuge, condemning them to death. When the capital of Kigali fell to Tutsi rebels, putting an end to the genocidal campaign, RTMC staff fled to Zaire (now the Democratic Republic of the Congo), where the radio station continued to operate using a mobile transmitter.

In December 2003 the three media executives were convicted of genocide, incitement and conspiracy to commit genocide, and CRIMES AGAINST HUMANITY, and sentenced to terms ranging from 35 years to life. At no point were they accused of personally taking part in the genocide, but journalists and media watchdogs were divided about the verdict. On the one hand, a representative for the COMMITTEE TO PROTECT JOURNALISTS, an advocacy group for press freedom, thought that no issue of free speech was involved. "To me, this was essentially a form of military communication to coordinate these attacks [against Tutsis]," said Joel Simon, the group's deputy director. "It is speech that helped make it possible to carry out the geno-

cide." Other advocates of free speech felt that the tribunal had gone too far. The three had never identified individuals to be targeted by name, they pointed out, even though no one denied that the rhetoric broadcast by RTMC or the articles appearing in the pages of *Kangura* were not incendiary. "This is dangerous stuff," said John Floyd, who defended Ngeze. "This isn't just a question of press freedom. This is an issue of intellectual freedom. This would be like prosecuting the publisher of the *Washington Post* for an op-ed article. If these three are found guilty, then press freedom around the world is in peril." Some legal experts, while unwilling to adopt Floyd's position, maintain that the 357-page legal judgment was overly broad in the way that it defined hate speech and that its reasoning could be used by repressive governments to suppress criticism. These legal scholars pointed to the tribunal's assertion that under international law, countries have the right to limit freedom of speech to protect national security and public order and an obligation to restrict speech that advocates "national, racial, or religious hatred that constitutes incitement to discrimination, hostility, or violence."

See also RWANDA, GENOCIDE IN.

Further Reading:
Bloxham, Donald. *Genocide on Trial: War Crimes Trials and the Formation of Holocaust History and Memory.* Oxford: Oxford University Press, 2003.

Dormann, Knut, and Louise Doswald-Beck. *Elements of War Crimes under the Rome Statute of the International Criminal Court: Sources and Commentary.* Cambridge: Cambridge University Press, 2003.

Hinton, Alexander Laban, and Robert Jay Lifton. *Why Did They Kill?: Cambodia in the Shadow of Genocide.* California Series in Public Anthropology, vol. 11. Berkeley: University of California Press, 2004.

Shelton, Dinah, ed. *International Crimes, Peace, and Human Rights: The Role of the International Criminal Court.* Ardsley, N.Y.: Transnational Publishers, Inc., 2000.

India, human rights violations in

The largest democracy in the world, with a population of over 1 billion, India still suffers from ethnic tensions, intractable insurgencies, violent sectarian disputes, and grave human rights abuses. Women face legal and societal discrimination, and there is widespread exploitation of indentured, bonded, and child labor as well as trafficking in women and children who are frequently forced into prostitution. Indigenous populations in rural areas and lower castes suffer from discrimination and violence. Muslims and Christians are also subject to harassment, threats, and attacks from Hindu extremists. Many of these problems stem from entrenched poverty and a hierarchical social structure that persists even in the face of an expanding economy.

In the 2004 parliamentary elections, the Congress Party won an unexpected victory, replacing the Hindu nationalist Bharatiya Janata Party (BJP). But no sooner were the celebrations over than the new government of Prime Minister Manmohan Singh had to try to confront the same problems that had brought down its predecessor. EXTRAJUDICIAL KILLINGS—including what the U.S. State Department describes as "faked encounter killings" as well as deaths in custody—were all too common. Human rights groups alleged that to cover up TORTURE, police often claimed the deaths had occurred as a result of combat operations.

In 2001 the National Human Rights Commission (NHRC) reported 1,305 deaths in custody, mostly of suspected rebels or criminals. Courts have been generally been slow to investigate or prosecute those responsible for the extrajudicial killings. To prove that suspects have been killed without DUE PROCESS, human rights groups cite the refusal of police officials to turn over the bodies of dead suspects they claimed to be killed in "encounters." The bodies are often cremated before families have a chance to view them. In Andhra Pradesh in 2001, the NHRC investigation found that 285 encounter deaths were allegedly committed by the police in connection with counterinsurgency operations against an indigenous group known as the Naxalites. The police in the state were also reported to have trained and armed a vigilante group known as the "Green Tigers" to combat the Naxalites. The Supreme Court has directed state human rights commissions and other civic rights protection committees to conduct surprise checks of police stations to monitor treatment of prisoners, but it is unclear whether these visits have curbed police abuse significantly.

According to the 2003 State Department *Country Report,* military and paramilitary forces have also been linked to abduction, torture, rape, arbitrary detention, and the extrajudicial killing of militants and noncombatant civilians, particularly in areas of insurgencies. Security forces have employed excessive use of force, especially in areas racked by insurgencies such as Jammu and Kashmir, which has become embroiled in a fierce conflict between Indian forces and Muslim militants reportedly backed by Pakistan. In the disputed province, the army and security forces have taken counterinsurgency measures against terrorists that are widely seen as repressive by human rights organizations. According to HUMAN RIGHTS WATCH, about 3,000 people are still missing in Kashmir after being arrested by security forces. The judiciary tends to acquiesce to the government in spite of abuses. In the northeast of the country, violent attacks against tribal groups by military and security forces have been justified as necessary to combat secessionist movements.

Special security legislation in these conflict areas has led to lengthy pretrial detention without charge, prolonged detention while undergoing trial, occasional limits on freedom of the press and freedom of movement, and harassment and arrest of human rights monitors. Human rights organizations point to one new law in particular, called the Prevention of Terrorism Act (POTA), which was enacted in March 2002. By creating what the U.S. State Department calls "an overly broad definition of terrorism," the act allows state authorities to detain suspects for up to three months without charge and up to three months more with the permission of a special judge. Human rights advocates fear that POTA will be used in a similar manner as a previous antiterrorism law, dropped in 1995, which had led to widespread and systematic curtailment of civil liberties and a period in which tens of thousands of people were detained and sometimes tortured because of their political beliefs. Although POTA has some safeguards to protect due process rights the earlier law did not have, human rights groups and journalists complain that it still poses a danger. The NHRC maintains that existing laws are quite adequate to deal with any threat to security. Already POTA has given license to security forces to detain hundreds of suspects indefinitely on suspicion of terrorism without any evidence. In addition to political opponents, POTA has been used against religious minorities, Dalits (a lower caste group), and tribal groups. In February 2003 alone, more than 300 people were arrested under the act. Even children have not been spared; human rights groups have charged that in 2003 POTA was used in Jharkhand state to detain 20 children, most of them students.

That children should be singled out by security forces is not very surprising in view of the discrimination against children that occurs on a daily basis. Hundreds of thousands of children as young as five are denied schooling and forced to work as bonded laborers in violation of the law. Many of these children are found in the silk industry, where they work up to 12 hours a day. Conditions in these factories are deplorable; children breathe smoke and fumes from the machinery and are in danger of infections from handling dead worms. By the time they reach adulthood, they are destitute, illiterate, and frequently crippled from years of sitting in a cramped position. Children are increasingly at risk of AIDS/HIV, which is spreading rapidly throughout the subcontinent. Thousands of children born with HIV face discrimination just as infected adults do. A law against homosexual acts has been used to harass health workers and educators trying to curb the spread of the disease.

Ignored by the rest of the world, a chronic civil war continues in the northeast region of the country, taking a toll of about 200 annually in the state of Manipur. Some 20 ethnic militias operate in Manipur, united only by their mutual distrust of the central government. In efforts to suppress the guerrillas, the authorities have carried out periodic embargoes of the state, stifling commerce and denying civilians desperately needed fuel and medicine. Human Rights Alert, an Indian human rights group, has documented 10 extrajudicial killings by Indian forces and paramilitaries in the state between July 2004 and September 2005. The Armed Forces Special Powers Act, applying only in the beleaguered north, confers immunity from prosecution for soldiers who commit human rights abuses.

India has only begun to take halting steps to grapple with the bloody legacy of mob violence against Sikhs (in 1984, 1992, and 1993) and against Muslims in the state of Gujarat in 2002, in which 2,000 people were killed and thousands more driven from their homes. As of 2004, most of the perpetrators had not been brought to justice for these atrocities. When suspects were charged in connection with the massacres in Gujarat, they were never prosecuted, and in many cases the charges were quietly dropped and cases dismissed. Similarly, those responsible for the illegal detention and extrajudicial execution of hundreds of people by security agencies in Punjab during a wave of Sikh secessionist violence have gone unpunished. Between 1984 and 1994, thousands of persons in Punjab "disappeared" and were believed to have been cremated. In cracking down on an insurgency in the state, police were also responsible for torture after offering cash bounties for the summary execution of suspected Sikh militants. Although the government claimed that the insurgency had been crushed and normalcy restored, police abuses continued. The identities of the perpetrators has long been known, but a decade later none had been charged, even though the Supreme Court has directed the NHRC to investigate 2,097 cases of illegal cremation. Human rights groups, alarmed by the failure of the government to adequately address reports of these abuses, are concerned that future cases won't be reported.

See also CHILDREN'S RIGHTS; GUJARAT, MASSACRES IN; KASHMIR AND JAMMU, HUMAN RIGHTS VIOLATIONS IN; RELIGIOUS PERSECUTION; TRAFFICKING IN PERSONS.

Further Reading:

Cohen, Stephen Philip. *India: Emerging Power.* Washington, D.C.: Brookings Institution Press, 2002.

Das, Gurcharan. *India Unbound: The Social and Economic Revolution from Independence to the Global Information Age.* New York: Anchor, 2002.

Talbott, Strobe. *Engaging India: Diplomacy, Democracy and the Bomb.* Washington, D.C.: Brookings Institution Press, 2004.

indiscriminate attacks

Indiscriminate attacks against a civilian population and individual civilians are prohibited by law. Additional Protocol I to the 1949 GENEVA CONVENTIONS declares that civilians "shall enjoy general protection against dangers arising from military operations." Further, the protocol prohibits threats of violence as well as violence when its primary purpose is "to spread terror among the civilian population." The protocol defines indiscriminate attacks as "(a) those which are not directed at a specific military objective; (b) those which employ a method or means of combat which cannot be directed at a specific military object; or (c) those which employ a method or means of combat the effects of which cannot be limited . . . and consequently, in each such case, are of a nature to strike military objects and civilians or civilian objects without distinction." Military objectives are defined by the protocol as "those objects which by their nature, location, purpose or use make an effective contribution to military action and whose total or partial destruction, capture or neutralization, in the circumstances ruling at the time, offers a definite military advantage."

The protocol sets out what specific types of attacks are considered indiscriminate:

(a) an attack by bombardment by any methods or means which treats as a single military objective a number of clearly separated and distinct military objectives located in a city, town, village or the other area containing a similar concentration of civilians or civilian objects;

(b) an attack which may be expected to cause incidental loss of civilian life, injury to civilians, damage to civilian objects, or a combination thereof, which would be excessive in relation to the concrete and direct military advantage anticipated.

The protocol also outlaws attacks against the civilian population or civilians as a reprisal. Civilians cannot be forced to become HUMAN SHIELDS by being relocated to installations or locations that might be subject to military attack. International law prohibits any attack that results in wanton destruction, which is defined as an attack that is not directed at military objectives and that results in widespread damage to civilian property. In addition, a belligerent is constrained from using weapons that cannot be properly targeted.

In assessing whether an indiscriminate attack has been carried out, one must also take into account such factors as the design of the weapon, the intention and professionalism of those using it, and the reliability of the intelligence that went into the decision to launch the attack. Even the time, weather, and visibility are considerations: If, for instance, an attack is undertaken even though civilians might be put into danger because of poor visibility or because more people might be on a road near a military objective due to the hour, a case could be made under international law that it constituted an indiscriminate attack. This means that a weapon can be defined as indiscriminate if it produces indiscriminate effects either because of its design or because of the way it is used, or both. A weapon cannot be used if it cannot be properly controlled. One example is the use by Iraq of Scud missiles aimed at Israeli cities during the 1991 Gulf War. The Iraqis were in violation of the law for two reasons. First, the objective of the missile attacks was not military; second, the missiles could not be aimed with any precision.

A belligerent is also forbidden from treating an area that contains both a military objective and civilian populations and property as a single military objective. Additional Protocol I states: "Parties to the conflict shall at all times distinguish between the civilian population and combatants and between civilian objects and military objectives and accordingly shall direct their operations only against military objectives." That way a whole city, for example, cannot be treated as a military target even though it may contain one or more military objectives. Under this prohibition, both the V-1 bombing of London by Germany and the fire-bombing of German cities during World War II by Allied warplanes would have been banned. International law does, however, acknowledge that COLLATERAL DAMAGE, in which civilians are injured or killed and civilian property destroyed, may result from an attack on a nearby military target. In that case, however, the law states that the harm that results to civilians or to civilian property must be proportionate to the importance of the military objective. That is to say, excessive force cannot be used against a military target if it is known that the consequences will inflict disproportionate harm on civilians. If the harm is considered excessive, then it is prohibited whether or not the attack is indiscriminate.

See also ADDITIONAL PROTOCOLS TO THE GENEVA CONVENTIONS; CIVILIAN IMMUNITY.

Further Reading:
Gutman, Roy, ed. *Crimes of War: What the Public Should Know.* New York: W. W. Norton & Company, 1999.
Jokie, Aleksander. *War Crimes and Collective Wrongdoing: A Reader.* London: Blackwell Publishers, 2001.
Neier, Aryeh. *War Crimes: Brutality, Genocide, Terror, and the Struggle for Justice.* New York: Crown, 1998.
Robertson, Geoffrey. *Crimes Against Humanity: The Struggle for Global Justice.* New York: New Press, 2003.

Indonesia, human rights violations in

Hopes that the collapse of the dictatorship of President SUHARTO would bring a measure of reconciliation and human rights improvements in Indonesia have largely gone unrealized. In the view of human rights organizations, the new president, Megawati Sukarnoputri, who took office in 2000, has not moved forcefully enough to curb human rights abuses, rein in the military, or bring an end to several violent ethnic and separatists conflicts. A surge in Islamic militarism in the largest Muslim nation on earth has stirred alarm in many Western capitals. The killings of more than 200 mostly Australian citizens in a Bali nightclub in 2002 underscored the growing threat of terrorism.

Indonesia has been racked by turmoil since gaining its independence from the Dutch in 1950 after a war lasting five years. It is a sprawling and ethnically diverse nation, occupying some 13,000 islands. Until 1965 Indonesia was under the control of President Sukarno, Megawati's father. (Indonesians often use only one name.) In 1965 Sukarno was ousted after a military coup carried out by the palace guard; in the upheaval that followed, General Suharto, head of the army's strategic command, seized power. At the same time the army launched an operation aimed at suppressing communist influence. Within a matter of months 300,000–1,000,000 suspected communists and leftist supporters were killed in an unprecedented bloodbath. Hundreds of thousands were also rounded up and arrested on charges of fomenting the coup. Only about 800 suspects ever received a trial. Suharto instituted a program that he called the New Order (*Orde Baru*) and pursued a pro-Western policy that earned him economic, military, and political support from the United States. Although Sukarno's overthrow ushered in some human rights reforms, his successor's rule increasingly began to take on the trappings of a military dictatorship, Suharto's reign was characterized by EXTRAJUDICIAL KILLINGS, rapes, beatings, TORTURE, DISAPPEARANCES, and egregious abuses by the military and security forces. Some of the gravest violations of human rights have taken place in provinces where military and security forces have brutally suppressed separatist movements.

In a period of one year alone—between June 2000 and June 2001—the Indonesian Commission for Disappearances and Victims of Violence (KONTRAS) reported that police killed 740 persons. According to a 2001 U.S. State Department *Country Report*, security forces continue to rape and sexually exploit suspects taken into custody. The judiciary is weak, corrupt, and politically subservient. Police have been known to intimidate and assault journalists. Although over 40 parties participated in the 2000 presidential elections, the government still imposes limits on political assembly, though most demonstrations are allowed to proceed without hindrance. Much of the violence can be attributed to ethnic, religious, and territorial conflicts, but the country also faces a growing problem of criminal violence. In the absence of effective government, response mobs and vigilante groups have taken the law into their own hands.

Given the turbulent atmosphere and the government's ineptitude and corruption, human rights organizations—both Indonesian and international—have assumed a crucial role in exposing injustice. But because of the threat they pose to perpetrators of abuse, they have come under increasing pressure from the security forces. Some activists and humanitarian workers have been detained, threatened, or even killed. In June 2004 the government ordered the expulsion of Sidney Jones, a prominent American political analyst. At the same time the government placed 20 international and local nongovernmental organizations on a "watch list," contending that they represented threats to the country's security. Human rights groups believed that Jones's deportation was related to critical reporting about Indonesia's poor human rights record. It was not considered coincidental that the expulsion came just ahead of presidential elections scheduled for July.

That one of the prominent candidates in that election, former general WIRANTO, is accused of war crimes in East Timor is of special concern to human rights groups. Wiranto was chief of Indonesia's armed forces in 1999 when the Indonesian army and military-backed militias carried out numerous atrocities against East Timorese after they voted for independence. In February 2003 he was indicted for CRIMES AGAINST HUMANITY by the UN-sponsored Special Panels for Serious Crimes of the Dili District Court and named as a chief suspect by the Indonesian Human Rights Commission. The U.S. State Department has put Wiranto—a nominee of the Gokar Party, one of Indonesia's most important political forces—on a visa watch list, barring him from entry into the United States. "Gokar should be embarrassed to select someone who has been indicted for crimes against humanity as its presidential candidate," said a HUMAN RIGHTS WATCH executive. "If Gokar has really reformed itself after the massive rights violations of the Suharto years, it should be distancing itself from its dark past instead of embracing it." In the July 2004 election Wiranto came in third and was thus eliminated from contention.

In recent years the most serious and widespread human rights violations have come about because of insurgencies such as the one in East Timor, which has now achieved independence. That the East Timorese have fulfilled their aspirations under a UN-supervised vote is expected to encourage other separatist movements, which are seen as a political and economic threat to the central government. Although the central government is based in Java, the largest island in the archipelago, it could not survive without exports from the outer islands. In many cases, the indigenous populations of these islands have been exploited or shunted aside by the Javanese, generating resentment and frustration and sparking numerous rebellions. These insurgencies have in turn provoked a violent response by the military and security forces. The province of Aceh has been the scene of bitter fighting between a local insurgency, the Free Aceh Movement, and the military over the course of several years. Another insurgency has flared up periodically in Papua; in the easternmost province, a separatist group Organisasi Papua Merdeka (OPM, or Free Papua Movement) has been waging war against the government since the 1960s. In 2002 President Megawati tried to end the conflict by bestowing a large measure of autonomy on Papua. Nonetheless, security forces have continued to commit abuses, including forced disappearances and killings. The Moluccas have also seen bitter fighting in the late 1990s, much of it between Muslims and Christians in West Java and Ambon. By some estimates, three years of sectarian fighting have caused as many as 6,000 deaths and left 750,000 REFUGEES internally displaced. In 2002 representatives of Muslim and Christian factions signed a peace agreement intended to end the conflict. Yet another conflict broke out in the late 1990s in Kalimantan, the Indonesian section of Borneo. In this case, indigenous Davaks have been pitted against Madurese who have resettled on their island. Hundreds of Madurese have been killed in the conflict, and the government has been forced to evacuate thousands more.

The Indonesian government has gradually—and some say grudgingly—moved to address the issue of Islamic radicalism, a relatively new phenomenon in a country that had long nurtured a reputation for being religiously moderate and tolerant. The militant group JEMAAH ISLAMIYAH is affiliated with al-QAEDA; it is believed to be responsible for several attacks on Western citizens and interests, including the Bali bombing. Its spiritual leader, Abu Bakhar BASHIR, has been brought up on charges for inciting terrorist attacks. In addition to the Bali bombing, the group has been linked to bombings of churches, U.S. consulates, and embassies as well as assassination attempts against then-president Megawati.

In October 2004 the first directly elected president of Indonesia, former general Susilo Bambang Yudhoyono, took office promising a new commitment to democracy. "Indonesia will be a democratic country, open, modern, pluralistic and tolerant," he said, "We will try hard to form a clean and good government." However, it remained questionable whether his words would translate into concrete action. Only a few weeks later, in November, the only Indonesian jailed for human rights abuses in connection with East Timor's independence referendum was cleared on appeal. The convicted official, Abilio Soares, the last Indonesian governor of East Timor, had previously been sentenced to three years in prison. The Supreme Court based its ruling on the fact that as a civilian official, Soares could not be culpable since East Timor was then under Indonesian military control. Soares was the last of 14 former Indonesian officials convicted for human rights abuses in East Timor whose sentences have been quashed. Human rights groups denounced the ruling, and the departing U.S. ambassador called the failure to bring those responsible for the violence in East Timor a missed chance to revive military ties with Washington.

See also ACEH, WAR CRIMES IN; EAST TIMOR, WAR CRIMES IN.

Further Reading:

Aspinall, Edward. *The Aceh Peace Process: Why It Failed.* Washington, D.C.: East-West Center, 2003.

Bertrand, Jacques, and John Ravenhill. *Nationalism and Ethnic Conflict in Indonesia.* Cambridge: Cambridge University Press, 2003.

Brown, Colin. *A Short History of Indonesia: The Unlikely Nation?* London: Allen & Unwin, 2004.

Dunn, James, and Xanana Gusmao. *East Timor: A Rough Passage to Independence.* Seattle: University of Washington Press, 2004.

Jardine, Matthew. *East Timor: Genocide in Paradise.* The Real Story Series. Monroe, Me.: Odonian Press, 2002.

King, Peter. *West Papua and Indonesia since Suharto: Independence, Autonomy or Chaos?* Sydney, Australia: University of New South Wales Press, 2004.

Legge, J. D. *Sukarno: A Political Biography.* 3d ed. Burlington, Vt.: Butterworth-Heinemann, 2003.

Leith, Denise. *The Politics of Power: Freeport in Suharto's Indonesia.* Honolulu: University of Hawaii Press, 2002.

Pinto, Constancio, and Jardine Matthew. *East Timor's Unfinished Struggle: Inside the Timorese Resistance.* Cambridge: South End Press (November 1, 1996).

Schwarz, Adam. *A Nation in Waiting: Indonesia's Search for Stability.* Philadelphia: Westview Press, 1999.

Sjamsuddin, Nazaruddin. *The Republican Revolt: A Study of the Acehnese Rebellion.* Singapore: Institute of Southeast Asian Studies, 1988.

Sukma, Rizal. *Security Operations in Aceh: Goals, Consequences, and Lessons.* Washington, D.C.: East-West Center, 2004.

Taylor, Jean. *Indonesia: Peoples and Histories.* New Haven, Conn.: Yale University Press, 2003.

Vatikiotis, Michael R. *Indonesian Politics under Suharto: The Rise and Fall of the New Order.* London: Routledge, 1999.

Inter-American Court of Human Rights

The Inter-American Court of Human Rights (IACHR) was established in 1978 by the AMERICAN CONVENTION ON HUMAN RIGHTS, under the aegis of the ORGANIZATION OF AMERICAN STATES (OAS), with the objective of ensuring the observance of the rights and freedoms throughout the Americas. The idea of such a court was in the works for

many decades. The Ninth International Conference of American States held in Bogotá, Colombia, in 1948 adopted a resolution stating that the protection of these rights "should be guaranteed by a juridical organ, inasmuch as no right is genuinely assured unless it is safeguarded by a competent court" and that "where internationally recognized rights are concerned, juridical protection, to be effective, should emanate from an international organ."

The court has two basic functions: On the one hand, its purpose is judicial insofar as it interprets provisions of the American Convention on Human Rights in cases brought to it by member nations; on the other hand, it serves in an advisory capacity, interpreting the convention or other relevant treaties on the request of a member state. The court can only rule, however, when a member state agrees that it has authority over a case. Many Latin American countries, which have a checkered history of adherence to human rights, have proven reluctant or even hostile to the idea of allowing a regional tribunal to assume jurisdiction over cases involving allegations of TORTURE, DISAPPEARANCES, EXTRAJUDICIAL KILLINGS, and corruption in their territory. On occasion some states, including Peru and Trinidad and Tobago, have actually withdrawn from the IACHR's jurisdiction. Access to the court is limited by the fact that states have to agree to allow cases to be heard. If one party disputes the court's jurisdiction, the case cannot go forward. Nor can individuals seek redress for their grievances by appealing directly to the court. They can, however, file their complaints with the Inter-American Commission on Human Rights, which is affiliated with the court. As a result the IACHR has been able to render only one-tenth of the judgments handed up the much-stronger European Court of Human Rights, which sits in Strasbourg. In addition, the Inter-American Court has a budget that is only four percent of its European counterpart, with one-tenth of its personnel.

Further Reading:

Fawcett, Louise, and Andrew Hurrell. *Regionalism in World Politics: Regional Organization and International Order.* Oxford: Oxford University Press, 1996.

Guillermoprieto, Alma. *Looking for History: Dispatches from Latin America.* New York: Vintage, 2002.

Skidmore, Thomas F., and Peter H. Smith. *Modern Latin America.* Oxford: Oxford University Press, 2000.

Williamson, Edwin. *The Penguin History of Latin America.* New York: Penguin Books, 1993.

Internal Displacement Project (Global IDP Project)

The Global IDP Project is an international nongovernmental organization (NGO) that campaigns to improve the lives and protect the rights of INTERNALLY DISPLACED PERSONS

(IDPs) who have been forcibly resettled within their own country by conflict or because of human rights violations. The project tracks internal displacement throughout the world and provides the results of its research and analyses to policy makers, humanitarian organizations, and the general public. It seeks to bring more states into accordance with the UNITED NATIONS GUIDING PRINCIPLES ON INTERNAL DISPLACEMENT, which sets out standards for the humane treatment of IDPs and specifies the obligations of states toward this population. The project was founded by the Norwegian Refugee Council (NRC) in 1996 primarily in response to the growing problem of displacement as a result of internal conflicts in the 1990s. The NRC was particularly concerned about the lack of information about IDPs and in 1998 published the first global survey of internal displacement. Subsequently the IDP entered into negotiations with the UN to create an electronic Internet archive on internal displacement. That archive was launched in December 1999.

See also TRANSFER OF CIVILIANS.

Further Reading:

Feller, Erika, Volker Turk, and Frances Nicholson, eds. *Refugee Protection in International Law: UNHCR's Global Consultations on International Protection.* Cambridge: Cambridge University Press, 2003.

Fritz, Mark. *Lost on Earth: Nomads of the New World.* New York: Routledge, 2000.

Groenewold, Julia, and Doctors Without Borders. *World in Crisis: The Politics of Survival at the End of the Twentieth Century.* London: Routledge, 1996.

Helton, Arthur C. *The Price of Indifference: Refugees and Humanitarian Action in the New Century.* A Council on Foreign Relations Book. Oxford: Oxford University Press, 2002.

Hyndman, Jennifer. *Managing Displacement: Refugees and the Politics of Humanitarianism.* Minneapolis: University of Minnesota Press, 2000.

Ingleby, David, ed. *Forced Migration and Mental Health: Rethinking the Care of Refugees and Displaced Persons.* New York: Plenum US, 2004.

Lischer, Sarah Kenyon. *Dangerous Sanctuaries: Refugee Camps, Civil War, and the Dilemmas of Humanitarian Aid.* Cornell Studies in Security Affairs. Ithaca, N.Y.: Cornell University Press, 2005.

internally displaced persons

The numbers of people displaced in their own countries have increased dramatically in the past 50 years as a result of conflict. In 2001 there were an estimated 20–25 million people classified as internally displaced persons (IDPs), compared to about 14.9 million REFUGEES who have been

Displaced ethnic Albanian children living in a makeshift shelter in the woods near Nekovce, Kosovo *(United Nations)*

forced across international borders. A refugee is considered someone with a well-founded fear of persecution based on his or her race, religion, nationality, or political beliefs who is constrained from returning home by war, civil conflict, political strife, or gross human rights abuses. By contrast, IDPs are uprooted from their homes in their own countries. INTERNATIONAL HUMANITARIAN LAW forbids this kind of forced relocation. The 1949 Geneva Convention specifically prohibits the mass expulsions of civilians such as were carried out by Nazi Germany during World War II. Article 49 of the Convention declares that "individual or mass forcible transfers . . . are prohibited, regardless of their motive."

The law against internal displacement is not absolute. Additional Protocol II of 1977, which applies in internal conflicts, allows forced civilian displacement under certain limited circumstances: when displacement is necessary for the civilians' safety or when their removal is required for "imperative military reasons." Article 17 of the protocol states that civilians cannot be forced from their "whole territory" because a conflict is taking place there. The article does not, however, define what is meant by "territory." In its *Commentary to the Additional Protocols,* the INTERNATIONAL COMMITTEE OF THE RED CROSS (ICRC) states that the article's intent is to minimize civilian displacement that is politically motivated. When civilians must be moved for their own safety or for military necessity, their evacuations must be carried out with adequate protection and under hygienic and humane conditions, and they should be as brief as possible. (The same standard applies to international conflicts.) Protection must be extended to IDPs once they are resettled because they are frequently at risk of killings, rape, and discrimination. Women and children are particularly vulnerable; according to the Red Cross, they make up to 80 percent of the internally displaced.

Displaced persons are also likely to be politically disenfranchised, especially if they have traveled long distances to their temporary homes, separating them from the tribe or ethnic group they relied on for support. They are also usually deprived of any political influence and lack representation, and consequently their plight may go ignored by the government. Indeed, the government may be responsible for their forced relocation, which is the case in Colombia, for instance. This is an area of special concern to the International Committee of the Red Cross, which sees its mandate as protecting and assisting all victims in conflict situations, including IDPs.

Article 25 of the UNIVERSAL DECLARATION OF HUMAN RIGHTS states that all people are entitled to a standard of living that is adequate for the health and well-being of the individual and his or her family. These rights are granted to IDPs, too, whether in transit or in the temporary shelter when they are resettled. They must have access to sufficient supply of nutritional food, water, housing, clothing, health care, and sanitation. Further, the food should be appropriate for the diets of pregnant women, children, and the elderly. In addition, displaced persons have other rights, as indicated in Article 22 of the Universal Declaration, which recognizes the right to realization of the "economic, social and cultural rights indispensable for (one's) dignity." Article 225 of the Universal Declaration provides that adequate medical care should be provided to IDPs because this is a particularly vulnerable population which often suffers from exhaustion, illness, and war-related injuries. Moreover, humanitarian law states that displaced persons have a right to education while they are living in temporary shelter. This provision is not only relevant to children who no longer have access to their schools but to adults who may need specialized education, particularly when they have lost their source of income and livelihood.

International humanitarian law does not specifically address the right of displaced persons to return voluntarily and in safety to their place of residence. However, such a right can be deduced from guarantees found in other treaties ensuring the freedom of movement and the right to choose one's residence.

The problem of displaced persons is getting worse, not better. The reason is not hard to find: "Recent conflicts have been characterized by an increasing targeting of civilians, either as a strategy of warfare or even as the very objective of the parties involved," the ICRC says. "Consequently, the internally displaced now often constitute a considerable part of the affected population." Moreover, many states are not living up to their commitments relating to treatment of IDPs. Legal and humanitarian experts agree that the existing law is insufficient as well. There are, for example, differing interpretations of "imperative military reasons"—one of the two exemptions that permit the relocation of civilians—and there are few inhibitions on the behavior of a state in this regard. "Lack of political will is ultimately the issue," stated Francis Deng, the UN representative on IDPs. "Even if you had fine principles, fine laws, but you don't have the will to enforce them, then it's as good as a dead letter." There is also a question of status: Unstable political conditions can raise the issue of sovereignty, a situation which has arisen in Somaliland. Somaliland has declared itself an independent state although the rest of the world considers it an integral part of Somalia. As a result, the Somaliland government looks upon the displaced population in its territory as refugees and thus the responsibility of the UNITED NATIONS HIGH COMMISSIONER FOR REFUGEES. But the United Nations looks upon them as internally displaced persons who ought to be the responsibility of the state.

See also ADDITIONAL PROTOCOLS TO THE GENEVA CONVENTIONS; DISPLACED PERSONS CAMPS; GENEVA CONVENTIONS; SOMALIA, HUMAN RIGHTS VIOLATIONS IN; TRANSFER OF CIVILIANS; UNITED NATIONS GUIDING PRINCIPLES ON INTERNAL DISPLACEMENT.

Further Reading:
Feller, Erika, Volker Turk, and Frances Nicholson, eds. *Refugee Protection in International Law: UNHCR's Global Consultations on International Protection.* Cambridge: Cambridge University Press, 2003.
Fritz, Mark. *Lost on Earth: Nomads of the New World.* New York: Routledge, 2000.
Groenewold, Julia, and Doctors Without Borders. *World in Crisis: The Politics of Survival at the End of the Twentieth Century.* London: Routledge, 1996.
Helton, Arthur C., *The Price of Indifference: Refugees and Humanitarian Action in the New Century.* A Council

on Foreign Relations Book. Oxford: Oxford University Press, 2002.

Hyndman, Jennifer. *Managing Displacement: Refugees and the Politics of Humanitarianism.* Minneapolis: University of Minnesota Press, 2000.

Ingleby, David, ed. *Forced Migration and Mental Health: Rethinking the Care of Refugees and Displaced Persons.* New York: Plenum US, 2004.

Lischer, Sarah Kenyon. *Dangerous Sanctuaries: Refugee Camps, Civil War, and the Dilemmas of Humanitarian Aid.* Cornell Studies in Security Affairs. Ithaca, N.Y.: Cornell University Press, 2005.

Moorehead, Caroline. *Human Cargo: A Journey among Refugees.* New York: Henry Holt and Co., 2005.

Ogata, Sadako, and Annan, Kofi. *The Turbulent Decade: Confronting the Refugee Crises of the 1990s.* New York: W. W. Norton & Company, 2005.

International Action Network on Small Arms (IANSA)

The International Action Network on Small Arms (IANSA) is a nongovernmental organization (NGO) whose primary mission is to bring attention to and put a halt to the proliferation and misuse of small arms, which are the primary type of weapons used in internal conflicts throughout the world. Founded in 1998, IANSA is made up of a wide range of organizations concerned with small arms, including policy-development organizations, national gun-control groups, research institutes, aid agencies, human rights groups, and people who have been victimized by small arms. It has spearheaded the establishment of five regional NGO networks covering more than 30 nations which are involved in such activities as public education and advocacy and arms export control campaigns. IANSA was a principal participant and organizing force in the July 2001 United Nations Small Arms Conference in New York, the first world gathering on small arms and light weapons. The organization focuses on several issues, including gender (men are disproportionately users of small arms and women disproportionately their victims); arms brokers who facilitate the spread of illicit arms to conflict areas such as Colombia, Angola, and Sierra Leone; monitoring traffic in small arms to identify their source and curb their distribution; child soldiers (more than 300,000 minors under 18 are fighting in wars in 30 countries); monitoring weapons collection and destruction programs; and working for more effective arms controls. IANSA is supported by the governments of Britain, Belgium, Sweden, and Norway in addition to several large philanthropic foundations.

See also ARMS, TRAFFICKING IN AND CONTROL MECHANISMS; WEAPONS IN THE CONDUCT OF WAR.

Further Reading:
Prokosch, Eric. *The Technology of Killing: A Military and Political History of Anti-personnel Weapons.* London: Zed Books, 1995.

U.S. Congressional Budget Office. *Convention on Prohibitions or Restrictions on the Use of Certain Conventional Weapons.* Report to Accompany Treaty Doc. 103–25. Washington, D.C.: U.S. Government Printing Office, 1995.

International Commission on Missing Persons

The International Commission on Missing Persons (ICMP) was established on June 29, 1996, at a meeting of the G-7 (Group of 7) in Lyon, France, when President Bill Clinton announced its formation. Its objective is to locate and identify people missing as a result of armed conflicts and other hostilities and violations of human rights. The ICMP was created specifically to investigate and resolve cases involving an estimated 10,000 people who had disappeared from Bosnia and Herzegovina during the 1992–95 war. The ICMP was given a mandate to work with all the governments involved in the conflict without regard to the victims' ethnic or religious origins. The initiative took on added importance because until the hundreds of thousands of family members affected learned what became of their loved ones, it would be difficult to rebuild societies shattered by the war.

Since its founding, the ICMP has carried out several forensic investigations intended to exhume bodies interred in anonymous and mass graves and then identify the remains, using DNA and other evidence. Family members are interviewed in an attempt to determine the circumstances involving the disappearances and blood samples collected so that the DNA can be matched by forensic analysis against samples from the remains. The commission's mandate later extended to Kosovo, where several hundred Albanian Kosovars disappeared in 1998–99 war. Over 5,500 blood samples have been collected in Kosovo since early 2002. By May 2003 the bodies of 37 Kosovar Albanians exhumed in Serbia were repatriated to their families in Kosovo.

See also BOSNIA AND HERZEGOVINA, HUMAN RIGHTS VIOLATIONS IN; DISAPPEARANCES; FORENSIC MEDICINE AND HUMAN RIGHTS; KOSOVO, WAR CRIMES IN.

Further Reading:
Ferllini Timms, Roxana. *Silent Witness: How Forensic Anthropology Is Used to Solve the World's Toughest Crimes.* Buffalo, N.Y.: Firefly Books Ltd, 2002.

Cox, Margaret, and Jon Sterenberg. *Forensic Archaeology, Anthropology and the Investigation of Mass Graves.* London: CRC Press, 2006.

International Committee of the Red Cross (ICRC)

The International Committee of the Red Cross (ICRC) is an international nongovernmental organization headquartered in Geneva, Switzerland, that seeks to alleviate suffering and aid victims of war and natural disasters. It is mandated by the international community to act as the guardian of INTERNATIONAL HUMANITARIAN LAW. As a neutral body, the ICRC representatives are guaranteed the right to visit PRISONERS OF WAR (POWs) to ensure that they are being treated in accordance with international law. The ICRC lists as its fundamental principles "humanity, impartiality, neutrality, independence, voluntary service, unity, and universality." The organization received a Nobel Peace Prize in 1917 and 1944 and shared a third Nobel Peace Prize in 1963 with the League of Red Cross Societies.

The ICRC was founded in 1875 by Jean-Henri DUNANT, a Swiss businessman and writer, in response to carnage he witnessed in the Battle of Solferino (1859) between French and Austrian forces. After observing how thousands of wounded soldiers were left to die, he conceived of an organization that would minister to the wounded of all sides to a conflict. By 1863, galvanized by his crusade, the Geneva Society for Public Welfare helped found the International Committee for the Relief of the Wounded, which later evolved into the ICRC. A year later an international conference of 13 nations met in Geneva to discuss the care of the sick and wounded in war. The conference culminated in the first Geneva Convention.

The ICRC is one component of a vast network that encompasses 178 national Red Cross and Red Crescent societies and the International Federation of Red Cross and Red Crescent Societies. (The Red Crescent was adopted in place of the Red Cross in Muslim countries.) These national societies are autonomous organizations that carry out their humanitarian activities in accordance with their own statutes, subject to national law. The governing body of the ICRC, known as the Committee, consists of 25 members, all of whom are Swiss, both because the organization was founded in Switzerland and because Switzerland has a long tradition of neutrality. The ICRC maintains that its neutral stance is "not an end in itself, but rather a means towards an end, which is: to be able to act on behalf of people protected by humanitarian law and to make a positive difference to those who are affected by armed violence." This neutral stance allows the ICRC to deal with authorities in the position to alleviate suffering. "*Not* taking sides in an armed conflict is vital in enabling ICRC to reach out to those who need its help." The ICRC asserts that this position does not imply any approval of or support for authorities that violate international humanitarian law. Other organizations, notably DOCTORS WITHOUT BORDERS, have taken issue with the ICRC's strict adherence to neutrality, arguing that in some cases, a position of neutrality is impossible to maintain in the face of serious violations of human rights by one party to the conflict. Even so, the changing character of international conflicts, marked by terrorism and abductions of and indiscriminate attacks on civilians and aid workers alike, has also affected representatives of the ICRC. In 2003 five ICRC staff members lost their lives in violence in Afghanistan and Iraq.

When conflict breaks out, the ICRC and the national society in the affected territory collaborate on procedures to help the victims. According to a 1997 accord, ICRC is responsible for dealing with humanitarian crises in conflict areas. The ICRC not only seeks to uphold humanitarian standards for civilians but also tries to ensure that injured or captive combatants are treated in accordance with international law. In 2003 more than 12,000 ICRC staff worldwide visited both civilians deprived of their liberty and POWs, to provide basic assistance. In addition, the ICRC works to restore family ties that have been ruptured because of war or natural disaster. Because of its role in conducting inspections of conditions in prisons and detention centers, the ICRC acts as an intermediary between the captor and the captive, a role that provides the organization with the ability to improve the treatment of the person deprived of his or her liberty. The ICRC does not release its findings to the public but does work behind the scenes to influence authorities and policy makers. The organization's official Web site emphasizes its unique role in conflict situations: "The wide-reaching respect for the ICRC as the impartial guardian of international humanitarian law means that it is allowed to monitor situations in thousands of places of detention worldwide where no other organization goes."

See also GENEVA CONVENTIONS.

Further Reading:

Berry, Nicholas O. *War and the Red Cross: The Unspoken Mission.* New York: St. Martin's Press, 1997.
Moorehead, Caroline. *Dunant's Dream: War, Switzerland, and the History of the Red Cross.* New York: Carroll & Graf Publishers, 1999.

International Convention on the Prevention and Punishment of the Crime of Genocide

See GENOCIDE CONVENTION.

International Court of Justice (World Court)

The International Court of Justice (ICJ)—better known as the World Court—is the principal judicial organ of the United Nations. The court, which began work in 1946, sits in The Hague in the Netherlands. It was formed to replace the Permanent Court of International Justice, which had been in operation since 1922. Its statute is similar to that of the Permanent Court's and constitutes an integral part of the Charter of the United Nations. The court has two basic roles: to settle legal disputes submitted by member states and to provide advisory opinions on legal questions referred to it by "duly authorized" international organs and agencies. Only states that are members of the United Nations—191 in 2004—are permitted to bring disputes before the World Court. The importance of many of these cases is evident from a sampling of the court's 2004 docket:

- Application of the Convention on the Prevention and Punishment of the Crime of Genocide (*Bosnia and Herzegovina v. Serbia and Montenegro*)
- Armed activities on the territory of the Congo (*Democratic Republic of the Congo v. Uganda*)
- Application of the Convention on the Prevention and Punishment of the Crime of Genocide (*Croatia v. Serbia and Montenegro*)
- Frontier Dispute (Benin/Niger)
- Armed Activities on the Territory of the Congo (*Democratic Republic of the Congo v. Rwanda*)

The court is composed of 15 judges elected to nine-year terms by the UN General Assembly and Security Council; it may not include more than one judge from any one country. The court hears oral arguments and then deliberates in private and announces its judgment in public. Judgments are final and cannot be appealed. In the event that one party fails to comply with the judgment, the injured party can appeal for recourse to the UN Security Council.

The court renders its judgments in accordance with international treaties and conventions in force, international custom, and the general principles of law as well as expert opinions. Between 1946 and 2004, the court delivered 88 judgments on territorial disputes, nonuse of force, noninterference in the internal affairs of nations, diplomatic relations, hostage-taking, the right of ASYLUM, nationality, rights of passage, and economic rights. In its advisory capacity, the court decides which states or organizations might provide useful input and gives them the opportunity of presenting written or oral statements. In principle, these advisory opinions are "consultative in character," which means they are not binding as such on the states or organizations that requested an opinion. In some cases, however, they may become binding. The court has given 25 Advisory Opinions since 1946 on such issues as the construction of a security wall on occupied Palestinian territory by Israel, reparation for injuries suffered in the service of the United Nation, the territorial status of South-West Africa (Namibia) and Western Sahara, the status of human rights rapporteurs, and the legality of the threat or use of nuclear weapons.

See also VIENNA CONVENTION ON DIPLOMATIC RELATIONS.

Further Reading:
Kwiatkowska, Barbara. *Decisions of the World Court Relevant to the UN Convention on the Law of the Sea: A Reference Guide.* New York: Kluwer Academic Publishers, 2002.
Na, A. *Rosenne's The World Court: What It Is and How It Works.* Geneva, Switzerland: United Nations Publications, 2004.

International Covenant on Civil and Political Rights (ICCPR)

The International Covenant on Civil and Political Rights (ICCPR), which was adopted by the United Nations General Assembly and entered into force on March 23, 1976, set out specific rights for individuals that all states must respect, including freedom of expression, freedom from discrimination, and freedom of movement. These rights are inalienable and must be recognized without distinction of any kind, such as race, color, sex, language, religion, political or other opinion, national or social origin, property, birth, or other status. The covenant confers on individuals a number of rights that are not enumerated in the 1948 UNIVERSAL DECLARATION OF HUMAN RIGHTS, including the right of all peoples to self-determination and the right of ethnic, religious, or linguistic minorities to enjoy their own culture, practice their own religion, and use their own language. The covenant omits some rights in the Universal Declaration, among them the right to own property and the right to asylum.

The covenant also provides for the establishment of a Human Rights Commission to assess how well state parties are promoting the rights of their citizens described in the treaty. This committee has the right to investigate allegations against one state party that it is not in compliance that are brought by another state party. The covenant has a second Optional Protocol, which entered into force in 1991, intended to promote the abolition of the death penalty worldwide. The Optional Protocol has won support in Western Europe and among some countries in Latin America, though not in the United States.

See also ASYLUM, POLITICAL; SLAVERY.

International Criminal Court (ICC)

The International Criminal Court (ICC) was established by the ROME STATUTE OF THE INTERNATIONAL CRIMINAL COURT on July 17, 1998. The ICC grew out of a United Nations conference with 120 states participating. The court sits in The Hague, the capital of the Netherlands. It is the first international court based on a treaty and is intended "to promote the rule of law and ensure that the gravest international crimes do not go unpunished." The Rome Statute entered into force on July 1, 2002, after 60 states had either ratified or acceded to it. Countries that do not ratify or accede to the treaty are under no obligation to cooperate with it, and it is unclear whether crimes committed in those countries come under the ICC's jurisdiction.

As of 2005, 139 governments had signed the treaty creating the International Criminal Court, and 97 governments had ratified it. Of the 15 Security Council members, the four European nations and five others have ratified it, and Russia, Algeria, the Philippines, and Japan have signed the founding treaty. Only China and the United States have done neither. The Bush administration opposes the court because it fears that it might be used to bring politically motivated cases against U.S. officials or military personnel. "We don't want to be party to legitimizing the ICC," Pierre-Richard Prosper, the U.S. ambassador at large for war crimes, said in January 2005 after a UN commission recommended that perpetrators of atrocities in Darfur, Sudan, be handed over to the court. The United States had gained immunity for its troops from the court's authority in 2002 and 2003, but in 2004 it was forced to withdraw a Security Council resolution to extend the exemption for another year because of international uproar over abuses committed by U.S. intelligence and military personnel at Abu Ghraib prison in Iraq.

The idea for such a court is not new: Proposals were floated to establish an international body in the late 19th century and again after the end of World War II. However, nothing came of the attempts to create an international court until the 1990s. Surprisingly, the initiative for the court came from the tiny Caribbean state of Trinidad and Tobago, which sought an international forum to fight drug trafficking. But what galvanized many nations to finally establish such an international court came about because of the revulsion over ethnic cleansing in the former Yugoslavia and the GENOCIDE in Rwanda.

It should be noted that the ICC cannot prosecute war crimes or CRIMES AGAINST HUMANITY retroactively; it can assert jurisdiction over only those crimes which are committed in the present. The court has jurisdiction over both crimes committed by residents of a state that is party to the treaty and over crimes that take place in territory of a signatory state even if the perpetrator is a citizen of a state that has declined to ratify or accede to the treaty. In principle at least, this mandate allows the court to try some cases involving the actions of U.S. military personnel in Bosnia, for example. The Rome Statute establishing the ICC also gives wide latitude to a prosecutor who can initiate cases on his or her own authority based on the belief that an independent prosecutor would be free from political restraints.

In an essay written for the CRIMES OF WAR PROJECT, Anthony Dwarkin explains the role the treaty's negotiators envisioned for a prosecutor: "It is easier to think that an independent prosecutor might pursue a case against a citizen of a powerful country than to imagine the government of another country doing it, at the risk of economic or diplomatic (even perhaps military) reprisal."

However, the ICC is limited in the types of cases that can be put before it. Unless the UN Security Council votes to hand over a case to the ICC, crimes committed by a government against its own people—such as the Rwandan genocide of 1994—may never be brought up before the ICC. That is because citizens of countries that have not ratified the Rome Statute cannot be prosecuted for actions they commit within their own territory, barring action by the Security Council. Moreover, the ICC cannot supercede the jurisdiction of national courts—unlike the special tribunals set up by the United Nations for Yugoslavia, Rwanda, and Sierra Leone—but they do have the ability to pursue cases when the countries involved fail to do so with the proviso that those countries are party to the Rome Statute. This principle—called "complementarity"—effectively makes the ICC into a court of last resort. The Rome Statute gives the ICC authority only in the event that a party to it shows itself "unwilling or unable genuinely to carry out the investigation or prosecution."

The Rome Statute leaves it up to the ICC to determine whether a state is genuinely pursuing a particular case or not. A national court would be found derelict only under certain circumstances, according to the provisions of the statute—for instance, if a state is clearly trying to evade the requirements of justice or handling a case with "the purpose of shielding the person concerned from criminal responsibility." There are, however, some cases where the ICC is expected to give deference to states in the interest of national reconciliation and peace. After majority black rule came to South Africa, for example, the government established a TRUTH AND RECONCILIATION COMMISSION, which was empowered to provide AMNESTY on individuals who had committed crimes under the APARTHEID regime in exchange for an admission of culpability. Philippe Kirsch, the first president of the ICC, has stated that "some limited amnesties may be compatible" with the ICC's obligations to investigate and prosecute crimes under the Rome Statute. But this is not to say that general amnesties pushed through by authoritarian regimes to immunize their own officials are likely to be allowed by the ICC; such amnesties had been enacted under General Augusto PINOCHET during his rule in Chile and under Argentina under military dictatorship. (Both amnesties have subsequently been nullified by national courts after the restoration of democracy in those countries.)

Because the ICC is so new, it is difficult to predict what kind of cases it will eventually hear, but international law experts believe that those states most likely to resort to the ICC will be politically unstable. Governments of such countries as Colombia, Afghanistan, or the Democratic Republic of the Congo, which do not have firm control over their own territory, may use the court, as Dwarkin points out, to shore up the domestic rule of law "almost as a declaration of the values that they hope will come to be associated with their own administrations."

How the ICC deals with aggression is also unclear. Although aggression was considered one of the most important charges leveled against Nazi war criminals at the NUREMBERG TRIALS, it has not figured prominently in the development of international criminal law. When the United Nations was establishing tribunals for the former Yugoslavia and Rwanda, for instance, aggression was not listed among the possible charges that could be brought against defendants, although both the war in Yugoslavia and genocide in Rwanda involved aggression on a massive scale. The Rome Statute does confer jurisdiction over aggression on the ICC, but only after an amendment is passed to the statute defining aggression and setting the conditions under which a case can be prosecuted for committing it. This will not happen for some time, since the statute also states that no amendment can be passed for seven years after the statute took effect. For now it is necessary for Security Council to find that an act of aggression has occurred.

In October 2005 the ICC issued its first arrest warrants for five members of Uganda's Lord's Resistance Army (LRA), a notorious rebel group known for abducting up to 30,000 children and turning them into soldiers, forced laborers, and sex slaves. The group has killed thousands of civilians and forced more than a million to flee their homes. Among the five whose arrest was sought was the LRA's leader, JOSEPH KONY, who was believed to be hiding across the border from Uganda in Sudan, which has aided the group in an ongoing conflict with Uganda.

See also DARFUR, WAR CRIMES IN; IRAQ, HUMAN RIGHTS VIOLATIONS IN POST-SADDAM; RWANDA, GENOCIDE IN; UNIVERSAL JURISDICTION; VICTIMS TRUST FUND; YUGOSLAVIA, WAR CRIMES IN.

Further Reading:
Ball, Howard. *Prosecuting War Crimes and Genocide: The Twentieth-Century Experience.* Lawrence: University Press of Kansas, 1999.
Bass, Gary Jonathan. *Stay the Hand of Vengeance: The Politics of War Crimes Tribunals.* Princeton, N.J.: Princeton University Press, 2001.
Beigbeder, Yves, and Theo van Boven. *Judging War Criminals: The Politics of International Justice.* Sidney, Australia: Palgrave Macmillan, 1999.
Bloxham, Donald. *Genocide on Trial: War Crimes Trials and the Formation of Holocaust History and Memory.* Oxford: Oxford University Press, 2003.
Cooper, Belinda, and Richard Goldstone. *War Crimes: The Legacy of Nuremberg.* New York: TV Books Inc., 1999.
Dormann, Knut, and Louise Doswald-Beck. *Elements of War Crimes under the Rome Statute of the International Criminal Court: Sources and Commentary.* Cambridge, U.K.: Cambridge University Press, 2003.
Falk, Richard A. *Crimes of War: A legal, political-documentary, and psychological inquiry into the responsibility of leaders, citizens, and soldiers for criminal acts in wars.* New York: Random House, 1971.

International Criminal Tribunal for Rwanda

The International Criminal Tribunal for Rwanda (ICTR) was created by the United Nations Security Council on November 8, 1994, to prosecute the perpetrators of a genocidal campaign carried out in Rwanda earlier that year. Some 800,000 people, predominantly members of the Tutsi tribal group, were systematically slaughtered by Hutu militants. The tribunal, located in Arusha, Tanzania, is one of three special tribunals established by the United Nations to try war crimes. (The other two are the INTERNATIONAL CRIMINAL TRIBUNAL FOR THE FORMER YUGOSLAVIA and the SPECIAL COURT FOR SIERRA LEONE.) The ICTR was given a mandate to investigate and try cases of GENOCIDE and other serious violations of INTERNATIONAL HUMANITARIAN LAW committed in the territory of Rwanda or in neighboring countries between January 1, 1994, and December 31, 1994.

The tribunal consists of three parts: the Trial Chambers and the Appeals Chamber; the Office of the Prosecutor; and the Registry, which is responsible for providing overall judicial and administrative support to the Chambers and the Prosecutor. The ICTR began its first trial in January 1997, and as of April 2004 it has handed down 15 judgments involving 21 accused; another 21 were still on trial. Among the most notable cases to be heard involved a *bourgmestre* (mayor) named J. P. Akayesu. His case stands out because it was the first time that an international tribunal was obliged to interpret the definition of genocide as defined in the 1948 Convention for the Prevention and Punishment of the Crime of genocide. This convention describes genocide as "the act of committing certain crimes, including the killing of members of the group or causing serious physical or mental harm to members of the group with the intent to destroy, in whole or in part, a national, racial or religious group, as such."

The ICTR carved out significant legal precedent by determining that rape and sexual violence—which was an integral part of the operations against the Tutsis—could constitute genocidal acts if they were committed with the intent to destroy a particular group of people, as was clearly the case in Rwanda. Other noteworthy precedents were established by the conviction of Jean Kambanda, former prime minister of Rwanda, who had pled guilty, though he later recanted. It was the first time that one of the accused had acknowledged his culpability for the crime of genocide before an international tribunal, and it was the first time that the head of a government was convicted of genocide. (Genocide also figures in the charges against former Yugoslav president Slobodon MILOŠEVIĆ, who was forced to stand trial before the International Criminal Tribunal for Yugoslavia, which sits in The Hague.)

In 2003 the ICTR rendered the highest number of judgments in a year involving eight cases. Three of the convictions that year drew particular attention because the defendants—two radio broadcasters and a newspaper executive—were not charged with inflicting bodily harm on any individual. Instead they were found guilty of INCITEMENT TO GENOCIDE by using the media to demonize the Tutsis, inflame the Hutus before to the genocide, and direct murderous mobs to locations where Tutsis had taken refuge. This was the first such case to be heard by an international tribunal since the conviction of Julius STREICHER, the editor of a notorious anti-Semitic magazine, at the NUREMBERG TRIALS. Although the judges noted the importance of freedom of speech, they maintained in their ruling that it was "critical to distinguish between the discussion of ethnic consciousness and the promotion of ethnic hatred." Nonetheless, the verdict was criticized by some First Amendment lawyers and scholars who raised concerns that authoritarian regimes might be tempted to use the court's reasoning in this case to suppress criticism and dissent in their own countries.

The ICTR has been beset by delays and financial problems. In 2004 the court reported a severe shortage of funds because 140 members of the United Nations had failed to honor their financial commitments, with the result that of the $212 million pledged for the court's operations, only $62 million has actually been received. Moreover, the mandate of the tribunal is set to expire at the end of the decade, and the prosecutor's office has expressed doubts whether there is adequate time to hear all the cases still pending. By March 2005 the court had convicted 21 people and acquitted three. Of those, only four had pleaded guilty. At the time 25 people were on trial and another 18 others were waiting to have their cases heard.

See also GENOCIDE CONVENTION; RWANDA, GENOCIDE IN.

Further Reading:
Barnett, Michael. *Eyewitness to a Genocide: The United Nations and Rwanda.* Ithaca, N.Y.: Cornell University Press, 2003.
Dallaire, Romeo, and Brent Beardsley. *Shake Hands with the Devil: The Failure of Humanity in Rwanda.* New York: Carroll & Graf, 2004.
Gourevich, Philip. *We Wish to Inform You That Tomorrow We Will Be Killed with Our Families: Stories from Rwanda.* New York, Picador, 1999.
Mamdani, Mahmood. *When Victims Become Killers: Colonialism, Nativism, and the Genocide in Rwanda.* Princeton, N.J.: Princeton University Press, 2002.
Melvern, Linda. *A People Betrayed: The Role of the West in Rwanda's Genocide.* London: Zed Books, 2000.
Peterson, Scott. *Me against My Brother: At War in Somalia, Sudan and Rwanda.* London: Routledge, 2001.
United Nations War Crimes Commission. *Law Reports of Trials of War Criminals: Four Genocide Trials.* Boulder, Colo.: Lynne Rienner Publishers, 1992.

International Criminal Tribunal for the former Yugoslavia (ICTY)

In May 1993, the United Nations Security Council established the International Criminal Tribunal for the former Yugoslavia (ICTY) to try those individuals responsible for violations of INTERNATIONAL HUMANITARIAN LAW in the territory of the former Yugoslavia in three wars beginning in 1991 and ending in 1999. The ICTY, which sits in The Hague, is the United Nations' first special tribunal. (Two others have been established: one to prosecute war crimes in Rwanda and another to try war crimes in Sierra Leone.) Slobodan MILOŠEVIĆ, the former president of Yugoslavia who went on trial on February 12, 2002, is the highest-profile defendant to be tried by the tribunal. As a special international court of this kind, it has charted new waters and inevitably drawn fire from critics who accuse it of being used as a political tool. By insisting that countries involved in the wars turn over accused war criminals for trial, it has also inflamed nationalists who oppose any cooperation with the ICTY.

UN Security Council Resolution 827 establishing the court was passed on May 25, 1993, while the war in Croatia and Bosnia and Herzegovina was still raging. The tribunal was given a mandate to bring to justice persons allegedly responsible for serious violations of international humanitarian law, deter similar crimes, provide justice to the victims, and contribute to the reconciliation of the war-torn region. Four categories of offenses fell under the tribunal's jurisdiction with the proviso that they occurred on the territory of the former Yugoslavia since 1991:

- grave breaches of the 1949 Geneva Conventions
- violations of the laws or customs of war
- genocide
- crimes against humanity

To carry out the prosecutions, the ICTY was given authority over national courts, an important consideration in light of the reluctance of many courts to prosecute nationals on their own initiative. Only individuals can be prosecuted, not organizations, political parties, administrative entities, or other legal subjects. This contrasts with the mandate of the NUREMBERG TRIALS in which organizations such as the SS and GESTAPO were held liable for war crimes along with the officials who perpetrated them.

Fifteen permanent judges sit on the tribunal; they are divided equally among the three Trial Chambers and the one Appeals Chamber. In addition to hearing testimony and legal arguments and ruling on the guilt or innocence of defendants, judges also draft and adopt legal instruments relating to the function of the tribunal, such as rules of procedure and evidence. Many of the legal issues that judges on the ICTY have been grappling with have not been dealt with since the Nuremberg and TOKYO TRIALS of World War II war criminals.

By May 2005, 128 people had appeared before the tribunal, and judgments had been rendered on 50, of whom 48 were found guilty and two were acquitted; another three were acquitted at the appeals stage. Some 20 arrest warrants had been issued for suspects still at large.

One of the ICTY's most significant rulings came in April 2004 when the court determined that the 1995 Srebrenica

War criminal Dragan Nikolić of Bosnia arriving at the Hague War Crimes Tribunal, February 2005 *(Robin Utrecht/Landov)*

massacre in Bosnia was GENOCIDE. Legal experts hailed the ruling as a historic decision with implications for the fate of other defendants, including the Yugoslav strongman Slobodan Milošević. In the worst atrocity in Europe since World War II, Serb forces massacred 7,000 Muslim men and boys in Srebrenica. Establishing that Milošević is guilty of genocide as well has turned out to be more problematic. In two years 300 witnesses, including high-level officials in his regime, have testified during his trial. (Milošević is defending himself at his own insistence.) In spite of this testimony, supplemented by voluminous documentation, many legal experts were fearful that the prosecution had failed to make the case for genocide, in part because the UN tribunal has set the bar for doing so extremely high. In order to prove genocide, prosecutors would need to show that Milošević specifically intended to destroy Bosnian Muslims as a people. Without access to a direct order in Milošević's name, this standard is difficult to meet.

The case is also jeopardized by the failure of the Yugoslav authorities to turn over important military documents that might implicate Milošević to the court's chief prosecutor, Carla DEL PONTE. According to Resolution 1503, adopted by the Security Council, the ICTY (and the Rwanda tribunal) must end its investigations by the end of 2004, complete its trials by end of 2008, and conclude all its work by 2010. Del Ponte has expressed doubt whether the tribunal will be able to complete its work before the deadline, citing a number of incomplete cases and the failure to apprehend a number of fugitives for whom warrants have been issued. The pressure of time, it is believed, might force prosecutors to drop cases involving lower-level suspects, leaving them for national courts, in order to concentrate on those who are most implicated in war crimes and CRIMES AGAINST HUMANITY.

In March 2005 the ICTY issued its final indictment after 12 years in existence. The indictment charged former interior minister Ljube Boskovski of Macedonia and a former senior police officer, Johan Tarculovski, with crimes that include the murder of civilians and wanton destruction during an ethnic Albanian guerrilla insurgency in Macedonia, which was also a part of the former Yugoslav Federation before winning independence.

See also BOSNIA AND HERZEGOVINA, HUMAN RIGHTS VIOLATIONS IN; CROATIA, HUMAN RIGHTS VIOLATIONS IN; GOTOVINA, ANTE; KARADŽIĆ, RADOVAN; MACEDONIA, HUMAN RIGHTS VIOLATIONS IN; MERON, THEODOR; SERBIA, HUMAN RIGHTS VIOLATIONS IN; SESELJ, VOJISLAV; SREBRENICA, MASSACRE IN; WAR CRIMINALS OF THE FORMER YUGOSLAVIA; YUGOSLAVIA, WAR CRIMES IN.

Further Reading:

Bassiouni, M. Cherif. *Sexual Violence: An invisible weapon of war in the former Yugoslavia.* Chicago: International Human Rights Law Institute, DePaul University, 1996.

Clark, Wesley K. *Waging Modern War: Bosnia, Kosovo, and the Future of Combat.* New York: Public Affairs.

Glenny, Misha. *The Fall of Yugoslavia: The Third Balkan War.* New York: Penguin Books, 1996.

Hagan, John. *Justice in the Balkans: Prosecuting War Crimes in the Hague Tribunal.* Chicago Series in Law and Society. Chicago: University of Chicago Press, 2003.

Harris, Nathaniel. *The War in Former Yugoslavia.* London: Hodder & Stoughton, 1997.

Hazan, Pierre, and James Thomas Snyder. *Justice in a Time of War: The True Story behind the International Criminal Tribunal for the Former Yugoslavia.* Eugenia and Hugh M. Stewart Series on Eastern Europe. Austin: Texas A&M University Press, 2004.

Honig, Jan Willem, and Norbert Both. *Srebrenica: Record of a War Crime.* New York: Penguin Books, 1997.

Kim, Julie. *War in the Former Yugoslavia: Chronology of Events August 16, 1992–May 30, 1993.* CRS Report for Congress. Washington, D.C.: Foreign Affairs and National Defense Division, Congressional Research Service, the Library of Congress, 1993.

Kipp, Jacob W. *International Ramifications of Yugoslavia's Serial Wars: The Challenge of Ethno-national Conflicts for a Post-Cold-War, European Order.* Fort Leavenworth, Kans.: European Military Studies Office, 1993.

Mertus, Julie. *Former Yugoslavia: War Crimes Trials in the Former Yugoslavia.* Helsinki: Human Rights Watch/Helsinki, 1995.

Naimark, Norman, and Holly Case. *Yugoslavia and Its Historians: Understanding the Balkan Wars of the 1990s.* Stanford, Calif.: Stanford University Press, 2003.

Rhode, David. *Endgame: The Betrayal and Fall of Srebrenica.* New York: Farrar, Straus & Giroux, 1997.

Rogel, Carole. *The Breakup of Yugoslavia and the War in Bosnia.* Westport, Conn.: Greenwood Press, 1998.

Rossanet, Bertrand de. *War and Peace in the Former Yugoslavia.* Boston: Martinus Nijhoff, 1997.

United Nations War Crimes Commission. *Law Reports of Trials of War Criminals: Four Genocide Trials.* Boulder, Colo.: Lynne Rienner Publishers, 1992.

International Humanitarian Fact-Finding Commission

The International Humanitarian Fact-Finding Commission, a permanent international body, was established by Article 90 of Additional Protocol I to the GENEVA CONVENTIONS of 1949, which affords rights and protections to the victims of armed conflicts. At the same time, the commission is also empowered to bring states into compliance with the guarantees provided by the Additional Protocol. The commission was formally constituted in 1991. It is based in Berne, Switzerland, and is composed of 15 independent individuals elected by the member states. (More than 60 states have recognized the commission's authority.) Its main purpose is to investigate allegations of serious breaches and violations of INTERNATIONAL HUMANITARIAN LAW in times of armed conflict. The president of the commission, Sir Kenneth Keith, acknowledges that the collection of facts relating to conflicts carries the danger of opening old wounds. Nonetheless, he stresses the importance of the commission's role: "For those who have experienced injustices and personal suffering, it is essential that the facts be established, that the causes of violations be recognized, and that appropriate measures be undertaken to prevent them from recurring."

See also ADDITIONAL PROTOCOLS TO THE GENEVA CONVENTIONS.

international humanitarian law (IHL)

International humanitarian law (IHL) refers to a body of humanitarian principles that are embodied in a number of international treaties that apply to armed conflict. The most important of these treaties—the four GENEVA CONVENTIONS of 1949 and the ADDITIONAL PROTOCOLS TO THE GENEVA CONVENTIONS of 1977—cover both international conflicts and such internal conflicts as insurrections and civil war. IHL is specifically concerned with, on the one hand, the conduct of belligerents during a conflict and, on the other hand, the protections of noncombatants, including civilians, the sick and wounded, and PRISONERS OF WAR. IHL differs from human rights in some respects. Human rights law applies to the rights of human beings—the right to free expression, for example, or the right to privacy—while IHL relates to armed conflict. Human rights are inviolable, and the laws guaranteeing them are applicable in times of peace and war. IHL applies only in times of war, whether international or internal. The Fourth Geneva Convention, for instance, makes it a crime for an OCCUPYING POWER to murder civilians under its control during an armed conflict or to restrict them from going about their normal lives as long as security concerns are met. The protection of civilians is given further weight in Additional Protocol I, Article 4, which states: "In order to ensure respect for and protection of the civilian population and civilian objects, the Parties to the conflict shall at all times distinguish between the civilian population and combatants and between civilian objects and military objectives and accordingly shall direct their operations only against military objectives." Protocol I also forbids belligerents from indiscriminate attacks on civilians, a prohibition that would include CARPET BOMBING or reprisal killings.

Under IHL the use of force must be proportionate to the importance of the military objective being targeted, and belligerents are required to avoid putting civilians at risk as much as possible. But it is important to note that IHL does not make war itself illegal—or as the writer Lawrence Weschler puts it, IHL is "determinedly agnostic on the question of the legality of war itself"—which means that not all civilian deaths, which might occur as a result of an attack on a military object—what is known as COLLATERAL DAMAGE—are unlawful during war. The first international treaties to form the existing framework of IHL were, however, concerned less with civilians in armed conflict, although they were not altogether ignored, and more with the combatants themselves. Negotiators of the early Geneva and HAGUE CONVENTIONS in the latter 19th and early 20th centuries wanted to ensure protections for combatants who were either wounded on the battlefield or taken prisoner, as well as to safeguard hospitals, ambulances, and medical personnel. These protections were expanded under the Second Geneva Convention to cover sailors shipwrecked at sea and hospital ships. Protections are also conferred on combatants who are no longer able to fight and on soldiers who surrender. Combatants who are ill or injured are entitled to proper medical care. The Third Geneva Convention covered the treatment of prisoners of war who were to be assured of medical care, adequate nutrition, and housing. The convention further restricts the captor power from threatening or mistreating prisoners of war, who are obliged only to provide their name, rank, and serial number. Civilians who are authorized to accompany a military unit, including chaplains and war correspondents, are also covered by these provisions. But these protections do not extend to mercenaries or spies.

The most significant protections conferred on civilians is found in Fourth Geneva Convention, which was in many ways a response to the atrocities of World War II and incorporate many of the standards of justice established by the NUREMBERG TRIALS of Nazi war criminals shortly after the end of the war. While the earlier Geneva conventions were largely concerned with international conflicts, the Fourth Geneva Convention of 1949 specifically relates to internal conflicts, which would include crimes committed by a state against its own citizens. The Fourth Convention protects civilians against INDISCRIMINATE ATTACKS, murder, TORTURE, PILLAGE, reprisals, indiscriminate destruction of property UNLAWFUL IMPRISONMENT, and being taken hostage. With rare exceptions, a power cannot force civilians from their homes or remove them to another location whether within its sovereignty or across a border. Special protections are offered to the sick, the elderly, women, and children. Civilians are entitled to adequate shelter, access to food and water, and medical care. The INTERNATIONAL COMMITTEE OF THE RED CROSS (ICRC) is officially designated as the neutral body responsible for ensuring that the provisions of the conventions are carried out. Subse-

quent treaties, including the Additional Protocols, strengthened and extended the protections of civilians to vital civilian installations such as dams and electric power and water plants; cultural property (libraries, museums, and historic and archaeological sites); and civic and religious institutions, including churches, mosques and synagogues. (However, the prohibitions against targeting civilian, cultural, or religious property were not absolute; such a location could become a military target if the opposing side was using it for military purposes.)

As recent wars and genocidal episodes have vividly illustrated—among them, three wars in the former Yugoslavia in the 1990s and the slaughter of Tutsis and moderate Hutus in Rwanda in 1994—enforcement of IHL continues to be a serious problem, even though the majority of nations have ratified the Geneva Conventions and other treaties that make up IHL. There are, to be sure, moral incentives to abide by the provisions of these accords. Parties to a conflict have a vested interest in treating prisoners of war well, for instance, because they would want to see their own soldiers treated well if they fell into enemy hands. Moreover, world opinion can constrain a state or an occupying power from violating IHL, especially at a time when even authoritarian regimes have difficulty suppressing news or keeping citizens from learning about what is happening abroad. Economic sanctions, while not always effective, can have a positive impact, and some countries, in fact, have curbed abuses because of the threat that trade or international aid will be cut off.

Legal action, too, can force countries to conform to IHL, especially if it is initiated by the United Nations Security Council, because of the political and military power of its permanent members: the United States, the United Kingdom, Russia, France, and China. In recent years the United Nations has established special tribunals to prosecute war criminals responsible for atrocities in Rwanda, the former Yugoslavia, and Sierra Leone. The legal precedents emerging from the rulings in these cases are likely to add to the growing body of IHL. National courts, too, are playing an important part in this process. For example, high courts in Argentina and Chile have stripped former political leaders and military officials of immunity so that they can be held accountable for crimes committed during the "dirty wars" of the 1970s. When all else fails, military force can be applied to enforce IHL, but because of political discord and bureaucratic wrangling, these interventions happen relatively rarely.

International humanitarian law did not suddenly spring into existence in the late 19th century. To some degree, IHL has been in effect, whether as codified law or CUSTOMARY LAW, probably for as long as armies have been waging war. As early as 500 B.C., the famous Chinese writer Sun Tzu discussed proper behavior on the battlefield in *The Art of War*. The concept of chivalry in medieval Europe is an example of

IHL; so are the samurai codes of Tokugawa Japan (1603–1867). These codes, too, called for the proper treatment of prisoners and set out the rules of combat on the battlefield, although they were limited; for instance, Crusaders did not feel any need to treat captured Muslim opponents the same way that they would treat captured Christian ones.

The groundwork for modern IHL was developed in 16th and 17th centuries in the writings of philosophers and scholars, including Montaigne, Rousseau, and GROTIUS. In many ways, IHL has evolved out of war itself: As technology made conflict increasingly deadly and expanded war to civilian population centers, there arose a need for new laws to deal with previously unimaginable circumstances. In June 1859 nearly 40,000 soldiers were killed when the Austrian army clashed with a French-Italian force during the Battle of Solferino. Among the witnesses to this carnage was a Swiss businessman named Jean-Henri DUNANT, who was so "seized with horror and pity" that he wrote a book about it in which he called for a neutral body to tend to the wounded on the battlefield in future conflicts. He realized his vision first in the creation of the ICRC in 1863 and then in an international conference that culminated in the Geneva Convention of 1864 "for the amelioration of the conditions of the wounded in armies in the field." A similar effort was underway in the United States, which resulted in the LIEBER CODE, a set of rules regarding military engagement drafted by New York professor Francis Lieber; Abraham Lincoln made the Lieber Code binding on all Union forces during the Civil War. The next major developments in establishing IHL came in 1899 and 1907 with the two Hague Conventions, which outlawed certain types of weapons and warfare. The next convention followed in 1925 (under the auspices of the LEAGUE OF NATIONS) and 1929 (under the auspices of the ICRC), both of which looked back to World War I. The 1925 Geneva Protocol, for instance, prohibited the use of poisonous gases, which had been used by German forces on battlefields of France.

The NUREMBERG TRIALS (and to a lesser extent, the TOKYO TRIALS of Japanese war criminals) made new law by trying high-ranking Nazi officials on charges of crimes against peace, GENOCIDE, and CRIMES AGAINST HUMANITY. (In fact, the very word *genocide* was not coined until World War II.) The next major conference, which resulted in the Geneva Conventions of 1949, was influenced by the bitter lessons learned from World War II. Subsequent conventions under UN auspices have dealt specifically with the protection of cultural property, defined and outlawed genocidal acts, and defined and outlawed acts of torture. The two 1977 protocols were drafted in response to the proliferation of insurgencies and civil conflicts raging in many parts of the developing world.

Almost half a century would have to pass before severe violators of international humanitarian law would face an international tribunal for the kind of crimes that Nazi officials were convicted of committing—first in the INTERNATIONAL CRIMINAL TRIBUNAL FOR THE FORMER YUGOSLAVIA, then in the INTERNATIONAL CRIMINAL TRIBUNAL FOR RWANDA and the SPECIAL COURT FOR SIERRA LEONE. In 1999 a new INTERNATIONAL CRIMINAL COURT (ICC) was established to hear cases involving war crimes, crimes against humanity, and other grave violations of international humanitarian law. The authority of the ICC has been recognized by many but by no means all states; the most significant exception is the United States, which opposes the court's authority on the grounds that American officials or military personnel might face politically motivated prosecutions by the court. Advocates of the ICC dismiss these fears, noting that the court is empowered to hear cases only after a national court has proven unable or unwilling to do so.

See also CRIMES OF WAR PROTECT; CULTURAL PROPERTY, PROTECTION OF; HUMANITARIAN INTERVENTION; MILITARY NECESSITY; TERRORISM AND INTERNATIONAL HUMANITARIAN LAW.

Further Reading:
Cooper, Belinda, and Richard Goldstone. *War Crimes: The Legacy of Nuremberg.* New York: TV Books Inc., 1999.

Dormann, Knut, and Louise Doswald-Beck. *Elements of War Crimes under the Rome Statute of the International Criminal Court: Sources and Commentary.* Cambridge: Cambridge University Press, 2003.

Falk, Richard A. *Crimes of War: A legal, political-documentary, and psychological inquiry into the responsibility of leaders, citizens, and soldiers for criminal acts in wars.* New York: Random House, 1971.

Holzgrefe, J. L., and Robert O. Keohane, eds, *Humanitarian Intervention: Ethical, Legal and Political Dilemmas.* Cambridge: Cambridge University Press, 2003.

Kennedy, David. *The Dark Sides of Virtue: Reassessing International Humanitarianism.* Princeton, N.J.: Princeton University Press, 2004.

Orford, Anne, James Crawford, and John Bell, eds. *Reading Humanitarian Intervention: Human Rights and the Use of Force in International Law.* Cambridge Studies in International and Comparative Law. Cambridge: Cambridge University Press, 2003.

Welsh, Jennifer M. *Humanitarian Intervention and International Relations.* Oxford: Oxford University Press, 2004.

International Labor Organization (ILO)

The International Labor Organization (ILO) is a United Nations agency that seeks the recognition and promotion of social justice and human and labor rights. Founded in 1919, the ILO enjoys a special place in history since it is the only major creation of the Treaty of Versailles, which brought the LEAGUE OF NATIONS into being, and still survives to this day. The ILO also became the first specialized agency of the United Nations in 1946 shortly after the world body itself was created. The ILO is composed of representatives from the government, business, and labor force of its member countries. In its Declaration on Fundamental Principles and Rights at Work, the ILO sets forth its basic principles:

- freedom of association and the effective recognition of the right to collective bargaining
- the elimination of all forms of forced or compulsory labor
- the effective abolition of child labor
- the elimination of discrimination in the workplace

It should be noted that member states are not bound by the Declaration. However, the ILO has been involved in drafting several conventions dealing with workers' rights, which do impose obligations on their signatories. The subjects covered by these conventions range from work hours and the ability to organize unions to child labor and minimum wage. Even though many countries have in principle accepted the idea of independent unions or the abolition of child labor they have continued to violate their obligations in practice.

Accordingly, the ILO actively promotes the development of independent employers' and workers' organizations and provides training and advisory services to those organizations. At the same time it has launched a worldwide campaign for ratification of the Convention and Recommendation banning child labor, which includes luring children into prostitution or recruiting them in the military.

International Military Tribunal   *See* NUREMBERG TRIALS.

International Military Tribunal for the Far East
See TOKYO TRIALS.

International Monitor Institute
The International Monitor Institute (IMI) is a research organization established to document and compile visual and audio evidence of human rights violations around the world. The IMI makes its database available to the public, nongovernmental organizations, governments, and policy makers. The institute was founded in 1993 in response to a request for help in organizing some 600 hours of film and video by the United Nations Commission of Experts. A Los

Angeles–based documentary production company, Linden Productions, resolved the dilemma by developing a method to organize, synopsize, and index the material. The result was a system that allowed researchers to easily search and access the collection.

The ICC began life as the Balkan Archives, which documented crimes in the Balkan wars of the 1990s. By researching the archives, prosecutors with the UN INTERNATIONAL CRIMINAL TRIBUNAL FOR THE FORMER YUGOSLAVIA have been able to gather evidence to bring cases against war criminals. The recognition that such a resource could help identify and prosecute individuals responsible for abuses elsewhere has led to the creation of similar archives for other regions, including Myanmar (Burma), Cambodia, Kurdistan, Rwanda, and Iraq—an initiative that developed into the IMI. Other archives have been established on specific subjects such as CHEMICAL WEAPONS. Today the IMI is a repository of over 5,000 hours of video, film, and radio reports in addition to over 600 photographs and slides.

Iran, human rights violations in
The history of human rights abuses in Iran extends back decades. The Pahlavi dynasty that took power in the 1920s had a terrible human rights record, including the regular use of TORTURE against detainees. Dissent was ruthlessly suppressed, especially by the shah of Iran's notorious security police, Savak. The Kurdish minority was harassed and persecuted, and religious Islamic figures as well as leftists who were perceived as a threat to the regime were arrested or exiled. Women, however, benefited from the shah's campaign to westernize the country and enjoyed many freedoms that were subsequently stripped away by the mullahs who succeeded him.

However, as was the case with the French and Russian revolutions in 1789 and 1917, respectively, the repression of the ancien régime soon paled into insignificance compared to the tyranny instituted by the new revolutionary Islamic regime, which came into power in 1979. The new rulers soon devoured their own, with moderate politicians replaced by hard-line Islamist ideologues. Beginning in 1980, the eight-year war with Iraq—started by Saddam HUSSEIN—paradoxically reinforced the Islamic regime, as it was able to call upon the innate patriotism of the Iranian people. (In addition, unlike 85 percent of the world's Muslims, who are Sunni, most Iranians follow the Shia version of that faith.)

The Iranian regime remains strongly theocratic. Above the elected president is a supreme head, a position held since 1989 by Ayatollah Khameini, the successor of the original leader, Ayatollah Khomeini. While women are eligible to vote for candidates for parliament—the Majlis—all candidates have to be vetted by the Guardian Council, a clerical Islamist body that can veto people deemed insufficiently Islamic.

The Revolutionary Guards, which are charged with enforcing Islamic discipline, are controlled by the clergy, not the parliament. (Technically speaking, Islam has no clergy, but Shiite Islam has much closer equivalents than its Sunni counterpart to the Christian clergy of the West.) The hard-liners have also supported Islamic terror abroad, notably in Lebanon and Palestine.

At home the security forces carry out systematic abuses, including arbitrary arrest and detention, EXTRAJUDICIAL KILLINGS and summary executions, DISAPPEARANCES, and widespread use of TORTURE and other degrading treatment. The justice system is characterized by unfair trials and a lack of DUE PROCESS. Some detainees have been held in secret and denied access to relatives, legal representation, and even medical care for varying periods. The state also infringes on citizens' privacy and restricts freedom of speech, press, assembly, association, religion, and movement. Scores of publications deemed critical of the Islamic government are closed down, and satellite television is illegal (although many people have dishes that they use in secret), Internet sites are filtered, and journalists imprisoned. Practitioners of the Baha'i faith, an offshoot of Islam, suffer from persecution, and at various times Jews have been arrested on charges of espionage, which have proved so flimsy that most were later freed without being tried. AMNESTY INTERNATIONAL estimates that at least a dozen political prisoners arrested in 2003 were detained without charge, trial, or regular access to their families and lawyers. Political prisoners were among the 108 convicted prisoners executed in 2003, and in the same year at least four prisoners were sentenced to death by stoning. (The head of the judiciary has reportedly called for an alternative to this practice.) At least 197 people were sentenced to be flogged, and 11 were sentenced to amputation of fingers and limbs. It is possible that the actual numbers are higher. Prisoners of Arabic and Kurdish origins appear to have been specifically marked for execution to deter dissent from their communities. Hundreds of students were arbitrarily arrested for participating in protests in 1999 and 2003 and mistreated while in custody. Families who have complained about the treatment of imprisoned relatives have also been subject to harassment and intimidation.

In the late 1990s widespread popular discontent with the hard-liners led to the election of a pro-reform parliament and the ascension of a reformist leader as president, Mohammed Khatami. There were even pro-American riots after the attacks of September 11, 2001. However, there has been widespread disenchantment with Khatami, who was constrained by the mullahs from aggressively carrying out liberalization. The Guardian Council, Iran's highest governing body, vetoed two bills introduced by the presidency and passed by Parliament in 2002, one which would have allowed the president to overturn court decisions he deemed unconstitutional and the other of which would have removed the Guardian Council's powers to select candidates for general election. The council has also rejected a parliamentary bill providing for Iran's accession to the UN CONVENTION AGAINST TORTURE, citing financial and constitutional reasons. In 2004 the Guardian Council purged so many moderate candidates in parliamentary elections that many voters boycotted the election, which had the effect of handing the conservatives a victory.

In recognition of the struggle for human rights in Iran, the Nobel Committee awarded the Peace Prize in 2004 to lawyer Shirin Ebadi for her activism, especially on behalf of the rights of women and children. She is a member of the Iranian Jurists Association for the Defense of Human Rights, whose founding members included five lawyers who had previously been imprisoned and banned from practicing law for various periods by the Revolutionary Court. Not surprisingly, the fractious government responded with mixed signals to the award: Khatami lauded her, while many mullahs voiced misgivings, seeing the bestowal of the prize as a Western plot to undermine their power.

In advance of presidential elections in June 2005, the Iranian Supreme Court freed a prominent dissident, Abbas Abdi, who had been jailed for two years for releasing a poll showing that a majority of Iranians favored better relations with the United States. (He was convicted of the crime of "selling secrets to the enemy.") At the same time, the head of the judiciary, Ayatollah Mahmoud Shahroudi, made a startling admission, saying that prisoners had been victims of police abuse while in custody. He called these abuses a "great injustice," adding that he had obtained evidence showing that investigators had used force to exact confessions. Although most Iranians were already aware of these violations of human rights, it was the first time that such a highly placed member of the judiciary had publicly acknowledged the practice. Whether it was only a symbolic step or represented a determination on the government's part to curb such abuses remained unclear.

Reformers were dealt a setback when the Guardian Council, the supreme authority of the country, eliminated liberal candidates from running in the presidential elections. Disillusionment with Khatami and the absence of any reformer on the ballot prompted large numbers of Iranians to stay away from the polls, handing a victory to hard-liner Mahmoud Ahmadinejad in a run-off election in June 2005. A populist and former mayor of Tehran, he was swept into office largely on the strength of his promises to ease the economic burden of millions of poor Iranians.

Ahmadinejad can rely on a secure majority in parliament as well as the backing of the mullahs.

Further Reading:

Karsh, Efraim. *The Iran-Iraq War 1980–1988.* London: Osprey Publishing, 2002

Keddie, Nikki R. *Modern Iran: Roots and Results of Revolution.* New Haven, Conn.: Yale University Press, 2003.

Pollack, Kenneth. *The Persian Puzzle: The Conflict Between Iran and America.* New York: Random House, 2004.

Sciolino, Elaine. *Persian Mirrors: The Elusive Face of Iran.* New York: Free Press, 2001.

Iraq, human rights violations in post-Saddam

The chaos that enveloped Iraq after a U.S.-backed coalition toppled Saddam HUSSEIN in April 2003 has contributed to a persistent pattern of human rights abuses by authorities, including the Iraqi interim government and U.S. occupying forces. According to human rights organizations, with some support from the U.S. State Department's annual *Country Report* on Iraq, Iraqis were subject to beatings with rubber hoses and metal rods, TORTURE, and electric shock. Detainees were often kept blindfolded and handcuffed for days or placed in isolation and deprived of food and water. Iraqi police were also accused of seeking bribes from families to release prisoners or allow them access to prisoners. (It should be noted that these abuses are separate from any committed by American military and intelligence personnel at the Abu Ghraib prison and other detention facilities in Iraq that have received wider attention.)

What makes the situation even worse is that many of the police officers, intelligence agents, and jailers responsible for the abuses are the people who held the same position under Saddam's Baathist regime. A lack of manpower and experience has accounted for their retention, especially in light of relentless insurgent attacks. HUMAN RIGHTS WATCH charged in a January 2005 report that these officers are "committing systematic torture and other abuses" of detainees. "Many of the same people who worked in Saddam's time are still doing those jobs today. So there is a continuity of personnel and of mind-set," stated a representative of the human rights group. The problem is one that the government has acknowledged. The "shortcomings" of the security forces, said the Iraqi human rights minister Bakhtiar Amin, were due to the legacy of the old regime.

Human Rights Watch additionally accused interim prime minister Ayad Allawi of "actively taking part, or is at least (being) complicit, in these grave violations of fundamental human rights." (Allawi stepped down in 2005 after a newly elected, predominantly Shiite government was sworn in.) Legal safeguards, the group asserted, were being largely ignored. People were arrested without warrants and held for days, weeks, or longer without charges being brought. Suspects were frequently denied access to lawyers, and there was evidence of mistreatment of child prisoners. Police ignored summonses from judges, and some judges who insisted on formalities being observed were removed from their posts.

The interim government, for its part, noted that the priority was to ramp up security to combat the insurgency. Within the first four months of 2004 alone, some 1,300 police officers and thousands of civilians were killed, and the monthly death tolls continued to mount. All the same, Human Rights Watch contended that the unstable security situation could not justify mistreatment of detainees. The group's report, based on interviews with 90 current and former detainees, indicated that a sizable number were tortured or ill-treated and stated that these accounts were backed up by evidence of physical abuse. "I was beaten with cables and suspended by my hands tied behind my back," a 30-year-old Baghdad resident told the human rights investigators, "I saw young men there lying on the floor while police [stepped] on their heads with boots. It was worse than Saddam's regime." Many of the detainees were later released for lack of evidence. Human Rights Watch did point out that the abuses, as bad as they were, could not be compared to the considerably worse kinds of torture inflicted on victims of Saddam's torturers, which included mock executions, disfigurement with acid, and sexual assault of family members in front of detainees.

In most cases the abuses after the fall of Saddam have taken place without any interference from U.S. authorities. There was at least one exception. On June 29, 2004, scouts from an Oregon Army National Guard unit observed Iraqi guards abusing detainees. According to Captain Jarrell Southal of the National Guard unit, his men had observed bound prisoners in an Interior Ministry compound "writhing in pain" and complaining of lack of water. The National Guard intervened to help the detainees and placed the Iraqi guards under arrest.

The human rights abuses blamed on the fledgling Iraqi government have not received the same intensive media attention as those in which U.S. and allied occupation forces are involved. The most egregious abuses attributed to U.S. military and intelligence personnel have taken place in prisons and other detention facilities, especially at the notorious prison of Abu Ghraib. Under the Baathist regime of Saddam Hussein, Abu Ghraib was one of the most notorious torture and human rights abuse centers. Mistreatment of prisoners was to continue, albeit on a nonlethal scale, after the American occupation of Iraq in 2003. The interrogation center, where most of the abuses occurred, was set up in September 2003 in response to the growing insurgency; it held some 600 prisoners designated as "security detainees" because they were suspected of knowing about attacks against U.S. and coalition forces.

By the middle of 2005, several U.S. service personnel had been tried and most of them convicted of the human rights abuses of Iraqi prisoners. Two high-ranking officers were reprimanded, demoted, or fined: Colonel Thomas M. Pappas, commander the 205th Military Intelligence Brigade at the prison in late 2003, and Brigadier General Janis L. Karpinski, who commanded the military police unit in charge of Abu Ghraib around the same time. In August 2004 a high-level army inquiry by Major General George R. Fay and Lieutenant General Anthony R. Jones had recommended punishment for Colonel Pappas and Lieutenant Colonel Steven L. Jordan, who was in charge of the prison's interrogation center and reported to Colonel Pappas. Karpinski was demoted one rank, to colonel, for dereliction of duty; she has said that she was being made a scapegoat. There was little indication that anyone higher up the chain of command, whether military or civilian, would be implicated or tried for the mistreatment of prisoners. The abuses were initially documented in three reports, one by General Antonio Taguba, another by an independent panel chaired by former Defense Secretary James Schlesinger, and the third for the army by Fay and Jones.

Abu Ghraib was one of three facilities used by the U.S. military to hold Iraqi detainees. In early 2005 the number of those in custody at all three prisons was estimated to be 9,000. In March 2005 the Pentagon announced that 26 detainees had died as a result of criminal homicide in U.S. military facilities in both Iraq and Afghanistan, including Abu Ghraib. (Another 11 homicides were considered justifiable.) However, fewer than 10 lower-ranking military personnel had been tried for any abuses of detainees, most of whom received nonjudicial sentences such as demotion or dishonorable discharge.

The human rights abuses at Abu Ghraib first came to light with the publication of photographs taken by some of the U.S. personnel involved in the abuses. A substantial INTERNATIONAL COMMITTEE OF THE RED CROSS (ICRC) investigation in 2003 noted that Iraqi prisoners were being subjected to the following:

- hooding—with bags put over the eyes, sometimes also with the prisoner being beaten
- handcuffing with flexi-cuffs, which can harm circulation or cause skin lesions
- beatings with hard objects
- pressing the face into the ground with boots, threats of worse treatment (such as execution, or being sent to Guantanamo)
- being stripped naked and held in solitary confinement

- being held naked outside the cell, as shown in the notorious photographs of acts of humiliation; often sexual, with women guards present or actively participating
- being attached to walls in painful positions, often over the course of days
- exposure while hooded to loud music or excessive heat/sunshine
- being forced to remain for long periods in humiliating positions

The infamous photographs also showed prisoners being forced to perform or imitate obscene sexual acts, with women present, which was considered especially humiliating by the victims in the shame-orientated Arab culture. Revelations of mistreatment of Iraqi prisoners by U.S. soldiers have surfaced since the abuses at Abu Ghraib first came to light. In September 2005 three former members of the Army's 82nd Airborne Division claimed that soldiers in their battalion in Iraq used beatings and other forms of abuse in 2003 and 2004 in an effort to collect intelligence about the growing insurgency. According to statements given separately to HUMAN RIGHTS WATCH by the three—a captain and two sergeants—Iraqi prisoners were stacked in pyramids, exposed to extremes of temperature, and deprived of sleep at Camp Mercury, a forward operating base near Falluja, a Sunni city and hotbed of insurgency until a U.S.-led assault in April 2004. "We would give them blows to the head, chest, legs and stomach, and pull them down, kick dirt on them," one sergeant told Human Rights Watch "This happened every day." Between the initial Abu Ghraib disclosures in early 2004 and September 2005 the army had opened more than 400 inquiries into detainee abuse in Iraq and Afghanistan and punished 230 soldiers and officers.

Several British soldiers have also been indicted for similar human rights abuses, which occurred in the southern Iraqi city of Basra during was called Operation Breadbasket, an initiative designed to prevent the widespread looting after the fall of the Baathist regime. Several critics have pointed out that the abuse of prisoners in Abu Ghraib might be attributed to the decision to remove Geneva Convention rights from the prisoners taken in Afghanistan and subsequently detained in Guantánamo Bay, Cuba. The ICRC also noted that perhaps as many as 70 percent of Iraqis seized by U.S. troops later turned out to be innocent.

See also AFGHANISTAN, HUMAN RIGHTS VIOLATIONS IN; GUANTÁNAMO DETAINEES.

Further Reading:
Bodansky, Yossef. *The Secret History of the Iraq War.* New York: Regan Books, 2004.

Cordesman, Anthony H. *The Iraq War: Strategy, Tactics, and Military Lessons.* Washington, D.C.: Center for Strategic and International Studies, 2003.

Danner, Mark. *Torture and Truth: America, Abu Ghraib, and the War on Terror.* New York: New York Review Books, 2004.

Hersh, Seymour M. *Chain of Command: The Road from 9/11 to Abu Ghraib.* New York: HarperCollins, 2004.

Keegan, John. *The Iraq War.* New York: Knopf, 2004.

MacKey, Sandra. *The Reckoning: Iraq and the Legacy of Saddam Hussein.* New York: W. W. Norton & Company, 2003.

Iraq, war crimes in   *See* HUSSEIN, SADDAM AL-TIKRITI.

Irian Jaya, human rights violations in

See INDONESIA, HUMAN RIGHTS VIOLATIONS IN.

irregulars

Irregulars are defined as combatants who are not full-time members of an organized army; these include paramilitary groups, militias, resistance fighters, and volunteer corps. In Colombia's civil war, for instance, several opposing groups of irregulars—paramilitaries and two rebel movements—are engaged in the conflict in addition to the national army. Irregulars can, however, be part-time members of a country's armed forces. Switzerland's army, for instance, is made up to a large extent of uniformed militias. Irregulars who fight against the occupation of a country are often called partisans, whether they operate within the occupied territory or outside it.

Irregular forces are usually formed because of ideological or religious causes or because of a breakdown in society which leads to lawless conditions. Sometimes irregulars are constituted simply to make money, which is the case with mercenaries. Irregulars frequently shun formal uniforms and tend to melt into civilian populations, making it more difficult to distinguish them. International law does recognize irregulars as lawful combatants, thereby entitling them to prisoner-of-war status, within certain limitations. For one thing, they must be identifiable as combatants—that is, they cannot conduct operations disguised as civilians. For another, some type of command structure must exist. Irregulars cannot operate on their own or in ad hoc groups independent of any authority, and they are generally expected to obey international laws governing behavior in armed conflict. If irregulars do not comply with these standards, they may be arrested and tried as criminals.

In international conflicts, mercenaries are not protected by international law and are not entitled to be treated as PRISONERS OF WAR according to the legal definition found in Additional Protocol I to the GENEVA CONVENTIONS of 1949. In internal wars, a government is not obliged to treat armed insurgents as prisoners of war and may try them for treason or other crimes. But the freedom of governments to act against irregulars in internal conflicts is not unlimited. If an irregular is put on trial, the state is obliged to ensure that the trial is conducted in a "regularly constituted court, affording all the judicial guarantees which are recognized as indispensable by civilized people" as described by ARTICLE 3 COMMON TO THE GENEVA CONVENTIONS of 1949.

See also ADDITIONAL PROTOCOLS TO THE GENEVA CONVENTIONS.

Further Reading:
Gutman, Roy, ed. *Crimes of War: What the Public Should Know.* New York: W. W. Norton & Company, 1999.

Isayama, Harukei   *See* WAR CRIMINALS OF JAPAN.

Ishii, Chujo Shiro   *See* MANCHURIA, JAPANESE WAR CRIMES IN.

Israel   *See* PALESTINE, HUMAN RIGHTS VIOLATIONS IN; SABRA AND SHATILLA, MASSACRE IN.

Ivory Coast, human rights violations in

For decades the West African nation of Ivory Coast (Côte d'Ivoire) held an enviable reputation for stability and economic growth. All that changed in 1999 as long-festering ethnic and political tensions erupted into violence. Throughout the 1970s and 1980s the country was dominated by President Félix Houphouët-Boigny, one of the longest-living leaders on the continent. Opposition to his conservative, pro-business regime was generally muted so long as the economy of the former French colony continued to flourish. But Houphouët-Boigny began to show increasing signs of megalomania as he aged, which was manifested in grandiose building programs that the nation could ill afford.

In 1993 Houphouët-Boigny died in his seventh five-year term. After 33 years of one-man rule, there was no process in place for a smooth transition. His successor, Henri Konan Bédié, sought to consolidate his power by neutralizing his political opponents. He promulgated a law preventing his principal rival, Alassane Ouattara, a former World Bank and IMF official, from running for office on the grounds that his parents were not both born in the

Ivory Coast. There was more at issue than politics, though. Bédié's move was seen as a power grab that favored the mainly Christian south (Bédié's base) at the expense of the Muslim north of the country. Bédié played an anti-Muslim hand as much as he could, even castigating northerners as "foreigners"; there were "pure" and "impure" Ivorians. He badly miscalculated: In December 1999 his government was toppled in the first coup in the country's history. The man who replaced him, however—General Robert Gueï, also a Christian from the south—continued the same anti-Muslim policies, barring candidates who were not of Ivorian descent in the next scheduled presidential election.

Gueï's ability to control his own destiny was uncertain. According to some reports, Ivorian soldiers held his government hostage, demanding $9,000 each for their role in making him leader of the country. Even with Muslims boycotting the election, Gueï still lost to Laurent Gbagbo. When Gueï tried to annul the results in July 2000, he, too, was ousted from power in a popular uprising, and Gbagbo, who was also a Christian, declared himself the winner. In the days following the disputed election, clashes broke out between supporters of Gueï and the new regime on the one hand and between Christian supporters of Gbagbo and Muslim supporters of Ouattara on the other. The death toll reached 350 before Gbagbo and Ouattara both pledged that they would work for national reconciliation. About 60 bodies turned up in the outskirts of the capital, Abidjan, most of them shot in the head; it appeared that they were supporters of Ouattara's Rally of the Republicans party. UN secretary-general Kofi Annan established a commission of inquiry to investigate the killings. The commission found that security forces were to blame and called on the government to prosecute those responsible. According to an account from one survivor of the massacre, two security officers ordered all the men to lie on the ground and say their prayers. Then they began to open fire. "One kid was crying," recalled the survivor. "He begged them not to shoot him saying he was still in school. 'They didn't listen.'" The bodies were later doused with gasoline and burned.

Despite Gbagbo and Ouattara's pledge, no one seemed in much of a hurry to reach an accommodation. In September 2002 another military coup attempt occurred, and though it failed it precipitated an unprecedented surge of violence in the country that went on for months. The government continued to target the "impure" Ivorians: immigrants and Muslims. Troops burned down immigrant houses and mosques. Paramilitary forces publicly beat immigrants in the streets after stripping and robbing them. Immigrants found in the capital were at risk of being molested by gangs of machete-wielding youth. Nearly 1,200 civilians are believed to have been killed in the resulting turmoil. All sides in the conflict were blamed for atrocities and other grave human rights abuses. By 2003 no

fewer than three ethnic-based rebel groups were vying for control in the north and west of the country. At one point they were even poised to move on Abidjan.

In a French-brokered peace accord in early 2003, Gbagbo agreed to include rebel representatives in a new coalition government in return for the rebels' disarmament, but this never happened and the rebels remained shut out of power. In February 2003 the government called on the INTERNATIONAL CRIMINAL COURT in The Hague to investigate human rights abuses that had occurred in the aftermath of the thwarted coup attempt of the previous September. The Gbagbo regime claimed that rebels had massacred between 60 and 100 detained gendarmes and their children in the city of Bouake, a charge rebels denied. Nonetheless, there is good evidence that the rebels did carry out such a massacre, burying the victims in mass graves. Human rights violations were frequently observed in rebel-held territory that included arbitrary arrest and the forcible conscription of civilians.

The government maintained that it was in no position to conduct its own investigation because it lacked the manpower. If, however, the Ivorian authorities were hoping to deflect criticism from their own violations of human rights they were quickly disabused of the notion. The United Nations, which oversees the court, was also looking into reports of killings of alleged rebel supporters by government death squads in loyalist territory and exploring possible links between high-level officials and the gunmen. Allegations of death squad activity on the part of the government persisted. In February 2003 the then UNITED NATIONS HIGH COMMISSIONER FOR HUMAN RIGHTS Sergio Vieira de Mello (who would later die in a bombing in Baghdad) condemned the death squads and anti-Muslim propaganda that he said was stoking the fires of hatred and xenophobia. Gbagbo adamantly defended his human rights record, insisting there were no death squads and threatening to sue the French newspapers *Le Monde* and *La Croix* for carrying reports saying that death squads did exist. Ivory Coast, he contended, was not "governed by an assassin." The United Nations begged to differ; its Human Rights office issued a report asserting that individuals close to the government, including the presidential guards, and members of Gbagbo's Bete tribe were in fact linked to death squads. Approximately 200 EXTRAJUDICIAL KILLINGS are thought to have been carried out by the death squads in addition to several DISAPPEARANCES of government opponents. To complicate matters, the western part of the country was caught up in fighting between various Liberian groups in what was basically a proxy war, a result of a spillover of the chronic strife in Liberia.

A French-mediated peace treaty brought an end to the eight-month civil war, a conflict that had taken the lives of hundreds and displaced nearly a million people. To prevent war from breaking out again, French troops are deployed in a buffer zone separating the Muslim north from the Christian south. Even so, tensions remained high, demobilization of combatants had yet to make much progress, and violence continued throughout 2004, threatening the fragile peace accord. There are still reports of massacres in rebel-held territory in the north which have been confirmed by UN and AMNESTY INTERNATIONAL investigators. In one case, 75 bodies were pulled out of a container where they had apparently been imprisoned and suffocated to death—an incident labeled a "massacre" by the UN Security Council. The deaths occurred in a flare-up of factional fighting in June 2004. The government of President Laurent Gbagbo has been blamed for atrocities even after the cease-fire went into effect. Troops and militias loyal to the government have been accused of numerous abuses, including the killings of at least 120 people during and after an attempted March opposition rally in the commercial capital, Abidjan.

See also LIBERIA, HUMAN RIGHTS VIOLATIONS IN.

Izieu, children of

Until April 1944, over 40 Jewish refugee children ages four to 17 were safely quartered in an abandoned farmhouse in the remote village of Izieu in central France; they were under the supervision of seven adults. Their Jewish identity was concealed for their protection, and from most accounts their lives in Izieu were almost idyllic. The Children's House had been established in 1943 by a former Red Cross nurse, Sabina Zlatin, who codirected the home with her husband, Miron. In spite of their precautions, the house was raided by the GESTAPO, acting on the orders of Klaus BARBIE, who headed the German secret police in Lyon. No one was prepared for the raid, which took place on April 6, 1944, a French holiday, and only one person was able to escape. (Sabina Zlatin was in Montpellier at the time, seeking a safer refuge for the children.) Forty-four children and their seven supervisors were hauled off and thrown into trucks. The children were taken directly to the "collection center" in Drancy and placed on the first available train to an extermination camp in Poland. Forty-two children and five adults were gassed in Auschwitz. Two of the oldest children and Miron Zlatin were transported to Tallinn, Estonia, where they were executed. Not a single child from the Children's House survived, and only one adult did—27-year-old Lea Feldblum, who led the children to the selection point where she was forcibly separated from them by the Gestapo and sent to a prison camp.

At Barbie's trial a survivor of Auschwitz spoke of the absence of children at the camp. "I asked myself where were the children who arrived with us? In the camp there wasn't a single child to be seen. Then those who had been there for a while informed us of the reality. 'You see that chimney, the one smoke never stops coming out. . . . [Y]ou smell that odor of burned flesh. . . .'"

Further Reading:
Bower, Tom. *Klaus Barbie, the Butcher of Lyons.* New York: Pantheon Books, 1984.
Dabringhaus, Erhard. *Klaus Barbie: The Shocking Story of How the U.S. Used This Nazi War Criminal as an Intelligence Agent.* New York: Acropolis Books, 1984.
Klarsfeld, Serge. *The Children of Izieu: A Human Tragedy.* Farmington Hills, Mich.: Holocaust Library, 1995.

Jackson, Robert Houghwout (1892–1954) *U.S. prosecutor at the Nuremberg Trials*

Robert Houghwout Jackson would have earned a place in the history books as a U.S. Supreme Court justice, but he is best known for his role as the lead prosecutor at the NUREMBERG TRIALS. Born in Spring Creek, Pennsylvania, on February 13, 1892, Jackson never earned a college degree. What formal education in law that he received was a single year taking classes at Albany Law School. He spent the first 42 years of his life raising a family, practicing law, and becoming involved in Democratic politics in New York at a time when Franklin Delano Roosevelt was serving as governor. Shortly after being elected president, Roosevelt asked Jackson to move to Washington to become general counsel at the Internal Revenue Service. Two years later, in 1936, Jackson became U.S. assistant attorney general, and over the next four years he gained a reputation for pursuing antitrust cases. In 1940 Roosevelt appointed him attorney general, the highest post in the Justice Department. But he had barely had a chance to settle into his new position when a vacancy on the Supreme Court prompted Roosevelt to name Jackson as a justice.

In 1945, after the end of World War II, President Harry Truman asked Jackson to represent the United States as chief prosecutor at the Nuremberg Trials. Jackson had long been an advocate of holding such trials. He maintained that only a legal proceeding could establish the guilt or innocence of the high-ranking Nazi officials and that it would not serve justice to simply execute the worst offenders without a trial as some Allies preferred. Truman believed that someone with Jackson's reputation and credentials was necessary to lead the prosecution team. For Jackson this was an unprecedented opportunity to establish a set of standards that would apply to aggressive war, crimes against peace, and CRIMES AGAINST HUMANITY. (Until this point, INTERNATIONAL HUMANITARIAN LAW had largely been concerned with behavior of belligerents in international conflicts but said little about a government violating the rights of its own citizens.)

Granted a leave of absence from the High Court, Jackson helped draft the London Charter of the International Military Tribunal, which formed the legal framework for the tribunal's mandate and established new standards in international law. Jackson worked for two months in summer 1945 to reach an agreement that would satisfy the U.S., British, French, and Soviet governments. The London Charter was signed on August 8, 1945. A little over a year later, the International Military Tribunal began hearing cases in Nuremberg. Jackson, an aggressive prosecutor who did not mince words, proved worthy of Truman's trust. At one point he called Hermann GÖRING "half militarist, half

Justice Robert H. Jackson *(Library of Congress)*

gangster." The trials established several significant precedents, including the principle that an individual could be found guilty of crimes even if he were only carrying out the policies of the state, as long as he was aware of the consequences of his action. Henceforth a person could not use the defense that he was "only following orders."

Many of the standards that guided the Nuremberg Trials were later incorporated into the GENEVA CONVENTIONS of 1949. With the conclusion of the trials, Jackson returned to the Supreme Court. In 1954 he joined the unanimous opinion of the landmark *Brown v. Board* decision that outlawed school segregation. Not long afterward, at the age of 62, he suffered a fatal heart attack. The epitaph on his grave in Frewsburg, New York, is as accurate as it is succinct. It reads: "He kept the ancient landmarks and built the new."

Further Reading:

Bosch, William J. *Judgment on Nuremberg: American Attitudes toward the Major German War-Crime Trials.* Durham: University of North Carolina Press, 1970.

Gilbert, G. M. *Nuremberg Diary.* New York: Da Capo Press, 1995.

Goldensohn, Leon, and Robert Gellately, eds. *The Nuremberg Interviews.* New York: Knopf, 2004.

Marrus, Michael R. *The Nuremberg War Crimes Trial of 1945–46: A Documentary History.* Bedford Series in History and Culture. Sidney, Australia: Palgrave Macmillan, 1997.

Maser, Werner. *Nuremberg: A Nation on Trial.* New York: Scribner, 1979.

Persico, Joseph. *Nuremberg: Infamy on Trial.* New York: Penguin Books, 1995.

Rice, Earle. *The Nuremberg Trials.* Famous Trials Series. San Diego, Calif.: Lucent Books, 1997.

Taylor, Telford. *The Anatomy of the Nuremberg Trials: A Personal Memoir.* New York: Little Brown & Co, 1993.

———. *Nuremberg Trial: War Crimes and International Law.* New York: Carnegie Endowment for International Peace, 1949.

Tusa, Ann, and John Tusa. *The Nuremberg Trials.* New York: Cooper Square Publishers, 2003.

Jamaica, human rights violations in

The Caribbean nation of Jamaica has significantly improved its human rights record since the tumult of the late 1970s and early 1980s. Recent elections have taken place peacefully in sharp contrast to the violence that marred the 1980 vote, which had claimed 800 lives. Nonetheless, serious problems persist. According to the U.S. State Department, unlawful killings remain a problem. Many of the killings by police have occurred while apprehending criminals. In 2002, 149 deaths were recorded during "encounters" between police and suspects, including those of 16 police officers, down from 163 such deaths in 2001. Not all of these deaths were likely to have been unlawful, even though allegations of "police murder" are frequently made. The government has, however, taken steps to investigate these reports and institute criminal investigations.

Crime is a terrible problem in the country, with an alarmingly high homicide rate exceeding 40 per 100,000 persons. Many inner cities have fallen under the control of armed gangs, some of them better equipped than the police and capable of carrying out targeted assaults against police and their families. Civil order is also threatened by vigilantism and spontaneous mob killings in response to the crime. At least 11 vigilante killings were recorded in 2002; some of the victims were specifically targeted, while others were killed as a result of spontaneous mob action. In one case a mob beat to death a man accused of committing several rapes and robberies; in another incident a mob stabbed a bus driver 56 times and slashed his throat after he and a passenger got into an altercation. Human rights advocates contend that the police do not take these cases seriously and never make any attempt to arrest the perpetrators.

Prison guards are still implicated in the TORTURE and abuse of prisoners and detainees, even though torture is prohibited by law and the government has tried to remove abusive guards. Juvenile detainees continue to be housed in adult prisons, even though this practice, too, is banned by law. According to a report by HUMAN RIGHTS WATCH, many children—often as young as 12 or 13—are detained for six months or more in filthy and overcrowded police lockups, putting them at risk of abuse by other inmates and their guards.

Janković, Gojko   *See* WAR CRIMINALS OF THE FORMER YUGOSLAVIA.

Japanese war crimes   *See* CHINA, HUMAN RIGHTS VIOLATIONS IN; MANCHURIA, JAPANESE WAR CRIMES IN; TOKYO TRIALS; WAR CRIMINALS OF JAPAN.

Jedwabne, massacre in

On July 10, 1941, Polish inhabitants of the town of Jedwabne massacred nearly 1,600 Jewish residents after the town was occupied by German forces. Only about a dozen Jews survived. The massacre would have remained an obscure incident—one of countless atrocities committed during World War II—were it not for the 2001 publication of the book *Neighbors*, by Jan Gross, which recounted the horrific episode. The revelations caused a great deal of furor and self-examination among Poles.

The massacre was precipitated by the arrival of a small detachment of German troops, who reached the town on June 23, 1941. German racial policies encouraged pogroms against Jews and other "undesirables" in areas that fell under their control. Their appearance in Jedwabne triggered a few outbursts of violence against Jews: One man was stoned to death, and another was stabbed and his eyes and tongue cut out. The surge in killings that took place several days later, however, seemed to take even the Nazi occupiers by surprise. "Was eight hours not enough for you to do with the Jews as you please?" one commander asked the Polish leadership of the town. The mayor insisted that the killings had to go on. "We have to destroy all the Jews," the mayor was quoted as saying, "no one should stay alive." Although the mayor orchestrated the killings, "people were free to improvise," Gross writes. Most of the victims were burned alive in a barn. "As for the little children," one witness said, "they roped a few together by their legs and carried them on their backs, then put them on pitchforks and threw them onto smoldering coals." According to Gross, half of the town's adult male population took part in the killings of their neighbors. The Germans limited their role to photographing the event.

On the 60th anniversary of the Jedwabne massacre, Polish president Aleksander Kwasniewski officially apologized for the part Poles played in the 1941 pogrom. Addressing a crowd of thousands, he declared, "We know with all certainty that among the persecutors and butchers there were Poles. Here in Jedwabne, citizens of the Polish Republic died at the hands of other citizens. . . . Because of that crime we should beg the forgiveness of the shades of the victims and their families. I therefore apologize here today, as a citizen and as the president of the Polish Republic. I apologize on my own behalf and on behalf of those Poles whose consciences have been stirred by that crime, who believe that one cannot be proud of Polish history's greatness without simultaneously feeling pain and shame at the evil committed by Poles against others."

Further Reading:

Gross, Jan. *Neighbors: The Destruction of the Jewish Community in Jedwabne, Poland.* New York: Penguin, 2002.

Jelisić, Goran   *See* WAR CRIMINALS OF THE FORMER YUGOSLAVIA.

Jemaah Islamiyah

Jemaah Islamiyah (JI) is a militant Islamist group active in several Southeast Asian countries. Its avowed mission is to establish a Muslim fundamentalist state in the region. There is some evidence that the group has links to al-QAEDA, although the exact nature of the association is unclear. JI has been linked to attacks or plots against U.S. and Western targets in Indonesia, Singapore, and the Philippines. Documents seized in raids by police indicate that the group also targeted leaders and senior officials of nations in the region, including President Megawati Sukarnoputri of Indonesia. The most spectacular strike attributed to JI occurred on October 12, 2002, when bombs killed 202 people, mostly Australians, at a Bali nightclub. The group is also suspected of a car bombing of the J. W. Marriott hotel in Jakarta that killed 12 in August 2002.

The terrorist network extends across Indonesia, Malaysia, the Philippines, Singapore, and Thailand. Smaller cells may also exist in Cambodia and Vietnam; there is even some possibility that it has managed to infiltrate Australia. An outgrowth of a militant Muslim movement known as Darul Islam, the IJ was formed in the mid-1980s by two Indonesian clerics, Abdullah Sungkar and Abu Bakar BASHIR. The former took charge of the group's political and strategic operations, while the latter assumed the role of spiritual leader. It is believed that Sungkar established relations with al-Qaeda in the mid-1990s, which caused IJ to take on a more militant cast. Although the authorities are divided on the number of hard-core JI members, the consensus view is that it ranges from several hundred to several thousand. The U.S. State Department estimates that IJ has 200 members in Malaysia alone. However, its vision of a fundamentalist Islamic state that would dominate Southeast Asia is not one widely embraced among the region's 300 million Muslims. In recent years several of its leaders, including its operational chief, Nurjaman Riduan Ismuddin, also known as Hambali, and Abu Bakar Bashir have been arrested and large caches of weapons and explosives seized. There are also reports that internal dissension has weakened the group's ability to coordinate attacks across the region, although it is believed to have retained an ability to carry out terrorist strikes.

Further Reading:

Burke, Jason. *Al-Qaeda: Casting a Shadow of Terror.* London: I.B.Tauris, 2004.
———. *Al-Qaeda: The True Story of Radical Islam.* London: I.B.Tauris, 2004.
Gunaratna, Rohan. *Inside Al Qaeda: Global Network of Terror.* New York: Berkley Publishing Group, 2003.
Mayer, Ann Elizabeth. *Islam and Human Rights: Tradition and Politics.* Philadelphia: Westview Press, 1998.
Zayy-at, Montassar al-. *The Road to Al-Qaeda: The Story of Bin Laden's Right-Hand Man.* Critical Studies on Islam. Translated by Ahmed Fekry. Edited by Sara Nimis. Ann Arbor, Mich.: Pluto Press, 2004.

Jiang Yanyong (Chiang Yen-Yung) (1931–) *Chinese human rights advocate*

A nationally known Chinese surgeon, Jiang Yanyong broke with the Communist Party to bring attention to the emerging outbreak of Severe Acute Respiratory Syndrome, or SARS, a deadly viral epidemic that broke out in Asia in 2003. Until the emergence of SARS in China, Jiang Yanyong had been a loyal member of the Communist Party. Alarmed by the official suppression of news of the outbreak, Jiang, then 72, leaked word of the epidemic to the media. Jiang was spurred to action when he watched the health minister go on national television to assure the world that there were only a handful of SARS cases and that there was no public health hazard. "As a doctor," he wrote in a letter posted on a Web site, "I have a responsibility to aid international and local efforts to prevent the spread of SARS."

The news soon spread around the world, as Jiang had intended. The World Health Organization (WHO), based in Geneva, issued a travel advisory warning travelers to shun certain parts of China. Other physicians were motivated to come forward with what they knew, although, unlike Jiang, only under conditions of anonymity. Jiang's initiative forced the government to acknowledge the extent of the epidemic and to take concerted action to contain it. Jiang used his fame as a crusading physician to bring attention to the government's continuing failure to acknowledge its responsibility for the 1989 Tiananmen Square massacres of prodemocracy demonstrators. In February 2004 he wrote a letter to Communist Party officials, demanding an admission of guilt in the killings. Jiang himself had treated scores of people injured in the crackdown. After he provided copies of the letter to the foreign press, the government arrested Jiang and his wife. His detention—in advance of the 16th anniversary of the Tiananmen Square uprising—stirred international outrage, and a month later, in late July 2004, the government released the couple.

See also CHINA, HUMAN RIGHTS VIOLATION IN.

Jodl, Alfred (1890–1946) *Nazi general*

Alfred Jodl was a high-ranking German general who, as head of the armed forces operations staff, orchestrated much of the planning and conduct of Nazi Germany's military campaigns during World War II. He was convicted of war crimes and GENOCIDE at the NUREMBERG TRIALS after the war. Born in Würzburg, Germany, on May 10, 1890, Jodl was groomed for a military career. After attending cadet school, he joined a field military regiment in 1910 as an artillery officer. When war broke out, he was sent to the western front, where he was wounded twice. Following the war, Jodl stayed in the army, whose size was severely limited by the terms of the armistice. In 1923 he made the acquaintance of the head of the fledgling NSDAP (National Socialist Party), Adolf HITLER. Like Hitler, he believed that the Versailles treaty, which ended the First World War, was a straitjacket from which Germany must escape. In 1935, two years after the Nazis came to power, Jodl won a promotion as chief of the National Defense Section in the High Command of the armed forces.

In August 1939 Jodl was promoted to chief of operation staff of the High Command. From that point on he provided advice and technical information to Hitler as preparations for war intensified. In September 1939 he took part in the German invasion of Poland that marked the beginning of the Second World War. Working closely with Wilhelm Keitel, the High Command chief of staff, he became instrumental in conducting all of Germany's military campaigns (with the exception of the launch of the Soviet invasion in the second half of 1941). He explicitly stated that his aims were the same as Hitler's and proved as good as his word: In carrying out military operations, Jodl showed no compunction about ordering the shooting of HOSTAGES. In Norway he was responsible for the forcible evacuation of civilians and had their homes burned to prevent them from helping the Soviets—clear violations of international law. He condoned an order providing for the execution of enemy civilians found guilty of offenses against German troops without a military trial. At the same time he ensured that German troops would never face punishment if they killed civilians.

In July 1944 Jodl came close to being killed in a failed assassination attempt on Hitler's life. In his last official act, he signed Germany's unconditional surrender to the Allies in May 1945 in Reims, France. He was subsequently arrested and transferred to an American prisoner-of-war camp before being put on trial in Nuremberg on charges of conspiracy to commit crimes against peace; planning, initiating, and waging wars of aggression; war crimes; and CRIMES AGAINST HUMANITY. He pleaded not guilty "before God, before history and my people." Found guilty on all four charges, he was sentenced to death and was hanged on October 16, 1946. His complicity in GENOCIDE and other crimes was not accepted by many Germans, however, and in 1953 a German arbitration board posthumously acquitted Jodl of all charges.

Jordan, human rights violations in

Jordan is one of several artificial countries created by Britain in the 1920s in the aftermath of the defeat of the Ottoman Empire in 1918. Unlike Iraq, another artificial state, whose royal family was massacred in 1958, the British-imposed Hashemite monarchy has survived, with King Hussein spending decades delicately poised on his

Children playing in the streets of the Baqa'a refugee camp, Amman, Jordan *(Stephenie Hollyman/United Nations/DPI)*

throne while the Middle East around him was embroiled in turmoil.

In 1948 Jordan, which originally was a Bedouin Arab state, found itself playing grudging host to thousands of Palestinian refugees fleeing the forces of the new Jewish state of Israel. There is considerable dispute over how many Palestinians were forced to leave and how many were driven out because of fear for their safety. Nonetheless, the presence of so many Palestinians in Jordan has been a source of friction and at times jeopardized the stability of the state. The monarchy's main source of security remains the Bedouin-based armed forces—King Hussein ruthlessly suppressed Palestinian dissent, especially during the early 1970s when a Palestinian uprising threatened to topple the regime—but the present, Western-educated, King Abdullah II has wisely married a Palestinian wife, Queen Rania, and sought to allay resentment. Tensions between the indigenous and Palestinian population, however, continue to make Jordan a politically fragile state.

Jordan has been called a "façade democracy," based on limited parliamentary elections which have been held since 1989. However, real power rests in the monarchy. In the past, the U.S. State Department has accused the Jor-

danian security forces—the General Intelligence Directorate and the Public Security Directorate—of extensive human rights abuses. In spite of a continuing number of deaths in police custody, human rights observers have noted an improvement in the human rights situation since 2003, when 245 political prisoners were released. Nonetheless, the legal system has been slow to prosecute so-called "honor killings" in which women are murdered—often in brutal circumstances—for alleged crimes against the honor of the husband's family. It should be noted, though, that educated, professional women enjoy considerably more freedom in Jordan than in neighboring Arab states.

See also PALESTINE, HUMAN RIGHTS VIOLATIONS IN.

journalists, protection of

Under INTERNATIONAL HUMANITARIAN LAW, accredited journalists accompanying an enemy armed force are protected under the Third Geneva Convention. Journalists are considered a legitimate part of the military unit. For instance, reporters embedded with the U.S.-backed coalition in the 2003 invasion of Iraq were accorded legal protections, but so were nonembedded reporters who covered the war as long as they were working for a legitimate news source.

If captured, journalists are to be treated like PRISONERS OF WAR (POWs). The Third Geneva Convention explicitly classifies war correspondents along with other essential, though nonuniformed personnel—chaplains or civilian contractors, for instance. Reporters can be detained only for "imperative reasons of security." Although they cannot be subject to interrogation (no more than POWs) the captor does have the right to confiscate their notes or film.

Distinguishing a correspondent from a combatant has become a more critical issue in recent years. Until the Vietnam War, war correspondents often wore army fatigues in war zones. However, Additional Protocol I of 1977 cautions journalists that they may not be assured of the Geneva protections if their clothing resembles the uniforms worn by combatants. Additional Protocol 1 further calls for governments to issue official identity cards to journalists. In spite of the rights conferred by international humanitarian law, war correspondents have been injured, killed, or kidnapped in increasing numbers in conflicts in many parts of the world, especially in Afghanistan, Iraq, and Chechnya. A record number of journalists were killed in 2003—more than in any other year in nearly a decade and nearly double the number in 2002. According to the COMMITTEE TO PROTECT JOURNALISTS, 36 were killed in 2003 as a direct result of their work. Of these, 19 were killed in Iraq, 13 by hostile acts (the others died in accidents); this was the highest casualty rate for any single country since 24 journalists died covering the civil war in Algeria in 1995. The toll of journalists killed in wartime mounted in 2004 because of the Iraqi war. By year's end, 54 journalists had been killed throughout the world—23 in Iraq alone, most of them Iraqis. By September 2005 about 40 journalists had been killed including almost 20 in Iraq. Reporters Without Borders declared Iraq the deadliest in the world for the profession. The Philippines recorded the next largest toll—eight killed in 2004 and 48 altogether from 1986, when democracy was restored, to 2004.

See also ADDITIONAL PROTOCOLS TO THE GENEVA CONVENTIONS; GENEVA CONVENTIONS.

Further Reading:
Garrels, Anne. *Naked in Baghdad: The Iraq War as Seen by NPR's Correspondent Anne Garrels*. New York: Farrar, Straus and Giroux, 2003.

Gutman, Roy, ed. *Crimes of War: What the Public Should Know*. New York: W. W. Norton & Company, 1999.

just and unjust wars

A just war is considered to be one that is fought in self-defense under Article 51 of the United Nations Charter. A whole body of theory has evolved to describe when a war can be justified, but in general the premise is that there is a set of rules of combat mutually agreed upon between belligerents of equal status. By the same token, an unjust war is considered one that is characterized by illegal aggression.

The term *just war* has to some extent been replaced by *legitimate use of force*. Only if the belligerents are equally matched in a just war is it possible to wage a war predicated on certain explicit standards of conduct on the battlefield or to reach an equitable peace accord once the conflict has ended. Tactics should not be used, for instance, that would incite an endless cycle of vengeance. Some just-war theorists, however, argue that the principle of symmetry should be abandoned and that the rules of war should apply to all belligerents equally. The problem for just-war theorists is to derive consistent principles to deal with wars of all kinds.

Just war is guided by several principles which were first summed up by Hugo GROTIUS, the 17th-century Dutch philosopher who drew on the work of medieval Catholic theologians.

1. It must have a just cause.
2. It must be declared by a proper authority.
3. It must be instituted with the right intention.
4. It must be undertaken only as a last resort.
5. It must be undertaken with peace as a goal (not war for its own sake).
6. It must have a reasonable chance of success.
7. Its ends must be proportional to the means.

The principle that a state has to have a just cause—*jus ad bellum*—can be put another way; that is, a war is considered just if it is initiated in self-defense. Self-defense can, however, entail the use of aggressive force. Aggressive action is not necessarily an unjust war if it is undertaken in response to a violation of territory, an insult to national honor, a trade embargo, or even a threat to an ally. In 1967, for instance, Israel attacked Egypt in response to the pullout of a UN peacekeeping force and an Egyptian blockade of a major Israeli port. Aggressive war is considered permissible only if its purpose is to retaliate against a wrong already perpetrated by another party or to prevent such a wrong from recurring. Although this principle seems straightforward, it raises other concerns such as the relationship of a government to its people. If, for instance, a government effectively represents the people within its jurisdiction, it has more right to respond to a hostile action than if it is a government that rules its citizens under duress. For instance, Vichy France, the collaborationist state established by Nazi Germany in 1940, would have little authority to carry out a just war since its very legitimacy was disputed.

A just war has to have a reasonable chance of meeting with success. A war might prove too costly in terms of blood, money, or political capital to justify even if the belligerent contemplating action is stronger than its opponent. The objective of the war should also be proportional to the means employed to attain it. Under this principle, Country A might have the right to attack Country B to retake territory that B has seized from A. However, if Country A then proceeds to annex territory that originally belonged to B, it would be in violation of this principle. In that case Country A would potentially find itself in control of a hostile population and be in violation of international law. What began as a war for a just cause would have become an unjust war because of the result.

The concept of just wars has a long history. It is embodied in Roman law, Christian encyclicals, and scholastic tradition as well as the medieval notions of chivalry and honor. In contemporary times, however, what constitutes a just or unjust war is subject to varying interpretations and vigorous debate. It is difficult to consider just war exclusively in terms of two more or less equal belligerents in a world filled with national liberation struggles, internal conflicts, and jihads.

Further Reading:
Gutman, Roy, ed. *Crimes of War: What the Public Should Know*. New York: W. W. Norton & Company, 1999.

Orford, Anne, James Crawford, and John Bell, eds. *Reading Humanitarian Intervention: Human Rights and the*

Use of Force in International Law. Cambridge Studies in International and Comparative Law. Cambridge: Cambridge University Press, 2003.

Weissman, Fabrice. *In the Shadow of "Just Wars": Violence, Politics, and Humanitarian Action.* Ithaca, N.Y.: Cornell University Press, 2004.

Welsh, Jennifer M. *Humanitarian Intervention and International Relations.* Oxford: Oxford University Press, 2004.

Wheeler, Nicholas J. *Saving Strangers: Humanitarian Intervention in International Society.* Oxford: Oxford University Press, 2003.

K

Kaltenbrunner, Ernst (1903–1946) *chief of SS Intelligence*

Austrian-born Ernst Kaltenbrunner headed the Austrian SS and later became chief of SS Intelligence after the assassination of his predecessor, Reinhard HEYDRICH, in June 1942. He was convicted at the NUREMBERG TRIALS of several crimes, including mass murders of civilians in occupied regions, establishing CONCENTRATION CAMPS, and the killings of PRISONERS OF WAR. Born on October 4, 1903, Kaltenbrunner earned a law degree, following the example of his father, and set up practice in Linz. In 1932 he joined the Nazi Party, and two years he later became head of the Austrian SS. In the same year he was arrested in connection with the assassination of the Austrian chancellor, Engelbert Dollfuss, who had sought to keep the Nazi Party from gaining influence. Found guilty of conspiracy, Kaltenbrunner was sentenced to six months in prison.

In 1938, under intense pressure from Adolf HITLER, Austria was annexed to Germany—what is known as the Anschluss. Kaltenbrunner's star was in the ascendant; he became minister for state security as well as assuming a dual role as both chief of police and *Gruppenführer*, or commander in chief, of the SS in Vienna. When Heydrich was assassinated by Czech partisans in 1942, Kaltenbrunner was appointed to step into his shoes as head of the SD (Sicherheitsdienst), which gave him the control over the GESTAPO and the concentration camp system. In his latter role he was implicated in the extermination of several million Jews; in addition, he was responsible for the murder of captured Allied commandos and parachutists and prisoners of war. An impressive figure, standing nearly seven feet tall, with a face marked by dueling scars, he was reported to have derived considerable pleasure from the killings, taking a personal interest in the methods of extermination. A rabid anti-Semite, he endorsed the idea of using poison gas to exterminate Jews at an accelerated rate. On at least one occasion he observed executions at the gas chamber at Mauthausen, a concentration camp he had helped develop.

When news reached Kaltenbrunner in July 1944 that Hitler had been killed in an assassination attempt—a report that turned out to be false—he reacted calmly and asked whether anyone wished to play cards with him while they waited to learn about future developments. But there was no doubt about Kaltenbrunner's loyalty to Hitler; he took charge of the investigation into the conspiracy and arrested many of the plotters, who were later executed. In the final days of the war, as the Red Army was closing in on Berlin, Kaltenbrunner gave orders that all prisoners in the concentration camps were to be killed; he then tried to flee south, only to be captured by Allied troops. Brought up before the Nuremberg Tribunal, Kaltenbrunner was charged with 10 counts of war crimes and crimes against humanity. He was found guilty and hanged on October 16, 1946.

Further Reading:

Browder, George C. *Hitler's Enforcers: The Gestapo and the SS Security Service in the Nazi Revolution.* Oxford: Oxford University Press, 1996.

Butler, Rupert. *The Gestapo: A History of Hitler's Secret Police 1933–45.* Havertown, Pa.: Casemate Publishers and Book Distributors, 2004.

Hohne, Heinz Zollen. *The Order of the Death's Head: The Story of Hitler's SS.* Classic Military History. New York: Penguin, 2001.

Kambanda, Jean *See* RWANDA HUMAN RIGHTS VIOLATORS.

Karadžić, Radovan (1945–) *Bosnian Serb nationalist and war criminal*

Radovan Karadžić has become one of the world's most wanted men. As the leader of a Bosnian Serb nationalist organization, he faces trial in The Hague on charges of GENOCIDE and CRIMES AGAINST HUMANITY. He gained international notoriety for initiating a campaign of terror against Bosnian Muslims during the conflict that erupted following the breakup of the former Yugoslavia in the 1990s. In some respect Karadžić's background makes him an improbable war criminal: He was once a poet and a bohemian who practiced as a psychiatrist. A burly man with a memorable crown of white hair, he was born in Montenegro (still a part of Yugoslavia) in 1945. He was inculcated in Serbian nationalism at an early age; his father, Vuk, had fought with the Chetniks, the Serb nationalist guerrillas who had fought against both the Nazi occupiers and communist partisans. Young Radovan saw little of his father growing up since Vuk was serving a prison sentence for his Serbian activism during the war. His mother, Jovankas, has described Radovan as a serious boy who respected the elderly, lent her a hand at home, and was always willing to help his schoolmates do their homework—in other words, a model son.

During the early 1960s Karadžić moved to Sarajevo, a cosmopolitan and ethnically diverse city in Bosnia, where he pursued a bohemian lifestyle and wrote poetry. In 1967 he married a psychoanalyst, the daughter of an old and wealthy Serb family. The new bride was not welcomed by his poet friends, who thought she was unattractive and domineering and suspected that he had married her for money. During this period, Karadžić regularly read his poems on radio and television. One of his poems, published in 1971, was meant to evoke the resentments of impoverished Yugoslav peasants. It is entitled "Let's Go Down to the Town and Kill Some Scum."

In 1967 Karadžić fell under the influence of Dobrica Ćosić, a Serbian writer and politician, who encouraged him to become politically active on behalf of the Serbian cause. It was not until the death of Tito, who had ruled over the country since the end of World War II, that Yugoslavia began to splinter apart. The turning point came in 1989 when Slobodan MILOŠEVIĆ rallied restive Serbs in Kosovo. His fiery speech is widely considered to have unleashed a wave of Serb nationalism that over the next six years would lead to three successive Balkan wars. The precipitating cause of the crisis was the presence of significant Serbian populations in predominantly Muslim Bosnia-Herzegovina and Catholic Croatia. By declaring themselves independent states, Bosnia and Croatia were dividing the Serbs, a prospect that Milošević vowed to oppose by any means possible. In Karadžić Milošević had found an ideal disciple. A writer who knew Karadžić for many years described him in an interview with *Time* magazine as "like clay," and as "a person without personality . . . without character, who could be molded. . . ."

Karadžić joined Initiative for a Serbian Democratic Party, which Milošević had founded to advance Serbian nationalism in Bosnia. Its motto was "All Serbs in one nation." It did not take long before Karadžić rose to the leadership of the new party (later called the Serbian Democratic Party), which one reporter described as consisting "of little more than a collection of bullies and thugs." It wasn't difficult for Karadžić and his fellow nationalists to persuade Serbs that the Muslims were bent on installing an exclusionist Islamic republic in the heart of the Balkans. At the same time Croats were derided as "Nazis." But in Karadžić's estimation Serbs could do no wrong; they were peaceful and kind and incapable of hatred. When he was reminded that Bosnian Serbs only made up one-third of Bosnia's population, Karadžić was characteristically dismissive, contending that they had been a majority in the past. "Serbian graves must be counted as well."

In April 1992 thousands of residents of Sarajevo (which only a few years previously had played host to the Winter Olympics) marched through the city to demonstrate for peace. Karadžić's bodyguards climbed to the roof of his party headquarters and began firing into the crowd without provocation, killing six people. In weeks some 60,000 Serbs had fled the city, creating in effect a Muslim enclave. Serbian paramilitary units and regular Yugoslavian forces laid siege to the city, raining fire on the helpless inhabitants. But when pressed by diplomats or reporters, Karadžić adamantly denied that Serbs were responsible for committing atrocities. When several Bosnians were slaughtered in a particularly gruesome incident known as the Marketplace Massacre, Karadžić insisted that many of the bodies be removed from the morgue and placed in the square for propaganda purposes. He said that this could be proven because the bodies had ice in their ears. He even went so far as to accuse the Muslims of shelling themselves to arouse world opinion against the Serbs.

In a meeting with Karadžić at the time, former U.S. ambassador to Yugoslavia Warren Zimmerman observed the frequency with which the Serb used violent imagery in his language—words like *war*, GENOCIDE, *annihilation*, and *hell*. Serbs were "the eternal victims" who were only defending themselves against Croats and Muslims. But time was running out. Under international pressure, reinforced by NATO bombing, Milošević agreed to a peace settlement brokered by Washington in Dayton, Ohio, in 1995. The settlement, known as the DAYTON ACCORDS, ended the Bosnian war and paved the way for NATO peacekeepers to enforce a truce among the warring factions. Karadžić then went into hiding.

In July 1995 the United Nations indicted Karadžić and Bosnian Serb army chief Ratko MLADIĆ on charges relating to the long siege of Sarajevo (1992–95), which took the lives of 10,000 civilians in the city. Karadžić is also accused of using 284 UN peacekeepers as HUMAN SHIELDS in May and June 1995 and of organizing the 1995 massacre of more than 7,000 Muslim men and boys in Srebrenica. According to the official UN indictment, Karadžić and Mladić "between April 1992 and July 1995, in the territory of the Republic of Bosnia and Herzegovina, by their acts and omissions, and in concert with others, committed a crime against humanity by persecuting Bosnian Muslim and Bosnian Croat civilians on national, political and religious grounds." Further, they are being held accountable for being "criminally responsible for the unlawful confinement, murder, rape, sexual assault, TORTURE, beating, robbery and inhumane treatment of civilians; the targeting of political leaders, intellectuals and professionals; the unlawful deportation and transfer of civilians; the unlawful shelling of civilians; the unlawful appropriation and plunder of real and personal property; the destruction of homes and businesses; and the destruction of places of worship."

Before his disappearance, Karadžić denied the accusations, refusing to acknowledge the legitimacy of the INTERNATIONAL CRIMINAL TRIBUNAL FOR THE FORMER YUGOSLAVIA established by the United Nations to prosecute war crimes. "If The Hague was a real juridical body I would be ready to go there to testify or do so on television," he asserted, "but it is a political body that has been created to blame the Serbs." There is speculation that Karadžić took refuge in the mountainous region of the Republika Srpska, an autonomous Bosnian Serbian enclave, or that he is now living in Belgrade. Repeated searches of his hometown and suspected hiding places have failed to turn him up, heightening suspicions that he is being protected by a network of politically connected supporters.

See also BOSNIA AND HERZEGOVINA, HUMAN RIGHTS VIOLATIONS IN; CROATIA, HUMAN RIGHTS VIOLATIONS IN; SARAJEVO, SIEGE OF; SREBRENICA, MASSACRE IN; YUGOSLAVIA, WAR CRIMES IN.

Further Reading:

Clark, Wesley K. *Waging Modern War: Bosnia, Kosovo, and the Future of Combat.* New York: Public Affairs

Glenny, Misha. *The Fall of Yugoslavia: The Third Balkan War.* New York: Penguin Books, 1996.

Mertus, Julie. *Former Yugoslavia: War Crimes Trials in the Former Yugoslavia.* Helsinki, Finland: Human Rights Watch/Helsinki, 1995.

Hagan, John. *Justice in the Balkans: Prosecuting War Crimes in the Hague Tribunal.* Chicago Series in Law and Society. Chicago: University of Chicago Press, 2003.

Harris, Nathaniel. *The War in Former Yugoslavia.* London: Hodder & Stoughton, 1997.

Hazan, Pierre, and James Thomas Snyder. *Justice in a Time of War: The True Story behind the International Criminal Tribunal for the Former Yugoslavia.* Eugenia and Hugh M. Stewart Series on Eastern Europe. Austin: Texas A&M University Press, 2004.

Honig, Jan Willem, and Norbert Both. *Srebrenica: Record of a War Crime.* New York: Penguin Books, 1997.

Kim, Julie. *War in the Former Yugoslavia: Chronology of Events August 16, 1992–May 30, 1993.* CRS report for Congress. Washington, D.C.: Foreign Affairs and National Defense Division, Congressional Research Service, the Library of Congress, 1993.

Kipp, Jacob W. *International Ramifications of Yugoslavia's Serial Wars: The Challenge of Ethno-national Conflicts for a Post-Cold-War, European Order.* Fort Leavenworth, Kans.: European Military Studies Office, 1993.

Naimark, Norman, and Holly Case. *Yugoslavia and Its Historians: Understanding the Balkan Wars of the 1990s.* Stanford, Calif.: Stanford University Press, 2003.

Rhode, David. *Endgame: The Betrayal and Fall of Srebrenica.* New York: Farrar, Straus & Giroux, 1997.

Rogel, Carole. *The Breakup of Yugoslavia and the War in Bosnia.* Westport, Conn.: Greenwood Press, 1998.

Rossanet, Bertrand de. *War and Peace in the Former Yugoslavia.* Boston: Martinus Nijhoff, 1997.

Scharf, Michael P. *Balkan Justice: The Story behind the First International War Crimes Trial since Nuremberg.* Durham, N.C.: Carolina Academic Press, 1997.

Taylor, David. *The Wars of Former Yugoslavia.* Bloomington, Ind.: Raintree, 2003.

Kashmir and Jammu, human rights violations in

The dispute over Kashmir and Jammu has kept India and Pakistan at loggerheads ever since the two countries gained their independence from Great Britain in August 1947. The two nations have gone to war twice over Kashmir and periodically threaten to do so again. Now that both Pakistan and India have nuclear weapons, the prospect of renewed conflict has made the resolution of the crisis more imperative than ever before.

At the time of independence, Kashmir was carved up between the two nations. The far northern and western areas of the state are under Pakistan's control, while the Kashmir valley, Jammu, and Ladakh are under India's control. A cease-fire demarcation known as the Line of Control is monitored by the United Nations Military Observer Group on India and Pakistan (UNMOGIP). Although UN resolutions have called for a plebiscite to determine the final status of the territory, India has rejected it on the grounds that Kashmiris vote in national elections in India, eliminating any need for a plebiscite, a position that Pakistan opposes. A 1972 agreement called the Simla Accord put off the question of a "final settlement" until some unspecified future but obliged both parties to abide by the cease-fire. However, in the years since, violence has only increased, posing the threat of a new war between the two countries. Muslim militants backed by Pakistan have escalated their attacks, and Indian military and security forces have responded in kind. As of 1999, three major militant organizations were active in Kashmir: the Hizb-ul Mujahidin, Harakat-ul Ansar, and Lashgar-i Toiba. (A fourth group, the Jammu and Kashmir Liberation Front, declared a cease-fire in 1994.) Several newer groups have recently emerged. Although they have sustained considerable casualties in two decades of fighting, these groups are thought to number in the thousands, their numbers swelled by recruits from Afghanistan. By recruiting foreigners to join their ranks, these militant groups have in effect transformed the insurgency from one dedicated to self-determination (or alliance with Pakistan) to a campaign that is viewed as part of a larger radical Islamic war.

The roots of the current conflict can be traced back to 1986, when the Indian government suppressed a nonviolent movement seeking Kashmiri autonomy, setting the stage for the insurgency that has wreaked such havoc on the territory. With peaceful channels of dissent cut off, hundreds of Muslims joined militant groups that relied on Pakistan for arms and support. A split developed—and still persists—between those who wanted to see an independent Kashmir and those favoring accession to Pakistan. Over the next several years, some of these groups targeted Hindus in the Kashmir valley, forcing approximately 100,000 Hindu Kashmiris, known as "Pandits," to flee their homes. More than 350,000 Kashmiris, most of them Pandits, have become internally displaced since 1990 as a result of the conflict. Some 250,000 displaced Kashmiris now live in private homes or camps in or near the city of Jammu; another 100,000 are displaced elsewhere in India, and a smaller number from Indian-controlled Kashmir have taken refuge in Pakistan. Altogether it is estimated that the conflict has uprooted 350,000 Kashmiris from their homes, most of them Hindu Pandits.

The Indian government launched a campaign against the militant groups that resulted in widespread human rights violations: shootings of unarmed demonstrators, massacres of civilian, EXTRAJUDICIAL KILLINGS of detainees, and DISAPPEARANCES. The army, police, and paramilitary forces have been linked to arbitrary and unlawful deprivations of life, which have resulted in deaths in custody and faked encounter killings. Militant groups committed grave violations of human rights as well, threatening, abducting, and killing Hindu civilians and engaging in indiscriminate bombing attacks and sabotage. Militants have carried out assassinations of government officials, military personnel, civil servants, and suspected informers. To supplement its security forces, India has armed and trained local auxiliary forces made up of militants who have either surrendered or been captured. These auxiliary groups have also been linked to human rights violations, targeting human rights advocates and journalists. According to a nongovernmental

organization in Kashmir, paramilitaries were responsible for 200 rapes in 2000 as part of a systematic campaign to instill fear among civilians. Under various emergency acts, paramilitaries are protected from investigation or prosecution for certain types of crimes. In some cases, security forces have been implicated in killing militants who tried to give themselves up. According to one prominent human rights activist, Indian forces had orders to shoot any person who came within 12 miles of the Line of Control or to shoot those who are unable to quickly justify their presence in the area. Foreign militants are at further risk if they are caught by the army.

Significant numbers of civilians have been killed in security operations as well. According to the *Kashmir Times,* continuing violence in Kashmir led to the deaths of more than 900 civilians in 2001. Uncounted numbers of combatants and civilians have also disappeared—about 2,250 persons between 1994 and 2000. The government claims that some of these "disappeared" have slipped over the border into Pakistan to receive training in terrorist camps, though most of the disappeared are presumed dead. (In 2000 AMNESTY INTERNATIONAL put the figure lower, around 750.)

For victims or for their families, there is little recourse. Local police are under instructions not to open a case without permission from higher authorities. Moreover, a Special Powers Act provides that without New Delhi's approval, no "prosecution, suit, or other legal proceeding shall be instituted . . . against any person in respect of anything done or purported to be done in exercise of the powers of the act." This act basically confers blanket immunity on security personnel. Even though bodies of detainees are often returned to families riddled with multiple bullet wounds or bearing evidence of TORTURE, no action is ever taken against members of the security forces. While the Indian National Human Rights Commission (NHRC) has the right to conduct an inquiry into alleged security force abuses in Jammu and Kashmir, the organization has no statutory power to investigate them. In some instances, the government holds out an offer of financial compensation to families of victims without, however, actually delivering on its promise. Since 1990 action has been taken against only a few hundred members of the security forces for human rights violations or other crimes. Punishments ranged from reduction in rank to imprisonment for up to 10 years.

In 2005 violence in Kashmir dipped appreciably, mainly as a result of an ease in relations between India and Pakistan. The tentative rapprochement between the two antagonists has led to a diminishment in Pakistani support for Muslim militants operating in Kashmir. In September Indian Prime Minister Manmohan Singh took the unprecedented step of inviting a separatist alliance, the All Parties Hurriyat Conference, to talks. Although some separatist groups opposed any peaceful settlement that would maintain Indian sovereignty over the Himalayan region the move was viewed as an important diplomatic opening. As expected, however, the talks ended with no agreement.

See also INDIA, HUMAN RIGHTS VIOLATIONS IN; PAKISTAN, HUMAN RIGHTS VIOLATIONS IN.

Further Research:

Bose, Sumanira. *Kashmir: Roots of Conflict, Paths to Peace.* Cambridge, Mass.: Harvard University Press, 2003.

Ganguly, Sumit. *Conflict Unending.* New York: Columbia University Press, 2002.

Schofield, Victoria. *Kashmir in Conflict: India, Pakistan and the Unending War.* London: I. B. Tauris & Company, 2002.

Katyn Forest, massacre in

Katyn Forest was the site of a 1940 massacre of almost 4,200 captured Polish officers by Soviet secret police agents acting on Joseph STALIN's orders. The Soviets had taken the officers prisoner in 1939 after seizing part of Poland as a result of a secret agreement between Germany and the Soviet Union. The Soviet dictator apparently believed that the Polish officers constituted a pool of future leaders of Poland, and as such represented a threat to Soviet Communist domination. The executioners, who were attached to the NKVD, the Soviet secret police, then buried the bodies in an attempt to conceal evidence of the crime. For years afterward the Soviets blamed the killings on German forces that subsequently occupied the area during World War II.

The massacre came to light in a Radio Berlin broadcast on April 13, 1943, which announced "a horrific discovery" in Katyn Forest—located near the city of Smolensk—where German occupation authorities had turned up "a great pit filled with layers of bodies of Polish officers." The Soviets countered that the Germans were simply trying to shift the blame for their own crime. To bolster their claim, the Nazis established a panel to investigate the killings. The documents they removed from the 4,243 bodies they exhumed were dated no later than May 6, 1940, adding credence to estimates that they had been in the ground for three years—prior to the German invasion of the Soviet Union. The Germans produced witnesses who reported seeing Soviet troops in trucks transporting Polish prisoners in the direction of the forest. In September 1943 the Soviets regained the area and opened their own investigation, which, not unexpectedly, reached the opposite conclusion, naming the Nazis as the killers. After the war there was little interest on the part of the United States or Britain to confront its wartime ally with charges of involvement in the massacre. However, the U.S. House of Representatives initiated its own investigation, which issued a report on

December 22, 1952, concluding that, based on the evidence, the Soviets were guilty of the massacre. That conclusion was confirmed by the Soviet government itself in 1989 after communism collapsed. It was revealed that Stalin's plan to eliminate the Polish military leadership was even more far-reaching than anyone had previously suspected. In March 1940 he had given orders to execute some 25,700 Poles, including those found at the Katyn Forest site.

See also MASS GRAVES.

Further Reading:

Paul, Allen. *Katyn: The Untold Story of Stalin's Polish Massacre.* New York: Scribner, 1991.

Zawodny, J. K. *Death in the Forest: The Story of the Katyn Forest Massacre.* International Studies of the Committee on International Relations. Notre Dame, Ind.: University of Notre Dame Press, 1962.

Kazakhstan, human rights violations in

Kazakhstan, a former republic of the Soviet Union, occupies a strategic location in central Asia. By virtue of its oil wealth, it is potentially the richest of the republics carved out of the defunct USSR. Nonetheless, the country has been unable to exploit its natural resources because of poor infrastructure and a lack of pipelines. Kazakhstan is also bedeviled by high unemployment, inflation, poverty, prostitution, drug addiction, and HIV/AIDS. Many of the problems are a legacy of the Soviet era, including pollution and radioactive contamination left at defunct rocket launch sites. Corruption is rife; Transparency International, a watchdog agency that monitors corruption around the globe, rates Kazakhstan one of the most corrupt countries in the world, ranking it 122 out of 145. The larger the number, the more corrupt the country is considered, based on reports from business leaders and nongovernmental organizations.

In spite of its problems, Kazakhstan has also taken on greater importance after the attacks of September 11, 2001, led to greater involvement of U.S. military forces in the region. Although nominally a democracy, Kazakhstan has been dominated by its president, Nursultan Abish-uly Nazarbayev, ever since gaining independence in 1991. A deft politician, he has succeeded in tamping down ethnic tensions that have erupted into violence in other parts of the former Soviet Union. The country has paid a price for stability: In his decade and a half of rule, Nazarbayev has increasingly consolidated power in his hands. The principal opposition leader, former prime minister Akezhan Kazhegeldin, was prevented from running against him in the 1999 election, which awarded the president an additional seven-year term. Kazhegeldin subsequently went into exile and was convicted in absentia for alleged misconduct while he was prime minister. In 2000 the legislature, at

Nazarbayev's urging, gave the president powers for life; even if he leaves office he will still retain other influential positions in the government. In 2004 elections his party, the Otan, was returned to power amid charges by international observers that the elections were flawed. Opposition leaders accused the government of widespread vote rigging. The director of Kazakhstan's largest poll-monitoring organization went so far as to call the elections the most blatantly fraudulent since the nation gained independence. Opposition representation in Parliament disappeared. When the major opposition party, Bright Path, called for a protest demonstration in the capital, the government refused permission. Bright Path backed off, with its leaders saying that they did not want to risk violence.

In spite of constitutional guarantees, freedom of the press is problematic; opposition media is subject to censorship and harassment. It is a crime, for instance, to insult the president, and journalists are forbidden to report on the state of his health, his financial affairs, or private life. The government also controls the printing presses and most media outlets. Several members of the president's family run news agencies and TV stations. The International Federation of Journalists, based in Brussels, contends that the regime is waging "a war on independent journalism." The war can become lethal. In July 2004 a prominent journalist who had called for Nazarbaev's resignation and had announced his own intention to run for president in 2006 was struck down by a car and killed in a suspicious incident labeled an accident. Observers at the scene reported that his tape recorder was stolen from the body. The government has also used ruinous lawsuits to deter the media from reporting unfavorable stories.

According to HUMAN RIGHTS WATCH, nongovernmental organizations are frequently harassed and intimidated by security agencies. Although Kazakhstan enjoys friendly relations with the United States, the State Department noted in its 2004 *Country Report* that the government of Kazakhstan "severely limited citizens' right to change their government and democratic institutions remained weak . . . [and that it] . . . restricted freedom of assembly and association and limited democratic expression by imposing restrictions on the registration of political parties."

Further Reading:

Furgus, Michael, and Janat Jandosova, eds. *Kazakhstan: Coming of Age.* London: Stacey International Publishers, 2004.

George, Alexandra. *Journey into Kazakhstan: The True Face of the Nazabayev Regime.* Lanham, Md.: University Press of America, 2001.

Olcott, Martha Brill. *Kazakhstan: Unfulfilled Promise.* New York: Carnegie Endowment for International Peace, 2002.

Keitel, Wilhelm (1882–1946) *Nazi general*

As commander in chief of the High Command of the Armed Forces (OKW), Wilhelm Keitel was among the most important military figures in Nazi Germany. Born on September 22, 1882, in Hanover, Germany, Keitel was raised in an authoritarian Prussian culture that espoused unquestioning loyalty to the kaiser as the highest value. A military career was a natural choice, and by the time that World War I broke out, Keitel had attained the rank of captain in the German army. After the war ended, he remained in the army and continued to rise in its ranks, but he also forged links with right-wing extremist groups. He believed that the German army should be strengthened despite the terms of the Versailles treaty, which limited Germany's military forces. In 1929 he received the opportunity to realize his dream: He was appointed head of the army's organization department, where he became involved in a secret plan to triple the size of the army. After Adolf HITLER came to power in January 1933, Keitel fell into his orbit almost immediately, becoming one of his most ardent admirers. Hitler rewarded his loyalty by making him commander in chief of the OKW.

After the fall of France in 1940, Keitel was promoted to field marshal. Nonetheless, he did not invariably support all of Hitler's policies, advising against the western offensive in Europe and Operation Barbarossa (the invasion of the Soviet Union). Realizing that Hitler had no intention of reconsidering his decisions, he quickly backed down. Keitel was such a yes-man that other officers referred to him behind his back as "Lakaitel"—"the nodding ass." Even after it was clear that Hitler was leading Germany to its destruction, Keitel never wavered in his belief in his leadership, nor did he show any hesitation about imposing Hitler's genocidal policies in occupied territories. When Poland came under German rule in 1939, he issued orders to the SS and GESTAPO to exterminate Jews.

In 1941 Keitel signed one of the so-called *Nacht und Nebel* (night and fog) decrees, which applied to the occupied territories of Western Europe. The decree specified that civilians should be tried for offenses against the German state only if the death sentence was likely to be carried out within a few days of arrest; otherwise the accused would be taken to Germany and nothing further would be heard of them. That same year Keitel signed an order instructing German field commanders to execute communist officials as soon as they were captured. In July 1941 he authorized Heinrich HIMMLER, head of the SS, the power to implement racial policies in occupied regions of the Soviet Union. The order indicated that legal punishments were too cumbersome to impose over such a wide area and therefore the army should rely on terrorism to suppress any dissent and cow the civilian population. Keitel also signed orders for the execution of striking workers and the killing of partisans and called on German civilians to lynch any captured Allied pilots. One of his orders stated that for every German soldier killed in an uprising, 100 "Communists" must be killed in reprisal. (Anyone involved in an uprising was automatically considered a communist.)

After the war ended, Keitel was arrested and tried for war crimes, CRIMES AGAINST HUMANITY, and conspiracy to commit aggression (among other charges) before the NUREMBERG TRIALS established by the Allies to prosecute Nazi war criminals. He retained his loyalty to Hitler throughout the proceedings, although he believed that the führer had dishonored himself by committing suicide. Pleading not guilty, he contended that German officers and soldiers should not be prosecuted for war crimes because they had taken an oath to obey orders. He maintained that in any case he had opposed the invasion of the Soviet Union and had twice tried to resign, but that he could not simply abdicate his duties or show disloyalty to the führer, the army, or the state. Moreover, he said, he was "never permitted to make decisions." His defense failed to move the jurists, who found him guilty and sentenced him to death. He asked to be shot by firing squad as befitting a military officer, but the request was denied. He was executed on October 16, 1946—by hanging. His autobiography, *In Service of the Reich,* appeared posthumously.

Further Reading:

Bloxham, Donald. *Genocide on Trial: War Crimes Trials and the Formation of Holocaust History and Memory.* Oxford: Oxford University Press, 2003.

Browder, George C. *Hitler's Enforcers: The Gestapo and the SS Security Service in the Nazi Revolution.* Oxford: Oxford University Press, 1996.

Butler, Rupert. *The Gestapo: A History of Hitler's Secret Police 1933–45.* Havertown, Pa.: Casemate Publishers and Book Distributors, 2004.

Dawidowicz, Lucy. *A Holocaust Reader.* Library of Jewish Studies. Chicago: Behrman House Publishing, 1976.

Dwork, Deborah, and Robert Jan Van Pelt. *Holocaust: A History.* New York: W. W. Norton & Company, 2003.

Gilbert, Martin. *The Holocaust: A History of the Jews of Europe During the Second World War.* New York: Owl Books, 1987.

Hohne, Heinz Zollen. *The Order of the Death's Head: The Story of Hitler's SS.* New York: Penguin, 2001.

Kenya, human rights violations in

After decades of one-man rule, Kenya celebrated a restoration of democracy in 2002 with the election of Mwai Kibaki of the opposition National Rainbow Coalition (NARC) after his predecessor, President Daniel arap Moi, voluntarily decided not to run again. Whether Kibaki's government will be able to meet the high expectations of voters is unclear since there remains a big mess to clean up. The government's human rights record is still problematic, although the new administration has begun to make some needed reforms. The government impinges on fundamental rights including privacy, freedom of speech, press, assembly, and association. Police have forcibly broken up demonstrations and have harassed members of nongovernmental organizations (NGOs); they also continue to commit EXTRAJUDICIAL KILLINGS. In a 2002 report, the Standing Committee on Human Rights (SCHR), the governmental human rights body, cited the "widespread use of lethal, excessive, and unnecessary force on civilians by police." As evidence, the committee stated that in 2002 police had killed 117 suspected criminals, while another 11 suspects and detainees had died in police custody. The Kenya Human Rights Commission (KHRC), a human rights NGO, said that it had documented more than 1,000 cases of unlawful killings between 1992 and 2002. In their defense, police claim that the use of lethal force was justified because of a surge in criminal activity and the increasing use of heavy arms by criminals, pointing out that in 2002, 22 police officers were killed in the line of duty.

There is no question that there is a crime problem—according to the government, 95 persons were killed in mob violence alone during 2002, and 719 deaths had resulted from mob violence over the five preceding years—yet human rights groups claim that the police are at fault as well. Much of the mob violence, they say, has come about because the public lacks confidence that the police will act to stop crime or apprehend criminals, causing them to take the law into their own hands. "Mob justice" has also been used as a cover to settle old scores. Police corruption was systematic and widespread. In a survey conducted by the Public Service Integrity Program, Kenyans viewed the police as the most corrupt institution in the country. In spite of constitutional prohibitions, there are also reports of suspects being tortured by police, which according to the Independent Medico Legal Unit (IMLU), a human rights NGO, led to the deaths of 45 persons from torture while in police custody in 2002. Methods of TORTURE include hanging persons upside down for long periods, genital mutilation, electric shocks, and submerging people's heads in water. Arbitrary arrests and detentions are also common, and the security forces are known to target civic leaders and journalists.

In spite of the fact that some officers have been prosecuted for abuses, most of those who are responsible have not been investigated, let alone prosecuted. According to the SCHR, "there was a code of silence under which officers failed to report brutality, destroyed evidence, or threatened witnesses in an effort to cover up abuses, contributing to a climate of impunity." Even though officials sometimes chastise officers and remind them of their obligations under the law, their words seldom have much of an impact.

See also MAU MAU UPRISING; NGUGI WA THIONGO.

Khieu Samphan (1931–   ) *Khmer Rouge leader*
Khieu Samphan was the last leader of the Khmer Rouge, the radical Maoist movement that, in its five years of power (1975–79), was responsible for the deaths of as many as 2 million Cambodians. He is believed to have been born in 1931 and, like many other future Khmer Rouge leaders, won a government scholarship to study in France. In Paris, while studying for a doctorate in economics, he became enthralled by Marxism. Returning to Cambodia, he was elected twice to the National Assembly and even served as a cabinet member in the government of Prince Norodom Sihanouk, achieving a reputation as "Mr. Clean" because of his incorruptibility. But he shortly fell out of favor because of his leftist views and took refuge in the jungles of eastern Cambodia, where POL POT was forming the Khmer Rouge.

For the next several years, Khieu Samphan remained out of public sight, spawning rumors that security forces had killed him. But he resurfaced in 1975 when the Khmer Rouge took control over the country and occupied the capital of Phnom Penh. Although the Khmer Rouge operated in secrecy and did not identify its leadership, Khieu Samphan became the nominal head of state. Real power, however, remained in Pol Pot's hands. After the Khmer Rouge was driven out of Phnom Penh by the Vietnamese in 1979, Khieu Samphan acted as the front man for the group, which had relocated to an area close to the Thai border. As vice president in charge of foreign affairs, he represented the Khmer Rouge in UN-sponsored peace negotiations in 1991 that were supposed to lead to elections. He also represented the Khmer Rouge on the Supreme National Council of an anti-Vietnam coalition that also included pro-Sihanouk forces.

Since the collapse of the Khmer Rouge in 1998, Khieu Samphan has been living in retirement. No action has been taken by the government to bring him or any other former Khmer Rouge leaders to trial, although by 2004 progress was being made to establish a war crime tribunal. Like many of his old comrades, Khieu Samphan has expressed shock that the Khmer Rouge could have perpetrated mass murder. "I have found it so difficult to believe what people told me of what happened under the Khmer Rouge regime, but today I am very clear that there was GENOCIDE," he said in an interview, "I have been wondering, and I am still wondering, why the leaders killed the people like that. I never conspired with any senior Khmer Rouge leaders to kill the people of Cambodia. No! I never. Within the regime, I was only a leader in name." After seeing a docu-

mentary about the atrocities, he said he was even more stunned: "I never believed previously that people were killed when they stole one potato to stay alive." Later at a news conference he said he was "sorry, very sorry" for what had happened.

See also CAMBODIA, WAR CRIMES IN.

Further Reading:
Chandler, David. *A History of Cambodia.* Philadelphia: Westview Press, 2000.
———. *The Tragedy of Cambodian History: Politics, War, and Revolution since 1945.* New Haven, Conn.: Yale University Press, 1993.
Hinton, Alexander Laban, and Robert Jay Lifton. *Why Did They Kill?: Cambodia in the Shadow of Genocide.* California Series in Public Anthropology, vol. 11. Berkeley: University of California Press, 2004.
Kiernan, Ben. *How Pol Pot Came to Power: Colonialism, Nationalism, and Communism in Cambodia, 1930–1975.* New Haven, Conn.: Yale University Press, 2004.
———. *The Pol Pot Regime: Race, Power, and Genocide in Cambodia under the Khmer Rouge, 1975–79.* New Haven, Conn.: Yale University Press, 2002.
Pran, Dith, comp. *Children of Cambodia's Killing Fields: Memoirs by Survivors.* Edited by Kim DePaul. New Haven, Conn.: Yale University Press, 1999.
Short, Philip. *Pol Pot: Anatomy of a Nightmare.* New York: Holt Rinehart, 2005.
Ung, Loung. *First They Killed My Father: A Daughter of Cambodia Remembers.* New York: Perennial, 2001.

Khmer Rouge   *See* CAMBODIA, WAR CRIMES IN; IENG SARY; KHIEU SAMPHAN; NUON CHEA; TA MOK.

Kiang Kek Iev (Kang Kek Ieu, Deuch, Duch)
(1930–   ) *Cambodian secret police chief*
Kiang Kek Iev, better known by his nom de guerre Deuch, was the head of the secret police and established the notorious Tuol Sleng detention center in Cambodia, where 20,000 prisoners were put to death by the Khmer Rouge regime. Deuch, a former high school teacher, selected an abandoned high school outside of the capital of Phnom Penh as the site of the center. Most of those who were tortured and executed in the center were political prisoners: former members of the Khmer Rouge who had fallen out with the regime. Deuch once boasted that one of his prisoners would "make good fertilizer," and signed a death warrant for nine children to which he appended the notation "kill them all." Between 1975 and 1976, 2,404 "antiparty elements" were tortured and executed. In 1977 the toll rose

to 6,330; in the first six months of 1978, 5,765 people were put to death. So much is known about the torturers and their victims because the prison authorities insisted on keeping meticulous records about how they extracted confessions. The machinery of death was so efficient that only six (possibly seven) prisoners are known to have survived.

Once the Khmer Rouge was driven from Phnom Penh by the Vietnamese in 1979, thousands of soldiers took up residence in the north of Cambodia near the Thai border. Over the next several years, Deuch tried to reinvent himself, reportedly helping run a UN refugee camp in Thailand (although there are allegations that he continued to torture his fellow countrymen who had sought shelter at the camp). Subsequently he tried to slip back into Cambodian society, calling himself Hong Ben or Ta Pin. In a show of repentance, he converted to Christianity and found support from missionaries affiliated with the International Hope University who helped him find a job working for the American Refugee Committee. When his true identity was revealed and he was arrested, his employer expressed astonishment. "We are in a state of shock," a spokesperson for the Refugee Committee was quoted as saying. "He was our best worker." Now in prison, Deuch has said that he feels "very sorry about the killings and the past." It is believed that he is likely to stand trial when—and if—a tribunal is established to prosecute war crimes committed by the Khmer Rouge.

See also CAMBODIA, WAR CRIMES IN.

Further Reading:
Hinton, Alexander Laban, and Robert Jay Lifton. *Why Did They Kill?: Cambodia in the Shadow of Genocide.* California Series in Public Anthropology, vol. 11. Berkeley: University of California Press, 2004.
Kiernan, Ben. *The Pol Pot Regime: Race, Power, and Genocide in Cambodia under the Khmer Rouge, 1975–79.* New Haven, Conn.: Yale University Press, 2002.
Pran, Dith, comp. *Children of Cambodia's Killing Fields: Memoirs by Survivors.* Edited by Kim DePaul. New Haven, Conn.: Yale University Press, 1999.

Kimberly Process   *See* CONFLICT DIAMONDS.

Kim Il Sung (Kim Sŏng-ju) (1912–1994) *North Korean dictator*
Kim Il Sung ruled Communist North Korea with an iron hand from 1946 until his death in 1994, turning it into the most isolated state in the world. He was born Kim Sŏng-ju into a peasant family in a North Korean village near Pyongyang. Korea at the time was under Japanese occupation, and his family's active opposition to the Japanese led

Former guerrilla leader and founder of North Korea Kim Il Sung *(Adrian Bradshaw/Landov)*

them to flee to Manchuria (under Chinese control) when he was still a child. However, the Japanese were gradually expanding their influence in Manchuria. In 1931 Kim became active in an anti-Japanese guerrilla group led by the Communist Party of China. His education came to an abrupt end when he was arrested and briefly imprisoned for his subversive activities. He proved an adept leader and became a commander of the guerrillas before the Japanese drove them out of northern China. In 1941 Kim fled Manchuria, now occupied by the Japanese, for the Soviet Far East. He received more formal military training at a camp near Khabarovsk and eventually became a major in the Red Army. In September 1945, a month after the end of World War II, Kim accompanied Soviet forces when they moved into Korea. The Soviets installed him as head of the Provisional People's Committee but not as the head of the

Communist Party, which was based in Seoul in South Korea, then occupied by U.S. forces. In 1948 he became the first premier of North Korea, which was formally known as the Democratic People's Republic of Korea (DPRK). In 1949 the two communist parties merged and became the Korean Workers Party (KWP), with Kim as party chairman.

With Soviet backing, Kim instituted a campaign of subversion to forcibly reunify the two Koreas, and on June 25, 1950, he launched an invasion of the South. There is some dispute among historians as to the extent of Soviet or Chinese support for an invasion; there is evidence to suggest that it was undertaken at Kim's initiative and his two allies only reluctantly acquiesced. At first DPRK forces enjoyed considerable success, capturing Seoul, the capital of the south, but a counteroffensive by UN forces pushed the North Korean troops far into their own territory, forcing Kim's government to take refuge in China. Kim was rescued by a massive intervention of Chinese troops that began in September 1951. After a bitter, seesawing conflict, the war ended in a stalemate. An armistice was signed, but relations between North and South Korea remained tense. Kim continued to harbor hopes for forcible reunification, and throughout his rule he carried out a campaign of sabotage, terrorism, and assassination in an unsuccessful attempt to topple the leadership of the Republic of Korea. He purged all rivals, established an austere and militarized society, and directed a disproportionate amount of the budget to a buildup of the military-industrial complex. All agriculture was collectivized. Heavy industry was emphasized, much of it devoted to manufacturing arms. He fostered a cult of personality—even encouraging people to impute supernatural powers to him—and was universally known as Great Leader. (His son KIM JONG IL, who would succeed him, is known as Dear Leader.) Contact with the outside world—even with family members in South Korea—was forbidden, so people had no way of knowing how impoverished and deprived they actually were.

Although Kim espoused an ideology of self-reliance called *juche*, North Korea could not have survived without regular infusions of Soviet and Chinese aid. In spite of his dependence on China and the USSR, Kim pursued an erratic and independent policy, tightening relations with one at the expense of the other at various points in his rule. Eventually, though, both countries began to become disillusioned with North Korea, especially after the collapse of communism in the Soviet Union. The economy continued to deteriorate even as South Korea's burgeoned, but the arms industry was never allowed to falter. Under Kim, North Korea emerged as one of the greatest threats to the United States, and from the 1970s on, it carried on a brisk traffic in advanced weapons systems, which it sold to Libya, Iran, Syria, and other countries that opposed American interests. In 1994 the United States had become so con-

cerned about the potential for North Korea to strike South Korea and Japan with missiles that then-president Jimmy Carter initiated negotiations with North Korea intended to freeze the missile program in exchange for an easing of sanctions. But before the talks could get underway, Kim Il Song succumbed to a heart attack on July 8, 1994, in the capital Pyongyang; he was 82. Hundreds of thousands of North Koreans turned out for his funeral; many were weeping. Within a few years his eldest son by his first marriage—Kim Il Sung was married twice—took power in accordance with his father's wishes.

See also NORTH KOREA, HUMAN RIGHTS VIOLATIONS IN.

Further Reading:
Harrold, Michael. *Comrades and Strangers: Behind the Closed Doors of North Korea.* New York: John Wiley & Sons, 2004.
Martin, Bradley K. *Under the Loving Care of the Fatherly Leader: North Korea and the Kim Dynasty.* New York: Thomas Dunne Books, 2004.
Vollertsen, Norbert, *Inside North Korea.* London: Encounter Books, 2005.

Kim Jong Il (1942–   ) *North Korean dictator*
The enigmatic North Korean strongman Kim Jong Il formally inherited his power in 1997, three years after the death of his father KIM IL SUNG. Diplomats have described the younger Kim, who had a reputation as a playboy and film buff, as "a vain, paranoid, cognac-guzzling hypochondriac." A diminutive man, he is also reputed to wear platform shoes to make himself appear taller. Whether his eccentricities conceal a cunning political mind at work or are indicative of a pathological condition is a subject of vigorous debate, especially because evidence continues to mount that North Korea is developing a capacity to create nuclear weapons. Former U.S. secretary of state Madeleine Albright, who met Kim, found him very well informed—"on top of his brief" and "not delusional." She did note that his comments about his plans for the North Korean economy struck her as illogical. There is also some dispute among experts as to whether he can exercise as much power as his father had. "I know I'm an object of criticism in the world," Kim has said, "but if I am being talked about, I must be doing the right things."

The cult surrounding "Dear Leader," as he is called (his father was called "Great Leader"), began virtually at Kim's birth in 1941 in Siberia while his father was in exile in the former Soviet Union. (The Korean peninsula was under Japanese domination until the end of World War II.) According to official communist accounts, however, he was born in 1942 in a log cabin at a communist guerrilla base on Mt. Paektu, North Korea's highest mountain, a story put out to strengthen the younger Kim's connection to the state. His birth was supposed to have been signaled by a double rainbow and a bright star in the sky. Kim attended Kim Il-Sung University and graduated in 1964. He subsequently became the head of North Korea's special forces, a position he held for much of the 1970s and 1980s. Some defectors have linked him to the 1986 bombing of a Korean Airlines jet in which 115 South Korean passengers died. In 1980 he was officially designated as Kim Il Sung's successor as head of the Korean Workers' Party. In 1991 he assumed control over the armed forces although he had no military experience.

While relaxing some economic restrictions imposed by his father, Kim Jong Il continues to maintain a firm hold over his people. There is no freedom of assembly, religion, or press. Even radios sold can only receive state radio broadcasts, and any tampering with them is punishable. Extrajudicial killings and disappearances continue to occur. Citizens can be detained arbitrarily and locked up in harsh conditions for "crimes against the revolution," including defection, attempted defection, slander of the policies of the party or state, listening to foreign broadcasts, writing "reactionary" letters, and possessing "reactionary printed matter." Capital punishment is frequently employed, and all assets belonging to the convicted individual are confiscated by the state. In spite of international aid, about 1.3 to 2 million North Koreans have perished from starvation. Refugees fleeing persistent poverty and famine—often seeking refuge in China—are confined to labor camps if they are repatriated. Some 200,000 people were believed to be interred in these camps as of 2005. Criminal law makes the death penalty mandatory for activities "in collusion with imperialists" aimed at "suppressing the national liberation struggle." Some prisoners are sentenced to death for such alleged "crimes" as "ideological divergence," "opposing socialism," and other "counterrevolutionary crimes." People have been executed for stealing cattle or electric wire. In some cases, executions reportedly were carried out at public meetings attended by workers, students, and schoolchildren. In 2004 there were reports that his favorite mistress, a former movie actress, had died of natural causes, which reportedly caused Kim to fall into a depression. Subsequently his portrait was taken down in many North Korean embassies around the world, stirring rumors that his power had eroded and there are unconfirmed reports of attempts against his life. However, there is no evidence that he has lost any control over North Korea. If he has one talent it is to keep the world guessing as to what he intends to do next.

See also NORTH KOREA, HUMAN RIGHTS VIOLATIONS IN.

Further Reading:
Breen, Michael. *Kim Jong-Il: North Korea's Dear Leader.* New York: John Wiley & Sons, 2004,
Harrold, Michael. *Comrades and Strangers: Behind the Closed Doors of North Korea.* New York: John Wiley & Sons, 2004.
Martin, Bradley K. *Under the Loving Care of the Fatherly Leader: North Korea and the Kim Dynasty.* New York: Thomas Dunne Books, 2004.
Vollertsen, Norbert, *Inside North Korea.* London: Encounter Books, 2005.

Kimura, Heitaro *See* WAR CRIMINALS OF JAPAN.

Klarsfeld, Serge (1935–) *Nazi hunter*
Serge Klarsfeld and his wife, Beate, have gained an international reputation as intrepid and dogged hunters of Nazi war criminals who escaped justice after World War II. Without their efforts, it is doubtful whether Klaus BARBIE, "the Butcher of Lyon," would ever have been tried or punished for his crimes. Born in Bucharest in 1935, Serge, who is Jewish, only narrowly escaped being arrested by the GESTAPO in Nice in 1943. His father, however, was not so lucky and was killed in Auschwitz. Serge met his future wife in the Paris Metro in the 1960s; he was a law student at the time and she was working as an au pair. Individually and together, the couple has pursued innumerable legal cases against Nazi criminals who were active in occupied and Vichy France, including Lischka and Alois BRUNNER, René BOUSQUET, Jean Leguay, Maurice PAPON, and Paul TOUVIER. Their efforts also prodded the French government to acknowledge France's culpability for many of the crimes committed on its soil.

The Klarsfelds were especially determined to find Klaus Barbie, who had terrorized Vichy France and ordered the DEPORTATIONS of 7,000 Jews to the CONCENTRATION CAMPS and the killing of another 4,000 non-Jews.

Renowned Nazi hunters Beate and Serge Klarsfeld *(Bettmann/Corbis)*

The Klarsfelds tracked him down to Peru, where he was posing as a businessman. Later he fled to Bolivia, where he was apprehended. The campaign to bring Barbie to justice culminated in his extradition to France in 1983; he was subsequently sentenced to life in prison.

What astonishes Serge Klarsfeld is the absence of any discernible guilt among the war criminals he has encountered. "They go on with their lives as if nothing had happened," he said in an interview. "When the war ended, ninety percent of them remained in Europe. The most amazing thing about them—and this doesn't vary—is how self-centered they are. All of them look 10 years younger than their peers. They have no conflicts and certainly no guilt." When the Klarsfelds exposed the former head of the Paris Gestapo, who had become the president of the Tribunal for Social Affairs in Lower Saxony, the judge complained that he might lose half of his pension if he were put on trial.

The Klarsfelds are unafraid to court controversy or create a stir if it will arouse public awareness. In the 1960s Beate slapped German chancellor Kurt-George Kiesinger because he had worked in the Nazi propaganda system. "We Germans have a special responsibility," she has said, explaining why she as a German would risk so much for Jews. "When I learned what had happened [in the war], I decided that in order not to be ashamed of my people, and to atone for the crimes perpetrated in their name, it was not enough to tell the victims that I merely sympathized." Hunting Nazi war criminals is not without its risks; Beate has been imprisoned and taunted and her car bombed, while Serge has been arrested in Germany and Syria. The two have worked on behalf of current human rights cases in countries like Iran and Bosnia. They have also devoted much of their work to documenting the Holocaust and commemorating the victims. "You might say that I am more of a hunter of Jewish souls," Serge said, "because for more than 20 years we have been looking for the traces of those Jews who perished. The victims have always been more important to me than their executioners."

Further Reading:

Klarsfeld, Serge. *Remembering Georgy: Letters from the House of Izieu.* New York: Aperture, 2001.
Klarsfeld, Serge, and Susan Sarah Cohen, eds. *French Children of the Holocaust: A Memorial.* New York: New York University Press, 1996.

Koch, Erich (1896–1986) *Ukrainian civil servant*

Erich Koch is known as the "Butcher of Ukraine" for good reason: As the head of the civil administration (*Reichskomissar*) of occupied Ukraine during World War II, he supervised the DEPORTATIONS of some 2.5–3 million Ukrainians to Germany to work as forced laborers. In addition to the thousands of Ukrainians who perished under brutal conditions, Koch also helped organize the extermination of 700,000 Ukrainian Jews. Even he acknowledged his reputation for cruelty, once describing himself as a "brutal dog." When he arrived in the Ukraine, he declared that his mission was to "suck from Ukraine all the goods we can get hold of, without consideration for the feeling or the property of the Ukrainians." He was equally blunt about his regard for the population he was ruling: "If I find a Ukrainian who is worthy of sitting at the same table with me, I must have him shot." True to his promise, the Ukraine suffered from more human and economic devastation than any other territory conquered by Germany during the war.

The future "Butcher of the Ukraine" was born in Elberfeld, Germany, on June 19, 1896. He fought in World War I and became a railway clerk after the war. In 1922 he joined the fledgling National Socialist German Workers Party (NSDAP); six years later he was appointed *Gauleiter* (district leader) of the Nazi Party in East Prussia, and in 1930 he was elected to the Reichstag (parliament). In 1941 Adolf HITLER sent him to the Ukraine, and at once he began a campaign of terror. Ukrainians, he said, "must be handled with the whip like the Negroes." He meant this literally; during the first year of the war, Koch encouraged the use of whips on Ukrainians although he later banned the practice, preferring more decisive methods of punishment.

Koch was ordered to find 450,000 workers a year for German industry by "ruthless" means. Documents uncovered after the war made it clear that these laborers would be "worked to death" as *Ostarbeiter* (slave laborers). At one point some 40,000 Ukrainians were being sent to Germany each month, but even so they were dying so rapidly that there was a pressing need for more. To meet the growing demand, German troops scoured Ukrainian cities abducting young men. Some historians estimate that as many as 2.5 million Ukrainians were forced into slave labor in Germany during the war. They were used to sustain agriculture, mining, metal production, and railroads—and most importantly, the arms industry. The removal of such large numbers was also part of a systematic policy to depopulate the country; those who were not press-ganged into FORCED LABOR succumbed to starvation or else were deported to CONCENTRATION CAMPS.

Kiev, Ukraine's largest city, was devastated by famine, and under Koch it lost its status as capital to Rivne, a small town to the west. Hitler also made it a policy to extinguish Ukrainian culture and education. In 1942, on a visit to the Ukraine, Hitler declared that Ukrainians, whom he regarded as subhuman, "should be given only the crudest kind of education necessary for communication between them and their German masters." Koch followed his directive: "I expect the General Commissars to close all schools and colleges with students over 15 years of age and send all teachers and students, irrespective of sex, in a body to Germany for work. . . . I require that no school except four-grade elementary schools should function." In January 1942 all schools above grade four were closed, as were all universities. "The entire Ukrainian intelligentsia must be decimated," declared SS leader Heinrich HIMMLER. Koch made certain that this was done.

After the Red Army retook the Ukraine in 1944, Koch returned to East Prussia. When Germany fell to the Allies in 1945, he went into hiding and remained at large until he was captured by the British army in Hamburg in May 1949. The Soviet Union demanded that he be extradited to stand trial for war crimes he committed on its territory, but instead the British turned him over to the Polish government. He went on trial in Poland in October 1958 for the killings of 400,000 Poles—his crimes in the Ukraine were not considered by the Polish court—and sentenced to death. However, his sentence was later commuted to life imprisonment. He died in prison on November 12, 1986.

See also UKRAINE, HUMAN RIGHTS VIOLATIONS IN.

Further Reading:

Berkhoff, Karel C. *Harvest of Despair: Life and Death in Ukraine under Nazi Rule.* Cambridge, Mass.: Belknap Press, 2004.

Piotrowski, Tadeusz, ed. *Genocide and Rescue in Wolyn: Recollections of the Ukrainian Nationalist Ethnic Cleansing Campaign against the Poles during World War II.* Jefferson, N.C.: McFarland & Company, 2000.

Kony, Joseph (c. 1958–   ) *Ugandan insurgent leader*

The founder of what is widely considered the most ruthless guerrilla group in Africa, Joseph Kony has spearheaded an insurgency that has terrorized northern Uganda for almost two decades. Kony advocates a decidedly idiosyncratic brand of Christian fundamentalism and purports to be a spirit medium. His group, the Lord's Resistance Army (LRA), has been responsible for killing tens of thousands, displacing well over a million people, and forcibly abducting children—estimates range up to 34,000—for use as soldiers, sex slaves, or forced laborers. He has reportedly called for the destruction of Christian missions and the slaughter of priests and missionaries. In a BBC report of May 2003, Kony was said to become possessed, and "whatever Kony says when he is possessed comes exactly true." He has been reputed to have accurately predicted the outcome of battles involving his forces. When Kony is in these states, the children are supposed to sing and worship.

Kony formed the LRA in the mid-1980s after the current leader, President Yoweri Museveni, came to power in Kampala. He exploited the resentment of the northern Ugandan Acholi people against Museveni for ousting the previous Ugandan leader, Milton Obote, who had Acholi roots. But Acholi support of the uprising would not endure long, as the civilians in the north became the principal victims of Kony's increasingly fanatical campaign against government forces.

Kony is not the first leader of an insurgency in the north to spread a spiritual message through the barrel of a gun. In 1985 the Holy Spirit Movement, led by a self-styled "prophetess" named Alice Lakwena, launched an uprising against the government. At its peak the movement boasted 7,000 troops. Lakwena's soldiers went to the front convinced that they were impervious to bullets, but after one battle in 1987 in which 400 Spirit soldiers were killed, the illusion became more difficult to sustain. The group scattered, and Lakwena sought refuge in Kenya, where she was briefly imprisoned.

The LRA, however, has proven a much more formidable threat than its predecessor. It is well-armed—soldiers are known to have shoulder-rockets—and military operations mounted by Kampala to crush it have so far failed to curtail its depredations or the epidemic of child abductions. Moreover, Sudan has also played a part in subsidizing the guerrillas, largely in response to Ugandan backing for a Sudanese insurgency. (A provisional peace agreement between rebels in the south and the government in Khartoum reached in late 2003 might lead to a change in Sudanese attitudes toward the LRA.)

Some witnesses have described Kony as a devoutly religious man. "We prayed a lot," recounted a former captive who met him once. "We used to say the Lord's Prayer. The objective of the prayers was to help us with the war so we could one day win and come out of our present difficult situation and live decently." Other captives have confirmed his religious character, saying that he conducts spiritual prayer sessions that are an exercise in syncretism, blending Catholic, Protestant, and even Islamic liturgy. On Fridays (the Muslim Sabbath) and Sundays, prayers were said three times a day. "Some days we would be told to pray against something bad that was about to happen," recalled one former captive. "When the government was about to attack us in Sudan, Kony said he had seen a vision from the Holy Spirit that UPDF [Uganda People's Defense Force] was preparing to attack us."

Kony seems to have a special predilection for children. In addition to abducting thousands of children of other parents, he has reportedly fathered 30–100 of his own. Unsurprisingly, his children are said to receive better treatment—including better food and school education—than the young abductees. "The rest of us only ate the beans and millet we cultivated," said a former abductee.

"Kony is not mad," said a leader of a local district council who has met Kony once. "He knows what he is doing, very well. For him this war has become a way of life and he is gaining a lot from it." In October 2005 the International Criminal Court issued an arrest warrant for Kony and four other leaders of his group.

See also CHILDREN'S RIGHTS, UGANDA, HUMAN RIGHTS VIOLATIONS IN.

Kosovo, war crimes in

In 1999 Serbian armed forces and paramilitary units moved to forcibly expel the predominantly Albanian population—some 1.8 million people—from the province of Kosovo in response to an uprising by an insurgent nationalist group. The ethnic cleansing and other atrocities that ensued led to a NATO air campaign that brought an end to the war. Estimates of the number of Albanians killed in the war range from 10,000 to 15,000. The conflict in Kosovo was the third war in the former Yugoslavia (after the wars in Bosnia and Croatia) orchestrated by Serbian strongman Slobodon MILOŠEVIĆ, who was subsequently deposed, arrested, and compelled to stand trial in The Hague for war crimes.

Efforts by the Serbs to crush the Kosovo Liberation Army (KLA), the Albanian insurgent group, began several months earlier in September 1998. Initially the government managed to rout the guerrillas from their strongholds. After 45 Albanians were massacred in the campaign, Belgrade temporarily halted its offensive in the face of mounting international criticism. Nonetheless, Yugoslavia continued to build up its forces in the province while supplying arms to local Serbs in preparation for a renewal of hostilities. Efforts by the ORGANIZATION FOR SECURITY AND COOPERATION IN EUROPE (OSCE) to broker a peace accord continued in Rambouillet, France, but it appears in retrospect that the Serb regime was using negotiations to build up its strength on the ground. A peacekeeping team called the Kosovo, Verification Mission (KVM) was deployed in Kosovo, but under Serb pressure they were forced to evacuate along with nongovernmental organizations on March 20. No sooner had they departed than Serb forces attacked several Albanian villages. According to the OSCE, "the level of incidents of summary and arbitrary killing escalated dramatically" once the peacekeeping mission had been forced to leave the territory.

By March 1999 the conflict had already cost the lives of an estimated 1,500–2,000 civilians and combatants. What had begun as an operation against the KLA soon expanded to encompass virtually the entire ethnic Albanian population, a clear violation of INTERNATIONAL HUMANITARIAN LAW. Over 200,000 Albanian civilians were internally displaced, while another 70,000 Albanians fled the province, seeking refuge in neighboring countries (principally Albania and Macedonia) or in Montenegro, which was still part of Yugoslavia. About 100,000 Yugoslav nationals, mostly

Kosovar Albanians, took refuge in Western Europe. Before the war came to an end in June 1999, 800,000 Albanian Kosovars, or approximately 80 percent of the population, had been uprooted from their homes. The countryside was devastated, with thousands of ethnic Albanian villages in Kosovo destroyed in part or in whole by burning or shelling.

To force Serb forces to withdraw, NATO instituted a bombing campaign that focused on targets in the Federal Republic of Yugoslavia, including the capital of Belgrade. (An errant bomb struck the Chinese embassy, killing three. NATO cluster bombs were also responsible for a few civilian deaths.) Rather than bringing an immediate end to hostilities, the air war—at least at first—seemed to have the opposite effect by intensifying the conflict. Expulsions were stepped up, and many of the refugees were subjected to brutal treatment—robbery and beatings were common—as they fled. Thousands of adult males were detained for weeks or months; many were tortured and in some cases executed. Several massacre sites have been exposed subsequently despite Serb efforts to conceal the evidence of their crimes. Some of the victims were children. Rape was used systematically as a war tactic; HUMAN RIGHTS WATCH documented nearly 100 cases of sexual assault by Yugoslav soldiers or security members, but the number is likely to be much higher. In addition, Serbs deliberately singled out prominent Kosovar Albanians—politicians, doctors, and human rights activists as well as individuals who had cooperated with the OSCE—for assassination. One of the first victims of such assassinations was a well-known human rights lawyer and his two sons.

It took the outside world some time to realize the extent of the atrocities. Unlike Croatia or Bosnia, both of which had substantial Serbian populations, Kosovo was almost entirely made up of Albanians, so observers were slow to appreciate the possibility that Milošević was intent on depopulating the province. The belief that the initiation of the NATO bombardment would impel the Yugoslav president to halt military operations also proved to be illusory. Serb forces moved against Albanians in the two major cities—Pec in the southwest and the capital, Pristina—only after the NATO campaign had begun. There is some evidence—much of it compiled from the accounts of REFUGEES—that Serb forces took out their resentment against NATO—which they were unable to attack—on Albanian Kosovar civilians. Some observers theorize that the ethnic cleansing in Kosovo was intended to destabilize neighboring Albania and Macedonia (about a quarter of the country's population is Muslim) by flooding the two nations with hundreds of thousands of refugees. In any case, the pace of expulsions was staggering: By March over half a million Albanian Kosovars had been forced from their homes, and a month later the refugee population had swollen to nearly 800,000. Not only were their homes destroyed but the Serbs made every effort to strip the Albanians of any proof of their identities, seizing ID cards, passports, and birth certificates, even license plates of their cars.

The Serbs—and to a lesser extent the KLA—ensured that the country would remain dangerous even after the war by planting mines and other ordinance. In just 17 months after the war ended in June 1999, 103 people were killed and 394 wounded because of accidents involving mines and unexploded ordinance.

Ultimately the NATO air campaign did succeed in halting the war which formally came to an end on June 12, 1999. The province—still technically a part of Yugoslavia—was placed under the control of the United Nations, and a peacekeeping mission was dispatched to the territory to maintain an uneasy peace. Thousands of Albanian Kosovars returned to their homes, although in many instances their homes were no longer habitable. The uncertain legal status of the province continues to cause tensions. The Albanians still seek independence, while the Serb minority prefers to keep the province under Yugoslavian authority. In spite of the presence of UN peacekeepers, clashes between the two ethnic groups erupt periodically. In a twist of history, it is often the Serb civilians who are targeted; in March 2004, for instance, a Serb village was totally destroyed by an Albanian mob—over 400 homes and 30 churches burned to the ground—and the inhabitants were forced to flee. Before order could be restored to the affected area, 28 people had died. Critics contend that the United Nations had become too complacent and had not fully understood just how tense relations between Albanians and Serbs actually are. By the end of 2004, the future of Kosovo remained indeterminate.

In October 2004 parliamentary elections, intended to resolve Kosovo's future status, dashed hopes for advocates of reconciliation between the Albanian and minority Serb populations. In the second general election held since UN peacekeepers moved into the province after the war ended, the results showed that the two populations remained at odds. Whereas Albanians went to the polls in large numbers, Serbs mostly stayed away. In December 2004 a former KLA guerrilla leader in the war, Ramush Haradinaj, was appointed prime minister, dealing another blow to hopes of reconciliation. His appointment came only weeks after he was questioned by the INTERNATIONAL CRIMINAL TRIBUNAL FOR THE FORMER YUGOSLAVIA on suspicion that he was responsible for war crimes during the war. Belgrade accused him of participating in atrocities in western Kosovo—killing Serbs and suspected Albanian collaborators—while commanding a contingent of KLA fighters.

See also BOSNIA AND HERZEGOVINA, HUMAN RIGHTS VIOLATIONS IN; CROATIA, HUMAN RIGHTS VIOLATIONS IN; RAPE AS A TACTIC OF WAR; RELIGIOUS PERSECUTION; SER-BIA, HUMAN RIGHTS VIOLATIONS IN; YUGOSLAVIA, WAR CRIMES IN.

Further Reading:
Clark, Wesley K. *Waging Modern War: Bosnia, Kosovo, and the Future of Combat.* New York: Public Affairs, 2001.

Ignatieff, Michael. *Virtual War: Kosovo and Beyond.* New York: Picador, 2001.

Judah, Tim. *Kosovo: War and Revenge.* New Haven, Conn.: Yale University Press, 2002.

Malcolm, Noel. *Kosovo: A Short History.* New York: HarperPerennial, 1999.

Mertus, Julie. *Kosovo: How Myths and Truths Started a War.* Berkeley: University of California Press, 1999.

Krajisnik, Moncilo   See WAR CRIMINALS OF THE FORMER YUGOSLAVIA.

Kramer, Josef (1906–1946) *SS concentration camp commandant*

Josef Kramer was one of 44 officers, guards, and trustees at the Belsen or Auschwitz CONCENTRATION CAMPS indicted by the Nuremberg Tribunal for murders and other offenses against inmates. He was also charged with having "knowingly participated in a common plan to operate a system of ill-treatment and murder in these camps." Even in the face of abundant documentation and eyewitness testimony, the defendants argued that the mistreatment and murder of inmates did not fall under the definition of war crimes and that because the concentration camp system was legal, under existing German law no crime had been committed.

Born in Germany in 1906, Kramer joined the SS (Schutzstaffel) and then in 1934 joined the concentration camp service. He first served at the Natzweiler camp before being appointed commandant of Auschwitz and later Belsen. During his time at Belsen, the population of inmates increased from 15,000 to almost 50,000. Allied forces found over 13,000 corpses when they liberated the camp in 1945. Kramer was found guilty and executed on October 1, 1946.

See also NUREMBERG TRIALS.

Further Reading:
Dawidowicz, Lucy. *A Holocaust Reader.* Library of Jewish Studies. Chicago: Behrman House Publishing, 1976.

Dwork, Deborah, and Robert Jan Van Pelt. *Holocaust: A History.* New York: W. W. Norton & Company, 2003.

Gilbert, Martin. *The Holocaust: A History of the Jews of Europe during the Second World War.* New York: Owl Books, 1987.

Rees, Laurence. *Auschwitz: A New History*. New York: PublicAffairs, 2005.

Kristić, Radislav   *See* WAR CRIMINALS OF THE FORMER YUGOSLAVIA.

Krupp, Gustav von Bohlen (1870–1950) *German industrialist and Nazi supporter*

Gustav von Bohlen Krupp headed the major German arms manufacturing company that bore his family name during Nazi rule. He was both a principal supplier of arms to the Nazi war machine and a beneficiary of slave labor made up of concentration camp inmates, which he used to churn out weapons. It was only because of his advanced age that he escaped being tried on charges of war crimes at the NUREMBERG TRIALS.

Although he was not born a Krupp, he acquired his name by permission of Kaiser Wilhelm II after marrying Bertha Krupp, the daughter of Friedrich Alfred Krupp, the arms manufacturer, in 1906. (Krupp was then 36 years old.) He had made a very profitable marriage: The Krupps had established an industrial dynasty that had its roots in the first major steelworks in Germany, founded in 1811. The Krupps expanded their empire over subsequent decades until it had become Germany's largest and one of the world's largest arms manufacturers. By the beginning of World War I, Krupp had already taken over the management of the company, and he presided over the introduction of a heavy-caliber howitzer known as Big Bertha (named for his wife), which was used to shell the Belgian fortress of Liège during the war.

Initially Krupp opposed Adolf HITLER, but he was persuaded to change his views when Hitler assured him that the Nazis were intent on breaking the back of labor unions and suppressing the leftist opposition, positions that Krupp favored. The Nazi government also promised to vastly increase its expenditures on arms, which would clearly benefit his company. As chairman of the Association of German Industrialists, Krupp was also in a good position to convert other business leaders as well. In 1933, shortly after assuming power, Hitler appointed Krupp chairman of the Adolf Hitler Spende, a special fund managed by Hitler's deputy, Martin BORMANN; the funds were to be channeled into the coffers of the Nazi Party in exchange for favors that would be conferred on the industrialists who had contributed to it. Until 1933, Germany had been constrained by the terms of the Versailles treaty from manufacturing arms on a large scale. However, after 1933, Hitler moved to secretly ramp up arms production regardless of the treaty. Krupp later recalled how he would accompany Hitler on inspection tours of his factories where, he said, he could "experience how the workers of Krupp cheered him in gratitude."

Under Krupp's direction, tanks began to roll off the assembly lines, although the effort was, on paper at least, a part of the Agricultural Tractor Scheme. Krupp's factories were also gearing up to produce other new weapons systems, which were developed and tested in Sweden and Holland so as to avoid drawing attention to the German arms buildup. Once World War II broke out, Krupp expanded his enterprises into newly occupied countries in Europe. "In the years after 1933 we worked with an incredible intensity and when the war did break out the speed and results were again increased," he recalled. "We are all proud of having thus contributed to the heretofore magnificent successes of our army."

To keep his factories running, Krupp appropriated more than 100,000 concentration camp inmates for slave labor. One of his factories was built inside Auschwitz. Estimates of the number of slave laborers who died as a result of mistreatment and disease run as high as 70,000. Krupp formally relinquished control of day-to-day operations of the factories in 1943 in favor of his son Alfred. After the war the victorious Allies made plans to try him for war crimes, noting that he had directly participated in the Nazi conspiracy. Krupp could hardly deny his complicity. Among the documents that fell into Allied hands was one in which he proclaimed, "I have always considered it to be an honor as well as an obligation to be the head of an arms factory and I know that the employees of Krupp share these feelings. Thanks to the educational work of the National Socialist Government this is the case all over Germany. I know that the things I have said here about the armament worker in particular hold true for every German worker. With these men and women who work for the cause with all their hearts, with cool heads and skilled hands we will master every fate." Because of his age, the decision was made not to try him at Nuremberg, though he was still technically under indictment at the time of his death in Austria on January 16, 1950.

See also CONCENTRATION CAMPS; FORCED LABOR.

Further Reading:

Rees, Laurence. *Auschwitz: A New History*. New York: PublicAffairs, 2005.

Kurdistan (Iraq), suppression of

The Kurds were the largest ethnic group *not* to obtain their own state in the post-1918 settlements in the Middle East that created Iraq. One of the oldest peoples in that region, and possibly descended from Hittites of biblical times, they are an Indo-European people surrounded largely by Arabs. Saladin, the medieval commander who fought off the Western crusaders in the 12th century, is perhaps the best-known Kurd in history. Today the estimated 26 million Kurds live in several different countries, principally in northern Iraq, southeastern Turkey, and western Iran, but also in Syria and other neighboring countries as well as the Soviet Union and Europe. More than half of the Kurdish population lives in Turkey, and another 17 percent is found in western Iraq. Approximately 850,000 Kurds live in Europe.

A large portion of Kurdistan was returned to Turkish control after World War I. Periodic separatist uprisings in Turkish Kurdistan—in 1925, 1945, and 1984–99—have led to brutal repression, thousands of deaths, and the internal displacement of thousands more. Because Britain was concerned about a possible Turkish seizure of the Mosul oil fields, London decided to incorporate the southern Kurdish area, under British League of Nations Mandate, into the new Iraqi state.

Although the Kurds and the new Iraqi ruling elite were all Sunni Muslim, the Kurds were never happy under Arab rule, which persisted, in effect, until the Kurdish areas in Iraq became autonomous under Western protection following the first Gulf War (1991). The Kurdish separatist struggle in Iraq predates Saddam HUSSEIN's rule, however. Fighting between Kurdish insurgents and forces loyal to Baghdad broke out in the 1960s and persisted until 1970, when the central government agreed to provide the Kurds with greater autonomy. Fighting resumed only a few years later when it appeared that Baghdad had little intention of abiding by its promises. Iraq had further reason to view the Kurds with suspicion because of their alliance with Iran at a time when the two neighbors were already engaged in violent clashes. Iran withdrew its support from the Kurds once the two countries agreed to a peace agreement, and the revolt was crushed. Iraq continued to suppress the Kurds. When full-scale war erupted between Iraq and Iran in 1980, the Kurds again seized the opportunity to rebel against Baghdad. This time Iraq responded with even greater ferocity and, in one of the most notorious episodes in the eight-year war, used gas against the Kurdish town of HALABJAH, killing as many as 5,000 civilians and turning thousands more into REFUGEES.

In 1991, after Iraq's defeat by U.S.-led coalition forces in the First Gulf War, the Kurds tried yet again to throw off the shackles of Saddam's regime. Once again their uprising was ruthlessly put down by Iraqi forces, and more than a million Kurds fled to Turkey, Iran, and the mountainous areas of northern Iraq. In response, the United States and its allies imposed a no-fly zone over Kuwait, carving out a protected enclave beyond the reach of Iraqi forces. Relief supplies were ferried in by coalition forces and private relief agencies to sustain the refugees with food, medicine, and shelter. For the first time the Kurds had a state of their own, although hardly on the terms they had imagined, since their autonomy was entirely dependent on outside forces. Even if Iraqi forces were kept at bay by Allied warplanes, the region was beset by violent factional fighting between the two major Kurdish parties. In 1996 leaders of one of the parties—the Kurdish Democratic Party—called on their old enemy for support, which led to an incursion of 30,000 Iraqi troops. The violence between the two parties threatened an all-out civil war, and it appeared likely that Saddam would be its beneficiary. However, a peace deal was worked out in the late 1990s put an end to factional fighting, with each party asserting control over a portion of the enclave.

The U.S.-led invasion of Iraq in 2003 spurred renewed hopes of independence among many Kurds who had championed American intervention all along. Tensions between Kurds and Iraqi Arabs have persisted even after the overthrow of Saddam Hussein. Both Kurds and Baghdad claim the Mosul oil fields, among the richest in Iraq. The Kurds believe that they have history on their side. As part of his policy to Arabize Mosul, Saddam had uprooted half of its population, mainly Kurds, in violation of international law. With the collapse of his rule, Kurds are demanding a right to reclaim a city they maintain is rightfully theirs and ought to become their capital. A significant percentage of the Kurdish population, however, appeared ready to accept autonomy in view of the vigorous opposition of Washington to any breakup of Iraq. (There is concern, too, that the Shiite south might secede as well.) Turkey and Iran would both protest vehemently against the establishment of an independent Kurdistan, fearing that the existence of such a state might unleash Kurdish insurgencies in their own countries.

See also IRAQ, HUMAN RIGHTS VIOLATIONS IN POST-SADDAM; SYRIA, HUMAN RIGHTS VIOLATIONS IN; TURKEY, HUMAN RIGHTS VIOLATIONS IN.

Kyrgyzstan, human rights violations in

A former Soviet republic in central Asia, Kyrgyzstan is still struggling to achieve a democracy and a free market economy. Its path to modernity has been hampered by several factors, including poverty and ethnic tensions over resources and housing. The ethnic conflict has been exacerbated by discrimination by the dominant Kyrgyz speakers against the Uzbeks. By failing to make a full transition from communism to capitalism, the country has seen the closing of many of its factories and an alarming rise in unemployment, with such dire repercussions as widespread malnutrition. After presidential and parliamentary elections in 2000, considered flawed by international observers, the government has intensified its campaign against critics and opposition groups, harassing and imprisoning opposition leaders and shutting down opposition newspapers. In the first part of 2002, antigovernment protests broke out in various parts of the country, set off by an accord with China, which had ceded some territory along its border, and the arrest of two prominent opposition leaders. In March, police opened fire on hundreds of demonstrators in a southern province, killing five. The violence led to the resignation of the government. Nonetheless, in May, when protesters gathered in front of the parliament building in the capital, the police responded by locking up some 90 peaceful demonstrators, a move that prompted a representative of HUMAN RIGHTS WATCH to charge that the country was "going down the road of intolerance and brutality," adding that the arrests were only part of a broader pattern of abuse.

The president, former physicist Askar Akayev, had at one point enjoyed a reputation as being one of the more liberal leaders of the former Soviet Union. But by the mid-1990s he was already moving to assert his grip on the nation by orchestrating a referendum which extended his powers at the expense of Parliament. In October 2000 he won a third term in elections seen as flawed by outside observers, and in the wake of the 2003 protests, he organized another referendum which further consolidated his power. Akayev

has asserted that the crackdown is necessary to combat Islamic militancy, and he has moved to bolster his credentials with the Washington by cooperating with the U.S. military operations in the region. Critics contend that he is only using the war on terrorism as a pretext to justify his efforts to suppress his detractors. He has announced that he will not run for the presidency again when his term expires in 2005; however he has taken the precaution to have Parliament pass a law granting him immunity for life.

Although freedom of the press was traditionally more honored in Kyrgyzstan than in its neighbors, the situation has begun to change for the worse: The opposition press is subject to increasing pressure, editorial content is subject to censorship and self-censorship, and the threat of legal action and onerous fines has stifled dissent. In March 2005, after parliamentary elections that were tainted by allegations of fraud, protests broke out in the south of the country and spread to the capital of Bishkek. Before the opposition had a chance to consolidate, mobs of youths had looted the presidential palace. Within days the regime had fallen, and Akayev had been driven into exile. The principal opposition leader, Kurman Ben Bakiyov, was elected president in 2005.

L

Laos, human rights violations in

The human rights record of Laos is poor. Security forces are known to abuse detainees; people who are suspected of being insurgents are singled out for especially harsh treatment. Arbitrary arrest and detention are commonly employed by police. According to the U.S. State Department in its 2004 *Country Report,* prisoners are sometimes tortured and confined in prisons in such deplorable condition that they can be life-threatening. Although TORTURE is forbidden by law, police have been known to beat suspects and burn them with cigarettes; in some cases, detainees were held in leg chains or wooden stocks. The judiciary system of the impoverished Indochinese nation is ineffective and subject to influence by the Communist government; suspects are forced to endure lengthy pretrial detention, and there is a decided lack of DUE PROCESS. Many prisoners have been held incommunicado and families denied access to them. Citizens' rights of free speech and privacy are curtailed. Freedom of religion, too, is restricted; several people have been imprisoned for their religious beliefs, and ethnic minority Protestant communities have come under pressure to repudiate their faith. Possibly the most egregious violations of human rights have arisen because of insurgent activity among the ethnic Hmong. The heightened level of insurgency has led to scores of civilian and military casualties. Human rights abuses and atrocities have also been perpetrated by the insurgents: In two incidents in 2003, insurgents fired on civilian buses, killing several people on each occasion. Several bombings have occurred throughout the country, including the central bus station in the capital of Vientiane, which have been attributed to rebel groups.

See also HMONG, PERSECUTION OF.

Lawyers Without Borders

A U.S.-based nonprofit organization, Lawyers Without Borders is dedicated to providing legal aid where it is needed throughout the world. It works with nongovernmental organizations (NGOs) to protect "the integrity of the legal process." According to its website, its mission "is to create a global association of lawyers dedicated to the promotion and protection of human justice via pro bono service." In July 2003 it was granted special consultive status by the Economic and Social Council of the United Nations (ECOSOC), a designation that will allow it to observe the proceedings of the UN Security Council and comment on its work as well as collaborate with other NGOs under the auspices of the United Nations.

Further Reading:
Shelton, Dinah. *Remedies in International Human Rights Law.* Oxford: Oxford University Press, 2001.
Steiner, Henry J., and Philip Alston. *International Human Rights in Context: Law, Politics, Morals.* Oxford: Oxford University Press, 2000.
Welch, Claude E., Jr. *Ngos and Human Rights: Promise and Performance.* Pennsylvania Studies in Human Rights. Philadelphia: University of Pennsylvania Press, 2000.

Lazarević, Vladimir   *See* WAR CRIMINALS OF THE FORMER YUGOSLAVIA.

Leadership Corps   *See* NAZI PARTY, LEADERSHIP CORPS OF.

League of Nations

Established at the end of World War I by the victorious Allied powers, the League of Nations was founded "to promote international co-operation and to achieve international peace and security." It was the first political international organization in history. The Covenant of the

League of Nations, setting forth its mission and organization, was approved as part of the Versailles treaty, which ended the war. Although the League was espoused by President Woodrow Wilson, who won the 1919 Nobel Peace Prize for his efforts, the U.S. Congress refused to ratify the Versailles treaty, which nonetheless entered into force on January 10, 1920. The League's original members were Belgium, Bolivia, Brazil, the British Empire, Canada, Australia, South Africa, New Zealand, India, China, Cuba, Ecuador, France, Greece, Guatemala, Haiti, Hejaz (now part of Saudi Arabia), Honduras, Italy, Japan, Liberia, Nicaragua, Panama, Peru, Poland, Portugal, Romania, Serb-Croat-Sloven State (later Yugoslavia), Siam (now Thailand), Czechoslovakia, and Uruguay. On November 15, 1920, the delegates gathered for the First Assembly of the League in its new Geneva headquarters. In one of its first acts, the League settled a territorial dispute between Sweden and Finland and resolved the division of Upper Silesia (present-day Poland).

Although the League of Nations has become practically synonymous with failure, it did have some early successes, bailing out Austria from economic calamity, preventing a war between Greece and Bulgaria, and lending assistance to refugees. The League also worked to ban white slave traffic and the opium trade. In addition, it is credited with undertaking pioneering work in surveys of health and providing financial aid to states in dire need. But when member states resisted its edicts—Poland refused to abide by the League's decision on a territorial dispute with Lithuania—the League was powerless to enforce its will. It was compelled to stand by helplessly when the French invaded the Ruhr (the industrial region of Germany) in 1923 and failed to prevent the Chaco War of 1932–36 between Bolivia and Paraguay or Japan's invasion of Manchuria in 1931. Two years later, in a show of contempt, Japan withdrew from the League. Germany followed suit the same year. In 1935, in another blow, Italy invaded Abyssinia even in the face of economic sanctions imposed by the League. In 1936 Adolf HITLER repudiated the Treaty of Versailles and proceeded to flout its provisions by remilitarizing the Rhineland. The League could do nothing to forestall the Spanish civil war, which broke out in 1936, or prevent Japan from going to war with China in 1937.

When the Soviet Union invaded Finland in December 1939, all the League could do was condemn the act of aggression. Thereafter the League effectively collapsed as an organized body, and its staff was reduced to a bare minimum. Only one component of the League—the INTERNATIONAL LABOR ORGANIZATION—continued to function through the war and survives to this day as part of the United Nations. The League of Nations dissolved itself on April 18, 1946. The concept of an international organization was not dead, however. On January 1, 1942, President Franklin D. Roosevelt had used the term *United Nations* for the first time. Then, at the end of the war, on June 25, 1945, the representatives of 50 countries meeting in San Francisco adopted the Charter of the United Nations, which formally came into existence the following October, when the signatory countries ratified the charter. All assets of the League of Nations were transferred to the new organization.

Further Reading:
Knock, Thomas J. *To End All Wars: Woodrow Wilson and the Quest for a New World Order.* Princeton, N.J.: Princeton University Press, 1995.
Ostrover, Gary B. *League of Nations 1919*, Vol. 1. Chicago: Avery, 1996.
United Nations Library. *League of Nations 1920–1946: Organization of Accomplishments.* New York: United Nations Publications, 1996.

Lebanon   See SYRIA, HUMAN RIGHTS VIOLATIONS IN.

legitimate military targets

Certain types of targets are considered legitimate or lawful under international law. It is important to distinguish lawful targets from other installations, buildings, and sites that are principally dedicated to civilian use and thus are off-limits (with some exceptions). The definition is found in Additional Protocol I to the GENEVA CONVENTIONS, Article 52, which states that a legitimate military target is one "which by [its] nature, location, purpose, or use makes an effective contribution to military action and whose total or partial destruction, capture or neutralization, in the circumstances ruling at the time, offers a definite military advantage." No attack can take place, however, if it is not justified by military necessity. An enemy force can be legitimately attacked; so can installations principally used by an enemy force such as barracks, fuel dumps, storage yards for vehicles, airfields, rocket launch ramps, and naval bases. Under INTERNATIONAL HUMANITARIAN LAW, the parties to a conflict are obliged to separate their military from civilians as much as possible, although in practice this is not always easily done. There are exceptional cases: Medical personnel and war correspondents in a military entourage, for instance, are protected from attack (although it is not considered a crime if they are killed or injured as a consequence of an attack on nearby troops). PRISONERS OF WAR, the ill, and those considered out of combat (HORS DE COMBAT) are also no longer considered lawful military targets.

Legitimate military targets also include facilities that sustain the ability of a belligerent to conduct war, such as munitions factories, storage facilities, and transportation and communication systems (railway lines, roads, bridges, tunnels, and canals) that serve the military. Research facilities involved in the development of weapons or other war matériel fall under this category. Any system or installation that provides a belligerent with a defensive capacity is also a lawful target—for example, oil pipelines, coalfields, fuel delivery trucks, and electric or gas plants that mainly provide power to the military. Broadcasting facilities and telegraph exchanges can also be legitimately targeted under certain circumstances: U.S. warplanes, for instance, struck broadcasting facilities in Baghdad before the ground invasion of Iraq in 2003 to deny Saddam HUSSEIN's regime a propaganda outlet. Attacks on nuclear plants, dams, and other installations that primarily serve the civilian population and whose destruction could create massive destruction disproportionate from any military gain are—with few exceptions—impermissible. Proportionality is a crucial consideration before an attack is considered justified under international law.

In the confusion of war, of course, many situations arise that make it difficult to distinguish between buildings or facilities that are intended principally for civilian use and those which have a military function. According to Article 52 of Additional Protocol I, "In case of doubt whether an object which is normally dedicated to civilian purposes, such as a place of worship, a house, or other dwelling or a school, is being used to make an effective contribution to military action, it shall be presumed not to be so used." However, there are occasions when a belligerent will appropriate a protected building—a church or museum, for instance—for defensive purposes. Hospitals are a trickier matter since they still enjoy immunity even if military guards are present on the premises. However, if soldiers are firing from hospital windows, the opposing force has the legitimate right to retaliate. Under those circumstances, the location would be considered a legitimate military target. Regardless, the opposing force is obliged to exercise restraint whenever there is a risk of significant loss of civilian life or destruction of civilian property. Again, if the destruction is likely to be disproportionate to the military objective achieved, the site should not be attacked. If the harm is "excessive in relation to the concrete and direct military advantage anticipated," it is a war crime.

See also ADDITIONAL PROTOCOLS TO THE GENEVA CONVENTIONS; CIVILIAN IMMUNITY; DAMS AND DIKES, PROTECTION OF.

Further Reading:
Falk, Richard A. *Crimes of War: A legal, political-documentary, and psychological inquiry into the responsibility of leaders, citizens, and soldiers for criminal acts in wars.* New York: Random House, 1971.

Goldstone, Richard. *For Humanity: Reflections of a War Crimes Investigator.* Castle Lectures Series. New Haven, Conn.: Yale University Press, 2000.
Gutman, Roy, ed. *Crimes of War: What the Public Should Know.* New York: W. W. Norton & Company, 1999.

Lemkin, Raphael (1901–1959) *legal scholar*

The Polish legal scholar Raphael Lemkin is best known for having coined the word GENOCIDE to describe the extermination of a group of people based on their nationality, religion, or ethnicity. Lemkin, who was Jewish, was born in eastern Poland, then part of czarist Russia, in June 1901. He studied at the University of Lwów before deciding on a career in law. He then went on to earn law doctorates at the University of Heidelberg and University of Lemberg. He later served as a public prosecutor and helped draft the criminal code of newly independent Poland.

Lemkin was shaken by recurring accounts of massacres of peoples around the world—especially the extermination of nearly 1.5 million Armenians by the Ottoman Turks in 1915 and the 1914–18 massacre of approximately 100,000 Christian Assyrians by Iraqis—and resolved to do something to prevent similar atrocities from happening again. He began to look at these "acts of barbarism" from a legal perspective, viewing them as crimes that should be punished. In 1933 he proposed to the Legal Council of the LEAGUE OF NATIONS meeting in Madrid that any attempt to annihilate an entire people should be outlawed. Even his own government did not back the proposal, and it failed to win approval. (The Poles did not wish to offend Nazi Germany while it was pursuing a policy of conciliation.) Lemkin, however, continued to press his proposal. The German invasion of Poland in September 1939, which began World War II, led to the very sort of catastrophes that he had foreseen. Lemkin slipped out of Poland and sought refuge in Sweden, where he resumed his career teaching law at the University of Stockholm. He and his brother Elias were the only two members of his family—which numbered over 40—to survive the war.

Throughout the war, Lemkin studied Nazism from the perspective of jurisprudence. He examined the decrees that the Nazis had issued to justify their actions in occupied Europe and used as a legal basis to exterminate Jews, Rom (Gypsies), and other people labeled "undesirable." Lemkin called these premeditated criminal acts "genocide," from the Greek prefix *genos*, meaning race, and the Latin suffix *cide*, meaning killing. In 1944 he published a seminal book called *Axis Rule in Occupied Europe.* His analysis served as a foundation for the legal framework of the NUREMBERG TRIALS, established by the victorious Allies to prosecute Nazi war criminals. Lemkin subsequently served as legal adviser to the U.S. chief prosecutor at the tribunal, Robert JACKSON.

Although genocide was one of the principal charges leveled against war criminals, Lemkin was not satisfied. Genocide was still considered a crime that could only take place in times of war and was not applicable in times of peace. At the Paris peace conference in 1946, Lemkin presented a proposal that would make acts of genocide punishable under international law under all circumstances, but his proposal was rejected, just as it had been a decade before. Without any organization or funding, or even an office, Lemkin persisted with his crusade nonetheless. His efforts were rewarded in 1946 when a similar resolution was approved by the newly created United Nations. On December 9, 1948, the UN General Assembly unanimously adopted the Convention on the Prevention and Punishment of the Crime of Genocide. Lemkin went on to hold several prestigious positions in the U.S. government as an adviser to the Bureau of Economic Warfare, the War Department (now the Defense Department), and the State Department. Lemkin settled in the United States and taught at Princeton, Yale, and Rutgers in the last decade of his life. Until his death in 1959, he continued to advocate for the ratification of the Genocide Convention. He was nominated twice for the Nobel Peace Prize and received numerous awards and honors.

Leopold II (1835–1909) *Belgian king*

King Leopold II of Belgium was known in his country as the King Builder for commissioning many monumental buildings, including museums and the Antwerp train station, but in the Congo, which he exploited as a personal fiefdom, he acquired a reputation as a mass murderer. Leopold believed that the key to Belgium's importance on the world stage was in acquiring colonies, and when he failed to persuade his people to embark on a colonization drive, he undertook to obtain a colony for himself. In 1876 he organized a private holding colony, which operated under the cover of an international scientific and philanthropic association. Three years later he hired the Anglo-American journalist and explorer Henry Morton Stanley to establish a colony in the Congo. Over the next four years, Stanley led several expeditions into the Congo and set up a number of outposts as a preliminary step to staking claim to the region. But before Leopold's dream could be realized, an effective transportation system had to be created. Stanley hit upon the idea of using steamboats, shipping them first in pieces to the port of Stanley Pool (later Leopoldville and now Kinshasa), and then transporting them by land 250 miles north, borne on the heads of porters, to the Congo River. From that point the ships could navigate freely for several hundred miles deep into the rain forests of southern Congo. Leopold backed the scheme and financed a small armada of steamships.

After considerable diplomatic wrangling at the Berlin Conference of 1884–85, Leopold secured the Congo Free State as his own personal preserve, which gave him title over a territory 76 times larger than Belgium and larger than all of Europe. To maintain order, an army was established called *Force Publique,* made up of Congolese and non-Congolese soldiers and commanded by Belgian officers; cannibals were recruited as well as part of a deliberate policy to keep the populace terrorized. At its peak the force numbered 20,000. The attitude of the colonists toward the Congolese was exemplified by the statement of one white man who declared that "only the whip can civilize the black."

After acquiring a monopoly on the colony's most important commodities—rubber and ivory—Leopold issued a decree requiring the Congolese to supply these products without any compensation. Anyone who defied these orders or failed to supply his quota was liable to have his hands lopped off. Mutilation became so commonplace that a Belgian captain adorned his flower beds with the heads of 21 natives killed in a punitive expedition. Villages were burned and children murdered as routine punishments. Under Leopold's regime, millions of Congolese were murdered or perished from disease or brutal conditions imposed by their oppressors. The harsh methods had their desired effect, however, increasing exports to such an extent that Leopold had to falsify accounts and trade statistics in order to conceal his enormous profits. He used his windfall to purchase more properties, reconstruct palaces, and build new monuments. He then went on a buying spree, forming companies to negotiate lucrative business deals in China, Morocco, Greece, the Philippines, and Bolivia.

Leopold's depredations did not escape the attention of the outside world. The atrocities in the Congo inspired Joseph Conrad's famous novel *Heart of Darkness* and provoked widespread outrage in the West. A protest campaign spearheaded by religious leaders in the early 1900s finally forced the Belgian parliament to take action, and in 1908, a year before his death, Leopold was compelled to cede his property to the nation. Henceforth, the Belgian Free State was to be known—until its independence in 1960—as the Belgian Congo.

See also DEMOCRATIC REPUBLIC OF THE CONGO, HUMAN RIGHTS VIOLATIONS IN.

Further Reading:
Edgerton, Robert. *The Troubled Heart of Africa: A History of the Congo.* New York: St. Martin's Press, 2002.
Hochschild, Adam. *King Leopold's Ghost.* Boston: Mariner Books, 1999.

Wrong, Michela. *In the Footsteps of Mr. Kurtz: Living on the Brink of Disaster in Mobutu's Congo*. New York: HarperCollins Publishers, 2001.

levée en masse

The *levée en masse,* or mass uprising, is a call to arms; historically, it is a means to inspire patriotism and swell the ranks of a national army to meet a threat posed by potential or actual enemies. The first documented *levée* took place in 1792 when the new regime in France believed that the gains of the French Revolution of 1789 were threatened by European powers eager to restore the old regime of the Bourbon monarchy. To defend the country's borders against the coalition of European adversaries, the revolutionary regime invoked emergency powers to draft virtually all men of military age into the army. Subsequently Napoleon relied on *levées* to mobilize forces for national defense. Poland, too, relied on *levées* to recruit as many men as possible against the Nazi invaders.

The term acquired legal status in the Brussels Conference in 1874. A *levée* does not refer to an uprising by people against its own government but instead entails organized resistance against an invader. *Levée en masse* implies that the population takes up arms already in its possession and that this uprising occurs spontaneously. The concept of a *levée* also appeals to Second Amendment advocates who view it as a legal justification for maintaining arms free from government control or interference. Under certain circumstances, individuals who join a *levée* are entitled to status as combatants and, if captured, are accorded the same rights as PRISONERS OF WAR. However, to be granted these privileges, a participant in a *levée* can only be engaged in conflict against an invading force. In the event that a territory is occupied, only members of an armed force who have not surrendered are considered legitimate combatants under international law. Civilians under occupation do not have the same rights if they take up arms. Nonetheless, even civilians who support a resistance movement would be protected against COLLECTIVE PUNISHMENT by an OCCUPYING POWER under the Fourth Geneva Convention.

Further Reading:
Gutman, Roy, ed. *Crimes of War: What the Public Should Know*. New York: W. W. Norton & Company, 1999.

Ley, Robert (1890–1945) *Nazi labor organizer*

The son of poor peasants and a chemist by trade, Robert Ley was responsible for turning organized labor into a tool of Nazi power. Born in 1890, he became a military aviator during World War I but spent most of that conflict as a prisoner of war after being shot down over France. After the

war he briefly worked as a chemist but was fired because of his drinking. Like other disaffected young men of his time, he joined Adolf HITLER's Social Democratic German Workers Party (NSDAP) in 1925, becoming one of its first members. He rose in the ranks of the Nazi Party and began publishing a Nazi journal, *Westdeutscher Beobachter.*

Shortly after taking power in 1933, the Nazis proclaimed May Day (May 1) as the Day of National Labor and organized a massive demonstration by workers in Berlin. But far from supporting labor, the Nazi Party had secretly issued an order 10 days earlier to purge the union leaders—placing them under "protective custody"—and seizing their offices and guns. Ley was the official who was responsible for carrying out the order, which was carried out the next day—May 2nd—by SS and SA troops. Shortly afterward all unions were integrated into a single organization under Nazi command called the *Deutsche Arbeitsfront (DAF),* which Ley headed. The new regime outlawed collective bargaining; henceforth, wages were set by labor representatives answerable only to the DAF. Two years later, in 1935, under a new set of labor laws—the so-called Strength through Joy program (*Arbeitsbuch*)—industrial workers were compelled to remain with a single employer and no longer had the option of looking for another job.

Even as he was depriving them of their rights, Ley organized various recreational and leisure time activities to divert workers who were increasingly being used to build vehicles for the army and ships for the navy. He remained an ardent supporter of the Nazis even as the German army was close to defeat. Albert SPEER, Hitler's architect, later recalled a conversation with Ley in the autumn of 1944, held in Ley's private railway car: "As usual, our conversation took place over glasses of strong wine. His increased stammering betrayed his agitation. 'You know we have this new poison gas—I've heard about it. The Fuehrer must do it. He must use it. Now he has to do it!' " While he waited in prison for his trial at Nuremberg to begin, Ley wrote a statement denouncing anti-Semitism and then hanged himself in his cell on October 25, 1945.

Further Reading:
Russell of Liverpool, Edward Frederick Langley Russell, Baron. *The Scourge of the Swastika: A Short History of Nazi War Crimes*. London: Greenhill Books/Lionel Leventhal, 2002.

Liberation Tigers of Tamil Eelan   See TIGERS, TAMIL.

Liberia, human rights violations in

Liberia has the distinction of being the oldest republic in Africa. Founded by freed American slaves in 1847, the country was long dominated by their descendants. That all changed in 1980 when the president, William Tolbert, was overthrown. Tolbert's ouster—and his subsequent execution—marked the beginning of two decades of civil war, rebellions, and coups in which all parties to the conflict committed atrocities and human rights abuses. Of Liberia's estimated 3,317,000 people, almost 300,000 were forced by the violence to seek refuge in other countries. But any safety to be found with Liberia's neighbors—Sierra Leone, Ivory Coast, or Guinea—was illusory. The wars that consumed Liberia would eventually spill over its borders, and wherever the violence spread the principal victims were mostly civilians.

Tolbert, the last leader who came from the country's aristocracy, owed his removal from office (and his death) to a master sergeant by the name of Samuel K. Doe. Doe formed a so-called People's Redemption Council and proceeded to suspend parliament, ruling by dictatorial decree. Pressured by the United Nations, however, he relaxed his grip to some extent and in 1984 permitted political parties to compete for a presidential election a year later. He had no problem tolerating rival parties so long as none had any possibility of winning. To run the country's finances, Doe chose an ambitious American-educated young man named Charles TAYLOR. Taylor soon betrayed Doe's trust, fleeing to the United States on charges of embezzling $1 million. When he returned to Liberia a year later, it was with the intention of overthrowing his former patron. He formed an opposition movement, the National Patriotic Front of Liberia (NPFL), which was soon splintered by factionalism.

The uprising against the government began in 1989. Within a matter of weeks, the 10,000-man army mustered by the NPFL was in control over most of the countryside. When the rebels were not fighting government forces, they were fighting each other. Alarmed at the spread of the conflict, a peacekeeping force—the ECOWAS MONITORING GROUP (ECOMOG) led by Nigeria—was sent to Liberia to restore order, but it was helpless to stop the conflict. A rival of Taylor's named Prince Johnson managed to abduct Samuel Doe from under the eyes of the peacekeepers. Not content with simply executing the former president, Johnson's men beat and mutilated him before putting him to death. Prince Johnson made certain that the grisly proceedings were videotaped for posterity. In months the conflict expanded to include no fewer than five different parties—ECOMOG, the Liberian army, the NPFL, its offshoot the Independent National Patriotic Front of Liberia (INPFL), and the United Liberation Movement of Liberia for Democracy (ULIMO), made up of Doe loyalists. To fund his ragtag army, Taylor looked to the diamond-rich eastern districts of neighboring Sierra Leone. To capture the mines, he formed a perfidious alliance with a former Sierra Leone corporal, Foday SANKOH. Within a few years,

diamonds from the mines captured by Sankoh's forces were being exported in significant numbers into territory occupied by Taylor.

By 1991 there were only two major combatants left: the peacekeepers who controlled little more than the capital of Monrovia and Taylor's NPFL, which held the rest of the country. An attempt at a peace agreement in 1993 lasted barely a year before war resumed, this time with new factions contributing to the chaos. The violence continued on and off until a cease-fire was reached in August 1996 under the auspices of ECOMOG. By then the conflict had claimed 150,000 Liberian lives, and over a million people had been displaced. By July 2000 there were already five outbreaks of fighting since the 1997 elections that were supposed to bring peace to the country.

The cease-fire paved the way for what was supposed to be a restoration of democracy, but true power remained in the hands of Charles Taylor. The end of the war had transformed him from a rebel leader in the bush to a political force to be reckoned with. In 1997 he won the presidency in an election whose fairness was in some dispute. The shaky peace did not endure for long, however, and soon Taylor was faced with armed uprisings in the countryside that he was quick to blame on the government of nearby Guinea. In the subsequent fighting, Liberian government forces were accused by the United Nations of "war crimes and other serious human rights abuses, including summary executions of scores of civilians, widespread rape of girls and women, and looting and burning of villages." In the course of the conflict, hundreds of civilians were forcibly conscripted and sent to the battlefield, mostly to serve as cannon fodder. The rebels, known by their acronym LURD (Liberians United for Reconciliation and Democracy) were also culpable, though perhaps to a lesser degree. LURD was charged with summary executions of suspected government collaborators, rape, and recruiting child soldiers. Tens of thousands of REFUGEES driven from their homes by the fighting were at risk for extortion for money and food by government soldiers manning checkpoints along the roads.

Of all the human rights abuses that went on in these years, the conscription of children stands out in particular because it underscores the difficulty of returning so many young people into society now that Liberia has achieved some measure of peace and civil order. "[W]e learned to fire, to take cover and how to kill," recalled one boy who was forced into LURD's ranks. "We were made to crawl under barbed wire while they were shooting at us, we were forced to advance towards the gun fire. This was to make us brave. . . . Sometimes we were made to man checkpoints. Other times we would go out on the front. During the fighting, I was very afraid. I killed many people, I saw friends dying all around me, it was terrible." In general, the older boys—14 or 15—did the fighting while the younger children were kept as support troops, but there were instances where boys and girls as young as nine and 10 bore arms. Children were also made to do forced labor or to serve as spies, infiltrating behind enemy lines. Almost every conscripted child was given a nom de guerre—a fighting name—as another means of brainwashing these young soldiers, depriving them of any link with their families. One boy, for instance, took the name of "Mother's Blessing" because his commander told him that his mother had blessed him to fight against government troops before succumbing to enemy fire. In fact, his mother was very much alive. Other monikers were inspired by a child's distinguishing trait. "Laughing and Killing" was given to a boy who would laugh whenever he shot an enemy soldier to death. "Disgruntled" never displayed enthusiasm on the battlefield, whereas "Captain No Mercy" killed anyone who dared to disobey orders.

In 2001 the United Nations imposed economic sanctions against Liberia in response to Taylor's continuing human rights abuses and support of rebellions in Sierra Leone, Guinea, and the Ivory Coast. Taylor also found himself under pressure from LURD forces, which had now taken substantial territory in the countryside and were threatening Monrovia, the capital. Nonetheless, Taylor held on even after being indicted on 17 counts of human rights violations by the United Nation's SPECIAL COURT FOR SIERRA LEONE, investigating war crimes committed in that country by Taylor's protégé, Foday Sankoh. As rebel forces occupied part of the capital, pressure steadily mounted on Taylor to resign. There were calls for action by the United States (which was thought to have a special relationship with Liberia because the country was founded by African Americans), but the Bush administration preferred to use diplomacy to force Taylor's exit. The United States did make a show of force, however, deploying three warships in Monrovia's harbor. Hundreds of the city's war-weary residents turned out to hail a small contingent of U.S. Marines when they were sent to reinforce security at the American embassy. Although human rights organizations demanded Taylor's arrest, it appeared uncertain whether he would ever step down unless he could be assured of eluding punishment.

In August 2003, after difficult negotiations, Nigeria agreed to give Taylor sanctuary. Even then it took three days for Taylor to finally leave office and go into exile. Many human rights activists still hope that the Nigerian government will ultimately decide to hand him over for trial. Shortly after his departure, a Liberian businessman named Charles Gyude Bryant was sworn in as head of a two-year transitional government. The country has only just begun to take the first tentative steps toward the daunting task of reconstruction.

See also CONFLICT DIAMONDS; CHILDREN'S RIGHTS; IVORY COAST, HUMAN RIGHTS VIOLATIONS IN; SIERRA LEONE, HUMAN RIGHTS VIOLATIONS IN.

Further Reading:
Adebajo, Adekeye. *Building Peace in West Africa: Liberia, Sierra Leone, and Guinea-Bissau.* International Peace Academy Occasional Paper Series. Boulder, Colo.: Lynne Rienner Publishers, 2002.
———. *Liberia's Civil War: Nigeria, Ecomog, and Regional Security in West Africa.* Boulder, Colo.: Lynne Rienner Publishers, 2002.
Ellils, Stephen. *The Mask of Anarchy: The Destruction of Liberia and the Religious Dimension of an African Civil War.* New York: New York University Press, 2001.
Kulah, Arthur F. *Liberia Will Rise Again: Reflections on the Liberian Civil Crisis.* Nashville: Abingdon Press, 1999.
Mohammed, Amos. *The Role of the Economic Community of the West African States: Ecowas—Conflict Management in Liberia.* Bloomington, Ind.: AuthorHouse, 2003.
Pham, John-Peter. *Liberia: Portrait of a Failed State.* London: Reed Press, 2004.

Libya, human rights violations in

In January 2003, in a move that outraged the U.S. government and human rights groups alike, Libya took over the chairmanship of the UNITED NATIONS HUMAN RIGHTS COMMISSION. HUMAN RIGHTS WATCH demanded to know how a country known for its flagrant violations of human rights could be allowed to assume charge of a commission whose purpose was to monitor violations of human rights throughout the world. In addition, Libya would be in a position to block any action taken against itself. Libya apparently benefited from an agreement to finance the African Union (the successor of the Organization of African Unity); in return, several African members of the United Nations backed Libya's chairmanship. But the United States and Great Britain, which had opposed the appointment, had cause to welcome Libya back into the international fold several months later when the Libyan government announced that it was abandoning its nuclear weapons program. Even Human Rights Watch conceded that Libya had made some progress in human rights.

Libya has been under the dominion of Colonel Muammar al-Gadhafi since he seized power in a coup in 1969. An erratic, temperamental figure, Gadhafi was considered an international pariah for his sponsorship of terrorist groups around the world. Libyan agents were implicated in the bombing of Pan Am 103 over Lockerbie, Scotland, on the night of December 21, 1988. Libya was also involved in the 1989 bombing of UTA flight 772 over Chad, which killed 171 persons, and the 1988 bombing of the La Belle discotheque in then-West Berlin, killing American servicemen. There is little question that Gadhafi was eager to make a deal with the West to remove sanctions on Libya, which led to his repudiation of terrorist organizations he had previously supported. It is also likely that as the United States ratcheted up its campaign against terrorist groups after the attacks of September 11, 2001, Gadhafi decided to rethink his policies. Sanctions against Libya were lifted in September 2003.

At home Libya still retains the trappings of one-man rule. Its human rights record is poor, and citizens' rights are severely curtailed, particularly when it applies to their ability to change the government. Political opposition is not permitted, and Islamic groups are particularly targeted for persecution. According to the U.S. State Department, security personnel routinely torture suspects and detain them illegally. The methods of TORTURE include clubbing suspects, applying electric shocks or corkscrews to their backs, pouring lemon juice into open wounds, breaking fingers, suffocating with plastic bags, starvation, burning with cigarettes, beating on the soles of the feet, and using attack dogs. Political prisoners are kept incommunicado indefinitely in unofficial detention centers managed by members of the Revolutionary Committees that act as an arm of Gadhafi's regime. Detainees have been held for years without any official charges being brought. Some human rights groups put the number of political detainees as high as 2,000. (In an AMNESTY, Gadhafi announced the release of 3,000 prisoners, but it is unknown how many might have been political prisoners, because international human rights monitors are denied access to them.)

The government has instituted what is called a Purge Law intended to punish economic crimes. Under the law, merchants and businessmen have been locked up on charges that include trading in foreign goods, corruption, and financing illegal Islamic organizations. Enforcement is the responsibility of so-called purification committees. The judiciary is entirely under the thumb of the government, and security forces have the right to impose their own sentences without any trial. Citizens have no rights of privacy to speak of and are not even permitted to own private property. Security forces are known to enter private residences without warrants, and the government is entitled to confiscate or destroy property belonging to "enemies of the people" or those who "cooperate" with foreign powers. The freedoms of speech, press, assembly, association, and religion are restricted. Some carefully controlled criticism in the press is allowed, but apparently only for the purpose of testing public reaction or weakening a political opponent. Worker rights are curbed as well, FORCED LABOR is practiced, and foreign workers, mostly from sub-Saharan Africa, are often mistreated. To maintain power, the Gadhafi regime relies on an elaborate security apparatus made up of security agencies and Revolutionary Committees; according to one estimate, 10–20 percent of the country's population is involved in surveillance activity. Families or communities are liable to punishment if they fail to inform on criminal or seditious elements. The crimes include "obstructing the people's power, instigating and practicing tribal fanaticism, possessing, trading in or smuggling unlicensed weapons, and damaging public and private institutions and property." Whole towns, villages, local assemblies, and tribes can be punished if they are accused of abetting or even sympathizing with perpetrators of crimes. The law specifies that communities could be punished by being denied food, official documents, or utilities such as water and electricity. What is called the "Code of Honor" allows the punishment of relatives of an individual convicted of certain crimes, particularly political dissidence.

Further Reading:
El-kikhia, Mansour O. *Libya's Qaddafi: The Politics of Contradiction.* Tallahasee: University Press of Florida, 1998.
Simmons, Geoff. *Libya and the West: From Independence to Lockerbie.* London: I. B. Tauris, 2004.

Lidice, massacre in

The annihilation of the Czech town of Lidice is among the most notorious massacres committed in German-occupied Europe during World War II. The massacre took place as a reprisal for the assassination of Reinhard HEYDRICH, *Reichsprotektor* of Czechoslovakia, on May 27, 1942, by two Czechs. The Germans were determined to exact revenge for the slaying of the most important Nazi official in Czechoslovakia, and well over a thousand people were killed in the capital, Prague. Reprisals were conducted in the countryside as well. In one village, Lezaky, every adult was killed when the Germans discovered a transmitter belonging to Heydrich's assassins. Of the children who were deported from the village to Germany for "re-education," only two survived.

On June 9, 10 truckloads of SS forces reached Lidice, 10 miles outside of Prague. The town was cordoned off, and no one was allowed to leave. When a 12-year-old boy and a peasant woman tried to escape, they were shot. All the men and boys over 16 years old—in addition to several women—were rounded up and locked in a barn. The next day they were taken out and shot behind the barn—10 at a time. By the time the SS was finished, 192 men and boys and 71 women lay dead. Another 19 men and seven women who escaped the initial onslaught were captured and sent to Prague, where they were killed. The 195 women who survived were deported to the Ravensbrück concentration camp in Germany, where 49 died by gassing or mistreatment. Ninety children were sent to a concentration camp where they were selected by "racial experts" for distribution to German parents. To conceal evidence of their crime, the SS dynamited the bodies and burned the town, bulldozing the rubble so thoroughly that no structure was left intact. In the hope of eradicating its memory altogether, the name of Lidice was expunged from all official records. The town was never rebuilt, but it has not been forgotten.

See also COLLECTIVE PUNISHMENT.

Further Reading:

Bradley, J. J. *Lidice: Sacrificial Village.* Ballantine's Illustrated History of the Violent Century. Human Conflict no. 2. New York: Ballantine Books, 1972.

MacDonald, C. A. *The Killing of Reinhard Heydrich: The SS "Butcher of Prague."* New York: Da Capo Press, 1998.

Whiting, Charles. *Heydrich: Henchman of Death.* Barnsley, U.K.: Leo Cooper, 1999.

Lieber Code (Instructions for the Government of the Armies of the United States in the Field)

Introduced while the American Civil War was still raging, the Lieber Code set forth established standards for behavior on the battlefield. Until the Lieber Code, no legal rules of warfare existed in the United States or anywhere else. A need for such a code was obvious early in the war. In July 1861, after the Battle of First Manassas, Union soldiers plundered and burned private homes in the northern Virginia countryside. In response to these outrages, General George McClellan, general of the Army of the Potomac, wrote to President Abraham Lincoln, asking him to see to it that the war was conducted according to "the highest principles known to Christian civilization" and to avoid targeting the civilian population to the extent that that was possible. Although Lincoln sacked McClellan a few months later and ignored his letter, he seemed to have realized that the general's concerns were justified.

The Lieber Code takes its name from its author, the law professor Francis Lieber, who drafted it at Lincoln's behest in 1863. It anticipated and influenced the work of the First Geneva Convention. (The international conference that would draft the Convention did not meet until later in 1863.) The Lieber Code was important for distinguishing behavior by combatants toward belligerents and noncombatants insofar as civilians were entitled to certain protections in times of armed combat. The code further specified standards of treatment for PRISONERS OF WAR by the capturing army. Moreover, all soldiers were to be treated equally, regardless of "class, color, or condition." The code is especially noteworthy for its concern with the treatment of African-American soldiers fighting for the

Union who might be captured by the Confederate Army and be treated as renegade slaves. After Lincoln approved its provisions, the adjutant general issued the Lieber Code as General Order 100 on April 24, 1863.

Lieber was an interesting choice to create rules of warfare. A German legal scholar, he had previously served as an adviser to Otto von Bismarck, the architect of German unification, and was a strong advocate of centralized government authority. He had no love for the American federalist system, enshrined in the Constitution, denouncing the founding fathers for having created "confederacies of petty sovereigns," and he dismissed the Jeffersonian philosophy of government as a collection of "obsolete ideas." Although the Lieber Code called for protections of civilians during armed conflict, its author had left a loophole, allowing Union commanders to ignore the code if "in their discretion" they believed that the situation on the battleground made it imperative. In light of ensuing events—including Sherman's destruction of Atlanta—it appears that Union forces frequently took advantage of the loophole.

See also CIVILIAN IMMUNITY; SLAVERY.

Further Reading:

Hartigan, Richard Shelly, ed. *Lieber's Code and the Law of War.* New Brunswick, N.J.: Transaction Pub, 1983.

limited war

Limited war is defined as armed conflict that does not rise to the level of total or general war, involving the engagement of the military forces of two or more nations. A state may make it clear before a conflict begins that it intends to exercise restraint in the pursuit of its military objectives, whether by its actions or by a unilateral declaration. The state may, for instance, wish to limit the conflict to a certain defined territory or make it known that it will not use the most powerful weapons at its disposal. By the same token, a state may declare that it will not seek to destroy certain installations or capacities of its enemy—its air force, for example, or a military communications system. In some instances a state may strike at only selected targets viewed as especially threatening—for instance, enemy installations or military bases, knowing that the enemy does not have the ability to retaliate. So in that sense, the war will be limited because only one party to the conflict is in a position to wage war. INTERNATIONAL HUMANITARIAN LAW applies regardless of whether a conflict is limited or total. Usually a limited war is meant to be of short duration, even if this does not always turn out to be the case.

For many years U.S. and British aircraft bombed Iraqi radar and antimissile systems to enforce no-fly zones over Iraqi Kurdistan without suffering a single downed plane—an example of a limited war. As a rule, in limited wars only two states are involved; that is, allies of each state do not enter the conflict as well. The Falklands War of 1982, between Great Britain and Argentina, could be considered a limited war. In that case, Britain was interested only in pushing out Argentine forces that had taken over the Falklands (Malvinas to Argentines), which Britain controlled and which Argentina claimed. Britain, which won the war, had no territorial designs on Argentina, nor did it set out to change the government, although that was an indirect result of the conflict.

History is replete with examples of TOTAL WAR, in which one side is determined to conquer the other, seize its territory, destroy its military capacity, subdue its population, and exploit its natural resources. Very simply, in total war empires and states see little reason to show any restraint in their exercise of force or in its objectives. Arguably, World War II represents the apogee of total war, as the objective of the Allies was the complete defeat and unconditional surrender of the Axis powers of Germany, Italy, and Japan. But after World War II, total war became much more difficult to wage. Certainly the threat of nuclear weapons being used in a third world war led to the imposition of a large measure of restraint—not only on the nuclear powers but also on their allies, many of which were engaged in limited "proxy" wars throughout the world. Neither the United States nor the Soviet Union was eager to see limited wars dragging them into a Third World War. This was particularly the case in the Middle East, where the conflict between Israel and the Arab states periodically threatened to embroil the two superpowers.

Limited wars became almost a fixture of the cold war, beginning with the Korean War of 1950–53. The Korean War was the first time that U.S. political and military leadership confronted a situation where outright victory by North Korea, backed by China, or South Korea, backed by the United States, was not feasible but rather concluded in a stalemate after three years. A generation later, the United States fought another limited—and frustrating—war in Vietnam. Again victory proved impossible to achieve, barring the possible use of nuclear weapons, a step that no U.S. president was willing to take.

Further Reading:

Falk, Richard A. *Crimes of War: A legal, political-documentary, and psychological inquiry into the responsibility of leaders, citizens, and soldiers for criminal acts in wars.* New York: Random House, 1971.

Gutman, Roy, ed. *Crimes of War: What the Public Should Know.* New York: W. W. Norton & Company, 1999.

Jackson, Nyamuya Maogoto. *War Crimes and Realpolitik: International Justice from World War I to the 21st Century.* Boulder, Colo.: Lynne Rienner Publishers, 2004.

Jokie, Aleksander. *War Crimes and Collective Wrongdoing: A Reader* London: Blackwell Publishers, 2001.

Lome Peace Accords *See* SANKOH, FODAY; SIERRA LEONE, HUMAN RIGHTS VIOLATIONS IN.

London Charter *See* NUREMBERG CHARTER.

López Rega, José (1916–1989) *Argentine secret police chief*

The former Argentine social welfare minister under Juan Perón and later his wife, Evita, José López Rega became known popularly as "El Brujo" (wizard or warlock). Perón, Argentina's strongman, was president twice from 1946 to 1955 and from 1973 to 1974. Under López Rega, the position of social welfare minister was a euphemism for the interior ministry, which put him in charge of the secret police. In that capacity he packed Perón's personal bodyguard with a group of men from around the world who were known as ultrarightists, including Cuban-American militants from the extremist group Alpha 66, gunmen from Italy's Ordine Nuovo, Croatian fascist USTACHE, and several Corsican gangsters who were involved in the infamous French Connection heroin conspiracy. Another handpicked recruit was Ciro Ahumada, an ex-leader of the ultraright French Secret Army Organization (OAS), which carried out a terrorist campaign to prevent President Charles de Gaulle from granting Algeria its independence from France.

López Rega's closest ally was his top deputy, Lieutenant Colonel Jorge Osinde, Perón's intelligence chief from his first administration. In the early 1970s the two men worked together to restore Perón to power. López Rega became an increasingly dominant figure even as Perón's influence began to fade. After Perón's death, López Rega became an advisor to his wife Evita, who assumed the presidency for two years. An occult follower, López Rega put up a monument to witchcraft in Buenos Aires (since dismantled) and was said to have cursed the country after he was pushed out of power in a military coup in 1976.

See also ARGENTINA, HUMAN RIGHTS VIOLATIONS IN.

M

MacBride, Sean (1904–1988) *human rights activist*
Dr. Sean MacBride was awarded the Nobel Peace Prize in 1974 and later the Lenin Prize from the Soviet Union and the American Medal of Justice for his work on behalf of human rights. His achievement is all the more remarkable in view of the fact that earlier in his life he was a nationalist who had fought against British rule of Ireland.

Born on January 26, 1904, MacBride was nurtured on the milk of Irish nationalism. His father, John MacBride, was executed by the British for participating in the Easter Rebellion in 1916; his mother, Maud Gonne MacBride, a fiery beauty and passionate nationalist in her own right, was immortalized in the poems of W. B. Yeats. MacBride spent his first years in France; upon returning home in 1918, he joined the Fianna, an Irish nationalist party. In 1921 he was involved in the negotiations with the British that resulted in the partition of Ireland. He continued to fight against British rule in the north of the country, and in 1936 he became chief of staff of the Irish Republican Army (IRA). After World War II, however, he abandoned militancy and began a political party, Clann na Poblachta, which won enough seats in the 1947 parliamentary elections to earn him a place in the government as minister for external affairs. In that capacity he was among the drafters of the EUROPEAN CONVENTION FOR THE PROTECTION OF HUMAN RIGHTS, which guaranteed international protection for human rights. As president of the Committee of Ministers of the Council of Europe from 1949 to 1950, MacBride was a driving force to gain acceptance of the convention, which was signed into law in Rome in November 1950. He devoted the rest of his life to the advocacy of the principles enshrined in the convention. A cofounder of AMNESTY INTERNATIONAL, he went on to serve as UN commissioner for Namibia (former South-West Africa) with the rank of assistant secretary general.

In awarding MacBride the Peace Prize in 1974, the Nobel Committee cited him for having "mobilized the conscience of the world in the fight against injustice." In 1979 he acted as a mediator in efforts to secure the release of American hostages being held in the U.S. embassy in Teheran. In addition to his other posts, he served as president of the International Board of Amnesty International, secretary general of the International Commission of Jurists, and chairperson and later president of the International Peace Bureau. He was also the author of what became known as the MacBride Principles, which were intended to ensure that U.S. companies operating in Northern Ireland comply with equal employment opportunities for Catholics. He died in Dublin on January 15, 1988.

Further Reading:
Steiner, Henry J., and Philip Alston. *International Human Rights in Context: Law, Politics, Morals.* Oxford: Oxford University Press, 2000.
Welch, Claude E., Jr. *Ngos and Human Rights: Promise and Performance.* Pennsylvania Studies in Human Rights. Philadelphia: University of Pennsylvania Press, 2000.

Macedonia, human rights violations in

A former Yugoslav republic, Macedonia emerged, largely unscathed, from the Balkan wars that broke out in the 1990s. However, the country has not managed to escape the violent ethnic conflict that sparked the conflict. Macedonia is divided along ethnic and religious lines: dominant Orthodox Christian Slavs (67 percent) and Albanian Muslims (25 percent). In 2001 Albanian insurgents rebelled in an effort to gain greater autonomy. The violence was precipitated by the war in neighboring Kosovo, which, while mostly populated by Albanians, was controlled by Slavic Serbia. Many Albanian Kosovar fighters and thousands of civilians fleeing the fighting took refuge in Macedonia, provoking a refugee crisis and fueling unrest among indigenous Albanians. After some initial successes on the battlefield, Macedonian forces were driven back by the Albanian National Liberation Army (NLA), which seized territory in the north and west of the country. The fighting was brought to an end by the intervention of the European Union and NATO. A peace accord, known as the Ohrid agreement, granted Albanians more political rights in exchange for the rebels laying down their arms. Although the agreement was bitterly opposed by Macedonian nationalists, both parties to the conflict have upheld its terms.

During the rebellion, human rights groups observed abuses by both Macedonian security forces and the insurgent NLA. Macedonian forces illegally detained Albanian men fleeing the violence and subjected them to maltreatment intended to exact confessions, actions HUMAN RIGHTS WATCH described as tantamount to TORTURE. Police were charged with systematically beating Albanian male civilians, including teenagers and the elderly. Similar abuses were reported against some Macedonian Slavs. On the other hand, Albanian rebels were accused by human rights groups of torture, sexual abuse, and mutilation of Macedonian Slav civilians. The NLA was also implicated in a pattern of abductions and illegal detentions.

See also KOSOVO, WAR CRIMES IN.

Majid, Ali Hassan al- (Chemical Ali) (1941–) *Iraqi war criminal*

Ali Hassan al-Majid earned the sobriquet by which he is best known, "Chemical Ali," for ordering an attack in 1988 using outlawed CHEMICAL WEAPONS, which are believed to have killed up to 5,000 Kurds in northern Iraq. He was the king of spades in the famous deck of cards of the 55 most-wanted Iraqi officials following the U.S. invasion in 2003. A cousin of Saddam Hussein, al-Majid held several important positions in his regime, serving as a general and as a close presidential adviser, or as Saddam's "hatchet man," in the words of a HUMAN RIGHTS WATCH report. During the 2003 U.S. invasion, al-Majid disappeared from sight for several months, and at one point it was thought that he had died in an American bombing strike on his home. However, after U.S. forces took Baghdad, he was captured in August 2003.

As secretary general of the Northern Bureau of Iraq's Baath Party, Ali Hassan al-Majid was in charge of all state agencies in the Kurdish region in northern Iraq from March 1987 to April 1989, giving him control of the army's I and V Corps, the general security directorate, and military intelligence. In orders dated June 20, 1987, he directed army commanders "to carry out special bombardments [a reference to chemical weapon use] . . . to kill the largest number of persons present in . . . prohibited zones"— meaning the Kurds, whom Saddam considered *insurrectionists*. The operations against the Kurds were known as the Anfal campaign; the name was derived from a Koranic

verse that justified the pillaging of infidel property. The Anfal campaign was launched just as the 1980–88 Iraq-Iran war was coming to an end. Some 100,000 civilians were killed or "disappeared," and many Kurdish villages and farms destroyed as a result of the Anfal campaign. Iraqi intelligence documents confiscated by U.S. military authorities leave no doubt that the campaign was systematic and conducted under al-Majid's direct supervision. He proved so effective at suppressing the Kurds that he was put in charge of Iraq's military occupation of Kuwait in 1990. He subsequently had a principle role in the campaign against an uprising by Iraq's Marsh Arabs during the 1990s in which the marshes were drained and almost a quarter of a million people were displaced, annihilating a culture that had thrived in the region for centuries. Each of these campaigns was characterized by executions, arbitrary arrests, "disappearances," torture, and other atrocities.

In 2004, al-Majid was one of 12 Iraqi officials (including Saddam Hussein) who went before an Iraqi court to hear the charges against them. As expected, one of the principal charges against him was the gassing of Kurds. He was reported as expressing surprise that the charges against him weren't even more numerous. The court set no date for his trial.

See also KURDISTAN, SUPPRESSION OF.

Further Reading:

Aburish, Said K., and Aburish Said. *Saddam Hussein.* London: Bloomsbury Publishing, 2001.
Coughlin, Con. *Saddam: King of Terror.* New York: Ecco, 2002.
Dodge, Toby. *Inventing Iraq: The Failure of Nation-Building and a History Denied.* New York: Columbia University Press, 2003.

Malaysia, human rights violations in

Among the most prosperous countries in Asia, Malaysia is a multiethnic, multireligious country; the minority Chinese dominate the economy and constitute the wealthiest community whereas the indigenous Malays dominate the political landscape. Indians are among the poorest of the three. It is a constant challenge to the country's leadership to maintain harmony among the many groups that make up this nation of over 25 million.

Until recently Malaysia was ruled by the autocratic prime minister Mahathir bin Mohamad, who only stepped down in October 2003 after 22 years in power, making him Asia's longest-serving elected leader. His successor, Abdullah Ahmad Badawi, is a more self-effacing leader who, upon taking office, was forced to cope with a rising Islamic fundamentalist movement. In a significant departure from his predecessor, he released former deputy prime minister

Anwar Ibrahim from prison. Freeing Malaysia's best-known opposition figure was considered a milestone in the struggle for human rights in Malaysia. Anwar had been arrested in September 1998 on charges of corruption and sodomy widely seen as politically motivated; until his arrest, he had been thought to be Mahathir's successor. Initially held under Malaysia's Internal Security Act, he was beaten by the national chief of police. After two separate trials in 1999 and 2000, he was sentenced to consecutive terms of six and nine years, respectively. Both trials were considered unfair by human rights groups; the prosecution frequently changed its charges, and government witnesses offered contradictory statements. The verdict was overturned by the nation's high court after Abdullah Badawi was elected. The sodomy conviction of a codefendant, Sukma Darmawan, was thrown out at the same time. Although Anwar's case is a "barometer" of Malaysia's commitment to freedom, HUMAN RIGHTS WATCH and other groups have called attention to about 100 lesser-known cases where detainees have been held under the Internal Security Act. Many of these are suspected militants who have remained in custody for up to three years without charges or trials. There have also been reports that these detainees have suffered from physical and psychological abuse. Some were forced to stand seminaked for long periods and subjected to sexually humiliating interrogations. Human rights groups also expressed the hope that Anwar's release might signal greater judicial independence than was seen under Mahathir's administration. "At some point, the Malaysian courts will again be called upon to render justice in a politically charged case," said a representative of Human Rights Watch when Anwar's conviction was overturned. "They must be able to hear cases free of outside pressure. That didn't happen with Anwar until today."

Like many other countries, the Malaysian government has used the global war against terrorism instituted after the attacks of September 11, 2001, as a pretext to curtail its commitments to human rights. In 2003, 11 persons died in police custody. The government-sponsored Human Rights Commission of Malaysia (Suhakam) contended that in addition to deaths that occurred in police custody, it had received "numerous" complaints of police brutality and negligence. Although no constitutional provision or law specifically prohibits TORTURE, there are laws that prohibit "committing grievous hurt," which does encompass torture. When investigations are carried out by the government, however, it does not issue reports on its findings. The Bar Council has expressed its distress with the situation and called for an investigation of a "number" of allegations of police abuse.

The 2004 U.S. State Department *Country Report* on Malaysia, covering events of the previous year, gives Malaysia credit for adhering to human rights, though it said that some problems remained. The government itself has acknowledged that it restricts certain political and civil rights in order to maintain social harmony and preserve political stability. Limits have been placed on freedom of the press, freedom of association, and freedom of assembly. There is also some discrimination against nonethnic Malays. Because of its geographical location, Malaysia is both a source and destination for trafficking in women and girls for the purposes of prostitution.

Further Reading:

Crouch, Harold. *Government and Society in Malaysia.* Ithaca, N.Y.: Cornell University Press, 1996.

Gomez, Edmund Terence, and K. S. Jomo. *Malaysia's Political Economy: Politics, Patronage and Profits.* Cambridge: Cambridge University Press, 1997.

Manchuria, Japanese war crimes in

Japan's territorial ambitions in Manchuria in northern China extend back to the Russo-Japanese War (1904–05) from which Japan emerged victorious. Manchuria was a military prize because of its coal, iron, and other mineral resources. In 1931 Japan installed the last emperor of China as the head of a puppet state called Manchukuo. However, the Japanese did not fully occupy Manchuria until 1937, when Japanese forces defied the League of Nations and invaded the region. Over the next several years the Japanese military proceeded to initiate a secret BIOLOGICAL WEAPONS program. The most notorious biological research facility, put into operation in 1939, was known as Unit 731 and based in Pingfan, Manchuria. The existence of Unit 731 and other similar units did not become known until nearly four decades after the war. The compound of 150 buildings housed a laboratory, an autopsy room, and a prison for the human subjects referred to as "logs," "monkeys," or "lumber." The prisoners were made up of criminals and political dissidents rounded up by the feared military police and other security forces.

Unit 731 was directed by a brilliant and flamboyant Japanese army microbiologist named Chujo Shiro Ishii. He called his work *Himitsu ni Himitsu*—"Secret of Secrets." An ultranationalist, he rose rapidly in the ranks of the military with the help of influential friends, eventually winning an assignment to Manchuria. His first command was codenamed the "Togo Unit," where, in one of their first biological experiments, the Japanese introduced bubonic plague into China's eastern Zhejiang province, killing 400 villagers in September 1942. Ishii later took over Unit 731, which was developing germ bombs that were intended to be dropped from warplanes on China. The unit was responsible for contaminating Manchuria's water supply with typhus. Every few days Ishii and his associates would draw

500 cc of blood from the prisoners until they became enfeebled from losing too much blood at which point he executed them by lethal injection. Ishii was particularly interested in developing biological weapons based on anthrax, glanders, and plague, all very contagious agents. He forced prisoners to consume drinks tainted with cholera, heroin, and castor oil seeds. After injecting prisoners with these agents, Ishii would carry out dissections rather than waiting for them to die. He did not confine his experiments to microbes; he also experimented with phosgene gas and potassium cyanide and used electricity to burn prisoners whom he later killed with poison. Frostbite experiments constituted another area of interest. Naked prisoners, male and female, were subjected to subfreezing temperatures; to ensure that the freezing was complete, the researchers pounded them with sticks until the impact produced a hollow sound. The prisoners were subsequently "defrosted" by a variety of means. Other experiments involved hanging prisoners upside down to determine how long it would take them to die.

A methodical record keeper, Ishii made certain to document these experiments in exhausting detail. As the war was coming to an end, he swore his officers to an oath of secrecy about their work at Unit 731. The facility itself was destroyed; so were most of the records of the experiments. Some of the dossiers survived, though, and came into the possession of Allied intelligence officials who were interested in learning about the research, fearing that the Americans had fallen too far behind the Japanese in the field of biological warfare. In 1948 the Allies offered Ishii and other top officials of Unit 731 immunity in exchange for their data, making it all but impossible for attorneys at the TOKYO TRIALS to prosecute them.

With characteristic bravado, Ishii delivered papers on the results of his research at distinguished scientific conferences. He never mentioned that the subjects of his research were human, but it was well known in Japanese scientific circles. He even went so far as to patent 200 of his discoveries, which earned him a considerable sum of money. At one point Ishii reportedly traveled to the United States after the war to give a talk. The role the United States played in cover-up of Unit 731 did not come to light until the publication of an article on the subject by John W. Powell, Jr., in the *Bulletin of Atomic Scientists*. But the American public did not really learn about the experiments and the deal the United States had reached with Ishii until 1992, when segments on Unit 731 were aired on CBS's *60 Minutes* and ABC's *20/20*.

In spite of the renewed attention, legal actions against the criminals of Unit 731 have made little progress; Japanese courts routinely reject lawsuits by victims of such experiments or their families, although appeals continue to be lodged. The Japanese government has also resisted calls to make financial restitution to survivors and their families. No Japanese government has ever acknowledged the guilt of physicians who participated in these experiments, although Japan had ratified the 1906 Hague Convention, which provides that "officers, soldiers, and other persons officially attached to armies, who are sick or wounded, shall be respected and cared for, without distinction of nationality, by the belligerent in whose power they are."

See also MATSUOKA, YOSUKE.

Further Reading:

Daws, Gavin. *Prisoners of the Japanese: POWS of World War II in the Pacific.* New York: Perennial, 1996.

Harris, Sheldon. *Factories of Death: Japanese Biological Warfare 1932–45 and the American Cover-Up.* London: Routledge, 1995.

Li, Peter, ed. *Japanese War Crimes: The Search for Justice.* New Brunswick, N.J.: Transaction Publishers, 2003.

Maga, Timothy P. *Judgment at Tokyo: The Japanese War Crimes Trials.* Lexington: University Press of Kentucky, 2001.

Mendelsohn, John. *The Preservation of Japanese War Crimes Trials Records in the National Archives.* Washington, D.C.: National Archives and Records Administration, 1982.

Minear, Richard R. *Victors' Justice: The Tokyo War Crimes Trial.* Michigan Classics in Japanese Studies. Ann Arbor: University of Michigan Center for Japanese Studies, 2001.

Piccigallo, Philip R. *The Japanese on Trial: Allied War Crimes Operations in the East, 1945–1951.* Austin: University of Texas Press, 1980.

Rees, Laurence. *Horror in the East: Japan and the Atrocities of World War II.* New York: Da Capo Press, 2002.

Russell of Liverpool, Edward Frederick Langley Russell, Baron. *Knights of the Bushido: A Short History of Japanese War Crimes.* London: Greenhill Books, 2005.

Tanaka, Yuki. *Hidden Horrors: Japanese War Crimes in World War II.* Philadelphia: Westview Press, 1998.

Martens Clause

The Martens Clause is named for Professor Friedrich von Martens, the Russian delegate at the Hague Peace Conferences of 1899. The clause is intended to address the issue of the status of civilians who take up arms against an OCCUPYING POWER. The larger states maintained that these civilians should be subject to execution, while the smaller states argued that they should be treated as lawful combatants who, if captured, should be treated as PRISONERS OF WAR. The Martens Clause states: "Until a more complete code of the laws of war is issued, the High Contracting Parties think it right to declare that in cases not included in the Regulations adopted by them, populations and belligerents remain under the protection and empire of the principles of international law, as they result from the usages established between civilized nations, from the laws of humanity and the requirements of the public conscience."

Ever since the clause's adoption, humanitarian lawyers have debated how its principles should be applied. For instance, some human rights advocates argue that the Martens Clause bans the use of nuclear weapons, a view that is rejected by the nuclear powers. The GENEVA CONVENTIONS of 1949 and the 1979 ADDITIONAL PROTOCOLS TO THE GENEVA CONVENTIONS have restated the Martens Clause. The International Law Commission has affirmed that the clause "provides that even in cases not covered by specific international agreements, civilians and combatants remain under the protection and authority of the principles of international law derived from established custom, from the principles of humanity and from the dictates of public conscience." That is to say, the clause is a part of CUSTOMARY LAW, which carries the force of law even when the protections in the clause are not cited in a particular treaty.

See also HAGUE CONVENTIONS.

Martić, Milan   *See* WAR CRIMINALS OF THE FORMER YUGOSLAVIA.

mass graves

Mass graves are often used to inter victims of atrocities during wartime. In recent years such graves have been uncovered in post-HUSSEIN Iraq, Argentina, Guatemala, El Salvador, Honduras, Ethiopia, Mexico, the former Yugoslavia, and Rwanda. Forensic examination of the remains in these graves can identify how the crimes were carried out and lead to the prosecution of those responsible. The discovery of mass graves also provides incontrovertible evidence of EXTRAJUDICIAL KILLINGS, TORTURE, and other crimes that in many cases the perpetrators denied had ever occurred. The discovery of mass graves in South America, for instance, has revealed the extent of the killings carried out by former military regimes against suspected dissidents during the "dirty wars" of the 1970s. After the U.S.-led invasion of Iraq in 2003, forensic investigators fanned out across Iraq to uncover mass graves. Early findings suggest that at least 400,000 people were killed and buried in such graves under the dictatorship of Saddam Hussein. Evidence gathered from these sites is expected to be used against the ousted strongman when he is brought to trial.

To establish a crime of GENOCIDE, it is necessary first to prove intent—for example, that individuals belonging to a particular religion, race, or ethnic group, were singled out for persecution, torture, or execution. To the extent that investigators can show that the victims discovered in a mass grave were all members of a particular class and were deliberately executed, the easier it is for prosecutors to determine a finding of genocide. Indeed, as Elizabeth Neuffer points out in an essay on the subject in the CRIMES OF WAR PROJECT, the very existence of mass graves can constitute a violation of INTERNATIONAL HUMANITARIAN LAW (IHL)—specifically, the Third and Fourth GENEVA CONVENTIONS and Additional Protocol I—which requires belligerents to comply with certain standards regarding the disposal of enemy dead. Deceased PRISONERS OF WAR or combatants must be buried in marked graves, their location mapped, and the INTERNATIONAL COMMITTEE OF THE RED CROSS notified of the death.

International law has not to date addressed the right to exhume mass graves. In 1973, however, the United Nations General Assembly adopted a resolution (3074) which calls on member states to cooperate with war crimes investigations. Additional Protocol I also requires parties to a conflict to conduct searches for missing persons after the end of hostilities. An individual state is not required to allow outside investigators to examine suspected mass graves. As Neuffer notes, not all mass graves can necessarily be considered evidence of atrocities; victims of a plague, for instance, may be buried hurriedly in a mass grave because of the danger of infection and the numbers of deaths involved. When they are crime scenes, though, mass graves must be protected from tampering.

To appreciate the difficulty that forensic anthropologists and other investigators confront when they investigate mass graves, one must take into consideration the fact that each human skeleton consists of about 200 bones and 32 teeth, any one of which can provide a knowledgeable researcher with evidence of a crime. Moreover, investigators need to collect evidence found with the remains—bullets, blindfolds, and binds, for instance, that were used by the perpetrators as well as clothing and personal possessions belonging to the victims that might help identify them and determine the circumstances under which they were executed. How the victim was killed is also difficult to resolve if a great deal of time has gone by since the execution was committed, depending on the state of decomposition. Dental records and DNA samples are often employed in the absence of other evidence. In Rwanda identification of many of the victims has proven impossible because of the numbers of the victims and the lack of records which could be used to aid in identifying them.

See also ADDITIONAL PROTOCOLS TO THE GENEVA CONVENTIONS. PHYSICIANS FOR HUMAN RIGHTS.

Further Reading:

Ferllini Timms, Roxana. *Silent Witness: How Forensic Anthropology Is Used to Solve the World's Toughest Crimes.* Buffalo, N.Y.: Firefly Books Ltd, 2002.

Gutman, Roy, ed. *Crimes of War: What the Public Should Know.* New York: W. W. Norton & Company, 1999.

Cox, Margaret, and Jon Sterenberg. *Forensic Archaeology, Anthropology and the Investigation of Mass Graves.* London: CRC Press, 2006.

Matsui Iwane (1878–1948) *Japanese general*

General Matsui Iwane was the Japanese commander largely responsible for the Nanjing (Nanking) massacre in 1937–38—also known to history as the Rape of Nanking ("Nanjing Datusha" in Chinese)—the worst single massacre of unarmed civilians by soldiers in 20th-century history. Between 200,000 and 350,000 Chinese civilians and soldiers who had laid down their arms were slaughtered by Japanese invaders over a period of less than two months. In addition, anywhere between 20,000 and 80,000 Chinese women and girls were raped, many of whom were later killed or forced to become sex slaves—one of the worst episodes of mass rape ever documented.

As commander of the Japanese expeditionary force, Matsui was given orders to "kill all captives" in Nanjing on December 5, 1937, after Chinese troops defending the city had refused to withdraw; Nanjing fell on December 13, and Matsui led the victorious Japanese into the city four days later. He remained for another week before being incapacitated by tuberculosis. During the time he was still in charge of the troops, he did nothing to stop the slaughter, which went on for the next six weeks. Matsui retired in 1938 and withdrew from active military duty at the war's end. However, he was considered one of the 14 Class A war criminals to be brought before the International Military Tribunal for the Far East established by the Allies, known as the TOKYO TRIALS. He was convicted for his role in the Nanjing and massacre executed. Even today, ultranationalists in Japan regard him as a martyr. He is buried at Yasukuni Shrine, which is dedicated to Japan's war dead and is also Japan's most revered Shinto temple.

See also NANJING (NANKING), MASSACRE IN.

Further Reading:

Honda, Katsuichi, and Frank Gibney, eds. *The Nanjing Massacre: A Japanese Journalist Confronts Japan's National Shame.* Studies of the Pacific Basin Institute. Armonk, N.Y.: East Gate Book, 1999.

Matsuoka Yosuke (1877–1946) *Japanese foreign minister and nationalist*

A former Japanese foreign minister during World War II, Matsuoka Yosuke was tried for war crimes after the end of World War II. Matsuoka stands out among other members of the Japanese military clique that exercised power in the 1930s and 1940s because he spent several years studying in the United States, graduating from Oregon University in 1900. He began his diplomatic career as consul in Shanghai. In 1927 he was appointed vice president of the Southern Manchuria Railway Company, an important position given Japan's territorial designs on the region. Matsuoka was an ardent supporter of annexing Manchuria to Japan; he espoused the view that mineral-rich Manchuria was "the Lifeline of Japan." In 1932 he was placed in charge of the Japanese delegation to the LEAGUE OF NATIONS. When the League strenuously protested Japan's invasion of Manchuria in 1937, he led the walkout of the Japanese delegation, an act that was widely applauded at home. His service was rewarded by an appointment to head the Southern Manchurian Railway Company.

In 1940 Matsuoka became minister of foreign affairs. In that capacity he promoted closer relations between Nazi Germany and Japan, advocating a policy known as the Greater East-Asian Co-prosperity Sphere, which served as a justification for Japanese dominance of the region. In a major diplomatic coup, Matsuoka brokered a neutrality accord with the Soviet Union in early 1941, although only a couple of months later he lobbied futilely for Japan to join Hitler's invasion of the Soviet Union. (The USSR only declared war against Japan a few weeks before the war ended.) Matsuoka was one of 27 Class A war criminals to be tried by the Allies, but he died of natural causes before he could be sentenced in 1946.

See also MANCHURIA, JAPANESE WAR CRIMES IN.

Further Reading:

Li, Peter, ed. *Japanese War Crimes: The Search for Justice.* Brunswick, N.J.: Transaction Publishers, 2003.

Maga, Timothy P. *Judgment at Tokyo: The Japanese War Crimes Trials.* Lexington: University Press of Kentucky, 2001.

Mendelsohn, John. *The Preservation of Japanese War Crimes Trials Records in the National Archives.* Washington, D.C.: National Archives and Records Administration, 1982.

Minear, Richard R. *Victors' Justice: The Tokyo War Crimes Trial.* Michigan Classics in Japanese Studies. Ann Arbor: University of Michigan, Center for Japanese Studies, 2001.

Piccigallo, Philip R. *The Japanese on Trial: Allied War Crimes Operations in the East, 1945–1951.* Austin: University of Texas Press, 1980.

Rees, Laurence. *Horror in the East: Japan and the Atrocities of World War II.* New York: Da Capo Press, 2002.

Russell, of Liverpool, Edward Frederick Langley Russell, Baron. *Knights of the Bushido: A Short History of*

Japanese War Crimes London: Greenhill Books, 2005.

Tanaka, Yuki. *Hidden Horrors: Japanese War Crimes in World War II.* Philadelphia: Westview Press, 1998.

Mau Mau uprising

The Mau Mau was an indigenous Kenyan insurgency directed against the British colonial power. Although it was crushed in the mid-1950s, it paved the way for eventual independence of the East African nation. The derivation of the phrase *Mau Mau* is in dispute. One theory holds that it comes from the mountain range bordering the western side of the Rift Valley, another that it is the cry of war of the Kikuyu, Kenya's largest tribe, and still another that it is an acronym for a Swahili phrase that means, "Let the white man go back abroad so the African can get his independence."

Known as the Movement or the Unifier, the Mau Mau rebellion was officially the creation of the Kikuyu Central Association (KCA). Initially the rebellion—which relied on a core of Kikuyu for its support though members of other tribes participated in it—targeted other Africans considered collaborators for working for the British. In one attack, Mau Mau guerrillas killed 93 Africans and as many as 1,800 altogether. But it was the attacks on white-owned farms—about 100 Europeans were killed—that terrorized European settlers, many of whom left the country. The British responded by imposing a brutal crackdown, and by 1953 the rebellion had virtually sputtered out, partly as a result of internal discord.

In 1955, of the 120,000 insurgents who had joined the Mau Mau, only about 15,000 were still alive and free. Official figures at the time put guerrilla losses at 11,000 and suspected African collaborators at 2,000. The British claimed that they had arrested another 30,000. Historians, however, have put the total deaths and detentions much higher: 14,000–30,000 guerrillas killed and from 80,000 to 100,000 arrested. The Mau Mau had accelerated the push for independence, which was finally achieved in 1963, but the legacy of the insurgency continues to haunt Kenya's former rulers. Five decades after the Mau Mau uprising, veterans of the movement took steps to reopen the books on alleged British abuses of Kenyans during the insurgency in the hope of gaining restitution from the British government. By 2003 lawyers had taken 6,000 depositions from Kenyans who reported that they had suffered from a variety of abuses, including rape, castration, TORTURE, whipping, indiscriminate killing, and theft of property. According to Caroline Elkins of Harvard University, who wrote a book about the alleged abuses, British security forces may have killed as many as 50,000 guerrillas, an estimate much higher than any previously given and a figure that has been disputed by other historians. The scale of abuses, if proven, would require the "rewriting of British imperial history" in the words of a BBC report.

See also KENYA, HUMAN RIGHTS VIOLATIONS IN.

Further Reading:

Elkins, Caroline. *Imperial Reckoning: The Untold Story of Britain's Gulag in Kenya.* New York: Henry Holt & Co., 2005.

Mauritania, human rights violations in

Bounded by the Atlantic Ocean and the Sahara Desert, Mauritania is a vast country with relatively few people; its population is fewer than 2 million. The country straddles a cultural divide that is also in part accountable for some of its most serious problems, since it links Arab Maghreb with western sub-Saharan Africa. Traditionally, the Arab-Berber north of the country has dominated the African south. Until the mid-1990s Mauritania was under one-party control. Opposition to the regime was suppressed, and arbitrary arrests and illegal detentions were frequent. Ethnic disputes often arose between the Arabs and African laborers and peasants who had migrated from neighboring Senegal seeking work. No matter how long they remained in the country, the Senegalese were not entitled to citizenship. These tensions flared into riots in 1989 in Mauritania and Senegal. The Mauritanian authorities reacted by deporting some 12,000 Senegalese back home. Black Mauritanians did not fare much better. In 1990 and 1991, 500 black Mauritanian soldiers were arrested on charges of plotting an uprising, and many were either arrested and deported without a trial or else killed.

In 1992 the government relaxed its grip on power and allowed political parties. Elections held in 1992 and 1993, however, were marred by accusations of fraud and boycotts by some opposition parties. A process of Arabization of the country appears to be underway. Arabic, for instance, is now compulsory in schools, and it is the only language taught in most of the schools over the objections of many black Mauritanians. According to human rights activists, the government restricts freedom of movement, especially involving travel by black Africans, and continues its practice of conducting arbitrary arrests and arbitrary detentions. In a new crackdown against dissidents, security forces rounded up dozens of religious leaders, opposition politicians, and human rights activists. Most were subsequently released but still faced charges of treason that many international watchdog agencies have denounced as groundless. "The government put forward no credible evidence that those arrested had been involved in any terrorist activities," charged the executive director of the Africa Division of HUMAN RIGHTS WATCH. "It seems that this is yet another example of a government opportunistically using the language of counter-terrorism to crack down on legitimate dissent."

Mauritania has also come under fire from international critics for condoning conditions that in most respects resemble SLAVERY. In a scathing report issued in 2002, the International Confederation of Free Trade Unions (ICFTU) condemned the government for the practiced of child labor and FORCED LABOR. Although Mauritania is a signatory to accords outlawing child labor, the report cites evidence that in 2000, 68,000 children ages 10–14 are working in agriculture and fishing and herding. Although "forced labor is not a widespread occurrence," the report said, "many workers remain in a situation tantamount to forced labor, as a consequence of established slavery." In fact, slavery is a shockingly recent phenomenon in Mauritania's history; it persisted until the early 1980s, when it was finally banned. International observers say that while the incidence of overt slavery has diminished significantly in the decades since then, the country is still haunted by its consequences, and many impoverished Mauritanians, mostly black African, remain in conditions that are almost indistinguishable from slavery. In spite of efforts by labor advocates to change government policy, forced labor practices continue unabated. "There has been no progress on this subject in recent years," the ICFTU report concluded. In August 2005 Mauritania's authoritarian leader Ould Taya was ousted in a military coup while he was out of the country, marking the end to 21 years of one-man rule. The Military Council for Justice and Democracy, as the junta was named, pledged a return to democracy, a promise that was greeted with skepticism. Nonetheless, some opposition leaders expressed hope that the military would keep its word.

See also CHILDREN'S RIGHTS.

Further Reading:

Gerteiny, Alfred G. *Islamic Influences on Politics in Mauritania*. Boston: African Studies Center, Boston University, 1971.

Handloff, Robert L. *Mauritania: A Country Study*. Area Handbook Series. Washington, D.C.: Government Printing Office, 1990.

Morrow, James. *Mauritania*. Modern Middle East Nations and Their Strategic Place in the World. Philadelphia: Mason Crest Publishers, 2004.

Waltz, Susan Eileen. *Human Rights and Reform: Changing the Face of North African Politics*. Berkeley: University of California Press, 1995.

Meakić, Zeljko　*See* WAR CRIMINALS OF THE FORMER YUGOSLAVIA.

Médecins Sans Frontières　*See* DOCTORS WITHOUT BORDERS.

medical experiments

Nonconsensual medical experiments on human beings are crimes under international law and the laws of most nations. The GENEVA CONVENTIONS of 1949 defined medical experiments on PRISONERS OF WAR (POWs) and protected persons—civilians under the control of an OCCUPYING POWER—as a grave breach. The 1998 ROME STATUTE OF THE INTERNATIONAL CRIMINAL COURT stated that medical experiments are war crimes, whether they occur in an international armed conflict or an internal one. The statute defined the crime as: "Subjecting persons who are in the power of an adverse party to physical mutilation or to medical or scientific experiments of any kind which are neither justified by the medical, dental or hospital treatment of the person concerned nor carried out in his or her interest, and which cause death to or seriously endanger the health of such person or persons."

These legal prohibitions were seen as necessary to prevent a recurrence of the horrifying medical experiments that were conducted by both Nazi Germany and Japan during World War II. In what was called the DOCTORS' TRIAL (October 1946–April 1949), 24 Nazi physicians and other medical officials were charged with involvement in "medical experiments without the subjects' consent, upon civilians and members of the armed forces of nations then at war with the German Reich and who were in the custody of the German Reich . . . in the course of which experiments the defendants committed murders, brutalities, cruelties, tortures, atrocities, and other inhuman acts." Most of the subjects were inmates of CONCENTRATION CAMPS. In some experiments, subjects were placed in chambers meant to simulate high-altitude conditions; forced to remain in tanks of ice water for periods of three hours; injected with malaria, epidemic jaundice, spotted fever, streptococcus, gas gangrene, and tetanus; deliberately exposed to mustard gas; forced to endure transplants of bones, muscles, and nerves removed from other subjects; and sterilized by means of X-ray, surgery, and drugs. At the Buchenwald concentration camp, inmates were administered poison intravenously or shot with poison bullets. Most of these experiments resulted in death or severe injury. The Japanese, too, systematically carried out a program of medical experimentation on POWs and civilians in areas they occupied. Subjects were vivisected without anesthesia, infected with different pathogens, or used to demonstrate surgical techniques, after which they were liable to be shot. In some cases, tourniquets were applied to the arms and legs of American POWs for seven or eight hours, which could cause death once the tourniquets were removed. In

June 1945, eight American airmen underwent vivisection at Kyushu Imperial University, one of Japan's most prestigious medical schools, lethal procedures in which doctors removed their lungs, hearts, livers, and stomachs. In Japanese-occupied Manchuria, the Japanese army established a special medical group—Unit 731—to carry out a series of barbaric medical experiments on captured Chinese civilians.

The crimes of Nazi and Japanese physicians led to the development of a Nuremberg Code governing medical experiments in war or in peacetime. The code declared that voluntary, informed consent from a human subject was necessary before any experiment could be undertaken. No deceit or coercion can be employed, and the subject must be apprised of all inconvenience and hazards to health that might result. The experiment must also be designed for the good of society. In addition, there must be no alternative to human experimentation such as animal experiments. All unnecessary physical and mental suffering and injury should be avoided, and any experiment that is likely to cause death or disabling injury should not take place at all. Subjects should be able to withdraw their consent at any time; similarly, physicians or scientists conducting the experiments have an obligation to stop them if it appears likely that death, injury, or disability will result.

See also Brandt, Karl; Clauberg, Carl; Manchuria, Japanese war crimes in; Mengele, Josef; Oberhauser, Herta.

Further Reading:

Gutman, Roy, ed. *Crimes of War: What the Public Should Know.* New York: W. W. Norton & Company, 1999.

Harris, Sheldon. *Factories of Death: Japanese Biological Warfare 1932–45 and the American Cover-Up.* London: Routledge, 1995.

Lagnado, Lucette Matalon, and Sheila Cohn Dekel. *Children of the Flames: Dr. Josef Mengele and the Untold Story of the Twins of Auschwitz.* New York: Penguin Books, 1992.

Lifton, Robert. *The Nazi Doctors: Medical Killing and the Psychology of Genocide.* New York: Basic Books, 2000.

Rees, Laurence. *Horror in the East: Japan and the Atrocities of World War II.* New York: Da Capo Press, 2002.

Tanaka, Yuki. *Hidden Horrors: Japanese War Crimes in World War II.* Philadelphia: Westview Press, 1998.

medical personnel, protection of

Military attacks against medical personnel units are prohibited by the Fourth Geneva Convention of 1949. Article 20 of the convention states: "Persons regularly and solely engaged in the operation and administration of civilian hospitals . . . shall be respected and protected." The convention additionally forbids the destruction, closure (whether temporary or permanent), or interruption of the supply of food, water, medicines, or electricity to civilian hospitals and clinics. However, this prohibition can be waived if hospitals or medical units are put to use by a belligerent for military purposes, in which case they are liable to attack so long as the force used is proportionate to the military value of the facility. International humanitarian law (IHL) also confers protections on medical personnel—physicians, medics, nurses, ambulance drivers, etc.—but they must identify themselves as physicians or health-care workers, respect medical ethical principles, and provide treatment to all victims in need without discrimination. This means that a doctor, for example, cannot give priority to an injured soldier from his own side in preference to a more seriously injured enemy soldier. Medical personnel are also constrained from barring arms unless they are required for self-defense. IHL does not afford legal protections to physicians and health-care workers who act in a nonmedical capacity.

See also civilian immunity; Geneva Conventions.

Further Reading:

Gutman, Roy, ed. *Crimes of War: What the Public Should Know.* New York: W. W. Norton & Company, 1999.

Memorial

Memorial is a Russian nongovernmental organization established to expose past political and civil human rights abuses in the former Soviet Union and advocate for human rights in present-day Russia. At the same time Memorial seeks "to introduce constructive proposals in government aimed at overcoming the totalitarian legacy and creating guarantees against its restoration." Memorial has created an information center and a map of the gulag, the notorious system of labor camps where millions of people were imprisoned for years under Joseph Stalin. The organization has exposed atrocities committed by the MVD (former Soviet secret police) troops in Chechnya and restored a cemetery of an NKVD (the precursor of the KGB and MVD) camp, where prisoners from Poland, Germany, Italy, Romania, and Russia are buried. Plans are being made to erect memorials at other camp cemeteries. Memorial also organizes humanitarian aid to freed political prisoners who survived the camps. In an attempt to prevent a repetition of the past, Memorial representatives have conducted classes in human rights in secondary schools.

Further Reading:

Applebaum, Anne. *Gulag: A History.* New York: Doubleday, 2004.

Khlevnink, Oleg. *The History of the Gulag: From Collectivization to the Great Terror.* Translated by Vadim A.

Staklo. *Annals of Communism Series.* New Haven: Yale University Press, 2004.

Kizny, Tomasz. *Gulag: Life and Death inside the Soviet Concentration Camps 1917–1990.* London: Firefly Books Ltd., 2004.

Solzhenitsyn, Aleksandr. *The Gulag Archipelago.* New York: HarperCollins, 1978.

Mengele, Josef (1911–1979) *Nazi medical experimenter and torturer*

Josef Mengele, the notorious doctor of Auschwitz, is known for good reason as the "Angel of Death." The son of a prosperous Bavarian industrialist, he was born on March 16, 1911. Those who knew him when he was growing up described him as a serious young man with ambition and intelligence. At the Frankfurt University Institute of Hereditary Biology and Racial Hygiene, Mengele chose to concentrate on physical anthropology and genetics. He pursued his medical studies at the Anthropological Institute at the University of Munich. His dissertation was entitled "Racial-Morphological Examination of the Anterior Portion of the Lower Jaw in Four Racial Groups." He published articles on twins and genetic abnormalities and the "irregular, dominant hereditary process." In retrospect, they hinted at the types of MEDICAL EXPERIMENTS he would later conduct on concentration-camp inmates.

Although it seemed Mengele was preparing for a career in academia, he had other ambitions in mind. Attracted at a young age to fascism, he joined the SA, a Nazi paramilitary group, in 1923, and in 1937—four years after Adolf HITLER came to power—he was accepted as a member of the Nazi Party, after which he applied for membership in the SS. In 1939 he served for six months with a mountain light-infantry regiment; beginning in 1940, as part of the reserve medical corps, he served three years with a Waffen SS unit. He was wounded in the Soviet Union and declared unfit for combat, but because of the bravery he displayed on the battlefield, he was awarded the Iron Cross and promoted to captain.

In 1943 Mengele arrived at Auschwitz. Prisoners recall him as an attractive man, always well groomed and meticulously dressed, with an aristocratic bearing. There are credible reports that he would stand at the railway platforms and make decisions about the detraining detainees as to who would live and who would be sent to the gas chambers. At one point, informed that one block was infested with lice, he solved the problem by ordering the gassing of all 750 women quartered on the block. But his notoriety is mainly due to his unspeakable medical experiments on inmates. Mengele performed surgery without anesthesia, injected his subjects with lethal germs, undertook sex-change operations, and removed organs and limbs. He was

Former Nazi medical officer Joseph Mengele *(Bettmann/Corbis)*

also known to put chemicals into the eyes of children in an attempt to change their eye color.

But no group of subjects interested Mengele more than twins. He began his experiments on twins in 1944, placing them in a special barracks. About 1,500 sets of twins passed through Auschwitz during Mengele's tenure. One twin would be the "control" and the other the experimental subject. If one twin took sick and went to the infirmary, the other would disappear soon afterwards, executed with a shot of phenol. "Three times a week we were marched to Auschwitz to a big brick building, sort of like a big gymnasium," one of the surviving twins recounted. "We would have to sit naked . . . and people in white jackets would observe us and write down notes. They also would study every part of our bodies." On one occasion Mengele put 14 pairs of Rom (Gypsy) twins to sleep simultaneously, injected chloroform into their hearts, killing them instantly, after which he dissected them, meticulously noting each body part. He also sewed twins together to create Siamese twins. Nonetheless, a number of the twins recall Mengele as a gentle, kindly man who gave them chocolates. Others saw through his affable guise, but nearly all of them knew that it was important to keep on his good side.

Of the 3,000 children—twins and nontwins—Mengele had experimented on, only about 200 were alive when the camp was liberated by the Soviet army on January 27, 1945. Before then, though, Mengele managed to escape, disguised as a member of the regular German infantry. He was captured by the Allies but only remained in custody as a prisoner of war a brief time before being released because no one was aware of who he was. In 1949, using an Italian residency document with a false name, Mengele obtained a passport and received permission to enter Argentina. He had chosen that country because he felt he could count on the support of Nazi sympathizers, and his father had done business there in the past. After settling in Argentina, he divorced his wife Irene and in 1958 married his brother Karl's widow, Martha. He maintained a quasi-normal lifestyle as a man with a regular job. The world had not forgotten him, though. He was tried in absentia by a Frankfurt court, which charged him with "hideous crimes" committed alone or with others "willfully and with bloodlust." He was indicted for several CRIMES AGAINST HUMANITY, including making selections for the gas chambers, administering lethal injections, shooting and beating victims, and perpetrating other forms of deliberate killing.

In spite of many attempts to track him down and bring him to justice, Mengele succeeded in living undiscovered for 35 years under various aliases. He relocated from Argentina to Paraguay and then to Brazil, where he died in 1979. He suffered a stroke while swimming and died after he was dragged to shore. However, his death remained unknown to the world until the 1980s, when Nazi hunters located his grave, which was marked "Wolfgang Gerhard." His family acknowledged that he was buried there and turned over his diaries and letters to investigators. Even so, suspicion persisted that he was still alive and his death was a hoax. In 1992, however, DNA was extracted from the bones and matched with DNA in blood samples from Mengele's son, confirming his identity.

See also ROM (ROMANY, GYPSIES), PERSECUTION OF.

Further Reading:
Goni, Uki. *The Real Odessa: How Peron Brought the Nazi War Criminals to Argentina.* London: Granta Books, 2003.
Lagnado, Lucette Matalon, and Sheila Cohn, Dekel. *Children of the Flames: Dr. Josef Mengele and the Untold Story of the Twins of Auschwitz.* New York: Penguin Books, 1992.
Lifton, Robert. *The Nazi Doctors: Medical Killing and the Psychology of Genocide.* New York: Basic Books, 2000.
Posner, Gerald. *Mengele: The Complete Story.* New York: Cooper Square Press, 2000.
Rees, Laurence. *Auschwitz: A New History.* New York: Public Affairs, 2005.

Mengistu Haile Mariam (1937–) *Ethiopian despot*
The former Ethiopian dictator Colonel Mengistu Haile Mariam seized power in 1974 in a violent coup and proceeded to establish a brutal reign under a junta known as the Dergue, a committee made up of junior officers. There is little available information about Mariam's early life. It is known that he was born in 1937 in the southern Ethiopian district of Walayta. His father was a soldier and his mother a servant. According to some accounts, he moved to Addis Ababa with his mother at an early age and grew up in the household of a prominent nobleman. He joined the army when he was young and served briefly as a private before attending Ethiopia's Holeta Military Academy, graduating in 1966 with the rank of second lieutenant. Assigned to the logistical and ordnance section of the Ethiopian army, he fell under the sway of Marxism and regularly referred to his fellow junior officers as "comrades," in the Soviet style. He became one of the leading figures of the future Dergue, which was composed of some 108 officers.

After taking power in 1974, Mengistu initiated a bloody campaign in which officials of the ousted emperor Haile Selasse were executed by firing squad; later the emperor himself and the patriarch of the dominant Ethiopian Orthodox Church were secretly killed. (There are allegations that Mengistu himself strangled the emperor to death.) At the same time he moved to purge rivals within the Dergue, executing them as well. In 1976, to inaugurate what he called the Red Terror, he appeared before a crowd in the capital, Addis Ababa, and held up a bottle filled with red liquid, which he said contained the blood of his enemies—"imperialists" and "counterrevolutionaries." Mengistu then orchestrated a wave of killings, targeting students and members of outlawed political parties. Thousands of young men and women were killed by *kebeles*, neighborhood watch committees which insisted on debiting the families of the victims for the price of the bullets used to execute them.

As the Soviet Union's principal ally in Africa, Mengistu was guaranteed a steady flow of arms to carry out his so-called counterinsurgency campaigns, which are believed to have cost the lives of thousands of people. When famine struck in 1984, the Mengistu regime sought to keep it secret from the outside world. Two secessionist insurgencies broke out around the same time, spearheaded by the Tigray and Eritrean People's Liberation Fronts. Subsequently the Dergue forcibly evicted hundreds of thousands of villagers from northern Ethiopia, relocating them to the south, ostensibly because they would be assured of richer food sources. In fact, the Dergue was determined to empty villages in rebel-infested areas to deny insurgents support.

In 1991 the Dergue was ousted by the Ethiopian People's Revolutionary Democratic Front (EPRDF), a coalition of regional and ethnic rebel groups. It is believed that in its 17 years in power, the Dergue was responsible for a minimum of 150,000 and possibly as many as half a million civilian deaths. The new regime set up a Special Prosecutor's Office (SRO) to investigate the crimes committed during Mengistu's reign. Over the next six years the SRO brought charges against more than 70 leading Dergue figures; altogether 5,198 people were charged for GENOCIDE, war crimes, and CRIMES AGAINST HUMANITY, of whom 2,246 were already in detention and another 2,952 were charged in absentia. Mengistu himself managed to elude justice by fleeing to Zimbabwe after the Dergue was toppled; 14 years later he was still living in exile.

About 200 cases have been heard by the courts—each of them with multiple defendants—with most of the focus on high-level officials who had given the orders. Human rights advocates have criticized the justice system for lengthy pretrial detentions and excessive delays in the investigating the cases. Lawyers for the defendants have complained about a lack of due process and restrictions on their access to clients. In the meantime, evidence of crimes committed during the Dergue era continues to be uncovered. In one instance, the bodies of 87 students were found near a provincial city, all of whom had been executed without trial.

See also ERITREA, HUMAN RIGHTS VIOLATIONS IN.

Further Reading:
Marcus, Harold G. *A History of Ethiopia*, updated ed. Berkeley: University of California Press, 2002.
Pausewang, Siegrfried, Kjetil Tronvoll, and Lovise Aaeln, eds. *Ethiopia since the Derg: A Decade of Democratic Pretension and Performance*. London: Zed Books, 2003.

mercenaries

Mercenaries—soldiers for hire—have been employed for hundreds of years. In the 18th and 19th centuries the Swiss hired out battalions to other European countries; the British used Hessian mercenaries during the American Revolution. More recently, mercenaries have been widely used in many of the postcolonial conflicts in Africa. The 1989 United Nations Convention on the Recruitment, Use, Financing and Training of Mercenaries defines a mercenary as any person who "is specially recruited locally or abroad in order to fight in an armed conflict; is motivated to take part in the hostilities essentially by the desire for private gain and, in fact, is promised, by or on behalf of a party to the conflict, material compensation . . .; is neither a national of a party to

the conflict nor a resident of territory controlled by a party to the conflict; is not a member of the armed forces of a party to the conflict. . . ." The convention also considers a person a mercenary if he or she is specifically recruited to participate in an effort to overthrow a government, undermine a state, or threaten its territorial integrity and is neither a national of the state or a member of its armed forces.

In 1968 the United Nations General Assembly and the Organization for African Unity enacted laws against mercenaries, outlawing their use in wars of national liberation. In 1977 the Security Council adopted a resolution condemning the recruitment of mercenaries to overthrow governments of any member state. Additional Protocol I to the GENEVA CONVENTIONS denies mercenaries combatant status or the rights of prisoners of war if captured. That means that mercenaries can be treated as common criminals. However, the increasing use of private security contractors in battlefield situations has made it more difficult to define a mercenary. Some critics contend that the UN definition is too subjective and depends too much on the motives of the fighter in making the determination. Moreover, the UN Charter gives states the right to individual or collective self-defense if attacked. If a state does come under armed attack and cannot depend on an outside force—such as the United Nations—to help it, the state may feel it has no choice but to hire mercenaries. The increasing reliance, too, on private security services has also made it difficult to ban the use of mercenaries outright.

Some critics of the UN ban suggest that mercenaries should enjoy combatant status under international law because that will make them more likely to abide by the Geneva Conventions and other treaties. In their view, private contractors hired to carry out military or security duties would become more accountable to the government that hires them. In 1999 the UNITED NATIONS HUMAN RIGHTS COMMISSION issued a "Report on the question of the use of mercenaries as a means of violating human rights and impeding the exercise of the right of peoples to self-determination" in which it stated that "mercenaries base their comparative advantage and greater efficiency on the fact that they do not regard themselves as being bound to respect human rights or the rules of INTERNATIONAL HUMANITARIAN LAW. . . . The participation of mercenaries in armed conflicts and in any other situation in which their services are unlawful may jeopardize the self-determination of peoples and always hampers the enjoyment of the human rights of those on whom their presence is inflicted." By relying on private military contractors (PMCs), the report said, the boundaries are blurred between combat and noncombat operations. For example, the DynCorp, a private security firm, provides bodyguards for Afghan president Hamid Karzai, and the Northrop Grumman Corporation has been paid $1.2 billion to fly planes that spray coca fields in Colombia and monitor smuggling. Although U.S. federal law bans American soldiers from participating in Colombia's war against a leftist insurgency and from training army units with ties to right-wing paramilitaries, these restrictions do not apply to PMCs.

The Pentagon has also used PMCs in Bosnia, Nigeria, Macedonia, and, most significantly, in Iraq. The *New York Times* called private military contractors the "new business face of war" because they provide "stand-ins for active soldiers." By 2004 the U.S. Defense Department had hired about 35 PMCs, including Kellogg Brown & Root, DynCorp, Vinnell, SAIC, ICI of Oregon, Logicon, and MPRI (Military Professionals Resources Inc.), which boasts of having "more generals per square foot than in the Pentagon." According to a July 2003 edition of *Soldier of Fortune* magazine (which covers the mercenary world), for-profit military companies do an estimated $100 billion in business worldwide annually.

The U.S. government's use of PMCs is grounded in the combined marque and reprisal and commerce clauses of the Constitution, which give Congress the power to regulate privateering, and the Arms Export Control Act, of 1979 which allowed Congress to delegate a large portion of its privateering power to the executive branch. Supreme Court rulings have also supported the government's ability to hire PMCs. Some members of Congress, though, are troubled by the Pentagon's use of PMCs. "Under a shroud of secrecy, the United States is carrying out military missions with people who don't have the same level of accountability," said Representative Jan Schakowsky (D, Ill.), "We have individuals who are not obligated to follow orders or follow the Military Code of Conduct. Their main obligation is to their employer, not to their country."

See also ADDITIONAL PROTOCOLS TO THE GENEVA CONVENTIONS.

Further Reading:
Gutman, Roy, ed. *Crimes of War: What the Public Should Know.* New York: W. W. Norton & Company, 1999. Universities Field Staff International (1989)

Meron, Theodor (1930–) *international jurist*
Theodor Meron, the president of the International Criminal Tribunal for the Former Yugoslavia (ICTY), is one of the few jurists to have personally experienced human rights violations: As a Jewish teenager he was held in a Nazi labor camp during World War II. Although he is reluctant to talk about his imprisonment, he does acknowledge that the ordeal influenced him to undertake a career in law in order to "explore the means to avoid mistreatment, to focus on ways to protect human dignity." In an interview with the *New York Times,* he explained that his "hunger for learn-

ing" was heightened because of having been deprived of an education from the age of nine to 15.

Born in 1930 in Poland, Meron has steeped himself in the laws of war and is an enthusiast of Shakespeare, who had much to say about man's inhumanity to man. (Meron has written two books on Shakespeare—*Henry's Wars and Shakespeare's Laws* [1993] and *Bloody Constraint: War and Chivalry in Shakespeare* [1998].) Now a U.S. citizen, he was a professor of international law at New York University before being elected to his position on the tribunal. Meron believes that while crimes against humanity may not have diminished significantly over the years, there is at least a growing recognition on the part of the international community that the guilty should be brought to justice and their crimes exposed. Specifically, he has expressed hope that some of the cases still pending in connection to the Balkan wars of the 1990s could be tried in the countries where the war crimes took place—Serbia, Bosnia, and Croatia—rather than in a neutral country such as the Netherlands. In 2005 he declared that this goal was closer at hand thanks to initiatives taken by the countries involved. For instance, Bosnia and Herzegovina enacted legislation to formally establish a body known as the War Crimes Chamber to try suspected war criminals.

In March 2005 Meron paid an unprecedented visit to Serb authorities in Belgrade who in the past had shown little sign of cooperation with the tribunal. On this occasion, though, he praised the government for having facilitated the surrender of a number of individuals indicted by the ICTY, which he said had created a favorable climate for increased cooperation between Serbia and the tribunal. Nonetheless, he pointed out that the ICTY would not be satisfied until three of the most wanted men—Ratko MLADIĆ, Radovan KARADZIĆ, and Ante GOTOVINA—were brought to justice. Meron has also championed the role of the ICTY in lending its resources to the national tribunals being established in the region through various training programs, the transfer of documents, and expertise. That help will make it possible for courts in Bosnia, Serbia, and Croatia to continue the investigation and prosecution of war criminals once the ICTY's mandate expires in 2008. "We must remember," Meron said, "without this tribunal, what would have followed is impunity."

See also BOSNIA AND HERZEGOVINA, HUMAN RIGHTS VIOLATIONS IN; CROATIA, HUMAN RIGHTS VIOLATIONS IN; SERBIA, HUMAN RIGHTS VIOLATIONS IN; YUGOSLAVIA, WAR CRIMES IN.

Further Reading:
Meron, Theodor. *Henry's Wars and Shakespeare's Laws.* Oxford: Oxford University Press 1993);
———. *Human Rights and Humanitarian Norms as Customary Law.* Oxford: Oxford University Press, 1989.

———. *War Crimes Law Comes of Age: Essays.* Oxford: Oxford University Press, 1999.

Mexico, human rights violations in

Mexico suffered its most violent period in modern history during a DIRTY WAR that was seldom fought in the open and was characterized by rampant human rights violations. The war began in the late 1960s and continued until the 1980s. During that time government agents abducted, tortured, murdered, or "disappeared" hundreds of Mexicans; there are 350 documented cases according to the National Commission on Human Rights, a government agency, but doubtless many more have occurred that have not been exposed. Ostensibly, the dirty war pitted the government against leftist subversives and insurgents, but in fact many innocent civilians ended up being drawn into the conflict and sometimes paying with their lives. Although the administration of President Vicente Fox has made some progress investigating human rights violations by government police and security forces, abuses still occur, and it is debatable whether most of the worst offenders will ever be brought to justice.

The dirty war, which was carried on under the administrations of Presidents Luis Echeverría and José López Portillo, was one in which Mexican police forces routinely resorted to "systematic beatings, near drowning and electric shocks" in the words of an AMNESTY INTERNATIONAL report. As in the case of other dirty wars in Latin America, notably in Uruguay, Argentina, and Chile, the government responded to leftist insurgencies by sweeping up many civilians in dragnets, even though their ties to guerrillas or subversive organizations were often either tenuous or nonexistent. Sometimes a blood relationship with a suspect was sufficient for the police to detain a person. There is some evidence that prisoners were executed after their torturers had extracted all the information from them that they could. Sometimes the killings took place out in the open, though. In 1968 troops opened fire on student protesters in the plaza at Tlatelolco. Human rights investigators say hundreds were killed in that incident, but the true number is unknown.

Even though the United States was aware of many of these abuses, Washington was slow to respond both for fear of jeopardizing relations with Mexico and because through the early 1970s, human rights was not given a high priority by the Nixon or Ford administrations. "Important point in Embassy's opinion, however," wrote the U.S. ambassador at the time, "is that GOM [Government of Mexico] . . . appears to be responding—however heavy-handedly—to legitimate and serious provocation by armed opponents who seek its overthrow and who in the last several years have come to constitute a genuine threat to public order in several parts of the country."

U.S. policy toward human rights abuses in Mexico underwent a dramatic shift during the Carter administration. In late 1978, after President Carter ordered a comprehensive review of relations between the two countries, the National Security Council (NSC) acknowledged in a secret annex to the report that grave abuses by the Mexican forces had taken place. The NSC singled out one paramilitary group in particular for some of the worst outrages known as the WHITE BRIGADES. Nonetheless, the United States was still reluctant to take concerted action to prod the Mexican government into improving its human rights record, believing that it would be "ill-advised and counterproductive." It was agreed that the White House would continue its old policy of "quiet diplomacy."

Human rights abuses persisted into the 1990s under the administration of President Carlos Salinas de Gortari. In May 1990, just as the United States, Mexico, and Canada were about to open negotiations on the creation of the North American Free Trade Agreement (NAFTA), a human rights advocate, Dr. Norma Corona Sapién, was slain by unidentified gunmen in Culiacán, capital of the Mexican state of Sinaloa. Her killing was linked by human rights organizations to her investigation of the TORTURE and killings of a Mexican lawyer and three Venezuelan University teachers reportedly carried out by judicial police officers. Sapién's death prompted a national outcry. Eager to burnish Mexico's human rights image, especially with such important trade talks looming, Salinas promised to crack down on abuses and punish the perpetrators. One tangible result was the creation of the National Human Rights Commission (CNDH). But new government agencies and well-intentioned pieces of legislation failed to put a halt to the abusive practices. On the contrary, Sapién's killing only seemed to mark the beginning of a campaign to silence human rights advocates. This campaign was not only limited to harassment, threats, or intimidation; sometimes it could become lethal. In June 1995 Dr. Abraham Polo Uscanga, a former judge, "disappeared." Two weeks later his body turned up—in his office. He had been killed with a single shot in the back of the head. A former member of the Federal District Supreme Court, which has jurisdiction over the Mexico City metropolitan area, he had been openly critical of corruption in the judiciary and had acquitted eight people falsely accused of terrorism, some of whom had undergone torture.

Even the clergy was not safe. Only weeks after Polo's killing, unknown gunmen opened fire on a car carrying Roman Catholic bishop Arturo Lona Reyes, a well-known human rights defender. The bishop survived, and five suspects were arrested. The authorities claimed that the attack was a robbery attempt, but the evidence indicated that the assailants had made no effort to stop the car in advance and had simply started shooting directly at the bishop. According to Amnesty International, the principal victims of rights abuses remain Indian or peasant activists who seek land reform. While an attack on a bishop will raise a hue and cry around the world, attempts to intimidate or kill people without a high profile will generally be overlooked.

The growing involvement of the Mexican military in maintaining public security is a source of concern to human rights organizations. Throughout the 1990s, the size and budget of the army increased in response to scattered insurgencies. On New Year's Day 1994 the country was taken unaware by an uprising in the southern state of Chiapas, an audacious action carried out by a hitherto unknown guerrilla group called the Zapatistas (or more officially the Zapatista National Liberation Army). The government first reacted by using excessive force against the rebels and their Indian supporters but later adopted a policy of containment. Many instances of abuses by the army in the Chiapas uprising have been exposed, but little has been done to investigate them. In one incident in 1994, 11 people were killed during the army occupation of a hospital. But HUMAN RIGHTS WATCH questioned the army's investigation and suggested that it really had no stomach for identifying or prosecuting the murderers. In an investigation of cases in Chiapas involving the alleged torture and rape of civilians by soldiers, the Inter-American Commission on Human Rights faulted the government for failing to do more to ensure the protection of the victims' legal rights and declared that its "investigation into the facts related to this case by the military courts [had been] completely inappropriate."

Two years after the Zapitista uprising, a guerrilla group called the Popular Revolutionary Army began one of their own in the southwestern state of Guerrero and in other states. As a result of continuing tensions in both areas of the country, the army has become a more dominant presence in the Mexican countryside.

The army has also been pressed into service in the war against drugs. Law enforcement officials consider Mexico the principal route through which drugs travel on their way to the United States from South America; over 80 percent of the cocaine that feeds American drug habits passes through Mexico. But Mexico is more than a transshipment channel: It is also a major narcotics producer in its own right, supplying 29 percent of the heroin and 70 percent of the marijuana imported into the United States. In 1987 President Miguel de la Madrid declared drug trafficking to be a "national security problem." Nearly a decade later it was still a problem. In 1996 President Ernesto Zedillo invited the country's top military leaders to join the National Public Security Council, giving the military an unprecedented role in establishing policy regarding public security. Five years later it was hard to see how much had changed. Drugs were still being produced and still flowing into the United States. In January 2001 President Vicente Fox declared his intention to fight a "war without quarter" against drug traffickers. More than 20,000 soldiers now take part in counternarcotics operations. However, it is possible to argue that the army is as much a part of the problem as it is the solution. Because officers usually rely on information from political allies about which suspects to target, they have become entangled in local power struggles. In Guerrero state, for instance, these invidious alliances have given caciques—local political bosses—the power to enlist the army to help their cause by the simple expedient of denouncing their enemies as either drug dealers or guerrillas. Evidence is trumped up, but because of an absence of outside monitors, these abuses become very hard to prove. The largest number of complaints about army abuses addressed to the National Human Rights Commission by civilians relates to its conduct while performing counternarcotics operations.

The ascension of President Vicente Fox to office in December 2000 was seen as a new beginning for Mexico. Finally the country had a president who was not from the PRI (Institutional Revolutionary Party), the party that had dominated Mexican political life for most of the 20th century. Individuals who had previously enjoyed immunity from prosecution for their crimes under the old regime might finally be forced to face their accusers. Crimes hushed up would soon be brought to light, or that was the hope anyway. Indeed, Fox vowed to bring an end to the climate of impunity and promised that his administration would resolve several high-profile human rights cases involving the army that until then had seemed to be going nowhere. However, although he secured the release of two prisoners who had been tortured while in custody, critics said that he had done little to curb human rights abuses halfway through his term in office. (Mexican presidents are only allowed to serve one six-year term.)

Efforts to come to terms with a lurid and bloody past have encountered a number of stumbling blocks, not the least the failure of high officials in the PRI regime to cooperate with investigators. Nonetheless, the release of once-secret documents has shed a good deal of light on the government's complicity in committing atrocities that it had long avoided responsibility for. Investigators have taken a special interest in identifying the perpetrators of a 1968 massacre of student protesters in Tlatelolco, in Mexico City. Some of the recently disclosed documents indicate that as many as 360 snipers under government command were involved. Among them was a secret battalion of police known as the Falcons, which undertook another attack on student protesters in 1971.

President Gustavo Díaz Ordaz had ordered Echeverría, then his interior secretary, to create the Falcons. He wanted a clandestine unit that could suppress student dissent in place of uniformed personnel, wishing to avoid a repetition of the controversy in the wake of the massacre of students at Tlatelolco, in Mexico City in 1968. Echeverría saw no reason to dissolve them when he became president. According to documents that only came to light in 2005, the Falcons were given false identification, code words, and nicknames. They were forbidden to talk about their real work, which was defined as being "dedicated . . . to committing crimes, with the intention of distracting the attention of public opinion." But the Falcons were by no means the only unit under government control; federal and city police as well as secret service agents were all present in and around the plaza where the massacre took place. At the time, the government claimed that it was the students who had opened fire on the police, an assertion contradicted by the documents.

The confrontation between students and police took place on October 2, 1968, only 10 days before the start of the Olympics in Mexico City. Estimates on the number of people killed range from 38 to several hundred. The true number will probably never be known. Echeverría denied having anything to do with the shootings, but the documents reveal that several of the snipers fired down on the crowd from an apartment owned by his sister-in-law. When he was called into the office of the special prosecutor Ignacio Carrillo in February 2005, Echeverría refused to talk, contending that he had a constitutional right as an ex-president to remain silent. He has ignored further attempts by the prosecutor's office to question him.

There is, however, some grounds for at least cautious optimism. As special prosecutor, Carrillo has taken some concrete steps to investigate past abuses, and the judiciary has shown some degree of independence. In November 2003 the Mexican Supreme Court ruled that former officials could be prosecuted in disappearance cases, saying that no statute of limitations could apply when no body had been found. Scarcely had the ink had time to dry on the decision than the former chief of Mexico's secret police, Miguel Nazar Haro, was arrested in February 2004 on charges of kidnapping a leftist leader 29 years before whose body was never located. Nazar Haro thus became the first government official arrested for crimes committed during the dirty war. He had headed the Federal Security Directorate, which was both an intelligence agency and a secret police force. What is unclear is whether this arrest marks a renewed effort on the government's part to bring human rights violators to justice and investigate past abuses or whether it is simply an aberration.

In an especially bold move, the special prosecutor filed murder charges against former president Luis Echeverría and several former government officials and military officers in the killings of student protesters in 1971. Specifi-cally, the charges related to the slayings of at least 25 protesters demanding reforms of the education system whom the Falcons had attacked with clubs and chains. Castillo said that Echeverría would face charges of GENO-CIDE, defined in the Mexican penal code as "systematic crimes against the lives of members of any national group," including political dissidents. Human rights advocates, who had hailed the unprecedented initiative when it was announced in July 2004, had little time to savor their victory. The very next day an appeals court judge threw out the charges against the former president. That underscored the belief by human rights groups that the Fox administration had no interest in providing strong support to the special prosecutor, raising fears that the country's leader was backing away from his pledge to break with the past and bring about needed political and judicial reforms.

Nonetheless, in early February 2005 Carillo announced his intention to bring charges against two dozen former military and civilian officials for the 1968 student massacre at Tlatelolco. At the same time he also indicated that he would charge Echeverría in the new indictment even while the Mexican Supreme Court was reviewing the earlier decision to throw out the first indictment against the former president. The prosecutor also said that he would bring 30 additional indictments before the end of 2005.

See also NAZAR HARO, MIGUEL.

Further Reading:

Amnesty International. *Mexico: Human Rights in Rural Areas.* London: Amnesty International, 1986.

Brysk, Alison, ed. *Globalization and Human Rights.* Berkeley: University of California Press, 2002.

Cartwright, William, ed. *Mexico: Facing the Challenges of Human Rights and Crime.* Jefferson, N.C.: Transnational Pub., 1999.

Human Rights Watch, ed. *Unceasing Abuses Human Rights in Mexico One Year after the Introduction of Reform.* Americas Watch Report. New York: Human Rights Watch, 1991.

military necessity

INTERNATIONAL HUMANITARIAN LAW (IHL) recognizes the legal concept of military necessity in view of the undeniable fact that belligerents wage a conflict with the intent of winning and that military actions are governed by that objective. That means that under certain circumstances in a conflict situation, military necessity may dictate attacks that cause loss of life to civilians or to civilian property. However, IHL imposes three fundamental constraints on the exercise of force because of military necessity, since humanitarian concerns do come into play. For one thing, an attack must be directed toward a military objective; if no military purpose is served, then IHL forbids an attack. An attack to terrorize or demoralize a civilian population, for instance, is banned. The second constraint involves the principle of proportionality: An attack on a military objective cannot be disproportionate to its military value. This principle is of particular concern when there is a likelihood of inflicting COLLATERAL DAMAGE, whether to civilians or to public property. Finally, military necessity can never be used as a pretext to violate other international humanitarian law—denying food or medical provisions to a civilian population under SIEGE, for instance.

Moreover, military necessity can only be used for military purposes and not as an instrument to bring about political goals. However, this determination is not so easily made, as Françoise Hampson points out in her essay on the subject for CRIMES OF WAR PROJECT. "Is persuading the enemy to surrender a military or political goal?" she asks. "Is 'persuading' the enemy to surrender by aerial bombardment a military or political goal?" It is possible that a belligerent will simply transform a political objective into a military one to justify its actions. The situation on the ground, which during a conflict is in constant flux, can also change the definition of what constitutes "military necessity." What may be justified at one point might not be justified at another because the circumstances have changed—for example, an area previously occupied by an enemy force becomes populated by civilians because of an influx of REFUGEES.

The use of weapons—in terms of both numbers and type—is also governed both by the immediate demands of military necessity and the constraints of IHL. Weapons are banned by IHL if they cause "superfluous injury or unnecessary suffering." However, opinion among legal experts is divided as to whether nuclear weapons, for instance, are outlawed under every circumstance. An advisory opinion by judges on the INTERNATIONAL COURT OF JUSTICE suggested that a state might be justified in using nuclear weapons if its very survival were at stake and no other recourse were available.

Hampson also points out that the judgment of what constitutes military necessity most often rests with a field commander; yet given the chaotic conditions prevailing on a battlefield, a commander may not be in a position to adequately assess the situation to be able to weigh military and humanitarian considerations. Under such circumstances, a finding of criminal culpability becomes more difficult. However, no ambiguity arises when a commander knows in advance that the orders he or she is giving are illegal on their face regardless of military necessity. IHL does take into account the assignment of legal responsibility by introducing the concept of "imperative military necessity" which, while not outlawing certain acts entirely, does presume that they are likely to be unlawful, thus putting "a significant burden of proof on those invoking the exception." That is to say, the commanders would be considered guilty until proven innocent. The Fourth Geneva Convention, for instance, permits an occupation force to deport or intern protected persons—civilians, medical personnel, sick or wounded combatants, and prisoners of war—for "imperative military necessity" as long as their protection, health, and safety is ensured. However, the occupier would have to establish that its actions were motivated by military necessity in order to avoid being held to account for a breach of international law. In sum, military necessity can be invoked only if the objective is vital to a military victory or if the survival of the belligerent's force is at risk.

See also CIVILIAN IMMUNITY; GENEVA CONVENTIONS; NUCLEAR ARMS AND INTERNATIONAL LAW; PROTECTED PERSONS; WILLFULL KILLING.

Further Reading:
Gutman, Roy, ed. *Crimes of War: What the Public Should Know.* New York: W. W. Norton & Company, 1999.

Milošević, Slobodan (1941–2006) *Yugoslav dictator*
The future Yugoslav president was born in 1941 in Serbia, then a part of the Kingdom of Yugoslavia, only months after the German invasion of the country. However, Slobodan Milošević grew up in a new country known as the Socialist Federal People's Republic of Yugoslavia. While nominally a communist state, under the leadership of Marshal Josip Broz (Tito) it pursued an independent course rather than follow dictates from Moscow. The young Slobodan's early life was darkened by family tragedy: His father, a schoolteacher, committed suicide in 1962, and his mother followed suit 11 years later. Historians and psychologists have speculated for years on the influence that these events had on Milošević.

When Milošević decided to marry a high school classmate named Mirana Marković—she came from a family of Serbian communist activists—he was entering into a political collaboration as much as he was into a domestic partnership. She would become a forceful influence in the course of his rise to power. After joining the Communist Party in 1959, Milošević went on to earn a law degree from the University of Belgrade. Although he never put his degree to much practical use at the time—he served as a director of a major Belgrade bank instead—his knowledge of the subject would come in handy decades later when he chose to defend himself at his own war crimes trial.

April 24, 1987, marked a turning point in Milošević's life and, it could be said, in the turbulent history of Yugoslavia as well. On that day he appeared before a restive crowd of fellow Serbs who had laid siege to the town hall of Kosovo Polje. The crowd was protesting mistreatment at the hands of the Albanians who made up 90 percent of the population of the province. At the time Milošević was a minor Communist Party functionary, but he saw a chance to make a name for himself. "No one will ever beat you again!" he vowed to cheers and applause. His declaration of defiance almost instantly elevated him to national prominence as a defender of Serbian nationalism.

There is little question that Milošević would never have gained international fame—and so much opprobrium—were it not for the violent breakup of the former Yugoslavia in the 1980s. The republic that emerged in the rubble of World War II was practically the creation of Tito, the Yugoslav leader for 35 years, and it was Tito who held the country's disparate parts and ethnic groups together. (Serbia is mainly Eastern Orthodox, Croatia mainly Roman Catholic, Bosnia and Kosovo mainly Muslim.) It was a difficult task; the Balkans were so often engulfed in war and ethnic clashes that Winston Churchill once famously remarked that "the Balkans produce more history than they can consume." With Tito's death in 1980, though, efforts to maintain the unwieldy Federal Republic of Yugoslavia

Former Yugoslav president Slobodan Milošević during the war crimes tribunal at The Hague, 2004 *(Fred Ernst/Landov)*

began to falter. Tito had effectively laid the seeds of the country's future dissolution. Seeking to reduce the concentration of Serbs and thereby reduce their political influence, he had seen to it that one-third of the Serbian population was scattered outside their own province. It was a decision that would come back to haunt the country—and the world. With Tito gone, the Serbs began to demand their own homeland—but then so did the Croats, the Bosnian Muslims, the Slovenians, and the Albanians, all of whom had at one time called Yugoslavia home.

With the sudden collapse of the Soviet Union and the dismantling of its former Eastern bloc, Milošević was shrewd enough to exploit Serbian nationalism as a means to achieve the power he had sought as a rising communist star. Two years after rallying Serbs in front of the town hall in Kosovo, he fomented demonstrations that drove elected Albanian leaders out of office altogether. In December 1987 he ousted the president of Serbia, and two years later, with the aid of compliant Serbian parliament, he took the post for himself. His populist touch was undeniable: In Serbia's first post-Communist multiparty and direct presidential elections in 1990, he was reelected president by an overwhelming majority. But his increasing truculence stirred alarm among other nationalities who were not eager to become minorities in a Greater Serbia. Within two years of Milošević's ascension to power, Slovenia, Croatia, and Bosnia and Herzegovina all seceded, leaving behind only two republics: Serbia (including the province of Kosovo) and Montenegro. The divorce did not proceed peacefully. Serb minorities in Croatia and Bosnia and Herzegovina clamored for a Greater Serbia. (Slovenia escaped relatively unscathed because few Serbs lived in its territory.)

In 1991, encouraged by Serbia, the Serb minorities in Croatia and Bosnia openly rebelled. Yugoslav armed forces and Serbian militias came to the aid of their fellow Serbs, launching a campaign intended to uproot Bosnian and Croatian populations, killing those that they did not expel. The strategy to force peoples from their homelands came to be called ethnic cleansing, an especially sinister addition to the vocabulary of atrocity and GENOCIDE. At first the war went badly for the Bosnians and Croatians, who were overwhelmed by the far better-armed Serbian forces. In Bosnia, Serbs captured nearly 40 percent of the country. Sarajevo, only a few years earlier the host of the Winter Olympic Games, was turned into a horrific killing field as Serb artillery and snipers hidden in the surrounding hills indiscriminately rained fire down on the city's terrorized inhabitants.

The West was slow to react to the bloodiest conflict in Europe since 1945. But the daily carnage in Sarajevo carried live on television all over the world had its effect. NATO bombers were ordered to launch air strikes against Serb positions, which had the immediate effect of easing the stranglehold on Sarajevo. Meanwhile, on the ground, better-trained Croat and Bosnian troops began to beat back the Serbs, retaking much of the territory that they had yielded in the first months of the war. The reverses, coupled with the air strikes, forced Miloševic to the bargaining table. The Clinton administration corralled the leaders of the three belligerents—Miloševic, Bosnia's Alija Izetbegovic, and Croatia's Franjo TUDJMAN—at Wright-Patterson Air Force Base in Dayton, Ohio, keeping them there until they came to an agreement that was signed by the warring parties in December 1995 (known as the DAYTON ACCORDS).

The atrocities perpetrated on all sides during the four years of war were considered serious enough to establish a commission to investigate them and try those responsible. In March 1996 the United Nations International War Crimes Tribunal in The Hague quietly questioned Serbian soldiers about war crimes and issued arrest warrants for Bosnian Serb officers.

Although the United Nations lifted most of its sanctions, Yugoslavia's economy continued to erode, and with it so did Miloševic's power. But the Yugoslav strongman moved quickly to crush any dissent. He continued to tighten his grip on the media and the reins of political power, annulling the results of municipal elections whose results he did not like. In spite of the Dayton accords, he showed no sign of being chastened, and in 1998 he went to war again, this time over the Yugoslav province of Kosovo, where armed Albanian separatists threatened to mount open rebellion. The defeat of Serbs at the hands of the conquering Ottomans in the Battle of Kosovo in 1392 still rankled—Albanians were even branded as "Turks" because of their shared Muslim heritage—and the prospect of the province's loss inspired a new burst of Serbian nationalism. Once again the Balkans were plunged into war, and once again it was Miloševic who was responsible. Yugoslav forces swept through Kosovo on the pretense of wiping out the armed separatists—the Kosovo Liberation Front (KLA)—but in the process killing hundreds of Albanian civilians and uprooting an estimated 780,000 from their homes. Pretending to buckle under diplomatic pressure, Miloševic initially agreed to a partial troop withdrawal at a conference in Rambouillet, France, in March 1999, only to renege and resume fighting.

In late May the INTERNATIONAL CRIMINAL TRIBUNAL FOR THE FORMER YUGOSLAVIA (ICTY) unsealed an indictment accusing Miloševic and four other senior Yugoslav officials of committing war crimes in Kosovo. Characteristically, Miloševic shrugged off the charges. Losing patience, NATO responded with air strikes on Kosovo and, even more controversially, on military and industrial targets inside Serbia, including installations in Belgrade. Although NATO confined its attacks to the air—putting armed forces on the ground was thought too politically risky by the Clin-ton administration—the bombardment persuaded Miloševic to withdraw his troops from the beleaguered province. UN peacekeepers then moved in to secure the region and supervise the return of Albanian refugees.

In spite of this latest defeat, Miloševic continued to hold on to power, largely by playing the same nationalist card that had gotten him into power in the first place. He was so confident of his popularity, in fact, that he even went so far as to call for early elections for president in September 2000. But for the first time, his canny political instincts had deserted him. Exhausted by three wars and an economy that was in shambles, the Yugoslavs turned him out of office and elected a former constitutional law professor, Vojislav Koštunica, in his place. In a desperate attempt to cling to power, Miloševic manipulated the courts into annulling the results. This time, though, he had overplayed his hand. Hundreds of thousands of demonstrators took to the streets, and, bowing to pressure, Miloševic stepped down.

Now that Miloševic had been shorn of power, the ICTY tried to convince Belgrade to arrest him and send him to The Hague to stand trial. The new Koštunica administration rebuffed the attempt, but the Serbia government acted on its own initiative and took him into custody in March 2001. Miloševic was charged with embezzlement and abuse of power, but the Serb leaders had no wish to keep him. Three months later he was extradited to The Hague over the strenuous objections of the federal government and the Yugoslav Constitutional Court. Presumably the Serb government was motivated by the $1 billion in aid held out by Western Powers as an inducement.

Miloševic has the dubious distinction of being the first head of state ever to be tried for war crimes. The tribunal has indicted him in three cases labeled simply Kosovo, Croatia, and Bosnia. As laid out in the formal indictment, it is alleged that:

1. "Between 1 January 1999 and 20 June 1999, forces of the FRY [Federal Republic of Yugoslavia] and Serbia acting at the direction, with the encouragement, or with the support of the accused, executed a campaign of terror and violence directed at Kosovo Albanian civilians.

2. Miloševic participated in a "joint criminal enterprise" between at least 1 August 1991 and June 1992. The purpose of this enterprise was the forcible removal of the majority of the Croat and other non-Serb population from approximately one-third of the territory of the Republic of Croatia, an area he planned to become part of a new Serb-dominated state.

3. Miloševic exerted control over the elements of the Yugoslav People's Army ("JNA") and the Yugoslav Army ("VJ") which participated in the planning, preparation, facilitation and execution of the forcible removal of the majority of non-Serbs, principally

Bosnian Muslims and Bosnian Croats, from large areas of Bosnia and Herzegovina.

Much to the surprise and chagrin of the presiding judges, Milošević rejected any legal help and insisted on defending himself. The first trial, which focused on his culpability in war crimes committed in Kosovo, began in February 2002 and concluded the following September. Later that month the prosecution began the presentation of its case regarding Milošević's alleged crimes in Croatia and Bosnia and Herzegovina. At no point in the trial, even when confronted with victims of the crimes he was charged with having perpetrated, has Milošević shown any hint of remorse or admitted any guilt. His trial was bedeviled by the defendant's recurring illness, the death of one of the presiding judges, and courtroom tactics by Milošević that seemed intended to bring the proceedings to a standstill. On March 11, 2006, with the trial still not concluded, the Balkan dictator died in his prison cell.

See also BOSNIA, HUMAN RIGHTS VIOLATIONS IN; CROATIA, HUMAN RIGHTS VIOLATIONS IN; KOSOVO, WAR CRIMES IN; SARAJEVO, SIEGE OF; SERBIA, HUMAN RIGHTS VIOLATIONS IN; SLOVENIA, HUMAN RIGHTS VIOLATIONS IN; SESELJ, VOJISLAV; SLOVENIA, HUMAN RIGHTS VIOLATIONS IN; YUGOSLAVIA, WAR CRIMES IN.

Further Reading:

Bassiouni, M. Cherif. *Sexual Violence: An Invisible Weapon of War in the Former Yugoslavia.* Chicago: International Human Rights Law Institute, DePaul University, 1996.

Clark, Wesley K. *Waging Modern War: Bosnia, Kosovo, and the Future of Combat.* New York: Public Affairs.

Glenny, Misha. *The Fall of Yugoslavia: The Third Balkan War.* New York: Penguin Books, 1996.

Honig, Jan Willem, and Norbert Both. *Srebrenica: Record of a War Crime.* New York: Penguin Books, 1997.

Hagan, John. Justice in the Balkans: *Prosecuting War Crimes in the Hague Tribunal.* Chicago Series in Law and Society. Chicago: University of Chicago Press, 2003.

Harris, Nathaniel. *The War in Former Yugoslavia.* London: Hodder & Stoughton, 1997.

Hazan, Pierre, and James Thomas Snyder. *Justice in a Time of War: The True Story behind the International Criminal Tribunal for the Former Yugoslavia.* Eugenia and Hugh M. Stewart Series on Eastern Europe. Austin: Texas A&M University Press, 2004.

Kim, Julie. *War in the Former Yugoslavia: Chronology of Events August 16, 1992–May 30, 1993.* CRS Report for Congress. Washington, D.C.: Foreign Affairs and National Defense Division, Congressional Research Service, the Library of Congress, 1993.

Kipp, Jacob W. *International Ramifications of Yugoslavia's Serial Wars: The Challenge of Ethno-national conflicts for a Post-Cold-War, European order.* Fort Leavenworth, Kans: European Military Studies Office, 1993.

Mertus, Julie. *Former Yugoslavia: War Crimes Trials in the Former Yugoslavia.* Helsinki: Human Rights Watch/Helsinki, 1995.

Naimark, Norman, and Holly Case. *Yugoslavia and Its Historians: Understanding the Balkan Wars of the 1990s.* Stanford, Calif.: Stanford University Press, 2003.

Rhode, David. *Endgame: The Betrayal and Fall of Srebrenica.* New York: Farrar, Straus & Giroux, 1997.

Rogel, Carole. *The Breakup of Yugoslavia and the War in Bosnia.* Westport, Conn.: Greenwood Press, 1998.

Rossanet, Bertrand de. *War and Peace in the Former Yugoslavia.* Boston: Martinus Nijhoff, 1997.

Scharf, Michael P. *Balkan Justice: The Story behind the First International War Crimes Trial since Nuremberg.* Durham, N.C.: Carolina Academic Press, 1997.

Minami, Jiro *See* WAR CRIMINALS OF JAPAN.

Mladić, Ratko (1943–) *Serbian commander and indicted war criminal*

The onetime commander of Bosnian Serbian forces in the 1992–95 Bosnian war, Ratko Mladić remains a fugitive from justice, charged by the United Nations with war crimes relating to the siege of Sarajevo and the massacre of thousands of Muslim men and boys in the UN-protected enclave of Srebrenica, the worst atrocity in Europe since World War II. Mladić and Radovic KARADŽIĆ, the firebrand nationalist politician who was indicted by the United Nations on similar charges, are considered the prime movers of a campaign of terror against Bosnian Muslim civilians.

In 1991 Mladić was appointed commander of the IX Corps of the Yugoslav People's Army in the Republic of Croatia (which had broken away from Yugoslavia) and subsequently was given command of the Bosnian Serb army. Like Karadžić, Mladić believed in the idea of a Greater Serbia that would unite minority Serb populations in Croatia and Bosnia and Herzegovina with what remained of Yugoslavia, where Serbs constituted the majority. In 1992 Mladić's forces occupied the heights over the Bosnian capital of Sarajevo, whose population by then had swelled with REFUGEES fleeing Serbian assaults elsewhere in the country. Over the next three and a half years Yugoslav regulars and Serbian paramilitary forces held the city hostage, killing an estimated 10,000 civilians, mostly Bosnian Muslims, with artillery and rocket fire.

In July 1995 Serb forces under Mladić's command shelled an enclave of Srebrenica that had previously been designated as a UN-protected area. Five days later the outmatched Dutch peacekeepers withdrew rather than attempt to defend the civilians who had taken refuge there. Mladić entered the town with Serb camera crews in tow to record his triumph for posterity. The following day the women and children were separated from the men and boys and taken away by buses. Mladić's troops then proceeded to execute more than 7,500 Muslim males ranging in age from 12 to 77.

When the DAYTON ACCORDS in November 1995 put an end to the Bosnian war, Mladić returned to Belgrade. For the next several years he continued to live openly in the Yugoslav capital, eating in expensive restaurants and attending soccer games with the assurance that he enjoyed government protection even though he was charged with war crimes and human rights violations by the INTERNATIONAL CRIMINAL TRIBUNAL FOR THE FORMER YUGOSLAVIA. The arrest of his patron, former Yugoslavian strongman president Slobodan MILOŠEVIĆ, in 2001 caused him to go underground. His present whereabouts are unknown, but in 2004 Carla DEL PONTE, chief prosecutor for the tribunal, contended that he was still in Belgrade. The international warrant issued for his arrest declares that he is wanted for "assault, CRIMES AGAINST HUMANITY, crimes against life and health, grave breaches of the 1949 GENEVA CONVENTIONS, murder, plunder, violations of the laws or customs of war." In a somewhat gratuitous aside, the warrant also notes that Mladić "may be dangerous."

See also BOSNIA AND HERZEGOVINA, HUMAN RIGHTS VIOLATIONS IN; CROATIA, HUMAN RIGHTS VIOLATIONS IN; SARAJEVO, SIEGE OF; SERBIA, HUMAN RIGHTS VIOLATIONS IN; SREBRENICA, MASSACRE IN.

Further Reading:

Bassiouni, M. Cherif. *Sexual Violence: An invisible weapon of war in the former Yugoslavia.* Chicago: International Human Rights Law Institute, DePaul University, 1996.

Clark, Wesley K. *Waging Modern War: Bosnia, Kosovo, and the Future of Combat.* New York: Public Affairs

Glenny, Misha. *The Fall of Yugoslavia: The Third Balkan War.* New York: Penguin Books, 1996.

Mertus, Julie. *Former Yugoslavia: War Crimes Trials in the Former Yugoslavia.* Helsinki: Human Rights Watch/Helsinki, 1995.

Mobutu Sese Seko (Joseph Desire Mobutu, Mobutu Sese Seko Ngbender wa za Banga) (1930–1997)
Congolese dictator

Mobutu Sese Seko was the dictator of Zaire (now the Democratic Republic of the Congo) for three decades, an era marked by repressive rule and such rampant corruption that his regime became widely known as a kleptocracy. Born Joseph Desire Mobutu on October 14, 1930, the future leader was raised in the northern village of Lisala in what was then the Belgian Congo. He was educated at a Catholic mission school and between 1949 and 1956 served in the Belgian colonial army, rising to the position of sergeant major, the highest rank open to an African.

In June 1960 Congo achieved its independence. The first prime minister, Patrice Lumumba, appointed the ambitious Mobutu as his private secretary and then as his chief of staff of the army. Within months the country was embroiled in civil war when Moise Tshombe, head of the mineral-rich province of Katanga, launched a secessionist rebellion. Lumumba sought help from the United Nations to restore order, and consequently the organization became caught up in the war. A month later, in September 1960, Mobutu, with the clandestine support of the CIA, participated in a military coup to oust Lumumba. As an avowed leftist and nationalist favoring a nonaligned policy, Lumumba was viewed as a threat to U.S. interests in the context of the cold war. Mobutu, on the other hand, was considered someone that Washington could work with. (Lumumba was executed a year later.) The war with Katanga continued, however. Evidence later emerged that Belgium was seeking to regain a foothold in the Congo—and secure its resources—by backing Tshombe. In the ensuing tumult, Tshombe even managed to become prime minister himself until he was forced out in 1964 after rigged elections.

Mobutu seized the opportunity to stage a second coup in November 1965. He put Tshombe on trial in absentia; the court condemned him to death. (Tshombe was later abducted to Algeria and died in a prison there in 1969.) Within two years of taking power, Mobutu declared a policy of "Africanization," and in October 1971 he changed the name of the country to Zaire, the name of the Congo River centuries before. In keeping with his African-roots policy, he also changed his own name, calling himself Mobutu Sese Seko Kuku Ngbendu wa za Banga (officially translated as "the all-powerful warrior who, because of his endurance and inflexible will to win, will go from conquest to conquest leaving fire in his wake"). As a demonstration of his tribal roots, he took to wearing a leopard-skin hat, which became his sartorial signature. His obsession with names also manifested itself in a Nationality Law, which abolished the use of all European names for persons and places.

Mobutu consolidated his rule as a one-party state and seized European-owned businesses. Dissent was crushed and opponents jailed or executed. However, he did succeed—at least for a time—in fostering a sense of national unity among several tribal and ethnic groups. Because there was no official language—French, a legacy of the

Former leader of Zaire Mobutu Sese Seko *(Landov)*

Belgian colonists, was the only common language—Mobutu promoted the widespread use of four local languages. At the same time he moved to shore up relations with the United States and Europe, cutting a number of deals with Western companies to exploit the country's valuable copper deposits. Because he positioned himself as a staunch anticommunist, he was looked upon by Washington as a vital ally in the region. Mobutu took advantage of his position to amass a fortune, estimated in the billions of dollars, most of which he evidently cached away in secret Swiss bank accounts. (The International Monetary Fund has estimated that his fortune reached its peak of about $4 billion in the 1980s.)

Although Mobutu made some moves toward democratic reform in the 1980s, allowing the formation of a political opposition party, he harassed and imprisoned its leaders. In the waning years of his regime, he confronted a number of uprisings, which he always managed to put down, twice with the assistance of French troops. Nonethe-

less, his hold on power steadily weakened. With the end of the cold war, Mobutu's value to the West diminished significantly, and the U.S. Congress cut off direct aid to protest his human rights abuses. A rebellion in eastern Zaire, led by a former Lumumba supporter named Laurent Kabila, gathered force, and the economy went into a tailspin. Meanwhile Mobutu's health was worsening—he suffered from prostate cancer—and he spent more and more time away from the capital of Kinshasa, preferring to stay on the Riviera or withdraw into the palatial splendor of his home in his native village of Gbadolite. Eventually Kabila's rebels succeeded in breaking out of their stronghold in the east and routing Mobutu's forces, which included a number of foreign MERCENARIES. Defiant until the end, Mobutu finally conceded power in May 1997 and went into exile. He died in Morocco in September of the same year. At the time of his death, Mobutu owned palaces and villas in Zaire, Morocco, South Africa, France, Belgium, Switzerland, Spain, and Portugal. He had also managed to assemble an impressive wine collection, worth an estimated $2.3 million, which he stored in his castle in Portugal.

See also CONGO, DEMOCRATIC REPUBLIC OF THE, WAR CRIMES IN; LEOPOLD II.

Further Reading:

Edgerton, Robert. *The Troubled Heart of Africa: A History of the Congo.* New York: St. Martin's Press, 2002.

Wrong, Michela. *In the Footsteps of Mr. Kurtz: Living on the Brink of Disaster in Mobutu's Congo.* New York: HarperCollins Publishers, 2001.

Monteneros *See* ARGENTINA, HUMAN RIGHTS VIOLATIONS IN.

Montesinos, Vladimiro Ilyich (1946–) *Peruvian spymaster*

Vladimiro Ilyich Montesinos was the security chief and intelligence head for Peruvian president Alberto FUJIMORI during a decade of authoritarian rule. A former army captain, Montesinos was second only to Fujimori in the power he wielded and was widely regarded—and reviled—as Fujimori's Rasputin. His parents were both communists, which explains why they named their son—born in 1946—after Vladimir Ilyich Lenin. Far from living up to his namesake, though, Montesinos developed into a committed rightist ideologue.

Montesinos joined the army in 1966, but he was cashiered and imprisoned in 1977 on the suspicion that he had sold state secrets to the CIA at a time when Peru was dominated by a leftist government and was a beneficiary of Soviet aid. In prison he studied law, and on his release he opened a practice defending people accused of tax fraud and drug trafficking. He soon acquired several new friends in the cocaine trade in addition to befriending corrupt army and police officials. When one general was accused of massacring civilians in an operation against insurgents, he turned to Montesinos to defend him; the case was dismissed. Montesinos also proved a valuable asset to the National Intelligence Service, known by its acronym SIN. In 1990 Fujimori sought Montesinos's help in resolving a tax-evasion case which might have jeopardized his bid for the presidency. Montesinos obligingly took care of the problem. There were also allegations that he had arranged for Colombia's drug baron Pablo Escobar to contribute $1 million to Fujimori's electoral campaign in exchange for allowing Escobar's agents the use of Peru's air space to transport cocaine. Nine years later Montesinos was thought to have orchestrated a "dirty tricks" campaign to influence Fujimori's victory for a third term in violation of the 1993 constitution, which limited a president to two terms.

Even as Montesinos was becoming more involved in extortion, drug trafficking, and illegal arms trading, Fujimori was publicly commending him for intercepting a consignment of arms from Jordan supposedly intended for the insurgent group Revolutionary Armed Forces of Colombia (FARC). The Jordanian government reacted angrily, insisting that the shipment had been sold to the Peruvian government. It later emerged that Montesinos himself was in the process of selling arms to FARC. In another suspect arms deal, the spymaster sold two shoddy MIG-29 fighters to Ecuador (which had just fought a brief border war with Peru), pocketing a sizable commission in the process. Montesinos has also been linked to a notorious death squad called La Colina, which might be implicated in the 1991 slaying of 15 civilians attending a party in a Lima slum who were apparently mistaken for a terrorist gathering.

In September 2000 a video was aired on Peruvian television that showed Montesinos bribing a member of the Peruvian Congress to influence his vote. The video scandalized the country, as much of the tape implicated Peru's most powerful figures. The tape, stolen from Montesinos's office safe, was only one of about a thousand that the spymaster had made for purposes of blackmail and as a kind of insurance policy to forestall any attempt to undermine him. In the uproar that ensued, Fujimori tried to put as much distance as he could between him and his former confidant and ordered his arrest. Montesinos fled the country immediately and, shortly after being denied asylum in Panama, dropped out of sight.

In November 2000 Switzerland announced that it was freezing about $50 million in five bank accounts that were linked to Montesinos, lending weight to the belief that he had laundered money through the accounts. Other suspect accounts were subsequently identified in the Cayman Islands, Uruguay, New York, and elsewhere, totaling $274 million. Much of these funds, investigators believed, came from his drug-trafficking and arms deals, but it still represents only about a third of the $800 million looted from Peru's treasury during the 10 years Fujimori had been in power. In November 2000 Fujimori took refuge in Japan, his parents' country of origin, and resigned from the presidency. (Peru has unsuccessfully tried to extradite him to stand trial for money laundering and other charges.) On June 23, 2001, the fugitive Montesinos was arrested in Venezuela and extradited to Peru. A year later he was tried and convicted of illegally controlling Peru's intelligence agency and received a sentence of nine years in prison. He was later given an additional sentence of eight years after standing trial on embezzlement charges. But it is likely that Montesinos will be returning to court several times in the near future; he still faces some 70 trials on various charges.

See also COLOMBIA, HUMAN RIGHTS VIOLATIONS IN.

Morocco, human rights violations in

Morocco has made some progress in human rights especially since the ascension of King Mohamed VI, who assumed the throne in 1999 after the death of his father, Hassan II, who had held power since 1961. However, a wave of al-QAEDA terrorist attacks in May 2003 has apparently set back the country's democratization. The coordinated attacks on May 16 directed at Western and Jewish targets in Casablanca led to the deaths of 46 people, including 12 suicide bombers; about 100 were injured. A terrorist law enacted in 2003 defined *terrorism* broadly to encompass any act that might arouse fear or jeopardize public safety. The act also extended by 10 days the time that a suspect can be held before charges must be filed. HUMAN RIGHTS WATCH called the antiterrorism law a "major regression" in efforts to create a civil society. After the act went into effect, security forces rounded up more than 2,000 people for suspected involvement with terrorist groups. As of late 2003, 903 of the defendants had been convicted and 17 sentenced to death. Many of these arrests and detentions have been arbitrary, according to the U.S. State Department *Country Report* on Morocco.

In spite of violations of civil liberties, the United States regards Morocco as a close ally in the war against terrorism and has provided Rabat with military and development assistance. It has also granted the country the status of "major non-NATO ally." However, human rights violations are rampant. While police usually arrest suspects in public, they frequently fail to identify themselves or produce warrants. Several suspects have died in police custody, but no serious attempts have been made to investigate these cases. Because of the swelling prison population, it is difficult to ascertain the fates of many of the detainees. As a result, reports of politically motivated DISAPPEARANCES are impossible to verify. However, both the Moroccan Association for Human Rights (AMDH) and AMNESTY INTERNATIONAL contend that the practice of holding suspects incommunicado have amounted to "a period of disappearance." In such cases police are often in the habit of denying to families that they are holding the individuals. And while the Penal Code outlaws the use of TORTURE, human rights organizations have collected evidence indicating that security forces often ignore the law. The judiciary suffers from inefficiency and corruption and is subject to political influence. The government limits freedom of assembly and freedom of the press. About 1,000 Islamic candidates have been forced to withdraw from local elections because of their political beliefs. The government also imposes restrictions on labor unions and curtails the right to strike. The crackdown has failed to dampen enthusiasm for Islamic movements, though. On the contrary, they have become increasingly popular, not the least because they have established social welfare programs in areas where people consider the government's programs as inadequate.

Until the 2003 Casablanca bombings, the government was lauded by human rights organizations for releasing hundreds of political prisoners and easing restrictions on the press and political activity. King Mohamed VI even went so far as to establish the Justice and Reconciliation Commission to document abuses perpetrated under his father's regime and determine "the responsibility of state or other apparatuses in the violations and the incidents under investigation." This commission is supposed to investigate some 13,000 cases of alleged abuses prior to 1999 and arrange for out-of-court settlements in cases where proof of abuse is found. Although he was known as a "moderate" and pro-Western ruler, King Hassan had been responsible for a ruthless campaign to imprison or disappear thousands of suspected leftists, Islamists, and advocates of self-determination for Western Sahara, a region bitterly disputed by Morocco and Algeria. In the late 1980s, Hassan moved to liberalize society and pledged that incidences of forced disappearances would never recur. At that point 112 disappearances had been reported, some of which had taken place two decades previously. Human rights groups and families, however, maintain that there were many more disappearances besides these, many of them stemming from violence in the Western Sahara.

The Justice and Reconciliation Commission is subject to certain restrictions that might hamper its efforts. It cannot find any individuals culpable in cases of abuse. In addition, it has no power to compel testimony or obtain necessary documents. Its mandate specifies that it can investigate cases of "arbitrary detention" and "enforced disappearance," leaving open the question whether it can undertake any investigation of other types of abuses, including TORTURE, sham trials, and the shooting of demonstrators. Nor is it clear whether the commission will have the right to probe any human rights violations that occurred after the May 2003 terrorist strikes in Casablanca.

See also BERBERS, HUMAN RIGHTS ABUSES OF.

Further Reading:

McNamara, Ronald J. *Democracy and Human Rights in the Mediterranean Partner States of the Osce: Algeria, Egypt, Israel, Jordan, Morocco and Tunisia: Briefing of the Committee on Security and Cooperation in Europe.* Chicago: Diane Pub. Co., 2004.

Sherry, Virginia N. *Cleaning the Face of Morocco: Human Rights Abuses and Recent Developments/North Africa.* New York: Human Rights First, 1990.

Slyomovics, Susan. *The Performance of Human Rights in Morocco.* Pennsylvania Studies in Human Rights. Philadelphia: University of Pennsylvania Press, 2005.

Waltz, Susan Eileen. *Human Rights and Reform: Changing the Face of North African Politics.* Berkeley: University of California Press, 1995.

Mothers of the Plaza de Mayo (Grandmothers of the Plaza de Mayo)

The Mothers of the Plaza de Mayo (*Asociación Madres de Plaza de Mayo* in Spanish) is an association of women that has held demonstrations every Thursday at 3:30 P.M. in the famous Plaza de Mayo in Buenos Aires, Argentina, for over 20 years. (They are sometimes known as Grandmothers of the Plaza de Mayo.) They are mothers of children who were disappeared during the "dirty wars" of the 1970s. That tumultuous period was marked by a clandestine campaign by a succession of military juntas against leftist insurgents and suspected sympathizers. The women, dressed in black, march around a statue of liberty in front of the presidential palace. Many have used white handkerchiefs printed with the names of their vanished children or carry signs with their children's photographs.

For years the authorities denied all knowledge of the whereabouts or fate of the victims, who were often spirited away in unmarked cars in the dead of night. The mothers' weekly protest became the most vivid and powerful expression of resistance to the military regimes. After democracy was restored in 1982, the government proved more forthcoming with information. The military has acknowledged that more than 9,000 abductees are still unaccounted for; the Mothers of the Plaza de Mayo believe the number is closer to 30,000. The women recognize that most of their children have been tortured and are probably dead, yet they have refused any monetary compensation for their losses and continue to demand government accountability. Some of the mothers suffered the same fate as their children for opposing the military regimes, including the organization's founder, Azucena Villaflor de Vicenti. Sometime between December 8 and 10, 1977, along with 11 members and friends of the Mothers, she was kidnapped by Argentine government forces and never seen again. In December 2003 the president of Mothers of the Plaza de Mayo, Estela Barnes de Carlotto, was awarded a UN Human Rights Prize.

See also ARGENTINA, HUMAN RIGHTS VIOLATIONS IN.

Further Reading:

Arditti, Rita. *Searching for Life: The Grandmothers of the Plaza de Mayo and the Disappeared Children of Argentina.* Berkeley: University of California Press, 1999.

Davis, William Columbus. *Warnings from the Far South: Democracy versus Dictatorship in Uruguay, Argentina, and Chile.* New York: Praeger Publishers, 1995.

Goni, Uki. *The Real Odessa: How Peron Brought the Nazi War Criminals to Argentina.* London: Granta Books, 2003.

Lewis, Paul H. *Guerrillas and Generals: The Dirty War in Argentina.* New York: Praeger, 2001.

Moyano, Maria. *Argentina's Lost Patrol: Armed Struggle, 1969–1979.* New Haven, Conn.: Yale University Press, 1995.

Rombero, Luis Alberto. *A History of Argentina in the Twentieth Century.* University Park: Pennsylvania State University Press, 2002.

Mugabe, Robert   *See* ZIMBABWE, HUMAN RIGHTS VIOLATIONS IN.

Mullah Omar (Mohammed Omar) (1959–) *Taliban leader*

The onetime TALIBAN leader of Afghanistan, Mohammed Omar—better known as Mullah Omar—suddenly gained a high public profile after the September 11, 2001, attacks in New York and Washington, D.C. At the time, his regime was harboring Osama Bin Laden, the mastermind of the terrorist strikes, but Mullah Omar refused to hand him over to Washington even at the cost of his regime. Within months the United States had invaded Afghanistan, toppling the Taliban and sending Mullah Omar into exile.

Reporters who met the reclusive Mullah while he was in power say that he loved to tell war stories. Presumably he had a lot of them to tell: He had been wounded four times in the jihad against Soviet forces, which had invaded the country in 1979; one of the battles had deprived him of an eye. Calling himself Commander of the Faithful, Omar followed a fundamentalist branch of Islam that is so strict that even the playing of music or flying a kite was made illegal. Born in 1959, the son of a peasant farmer, he claimed to have started the Taliban movement after a dream in which Allah asked him to lead the faithful. The core of the Taliban (from *talib*, meaning "one who seeks") consisted of young students of Islam, many of whom were driven into exile in neighboring Pakistan after the Soviets took over the country. Omar himself studied the Koran in a fundamentalist school, or madrassa, in Pakistan. Although he might have been motivated by a dream, he had other reasons to try to wrest control over his native country. After the withdrawal of Soviet troops in 1989, Afghanistan had plunged into chaos as various warlords fought among themselves for domination. Omar has told interviewers that he was appalled by the lawless atmosphere that prevailed but was provoked especially by one incident in which mujahideen (veterans of the resistance against the Soviets) went on a rampage, raping several women who lived near Kandahar, Omar's family home.

Initially accompanied by only 30 followers from his Pashtun tribe, Omar went to war. More fighters soon joined him, and he began to acquire a kind of cult status, which he did nothing to discourage. On the contrary, in 1996, accepting the title of *amirul momineen* (commander of the faithful), he appeared before cheering Taliban followers wrapped in a coat said to have been worn by the prophet Mohammed. (His title was not accepted by Muslims outside of Afghanistan.) By 1998 he had secured control over most of the country, although at no point did the Taliban ever extend its power over all Afghani territory. Anti-Taliban fighters, collectively known as the Northern Alliance, continued to hold out. Omar ruled from Kandahar, never visiting the capital, Kabul. In the first years of the Taliban regime, he would routinely appear in local mosques, but over time he became increasingly reclusive, preferring to ride around in armed convoys of Landcruisers. He increasingly fell under the influence of the radical Saudi exile Osama Bin Laden, his deputy Ayman Zawahiri, and the Islamic jihad faithful that they had brought with them from Saudi Arabia and Egypt.

There were reports that the Taliban was divided about the course it should take, with some moderates favoring a more open policy. Nonetheless, it appeared that by late 2001 Omar was becoming increasingly beholden to Bin Laden and reliant on his generous subsidies. After the United States had satisfied itself that Bin Laden's al-QAEDA group was behind the terrorist attacks on 9/11, Washington demanded that Omar turn over Bin Laden or face an invasion. Omar was characteristically defiant. "America is very strong," he admitted in an interview with the Voice of America (VOA). But he went on to say that it would make no difference: "Even if it were twice as strong or twice that, it could not be strong enough to defeat us. We are confident that no one can harm us if God is with us." Asked by VOA if he would give up Bin Laden, he said, "No. We cannot do that. If we did, it means we are not Muslims . . . that Islam is finished. If we were afraid of attack, we could have surrendered him the last time we were threatened and attacked. So America can hit us again, and this time we don't even have a friend." The United States did, as he predicted, hit him, and by November 2001 Omar, Bin Laden, and other top Taliban officials were on the run, presumably taking refuge in the remote mountainous region on the border with Pakistan. Although there have been occasional reports of sightings since then, Mullah Omar was still at large as of early 2005, in spite of a bounty on his head of several million dollars offered by the United States.

See also AFGHANISTAN, HUMAN RIGHTS VIOLATIONS IN.

Further Reading:
Anderson, J. L., and Thomas Dworzak. *Taliban*. London: Trolley, 2003.
Burke, Jason. *Al-Qaeda: Casting a Shadow of Terror*. London: I. B. Tauris, 2004.
———. *Al-Qaeda: The True Story of Radical Islam*. London: I. B. Tauris, 2004.
Ewans, Martin. *Afghanistan: A Short History of Its People and Politics*. New York: Perennial, 2002.
Micheletti, Eric. *Special Forces in Afghanistan 2001–2003: War against Terrorism*. Paris: Historie & Collections, 2003.
Rashid, Ahmed. *Jihad: The Rise of Militant Islam in Central Asia*. New York: Penguin Books, 2003.
———. *Taliban: Militant Islam, Oil and Fundamentalism in Central Asia*. New Haven: Yale University Press, 2001.
Tanner, Stephen. *Afghanistan: A Military History from Alexander the Great to the Fall of the Taliban*. New York: Perseus Books Group, 2003.
Zayy-at, Montassor al-. *The Road to Al-Qaeda: The Story of Bin Laden's Right-Hand Man*. Critical Studies on Islam. Translated by Ahmed Fekry. Edited by Sara Nionis. Ann Arbor, Mich.: Pluto Press, 2004.

Müller, Heinrich (1900–?) *Gestapo chief*

Heinrich Müller (also spelled Mueller) was the chief of the GESTAPO from 1939 until the end of World War II in 1945. Although he remained in the shadows, he wielded immense power over the lives of hundreds of millions of people in parts of Europe occupied by the German army. For decades the German Office of Investigation of Nazis considered him its most wanted war criminal.

Born in Munich on April 28, 1900, Müller served as a pilot in World War I. After the war he joined the police in his native Munich, where he became known for pursuing communists. Although he proved to be an able investigator, he was indifferent to the norms of legal procedure. His reputation for getting results, however, attracted the interest of Heinrich HIMMLER and Reinhard HEYDRICH, who headed the SS, the Nazi elite police. After Adlof HITLER came to power in 1933, Himmler and Heydrich formed a national political police which they called the Geheime Staatspolizei (Gestapo). The following year Müller joined the SS. He won succeeding promotions until he was appointed chief of the Gestapo, known formally as Reich Main Security Office (RSHA) Amt IV. In his new position, Müller undertook to implement Nazi policies designed to crush Jews and other enemies of the state. One of his most trusted subordinates was Adolf EICHMANN, who ran the Gestapo's Office of Resettlement and then its Office of Jewish Affairs. Müller subsequently put Eichmann in charge of the deportation and extermination of the several million Jews in occupied Europe.

Müller was also behind a plot to blame Poland for starting World War II in 1939 by staging a phony Polish attack against a German radio station. In March 1944 he signed the "Bullet Order," which authorized the killings of escaped PRISONERS OF WAR. A committed Hitler loyalist, he earned a military decoration for his role in rounding up and torturing the participants in the July 20, 1944, plot to kill Hitler. As head of the Gestapo, he also masterminded counterespionage operations against the French Resistance and a Soviet spy network known as the Rote Kapelle (Red Orchestra). He organized the kidnapping of British intelligence officials and even plotted to abduct the duke of Windsor, a scheme that was never executed. As the war turned increasingly in favor of the Allies, he used his spy network to try to cause a rift between the Soviets and the United States and Great Britain.

After the war, some high-placed Nazi officials told their American captors that Müller might have been a Soviet agent, but most SS officers who were close to him asserted that such an accusation was absurd. According to witnesses later interviewed by West German police, Müller was last seen alive on May 1, 1945. At the time he refused to try to escape with other Nazi officials gathered at Hitler's Chancellery building. "We know the Russian methods exactly," Müller was reported to have said. "I haven't the faintest intention of . . . being taken prisoner by the Russians." While the search for Müller has continued intermittently over ensuing decades, it is not known whether he is alive or dead.

Further Reading:

Browder, George C. *Hitler's Enforcers: The Gestapo and the SS Security Service in the Nazi Revolution.* Oxford: Oxford University Press, 1996.

Butler, Rupert. *The Gestapo: A History of Hitler's Secret Police 1933–45.* Havertown, Pa.: Casemate Publishers and Book Distributors, 2004.

Douglas, Gregory. *Gestapo Chief: The 1948 Interrogation of Heinrich Muller, Volume 3.* San Jose, Calif.: R. James Bender Pub., 1998.

Hohne, Heinz Zollen. *The Order of the Death's Head: Story of Hitler's SS.* New York: Penguin, 2001.

Myanmar, human rights violations in

Myanmar (formerly Burma) has been ruled by a succession of military dictatorships since 1962. Dissent has been ruthlessly suppressed and Myanmar's most prominent political opposition leader, AUNG SAN SUU KYI, winner of the Nobel Peace Prize, was still under house arrest in early 2005. There is little question that she would be the country's president if democracy were restored. Her party, the National League for Democracy (NLD), gained a majority in parliament in elections in 1990, but rather than concede defeat, the military annulled the election. Since then security forces have rounded up and arrested members of the opposition; those that remain free are kept on a tight leash. AMNESTY INTERNATIONAL estimated that more than a thousand political prisoners were still being detained in early 2003. In spite of periodic negotiations between the army and San Suu Kyi, there are few signs that the military has any intention of voluntarily relinquishing power.

Myanmar also confronts serious ethnic problems, perhaps not surprising given the fact that the population is made up of 135 different ethnic groups. (The Burman is the largest, accounting for around 55 percent of the population.) Ethnic tensions have led to a number of insurgencies. Members of the Karen, for instance, have been fighting the government for more than 50 years. In its attempt to quell ethnic rebellions, the Myanmar army has become increasingly aggressive. According to human rights groups, the army has committed numerous human rights violations, including forced relocation, razing of villages, rape, TORTURE, and summary executions. The army has also made widespread use of conscription, forcing local villagers to work without pay growing food for soldiers, performing road maintenance, or serving as porters in military camps.

Myanmar has the dubious distinction of having more child soldiers than any other country in the world, accounting for approximately one-fourth of the 300,000 children currently believed to be involved in armed conflicts around the world. The United Nations secretary-general has placed Myanmar on a list of violators that flout international laws

Red Cross workers speaking with a detainee in a Myanmar prison *(J. P. Moret/ICRC)*

prohibiting the recruitment and use of children as soldiers. A 2002 investigation by HUMAN RIGHTS WATCH found that as many as 70,000 children under the age of 18 may be serving in the army. Another 6,000–7,000 serve in Myanmar's armed ethnic opposition groups; about 20 percent of the Karen insurgent army is composed of children under the age of 18. Army recruiters force boys as young as 11 into the army and regularly haul children off the street. Child soldiers are forced to commit human rights abuses against civilians. Children have rounded up villagers for FORCED LABOR, burned villages, and carried out executions. In an account reported by Human Rights International, a 14-year-old soldier reported that his unit had killed 15 women and children in operations in Shan State. The women were blindfolded, the boy said, and "then six of the corporals loaded their guns and shot them. They fired on auto. The women had no time to shout. I felt very bad because there were all these people in front of me, and they killed them all. After the mothers were killed they killed the babies. They swung them by their legs and smashed them against a rock."

See also CHILDREN'S RIGHTS.

Further Reading:
Diller, Janelle M. *The National Convention in Burma (Myanmar): An Ipediment to the Restoration of Democracy: a Report.* New York: International League for Human Rights, 1996.
Ross, James D. *Human Rights in Burma (Myanmar) since the May 1990 National Election.* New York: Lawyers Committee for Human Rights, 1991.

My Lai massacre

On March 16, 1968, the South Vietnamese village of My Lai became the site of the most infamous atrocity committed by U.S. forces in the Vietnam War. News of the massacre of civilians shocked the American public and led to intense questioning about the wisdom of the war. The village was located in the heavily infiltrated Vietcong (VC) district of Son My. A number of U.S. troops with Charlie Company conducting operations in the area had been wounded or killed in previous weeks by VC communist insurgents. Under the command of Lieutenant William Calley, members of Charlie Company were ordered to conduct a "search and destroy" mission. Although there was no evidence of the village having harbored Vietcong, the soldiers entered the village firing without encountering opposing fire. In the ensuing massacre, as many as 500 unarmed villagers were killed. Eyewitnesses gave accounts of elderly men being bayoneted and praying women and children being shot in the back of the head. Calley reportedly rounded up several villagers personally, ordered them into a ditch, and then proceeded to slaughter them with machine-gun fire.

Initially the incident was portrayed by the Pentagon as a battle and the killings attributed to combat casualties. A secret military investigation was instituted, and consequently Calley was charged with murder in September 1969. An unemployed college dropout in civilian life, Calley claimed at his trial that he had been ordered by his superior, Captain Ernest Medina, to kill the village population, but his defense failed. The evidence gathered against him was too compelling, and he was found guilty and sentenced to life. (He was released in 1974 and, after being dishonorably discharged from the army, found work in the insurance business.) No one else in Charlie Company was ever tried for participating in the massacre.

In spite of the military proceedings, the official cover-up continued, and the massacre did not become public knowledge until November 1969, when journalist Seymour Hersh published a story about the incident based on conversations with a Vietnam veteran named Ron Ridenhour, who had heard of the massacre from members of Charlie Company. A military commission was established to conduct a sweeping investigation of conditions among the armed forces serving in Vietnam; it found endemic failures in leadership, discipline, and morale, especially among draftees. The uproar over the massacres also had the effect of pushing the administration of President Richard M. Nixon into accelerating its efforts to withdraw U.S. troops from the region, which were finally completed in 1973.

See also TAYLOR, TELFORD; TIGER FORCE; VIETNAM, HUMAN RIGHTS VIOLATIONS IN.

Further Reading:
Bilton, Michael, and Kevin Sim. *Four Hours in My Lai.* New York: Penguin Books, 1993.
Hersh, Seymour. *My Lai 4: A Report on the Massacre and Its Aftermath.* New York: Random House Trade, 1970.
Olson, James S., and Roberts, Randy, eds. *My Lai: A Brief History with Documents (The Bedford Series in History and Culture).* Sydney, Australia: Palgrave Macmillan, 1998.
Taylor, Telford. *Nuremberg and Vietnam: An American Tragedy.* New York: Times Books, 1970.
Vietnam Veterans against the War. *The Winter Soldier Investigation: An Inquiry into American War Crimes.* Boston: Beacon Press, 1972.

N

Nagano, Osami   *See* WAR CRIMINALS OF JAPAN.

Nanjing (Nanking), massacre in

In November 1937, Nanjing (previously known as Nanking), the provisional capital of the Republic of China, came under siege by the Japanese Imperial Army. When the city fell in early December, the Japanese carried out a massacre that became known to history as the Rape of Nanking. It was the worst single massacre of unarmed civilians by soldiers in the 20th century.

After launching their assault in July 1937, the Japanese had successively driven Chinese forces under President Chiang Kai-shek from Beijing, Tianjin, and Shanghai. The Chinese retreated to Nanjing, where they held out for several weeks. When they initially rejected demands for surrender, the Japanese commander MATSUI Iwane was given orders not to take any prisoners alive. Before Nanjing fell, about half a million inhabitants—half the population—managed to escape. When the city finally capitulated on December 13, the Japanese troops laid it to waste and went on a rampage that continued for the next seven weeks. By the time the massacre was over, anywhere between 100,000 and 350,000 people—civilians and Chinese soldiers who had surrendered—had been killed; in addition, some 20,000 women and girls were raped, the second-largest mass rape recorded. Many were later killed, and still other women were forced to become sex slaves. Japanese soldiers engaged in killing contests to see who could kill the fastest. Victims were slaughtered in a variety of ways. Some were buried alive or nailed to wooden boards and then run over by tanks; others were crucified on trees or electric posts, flayed, and used for bayonet practice. There were reports of men having their eyes gouged out and noses and ears hacked off before being set ablaze and babies being bayoneted and flung into vats of boiling water. The rate of killings per day was in excess of 8,000.

In 1946, even as the International Military Tribunal for the Far East was conducting trials of war criminals in Japan, better known as the TOKYO TRIALS, China held a war-crimes trial of its own under the supervision of the United States. More than 1,000 eyewitnesses came forward to testify about the atrocities in Nanjing. Bringing to justice the many potential defendants was almost impossible given the lack of investigators and the chaotic conditions prevailing in postwar China. Nonetheless, 148 Japanese officers and soldiers—including the general in charge of Nanjing—received death sentences, and another 83 were sentenced to time in prison. In contrast to Germany, Japan has been slow to acknowledge its culpability for war crimes like the Nanjing massacres, a source of continual friction between China and Japan over half a century later.

See also RAPE AS A TACTIC OF WAR.

Further Reading:
Chang, Iris. *The Rape of Nanking: The Forgotten Holocaust of World War II.* New York: Penguin, 1998.
Honda, Katsuichi, and Frank Gibney eds. *The Nanjing Massacre: A Japanese Journalist Confronts Japan's National Shame.* Studies of the Pacific Basin Institute, Armonk, N.Y.: East Gate Book, 1999.

National Intelligence Directorate (DINA)

DINA is the acronym for *Departamento de Inteligencia Nacional* (Department of National Intelligence, or National Intelligence Directorate), the Chilean secret police agency under the military dictatorship of General Augusto PINOCHET. Officially established in a decree in 1973, two years after Pinochet seized power in a coup, DINA became a "state within a state"; all other intelligence agencies were subordinated to it.

DINA had two principal objectives: instilling terror in the population to ensure political security and gaining intelligence about enemies of the regime. In early 1974 its agents carried out the arrests of up to 250 people a week, most of whom had not been formally charged. The arrests were conducted secretly by men who arrived at the homes of the accused after curfew, wearing civilian clothes and refusing to identify themselves. They would blindfold the victims and take them away in unmarked pickup trucks. DINA agents were given unlimited power to arrest suspects without charges and to raid and search houses without warrants.

All authority in DINA was concentrated in its head, General Manuel CONTRERAS, who answered only to Pinochet himself. The core of the network was the General Command, a cadre of 30–40 men who were personally loyal to Contreras. The elite units of DINA were known as the Brigades of Arrests and Interrogation. These operated in squads of five or six persons under the command of a captain or major and used the names of Chile's traditional Indian tribes, such as Antumapu, Pehuenche, and Peldehue. Special safe houses were set up where interrogations could take place. Those detainees regarded as "incapable of rehabilitation" were tortured, sometimes for months, before being executed. The authorities, meanwhile, continued to deny any knowledge of the victims' whereabouts to desperate family members and friends. DINA issued no warrants and maintained no official arrest records; no bodies were ever taken to a morgue nor were death certificates filed.

DINA's largest and most secret divisions were known as the Government Service and Internal sections, which were given the responsibility for identifying and suppressing dissent within the government and in the civilian population as a whole. Operating out of a large complex of offices in downtown Santiago, DINA ran a vast network of spies and as many as 20,000–30,000 informants called *soplones,* or whisperers. With so many informants, people were naturally fearful of saying anything that could be considered seditious. In the early years of the Pinochet regime, DINA concentrated on leftists who had gone underground and taken up arms. Later, however, Contreras moved against socialists, communists, and other leftist supporters of former socialist president Salvador Allende. In 1975 he extended his dragnet to include members of the opposition Christian Democrats and even suspected opponents in the Catholic Church. Contreras retired from DINA in 1978, and the organization was disbanded after Pinochet gave up power in 1990.

See also CHILE, HUMAN RIGHTS VIOLATIONS IN.

Further Reading:
Constable, Pamela. *A Nation of Enemies: Chile under Pinochet.* New York: W. W. Norton & Company, 1993.
Dinges, John. *The Condor Years: How Pinochet and His Allies Brought Terrorism to Three Continents.* New York: New Press, 2004.
Dorfman, Ariel. *Exorcising Terror: The Incredible Unending Trial of Augusto Pinochet.* New York: Seven Stories Press, 2002.
Kornbluh, Peter. *The Pinochet File: A Declassified Dossier on Atrocity and Accountability.* A National Security Archive Book. New York: New Press, 2003.
Politzer, Patricia, and Diane Wachtel. *Fear in Chile: Lives under Pinochet.* New York: New Press, 2001.

Nazar Haro, Miguel (1927–) *Mexican police chief*
In February 2004 justice finally caught up with Miguel Nazar Haro, the former head of the Mexican secret police. At the age of 79, Nazar Haro was probably under the impression that he could live out his retirement in peace since no official of his prominence had ever been prosecuted for human rights abuses committed in the so-called dirty war between government security forces and suspected leftist sympathizers. At the height of the dirty war, during the late 1970s and early 1980s, Nazar Haro had headed the Federal Security Directorate, which served as both an intelligence agency and a secret police force. (The directorate was shut down in 1985.) In this position, Nazar Haro was able to cultivate important friends, including the CIA, to which he supplied information about leftists throughout Latin America. His work as a liaison for the U.S. Intelligence agency was considered so critical that even after he left his post, the CIA reportedly blocked his indictment in 1982 by a San Diego grand jury on charges of running an auto-theft ring. (He was alleged to have stolen hundreds of cars in California and resold them in Mexico.)

In 2004 Nazar Haro was charged in connection with the disappearance of Jesús Piedra Ibarra, the leader of a small guerrilla group called the 23rd of September League. Ibarra had been arrested in 1975, beaten, tortured, transported to a military camp in Mexico City, and held in secret for years. He was last seen alive in 1984; his body has never been found. For years the absence of a body made it difficult to bring charges against officials accused of having arranged the disappearance of the victim. But that changed in November 2003 when the Mexican Supreme Court ruled that an individual could be indicted for a disappearance even if no body was found, declaring that such a crime was not covered by any statute of limitations. Nazar Haro's arrest on a Mexico City freeway was the first case in which the high court's ruling was put into effect. The arrest was also seen as a triumph for the special federal prosecutor appointed by President Vincente Fox to investigate past human rights crimes attributed to security forces and the military during the dirty war and afterwards. Luis de la Barreda Moreno,

Nazar Haro's predecessor as secret police chief, faces similar charges and remains a fugitive.

See also MEXICO, HUMAN RIGHTS VIOLATIONS IN.

Nazi Party, Leadership Corps of

The Leadership Corps was the governing elite of the Nazi Party (National Socialist Party; NSDAP) with Adolf HITLER as its head. Membership at all levels was voluntary. According to Nazi doctrine, the Leadership Corps was "responsible for the complete penetration of the German Nation with the National Socialist spirit." The corps was placed in control of the German state, as Hitler bluntly made clear when he addressed a Nazi Party Congress in 1935: "It is not the State which gives orders to us, it is we who give orders to the State." In effect, the Nazi Party was seen as embodying the will of the German people. Thus, the NSDAP was not a party that simply occupied power and filled government positions with its members. Far from being under the rule of law, carrying out "single tasks of public administration," the NSDAP was supposed to be the "bearer of the German state-idea" in all areas of life. Under this doctrine, the distinction between party and state was virtually abolished, and the Nazi Party was also given the right to destroy all opponents.

In 1945 the Leadership Corps was indicted as a criminal organization by the International Military Tribunal conducted by the Allies at the NUREMBERG TRIALS. The indictment stated: "All the defendants, with divers other persons, during a period years preceding 8 May, 1945, participated as leaders, organizers, instigators or accomplices in the formulation or execution of a common plan or conspiracy to commit, or which involved the commission of, Crimes against Peace, War crimes, and CRIMES AGAINST HUMANITY, as defined in the Charter of this Tribunal, and, in accordance with the provisions of the charter, are individually responsible for their own acts and for all acts committed by any persons in the execution of such [a] plan or conspiracy."

The verdicts of the trial were announced on September 30 and on October 1, 1946; 12 defendants were sentenced to death by hanging, seven were sentenced to life imprisonment or to lesser terms, and three were acquitted. The last defendant convicted, Rudolf HESS, committed suicide in prison in August 1987.

Further Reading:

Buscher, Frank. M. *The U.S. War Crimes Trial Program in Germany, 1946–1955.* Contributions in Military Studies. Westport, Conn.: Greenwood Press, 1989.
Russell of Liverpool, Edward Frederick Langley Russell, Baron. *The Scourge of the Swastika: A Short History of Nazi War Crimes.* London: Greenhill Books/Lionel Leventhal, 2002.
Nesbit, Roy Conyers. *The Flight of Rudolf Hess: Myths and Reality.* New York: Sutton Publishing, 2003.
Padfield, Peter. *Hess: The Fuhrer's Disciple.* London: Cassell, 2001.
Weindling, Paul Julian. *Nazi Medicine and the Nuremberg Trials: From Medical War Crimes to Informed Consent.* Sydney, Australia: Palgrave Macmillan, 2005.

Nazi war crimes

See CIA WAR CRIMES ARCHIVE; FINAL SOLUTION; NUREMBURG TRIALS; WANNSEE CONFERENCE.

Nepal, human rights violations in

Since 1996 civil war has created a grave human rights crisis in the tiny Himalayan nation of Nepal. Up to 10,000 Nepalese, mostly civilians, have perished during the conflict. The war was sparked by a rebellion by Maoist insurgents that began in the remote countryside but now reaches into the capital of Katmandu. The rebels, who assert that they are fighting a "People's War," have gained sufficient strength to blockade Katmandu for days at a time, threatening the city's fuel and food supplies. Civilians are caught between the Maoists and security forces. They must choose between cooperating with the military or with the rebels, risking reprisals from one side or the other. According to human rights organizations, civilians are regularly executed, abducted, and tortured by both parties to the conflict. The government has announced a policy to "break the backbone" of the rebellion, which has led to EXTRAJUDICIAL KILLINGS and DISAPPEARANCES. The Maoists are, if anything, more culpable; villagers deemed supporters of the regime are classified as "class enemies" and put to death.

Although the Royal Nepal Army has expanded its ranks—by 2004 it was able to muster 72,000 men—it still has proven incapable of defeating the insurgents even though it is believed to have no more than 4,000 core members and some 15,000 militia supporters. The insurgents have also pressed children—about 8,000 in 2004 alone—into service. The army has largely been confined to the capital. Approximately two-thirds of the country has been abandoned by the police, allowing the Maoists to move freely and exert power over a large segment of the population. The fear of being swallowed up in the conflict has driven thousands of Nepalese to take refuge in India.

Vulnerable villagers are also subjected to intimidation and extortion. The insurgents are in the habit of imposing a "tax" on civilians. They have also recruited children as messengers or porters or as spies, clear violations of international conventions against the conscription of children in armed conflicts. Soldiers, too, have also been known to use extortion and blackmail or isolate whole villages in an effort to deny food and shelter to the rebels. "Rampant abuses have created a climate of intense fear in Nepal's villages," said a HUMAN RIGHTS WATCH representative. "Because of Nepal's geography and poverty, Nepalis under attack or threat usually have nowhere to turn to for protection or redress."

Human rights organizations as well as lawyers and journalists have come under fire from the government, which tends to brand them as Maoist sympathizers. There is little indication that the government intends to honor its public commitments to human rights. By the same token, Maoists have executed local activists whom they view as adversaries. When challenged by human rights organizations, the insurgents contend that their victims had stood in the way of liberating the country from oppressive rule. Both sides, however, maintain that they support the creation of a Human Rights Accord, which would pave the way for the deployment of impartial monitors to prevent future abuses.

The insurgency was fueled by the country's endemic and widespread poverty. According to the World Bank, 42 percent of the Nepalese live below the poverty line. The nation is also 85 percent rural. The country is run more like a feudal fiefdom than the parliamentary democracy the government claims it to be. In many respects, because of its misguided policies, the government is to blame for the insurgency's success. Most notably, Katmandu failed to institute land reform legislation once representative government was restored in 1990. Peasants began to protest against the excessive rents they were forced to pay to use the land. In response, the government sent military forces into the countryside—Operation Romeo and Operation Kilo Sera II—but far from suppressing peasant agitation, they only succeeded in winning recruits for the Communist Party of Nepal (Maoist), or CPNM. By abolishing the elected parliament, King Gyanendra marginalized other political factions. Students have grown increasingly vocal in protesting the monarchy and the government's policies. In April 2004 more than 1,000 people demonstrated for restoration of democracy. Police plunged into the crowd, injuring 150 protesters with truncheons, rubber bullets, and tear gas. As many as 25,000 protesters turned out subsequently in defiance of a ban on demonstrations. Nonetheless, the government postponed elections, and efforts at reconciliation have all but collapsed.

Deteriorating conditions in Nepal have caused increasing alarm in foreign capitals. The Bush administration warned that the country was in danger of becoming a "failed state" and placed the CPNM on the State Department's Watch List, labeling it a terrorist organization. The United States, India, Britain, and other countries have pro-vided military aid to the government to support the counterinsurgency. In addition, the United States has sent in military advisers. Human rights organizations have charged that the addition of 8,400 American M-16 submachine guns, Belgian FAL submachine guns, high-tech night-fighting equipment, and British helicopters has only succeeded in intensifying the conflict. According to the Nepal human rights group, Informal Sector Service Centre, 800 of the 1,100 deaths since the end of a seven-month cease-fire in August 2003 were inflicted by government forces. AMNESTY INTERNATIONAL issued a statement at the end of 2004, saying that the killings are occurring in "the context of a severe human rights crisis and a breakdown in the rule of law." According to statistics compiled by the group, the number of killings by both security forces and Maoist rebels increased significantly in 2004.

The Maoist insurgency and lack of democracy are not the only human rights crises facing Nepal. Ethnic tensions have also bedeviled the country. The Dalit ethnic group in particular has suffered grievous human rights abuses. These abuses stem from a caste-based system that has encouraged discrimination against the Dalits, who number 4.5 million, or 21 percent, of Nepal's population. While the Dalits have suffered from persecution for centuries, the Maoist insurgency has put them at further risk. Security forces tend to view them as supporters of the insurgents, and violence against the Dalits is seldom investigated by the police.

In January 2005, in what amounted to a coup, King Gyanendra suspended the government, imposed a state of emergency, and clamped down on civil liberties, including the right of assembly and freedom of speech. He also cut off communication with the outside world by phone or Internet and placed political opposition leaders under arrest. He declared that his decision was necessary because the politicians had failed to resolve the country's political crisis and said that instead he would govern for three years. Only in this way, he said, could the army effectively deal with the Maoist insurgency. Leaders of several governments, especially Nepal's neighbor India, denounced the king's move. Human rights groups warned that the coup represented a step backward after a 15-year experiment with democracy, and also pointed out that if the army—now 86,000 strong—was needed in the fight against the Maoists, then they should be put to better use than patrolling TV and newspaper offices to ensure that the media said nothing critical about the king. By September 2005 the king had lifted emergency rule but parliament remained suspended. After an emboldened citizenry took to the streets to demand elections, the foreign minister announced that local elections would be held in spring 2006 and parliamentary elections two years later. There was no indication, however, when restrictions on civil liberties imposed by the king might be loosened. Nor was there any indication that the government put in place after the January coup had made discernibly more progress against the Maoist insurgency than the previous democratically elected government had.

Further Reading:

Gregson, Jonathan. *Massacre at the Palace: The Doomed Royal Dynasty of Nepal.* New York: Miramax Books, 2002.

Hutt, Michael, ed. *Himalayan People's War: Nepal's Maoist Rebellion.* Bloomington: Indiana University Press, 2004.

Onesto, Li. *Dispatches from the People's War in Nepal.* Ann Arbor, Mich.: Pluto Press, 2005.

Neurath, Konstantin von (1873–1956) *German diplomat*

The German diplomat Konstantin von Neurath was already in the German government when Adolf HITLER came to power in 1933. However, Hitler initially kept him on because he was such a staunch advocate of Nazi foreign policy. His participation in the Nazi regime led to his being convicted for crimes against peace at the NUREMBERG TRIALS after World War II.

Born in Württemberg, Germany, in 1873, the son of a minor aristocrat, Neurath went on to study law in Tübingen and Berlin. In 1901, after briefly practicing law, he joined the civil service and worked for the Foreign Office, representing Germany in London and Constantinople. He enlisted in the army as an infantry officer in World War I; badly wounded in 1914, he was awarded the Iron Cross. On recovering, he returned to the diplomatic service. He was assigned to the embassy in Rome in 1921 and remained there for a decade during Benito Mussolini's ascent to power as head of a fascist government. (Neurath was not very impressed with the Italian brand of fascism.) In 1932, after a brief posting in London, he was recalled to Germany to become minister of foreign affairs under Franz von PAPEN. In 1938, five years after Hitler had come to power, Neurath was dismissed in favor of Joachim von RIBBENTROP. However, after Germany seized Czechoslovakia, he was appointed reich protector of Bohemia and Moravia in 1939. In that capacity he was responsible for dissolving the Czech parliament and its political parties as well as suppressing freedom of the press and imposing the racist NUREMBERG LAWS. He did not remain long in that position, because the Nazi regime felt that he had treated the Czechs too leniently, and he was replaced by the far more reliably brutal Reinhard HEYDRICH in 1941. Neurath concluded his career in the Nazi regime as a general in the SS.

Tried before the International Military Tribunal of War Criminals in Nuremberg, Neurath was found guilty of conspiracy, crimes against peace, war crimes, and CRIMES AGAINST HUMANITY. The charges were based on his having served the Third Reich as foreign minister and reich protector of Bohemia and Moravia in addition to other positions. The court ruled that he had committed crimes against peace by carrying out a foreign policy intended to break international treaties and having willingly acceded to Hitler's war plans. In his position as reich protector, the tribunal declared, he must have known "that war crimes and crimes against humanity were being committed under his authority." In 1946 he was sentenced to 15 years in prison, but he was released for reasons of ill health in 1954. He died two years later at the age of 83.

Further Reading:

Gilbert, G. M. *Nuremberg Diary.* New York: Da Capo Press, 1995.

Goldensohn, Leon, and Robert Gellately, eds. *The Nuremberg Interviews.* New York: Knopf, 2004.

Marrus, Robert and Michael R. Marrus. *The Nuremberg War Crimes Trial of 1945–46: A Documentary History.* Bedford Series in History and Culture. Sidney, Australia: Palgrave Macmillan, 1997.

Maser, Werner. *Nuremberg: A Nation on Trial.* New York: Scribner, 1979.

Persico, Joseph. *Nuremberg: Infany on Trial.* New York: Penguin Books, 1995.

Rice, Earle. *The Nuremberg Trials.* Famous Trials Series. San Diego, Calif.: Lucent Books, 1997.

Taylor, Telford. *The Anatomy of the Nuremberg Trials: A Personal Memoir.* New York: Little, Brown & Co, 1993.

Ngugi wa Thiong'o (1938–) *Kenyan human rights advocate and writer*

Ngugi wa Thiong'o is Kenya's best-known novelist and a leading human rights advocate who spent 22 years in exile for espousing his political views. Although he was a supporter of an indigenous insurgency against British rule in the 1940s, he subsequently attacked the country's postcolonial leaders for perpetrating a culture of inequality and injustice. In 1977 he wrote two works critical of the government: a novel entitled *Petals of Blood* and a play called *I Will Marry When I Want.* President Jomo Kenyatta was so infuriated that he not only jailed Ngugi but also ordered the destruction of the theater where the play had been performed. Even in prison, Ngugi refused to stop his attacks on an increasingly repressive regime, using toilet paper to write a play, *Devil on the Cross,* and a memoir, *Detained: A Writer's Prison Diary.* The government refused to allow him to return to his position teaching at the University of Nairobi upon his release.

On a visit to London in 1982, Ngugi learned that an order for his arrest had been issued by Kenyatta's successor, President Daniel arap Moi, and he decided to remain abroad. Although in exile, he continued to write and make his influence felt in his homeland. In a novel called *Matigari*, he depicted a character who roamed the countryside seeking justice. The government was so convinced that such a man actually existed that it ordered an arrest warrant for the character. In 2004 Ngugi returned home after a new government replaced Moi's regime in democratic elections. However, no sooner had he received a tumultuous welcome than he and his wife were assaulted by intruders while they slept in their hotel room. Ngugi was repeatedly burned with a lit cigarette, and his wife was raped. Although the incident was blamed on criminals, there were rumors that the attack—perpetrated on the very night of his homecoming—was not a coincidence but was actually an attack by political opponents.

See also KENYA, HUMAN RIGHTS VIOLATIONS IN.

Nicaragua, human rights violations in *See* SOMOZA DEBAYLE, ANASTASIO; SOMOZA GARCÍA, ANASTASIO.

Nigeria, human rights violations in

Since the death in 1999 of the country's strongman, Sani Abacha, Nigeria has begun to enjoy some of the benefits of freedom. Nonetheless, serious human problems remain, and ethnic and religious tensions hamper progress in many regions. Even though Nigeria's democratic leader, President Olusegun Obasanjo, has vowed to fight abuses and corruption, there are still reports of EXTRAJUDICIAL KILLINGS, deaths in custody, TORTURE, and cruel and inhuman or degrading treatment in police detention centers throughout the country. Many of these violations occurred in the course of anticrime operations. The lawless climate is aggravated by the proliferation of armed vigilante groups, especially in the south and southeast; these groups are blamed for torture, inhumane treatment, and DISAPPEARANCES of suspected criminals. In some cases the vigilante groups appear to be operating with the backing of state governments that have effectively "outsourced" law enforcement. In its 2003 annual report, for instance, AMNESTY INTERNATIONAL (AI) noted the extrajudicial killings of dozens of people in Anambra State by a vigilante group officially endorsed by a law passed in 2000 by the Anambra State House of Assembly. Police found that the vigilantes had set up five secret detention centers; at least 100 members of the group were arrested but released without charges.

According to AI, state-sanctioned vigilante groups in two other states were also responsible for extrajudicial executions, torture, and unlawful detention. Moreover, reports cited by AI indicate that politically motivated killings and "acts of harassment and intimidation" that have taken place throughout the country may be linked to officials in state and local governments as well as to political parties. At the same time the authorities have shown no willingness to bring to justice perpetrators of human rights violations. These violations include two incidents in which large groups of civilians were killed by the army in recent years— over 250 unarmed civilians in the town of Odi, Bayelsa State, in 1999 and more than 200 civilians in Benue State in 2001. The 10-member Judicial Commission of Inquiry has since been created by the federal government to investigate the causes of intercommunal violence in Benue and three other states, but its mandate did not include a probe of the massacre.

In a July 2005 report on police abuses, Human Rights Watch said that the number of people the police claimed as "killed in combat" had grown from 834 to 3,100 between 2000 and 2003. Many suspects taken into police custody were beaten, subjected to electric shocks, and raped, according to witnesses interviewed for the report. During the same period, however, the police force has more than doubled because of the rising threat of crime. But police receive poor training and often lack the technical facilities or tools to perform fingerprinting, for example, or conduct autopsies. The situation has gotten so dire that the United Nations appointed an official to investigate allegations of unlawful killings. There are some signs, however, that the government is finally taking action to curb the abuses. In the fall of 2005 the government convened an unprecedented commission of inquiry in response to the slayings of six people in the capital of Abuja. The police initially claimed that the six were robbers and tried to bury the bodies before they could be identified. It turned out that they were young people celebrating an engagement, and, in the course of a roadside dispute, the police had executed them. They then proceeded to plant guns and knives in the victims' bullet-riddled car and positioned the corpses around the vehicle to take photographs to support their case. Five of the seven officers involved have been charged; one vanished under mysterious circumstances and the other decided to cooperate with the commission. Nigerians hope that the investigation will become a precedent and not an aberration.

Ethnic and religious tensions have grown in the north of the country where twelve states with large Muslim populations have adopted strict Islamic law (sharia). These courts have handed down sentences of death and corporal punishments that include amputations of hands (for thievery and armed robbery) and flogging (for fornication, drinking alcohol, and other offenses). Premarital consensual sexual relations, for instance, is a crime punishable by 100 lashes. No case tried by these Islamic courts has stirred more international opprobrium than that of Amina Lawal, who was convicted of adultery and sentenced to death by stoning. (The man involved was not charged.) The judges were not swayed by the fact that as a result of her "crime" she had become the mother of a baby girl. When she appealed her conviction, however, she received significant support from a team of pro bono attorneys and international human rights organizations. Her acquittal in 2003 was greeted with widespread relief, but there is little evidence to indicate that the satisfactory resolution of her case has tempered verdicts in other Islamic court proceedings.

In recent years Nigeria has been wracked by ethnic and religious clashes that have left hundreds dead and thousands displaced. But religious and ethnic differences tell only part of the story and may actually camouflage the true source of the disputes, which often involve a fight over resources. In the central highlands, for example, the farmers are mostly Christian and herders are mostly Muslim. Tensions have been building for years between those who consider themselves indigenous to the area—mainly Christian tribes—and those whom they consider interlopers—namely, the herders, ethnic Fulani, and Hausa. In September 2001 what began as a political dispute in the Yelwa state capital of Jos degenerated into violence. The ensuing riots took the lives of a 1,000 Christians and Muslims in four days. The rift between the two communities, which had once lived in relative peace, was irreparable: Intermarriage was banned, and even the city's market was divided along religious and ethnic lines. The riots in Jos ignited violence in nearby villages, causing families to flee their homes and turning what was once Nigeria's breadbasket into a wasteland. Yelwa witnessed more pogroms over the next few months. In February 2002 Muslims burned Christians to death inside a Yelwa church; in May, Christian militias killed several Muslims, setting off a wave of revenge killings and leading to the declaration of a state of emergency by the national government.

Ethnic clashes have become endemic, too, in Nigeria's oil-rich Delta region. Not surprisingly, oil is at the root of the growing protests by the indigenous people, who protest that they are receiving little revenue from the oil while suffering environmental degradation resulting from its production. To protect the reserves, the central government has deployed army and naval troops to guard installations owned by foreign oil companies. Dozens of people have been killed in protests, and oil production has periodically been disrupted, at times contributing to higher oil prices worldwide. The violence escalated in 2003 and 2004 and has been increasingly characterized by indiscriminate killings of civilians and displacement of tens of thousands from their homes. To complicate matters further, criminal organizations have hired gangs of young men to steal crude oil, precipitating a struggle over the profits from the sale of the pilfered oil. According to HUMAN RIGHTS WATCH, two armed vigilante groups are the main perpetrators of the violence in the Niger Delta, and while they once had the sanction of the state government, they now operate independently. In one incident in Port Harcourt, the capital of Rivers state and the hub for oil operations, one of the groups mounted an attack that ended up killing at least 16 bystanders. When the army moved in, the group declared "all-out war" on the Nigerian state, putting additional pressure on jittery oil markets.

See also BIAFRA, WAR CRIMES IN; SOYINKA, WOLE.

Further Reading:
Achebe, Chinua. *The Trouble with Nigeria.* London: Heinemann, 1984.
Maier, Karl. *This House Has Fallen: Nigeria in Crisis.* Philadelphia: Westview Press, 2003.
Osaghae, Eghosa E. *Crippled Giant: Nigeria Since Independence.* Bloomington: Indiana University Press, 1998.

Nikolić, Ivan   *See* WAR CRIMINALS OF THE FORMER YUGOSLAVIA.

Niyazov, Separmurat   *See* TURKMENISTAN, HUMAN RIGHTS VIOLATIONS IN.

No Gun Ri (Korea), massacre in

Until 2001, the 1950 massacre of civilian REFUGEES in No Gun Ri during the Korean War was unknown to the American public. An investigation initiated by the Associated Press (AP) news agency in that year found that U.S. soldiers had opened fire on the refugees at a railway bridge on July 26, 1950. According to the AP investigation, which was confirmed by 12 former soldiers who had witnessed the event, American troops machine-gunned as many as 300 civilians. They had taken shelter under the bridge in an attempt to escape strafing by U.S. warplanes that had already killed about 100 people. This was at a time when American troops were retreating in the face of a North Korean onslaught. U.S. commanders feared that North Korean soldiers were infiltrating disguised as civilians and hiding out among the refugees. The officers gave orders to all units to "shoot civilians" as a precautionary measure. Six former members of the 1st Cavalry Division later admitted firing on the refugees under the bridge at No Gun Ri. One soldier described the event as "wholesale slaughter." Some soldiers, however, refused to obey the orders. The shooting went on for three nights.

The massacre of No Gun Ri was not the only attack on civilians in which U.S. forces were involved during the Korean War. In another incident, American aircraft reportedly firebombed 300 civilians trapped in a cave, even though some pilots voiced misgivings that they might be targeting innocent people. According to eyewitnesses and U.S. military documents, two strategic bridges used by refugees fleeing the Communist advance were ordered destroyed by American army officers in August 1950, killing hundreds of civilians. There are reports that the South Korean Defense Ministry had become aware of 40 cases where civilians were killed by U.S. forces during the war. South Korean soldiers and police, too, are thought to have executed more than 2,000 political prisoners without trial in the early weeks of the conflict. After the AP reports were published, the Clinton administration issued a formal apology for the No Gun Ri massacre, although in South Korea there were calls for a fuller investigation.

Further Reading:
Chinnery, Philip D. *Korean Atrocity!: Forgotten War Crimes, 1950–1953.* Annapolis, Md.: United States Naval Institute, 2001.

Nokmin (Avengers)

The Nokmin (Avengers) were established by Jewish survivors of the Holocaust to assist the illegal immigration of Jews to Palestine. However, the Nokmin expanded their mission to hunt down Nazi war criminals who had evaded justice after the war. The group was reportedly founded by three men: Israel Carmi, Chaim Laskov (later Israel Defense Forces chief of staff), and Abba Kovner. Disguised as British soldiers, they scoured Europe, even infiltrating prisoner-of-war camps run by British and American forces, summarily executing men identified as war criminals, including hundreds of SS soldiers involved in running the Nazi CONCENTRATION CAMPS. Initially they had handed over the men they captured to the Allied authorities, but in the chaotic aftermath of the war, many of the SS managed to escape, causing the Nokmin to change their tactics and simply kill the former Nazis they found. By some estimates the Nokmin assassinated as many as 1,000 war criminals before disbanding.

noncombatants   *See* CIVILIAN IMMUNITY; JOURNALISTS, PROTECTION OF; MEDICAL PERSONNEL, PROTECTION OF; PROTECTED PERSONS.

nondefended localities

Nondefended localities are places identified under Article 59 of the 1949 GENEVA CONVENTIONS that may not be attacked. In the overall context of the conventions, these are primarily civilian locales but also places without weapons. Such locations are places where:

(a) all combatants, as well as mobile weapons and mobile military equipment, must have been evacuated;
(b) no hostile use shall be made of fixed military installations or establishments;
(c) no acts of hostility shall be committed by the authorities to the population; and
(d) no activities in support of military operations shall be undertaken.

Police forces do not count as military personnel under Article 59.

The 1995 massacre at Srebrenica is a clear example of a flagrant breach of the convention, since the local people and UN peacekeeping forces had clearly surrendered and made apparent that they would not be taking hostile action against the Serb forces who were moving in to occupy the city. Any attack upon such a locality can thus be regarded as a war crime.

Further Reading:
Gutman, Roy, ed. *Crimes of War: What the Public Should Know.* New York: W. W. Norton & Company, 1999.
Jackson, Nyamuya Maogoto. *War Crimes and Realpolitik: International Justice from World War I to the 21st Century.* Boulder, Colo.: Lynne Rienner Publishers, 2004.
Jokie, Aleksander. *War Crimes and Collective Wrongdoing: A Reader.* London: Blackwell Publishers, 2001.

Noriega, Manuel (1938–) *Panamanian dictator*

General Manuel Noriega, former Panamanian strongman, is best known for provoking an invasion of his country by U.S. forces in 1989. He was subsequently tried and convicted on drug-trafficking charges and sentenced to 40-years in prison. Earlier in his colorful career, though, Noriega had enjoyed a close relationship with the United States and had reportedly collected $100,000 a year working for the CIA.

Born in Panama City, Noriega won a scholarship to study at the Chorrios Military Academy in Lima, Peru. On his return to Panama, he received a commission as a sublieutenant in the National Guard, where he became a close ally with the future Panamanian leader Omar Torrijos Herrera. Under Torrijos's patronage, Noriega's career prospered, and after Torrijos took power in a coup in 1968,

Noriega was appointed chief of military intelligence. After Torrijos's death in an airplane crash in 1981, Noriega became chief of staff to the head of the National Guard. Two years later he promoted himself to general, a position that allowed him to effectively take control of the government, although he never assumed the office of president. Under Noriega's dictatorial rule, the military increased its power and its size, corruption became rampant, and political dissent was curbed. Noriega was widely suspected of being implicated in the killing in 1985 of a leading critic of the military, Hugo Spadafora. When President Nicolás Ardito Barletta tried to investigate, Noriega had him thrown out of office.

Throughout much of this period, Noriega acted as a CIA asset. In 1976 he met with then-CIA director George Bush (later the 41st president of the United States) for the first time and apparently remained on a friendly basis with him for some years afterward. Initially Noriega provided help to the U.S. effort to support the contras in Nicaragua who were seeking to topple the leftist Sandinista regime; he allowed Panama to be used by the United States as a transshipment point for the CIA to fly in weapons to the contras. Eventually, though, he balked at further cooperation with the United States. In 1986 reports surfaced in the news that Noriega was involved in drug trafficking, money laundering, and serving as a double agent for both the CIA and Cuba's intelligence agency. For agents of the U.S. Drug Enforcement Agency (DEA), allegations of Noriega's involvement in illegal drugs were nothing new; the DEA had been investigating him for trafficking as early as 1975, though nothing had come of it.

Noriega became increasingly repressive, prompting increased protests and violence. In 1987 the U.S. Senate demanded that the Panamanian government oust him and investigate his activities. The United States suspended all aid to Panama. A year later a U.S. grand jury in Florida indicted Noriega on charges of racketeering, violating drug laws, and money laundering. U.S. officials charged that he had amassed as much as $200–$300 million from his illegal activities. He was said to have acquired an apartment in Paris, a helicopter, three Lear jets, and three yachts. Conveniently, he also had a bank of his own in Panama City.

As the United States ratcheted up its diplomatic pressure on Panama. Noriega stubbornly resisted calls for him to go. In fall 1989 he "annulled" the elections and declared himself head of state. After putting down an attempted coup by disaffected elements of the Panamanian Defense Forces, he accused the United States of "aggression . . . against the tranquility of our country." In December 1989 President George Bush authorized an invasion of Panama to oust Noriega. A contingent of 16,000 American soldiers took control of the country within a few days, though at the cost of 1,000 Panamanian lives. Noriega was arrested a

month later and sent to stand trial in Miami. At his 1991 trial, Noriega's attorneys argued that his fortune came not from drug dealing but from the CIA and that many of the witnesses against him were involved in illegal activities themselves and were hardly credible. Nonetheless, Noriega was found guilty of cocaine trafficking, racketeering, and money laundering; he received a sentence of 40 years in prison. It was the first time that a foreign head of state was found guilty of criminal charges by a U.S. court. In Panama he was later convicted in absentia for ordering the murder of Spadafora, his former critic, as well as for the killing of an army officer. He was sentenced to 20 years in prison for each crime.

Further Reading:

Albert, Steve. *The Case against the General: Manuel Noriega and the Politics of American Justice.* New York: Scribner, 1994.

Dinges, John. *Our Man in Panama: How General Noriega Used the United States—and Made Millions in Drugs and Arms.* New York: Random House, 1990.

Eisner, Peter. *America's Prisoner: The Memoirs of Manuel Noriega.* New York: Random House, 1997.

North Korea, human rights violations in

Arguably the most isolated country in the world, the Democratic Republic of Korea has a deplorable human rights record. North Korean citizens are deprived of nearly all fundamental rights: freedom of speech, freedom of the press, freedom of religion, freedom of assembly, and even freedom of residence. Radios, for instance, are manufactured so that they can only be tuned into state-run stations; it is a violation of the law to tinker with the radio to receive other broadcasts.

Communist North Korea has had only two leaders since its founding after World War II: the late KIM IL SUNG, known as "Great Leader," and his son KIM JONG IL, known as "Dear Leader." According to HUMAN RIGHTS WATCH, the population is divided into three groups: the core group, made up of the elite (28 percent); the "unstable," or "wavering" (45 percent); and the "hostile" (27 percent). These three groups are further subdivided into 51 classifications based on their loyalty to the Korean Workers Party (KWP). These classifications determine the access an individual has to employment, residence, food, and medical care as well as privileges including the right to patronize certain businesses and stores. For those who are suspected of disloyalty, the punishment may be execution or consignment to one of 12 camps reserved for political prisoners. These camps are now thought to hold about 200,000 people, or about 1 percent of the population. Families of dissidents may also be sent off to labor camps, where they frequently perish from starvation, exposure, or maltreatment.

Defectors and REFUGEES report that the regime executes political prisoners and other opponents, including repatriated defectors, suspected spies, and people accused of being involved in plots against the leadership. The death penalty is mandatory for activities "in collusion with imperialists" aimed at "suppressing the national liberation struggle." According to the 2003 U.S. State Department *Country Report*, people have been condemned to death for such ill-defined "crimes" as "ideological divergence," "opposing socialism," and the ambiguously classified "counterrevolutionary crimes." In some cases, executions were carried out at public gatherings of workers, students, and even schoolchildren. Border guards operate on shoot-to-kill orders, and there are reports that members of underground churches have been executed for practicing their faiths against the law.

Although funds and privileges are lavished on the military to maintain their loyalty, there are signs of dissension even in the army. In 1998 there were uncorroborated reports of a purge of several thousand members of the army—many of whom were killed—after a failed coup attempt. Agence France-Presse, the French press agency, said that in 1997 a four-star general who ran the Political Bureau of the Korean People's Army was executed along with several top officials before a crowd of thousands. The government, however, has insisted to AMNESTY INTERNATIONAL that only a handful of executions had taken place since 1985. The North Korean authorities do not limit their depredations to their own citizens; there were numerous abductions of Japanese citizens by North Korean agents between 1977 and 1983. Some of these abductees were later repatriated although only after spending years as prisoners in North Korea. There are also reports of kidnappings of South Koreans.

Until a tentative rapprochement between the two Koreas in the early 2000s, North Korea regularly staged confrontations with South Korea that sometimes led to violent clashes. The loss of economic assistance from the USSR after the collapse of communism there has only added to North Korea's woes. Starvation is probably the worst crisis facing the country. The forced collectivization of North Korea, coupled with drought, has resulted in recurrent famines that are estimated to have taken the lives of as many as 2 million people, with children bearing the brunt. Increasingly desperate North Koreans are willing to risk arrest and imprisonment by fleeing to China. (Because the border with South Korea is so well guarded, it is almost impossible to flee in the other direction.) Since 1994, when famine first broke out, thousands have defied the law to find sanctuary in China. The Chinese authorities have made it clear, though, that they do not welcome the influx of refugees and have frequently sent them back in violation of international law. China is a party to the 1951 UN Convention on the Status of Refugees and its 1967 Protocol, the Refugee Convention, which forbid states to push back migrants "to the frontiers of territories where [their] life or freedom would be threatened on account of . . . race, religion, nationality, membership of a particular social group or political opinion." Even those North Koreans who do manage to slip into China are forced to live underground for fear of exposure, eking out a living and risking exploitation.

In spite of the regime's adherence to the doctrine of *juche* (self-reliance), North Korea has been compelled to seek aid from international relief agencies to feed its population, but its suspicion of foreigners has made it difficult for the agencies to ensure that the food is properly distributed. Pyongyang has begun to relax its iron grip at least to some degree; in recent years, initiating diplomatic relations with 19 countries, including Britain and several European nations. It has also invited foreign investment: South Korean firms are engaged in several major projects in the North, among them a multimillion dollar industrial complex in the southwest of the country. This cautious economic liberalization has not, however, been matched by a similar political opening. Nor has the expanded diplomatic effort lessened suspicion that North Korea is pursuing a weapons-development program with an eye to producing nuclear weapons. Indeed, far from discouraging such suspicions, Pyongyang has periodically boasted that it already has a nuclear capacity. It is unknown whether North Korea is playing a game of brinkmanship for the purpose of extorting more aid in exchange for halting its nuclear program or the program is being pursued out of the regime's paranoia that only by acquiring nuclear weapons will it be able to stave off an attack by the United States.

Further Reading:

Breen, Michael. *Kim Jong-Il: North Korea's Dear Leader.* New York: John Wiley & Sons, 2004,

Harrold, Michael. *Comrades and Strangers: Behind the Closed Doors of North Korea.* New York: John Wiley & Sons, 2004.

Martin, Bradley K. *Under the Loving Care of the Fatherly Leader: North Korea and the Kim Dynasty.* New York: Thomas Dunne Books, 2004.

Vollertsen, Norbert. *Inside North Korea.* London: Encounter Books, 2005.

nuclear arms and international law

The legality of the use of nuclear arms remains in dispute. Several treaties, most of them dating back to the cold war, limit the production, stockpiling, and testing of nuclear weapons as well as their proliferation. In a 1997 advisory opinion, the INTERNATIONAL COURT OF JUSTICE (ICJ; more popularly known as the World Court), the principal judicial organ of the United Nations, concluded that the use of nuclear weapons would generally be contrary to the principles and rules of INTERNATIONAL HUMANITARIAN LAW. Even "in an extreme circumstance of self-defense," the ICJ said, humanitarian law should hold priority. At the same time the court rejected the argument that small targeted nuclear weapons—so-called bunker busters for their ability to penetrate hardened defenses deep underground—were legal under international law, either. Even so the ICJ refused to make a definitive determination, saying that "in view of the current state of international law, and of the elements of fact at its disposal, the Court cannot conclude definitively whether the threat or use of nuclear weapons would be lawful or unlawful in an extreme circumstance of self-defence, in which the very survival of a State would be at stake." The court did, however, find that if indeed there were circumstances in which using nuclear weapons would ever be legal, then they were limited only under "an extreme circumstance of self-defense, in which the very survival of a State would be at stake." The president of the court, Judge Bedjaoui, hastened to add, lest there be any misconceptions, that the ICJ's opinion could "in no way be interpreted as a partially-opened door through which it recognizes the legality of the threat or use of nuclear weapons." Nuclear weapons, the judge pointed out, were "blind weapons" that "destabilize, by their very nature, humanitarian law, the law of distinguishing in the use of weapons." Further, he argued that they represented "absolute evil" and have the effect of destabilizing humanitarian law "which radically exclude each other, the existence of one necessarily supposing the non-existence of the other." The court unanimously found that: "There exists an obligation to pursue in good faith and bring to a conclusion negotiations leading to nuclear disarmament in all its aspects under strict and effective international control." (The ICJ also took up a question raised by the World Health Organization, or WHO, which was whether the use of nuclear weapons by a state in war or other armed conflict would be in breach of its obligations under international law "in view of the health and environmental effects." The ICJ declined to respond to the WHO query because it was beyond the scope of the United Nations' jurisdiction.)

Some experts cite the HAGUE CONVENTIONS of 1907 as precedent for the ICJ's view. The conventions set forth the distinction between civilian and military objectives, specifying that belligerents must take measures to protect the former as much as possible even while targeting the latter. The Hague Draft Rules stated: "Aerial bombardment for the purpose of terrorizing civilian population, of destroying or damaging private property not of military character, or of injuring noncombatants is prohibited." One reading of this stipulation has led some legal scholars to contend that dropping the atomic bombs on Hiroshima and Nagasaki was illegal because the greatest impact was felt among a civilian population, notwithstanding any military objectives that the Allies sought to destroy. However, there is no comprehensive or universal prohibition against the use of nuclear weapons today, nor has any state with nuclear weapons (whether acknowledged or not) indicated any change in nuclear policy to take into account the ICJ's advisory opinion. Some legal scholars refer back to the principles of the NUREMBERG CHARTER, which formed the basis for the prosecution of Nazi war criminals at the end of World War II. These principles declared that individuals could not escape responsibility for their actions simply by asserting that they were only obeying orders. Nor, in this view, does the fact that no national law exists outlawing the use of nuclear weapons necessarily immunize a head of state or other government officials from being found culpable of ordering a nuclear strike if the Nuremberg Principles—promulgated by the United Nations in 1950—were to be applied.

See also NUREMBERG TRIALS; WEAPONS IN THE CONDUCT OF WAR; WEAPONS OF MASS DESTRUCTION.

Further Reading:
Feaver, Peter. *Guarding the Guardians: Civilian Control of Nuclear Weapons in the United States.* Cornell Studies in Security Affairs. Ithaca, N.Y.: Cornell University Press, 1992.
Krepon, Michael. *Strategic Stalemate: Nuclear Weapons and Arms Control in American Politics.* Sydney, Australia: Palgrave Macmillan, 1986.
Nichols, Gary W. and Milton L. Boykin eds. *Arms Control and Nuclear Weapons: U.S. Policies and the National Interest.* Contributions in Military Studies. Westport, Conn.: Greenwood Press, 1987.

Nuon Chea (1928–) *Khmer Rouge leader*

Nuon Chea was Brother Number Two in the leadership of the Khmer Rouge and the brother-in-law of Brother Number One, POL POT. Born into a wealthy Chinese-Cambodian family and educated in Thailand, Nuon Chea became Pol Pot's comrade—and brother-in-law—in the 1950s. As second in command of the radical Maoist group that held power in Cambodia from 1975 to 1979, he was in charge of the security forces that hunted down traitors to the regime. Researchers and historians believe that as the movement's ideologue, Nuon Chea was responsible for Khmer Rouge policies that led to the genocidal campaign that was supposed to create a self-reliant agrarian utopia. Instead it led to the deaths of almost 2 million people and ushered in a reign of terror.

After the collapse of the Khmer Rouge in 1998, Nuon Chea settled on the outskirts of Pailin, a town that was once a Khmer Rouge stronghold. Pailin also had the advantage of being rich in gems and timber, making it a source of revenue for the insurgents. Nuon Chea took up residence in a modest bungalow with his wife. In interviews with the press, he claims to have begun to practice Buddhism. Although no move has been made by the government of Hun Sen to bring him to trial for war crimes, he has declared that he would "gladly appear" before a UN-backed tribunal, but it seems that he does not think he would be found guilty. He admitted that he made "mistakes" but denied that he was guilty of GENOCIDE, even rejecting the idea that millions of people had perished because of the Khmer Rouge's brutal despotism. "People died but there were so many causes of their deaths. We have to know the situation, what the situation was like." He tried to excuse himself by appealing to his youthful idealism. "But I had my ideology," he stated. "I wanted to free my country. I wanted people to have well-being." Nevertheless, he also insisted that he failed to "use wisdom to find the truth of what was going on, to check who was doing wrong and who was doing right. I accept that error." In a 2002 interview with PBS's *Frontline,* when he was 77, Nuon Chea even went so far as to contend that the Khmer Rouge deserved some credit for its accomplishments "A person's not always wrong and not always right. Like the leaders—we did some wrong, but we also did some right. Just because you're wrong doesn't mean you're a bad person. If you do anything, you're going to make mistakes."

Nuon Chea's claims of innocence are dismissed by many analysts and historians of the Khmer Rouge era. "Nuon Chea, in my view, is more guilty of CRIME AGAINST HUMANITY—war crimes, TORTURE and mass murder—than any other single Cambodian," asserted Nate Thayer, a journalist who covered the Khmer Rouge for years. "We have far more documentary evidence against Nuon Chea than we do against Pol Pot." Some of that evidence was collected from the notorious detention center of Tuol Sleng, where 20,000 political prisoners were tortured and executed. Documents maintained by the authorities of the center indicate that Nuon Chea was responsible for ordering the arrests and approving the executions. "For every single person who came through Tuol Sleng, Nuon Chea was given a copy of the briefing of the torture and remarked on when it was appropriate to have them killed. We have overwhelming evidence he was involved at least in those 14,000 murders personally, that he personally ordered them."

See also CAMBODIA, WAR CRIMES IN.

Further Reading:

Chandler, David. *A History of Cambodia.* Philadelphia: Westview Press. 2000.

———. *The Tragedy of Cambodian History: Politics, War, and Revolution since 1945.* New Haven, Conn.: Yale University Press, 1993.

Gottesman, Evan. *Cambodia after the Khmer Rouge: Inside the Politics of Nation Building.* New Haven, Conn.: Yale University Press, 2004.

Hinton, Alexander Laban, and Robert Jay Lifton. *Why Did They Kill?: Cambodia in the Shadow of Genocide.* California Series in Public Anthropology, vol. 11. Berkeley: University of California Press, 2004.

Kiernan, Ben. *How Pol Pot Came to Power: Colonialism, Nationalism, and Communism in Cambodia, 1930–1975.* New Haven, Conn.: Yale University Press, 2004.

———. *The Pol Pot Regime: Race, Power, and Genocide in Cambodia under the Khmer Rouge, 1975–79.* New Haven, Conn.: Yale University Press, 2002.

Pran, Dith, comp. *Children of Cambodia's Killing Fields: Memoirs by Survivors.* Edited by Kim De Paul. New Haven, Conn.: Yale University Press, 1999.

Short, Philip. *Pol Pot: Anatomy of a Nightmare.* New York: Holt Rinehart, 2005.

Ung, Loung. *First They Killed My Father: A Daughter of Cambodia Remembers.* New York: Perennial, 2001.

Nuremberg Charter (Agreement for the Prosecution and Punishment of the Major War Criminals of the European Axis and Charter of the International Military Tribunal; London Charter)

The Nuremberg Charter, agreed upon in 1945 by the victorious Allies the United States, the Soviet Union, Great Britain, and France after World War II, established the principles that would be applied in bringing Nazi war criminals to justice. Formally known as the Agreement for the Prosecution and Punishment of the Major War Criminals of the European Axis and Charter of the International Military Tribunal (IMT), the Nuremberg Charter introduced the concept of CRIMES AGAINST HUMANITY in Article 6C. Crimes against humanity included "murder, extermination, enslavement, deportation, and other inhumane acts committed against civilian populations, before or during the war; or persecutions on political, racial or religious grounds in execution of or in connection with any crime within the jurisdiction of the Tribunal, whether or not in violation of the domestic law of the country where perpetrated."

Until the Nuremberg Charter, there was no separate crime in international law that addressed crimes committed by a state against its own civilian population (in contrast to war crimes and crimes against peace or wars of aggression). The charter is also significant because it affirmed that individuals were responsible for their own actions and could not use the defense that they were only obeying orders. The United States and its allies hoped that the charter would make war an international crime except when carried out in self-defense. The notion that wars of aggression should be considered crimes was such a break with precedent that a French delegate to the conference deliberating the terms of the Charter described it as "shocking," contending that it would amount to "ex post facto legislation"—that is, it would question the legality of past wars, even those fought by the Allies.

A second objective of the charter was to ensure that henceforth civilians received protections against brutal treatment regardless of whether the perpetrator was an invader or their own government. Third, the charter was meant to enshrine the principle that crimes were to be answered by justice and not by acts of revenge. Thus, the Nazi war criminals were to be tried in accordance with accepted norms of jurisprudence—the right to counsel, the right to mount a defense and appeal a verdict, and so forth—even though they never accorded the same rights to suspects when they were in power. Nonetheless, some critics still saw the NUREMBERG TRIALS as "victors' justice" since only the defeated were subject to trial. Of the 21 major Nazi war criminals tried, 18 were convicted, mostly of crimes against peace.

In spite of the Allied hopes, legal attempts to outlaw war have not met with much success and there have been few prosecutions for crimes against humanity. However, this category of crimes has been included in the statutes of the INTERNATIONAL CRIMINAL TRIBUNAL FOR THE FORMER YUGOSLAVIA (ICTY) and the INTERNATIONAL CRIMINAL TRIBUNAL FOR RWANDA (ICTR), both of which were established by the United Nations, and appears as well as in the statute of the INTERNATIONAL CRIMINAL COURT (ICC). Altogether there are no fewer than 11 international texts in which crimes against humanity are recognized, although their definition differs slightly both in terms of what constitutes a crime against humanity and its legal ramifications. Nonetheless, they all have certain elements in common insofar as (1) they refer to specific acts of violence against persons regardless of his or her citizenship or whether the acts were committed in wartime or peacetime, and (2) that these acts are motivated by a deliberate persecution of a particular group on the basis of its nationality, race, ethnicity, or culture.

Further Reading:
Bosch, William J. *Judgment on Nuremberg: American Attitudes toward the Major German War-Crime Trials.* Durham: University of North Carolina Press, 1970.
Gilbert, G. M. *Nuremberg Diary.* New York: Da Capo Press, 1995.
Goldensohn, Leon, and Robert Gellately, eds. *The Nuremberg Interviews.* New York: Knopf, 2004.
Maser, Werner. *Nuremberg: A Nation on Trial.* New York: Scribner, 1979.
Marrus, Robert, and Michael R. Marrus. *The Nuremberg War Crimes Trial of 1945–46: A Documentary History.* Bedford Series in History and Culture. Sidney, Australia: Palgrave Macmillan, 1997.
Persico, Joseph. *Nuremberg: Infamy on Trial.* New York: Penguin Books, 1995.
Rice, Earle. *The Nuremberg Trials.* Famous Trials Series. San Diego, Calif.: Lucent Books, 1997.
Taylor, Telford. *The Anatomy of the Nuremberg Trials: A Personal Memoir.* New York: Little, Brown & Co, 1993.
Taylor, Telford. *Nuremberg Trials: War Crimes and International Law.* New York: Carnegie Endowment for International Peace, 1949.
Tusa, Ann, and John Tusa. *The Nuremberg Trials.* New York: Cooper Square Publishers, 2003.

Nuremberg Laws (Nuremberg Decrees)

The Nuremberg Laws, enacted in 1935 by the Congress of the National Socialist German Workers Party (NSDAP, or Nazi Party), were designed to clarify who could be considered a German citizen while segregating Jews from society and depriving them of economic, political, and other rights. The laws were intended to ensure the purity of German blood and honor as conceived by the Nazis. The laws, passed on September 15, 1935, in Nuremberg, were supplemented by other laws that imposed additional restrictions on the Jews in Germany, depriving them of political rights.

Not all the delegates to the congress gathering in August 1935 were in favor of the state-sponsored discrimination against Jews, especially in the economic sphere. The economics minister, for instance, while offering no moral condemnation of limiting Jewish rights, nonetheless suggested that the Third Reich could benefit by using Jewish entrepreneurial talent that would henceforth be kept out of the labor market. The Nuremberg Laws, which were publicly announced at the annual rally of the Nazi Party, were improvised and hastily written—so quickly, in fact, that the drafters ran out of paper and had to resort to menu cards. So-called Jewish advisers were flown from Berlin to Nuremberg to offer their input. The first law—the Law for the Protection of German Blood and German Honor—banned marriages and extramarital intercourse between Jews and Germans or those of "related blood." Jewish households could not hire German females under age 45. It stated:

1. A citizen of the Reich is that subject only who is of German or kindred blood and who, through his conduct, shows that he is both desirous and fit to serve the German people and Reich faithfully.
2. The right to citizenship is acquired by the granting of Reich citizenship papers.

3. Only the citizen of the Reich enjoys full political rights in accordance with the provision of the laws.

The second law, called the Reich Citizenship Law, stripped Jews of their German citizenship and introduced a new distinction between "Reich citizens" and "nationals."

It is important to note that these racial purity laws did not classify a Jew by his or her religious affiliation; instead a Jew was a person with three or four Jewish grandparents, irrespective of whether that person followed the Jewish faith. That meant that many Jews who regarded themselves as secular German citizens were officially classified as Jews and stripped of their rights. Even Christian converts were defined as Jews. The Nuremberg Laws simply made official a policy of persecution that was already being applied. However, the Nazi regime was sensitive enough to international opinion that it moderated the enforcement of some of the laws in the weeks before the 1936 Olympic Games in Berlin, and signs prohibiting Jews from public venues were taken down.

Once the Olympics were over (no German Jews had been allowed to participate), the persecution of Jews was renewed on a larger scale than before. Over the next two years Jews were forced to register their property as a first step to driving them into destitution. The Germans proceeded to "Aryanize" Jewish businesses, turning them over to German managers and workers and throwing Jewish employees out of work. Jewish doctors and Jewish lawyers were forbidden to practice. Jews were also required to carry identity cards with a red J stamped on them. (Later Jews were forced to wear yellow stars.) If a Jew did not have a readily identifiable "Jewish" name, the Nazis assigned Jewish middle names: "Israel" for males, "Sara" for females. These discriminatory measures, as it turned out, only represented an initial phase in what became a systematic campaign to empty Europe of its entire Jewish population, first by forced migration and then by execution.

See also FRICK, WILHELM; STOCKART, WILHELM; WANNSEE CONFERENCE.

Further Reading:

Bloxham, Donald. *Genocide on Trial: War Crimes Trials and the Formation of Holocaust History and Memory.* Oxford: Oxford University Press, 2003.

Dawidowicz, Lucy. *A Holocaust Reader.* Library of Jewish Studies. Chicago: Behrman House Publishing, 1976.

Dwork, Deborah, and Robert Jan Van Pelt. *Holocaust: A History.* New York: W. W. Norton & Company, 2003.

Giblin, James Cross. *The Life and Death of Adolf Hitler.* New York: Clarion Books, 2002.

Gilbert, Martin. *The Holocaust: A History of the Jews of Europe during the Second World War.* New York: Owl Books, 1987.

Roseman, Mark. *The Wannsee Conference and the Final Solution: A Reconsideration.* New York: Metropolitan Books, 2002.

Nuremberg Medical Trial   *See* DOCTORS' TRIAL.

Nuremberg Trials (International Military Tribunal)

The trials of Nazi war criminals in the immediate aftermath of World War II at Nuremberg, Germany, stands out as a major achievement in the development of INTERNATIONAL HUMANITARIAN LAW. For one, it represented a commitment on the part of the victorious Allies to try individuals implicated in war crimes and GENOCIDE in a court of law. The objective was to see justice done rather than to seek revenge. For another, the trials led to the creation of a large body of international law designed to prevent similar abuses from recurring and establish mechanisms to punish offenders. Nuremberg also established the principle of individual responsibility: A defendant could no longer claim that he was not culpable of a crime because he was only following orders from a superior or a government.

The first indictments, announced on October 18, 1945, charged 24 individuals with a variety of crimes and atrocities, including the deliberate instigation of aggressive wars; extermination of racial and religious groups; murder and mistreatment of PRISONERS OF WAR; and the murder, mistreatment, enslavement, and deportation of hundreds of thousands of inhabitants of countries occupied by Germany during the war. The initial group of defendants was made up of some of the most powerful officials in the hierarchy of the Third Reich, most of whom were in the custody of one of the four prosecuting nations: the United States, the Soviet Union, Great Britain, and France. The choice of these defendants was based more on their prominence than on the evidence that had been gathered against them. Some were included because of the demands of one of the prosecuting nations. For example, Hans FRITZSCHE, a relatively minor official who had served in the propaganda ministry, was put on trial at the insistence of the Soviet Union. But most of the defendants were in fact major figures who had wielded vast power under Adolf HITLER: Hermann GÖRING, Rudolf HESS, Joachim von RIBBENTROP, Field Marshal Wilhelm KEITEL, Grand Admiral Erich RAEDER, and 18 other military leaders and civilian officials, in addition to the munitions maker Gustav KRUPP. Three of the accused individuals avoided trial: Robert LEY, the Nazi labor leader, hanged himself before the trial could begin; Krupp was found too weak to stand trial; and Hitler's powerful deputy, Martin BORMANN, had vanished. (Bormann was convicted and sentenced to death in absentia; his fate is unknown.) In addition, several institutions that

Courtroom of the Nuremberg Trials, 1945–1946 *(Library of Congress)*

formed part of the basic structure of the Nazi government were indicted as criminal organizations, including the SS (Schutzstaffel, or Defense Corps), the GESTAPO (Geheime Staatspolizei, or Secret State Police), the SA (Sturmabteilung, or Storm Troops), the Reich Cabinet (Reichsregierung), the Corps of the Political Leaders of the Nazi Party, and the general staff and high command of the German armed forces.

The groundwork for the Nuremberg Trials was established the previous August in London when the British, French, Americans, and Soviets signed the agreement known as the London Charter, also known as the NUREMBERG CHARTER, which created the Nuremberg court, officially the International Military Tribunal. The charter described the types of crimes that the tribunal would hear. While the Allies decided as well to try organizations like the

SS and SA, they made no attempt to define what was meant by the term *criminal organizations.* Nonetheless, by indicting these organizations, the Allies intended to implicate by association thousands of their members, even if it was impossible to bring them all to trial.

The trial rules for the tribunal were based on a combination of Anglo-American jurisprudence and continental civil law derived from the Napoleonic Code. The hybrid legal framework that resulted differed in significant respects from the legal system in place in the United States. In an American court, for instance, prosecutors must present sufficient evidence to indict an individual, whereas the tribunal did not require prosecutors to offer all the proof against defendants at the time they unsealed their indictments. In addition, hearsay evidence was allowed at Nuremberg in the form of testimony from individuals who would not be called upon as witnesses, whereas in most instances hearsay evidence cannot be admitted in an American court. The tribunal also allowed evidence to be admitted if it were only "probative," a lower standard than in U.S. courts, and did not allow defendants to confront or question their accusers, which is a right guaranteed by the U.S. Constitution. The defendants would have no right to a jury trial, and all decisions made by the judges were final and could not be appealed, although the defendants were entitled to ask the Control Council of Germany—the Allied occupation government—to reduce or change their sentences. Defendants could, however, select an attorney of their choice or else represent themselves if they wished. In a novel legal strategy, Lieutenant Colonel Murray Bernays, an attorney in the U.S. War Department, proposed an approach whereby the defendants would be tried as conspirators in planning and waging a war of aggression (which, among other things, entailed breaking international treaties). His proposal was eventually incorporated into the Nuremberg Charter.

The trial of the individual defendants was to take place first; only then would legal proceedings begin against the indicted criminal organizations. The Allies agreed to divide up the prosecution, with each power taking turns. The United States was given the most difficult task, proving Count One, the conspiracy charge. There were four counts altogether:

Count One: Conspiracy to Wage Aggressive War

The conspiracy charge was designed to circumvent the problem of how to find the defendants guilty of acts they had committed before the war. It was one of the most controversial aspects of the trial—the concept of conspiracy is not recognized in continental law—because to some historians, it sought to find a coherent policy (or organized plot) that might exist only in the minds of prosecutors. Moreover, pursuing conspiracy charges allowed lawyers for the defendants to argue that they had never participated in any conspiracy or at least known in advance that the scheme would lead to any serious criminal acts.

Count Two: Waging Aggressive War, or "Crimes against Peace"

The Nuremberg Charter defined this count as "the planning, preparation, initiation, and waging of wars of aggression, which were also wars in violation of international treaties, agreements, and assurances." The prosecution of this charge was put in the hands of the British. The prosecution was handicapped to some degree. On the one hand, there was no doubt that Nazi Germany had waged aggressive war or that it had broken international treaties, particularly the Kellogg-Briand Pact of 1928, which renounced war as an instrument of national policy (which was distinguished from a defensive war); however, the pact failed both to define "aggressive war" or to prescribe any penalties for violators. Moreover, in two cases—the Anschluss (the merger of Germany and Austria) and the invasion of Czechoslovakia—the charge could not be applied since Hitler had orchestrated events so as to accomplish his aims without force of arms. Moreover, the Soviet Union had violated the Kellogg-Briand Pact itself by invading Finland, Poland, and the Baltics and had in addition signed a nonaggression pact with Hitler to divide up Poland.

Count Three: War Crimes

The Nuremberg Charter defined war crimes as "murder, ill treatment or deportation to slave labor or for any other purpose of civilian population or in occupied territory, murder or ill-treatment of prisoners-of-war or persons on the seas, killing of hostages, plunder of public or private property, wanton destruction of cities, towns, or villages or devastation not justified by military necessity." The Soviet and French prosecutors, who were given this part of the case, had more precedent to rely upon than their American and British prosecutors had. Much of this precedent had been established in a series of treaties governing treatment of prisoners of war (POWs), setting the rules for the conduct of warfare, and banning certain types of armaments (dumdum bullets, poisonous gas, etc.), including the Geneva Conventions of 1864 and 1906 and the Hague Conventions of 1899 and 1907.

Count Four: Crimes against Humanity

War crimes were defined by the Nuremberg Charter as "murder, extermination, enslavement, deportation, and other inhumane acts committed against any civilian population before or during the war, or persecutions on political, racial, or religious grounds in execution of or in connection with any crimes within the jurisdiction of the International Military Tribunal, whether or not in violation of domestic law of the country where perpetrated." This was the charge applied to defendants who had organized and run the concentration camps and death camps and participated in Nazi death squads in Eastern Europe and the Soviet Union. The prosecution for this count was conducted by the French and Soviets. Until the Nuremberg Charter, there had been some debate as to whether crimes against humanity referred exclusively to crimes committed by a state against its own people or whether it could apply to international conflicts. The Nuremberg Charter decided the issue in favor of the latter, establishing an important precedent for international humanitarian law.

The first trial began on November 20, 1945, and judgments were handed down on September 30–October 1, 1946. In announcing the verdicts, the tribunal rejected two major claims by the defense: (1) that the defendants' rights had been violated because crimes of aggression had not previously been defined as crimes under international law, and (2) that they were not legally responsible for committing any crimes because they were acting under orders. The tribunal stated that "the true test . . . is not the existence of the order but whether moral choice [in executing it] was in fact possible." The evidence, said the tribunal, overwhelmingly proved that most of the defendants were guilty of systematic atrocities—including the extermination of 6 million Jews and thousands of Rom (Gypsies) and the forcible DEPORTATIONS of 5 million people from their homes in occupied Europe to serve as slave laborers in Germany.

Twelve defendants were sentenced to death by hanging, seven received prison terms ranging from 10 years to life, and three were acquitted, including Franz von PAPEN, the German diplomat, and Hjalmar Horace Greeley SCHACHT, the president of the German Central Bank. The convicted defendants sought clemency from the Control Council, but their appeals were rejected. The Allies acted quickly to carry out the death sentences, hanging 10 condemned to death on October 16, 1946. Only Göring escaped his punishment by committing suicide in prison a few hours before he was to be executed.

With the first trial over, the International Military Tribunal turned to the trial of the indicted criminal organizations. After the monthlong trial, the tribunal found three of the organizations guilty: the SS, the Gestapo, and the Corps of the Political Leaders of the Nazi Party. Three others were acquitted: the SA (whose power had vastly diminished before the war), the Reich Cabinet, and the general staff and high command of the German Armed Forces. In the case of the cabinet and the general staff, the judges determined that relatively few members were responsible for criminal acts and that these could be better prosecuted individually. The prosecution of criminal organizations was controversial because it raised the prospect of guilt by association, although no individual member was ever punished on the basis of the tribunal's convictions. (The Allied occupation authorities did, however, hold de-Nazification trials of individual members of these organization.)

Between 1946 and 1950, the Allies held 12 more trials of accused Nazi officials and supporters under the authority of Control Council Law No. 10, which was modeled on the Nuremberg Charter but provided for prosecuting the trials in each of the four zones of occupied Germany. Some 185 individuals were indicted in the 12 cases, including SS officials who had supervised concentration camps and participated in the extermination of Jews and other groups, doctors who had carried out immoral MEDICAL EXPERIMENTS on concentration camp inmates and POWs, judges who had used the color of law to murder, high military and civilian officials who had actively participated in Nazi criminal acts, and industrialists accused of looting and using slave labor. Several doctors and SS leaders were condemned to death by hanging,

and approximately 120 other defendants were given prison sentences of various durations; 35 defendants were acquitted. Although war-crimes charges were leveled against about 5,000 other Nazis, including concentration camp guards and soldiers, many of them managed to escape. Still others were arrested later and tried in courts of individual countries under national laws.

A similar tribunal set up to try Japanese war criminals became known as the TOKYO TRIALS. The International Military Tribunal for the Far East, as it was known, was made up of judges from 11 of the Allied nations, who sentenced seven of the 28 defendants to death and handed down prison sentences to the rest.

The legacy of the Nuremberg Trials is a mixed one. Until Nuremberg, jurisdiction over war crimes generally fell under national military courts. Nuremberg also established a precedent in which the concepts of conspiracy and collective guilt were introduced as prosecutable offenses. The Nuremberg and Tokyo trials represented the first organized attempt to apply principles of international law that often had scant legal precedent, if any. Although the fact that prosecutors had to improvise and face charges of using ex post facto law—trying crimes for which no law existed at the time that they were committed—the Nuremberg verdicts won widespread acceptance internationally. In 1950 the United Nations promulgated the so-called Nuremberg Principles—among them the concept that individuals cannot avoid responsibility for their actions by claiming they were acting under orders—which many countries have since adopted into the legal systems of most countries.

The Nuremberg Trials fulfilled another important function as well: providing what remains the most comprehensive account of the Nazi era, from Hitler's coming to power to the planning for war to the crimes committed in the prosecution of that war. There were bound to be misgivings on the part of some legal experts. The defendants, critics contended, were selected arbitrarily and implicated for violations of international law, which was binding on nations but not on individuals. Moreover, some detractors believed that an accused individual should only be tried under the laws of his or her own nation, not under a new regime and new laws that came about after the war. Proponents of the trials acknowledge that perfect justice could never be achieved under the circumstances but that the trials represented the best alternative available and were in any case far preferable to simply summarily executing Nazi war criminals without troubling with any legal formalities—an idea that even Joseph STALIN and Winston Churchill had entertained. (In 1944 Churchill had said that Nazi war criminals should be "hunted down and shot.") The promise of the Nuremberg Trials—that they might deter others from perpetrating atrocities or waging aggressive war—was short-lived. Atrocities on an alarming scale continued to occur—in Cambodia, Liberia, Rwanda, the former Yugoslavia, and Darfur, among other places—and yet the international community has yet to find a reliable means of intervening to stop them or providing a permanent means to punish their perpetrators.

See also BRANDT, KARL; DOCTORS' TRIAL; DÖNITZ, KARL; EINSATZGRUPPEN; FRANK, HANS; FRICK, WILHELM; FUNK, WALTHER; JACKSON, ROBERT; JODL, ALFRED; KALTENBRUNNER, ERNST; KRAMER, JOSEF; NAZI PARTY, LEADERSHIP CORPS OF; NEURATH, CONSTANTIN VON; POHL, OSWALD; ROSENBERG, ALFRED; SAUCKEL, FRITZ; SCHELLENERG, WALTER; SCHIRACH, BALDUR VON; SEYSS-INQUART, ARTHUR; SPEER, ALBERT; SS; STREICHER, JULIUS; TAYLOR, TELFORD.

Further Reading:

Bosch, William J. *Judgment on Nuremberg: American Attitudes toward the Major German War-Crime Trials.* Durham: University of North Carolina Press, 1970.

Gilbert, G. M. *Nuremberg Diary.* New York: Da Capo Press, 1995.

Goldensohn, Leon, and Robert Gellately, eds. *The Nuremberg Interviews.* New York: Knopf, 2004.

Maser, Werner. *Nuremberg: A Nation on Trial.* New York: Scribner, 1979.

Marrus, Robert, and Michael R. Marrus. *The Nuremberg War Crimes Trial of 1945–46: A Documentary History.* Bedford Series in History and Culture. Sidney, Australia: Palgrave Macmillan, 1997.

Persico, Joseph. *Nuremberg: Infamy on Trial.* New York: Penguin Books, 1995.

Rice, Earle. *The Nuremberg Trials. Famous Trials Series.* Farmington Hills: Lucent Books, 1997.

Taylor, Telford. *The Anatomy of the Nuremberg Trials: A Personal Memoir.* New York: Little, Brown & Co, 1993.

Taylor, Telford. *Nuremberg Trials: War Crimes and International Law.* New York: Carnegie Endowment for International Peace, 1949.

Tusa, Ann, and John Tusa. *The Nuremberg Trials.* New York: Cooper Square Publishers, 2003.

Nzapali, Sebastian (1951–) *Congolese war criminal*
Sebastian Nzapali, a former Congolese military officer, became the first person convicted under a new Dutch law permitting the prosecution of CRIMES AGAINST HUMANITY that were committed in another country. The Dutch law is based on the 1984 United Nations CONVENTION AGAINST TORTURE. Nzapali's case was considered exceptional because few countries actually apply laws that flow from the convention. (France and Switzerland have both held foreigners suspected of committing TORTURE in other countries, but the suspects were never tried, because they were either released for lack of evidence or managed to escape.) Nzapali had arrived in the Netherlands in 1998 seeking political asylum, but he was recognized and denounced by some of his victims. The Dutch dispatched investigators to the Congo to determine whether the allegations had any basis in fact. When they were convinced that Nzapali was implicated in torture, they placed him under arrest. Nzapali contended that he was persecuted himself and denied charges that he had tortured and raped people in 1996 when the Congo (then known as Zaire) was ruled by the late dictator MOBUTU SESE SEKO. Prosecutors established, however, that Nzapali had in fact committed torture and that he had acquired his nickname "The King of the Beasts" because he had treated prisoners like animals. In April 2004 the 51-year-old Nzapali was found guilty of torture (though not of rape) and sentenced to 70 months prison.

See also CONGO, DEMOCRATIC REPUBLIC OF THE, WAR CRIMES IN.

Further Reading:

Edgerton, Robert. *The Troubled Heart of Africa: A History of the Congo.* New York: St. Martin's Press, 2002.

Wrong, Michela. *In the Footsteps of Mr. Kurtz: Living on the Brink of Disaster in Mobutu's Congo.* New York: HarperCollins Publishers, 2001.

Oberheuser, Herta (1911–1978) *Nazi doctor*

Dr. Herta Oberheuser was the only female defendant to be charged with crimes based on MEDICAL EXPERIMENTS in CONCENTRATION CAMPS in the DOCTORS' TRIAL part of the NUREMBERG TRIALS. She was implicated in the murder of children by injecting them with oil and other substances; once they were dead, she would then amputate their limbs and remove their vital organs. Usually it took only three to five minutes for the injections to kill their victims, who were conscious almost until the last moment. She was also known to have inflicted wounds on her unwilling victims—to simulate the wounds German soldiers might sustain—and then to aggravate the resulting infections by rubbing in foreign objects, such as wood, rusty nails, crushed glass, dirt, or sawdust. She was sentenced to 20 years in prison but released after only a few years in 1952. She went back to medicine, becoming a family doctor in a small town until her medical license was revoked in 1958.

Further Reading:

Lifton, Robert. *The Nazi Doctors: Medical Killing and the Psychology of Genocide.* New York: Basic Books, 2000.

Obote, Milton (Apollo Milton Obote) (1945–2005) *Ugandan dictator*

Milton Obote was twice president of Uganda; his corrupt and dictatorial policies ultimately led to his ouster and exile—twice. Born on December 28, 1945, Obote became active in Ugandan politics when the country was still under British rule. After founding the Ugandan People's Congress, he took part in a coalition that took over the government of Uganda after it won its independence in 1963. Soon thereafter he became the country's second president. By keeping the military placated, Obote strengthened his control over Uganda, suppressing the opposition. He came to rely more and more on an illiterate soldier named Idi AMIN to advance his own ends, elevating Amin to positions of ever greater authority.

When Amin was implicated by Parliament in a gold and ivory smuggling scheme, Obote reacted by snubbing the legislators, convinced that he and Amin were above the law. However, when Parliament brought down his government with a vote of no confidence, he called upon Amin to launch a coup against his own government, had himself declared president, and passed a new constitution. Martial law was imposed to forestall any resistance. Over the next few years, though, Obote began to fear for his position—he escaped a number of assassination attempts—and became increasingly fearful of Amin. He formed an elite security unit to protect him and gave orders to arrest Amin on charges of financial malfeasance. Amin got wind of the order and seized the capital of Kampala, executing Obote's supporters. Obote fled to Tanzania, where he bided his time in exile while Uganda was plunged into chaos under Amin's bloody regime. Tensions between Tanzania and Uganda erupted into open warfare in 1978. Tanzanian troops moved into Uganda, toppled Amin (who went into exile in Saudi Arabia), and reinstalled Obote as the head of an interim government.

In 1980 Uganda held its first democratic elections in 18 years. When the vote did not favor Obote's party, as expected, Obote simply had the votes recounted to make him president. Obote's efforts to consolidate power antagonized a top military official, Colonel Yoweri Museveni, who launched a guerrilla war. As it became apparent that Museveni enjoyed popular support, Obote resorted to ever more brutal methods. He was accused of perpetrating massacres and carrying out a scorched earth policy, forcing as many as 20,000 civilians from their homes in areas with high levels of support for Museveni. The U.S. State Department claimed that his forces killed up to 200,000 in its campaign. (It is believed that some 300,000 people were killed altogether in the conflict.) And even briefly considered the idea of accepting military aid from North

Korea. Obote, who seemed to have learned nothing from history, became increasingly concerned about the loyalty of his own supporters, and while he was out of the country, he ordered the arrest of his top military advisers. The military struck first and took over Kampala, driving Obote into exile a second time—to Tanzania and then Zambia, but not before he looted much of Uganda's treasury. A year later Museveni assumed power. It is estimated that the war between Obote's and Museveni's forces cost as many as 300,000 lives.

See also UGANDA, HUMAN RIGHTS VIOLATIONS IN.

Further Reading:

Allen, John. *Idi Amin.* History's Villains. San Diego: Blackbirch Press, 2003.

Allen, Peter A. P. *Interesting Times: Life in Uganda under Idi Amin.* London: Book Guild, Limited, 2000.

Mutibwa, Phares. *Uganda since Independence: A Story of Unfulfilled Hopes.* London: Africa World Press, 1992.

occupying power

International law—in particular Section III of the Fourth Geneva Convention of 1949—establishes basic principles an occupying power should abide by in its treatment of populations that come under its control. A foreign territory is considered occupied only if the belligerent actually controls it. The obligations of an occupying belligerent do not forbid it from suspending or repealing local laws that are seen as a threat to its security or are in violation of the convention; however, with minor exceptions penal laws of the territory must remain in place. The earlier Hague Regulations Concerning the Law and Customs of War on Land also forbid altering local law.

An occupying power may take measures that it believes necessary to protect its security or communication system. Individuals resisting the occupier are liable to arrest and punishment; however, the Geneva Convention requires the occupying power to meet certain conditions: The detainee is entitled to a trial and has the right to seek counsel, summon witnesses in his or her defense, and appeal a verdict. If an occupier employs military courts, they must be nonpolitical judicial bodies and sit in the occupied territory rather than be employed simply as instruments of punishment to persecute resistors. If a death penalty is imposed, the convention calls for a six-month delay before it can be carried out; moreover, a third party—typically a government of an outside country charged with protecting civilians under occupation—must be notified. In addition, the convention bars TORTURE, murder, corporeal punishment, mutilation, and "any other measures of brutality." The convention also specifies that an occupying power may not "alter the status of public officials or judges in the occupied territories . . .

should they abstain from fulfilling their functions for reasons of conscience."

How, though, are the limitations enshrined in the Fourth Convention to be reconciled in cases such as occupied Iraq? The U.S.-led coalition that took over the country in 2003 has made it clear that it seeks to overhaul Iraq's political, judicial, and other state institutions that had previously served the dictatorship of Saddam HUSSEIN. It is possible to argue that the coalition is not, in fact, an occupying power—which would make the question moot—but in the absence of any alternative source of governance, it is difficult to imagine what other role the coalition has assumed for itself. In a 2003 essay on the subject, Thomas D. Grant, a public international lawyer and fellow of Wolfson College in Britain, writes: "The coalition in Iraq presents a case distinct from certain past cases of occupation, in the sense that, though the Iraqi state continues to hold all rights to its territory, there remains now no governmental organ that can exercise those rights—apart from the coalition itself." The Fourth Convention, he points out, does allow an occupying authority to make certain changes in laws to ensure good governance during the occupation. It should be kept in mind that an occupying power can make certain changes to ensure its own security. Because occupation was seen as temporary, however, the occupying power is not free to change laws to bring them into accord with its own judicial conceptions. Grant takes the view that it is possible to "carve out" from the Hague Resolutions and Fourth Convention the authority to overhaul laws of the occupied territory, which could be achieved by a United Nations Security Council resolution. Precedent has already been established during the transition to independence of East Timor (formerly a part of Indonesia) or in the creation of an autonomous Kosovo (formerly ruled by Serb-dominated Yugoslavia). In both instances, with UN sanction, existing laws were swept aside in the interests of reform, democracy, and political stability.

See also EAST TIMOR, WAR CRIMES IN; GENEVA CONVENTIONS; HAGUE CONVENTIONS; IRAQ, HUMAN RIGHTS VIOLATIONS IN POST-SADDAM; KOSOVO, WAR CRIMES IN.

Further Reading:

Falk, Richard A. *Crimes of War: A legal, political-documentary, and psychological inquiry into the responsibility of leaders, citizens, and soldiers for criminal acts in wars.* New York: Random House, 1971.

Gutman, Roy, ed. *Crimes of War: What the Public Should Know.* New York: W. W. Norton & Company, 1999.

Jackson, Nyamuya Maogoto. *War Crimes and Realpolitik: International Justice from World War I to the 21st Century.* Boulder, Colo.: Lynne Rienner Publishers, 2004.

Jokie, Aleksander. *War Crimes and Collective Wrongdoing: A Reader.* London: Blackwell Publishers, 2001.

Office of Special Investigations

The Office of Special Investigations (OSI), which operates within the U.S. Department of Justice, was established to uncover individuals involved in war crimes before and during World War II who might have slipped into the United States illegally or fraudulently. The OSI has helped deport nearly 100 former concentration-camp guards who worked for the Nazis since its inception. At the same time it has prevented 170 war-crimes suspects from entering the United States. It has also the responsibility for tracking down gold, jewelry, and money that the Nazis stole from victims of the Holocaust. Once a suspect is located, the OSI seeks to take appropriate legal action, which can entail exclusion, denaturalization, or deportation.

The OSI was formed in 1979 in response to reports that thousands of Nazi war criminals were living in the United States. Since then it has conducted hundreds of investigations and filed complaints against more than 70 Nazi war criminals, most of whom were Lithuanian, Latvian, or Ukrainian nationals who had collaborated with the Nazis. These criminals fall into several categories: Some were responsible for giving the orders for atrocities, while others were members of local police or administrators who carried out executions of Jews and others singled out for persecution. Additional cases involve individuals who had spread racist and inflammatory propaganda as well as German scientists who participated in unethical MEDICAL EXPERIMENTS on concentration-camp inmates. The OSI has pursued several important cases, including those of Andrija Artuković, minister of the interior of Croatia; Feodor Federenko, a Ukrainian guard at the Treblinka death camp; John Iwan Demjanjuk, the Ukrainian operator of the gas chambers at Treblinka; Valerian Trifa, leader of an Iron Guard (fascist) student group in Romania; and Arthur Rudolph, a Nazi rocket scientist involved in slave labor at the Dora-Mittelbau camp. Several of these men were expelled from the United States. The OSI also undertook the investigation of two special cases at the request of the U.S. government: Klaus BARBIE, "the Butcher of Lyon," and the notorious Dr. Josef MENGELE.

In addition to tracking down war criminals, the OSI has also sponsored research on fascist movements in Eastern Europe and the role played by local collaborators in Nazi war crimes. The OSI has come in for criticism, especially from European émigré groups who have protested against the use of newly opened Soviet archives to investigate cases, contending that the evidence is tainted and that the individuals named were targeted not because they were Nazis but because they were anticommunists. Critics also say that the OSI has concentrated too much on lower-level war criminals.

In recent years the OSI's workload has increased because of new information about suspects that has been disclosed by the opening of archives in the former Soviet Union and East-bloc countries. In 2005 its mandate was shifted to take into account the reality that fewer Nazi war criminals still remained alive to hunt down. As a result of legislation overhauling U.S. intelligence agencies, the OSI has been given a new mission to locate and prosecute individuals suspected of war crimes in current conflicts around the world, including the Balkans, Rwanda, and Cambodia, many of whom have come to the United States masquerading as REFUGEES. "For the first time since Nuremberg, the world is really getting serious about these kinds of cases," said Eli M. Rosenbaum, head of the OSI, when the changes were announced.

The new mission, included as part of the broad intelligence restructuring package recently passed by Congress and signed by President Bush, has Justice officials scrambling to assemble an operating plan and proposed budget for the tiny office. Currently, the OSI has 28 employees and $5 million in annual expenses. The expansion of the office was a reflection of growing worldwide concern over the fate of suspected war criminals from the Balkans, Cambodia, and elsewhere, many of whom have escaped prosecution by blending in with immigrant populations in the United States.

Okawa Shumei (1886–1957) *Japanese militarist*

Okawa Shumei, a staunch nationalist, political theorist, and propagandist, was indicted by the International Military Tribunal for the Far East (better known as the TOKYO TRIALS) for war crimes. An ultranationalist who had served as chief of the East Asian Economic Survey Bureau, he was actively involved in two rightist coups in 1931, and in 1932 he was imprisoned for the assassination of Premier Tsuyoshi Inukai. Okawa advocated a political philosophy known as "Asia for the Asians," which had a great deal of influence on the Kodoha, or "Imperial Way Faction," a right-wing association of mostly junior Imperial Army officers who saw Western influences as poisonous, opposed the dominance of the government by political powers, and sought to "restore" the emperor as an absolute ruler, with the army serving as the protector of Japanese values. The Kodoha movement was dismantled after a failed coup in 1936, but by then its ideas had gained currency in higher echelons of the government, and many of its adherents had acquired positions of power. The rightists who decided to carry out the war against the Allies were putting into practice policies that Okawa had espoused. Though he was not involved in the war itself, he was implicated for his role in inflaming the Japanese against the Allies and promoting a war to establish Japanese hegemony in Asia.

On the first day of his trial, at the reading of the indictments, Okawa went mad and began to beat the head of codefendant Hideki TOJO, the former prime minister. All charges against him were dropped, and he was committed to a psychiatric hospital, never to be tried. He was discharged in 1948 and died nine years later.

Olivera Castillo, Jorge (1961–) *Cuban dissident*

Jorge Olivera Castillo, head of an independent Havana news agency, is a well-known political dissident in Cuba who has been imprisoned for his activities on behalf of greater freedom. He was among 76 noted dissidents arrested in March 2003 and sentenced to several years imprisonment. However, he was released in late 2004 after serving about 20 months of his sentence. Olivera Castillo was accused of maintaining links with subversive press groups from 1991 on, particularly with Radio Martí, a U.S.-based radio outlet broadcasting in Cuba, as well as for having "an illegal email account." In addition, he was charged with possession of a typewriter and a Super-8 video camera that he had reportedly received from U.S. diplomats to help him with his work.

Born in 1961, Olivera Castillo was the director and editor of the independent, non–state-controlled news agency Habana Press. Previously he had worked for the state-controlled Cuban Institute of Radio and Television before being fired in 1992 for reportedly collaborating with dissident movements. Accustomed to being harassed and arrested for his political activities, he was detained for trying to escape from Cuba on a raft and at one point was evicted from his house by a neighborhood vigilante group and forced to sleep on park benches. He was held under house arrest in 1999 and denounced by name by Fidel Castro (also in 1999) as a threat to the security of the forthcoming Ibero-American Summit in Havana.

See also CUBA, HUMAN RIGHTS VIOLATIONS IN.

Omar, Mullah *See* MULLAH OMAR.

Operation Condor

Operation Condor was a clandestine campaign of terror in the mid-1970s supported by an alliance of rightist regimes in six Southern Cone nations: Argentina, Bolivia, Brazil, Chile, Paraguay, and Uruguay. Spearheaded by President Augusto PINOCHET, who had seized power in Chile in 1973, and launched that same year, it principally targeted leftist insurgents and political dissidents. In a period of seven years, under the pretext of keeping communism at

bay, agents working for Operation Condor are believed to have killed between 15,000 and 30,000 people considered as subversive. In fact, the operation was designed to maintain several dictatorships in power.

On one level—Phase I—Condor was set up to carry out abductions, DISAPPEARANCES, interrogations, and TORTURE; on another level—Phase II—it was designed to facilitate mutual cooperation among military intelligence services, which involved the coordination of political surveillance and exchange of information across borders. But its most clandestine activities—Phase III—were intended to crush prominent political dissidents in exile who might have the capacity to mobilize opposition against the military regimes. To carry this out, special commando teams were formed and sent on missions in South America, Europe, and the United States. In 1976 the CIA reported that it had received information that Condor intended to undertake "executive action" outside of the Southern Cone. That same year, on September 21, agents of Condor brazenly carried out the assassination of former Chilean ambassador and Pinochet opponent Orlando Letelier and his aide in the heart of Washington, D.C. The killings were perpetrated by a U.S. expatriate with ties to the Chilean intelligence agency DINA (NATIONAL INTELLIGENCE DIRECTORATE) acting under orders of the spymaster Manuel CONTRERAS. Condor assassins also targeted then-New York congressman Ed Koch (later New York's mayor), though the plot was never carried out. Condor was responsible for the slayings of Chilean Christian Democrat leader Bernardo Leighton and his wife in Rome and General Carlos Prats, former commander in chief of the Chilean army, in Buenos Aires. Other victims of Condor included the ex-president of Bolivia, Juan Jose Torres, and two Uruguayan legislators known for their opposition to the military regime in their country.

Operation Condor is noteworthy not only because of its clandestine nature and its violent excesses, but because it embraced a transnational ideology that trumped sovereignty. Many of those who championed Condor believed that they were engaged in a Third World War and that any means was permitted to defeat the enemy. Leftists were not the only victims: Labor activists and peasant leaders, priests and nuns, intellectuals, journalists, students, and teachers also fell afoul of the military juntas. Substantial evidence has emerged from declassified documents that the United States supported Condor as a legitimate counterterror organization and that the CIA worked closely with some of the security forces involved in its operation. The former chief of staff of Paraguay's armed forces claimed that the United States had made an arrangement with South American intelligence chiefs involved in Condor to "keep in touch with one another through a U.S. communications installation in the Panama Canal Zone which covers all of Latin

America," to allow them "to co-ordinate intelligence information among the southern cone countries."

Operation Condor eventually collapsed in the late 1970s as a result of internal tensions. Moreover, the dictatorships that had backed it had begun to crumble, and by the early 1990s none of the participating governments were still in power. But it took some time before the world learned about Operation Condor and longer still before at least some of the perpetrators of the crimes committed on behalf of Condor were brought to justice. Condor first came to light in December 1992 when a Paraguayan judge uncovered what was named a "terror archive"—dossiers on hundreds, perhaps thousands of men and women who had been abducted, tortured, and killed by the security forces of the six member states. Some of these archives have been used to prosecute the offenders. Over 200 international warrants have been issued for the arrest of military officials who participated in Condor.

See also ARGENTINA, HUMAN RIGHTS VIOLATIONS IN; BOLIVIA, HUMAN RIGHTS VIOLATIONS IN; BRAZIL, HUMAN RIGHTS VIOLATIONS IN; CHILE, HUMAN RIGHTS VIOLATIONS IN; URUGUAY, HUMAN RIGHTS VIOLATIONS IN.

Further Reading:

Constable, Pamela. *A Nation of Enemies: Chile under Pinochet*. New York: W. W. Norton & Company, 1993.

Davis, William Columbus. *Warnings from the Far South: Democracy versus Dictatorship in Uruguay, Argentina, and Chile*. New York: Praeger Publishers, 1995.

Dinges, John. *The Condor Years: How Pinochet and His Allies Brought Terrorism to Three Continents*. New York: New Press, 2004.

Dorfman, Ariel. *Exorcising Terror: The Incredible Unending Trial of Augusto Pinochet*. New York: Seven Stories Press, 2002.

Kornbluh, Peter. *The Pinochet File: A Declassified Dossier on Atrocity and Accountability*. A National Security Archive Book. New York: New Press, 2003.

Politzer, Patricia, and Diane Wachtel. *Fear in Chile: Lives under Pinochet*. New York: New Press, 2001.

Oradour, massacre in

Oradour-sur-Glane was the site of the worst atrocity that occurred on French soil in World War II. In early June 1944 an order was issued to the OKW (High Command of the Armed Forces of Germany) to the effect that henceforth active members of the French Resistance were to be treated as guerrillas who represented a "danger to the rear of our fighting troops." The danger was not exaggerated. In the town of Tulle in southern Normandy, the 2nd Waffen-SS Division *Das Reich* found 62 mutilated bodies of German soldiers who had surrendered to the Resistance. In reprisal, the SS, with the aid of the local prefect and the mayor, rounded up all the males in town. Twenty-one were released because of their youth; the remaining 99 were hanged. Then reports reached the German High Command that a German general had been captured by armed citizens in the town of Oradour who were threatening to burn him in public. The SS occupied the town on June 10—four days after D-Day—and rounded up the population. The men were separated from the women and children, locked in garages and barns, and shot. The women and children were imprisoned in a church that was burned to the ground; all but two women died in the blaze. There is some dispute whether the SS deliberately set the church afire or whether fires burning in neighboring houses spread to that building. (According to some accounts, the Resistance maintained an arsenal in the belfry, which exploded.)

The death toll from the massacre was compiled only after the war. It is estimated that 393 residents of the town, 167 people from the surrounding countryside, 33 people from Limoges, and 55 from other areas were killed during this rampage. The German casualty rate was far lower: one SS member killed, one SS wounded.

No official action was taken by the German authorities against the atrocities' perpetrators, who were judged to be guilty of no more than an "excess of zeal," while the dead were officially classified as the "enemy." In early 1953 a trial was held in Bordeaux to prosecute some of the individuals involved in the massacres. Most of those accused were Alsatian French. Because Alsace had a large German population—Alsace had been under German control at various point in history—and is the most Protestant province in France, the case had stirred a good deal of unease. Anxious to avoid antagonizing a region that the government hoped to reintegrate into France, the judges handed down relatively light sentences to the defendants. Moreover, many of the accused had served with the French colonial forces fighting in Indochina, and so there was little motivation to call them into account for the atrocities in either Oradour or Tulle. By 1958 those defendants who had been sentenced to prison were freed. Then General Charles de Gaulle (who would later become president) ordered a 100-year embargo on all files relating to the massacres. With improving relations between France and Germany, neither government had any wish to reopen the case.

Further Reading:

Browder, George C. *Hitler's Enforcers: The Gestapo and the SS Security Service in the Nazi Revolution*. Oxford: Oxford University Press, 1996.

Hohne, Heinz Zollen. *The Order of the Death's Head: The Story of Hitler's SS*. Classic Military History. New York: Penguin, 2001.

Organization for Security and Cooperation in Europe (OSCE)

The Organization for Security and Cooperation in Europe (OSCE) is the largest regional security organization in the world. It evolved from the Conference on Security and Cooperation in Europe, which resulted in the Final Act, a politically binding accord (though not a formal treaty), signed in Helsinki, Finland, in 1975 by the European nations (except Albania), Turkey, the United States, Canada, and the Soviet Union. In its earlier incarnation as the Conference on Security and Cooperation in Europe (CSCE), it served as a forum for a series of meetings and conferences to expand and review the commitments of participants in carrying out the HELSINKI ACCORDS. But with the end of the cold war in 1990, the organization began to play a greater role in shaping Europe. Henceforth the CSCE—and later the OSCE—would acquire permanent institutions and operational capabilities.

The OSCE is a cooperative body in which all 55 participating nations (based in Europe, North America, and central Asia) have equal rights. Its major focus is the maintenance of security in all its aspects: political, military, humanitarian, economic, and environmental. In fulfilling its mandate, the OSCE specializes in conflict resolution and crisis management, which requires it to deal with a wide range of issues, including arms control; confidence and security building; and policing, disarmament, counterterrorism, and economic and environmental activities. Decisions are reached by consensus but are not politically binding on members. Several treaties have come into force in recent years that seek to ensure security on the continent: the Treaty on Conventional Armed Forces in Europe (CFE), the Treaty on Open Skies, and the Document on Small Arms and Light Weapons. The OSCE is headquartered in Vienna, Austria, with regional offices in Copenhagen, Geneva, The Hague, Prague, and Warsaw.

Organization of American States (OAS)

The Organization of American States (OAS) is made up of 34 nations in the Western Hemisphere with democratically elected governments. The organization was founded in 1948 by 21 nations whose representatives signed the OAS Charter, which set out common goals while affirming each nation's sovereignty. The concept of the OAS actually dates back much further: The great Latin American liberator Simón Bolívar conceived of just such a hemispheric alliance "united in heart" in the 1820s. In the 1890s several nations in the region formed the Commercial Bureau of American Republics, which evolved into the Pan American Union, the precursor of the OAS. The Pan American Union subsequently expanded to include nations of the English-speaking Caribbean and Canada.

The formation of the OAS was accompanied by the adoption of the American Declaration of the Rights and Duties of Man, the first international statement of its kind. This declaration was based on the principle that individuals have certain essential rights that are derived not from their nationality or place of residence but rather from their very status as human beings. The OAS Charter begins the main body of the text with a ringing affirmation: "All men are born free and equal, in dignity and in rights, and, being endowed by nature with reason and conscience, they should conduct themselves as brothers one to another." But with rights come duties: "The fulfillment of duty by each individual is a prerequisite to the rights of all. Rights and duties are interrelated in every social and political activity of man. While rights exalt individual liberty, duties express the dignity of that liberty." Among the duties the Declaration cites are "duties of a juridical nature" that "presuppose others of a moral nature which support them in principle and constitute their basis."

The OAS defines its mission in the Inter-American Democratic Charter, adopted in 2002: "The peoples of the Americas have a right to democracy and their governments have an obligation to promote and defend it." The OAS seeks to promote democracy and good governance, strengthen human rights, foster peace and security, and expand trade. In addition, the OAS tries to encourage decentralization of governments, modernization of political parties, and the increasing role of civic society; and it seeks to ensure peace and security in the region. In this role it is committed to combating terrorism and resolving territorial disputes between members. Regional peace is seen as inseparable from the issue of human rights. The Declaration on Security in the Americas, issued in 2001, states: "Peace is a value and a principle in itself, based on democracy, justice, respect for human rights, solidarity, security, and respect for international law."

The OAS has established two principal mechanisms to address human rights: the Inter-American Commission on Human Rights, based in Washington, D.C., and the INTER-AMERICAN COURT OF HUMAN RIGHTS, located in San José, Costa Rica. Individuals who believe they are unable to find justice for human rights violations in their own countries have the right to appeal to the Inter-American Commission, which can recommend to the member state involved ways to redress the problem. The commission can also recommend that the case be heard by the Inter-American Court for a binding decision, but only if the member state accepts its jurisdiction. The commission also dispatches representatives to make on-site visits to analyze and report on human rights conditions, but they must be invited by the state.

Further Reading:

Fawcett, Louise, and Andrew Hurrell, eds. *Regionalism in World Politics: Regional Organization and International Order.* Oxford: Oxford University Press, 1996.

Guillermoprieto, Alma. *Looking for History: Dispatches from Latin America.* New York: Vintage, 2002.

Skidmore, Thomas F., and Peter H. Smith. *Modern Latin America.* Oxford: Oxford University Press, 2000.

Williamson, Edwin. *The Penguin History of Latin America.* New York: Penguin Books, 1993.

Oxfam

Oxfam is a nongovernmental organization dedicated to tackling problems associated with poverty and providing famine relief to devastated regions of the developing world. Oxfam began life during the Second World War to deal with the famine in Nazi-occupied Greece that resulted from an Allied blockade. Several famine-relief committees sprang up in Britain to persuade the government there to allow essential supplies to reach the civilian population. One of these committees, the Oxford Committee for Famine Relief, met for the first time on October 5, 1942. Among its founders were Canon T. R. Milford of the University Church and Gilbert Murray, a former professor of Greek at Oxford University. Unlike other famine committees that dissolved after the war, the Oxford Committee expanded its mandate to include "the relief of suffering in consequence of the war." The committee worked to bring food and clothing to Europeans recovering from the war and then, in 1949, expanded its activities to provide "the relief of suffering arising as a result of wars or of other causes in any part of the world." The Oxford Committee became formally known as Oxfam in 1965.

Oxfam sought to portray the peoples in the developing world as human beings, not faceless abstractions, and to educate the peoples of the developed world about the root causes of poverty. In Oxfam's view, the globe had sufficient resources to ensure adequate food and shelter for the worldwide population; what was lacking was political will to get them where they were most needed. In the 1960s Oxfam initiated several self-help programs to encourage Third World communities to improve their water, farming practices, and health care. Oxfam has also tried to prod governments and international bodies to respond to problems of trade imbalances, hunger, and endemic poverty. To raise funds, Oxfam relies on donors and some 22,000 volunteers in the United Kingdom who sell donated items and handicrafts from overseas. In the 1980s Oxfam concentrated most of its relief efforts on the Horn of Africa, devoting half of its budget to relief of the famine that was then laying waste to the region.

With a growth in income from donations, Oxfam has been able to dedicate its resources to "policy, research, and campaigning work to address the structural causes of poverty in the South, such as crippling debt burdens, unfair terms of trade, and inappropriate agriculture policies." Oxfam has been involved in providing emergency humanitarian aid to parts of the former Soviet Union and the former Yugoslavia, but its largest response to a humanitarian disaster to date has been in the Great Lakes region of central Africa (which encompasses eastern Zaire, Burundi, and Rwanda) in the mid-1990s. Oxfam recognized, though, that merely offering aid could only do so much given the political, economic, and social problems that ignited the crisis. For this reason the organization mounted an international lobbying campaign meant to galvanize the United Nations, the Organization of African Unity, and powerful governments into taking concerted action to bring peace to the region.

Further Reading:

Aall, Pamela R., Daniel Miltenberger, and George Weiss. *IGOs, NGOs, and the Military in Peace and Relief Operations.* Washington, D.C.: United States Institute of Peace Press, 2000.

Byman, Daniel, Ian Lesser, Bruce Pirnie, Cheryl Benard, and Matthew Waxman. *Strengthening the Partnership: Improving Military Coordination with Relief Agencies and Allies in Humanitarian Operations.* Santa Monica, Calif.: Rand Corporation (NBN), 2000.

Erskins, Toni. *Can Institutions Have Responsibilities: Collective Moral Agency and International Relations.* Global Issues Series. Sydney, Australia: Palgrave Macmillan, 2004.

Rieff, David. *A Bed for the Night: Humanitarianism in Crisis.* New York: Simon & Schuster, 2002.

Vaux, Anthony. *The Selfish Altruist: Relief Work in Famine and War.* London: Earthscan Publications, 2001.

P

Padilla, Jose (1972–) *alleged American al-Qaeda supporter*

Jose Padilla, an American citizen, came to international attention when he was arrested on May 8, 2002, at Chicago's O'Hare Airport on suspicion that he had plotted to detonate a "dirty bomb" (one that could spread radiation) and use natural gas to blow up apartment buildings in Washington, D.C., New York, and Florida. (No bomb or bomb-making components were found in his possession at the time of his arrest.) The U.S. government declared him to be an "enemy combatant" and had him transferred from civilian to military custody. He was held incommunicado in a South Carolina military brig without access to a lawyer from June 2002 until March 2004, when the Justice Department bowed to outside pressure and allowed a lawyer to see him.

The United States viewed Padilla as an enemy combatant taken in the war on terrorism that was launched in response to the September 11, 2001, attacks by al-QAEDA; as such, the Bush administration contended that he was not entitled to the constitutional protections accorded to other American citizens charged with a crime. In fact, Padilla was not formally charged with any crime at all. Specifically, the government contended that Padilla was "closely associated with Al Qaeda"; that he had engaged in "war-like acts, including conduct in preparation for acts of international terrorism"; that he had intelligence that could help the United States prevent future terrorist attacks; and that he was a continuing threat to U.S. security. Nonetheless, the government did not allege that Padilla was actually a member of al-Qaeda. According to a Justice Department report issued spring 2004, Padilla had admitted that he had attended al-Qaeda training camps where the plot to blow up apartment buildings was discussed. Because no lawyer was permitted to represent Padilla during his interrogation, any evidence gained at that time would not have been admissible in court. Nor was Padilla in a position to challenge an indictment since there was none.

In its report, the Justice Department stated that Padilla had not been mistreated but refused to confirm that the interrogation had complied with the Geneva Convention. There was no means to determine what had transpired during the interrogations since his appointed lawyer was under a gag order. A footnote in the report did shed some light on Padilla's defense: He contended that while he was in an al-Qaeda camp he had never sworn allegiance to the group and any talk of a plot was only a pretext so that he could leave Afghanistan and avoid having to fight.

The case began to make its way through the federal justice system. A panel of the second U.S. Circuit Court of Appeals issued a 2-1 ruling barring the president from declaring a U.S. citizen an "enemy combatant" without congressional authorization. The court ordered Padilla freed from military custody in 30 days, leaving open the option that he could be held pending a criminal trial in civilian courts. The Justice Department appealed, and the case—*Padilla v. Rumsfeld*—was argued before the U.S. Supreme Court. On June 28, 2004, the High Court ruled on narrow technical grounds that the Padilla case should be heard in a federal court in South Carolina rather than by a federal court in New York, where the suit had originally been filed. In its decision the court also said that Padilla had improperly named Secretary of Defense Donald Rumsfeld as the respondent, instead of the warden of the military brig where Padilla was held. On the same day the Supreme Court ruled more emphatically in a case related to another U.S. citizen, Yaser HAMDI, who, unlike Padilla, had been captured in Afghanistan.

Padilla's case came before the federal district court in South Carolina in early 2005. Although the decision was technical and did not rule on the merits of the case, many legal observers believed that it left the government with the choice of either charging him or freeing him. In March 2005 a federal district judge in South Carolina ruled that the government should release Padilla from the military brig where he was being held within 45 days, saying that the

Bush administration was not entitled to detain an American citizen for three years without bringing charges. In his opinion Judge Henry Floyd wrote, "The court finds that the president has no power, neither express nor implied, neither constitutional nor statutory, to hold petitioner as an enemy combatant." In September 2005 a Federal Circuit Court overturned an earlier decision by a U.S. District Court judge in South Carolina, where Mr. Padilla was imprisoned, in favor of the Bush administration. In the South Carolina decision, the judge held that the president had no authority to detain an American citizen arrested in the United States as an enemy combatant. The District Court ruled that Padilla must be treated no differently from any criminal suspect even if he was an al-Qaeda terrorist. The Fourth Circuit Court, however, maintained that since Congress had authorized the use of force against al-Qaeda, and since the Supreme Court had approved Congress's action, the Bush administration did have the authority to detain or to kill the enemy. Although it had not been proven in court that Padilla was, in fact, a terrorist the Federal Court ruled that his detention was legal. The ruling was appealed to the Supreme Court. In late 2005 the Bush administration moved to transfer Padilla for trial in a civilian court without waiving its right to charge him again as an unlawful combatant.

Further Reading:

Hersh, Seymour M. *Chain of Command: The Road from 9/11 to Abu Ghraib.* New York: HarperCollins, 2004.

Danner, Mark. *Torture and Truth: America, Abu Ghraib, and the War on Terror.* New York: New York Review Books, 2004.

Pakistan, human rights violations in

Since taking power in a military coup in 1999, Pervez Musharraf remains the undisputed leader of Pakistan six years later. Although he has allowed a certain measure of democracy, he has shown little inclination to step down or return the country to civilian rule. Pakistan, a poor country with nuclear arms, has become a frontline state in the war on terrorism. Before the 9/11 terrorist attacks on the United States, it was a principal backer of the fundamentalist TALIBAN regime in neighboring Afghanistan. After 9/11, Musharraf made common cause with the United States, turning on Pakistan's former allies. However, a large number of Pakistanis still support the aims of Islamic militancy as exemplified by the Taliban and al-QAEDA. Thousands of Taliban and al-Qaeda militants are believed to have taken refuge in the mountainous region bordering Afghanistan, where they are sheltered by tribes with a long history of defying the authority of the central government in Islamabad. In addition, hundreds of thousands of ordinary Afghans still remain in refugee camps in Pakistan after fleeing the Soviet occupation of their country during the 1980s. (The Soviets withdrew in 1989, but many REFUGEES refused to return home because of the unstable political climate.)

The increasing influence of Islamic militancy in the country has only heightened religious and ethnic tensions that were already present before the fall of the Taliban in 2001. Violence regularly flares up between adherents of Shiite and Sunni factions, with hundreds of people having been attacked and killed. (Pakistan is predominantly Sunni.) Although Musharraf has made some efforts to quell the sectarian violence and rein in militant groups, HUMAN RIGHTS WATCH and other human rights advocates contend that his rule has been marked by a rise in extremist activity and an increase in religious killings, partly because he has marginalized mainstream political groups and stifled political dissent. Opposition leaders and legislators have been harassed, beaten, subjected to blackmail, and arrested. Nor is there any sign of political liberalization. In December 2004 police disrupted a rally held by the Pakistan People's Party (PPP), arresting hundreds, including several legislators. The president of another opposition party, the Alliance for the Restoration of Democracy, was sentenced to 23 years in prison for reading an anti-Musharraf letter to journalists. The former speaker of the National Assembly was jailed for 10 years on charges of corruption. Human rights groups have criticized the judiciary, which Human Rights Watch has characterized as "emasculated."

The country has become increasingly militarized, a trend benefiting religious parties that have traditionally enjoyed close relations with the army. On the other hand, women and religious minorities have suffered. The laws pertaining to rape and honor killings of women are weak or seldom enforced, creating a climate of impunity for the perpetrators. According to government figures, about 1,000 women are victims of honor killings every year, usually committed by members of their families. At the same time, penalties for violating blasphemy laws have been stiffened, resulting in long prison terms and even the imposition of death sentences for Muslims who have questioned a strict interpretation of the Koran.

According to Human Rights Watch, Pakistan's collaboration with the United States in pursuing al-Qaeda and other Islamic militants has been "exemplified by a disregard for DUE PROCESS," as demonstrated by the number of arbitrary arrests and detentions. Concerns about military actions have also been raised by the Human Rights Commission of Pakistan (HRCP), the country's most prominent human rights group, which has criticized the government's reliance on security forces to deal with social and civil conflicts. The group charged that, in addition, the private sector was falling under military control, with officers being appointed to head large and small businesses. Two tribal regions, South Waziristan and Balochistan, have experienced a much deeper involvement of the military than in the past. In spring 2004, for example, some 25,000 troops moved into South Waziristan, a region where 200,000 Afghans had taken refuge, as part of a campaign to root out al-Qaeda terrorists. In the course of counterterrorism operations, the army displaced some 25,000 refugees, forcing them back over the border. Some of the refugees were only given two hours notice to pack up and leave. The incursions also took the lives of tribes living in the area, which resulted in violent clashes. (Most of the troops were later withdrawn from the area.)

The military has also committed abuses in Punjab, the country's breadbasket, where army and paramilitary forces allied with the army have killed and tortured farmers who refuse to cede land rights to them. These forces have even resorted to torturing children of farmers and have suppressed a farmers' movement. Punjab is considered especially important to the army because it draws more recruits from the province than anywhere else. Because the military claims on farmland—the most fertile in the country—have virtually no legal basis, the army has undertaken a campaign of murder, arbitrary detention, and TORTURE to force farmers into submission. According to Human Rights Watch, on two occasions the army laid siege to villages, depriving their inhabitants of food and water. Most of the abuses have been attributed to the Pakistan Rangers, a paramilitary unit that has set up detention centers—known as "torture cells"—to hold farmers until they sign agreements giving up title to their land. Musharraf's efforts to burnish Pakistan's reputation in the eyes of the world suffered a grave setback in September 2005 while he was attending the world summit at the United Nations. In comments to the press, which he subsequently denied making, he dismissed complaints about persistent abuse and rape of women in his country. Claiming rape, he told a *Washington Post* correspondent, had become a "moneymaking concern"; he added, "A lot of people say if you want to go abroad and get a visa for Canada or citizenship and be a millionaire, get yourself raped." Predictably his comment caused outrage among women's groups and human rights organizations. Musharraf was reacting specifically to recent reports of two high-profile cases that had attracted worldwide notoriety: one involved Mukhtar Mai, who was allegedly gang-raped in 2002 on orders of a village council, and the other Shazia Khalid, a physician apparently attacked inside a government hospital quarters in Baluchistan Province in 2005. In both cases the perpetrators received light sentences or were acquitted, or else were never apprehended at all. When Mai tried to go abroad to speak about the lack of rights for women in her country, Musharraf denied her permission (he later backed down

under pressure from Washington), saying, "I don't want to project the bad image of Pakistan." Khalid, for her part, said that she was forced to leave Pakistan because of death threats. When a government-sponsored conference on "violence against women" Musharraf decried nongovernmental organizations for participating and said that Pakistan should not be singled out since rape was a global problem.

See also AFGANISTAN, HUMAN RIGHTS VIOLATIONS IN; COLLECTIVE PUNISHMENT; RELIGIOUS PERSECUTION.

Further Reading:

Abbas, Hassan. *Pakistan's Drift into Extremism: Allah, the Army, and America's War on Terror.* Armonk, N.Y.: M. E. Sharpe, 2004.

Zayy-at, Montasser al-. *The Road to Al-Qaeda: The Story of Bin Laden's Right-Hand Man.* Critical Studies on Islam. Translated by Ahmed Fekry. Translated by Sora Nimis. Ann Arbor, Mich.: Pluto Press, 2004.

Burke, Jason. *Al-Qaeda: Casting a Shadow of Terror.* London: I. B. Tauris, 2004.

———. *Al-Qaeda: The True Story of Radical Islam.* London: I. B. Tauris, 2004.

Gunaratna, Rohan. *Inside Al Qaeda: Global Network of Terror.* New York: Berkley Publishing Group, 2003.

Weaver, Mary Anne. *Pakistan: In the Shadow of Jihad and Afghanistan.* New York: Farrar, Straus and Giroux, 2003.

Palestine, human rights violations in

Palestine entered a new era with the death of Yasser Arafat, longtime leader of the Palestinians, in 2004. He was succeeded in early 2005 by Mahmoud Abbas (known also by the nom de guerre Abu Mazen). Within months of his assuming, power talks began between Abbas and Israeli prime minister Ariel Sharon that offered the promise of a two-state solution, with an independent Palestine living in peace alongside Israel. Nevertheless, neutral sources have reported serious human rights abuses by both sides, including TORTURE. The Israel Defense Force (IDF) contends that any "physical pressure" applied to Palestinians taken into custody is sanctioned by Israel's Supreme Court, although it also claims that these methods, such as sleep deprivation, do not amount to inflicting physical pain.

Until Israel occupied the West Bank and Gaza in the Six-Day War of 1967, the West Bank had been part of Jordan and Gaza had been under the rule of Egypt. However, growing sentiment for an independent Palestinian state led to violent resistance that initially took the form of stone-throwing against Israeli forces. The first intifada (Arab for "uprising") began in 1987 and lasted until 1993; by the time it ended with the signing of the Oslo accords, which called for the creation of an independent Palestinian state, 1,162 Palestinians and 160 Israelis had been killed. The second and more violent intifada broke out in September 2000 and continued until the death of longtime Palestinian leader Yasser Arafat in 2005.

Throughout the four years of the intifada Palestinian militant groups maintained that any violence carried out against Israel was justified as a form of resistance to foreign occupation. This view received wide support from the Palestinian population. A number of militant organizations conducted suicide bombings and mortar attacks against Israeli civilians, with considerable loss of life. Three militant groups in particular—Hamas, Islamic Jihad, and the Al Aksa Brigades—took responsibility for most of these terrorist strikes. Israel retaliated by closing off West Bank cities and towns, invading refugee camps, and rounding up hundreds of young men suspected of links with the militants. In addition, Israel has used tactics that have been widely condemned by other governments and the United Nations, including targeted assassinations meant to decapitate the leadership of the militant groups. Israel has also engaged in practices such as demolishing the homes of families of suicide bombers—over 200 Palestinian homes in 2002 and 2003 alone—even in the absence of evidence that the families were aware of or supported the actions of the bombers. About 2,500 houses have been destroyed in this way, leaving more than 4,300 people homeless. The demolitions have been decried as COLLECTIVE PUNISHMENT, which is banned under INTERNATIONAL HUMANITARIAN LAW. In 2005 a special commission set up by the IDF concluded that demolitions should stop because they were only causing more resentment and doing little to deter future attacks.

American publications have documented that during the 2000–2004 period of the intifada, nearly 3,000 Palestinians were killed, 534 of them being children under 18. According to the *Journal of Palestinian Studies,* 119 people alone were killed in an IDF attack on the West Bank city Nablus in April 2002, and 600 between 2000 and 2004. The U.S. government also estimates that in the IDF's "targeted killings" of known Palestinian terrorists, 47 innocent civilian bystanders also lost their lives. Attacks by the IDF in response to terrorist attacks have resulted in the injuries of some 40,000 Palestinians; at least 2,500 have been left with permanent disabilities. More than 300 schools have been destroyed; 30 of them were converted into military posts. The U.S. government reckons that there are over 5,000 prisoners held by Israel, although several hundred were released as a goodwill gesture in the weeks following Abbas's election.

Neutral sources such as the U.S. State Department make clear that during the Second Intifada, which began in 2000, the security forces of *both* sides—the Israeli Defense Force and the Palestinian Authority—"committed numerous, serious human rights abuses." The violence had a profoundly disruptive effect on the Palestinian economy. The U.S. Agency for International Development (USAID) stated that up to 44 percent of Palestinian children were anemic, and other sources found that 60 percent of the Palestinians were living below the poverty level (of $2-a-day income), with a 43 percent unemployment rate. In response to attacks by Palestinian militants, the Israelis have imposed serious restrictions on the movements of Palestinian civilians and have often carried out mass arbitrary arrests. Israel forces established over 700 checkpoints, most of which were located on the West Bank (occupied by Israel since the Six Day War in 1967), and around 60 in Gaza. (The Sharon government announced that it intended to withdraw from Gaza and tear down settlements that have been home to about 8,000 Israeli settlers; this process began in August 2005.) To prevent the infiltration of suicide bombers, the Israeli government began a Security Wall, which is intended to separate Palestinian population centers from Israel. In an advisory opinion, the INTERNATIONAL COURT OF JUSTICE ruled in 2004 that the wall was illegal because its route would enclose large parcels of Palestinian-owned land on the Israeli side. Israel's Supreme Court has ordered the government to relocate segments of the wall to take into account some Palestinian claims. Although the wall appears to represent a unilaterally drawn border—which carves out a significant amount of the West Bank beyond the pre-1967 border known as the Green Line—the Israeli authorities insist that its purpose is only to safeguard its citizens and is not meant to be permanent.

Although Yasser Arafat routinely criticized terrorist strikes on Israeli civilians, there is little evidence that he took any steps to rein in the militants who carried out the attacks. Moreover, with over a dozen different security forces under the Palestinian Authority and other groups, such as Hamas, acting autonomously, Israel contended that the situation was close to anarchy and that it had no partner with whom to negotiate. In the four years of the Second Intifada, Palestinians have become disenchanted with a state of continual war, which has also brought economic devastation, corruption, and an upsurge in crime. Signaling their readiness to try another course, the Palestinian electorate gave Abbas almost 60 percent of the vote after he had renounced violent resistance against Israel. Indeed, shortly after he met Sharon in a summit hosted by Egypt in February 2005, he pronounced the intifada to be over.

Subsequently Abbas took some steps to rein in the militants, relying on diplomacy to bring Hamas and the Al Aksa brigades into the political process. (Islamic Jihad, another radical group, rebuffed Abbas's efforts.) His strategy has had mixed success. Violence has diminished, though tensions remain high, and Hamas has participated in local elections in Gaza and the West Bank, often beating moderates. Israel, however, continues to demand that Abbas crack down on the militants and disarm them. Suicide attacks against civilians have dropped off sharply since Abbas assumed the leadership of the Palestinian Authority but have not ceased altogether, and clashes regularly occur between Israeli security forces and Palestinian militants. Both sides, however, continued to exercise restraint rare for the region. In August 2005 Sharon defied the base of his right-wing Likud Party and ordered the evacuation of approximately 8,500 Jewish settlers from Gaza, a process that went more smoothly than even the most optimistic Israelis had dared hope. Although Gaza was handed over to the Palestinian Authority, the process was fraught with uncertainty. For one thing, it was unclear at the end of 2005 whether Hamas or the Palestinian Authority would govern Gaza; for another, Israel still controlled access to Gaza by air, sea, and land. Moreover, in the view of Palestinians and many Israelis, Sharon had used the Gaza pullout as a way of defusing international pressure (especially from the United States), allowing the Israeli government to put off consideration of a similar withdrawal of settlers from the West Bank, which in 2005 was home to about 250,000 Jews.

Further Reading:
Finkelstein, Norman G. *Image and Reality of the Israel-Palestine Conflict.* New York: W. W. Norton, 2003.
Roraback, Amanda. *Israel-Palestine in a Nutshell.* Santa Monica, Calif.: Enisen Publishing, 2004.
Said, Edward W. *The Question of Palestine.* New York: Vintage, 1992.
Smith, Charles D. *Palestine and the Arab-Israeli Conflict.* New York: Bedford/St. Martin's, 2004.

Papen, Franz von (1879–1969) *German diplomat*
As a former chancellor of Germany, Franz von Papen lent his prestige and support to the Nazis and helped them gain power. He was tried by the Allies after World War II and acquitted, though a German court subsequently convicted him as "a major offender" during the war. Unlike most Nazi officials, Papen could boast of an aristocratic lineage: He was born into an old Westphalian noble family on October 19, 1879, the son of a wealthy landowner. Papen joined the German army before the outbreak of World War I and was sent to Washington to serve as a military attaché. He was expelled a year later for initiating an illegal arrangement with a company in Bridgeport, Connecticut, to produce armaments for Germany, a violation of the U.S. Neutrality Act. After the war he became a leading figure in the Catholic Center Party (BVP) and in 1921 was elected to the Reichstag (parliament). He gained further influence by purchasing a controlling share of the party newspaper, the *Germania*, which he tried to use—unsuccessfully—to impose his reactionary views on the BVP. He was named chancellor by President Paul von Hindenburg in 1932 but opposition to his ultraconservative policies forced his ouster within months. Still, during his brief tenure he managed to do the Nazis several favors, lifting the ban on the SA (Sturmabteilung), the Nazi security police, and ousting Prussia's Social Democratic government.

Once out of power, Papen looked to Adolf HITLER to revive his political prospects. He used his connections with such industrialists as Hjalmar SCHACHT, Fritz Thyseen, and Gustav KRUPP and his son Arthur to convince Hindenburg to appoint Hitler as chancellor. The lobbying effort succeeded, and Hitler rewarded Papen by naming him vice chancellor. Papen assured Hindenburg that he would temper Hitler's more extremist policies, a promise that he could not possibly have kept even if he were sincere. Papen later served Hitler as ambassador to Austria, a position he held from 1934 to 1939. As ambassador, he was involved in plans to implement the Anschluss—the union of Germany and Austria under Nazi rule. From 1939 until 1944, Papen represented the Third Reich as ambassador to Turkey. Before the war ended, he retired to his native Westphalia, where he was arrested by Allied forces on April 10, 1945.

Papen was tried at the NUREMBERG TRIALS on charges of conspiring to start World War II and found not guilty. However, the new West German government put him on trial as a "major offender" for aiding the Nazi regime and sentenced him to eight years' imprisonment. Like many wealthy supporters of Hitler, he was forgiven within a short time and released in January 1949; all of his property and wealth, confiscated as part of his punishment, was returned to him, although he was forced to sacrifice his pension and deprived of a driver's license. Papen died on May 2, 1969.

Further Reading:
Goldensohn, Leon, and Robert Gellately, eds. *The Nuremberg Interviews.* New York: Knopf, 2004.
Marrus, Robert, and Michael R. Marrus. *The Nuremberg War Crimes Trial of 1945–46: A Documentary History. Bedford Series in History and Culture.* Sidney, Australia: Palgrave Macmillan, 1997.
Maser, Werner. *Nuremberg: A Nation on Trial.* New York: Scribner, 1979.
Rice, Earle. *The Nuremberg Trials. Famous Trials Series.* San Diego, Calif.: Lucent Books, 1997.
Taylor, Telford. *The Anatomy of the Nuremberg Trials: A Personal Memoir.* New York: Little, Brown & Co, 1993.
———. *Nuremberg Trials: War Crimes and International Law.* New York: Carnegie Endowment for International Peace, 1949.

Papon, Maurice (1910–) *French Nazi collaborator*
As head of the southwestern Gironde region of Vichy France during World War II, Maurice Papon was responsible for the DEPORTATIONS of as many as 1,500 Jews to CONCENTRATION CAMPS. But he managed to avoid having to answer for his crimes for several years, succeeding in masquerading as a member of the French Resistance after the war. His skill in covering his tracks was such that he was decorated by General Charles de Gaulle and even managed to become a cabinet minister.

Born in 1910, Papon entered public service at the age of 20. His advancement through the ranks of the civil service was not hampered by the Nazi occupation of France in 1940, and at the age of 31 he was appointed general secretary of the prefecture of the Gironde region. However, when he realized that the Germans were losing the war, he switched sides, informing on his former allies to the French Resistance, an act that later won him the Carte d'Ancien Combattant de la Résistance, a coveted decoration for fighting the German occupation. Under de Gaulle's government, Papon became prefet de police in Paris, a post he held until 1968. He then entered politics, becoming budget minister in the government of President Valéry Giscard d'Estaing in the 1970s.

In 1981 Papon's cover was blown when old documents were uncovered by accident in the Bordeaux town hall, including the deportation orders he had signed. Shortly after the papers were published in a popular magazine, charges were brought against him, but in 1987 they were dropped because of legal technicalities. The following year, new charges were brought, accusing him of CRIMES AGAINST HUMANITY (later changed to complicity in crimes against humanity). After spending years trying to stop the legal process from going forward, Papon was finally compelled to stand trial in October 1997. At that point he was the highest-ranking former Vichy official to be put in the dock. Specifically, he was charged with ordering the arrest and internment of hundreds of Jews, some of whom were eventually sent to their deaths in Auschwitz. (There were allegations by human rights advocates that the French government had deliberately delayed the legal proceedings out of fear that putting Papon on trial would bring to light the extent of French collaboration with the German occupiers during the war.) At his trial, Papon contended that he was a victim of mistaken identity and in any case, the meaning of the 50-year-old documents was subject to misinterpretation. In addition, he claimed to have no idea of what became of the Jews whose deportations he had ordered. He reminded the court that he had aided the Resistance and in this capacity had actually helped save Jews. His trial, which lasted six months, was the longest in French history.

On April 2, 1998, Papon, then 87, was found guilty, although the jury acquitted him on the most serious counts, agreeing with his defense attorney that he was unaware of the ultimate fate of the Jews whose deportation orders he had signed. He was sentenced to 10 years' imprisonment as well as 10 years' privation of his civic, civil, and family rights. He was also stripped of all decorations and ordered to pay a fine equivalent to nearly $800,000. Papon's trial assumed a larger importance because it forced the French public to come to terms with the fact that collaboration with the Nazis was hardly an aberrant phenomenon and that many thousands—some in important positions, such as the late president François Mitterrand—had not acquitted themselves honorably during the war.

Papua, New Guinea, human rights violations in
See INDONESIA, HUMAN RIGHTS VIOLATIONS IN.

Party of God   *See* UGANDA, HUMAN RIGHTS VIOLATIONS IN.

Pavelić, Ante (1889–1959) *Croatian Nazi collaborator*
Ante Pavelić—known as the Butcher of the Balkans—was the fascist dictator of the Nazi puppet state of Croatia during World War II and one of the founders of the Croatian fascist movement, the USTACHE (also Ustasha and Ustaše). He is responsible for instigating the mass murder of 80,000 Jews, 30,000 Rom (Gypsies), and over 500,000 Serbs. Nonetheless, he was never brought to justice for his crimes.

Born in Bosnia and Herzegovina on July 14, 1889, Pavelić studied law in Zagreb, Croatia's capital. As a young man he joined a nationalist party called the Pure Party of Rights, eventually becoming the party secretary. In 1927 he began his political career by running for the Zagreb city council. In 1929 he cofounded the Ustache and then fled to Italy to avoid arrest for subversive activities. When the Yugoslav king Alexander was assassinated, Pavelić and other members of the Ustache were arrested on charges of conspiring to kill him. Pavelić was extradited to Yugoslavia but soon released.

In 1941 the Germans invaded Yugoslavia and installed Pavelić as *poglavnik* (leader) of the Independent State of Croatia. As the head of Croatia he ordered, orchestrated, and instituted a campaign of terror against Serbs, Jews, Rom, and communist Croats. Although there was no legal definition of GENOCIDE at the time—the word itself did not come into general use until after World War II—Pavelić can be accused of committing genocide against the Serbs since the Ustache under his command was targeting a whole people on the basis of their ethnicity. Serbs were exterminated, expelled from Croatia, or else forced to convert to Catholicism. (Serbs are largely Eastern Orthodox.)

Pavelić enriched himself by plundering the wealth confiscated from concentration-camp inmates, Orthodox Christian churches, and Jewish synagogues as well as the property seized from Serbs, Rom, and Jews. All the same he had powerful allies in the Vatican and Franciscan Order and was personally received by Pope Pius XII.

As the war was coming to an end, Pavelić managed to slip away. Assisted by high-placed connections in the Vatican, he was spirited off to South America along with hundreds of other fugitive Nazis and Ustache members. He took up residence in Argentina, where he became a security adviser to President Juan and Eva Perón before retiring to Spain, another hospitable country then under the rule of Francisco Franco. He died peacefully in Spain in 1959. Some nationalist Croatians still regard Pavelić as a hero of Croatian independence in spite of his atrocities and seek the return of his body to Croatia. In 1998 a class action lawsuit was filed in San Francisco against the Vatican bank, the Order of the Franciscans, and surviving members of Ustache, demanding an account of the loot that Pavelić plundered.

See also CROATIA, HUMAN RIGHTS VIOLATIONS IN; ROM (ROMANY, GYPSIES), PERSECUTION OF.

Further Reading:
Goldstein, Ivo. *Croatia: A History.* Montreal: McGill-Queen's University Press, 2000.
Muñoz, Antonio J. *For Croatia and Christ: The Croatian Army in World War II, 1941–1945.* Bayside, N.Y.: Europa Books Inc., 2004.
Tanner, Marcus. *Croatia: A Nation Forged in War.* New Haven, Conn.: Yale University Press, 2001.

Perisić, Momcilo   *See* WAR CRIMINALS OF THE FORMER YUGOSLAVIA.

Peru, human rights violations in   *See* FUJIMORI, ALBERTO; MONTESINA, VLADIMIRO; SHINING PATH.

Philippines, human rights violations in
The Philippines, while a democratic country since 1984, confronts serious political and economic problems, most of them stemming from inequality in the distribution of wealth and entrenched poverty. Even maintaining a democratically elected government is fraught with difficulties. The run-up to elections can often be a period characterized by a surge in violence. The police reported that 64 people were killed during the 1998 elections. In the 2001 midterm elections, the price in blood was even worse: 132 people were killed. The trend has shown no sign of abating. Polit-ical violence poses a particular risk to ensuring that human rights are upheld. Human rights violations are especially rampant in rural areas of the country that have been wracked by Muslim and communist separatist insurgencies for several years.

The Philippines has also become a frontline country in the U.S.-backed war on terrorism because its territory has been used by Muslim extremists who appear to have at least ideological, if not logistical, links to other militant Islamic groups in the region. Elements of the security services are blamed for arbitrary, unlawful, and occasionally EXTRAJUDICIAL KILLINGS, as well as DISAPPEARANCES, TORTURE, and arbitrary arrest and detention. The Philippine National Police (PNP) have been blamed for some of the worst abuses of human rights of any government institution, according to the constitutionally mandated Commission on Human Rights (CHR). Extrajudicial killings by police and vigilantes authorized by local officials have been employed "as expedient means of fighting crime and terrorism" in the words of the 2004 U.S. State Department *Country Report.* These summary executions of suspects are known as "salvaging." Police and military spokesmen often try to explain away suspicious deaths of suspects as the "unavoidable" consequence of shootouts or an effort to stop them from escaping police custody. In rural areas, extralegal executions serve political ends as local officials rely on assassinations (some perpetrated by elements of the police or the military) to assassinate political rivals or members of their families.

According to the Task Force for Detainees of the Philippines (TFDP), a human rights activist group, torture of suspects is "ingrained" in the arrest and detention process. Detainees are routinely struck or threatened with guns; beatings were more common at the beginning of interrogations. Police often practice arbitrary arrests and detentions in spite of constitutional guarantees requiring a judicial determination of probable cause before an arrest warrant can be issued and a prohibition against holding prisoners incommunicado or in secret places of detention. In the first six months of 2003, the CHR investigated 72 cases of illegal arrest and detention—an increase of 24 percent from the number recorded during the same period in 2002. Many of those taken into custody are political detainees, although they are often charged for ordinary crimes; the TFDP and the Philippine Human Rights Information Center (Philrights, a nongovernmental organization) both estimated the total number of political prisoners in the country was approximately 200 by the end of 2003.

The legal system is ill prepared to redress the violations of human rights: Because they are underpaid, judges and prosecutors are susceptible to corruption and the influence of the powerful. There have been attempts to reform the judiciary and institute fairer and speedier trials, but even so, most Filipinos appear to believe that they have little hope of obtaining justice. Human rights activists, too, have a hard time making headway since they are often subject to harassment by the military and police. Although the Philippines has a free press, journalists are at grave risk if their reporting threatens powerful political or criminal interests; more journalists were killed as a result of deliberate assassinations in the Philippines in 2004 than in any other country but war-torn Iraq; nearly 50 have been killed since 1984, the year that democracy was restored.

Two significant insurgencies have also contributed to grave human rights abuses. The largest is led by the Philippine Communist Party (CPP) and its well-funded military wing, the New People's Army (NPA), which is active in various regions of the country. The NPA has been fighting the army for almost three decades. AMNESTY INTERNATIONAL (AI) has called attention to several reported extrajudicial executions that "appear to have taken place within the context of military anti-insurgency operations" against the NPA, which the group says are likely to have been carried out by Armed Forces of the Philippines (AFP). AI points to what it terms "a pattern of killings and 'disappearances' of left-wing opposition activists and human rights defenders." The military has also alarmed human rights groups by labeling members of legitimate political parties as belonging to "front organizations" for the NPA. Once such individuals are stigmatized, AI says, they are more likely to be targets of military action.

The other major insurgency is being spearheaded by the smaller Abu Sayyaf Group (ASG), which is seeking an Iranian-style Islamic state in Mindanao, an island in the southern Philippines inhabited by a large Muslim population. Abu Sayyaf, whose name means "Bearer of the Sword," broke with the less-extremist Moro National Liberation Front in 1991. Various Moro factions had been waging a separatist war with Manila throughout the 1970s, but in January 1987 the larger groups eventually reached peace agreements that allowed for greater autonomy for Mindanao. Some groups such as Abu Sayyaf, which operates almost exclusively in the southern islands, have never accepted the accord. Abu Sayyaf, which is said to number several hundred young Islamic radicals, has become a particular cause for concern for U.S. policymakers after the September 11, 2001, terrorist attacks since it maintains ties to a number of Islamic fundamentalist organizations around the world, including Osama Bin Ladin's al-QAEDA. It is thought that Ramzi Yousef, who was convicted of organizing the 1993 bombing of the World Trade Center in New York, also had some connection to the guerrilla group.

Fighting has broken out between the ASG and other Muslim insurgents, which has resulted in the displacement of about 350,000 persons from Mindanao in 2003 alone, according to the Department of Social Welfare and Development. There are credible reports of widespread human rights violations by the government forces as well as the ASG. The CHR investigated almost 100 killings in the first half of 2003 that had been committed by both insurgents and the army (the same number as 2002 for the same period). Terrorists carried out kidnappings and killings, including political assassinations and summary beheadings of hostages and local residents. Six summary executions of civilians by government forces were documented by the TFDP between January and June in 2003. The army has been charged by some groups with illegally detaining citizens, torching houses, uprooting residents from their homes, and even shelling villages suspected of being ASG strongholds. Both sides have used children as fighters.

Further Reading:
Barreveld, Dirk J. *Terrorism in the Philippines: The Bloody Trail of Abu Sayyaf, Bin Laden's East Asian Connection.* New York: Writers Club Press, 2001.

Schirmer, Daniel B., and Stephen Shalom. *The Philippines Reader: A History of Colonialism, Neocolonialism, Dictatorship, and Resistance.* Boston: South End Press, 1987.

Phoenix program

The Phoenix program (*Kế Hoạch Phụng Hoàng* in Vietnamese) was a covert intelligence operation run by the CIA during the Vietnam War from 1968 to 1972. The secret operation, which was assisted by the South Vietnamese, was intended to curb communist Vietcong (VC) infiltration in the south and eliminate its base of support. Many of the suspected VC sympathizers were killed in what one former Phoenix officer, testifying before Congress, called "a sterile depersonalized murder program," which he compared to "Nazi atrocities."

Some of the Phoenix operations involved intelligence gathering, while others were military in nature—for example, interdicting Vietcong assassination squads. As part of the program, Provincial Interrogation Centers (PICs) were established in South Vietnam's 44 provinces; South Vietnamese, North Vietnamese defectors as well as mercenaries from Cambodia and China were recruited to staff them. Overall administration, however, was handled by the CIA, with assistance from Green Berets and Naval SEALs (sea, air, and land teams). Later the program was taken over by the U.S. Army and armed forces of the Republic of Vietnam as part of the "Vietnamization" policy promoted by President Richard Nixon to expedite withdrawal of U.S. forces from the region. In congressional testimony, the U.S. ambassador to Vietnam, William Colby (later director of CIA), described the program as a vital part of a long-term strategy. "Since this is a sophisticated and experienced enemy," he said, "experts are also needed to combat it.

Thus, the Phoenix program started in mid-1968 to bring together the police, military, and the other government organizations to contribute knowledge and act against this enemy infrastructure. It secures information about the enemy organization, identifies the individuals who make it up, and conducts operations against them." He cited an example: "These operations might consist of two policemen walking down the street to arrest an individual revealed as a member of the enemy apparatus or they might involve a three-battalion attack on a jungle hideout of a district or province committee." As a result of Phoenix, he went on to say, communists were captured, turned themselves in, or were killed in firefights. "Our own government provides advisory assistance and support to this internal security program through the police, the administration, the information services and the intelligence services."

The Phoenix program was intended to meet a growing insurgency by the Vietcong (formally known as the National Liberation Front). The apparatus Colby referred to was responsible for killing more than 6,000 people in terrorist attacks, including some 1,200 targeted assassinations of village chiefs and officials in 1969 alone. The program, however, began to be used by the South Vietnamese government to eliminate political opponents, whether or not they were affiliated with the Vietcong. Corruption became rife as South Vietnamese officials working with the program demanded protection money to avoid arrest or released suspects in exchange for bribes. The program was also characterized by CIA-sanctioned assassinations in contravention to the GENEVA CONVENTIONS. U.S. military officials' "Body counts" of Vietcong cadres killed were notoriously unreliable, and many of those who were killed were labeled VC posthumously. Provincial chiefs also sought to meet quotas of VC killed or captured by resorting to schemes such as arresting the same person several times or asserting that soldiers killed in combat were eliminated as a result of the Phoenix program. The program was ultimately judged a failure, not least because of widespread abuse, corruption, and EXTRAJUDICIAL KILLINGS.

See also TIGER FORCE; VIETNAM, HUMAN RIGHTS VIOLATIONS IN.

Further Reading:
Taylor, Telford. *Nuremberg and Vietnam: An American Tragedy.* New York: Times Books, 1970.
Vietnam Veterans against the War. *The Winter Soldier Investigation: An Inquiry into American War Crimes.* Boston: Beacon Press, 1972.

Physicians for Human Rights

Physicians for Human Rights (PHR) is a nongovernmental advocacy group whose guiding philosophy is based on the belief that health is inseparable from human rights. In 1997 the group shared the Nobel Peace Prize with the International Campaign to Ban Landmines. PHR uses medical and scientific methods to investigate and expose violations of human rights throughout the world and tries to put a stop to them. The organization also supports a wide-ranging educational campaign for health professionals and nursing students to get them involved in human rights work. Since 1996 PHR has been active in seeking to prevent TORTURE, DISAPPEARANCES, and EXTRAJUDICIAL KILLINGS as well as working to improve health and sanitary conditions in prisons and detention centers. While supporting the idea of medical neutrality in conflict situations, PHR also works to ensure that physicians and other health-care workers do not participate in torture. Among its other activities, PHR lends its services to investigations of MASS GRAVES to recover the dead, determine the cause and manner of death, identify the remains, and gather evidence that might prove valuable in bringing perpetrators of massacres and other war crimes to justice.

Further Reading:
Aall, Pamela R., Daniel Miltenberger, and George Weiss. *IGOs, NGOs, and the Military in Peace and Relief Operations.* Washington, D.C.: United States Institute of Peace Press, 2000.
Byman, Daniel, Ian Lesser, Bruce Pirnie, Cheryl Benard, and Matthew Waxman. *Strengthening the Partnership: Improving Military Coordination with Relief Agencies and Allies in Humanitarian Operations.* Santa Monica, Calif.: Rand Corporation (NBN), 2000.
Erskins, Toni. *Can Institutions Have Responsibilities: Collective Moral Agency and International Relations.* Global Issues Series. Sydney, Australia: Palgrave Macmillan, 2004.
Rieff, David. *A Bed for the Night: Humanitarianism in Crisis.* New York: Simon & Schuster, 2002.
Vaux, Anthony. *The Selfish Altruist: Relief Work in Famine and War.* London: Earthscan Publications, 2001.

pillage

Pillage—the act of looting or plundering property—has long been associated as a justifiable reward for victory and compensation for assuming the risks of combat. Pillage is banned under international law. The Hague Convention of 1907 declared: "The pillage of a town or place, even when taken by assault, is prohibited." The GENEVA CONVENTIONS of 1949 reaffirmed the ban on pillage in the most succinct and emphatic way possible: "Pillage is prohibited."

During World War II the Nazis carried out a campaign of pillage possibly unrivaled in history, looting the patrimony of the nations they conquered and making off with thousands of artistic treasures from Europe's great museums. Even American troops were not immune from the temptation of pillage. It was only in 2004 that the U.S. government agreed to settle a lawsuit brought by Hungarian Jews over the looting of their valuables by American soldiers during World War II. The pillaged property included gold, silver, paintings, and furs, originally stolen from Jews by the Nazis before the end of the war. U.S. forces intercepted a train shipment of the goods but refused to turn it over to the original owners, who had survived the CONCENTRATION CAMPS, on the grounds that the property and valuables were "unidentifiable." Some of the items were appropriated by the U.S. Army and sold to soldiers, according to a 1999 report by the Presidential Advisory Commission on Holocaust Assets in the United States. In 2005 the U.S. government reached a settlement with the victims of the theft for $25 million.

International law distinguishes between *pillage*, which is defined as looting or plunder, and *requisitioning*, which is defined as the taking of "necessities" from a population for the use of an army of occupation. Until canning was invented, allowing armies to preserve and carry their food, armies would frequently seize food and provisions from the conquered populations. However, requisitioning has become more limited now that armies are better able to bring their own supplies with them. The Geneva Conventions specify that an army is legitimately entitled to requisition food or medical supplies but under two conditions: (1) the provisions must be intended only for the use of occupation forces—that is, the goods cannot be acquired for enrichment or profit, and (2) requisitioning can take place "only if the requirements of the civilian population have been taken into account." Fair value must be paid for the goods, in cash if possible. Nonetheless, international law does recognize that goods may be taken by an army "subject to the laws and customs of war," which can be interpreted as a justified basis under certain circumstances for seizing booty.

In spite of international laws outlawing pillage, the practice has continued: Iraqi forces pillaged Kuwait just before they were forced to withdraw by coalition forces in 1991, and Serb forces and militia groups pillaged Bosnia and Herzegovina and Croatia during the Bosnian War in the early 1990s as well as Kosovo during the 1999 war in that breakaway province.

Further Reading:
Gutman, Roy, ed. *Crimes of War: What the Public Should Know.* New York: W. W. Norton & Company, 1999.
Jackson, Nyamuya Maogoto. *War Crimes and Realpolitik: International Justice from World War I to the 21st Century.* Boulder, Colo.: Lynne Rienner Publishers, 2004.
Jokie, Aleksander. *War Crimes and Collective Wrongdoing: A Reader.* London: Blackwell Publishers, 2001.

Pinochet, Augusto (Augusto Pinochet Ugarte)
(1915–   ) *Chilean dictator*

The former dictator of Chile, General Augusto Pinochet Ugarte, came to power in a coup in 1973 and held power for the next 17 years. His rule was marked by brutality and a campaign of intimidation and terror designed to quash all dissent. It is believed that over 3,000 people were killed by his security forces, hundreds of thousands were tortured, and almost a million were driven into exile by fear and threats.

The future dictator was born into a middle-class family on November 26, 1915, in the Pacific coastal port of Valparaiso, Chile. He attended military school and graduated in 1936 as a sublieutenant in the infantry. Rising quickly in the ranks, he was a major by 1953, and that year he was made commander of a detention camp during a military crackdown on the Communist Party. It was an indication of things to come. At the beginning of 1972, he was appointed general chief of staff of the army, an elevation that came during a turbulent time. Protests were growing against the leftist government of Salvador Allende, who had been elected two years previously and whose socialist policies had wreaked havoc on the economy. Allende's government was also coming under pressure from the Nixon administration, which feared that Allende would turn Chile into another pro-Soviet Cuba. Plans were put in motion to destabilize the Allende government, and contacts were initiated between the Chilean military and U.S. intelligence agencies.

Unsuspecting, Allende sought to quell unrest in his armed forces by appointing Pinochet commander in chief

Chilean dictator Augusto Pinochet (left) with Salvador Allende, the president he overthrew in a violent military coup *(Landov)*

of the army in late August 1973. On September 11, 1973—only weeks later—the military staged a coup d'état. Allende reportedly committed suicide while defending himself in the besieged palace, and many of his top aides were arrested and subsequently put to death. The following day the four heads of the military services and the police designated Pinochet as president, a position he was to hold until 1990. Pinochet has stated in his memoirs that he was the mastermind of the coup, although other military officials have disputed this assertion, contending that he was more or less dragged into the plot just a few days before the coup actually took place. But there is no question that once in power he was quick to consolidate his rule and launch a campaign of terror to crush any opposition. At the same time he instituted a new economic regime, reversing the socialist policies of his ousted predecessor, returning nationalized businesses and industries to their owners, and lowering barriers to free trade. Inflation was brought under control, and the country acquired a reputation as a flourishing model of capitalism in Latin America, in contrast to the statist economies of many of its neighbors. But prosperity came at a high price. In 1988 Pinochet took a major gamble and announced a plebicite in which the Chileans could vote whether to extend his presidency an additional eight years. He evidently believed that he would have no trouble winning, but instead he lost. In 1990 he agreed to step down as president but only on the condition that he remain commander in chief of the army and that he serve as senator for life, a position that would confer immunity on him for any crimes committed while he held the presidency. With support from much of the military, Pinochet had little reason to think that he would ever have to stand trial. He was mistaken.

Pinochet had drawn the attention of the Spanish judge Manuel García-Castellon, who had earned a reputation for pursuing perpetrators of human rights abuses during the "dirty war" in Argentina (1976–83). Like his more famous colleague, Balthasar GARZÓN, Garcia-Castellon had pursued the fate of Spanish citizens who had been disappeared and presumably murdered by security forces. (In Spain judges also have a prosecutorial role in that they can bring charges as well as hear trials.) Just as Garzón investigated the 320 Spaniards who were killed in Argentina, Garcia-Castellon wanted to find out what happened to 100 Spaniards who were disappeared in Chile during Pinochet's military rule. He was particularly interested in clandestine alliances that had been formed between military juntas in Argentina, Uruguay, and Chile. In an effort to exterminate political opposition in these countries, agents would be sent across borders to carry out assassinations of political dissidents in what was known as OPERATION CONDOR.

In 1998 García-Castellon went to Washington in hope of obtaining secret files about Operation Condor from the FBI. He based his request on a 1990 legal assistance treaty that requires the exchange of information on legal cases between U.S. and Spanish law enforcement officials. Most of the material in FBI files concerned the 1976 car-bomb assassination of Orlando Letelier, a former Chilean diplomat who had been killed by Chilean agents in Washington D.C. Although García-Castellon reported that the FBI had offered its "full cooperation," he failed to obtain more information about the clandestine operation than was already known. Nor did the judge obtain much information about relevant files that might reside in other U.S. agencies, particularly the CIA, which had worked closely in the mid-1970s with DINA (National Intelligence Directorate), the Chilean secret police. Castellon-García did, however, meet with two DINA agents implicated in the Letalier assassination: Michael Townley (who was in a federal witness protection program) and DINA chief Manuel CONTRERAS, who was convicted in Chile in 1997 for masterminding the assassination plot. Contreras told García-Castellon that his actions had been sanctioned by Pinochet's government and insisted that the Chilean courts had had no right to try him.

It was from these interviews and the intelligence records he had gathered during his Washington visit that García-Castellon determined there was sufficient evidence to justify the interrogation of Pinochet. Pinochet, however, was adamant that no Spanish court could try him because of an amnesty program that he had implemented himself before giving up power in 1990. Recognizing that he did not have sufficient clout to pursue a case as controversial and charged as Pinochet's, García-Castellon handed off the prosecution to Garzón—who proved equal to the task.

In 1998 while in London, where he had gone to seek medical treatment, Pinochet was served with a warrant issued by Garzón and placed under house arrest. The charges included 94 counts of TORTURE and one count of conspiracy to commit torture that had occurred in the last 14 months of his rule. The time limit was dictated by a legal technicality: Britain had only signed the CONVENTION AGAINST TORTURE in 1988. Human rights advocates seized upon Pinochet's detention as a watershed, a sign that war criminals, no matter how powerful, could indeed be brought to justice. The Chilean government, fearing a military reaction, contended that Pinochet should only be tried in Chile. Others decried the arrest altogether, including former British prime minister Margaret Thatcher. There was also concern about Pinochet's age—he was 82 at the time—and his health. In the first legal action the lord chief justice, Lord Bingham, ruled that Pinochet was "entitled to immunity as a former sovereign from the criminal and civil process of the English courts."

Pinochet's case then went to the House of Lords, which in November 1998 ruled 3-2 that state immunity applied only to acts that were consonant with international law. Torture and abductions clearly were not legal functions of a sovereign, and thus Lord Bingham's justification was flawed. It began to look as though Pinochet would be extradited to Spain to stand trial, but only on torture charges relating to the period after December 8, 1988, the date on which Britain had ratified the torture convention. However, the British home secretary decided against extraditing Pinochet on humanitarian grounds.

On his return to Chile, the former dictator was greeted warmly by supporters when he stepped down from the plane, prompting the government to insist that he make no further public appearances. Chile was not the same country Pinochet had left two years before. He was no longer a dreaded or a powerful figure, and efforts began to bring him to justice on several fronts, including in Argentina, which sought his extradition for orchestrating the assassination of a political opponent in Buenos Aires. Several suits were filed in Chilean courts against him as well, his senatorial immunity was removed, and he was once more placed under house arrest. In July 2002 the Chilean Supreme Court, by a vote of 2-1, dismissed all the cases against him for medical reasons (moderate vascular dementia). The decision drew harsh criticism from many legal experts who believed that Pinochet was sufficiently in command of his faculties to defend himself.

Convinced that he would never have to be tried for his crimes, Pinochet retired to his estate in the countryside. Even after the bloody years of his dictatorship, Pinochet still had many supporters in Chile convinced that he had rescued the country from communism and paved the way for a dynamic economy regarded as one of the most prosperous in Latin America. For those who suffered from the repression or whose friends and relatives were tortured or killed, the failure to bring him to justice was a wound that would never heal. Pinochet's legal problems, though, were only beginning.

In May 2004 a Santiago court ruled that the former dictator could in fact be sued by families of the victims for his part in the repression of the 1970s and 1980s. This action occurred after Pinochet gave a television interview in which he appeared lucid, calling into question the Supreme Court's rulings that he was unfit for trial. One of the prosecution lawyers called the new ruling "a miracle." The Supreme Court was once again forced to decide whether Pinochet could be forced to stand trial. Chilean investigators reportedly began gathering evidence tying Pinochet to the 1974 assassination of General Carlos Prats, Pinochet's predecessor as commander of the Chilean army, and the 1976 Letelier assassination.

Before going to prison for 12 years in another case, Pinochet's former security chief, Manuel Contreras, threatened to expose misdeeds that he had personal knowledge of, saying, "General Pinochet needs to assume his responsibility." The family of Charles Horman, an American journalist who was abducted and presumably killed by Chilean secret police shortly after the coup, also announced their intention to pursue Pinochet in the courts. Even some supporters of Pinochet grew disenchanted with him when it was revealed that while in power he had secreted over $16 million in Chilean and foreign banks under five different aliases, belying the image of the austere, incorruptible general that he had tried to foster.

See also CHILE, HUMAN RIGHTS VIOLATIONS IN.

Further Reading:
Davis, William Columbus. *Warnings from the Far South: Democracy versus Dictatorship in Uruguay, Argentina, and Chile.* New York: Praeger Publishers, 1995.
Constable, Pamela. *A Nation of Enemies: Chile under Pinochet.* New York: W. W. Norton & Company, 1993.
Dinges, John. *The Condor Years: How Pinochet and His Allies Brought Terrorism to Three Continents.* New York: New Press, 2004.
Dorfman, Ariel. *Exorcising Terror: The Incredible Unending Trial of Augusto Pinochet.* New York: Seven Stories Press, 2002.
Kornbluh, Peter. *The Pinochet File: A Declassified Dossier on Atrocity and Accountability.* A National Security Archive Book. New York: New Press, 2003.
Politzer, Patricia, and Diane Wachtel. *Fear in Chile: Lives under Pinochet.* New York: New Press, 2001.

pogrom

A pogrom is an organized, often state-sanctioned massacre or persecution of a minority group, especially Jews. The word is derived from the Russian *pogromit*, which is variously translated as "outrage," "havoc," and "riot." As its etymology implies, the first pogroms took place in Russia in the late 19th and early 20th centuries, but their number—and intensity—increased after the assassination of Czar Alexander II in 1881. In 1903 crowds went on a three-day pogrom in Chişinău (now the capital of Moldova), resulting in the death of 45 Jews. Anti-Semitism was by no means new to Russia. What distinguished pogroms was their organization and direct or indirect government sponsorship. These pogroms played upon and exacerbated resentment against Jews and were frequently used to divert attention from political or economic problems. The abortive anti-czarist revolution of 1905, for example, precipitated a wave of violent pogroms, as the government tried to restore its credibility. If the czarist regimes did not actively encourage these attacks, they took few steps to put a stop to them. Soldiers and police looked the other way when inflamed crowds descended on the Jewish quarters or ghettoes. In some cases, they actively participated in the beatings, killings, looting, and arson. The pogroms hastened the migration of hundreds of thousands of Jews, who found sanctuary in the United States in the late 19th and early 20th century. Pogroms came to an end in Russia only with the 1917 revolution that brought the Bolsheviks to power. Pogroms continued to be carried elsewhere out, though. On November 9 and 10, 1938, the Nazis organized a nationwide pogrom—Kristallnacht (Night of the Broken Glass)—encouraging crowds to loot Jewish businesses and burn synagogues, setting the stage for a systematic campaign to eliminate the Jews from public and commercial life in Germany. There is evidence that the Soviet dictator Joseph STALIN intended to revive the pogrom in the USSR against Jews, just before he died in 1953.

Further Reading:

Klier, John Doyle, and Sholomo Lambroza, eds. *Pogroms: Anti-Jewish Violence in Modern Russian History.* Cambridge: Cambridge University Press, 1992.

Rubenstein, Joshua, Vladimir Naumov, and Laura E. Wolfson, eds. *Stalin's Secret Pogrom: The Postwar Inquisition of the Jewish Anti-Fascist Committee (Annals of Communism).* New Haven, Conn.: Yale University Press, 2001.

Pohl, Oswald (1892–1951) *Nazi economic czar*

Obergruppenführer Oswald Pohl was the head of the economic empire established by the SS (Schutzstaffel), the principal Nazi security force. Pohl was born in Duisburg, Germany, on May 30, 1892. Trained as a navy purser, he joined the NSDAP (National Socialist German Workers Party, later the Nazis) in 1926. He soon attracted the attention of SS chief Heinrich HIMMLER, who advanced his career. In 1942 Himmler appointed Pohl the chair of the SS Economic and Administrative Department (Wirtschaftsverwaltungshauptamt). This department consisted of five administrative divisions that handled the SS's financial and legal affairs, such as procurement and management of equipment, which included uniforms, buildings, and crematoria; the management of businesses run by the SS; and the Death's Head units (Totenkopfverbände), which administered the CONCENTRATION CAMPS. The Death's Head units routinely confiscated the possessions of Jews when they entered the camps, including watches, valuables, jewelry, money, and even hair and gold fillings. Pohl was also responsible for farming out slave labor to SS-affiliated companies such as I. G. Farben and Krupp.

Pohl was arrested in 1945 at the end of World War II and brought to trial by the Allies at Nuremberg. Together with 16 other SS officials, he was tried for crimes against concentration camp inmates and for exploitation of slave labor. Convicted and sentenced to death in November 1947, he was only executed in June 1951.

See also NUREMBERG TRIALS.

Further Reading:

Browder, George C. *Hitler's Enforcers: The Gestapo and the Ss Security Service in the Nazi Revolution.* Oxford: Oxford University Press, 1996.

Hohne, Heinz Zollen. *The Order of the Death's Head: The Story of Hitler's SS.* Classic Military History. New York: Penguin, 2001.

Pol Pot (Saloth Sar) (1925–1998) *Khmer Rouge leader*

As "Brother Number One," the leader of the Maoist Khmer Rouge movement, Pol Pot orchestrated a genocidal campaign in Cambodia that in a five-year period (1975–79) accounted for as many as 1.7 million deaths. Pol Pot was born Saloth Sar in 1925 (though experts have not completely agreed on his actual birth date) into a relatively prosperous farming family in central Cambodia. (The country was then under French colonial rule.) One of his brothers, Saloth Neap, recalled Pol Pot as a gentle and kind child, although he admitted that he had lost track of him until he spotted a poster of him identifying him as Brother Number One many years later. As a young boy, Pol Pot was sent to the capital of Phnom Penh, where he was raised by a cousin. He spent six years in a Buddhist monastery and became a monk for two years. Buddhism evidently lost its allure for him because he went on to study carpentry at a technical school. He still had time to become involved in politics and participated in the anti-French resistance. In 1946 he joined the Cambodian Communist Party.

Pol Pot earned a scholarship to study radio electronics in Paris, where his experiences reinforced his Marxist leanings. He hosted a series of communist cell meetings with other like-minded Cambodian students in his apartment in the Latin Quarter. His political activism might have proven too much of a distraction from his studies, because he failed his exams and lost his scholarship. By 1953 he was back in Phnom Penh. There he found a job teaching at a private school, a position he kept until 1963, but all during that time he was active in the underground Cambodian Communist Party, rising in its ranks and ultimately assuming its highest post in 1962 as secretary-general.

In 1963 Pol Pot and several of his confederates were forced to flee into the jungles in eastern Cambodia to avoid arrest. While in hiding he established a base in Kampong Thom, where he began to assemble a guerrilla force and plot a communist takeover of the country. It was in Kampong Thom, that the radical Khmer Rouge was born. There is some indication that he was influenced by the self-sufficient lifestyle of the hill tribes in the region. What struck

Pol Pot was that they did not need to rely on help from outsiders, were "untainted" by Buddhism, and conducted all their transactions without using money.

In 1970 a military coup backed by the United States overthrew Cambodia's leader, Prince Norodom Sihanouk. The Khmer Rouge began an offensive aimed at toppling the military regime, a war that played out against the backdrop of the Vietnam War, which had begun to engulf neighboring Cambodia as well. The Khmer Rouge gradually captured most of the country and by April 1975 stood at the gates of Phnom Penh. Once in power, the Khmer Rouge launched a radical utopian experiment intended to remake Cambodia into a completely self-reliant agrarian society. Although Pol Pot served as prime minister, the Khmer Rouge leadership maintained a chilling anonymity. As many as 3 million people were expelled from the cities and forced to farm in what became known as the "killing fields." Estimates of casualties vary, but most analysts believe that in the five years the Khmer Rouge ruled the country, nearly 2 million people were either killed outright for infractions as trivial as wearing glasses or speaking French (evidence that they were "intellectuals") or perished as a result of starvation and disease. Although Pol Pot seldom appeared in public, he is believed to have given the orders for the killings.

In 1979 increasing tensions between Cambodia and Vietnam led to war. Less than two weeks after its troops had crossed the Cambodian border, the Vietnamese took Phnom Penh, putting an end to the Khmer Rouge's five-year reign of terror. Pol Pot reconstituted his forces near the Thai border. No longer self-reliant, the Khmer Rouge now relied on China for arms and financial aid. It also retained diplomatic recognition from many Asian nations and the United States, which still considered the Khmer Rouge the legitimate government and the Vietnamese illegal occupiers.

Pol Pot retained his leadership position throughout the 1980s and early 1990s, but the exact nature of his authority is murky: In 1985 he was reportedly removed from military and political leadership and given an ill-defined defense position instead. Nonetheless, he is believed to have used his influence to bring the Khmer Rouge to the negotiating table in 1991, an action that was intended to lead to UN-sponsored elections. In 1992 Prince Sihanouk, who had once supported the Khmer Rouge, turned on them and gave his backing to the Hun Sen government installed by Vietnam. The Khmer Rouge withdrew from the peace process, boycotted the elections, and resumed fighting. But the guerrillas failed to make much headway, and dissension broke out in the Khmer Rouge ranks as to which direction it should take. The Hun Sen regime made it clear that it would not negotiate with the Khmer Rouge as long as Pol Pot was still in authority. In 1996 the Khmer

This photograph of Khmer Rouge leader Pol Pot hangs in the Tuol Sleng Museum *(Pablo San Juan/Corbis)*

Rouge split apart, and its moderate faction in the north, led by IENG SARY, defected to the government. But hardliners remained in their stronghold near the Thai border. In 1997 leaders of the hard-line faction mutinied against Pol Pot and arrested him. He was tried by a "people's tribunal" made up of his former comrades and sentenced to life imprisonment. Two months later, under house arrest in his jungle redoubt, he was permitted to give an interview to the press in which he declared, "My conscience is clear."

Certainly the "people's tribunal" was not the trial that Pol Pot's victims or human rights organizations wished for. Until this point, the United States had opposed a trial of Pol Pot for war crimes. "There's certainly a major American responsibility for this whole situation," asserted Cambodia scholar Stephen Heder in an interview with the *New York Times:* "A war-crimes trial could have posed a problem for the US because it could have raised questions about US bombing [in Cambodia] from 1969 through 1973."

Pol Pot would never have to face a war crimes trial, though. He died at 72—apparently of a heart attack—on April 15, 1998. According to one witness, his body was "burned like old rubbish."

See also CAMBODIA, WAR CRIMES IN.

Further Reading:

Chandler, David. *A History of Cambodia.* Philadelphia: Westview Press. 2000.

Coates, Karen J. *Cambodia Now: Life in the Wake of War.* Jefferson, N.C.: McFarland & Company, 2005.

Gottesman, Evan. *Cambodia after the Khmer Rouge: Inside the Politics of Nation Building.* New Haven, Conn.: Yale University Press, 2004.

Hinton, Alexander Laban, and Robert Jay Lifton. *Why Did They Kill?: Cambodia in the Shadow of Genocide.* California Series in Public Anthropology, vol. 11. Berkeley: University of California Press, 2004.

Kiernan, Ben. *How Pol Pot Came to Power: Colonialism, Nationalism, and Communism in Cambodia, 1930–1975.* New Haven, Conn.: Yale University Press, 2004.

———. *The Pol Pot Regime: Race, Power, and Genocide in Cambodia under the Khmer Rouge, 1975–79.* New Haven, Conn.: Yale University Press, 2002.

Pran, Dith, comp. *Children of Cambodia's Killing Fields: Memoirs by Survivors.* Edited by Kim DePaul. New Haven, Conn.: Yale University Press, 1999.

Short, Philip. *Pol Pot: Anatomy of a Nightmare.* New York: Holt Rinehart, 2005.

Ung, Loung. *First They Killed My Father: A Daughter of Cambodia Remembers.* New York: Perennial, 2001.

Priebke, Erich (1914–   ) *Nazi war criminal*

SS Hauptsturmführer Erich Priebke is a convicted war criminal who was tried for his responsibility for the March 1944 Ardeatine caves massacre in which German soldiers executed 335 Italian civilians in revenge for a bomb attack by a partisan communist group that had killed 33 German soldiers. Among the victims were 75 Jews, which made the massacre the largest single episode of the Holocaust in Italy during World War II. However, Priebke is believed to have been responsible previously for deporting 6,000–7,000 Italian Jews to Auschwitz and to have tortured political prisoners.

After Germany's defeat, Priebke was captured by the British and held in a prison camp, but he succeeded in escaping and fleeing to Argentina before he could be tried for his participation in the massacre. He remained in exile for the next 50 years without any attempt being made to bring him to justice. Then, in 1994, he decided it was safe enough for him to speak publicly about his role in the mas-

sacre, which brought renewed attention to an incident largely forgotten by the world. His interview on ABC television eventually led to a trial that would last for four years. In the interview with Sam Donaldson, Priebke maintained that he had only been following the orders of the GESTAPO chief in Rome, Lieutenant-Colonel Herbert Kappler. (Kappler was convicted in 1948 and sentenced to life in prison, but he managed to escape in 1977, only to die a few months later of cancer.) Priebke further asserted that in any case, the victims (ranging from 14-year-old boys to men in their 70s) were terrorists. Nonetheless, he did acknowledge that he had compiled the lists of those marked for death.

The interview stirred outrage among people who wondered how an unrepentant Nazi war criminal could have lived openly in Argentina for half a century. The Argentine authorities responded by placing him under house arrest, citing his advanced age and poor health to explain why they had not put him in prison. After 17 months of legal wrangling, the Argentine Supreme Court ordered Priebke extradited to Italy to stand trial. Priebke pleaded not guilty. While not denying his responsibility, he nonetheless insisted that the Italians who had attacked the German soldiers were to blame and that their execution should be considered a legitimate punishment. At the trial it emerged that Priebke had personally shot two of the victims, but the court found him not guilty because the statute of limitations made it impossible to convict him. He was not freed, however, since he faced trial in Germany as well. While Italian prosecutors appealed, Germany requested that he remain in prison until his extradition could be finalized. Then the Italian Supreme Court weighed in by repudiating the competence of the lower court that had acquitted him, although it declined to extradite him on the grounds that he was going to be tried for the same crime in an Italian court.

In his second Italian trial, Priebke was convicted and sentenced to 15 years in prison (with 10 years subtracted because of time already served in Italy and Argentina.) In 2004 some Italian demonstrators took to the streets to demand his release because of his advanced age. The demonstration stirred anger among Italian Jewish groups and city officials who had no wish to see him released. Priebke appealed, but the appellate court ruled that by committing first-degree murder, he should be imprisoned for the rest of his life. He showed no signs of contrition: "I gave Argentina 50 years of my life, and they don't want me. I fought for Germany during the war, now they want me put to trial for obeying orders." Still in prison in 2005, the 92-year-old Priebke is the oldest prisoner in Europe.

prisoners of conscience

The term *prisoners of conscience* is used by AMNESTY INTERNATIONAL (AI), a human rights organization, to refer to people who have been arrested or detained because of their political views or because they have been singled out on the basis of their race, religion, or ethnicity. According to AI, prisoners of conscience are those "who have not used, or encouraged the use of, violence; have not openly supported or recommended hatred for racial, religious or similar reasons to provoke people to discriminate, or to be hostile or violent; are detained or imprisoned because of their political, religious or other beliefs, or their ethnic origin, sex, color or similar reasons." Among those who fall into this category are individuals who have been arrested because they tried to hold a political demonstration or form a political party in a country where the exercise of democratic rights is banned. AI makes a distinction between prisoners of conscience and political prisoners. Under AI's definition, political prisoners are those who have been imprisoned because of their political background, which "may include being a member of a forbidden political party, or being involved in armed struggle against the government, or being victims of other kinds of systematic discrimination based on sex, race or other reasons." The principal difference, of course, is that a political prisoner, unlike a prisoner of conscience, "may have used or encouraged the use of violence."

Further Reading:

Benenson, Peter. *Persecution*. London: Penguin Books, 1961.

Winner, David. *Peter Benenson: Taking a Stand against Injustice—Amnesty International.* Milwaukee: Gareth Stevens Pub., 1992.

prisoners of war (POWs)

The treatment of prisoners of war (POWs) has long been a major concern of INTERNATIONAL HUMANITARIAN LAW (IHL). Although captured soldiers obviously lose their freedom, they do not lose their military status according to the Third Geneva Convention Relative to the Treatment of Prisoners of War. POWs, for instance, are expected to salute captor officers of a higher rank. Of paramount concern in IHL is the principle that POWs are entitled to humane treatment; the INTERNATIONAL COMMITTEE OF THE RED CROSS (ICRC) is mandated under Article 126 of the Geneva Convention to guarantee that POWs receive all the protections to which they are entitled. Although the ICRC has the obligation to visit POW camps to assess conditions under which POWs are being held, the convention also allows visits by other outside parties such as journalists and humanitarian aid workers. The convention also specifies that POWs must be placed in camps that do not jeopardize their health and safety; in other words, the camps cannot be located in areas where

the inmates are exposed to conflict or aerial bombardment. Prisoners must also be housed in humanitarian conditions that should meet the standards of the living quarters of the captor forces. They must be adequately fed and provided with competent medical care if they need it. The convention obliges the captor to ensure that the POWs are properly clothed, usually in their own uniforms. POWs also are guaranteed the ability to communicate with the outside world; under Article 71 they can correspond with families and are permitted to receive shipments of food, clothing, and other necessities.

There are provisions in the convention covering the use of force to impose discipline and prevent or punish escape attempts. Article 42 provides that the use of weapons against POWs is "an extreme measure" and that their use "shall always be preceded by warnings appropriate to the circumstances." Once hostilities cease, the Geneva Convention and Additional Protocol I of 1977 call for the immediate release and repatriation of all POWs. The protocol states that any "unjustifiable delay in the repatriation of prisoners of war or civilians" is a grave breach of international humanitarian law. There is no excuse to delay the release of POWs until a formal treaty is

Japanese prisoners of war being guarded by American soldiers during World War II *(Library of Congress)*

signed. However, a captor is not required to release or repatriate prisoners of war when there is a justifiable reason to believe that hostilities have not in fact ended—when, for example, a cease-fire is likely to be only temporary. Moreover, there are cases where POWs may not wish to be repatriated, as happened after the end of World War II, when many Soviet soldiers held in German POW camps balked against being returned to the Soviet Union. (Their resistance to repatriation was justified since thousands of returning POWs were labeled as traitors for having allowed themselves to be captured and shipped off to Siberian labor camps.) According to the ICRC, international law gives prisoners the right to refuse forcible repatriation.

See also ADDITIONAL PROTOCOLS TO THE GENEVA CONVENTIONS; GENEVA CONVENTIONS; GUANTÁNAMO DETAINEES.

Further Reading:

Berry, Nicholas O. *War and the Red Cross: The Unspoken Mission.* New York: St. Martin's Press, 1997.

Dormann, Knut, and Louise Doswald-Beck. *Elements of War Crimes under the Rome Statute of the International Criminal Court: Sources and Commentary.* Cambridge: Cambridge University Press, 2003.

Falk, Richard A. *Crimes of War: A legal, political-documentary, and psychological inquiry into the responsibility of leaders, citizens, and soldiers for criminal acts in wars.* New York: Random House, 1971.

Gutman, Roy, ed. *Crimes of War: What the Public Should Know.* New York: W. W. Norton & Company, 1999.

Jackson, Nyamuya Maogoto. *War Crimes and Realpolitik: International Justice from World War I to the 21st Century.* Boulder, Colo.: Lynne Rienner Publishers, 2004.

Moorehead, Caroline. *Dunant's Dream: War, Switzerland and the History of the Red Cross.* New York: Carroll & Graf Publishers, 1999.

private military contractors   *See* MERCENARIES.

prostitution, enforced   *See* TRAFFICKING IN PERSONS.

protected persons

INTERNATIONAL HUMANITARIAN LAW recognizes several different categories of individuals in conflict situations as "protected." Under certain circumstances, both combatants and noncombatants are entitled to protected status. The first three GENEVA CONVENTIONS of 1949 set forth standards for protection of combatants in international armed conflicts. *Combatants* are defined as members of an armed force who are also legitimate military targets. In addition to combatants, the conventions also protect associated military personnel including those who are HORS DE COMBAT—no longer able to fight; wounded and sick in the field; wounded, sick, and shipwrecked at sea; and prisoners of war.

The Fourth Geneva Convention of 1949 refers specifically to the protection of civilians. Whether combatants or civilians, the Fourth Convention states that all protected persons "shall in all circumstances be treated humanely, without any adverse distinction founded on race, color, religion or faith, sex, birth or wealth, or any other similar criteria." Protected persons must not be subjected to "violence to life and person, in particular murder of all kinds, mutilation, cruel treatment and TORTURE; taking of HOSTAGES; outrages upon personal dignity, in particular, humiliating and degrading treatment; the passing of sentences and the carrying out of executions without previous judgment pronounced by a regularly constituted court, affording all the judicial guarantees which are recognized as indispensable by civilized peoples."

Protected persons may not be killed, tortured, coerced, used as human shields, collectively punished or employed as subjects of MEDICAL EXPERIMENTS. The 1998 Rome Statute, which established the INTERNATIONAL CRIMINAL COURT, classified medical experiments as war crimes, whether they occur in an international armed conflict or an internal one. Protected persons cannot be forcibly transferred or deported from occupied territory, although there are exceptions in cases of emergencies or security concerns. Women must be "treated with all the regard due to their sex" and female prisoners of war are to be treated no differently from male prisoners of war. The Fourth Geneva Convention further prohibits "rape, enforced prostitution, or any form of indecent assault" directed against women. The wounded and sick, expectant mothers, the aged, children, clerics, and medical personnel are also entitled to special consideration.

The Fourth Geneva Convention classifies civilians into three categories: aliens in a territory that is engaged in an international conflict, persons residing in an occupied territory, and internees. Although the protected status of each of these groups differs to some extent, members of all groups are entitled to be treated with respect and given humanitarian treatment under all circumstances. Additional Protocol I of 1977 affirms the right of civilians to be protected against INDISCRIMINATE ATTACKS that fail to distinguish between combatants and noncombatants. Thus, any attack on a military objective is prohibited if it is known that it will also result in widespread civilian casualties disproportionate to the objective being targeted. Additional Protocol I also states that civilians under occupation are entitled to adequate food and medical supplies vital to its survival. Additional Protocol II applies the protections in Protocol I to internal conflicts, proscribing making civilians—as individuals or as a group—targets of attack. Attacks are banned against facilities—such as electric plants, dams, dikes, etc.—that are essential for the survival of the civilian population. Additional Protocol II (which technically is binding only on signatories) also calls upon military units to protect civilians and, when conducting operations, to distinguish between civilians and combatants.

See also CIVILIAN IMMUNITY; MEDICAL PERSONNEL, PROTECTION OF; ROME STATUTE OF THE INTERNATIONAL CRIMINAL COURT.

Further Reading:

Dormann, Knut, and Louise Doswald-Beck. *Elements of War Crimes under the Rome Statute of the International Criminal Court: Sources and Commentary.* Cambridge: Cambridge University Press, 2003.

Gutman, Roy, ed. *Crimes of War: What the Public Should Know.* New York: W. W. Norton & Company, 1999.

International Committee of the Red Cross. *International Law Concerning the Conduct of Hostilities: Collection of Hague Conventions and Some Other Treaties.* Geneva, Switzerland: International Committee of the Red Cross, 1989.

Protocol on Prohibitions or Restrictions on the Use of Mines, Booby-Traps and Other Devices

The Protocol on Prohibitions . . . emerged from the Anti-Personnel (AP) Mine Ban Convention (September 1995–May 1996) and was an outgrowth of the 1981 CONVENTION ON PROHIBITIONS OR RESTRICTIONS ON THE USE OF CERTAIN CONVENTIONAL WEAPONS Which May be Deemed to be Excessively Injurious or to Have Indiscriminate Effects. The AP Mine Ban Convention, which banned blinding lasers, fragments, and incendiary devices as well as the use of mines against civilians, defined an antipersonnel mine (APM) as "a mine designed to be exploded by the presence, proximity or contact of a person and that will incapacitate, injure or kill one or more persons." (Mines that are designed to be detonated by the presence, proximity, or contact of a vehicle rather than a person are not considered APMs.) By comparison, a booby trap is defined as a device "designed, constructed or adapted to kill or injure, and which functions unexpectedly when a person disturbs or approaches an apparently harmless object or performs an apparently safe act." "Other devices" are defined as "manually-emplaced munitions and devices including improvised explosive devices designed to kill, injure or damage and which are activated manually, by remote control or automatically after a lapse of time."

The AP II, as the protocol is known, makes each state party responsible for all mines, booby traps, or other devices it uses and obliges the state party to clear, remove, destroy, or maintain all mines, booby traps, and other devices in accordance with the protocol. Banned is any device falling into these categories that causes "superfluous injury or unnecessary suffering," and is intended against civilians or civilian "objects." The protocol mandates that mines should only be used for military purposes and against military objectives and, like bombs, should not be delivered by "indiscriminate means" or placed in such a manner as to inflict "excessive impact" on civilians disproportionate to the significance of the military objective being targeted. Warnings should be given whenever possible to civilians to protect them from being endangered by mines.

In December 1997 a more comprehensive effort was made at the Anti-Personnel Mine Ban Convention (also known as the Mine Ban Treaty, or Ottawa Convention), which sought to destroy or ensure the destruction of all APMs. The convention, which entered into force on March 1, 1999, became known as the CONVENTION ON THE PROHIBITION OF THE USE, STOCKPILING, PRODUCTION AND TRANSFER OF ANTI-PERSONNEL MINES AND ON THEIR DESTRUCTION.

Further Reading:

Cornish, Paul. *Anti-personnel Mines: Controlling the Plague of "Butterflies."* London: Royal Institute of International Affairs, 1994.

Harpviken, Kristian Berg, ed. *The Future of Humanitarian Mine Action (Third Worlds).* Sydney, Australia: Palgrave Macmillan, 2004.

Prokosch, Eric. *The Technology of Killing: A Military and Political History of Anti-personnel Weapons.* London: Zed Books, 1995.

U.S. Congressional Budget Office. *Convention on Prohibitions or Restrictions on the Use of Certain Conventional Weapons.* Report to Accompany Treaty Doc. 103–25. Washington, D.C.: U.S. Government Printing Office, 1995.

Protocol to the Hague Convention of 1954 for the Protection of Cultural Property in the Event of Armed Conflict, Second

The Second Protocol to the Hague Convention of 1954 for the Protection of Cultural Property in the Event of an Armed Conflict, adopted on March 26, 1999, affirms and elaborates on the 1954 Hague Convention, which sought to protect valuable cultural property in times of international conflict. The convention was drafted in response to the destruction of entire cities during World War II and set forth the standard that cultural property could be attacked only in case of "imperative military necessity." It suffered from a failure to define what was meant by "military necessity." In 1977 Additional Protocol I to the GENEVA CONVENTIONS took the position that only narrowly defined military objectives could be subject to attack, which meant that except in rare exceptions—for example, when a church or museum is used for military purposes by a belligerent and when no alternative to attacking the site is available—cultural property is immunized. The Second Protocol to the HAGUE CONVENTIONS took into account the enhanced protections offered by the Additional Protocols. The Second Protocol accords valuable cultural property additional protections so long as it is adequately protected under local law and is not used for military purposes or to shield military installations; these properties are placed on the List of Cultural Property under Enhanced Protection. Decisions as to which properties are entitled to inclusion on the list are made by the Committee for the Protection of Cultural Property in the Event of Armed Conflict, an intergovernmental committee established under the protocol. The protocol also criminalizes acts that violate the protections of cultural property conferred by the protocol and applies equally to international and internal conflicts.

See also ADDITIONAL PROTOCOLS TO THE GENEVA CONVENTIONS; CULTURAL PROPERTY, PROTECTION OF.

Further Reading:
Gutman, Roy, ed. *Crimes of War: What the Public Should Know.* New York: W. W. Norton, 1999.
International Committee of the Red Cross. *International Law Concerning the Conduct of Hostilities: Collection of Hague Conventions and Some Other Treaties.* Geneva, Switzerland: International Committee of the Red Cross, 1989.

public property, protection of
INTERNATIONAL HUMANITARIAN LAW outlaws the destruction of public property during armed conflict with certain important exceptions. The limited prohibition is found in Article 52 of the 1977 Additional Protocol I to the GENEVA CONVENTIONS. The protocol affirms that "civilian objects shall not be the object of attack or reprisals, and objects or installations ordinarily of civilian use are presumed to be civilian unless determined to be otherwise." However, the protocol does allow the destruction of "those objects which by their nature, location, purpose or use make an effective contribution to military action and whose total or partial destruction, capture or neutralization, in the circumstances ruling at the time, offers a definite military advantage." There are also exceptions for COLLATERAL DAMAGE—that is, unavoidable damage caused to property in the vicinity of a legitimate military objective. However, destruction cannot be wanton or indiscriminate.

The 1998 Rome Statute, which established the INTERNATIONAL CRIMINAL COURT, describes "extensive destruction and appropriation of property, not justified by military necessity and carried out unlawfully and wantonly" as a crime liable to be prosecuted. The Fourth Geneva Convention of 1949 prohibits the destruction of public property by an occupation force. Under those circumstances, the Fourth Convention states, the "extensive destruction and appropriation of property, not justified by military necessity and carried out unlawfully and wantonly" is a violation of international law. International law exempts public property from complete immunity if that property is appropriated for military purposes—for example, if a museum is used as a command post. But even in such cases, the damage inflicted on the property must be proportionate to its importance as a military objective. Again, the damage cannot be wanton—destroyed simply for the sake of destruction or a desire for revenge. This principle was put forward as early as the 1907 Hague Convention, which specified that destruction or seizure of property is prohibited unless it is "imperatively demanded by the necessities of war."

In practice, of course, it is often difficult to determine whether damage was proportional or wanton, since neutral observers are seldom present when an attack on property takes place. Only an assessment of the attack's military context of the attack would enable an outsider to determine whether a war crime has been committed or not. The bombed-out ruins of a church or a mosque, for instance, might be seen as evidence of a crime, but culpability might not be found if it turned out that the religious institution had been used by a belligerent to stage an ambush. In an opinion issued in 1994, the INTERNATIONAL COMMITTEE OF THE RED CROSS (ICRC) declared that belligerents "do not have an unlimited right regarding the choice of methods and means of warfare," adding that they are obliged to make "a clear distinction . . . between civilians and civilian objects on the one hand and combatants and military objectives on the other." Attacks on civilian property designed to spread terror in a civilian population are prohibited. The ICRC also emphasizes the concept of proportionality, declaring that "all attacks directed indiscriminately at military and civilian objectives and those which may be expected to cause incidental loss of human life, injury to civilians or damage to civilian objects which would be excessive in relation to the concrete and direct military advantage anticipated." International law has long called for the protection of "hospitals, ambulances, and any other object bearing the Red Cross," which are not to attacked or used for military purposes under any circumstances.

See also ADDITIONAL PROTOCOLS TO THE GENEVA CONVENTIONS; CIVILIAN IMMUNITY; MEDICAL PERSONNEL, PROTECTION OF; ROME STATUTE OF THE INTERNATIONAL CRIMINAL COURT.

Further Reading:

Falk, Richard A. *Crimes of War: A legal, political-documentary, and psychological inquiry into the responsibility of leaders, citizens, and soldiers for criminal acts in wars.* New York: Random House,1971.

Goldstone, Richard. *For Humanity: Reflections of a War Crimes Investigator.* Castle Lectures Series. New Haven, Conn.: Yale University Press, 2000.

Gutman, Roy, ed. *Crimes of War: What the Public Should Know.* New York: W. W. Norton & Company, 1999.

Jackson, Nyamuya Maogoto. *War Crimes and Realpolitik: International Justice from World War I to the 21st Century.* Boulder, Colo.: Lynne Rienner Publishers, 2004.

Jokie, Aleksander. *War Crimes and Collective Wrongdoing: A Reader.* London: Blackwell Publishers, 2001.

Meron, Theodor. *War Crimes Law Comes of Age: Essays.* Oxford: Oxford University Press, 1999.

Qaeda, al-

The most infamous terrorist organization of modern times, al-Qaeda was responsible for the 9/11 (2001) terrorist attacks on the World Trade Center and the Pentagon, which accounted for over 3,000 deaths. But while it was unknown to most of the world prior to those strikes, the movement had been conducting terrorist acts for many years. Al-Qaeda—whose name means "the base" or "the foundation" in Arabic—was founded in Peshawar, Pakistan, in 1988. Popular use of the name is credited by some to U.S. intelligence officials who found a reference to the al-Qaeda-al-Jihad ("the base of the jihad," or holy war) and assumed that al-Qaeda was the name of the group. (The leading figures of al-Qaeda do not refer to it as such.) Its ideology can be traced back to the Muslim Brotherhood, which arose in Egypt. Most of al-Qaeda's members subscribe to a strict Wahabi interpretation of Islam that is practiced in Saudi Arabia. Over the years al-Qaeda has expanded its list of grievances; whereas at first it claimed to be fighting to rid Saudi Arabia—home to Mecca, Islam's holiest site—of the American military presence established after the Gulf War in 1991, it later promoted a jihad to combat Western influence throughout the Muslim world. In a broader sense, some historians believe that al-Qaeda seeks to restore the caliphate, hearkening back to the 13th century, when Muslim hegemony extended throughout much of Asia and much of Europe. To achieve this goal al-Qaeda has vowed to overthrow authoritarian regimes in Egypt, Saudi Arabia, and Pakistan that have received strong support from the West. Israel is especially seen as an alien presence in the Middle East that must be eliminated.

The founder of al-Qaeda, Osama Bin Laden, a wealthy Saudi, is undoubtedly the most wanted man in the world. He received his military training in the war against the Soviets in Afghanistan during the 1980s. Bin Laden was among the mujahideen (holy warriors) who formed a paramilitary group called the Office of Services under Sheikh Abdullah Azzam. Ironically, like many other mujahideen, he had benefited from arms and financial assistance from the Central Intelligence Agency (CIA) and the Pakistani intelligence agencies, which had a common goal in seeing the Red Army driven out of Afghanistan after a decade of occupation. Just before the Soviet withdrawal in 1989, Bin Laden and Azzam parted company, reportedly because Bin Laden wanted to extend the conflict beyond Afghanistan. Over the next few years, Bin Laden devoted himself to building a financial and organizational structure for the group. In 1991 he was invited to establish a base in Sudan, which had come under the rule of an Islamic regime. For the next several years, al-Qaeda set up several businesses—trading companies, farms, construction firms, and diamond-smuggling enterprises—to build up its financial resources. The group also ran training camps where followers learned how to use weapons and plant explosives.

When al-Qaeda was linked to an attempted assassination of Egyptian president Hosni Mubarak in Addis Ababa, Ethiopia, Sudan expelled Bin Laden, but not before first offering to hand him over to the United States. However, at the time the Clinton administration had no legal basis to take him into custody. In 1996 Bin Laden returned to Afghanistan, where he entered into an alliance with the new Taliban regime there under Mullah Omar. The Taliban, which also followed a fundamentalist form of Islam, provided al-Qaeda with funds, arms, and—most importantly—protection. Al-Qaeda opened several training camps in its new home, recruiting militants from India, Chechnya, the Philippines, Kosovo, Yemen, Somalia, and Uzbekistan, as well as the Arab nations. Some recruits even found their way to Afghanistan from the United Kingdom and the United States. Bin Laden's principal deputy, Ayman al-Zawahiri, an Egyptian doctor, announced a fatwa (an Islamic decree) under the banner of "the World Islamic Front for Jihad Against the Jews and Crusaders," in which he declared that "to kill Americans and their allies, civilians, and military is an individual duty of every Muslim who is

able." Zawahiri, who was implicated in the assassination of Egyptian president Anwar Sadat, is considered the organizational genius of al-Qaeda; as of early 2005 he, like Bin Laden, has managed to avoid capture.

Al-Qaeda announced its debut on the world stage with a series of spectacular attacks, including a boat attack on the American naval vessel USS *Cole* in Yemen; the simultaneous bombings of the American embassies in Nairobi and Tanzania, which took over 300 lives in 1998; and the bombings of aircraft and movie theaters in the Philippines. In 1993 an attempt to blow up the World Trade Center in New York, which killed five people, made Americans aware of the terrorist threat from Islamic militants for the first time. Al-Qaeda is also blamed for the 1996 bombing of the Khobar Towers, which killed several U.S. military personnel, in Dhahran, Saudi Arabia. Al-Qaeda adherents volunteered for service in the war in Bosnia in the early 1990s and in the war in Chechnya between separatists and the Russian army.

After the 9/11 attacks, U.S. intelligence officials quickly identified al-Qaeda as the perpetrator, and Washington demanded that the Taliban surrender Bin Laden. Mullah Omar's refusal led to war in the fall of 2001. Within a matter of months, the Taliban and its al-Qaeda allies had been routed and largely driven out of the country. Both Mullah Omar and Bin Laden went into hiding, presumably in the isolated mountainous border region on the Afghan-Pakistani border. By the beginning of 2005 the two men were still at large in spite of the fact that the United States had placed a large price on their heads.

Although several top leaders of al-Qaeda have been captured or killed in the war on terrorism, as Washington has called it, most experts believe that the organization has metastasized, spawning several offshoots. Terrorist cells have sprung up in several countries, including Algeria, Morocco, Turkey, Egypt, Syria, Uzbekistan, Tajikistan, Iraq, Saudi Arabia, Kuwait, Indonesia, Kenya, and Tanzania. Cells have also been identified in France, the Netherlands, Germany, Britain, and Spain, finding sanctuary among supporters in Muslim émigré communities. According to *Jane's*, the respected British military journal, al-Qaeda has informal ties with at least 24 other terrorist groups, including the Egyptian Islamic Jihad, Abu Sayyaf, Jemaah Islamiyah, Hezbollah, Hesb' I Islami, Ansar al Islam, and the Islamic Group. Political observers also believe that many autonomous terrorist groups with no connection to al-Qaeda nonetheless claim an affiliation because it offers added prestige in the eyes of many disaffected people in the Arab world.

There is some debate as to how directly al-Qaeda can be linked to many of the terrorist acts that have occurred since the organization lost its base in Afghanistan, but there is some evidence that its adherents have been involved in bombings, kidnappings, and killings of Westerners in Indonesia, Morocco, Saudi Arabia, and Western Europe. Jemaah Islamiah, for instance, which is closely aligned with al-Qaeda, is believed to have been behind the nightclub bombing in Bali that killed over 200 mostly Australian youths in 2002. An al-Qaeda-affiliated Moroccan cell was implicated in the commuter train bombings in Madrid in March 2004 that killed 200 people. There is also considerable evidence to indicate that al-Qaeda militants have exploited the chaos in Iraq during the U.S. occupation there, carrying out roadside bombings, abductions, beheadings, and executions of Iraqis, Americans, and other foreigners. Al-Qaeda was also involved in the assassination of U.S. diplomat Laurence Foley in Jordan; a terrorist car bombing in Kenya; an abortive missile attack on an Israeli aircraft in November 2002; bombings of a foreign compound in Riyadh, Saudi Arabia; and the bombing of a synagogue in Istanbul in 2003. Whether Bin Laden has ordered all or some of these attacks, or whether he is aware of them in advance, is unknown. Many political observers believe that, as a fugitive, he is too isolated to be intimately involved in planning terrorist attacks but rather serves as an inspirational figure and advocate for those who do. Despite initial reports that he had been killed or was critically ill (he is said to have kidney disease) after he fled Afghanistan, Bin Laden subsequently resurfaced in a number of videos and audiotapes in which he exhorts his followers to continue the jihad and reminds the world that he hasn't gone away.

See also AFGHANISTAN, HUMAN RIGHTS VIOLATIONS IN; SAUDI ARABIA, HUMAN RIGHTS VIOLATIONS IN.

Further Reading:

Burke, Jason. *Al-Qaeda: Casting a Shadow of Terror.* London: I. B. Tauris, 2004.

———. *Al-Qaeda: The True Story of Radical Islam.* London: I. B. Tauris, 2004.

Gunaratna, Rohan. *Inside Al Qaeda: Global Network of Terror.* New York: Berkley Publishing Group, 2003.

Scheuer, Michael. *Imperial Hubris: Why the West Is Losing the War on Terror.* Washington, D.C.: Potomac Books, 2004.

Zayy-at, Montassar al-. *The Road to Al-Qaeda: The Story of Bin Laden's Right-Hand Man.* Critical Studies on Islam. Translated by Ahmed Fekry. Edited by Sarah Nimis. Ann Arbor, Mich.: Pluto Press, 2004.

R

Raeder, Erich (1876–1960) *Nazi naval commander*
Erich Raeder, German supreme naval commander from 1928 to 1943, was among the war criminals put on trial in Nuremberg at the end of World War II. The son of a headmaster, he was born in Schleswig-Holstein on April 24, 1876. He joined the Imperial Navy in 1894 and quickly rose in the ranks. In 1928 he was promoted to admiral and head of the German navy. While not a strong supporter of the Nazi Party, which took power in 1933, he backed Adolf HITLER's efforts to rebuild the navy and make Germany a great military power once again. In 1936, just before Raeder's 60th birthday, Hitler rewarded him with the title grand admiral.

In October 1939, shortly after the invasion of Poland, Raeder proposed to Hitler that the Germans invade Norway and Denmark, pointing out that without establishing naval bases in those countries, it would be impossible for Germany to successfully mount an attack against Great Britain. At the same time, Raeder advocated a policy of deploying greater numbers of U-boats and small surface vessels while establishing a strong German presence in North Africa and the Middle East that would allow Germany to dominate the Mediterranean. In Raeder's view, the planned assault on Britain—known as Operation Sea Lion—would also require the German air force, the Luftwaffe, commanded by Raeder's rival Hermann GÖRING, to gain air supremacy over Britain's Royal Air Force. However, the Luftwaffe's failure to meet this goal forced Hitler to cancel an invasion of the British Isles.

With the loss of the Battle of Britain, Hitler diverted his resources to an invasion of the Soviet Union (Operation Barbarossa), which Raeder opposed. As the German navy began to sustain a series of setbacks, Hitler became disillusioned with Raeder's performance and accused him of incompetence for failing to stop a large Allied convoy from reaching Europe. Raeder was subsequently demoted to the rank of admiral inspector of the German navy in January 1943. He resigned the following May and was succeeded as commander of the navy by Karl DÖNITZ, who was later appointed Hitler's designated successor just before the latter committed suicide in 1945, as the Allies were tightening their noose around Berlin. At the NUREMBERG TRIALS, Raeder was found guilty of conspiring to wage a "war of aggression" for promoting the remilitarization of the German navy and sentenced to life imprisonment. However, because of ill health his sentence was reduced, and he was released in 1955. He went on to write a memoir entitled *Mein Leben*. He died on November 6, 1960.

rape as a tactic of war
Rape and other forms of sexual violence have been used as a tactic of terror in many wars throughout history. The Nazis raped Jewish women on Kristallnacht (Night of Broken Glass) in November 1938 at the start of the pogrom against Jews. Soldiers of the Red Army raped thousands of German women in the waning days of the Second World War as they pushed into Berlin in revenge for German atrocities committed on Soviet territory. The Japanese raped Chinese women during the massacre of NANJING, and during Japan's colonial rule of Korea, Japanese soldiers exploited between 100,000 and 200,000 Korean women, turning them into sexual slaves called COMFORT WOMEN. The Pakistani army was implicated in rape that occurred during the nine-month war of Bangladeshi independence in 1971. According to International Planned Parenthood, an estimated 250,000–400,000 women in Bangladesh were raped in the war, resulting in an estimated 25,000 pregnancies. Some U.S. troops in the Vietnam War raped Vietnamese women, who suffered further violence after the war as thousands of boat people attempting to flee communist rule in frail boats were set upon by pirates. The UNITED NATIONS HIGH COMMISSIONER FOR REFUGEES reported that 39 percent of Vietnamese boat women between the ages of 11 and 40 were abducted or raped at sea in 1985. More recently, rape was employed as a deliberate strategy of terror in the 1980s and 1990s in

Liberia, Uganda, Ethiopia, Rwanda, Myanmar (Burma), and the former Yugoslavia. In Bosnia and Herzegovina, Muslim and Croat refugees uprooted by Serb forces in the Bosnian War reported that women were raped in public as part of a campaign of "ETHNIC CLEANSING," forcing families to flee their villages.

Rape is not only a crime directed against an individual but also targets the victim's family and community. In many cultures a woman who has been raped is stigmatized and considered a pariah; a child born to a woman who becomes pregnant by rape is especially at risk of being shunned by family and community. In that sense, rape is used to tear apart the bonds of family and society at large. Rape is also used as a manifestation of ethnic or nationalistic hatred. It has the additional effect of humiliating and shaming male members of the victim's family, since acts of sexual violence against women demonstrate the men's inability to protect their women. As a result, an enemy can traumatize a large number of people by targeting only a relatively few victims.

In spite of the frequency of its use as a tool of war, rape has been underreported and often overlooked by law-enforcement agencies. Nonetheless, rape has been considered a war crime for several centuries; as far back as 1474, Sir Peter von Hagenbach, an emissary of Charles the Bold of Burgundy, was convicted on charges of rape as well as murder and PILLAGE, tactics he used to subdue the Austrian town of Breisach. The LIEBER CODE, drafted by Francis Lieber at the request of Abraham Lincoln, made rape a capital crime for Union troops during the American Civil War. Article 46 of the regulations annexed to the 1907 Hague Convention calls for respect for "family honor and rights"; this provision was applied in the prosecution of Japanese officers for thousands of rapes committed by Japanese troops in Nanjing.

Although evidence of rape was introduced at the NUREMBERG TRIALS, none of the convicted Nazi war criminals was ever found guilty of that crime. The first time that rape was specifically cited as a war crime was at the TOKYO TRIALS of Japanese war criminals who were charged with violation of the laws and customs of war. Several Japanese officers were found guilty of allowing troops under their command to rape women in areas they conquered. Many legal experts contend that rape could be considered GENOCIDE if it is directed systematically at victims who belong to a particular race, ethnic or national group, as was the case in Rwanda and the former Yugoslavia. In January 1993, after a UN investigation revealed the prevalence of rape in the Bosnian War, the UNITED NATIONS HUMAN RIGHTS COMMISSION passed a resolution that identified rape as a war crime for the first time and called for an international tribunal to prosecute these crimes. As envisioned, this tribunal could try officers for ordering and committing rape; individuals who are in a position to stop rape and do not could also be held liable.

The most recent effort to make rape a crime under international law is found in the Rome Statute of 1998, adopted by delegates to a UN conference, which established the permanent INTERNATIONAL CRIMINAL COURT. The statute listed forced pregnancy as a war crime for the first time: "The unlawful confinement, of a woman forcibly made pregnant, with the intent of affecting the ethnic composition of any population or carrying out other grave violations of international law." The court's statutes also consider sexual slavery, enforced prostitution, and enforced sterilization treat to be CRIMES AGAINST HUMANITY as well as rape, whether they are committed in war or peacetime, as long as the acts are widespread or systematic in nature. If committed in an international conflict, these crimes may constitute a grave breach of Article 27 of the Fourth Geneva Convention of 1949, which states that women shall be protected against any attack on their honor, including rape, enforced prostitution, or any form of indecent assault. In addition, sexual violence can be considered an action willfully causing great suffering or serious injury to body or health, which is a grave breach under Article 147 of the Fourth Geneva Convention. If, on the other hand, these acts are committed during an internal conflict, it may be a serious violation of ARTICLE 3 COMMON TO THE GENEVA CONVENTIONS.

Women are not the only victims of rape. The INTERNATIONAL CRIMINAL TRIBUNAL FOR THE FORMER YUGOSLAVIA (ICTY) convicted Dusko Tadić, a Bosnian Serb, for violating Common Article 3, as incorporated into the statute of the Yugoslav tribunal, for forcing one detainee at Omarska camp, where he was a commanding officer, to bite off the testicle of another. A Bosnian Croat paramilitary chief named Anto Furundzija was found guilty by the ICTY for allowing a subordinate to rape a Bosnian Muslim woman. Furundzija's case was the first time a UN war crimes tribunal tried a case where rape was the major crime charged against a defendant. In its description of the crime, the tribunal chose to use the gender-neutral term *victim* in defining any person who had been raped or subjected to other forms of sexual violence.

See also BANGLADESH, HUMAN RIGHTS VIOLATIONS IN; BOSNIA AND HERZEGOVINA, HUMAN RIGHTS VIOLATIONS IN; ETHIOPIA, HUMAN RIGHTS VIOLATIONS IN; GENEVA CONVENTIONS; HAGUE CONVENTIONS; LIBERIA, HUMAN RIGHTS VIOLATIONS IN; MYANMAR, HUMAN RIGHTS VIOLATIONS IN; NANJING, MASSACRE IN; ROME STATUTE OF THE INTERNATIONAL CRIMINAL COURT; RWANDA, GENOCIDE IN; UGANDA, HUMAN RIGHTS VIOLATIONS IN; WOMEN'S RIGHTS, VIOLATIONS OF; YUGOSLAVIA, WAR CRIMES IN.

Further Reading:

Bloxham, Donald. *Genocide on Trial: War Crimes Trials and the Formation of Holocaust History and Memory.* Oxford: Oxford University Press, 2003.

Cooper, Belinda, and Richard Goldstone. *War Crimes: The Legacy of Nuremberg.* New York: TV Books Inc., 1999.

Dormann, Knut, and Louise Doswald-Beck. *Elements of War Crimes under the Rome Statute of the International Criminal Court: Sources and Commentary.* Cambridge: Cambridge University Press, 2003.

Falk, Richard A. *Crimes of War: A legal, political-documentary, and psychological inquiry into the responsibility of leaders, citizens, and soldiers for criminal acts in wars.* New York: Random House,1971.

Goldstone, Richard. *For Humanity: Reflections of a War Crimes Investigator.* Castle Lectures Series. New Haven, Conn.: Yale University Press, 2000.

Gutman, Roy, ed. *Crimes of War: What the Public Should Know.* New York: W. W. Norton & Company, 1999.

Jackson, Nyamuya Maogoto. *War Crimes and Realpolitik: International Justice from World War I to the 21st Century.* Boulder, Colo.: Lynne Rienner Publishers, 2004.

Jokie, Aleksander. *War Crimes and Collective Wrongdoing: A Reader.* London: Blackwell Publishers, 2001

Raznatovíc, Željko   *See* ARKAN.

Red Cross   *See* INTERNATIONAL COMMITTEE OF THE RED CROSS.

refoulement

Refoulement is a term that describes the involuntary return to their homelands of REFUGEES who have a legitimate fear of facing persecution. People who can legally claim refugee status are protected by international law from refoulement. This protection is found in the United Nations Convention Relating to the Status of Refugees and its 1967 Additional Protocol. Only when a person no longer claim refugee status is the prohibition against refoulement lifted.

Voluntary return is distinguished from refoulement by the absence of what are known as "push factors"—those influences that push a person to repatriate (go home). One push factor is coercion or force. Another push factor is denying a refugee the right to seek the advice or protection of a neutral body such as the INTERNATIONAL COMMITTEE OF THE RED CROSS. Reducing or denying essential services in the host country so as to force refugees to return would also be considered a push factor. However, refoulement can also be said to occur if a person claiming refugee status is kept in ignorance or is misinformed as to the actual conditions in his homeland and is convinced to return. The United Nations HIGH COMMISSIONER FOR REFUGEES (UNHCR) has stated in the Repatriation Handbook that "[o]nly an informed decision can be a voluntary decision." Some

human rights advocates have charged that Australia was wrong to try to repatriate detainees from Afghanistan temporarily settled on the Pacific island of Nauru both because the Afghanis were given no choice and because they had no access to objective and reliable information about what conditions obtained in Afghanistan. However, questions have been raised about exactly which persons should be considered immune from refoulement and who is entitled to claim refugee status. Would illegal aliens, for instance, have the same rights as those who are legally admitted to another country? In addition, the nature of many regional conflicts has made it more difficult, if not impossible, to distinguish between those who are legitimate refugees and those who are pretending to be refugees to escape punishment for crimes committed in the territory they have fled. This situation arose when hundreds of thousands of Hutus made their way across the border of then Zaire (now Democratic Republic of the Congo) after the 1994 genocide in neighboring RWANDA. Most of those who sought sanctuary were civilians but among them were Hutu militants responsible for many of the killings of Tutsi civilians in their native land. In the chaos the UNHCR officials had little way of knowing which people had committed crimes and which were should be guaranteed protection from refoulement because they had a legitimate fear of persecution if forced to return to Rwanda. The UNHCR decided to confer protected status on all the Hutus without making an effort to separate out the killers for fear of sending innocent refugees back. Two years later, though the Tutsi-led Rwandan army pushed into eastern Zaire and forced most of the refugees back anyway.

See also AFGHANISTAN, HUMAN RIGHTS VIOLATIONS IN; CONGO, DEMOCRATIC REPUBLIC OF THE, WAR CRIMES IN; RWANDA, GENOCIDE IN.

Further Reading:
Fritz, Mark. *Lost on Earth: Nomads of the New World.* New York: Routledge, 2000.

Groenewold, Julia, and Doctors Without Borders. *World in Crisis: The Politics of Survival at the End of the Twentieth Century.* London: Routledge, 1996.

Gutman, Roy, ed. *Crimes of War: What the Public Should Know.* New York: W. W. Norton & Company, 1999.

Helton, Arthur C. *The Price of Indifference: Refugees and Humanitarian Action in the New Century.* A Council on Foreign Relations Book. Oxford: Oxford University Press, 2002.

Hyndman, Jennifer. *Managing Displacement: Refugees and the Politics of Humanitarianism.* Minneapolis: University of Minnesota Press, 2000.

Ingleby, David, ed. *Forced Migration and Mental Health: Rethinking the Care of Refugees and Displaced Persons.* International and Cultural Psychology: Topics, Issues, and Directions. New York: Plenum US, 2004.

Lebanese refugees in Beirut, 1978 *(United Nations)*

Lischer, Sarah Kenyon. *Dangerous Sanctuaries: Refugee Camps, Civil War, and the Dilemmas of Humanitarian Aid.* Cornell Studies in Security Affairs. Ithaca, N.Y.: Cornell University Press, 2005.

Moorehead, Caroline. *Human Cargo: A Journey among Refugees.* New York: Henry Holt and Co., 2005.

Ogata, Sadako, and Kofi Annan. *The Turbulent Decade: Confronting the Refugee Crises of the 1990s.* New York: W. W. Norton & Company, 2005.

refugees

Refugees are defined as people who are forced to leave their homes in order to seek safety or refuge elsewhere. Many factors can lead to a person becoming a refugee, but conflict, persecution, economic deprivation, natural disas-ter, and harsh living and working conditions are among the major causes. The United Nations defines the term *refugees* more narrowly as "persons who are outside their country and cannot return owing to a well-founded fear of persecution because of their race, religion, nationality, political opinion, or membership in a particular social group."

At the beginning of 2002, the UNITED NATIONS HIGH COMMISSIONER FOR REFUGEES (UNHCR) estimated that there were more than 12 million refugees in the world. The refugee population has remained relatively stable for two decades. (In 1981 there were an estimated 10 million refugees.) Asia has played host to nearly 50 percent of the world's refugee population; Africa and Europe have offered sanctuary to just over 20 percent. Refugees are accorded certain protections under international law that are not granted to INTERNALLY DISPLACED PERSONS (IDPs) who have not crossed international borders. (Internally displaced persons are described by the UN as "persons who have been forced or obliged to flee or to leave their homes or places of habitual residence, in particular, as a result of, or in order to avoid the effects of, armed conflict, situations of generalized violence, violations of human rights, or natural or human-made disasters, and who have not crossed an internationally recognized state border." There are an estimated 20–25 million IDPs in the world, far greater than the number of refugees.) International law requires governments to grant asylum to refugees who have a legitimate fear of persecution if they are returned to their homelands. In principle, states are obliged to provide shelter, food, and other vital resources to refugees and are prohibited from repatriating them so long as conditions remain unsafe in their countries of origin.

For all intents and purposes, many refugees have become permanent inhabitants of their host countries; thousands of Afghans, for instance, remain in refugee camps in Pakistan, having taken refuge there in the 1980s after the Soviet invasion of their country. There are thought to be over 3.5 million Afghan refugees living abroad—the largest refugee population in the world—although some have begun to return since the overthrow of the TALIBAN regime in 2001. New refugee populations have been created (or else prevented from returning home) in recent years due to conflicts in Afghanistan, Iraq, Angola, Sudan, the Democratic Republic of the Congo, Burundi, and Bosnia and Herzegovina. Each of these conflict areas has added another 400,000 refugees to the total. A potential refugee crisis is brewing as a result of economic and political instability in Communist North Korea; many desperate North Koreans have tried to find refuge in China and Russia in the hope of eventually finding asylum in South Korea, the United States, or elsewhere. The Western Hemisphere has seen large influxes of refugees fleeing political oppression and destitution in Cuba and Haiti. The emergence of a refugee problem is often the first signal the world has of political dislocation in the country from which refugees are fleeing. Europe has also begun to grapple with a tide of African and central Asian refugees who risk their lives to make the treacherous sea crossing.

Like the United States, European countries have become increasingly restrictive and more discriminating about according refugee status. Ideas have been floated to "outsource" the refugee problem by establishing temporary havens outside of Europe for asylum seekers; one such zone, for instance, was proposed for Libya to prevent refugees from sub-Saharan countries from reaching European shores. In the United States, refugees from Haiti are at risk of being repatriated because they are deemed to be economic refugees seeking jobs rather than people who fear political violence. Cuban refugees, on the other hand, are granted refugee status under a program called humanitarian parole. The UN High Commissioner for Refugees, the leading international agency for refugee issues, has promoted three ways to protect refugees: voluntary repatriation, settlement in the host country, and third-country resettlement.

See also ASYLUM, POLITICAL; DISPLACED PERSON CAMPS; REFOULEMENT; RELIGIOUS PERSECUTION.

Further Reading:

Fritz, Mark. *Lost on Earth: Nomads of the New World.* New York: Routledge, 2000.

Groenewold, Julia, and Doctors Without Borders. *World in Crisis: The Politics of Survival at the End of the Twentieth Century.* London: Routledge, 1996.

Gutman, Roy, ed. *Crimes of War: What the Public Should Know.* New York: W. W. Norton & Company, 1999.

Helton, Arthur C. *The Price of Indifference: Refugees and Humanitarian Action in the New Century.* A Council on Foreign Relations Book. Oxford: Oxford University Press, 2002.

Hyndman, Jennifer. *Managing Displacement: Refugees and the Politics of Humanitarianism.* Minneapolis: University of Minnesota Press, 2000.

Ingleby, David, ed. *Forced Migration and Mental Health: Rethinking the Care of Refugees and Displaced Persons.* International and Cultural Psychology: Topics, Issues, and Directions. New York: Plenum US, 2004.

Lischer, Sarah Kenyon. *Dangerous Sanctuaries: Refugee Camps, Civil War, and the Dilemmas of Humanitarian Aid.* Cornell Studies in Security Affairs. Ithaca, N.Y.: Cornell University Press, 2005.

Moorehead, Caroline. *Human Cargo: A Journey among Refugees.* New York: Henry Holt and Co., 2005.

Ogata, Sadako, and Kofi Annan. *The Turbulent Decade: Confronting the Refugee Crises of the 1990s.* New York: W. W. Norton & Company, 2005.

Refugees International

A nongovernmental organization (NGO) established in 1979, Refugees International (RI) describes its mission as generating "lifesaving humanitarian assistance and protection for displaced people around the world" while working to put an end to conditions that create displacement in the first place. RI states that its foremost role is to act as "a witness to the suffering of the displaced." Representatives of the organization spend time in the field, gathering information from people affected by war as well as from NGOs and relevant agencies. Based in Washington, D.C., RI regularly sends representatives on assessment missions to regions where war-affected populations have been forgotten by the rest of the world. In 2004 RI was involved in 20 countries where displacement is a critical problem, including the Darfur region of Sudan, Ethiopia, Bangladesh, Liberia, Haiti, Uganda, and Cambodia. RI seeks to identify the most urgent needs of REFUGEES and the internally displaced and then find solutions for them. To do this, the organization conducts advocacy campaigns intended to influence various governments and the United Nations. It is funded by individuals, foundations, and corporations.

The concept of RI originated with Sue Mortan, an American expatriate living in Asia. In 1979 she became aware of the problem of displaced people when she witnessed some 40,000 Cambodians being forced back into their war-torn country after taking refuge on the Thai border in 1979. She envisioned Refugees International as a "global voice for the world's dispossessed." She later joined a handful of protesters in front of the White House, calling for the protection of Indonesian refugees. President Jimmy Carter subsequently ordered U.S. naval vessels to rescue "boat people" fleeing Vietnam in fragile fishing boats. RI grew out of that initial effort.

See also DISPLACED PERSON CAMPS.

Further Reading:
Aall, Pamela R., Daniel Miltenberger, and George Weiss. *IGOs, NGOs, and the Military in Peace and Relief Operations.* Washington, D.C.: United States Institute of Peace Press, 2000.
Byman, Daniel, Ian Lesser, Bruce Pirnie, Cheryl Benard, and Matthew Waxman. *Strengthening the Partnership: Improving Military Coordination with Relief Agencies and Allies in Humanitarian Operations.* Santa Monica, Calif. Rand Corporation (NBN), 2000.
Erskins, Toni. *Can Institutions Have Responsibilities: Collective Moral Agency and International Relations.* Global Issues Series. Sydney, Australia: Palgrave Macmillan, 2004.
Lischer, Sarah Kenyon. *Dangerous Sanctuaries: Refugee Camps, Civil War, and the Dilemmas of Humanitarian Aid.* Cornell Studies in Security Affairs. Ithaca, N.Y.: Cornell University Press, 2005.
Ogata, Sadako, and Kofi Annan. *The Turbulent Decade: Confronting the Refugee Crises of the 1990s.* New York: W. W. Norton & Company, 2005.
Rieff, David. *A Bed for the Night: Humanitarianism in Crisis.* New York: Simon & Schuster, 2002.
Vaux, Anthony. *The Selfish Altruist: Relief Work in Famine and War.* London: Earthscan Publications, 2001.

religious persecution

As a phenomenon, religious persecution has been going on since antiquity. It has probably accounted for more blood-shed than wars over ideology or resources. In many cases religious persecution is used as a cover for political or territorial objectives. In the Bosnian War of the early 1990s, for instance, Bosnian Muslims were targeted by Serbs because they had declared their independence (political), stood in the way of a greater Serbia (territorial), and subscribed to a faith that was introduced to the Balkans by Turkish invaders in the 14th century (religious). During the war, mosques were vandalized and sacked just as they were during the 1999 war in Kosovo, a separatist province with a majority Albanian Muslim population. Religious persecution is not always lethal, of course, but it almost always seeks to deprive a person practicing a certain faith of a number of rights, including the right to have an education, to work, or to own property.

Religious persecution became a focus of INTERNATIONAL HUMANITARIAN LAW (IHL) after World War II, during which millions of people had been slaughtered simply because they were Jewish. Freedom of religion was guaranteed in Article 13 of the United Nations Charter (1945), which declared: "The General Assembly shall initiate studies and make recommendations for the purpose of . . . promoting international cooperation in the economic, social, cultural, educational and health fields, and assisting in the realization of human rights and fundamental freedoms for all without distinction as to race, sex, language or religion." The right to practice one's faith without fear of persecution was also enshrined in the 1948 UNIVERSAL DECLARATION OF HUMAN RIGHTS. Article 18 of the declaration states: "Everyone has the right to freedom of thought, conscience and religion; this right includes freedom to change his religion or belief, and freedom, either alone or in community with others and in public or private, to manifest his religion or belief in teaching, practice worship and observance." In 1966 the UN General Assembly adopted two covenants that recognized a right to freedom of religion, including both freedom of belief and practice. In 1981 the United Nations expanded upon these protections by adopting the Declaration on the Elimination of All Forms of Intolerance Based on Religion or Belief, and by the subsequent creation of a special rapporteur on religious intolerance.

It is rare for the United Nations to intervene in a humanitarian crisis solely on the basis of religious persecution, although the organization has intervened in situations posing a threat to peace and security where religious rivalry or persecution was also taking place. The UN Truce Supervision Organization in Jerusalem (UNTSO) was deployed in 1948 to monitor the truce between Israelis, the majority of whom were Jews, and Arabs, the majority of whom were Palestinian Muslims. In 1949 the UN Military Observer Group (UNMOGIP) was deployed to maintain a cease-fire between India (predominantly Hindu) and Pakistan (predominantly Muslim). More recently, the United Nations intervened in East Timor, which is mainly populated by Christians and had been in the process of gaining its independence from Indonesia, which has the largest Muslim population of any country in the world.

Attempts to deter and prevent religious persecution are hardly limited to the United Nations. Many intra- and interreligious coalitions have brought together Christians, Jews, Muslims, Sikhs, Buddhists, and representatives of other religions. Such a coalition brought pressure on the U.S. Congress in the late 1990s to address religious repression in other countries. In October 1998 Congress unanimously passed the International Religious Freedom Act (IRFA), establishing an Office of International Religious Freedom in the State Department, which is responsible for producing an annual report on religious freedom and persecution in all foreign countries. The reports are intended for use in identifying countries that have "systematic, ongoing and egregious" violations of religious freedom. The reports are also to be used by the U.S. government in determining policies toward nations that practice or condone religious persecution. In recent years the renewed attention on religious persecution has put a spotlight on Chinese repression of Tibetan Buddhists, Christians, and followers of the Falon Gung and Russian persecution of certain groups, such as Jehovah's Witnesses, which do not have official state recognition. Efforts by the United States to mediate the 20-year civil war between the Muslim north and Christian south in the Sudan were also influenced by American Christian organizations.

Religious tensions are rising in many regions throughout the world, often fueled by economic deprivation, illegal emigration, and political discord. In recent years, for example, Western Europe has begun to experience a surge in violence against Muslim immigrants because of their perceived failure to adapt to the culture of their new homes. At the same time, some Muslim radicals have called for violence against Christians and Jews. Attempts by governments to neutralize religion as a factor in civil society often arouse as many passions as they are meant to allay. France, for instance, imposed a hotly debated policy banning the display of any religion by students in public schools, such as crucifixes, Jewish stars, or head scarves for Muslim girls. Some critics contend that these measures, however well intentioned, can also be seen as a form of religious persecution.

See also BOSNIA AND HERZEGOVINA, HUMAN RIGHTS VIOLATIONS IN; CHINA, HUMAN RIGHTS VIOLATIONS IN; EAST TIMOR, WAR CRIMES IN; INDIA, HUMAN RIGHTS VIOLATIONS IN; KOSOVO, WAR CRIMES IN; PAKISTAN, HUMAN RIGHTS VIOLATIONS IN; RUSSIA, HUMAN RIGHTS VIOLATIONS IN; SUDAN, HUMAN RIGHTS VIOLATIONS IN.

Further Reading:

Buergenthal, Thomas. *Religious Fundamentalisms and the Human Rights of Women.* Sidney, Australia: Palgrave Macmillan, 1999.

Mayer, Ann Elizabeth. *Islam and Human Rights: Tradition and Politics.* Philadelphia: Westview Press, 1998.

Vyver, Johan D. van der, and John Witte, Jr., eds. *Religious Human Rights in Global Perspective: Legal Perspectives.* Grand Rapids, Mich.: Wm. B. Eerdmans Publishing Company, 2000.

reparations

After the end of a war, reparations usually take the form of financial compensation paid by a defeated nation to the victors. Until the Thirty Years War of the 17th century, conquering armies generally took compensation in the form of booty, but monetary damages became more common during the Napoleonic Wars of 1792–1815. In 1871, after the Franco-Prussian War, the Prussians demanded that the defeated French pay about $1 billion in reparations (in today's dollars). After World War I, U.S. president Woodrow Wilson and the heads of France and Great Britain insisted on reparations from Germany that proved crippling: After making an initial payment of $250 million, Germany defaulted. Historians believe that the Allies made a grave mistake by demanding excessive reparations, which are thought to be one of the major contributing factors that led Germany to remilitarize and go to war again. After initially agreeing on a reparations policy for Germany after the Second World War, the Allies eventually went their separate ways. The Soviets obtained their reparations from East Germany, while West Germany (the Federal Republic of Germany) undertook to pay reparations to groups that had suffered egregiously from Nazi persecution, providing more than $700 million to Israel and to Jews who had survived the CONCENTRATION CAMPS or to their families elsewhere in the world. Japan and other Axis powers paid about $1.4 billion in reparations as well.

While there is established precedent for war reparations, the situation is more complicated when it comes to reparations as a remedy for human rights violations. Debate periodically flares up in the United States, for instance, about whether the U.S. government should pay reparations to descendants of African-American slaves. Many indigenous peoples have also asserted their rights to reparations, among them the Aboriginals of Australia. There is no question that indigenous peoples—a category that numbers about 600 million worldwide—have suffered from abuse, exploitation, and persecution at the hands of governments and corporations without receiving adequate compensation. Campaigns to obtain reparations, however, usually have met with limited success, if any. Most nations do not carry laws on their books obliging them to remedy human rights injustices or racial discrimination. The ability of victims to obtain compensation is constrained by statutes of limitation, the imposition of AMNESTY laws granting immunity to officials implicated in human rights violations, a failure on the part of the government concerned to acknowledge that an injustice was done, and the failure of the victims to forcefully make their cases or find sufficient funding to press their causes.

Although there is still no universally applicable code of laws pertaining to reparations, the UNITED NATIONS HUMAN RIGHTS COMMISSION has put forth a set of principles to assist victims of human rights violations; they are formally known as "The Draft Basic Principles and Guidelines on the Right to Remedy and Reparation for Victims of Violations of International Human Rights and Humanitarian Law." The Draft Basic Principles underscore the need for defined standards for the right to reparations in international law that "are amenable to universal application by all states, reflecting the various legal cultures and traditions of the world." The draft states further: "Having a single body of international principles and guidelines is the only way to guarantee the ultimate goal of reparation: the non-repetition of the act." But these principles are only recommendations and have no force in law.

See also ABORIGINALS (AUSTRALIA), MISTREATMENT OF.

Further Reading:
Cose, Ellis. *Bone to Pick: Of Forgiveness, Reconciliation, Reparation, and Revenge.* New York: Atria, 2004.
Gutman, Roy, ed. *Crimes of War: What the Public Should Know.* New York: W. W. Norton & Company, 1999.
Salzberger, Ronald P. *Reparations for Slavery: A Reader.* Evanston, Ill.: Rowman & Littlefield Publishers, Inc., 2004.

reprisal

Reprisal is a legal term in INTERNATIONAL HUMANITARIAN LAW (IHL) that refers to a particular kind of retaliation. It differs from retaliation, however, in that it is considered a self-enforcement mechanism rather than a form of punishment. Under IHL a reprisal can only be undertaken to force a belligerent to cease its violation of an international law, which has brought harm to the other party. If the same action were undertaken without a breach of international law already having been committed, it would simply be a breach of international law itself.

Reprisal must be a response, not an initiative. It can take the form of an equal injury to the offending party—effectively violating the same laws that the first party has broken already—or it can be disproportionate to the initial

harm and conducted with few if any constraints. The former type of reprisal is known as "in kind" and the latter as "not in kind." In general, reprisal by a belligerent for harm done by an adversary is in violation of international law. However, CUSTOMARY LAW has established some precedents allowing a "right of reprisal" as long as some basic "rules" are complied with. The right of reprisal requires subsidiarity (the failure to find redress by any other means), notice (official warning that retaliatory action is intended), and proportionality (the injury and suffering inflicted on the adversary cannot exceed that leveled by the enemy). The act of reprisal should also be temporary, lasting only as long as is necessary to cause the enemy to cease its violation.

As Frits Kalshoven points out in an essay for the CRIMES OF WAR PROJECT, the major problem with reprisals is that they are almost invariably directed against people who had nothing to do with the original violation that prompted the reprisal. Moreover, reprisals are seldom seen as justified by the party that is on the receiving end and can often lead to further reprisals by the other side. That is why for the most part international law has sought to ban reprisals as much as possible. Reprisal was explicitly cited in the 1929 Geneva Convention, which outlawed the practice against PRISONERS OF WAR. Subsequent treaties further limited the potential targets of reprisals. The GENEVA CONVENTIONS of 1949 broadened the protections against reprisals already in place for prisoners of war by prohibiting reprisals against civilians and objects (which would include vital installations such as dams and electric plants or cultural property). The prohibition is further elaborated on in Articles 51–55 of Additional Protocol 1 of 1977, although it is not mentioned in Additional Protocol II. Not all states that ratified Additional Protocol 1 have accepted a blanket ban against reprisals. The United Kingdom, for example, has taken the position that it would have the right to undertake "in kind" reprisals under certain circumstances. Reprisal has almost vanished from IHL, with one possible exception in which illegal methods of warfare are used against combatants.

See also ADDITIONAL PROTOCOLS TO THE GENEVA CONVENTIONS.

Further Reading:
Gutman, Roy, ed. *Crimes of War: What the Public Should Know.* New York: W. W. Norton & Company, 1999.
Jackson, Nyamuya Maogoto. *War Crimes and Realpolitik: International Justice from World War I to the 21st Century.* Boulder, Colo.: Lynne Rienner Publishers, 2004.
Jokie, Aleksander. *War Crimes and Collective Wrongdoing: A Reader.* London: Blackwell Publishers, 2001.

Ribbentrop, Joachim von (1893–1946) *German foreign minister*

Joachim von Ribbentrop, foreign minister of the Third Reich, was instrumental in forging a short-lived nonaggression pact with the Soviet Union in 1940. In spite of his claims that he was unaware of Nazi atrocities during World War II, he was found guilty of war crimes by the Allies at the NUREMBERG TRIALS and sentenced to death.

The son of a German army officer, Ribbentrop was born in Wesel, Germany, on April 30, 1893. He was educated at a Swiss boarding school and spent time in France and England, where he began working as a clerk with a German importing firm. He then moved to Canada to take up a job as a timekeeper on the Quebec Bridge and the Canadian Pacific Railroad. He continued his peripatetic existence, working as a journalist in New York and Boston, but when World War I erupted, he returned to Germany to join the army. In 1917, having sustained a war wound and acquired an Iron Cross for bravery, he entered the War Ministry; two years later he served as a delegate to the Paris Peace Conference to negotiate an end to the war. He spent the next several years making a considerable fortune in the wine business.

Although he joined the National Socialist German Workers Party (NSDAP) in 1921, Ribbentrop did not gain prominence in the Nazi hierarchy until 1933, when he became Adolf HITLER's foreign affairs adviser. In August 1936 Hitler named him ambassador to London. Ribbentrop's principal mission was to persuade the British to stay out of the war and make common cause with Germany against the Communist Soviet Union. He did not succeed in either objective, nor did he endear himself to the British public by posting SS guards in front of the German embassy or giving the Hitler salute to King George VI when he presented his credentials.

In 1938 Hitler appointed Ribbentrop as foreign minister, replacing Konstantin von NEURATH. In August 1938 he was deeply involved in negotiations with England and France to secure the annexation of Czechoslovakia. Hitler then called on Ribbentrop's diplomatic skills to forge a military alliance with Japan and Italy, which collectively became known as the Axis powers. In a deft bit of diplomatic maneuvering, Ribbentrop sent a telegram to Vyacheslav Molotov, the Soviet foreign minister, informing him about the pact and assuring him that the new alliance had no designs on his country, which, he said, was actually directed against the United States. (As it turned out, Molotov was already aware that the alliance had been formed, thanks to one of his spies.) Although Hitler intended to invade the Soviet Union, he realized that he needed a delaying action to give him time to advance his military buildup. Ribbentrop and Molotov met in Moscow to work out a nonaggression pact, which was signed on August 23, 1939. The pact remained in force until Germany launched its invasion of the Soviet Union in June 1941. The pact also contained a secret appendix that carved up Estonia, Latvia, Lithuania, and Poland between the two powers.

Ribbentrop played a comparatively minor role for the duration of the war. He was arrested in June 1945 by British troops and put on trial by the Allies at Nuremberg, charged with conspiring and waging aggressive war, war crimes, and CRIMES AGAINST HUMANITY. Although he maintained that he did not know about the CONCENTRATION CAMPS or the Nazi extermination program, the judges were not persuaded. He was convicted and hanged in 1946.

Further Reading:

Bloch, Michael. *Ribbentrop: A Biography.* New York: Crown, 1993.

Goldensohn, Leon, and Robert Gellately, eds. *The Nuremberg Interviews.* New York: Knopf, 2004.

Maser, Werner. *Nuremberg: A Nation on Trial.* New York: Scribner, 1979.

Marrus, Robert, and Michael R. Marrus. *The Nuremberg War Crimes Trial of 1945–46: A Documentary History.* Bedford Series in History and Culture Sidney, Australia: Palgrave Macmillan, 1997.

Weitz, John. *Joachim von Ribbentrop: Hitler's Diplomat.* London: Weidenfeld and Nicolson, 1992.

Ríos Montt, José Efraín (1926–) *Guatemalan dictator*

General Efraín Ríos Montt headed Guatemala from March 1982 to August 1983, a turbulent period during which the military conducted a brutal war against a leftist insurgency. A born-again evangelical Protestant, Ríos Montt was once quoted as saying that "a Christian has to walk around with his Bible and his machine gun." In 1954 he was involved in the CIA-backed ouster of leftist-leaning President Jacob Arbenz, declaring that Arbenz was holding the country "in the grip of a Russian-controlled dictatorship." After nearly three decades of successive dictatorships, Rios Montt assumed power in a 1982 coup. In 2001 The Asociacion para la Justicia y Reconciliacion, a Guatemalan organization set up to investigate abuses committed in the Guatemalan civil war, charged that Ríos Montt had promoted what amounted to a genocidal policy to destroy ethnic Maya communities that were seen by the military as providing a base for the insurgents. According to the association, the policy of eliminating leftist sympathizers led to attacks—directed at both Maya and non-Maya peoples—that "included inhumane killings, exterminations, extra-judicial executions, forced DISAPPEARANCES, TORTURE, rape, cruel treatment, mutilations, and persecution on such a massive scale that they constitute CRIMES AGAINST HUMANITY."

This policy, said the association, resulted in mass murder and mass displacement of the targeted communities "which forced them into sub-human conditions." It is not clear whether Ríos Montt directed these attacks, but it is reasonable to assume that he had some knowledge of them. Nonetheless, after Ríos Montt came to power, the U.S. ambassador at the time declared that Guatemala "has come out of the darkness and into the light." President Reagan later maintained that Ríos Montt had been given "a bum rap" by human rights groups and was actually only cleaning up the mess left by his predecessor, General Romeo Lucas Garcia. Ríos Montt attempted a political resurrection in 2003 when he tried to run for president, but the effort failed when he came in third—much to the relief of human rights advocates.

See also GUATEMALA, HUMAN RIGHTS VIOLATIONS IN.

Further Reading:

Archdiocese of Guatemala. *Guatemala: Never Again!* Maryknoll, N.Y: Orbis Books, 1999.

O'Kane, Trish. *Guatemala: A Guide to the People, Politics, and Culture.* London: Latin America Bureau, 1999.

Wilkinson, Daniel. *Silence on the Mountain: Stories of Terror, Betrayal, and Forgetting in Guatemala.* Boston: Houghton Mifflin, 2002.

Rom (Roma, Romany, Gypsies), persecution of

The Rom, also known as Roma or Romany and commonly misidentified as Gypsies, settled in Europe as early as the 14th century after migrating from the Indian subcontinent. They have long suffered from persecution, and never more so than under German occupation during World War II. It is estimated that as many as 1.5 million Rom perished between 1935 and 1945 at the hands of the Nazis. Even today, though, Rom face discrimination and harassment that contribute to high rates of poverty and unemployment. When he came to power in Germany in 1933, Adolf HITLER did not need to introduce new laws directed against the Rom; he only built upon so-called "anti-Gypsy" laws that had originated in the Middle Ages. However, he was confronted with an ideological dilemma: His well-known antagonism toward the Jews was based on the fact that they were non-Aryan, but because of their descent from Indians—the quintessential Aryans—the same could not be said about the Rom. The Nazis resolved this particular conundrum by simply denying the truth and insisting that the Rom were not of Aryan origin at all but were instead "subhuman beings" and members of a "lower race."

In September 1935 the Nazis enacted the racist NUREMBERG LAWS, which were intended to remove Jews from the political, social, and economic life of the country. Two years later the laws were applied to the Rom as well.

Under these laws, the Rom were also forbidden to intermarry people who were classified as Aryans. An individual was classified as a Rom if two grandparents had Romany blood. Like Jews, the Rom were placed in CONCENTRATION CAMPS—initially at Dachau, Dieselstrasse, Mahrzan, and Vennhausen—as early as 1937. Subsequently Rom were imprisoned at Buchenwald, where thousands were worked to death, tortured, shot, or hanged. Rom were frequently sterilized, a practice that began as early as 1933. When the Nazis determined on the Entlösung, or FINAL SOLUTION, only two groups were singled out for complete destruction: Jews and Rom. After 1938, Rom were deported from many parts of occupied Europe, including the Baltic states, Poland, Austria, Czechoslovakia, France, Italy, and Hungary and sent to concentration camps for extermination. But some Rom still remained at large, prompting the Nazis to conduct roundups of Rom in February 1943. As a result of these dragnets, over 10,000 Rom were placed in Sachsenhausen, and 16,000 were sent to Auschwitz. At both camps the Rom were brutalized and killed in a variety of ways and were also sent to the gas chambers for the first time.

Notwithstanding the systematic campaign to annihilate the Rom, their plight was ignored by Allied prosecutors at the NUREMBERG TRIALS. In fact, no war crime tribunals after the war ever investigated the atrocities that led to the deaths of so many Rom. This is not to say that there has not been official recognition of Rom suffering during the war; the U.S. Holocaust Memorial Council, for instance, has acknowledged that, like the Jews, the Rom were victims of a genocidal campaign by the Nazis. The distinguished writer Elie Wiesel, a Jewish survivor of Auschwitz, spoke about the Rom when he accepted the 1986 Nobel Peace Prize: "We have not done enough to make other people listen to your voice of sadness. I can promise you we shall do whatever we can from now on to listen better."

Nonetheless, persecution of the Rom persists in Europe, often fostered by neo-Nazis and other right-wing extremists. In the 1990s, for instance, neo-Nazis claimed responsibility for planting a pipe bomb in an Austrian village that killed four Rom. In another incident, racists attacked a hostel housing Rom asylum seekers in Rostock, Germany. The Rom have also found themselves in the middle of the ethnic conflicts in the former Yugoslavia; in 1994 they were persecuted by Serbs during the Bosnian conflict; then in 1999 they were persecuted by ethnic Albanians in the breakaway province of Kosovo because some of them were accused of taking sides with the ethnic Serbs. The Rom also suffer from routine discrimination and are often barred from restaurants, swimming pools, and discotheques. When Rom attempt to flee from countries where they face persecution, they may find themselves subjected to restrictive asylum policies that prevent them from finding refuge.

In spite of violence directed against the Rom, the United Nations did not formally address the issue until a resolution was adopted in 1991 that acknowledged, "in many countries, various obstacles exist to the full realization by persons belonging to the Roma community of their civil, political, economic, social and cultural rights and that such obstacles constitute discrimination directed specifically against that community, rendering it particularly vulnerable." A subsequent resolution entitled "Protection of Roma (Gypsies)," adopted the same year, urged the special rapporteur on minorities to give special attention to conditions in Rom communities. In the mid-1990s, as part of this effort, the Office of the UNITED NATIONS HIGH COMMISSIONER FOR REFUGEES (UNHCR) conducted a survey of Rom communities in Europe. The results were alarming: UN investigators found that persecution against the Rom in central and eastern Europe had the potential of becoming "one of the greatest destabilizing factors in Europe since the 1920s and 1930s." They identified three factors contributing to the problems afflicting the Rom: "increasing economic deprivation, increasing social instability, and the surfacing of long-suppressed ethnic hostilities . . . fuelled by the 'skinhead' syndrome that has made its way from Western Europe."

See also KOSOVO, WAR CRIMES IN; YUGOSLAVIA, WAR CRIMES IN.

Further Reading:

Bancroft, Angus. *Roma and Gypsy—Travellers in Europe: Modernity, Race, Space and Exclusion.* Research in Migration and Ethnic Relations. Aldershot, U.K.: Ashgate, 2005.

Lieseois, J. *Roma Gypsies: A European Minority.* Minority Rights Group Reports. London: Minority Rights, 1995.

Rome Statute of the International Criminal Court

The INTERNATIONAL CRIMINAL COURT (ICC), described as "the first ever permanent, treaty based, international criminal court established to promote the rule of law and ensure that the gravest international crimes do not go unpunished," was established by the Rome Statute on July 17, 1998. It was adopted by delegates of 120 countries participating in the United Nations Diplomatic Conference of Plenipotentiaries on the Establishment of an International Criminal Court. The statute set out the ICC jurisdiction, structure, and functions. It entered into force on July 1, 2002, after being ratified by 60 nations. Any individual implicated in a crime under the statute after that date became liable to being brought before the ICC, which sits in the Hague in the Netherlands. It should be noted that the ICC is separate from two ad hoc UN tribunals—the INTERNATIONAL CRIMINAL TRIBUNAL FOR THE FORMER YUGOSLAVIA and the INTERNATIONAL CRIMINAL TRIBUNAL FOR RWANDA.

See also WAR CRIMES, CATEGORIZATION OF.

Further Reading:

Dormann, Knut, and Louise Doswald-Beck. *Elements of War Crimes under the Rome Statute of the International Criminal Court: Sources and Commentary.* Cambridge: Cambridge University Press, 2003.

Romano, Cesare, Andre Nollkaemper, and Jann K. Kleffner. eds. *Internationalized Criminal Courts and Tribunals: Sierra Leone, East Timor, Kosovo, and Cambodia.* International Courts and Tribunals Series. Oxford: Oxford University Press, 2004.

Rosenberg, Alfred (1893–1946) *Nazi ideologue*

Alfred Rosenberg was the official National Socialist ideologist who was charged by the tribunal at the NUREMBERG TRIALS after the war with being "an essential part of the conspirator's program for seizure of power and preparation for aggressive war." A rabid anti-Semite, he also provided the Nazis with a philosophical basis for some of their most pernicious policies, including the theory of racism, lebensraum (the removal of non-Aryan people from German-occupied territory), the abolition of the Versailles treaty, and persecution of the Jews and Christian churches. As early as 1918, he gave a speech about the "Jewish problem," which represented his first foray into politics. "For Germany the Jewish Question is only then solved when the Last Jew has left the Greater German space," he wrote years later when Germany was already at war. "Since Germany with its blood and its nationalism has now broken for always this Jewish dictatorship for all Europe and has seen to it that Europe as a whole will become free from the Jewish parasitism once more, we may, I believe, also say for all Europeans: For Europe the Jewish question is only then solved when the last Jew has left the European continent."

Rosenberg was born to ethnic German parents in Tallinn, Russia (now Estonia), on January 12, 1893. As a student of architecture at the Riga Technical Institute, he joined a pro-German student group. A supporter of the Whites—the anti-Bolshevik forces—during the Russian Civil War, he fled to France when the Communists came to power. In 1918 he relocated to Germany, where he joined the nascent National Socialist German Workers Party (NSDAP) in January 1919—nine months before Adolf HITLER—becoming editor of the party newspaper *Voelkischer Beobachter* (National observer). His first publication in 1922 was entitled "Nature, Basic Principles, and Aims of the NSDAP," which set forth Nazi political objectives. He befriended Hitler and visited the future führer when he was imprisoned after the Beer Hall Putsch, an abortive coup attempt in 1923 against the government of Bavaria. Some biographers believe that Rosenberg helped Hitler write his memoir, *Mein Kampf* (*My Struggle*). While Hitler remained in prison, Rosenberg briefly served as head of the Nazi Party. Although Rosenberg was flattered by his appointment, there is some indication that Hitler chose him because he believed Rosenberg had a weak character and thus could pose no threat to his leadership once he was freed.

In 1929 Rosenberg founded the Militant League for German Culture. When the Nazis came to power in 1933, he hoped to become foreign minister but was passed over in favor of Joachim von RIBBENTROP. Instead he became the Nazi's chief ideologue when, in January 1934, Hitler made him responsible for the spiritual and philosophical education of the Nazis and allied groups. In 1940 he became head of the Hohe Schule (literally "high school"), the Center of National Socialist Ideological and Educational Research. When Operation Barbarossa—the code name for the German invasion of the Soviet Union—appeared to be going well, he received an additional appointment as minister for the eastern territories (though he had to share his responsibilities with Hermann GÖRING, Heinrich HIMMLER, and Erich KOCH). Nonetheless, he took advantage of his position to plunder money and valuables from Jews in Poland and occupied parts of the USSR. In advocating the policy of lebensraum, Rosenberg wrote, "The understanding that the German nation, if it is not to perish in the truest sense of the word, needs ground and soil for itself and its future generations, and the second sober perception that this soil can no more be conquered in Africa, but in Europe and first of all in the East-these organically determine the German foreign policy for centuries." He also sought to substitute a pagan-oriented mythology in place of Christianity: "Today, a new faith is awakening—the Myth of the Blood, the belief that the divine being of mankind generally is to be defended with the blood. The faith embodied by the fullest realization, that the Nordic blood constitutes that mystery which has supplanted and overwhelmed the old sacraments." By the same token, he advocated the persecution of Christian churches: "We now realize that the central supreme values of the Roman and the Protestant Churches, being a negative Christianity, do not respond to our soul, that they hinder the organic powers of the peoples determined by their Nordic race, that they must give way to them, that they will have to be remodeled to conform to a Germanic Christendom."

But no issue obsessed Rosenberg as much as the "Jewish Question." He sent representatives to the WANNSEE CONFERENCE to determine how the FINAL SOLUTION was to be carried out, a policy that had as its aim the destruction of the entire Jewish population of Europe. He also proposed an Anti-Jewish Congress, to be held in June 1944, but it was cancelled because of the war. At one point, when 100 Frenchmen were about to be executed in REPRISAL for attacks on German soldiers, Rosenberg proposed instead that 100 Jewish bankers be substituted for the purpose of "awakening the anti-Jewish sentiment," in the words of the Nuremberg Tribunal indictment.

At the end of the war Rosenberg was captured by Allied troops. He was charged by the Nuremberg Tribunal with "conspiracy to commit crimes against peace; planning, initiating and waging wars of aggression; war-crimes; CRIMES AGAINST HUMANITY." Found guilty on these charges, he was sentenced to death and executed with several other codefendants on October 16, 1946.

Further Reading:

Dawidowicz, Lucy. *A Holocaust Reader*. Library of Jewish Studies. Chicago: Behrman House Publishing, 1976.
Dwork, Deborah, and Robert Jan Van Pelt. *Holocaust: A History*. New York: W. W. Norton & Company, 2003.
Gilbert, Martin. *The Holocaust: A History of the Jews of Europe during the Second World War*. New York: Owl Books, 1987.
Roseman, Mark. *The Wannsee Conference and the Final Solution: A Reconsideration*. New York: Metropolitan Books, 2002.

Russia, human rights violations in

At the end of 2004 the Russian Federation appeared to be reverting to a form of authoritarianism after a relatively brief flirtation with democracy. New policies instituted by President Vladimir Putin have concentrated more power in the Kremlin; the Duma, or parliament, is overwhelmingly controlled by his political party. Most of the major television outlets—the principal source of news for most Russians—are now run by the state. Investigative journalists have been harassed, and some have been killed under mysterious circumstances. In such a political climate, it is not surprising to find that Russia's human rights record has worsened in many areas, but nowhere more than in Chechnya, where Russia has fought two wars since the early 1990s to end a separatist insurgency. Sporadic efforts to resolve the conflict have, however, failed. The war continues to account for atrocities, DISAPPEARANCES, and other forms of abuse in which both sides are complicit. The violence has spread from Chechnya to other parts of Russia, including Moscow, which has suffered from a number of terrorist attacks, most of them connected to the war. Security forces have engaged in TORTURE and violence, and the Federal Security Service (FSB), the successor of the KGB, operates with only limited oversight by the Procurator (chief prosecutor) and the courts. According to the Observatory for the Protection of Human Rights Defenders, a human rights nongovernmental organization (NGO), Putin's policy of "controlled democracy"—creating a strong centralized state—is being justified by the need to combat terrorism in Chechnya.

Security forces, which previously were charged with maintaining civil order, are becoming increasingly militarized as they are called upon to take part in conflicts like the one in Chechnya. Although the Code of Criminal Procedure bans arbitrary arrests or protracted detentions, abuses persist. Security forces continue to infringe on citizens' privacy rights. In general, the government has taken step to circumscribe rights that citizens had only begun to enjoy since the fall of communism in 1990. In July 2003, for instance, a new law was passed by the Duma that imposed several new limits on demonstrations, banning them altogether near government buildings, although some of the more stringent restrictions were subsequently modified. Regional and local authorities have shown even more of a disregard for human rights than the Kremlin, in some cases suppressing freedom of assembly and imposing restrictions on select religious groups, such as Jehovah's Witnesses, that do not have official recognition. (The Russian Orthodox Church is the dominant faith.) Members of certain ethnic groups have been singled out for persecution and attack by racists, resulting in beatings and killings. Victims of bigotry are more likely to be dark-skinned; those people who are Rom (Gypsies) or come from the Caucasus, central Asia, or Africa are particularly at risk. In many instances officials not only condone persecution of ethnic minorities but practice it themselves. People from the Caucasus are routinely harassed by security forces and often detained at checkpoints near the border with Chechnya. Chechen men are regularly the victims of targeted security operations known as night raids. Activities of NGOs—especially human rights groups trying to gain access to Chechnya—also suffer from harassment and restrictions. But human rights activists elsewhere in the country come under pressure as well, particularly in St. Petersburg, where legal proceedings have been instituted against NGOs as a means of shutting them down.

Political opposition figures have been assassinated, but there is little evidence that the government has seriously tried to identify, much less pursue, the perpetrators. The constitution bans the use of torture, violence, or other types of mistreatment of suspects by police, but human rights groups report that torture and beatings by police and other security forces continue nonetheless. The authorities have been slow to punish the guilty, in part because neither the criminal code nor the constitution offers a definition of torture, making it more difficult to bring charges. Human rights activists are also concerned about the confinement of individuals in psychiatric hospitals because of their political or religious beliefs, a practice that was common in the Soviet era as well. At one point, according to the Independent Psy-

chiatric Association of Russia, 10 Jehovah's Witnesses were incarcerated in a psychiatric hospital where doctors purportedly tried to "return to them their mental health."

As an institution, the military is rife with abuse; there is almost an epidemic of violent hazing—called *dedovshchina*—of new recruits that have resulted in deaths and severe injuries. In 2001 the chief military prosecutor announced that approximately 2,000 hazing incidents had been reported in the first half of the year. Threats of beatings have been used to extort money from recruits.

See also CHECHNYA, WAR CRIMES IN; RELIGIOUS PERSECUTION; ROM (ROMA, ROMANY, GYPSIES), PERSECUTION OF.

Further Reading:

Billington, James H. *Russia in Search of Itself*. Washington, D.C.: Woodrow Wilson Center Press, 2004.

Campbell, Ben Nighthorse, ed. *Troubling Trends: Human Rights in Russia Hearing before the Commission on Security and Cooperation in Europe*. Chicago: Diane Pub Co, 2003.

Meier, Andrew. *Chechnya: To the Heart of a Conflict*. New York: W. W. Norton & Company, 2004.

Orr, Michael. *Russia's Wars with Chechnya 1994–2003*. Essential Histories. London: Osprey Publishing, 2005.

Politkovskya, Anna. *A Small Corner of Hell: Dispatches from Chechnya*. Chicago: University of Chicago Press, 2003.

Tishkov, Valery, and Mikhail Gorbachev. *Chechnya: Life in a War-Torn Society*. California Series in Public Anthropology. Berkeley: University of California Press, 2004.

Weiler, Jonathan. *Human Rights in Russia: A Darker Side of Reform*. Boulder, Colo.: Lynne Rienner Publishers, 2004.

Witte, John, and Michael Bourdeaux. *Proselytism and Orthodoxy in Russia: The New War for Souls*. Religion & Human Rights Series. Maryknoll, N.Y.: Orbis Books, 1999.

Rwanda, genocide in

In 100 days in 1994, some 800,000 people, mainly members of the Tutsi ethnic group, were slaughtered in the East African nation of Rwanda, making it one of the worst atrocities in the bloody history of the 20th century. (Estimates of deaths range from approximately 800,000 to 1 million, or one in every 16 people living in Rwanda at the time.) The violence came about as a result of simmering tensions between the majority Hutus, who make up 85 percent of Rwanda's population of 7.2 million (as of 1994), and the Tutsis, who had traditionally enjoyed elite status. The Belgian colonial rulers contributed to the problem by rewarding the Tutsis with privileges and a Western education while denying political and economic power to the Hutus. The Belgians issued identity cards to distinguish the two groups, an act that would have chilling ramifications nearly a century later.

In the 1950s Hutu resentment against the Tutsis burst into violence; by 1963, after Rwanda had become independent, the Hutus were firmly in control of the country. Tutsis were massacred and subjected to discrimination and persecution. Many Tutsis went into exile in neighboring Uganda, where they formed the Rwandan Patriotic Front (RPF). In the early 1990s the RPF invaded the country, setting off a civil war lasting six months that ended only with a cease-fire—formally called the Arusha Accords—in 1991. In spite of the agreement, animosities between the ethnic groups only deepened: By early 1994 the situation had deteriorated to such an extent that humanitarian agencies began to evacuate their employees. The commander of the United Nations peacekeeping force, deployed in the country to supervise the Arusha Accords, recognized the danger and requested authorization from UN headquarters in New York to take action to prevent the conflict from exploding. But the United Nations failed to respond in any meaningful way.

The event that precipitated the subsequent GENOCIDE occurred on April 6, 1994, when the plane carrying President Habyariman, a moderate Hutu, and his Burundian counterpart was brought down by a rocket under mysterious circumstances. Habyariman had been involved in negotiations to reach an accord that would have diminished the political influence of Hutu extremists, leading to suspicion that they were responsible for the attack. In any case, the assassination served as a pretext to launch a massacre by Hutu militants that had been planned far in advance. For months Hutu propagandists had made wide use of radio and television broadcasts to incite violence against Tutsis. In late 1993 and early 1994, two Hutu radical political parties—the National Republican Movement for Democracy (MRND) and the Coalition for the Defense of the Republic (CDR)—had aggressively recruited unemployed young men to fill the ranks of their militias. At the same time the militias acted to procure arms from South Africa and Egypt and sought advisory assistance from the French military mission. (The French were longtime allies of the Hutus.) In February 1994 Hutu militants assassinated a moderate Hutu minister and killed several of his supporters.

Once the genocidal campaign was launched, checkpoints were set up throughout the capital of Kigali, and Rwandan army soldiers went from house to house killing Tutsis and moderate Hutus. Acting together with the Presidential Guard the militias succeeded in killing an estimated 20,000 people in the capital and its immediate environs within a week. No sooner had a group of Hutu politicians close to the late president formed a new government than the Tutsi-backed RPF in exile resumed the civil war. Two weeks into the massacres, the interim prime minister was assassinated, in addition to the 12 Belgian soldiers guarding him. The UN peacekeeping mission proved ineffective to forestall the atrocities. After Belgium announced the withdrawal of its 400-man peacekeeping contingent, the Hutu extremists decided to extend their genocidal campaign beyond the capital to the east and the southwest. Militias fanned out into the countryside to continue their killings; if local Hutus refused to collaborate in the bloodbath they, too, were killed. Local Hutu officials and broadcasters, however, often volunteered to help, directing the militias to Tutsi homes or to churches and schools where Tutsis had taken refuge. Survivors were frequently set upon and killed with machetes. In some localities, thousands were massacred within a matter of hours.

The militias would generally begin their "work" at eight in the morning and finish their slaughter by four in the afternoon and then resume the following day until all Tutsis in the community were killed. The objective was ethnic extinction. Those who tried to flee the targeted communities were stopped at barricades set up in the roads where soldiers or militiamen would demand to see their identity papers. If people were found to be registered as Tutsis, they would be killed immediately. Rape was widely employed as a means of warfare; many Tutsi women were gang-raped, sometimes for weeks at a time by men who had murdered their families. As many as 7,300 rape victims later died from AIDS; it is estimated that as many as 14,000 women have been infected. (A total of 500,000 people, or nearly 9 percent of the adult population of Rwanda, is HIV-positive.)

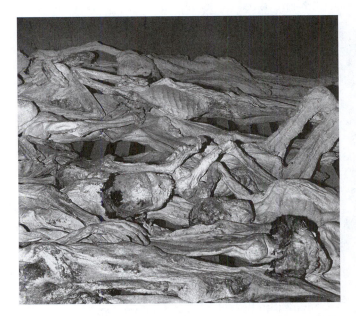

The remains of some victims of the Hutu-Tutsi massacre, Rwanda *(Exile Images)*

By mid-May 1994 Hutu militia leaders were exhorting their forces to finish "cleaning up" those Tutsis and moderate Hutus who had managed to survive the first wave of attacks. Catholic priests and nuns were not spared (though some of them actually took part in the massacres). The most widely listened-to Hutu radio station, RTLM, even went so far as to remind the extremists that Tutsi children, too, should be targeted. There were, to be sure, some Hutu officials and military commanders who refused to participate in the slaughter or tried—even at risk of their own lives—to protect Tutsi civilians. But their efforts, heroic as they were, were not enough to impede the savagery.

As the massacres continued, forces of the RPF were beginning to make significant gains on the battlefield against the Rwandan Hutu army. Attempts to broker a cease-fire came to naught, and by July 4 the RPF, under the command of Paul Kagame, had taken control of Kigali, spurring a mass exodus of almost 2 million Hutu soldiers and civilians into neighboring Zaire (now the Democratic Republic of the Congo), Burundi, and Tanzania. Hundreds of thousands of Hutu REFUGEES were crowded into squalid camps, dying in large numbers from disease, starvation, or lack of water. The same Hutu leaders who had instituted the genocide in the first place asserted control over the camps, supervising the distribution of food, water, and medical supplies to ensure their power. At the same time they announced their intention to return to Rwanda to complete their "work" of slaughtering Tutsis.

Although the UN Security Council had adopted a resolution on April 30, 1994, shortly after the massacres began, condemning the killings, the word *genocide* never appeared in it. Nearly three weeks later the Security Council authorized the deployment of a peacekeeping mission of 6,800 soldiers, called UNITED NATIONS ASSISTANCE MISSION IN RWANDA UNAMIR II. It was not until late June, however, after a great deal of bureaucratic wrangling, that a contingent of French troops actually reached Rwanda and established a so-called safe zone in the southwestern region of the country. Even then they were not permitted to use force. The United States remained on the sidelines, and the Clinton administration refused to publicly characterize the violence as genocide, even though the word was used in internal State Department documents that were later declassified.

Three years later, on July 1, 1997, the UN Security Council voted to establish a commission of experts to consider the idea of setting up an international tribunal to try those accused of perpetrating atrocities. Ironically, Rwanda, now led by a Tutsi government, voted against the resolution on the grounds that the proposed tribunal would not be able to use the death penalty; Rwanda did, however, agree to cooperate with the tribunal. Resolution 955, setting up the INTERNATIONAL CRIMINAL TRIBUNAL FOR RWANDA, was passed on November 8, 1994. The course of justice, though, has been painfully slow; after eight years the tribunal, based in Arusha, Tanzania, had only convicted 18 defendants. On their own the Rwandan authorities have arrested 120,000 individuals suspected of participating in the atrocities, but it lacks the capacity to put them on trial. For that matter, there is hardly any room to hold so many prisoners. Recognizing that it would take about a century to process all the accused, the government has released thousands of suspects, angering humanitarian groups. Some 5,000 have been rearrested on more serious charges than those originally leveled against them. To try to bring as many to justice as possible, the government has resorted to mass trials. In the biggest one, 105 were convicted and 37 acquitted.

See also ARMS, TRAFFICKING IN AND CONTROL MECHANISMS; RAPE AS A TACTIC OF WAR; UGANDA, HUMAN RIGHTS VIOLATIONS IN.

Further Reading:

Barnett, Michael. *Eyewitness to a Genocide: The United Nations and Rwanda.* Ithaca, N.Y.: Cornell University Press, 2003.

Gourevich, Philip. *We Wish to Inform You That Tomorrow We Will Be Killed with Our Families: Stories from Rwanda.* New York, Picador, 1999.

Dallaire, Romeo, and Brent Beardsley. *Shake Hands with the Devil: The Failure of Humanity in Rwanda.* New York: Carroll & Graf, 2004.

Mamdani, Mahmood. *When Victims Become Killers: Colonialism, Nativism, and the Genocide in Rwanda.* Princeton, N.J.: Princeton University Press, 2002.

Melvern, Linda. *A People Betrayed: The Role of the West in Rwanda's Genocide.* London: Zed Books, 2000.

Peterson, Scott. *Me against My Brother: At War in Somalia, Sudan and Rwanda.* London: Routledge, 2001.

Temple-Rason, Dina. *Justice on the Grass: Three Rwandan Journalists, Their Trial for War Crimes, and a Nation's Quest for Redemption.* New York: Free Press, 2005.

Rwandan human rights violators

Although it is well known that the 1994 atrocities in Rwanda took the lives of some 800,000 ethnic Tutsis and moderate Hutus, few people would recognize the names of the murderers. The United Nations–sponsored tribunal established in Arusha, Tanzania, to try suspects implicated in the genocidal campaign has convicted several individuals, but the caseload far outstrips its ability to bring to justice many of the worst offenders. Thousands more still await trial inside Rwanda, but the court system there is unequal to the task of giving the multitudes of defendants a fair trial. Nonetheless, a number of the perpetrators have been brought to justice, and it is instructive to make note of three of the cases because of the light they shed on the crimes that were carried out and the reasoning that underlay the court's judgments.

Akayesu, Jean-Paul

Jean-Paul Akayesu, a former official in Rwanda, had the dubious distinction of being the first suspect to stand trial for war crimes under the auspices of the newly formed INTERNATIONAL CRIMINAL TRIBUNAL FOR RWANDA (ICTR). More importantly, though, his conviction was an acknowledgment that sexual violence against women was a war crime. The ruling was the first time that an international court punished sexual violence in a civil war and the first time that it was determined that rape was used as an act of GENOCIDE as well as an act of TORTURE.

Born in 1953, Akayesu, a Hutu, was a teacher and school inspector before becoming a burgomaster, or mayor, of the commune of Taba, a position he was holding in April 1994 when genocidal warfare broke out in Rwanda, mainly perpetrated by Hutu extremists against the minority Tutu population. As mayor, Akayesu was responsible for maintaining law and public order in his commune, but instead he stood by as at least 2,000 Tutsis were killed in Taba between April 7 and the end of June. Many of the victims were fleeing killings elsewhere. Women were raped and threatened; those who were allowed to live suffered emotional and physical trauma. The killings were so widespread and so flagrant that there is no question of his not being aware of them.

Akayesu was arrested in Zambia in 1996 on a warrant issued by the United Nations, which had established the criminal court to prosecute war crimes. During his initial nine-hour interrogation, he insisted on his innocence. Nonetheless, the court had sufficient evidence to charge him with 12 counts of genocide, CRIMES AGAINST HUMANITY, and violations of ARTICLE 3 COMMON TO THE GENEVA CONVENTIONS, governing a state's treatment of civilians. It was only later that the indictment was amended to include rape charges as well and then only as a result of concerted pressure by nongovernmental organizations.

The trial lasted from January to May 1997, during which over 30 witnesses testified about the mass killing in Taba while Akayesu was in power. Four witnesses appeared to testify about sexual violence, reporting incidents of gang rape and murder. They agreed that Akayesu had done nothing to stop the rapes or killings of women. At one point a witness recalled him saying to the rapists, "Don't complain to me now that you don't know what a Tutsi woman tastes like."

Although rape is a violation of the 1949 GENEVA CONVENTIONS, the 1948 GENOCIDE CONVENTION, the 1984 CONVENTION AGAINST TORTURE, and it is considered a crime against humanity under international CUSTOMARY LAW, military or political authorities often have dismissed the gravity of the offense, labeling it an aberrant act of individual soldiers rather than as a willful pattern of terror. Akayesu mounted a vigorous defense, calling several witnesses and even taking the stand himself, but on October 2, 1998, the ICTR found him guilty and sentenced him to three life sentences for genocide and crimes against humanity and to 80 years for other violations, including rape and encouraging widespread sexual violence.

Gacumbitsi, Sylvestre

Former Rwandan mayor Sylvestre Gacumbitsi is one of several suspects implicated and tried for the 1994 genocide in his country. A Hutu, Gacumbitsi was tried by the ICTR and found guilty of organizing the killings of 20,000 people (though not of genocide), mostly ethnic Tutsis. He was sentenced to 30 years' imprisonment. According to the indictment, he lured his victims into a church, at Nyarubuye parish on April 5th 1994, where he promised them that they would be safe from marauding Hutu militants. He then proceeded to distribute weapons and urged Hutus to kill and rape Tutsis who had lived together as neighbors for years. He also was responsible for using rape as a weapon of war: He went around announcing through a megaphone that all Tutsi women were to be raped and "sexually degraded." Apparently he felt he should set an example. One witness testified that Gacumbitsi had raped her. After the genocide ended, leaving 800,000 Tutsis and moderate Hutus dead, he sought refuge in Tanzania, where he was identified by a television news crew. He was arrested shortly afterward in June 2001. In June 2004 Gacumbitsi was found guilty of genocide, extermination, and rape by the International Criminal Tribunal for Rwanda in Tanzania.

Kambanda, Jean

Jean Kambanda, the former prime minister of Rwanda, became the first leader of a government to be convicted of genocide. He was sentenced by the ICTR in September 1998 for crimes committed during the genocidal campaign by Hutu extremists four years earlier in which about 800,000 people were killed. Initially he had pleaded guilty and was sentenced to life imprisonment in 1999. In his appeal Kambanda claimed that he had been forced into pleading guilty, a defense the appeals court rejected in upholding the verdict.

See also RAPE AS A TACTIC OF WAR; RWANDA, GENOCIDE IN.

Further Reading:

Barnett, Michael. *Eyewitness to a Genocide: The United Nations and Rwanda.* Ithaca, New York: Cornell University Press, 2003.

Dallaire, Romeo, and Brent Beardsley. *Shake Hands with the Devil: The Failure of Humanity in Rwanda.* New York: Carroll & Graf, 2004.

Gourevich, Philip. *We Wish to Inform You That Tomorrow We Will Be Killed with Our Families: Stories from Rwanda.* New York: Picador, 1999.

Mamdani, Mahmood. *When Victims Become Killers: Colonialism, Nativism, and the Genocide in Rwanda.* Princeton, N.J.: Princeton University Press, 2002.

Melvern, Linda. *A People Betrayed: The Role of the West in Rwanda's Genocide.* London: Zed Books, 2000.

Peterson, Scott. *Me against My Brother: At War in Somalia, Sudan and Rwanda.* London: Routledge, 2001.

S

Sabra and Shatilla, massacre in

In June 1982 Israel's prime minister Menachem Begin ordered an invasion of Lebanon, which had increasingly fallen under the influence of the Palestinian Liberation Organization (PLO), then regarded as the greatest threat to Israel's security. Begin, together with Defense Minister Ariel Sharon (later prime minister), believed that intervention would allow Israel to manipulate events in its favor by eliminating the PLO's base of operations—it was recruiting more members from Palestinian refugee camps in the country—while installing a sympathetic regime that would make peace with Israel. At the time, Lebanon was embroiled in a civil war that divided the country largely along ethnic lines. Israel, however, looked on the Maronite Christians as their allies and proxies who still wielded considerable economic and political power, although they were outnumbered by Muslims.

On June 6, 1982, the Israel Defense Force (IDF) pushed over the border and moved all the way to the capital of Beirut, laying siege to the PLO stronghold in West Beirut for two months. The United States devised a plan to evacuate the PLO fighters from Lebanon, and a multinational force was dispatched to carry the evacuation out in August. Under the plan, the PLO, led by Yasser Arafat, left Lebanon for more hospitable quarters in Tunisia. Proclaiming that it had accomplished its mission, the force pulled out in September. Nonetheless, Israel contended that 2,000 PLO guerrillas remained in refugee camps and applied pressure to Lebanon's new president, Bashir Gemayel, a Maronite Christian, to send his forces into the camps to root them out.

On September 14, 1982, Gemayel was killed when a powerful bomb went off, destroying the headquarters of his Phalangist Party in East Beirut, a district largely under Christian control. The next day the IDF violated the evacuation agreement and entered Muslim West Beirut. The IDF provided military protection for members of Gemayel's Lebanese Forces, a Phalangist militia, and Saad Haddad's South Lebanon Army. These troops proceeded to enter the Sabra and Shatilla refugee camps, which housed 30,000 Palestinians and some Lebanese; Israeli tanks surrounded the camps, cutting off all access. Beginning on September 16, for the next 38 hours the militia carried out a massacre that, according to the INTERNATIONAL COMMITTEE OF THE RED CROSS (ICRC), left 2,400 dead. Some analysts believe that the figure might be higher; Palestinian sources put the number at closer to 3000. Nor is there any way to be certain how many, if any, of the victims were PLO fighters.

Although Israeli forces had not done any of the killings, Israel was widely criticized for failing to take any action to stop the Phalangists even when it was clear what was happening within the camps. Indeed, there is some evidence to indicate that the IDF was closely collaborating with the militias. An Israeli commission of inquiry was established which concluded that several leading figures, including Begin, Sharon, and IDF generals, bore "indirect responsibility" for the massacres, based on the fact that Israeli troops had not directly participated in the killings.

See also WALLEYN, LUC.

safe havens

The term *safe haven* applies to an area that is designated off-limits for military targeting. The term does not have specific legal standing, but the Fourth Geneva Convention of 1949 concerning the Protection of Civilian Persons in Times of War and Additional Protocol I do provide for three types of protected areas: hospital zones, neutralized zones, and demilitarized zones. For demilitarization to take place, however, the belligerents must agree to set aside such a zone. Article 14 states that the parties concerned may "conclude agreements on mutual recognition of the zones and localities they have created." The convention does not indicate how these agreements are to be made, leaving it up to the belligerents. Article 15 states that any party to a conflict may propose to establish "neutralized zones intended to shelter from the effects of war" the "wounded and sick combatants or non-combatants" and "civilian persons who take no part in hostilities." Articles 23 and 59 state that parties shall permit "the free passage of all consignments of essential foodstuffs, medical supplies, and clothing to these zones."

The treatment of REFUGEES was specifically addressed by the 1951 United Nations Refugee Convention, which establishes the obligation of states toward refugees and describes the rights they enjoy; the treaty was a formal recognition that states could take in refugees fleeing persecution in their home countries. Until World War II the body of international law protected civilians only in situations where they were threatened by forces of a belligerent state. Article 33 of the convention states that "no Contracting State shall expel or return a refugee in any manner whatsoever to the frontiers of a territory where his life or freedom would be threatened on account of his race, religion, nationality, membership of a particular social group or political opinion."

The concept of safe havens—also known as corridors of tranquility, humanitarian corridors, neutral zones, security zones, and safety zones predates the 1949 Geneva Convention and the 1951 Refugee Convention. A safe haven was established in Shanghai in the 1930s, for instance, while war was waging between China and Japan. Both belligerents agreed to the protected area, which eventually offered sanctuary to about 1 million Chinese. The UN Security Council and other bodies have attempted to establish safe havens in many recent conflicts as well. The principal reason for such safe havens is to protect refugees and INTERNALLY DISPLACED PERSONS. Another reason is to prevent refugees from seeking sanctuary across an international border. During the GENOCIDE in Rwanda, for instance, safe havens, called *zones humanitaires sûres* (safe humanitarian zones) were set up in southwestern Rwanda to prevent potential refugees from fleeing to Zaire.

In principle, these safe havens are to remain free of military occupation. The Kurdish area of northern Iraq is a good example of a successful safe haven. Established after the 1991 Gulf War and protected from Iraqi incursion by U.S. and British warplanes, the area enjoyed relative peace and autonomy until the fall of Saddam HUSSEIN in 2003. It also afforded sanctuary for approximately 400,000 Kurdish refugees who had fled over the border to Turkey to escape Saddam's forces in the aftermath of a failed Kurdish uprising.

Many safe havens have proven to be tragic deceptions. In 1993 during the Bosnian War, the UN Security Council designated six safe havens in Bosnia and Herzegovina that were intended to shelter Muslim civilians from depredations of Serb forces. However, there was no attempt to define the borders of these safe havens or to ensure the protection of refugees in these areas. In July 1995 UN troops, mainly composed of Dutch soldiers, abandoned designated safe havens in Srebrinca and Zepa rather than defend them against Serb forces and paramilitary units. The Serbs proceeded to expel the Muslim women and children before killing nearly 7,000 youths and adult men. It was the worst atrocity in Europe since World War II and underscored the problems of setting up a safe haven without also providing the means with which to protect it.

See also ADDITIONAL PROTOCOLS TO THE GENEVA CONVENTIONS; BOSNIA AND HERZEGOVINA, HUMAN RIGHTS VIOLATIONS IN; Geneva conventions; KURDISTAN (IRAQ), SUPPRESSION OF.

Further Reading:
Feller, Erika, Volker Turk, and Frances Nicholson, eds. *Refugee Protection in International Law: UNHCR's Global Consultations on International Protection.* Cambridge: Cambridge University Press, 2003.

Fritz, Mark. *Lost on Earth: Nomads of the New World.* New York: Routledge, 2000.

Groenewold, Julia, and Doctors Without Borders. *World in Crisis: The Politics of Survival at the End of the Twentieth Century.* London: Routledge, 1996.

Helton, Arthur C. *The Price of Indifference: Refugees and Humanitarian Action in the New Century.* A Council on Foreign Relations Book. Oxford: Oxford University Press, 2002.

Hyndman, Jennifer. *Managing Displacement: Refugees and the Politics of Humanitarianism.* Minneapolis: University of Minnesota Press, 2000.

Ingleby, David, ed. *Forced Migration and Mental Health: Rethinking the Care of Refugees and Displaced Persons.* New York: Plenum US, 2004.

Lischer, Sarah Kenyon. *Dangerous Sanctuaries: Refugee Camps, Civil War, and the Dilemmas of Humanitarian Aid.* Cornell Studies in Security Affairs. Ithaca, N.Y.: Cornell University Press, 2005.

Moorehead, Caroline. *Human Cargo: A Journey among Refugees.* New York: Henry Holt and Co., 2005.

Ogata, Sadako, and Kofi Annan. *The Turbulent Decade: Confronting the Refugee Crises of the 1990s.* New York: W. W. Norton & Company, 2005.

Sakai Takashi (1887–1946) *Japanese war criminal*
Sakai Takashi served as a Japanese military commander in China first during Sino-Japanese hostilities that erupted in 1931 and then during World War II. After the war he was tried for war crimes and CRIMES AGAINST HUMANITY as well as crimes in violation of Chinese law. Sakai was also governor-general of Hong Kong for the occupation authorities. Born in 1887, he was among the high officials in the

Japanese military who promoted Japan's aggression against China. In 1931, after the Mukden incident (a staged provocation that provided the pretext for Japan's attack on Manchuria), he formed a terrorist group to foment disorder in Beijing (then Peking) and Tianjin (then Tientsin); the group carried out assassinations of various Chinese officials, politicians, and newspaper reporters.

In May 1934 Sakai threatened to attack Beijing using artillery and air forces, and he demanded the dismissal of the heads of the local Chinese authorities in the province of Hopei as well as the withdrawal of all Chinese troops from the province. As a commander of the Japanese Twenty-third Army operating in South China, he organized a puppet government and formed a so-called Peace Army in an effort to overthrow the Chinese government. Later, as regimental commander of the 29th Infantry Brigade in China, he was involved directly or indirectly in acts of atrocity, including the massacre of over 100 civilians in Guangdong (Kwang-tung) and Hainan by shooting, bayoneting, and drowning. Women were raped and mutilated, their bodies fed to dogs. Troops under Sakai's command forcibly evicted civilians from their homes, plundered their produce and animals, and burned down their houses. Sakai also allegedly ordered the execution of more than 100 PRISONERS OF WAR, many of whom were already wounded. In December 1941 he ordered the execution of 20 members of a British medical unit; seven nurses were raped and mutilated as well.

Following the war, Sakai was tried in China under the Chinese Rules governing the Trial of War Criminals that were in force at the time. While he initially pleaded not guilty, he later asked for the charges to be amended, acknowledging that while he might have been guilty of having taken part in a war of aggression and had committed a crime against peace, he contended that he had acted under orders of his government. He also asserted that he had no knowledge of any atrocities, which he attributed to subordinates. Nonetheless, his pleas to have the charges changed were rejected, and he was found guilty "of participating in the war of aggression" and "of inciting or permitting his subordinates to murder prisoners of war, wounded soldiers and non-combatants; to rape, plunder and deport civilians; to indulge in cruel punishment and torture; and to cause destruction of property." He was also found guilty of participation in a war of aggression, a crime against peace, war crimes, and crimes against humanity. Sakai was sentenced to death and executed in 1946.

See also MANCHURIA, JAPANESE WAR CRIMES IN.

Further Reading:

Daws, Gavin. *Prisoners of the Japanese: POWs of World War II in the Pacific.* New York: Perennial, 1996.

Li, Peter, ed. *Japanese War Crimes: The Search for Justice.* New Brunswick, N.J.: Transaction Publishers, 2003.

Maga, Timothy P. *Judgment at Tokyo: The Japanese War Crimes Trials.* Lexington: University Press of Kentucky, 2001.

Mendelsohn, John. *The Preservation of Japanese War Crimes Trials Records in the National Archives.* Washington, D.C.: National Archives and Records Administration, 1982.

Minear, Richard R. *Victors' Justice: The Tokyo War Crimes Trial.* Michigan Classics in Japanese Studies. Ann Arbor: University of Michigan, Center for Japanese Studies, 2001.

Piccigallo, Philip R. *The Japanese on Trial: Allied War Crimes Operations in the East, 1945–1951.* Austin: University of Texas Press, 1980.

Rees, Laurence. *Horror in the East: Japan and the Atrocities of World War II.* New York: Da Capo Press, 2002.

Russell, of Liverpool, Edward Frederick Langley Russell, Baron. *Knights of the Bushido: A Short History of Japanese War Crimes.* London: Greenhill Books, 2005.

Tanaka, Yuki. *Hidden Horrors: Japanese War Crimes in World War II.* Boulder, Colo.: Westview Press, 1998.

sanctions

Sanctions, which are often (though not always) economic in nature, are a controversial weapon to force a law-breaking state to abide by international law or punish it for past violations. Many political analysts are convinced that they are ineffective at achieving their purpose and, in addition, impose unjustified suffering on civilian populations in the affected countries. The use of economic sanctions gained worldwide attention after the 1991 Gulf War. Until the 2003 U.S.-backed invasion, sanctions had been imposed on Iraq as punishment for its earlier invasion of Kuwait. It is debatable whether those sanctions accomplished the objectives members of the United Nations Security Council envisioned in light of the ease with which the Saddam HUSSEIN regime was able to violate them.

In addition to economic sanctions—a trade embargo, for example—sanctions can take the form of diplomacy—for example, diplomatic relations are suspended or officials in the government of an outlaw state may be denied the right to travel outside of their country. In recent years the Security Council has imposed some form of trade sanctions on Angola, Haiti, Liberia, Libya, Rwanda, Somalia, and the countries of the former Yugoslavia as well as Iraq. The Security Council can act under Chapter VII of the UN Charter to decide whether any threat to the peace, breach of the peace, or act of aggression warrants the imposition of mandatory sanctions to force a state to alter its behavior. In certain cases military force can be employed to enforce sanctions. Economic sanctions often take a long time to prove effective, and states can evade them by smuggling and resorting to black markets. Nonetheless, in some instances they have proven effective; both Serbia and Libya significantly changed policies inimical to the international community under the pressure of economic sanctions. Countries such as Myanmar, which are poor and isolated to begin with and thus are less reliant on trade, are less susceptible to sanctions.

There is also a legal basis for sanctions in Article 41 of the UN Charter that provides for economic and other kinds of nonmilitary measures for maintaining or restoring international peace and security. It should be noted, however, that the term *sanctions* is not mentioned in the text. Once the United Nations agrees on the imposition of sanctions on a country, all member states are bound to comply with them.

Sanctions may be partial or comprehensive. Even the most stringent sanctions make allowances, and exceptions are usually made for humanitarian purposes—for instance, ensuring that medicines and food are delivered to states under sanction. In the case of Iraq, an "oil for food program" was instituted in which the United Nations allowed the oil-rich country to sell a certain amount of oil each year—approximately $2 billion worth—in exchange for food. (The program was later revealed to be riddled by massive corruption.) Even the United States did not abide by the embargo of Iraq, turning a blind eye to oil smuggling by its allies Turkey and Jordan.

Not all sanctions enjoy UN approval. Some states may unilaterally impose sanctions on another state, which is the case with the United States' long-standing embargo of Cuba. Although the world leader has maintained its sanctions against the Castro regime for decades, other countries—including Canada, members of the European Union, and most states in Latin America—continue to do business with Cuba. Some legal scholars believe that sanctions impose what amounts to COLLECTIVE PUNISHMENT (which is otherwise outlawed by international law) since the civilian population of a sanctioned state is deprived of its economic lifeblood because of actions committed by a government over which it has little or no control. In an essay on the subject, Dr. Hans Köchler points out what he perceives is a contradiction between two lofty goals advocated by the United Nations: maintaining international peace and security on the one hand and human rights on the other. Sanctions aimed at the former, he maintains, come at the price of the latter.

Economic sanctions are often viewed as a preliminary step before taking military action, as provided for in Article 42. It is up to the UN Security Council, however, to determine whether military action is required based on its assessment that a threat to peace, a breach of peace, or an act of aggression exists. Where force is contemplated, the Security Council authorizes its member states to "use all necessary means to restore international peace and security." Humanitarian considerations are not cited. Moreover, Köchler says, the decision of what violations require sanctions is left in the hands of powerful member states that sit on the Security Council: China, France, Russia, the United Kingdom, and the United States. In 2003 the United States argued—unsuccessfully—that Iraq was in breach of the sanctions because it was developing weapons of mass destruction, and therefore military force was required to enforce the sanctions.

Some governments may be involved in egregious violations of human rights but avoid sanctions, whereas other governments may be less culpable in this regard and come under a sanctions regime. Governments that perpetrate grave human rights abuses on civilians do not always represent a threat to international peace or security, after all. Other forms of sanctions also exist that are not quite so extreme. International organizations have established procedures for applying pressure on states that do not comply with their human rights obligations. Many international treaties require member states to report on their compliance, and if they are found in violation they may be suspended from the organization and come under fire in the media. Shame can also be used to enforce sanctions, even if they do not have the force of law. Regimes may suffer a blow to prestige and a severe loss of business because of human rights campaigns, for instance, even in the absence of formal sanctions.

Further Reading:

Arnove, Anthony, ed. *Iraq under Siege, Updated Edition: The Deadly Impact of Sanctions and War.* Boston: South End Press, 2002.

Collins, Joseph. J., and Gabrielle D. Bowdoin. *Beyond Unilateral Economic Sanctions: Better Alternatives for U.S. Foreign Policy (Csis Report).* Washington, D.C.: Center for Strategic and International Studies, 1999.

Gutman, Roy, ed. *Crimes of War: What the Public Should Know.* New York: W. W. Norton & Company, 1999.

Sankoh, Foday (1937–2003) *Sierra Leone guerrilla leader*

A firebrand and polarizing political figure, Foday Sankoh brought terror to his home country of Sierra Leone on an unparalleled scale in the 1990s. Adjectives such as *charismatic* and *ebullient* were regularly used to describe him. One reporter called him a "tubby leader," a characterization that made him sound more like a lovable clown than a murderous thug.

In the 1970s Sankoh began making a name for himself as a student leader in the small West African nation. He served as an army corporal and later as a TV cameraman before briefly being imprisoned for antigovernment activities. He then went into exile in Libya, where he befriended other political dissidents. At the time Libya, under Colonel Muammar al-Gadhafi, was a hotbed of revolutionary fervor, a refuge for exiles from all over West Africa. Sankoh's fellow revolutionaries looked up to him because he was a decade older than most of them; they called him Papei (Papa).

In 1987 Sankoh returned to Sierra Leone. After receiving military training he slipped into the bordering country of Liberia. There he befriended Charles TAYLOR, a like-minded Liberian revolutionary with no more moral scruples than he had. Taylor was plotting his own ascent to power in Liberia and was happy to lend a helping hand to Sankoh in his effort to seize power in Sierra Leone. It would take Taylor eight years—and a vicious campaign of terror—to achieve his ambition: the presidency of Liberia. In 1991, under Taylor's patronage, Sankoh formed the Revolutionary United Front (RUF) in Sierra Leone. If initially Sankoh railed against corruption among Sierra Leone's elite, he soon dropped all pretense of revolutionary reform. All that truly interested him was seizing power and wealth—in the form of diamonds. He launched his campaign in the countryside, initially focusing his efforts on the eastern districts where the diamond mines were located. His forces abducted and raped children; there are reports that some even engaged in cannibalism when food ran short. But if there was one horrifying practice that distinguished Sankoh's depredations, it was the amputation of limbs. Sankoh persisted in denying that these atrocities were sanctioned or indeed that they were taking place at all. Critics who dared to cross Sankoh by telling the truth sometimes paid with their lives. The brutal campaign met with success, and Sankoh was able to consolidate control over the diamond-producing areas, providing him with a base from which to threaten the capital of Freetown. Meanwhile government forces bottled up in Freetown were on the verge of collapse. In 1992 a young army officer, Valentine Strasser, took power in a coup backed by mercenaries. But Taylor continued to support the RUF, using the diamond wealth to subsidize its ragtag, drug-addled army.

Sierra Leone enjoyed a brief fling with democracy with the election of Ahmed Tejan Kabbah, who had the backing of Nigeria, but he, too, was soon overthrown in yet another military coup. A Nigerian peacekeeping mission restored Kabbah to power, but their presence failed to quell the civil war, which was further complicated by other factions and militia groups with agendas of their own. Sankoh's luck appeared to run out when he was captured and sentenced to death. After he announced that he had rediscovered God, his fortunes took another turn when a peace accord, brokered by the United States, was struck between the government and the RUF in 1999. Instead of being put to death, he was elevated to a high-ranking position in a coalition government. Under the terms of the Lome accord, as the peace agreement was called, RUF soldiers were to be integrated with the regular army. Sankoh was even allowed to regain control over the diamond mines. The fragile peace did not last very long, however, as RUF forces challenged the United Nations, capturing 500 peacekeepers. As the former colonial power, Great Britain felt a special responsibility for Sierra Leone and dispatched troops to rescue the trapped UN soldiers. In the chaos, Sankoh tried to escape Freetown but was recognized and captured. Gradually the United Nations asserted control over Freetown and portions of the countryside. A disarmament program was instituted, and by 2002 nearly 50,000 RUF fighters had laid down their arms. A SPECIAL COURT FOR SIERRA LEONE was established under UN auspices to try the worst offenders on all sides. However, Foday Sankoh, the man most responsible for the carnage of the last decade, escaped justice one last time, dying in prison of natural causes in July 2003.

See also CONFLICT DIAMONDS; LIBERIA, HUMAN RIGHTS VIOLATIONS IN; SIERRA LEONE, HUMAN RIGHTS VIOLATIONS IN.

Further Reading:

Ferme, Mariane C. *The Underneath of Things: Violence, History, and the Everyday in Sierra Leone.* Berkeley: University of California Press, 2001.

Jackson, Michael. *In Sierra Leone.* Durham, N.C.: Duke University Press, 2004.

Richards, Paul. *Fighting for the Rain Forest: War, Youth, and Resources in Sierra Leone.* African Issues Series. London: Heinemann, 1996.

Romano, Cesare, Andre Nollkaemper, and Jann K. Kleffner, eds. *Internationalized Criminal Courts and Tribunals: Sierra Leone, East Timor, Kosovo, and Cambodia.* International Courts and Tribunals Series. Oxford: Oxford University Press, 2004.

Voeten, Teun. *How de Body? One Man's Terrifying Journey through an African War.* New York: Thomas Dunne Books, 2002.

Sant'Anna di Stazzema, massacre in

The Tuscan village of Sant'Anna di Stazzema was the site of a massacre of 560 people—mostly women, children, and the elderly—by Nazi SS forces during World War II. The killings took place on August 12, 1944, shortly after Italian dictator Benito Mussolini had been deposed. The SS rounded up civilians in nearby villages to prevent them from lending support to the partisans who were harassing the retreating German forces. Feeling they were likely to be arrested and killed, the men in Sant'Anna di Stazzema decided to flee under the mistaken assumption that the SS would leave the women and children alone. An inquiry conducted by the U.S. Army in October 1944 turned up evidence of charred remains in houses that had been burned, but the SS officers involved were never pursued. Further investigation was hampered for political reasons. The Allies had determined only to try higher-ranking Nazi officials, and Italy, eager to establish close relations with West Germany, had no motivation to risk opening old wounds. Therefore, although the victims were memorialized, no serious attempts were made to bring the perpetrators to justice until 2004, when Italian military prosecutors decided to reopen the case by charging seven former SS officers for their involvement in the atrocity. The trial of the first three defendants began in absentia in spring 2004. In June 2005, after a yearlong trial, 10 former members of the Nazi SS accused of taking part in the massacre were found guilty in absentia and sentenced to life in prison. All the defendants, now in their eighties, remained in Germany, which, as a matter of principle, will not extradite its own citizens. However, a court in Stuttgart was conducting its own investigation of the event in preparation for a possible trial in Germany.

Further Reading:

Browder, George C. *Hitler's Enforcers: The Gestapo and the SS Security Service in the Nazi Revolution.* Oxford: Oxford University Press, 1996.

Hohne, Heinz Zollen. *The Order of the Death's Head: The Story of Hitler's SS.* Classic Military History. New York: Penguin, 2001.

Sarajevo, siege of

Until 1992 Sarajevo, now the capital of Bosnia and Herzegovina, was a lively cosmopolitan city where Muslims, Christians, and Jews lived together in peace. In 1984 it played host to the Winter Olympics. Founded in the 15th century, Sarajevo takes its name from the Turkish word *serai*, which means "palace." On June 28, 1914, the archduke of Austria, Francis Ferdinand, was assassinated by a Serbian nationalist, an event that triggered the outbreak of the First World War. Violence again struck the city in spring 1992 when Bosnia and Herzegovina declared its independence from Yugoslavia, setting off another war. Serbs opposed the independence of Bosnia and neighboring Croatia because it would make the Serb populations a minority in both those republics. (Serbs enjoyed a majority status only in Serbia proper.) The conflict was worsened by religious and ethnic rifts: The Serbs belonged to the Eastern Orthodox Church whereas most of the Bosnians were Muslims. While the Muslims were predominantly secular,

many Serbs regarded them as descendants of the reviled Turks whose armies had pushed into the Balkans in the 14th century.

At the start of the conflict, Serbian forces, aided by Bosnian Serb paramilitary units, attacked the Bosnian army. Initially the Serbs enjoyed considerable success on the battlefield, seizing nearly all Bosnian towns except for Sarajevo. Then, on April 6, 1992, Serb militants opened fire on peace demonstrators, killing five and injuring 30. On May 1 Serb mortars delivered the opening salvo of a SIEGE that would last for four years. That the United Nations had declared Sarajevo a safe haven made no difference. The Bosnian Serb Romanija Corps, under the command of General Stanislav Galic, proceeded to besiege the city, blockading all roads and shutting down the airport to deny Sarajevo's approximately half a million residents food, medicine, water, and electricity. Red Cross trucks given clearance to enter Sarajevo were often seized or destroyed. The Serbs set up artillery on the mountains surrounding the city, allowing them to shell it at will.

During the siege Sarajevo was pounded with an average of 329 shells a day, reaching a high of 3,777 shell impacts. It was only the reopening of the airport in June 1993 and a United Nations airlift that kept the inhabitants from starving to death. But the killings continued unabated, and the most routine actions became perilous. For example, on June 1–15, 1992, 15 people had been killed and another 80 wounded in a mortar attack during a soccer game. But a year later, 12 people were killed while waiting in line to get water. But the incident that caused the most outrage throughout the world occurred on February 5, 1994, when a mortar shell killed 66 and wounded 140 others in the Sarajevo marketplace. Even maternity wards were not spared. By the time the siege ended on February 29, 1996, after a cease-fire had been put into place, an estimated 10,000–12,000 people had been killed and another 50,000 wounded. Hardly a single structure had escaped damage or destruction. Today the population is about 220,000, less than half of what it was before the war.

See also BOSNIA AND HERZEGOVINA, HUMAN RIGHTS VIOLATIONS IN; YUGOSLAVIA, WAR CRIMES IN.

Further Reading:

Clark, Wesley K. *Waging Modern War: Bosnia, Kosovo, and the Future of Combat.* New York: Public Affairs.

Glenny, Misha. *The Fall of Yugoslavia: The Third Balkan War.* New York: Penguin Books, 1996.

Hagan, John. *Justice in the Balkans: Prosecuting War Crimes in the Hague Tribunal.* Chicago Series in Law and Society. Chicago: University of Chicago Press, 2003.

Harris, Nathaniel. *The War in Former Yugoslavia.* London: Hodder & Stoughton, 1997.

Mertus, Julie. *Former Yugoslavia: War Crimes Trials in the Former Yugoslavia.* Helsinki: Human Rights Watch/Helsinki, 1995.

Rossanet, Bertrand de. *War and Peace in the Former Yugoslavia.* Boston: Martinus Nijhoff, 1997.

Saravia, Alvaro (1946–) *alleged Salvadoran assassin*

Alvaro Saravia, a Salvadoran national, was named in a civil suit as the man who participated in the assassination of Archbishop Óscar Romero in 1980 while the cleric was celebrating mass in San Salvador, the capital of El Salvador. Romero, an outspoken opponent of the right-wing death squads and their political allies then in power, was killed to silence his voice. His slaying had been ordered by the founder of El Salvador's rightist party, Roberto D'AUBUISSON, who died in 1992. No Salvadoran court has ever conducted an investigation into Romero's death. (An AMNESTY law makes prosecutions of war criminals all but impossible and has effectively nullified the findings of a UN-sponsored truth commission, which had implicated D'Aubuisson and Saravia.)

The effort to bring Saravia to justice took place in 2004 in an unlikely venue—Fresno, California—under the Alien Tort Claims Act of 1789, which allows nationals of a foreign country to bring a civil suit against another foreign national for certain types of crimes committed elsewhere in the world. The suit asserted that the former Salvadoran air force captain had actively abetted the assassination by obtaining the gun, arranging for the killer's transportation to the chapel, and paying him off. The suit, which was filed by the Center for Justice and Accountability, a human rights organization, on behalf of a relative of the archbishop, sought damages for EXTRAJUDICIAL KILLINGS and CRIMES AGAINST HUMANITY. Because it was a civil trial, the defendant could only be punished by being fined. Saravia was found guilty, although it was difficult to say when, if ever, the monetary damages assessed could be collected. A legal U.S. resident, Saravia had gone into hiding before the trial had begun. According to declassified State Department and CIA documents, the U.S. administration was aware of his alleged involvement in the Romero slaying shortly after it occurred, raising questions as to why he had been permitted to settle in the United States.

See also EL SALVADOR, WAR CRIMES IN.

Further Reading:

Armstrong, Robert. *El Salvador: The Face of Revolution.* Boston: South End Press, 1982.

Wood, Elisabeth Jean, Peter Lange, et al., eds. *Insurgent Collective Action and Civil War in El Salvador.* Cambridge Studies in Comparative Politics. Cambridge: Cambridge University Press, 2003.

Sauckel, Fritz (1894–1946) *Nazi war criminal*

As Nazi plenipotentiary general for labor mobilization from 1942 to 1945, Fritz Sauckel was responsible for mobilizing the slave labor force to sustain the military and industrial power of the Third Reich during World War II. He was tried by the victorious Allies at the NUREMBERG TRIALS and convicted as a war criminal.

Born in Hassfurt am Main on October 27, 1894, Sauckel worked as a young man on Norwegian and Swedish merchant ships. During World War I he was captured and interned in a French prisoner-of-war camp. He was an early adherent of the Nazis, joining the party shortly after its inception in 1921. After the Nazis took power in Germany in 1933, Sauckel was made governor of Thuringia; he also held the rank of honorary general in the elite Nazi paramilitary units, the SA and the SS. In 1942 he was put in charge of the labor mobilization effort, and in this capacity he organized the deportation of 5 million people from occupied European territories to work as slave labor in Germany. He gave specific orders that they were to be exploited "to the highest degree possible at the lowest conceivable degree of expenditure." Special protection squads were used to press-gang laborers into SLAVERY. Sauckel was also responsible for the executions of thousands of Polish Jews.

At his trial before the International Military Tribunal at Nuremberg, Sauckel maintained his innocence and denied any knowledge of the CONCENTRATION CAMPS. He expressed his shock at learning of the widespread atrocities carried out by the Nazis. In spite of his profession of innocence, he was found guilty and hanged on October 16, 1946.

Further Reading:

Ferencz, Benjamin B., and Telford Taylor. *Less Than Slaves: Jewish Forced Labor and the Quest for Compensation.* Bloomington: Indiana University Press, 2002.

Jaskof, Paul B. *The Architecture of Oppression: The SS, Forced Labor and the Nazi Monumental Building Economy.* London: Routledge, 2000.

Saudi Arabia, human rights violations in

Saudi Arabia is a recent country that came into being in 1932 as the result of the conquests of King Abdul Aziz Al Saud, better known in the West as Ibn Saud. It is one of the most repressive regimes on earth, and U.S. State Department reports describe its human rights record as poor, despite close American-Saudi ties. The home of 15 out of the 19 of the 9/11 (2001) bombers and of al-QAEDA founder Osama Bin Laden, Saudi Arabia is a monarchical dictatorship and the most restrictive of all Islamic countries.

In the 18th century the Al Saud clan, then rulers of the Najd region of central Arabia, came together with the Islamic religious reformer Al-Wahhab. Wahhab followed the hard-line Hanbali school of Islam, the severest of the four main schools of Sunni Islam (the version of that faith followed by 85 percent of Muslims worldwide). In the early 20th century, the Al Saud family and the Wahhabi sect of Hanbali Islam again combined, with Ibn Saud leading campaigns of conquest that resulted in his capture of most of the Arabian peninsula by 1924. This context is important, since the majority of Muslims outside of Arabia do not follow the austere Hanbali/Wahhabi interpretation of that faith, and would therefore reject the radical, often extreme, version that prevails in Saudi Arabia. (Leading moderate Islamic thinkers such as Akbar Ahmed have argued that much of Saudi Islam is in fact more cultural than strictly Islamic, especially in the treatment of women and of religious minorities.)

As well as being a dictatorship, ruled by the Al Saud family, Saudi Arabia is highly repressive religiously. Islamic law, sharia, is rigidly enforced, and all the ancient punishments are still enforced. For example, there was enormous controversy 20 years ago when a Saudi princess was executed for committing adultery, a crime that still carries the death penalty. Thieves often have their right hand and left foot amputated. Beheading is not infrequent, and Islam is the only religion permitted in the country. Even the Shiite minority (the sect of Islam prevalent in Iran and predominant in Iraq) is harassed, even though—or perhaps because—Shiites live primarily in the oil-producing provinces. In the closed-court justice system, most defendants are not entitled to legal representation. The U.S. government's human rights reports on Saudi Arabia also note that the jails are mainly unsanitary. Furthermore, in legal proceedings the testimony of a woman is half the value of that of a man. While other Muslim countries often use sharia law for family issues, in Saudi Arabia it is the sole legal code for the country.

Limited local elections were allowed for the first time ever in 2005, but, unlike several Persian Gulf states and Iran, where women may vote, no woman was permitted to vote. While many Islamic countries permit women to go alone outdoors and wear a head scarf without facial covering, in Saudi Arabia women are not allowed out alone without a male relative, and they may not drive. They also have to cover their faces entirely when in public. Except for the brief time of TALIBAN rule in Afghanistan, the Saudi regime is drastically more restrictive than any other Islamic country. The U.S. State Department human rights reports point out that spousal violence against women is common and that persecuted women are not allowed by law to leave the country, even if they are fleeing their abusive husbands.

While many Middle Eastern countries have secret police to crush political dissent, Saudi Arabia also has a unique police force, which is charged with the zealous enforcement of the Hanbali/Wahhabi code of Islam. The *mutawwa'in*—police for the repression of vice—ensure obedience to the religious observances, from the absolute prohibition on alcohol to the subjection of women. In a notorious recent case, girl pupils fleeing a burning school were forced back into the flames by these police so that they would not be seen in public without head and face coverings. Several girls died as a result, and an embarrassed Saudi regime was then obliged to transfer the supervision of girls' schools from the religious authorities to the education ministry.

The security forces, however repressive, have been unable to stop terrorist attacks by Islamic militants who have targeted foreigners in Riyadh, Jidda, and elsewhere. Several Saudis have lost their lives in the attacks as well. Many of the attacks appear designed to scare off foreign investment and damage the oil industry, which is dependent on foreign workers and provides the major source of revenue for the country. While Osama Bin Laden has vowed the destruction of the Saudi monarchy, it is unknown whether the terrorist groups implicated in these attacks are directly connected to al-Qaeda or are merely claiming an affiliation. For several years wealthy Saudis provided funding for the jihadis—holy warriors—who fought the Soviets in Afghanistan and subsidized the madrassas (religious Islamic schools) in Pakistan and elsewhere, fostering Islamic militancy in the belief that they were buying immunity for themselves. But that illusion has been shattered now that the terrorists have shown their willingness to strike on Saudi soil.

In August 2005 King Fahd died after a long illness. He was succeeded by his more reform-minded half brother, Crown Prince Abdullah. But whether Abdullah—or any of the other members of the royal family—will be able to meet growing demands for representative government remains unclear. Although the Saudi authorities are beginning to take some small steps toward opening up the government, hitherto the monopoly of the royal family, it may be a case of too little too late.

Further Reading:

AbuKhalil, As'ad. *The Battle for Saudi Arabia: Royalty, Fundamentalism, and Global Power.* New York: Seven Stories Press, 2004.

Bradley, John R. *Saudi Arabia Exposed: Inside a Kingdom in Crisis.* Sidney, Australia: Palgrave Macmillan, 2005.

Long, David E. *The Kingdom of Saudi Arabia.* Tallahassee: University Press of Florida, 1998.

Sawoniuk, Anthony (1921–) *Nazi war criminal*

Anthony Sawoniuk was the first of 376 suspected war criminals tried in Britain for war crimes in World War II under the 1991 War Crimes Act. In 1999 Sawoniuk, then 78, was found guilty of killing one unnamed Jewish woman. A former railway ticket collector and pensioner, Sawoniak said that he was innocent of any wrongdoing and claimed to be the victim of a conspiracy. He contended that the murders he was implicated for were the Germans' responsibility. His trial is significant because it was the first time that a British jury had traveled abroad to view a crime scene (in Belarus) and because the defendant was the first U.K. citizen accused of war crimes to speak in his own defense in a criminal court.

Sawoniuk was identified as a suspect in 1988 as a result of information turned over to the British government by the former Soviet government. An inquiry into his conduct during the war did not begin, however, until 1994. He was ultimately charged with war crimes that had taken place in 1942 in the village of Domachevo in Belarus, a former Soviet republic, when Belarus was occupied by the Nazis. A witness said that he had seen Sawoniuk, known then as "Andrusha," order three Jews—two men and a woman—to undress in front of an open grave before shooting them in the back of the head. There was testimony that he might have killed as many as 15 Jews at the time, using a submachine gun. The prosecution alleged that Sawoniuk had led "search and kill" police squads, which hunted down Jews trying to escape the Nazis. He was "not only prepared to do the Nazis' bidding," the lead prosecutor said, "but carried out their genocidal policy with enthusiasm."

Schacht, Hjalmar Horace Greeley (1877–1970)
German banker

Hjalmar Schacht was a leading German financier who served as minister of economics under Adolf HITLER before falling out of favor with the führer. He was exonerated on war crime charges by the tribunal at the NUREMBERG TRIALS after the war, although he was later found guilty for other offenses by a German court.

Born on January 22, 1877, the son of a salesman who had lived in the United States, Schacht was named for the fiery American journalist Horace Greeley, who had campaigned against slavery before the Civil War. Schact studied medicine, philology, and political science before turning to economics and went on to hold a number of executive positions in the banking industry, becoming director of the German National Bank in 1916. His advancement continued after the end of World War I; in 1923 he became Reich currency commissioner at a time when hyperinflation was threatening the stability of the Weimar Republic. As a reward for bringing inflation under control, he was appointed president of the Reichsbank, though he resigned in 1930 because of his opposition to ruinous REPARATIONS to the Allies that Germany had agreed to pay under the Versailles treaty. His conversion to National Socialism (Nazism) occurred after reading Hitler's memoir, *Mein Kampf.*

In early 1931 Schacht was introduced to Hitler, who persuaded him to raise funds for the Nazis, using his contacts with prominent industrialists like Albert Voegler of the United Steel Works and the arms manufacturers Gustav KRUPP and Alfried Krupp. Schacht did not confine his support to fundraising. In 1932 he collected the signatures of industrialists for a letter addressed to Chancellor Paul von Hindenburg, requesting that he appoint Hitler as chancellor. After Hitler's ascension to power, Schacht organized the Association of German Industrialists, which put up 3 million marks for the Nazi election campaign. On Hitler's behalf he traveled to the United States, making over 40 speeches in public and on the radio in which he reassured his listeners that Hitler was committed to restoring democracy to Germany. He even succeeded in meeting President Franklin Roosevelt, who thought the banker was "extremely arrogant."

In 1934 Hitler made Schacht his minister of economics. Schacht's economic views were shaped more by the seminal British economist John Maynard Keynes and the tenets of Roosevelt's New Deal than by Nazi ideology. He convinced Hitler to support a massive public-works program that resulted in the construction of the *Autobahnen,* Germany's famous highway system. Schacht shared the anti-Semitism of the other Nazi officials; in one speech he maintained that "the Jews must realize that their influence in Germany has disappeared for all time." However, unlike many Nazis, he was opposed to violent means to solve "the Jewish problem." Instead he worked out an arrangement with the World Zionist Organization to allow Jews to emigrate to Palestine (then under British mandate) in exchange for 15,000 reichmarks each. Some 170,000 Jews ultimately left for Palestine as part of the deal, which allowed them to escape the CONCENTRATION CAMPS. Schacht also repudiated the rabid anti-Semitic articles in *Der Stürmer,* published by Nazi propagandist Julius STREICHER, condemning what he termed "unlawful activities" against Jews. He pointed out that many Jews had fought bravely for Germany during the First World War and ought to be treated fairly.

Although Schacht negotiated bartering agreements with countries in the Balkans and Middle East to provide Germany with raw materials to rebuild its military strength, he harbored misgivings about the vast sums of money being spent on Germany's remilitarization. He cautioned Hitler that the expenditures on arms posed a risk of reigniting inflation. His words fell on deaf ears. Hitler's trusted deputy, Hermann GÖRING, who ran the economy (and was nominally

Schacht's superior), supported Germany's rearmament. He told Schacht, "If the Führer wishes it then two times two are five." In 1937 Schacht resigned as minister of economics over disagreements about rearmament but remained in Hitler's government as minister without portfolio. In 1944, however, he was arrested and placed in Dachau concentration camp on suspicion of participating in the failed attempt on Hitler's life in July 1944. Two of the conspirators had, in fact, approached Schacht, hoping to enlist him in the plot, but he had rebuffed their overtures.

Schacht survived the war, after which he fell into the custody of the Allies and was put on trial at Nuremberg, charged with CRIMES AGAINST HUMANITY. Acquitted, he was nonetheless subsequently rearrested on other charges and convicted by a German court. He was sentenced to eight years' imprisonment but was freed in 1948. In 1953 he established a private bank in Düsseldorf and went on to write an autobiography, *Confessions of the Old Wizard*. He also served as an economic adviser to a number of foreign governments including, that of President Gamal Nasser in Egypt. Schacht died in Munich on June 4, 1970.

Schellenberg, Walter (1910–1952) *Nazi official*

Walter Schellenberg was deputy director of the SS (security police) during the Third Reich and later became actively involved in counterintelligence activities. In contrast to other top Nazi officials tried at the NUREMBERG TRIALS for war crimes, he testified against the regime that he had served, sparing himself a long prison sentence.

Born on January 16, 1910, in Saarbruecken, Germany, Schellenberg studied medicine and law at the University of Bonn. In 1933, shortly after Adolf HITLER had come to power, Schellenberg decided to join the SS, the elite Nazi security police, motivated more by ambition than by ideology. Clever and intelligent, he cultivated friendships with powerful Nazi officials, including SS head Heinrich HIMMLER and Admiral Wilhelm Canaris, chief of the Abwehr (military intelligence). After the Germans occupied Czechoslovakia, Schellenberg became allied with Reinhard HEYDRICH, deputy chief of the GESTAPO and protector of Bohemia and Moravia. As a counterintelligence officer, he was involved in the planning of a plot to kidnap King Edward VIII of England—a plan that was never carried out. He was more successful in penetrating the fabled Soviet spy ring called the Red Orchestra. After the failure of the assassination attempt on Hitler's life on July 20, 1944, Schellenberg was given orders to arrest his old friend Admiral Canaris, who was suspected of involvement in the plot. (Canaris was subsequently released, only to be arrested again by the Allies.)

In 1944, recognizing that the Third Reich would shortly collapse, Schellenberg sought to ingratiate himself with the Allies by traveling to Stockholm, where he tried to start peace negotiations on behalf of Himmler, who was his superior. The negotiations went nowhere, and in June 1945 he was arrested by the Allies and subsequently tried at Nuremberg for war crimes. However, by testifying against his former associates, he received a sentence of only six years. Released in 1950, he went on to write his memoirs, in which he contended that his spy network had managed to penetrate England, unaware that all his spies had been turned by MI5, the British secret service. Schellenberg died in Turin, Italy, on March 31, 1952.

Further Reading:
Whiting, Charles. *Heydrich: Henchman of Death.* Barnsley: Leo Cooper, 1999.

Schirach, Baldur von (1907–1974) *Nazi youth leader*

Baldur von Schirach served as youth leader of the Nazi Party and later as gauleiter of Vienna. He was charged with and convicted of war crimes at the NUREMBERG TRIALS, although he was one of the few Nazi officials to repudiate Hitler. Schirach was born in Berlin on March 9, 1907. At the age of 10 he became a member of the Young Germans' League, where he developed the racist views that would guide him throughout his life. In 1925 he joined the National Socialist German Workers Party (NSDAP), and only a year later he was introduced to the party's head, Adolf HITLER. Hitler took Schirach under his wing and in 1929 appointed him head of the Nazi Students' Union, later promoting him to the head of the Hitler Youth in 1933. As the youth leader Schirach composed prayers in praise of the führer that had to be recited by members of Nazi youth organizations before their meals. In 1940 he joined the German army and won an Iron Cross fighting in France. That same year Hitler made him gauletier (district leader) of Vienna; in that capacity he supervised the deportation of Jews from the Austrian capital to death camps in Poland.

After his capture by Allied troops at the end of the war, Schirach claimed that he was unaware of the purpose of the CONCENTRATION CAMPS and so could not have known that he was sending Jews off to be exterminated. He even presented evidence that he had lodged a protest with Martin BORMANN, Hitler's influential deputy, regarding the brutal treatment of Austrian Jews. Nonetheless, he was convicted and sentenced to 20 years in prison. He died on August 8, 1974.

scorched earth

Scorched earth is a military tactic used to destroy resources in an attempt to deprive an enemy force of its ability to wage war. The term is derived from the practice of burning crops—e.g., scorching the earth—to deny an opponent from living off the land. But the term is equally applicable to the destruction of industrial infrastructure and communication or transportation networks and facilities. A scorched earth policy is by no means limited to invading forces; defenders have been known to destroy their own resources to prevent them from falling into the hands of the enemy. This tactic was famously employed by the Russians during the Napoleonic invasion of 1812; rather than allow the French to seize the capital, the czarist armies burned Moscow to the ground. Denied booty and food, the French troops were forced to retreat. The Russian forces stood by while a bitter Russian winter took its toll. Weaker forces often rely on scorched earth tactics to undermine a more powerful enemy. For example, Spanish guerrillas carried out scorched earth tactics in the Peninsular War (1808–14), allowing them to overcome the much larger French army. General Sherman's March to the Sea in the American Civil War is another well-known example; it was during that campaign that Atlanta was burned to the ground by Union forces. In the Sino-Japanese War (1937–45), the Chinese destroyed dams and levees, flooding their own territory to forestall the advance of Japanese forces. German forces used similar tactics at the end of World War II, destroying rail networks in Europe as they retreated before the Allied advance. In the two-decades-old civil war in Sudan, both government and guerrilla forces in the south of the country looted livestock and destroyed houses, clearing out civilian populations to ensure access to oil resources in violation of the GENEVA CONVENTIONS. Arab militias in the DARFUR region of western Sudan have also carried out a scorched earth policy to drive out an indigenous black African population.

Further Reading:

Carell, Paul. *Scorched Earth: The Russian-German War 1943–1944*. Atglen, Pa.: Schiffer Publishing, 1994.

Power, Samantha. *"A Problem from Hell": America and the Age of Genocide*. New York: HarperPerennial, 2003.

Prunier, Gerard. *Darfur: The Ambiguous Genocide*. Ithaca, N.Y.: Cornell University Press, 2005.

Zamoyski, Adam. *Moscow 1812: Napoleon's Fatal March*. New York: HarperCollins, 2004.

Serbia, human rights violations in

Serbia and Montenegro (SaM) is a constitutional republic consisting of the relatively large Republic of Serbia and the much smaller Republic of Montenegro. The two republics are all that remains of the former Federal Socialist Republic of Yugoslavia. Serbia is still recovering from the Balkan wars of the 1990s and the authoritarian regime of the former president Slobodan MILOŠEVIĆ, and its political stability remains at risk. In March 2003 the assassination of Prime Minister Zoran Djindjic prompted the government to impose a 42-day state of emergency. Although the government has generally reined in security forces, there are still maverick elements of the police that commit human rights abuses, which increased during the emergency. Abuses encompassed beatings, arbitrary arrests, detentions, and TORTURE, reported forms of which included asphyxiation with a plastic bag, electric shock, and mock executions. During the security sweeps, more than 10,000 individuals were detained; approximately 2,000 remained in custody by the end of the year. Djindjic's assassination, carried out by a group of nationalist paramilitaries and organized criminals, was viewed as a botched attempt to topple the government. Suspects were quickly rounded up, and the conspirators went on trial in December 2003.

The justice system is susceptible to political influence, and defendants face the prospect of lengthy trials. In a marked departure from the Milošević era, the parliament has enacted legislation to establish a special domestic war-crimes court and appoint a special prosecutor. Until recently the Serbian government failed to investigate or prosecute suspected war criminals who were involved in the Bosnian War or the Kosovo War. The parliament has also demonstrated greater willingness to cooperate with the INTERNATIONAL CRIMINAL TRIBUNAL FOR THE FORMER YUGOSLAVIA (ICTY), which resulted in four voluntary surrenders of indicted officials and paved the way for the arrest and transfer of another five to The Hague, where the court sits. In addition, the government handed over documents to the ICTY relevant to the prosecution of former Serb officials and permitted witnesses to testify. Even so, the ICTY has expressed misgivings about the willingness of Serbian authorities to bring the worst offenders to justice, noting that one of the most notorious individuals indicted by the tribunal—General Ratko MLADIĆ—has been at large in Serbia for almost a decade. Meanwhile, the government continues to make progress in identifying exhumed bodies of victims killed during the war. In 2001, for instance, Serb authorities discovered hundreds of bodies of ethnic Albanians in a mass grave; it is assumed that the victims were killed in Kosovo during a secessionist war in 1999 and then transferred to Serbia to conceal evidence of the slayings. Almost 200 bodies were identified by the Serbian government, in cooperation with international organizations and the International Commission on Missing Persons (ICMP), and repatriated to Kosovo.

After Milošević's ouster in 2000, Serb authorities have taken steps to investigate several high-profile political killings that appear to have a criminal dimension. Two former police officers and five accomplices went on trial for the 2002 killing of former Belgrade police chief Bosko Buha. During the trial a Belgrade police inspector offered sensational disclosures implicating other members of the police in other crimes. A former official was also sentenced to seven years imprisonment for the attempted murder of Vuk Drašković, a political opposition leader during the Milošević era.

See also BOSNIA AND HERZEGOVINA, HUMAN RIGHTS VIOLATIONS IN; KOSOVO, WAR CRIMES IN; YUGOSLAVIA, WAR CRIMES IN.

Further Reading:

Hagan, John. *Justice in the Balkans: Prosecuting War Crimes in the Hague Tribunal.* Chicago Series in Law and Society. Chicago: University of Chicago Press, 2003.

Hazan, Pierre, and James Thomas Snyder. *Justice in a Time of War: The True Story Behind the International Criminal Tribunal for the Former Yugoslavia.* Eugenia and Hugh M. Stewart Series on Eastern Europe. Austin: Texas A&M University Press, 2004.

Mertus, Julie. *Former Yugoslavia: War Crimes Trials in the Former Yugoslavia.* Helsinki: Human Rights Watch/Helsinki, 1995.

Rossanet, Bertrand de. *War and Peace in the Former Yugoslavia.* Boston: Martinus Nijhoff, 1997.

Seselj, Vojislav (1954–) *Serbian paramilitary commander*

Vojislav Seselj (pronounced SHESH-el), a former Serbian officer, was indicted by the INTERNATIONAL CRIMINAL TRIBUNAL FOR THE FORMER YUGOSLAVIA (ICTY) in The Hague on war crimes charges relating to the Slovenian, Bosnian, and Croatian wars of the 1990s. Under Seselj's direction, several paramilitary groups known as Seselj's Men and the White Eagles carried out persecutions, plunder, and killings of non-Serbian civilians. Although these groups had the support of the then Yugoslav leader Slobodan MILOŠEVIĆ, the two were bitter political rivals. If anything, Seselj was more intemperate than Milošević. He once threatened to blow up a nuclear power plant in the breakaway province of Slovenia (now an independent state) and warned that the Serbs would launch missile strikes in Italy, Austria, and Croatia in retaliation for NATO air strikes on Belgrade, the Yugoslav capital. While he has denied any complicity in the crimes of which he stands accused, he voluntarily turned himself into The Hague.

Born in 1954 in eastern Herzegovina (then a part of Yugoslavia), Seselj had a brilliant academic career: He was the youngest student ever to earn a Ph.D. in Yugoslavia. Subsequently he taught at the University of Michigan and at Sarajevo University. His exposure to American values, however, did not seem to have instilled him with democratic values. An ardent Serb nationalist, he wrote an article advocating the formation of a Serb state to replace the mul-

tiethnic Yugoslavia, then under communist rule. For his temerity he was sentenced to two years in prison. In 1990, as Yugoslavia began to disintegrate, he founded the Radical Party (SRS) and joined a parliamentary alliance with Milošević's party. The alliance, however, quickly collapsed over Milošević's apparent readiness to withdraw military support to Bosnian Serbs who were fighting to create an independent state of their own. Milošević called his one-time ally "the personification of violence and primitivity," strong charges coming from a man who would later be charged by the ICTY with war crimes.

The two men, however, patched up their differences when the third Balkan war of the 1990s threatened to erupt in the province of Kosovo. Ethnic tensions had been brewing in the province between Serbs and the Albanians who made up the majority of the population. "Their country is Albania and they should live there," Seselj declared. "The only Albanians who should live here (Kosovo) are the ones who think of Serbia as their fatherland."

Imprisonment has not mellowed the former warlord. Even though he remains behind bars, he succeeded in winning a seat in the Yugoslav parliament in elections held in 2003, using a prison phone to communicate with a Belgrade radio station, which then broadcast his words to supporters. He has repudiated the UN-sponsored ICTY as an "American tool against Serbs," which he says he "will blast to pieces." Nor has he shown any deference to the judges, comparing them to Nazis and demanding that they change their red-and-black courtroom robes because they reminded him of the Roman Catholic Inquisition. Although other defendants facing trial at The Hague have shown intemperate behavior during the court proceedings—Milošević in particular—none has proven quite so troublesome as Seselj. "Other accused have their ways of being difficult," said a tribunal spokesman, "but we have not seen such extreme verbal assaults before." His disruptive tactics have caused court officials to openly speculate whether a fair trial is even possible.

See also BOSNIA AND HERZEGOVINA, HUMAN RIGHTS VIOLATIONS IN; CROATIA, HUMAN RIGHTS VIOLATIONS IN; SERBIA, HUMAN RIGHTS VIOLATIONS IN; SLOVENIA, HUMAN RIGHTS VIOLATIONS IN.

Further Reading:

Hagan, John. *Justice in the Balkans: Prosecuting War Crimes in the Hague Tribunal.* Chicago Series in Law and Society. Chicago: University of Chicago Press, 2003.

Hazan, Pierre, and James Thomas Snyder. *Justice in a Time of War: The True Story behind the International Criminal Tribunal for the Former Yugoslavia.* Eugenia and Hugh M. Stewart Series on Eastern Europe. Austin: Texas A&M University Press, 2004.

Kim, Julie. *War in the Former Yugoslavia: Chronology of Events August 16, 1992–May 30, 1993.* CRS report for Congress. Washington, D.C.: Foreign Affairs and National Defense Division, Congressional Research Service, the Library of Congress, 1993.

Kipp, Jacob W. *International Ramifications of Yugoslavia's Serial Wars: The Challenge of Ethno-national Conflicts for a Post-Cold-War, European order.* Fort Leavenworth, Kans.: European Military Studies Office, 1993.

Naimark, Norman, and Holly Case. *Yugoslavia and Its Historians: Understanding the Balkan Wars of the 1990s.* Stanford, Calif.: Stanford University Press, 2003.

Rogel, Carole. *The Breakup of Yugoslavia and the War in Bosnia.* Westport, Conn.: Greenwood Press, 1998.

Rossanet, Bertrand de. *War and Peace in the Former Yugoslavia.* Boston: Martinus Nijhoff, 1997.

Scharf, Michael P. *Balkan Justice: The Story behind the First International War Crimes Trial since Nuremberg.* Durham, N.C.: Carolina Academic Press, 1997.

Seyss-Inquart, Arthur (Arthur Zajtich) (1892–1946)
Nazi official

Arthur Seyss-Inquart served the Nazi regime during World War II as an official in Austria and occupied Poland before becoming *Reichskommissar* for the Occupied Netherlands. Under his rule nearly the entire Jewish population of the Netherlands was deported to CONCENTRATION CAMPS. After the war he was tried by the Allies at the NUREMBERG TRIALS, found guilty of war crimes, and sentenced to death.

The son of a teacher, Seyss-Inquart was born Arthur Zajtich in Stonarov, Moravia (then part of the Austro-Hungarian Empire), on July 22, 1892. He fought for the Austrian army in World War I and received several decorations for bravery in combat. He went on to obtain a degree in law from the University of Vienna and open a law practice in Austria. He soon became drawn to right-wing ideology and joined the Austrian National Socialist (Nazi) Party, which favored the union (*Anschluss*) of Austria and Germany. "The National Socialist Party in Austria never tried to hide its inclination for a greater Germany," he declared in a speech. "That Austria would one day return to the Reich was a matter of course for all National Socialists and for true Germans in Austria." Seyss-Inquart became state chancellor in the Austrian government of Kurt von Schuschnigg, but when Schushnigg was forced to resign after rejecting Adolf HITLER's demands for a more pro-Nazi government, Seyss-Inquart replaced him as the head of a National Socialist cabinet; he later said that he had called on Hitler for armed assistance to save Austria from plunging into civil war. Seyss-Inquart subsequently drafted

a law that reduced Austria to the level of a German province but continued to head the new Ostmark, as the province was known, answering to the chief minister Ernst KALTENBRUNNER. Seyss-Inquart was also given the honorary SS rank of *Gruppenführer,* which he held as well as minister without portfolio in Hitler's government.

In 1940 Seyss-Inquart was appointed deputy governor of Poland (occupied the year before) under Governor-General Hans FRANK. In his new capacity, he was involved with relocating Polish Jews into ghettoes (from which they would eventually be deported to extermination camps) and what was euphemistically called the "extraordinary pacification" of the remnants of Polish resistance. In May 1940, after the Germans had seized the Low Countries, Seyss-Inquart moved on to the Netherlands, charged with forging a closer economic relationship with Germany. As *Reichskommissar,* he was effectively in control of the Netherlands; to bolster his position he backed a right-wing party, the Dutch NSB, which formed a paramilitary unit known as the Landwacht. At the same time he locked up officials of other political parties that were banned. He extended his control into the cultural sphere "right down to the chess players' club" under a policy called the *Kulturkammer* and carried out orders to extract 50 million marks a month from the country to compensate Germany for the costs of occupation. He ruthlessly suppressed "terror," as he termed the resistance, and directly ordered the execution of 800 people (although estimates range up to 3,500), among them political prisoners and Dutch men executed in reprisal killings, under the "Hostage Law." In addition, he supervised a FORCED LABOR recruitment campaign, drafting 530,000 Dutch civilians to work for the Germans; almost half of them were shipped to Germany to work in factories there. Ultimately insistent demands for more labor grew too much even for Seyss-Inquart, and when in 1944 Berlin asked for an additional 250,000 laborers, he was able to muster only 12,000.

An avowed anti-Semite, Seyss-Inquart had conducted a purge of all Jews in the government, the press, and the major professions shortly after arriving in the Netherlands. He then organized a registration campaign to document all Jews (about 140,000) in the country; by 1941 thousands of Jews had been herded into ghettoes in Amsterdam or camps at Westerbork and Vught. The first DEPORTATIONS occurred in February 1941, when 1,000 Dutch Jews were sent to the Buchenwald and Mauthausen concentration camps. Subsequently most Dutch Jews were deported to Auschwitz. In September 1944, as the Allies were approaching the Netherlands, Jews were relocated from Westerbork and sent to their deaths at Theresienstadt in Czechoslovakia. Of the 140,000 Jews who were registered before the war, only 13,400 survived—5,400 who had returned from the camps and others who had emerged from hiding.

In the final months of the war, Seyss-Inquart helped carry out a brutal scorched earth policy to destroy Dutch harbor facilities and flood the country, devastating its agricultural industry and causing widespread famine, which is believed to have led to the deaths of 30,000 people. Seyss-Inquart remained head of the Netherlands until the bitter end. Captured by the Allies in May 1945, he was tried before the Nuremberg Tribunal on charges of conspiracy to commit crimes against peace; planning, initiating, and waging wars of aggression; war crimes; and CRIMES AGAINST HUMANITY. He was found guilty on all counts and hanged along with several other Nazi officials on October 16, 1946.

Further Reading:

Beigbeder, Yves, and Theo van Boven. *Judging War Criminals: The Politics of International Justice.* Sidney, Australia: Palgrave Macmillan, 1999.

Bloxham, Donald. *Genocide on Trial: War Crimes Trials and the Formation of Holocaust History and Memory.* Oxford: Oxford University Press, 2003.

Cooper, Belinda, and Richard Goldstone. *War Crimes: The Legacy of Nuremberg.* New York: TV Books Inc., 1999.

Dawidowicz, Lucy. *A Holocaust Reader.* Library of Jewish Studies. Chicago: Behrman House Publishing, 1976.

Dwork, Deborah, and Robert Jan Van Pelt. *Holocaust: A History.* New York: W. W. Norton & Company, 2003.

Gilbert, Martin. *The Holocaust: A History of the Jews of Europe During the Second World War.* New York: Owl Books, 1987.

Shattuck, John (1942–   ) *American diplomat and human rights advocate*

Former assistant secretary of state for democracy, human rights, and labor in the Clinton administration, John Shattuck has been an outspoken advocate for human rights. He deplored the failure of the United States to intervene and stop the GENOCIDE in Rwanda in 1994. In an interview for the PBS program *Frontline*, Shattuck blamed bureaucratic bungling and political concerns for Washington's inaction. Policy makers were already on "overload," he said, when the genocide broke out: "I discovered that [Secretary of State Warren] Christopher was totally preoccupied with China and the Middle East. . . . One of the untold stories about Rwanda is the terrible tragedy of the timing. . . . Had the genocide occurred a year and a half later, the response might well have been different." In another interview he elaborated on the wisdom of intervention in humanitarian crises such as Rwanda's: "You want to save lives at first if genocide is under way, and there are instances in which

intervention, including military intervention, is absolutely essential. It should have been done in Rwanda. It was belatedly done in Bosnia. It was done in Afghanistan. It was done in Kosovo. It was done the wrong way in Iraq, but it needed to be done. You also cannot assume that any model of democracy, certainly our own model, but even any other model, is necessarily going to work in another country. So you'd better listen closely to what you're hearing."

Shattuck, who later served as U.S. ambassador to the Czech Republic, is the author of the book *Freedom on Fire: Human Rights Wars and America's Response.* In 2000 he was named the chief executive officer of the John F. Kennedy Library and Foundation at Harvard University, where he has taught law. A graduate of Yale Law School with an M.A. in law from Cambridge University, he previously served as executive director of the American Civil Liberties Union Washington, D.C., office and national staff counsel from 1971 to 1984.

See also RWANDA, GENOCIDE IN.

Further Reading:

Shattuck, John. *Freedom on Fire: Human Rights Wars and America's Response.* Cambridge, Mass.: Harvard University Press, 2003.

Shimada Shigetaro (1883–1976) *Japanese naval commander and militarist*

Admiral Shimada Shigetaro was a navy minister and a member of the Supreme War Council in Japan during World War II. Classified as a Class A war criminal, he was convicted by the International Military Tribunal for the Far East (the TOKYO TRIALS) for his actions during World War II.

Born in 1883, Shimada served as vice chief of the naval staff and commander of Japan's China Fleet before becoming minister of the navy, a position he held from 1941 to 1944. Naval forces under his command carried out massacres of Allied PRISONERS OF WAR and killed survivors of torpedoed Allied ships. Prisoners and civilians alike were also interned aboard ships—known as hell ships—under deplorable conditions. Ironically, Shimada and many other top naval officials had initially opposed Japan going to war with the United States. But in the interest of national unity, Shimada eventually acquiesced to the army, which was strongly in favor of war. He declared that the destruction of "harmony" between the army and navy was far worse than the prospect of war, which ultimately proved ruinous to Japan.

At the Tokyo Trials Shimada was one of several Class A war criminals who, the indictment charged, had "contemplated and carried out . . . murdering, maiming and ill-treating prisoners of war [and] civilian internees . . . forcing them to labor under inhumane conditions . . . plundering public and private property, wantonly destroying cities, towns and villages beyond any justification of military necessity; (perpetrating) mass murder, rape, PILLAGE, brigandage, TORTURE and other barbaric cruelties upon the helpless civilian population of the over-run countries." Shimada was found guilty on five counts and sentenced to prison. He was paroled in 1955 and died in 1976.

Further Reading:

Daws, Gavin. *Prisoners of the Japanese: POWs of World War II in the Pacific.* New York: Perennial, 1996.

Lamont-Brown, Raymond. *Ships from Hell: Japanese War Crimes on the High Seas.* Phoenix Mill: Sutton Publishing, 2002.

Shining Path (Sendero Luminoso)

The Shining Path (Sendero Luminoso in Spanish) was a radical Maoist insurgency that terrorized Peru throughout the 1980s. At its height the Shining Path was the most formidable guerrilla group in Latin America. Approximately 30,000 Peruvians, most of them civilians, were killed by both guerrillas and government forces in 15 years of conflict. The group, which was founded by a former philosophy professor, Abimael Guzmán Reynoso, in the late 1960s, grew out of the Peruvian Communist Party but eventually abandoned the facade of political legitimacy and turned to terrorism in 1980. Guzmán organized his guerrilla force for over a decade before he was prepared to launch its first strikes. The Shining Path's objective was to destroy the state, demolish all of its institutions, and install a communist peasant revolutionary regime in its place. Perhaps only Cambodia's Khmer Rouge rivaled the Shining Path in its drive to radicalize a nation. And like the Khmer Rouge, the Peruvian group adhered to a policy of self-reliance that led the group to shun all outside assistance, even from communist nations.

In 1980 the Shining Path signaled their forthcoming campaign of terror by stringing up dead dogs on lampposts in every city in Peru. The gruesome sight made a chilling impression on the population. By the mid-1980s, the guerrillas, who now numbered several thousand, had taken control over large parts of the Peruvian countryside. They then began to stage dramatic attacks in major cities, stirring fears that the insurgents might be in a position to overrun the whole country. The worst single incident took place in July 1992, when two car bombs went off in the middle-class district of Miraflores in Lima, killing 20 people and injuring more than 250 others.

In 1992 then-President Alberto FUJIMORI declared martial law, setting the stage for a military crackdown that resulted in numerous human rights violations. The army began to score several successes. In 1992 Guzmán, who had

practically become a mythical figure in the minds of many Peruvians due to his ability to elude detection, was captured. His arrest, together with the apprehension of most of the Shining Path's leaders, dealt a blow to the guerrillas from which they never recovered. Guzmán was tried and sentenced to life in prison. However, elements of the Shining Path have continued to wage war against the government on a lesser scale. There are reports that the rump faction, which is down to a few hundred members, has become involved in narcotrafficking and kidnapping for ransom to raise funds for its operations—a departure from earlier policy under Guzmán's leadership. Several of its members were taken captive as recently as 2003.

Further Reading:

Gorriti Ellenbogen, Gustavo. *The Shining Path: A History of the Millenarian War in Peru.* Translated by Robin Kirle. Chapel Hill: University of North Carolina Press, 1999.

Palmer, David Scott, ed. *The Shining Path of Peru.* Sidney, Australia: Palgrave Macmillan, 1991.

Stern, Steve, ed. *Shining and Other Paths: War and Society in Peru 1980–1995.* Durham, N.C.: Duke University Press, 1998.

siege

As a military tactic, a siege of a city held by a belligerent force is not, at least in theory, explicitly outlawed by INTERNATIONAL HUMANITARIAN LAW: The capture of a city defended by an enemy could be considered a legitimate military objective. Sieges are generally employed to wear away the enemy's defenses while depriving the city's inhabitants of needed resources, including food, which will hasten its surrender. Until the end of World War II, sieges were justified under the doctrine of military necessity. The Regulations to the Hague Conventions of 1907, however, banned bombardment of "undefended" cities. Postwar treaties, notably the GENEVA CONVENTIONS of 1949 and the ADDITIONAL PROTOCOLS TO THE GENEVA CONVENTIONS of 1977, have imposed such restrictions on the infliction of harm on civilian populations "as a method of combat" that sieges are implicitly banned, though it should be noted that neither the conventions nor the additional protocols specifically mention sieges.

If in the past starvation was seen as a means of forcing the surrender of a besieged city, that practice is no longer considered acceptable. The Fourth Geneva Convention allows a force to bar food from reaching a civilian population if that food will also be used by enemy military forces. However, Additional Protocol I, which covers international conflicts, appears to negate that exception. It states that all efforts must be made to distinguish between military personnel and civilian populations, and military operations should be "directed only against military objectives." The protocol prohibits the starvation of civilians, even if some food delivered by relief agencies falls into the hands of troops defending the city. Moreover, a belligerent is barred from targeting property vital to civilian survival, such as electric plants, a further impediment to laying siege to a city. Protocol II, which covers internal conflicts, echoes this provision: "[T]he civilian population as such, as well as individual civilians, shall not be the object of attack."

In spite of these prohibitions, sieges continue to be employed as a method of warfare—for instance, in Iraq by U.S. forces and in Chechnya by Russian forces. But the true horror of a siege was driven home by the four-year siege of Sarajevo (1992–96) by Serb forces during the Bosnian War. Artillery attacks and snipers positioned in the mountains above Sarajevo killed 10,000–12,000 people and injured another 50,000, almost all of them civilians. Hardly a single building was left intact. During the siege, Serbs tried to starve the city out; only extraordinary efforts by UN relief agencies managed to prevent famine. The INTERNATIONAL CRIMINAL TRIBUNAL FOR THE FORMER YUGOSLAVIA found the commander of Bosnian Serb forces besieging the city guilty of deliberately targeting civilians, leaving little doubt that in most cases sieges are likely to violate the norms of international humanitarian law.

See also BOSNIA AND HERZEGOVINA, HUMAN RIGHTS VIOLATIONS IN; SARAJEVO, SIEGE OF; STARVATION AS A TACTIC OF WAR.

Further Reading:
Gutman, Roy, ed. *Crimes of War: What the Public Should Know.* New York: W. W. Norton & Company, 1999.
Hagan, John. *Justice in the Balkans: Prosecuting War Crimes in the Hague Tribunal.* Chicago Series in Law and Society. Chicago: University of Chicago Press, 2003.
Harris, Nathaniel. *The War in Former Yugoslavia.* London: Hodder & Stoughton, 1997.
Hazan, Pierre, and James Thomas Snyder. *Justice in a Time of War: The True Story behind the International Criminal Tribunal for the Former Yugoslavia.* Eugenia and Hugh M. Stewart Series on Eastern Europe. Austin: Texas A&M University Press, 2004.
United Nations War Crimes Commission. *Law Reports of Trials of War Criminals: Four Genocide Trials.* Boulder, Colo.: Lynne Rienner Publishers, 1992.

Sierra Leone, human rights violations in

Sierra Leone, a former British colony in West Africa, holds an especially grim distinction in the annals of war crimes and human rights violations. Once one of the most beauti-

ful countries on the continent, Sierra Leone now lies in shambles as a result of a brutal civil war that engulfed the country over a 10-year period that spanned most of the 1990s. In a campaign of violence that shocked the world, rebels mutilated civilians, lopping off limbs and even lips to intimidate supporters of the government. It is believed that nearly 20,000 people were maimed in this way. The war cost the lives of 75,000 and displaced 2 million people. No one knows how many women were raped. An estimated 5,400 children were abducted by rebels and forced to become sexual slaves or pressed into combat.

By nearly every measure of civilization—health, mortality rates, sanitation, education, infrastructure, and so on—Sierra Leone now ranks almost dead last. Average life expectancy is only 38, infant mortality rate is 164 per thousand, and nearly two-thirds of the adult population is illiterate. The capital, Freetown, has been plundered, and most of the country's educated people have fled—a particularly bitter irony in a country that had boasted West Africa's first university. While rich in such natural resources as iron ore and bauxite, Sierra Leone is best known for its diamond reserves. These so-called CONFLICT DIAMONDS have turned out to be a curse, however: Without them the civil war might never have been fought or funded. (Legal exports of diamonds before the war were about $60 million annually.)

The war actually began in neighboring Liberia in 1991 and then proceeded to spill over the border when Liberian insurgents began to occupy parts of Sierra Leone. Although government troops succeeded in repelling these Liberian groups, they soon found themselves facing a Liberian-sponsored indigenous insurgency known as the Revolutionary United Front (RUF) under the leadership of Foday SANKOH. Although a peace accord was reached between the warring factions in 1992, the country continued to be rocked by a series of coups and insurrections. In 1997, after a military coup toppled President Ahmed Kabbah, the stage was set for a second round of fighting. The crisis spurred the country's West African neighbors to intervene. In February 1998, Nigerian troops dispatched by ECO-MOG (ECOWAS MONITORING GROUP) occupied Freetown and began an offensive against Sankoh and the RUF. A month later Kabbah was restored to power.

The presence of the peacekeepers failed to subdue the rebellion, however, and in January 1999 the RUF and other rebel factions launched an attack on the capital that left thousands of civilians dead. There is no more telling indication of the rebel intentions than the code name they assigned the offensive against Freetown: Operation No Living Thing. The assault lived up to its billing, taking the lives of 6,000 civilians in just two weeks. Many of the worst atrocities were committed by children soldiers, who burned homes and hacked limbs with casual savagery. One of the terrorists was a girl who proudly called herself Queen Cut Hands. Even though the rebels were eventually forced to retreat from the capital, they did not go far and continued to dominate the rural areas. They also maintained their control over the diamond mines, providing them a source of wealth to buy more arms.

By this time the Nigerians were running out of money to support the peacekeeping mission, forcing the hand of the British, the country's former colonial power, which was prepared to use force to restore order. The United States, however, opposed a military solution and called for negotiations. The Reverend Jesse Jackson was sent as a special envoy to broker a cease-fire agreement in late 1999 which became known as the Lome Peace Accords. By the terms of the accords, Sankoh—who had been condemned to death in 1998—was elevated to the vice presidency, effectively giving him control over the diamond mines. Even more dismaying to human rights groups, the accord also provided for a blanket AMNESTY for all human rights abuses committed up to the date the agreement was signed.

International law—specifically Article 6 of Additional Protocol I to the GENEVA CONVENTIONS—encourages granting amnesty as a way of bringing about reconciliation after a conflict. However, legal experts disagree as to whether any amnesty can be applied to serious war crimes, such as those perpetuated by the RUF. This is the position taken by human rights organizations, and UN secretary general Kofi Annan declared that the United Nations would not be bound by the Lome accord.

In spite of the accord, peace did not hold in Sierra Leone. In spring 2000 RUF soldiers, many of them high on crack, marijuana, speed, and cheap gin, clashed with UN peacekeepers. The campaign of terror resumed. In May 2000, less than a year after the peace agreement, the RUF launched another assault on Freetown. Once again the capital descended into chaos. In the countryside, 500 UN peacekeepers were taken hostage by the rebels and were freed only because of an audacious rescue mission by British troops. Sankoh was caught as he attempted to flee Freetown.

In August 2000 the UN Security Council voted to establish a SPECIAL COURT FOR SIERRA LEONE under the joint jurisdiction of the Sierra Leone government and the United Nations to prosecute individuals charged with war crimes. Although the rebel groups were most culpable, all parties to the conflict, including soldiers of ECOMOG, the Nigerian-led peacekeeping mission, became implicated in human rights abuses. A second ceasefire in 2001 proved more enduring, and the United Nations was able to disarm 45,000 RUF fighters.

See also ADDITIONAL PROTOCOLS TO THE GENEVA CONVENTIONS; CHILDREN'S RIGHTS; LIBERIA, HUMAN RIGHTS VIOLATIONS IN.

Further Reading:
Ferme, Mariane C. *The Underneath of Things: Violence, History, and the Everyday in Sierra Leone.* Berkeley: University of California Press, 2001.
Jackson, Michael. *In Sierra Leone.* Durham, N.C.: Duke University Press, 2004.
Richards, Paul. *Fighting for the Rain Forest: War, Youth, and Resources in Sierra Leone.* African Issues Series. London: Heinemann, 1996.
Romano, Cesare, Andre Nollkaemper and Jann K. Kleffner, eds. *Internationalized Criminal Courts and Tribunals: Sierra Leone, East Timor, Kosovo, and Cambodia.* International Courts and Tribunals Series. Oxford: Oxford University Press, 2004.
Voeten, Teun. *How de Body? One Man's Terrifying Journey through an African War.* New York: Thomas Dunne Books, 2002.

slavery

According to the United Nations *slavery* is a term that applies to a variety of human rights violations and is not limited to traditional slavery and the slave trade. The contemporary definition of slavery includes "the sale of children, child prostitution, child pornography, the exploitation of child labor, the sexual mutilation of female children, the use of children in armed conflicts, debt bondage, the traffic in persons and in the sale of human organs, the exploitation of prostitution, and certain practices under APARTHEID and colonial régimes." Though broad, this definition attempts to deal with the myriad ways that people are being exploited even if they receive a small amount of money. Debt bondage, for instance, is considered slavery since a person is not free to leave a job until money owed by the worker is repaid. Often slavery is practiced in secrecy, which makes it more difficult to uncover, punish, or put a stop to it. Not surprisingly, the people most likely to be enslaved are the poorest and most vulnerable.

In spite of its clandestine nature, the various forms of slavery are known to be widespread. For instance, according to the INTERNATIONAL LABOR ORGANIZATION (ILO), a United Nations body, as many as 100 million children alone are in FORCED LABOR. Modern attempts to abolish slavery extend back to the early 19th century: The British banned slavery throughout its empire in 1837. In the United States the LIEBER CODE, which governed the conduct of the Union Army during the Civil War, outlawed the enslavement of any prisoner. The Emancipation Proclamation, issued by President Abraham Lincoln on January 1, 1863, abolished slavery in the United States even though slavery persisted in Southern states until the Civil War ended in 1865.

The first treaty of the 20th century addressing the issue was the Slavery Convention of 1926, drawn up by the

LEAGUE OF NATIONS. This convention broadened the definition of slavery to include the practices and institutions of debt bondage, servile forms of marriage, and the exploitation of children and adolescents. Article 1 states that enslavement "is the status or condition of a person over whom any or all of the powers attaching to the right of ownership are exercised." The slave trade is defined by the convention as "all acts involved in the capture, acquisition or disposal of a person with intent to reduce him to slavery; all acts involved in the acquisition of a slave with a view to selling or exchanging him; all acts of disposal by sale or exchange of a slave acquired with a view to being sold or exchanged and, in general, every act of trade or transport of slaves." The United Nations, the successor to the League, adopted the Slavery Convention in 1953. By 1993 some 86 states had ratified the convention, which obliges signatories to prevent and suppress the slave trade and to abolish slavery in all its forms.

There are other agreements that deal with various forms of slavery. The UNIVERSAL DECLARATION OF HUMAN RIGHTS of 1948 declares: "No one shall be held in slavery or servitude: slavery and the slave trade shall be prohibited in all their forms." The declaration is not a binding treaty, so over the next several years the United Nations enacted a series of agreements that banned various forms of slavery. For example, the 1949 Convention for the Suppression of the Traffic in Persons and of the Exploitation of the Prostitution of Others, targets the procurer and not the prostitution. This convention calls on parties to the accord to curb the traffic in persons of either sex for the purpose of prostitution. Other accords include the INTERNATIONAL COVENANT ON CIVIL AND POLITICAL RIGHTS, the International Covenant on Economic, Social and Cultural Rights, the Convention on the Elimination of All Forms of Discrimination against Women, and the CONVENTION ON THE RIGHTS OF THE CHILD. The latter, which entered into force in 1990, is considered potentially one of the most effective means of combating slavery because of the sheer number of children who are forced into slavery, prostitution, or combat around the world.

The 1977 Additional Protocol II to the GENEVA CONVENTIONS is the first accord explicitly banning slavery in internal armed conflict. Article 4 states: "Slavery and the slave trade in all their forms . . . are and shall remain prohibited at any time and in any place whatsoever." Although the United States and other countries did not ratify this protocol, the prohibition against slavery is considered binding nonetheless, based on CUSTOMARY LAW. Most recently, the 1998 ROME STATUTE OF THE INTERNATIONAL CRIMINAL COURT termed enslavement a crime against humanity when it is systematically directed at a civilian population. The statute uses the 1926 Slavery Convention in defining enslavement as "the exercise of any or all of the powers attaching to the right of ownership over a person and includes the exercise of such power in the course of TRAFFICKING IN PERSONS, in particular women and children."

See also ADDITIONAL PROTOCOLS TO THE GENEVA CONVENTIONS; CHILDREN'S RIGHTS.

Further Reading:

Dormann, Knut, and Louise Doswald-Beck. *Elements of War Crimes under the Rome Statute of the International Criminal Court: Sources and Commentary.* Cambridge: Cambridge University Press, 2003.

Meltzer, Milton. *Slavery: A World History.* New York: Da Capo Press, 1993.

Slovenia, human rights violations in

Of all the newly independent countries that once constituted the former Yugoslavia, Slovenia has emerged with the fewest scars. Slovenia was the first to formally break away from the federation in 1991, precipitating a brief war. After 10 days of fighting, the Yugoslav forces withdrew in defeat. Unlike Bosnia and Croatia, which also declared independence, Slovenia had a small Serb population, with the result that Belgrade did not envision it as an integral part of a "greater Serbia."

According to recent U.S. State Department reports, Slovenia receives fairly high marks for upholding human rights. There are some allegations of police brutality and self-censorship in the media because of political or economic pressure. The most serious human rights problems are a direct consequence of the war: More than 18,000 non-Slovenes lost their citizenship after Slovenia declared its independence. While ethnic Slovenes were automatically given citizenship, those people belonging to other ethnic groups had to apply for citizenship. Anyone who failed to do so within a year lost his citizenship, becoming in effect one of the "erased," who were deprived of their right to permanent residency, pensions, and health benefits. At least seven committed suicide in despair; thousands more were made homeless or were arrested for minor offenses, such as jaywalking, and then deported because they lacked proper papers. In 2004 a referendum was held to determine whether these legal "nonpersons" could be restored to citizenship. But the vast majority of Slovenes, responding to fears of illegal immigration and galvanized by nationalist sentiment, voted against restoring Slovene citizenship to nonpersons. "It is a shame that they were erased, but the country will go bankrupt if it has to pay compensation," said one voter. "We've come too far to let the country go down the drain just like that." A minority of Slovenes, however, viewed the vote as a manifestation of racism, intolerance, and xenophobia.

See also YUGOSLAVIA, WAR CRIMES IN.

Further Reading:
Glenny, Misha. *The Fall of Yugoslavia: The Third Balkan War.* New York: Penguin Books, 1996.
Kim, Julie. *War in the Former Yugoslavia: Chronology of Events August 16, 1992–May 30, 1993.* CRS report for Congress. Washington, D.C.: Foreign Affairs and National Defense Division, Congressional Research Service, the Library of Congress, 1993.

Solzhenitsyn, Aleksandr Isayevich (1918–)

Russian novelist and dissident

Aleksandr Solzhenitsyn, who won the Nobel Prize in literature in 1970, is probably as well known for his fearless opposition to the now-defunct Soviet regime as he is for his large body of writing. His best-known works, the novels *One Day in the Life of Ivan Denisovich* and *The First Circle* and the nonfiction *The Gulag Archipelago,* are all based on his harrowing experiences as a prisoner in the Siberian GULAGS, the notorious Soviet prison camps where millions perished under the brutal dictatorship of Josef STALIN.

Solzhenitsyn was born in 1918 into a Cossack intellectual family in the northern Caucasus Mountains. After receiving a degree in mathematics and physics from the University of Rostov-on-Don and taking correspondence courses in literature at Moscow State University, he joined the Red Army and fought in World War II, achieving the rank of captain of artillery and receiving two decorations for valor. But no sooner had the war ended than he was arrested in 1945 when it was discovered that he had written a letter critical of Stalin—"the man with the mustache." He spent the next eight years in the gulag and in labor prisons, but because of his advanced education he escaped having to endure hard labor.

In 1950 Solzhenitsyn was transferred to a political prison, where he performed manual labor. During this period he became ill with stomach cancer, which was successfully treated. His hospital experience formed the basis of his novel *The Cancer Ward.* Although he made a living as a teacher following his release, he continued to write in secret to avoid further problems with the regime. Stalin's death and the ascension to power of Premier Nikita Khrushchev ushered in a new, more open political era. In the more relaxed atmosphere, Solzhenitsyn published *One Day in the Life of Ivan Denisovich,* first in serial form in the literary journal *Novyi Mir,* then as a book in 1962. An immediate sensation, the novel was acclaimed not only because of its literary quality but also because of its subject matter: Until this point, writers had steered clear of the subject of the gulag and Stalinist repression. The book was published abroad and gained its author international acclaim. At the time Solzhenitsyn was 42. The thaw lasted only a few years, however, and it became increasingly diffi-cult for him to get his words in print except by means of illegal samizdat—self-published writing surreptitiously passed from reader to reader. Between 1963 and 1966 he succeeded in publishing only four stories.

In 1965 many of Solzhenitsyn's manuscripts were confiscated by the KGB, but even so he managed to smuggle some of his work to the West. When he was awarded the Nobel Prize in 1970, he refused to go to Stockholm to accept the honor for fear that he would not be allowed to return home. In 1971 he published *August 1914,* a novel about czarist Russia during World War I. Two years later *The Gulag Archipelago,* the first book of his three-volume chronicle of the Soviet labor camps, appeared, earning its author even wider recognition abroad. At home, though, he was viewed by the Communist regime as a dangerous dissident, and in 1974 he was detained on charges of treason, stripped of his citizenship, and then sent into exile. He lived first in Switzerland and later settled in Vermont, a state he found congenial because of its climate and relative isolation. He devoted himself to his work, turning out several new books, among them *The Red Wheel,* an epic about the Russian Revolution, which was part of a series that also included the earlier *August 1914* (which he revised), *October 1916, March 1917,* and *April 1917.*

In 1990 the new leader of the Soviet Union, Mikhail Gorbachev, offered to restore Solzhenitzyn's citizenship; a year later charges of treason against him were dropped. In 1994 Solzhenitsyn returned from exile and made a spectacular whistle-stop train tour through Siberia. No longer a pariah, he was greeted by President Boris Yeltsin, now the head of a new postcommunist Russia, and given the opportunity to deliver an address to the Russian Duma (parliament). But Solzhenitsyn did not fit into the new Russia anymore than he had the old Soviet Union or, for that matter, the United States. Calling for a revival of Holy Russia under the Russian Orthodox Church, he decried what he termed the "spiritual exhaustion" of Western culture, where "mediocrity triumphs under the guise of democratic restraints." In a controversial speech given to students at Harvard University in 1978, he declared, "We [Russians] have been through a spiritual training far in advance of Western experience. The complex and deadly crush of life has produced stronger, deeper, and more interesting personalities than those generated by standardized Western well-being."

Further Reading:
Solzhenitsyn, Aleksandr. *August 1914.* New York: Farrar, Straus & Giroux, 2000.
———. *The Cancer Ward.* New York: Farrar, Straus & Giroux, 1991.
———. *The First Circle.* Evanston, Ill.: Northwestern University Press, 1997.

———. *The Gulag Archipelago.* New York: HarperCollins, 1978.

———. *One Day in the Life of Ivan Denisovich.* New York: Signet Classics, 1999.

Somalia, human rights violations in

Since the pullout of United Nations troops in March 1995 amid violence and chaos—an event made famous by the book and movie version of *Blackhawk Down*—Somalia has been largely abandoned by the international community. Whatever order exists in the country depends on Islamic law (sharia) and clan loyalty. However, as 2004 came to an end, negotiations conducted in Kenya among various elements of Somali civil society held out the promise of a restoration of a functioning government. Under the tumultuous conditions that have prevailed for the last decade, though, thousands of civilians have suffered from grave human rights abuses; according to a report by HUMAN RIGHTS WATCH, these abuses include "killings of civilians through the indiscriminate use of heavy weapons, the deliberate, targeted killing of civilians, execution-style killings of captives, rape and other cruel and degrading treatment, and forced displacement and controls on freedom of movement." The pattern of these abuses, the human rights group says, reflects clan rivalries that fueled and exacerbated a famine in 1991–92, leading to the intervention of UN forces, spearheaded by the United States. (President George H. W. Bush authorized the deployment of U.S. forces as part of the UN mission.)

Initially, after the UN withdrawal in 1995, the warlords defied expectations by cooperating with one another through a so-called Peace Committee, which administered the harbor and airport in the capital of Mogadishu. The accord broke down, but even so, the country never descended into the state of anarchy that existed before to the abortive UN mission. Traditional sources of authority—predominantly clan leaders—have managed to maintain a precarious peace ever since. But any calm is contingent on the willingness of warlords to refrain from resorting to violence.

The power of the warlords reaches into many parts of society, blurring the lines between nation and clan. Followers of these warlords, for example, also hold multiple positions—as militiamen, contract guards, or police officers, for example—while retaining their ultimate loyalty to the warlord. Human rights groups hope that a general weariness with perpetual conflict may have an ameliorative effect on the warlords and temper their readiness to use violence on a massive scale. Already civil war has led to hundreds of thousands of deaths from mass killings and the destruction of infrastructure vital to survival, including the water systems and the means of production. EXTRAJUDICIAL KILLINGS still characterize clan rivalries, and bodies are publicly displayed as a warning. When warnings go unheeded, warlords have killed clan elders and other traditional leaders who have sought to bring about reconciliation among factions that may threaten their power.

The clan rivalries have also resulted in whole communities being uprooted from their homes and threatened with death if they return. Women are especially at risk from these forced expulsions. Several hundred thousand Somalis have been forced to flee to neighboring countries where they have been settled temporarily in camps, while hundreds of thousands more have been internally displaced. It is only because of abundant rainfall and good harvests in recent years that thousands more have escaped starvation and death. According to Human Rights Watch, those civilians who are most at risk must rely for protection on application of sharia law in the absence of a national judicial system, although in their interpretation of Islamic law, Somali religious authorities mete out draconian punishments—known as *hudud*—that include summary executions and amputations. Compensation for victims of abuses often rests on clan identity. "The only human rights protection is the structure of the clan, in the sense that it is the clan that protects rights," noted a relief agency official.

Over the last several years elders, businessmen, women's groups, intellectuals, and religious leaders have gathered in Somalia and outside the country in an attempt to establish a new government and reach a political settlement. While these conferences have excluded or marginalized the warlords, it is unclear whether a permanent political settlement can take hold without their acquiescence.

In January 2005 several of Somalia's feuding factions managed to hammer out a peace deal in Nairobi, Kenya, which some observers saw as the best chance in a decade for the restoration of some kind of normalcy to the strife-ridden country. The accord called for a five-year transitional government, a new constitution, and a national census. A new parliament was also to be formed. However, making the transition—politically but also geographically—has proved problematic. The capital, Mogadishu, remains violent, and opponents of the treaty have made it clear that they are in no hurry to lay down their arms or relinquish power. Meanwhile, Western governments have taken a renewed interest in the country because of the infiltration of Islamic militants who are thought to have taken advantage of the lawlessness prevailing in the country to set up training camps and plot terrorist attacks.

See also INTERNALLY DISPLACED PERSONS.

Further Reading:
Clarke, Walter, and Jeffrey Herbst, eds. *Learning from Somalia: The Lessons of Armed Humanitarian Intervention.* Boulder, Colo.: Westview Press, 1997.

Menkhaus, Ken. *Somalia: State Collapse and the Threat of Terrorism.* London: International Institute for Strategic Studies, 2004.

Peterson, Scott. *Me against My Brother: At War in Somalia, Sudan and Rwanda.* London: Routledge, 2001.

Razack, Sherene H. *Dark Threats and White Knights: The Somalia Affair, Peacekeeping, and the New Imperialism.* Toronto: University of Toronto Press, 2004.

Somoza Debayle, Anastasio (1925–1980)

Nicaraguan despot

The Nicaraguan dictator Anastasio Somoza Debayle was the third member of a political dynasty begun by his father, Anastasio SOMOZA GARCÍA. Born in 1925, he was educated in the United States, graduating from West Point in 1946. Somoza became the director of the National Guard in 1955, shortly after his father's assassination and the assumption of power by his older brother Luis Somoza Debayle as president. In his new position he led a bloody campaign against political opponents in revenge for his father's killing. Dissidents were tortured and imprisoned and civil liberties suspended. Somoza became president in 1967, shortly before his brother Luis succumbed to a heart attack. Although he did not run for the presidency in 1972 because of a law banning reelection of the president (which had been restored by Luis), he remained the dominant power behind the throne as head of the National Guard, using it as his base of power, like his father.

Known as "the vampire dictator," Somoza is reported to have made $12 million a year buying donated blood and selling it abroad at a 300 percent markup. An opportunist who became accustomed to outflanking his adversaries, he confronted growing opposition spearheaded by Pedro Joaquín Chamorro Cardenal, publisher of the newspaper *La Prensa,* as well as from outspoken prelates in the Catholic Church. Then in December 1972 the capital of Nicaragua, Managua, was hit by a devastating earthquake that killed an estimated 10,000 people and left 50,000 families homeless while destroying much of the city. The National Guard looted the ruins, and Somoza exploited the chaotic situation, declaring himself the country's leader again. It was later revealed that the Somozas embezzled much of the international aid—about $30 million in relief supplies—that poured into the country after the disaster.

Somoza imposed martial law and intensified political repression. In 1974, even in the face of opposition from his own party, he won election as president. A couple of months later an armed Marxist group known as the Sandinista National Liberation Front (FSLN) took several high government officials hostage, among them relatives of Somoza. After procuring a ransom of $1 million, the insurgents secured the release of political prisoners and flew with

Nicaraguan despot Anastasio Somoza *(Bettmann/Corbis)*

them to refuge in Cuba. Somoza responded to this humiliation with a further crackdown that included the TORTURE and murder of FSLN supporters. A state of siege was declared, and the country was plunged into civil war. Prodded by President Richard Nixon's administration, Somoza lifted the state of siege, which paved the way for a resumption of protests. An anti-Somoza alliance of businessmen and academics known as Los Doce (the Group of Twelve) sprang up and established ties with the Sandinistas.

The assassination in 1978 of the publisher Chamorro Cardenal triggered a public outcry and led to mass demonstrations against the Somoza regime. Characteristically, Somoza responded by a renewed crackdown, while boasting that he would remain in power until his term ended in 1981. In reaction, the Sandinistas carried out attacks throughout the country. The Somoza regime had outworn its welcome, and the United States washed its hands of the dictator, suspending all military aid. Somoza resorted to the international markets to buy the weapons he needed to fight the mounting insurgency. The country, which had never recovered from the earthquake, was practically bankrupt. Capital fled the country, inflation soared, and so did unemployment. More opposition groups joined Los Doce, forming what was called the Broad Opposition Front (FAO). The FAO then tried to resolve the crisis, but the Sandinistas were not about to wait: In August 1978 they seized the national palace and took nearly 2,000 officials and members of the Nicaraguan congress hostage for two days. The National Guard lost its nerve, and Somoza was forced to accede to most of the rebel demands, which included releasing 60 FSLN members from prison and providing safe passage for the hostage takers to Panama and Venezuela. Somoza was also compelled to allow the media to publish a Sandinista declaration.

At the end of 1978 the ORGANIZATION OF AMERICAN STATES Inter-American Commission on Human Rights issued a report charging the National Guard with a large number of human rights abuses, a move that was followed shortly by a UN resolution condemning the Nicaraguan government. By June 1979 virtually all of the country had fallen under the control of the Sandinistas, with the exception of the capital. Somoza tried to hang on to power—at one point he went so far as to bomb Managua—but he was finally forced to capitulate on July 17, bringing an end to the Somozas' 47-year rule. He fled to Miami and then to Paraguay; many members of the National Guard went into exile as well. In September 1980 Somoza was assassinated in Asunción, Paraguay's capital, reportedly by a leftist Argentine group. The civil war is thought to have cost as many as 50,000 lives; another 120,000 went into exile, and 600,000 were made homeless.

Further Reading:

Alegria, Claribel, and Darwin Flakoll. *Death of Somoza.* Willimantic, Conn.: Curbstone Press, 1996.

Diederich, Bernard. *Somoza and the Legacy of U.S. Involvement in Central America.* Princeton, N.J.: Marcus Wiener, 1989.

Walter, Knut. *The Regime of Anastasio Somoza, 1936–1956.* Chapel Hill: University of North Carolina Press, 1993.

Somoza García, Anastasio (1896–1956) *Nicaraguan dictator*

Anastasio Somoza García, the patriarch of the Somoza dynasty that dominated Nicaraguan political life for several decades, owed his presidency to the U.S. Marines, who had invaded Nicaragua in 1912 and stayed until 1933 to ensure political stability in the region under a pliable regime. The marines additionally formed the country's National Guard, which provided a base of support for three generations of Somoza rule. When the marines withdrew, they gave command of the National Guard to Somoza, who was characterized by General Smedley But-

ler, the marine commander, as "a high-class muscle man for big business, for Wall Street, and for the banks." It was President Franklin Delano Roosevelt who famously declared, "Somoza may be a son of a bitch, but he's our son of a bitch." The U.S. moves to install a government to its liking inspired armed resistance under the leadership of a Liberal Party general, Augusto César Sandino. Although he negotiated a peace agreement with the U.S.-backed government, he was still considered a threat, and in 1934 he was assassinated by National Guard officers. But for many Nicaraguans, Sandino remained a symbol of nationalism, and several years later his name was appropriated by a revitalized leftist movement, the Sandinistas.

Somoza used his post as a springboard to win the presidency; he then proceeded to use the power of patronage to employ several members of his family in top government and military positions. His party, the Liberal Nationalists, enjoyed complete authority over the country, secure in the knowledge that it had the support of Washington. (Somoza García even had Roosevelt's birthday made a national holiday to curry favor with the United States.) Within a short time the National Guard was able to secure a virtual monopoly over most government-owned enterprises, including the national radio and telegraph networks, health services, and the national railroads. To solidify his power, Somoza had the constitutional ban on presidential reelection removed, allowing him to remain in office for as long as he chose.

As the country became a source of produce for the U.S. war effort, Nicaragua's economy flourished during World War II, though the Somozas managed to skim off most of the profits. During the war, Somoza confiscated German-owned property, which he then sold off at rock-bottom prices to cronies and members of his family. By the late 1940s he had become Nicaragua's largest landholder, giving him the right to most of the country's cattle ranches and coffee plantations. The Somoza family also either owned or controlled all the banks, the national airlines, a cement factory, textile plants, several large electric power companies, and extensive rental property in the cities. Somoza García's wealth during this period is thought to have been close to $60 million, which would probably run close to $1 billion today. It was the largest fortune ever amassed in the country's history.

Growing dissent to Somoza's rule caused him to step down and run Nicaragua through a number of proxies who served as nominal heads of state. His real power lay in the National Guard in any case. In 1950, though, he cut a deal with the opposition Conservatives to return to the presidency. Although he succeeded in bringing stability and a degree of prosperity to Nicaragua during the postwar years, his rule continued to be characterized by corruption and favoritism. When other elite families protested his authoritarian regime, he had them exiled. At the same time, to perpetuate his political dynasty, he groomed his two sons, Luis Somoza Debayle and Anastasio SOMOZA DEBAYLE, to take the reins of power, making the former director of the National Guard and the latter its commander. On September 21, 1956, Somoza García was fatally shot by a 27-year-old Nicaraguan poet. He died eight days later and was succeeded as president by his son Luis.

Further Reading:
Diederich, Bernard. *Somoza and the Legacy of U.S. Involvement in Central America.* Princeton, N.J.: Marcus Wiener, 1989.
Walter, Knut. *The Regime of Anastasio Somoza, 1936–1956.* Chapel Hill: University of North Carolina Press, 1993.

Souaidia, Habib (1972–   ) *Algerian dissident and writer*
Habib Souaidia, a former Algerian officer, was forced to flee to France after writing a book published in 2001 called *La Sale Guerre* (The dirty war), which exposed acts of TORTURE, EXTRAJUDICIAL KILLINGS, and other grave human rights abuses perpetrated by militias, security forces, and the army in the war against Islamic insurgents during the civil war in Algeria in the 1990s. Even after the violence abated, thousands of families still have no idea what became of family members who disappeared during the conflict. A parachute officer in the special forces, Souaida had been involved in fighting Islamic militant groups. He suffered from nightmares and flashbacks as a result of his experiences but was unable to obtain psychiatric help in Algeria because as a former officer he was not considered one of the "victims." Because his book revealed injustices committed by the government, he feared for his life. After living on the run, he finally managed to reach France in April 2000. "I was afraid of being turned away at the border," he told interviewers. "If I had been sent back it would have meant being killed or being sent back to prison." Even then he was compelled to wait for eight months before he was permitted to stay in France.

See also ALGERIA, HUMAN RIGHTS VIOLATIONS IN.

Further Reading:
Sammakia, Nejla. *Algeria, Elections in the Shadow of Violence and Repression.* New York: Human Rights Watch/Middle East, 1997.
Waltz, Susan Eileen. *Human Rights and Reform: Changing the Face of North African Politics.* Berkeley: University of California Press, 1995.
Whitley, Andrew. *Human Rights Abuses in Algeria: No One Is Spared.* New York: Human Rights Watch, 1994.

South Africa, human rights violations in
See APARTHEID; BASSOUN, WOUTER; TRUTH AND RECONCILIATION COMMISSION; TUTU, DESMOND.

Soyinka, Wole   (Akinwande Oluwole Soyinka)
(1934–   ) *Nigerian writer and human rights advocate*
The Nigerian Nobel laureate Wole Soyinka is known in his native country as much for his human rights activism and political dissidence as he is for his books, poems, and plays. Born in 1934, he has been imprisoned or forced into exile because of his political views. He spent three years in prison (1969–70) as the Nigerian civil war raged, and during that time he wrote a prose work and several poems that were compiled in a collection called *Poems from Prison.* Soyinka won the Nobel Prize in Literature in 1986 for plays and poems that depicted "the drama of existence," in the words of the Swedish Academy. His fame failed to protect him, however, and eight years later he was forced to flee the country, shortly after General Sani Abacha took power, introducing a brutal dictatorship. Soyinka was tried in absentia for treason in 1997. He returned to Nigeria only after Abacha's death and the collapse of his regime. Although democracy was restored, he continues to agitate for political rights. In a political demonstration in 2004, which turned violent, police briefly detained him as an instigator. He castigated the government for failing to uphold democratic principles. "We cannot claim we are running a democracy when we cannot assemble on the street," he said.

See also NIGERIA, HUMAN RIGHTS VIOLATIONS IN.

Further Reading:
Soyinka, Wole. *Ake: The Years of Childhood.* New York: Vintage, 1989.
———. *Climate of Fear: The Quest for Dignity in a Dehumanized World.* Reith Lectures. New York: Random House Trade Paperbacks, 2005.
———. *Death and the King's Horseman.* New York: W. W. Norton & Company, 2002.

Special Court for Sierra Leone
In June 2000 the government of Sierra Leone asked the United Nations to set up an international tribunal for CRIMES AGAINST HUMANITY in order to try rebel leader Foday SANKOH and others implicated in atrocities committed during the civil war in that country. Unlike similar special UN tribunals for Rwanda and the former Yugoslavia, which are located in Tanzania and The Hague, respectively, the Special Court for Sierra Leone is based in the country where the crimes were committed. The Special

Court is supposed to operate on a budget one-fifth of that for Rwanda and the former Yugoslavia—about $60 million for its first three years.

The Special Court is composed of lawyers and judges from Sierra Leone and abroad. Its mandate covers all the atrocities that occurred over 10 years of civil strife. It also covers the prosecution of leaders of the Revolutionary United Front (RUF), an insurgent movement responsible for killing and maiming thousands of civilians, as well as other actors in the war who had "the greatest responsibility" for war crimes, including government officials, members of the Sierra Leone military and police forces, and ECO-MOG (ECOWAS MONITORING GROUP—the Nigerian-led peacekeeping force). However, a decision was made not to try any juveniles under the age of 15, although many children were pressed into combat by all parties to the conflict. Even children who had perpetrated atrocities, it was believed, should be considered victims and not perpetrators of crimes. The Geneva Conventions prohibit the use of children as soldiers.

Of the 12 men originally indicted, Sankoh was clearly the most important defendant but he cheated justice by dying of natural causes in prison in July 2003. As of September 2005, 11 persons associated with all three of the country's former warring factions had been indicted and charged with war crimes, crimes against humanity, and other serious violations of international humanitarian law. Specifically, the charges include murder, rape, extermination, acts of terror, enslavement, looting and burning, sexual slavery, conscription of children into an armed force, and attacks on United Nations peacekeepers and humanitarian workers, among others.

See also SIERRA LEONE, HUMAN RIGHTS VIOLATIONS IN.

Further Reading:

Ferme, Mariane C. *The Underneath of Things: Violence, History, and the Everyday in Sierra Leone.* Berkeley: University of California Press, 2001.

Jackson, Michael. *In Sierra Leone.* Durham, N.C.: Duke University Press, 2004.

Richards, Paul. *Fighting for the Rain Forest: War, Youth, and Resources in Sierra Leone.* African Issues Series. London: Heinemann, 1996.

Romano, Cesare, Andre Nollkaemper, and Jann K. Kleffner, eds. *Internationalized Criminal Courts and Tribunals: Sierra Leone, East Timor, Kosovo, and Cambodia.* International Courts and Tribunals Series. Oxford: Oxford University Press, 2004.

Voeten, Teun. *How de Body? One Man's Terrifying Journey through an African War.* New York: Thomas Dunne Books, 2002.

Speer, Albert (1905–1981) *Nazi architect*

Albert Speer, Adolf HITLER's principal architect and later the head of the Third Reich's armaments production, is one of the most complex and problematic Nazi war criminals to be tried at the NUREMBERG TRIALS. In contrast to other notorious Nazi officials such as Joseph GOEBBELS and Heinrich HIMMLER, Speer freely acknowledged his guilt, although he contended that he was unaware of the Holocaust until his trial after the war. As one commentator put it, "Speer existed in what the Dutch Protestant theologian Willem Visser't Hooft has called 'a twilight between knowing and not knowing.'"

One of Speer's biographers called him a "frustrated romantic," emotionally crippled by an unhappy childhood. He was born in Mannheim, Germany, in 1905. While his was a life of privilege, the atmosphere at home was cold and distant. "Father and I never talked about our feelings," Speer recalled in one of his memoirs. "That was his way, and I have inherited from him." He initially hoped to become a mathematician but instead followed his father and grandfather's path and studied architecture. In 1931, shortly after completing his studies, he attended a Nazi Party rally where he first heard Hitler speak. He was mesmerized. Speer's intense attraction to Hitler has been characterized by biographers as "a sublimated, nonsexual but homoerotic devotion." "I am ashamed of it now," Speer acknowledged after the war, "but at the time, I found him deeply exciting." Hitler reciprocated his interest, seeing in the young architect a tabula rasa whom he could mold as he chose.

For his first commission, Speer was hired by Joseph Goebbels, the Nazi propaganda minister, to renovate the Propaganda Ministry. Goebbels found the results so impressive that he recommended him to Hitler, who put Speer to work renovating the Chancellery in Berlin, the official seat of power. By 1934, shortly after the Nazis had come to power, Speer was promoted to chief architect for the party. He then undertook one of his best-known commissions: the design of the parade grounds at Nuremberg where the Nazis orchestrated mass rallies. The grounds were inspired by ancient Greek temple architecture but constructed on a massive scale that was capable of holding 250,000 people. At a rally in 1934, to enhance the drama, he deployed 150 antiaircraft searchlights around the parade grounds, creating what one diplomat in attendance called "a cathedral of light." The rallies set against Speer's grandiose backdrop became known to the rest of the world thanks to Leni Riefenstahl's powerful propaganda film *Triumph of the Will.*

Strongly influenced by the legacy of classical Greek and Roman architecture, Speer derived a theory of his own that he called the theory of "ruin value." That is to say, every structure that was to be built to commemorate the

Third Reich's glory should be so constructed that even after the passage of centuries it would produce aesthetically pleasing ruins. Hitler, who had declared that the Third Reich would endure for a thousand years, enthusiastically endorsed Speer's theory of built-in obsolescence. The führer decided to give Speer even more of an opportunity to put his theory into practice. Speer was now given the daunting assignment of reconstructing Berlin, which Hitler envisioned as the capital of a great state called Germania. The first step in carrying out this mammoth project was to design a new stadium that would play host to the 1936 Olympic games. He then went on to design a new Chancellery that, had it been built, would have contained a hall twice the size of the famous Hall of Mirrors in the Versailles palace. But the outbreak of World War II in 1939 put a halt to these grandiose plans. There were more pressing concerns for Germany, such as cranking out the tanks, planes, and guns to keep the war going.

In 1942 Hitler tapped Speer to take on a new responsibility, appointing him minister of armaments and war production. Speer proved that he could be just as capable and as diligent in his new capacity as he was as an architect. He displayed no compunction about using slave labor to increase production, even though he recognized that Germany had no chance of winning the war. "I'm not happy to face it," Speer recounted, "but in the context of my life then, these workers' only significance was what they could produce towards our war effort; I didn't see them as human beings, as individuals." If he objected to mistreatment of the slave laborers, it was not out of any humanitarian concerns. Rather, he was concerned that if his workers were abused, efficiency would suffer. Speer was an exemplary administrator; production levels at his factories continued to rise, reaching a peak in 1944 during the heaviest Allied bombing of the war. Historians believe that if Speer had not been quite so dedicated and proficient, Germany might not have been able to fight on as long as it did. Some experts estimate that Speer's efforts caused the war to last for a full year longer than it would otherwise, which also gave the Nazis more time to carry out mass exterminations.

But Speer's loyalty to Hitler had its limits. As the Allies encircled Berlin in 1945, Hitler gave an order to conduct a scorched-earth policy and raze every industrial facility so as to deny the victors the chance to gain any benefit. Speer recognized that if this order were carried out, it would impede any prospect for the country's postwar recovery, and he actively sought to undermine the führer's command. He went even further and plotted Hitler's assassination, though Hitler later saved him the trouble by taking his own life, apparently unaware that his former protégé had turned against him. In fact, he continued to look on Speer as a close friend, and the architect was one of the last people he spoke to before committing suicide.

Brought up on charges of war crimes before the International Military Tribunal at Nuremberg, Speer made no attempt to deny his culpability. He was, in fact, the only prominent member of the upper echelons of the Nazi Party to acknowledge carrying out Hitler's orders. Nonetheless, he denied that he had any knowledge of the mass extermination of Jews and other victims and said that until he heard testimony at the trial, he was unaware of the existence of the CONCENTRATION CAMPS. "Of the dreadful things, I knew nothing," he wrote to his daughter in 1952. Speer received special leniency from the court because of his reputation for incorruptibility and his willingness to take responsibility for his actions. He also had help from an unexpected source: His name had appeared in a list drawn up of future government officials by the July 20, 1944, conspirators who had tried unsuccessfully to assassinate Hitler and replace him with a de-Nazified government that could sue for peace. His inclusion on the list, Speer later said, might have saved his life.

The tribunal sentenced Speer to 20 years in Spandau prison in West Berlin, mainly on charges of having used slave labor. He resolved to use his imprisonment to transform himself into a "new man," an endeavor that was assisted by the prison chaplain, Georges Casalis. "When I met Speer," Casalis told Speer's biographer Gitta Sereny, "he was the most tortured man I had ever met. By the time I left Spandau (three years later), I saw him as the most repentant." Speer described Spandau as less a prison for him than "a refuge." He used the time to write, managing to turn out some 1,200 pages of a memoir, using toilet paper and cigarette papers. He later drew on these pages for two books published after he was released in 1966, *Inside the Third Reich* and *Spandau: The Secret Diaries*, which became international best-sellers. "You simply cannot understand what it is like to live in a dictatorship," he wrote in one account, "you can't understand the game of danger, but above all you cannot understand the fear on which the whole thing is based. Nor, I suppose, have you any concept of the charisma of a man such as Hitler." He claimed to have learned his lesson: "I am beginning to grasp that there is only one type of valid loyalty: toward morality." Critics charged, however, that his books were self-serving and that he downplayed his own role in Nazi atrocities.

Speer spent his remaining years trying to refurbish his image. "He worked hard at being penitent," as one writer put it. Albert Speer died in a London hospital on September 1, 1981—42 years to the day after Hitler's invasion of Poland marked the beginning of World War II.

Further Reading:
Sereny, Gitta. *Albert Speer: His Battle with Truth.* New York: Vintage, 1996.

Speer, Albert. *Inside the Third Reich.* New York: Simon & Schuster, 1997.

Van Der Vat, Dan. *The Good Nazi: The Life and Lies of Albert Speer.* Boston: Houghton Mifflin, 1997.

Srebrenica, massacre in

Srebrenica, a previously obscure town in eastern Bosnia and Herzegovina, became the site in 1995 of the worst atrocity in Europe since the end of World War II during the Bosnian War. The war was fought between Serbs, who made up the two remaining countries in the former Yugoslavia—Serbia and Montenegro on the one hand and Croatia and Bosnia on the other—both of which had declared their independence. Because of its large concentration of Muslims, the United Nations had declared the enclave of Srebrenica a safe haven that was guarded by a Dutch peacekeeping force. However, when confronted by Bosnian Serb forces in July 1995, the UN contingent withdrew: Women and young children were expelled from the area, and the occupiers proceeded to massacre as many as 7,800 Muslim men and boys between July 13 and 15.

Since the end of the war, some 1,200 of the victims have been identified by DNA analysis. Several Serbian officers involved in the killings have subsequently been tried and convicted by the INTERNATIONAL CRIMINAL TRIBUNAL FOR THE FORMER YUGOSLAVIA, sitting in The Hague. In a belated but welcome acknowledgment of responsibility, the Bosnian Serb government established after the war released a report in November 2004 that provided details of how the massacre was plotted and carried out. While the full contents of the report were not made public, it was said to contain the names of possible perpetrators. Srebrenica has also come to symbolize the failure of the international community to live up to its commitments to protect vulnerable populations in time of war. In the final months of 2005 the identities of thousands of Bosnian Serb soldiers, police officers, and officials involved in the massacres were revealed as a result of a two-year investigation by the Bosnian Serbian officials. A list of names of some 17,000 Bosnian Serbs who participated in the killings was made available to a war crimes tribunal in Bosnia and Herzegovina which said that based on the new evidence it would increase the number of its prosecutions. As many as 90 additional suspects were expected to be indicted. In a separate incident, five Serb paramilitaries were indicted for war crimes after a video surfaced that showed the men—members of the notorious Scorpions unit—executing six Srebrenica Muslim civilians. If convicted, they could face up to 50 years in prison. (Serb law does not permit the death penalty.)

See also BOSNIA AND HERZEGOVINA, HUMAN RIGHTS VIOLATIONS IN; SAFE HAVENS; YUGOSLAVIA, WAR CRIMES IN.

Further Reading:

Glenny, Misha. *The Fall of Yugoslavia: The Third Balkan War.* New York: Penguin Books, 1996.

Mertus, Julie. *Former Yugoslavia: War Crimes Trials in the Former Yugoslavia.* Helsinki: Human Rights Watch/Helsinki, 1995.

Honig, Jan Willem, and Norbert Both. *Srebrenica: Record of a War Crime.* New York: Penguin Books, 1997.

Rhode, David. *Endgame: The Betrayal and Fall of Srebrenica.* New York: Farrar, Straus & Giroux, 1997.

Rossanet, Bertrand de. *War and Peace in the Former Yugoslavia.* Boston: Martinus Nijhoff, 1997.

Sri Lanka, human rights violations in

The human rights situation on the island nation of Sri Lanka is inextricably linked to the civil war that has embroiled the country since 1983. The war between the government and ethnic Tamil insurgents has been characterized by atrocities, TORTURE, mistreatment of civilians, and forced conscription of children. A cease-fire was agreed upon in February 2002, but killings and abuses continue to occur, although not to the same degree as in the past.

The source of the conflict stems in large part from ethnic tensions between the majority Singhalese (who mainly follow Buddhism) and the Tamil minority (who practice Hinduism). The conflict between the government and the Liberation TIGERS of Tamil Eelam (LTTE), the major Tamil insurgent group, has resulted in the killing of more than 60,000 people. Both sides in the war are implicated in numerous human rights violations. Until the cease-fire, security forces were responsible for killing prisoners they took in addition to other EXTRAJUDICIAL KILLINGS, which they defend by claiming that the victims were Tiger guerrillas felled in combat. Military and police personnel also tortured detainees. The contested areas in the north became especially perilous for civilians, and freedom of movement was restricted. Torture and arbitrary arrests and detentions, already widespread, became more frequent with the passage of New Emergency Regulations (ER) which, according to the U.S. State Department, further "eroded due process protections."

Even though the violence has abated since the cease-fire, the government has made little progress toward investigating past abuses or bringing those responsible for them to justice. Censorship has limited the ability of the media—domestic or foreign—to investigate or expose government culpability in abuses. Security forces have been known to harass journalists, although this situation, too, has eased since the cease-fire took hold. Many of the worst abuses have been blamed on proxy forces made up of defectors who have been recruited by the security forces to identify and hunt down their former comrades. These militias have been blamed for numerous extrajudicial killings and DISAP-

PEARANCES, although two of the groups were supposed to have been disarmed.

If anything, the Tigers are responsible for even more human rights violations, and the U.S. State Department has labeled them a terrorist group. According to HUMAN RIGHTS WATCH, the Tigers targeted and killed several people with links to Tamil political parties opposed to the LTTE even after the cease-fire took effect; many other Tamil opponents have been abducted without any indication as to their fate. In the past the Tigers staged spectacular terrorist acts, including suicide bombings—which the group introduced to the world as an innovative guerrilla tactic—killing 170 civilians in such bombings during a nine-month period at the height of the conflict.

Both the LTTE and the government have recruited child soldiers—as young as 11—but the Tigers are probably more culpable in this respect. In one survey conducted in the 1990s, 40–60 percent of LTTE soldiers killed in battle were children under the age of 18. Children have also been used by the Tigers as suicide bombers. In 2002 UNICEF documented over 3,500 cases of child recruitment after the cease-fire, and the total is likely to be much higher. In a number of instances families were threatened if they didn't surrender their children for "the cause" while in other cases they gave them up voluntarily because they were unable to care for them. Children have also been known to voluntarily join the LTTE because their families have suffered at the hands of government forces. The treatment of child recruits by LTTE is brutal, and those who try to escape are beaten in front of their peers as a warning. In June 2003 the LTTE signed an Action Plan for Children Affected by War that obliged it to cease its recruitment of child soldiers and free the children it held. Although LTTE did release 831 children, by November 2004 it had recruited or rerecruited 1,700 more.

See also CHILDREN'S RIGHTS.

Further Reading:
De Votta, Neil: *Blowback: Linguistic Nationalism, Institutional Decay, and Ethnic Conflict in Sri Lanka.* Contemporary Issues in Asia and the Pacific. Stanford, Calif.: Stanford University Press, 2004.
Tambiah, Stanley Jeyaraja. *Buddhism Betrayed?: Religion, Politics, and Violence in Sri Lanka.* A Monograph of the World Institute for Development Economics Research. Chicago: University of Chicago Press, 1992.
Winslow, Deborah, and Michael Woost, eds. *Economy, Culture, and Civil War in Sri Lanka.* Bloomington: Indiana University Press, 2004.

SS (Schutzstaffel)

The SS was possibly the most feared security police force in the Nazi state terror apparatus. SS is the abbreviation for the German word *Schutzstaffel*, which means "defense corps." Initially, the SS served as an elite bodyguard for Adolf HITLER, answerable to the SA (Sturmabteilung, or storm troops), the Nazi paramilitary unit. However, the SS began to expand in size and power, becoming both a police force and an army within the regular army; the Waffen SS, also took primary responsibility for manning the CONCENTRATION CAMPS.

The SS originated in Bavaria in the 1920s, a decade before the Nazis came to power. Under the direction of Heinrich HIMMLER, the force developed into an efficient killing machine for the purpose of implementing Nazi racial policies. In June 1931 Himmler joined forces with Reinhard HEYDRICH. A year after Hitler came to power in 1933, the two men helped Hitler consolidate power in the SS by eliminating the rival SA as a viable force in a bloody purge known to history as the Night of the Long Knives. At the same time Himmler moved to infiltrate and reorganize the German police system and create a new security police. Under this scheme the political police—the GESTAPO (Geheime Staatspolize, or secret state police)—was put under Heydrich's control, and the Ordnungspolizei (or Orpo, the ordinary criminal police) was put under the charge of Kurt Dalugue. The SS proceeded to set up the first ghettoes in Poland and formed the EINSATZGRUPPEN, the extermination squads that followed the German army into occupied areas of Europe and the Soviet Union, killing Jews, Slavs, and others considered subhuman. There was, in addition, an economic component to the SS; under Obergruppenführer Oswald POHL, the SS built up a vast network of enterprises based on slave labor, extortion, and murder.

Himmler selected Theodor Eicke to recruit personnel for the concentration camps. Eicke would prove more ruthless than the Bavarian police guards who were originally assigned to the camps. He formed the Totenkopfverbaende (SS Death's Head Battalion) by scouring the streets of Berlin, Hamburg, and Munich for unemployed thugs. He then dressed them in the black SS uniform but with the addition of a red fez with the design of a human skull beneath the swastika and a black silk tassel.

By 1939 the SS had been organized into four major branches: (1) the General SS, members of which served part-time on a voluntary basis; (2) the SD, or Security Service; (3) the Waffen SS; and (4) the Death's Head concentration-camp guard units. At the same time, the state police and Gestapo were merged into the Reich Main Security Office (Reichssicherheitshauptamt, or RSHA) under Heydrich's command.

At the NUREMBERG TRIALS the Allies took the unusual step of trying Nazi military and security bodies, indicting them as criminal organizations: the SS, the Gestapo, the SA, and the General Staff and High Command of the German armed forces. There were three cases that specifically focused on activities undertaken by SS personnel in which 56 "full-time" SS defendants were indicted. ("Full-time" SS officers were distinguished from "honorary" SS officers.) In the first (*United States v. Oswald Pohl et al.*), three of the defendants, including Pohl, were sentenced to death, with one sentence subsequently changed to a term of life imprisonment; 11 were given sentences ranging from 10 years to life; and three were acquitted. In the second case (*United States v. Ulrich Greifelt et al.*), eight of the defendants were sentenced to prison for periods ranging from life to 15 years, five were found guilty of membership in the SS, and one defendant was acquitted. In the third, known as the Einsatzgruppen Case, 14 were sentenced to death, two were sentenced to life imprisonment, and five others were sentenced to imprisonment for terms ranging from 10 to 20 years.

Further Reading:

Browder, George C. *Hitler's Enforcers: The Gestapo and the SS Security Service in the Nazi Revolution.* Oxford: Oxford University Press, 1996.

Hohne, Heinz Zollen. *The Order of the Death's Head: The Story of Hitler's SS.* Classic Military History. New York: Penguin, 2001.

Whiting, Charles. *Heydrich: Henchman of Death.* Barnsley, U.K.: Leo Cooper, 1999.

Stalin, Joseph (Josif Vissarionovich Dzhugashvili)
(1879–1953) *Soviet dictator*

The future dictator of the Soviet Union was born Josif Vissarionovich Dzhugashvili to illiterate peasant parents in Georgia in the southern Caucuses. Some historians have attributed his tyrannical temperament to the frequent beatings he received from his father when he was growing up. His mother encouraged him to become a priest in the Russian Orthodox Church, and he studied for the priesthood until he was almost 20. However, he fell under the sway of Karl Marx rather than God, and he was expelled from the seminary in 1899. He then became involved in the socialist underground, distributing Marxist propaganda and serving as a labor agitator. Dzhugashvili was arrested by the czarist police in 1903 and sentenced to imprisonment in Siberia, but he was back in Georgia within a year. When the Social Democrats split into two factions (Mensheviks and Bolsheviks), he joined the more militant Bolsheviks under the leadership of Vladimir Lenin. In 1908 he was arrested again and sent into exile but managed to escape. The next several years were marked by other arrests, narrow escapes, and secret trips abroad on behalf of Lenin to raise support for the Bolsheviks. During this period Dzhugashvili assumed the pseudonym Stalin (meaning "man of steel")

Stalin (left) with top Soviet leader Sergey Kirov (later assassinated) *(Library of Congress)*

and was elevated by Lenin to the Central Committee, the highest body of the Bolshevik Party (later the Communist Party).

In 1913 Stalin was again arrested and again exiled to Siberia, to be freed only when the monarchy was toppled by revolution in 1917. He then established a base in Petrograd (now St. Petersburg) and became editor of *Pravda*, the Communist Party's mouthpiece. In 1919 he was elected a member of the Politburo, the Communist Party's most important decision-making body. He also became head of the Commissariat for Nationality Affairs, a position that was of crucial importance because the new Soviet regime was struggling to maintain control over the country's disparate ethnic groups and nationalities in the midst of civil war, which lasted from 1918 to 1921. Stalin was directly involved in planning military strategy against counterrevolutionary forces—the Whites—as well as against Polish forces in the war between Russia and Poland (1920–21). His decisions were disastrous and put him at loggerheads with Leon Trotsky, the commissar of war and heir apparent to Lenin.

After the Communist victory, Stalin quietly built up organizational strength. In 1923 he was elected general secretary of the Communist Party, a position he used as his power base. Lenin, who was seriously ill at this point, was beginning to harbor deep misgivings and wrote a "testament" in which he cautioned against allowing Stalin to succeed him. But Stalin continued his inexorable rise to power after Lenin's death in 1924. For the next few years he was obliged to outmaneuver a number of rivals, including Nikolai Bukharin, Lev Kamenev, and Grigory Zinovyev. But it was only after he had succeeded in marginalizing Trotsky, who was forced into exile, that he was able to secure uncontested power. (Trotsky was assassinated on Stalin's orders in Mexico City in 1940.) Thereafter, from 1928 until his death in 1953, Stalin was effectively in complete control over the party and the country.

With the economy in a state of decline, Stalin abandoned Lenin's New Economic Policy, which allowed some free-market commerce, in favor of a policy of collectivization of the agricultural sector to raise output and bolster efficiency. Although the policy was promoted as a boon to peasants, it was vigorously resisted by small farmers, known as kulaks, who were now being called upon to sacrifice their land and become members of a collective farm. The new policy threatened not only their livelihood but a traditional way of life that had endured for generations. Stalin forcibly suppressed opposition, characterizing the kulaks as capitalist parasites and using special Shock Brigades to bring them to heel. The kulaks were either shot or sent to Siberia.

Between 1929 and 1933, as collectivization was being carried out, millions of people lost their lives—5 million in the Ukraine alone, according to some estimates—mostly on account of a famine that resulted from the massive disruption to agricultural production. At the same time, Stalin moved rapidly to industrialize Russia—regarded as one of the poorest nations in Europe before 1914—introducing a succession of five-year plans. The ramped-up production levels did yield extraordinary gains that exceeded Germany's pace of industrialization in the 19th century and Japan's earlier in the 20th century. To subsidize this ambitious program, Stalin relied to a great degree on wealth he appropriated from the people. However ruthless his regime, he is also credited with improving the health of the Soviet populace with aggressive immunization campaigns against typhus, cholera, and malaria and improving and expanding the educational system.

In the early 1930s Stalin consolidated absolute power by carrying out purges of political opponents, real or imagined—among them many old Bolsheviks. Between 1936 and 1937—a period known as the Great Terror—several once-powerful Communist Party officials were convicted in "show trials" and either shot or sent to the GULAG—the camps in Siberia and elsewhere. There were four major purge trials during these years: the Trial of the Sixteen; the Trial of the Seventeen; the Trial of the Red Army Generals; and finally, in March 1938, the Trial of the Twenty-One. The KGB, the successor to the NKVD (the Soviet secret police under Stalin), estimated that 681,692 people were shot between 1937 and 1938, although this figure might be an undercount. Millions of people were arrested, often in the dead of night, on the basis of trumped-up charges or none at all. (Historians are divided as to how many million victims there actually were, with estimates ranging from eight to 20 million; some put the number as high as 50 million.) Stalin is thought to have personally signed as many as 40,000 death warrants of political opponents.

For all his cunning, Stalin appears to have been taken in by Adolf HITLER's assurances that the Germans had no territorial designs on the Soviet Union. In 1939 he agreed to a nonaggression pact with Nazi Germany (the Molotov-Ribbentrop Pact), which also contained a secret appendix that carved up Poland between the Soviet Union and Germany and allowed the USSR a free hand in the Baltic nations of Estonia, Latvia, and Lithuania. In 1940 Stalin effectively decapitated the Polish leadership, ordering the execution of thousands of Polish officers in Katyn Forest after they had been captured by the Red Army, which had seized its share of the country under the terms of the nonaggression pact. The Kremlin later tried to cover up responsibility and laid the blame on the Germans for the atrocity.

In 1941 the Germans, taking Stalin by surprise, launched Operation Barbarosa, the code name for their invasion of the Soviet Union. Initially Germany scored major gains. The Red Army was at a disadvantage because its leadership had been crippled by Stalin after he had purged so many of his top generals. There is no doubt that the Soviets suffered the most during World War II and yet were responsible in large part for Germany's ultimate defeat. Approximately 22 million people (13 percent of the Soviet population)—7 million of them civilians—were killed in the war. Ironically, German aggression united the Soviet people behind Stalin against a common invader, even after so many years of misrule. Stalin cleverly played the nationalist card, downplaying ideology, to mobilize resistance to the invader. The 1943 surrender of General von Paulus's Sixth Army to the Red Army at Stalingrad is generally considered the turning point of the war, making the German defeat inevitable.

Even before the end of the war, Stalin began to plan for the expansion of Soviet influence well beyond the borders of the USSR. As a vital wartime ally, he wrested concessions from an ailing President Franklin Roosevelt that allowed the Soviets to carve out a sphere of influence in Eastern Europe after the war. Between 1945 and 1948, the Soviets extended their influence over East Germany, Poland, Czechoslovakia, Hungary, Romania, and Bulgaria. (An independent communist regime under Josip Broz [Tito] was established in Yugoslavia.) These puppet "people's republics" formed a military alliance known as the Warsaw Pact, which was dominated by Moscow. In a famous speech in Fulton, Missouri, British prime minister Winston Churchill declared that an "iron curtain" had descended across Europe. The phrase stuck. What became known as the cold war between the Communist empire and the West had begun.

In the early 1950s Stalin increasingly showed signs of mental and physical disability. His megalomania was only matched by his paranoia. Those closest to him were fearful, never knowing when he would single them out for disloyalty, which could mean either imprisonment or execution. In early 1953 he ordered the arrests of several Kremlin doctors whom he accused of plotting against his life. As many of these doctors were Jewish, his action raised fears that he was about to initiate an anti-Semitic campaign throughout the country. But if he were planning such a pogrom, he never lived long enough to order it. On March 1, 1953, Stalin collapsed after an all-night dinner whose guests included Lavrenti Beria, head of the secret police, and Nikita Khrushchev, who would later become Soviet premier. He died four days later, having never regained consciousness. Officially the cause of death was a cerebral hemorrhage, but Vyacheslav Molotov, the foreign minister, claimed in his memoirs that Beria had poisoned Stalin.

Since Stalin's death, historians have quarreled about how he should be judged. For example, in his biography *Stalin: Breaker of Nations,* Robert Conquest found that there was "something in [Stalin's] character best thought of as an absence of life in its fullest sense." He characterized Stalin as a "vast, dark figure looming over the century," who was incapable of any sort of sympathetic human relationship. On the other hand, Robert Service in his portrait of the Soviet dictator, *Stalin: A Biography,* argues that while indeed Stalin was "as wicked a man as has ever lived" and someone who suffered from a "dangerously damaged" personality, he was nonetheless "hard-working," "capable of kindness to relatives," a "ruler of great assiduity," a "fluent and thoughtful writer," and "a delightful purveyor of jokes and mimicry." In addition, Service finds him "a thoughtful man" who "tried to make sense of the universe as he found it." Service allows that he could be guilty of trying to humanize Stalin but points out that "[i]f the likes of Stalin, Hitler, Mao and Pol Pot are represented as having been 'animals,' 'monsters' or 'killing machines,' we shall never be able to discern their successors."

In Russia, too, Stalin's reputation has undergone a resurrection of sorts. Denounced by Khrushchev for his excesses at a famous speech delivered in secret to the 20th Communist Party Congress, Stalin has enjoyed renewed popularity among some Russians who see him as a symbol of former Soviet glory. In 2005 the government announced a plan to erect a statue of Stalin in Moscow after a long period in which his once-ubiquitous image had been stripped from practically all public places. The backers of legislation to raise the statue maintained that Stalin should be honored for his leadership in World War II.

See also KATYN FOREST, MASSACRE IN.

Further Reading:
Applebaum, Anne. *Gulag: A History.* New York: Anchor, 2004.

Conquest, Robert. *Stalin: Breaker of Nations.* New York: Penguin Books, 1992.

Khlevniuk, Oleg. *The History of the Gulag: From Collectivization to the Great Terror.* Annals of Communism Series. Translated by Vadim A. Staklo. New Haven, Conn.: Yale University Press, 2004.

Kizny, Tomasz. *Gulag: Life and Death inside the Soviet Concentration Camps 1917–1990.* London: Firefly Books Ltd, 2004.

Montefiore, Simon Sebag. *Stalin: The Court of the Red Tsar.* New York: Knopf, 2004.

Radzinsky, Edvard. *Stalin: The First In-Depth Biography Based on Explosive New Documents from Russia's Secret Archives.* New York: Anchor, 1997.

Service, Robert. *Stalin: A Biography.* Cambridge, Mass.: Belknap Press, 2005.

Solzhenitsyn, Aleksandr. *The Gulag Archipelago.* New York: Harpercollins, 1978.

Ulam, Adam B. *Stalin: The Man and His Era.* Boston: Beacon Press, 1987.

starvation as a tactic of war

As a tool of war, starvation is prohibited under INTERNATIONAL HUMANITARIAN LAW. The ADDITIONAL PROTOCOLS TO THE GENEVA CONVENTIONS ban the starvation of civilian populations in both international and internal conflicts. However, the law also imposes no obligation on one party to a conflict to ensure the supply of food or other provisions to its adversary. How these two apparently opposing positions are to be reconciled has been an ongoing source of dispute among legal scholars and international bodies. The INTERNATIONAL COMMITTEE OF THE RED CROSS (ICRC) takes the unequivocal position that there is no justification for denying food to those who need it, regardless of the possibility that some of that food might be used by an enemy force. The ICRC's view, however, is a minority one. More specifically, the issue hinges on "the right of passage" through a battlefront. Article 23 of the Fourth Geneva Convention of 1949 refers to free passage for "children under fifteen, expectant mothers and maternity cases." Other civilians may also enjoy the right of free passage if the territory they inhabit is deemed "inadequately supplied."

Further limits on using starvation as a means of warfare are found in Additional Protocol I, covering international armed conflict, which prohibits the targeting or destruction of "objects indispensable to the survival of the civilian population," a provision applying to food and to the means of producing food—for example, a flour plant, reservoir, or farm. A belligerent is enjoined by the protocol from taking any action "which may be expected to leave the civilian population with such inadequate food or water as to cause starvation or force its movement." Protocol I also permits "relief actions which are humanitarian and impartial in character and conducted without any adverse distinction shall be undertaken," although this provision does add the qualification that both parties to the conflict must agree to it. Protocol II provides for similar protections for civilian in an internal armed conflict. Relief operations "which are of an exclusively humanitarian and impartial nature" can be undertaken when a civilian population is suffering "undue hardship" due to a lack of food or medical supplies "essential to its survival." Relief actions conducted "without any adverse distinction" shall be undertaken subject to the consent of the state involved. Even though the United States is not a party to either protocol, it subscribes to the prohibition of starvation as a military tactic.

See also GENEVA CONVENTIONS; SIEGE.

Further Reading:

Gutman, Roy, ed. *Crimes of War: What the Public Should Know.* New York: W. W. Norton & Company, 1999.

Stockholm Declaration on Genocide

The Stockholm Declaration on Genocide, announced on January 28, 2004, emerged from a three-day intergovernmental conference sponsored by the United Nations that was entitled "Preventing GENOCIDE: Threats and Responsibilities." Attended by delegates from 58 nations, it was the first major international conference on genocide since the United Nations adopted the GENOCIDE CONVENTION in 1948. The declaration called for collective efforts of the international community to prevent genocide, ethnic cleansing, and mass killings. The declaration also obliged state members to identify and report possible threats of genocide and take effective measures to stop it from happening.

This was the fourth conference held by the United Nations on genocide in recent years. The first conference, held in January 2000, called "The Holocaust", resulted in the Stockholm Declaration on Holocaust Education, Remembrance and Research. The second in 2001 was titled Combating Intolerance and the third, in 2002, the Conference on Truth, Justice and Reconciliation. The preamble from the Stockholm Declaration states: "Recalling our responsibility to fight the evils of genocide, ethnic cleansing, racism, anti-Semitism, Islamophobia and xenophobia, we, the participants of the Stockholm International Forum 2004: Preventing Genocide: Threats and Responsibilities, conscious of our obligations and responsibilities under international law including human rights and INTERNATIONAL HUMANITARIAN LAW, deeply concerned with the repeated occurrence of genocide, mass murder and ethnic cleansing in recent history as well as with the widespread occurrence of impunity for such crimes, are committed to doing our utmost for the prevention of these scourges in order to build a more secure future for us all."

St. Petersburg Declaration   *See* WEAPONS IN THE CONDUCT OF WAR.

Streicher, Julius   (1885–1946)   *Nazi propagandist*

Julius Streicher was a Nazi propagandist whose virulent anti-Semitic tirades earned him a reputation as Nazi Germany's most prominent Jew baiter. Although he was never charged with actively participating in Nazi killings, he was convicted for CRIMES AGAINST HUMANITY at the NUREMBERG TRIALS for his role in inciting hatred.

The son of a teacher, Streicher was born on February 12, 1885. He joined the German army during World War I and was awarded an Iron Cross for bravery. In 1919 he helped found an anti-Semitic organization called Wistrich, which was later integrated into the National Socialist German Workers Party (NSDAP), better known as the Nazis. Adolf HITLER cited Streicher for turning the party over to him in his memoir *Mein Kampf.* In 1923 Streicher founded the anti-Semitic newspaper *Der Stürmer,* which would eventually have a circulation of 800,000. In 1933 he started another daily, *Fränkische Tageszeitung.* He also became a publisher of magazines and books, all of which carried the same racist message. Jews, he wrote, were responsible for all the problems that ailed Germany, including depression, unemployment, and inflation. He accused Jews of being heavily involved in prostitution as well. "We know that the Jew, whether he is baptized as a Protestant or as a Catholic, remains a Jew," he asserted. "Why cannot you realize, you Protestant clergymen, you Catholic priests, you who have scales before your eyes and serve the god of the Jews who is not the God of Love but the God of Hate. Why do you not listen to Christ, who said to the Jews, 'You are children of the devil.' " In a speech he gave on another occasion, he asserted, "The Jew seeks domination not only among the German people but among all peoples. The communists pave the way for him. Do you not know that the God of the Old Testament orders the Jews to consume and enslave the peoples of the earth?" He credited Hitler for his commitment to target the Jews: "You may think about Adolf Hitler as you please, but one thing you must admit. He possessed the courage to attempt to free the German people from the Jew by a national revolution. That was action indeed."

Streicher did not only direct his anti-Semitic rants at adults; he also wanted to ensure that children too were inculcated in hatred against Jews. Accordingly, his publishing firm released an anti-Semitic children's book, *Der Giftpilz* (The poisonous mushroom). Even ardent Nazis had misgivings about Streicher's propaganda, not necessarily because of its anti-Semitism but because he also filled the pages of his papers with pornography and sensationalism. Because of his anti-Semitic credentials, Streicher was appointed chairman of the central committee directing the organization of a boycott against all Jewish-owned businesses in Germany. "Jewry will realize whom it has challenged," he declared on the eve of the boycott in late March 1933. He also published an article entitled "Defeat the Enemy of the World! by Julius Streicher, official leader of the central committee to combat the Jewish atrocity and

boycott campaign," in which he stated, "Jewry wanted this battle. It shall have it until it realizes that the Germany of the brown battalions is not a country of cowardice and surrender. Jewry will have to fight until we have won victory." The "brown battalions" refers to the SA (Sturmabteilung), the Nazi paramilitaries who wore brown shirts and in fact were known as Brown Shirts. (The SS were known as Black Shirts for their characteristic uniforms.)

In spite of his prominence as a propagandist, Streicher held only a few official positions in the Nazi hierarchy—as a member of the Reichstag (parliament) from 1933 (the

Julius Streicher (center) with other members of the Nazi Party during a rally in Nuremberg *(Library of Congress)*

year the Nazis came to power) until 1945 and as *Ober-gruppenführer* in the SA. In 1940 Streicher finally went too far and defamed Hermann GÖRING, Hitler's top deputy, in his papers, losing all of his party offices as a result. However, he did not fall out of favor entirely, because he remained on good terms with Hitler. After the war he was tried by the Nuremberg Military Tribunal and found guilty of crimes against humanity. Before he was hanged on October 16, 1946, his last words were "Heil Hitler."

Further Reading:

Bytwerk, Randell I. *Bending Spines: The Propagandas of Nazi Germany and the German Democratic Republic.* Rhetoric and Public Affairs Series. East Lansing: Michigan State University Press, 2004.

———. *Julius Streicher: Nazi Editor of the Notorious Anti-Semitic Newspaper Der Sturmer.* New York: Cooper Square Press, 2001.

Read, Anthony. *The Devil's Disciples: Hitler's Inner Circle.* New York: W. W. Norton, 2004.

Strössner, Alfredo (1912–) *Paraguayan dictator*

Alfredo Strössner was president of Paraguay from 1954 to 1989, one of the longest-lasting dictators in Latin American history. Born to a German Paraguayan family in 1912, he became a commissioned officer in 1932 and fought in the Chaco War between Paraguay and Bolivia over disputed territory (1932–35). He later participated in a civil war in 1947, which pitted the government against a leftist insurgency. In 1951 he was appointed commander in chief of the armed forces, and in 1954 he orchestrated the coup that brought him to power. He not only maintained control over the armed forces but went on to manipulate his "reelection" in the next seven presidential elections (1958, 1963, 1968, 1973, 1978, 1983, and 1988). An admirer of the Nazis, he opened his country's doors to wanted Nazi war criminals—among them the notorious Auschwitz doctor, Josef MENGELE, who was granted citizenship and allowed to practice as a doctor in the capital of Asunción. One correspondent described Strössner's administration as the "poor man's Nazi regime."

In the 1950s Strössner welcomed a delegation of TORTURE experts from Argentina who trained Paraguayans in their methods. Over the years he also played host to Croatian fascists and right-wing nationalists who gathered in the capital for the congress of the Anti-Communist League in 1971. The Paraguayan army carried out its own type of ethnic cleansing, targeting the indigenous Ache Indians, whom the dictator claimed were standing in the way of progress. "Progress" meant depriving the Ache of their land so that international corporations could exploit them for timber, mineral wealth, and grazing rights. Indians were killed and uprooted from their lands; some were sold into SLAVERY and others corralled on reservations under the supervision of American fundamentalist missionaries.

At the same time, Strössner brought a measure of economic stability to the country. In cooperation with Brazil, he built the Itaipú dam on the Paraná River; its power plant, the world's largest hydroelectric station, provided a new revenue source from the export of electricity. Yet prosperity came at the expense of the workers who saw their wages erode. Strössner kept a lid on political opposition (though he allowed greater dissent toward the end of his tenure). Nonetheless, his firm stance against communism won him many high-placed friends in Washington. President Richard Nixon described Paraguay as a "model of democracy for Latin America," and the U.S. House of Representatives passed a resolution authorizing U.S. troop movements to Paraguay in the event of a communist threat—which never materialized. The United States provided nearly $150 million in aid between 1962 and 1975 and trained more than 1,000 Paraguayan troops at U.S. installations.

Corruption flourished under Strössner's regime. In 1971 high-ranking officials in the government were implicated in a drug-smuggling scheme using Paraguay as a transit point. Yet in spite of Strössner's heavy-handed methods, he could not stifle all dissent. Beginning in the 1970s, leaders of the Catholic Church began to express misgivings about the regime's unsavory human rights record and called for social reform. Strössner responded by persecuting the church. His security forces stormed Catholic universities, arresting teachers and beating students. Church activists were arrested and Jesuits expelled from the country. Priests driven from their churches took up residence in impoverished neighborhoods where they continued to work for change, encouraging the poor to assert their rights.

By the 1980s, even the U.S. government no longer regarded Strössner as a valuable ally and began to openly repudiate his abuses of civil rights and habit of turning a blind eye to drug smuggling through Paraguayan territory. In 1988 a coup launched by a top general, Andres Rodriguez, toppled Strössner, who went into exile in Brazil. Sixteen years later he was still living comfortably in exile. There are reports that he lives in a well-guarded mansion and enjoys fishing and watching television in his spare time.

Further Reading:

McKewen, Darren. *Transition from Stroessner: The 1989 Paraguayan Elections: Post-election Report.* CSIS Latin American Election Studies Series. Washington, D.C.: Center for Strategic & International Studies, 1989.

Sanders, Thomas Griffen. *The Fall of Stroessner: Continuity and Change in Paraguay.* Berkeley, Calif.: Universities Field Staff International, 1989.

Struger, Pavle *See* WAR CRIMINALS OF THE FORMER YUGOSLAVIA.

Stuckart, Wilhelm (1902–1953) *drafter of the Nuremberg laws*

A member of the Nazi SS, Wilhelm Stuckart was responsible for drafting the notorious NUREMBERG LAWS (1936), which were designed to segregate Jews, deprive them of an ability to make a living, and prohibit them from intermarrying with Germans classified as Aryans. A lawyer by profession, Stuckart had previously served as a mayor of Stettin and as permanent secretary in the Prussian Ministry of Culture. After 1935 he was appointed state secretary (second in command) in the Reich Ministry of the Interior. A supporter of the FINAL SOLUTION—the Nazi policy to annihilate the entire Jewish population of Germany and occupied Europe—he represented the Reich Ministry of the Interior at the 1942 WANNSEE CONFERENCE, a gathering of high-ranking Nazi officials to determine how this policy should be implemented. Stuckart proved more moderate than many of his colleagues, arguing that those Jews who had some non-Jewish blood should be spared extermination. After the war, he was sentenced by the Allies to three years and 10 months in prison. He died in a traffic accident in 1953.

Further Reading:

Dawidowicz, Lucy. *A Holocaust Reader.* Library of Jewish Studies. Chicago: Behrman House Publishing, 1976.

Dwork, Deborah, and Robert Jan Van Pelt. *Holocaust: A History.* New York: W. W. Norton & Company, 2003.

Gilbert, Martin. *The Holocaust: A History of the Jews of Europe during the Second World War.* New York: Owl Books, 1987.

Roseman, Mark. *The Wannsee Conference and the Final Solution: A Reconsideration.* New York: Metropolitan Books, 2002.

Sudan, human rights violations in

Sudan, which formally became independent in 1956, has never been a truly unified state. The north is largely Arab and Muslim while the southern part of the country is dominated by animist and Christian populations. Power resides in the north, the location of the capital, Khartoum, but the country's wealth, mainly in the form of oil, is found in the south. Southerners believed that they were being unfairly treated by Khartoum, denied both the political and the economic power they were entitled to. In 1963 rebels in the south formed the Land Freedom Army and began to mount attacks against the central government, triggering a civil war. In 1969 a coup brought to power a pro-Soviet leader, Colonel Jaafar Nimeiry. Three years later Nimeiry agreed to end the civil war and allow the south more autonomy. Nimeiry, however, began to adopt a more pro-Arab policy and advocated the imposition of strict Islamic (sharia) law, stirring resentment in the south and setting the stage for a renewal of the conflict. Several guerrilla groups emerged in the south, led by the Sudanese People's Liberation Army (SPLA). In 1984 the Nimeiry regime, weakened by war, a severe food shortage and a debt crisis, was ousted in a coup by Brigadier Omar Hassan al-Bashir. Bashir proceeded to set up a military government, clamped down on political opposition, and intensified efforts to bring the south to heel. The situation continued to deteriorate; in 1994, 100,000 refugees fled Sudan for temporary shelter in neighboring Uganda. To get food and other necessities to the peoples in beleaguered regions of the south, international aid groups negotiated with the government to create safety zones where aid could be airlifted in without risk of attack. By the mid-1990s the SPLA, led by John Garang, a former officer in the Sudanese army, controlled most of southern Sudan and a number of important towns. For its part, the government controlled Juba, the most important city in the south, as well as several strategically important southern towns along the Nile. Various international efforts to broker a halt to the fighting achieved little success until the parties to the conflict, meeting in Nairobi, finally agreed in 2004 to a peace accord, which included a power-sharing arrangement. In addition, the accord held out the prospect of eventual secession by the south if its inhabitants chose to go their own way. Garang's death in a helicopter accident in 2005 complicated, but did not derail, the peace accord. Ironically, the apparent resolution of the civil war between north and south took place at the same time a new civil war—in a region of western Sudan known as Darfur—was spiraling out of control. In Darfur government-backed Arab militias were pursuing a brutal campaign to drive out black African farmers from their lands, killing tens of thousands of people, burning villages, and stealing livestock. In spite of the crisis in Darfur the Bashir government and the SPLA began to implement the terms of the accord. Even the death only a few months later of the charismatic Garang in a helicopter crash—an apparent accident—failed to derail the agreement. By late summer 2005 top SPLA officials had joined Bashir's government.

Nonetheless, it will require a concerted effort on all sides—and there are serious policy differences among the various guerrilla groups in the south as well—to ensure that the accord takes firm hold. The cost of recovery from the long years of fighting is certain to be enormous and require a generous infusion of international aid. Moreover, it is unclear whether Khartoum would ever allow the south to secede in view of its oil resources.

The war in the largest country in Africa, with a population of about 30 million, has claimed an estimated 2 million people—about 1 out of every 5—and uprooted 4 million others—almost one in five of the entire Sudanese population. Much of the population remains internally displaced, and hundreds of thousands have taken refuge in other countries. Under the terms of the peace accord, inhabitants of the south have the right to hold a referendum on independence within six years. However, there is no provision for accountability; those responsible for the worst atrocities will apparently face no charges. These atrocities have been committed by all sides in the conflict. The government in the north has systematically prevented food supplies from reaching civilian populations in the south in an effort to starve them, conducting a SCORCHED EARTH policy, displacing whole villages and forcing their inhabitants to take refuge in areas where it is impossible to survive. Those civilians in oil-rich regions have been singled out as targets and subjected to aerial bombardment, strafing of their villages by helicopter gunships, extrajudicial executions of male civilians, massacres, rapes, and abductions, according to AMNESTY INTERNATIONAL. Government troops have been accused of slitting the throats of women and children or nailing them to trees with iron spikes. Rebel forces of the Sudan People's Liberation Army have also been implicated in crimes including summary executions, rape, and the destruction of homes to terrorize civilian populations. The accord does not call for establishing a truth commission (as was the case in South Africa after APARTHEID), nor is there any mention of compensation for the victims. Human rights groups point out that having escaped punishment for past abuses, architects of the atrocities in the civil war are likely to believe that they can perpetuate more crimes in Darfur with the same sense of impunity. According to Amnesty International, the major difference between the results of the scorched earth policy pursued during the civil war and the ethnic cleansing going on in Darfur is only the rate at which the abuses are taking place. While in the north-south conflict it took 20 years to displace 4 million people, government troops and Arab militias needed only two years to push 1.6 million people out of their homes in Darfur.

Civilians have borne the brunt of the war between the army—the Popular Defense Force (PDF)—and the largest armed opposition force, the Sudan People's Liberation Army (SPLA). (To replenish the ranks of the PDF, a government conscription law makes military training mandatory for university admission or gaining employment.) But another war was being waged simultaneously; the "other" war, which accounted for the majority of casualties in recent years, took place between various militias allied with the government or with the SPLA. What made the conflict more difficult to comprehend was the tendency of these militias to change sides depending on their interests, the prospect of acquiring more power, or simply because one side offered a more reliable source of arms. Amnesty International says that in the last years of the war, more civilians were being killed as a result of interfactional fighting among southerners than in clashes with government forces. More blame for civilian atrocities attaches to the government, however: Its forces have used helicopter gunships and high-altitude bombardment on populated areas in the south, causing thousands of villagers to abandon their homes. To ensure that the villagers would not return, the army regularly destroyed their crops and stole their livestock.

Race and religion only go so far in explaining why the civil war broke out or why it lasted so long. Oil plays a large role as well: Most of the oil lies in the south, and most of the refineries are located in the north. (Competition for resources also largely accounts for the Darfur conflict, where grazing land is at issue.) When the war began in 1984, one of the first attacks staged by the SPLA targeted Chevron workers. (The giant oil company was planning to build an oil pipeline from oil fields in the south to refineries in Port Sudan in the north.) According to Amnesty International, it is no coincidence that southerners living in oil-rich areas have suffered the worst excesses committed by government forces. A special brigade was even set up to protect oilfields; known as the oil brigade, its fighters are mujahideen—holy warriors—and they are promised martyrdom if they die in combat.

In 1999, Amnesty International says, fighting intensified in areas where foreign petroleum companies had staked exploitation rights. Amnesty and other human rights groups were denied access to the affected areas to investigate complaints of aerial bombardment and strafing of villages and the forcible displacement of populations. The army and allied militias have also perpetrated numerous other atrocities, including rape, mass murders, slitting children's throats, nailing women and children to trees with iron spikes, and crushing people to death with tanks.

See also DARFUR, WAR CRIMES IN; RELIGIOUS PERSECUTION.

Further Reading:

Dodge, Cole P., and Magne Raundelen. *Reaching Children in War: Sudan Uganda and Mozambique*. London: Taylor & Francis, 1992.

Johnson, Douglas Hamilton. *The Root Causes of Sudan's Civil Wars*. Bloomington: Indiana University Press, 2003.

Jok, Madut Jok. *War and Slavery in Sudan*. Philadelphia: University of Pennsylvania Press, 2001.

Peterson, Scott. *Me against My Brother: At War in Somalia, Sudan and Rwanda*. London: Routledge, 2001.

Rone, Jemera. *Famine in Sudan, 1998: The Human Rights Causes.* New York: Human Rights Watch, 1999.

Salam, A. H. Abdel, and Alexander De Waal, eds. *The Phoenix State: Civil Society and the Future of Sudan.* London: Red Sea Press, 2000.

Suharto (Soeharto) (1921–) *Indonesian dictator*

The second president of Indonesia, General Suharto was an authoritarian whose term extended for 32 years (1967–98). Under his rule the country became increasingly militarized and nationalistic, and he used his domination of the country's levers of power to enrich both himself and his family. Suharto—like many Indonesians he uses only one name—was born on June 8, 1921. His parents were poor farmers in central Java, the main island of the sprawling Indonesian archipelago; at the time the country was under Dutch colonial rule. When Japan invaded and drove out the Dutch during World War II, Suharto joined the collaborationist Japanese "self defense corps" and became a battalion commander. When the war ended, the Dutch tried to restore their colonial rule, and armed resistance broke out. Suharto became actively involved in the struggle to throw off Dutch rule, and after Indonesia finally gained its independence in 1949, he rose in the ranks of the new Indonesian army.

In 1963 Suharto led Indonesian forces in a campaign to force the Dutch out of West Irian (now Papua Province). He was subsequently appointed head of a strategic command that was supposed to restore order in the event of a national emergency. The chance to respond to such an emergency arose in 1965 with the outbreak of a leftist uprising. Suharto put down the rebellion at the costs of thousands of lives and, exploiting the crisis, prevailed on Indonesia's first president, Sukarno, to transfer power to him. (Sukarno was placed under house arrest and died in 1970.) Suharto built a strong centralized government, with his political party, the New Order, providing his power base. He had grand designs for Indonesia—politically, economically, and territorially.

In 1975 Indonesian forces annexed East Timor after Portugal, the former colonial power, pulled out. Suharto encouraged Indonesians from Java to move to other parts of the country predominantly populated by ethnic minorities such as East Timor, in a policy of "transmigration" intended to assert centralized authority over the archipelago. He allowed the military free rein and permitted a climate of corruption. In doing so he set the stage for a wave of separatist uprisings that continued to bedevil Indonesia long after he left office.

A staunch anticommunist, Suharto formed close relations with the West and proceeded to develop Indonesia's economy, opening it up to foreign investment. While the economy flourished, the benefits were not distributed equally, and much of the population remained mired in poverty as Suharto's family and friends reaped much of the profits. Meanwhile Suharto used his power to build up his own financial empire. He began by acquiring several flour mills, but by the end of his reign he and his six children could claim the ownership of banks, automobile manufacturers, and cigarette companies. It is believed that he and his children took a considerable portion of an International Monetary Fund (IMF) loan of $43 billion for themselves.

At no point in his long rule did Suharto give any indication of when or if he planned to step down. In 1997 an economic crisis—the "Asian meltdown"—caused the Indonesian currency to plummet and food and fuel prices to rise. The crisis prompted calls for Suharto—about to begin his seventh term—to leave office, but he ignored them. The IMF concluded that no financial rescue package was likely to restore Indonesia's health so long as Suharto remained in power. In 1998 thousands of protesters, many of them university students, took to the streets. In May police fired on a demonstration, resulting in an estimated 500 deaths and setting off two days of rioting, looting, and arson. Even the president's supporters realized that the time had come for him to go, and on May 21 he submitted his resignation. In spite of various attempts by government prosecutors to investigate corruption or human rights abuses during his three decades of rule, Suharto and his sons have never been compelled to stand trial. He is still ranked as the one of the richest people in the world, with estimates of his family's wealth as high as $16 billion.

See also EAST TIMOR, WAR CRIMES IN; INDONESIA, HUMAN RIGHTS VIOLATIONS IN.

Further Reading:
King, Peter. *West Papua and Indonesia since Suharto: Independence, Autonomy or Chaos?* Sydney, Australia: University of New South Wales Press, 2004.

Leith, Denise. *The Politics of Power: Freeport in Suharto's Indonesia.* Honolulu: University of Hawaii Press, 2002.

Schwarz, Adam. *A Nation in Waiting: Indonesia's Search for Stability.* Philadelphia: Westview Press, 1999.

Taylor, Jean. *Indonesia: Peoples and Histories.* New Haven, Conn.: Yale University Press, 2003.

Sullivan Principles (Global Sullivan Principles for Corporate Social Responsibility)

The Sullivan Principles, announced in 1977, were intended to put pressure on U.S. companies doing business in South Africa, then under APARTHEID rule, to treat African employees the same way they would American workers. Revised and "relaunched" in 1999, they were called the Global Sullivan Principles for Corporate Social Responsibility. The Sullivan Principles derive their name from the

Reverend Leon Sullivan, who created them. In 1971 Sullivan had managed to secure a place on the board of directors at General Motors, which at the time was the largest employer of blacks in South Africa. Sullivan used his position to prod the board to bring pressure to bear on the South African government to reform its apartheid system based on strict segregation of the white minority and black majority. "Starting with the workplace, I tightened the screws step by step and raised the bar step by step," he told an interviewer. "Eventually I got to the point where I said that companies must practice corporate civil disobedience against the laws and I threatened South Africa and said in two years '[Nelson] Mandela must be freed, apartheid must end, and blacks must vote or else I'll bring every American company I can out of South Africa.'"

When Nelson Mandela, the imprisoned leader of the African National Congress, was not freed and apartheid did not end, Sullivan mounted a successful public-relations campaign to bring attention to the principles that bear his name. Thanks to his efforts, more than 100 foreign companies pulled out of South Africa, threatening its economy and hastening the end of the apartheid system. According to Sullivan, the revised 1999 Global Principles call on multinational companies to "encourage companies to support economic, social and political justice wherever they do business." The principles are meant to apply to companies of any size operating in any part of the world. They have been endorsed and implemented by about 100 companies that agree to make a commitment to the principles and demonstrate their compliance. Sullivan, who was awarded the Presidential Medal of Freedom by President George H. W. Bush, died in 2001 at the age of 78.

See also VOLUNTARY CODES OF CONDUCT.

Syria, human rights violations in

Since the death in 2000 of President Hafiz al-Assad, who dominated the country for 30 years, Syria has undergone a gradual loosening of restrictions but there is scant evidence that democratization will occur any time in the near future. After Assad died, the reins of power passed to his son Bashar, a London-trained ophthalmologist, who subsequently freed hundreds of political detainees and allowed political debates. This flirtation with liberalization did not last long, however; more recently the government has moved to suppress dissent. Nonetheless, opponents of autocratic rule, drawing encouragement from the example of Saddam HUSSEIN's downfall in neighboring Iraq, have become more vocal. If their intention was to test the limits of freedom, these critics quickly found them. In April 2004 a Syrian military court sentenced 14 human rights advocates to three months in prison on the grounds that they belonged to an outlawed organization and had attended a lecture in which speakers called on the government to rescind its emergency law (which has been in effect since the country's revolution in 1963). AMNESTY INTERNATIONAL condemned the judgment, which was subject to appeal. Only a month before, on the 41st anniversary of the Baathist Party coming to power, 25 protesters against the emergency law audaciously demonstrated in front of the Parliament. Reformers said that they had collected 17,000 signatures in support of dismantling the emergency law. The police moved in on the demonstrators, shredding banners and destroying reporters' notebooks.

The Baathist Party, which has about 2 million members, constitutes a parallel or shadow government, but the younger Assad has taken some steps to strip the party of its power and consolidate it in the government. (Until the U.S.-led invasion of Iraq, that country had also been led by the Baathist Party, though the Iraqi and Syrian regimes seldom found common cause.) The regime has responded far more aggressively—and violently—to Kurdish dissent. The toppling of Saddam Hussein's regime has galvanized Syria's minority Kurdish population of 1.5 million (out of 17 million), spurring hopes of greater freedom. Some 200,000 Kurds have been denied Syrian citizenship, which means that they cannot vote or register their land. The government's repression of Kurdish rights stems from fears that Kurds may seek a state of their own. In late March 2004 Kurdish demonstrators in northeastern Syria were fired on by security forces. The riot was precipitated by events at a soccer match when some soccer fans began waving a Kurdish flag and held signs blessing President George W. Bush while chanting, "We will sacrifice our lives for Bush." Opposing fans responded with taunts, and soon fighting broke out. Police were summoned but their presence only exacerbated the unrest. According to Kurdish sources, 14 or 15 people were killed and 60 wounded in two days of rioting. The news set off more demonstrations by Kurds and students in the capital, Damascus. Riot police were deployed around the university and in a largely Kurdish suburb. Syrian human rights organizations rallied to support Kurdish protests, asserting that blame for the killings of unarmed demonstrators rested solely with the security forces. These organizations called for negotiations to ensure greater rights for the Kurdish people rather than resort to a violent crackdown.

The assassination of former Lebanese prime minister Rafik Hariri in February 2005 precipitated widespread protest against Syria's hegemony over its neighbor. Hariri had been a longtime opponent of the Syrian military deployment in Lebanon, which was originally intended to impose peace after a decade of civil war. Although the Syrians had agreed in principle to withdraw the troops—numbering about 14,000 in 2005—Damascus has continued to stall. In addition to maintaining its troops on Lebanese soil, Syria has exercised political power over Beirut, securing a third term for the pro-Syrian president, which required a change in the constitution. A month after Hariri's slaying, investigators had yet to identify the perpetrators, although many Lebanese attributed the killing to Syria in light of Hariri's plans to run for office again. Unprecedented demonstrations against Syria erupted in Beirut, and both the French and the American governments called upon Syria to pull out its forces and intelligence agents. Even Saudi Arabia and other Arab governments, which traditionally might have been expected to back Damascus, urged Assad to leave Lebanon. Since Syria has reaped considerable economic benefits from Lebanon—some $4 billion annually in revenue from migrant laborers repatriating money as well as involvement in drug smuggling—Damascus is understandably reluctant to loosen its long-standing ties. Whether the younger Assad could survive any decision to relinquish Lebanon is also in doubt. The consequences of the Lebanese crisis were already being felt in Syria, however, as the Assad regime adopted a defensive posture, cracking down on hard-won freedoms. In late spring 2005 Syria bowed to international pressure and pulled its troops out of Lebanon, though it was believed that it had left many intelligence agents behind to monitor developments. In September a United Nations inquiry into Hariri's assassination resulted in the arrests of four Lebanese security officials with close ties to Syria, further strengthening suspicions that Damascus was implicated in the slaying in spite of official denials. Speculation was rife in the Syrian capital that high-level figures in the regime, perhaps even Assad himself, might be named as suspects by the UN team, a possibility that might trigger a major political crisis.

See also KURDISTAN, SUPPRESSION OF.

Further Reading:

George, Alan. *Syria: Neither Bread nor Freedom.* London: Zed Books, 2003.

Hinnebusch, Raymond. *Syria: Revolution from Above.* London: Routledge, 2002.

Leverett, Flynt. *Inheriting Syria: Bashar's Trial by Fire.* Washington, D.C.: Brookings Institution Press, 2005.

T

Tachibana, Yoshio   *See* WAR CRIMINALS OF JAPAN.

Tadić, Dusan   *See* WAR CRIMINALS OF THE FORMER YUGOSLAVIA.

Taliban

The Taliban (derived from the Arabic for Students of Islamic Knowledge Movement) ruled Afghanistan from 1996 until 2001. After taking control of 90 percent of Afghan territory with the backing of neighboring Pakistan, the Taliban imposed a strict fundamentalist strain of Islam on the country. in 1996 Taliban leader MULLAH OMAR allowed the al-QAEDA leader Osama Bin Laden to establish camps in Afghanistan to train and arm Islamic militants. In December 2001 the Taliban was driven from power by American forces after Mullah Omar refused to hand over Bin Laden, who had orchestrated the 9/11 (2001) attacks on New York and Washington, D.C.

Originally the Taliban were made up of mujahideen (holy warriors), who had fought the Soviet occupation of their country for 10 years. However, unlike other mujahideen who fought for various warlords, the Taliban drew their recruits from religious students, many of whom studied in the Islamic madrassas, or religious schools, in Pakistan. With arms clandestinely supplied by Pakistan, the Taliban overcame rival factions and seized power, taking the capital of Kabul in 1996. (Mullah Omar nonetheless continued to rule from his tribal stronghold in Kandahar.) Initially the Taliban enjoyed considerable popularity as it succeeded in restoring order to a country that had been plunged into near anarchy by factional and tribal fighting. But order came at a high cost: The Taliban introduced sharia, or Islamic, law, which banned television, the playing of music, the Internet, and even kite flying, which were denounced as frivolous or heretical. Women were forced to wear burkas—garments that covered them from head to toe—and were barred from public life. Girls could not attend school, and women were not permitted to work. Violators could be beaten, stoned to death, or shot by special vice police.

Throughout the years of Taliban rule, the country never knew peace. The Taliban were unable to dislodge their opposition, known as the Northern Alliance, nominally headed by the former president Burhanuddin Rabbani. In spite of successive Taliban offensives, the Northern Alliance managed to cling to about 10 percent of Afghan territory in the north. The Taliban were mainly Sunni Pashtuns (the largest of Afghanistan's several tribes), whereas the Northern Alliance was composed of Tajiks, Hazara, Uzbeks, and Turkmen. In its six years in power, the Taliban was only recognized by three countries—Saudi Arabia, Pakistan, and the United Arab Emirates. Nor did it win any friends by ordering the destruction of the 2000-year-old Buddhist statues of Bamian in March 2001, declaring that representations of the human figure were contrary to teachings of the Koran. (Many other precious Afghan antiquities were destroyed for the same reason.) Nevertheless, the Taliban might have remained in power longer if it had not been so quick to embrace Bin Laden's terrorist organization. In addition to a common ideology, the Taliban was also beholden to Bin Laden because they needed his money.

By the time the United States invaded Afghanistan, the Taliban had already split into opposing factions. Although most of the Taliban fighters surrendered or took flight across the border into Pakistan, its leaders retain an ability to make trouble for the new Afghani authorities. Taliban insurgents regularly stage guerrilla attacks, kidnapping and killing government officials, aid workers, and construction crews. Schools for girls have been bombed or forced to close because of threats. At the same time, the newly elected government of Hamid Karzai has made overtures to more moderate Taliban elements, raising the prospect that some former Taliban fighters could eventually be incorporated into the government and security forces.

See also AFGHANISTAN, HUMAN RIGHTS VIOLATIONS IN; HAZARA, PERSECUTION OF.

Further Reading:
Anderson, J. L., and Thomas Dworzak. *Taliban.* London: Trolley, 2003.
Burke, Jason. *Al-Qaeda: Casting a Shadow of Terror.* London: I. B. Tauris, 2004.
———. *Al-Qaeda: The True Story of Radical Islam.* London: I. B. Tauris, 2004.
Rashid, Ahmed. *Jihad: The Rise of Militant Islam in Central Asia.* New York: Penguin Books, 2003.
———. *Taliban: Militant Islam, Oil and Fundamentalism in Central Asia.* New Haven, Conn.: Yale University Press, 2001.
Zayy-at, Montasser al-. *The Road to Al-Qaeda: The Story of Bin Laden's Right-Hand Man.* Critical Studies on Islam. Translated by Ahmed Fekry. Edited by Sara Nimis. Ann Arbor, Mich.: Pluto Press, 2004.

Tamenori, Soto   *See* WAR CRIMINALS OF JAPAN.

Tamil Tigers   *See* TIGERS, TAMIL.

Ta Mok (Chhit Choeun) (1926–) *Khmer Rouge leader*

Chhit Choeun was a leader of the Khmer Rouge, a fanatic communist insurgency that terrorized Cambodia—in and out of power—for decades. His reputation for savagery is underscored by his nom de guerre Ta Mok, which means "Grandfather Butcher." Ta Mok, a onetime Buddhist monk, played a critical role in the murder of between 1.5 and 2 million people who perished during the four years the Khmer Rouge ruled Cambodia. His power base lay with tribes in the southwestern part of Cambodia, and in 1975 he joined in an alliance with POL POT, the leader of the Khmer Rouge. He even supplied Pol Pot—otherwise known as "Brother No. 1"—with his bodyguards. (He also surrounded himself with bodyguards, all of whom were women.) Over the next two years, Ta Mok provided Pol Pot with the backing he needed to eliminate all internal opposition and enabled him to initiate a campaign of terror against the local population. Elements of Ta Mok's party fanned out from their base in the southwest into other parts of the country to carry out a purge of Pol Pot's enemies within the Khmer Rouge. In 1975 the guerrillas seized the capital, Phnom Penh, and proceeded to unleash a reign of terror. Ta Mok was given control over the army, and his chief lieutenant, Mit Deuch, was appointed head of the secret police.

In 1979 the Vietnamese invaded Cambodia and defeated the Khmer Rouge, which soon resumed guerrilla warfare from bases in the mountainous north. As commander of the northern zone, Ta Mok continued to exercise considerable influence in the Khmer Rouge insurgency. By 1997, though, internal dissension had erupted in the leadership. Ta Mok and two other top Khmer Rouge leaders, Nuon Chea and Khieu Samphan, turned against Pol Pot and placed him under house arrest. (Pol Pot died soon afterward.) But in 1998, other elements of the Khmer Rouge rebelled against Ta Mok, the last major Khmer Rouge leader still at large, and in March that year he was captured by the Cambodian army on the Thai border. Within two days he was charged under a 1994 law banning the Khmer Rouge, but by 2000 the 74-year-old still had not been brought to trial. Hun Sen, the Cambodian prime minister, warned that Ta Mok might implicate important political leaders who had had ties with the Khmer Rouge and in the process jeopardize moves toward national reconciliation. Hun Sen did, however, say that he supported a proposal for a tribunal to try former Khmer Rouge leaders with the assistance of the United Nations, but by 2004 efforts to organize such a tribunal were being hampered by the government's demands. Human rights organizations continued to voice concerns that without international involvement, the trial of Ta Mok and his colleagues would not be seen as fair. Cambodia "deserves better than a show trial," AMNESTY INTERNATIONAL declared. In an interview from prison, Ta Mok has said that he knew only "a fraction" of what went on during the years that the Khmer Rouge ruled the country. Then he went on to say, "Sometimes I think we are cursed. Everybody takes from this country. So few people give anything. Everybody betrays us in the end."

See also CAMBODIA, WAR CRIMES IN.

Further Reading:
Hinton, Alexander Laban, and Robert Jay Lifton. *Why Did They Kill?: Cambodia in the Shadow of Genocide.* California Series in Public Anthropology, vol. 11. Berkeley: University of California Press, 2004.
Kiernan, Ben. *How Pol Pot Came to Power: Colonialism, Nationalism, and Communism in Cambodia, 1930–1975.* New Haven, Conn.: Yale University Press, 2004.
———. *The Pol Pot Regime: Race, Power, and Genocide in Cambodia under the Khmer Rouge, 1975–79.* New Haven, Conn.: Yale University Press, 2002.
Pran, Dith, comp. *Children of Cambodia's Killing Fields: Memoirs by Survivors.* Edited by Kim DePaul. New Haven, Conn.: Yale University Press, 1999.
Short, Philip. *Pol Pot: Anatomy of a Nightmare.* New York: Holt Rinehart, 2005.
Ung, Loung. *First They Killed My Father: A Daughter of Cambodia Remembers.* New York: Perennial, 2001.

Tatoune, Jean *See* HAITIAN HUMAN RIGHTS VIOLATORS.

Taylor, Charles Ghankay (Charles MacArthur Dapkana Taylor) (1948–) *Liberian dictator*

Until he was unceremoniously sent into exile, Charles MacArthur Dapkana Taylor was one of Africa's most feared despots. Had he only terrorized his native Liberia—first as the leader of a savage insurgency and then as the country's president—he would have deserved his ignominious reputation. But he was also instrumental in instigating a reign of terror in the neighboring West African state of Sierra Leone.

The creation of former slaves sent to America in 1847, Liberia is the oldest black African republic. Unfortunately, its historic distinction has been overshadowed by corruption, exploitation, and repression. In the early 1990s Taylor was merely one of several warlords competing for power, but he proved more adept—and ruthless—than his rivals. The disintegration of the state had begun in 1980 with a coup led by an army master sergeant named Samuel Doe. Until then Liberia had been dominated by the descendants of the freed African-American slaves. Taylor was born into one of these aristocratic families in 1948 but later, perhaps to make his name sound more "African," adopted Ghankay as his middle name. Following the example of other sons and daughters of the Liberian elite, he was sent to the United States to pursue his studies, returning home shortly after Doe's successful coup.

Doe saw in Charles Taylor a useful ally. Taylor, however, had no loyalties other than to himself. He was determined to back Doe only so long as it suited him. Unwisely, Doe put him in charge of the General Services Agency, which allowed Taylor to control—and plunder—much of the country's budget. Accused of stealing $1 million, he fled to the United States. But far from finding refuge, he was detained in the Plymouth County House of Correction in Massachusetts, under a Liberian extradition warrant. While he insisted on his innocence, he did not stick around to face charges. How he escaped prison is in dispute. There are stories that he managed to saw through the bars, but some conspiracy theorists maintain that his escape was abetted by Americans who were interested in using him to rid Liberia of Doe's corrupt regime.

On Christmas Eve 1989, not long after his return, Taylor launched an insurrection intended to bring down his former patron. A shrewd tactician, he had already built up a vast and far-flung network of supporters and foreign allies. He counted among his friends the radical Colonel Muammar al-Gadhafi of Libya and the conservative Felix Houphouet-Boigny, then ruler of Ivory Coast, as well as a host of shady businessmen and arms dealers. Taylor was by no means alone in his quest to topple Doe. Other factions, equally as murderous, were also competing for power. Doe was finally abducted by elements of a rival force and executed.

Liberians who had hoped that Doe's death would restore order to the country were grievously mistaken. The next five years were marked by tribal and factional violence that brought ruin to the country. When a Nigerian-brokered peace accord was reached in 1995, Taylor had emerged as de facto ruler. Two years later he officially consolidated power, winning election for president though there is considerable evidence that he secured his victory only by intimidating his opponents. In the immediate aftermath of the elections, he made a show of instituting democratic government, bringing rival political leaders into his government. By 1999, however, with the withdrawal of Nigerian peacekeepers, he reverted to form, cracking down on opponents and shutting down independent newspapers and radio stations.

Taylor was not content simply to rule one country. He had designs on the diamond wealth of neighboring Sierra Leone as well. To this end he sponsored a civil war spearheaded by Foday SANKOH, a former corporal and TV cameraman whose violent temperament matched his own. Diamond wealth fueled the conflict in Sierra Leone even as it allowed Taylor to maintain his grip on power in Liberia's capital, Monrovia.

Braggadocio has always been one of Taylor's most outstanding traits. In 1999 he went before a prayer meeting clad from head to toe in white to repudiate accusations by the United Nations that he was an arms dealer. A lay preacher in the Baptist Church, he prayed for forgiveness even as he continued to insist on his innocence. He freely gave interviews to the BBC, though he largely remained out of sight of his own people. When a BBC commentator pointed out that many people in the world considered him a murderer, he countered by saying that Jesus Christ had also been accused of being a murderer in his time.

Opposition to Taylor erupted into civil war. A rebel group called Liberians United for Reconciliation and Democracy (LURD) rose up in the countryside, and soon government forces were in retreat. By 2002 Taylor's control was reduced to the environs of Monrovia. He blamed Guinea, a neighboring state, for supporting the rebels and ordered retaliatory strikes aimed at Guinea border towns, widening the war and precipitating a refugee crisis.

In June 2003 Taylor was indicted on 17 violations of INTERNATIONAL HUMANITARIAN LAW, war crimes, and CRIMES AGAINST HUMANITY by the SPECIAL COURT FOR SIERRA LEONE. The charges stemmed from Taylor's involvement in the decade-long civil war in Sierra Leone, which ended in 2002. Specifically, the indictment found him in violation of Article 6.1 and 6.3 of the court's statute, which allows high-ranking officials to be held individually criminally responsible. Taylor was held accountable for attacks meant to terrorize civilian populations, which, according to the indictment, included "unlawful killings, physical and sexual violence against civilian men, women, and children, abductions and looting and destruction of civilian property." Taylor was also charged with several additional crimes, including sexual slavery, FORCED LABOR, forced combat training for children, and using physical mutilation as a form of intimidation.

Taylor ignored the indictments, but he could not ignore the mounting threat to his regime from rebel forces. Monrovia itself became engulfed in chaos as rebels moved on the capital. Under international pressure, he finally agreed to leave office but, fearing arrest, made his resignation contingent on an offer of sanctuary from another government. Although human rights organizations vehemently objected to any agreement that would allow him to go free, the Bush administration tacitly supported exile. Otherwise it was believed that he would make a last stand, subjecting the Liberian population to even more suffering. In August 2003, after days of hesitation, he finally stepped down, but he refused to climb aboard the plane waiting to spirit him into exile in Nigeria before holding a press conference. Declaring that he would one day return to reclaim power, he gave every indication that Liberians would welcome him back. Diplomatic efforts have continued to have Taylor extradited from Nigeria to stand trial, but as of mid-2005 the Nigerian government had rebuffed all calls to arrest him.

See also CONFLICT DIAMONDS; LIBERIA, HUMAN RIGHTS VIOLATIONS IN; SIERRA LEONE, HUMAN RIGHTS VIOLATIONS IN.

Further Reading:
Adebajo, Adekeye. *Building Peace in West Africa: Liberia, Sierra Leone, and Guinea-Bissau.* International Peace Academy Occasional Paper Series. Boulder, Colo.: Lynne Rienner Publishers, 2002.

———. *Liberia's Civil War: Nigeria, ECOMOG, and Regional Security in West Africa.* Boulder, Colo.: Lynne Rienner Publishers, 2002.

Ellils, Stephen. *The Mask of Anarchy: The Destruction of Liberia and the Religious Dimension of an African Civil War.* New York: New York University Press, 2001.

Kulah, Arthur F. *Liberia Will Rise Again: Reflections on the Liberian Civil Crisis.* Nashville, Tenn.: Abingdon Press, 1999.

Mohammed, Amos. *The Role of the Economic Community of the West African States: ECOWAS—Conflict Management in Liberia.* Bloomington, IN: Authorhouse, 2003.

Pham, John-Peter. *Liberia: Portrait of a Failed State.* London: Reed Press, 2004.

Taylor, Telford (1908–1998) *American prosecutor*
Telford Taylor achieved fame as a lead prosecutors of Nazi war criminals at the second round of NUREMBERG TRIALS after World War II. But Taylor, an army colonel at the time of the first trials, was more than a prosecutor since he also helped draft the rules for how such war criminals as Hermann GÖRING and Rudolf HESS were to be prosecuted. Until Nuremberg there was little precedent to rely upon for such proceedings.

Taylor was born on February 24, 1908, in Schenectady, New York. He showed promise as a jazz musician but found his true calling in government after graduating from Harvard Law School in 1932. It was not long before he entered government service, and over the next several years he held various legal posts in the Department of Interior, the Agricultural Adjustment Administration, the Senate Interstate Commerce Committee, the Department of Justice, and the Federal Communications Commission. When the United States entered World War II, he joined Army Intelligence. In 1943, promoted to lieutenant colonel, he became military attaché in the U.S. Embassy in London. He was a full colonel by 1944 at a time when Allied leaders were deliberating over how to deal with Nazi war criminals.

In the first group of Nuremberg Trials, Taylor served as assistant to Robert H. JACKSON, the principal prosecutor for the Allies (Britain, France, the United States, and the Soviet Union). Before Nuremberg, some suspected war criminals were tried in national courts under a variety of laws. There was strong resistance among many Allied leaders to try Nazi officials in an international forum. British prime minister Winston Churchill was in favor of simply shooting Nazi leaders without a trial once they were caught and identified. Joseph STALIN, the Soviet dictator, also supported the idea of executing war criminals without troubling with legal formalities. Taylor, on the other hand, argued for an international trial, cautioning against holding "a scattering of small trials" because they would carry no weight "whereas the world's eyes and ears would be fastened on a big international trial." In the end, his was a view that prevailed. Both Taylor and Jackson also believed that it was possible to distinguish gradations of guilt even when confronted with suspects who had committed reprehensible acts. In other words, an industrialist who made profits off slave labor was not necessarily as culpable as a Nazi officer who had given the orders to execute thousands of civilians or a doctor who had performed MEDICAL EXPERIMENTS on helpless children. Above all, the prosecutors—both Americans—were anxious that the trials not be considered a sham that allowed the victors to take revenge against the defeated. Taylor also believed that the trials could bring to an end a tragic chapter in Germany's history and pave the way for Germany to regain its former place in longest sentence, which was given to Hess. Hess was held in Spandau Prison in Berlin for over 40 years—the only prisoner in the facility—until he killed himself at age 93. "Such long-continued incarceration," Taylor noted, was itself "a crime against humanity."

When he returned to the United States Taylor practiced law, but when the Korean War broke out he agreed to become administrator of the Small Defense Plants Administration at President Truman's behest. In the early 1950s he became an outspoken critic of Senator Joseph McCarthy, who conducted a vitriolic anticommunist campaign that Taylor denounced as "a vicious weapon of the extreme right against their political opponents." McCarthy, Taylor said at a speech at West Point in 1953, was "a dangerous adventurer." In response, McCarthy intimated that Taylor had somehow become linked with communists himself, an allegation that had no basis in fact. Taylor, undeterred, continued to criticize the senator.

In the late 1960s, Taylor, now a professor of law at Columbia University, proved to be just as vigorous in his opposition to U.S. policy in Vietnam. In 1971 he called for a national commission to investigate the origins and prosecution of the war. In 1972 he repudiated the bombing of Hanoi by American warplanes as "immoral and senseless." A year later he joined a delegation (which included folk singer Joan Baez) that traveled to North Vietnam, where he visited prisoner-of-war camps. Not unexpectedly, he weighed in on the trial of Lieutenant William Calley, who was charged with ordering a massacre of unarmed Vietnamese civilians in My Lai. Taylor argued that Calley—the only individual convicted in the atrocity—had been made a scapegoat and that officials in the White House and Pentagon should also be held accountable. In the 1980s, in a departure from his usual assignments, Taylor's services were called upon by the National Basketball Association as a special master to resolve legal disputes.

Taylor was the author of several books that include *Grand Inquest: The Story of Congressional Investigations, Sword and Swastika, The March of Conquest, The Breaking Wave,* and *Munich: The Price of Peace.* A few years before his death on May 22, 1998, he commented on the war then raging in Bosnia, characterized by the worst atrocities in Europe since the Second World War. "We must never forget that the record on which we judge these defendants is the record on which history will judge us tomorrow," he declared. "To pass these defendants a poisoned chalice is to put it to our lips as well. . . . The wrongs which we seek to condemn and punish have been so calculated, so malignant, and so devastating, that civilization cannot tolerate their being ignored, because it cannot survive their being repeated. . . ."

See also MY LAI MASSACRE.

American brigadier general Telford Taylor, who prosecuted top Nazis at the Nuremberg Trials *(Library of Congress)*

the international community. Germany would not be treated as a pariah state, Taylor believed, if there were not to be a recurrence of the same conditions that led to the Second World War.

Twenty-two top Nazi officials were brought to trial; 19 were convicted and 12 sentenced to death. (Göring escaped execution by committing suicide.) After the first round of trials ended in 1946, Jackson left his post and Taylor was promoted to brigadier general and appointed lead prosecutor in his place. In the second round of trials, Taylor indicted 23 German doctors and scientists—"infantile sadists" in his words; the only science they knew, he said, was the "science of inducing death." Taylor also prosecuted a number of Nazi officials and judges, industrialists, and SS officers. These trials ended in 1949—not entirely successfully from Taylor's point of view; Alfred KRUPP, head of I. G. Farben Chemical, who was accused of using slave labor in his factories, won acquittal because of a lack of evidence. Nonetheless, Taylor did win several convictions of other defendants including 13 SS officers. Thirty-seven defendants were sentenced to death, and 64 others received prison sentences although some were subsequently commuted. Taylor later had cause to regret the

Further Reading:

Ferencz, Benjamin B., and Telford Taylor. *Less Than Slaves: Jewish Forced Labor and the Quest for Compensation.* Bloomington: Indiana University Press, 2002.

Taylor, Telford. *The Anatomy of the Nuremberg Trials: A Personal Memoir.* Knopf, 1992.

———. *Munich: The Price of Peace.* New York: Random House, 1980.

———. *Nuremberg and Vietnam: An American Tragedy.* New York: Times Books, 1970.

terrorism and international humanitarian law

The September 11, 2001, terrorist attacks on the United States and the subsequent war on terror have confronted advocates of INTERNATIONAL HUMANITARIAN LAW (IHL) with a dilemma. How is it possible to justify applying the same laws to terrorists that govern the treatment of legitimate combatants and PRISONERS OF WAR (POWs)? On the one hand, the GENEVA CONVENTIONS and other relevant treaties establish rights for prisoners of war and the treatment of enemy combatants. On the other hand, terrorists and terrorist organizations are not parties to these agreements and willfully violate protections for civilians set out by many of these same accords. The Bush administration, for instance, has taken the view—disputed by many human rights advocates and called into question by several U.S. federal courts—that terrorists have no rights under the Geneva Conventions, the 1977 ADDITIONAL PROTOCOLS TO THE GENEVA CONVENTIONS, or the protections guaranteed to citizens under the U.S. Constitution. The U.S. Justice Department has even sought to treat American citizens suspected of supporting or participating in terrorist organizations as exempt from constitutional guarantees such as DUE PROCESS.

There are several explicit references to terrorism in IHL, even though it does not provide a definition of terrorism. The Fourth Geneva Convention of 1949 (Article 33) states that "Collective penalties and likewise all measures of intimidation or of terrorism are prohibited." Additional Protocol I (Article 51) states: "The civilian population as such, as well as individual civilians, shall not be the object of attack. Acts or threats of violence the primary purpose of which is to spread terror among the civilian population are prohibited," Additional Protocol II (Articles 4 and 13) prohibits "acts of terrorism" against persons not or no longer taking part in hostilities. Terrorism would also be classified as COLLECTIVE PUNISHMENT of civilians, a practice outlawed by IHL as well. (IHL does, however, include qualifications that permit attacks on military objectives or measures undertaken for military security that may have a negative impact on civilians.) The basic criterion relating to the treatment of civilians in combat is based on adherence to the "principle of distinction." This principle, considered the cornerstone of IHL, requires belligerents to distinguish between military and civilian objectives and protects civilians in wartime from deliberate targeting, deportation (with a few limited exceptions), and hostage taking, as well as protecting property vital to civilians from intentional destruction such as dams, power plants, and irrigation systems.

In peacetime, acts against a civilian population or civilian property would be classified as war crimes. Under the principle of UNIVERSAL JURISDICTION, war crimes can be prosecuted by any state even if its citizens were not directly involved and the act did not take place on its territory. In that respect, terrorism does not constitute a legally recognized armed conflict. IHL recognizes that there must be parties to a conflict. These parties may be states, but they can also be rebel groups if they meet certain criteria: They must have a military organization, for instance, and have a formal command structure. IHL applies equally to all parties to a conflict, whether aggressor or defender. It requires all belligerents to adhere to provisions protecting civilians. This implies parity between the adversaries and, in addition, makes a distinction between law enforcement and military action. Suppression of a violent protest by police and security forces, for instance, would not be covered by IHL because the protesters did not meet the criteria for an insurgent group.

The INTERNATIONAL COMMITTEE OF THE RED CROSS (ICRC) has weighed in on the application of IHL to the war on terrorism. It has issued a fact sheet (though not an institutional opinion), indicating that the war launched by the United States against Afghanistan in the wake of the 9/11 attacks was an armed conflict under the definition of IHL, specifically the Fourth Geneva Convention, as well as the rules of CUSTOMARY LAW. But waging a "war on terrorism," in the ICRC's assessment, does not necessarily meet the definition of an armed conflict because the element of parity is absent—that is, there are not two recognizable parties to the conflict. Most incidents of violence described as "terrorist," says the ICRC, are "perpetrated by loosely organized groups (networks), or individuals that, at best, share a common ideology." According to the ICRC, that makes it "doubtful" whether these groups and networks can be characterized as a "party" to a conflict within the meaning of IHL. This therefore suggests that such acts should be treated as crimes better addressed by either international or domestic law enforcement. In other words, the ICRC suggests, these acts are not covered by IHL because they do not take place in the context of armed conflict. By the same token, measures taken by states to combat or prevent terrorism do not amount to military actions in an armed conflict, but rather involve measures undertaken by the judiciary and police as well as policies and tactics adopted by international law-enforcement agencies such as Interpol. Many antiterrorism measures do not entail combat at all but instead focus on eliminating sources of financial support for terrorists or ensuring the security of computer networks. " 'Terrorism' is a phenomenon," says the ICRC. "Both practically and legally, war cannot be waged against a phenomenon, but only against an identifiable party to an armed conflict."

In spite of the fact that terrorists and terrorist groups are not a party to an armed conflict under IHL, states nonetheless have the obligation to treat terrorists who are arrested or captured according to a national or international legal framework. In the view of the ICRC, those combatants who were captured during the war in Afghanistan, for instance, ought to be protected by IHL, meaning that they should be treated like prisoners of war in any armed conflict. This position is distinctly at odds with the one taken by the Bush administration, which views even fighters for the former TALIBAN regime taken in the war as "unlawful" combatants who are not entitled to rights and protections of prisoners of war. This policy considers the Taliban as allies of terrorists—specifically al-QAEDA—and not as soldiers in the service of a legitimate government. The U.S. military describes an unlawful combatant as an individual who is not authorized to take a direct part in hostilities but participates all the same and who, if captured, may be tried and punished. Such individuals could be civilians who engage in war without authorization; noncombat members of the military, such as medics or chaplains, who engage in combat; and soldiers who fight out of uniform. Under the policy promulgated by the United States, these captives may be detained indefinitely; thus, provisions of IHL calling for the repatriation of POWs after hostilities cease would not apply because it is impossible to determine when, if ever, a war on terrorism could be declared over.

If the status of a POW is in doubt, the Third Geneva Convention calls for a competent tribunal to be established to settle the question. The ICRC also notes that a POW can be tried for war crimes and may be held until the sentence is served regardless of whether hostilities have ended. The Fourth Geneva Convention does make a distinction between combatants and enemy nationals such as mercenaries or civilians who do not carry arms openly or wear a uniform (saboteurs, spies, etc.)—so-called unprivileged or unlawful belligerents. If arrested, these enemy nationals would not be considered prisoners of war but under IHL and would be tried for violations of domestic law and imprisoned until the sentence has been fulfilled. Nonetheless, individuals in this category are still entitled to a fair tiral.

ARTICLE 3 COMMON TO THE GENEVA CONVENTIONS and customary law also offer protections to individuals detained in noninternational armed conflicts, as was the case with Afghanistan after the Taliban was defeated in spring 2002. IHL and relevant criminal domestic laws apply to those detainees, who also have the right to a fair trial for any crimes of which they are accused. According to the ICRC, "no person captured in the fight against terrorism can be considered outside the law; there is no such thing as a 'black hole' in terms of legal protection." By the same token, under the Geneva Conventions, the ICRC must be granted access to persons detained in an international armed conflict, whether they are POWs or persons protected by the Fourth Geneva Convention. In that regard, the ICRC has called for a formal determination of the status of the individuals held at the U.S. base in Guantánamo Bay who are accused of terrorist activities.

See also GUANTÁNAMO DETAINEES.

Further Reading:
Burke, Jason. *Al-Qaeda: Casting a Shadow of Terror.* London: I. B. Tauris, 2004.
———. *Al-Qaeda: The True Story of Radical Islam.* London: I. B. Tauris, 2004.
Danner, Mark. *Torture and Truth: America, Abu Ghraib, and the War on Terror.* New York: New York Review Books, 2004.
Gunaratna, Rohan. *Inside Al Qaeda: Global Network of Terror.* New York: Berkley Publishing Group, 2003.
Hersh, Seymour M. *Chain of Command: The Road from 9/11 to Abu Ghraib.* New York: HarperCollins, 2004.
Micheletti, Eric. *Special Forces in Afghanistan 2001–2003: War Against Terrorism.* Paris: Historie & Collections, 2003.
Scheuer, Michael. *Imperial Hubris: Why the West Is Losing the War on Terror.* Washington, D.C.: Potomac Books, 2004.
Zayy-at, Montasser al-. *The Road to Al-Qaeda: The Story of Bin Laden's Right-Hand Man.* Critical Studies on Islam. Translated by Ahmed Fekry. Edited by Sara Nimis. Ann Arbor, Mich.: Pluto Press, 2004.

Thailand, human rights violations in

Although it is a democracy, Thailand's government still has a mixed record on human rights. There have been numerous cases of EXTRAJUDICIAL KILLINGS by police, especially in connection with an antidrug campaign. In the south of the country, the police and security forces have brutally suppressed dissent, killing about 650 Muslims in 2004, stirring widespread outrage in a region that is home to a large Muslim population. (The majority of Thais are Buddhists.) There is some question about the commitment of the government of Prime Minister Thaksin Shinawatra to freedom of the press in view of the fact that his family controls the Shin Corporation, the country's biggest media and communications company, which owns the major television channels and satellite and mobile phone networks.

Probably no event in recent years has drawn attention to Thailand's human rights problems more than the deaths of 78 Muslim protesters who died in police custody in October 2004. The victims were suffocated or crushed to death while being transported to police headquarters after being arrested for taking part in a political demonstration. Eyewitnesses reported seeing the protesters being beaten after they were arrested and then thrown face down into military trucks and piled four or five high. Security forces shot and killed another seven protesters at the demonstration itself. (Another 1,200 were still being detained weeks later without access to legal representation.) This was by no means the first incident in which security forces used excessive force: The previous April they had killed some 110 Muslim militants armed only with machetes who had taken refuge in a mosque. Human rights groups decried the killings, insisting that lethal force was not necessary to subdue the insurgents, most of whom were in their teens or early 20s. Earlier, in March 2004, Somchai Neelapajit, a prominent human rights lawyer for Thai Muslims facing terrorism charges, was disappeared and, according to HUMAN RIGHTS WATCH, most likely to have been tortured and killed. "Each incident fostered the atmosphere of impunity in which security forces in Narithawit [southern Thailand] seemed to be operating," Human Rights Watch said in an open letter to the prime minister, demanding investigations into the incidents and the prosecutions of those found culpable.

The pattern of abuses by security forces also extends to the so-called war on drugs, which has accounted for at least 2,275 extrajudicial executions by security forces, according to Human Rights Watch. When he took office in February 2001, Prime Minister Thaksin Shinawatra declared the "prevention and suppression" of narcotic drugs as one of his top priorities. Two years later the antidrug campaign officially began, but it soon devolved into a spree of violence characterized by wholesale killings by security forces, arbitrary arrest, intimidation of human rights advocates, and the blacklisting of several thousand people. The government was quick to blame the killings on drug gangs, a claim that is belied by credible reports received by human rights organizations. The drug war also jeopardized Thailand's relatively successful fight against HIV/AIDS by creating such a climate of fear that drug users were driven underground rather than seeking help and risking imprisonment or worse. Some people taken into custody reported that drugs had been planted on them by police and that they were forced to make confessions in order for the police to fulfill arrest quotas.

Further Reading:
Baker, Christopher, and Pasuk Phongpaichit. *A History of Thailand.* Cambridge: Cambridge University Press, 2005.

Slagter, Robert, and Harold Kerbo. *Modern Thailand.* Comparative Societies Series. Boston: McGraw-Hill, 2000.

Tibet   *See* CHINA, HUMAN RIGHTS VIOLATIONS IN.

Tiger Force

U.S. involvement in Vietnam, which cost the lives of 50,000 Americans and as many as 2 million Vietnamese combatants and civilians, lasted from the early 1960s and ended in 1975. Because of the clandestine nature of the war, making it difficult to tell friend from foe, U.S. forces resorted to various strategies to combat an elusive enemy. Some of the methods relied on ambushes, booby traps, and strikes on suspected bases of guerrilla support—in other words, the same tactics that the Vietcong insurgents were using to attack U.S. and South Vietnamese forces. However, the result was that in certain instances, American troops committed illegal acts. Revelations of atrocities by American troops on a hitherto unknown scale, though, surfaced only in October 2003—30 years after the United States withdrew its troops from Indochina—thanks to a series of Pulitzer Prize–winning articles in the *Toledo Blade.* Until then most Americans believed that the 1968 massacre of approximately 400 Vietnamese civilians in the village of My Lai was an anomaly rather than part of a larger pattern.

A year before the MY LAI MASSACRE, the U.S. Army had set up a special task force to conduct operations against communist Vietcong insurgents in the Central Highlands, a region of South Vietnam that was the site of intense fighting at the time. One of the principal components of the task force was a platoon known as the Tiger Force, a 45-man unit detached from the 101st Airborne Division. In the short period of its existence, the Tiger Force was responsible for such atrocities as intentionally blowing up women and children in underground bunkers, shooting farmers while they were at work in their fields, and torturing and executing prisoners before lopping off their ears and scalps for souvenirs. It is believed that the Tiger Force might have killed several hundred people. One medic reported that 120 civilians had been killed in a single month. Attempts by two soldiers to halt the killings went ignored by the commanders. According to the *Toledo Blade,* the atrocities occurred over a period of seven months in 1967.

An internal army investigation into the atrocities went on for four and a half years (February 1971–June 1975)—the longest such probe related to the army's actions in Vietnam—and reached all the way to the White House. Although investigators found 18 soldiers culpable of 20 war crimes, including murder, assault, and dereliction of duty, no one was ever charged, nor was the public made aware of the investigation. The investigation suffered from delays and inaction: A year passed before witnesses were even interviewed, and five of the soldiers implicated were allowed to leave the army quietly. Although a March 2, 1973, White House memo described the case and referred to five "unidentified members of Tiger Force" under investigation for crimes ranging from murder to body mutilation, there was little interest in the administration of President Richard M. Nixon to follow up on the investigation, especially after American disengagement from the region. By the time the Ford administration took office, the climate had changed completely. "No one wanted to hear about war crimes then," said Dr. David Anderson, editor of a book about war crimes called *Facing My Lai,* adding, "It would have been embarrassing."

Altogether the U.S. Army conducted 242 war-crimes investigations stemming from the Vietnam War; 21 cases, or about a third of the total, were substantiated and led to convictions based on charges ranging from beating prisoners to murdering civilians. Ten soldiers received prison terms ranging from 30 days to 20 years, though many sentences were later reduced.

See also PHOENIX PROGRAM; VIETNAM, HUMAN RIGHTS VIOLATIONS IN.

Further Reading:

Anderson, David, ed. *Facing My Lai: Moving Beyond the Massacre.* Lawrence: University of Kansas Press, 1998.
Bilton, Michael, and Kevin Sim. *Four Hours in My Lai.* New York: Penguin Books, 1993.
Hersh, Seymour. *My Lai 4: A Report on the Massacre and Its Aftermath.* New York: Random House, 1970.
Olson, James S., and Randy Roberts. *My Lai: A Brief History with Documents.* The Bedford Series in History and Culture. Sydney, Australia: Palgrave Macmillan, 1998.
Taylor, Telford. *Nuremberg and Vietnam: An American Tragedy.* New York: Times Books, 1970.
Vietnam Veterans against the War. *The Winter Soldier Investigation: An Inquiry into American War Crimes.* Boston: Beacon Press, 1972.

Tigers, Tamil (Liberation Tigers of Tamil Eelam)

The Liberation Tigers of Tamil Eelam (LTTE), popularly known as the Tamil Tigers, have been fighting for independence for the northern part of Sri Lanka since their founding in 1976. The Tigers sprang up in response to discrimination by the majority Sinhalese. The Tigers began a civil war with the Sri Lankan government in 1983, relying on guerrilla tactics characterized by acts of terror, atrocities, child recruitment, and numerous human rights abuses. Government forces have also been implicated in atrocities and egregious human rights violations. By 2004 a tenuous cease-fire had taken hold on the island, although a political settlement still seemed distant.

The Tigers are responsible for introducing a new terrorist tactic to the world: suicide bombings. A special unit, the Black Tigers, staged spectacular suicide bombings—a number in the capital, Colombo—long before such terrorist acts occurred in the Middle East. Those men and women who join the Black Tigers carry cyanide capsules in the event of capture. The Tigers have been accused of the ethnic cleansing of the Jaffna peninsula, driving out all ethnic groups who were non-Tamil. In addition, they have been charged with targeting Sinhalese civilians and villages. In one incident in 1999, Tiger units reportedly hacked women and children to death.

The Tigers have formed a highly organized structure that includes an intelligence unit, a naval unit (the Sea Tigers), and women's political and military wings. The core of the Tamil Tigers is said to consist of about 10,000 fighters who are well armed with artillery, surface-to-air missiles, and rocket launchers. The group also relies on a vast network of informants and supporters and has established an international presence to advocate for Tamil independence. Although the Tamils mainly operate out of the northern and eastern coastal areas of Sri Lanka, they have carried out attacks throughout the island. Based in the Wanni region, the group is commanded by the reclusive Velupillai Prabhakaran.

See also SRI LANKA, HUMAN RIGHTS VIOLATIONS IN.

Further Reading:

De Votta, Neil. *Blowback: Linguistic Nationalism, Institutional Decay, and Ethnic Conflict in Sri Lanka.* Contemporary Issues in Asia and the Pacific. Stanford, Calif.: Stanford University Press, 2004.
Tambiah, Stanley Jeyaraja. *Buddhism Betrayed?: Religion, Politics, and Violence in Sri Lanka.* A Monograph of the World Institute for Development Economics Research. Chicago: University Of Chicago Press, 1992.
Winslow, Deborah, and Michael Woost, eds. *Economy, Culture, and Civil War in Sri Lanka.* Bloomington: Indiana University Press, 2004.

Togo, human rights violations in

Until recently human rights conditions in the West African state of Togo have been problematic. Until his death in February 2005, President Gnassingbé Eyadéma had led Togo for 38 years, since seizing power in a coup in January 1967. In principle, the country is democratic: Political parties were legalized in 1991, and a democratic constitution was adopted in 1992. Nonetheless the government has suppressed political dissent, and elections are not considered fair. Several hundred people were killed after disputed elections in 1998; an investigation into the affair by a joint United Nations–Organization of African Unity (now the African Union) committee found in 2001 that the government had systematically violated human rights. The press is similarly stifled: The one major television outlet is state-owned, and journalists working for independent publications are often harassed and threatened with legal action if they write articles opposed to government policies.

Ten years of economic sanctions by the European Union (EU) that began in the mid-1990s led Eyadéma to relax his grip on power and take some steps toward EU-demanded political reforms. In 2004 he announced an amnesty for over 500 of the country's 3,200 prisoners, though most were common criminals. AMNESTY INTERNATIONAL identified seven of the released prisoners as members of the opposition party, the Union of Forces for Change (UFC), who were arrested after they had protested the barring of their candidate, Gilchrist Olympio, from taking part in presidential elections. Although the regime insists that it holds no political prisoners, the U.S. State Department in its annual *Country Report* has confirmed that political opponents are in fact incarcerated in Togolese prisons.

Trafficking in children represents another significant problem for the country. Child welfare groups say that Togo has failed to enact strict laws against the practice of exploiting children as prostitutes or as forced laborers. In the capital of Lomé, there is even an area known as the Child Market, where girls as young as nine are sold for sex, sometimes for as little as a dollar. Many of the children are abandoned, while others have been separated from their families. According to a report by HUMAN RIGHTS WATCH, the police do nothing to stop the trade.

Hopes that democracy would be restored to Togo after the death of Gnassingbé Eyadéma were shattered when the army announced that his 39-year-old son, Faure Gnassingbé, would assume power. The move was seen as a coup since it was in violation of the constitution, which calls for the speaker of the parliament as first in the line of succession. The African Union and other governments, including Washington, denounced this attempt to circumvent the law, and within days demonstrations broke out in the capital that led to three deaths. Under intense pressure, Faure Gnassingbé stepped down only weeks after his appointment, but only months later he won election to the presidency in an election disputed by the opposition. Days of rioting followed in which several people were killed. Whether Gnassingbé would be able to steer the country in a democratic direction, or whether he would even want to, remained unclear. Calls by President Gnassingbé for the return of refugees who had fled the country in the aftermath of post-election violence have gone unheeded. Nearly six months later, some 38,000 people remained in refugee camps in Benin and Ghana, fearful of being harassed or arrested by security forces if they set foot in Togo.

Tojo Hideki (1884–1948) *Japanese nationalist leader*

The best-known Japanese war criminal, Tojo Hideki served as Japan's minister of war and prime minister during World War II; for most of the war, he was for all practical purposes the country's dictator. As the official in command of Japanese occupation forces in China, he is responsible for the murder of almost 4 million Chinese. He also approved a secret program to conduct MEDICAL EXPERIMENTS on PRISONERS OF WAR and Chinese captives. After the war he was tried by the International Military Tribunal for the Far East—the TOKYO TRIALS—convicted, and condemned to death.

Tojo was born in Tokyo on December 30, 1884. After joining the Japanese army, he quickly rose in the ranks, becoming major general in 1933 and, in 1937, chief of staff of the Kwantung Army in Manchuria, which Japan had seized from China. After a brief six-month stint as vice min-

Former Japanese general and premier Tojo Hideki
(Bettmann/Corbis)

ister of war in 1941, he rejoined the military, this time as the commander of the army's aviation division. A fervent right-wing nationalist, he was an admirer of Adolf HITLER and an advocate of preemptive air strikes on China and the Soviet Union, countries he saw as long-term threats to Japanese interests. He opposed efforts by the foreign minister, Shignori Togo, to withdraw Japanese troops from China and Korea, which Japan had ruled as a colonial power since 1905.

In 1941 Tojo was appointed prime minister by Emperor Hirohito; he was also given the position of war minister, which put him in charge of the Japanese army, and additionally held the positions of home minister and foreign minister. Within two months he approved the attack on U.S. forces in Hawaii. (The actual decision to attack Pearl Harbor was made by Admiral Isoroku Yamamoto.) Tojo personally took charge of the Battle of the Pacific against U.S. forces, but by July 1944, after Japan suffered the loss of the strategically important island of Saipan, he resigned and disgraced, made a failed attempt to commit suicide. The postwar military tribunal established by the Allies found him guilty of waging wars of aggression in violation of international law as well as waging unprovoked war against China, the United States, the British Commonwealth, the Netherlands, and France (the latter three were colonial powers in Asia). In addition, Tojo was convicted for ordering, authorizing, and permitting inhumane treatment of prisoners of war and civilians. He was sentenced to death on November 12, 1948, and executed by hanging.

Further Reading:

Browne, Courtney. *Tojo: The Last Banzai.* New York: Da Capo Press, 1998.

Daws, Gavin. *Prisoners of the Japanese: POWs of World War II in the Pacific.* New York: Perennial, 1996.

Harris, Sheldon. *Factories of Death: Japanese Biological Warfare 1932–45 and the American Cover-Up.* London: Routledge, 1995.

Hoyt, Edwin. *Warlord: Tojo against the World.* New York: Cooper Square Press, 2001.

Li, Peter. *Japanese War Crimes: The Search for Justice.* New Brunswick, N.J.: Transaction Publishers, 2003.

Maga, Timothy P. *Judgment at Tokyo: The Japanese War Crimes Trials.* Lexington: University Press of Kentucky, 2001.

Tokyo Trials (International Military Tribunal for the Far East)

The International Military Tribunal for the Far East (IMTFE) began trying Japanese war criminals in Tokyo, Japan, on May 3, 1946, about half a year after the International Military Tribunal began trying Nazi war criminals in Germany (the NUREMBERG TRIALS). The tribunal held its final session on November 12, 1948. The trials of what were called Class A Japanese war criminals are known as the Tokyo Trials. The charges covered crimes committed by Japanese officials as far back as 1928 (involving the assassination of a Manchurian warlord) and up to the Japanese surrender to the Allies in August 1945. Judges from 11 nations served on the tribunal. The legal basis for the Tokyo Trials can be found in a number of agreements reached while the war was still in progress. These included the Cairo Conference, at which the United States, Great Britain, and China issued a declaration on December 1, 1943, that "the purpose of this war is to stop and punish Japanese aggression"; and the fifth article of the Potsdam Declaration of July 1945, signed by the same three Allies, which stated that "justice shall be meted out to all war criminals including those who have visited cruelties upon our prisoners." Specific provisions relating to the arrest and treatment of war criminals were enumerated in the Instrument of Japanese Surrender of September 2, 1945. The legal framework for the tribunal itself stems from a recommendation by the new Commission of Crimes of the United Nations (established at London in summer 1943).

The Moscow Conference of foreign ministers of the "Big Four"—the United States, the Soviet Union, Great Britain, and China—decided to establish the tribunal in Tokyo. The Tokyo Trials drew upon the guiding principles of the Nuremberg Trials, which would make the accused liable to such charges as crimes against peace, CRIMES AGAINST HUMANITY, and war crimes and aggressive war, although there was to be no imposition of "collective guilt," which was the case regarding Nazi crimes. One judge was chosen from each of the 11 nations represented on the tribunal. Of the 70 Class A war criminal suspects arrested after 1945, 28 were brought to trial before the IMTFE; nine were political or civilian officials and 19 were military officials. They were charged with a military campaign that "contemplated and carried out . . . murdering, maiming and ill-treating prisoners of war (and) civilian internees . . . forcing them to labor under inhumane conditions . . . plundering public and private property, wantonly destroying cities, towns and villages beyond any justification of military necessity; (perpetrating) mass murder, rape, pillage, brigandage, TORTURE and other barbaric cruelties upon the helpless civilian population of the over-run countries." In a statement issued to the press, Joseph Keenan, the chief prosecutor representing the United States, declared that "war and treaty-breakers should be stripped of the glamour of national heroes and exposed as what they really are—plain, ordinary murderers."

The prosecutors presented evidence to prove that the Japanese had planned the war as early as 1931 and went on to show that many of the accused were responsible for (or were aware of) such atrocities as the rape of Nanjing (Nanking) in 1937, in which as many as 300,000 Chinese were killed by Japanese invaders and 20,000 women raped, and the 1942 Singapore massacre in which Japanese forces systematically killed at least 5,000 ethnic Chinese civilians (and perhaps several thousand more) in an avowed effort to hunt down guerrillas. American and British prosecutors were able to establish from documentary evidence that the Japanese had determined on attacks against both nations without any legal justification: No treaty had been broken, and Japan was not being threatened by either nation. In addition, prosecutors pressed the case that Japanese officials were instrumental in the trafficking of opium in occupied China with the purpose of weakening Chinese morale and providing revenues for the Japanese war machine.

When the trial finally drew to an end after two and a half years, the tribunal found 25 guilty, many on multiple counts. Seven were sentenced to death by hanging, the most prominent of whom was TOJO Hideki, the former prime minister, who was responsible for launching the attack on Pearl Harbor in 1941. Sixteen were sentenced to life in prison and two others to lesser terms. (Two of the original 28 died of natural causes during the trial, and one suffered a mental breakdown and was committed to a psychiatric institution before being released in 1948.) Three of those sentenced to life imprisonment died in prison; the remaining 13 were paroled between 1954 and 1956.

That still left more than 40 Class A criminals who remained in Tokyo's Sugamo prison awaiting trial. Many of these were other military and diplomatic officials as well as industrialists and financial figures who had helped finance the war and had engaged in munitions manufacture and drug trafficking. Most of these prisoners were released in 1947 and 1948 by General Douglas MacArthur, supreme commander of occupied Japan. Critics of the United States' handling of Japanese war criminals after the war are especially upset that so many were able to escape justice. Indeed, several of the accused who were never tried returned to politics in postwar Japan. Emperor Hirohito was removed from a list of war criminals and kept on the throne in the interest of reconciliation, even though former prime minister Tojo had admitted that he had consulted with the emperor about the sneak attack on Pearl Harbor, that the emperor "had consented, though reluctantly, to the war," and that "none of us would dare act against the Emperor's will."

See also MANCHURIA, JAPANESE WAR CRIMES IN; MATSUI IWANE; NANJING, MASSACRE IN; OKAWA SHUMEI; SHIMADA SHIGETARO.

Further Reading:
Daws, Gavin. *Prisoners of the Japanese: POWs of World War II in the Pacific.* New York: Perennial, 1996.

Harris, Sheldon. *Factories of Death: Japanese Biological Warfare 1932–45 and the American Cover-Up.* London: Routledge, 1995.
Lamont-Brown, Raymond. *Ships from Hell: Japanese War Crimes on the High Seas.* Phoenix Mill, U.K.: Sutton Publishing, 2002.
Li, Peter. *Japanese War Crimes: The Search for Justice.* New Brunswick, N.J.: Transaction Publishers, 2003.
Maga, Timothy P. *Judgment at Tokyo: The Japanese War Crimes Trials.* Lexington: University Press of Kentucky, 2001.
Mendelsohn, John. *The Preservation of Japanese War Crimes Trials Records in the National Archives.* Washington, D.C.: National Archives and Records Administration, 1982.
Minear, Richard R. *Victors' Justice: The Tokyo War Crimes Trial.* Michigan Classics in Japanese Studies. Ann Arbor: University of Michigan Center for Japanese Studies, 2001.
Piccigallo, Philip R. *The Japanese on Trial: Allied War Crimes Operations in the East, 1945–1951.* Austin: University of Texas Press, 1980.
Rees, Laurence. *Horror in the East: Japan and the Atrocities of World War II.* New York: Da Capo Press, 2002.
Russell, of Liverpool, Edward Frederick Langley Russell, Baron. *Knights of the Bushido: A Short History of Japanese War Crimes.* London: Greenhill Books, 2005.
Tanaka, Yuki. *Hidden Horrors: Japanese War Crimes in World War II.* Philadelphia: Westview Press, 1998.

torture

Torture is universally prohibited under INTERNATIONAL HUMANITARIAN LAW. The 1984 Convention for the Prevention of Torture and Inhuman or Degrading Treatment or Punishment (known as the CONVENTION AGAINST TORTURE) states: "No exceptional circumstances whatsoever, whether a state of war or a threat of war, internal political instability or any other public emergency, may be invoked as a justification of torture." The convention defines torture as "any act by which severe pain or suffering, whether physical or mental, is intentionally inflicted on a person for such purposes as obtaining from him or a third person information or a confession." Torture may be "inflicted by or at the instigation of or acquiescence of a public official or other person acting in an official capacity." The legal definition of torture also includes the punishment of a detainee for an act he or another person committed as well as intimidation based on discrimination.

The Torture Convention is only one of several international agreements that address torture. Legal constraints against the practice can also be found in the INTERNATIONAL COVENANT ON CIVIL AND POLITICAL RIGHTS; the

CONVENTION ON THE RIGHTS OF THE CHILD; and the European, African, and Inter-American Conventions on Human Rights. ARTICLE 3 COMMON TO THE GENEVA CONVENTIONS of 1949 emphasizes that torture is forbidden during internal or international conflicts. It outlaws "violence to life and person, in particular murder of all kinds, mutilation, cruel treatment and torture," and "outrages upon personal dignity, in particular humiliating and degrading treatment" are banned under any circumstances. The prohibition is especially applicable to PRISONERS OF WAR and civilians, but it extends even to common criminals. Torture is also banned by CUSTOMARY LAW—law that is based mainly on precedent and morality rather than on codified rules. Torture is specifically prohibited in armed conflict, whether international or internal. Article 44 of the Hague Regulations of 1907 on customs of war declares that "a belligerent is forbidden to force the inhabitants of territory occupied by it to furnish information about the army of the other belligerent, or about its means of defense."

International law does make some attempt to distinguish between torture and inhumane treatment; the former frequently makes use of force with the intent to inflict pain to extract information from a detainee, while the latter is aimed at robbing a detainee of his dignity. In practice, however, it is difficult to make such a determination, as the abuses by U.S. soldiers at the Iraqi prison of Abu Graibh vividly demonstrate. In that case prisoners were often publicly humiliated; most legal experts reflected public opinion by labeling such abuses as torture even in the absence of overt physical force. Leaving a person naked, for instance, constitutes a form of torture although no force is employed. International law recognizes that in many instances torture is not used to elicit information but rather as a means of revenge to cause suffering. Individuals who engage in torture may also do so because they derive sadistic pleasure from it. Torture can also take the form of sexual assault. Article 27 of the Fourth Geneva Convention states that women must be protected against "rape, enforced prostitution, or any form of indecent assault" in conflict.

Although most nations have laws on their books forbidding torture, the practice is carried on routinely in many parts of the world. Security forces engaged in combating insurgencies or antiterrorism campaigns are particularly likely to resort to torture. To conceal evidence of their activities, police and security forces also torture suspects while holding them incommunicado, denying the detainee all contact with the outside world. Various means of torture can be employed without leaving marks, although the pain can be just as excruciating as the pain from methods that leave bruises and scars. In many countries—especially in Latin America during the "dirty wars" of the 1970s and early 1980s—political and military leaders engaged in widespread torture enact AMNESTY laws while they are still in power in an attempt (not always successful) to evade the legal consequences of their actions.

See also CONVENTION AGAINST TORTURE; GENEVA CONVENTIONS; IRAQ, HUMAN RIGHTS VIOLATIONS IN POST-SADDAM; RAPE AS A TACTIC OF WAR.

Further Reading:
Greenberg, Karen J., and Johsua L. Dratel, eds. *The Torture Papers: The Road to Abu Ghraib*. Cambridge: Cambridge University Press, 2005.

Gutman, Roy, ed. *Crimes of War: What the Public Should Know*. New York: W. W. Norton & Company, 1999.

Jackson, Nyamuya Maogoto. *War Crimes and Realpolitik: International Justice from World War I to the 21st Century*. Boulder, Colo.: Lynne Rienner Publishers, 2004.

Jokie, Aleksander. *War Crimes and Collective Wrongdoing: A Reader*. London: Blackwell Publishers, 2001.

Levinson, Sanford, ed. *Torture: A Collection*. Oxford: Oxford University Press, 2004.

total war

The phrase *total war* has at least three different meanings. In one construction, total war entails the state's mobilization of all resources—political, military, and economic—to defeat an enemy. In a second interpretation, total war refers to the announced intent of a state to bring the conflict against the enemy to any part of the world, using any means at its disposal, which could mean resorting to illegal weapons of mass destruction (BIOLOGICAL WEAPONS, for instance) or engaging in a scorched-earth policy. In a third meaning, total war refers to a state's determination to conduct military operations on any part of an enemy's territory and incapacitate its industrial and agricultural base. World War II would meet the criteria for total war under any of these definitions. (Great Britain used the term to apply to both world wars.)

Total war is distinguished from LIMITED WAR; the latter is waged only to achieve objectives that are more circumscribed—taking back occupied territory, for example, or destroying an enemy's air force in a preemptive action—and is generally fought for only so long as needed to reach the objective. Total war, on the other hand, may go on for years if necessary to entirely destroy the enemy. This was the case with the Allied war against Germany in World War II: The Allied leaders had made the determination to settle for nothing less than unconditional surrender and occupation of all of Germany, ruling out any negotiated settlement.

INTERNATIONAL HUMANITARIAN LAW (IHL) does not necessarily outlaw total war under any of its three definitions, although it does ban specific practices in conducting any war such as the use of illegal weapons. These restrictions have the effect of making it more difficult for a belligerent to carry out a total war for which the goal is the complete destruction of an enemy's military and industrial infrastructure, for example. Similarly, IHL forbids targeting of civilian populations and calls for restraint in attacking military objectives if an attack is likely to cause wanton destruction of civilian property and a loss of civilian life disproportionate to the value of the military installation. In other words, total law does not give a belligerent license to employ whatever method it chooses to bring about an adversary's defeat. Any nation that announced it was prepared to take any measure to achieve a victory would be in grave breach of international law and subject to penalties by the United Nations Security Council that could range from sanctions to military action. Nor can total war be offered as an excuse for staging REPRISALS against civilians or civilian property that are banned by both the GENEVA CONVENTIONS of 1949 and Additional Protocol I of 1977.

See also ADDITIONAL PROTOCOLS TO THE GENEVA CONVENTIONS.

Further Reading:
Gutman, Roy, ed. *Crimes of War: What the Public Should Know.* New York: W. W. Norton & Company, 1999.
Marwick, Arthur, Wendy Simpson, and Clive Emsley, eds. *Total War and Historical Change: Europe, 1914–1955.* London: Open University Press, 2001.

Touvier, Paul (1915–1996) *French Nazi collaborator*

Paul Touvier has the dubious distinction of being the only Frenchman to be convicted of war CRIMES AGAINST HUMANITY. During World War II, while he was a member of a pro-Nazi militia established by the collaborationist regime of Vichy France, he had ordered the execution of seven Jews. Touvier was so loyal to his German superior, the notorious Klaus BARBIE, the Lyon GESTAPO chief, that he became known as "the French Barbie" as well as "the hangman of Lyon." In addition to the executions of the seven Jews, there is evidence to suggest that he was responsible for many other crimes, including the killings of a prominent human rights advocate and his wife in 1944 and the deportation of 57 Spanish refugees who were rounded up in a Gestapo raid.

When the war ended, Touvier dropped out of sight. He was convicted in absentia of treason, collaboration, and helping TORTURE and execute members of the Resistance; he was sentenced to death. Relying on fake identity cards, Touvier survived under cover by passing counterfeit money and even selling bootleg chocolate to candy stores. In 1947 he was arrested while trying to rob a bakery but managed to escape once more. When the statute of limitations for the

crimes with which he was charged expired, Touvier surfaced again. French president Georges Pompidou then granted him what amounted to a pardon, which allowed Touvier to return to Lyon and recover his property. The restoration of Touvier's legal status aroused a nationwide protest that only intensified when it was learned that the property he claimed had been seized from him had actually belonged to deported Jews. The protests led to an indictment in 1973 on charges of crimes against humanity, which are not liable to the statute of limitations. Touvier thereupon went into hiding again.

Aided by rightist Catholics, Touvier, remained elusive until he was captured on May 24, 1989, in a Catholic monastery in Nice that was operated by adherents of the excommunicated Marcel Lefebvre, a rabid conservative cleric. At the time of his arrest, Touvier declared, "I regret nothing." He later claimed at his trial that the Germans had demanded the lives of 100 Jews in retaliation for the assassination of the Vichy minister of information, but by bargaining with the Gestapo, Touvier had succeeded in sparing all but the seven he was charged with executing. The argument failed to persuade the jury. "I have never forgotten the victims . . ." he said when he was sentenced. "I think of them every day, every evening." He died in prison at age 81.

Further Reading:
Wexler, Leila Sadat. *The Trial of Vichy Collaborator Paul Touvier for Crimes against Humanity in France.* St. Louis: Washington University School of Law, 1994.

trafficking in persons

Trafficking in persons is a transnational criminal enterprise that is estimated to involve anywhere from 700,000 to 4 million people, primarily women and children. Many of the trafficked persons, whom criminal networks lure from their homes with the prospect of well-paying jobs, find themselves coerced into prostitution, domestic servitude, or farm or factory labor. Trafficking in persons is a crime under international law and the laws of most nations. It is characterized by the movement of people across or within borders; the use of threats, intimidation, or deception; and compelling victims into a situation against their will for the purposes of exploiting them. Traffickers ensure compliance with their demands even after the victim reaches his or her destination through a variety of means: debt-bondage, passport confiscation, physical and psychological abuse, rape, and TORTURE. The threat of arrest and deportation constantly hangs over the victim, who may also fear retaliation against his or her family. Trafficking of persons should not be confused with the smuggling of illegal migrants who, while often subject to exploitation, nonetheless undertake their journeys voluntarily.

In many respects, trafficking of persons is considered as a modern form of SLAVERY, and indeed it may result in putting its victims in situations that are indistinguishable from slavery. Trafficking in persons is often carried out by criminal networks and abetted by a climate of corruption. The practice also feeds into other types of criminal activity ranging from document fraud and bribery to child prostitution and indentured servitude. According to statistics compiled by the Congressional Research Service in 2000, the majority of victims originate in Asia: more than 225,000 from Southeast Asia and more than 150,000 from South Asia every year. About 100,000 trafficked persons come from states of the former Soviet Union, which provides the largest source of prostitution, and more than 75,000 come from Eastern Europe. An estimated 100,000 people are trafficked from Latin America and the Caribbean, and over 50,000 are from Africa. The most common destinations for trafficked persons are large cities, tourist resorts, and military bases.

Several misconceptions surround trafficking of persons. For one, traffickers include women as well as men. For another, not all women are trafficked for prostitution (many become domestic servants), and not all victims of trafficking are uneducated or from rural areas. On the contrary, many have had a secondary or postsecondary school education; many trafficked women from Russia and Eastern Europe hold college degrees and have lived in major cities. In Hong Kong a large number of Filipinas in domestic servitude were once teachers and nurses.

Trafficking of persons is increasingly recognized as an international problem requiring urgent action. In November 2000 the United Nations General Assembly adopted the Protocol to Prevent, Suppress and Punish Trafficking in Persons, Especially Women and Children, Supplementing the United Nations Convention Against Transnational Organized Crime; within a month the protocol was signed by 101 countries. Intended to "prevent and combat" trafficking in persons, the TRAFFICKING PROTOCOL, as it is called, covers specific criminal offenses and sets out measures that state parties are required to take to facilitate cooperation to stop the practice. It also sets out actions to protect and assist victims. The protocol is only the most recent of several other international human rights treaties to address trafficking, which include the United Nations Supplementary Convention on the Abolition of Slavery, the Slave Trade, and Institutions and Practices Similar to Slavery. In addition, the UN Convention on the Elimination of All Forms of Discrimination against Women calls for all parties to take measures "to suppress all forms of traffic in women and exploitation of prostitution of women." Many nations have become more aggressive about tackling the problem of trafficking as well. The U.S. Department of Justice prosecuted 76 traffickers in 2001 and 2002, three times

as many as in the previous two years and by 2003 had opened another 125 trafficking investigations, nearly twice as many as in January 2001. In 2003 the United States Agency for International Development (USAID) provided over $15 million for specific antitrafficking activities in 36 countries, an increase of more than 50 percent over USAID antitrafficking funding for 2002.

See also CHILDREN'S RIGHTS; WOMEN'S RIGHTS, VIOLATIONS OF.

Further Reading:

Farley, Melissa, ed. *Prostitution, Trafficking, and Traumatic Stress.* Binghamton, N.Y.: Haworth Maltreatment & Trauma Press, 2004.

Powell, Colin, and Nancy Raphel, eds. *Trafficking in Persons Report, 2002.* Chicago: Diane Pub. Co., 2003.

Rijken, Conny. *Trafficking in Persons: Prosecution from a European Perspective.* Cambridge: Cambridge University Press, 2003.

Thomas, Dorothy Q., and Thomas Sidney Jones, eds. *A Modern Form of Slavery: Trafficking of Burmese Women and Girls into Brothels in Thailand.* New York: Human Rights Watch, 1994.

Trafficking Protocol

The United Nations' Trafficking Protocol, opened for signature in December 2000, is an international agreement that addresses all forms of TRAFFICKING IN PERSONS, FORCED LABOR, SLAVERY, and servitude. Its full title is Protocol to Prevent, Suppress and Punish Trafficking in Persons, Especially Women and Children, Supplementing the United Nations Convention against Transnational Organized Crime. *Trafficking* is taken to mean "recruitment, transportation, transfer, harboring or receipt of persons" by improper means (such as force, abduction, fraud, or coercion) for an improper purpose, which would include forced or coerced labor, servitude, SLAVERY, or sexual exploitation.

One of three related agreements developed by the United Nations Crime Commission, the Trafficking Protocol contains the first definition of trafficking in international human rights law. The protocol is intended to "prevent and combat" trafficking in persons and calls for international cooperation against such trafficking. It provides for criminal offenses and control and cooperation measures against traffickers and also sets forth some measures to protect and assist the victims. The protocol covers a range of cases that must meet two criteria: that an element of duress is involved and that it must be international in nature. This means that a person must be taken across a national border against his or her will or that a transnational group—usually a criminal organization—is exploiting the person within a country's borders.

The protocol deliberately fails to clarify the meaning of such terms as *exploitation of the prostitution of others* and *sexual exploitation* so that even governments that legally tolerate prostitution would feel free to sign it. The two other related accords—the Convention Against Transnational Organized Crime and the Smuggling Protocol—are primarily meant as law-enforcement instruments designed to ensure cross-border cooperation and encourage all signatories—over 120 states—to put laws on their books that cover the crimes cited in the protocol if they have not already done so. Countries that have signed the protocol have taken different positions on its application, with some arguing that its major focus should be directed to women and children since they are most likely to be exploited and trafficked. Others contend that it should not discriminate among classes of victims since the protocol only refers to all "persons," even if it is taken to generally apply to women and children.

Another difficulty arises in determining the nature of force and coercion. Children cannot freely consent to participate in sexual activity or perform labor. But for adults the situation is much less clear: It is not always possible to distinguish between consensual acts and acts that are performed because of deception, fraud, abduction, force, or threat. It is also difficult to assess on the basis of the protocol what degree of international or organized crime involvement is required to invoke its provisions. It is thought that if there is only a marginal involvement, then the violation can be more efficiently dealt with by local or national law-enforcement authorities without recourse to the protocol. In cases where entirely domestic crimes are committed by a transnational crime group, however, it is more difficult to determine whether the protocol should or should not apply.

Further Reading:
Farley, Melissa, ed. *Prostitution, Trafficking, and Traumatic Stress.* Binghamton, N.Y.: Haworth Maltreatment and Trauma Press, 2004.
Powell, Colin, and Nancy Raphel, eds. *Trafficking in Persons Report, 2002.* Chicago: Diane Pub. Co., 2003.
Rijken, Conny. *Trafficking in Persons: Prosecution from a European Perspective.* Cambridge: Cambridge University Press, 2003.
Thomas, Dorothy Q., and Thomas Sidney Jones, eds. *A Modern Form of Slavery: Trafficking of Burmese Women and Girls into Brothels in Thailand.* New York: Human Rights Watch, 1994.

transfer of civilians

INTERNATIONAL HUMANITARIAN LAW (IHL) prohibits the forcible transfer of civilians by an OCCUPYING POWER under all but the most exigent circumstances. An occupier can relocate civilians if necessary for "imperative military reasons" under Article 17 of the 1977 Additional Protocol II to the GENEVA CONVENTIONS, which states: "Should such displacements have to be carried out, all possible measures shall be taken in order that the civilian population may be received under satisfactory conditions of shelter, hygiene, safety and nutrition." Nonetheless, the evacuation of the civilian population must be temporary, and those who have been relocated must be returned to their homes as soon as conditions permit. Individuals who are moved in this way are known as INTERNALLY DISPLACED PERSONS, or IDPs.

Following World War II, the forcible removal of civilians became an issue of particular importance for policy makers because of the Nazi practice of deporting civilians from occupied countries—whether to death camps or for work as forced laborers in German industry and agriculture—while settling Germans in the territory they had been uprooted from. The NUREMBERG TRIALS after the war indicted several Nazi officials for carrying out the forcible transfer of civilians, making it a crime against humanity. The final judgments, however, mentioned only the DEPORTATIONS and not the resettlement. The law regarding deportations of civilians has not, however, kept up with recent developments. For instance, it is difficult to find laws in IHL that cover a situation in which a state transfers its own nationals from refugee or IDP centers in parts of their territory that are relatively free from violence and puts them in harm's way by moving them closer to the front lines.

See also ADDITIONAL PROTOCOLS TO THE GENEVA CONVENTIONS.

Further Reading:
Feller, Erika, Volker Turk, and Frances Nicholson, eds. *Refugee Protection in International Law: UNHCR's Global Consultations on International Protection.* Cambridge: Cambridge University Press, 2003.
Gutman, Roy, ed. *Crimes of War: What the Public Should Know.* New York: W. W. Norton & Company, 1999.
Hyndman, Jennifer. *Managing Displacement: Refugees and the Politics of Humanitarianism.* Minneapolis: University of Minnesota Press, 2000.
Ingleby, David, ed. *Forced Migration and Mental Health: Rethinking the Care of Refugees and Displaced Persons.* New York: Plenum US, 2004.
Lischer, Sarah Kenyon. *Dangerous Sanctuaries: Refugee Camps, Civil War, and the Dilemmas of Humanitarian Aid.* Cornell Studies in Security Affairs. Ithaca, N.Y.: Cornell University Press, 2005.

Trujillo, Rafael Molino (1891–1961) *Dominican despot*
Rafael Trujillo controlled the Dominican Republic for three decades (1930–61) either as its president or as its military

strongman. His long rule came to an end only by means of assassination. Trujillo was born into a poor, mixed-race family on October 24, 1891. His future course was set at the age of 18 when he joined the Dominican National Guard, a force established by the U.S. Marines, which had occupied the island in 1916 to protect American economic and political interests in the country. (The Dominican Republic shares the island of Hispaniola with Haiti.) Trujillo rose so rapidly in the ranks of the National Guard that when the marines pulled out in 1924, they left him in charge. He used his power base in the National Guard to run for president in 1930, in which he claimed—fraudulently—to have received 95 percent of the vote. He then set about suppressing all dissent, establishing a secret police force called SIM (Military Intelligence Service), and banishing political opponents. SIM was given a free hand to murder and TORTURE. In one particularly gruesome incident, Trujillo ordered the massacre of thousands of black Haitian migrant workers.

An admirer of the Spanish dictator Francisco Franco, Trujillo encouraged a cult of personality, renaming the capital Santo Domingo Ciudad Trujillo, which he rebuilt extensively after it was devastated by a hurricane. Neon signs greeted visitors to the city with the proclamation "God and Trujillo." He renamed the highest mountain of the country Pico Trujillo (Trujillo Peak). Even gestures that appeared selfless—such as permitting Jewish refugees from Nazi Germany to settle in the Dominican Republic when they were being barred from other nations—were seen as public relations stunts. In the meantime he went about enriching himself and his family, taking over plantations and businesses. By the late 1950s it was estimated that Trujillo's family controlled nearly all the wealth in the country. At the same time he made sure to ingratiate himself with Washington, welcoming American business investment and, after the end of World War II, embracing a staunch anticommunist policy.

From 1949 on, opponents of the Trujillo regime made several attempts to oust him. On June 14, 1949, exiled Dominicans launched an abortive strike—known as the Luperion invasion—using 14 sea planes. The insurgency was crushed, and rebels who survived were rounded up, tortured, and executed at a military base. (Nonetheless, the invasion inspired the anti-Trujillo June 14th Movement.) Various anti-Trujillo conspiracies subsequently sprang up—some included Trujillo's relatives—but SIM agents usually succeeded in penetrating them before they had any chance of succeeding. Trujillo saw opposition everywhere and even took on the Catholic Church. SIM agents arrested five priests, accusing them of conspiracy and bomb making. The Catholic Church sent a pastoral letter to the dictator calling on him to halt the "excesses, dry the tears, heal the wounds."

Trujillo had no intention of stopping the excesses or healing any wounds, but in two cases, the secret police overplayed their hand. In the first they arrested two activists—Maria Teresa and Minerva Mirabel—and their husbands while they were driving home, then beat them and strangled them to death in a sugarcane patch. The brutal slayings of the Mirabel sisters provoked an international outcry, no doubt helped by the fact that they were both attractive and photogenic. In the second case, a critic of the regime, Jesus de Galindez, disappeared in New York and was never seen again. The disappearance occurred only days before the publication of his book *The Age of Trujillo*, which exposed the inner workings of the regime based on his personal experience. There was strong suspicion that Trujillo's agents had kidnapped Galindez, spiriting him away to the island before killing him.

When Trujillo received word that Venezuelan president Romulo Betancourt had lent support to Dominican rebels in exile, he tried to have Betancourt assassinated as well. The attempt failed, but it brought renewed attention to Trujillo's clumsy efforts to intervene in the affairs of other countries. In 1960 the ORGANIZATION OF AMERICAN STATES (OAS) imposed harsh sanctions against the country and severed diplomatic ties. By this time Washington had wearied of the Dominican dictator, and the CIA began to slip arms to rebels plotting Trujillo's assassination. On May 30, 1961, they succeeded: Trujillo was ambushed and killed while he was riding on a deserted highway. But his death did not bring about the immediate end of his regime. The next day his son, Ramfi Trujillo, took power, and within a month almost all of the assassins were apprehended. Some were tortured and committed suicide; others were dragged out of prison and taken to the younger Trujillo's hacienda, where they were tied to trees, shot, cut up, and fed to sharks at a nearby beach. By then, though, anti-Trujillo riots had broken out in the capital, forcing Ramfi Trujillo to flee the country under U.S. military protection. (Ramfi lived out his exile as an international socialite, dying in 1969 from injuries sustained in a car accident.) To keep the situation from descending into chaos, the U.S. Atlantic fleet put into Santo Domingo's harbor, reasserting Washington's interests on the island just as it had several decades before. Even in death, though, the Dominican Republic was a dangerous place for Rafael Trujillo. He was buried, not in Dominican soil, but in Père Lachaise Cemetery in Paris.

See also DOMINICAN REPUBLIC, HUMAN RIGHTS VIOLATIONS IN.

Further Reading:

Diederich, Bernard. *Trujillo: The Death of the Dictator.* Princeton, N.J.: Markus Wiener Pub., 1999.
Roorda, Eric Paul. *The Dictator Next Door: The Good Neighbor Policy and the Trujillo Regime in the Dominican Republic, 1930–1945.* Durham, N.C.: Duke University Press, 1998.

Truth and Reconciliation Commission

The Truth and Reconciliation Commission was established in South Africa to investigate human rights abuses that occurred under the defunct white supremacist APARTHEID regime between 1960 and 1994. The commission oversees three committees dealing with human rights violations, reparations, and AMNESTY. The commission was created by the 1995 Promotion of National Unity and Reconciliation Act with a mandate to investigate and provide "as complete a picture as possible of the nature, causes and extent of gross violations of human rights." The act allows the commission to provide amnesty "to those who make full disclosure of all the relevant facts relating to acts associated with a political objective committed in the course of the conflicts of the past." Applications for amnesty have come from police and rightist extremists active in the apartheid regime as well as from black militants who fought against it.

The apartheid government of South Africa, which was in power for 50 years, was based on a strict policy of racial separation. The major source of resistance came from the African National Congress (ANC), which was outlawed under apartheid; its leaders were either arrested or forced to go underground. Nonetheless, the regime was compelled to secure its power by increasingly brutal methods, including TORTURE and EXTRAJUDICIAL KILLINGS. The ANC and other black activists were also implicated in human rights abuses and terrorism, though to a lesser degree.

In the early 1990s the white leadership acknowledged that majority rule could not be put off indefinitely. ANC leader Nelson Mandela was released from prison after 27 years, and in 1994 he became president in the country's first free election. A number of black leaders called for a tribunal to try officials of the apartheid regime for their crimes, guided by the precedent of the International Military Tribunal set up by the Allies to try Nazi officials for war crimes (the NUREMBERG TRIALS). Mandela's government took the position, though, that such a tribunal would only aggravate existing tensions and deepen the racial divide. The government felt that the country's bitter wounds would have a better chance of healing if the priority was given to exposing the truth about abuses rather than punishing the perpetrators. The result was the Truth and Reconciliation Commission, which opened its first sessions in April 1996. The commission was charged with identifying victims of gross human rights violations and ensuring that they received appropriate support and compensation. The commission's longtime chair was Archbishop Desmond TUTU. In the two years of the commission's existence, it received over 7,000 applications for amnesty; of these, 4,500 were rejected, and only about 125 have been granted. Some 21,000 victims of apartheid were willing to come forward to testify.

The Truth and Reconciliation Commission has not been without its critics: Many South Africans, including some ANC members, contended that the commission was too lenient in granting amnesty to white officials responsible for killing and torturing blacks. However, the commission has won wide support from human rights groups, and it has become a model for similar commissions in other countries that have recently thrown off tyrannical regimes.

See also GOLDSTONE, RICHARD J.

Further Reading:
Edelstein, Jillian. *Truth and Lies: Stories from the Truth and Reconciliation Commission in South Africa.* New York: New Press, 2002.
James, Wilmot Godfrey, and Linda van de Vijver, eds. *After the TRC: Reflections on Truth and Reconciliation in South Africa.* Athens: Ohio University Press, 2001.
Wilson, Richard A. *The Politics of Truth and Reconciliation in South Africa: Legitimizing the Post-Apartheid State.* Cambridge Studies in Law and Society. Cambridge: Cambridge University Press, 2001.

Tudjman, Franjo (1922–1999) *president of Croatia*

Franjo Tudjman, the autocratic president of Croatia during the war in Bosnia, liked to be known as "father of his country," but he was also a racist and anti-Semite with fascist inclinations. Under his rule, Croatian forces forced 400,000 Serbs out of Croatia during the Bosnian War in what amounted to ethnic cleansing.

Tudjman was born in the northern Croatian region of Zagorje on May 14, 1922. While attending secondary school in the Croatian capital of Zagreb from 1934 to 1941, he became an ardent nationalist and joined an antifascist movement, actions that led to his imprisonment. After the war he held top positions in the Ministry of National Defense and the Yugoslav People's Army (where he was the youngest major general in its history). In 1961 Tudjman left the military to establish the Institute for the History of the Labor Movement in Croatia. After earning a graduate degree in political science, he spent the next several years turning out several books on history, mythologizing the medieval origins of Croatia while downplaying the atrocities of the fascist organization USTACHE, which had been allied with the Nazis during World War II. In one book Tudjman wrote that 30,000 Serbs, Jews, Rom (Gypsies), and others had been killed in a Ustache camp when the true number was closer to 800,000. He characterized Ustache excesses as "positive achievements" that were "the expression of the historical efforts of the Croatian people." His distortion resulted in a brief prison sentence. No one could accuse him of a lack of industry, though: He found time to work as a senior lecturer on "Socialist Revolution and Contemporary National History of Croatia" at the Faculty of Political Sciences in Zagreb, serve as a representative in the Croatian Parliament, and edit a magazine as well as two encyclopedias.

In 1971 Tudjman was imprisoned for nine months for participating in a nationalist movement known as Croatian Spring, which advocated Croatian independence from Yugoslavia, of which it was then a part. By this time he had become a leading figure in the nationalist movement. In February 1981 the Communist government of Yugoslavia imprisoned him for giving interviews to Swedish, German, and French radio and television outlets advocating Croatian independence; he was released in May 1984 for health reasons. Three years later, after obtaining a passport for the first time in 17 years, he traveled throughout the United States and Canada, calling for Croatian independence. His vision of a free Croatia, however, also entailed the expulsion of Serb and Muslim minorities. Nor was Tudjman content to limit the state to its existing borders within the Yugoslav federation; Croatian territory, he believed, should be extended into part of Bosnia and Herzegovina (with Bosnian Serbs getting the rest), in effect depriving the Muslim majority there of any homeland at all. In his view, Catholic Croatia was the bulwark defending the West from the Orthodox Christian Serbs and Muslim Balkans.

In 1989 Tudjman established a political party called the Croatian Democratic Union (HDZ) and became its president. In 1991, after a referendum, Croatia declared itself independent in defiance of Belgrade. The Serbs reacted with predictable fury when they suddenly found themselves a beleaguered minority in Croatia and Bosnia and Herzegovina, which also broke away from the former Yugoslavian federation. Tudjman's party adopted some of the symbols of the Ustache, basing the design of its new flag on that of the Ustache flag and renaming streets and squares after Croatian nationalist "heroes."

The Bosnian War developed into a three-sided conflict among Croats, Serbs, and Muslims with so many shifting alliances that at one point Croats and Serbs were fighting together against Bosnian Muslims in one part of Bosnia, while in another Croats and Bosnians were lined up against Serb forces. In 1992 Croat forces initially targeted Muslims, massacring civilians in the Mostar region. Tudjman extended Croatian influence in Bosnia by sponsoring and subsidizing the Croatian Defense Council (the HVO militia), which was responsible for killing Muslims and torching Serb churches. Two years later, however, the Croatian and Muslim forces formed an alliance against Serbs with the backing of the United States and Western European powers.

"Tudjman almost certainly did not care that he was a monster because, unlike Milošević, he was our monster," commented the author Misha Glenny, describing Tudjman's relationship with the Western powers. After all, for the West, the principal antagonist was the Serb dictator, Slobodan MILOŠEVIĆ, who had instigated the war. In 1995 the Croatians launched two offensives—dubbed "Lightning" and "Storm"—against the predominantly Serbian-inhabited regions of West Slavonia and Krajina, bombarding Knjin, the Serbian "capital" of Krajina. Approximately a quarter of a million Serbs were driven from their homes or murdered. A UN report described the carnage: "New evidence for the atrocities continues to emerge, on average, six corpses a day. . . . [T]he corpses, some fresh, others decayed, are predominantly old men. Many were shot in the back of the head or had their throats cut, others were mutilated. . . . The crimes were committed by the Croatian army, the Croatian police and Croatian civilians. No efforts were observed of them being ordered to stop, and everything points to a policy of scorched earth."

Before the war, Croatia's population had been about 12 percent Serb. After Tudjman's campaign, only a scattering of Serbs remained. With the military support of NATO, Croatian forces occupied large sections of northwest Bosnia as well, pushing out hundreds of thousands of Serbs who lived in that region. In 1994 the United States intervened to impose a cease-fire. Tudjman was pressured into participating in the American-sponsored Dayton, Ohio, talks that led to the DAYTON ACCORDS, ending the Bosnian War.

Throughout Tudjman's 10-year regime, Croatia suffered from economic devastation and corruption. Unemployment reached 20 percent. Members of Tudjman's family appropriated formerly state-owned property for themselves. Dissent was suppressed, and journalists who dared to openly challenge Tudjman were harassed. There were no fewer than nine different security agencies to ensure that people towed the line, including one directly under the control of Tudjman's son, Miroslav. As long as Tudjman remained in power, the European Union (EU) refused to consider Croatia for candidate status for EU membership. The Western powers became increasingly disillusioned with Tudjman, viewing with alarm his calls for the "independence" of a Croatian enclave in Bosnia and Herzegovina, which would threaten hard-won political stability throughout the region. Tudjman died after a long illness on December 11, 1999, opening the way for the creation of a truly democratic state.

See also BOSNIA AND HERZEGOVINA, HUMAN RIGHTS VIOLATIONS IN; CROATIA, HUMAN RIGHTS VIOLATIONS IN; YUGOSLAVIA, WAR CRIMES IN.

Further Reading:

Bassiouni, M. Cherif. *Sexual Violence: An Invisible Weapon of War in the Former Yugoslavia*. Chicago: International Human Rights Law Institute, DePaul University, 1996.
Clark, Wesley K. *Waging Modern War: Bosnia, Kosovo, and the Future of Combat*. New York: Public Affairs.

Glenny, Misha. *The Fall of Yugoslavia: The Third Balkan War.* New York: Penguin Books, 1996.

Harris, Nathaniel. *The War in Former Yugoslavia.* London: Hodder & Stoughton, 1997.

Kim, Julie. *War in the Former Yugoslavia: Chronology of Events August 16, 1992–May 30, 1993.* CRS Report for Congress. Washington, D.C.: Foreign Affairs and National Defense Division, Congressional Research Service, the Library of Congress, 1993.

Mertus, Julie. *Former Yugoslavia: War Crimes Trials in the Former Yugoslavia.* Helsinki: Human Rights Watch/Helsinki, 1995.

Rossanet, Bertrand de. *War and Peace in the Former Yugoslavia.* Boston: Martinus Nijhoff, 1997.

Tunisia, human rights violations in

Once considered among the freest and most open countries in the Middle East, Tunisia has in recent years become transformed into a quasi-police state, according to many human rights advocates. The North African nation won independence from France in 1956 and until 1987 enjoyed the relatively enlightened rule of Habib Bourguiba, an adherent of secularism who introduced compulsory education, encouraged the emancipation of women, and abolished polygamy. Nonetheless, he eventually became a dictator whose party dominated all political life in the country.

Seen as increasingly senile and unfit to rule, Bourguiba was ousted in a coup in 1987 by Zine El Abidine Ben Ali, who has retained the leadership of Tunisia ever since. Under Ben Ali's rule, practically all dissent has been crushed. The first targets were Islamic fundamentalists in the early 1990s, but the security forces soon moved on to human rights advocates, opposition leaders, and journalists who dared to criticize the regime. The media have been turned into a tool of government propaganda, and little dissent is allowed to be aired, even though the constitution calls for freedom of the press. Journalists are kept under surveillance and are at risk of harassment, imprisonment, or exile. Editions of foreign papers are frequently seized if they carry stories critical of the government. Estimates of the number of political prisoners incarcerated in Tunisian jails range from 500 to 1,000. Most are Islamists who are labeled as terrorists without any evidence to support the accusation. Their trials—usually for charges relating to nonviolent political activities—are deplored by human rights organizations as unjust. "In Tunisia opponents or perceived opponents of the government are subjected to abuse within a justice system resembling one from a Kafka novel," an AMNESTY INTERNATIONAL representative declared. "Confessions are coerced out of detainees, at trial defendants' files are confiscated from lawyers or tampered with, and political prisoners are subjected to a harsh prison regime, including solitary confinement."

The Tunisian judiciary has little independence and is quick to convict political dissidents on the basis of dubious evidence and ignore allegations of torture by police. According to credible reports, some of the tortured prisoners are subjected to include "sleep deprivation for 8 consecutive days and nights; ice cold shower with the person bound hand and foot; needles stuck into the nape of the neck; beatings; suspension of the person and blows carried out with a stick to the soles of the feet; suspension from the ceiling, completely naked, hands tied in front or behind the back and the application of electric shocks to the sensitive parts of the body, including genital organs, often causing loss of consciousness, which is extremely dangerous in this suspended position; tightening of a cord placed around the testicles whilst the person is suspended, naked and tied-up." Another torture method is to plunge the prisoner "naked and tied up, into a bath of foul water and detergent, holding the head under the water until near suffocation, then quickly pulling the head out of water before plunging it straight back, and so on again. . . ." One especially gruesome type of torture is called "roasting," which entails "tying the person in an outstretched position by the hands and feet to an axle fastened between two tables, and then turning the person like a chicken on a spit in such a way that the head hits the floor with every turn, all the while drenching the person in ice cold water and slapping the back of the neck constantly, as if one were playing an instrument called the 'Darbouka,' applying high intensity electric shocks at rapid intervals."

In spite of the government's human rights violations, the United States has been reluctant to criticize the Ben Ali regime. In fact, Washington has praised the Tunisian president for his cooperation in combating terrorism. The United States has shown no indication of curtailing its modest military aid program to Tunisia, and the two countries have conducted joint military exercises. One member of a visiting congressional delegation called Ben Ali a statesman who has "done a tremendous job in Tunisia and who is well respected back home as well as here in the Arab world." On a December 2003 stopover in Tunis, the capital, Secretary of State Colin Powell acknowledged that the government might do more to bring about "more political pluralism and openness" but nonetheless expressed his support for Ben Ali's leadership.

Newspapers regularly refer to Ben Ali as the "Architect for Change," although any change that might bring about a relaxation of the president's grip on power appears remote. In a referendum that allowed him the right to stand for reelection to a fourth term in October 2004, he claimed to have received 99 percent of the vote. The same referendum also conferred on him immunity from prosecution for life.

Further Reading:
Charrad, M. *States and Women's Rights: The Making of Postcolonial Tunisia, Algeria, and Morocco.* Berkeley: University of California Press, 2001.

King, Stephen J. *Liberalization against Democracy: The Local Politics of Economic Reform in Tunisia* Bloomington: Indiana University Press, 2003.

McNamara, Ronald J. *Democracy and Human Rights in the Mediterranean Partner States of the Osce: Algeria, Egypt, Israel, Jordan, Morocco and Tunisia: Briefing of the Committee on Security and Cooperation in Europe.* Chicago: Diane Pub. Co., 2004.

Perkins, Kenneth. *A History of Modern Tunisia.* Cambridge: Cambridge University Press, 2004.

Tupamaros   *See* URUGUAY, HUMAN RIGHTS VIOLATIONS IN.

Turkey, human rights violations in

In its quest for membership in the European Union (EU), Turkey has been obliged to undertake several major political reforms and put a troubling past behind it. Sufficient progress had been made by 2004 for the EU to agree to open talks that might eventually lead to Turkey's ascension. The government, under the moderate Muslim Justice and Development Party (AKP), has resolved to make further changes to bolster its candidacy. Nonetheless, the extent of the reforms it has already instituted cannot be underestimated. In the early 1990s, for instance, state forces were still committing EXTRAJUDICIAL KILLINGS and DISAPPEARANCES, or political killings carried out by groups with ties to the military, on almost a daily basis. Deaths in police custody occurred on an average of one a week. Such abuses have been stopped for the most part.

According to human rights groups, two issues still require urgent action: failure to sufficiently curb TORTURE and mistreatment by police and the resolution of an insurgency by Turkish Kurds that has left hundreds of thousands of people internally displaced. According to HUMAN RIGHTS WATCH, torture is still practiced, although changes in the law have reduced its frequency. The system of detention and interrogation, the group says, "encouraged torture and protected the perpetrators." Over the last 20 years, more than 400 Turkish citizens died in custody, apparently as a result of torture, with 45 deaths in 1994 alone. However, there were no reports of deaths by torture in 2004. Legal reforms enacted since Turkey initiated its bid for EU candidacy now guarantee detainees the right to legal counsel, but there are reports that prisoners are still denied access to lawyers and suffer from beatings and intimidation in prison. Even as recently as 2004, Human Rights Watch reported that hundreds of Turkish citizens had complained of torture or ill-treatment to prosecutors, the official government human rights body, and independent human rights associations. Much of the abuse appears to stem from a lack of supervision at local police stations. A culture of impunity still persists, and there is no regular monitoring system in place to ensure that the rights of detainees are being upheld. The EU Commission summed up the situation in a report in 2004: "Although torture is no longer systematic, numerous cases of ill-treatment including torture still continue to occur and further efforts will be required to eradicate such practice."

A long-running bloody conflict with Kurdish insurgents fighting for independence has posed a challenge to a succession of Turkish civilian and military governments. The separatist movement—led by a guerrilla group known as the Kurdish Workers Party (PKK)—came into existence in the early 1990s, largely in reaction to the government's suppression of the rights of the country's 12 million Kurds, including banning of the use of the Kurdish language in national media or in Kurdish schools. In a decade of war, which was mostly concentrated in the southeast of the country near the Iraqi border, over 380,000 Kurdish villagers were displaced. Turkish soldiers and security forces uprooted the villagers, destroying their homes, crops, and livestock. These operations also involved extrajudicial killings and disappearances. The military has deployed so many troops in the region that the rebellion has largely been brought to an end. But the PKK has been reported to be still operating out of bases in northern Iraq, beyond the control of U.S. occupation forces there.

Ankara has cautiously begun to take some steps to improve relations with the Kurds. In 2003, for instance, state-run Turkish television for the first time aired a broadcast in Kurmandji, the most widely spoken Kurdish dialect. In addition, an appeals court ordered the release of four Kurdish dissidents who had spent nearly a decade in prison on charges of belonging to the PKK. The government also claims to have permitted the return of about a quarter of the displaced Kurds to their homes, though this report could not be independently substantiated. According to the BBC, Kurds are in fact being allowed to resettle near their old homes, but only if they promise to join a state-run village guard system. In spite of these gestures, Turkish and Kurdish intellectuals and lawyers continue to voice misgivings about the government's treatment of the Kurdish issue and charge that Ankara is trying to stifle dissent, citing the arrest of eight Kurdish MPs who were sentenced to 15 years on charges of promoting Kurdish separatism. In one case, prosecutors threatened to bring charges of separatism against Yasar Kemal, arguably the country's most important author, for writing an article accusing Turkey of oppressing its Kurdish population.

Turkey has taken significant strides in addressing human rights abuses, in large part because of pressure from the European Union, which Turkey is eager to join. However, the government and judiciary have shown themselves willing to put human rights concerns aside when it comes to any mention of the country's role in driving out and killing Armenians during World War I. Twice a conference on the Armenian genocide was canceled under pressure from Turkish authorities. Justice Minister Cemil Cicek condemned the meeting as "treason" and a "stab in the back of the Turkish nation." However, when a court ordered the conference canceled a second time in September 2005 (it had done so in May), some members of the government reacted with dismay. "There's no one better at hurting themselves than us," Foreign Minister Abdullah Gul said, and Prime Minister Recep Tayyip Erdogan declared that the court decision was not worthy of a democratic country. Nonetheless, prosecutors continue to single out prominent individuals for speaking out about the events of a century earlier. The country's best-known writer, Orhan Pamuk, was charged in 2005 for remarks he made to a Swiss newspaper in which he said that "one million Armenians were killed in these lands and nobody but me dares to talk about it." He, too, was charged with committing "treason," and at least in one instance, a local official ordered his works seized and destroyed.

See also KURDISTAN (IRAQ), SUPPRESSION OF.

Further Reading:

Amnesty International. *Turkey: No Security without Human Rights.* London: Amnesty International, 1996.

Dalacoura, Katerina. *Engagement or Coercion?: Weighing Western Human Rights Policies towards Turkey, Iran, and Egypt.* London: Royal Institute of International Affairs, 2004.

Kinzer, Stephen. *Crescent and Star: Turkey between Two Worlds.* New York: Farrar, Straus & Giroux, 2002.

Turkmenistan, human rights violations in

An independent central Asian republic, Turkmenistan was formerly a part of the Soviet Union until its breakup in 1991. Since 1999 the country has been dominated by President Saparmurat Niyazov, who gained power in flawed elections and has fostered a cult of personality. His image is so ubiquitous that he appears on the labels of vodka bottles and pops up in the top right corner on national television. The capital of Ashkhabad is dominated by a rotating 36-foot-tall, gold-leaf statue of the president atop a 250-foot base. He has even renamed months of the year after himself, his mother, and his 2005 "inspirational" work *The Book*

of Spirit. Niyazov seems to have used his office as a platform from which to promote his literary ambitions, giving readings of his poetry collections on national TV, even interrupting cabinet meetings to recite his poems.

Turkmenistan is a one-party state in which Nyazov's party—the Democratic Party of Turkmenistan (DPT)—enjoys absolute monopoly in the Majlis, or parliament. All other political activity is banned, and political opposition is stifled. The only individuals allowed to run for office are chosen by Niyazov. The president also chooses judges for five-year terms without troubling with legislative review. He regularly dismisses cabinet members and other government officials on charges of corruption, has them tried in secret trials, and frequently imprisons or sentences them to internal exile. These actions, however, have little effect in reducing corruption, which is rampant. The economy is strictly regulated by the government, which limits access to opportunity and access to industry and services. The agricultural sector is also dominated by a state command-and-control system based on the old Soviet model. Citizens must carry internal passports, which indicate their place of residence and movements in and out of the country. There is no freedom of assembly. Freedom of the press exists only on paper but is prohibited in practice. All media are in the hands of the government. To prevent citizens from learning what is going on in the outside world, the government also restricts access to satellite television and foreign newspapers and magazines.

Freedom of religion, too, is guaranteed by the constitution, but that freedom is mainly enjoyed by members of the Sunni Islamic majority (89 percent of the population) and the Russian Orthodox Church. The government closely monitors any expression of religious faith, and even a religion that can claim only five adherents must register. However, in addition to the Sunnis and Russian Orthodox Church, only four minority faiths have registered successfully. Members of other religious congregations are prohibited from gathering publicly, proselytizing, or disseminating religious materials.

In November 2002 the president's motorcade came under armed attack. The abortive assassination attempt provided Niazov with the pretext to launch a campaign against dissidents. According to the U.S. State Department, security forces committed numerous human rights abuses in carrying out their sweep of dissidents, including TORTURE and the punishment of suspects' families. Although the government denied charges of abuse, it refused to allow independent observers to attend the trials of the accused and denied access to members of a fact-finding mission of the ORGANIZATION FOR SECURITY AND COOPERATION IN EUROPE. Nor was the INTERNATIONAL COMMITTEE OF THE RED CROSS permitted to visit political prisoners.

Further Reading:
Edgar, Adrienne Lynn. *Tribal Nation: The Making of Soviet Turkmenistan.* Princeton, N.J.: Princeton University Press, 2004.
Habeeb, William Mark. *Turkmenistan.* Philadelphia: Mason Crest Publishers, 2005.

Tutu, Desmond (1931–   ) *South African antiapartheid activist and human rights defender*

The Anglican archbishop Desmond Tutu won the 1984 Nobel Peace Prize for his advocacy of human rights and racial justice in South Africa during the era of APARTHEID, the white supremacist system of government that ruled South Africa for half a century until 1994. In spite of arrests and intimidation, he continued to lead protests and draw attention to the inequalities in a country where the black majority was denied basic civil freedoms. For many years, while Nelson Mandela, the leader of the opposition African National Congress, was in prison, Archbishop Tutu was the most prominent foe of apartheid who did not take part in violent resistance. After South Africa's first free elections in which Mandela was elected president Tutu was appointed chair of the TRUTH AND RECONCILIATION COMMISSION, which provided a public forum for the disclosure of crimes committed by officials and military leaders as well as by black militants.

Tutu was born in 1931 in Klerksdorp, Transvaal, South Africa. He started out training to be a teacher but later turned to the study of theology. He was ordained as a priest in 1960 and obtained a Master of Theology in England in 1962. In 1975 he was appointed dean of St. Mary's Cathedral in Johannesburg, becoming the first black to hold that position. He was bishop of Lesotho from 1976 to 1978, and in 1978 he became the first black general secretary of the South African Council of Churches. In awarding the Peace Prize to Tutu, the Nobel Committee cited "the courage and heroism shown by black South Africans in their use of peaceful methods in the struggle against apartheid." In 1986 he was named archbishop of Cape Town, a position he gave up so that he could take over the chair of the Truth and Reconciliation Commission.

Further Reading:
Edelstein, Jillian. *Truth and Lies: Stories from the Truth and Reconciliation Commission in South Africa.* New York: New Press, 2002.
James, Wilmot Godfrey, and Linda van de Vijver, eds. *After the TRC: Reflections on Truth and Reconciliation in South Africa.* Athens: Ohio University Press, 2001.
Tutu, Desmond. *God Has a Dream: A Vision of Hope for Our Time.* New York: Doubleday, 2004.
Wilson, Richard A. *The Politics of Truth and Reconciliation in South Africa: Legitimizing the Post-Apartheid State.* Cambridge Studies in Law and Society. Cambridge: Cambridge University Press, 2001.

U

Uganda, human rights violations in

A former British colony, Uganda emerged relatively recently from decades of oppressive despotism. During nearly a decade in power (1971–79) Idi AMIN achieved a reputation for brutality and capriciousness on the international stage, distinguishing himself from other tyrants by his showmanship and outrageous remarks. Once, for instance, he praised Adolf HITLER for killing Jews. He was finally ousted in 1980 by the former Ugandan leader Milton OBOTE, whose regime turned out to be as corrupt and dictatorial as the one it had replaced. International human rights organizations estimate that up to half a million people were killed in state-sponsored killings during this period.

In July 1985 Obote, too, was forced from power by disaffected elements of the army. After a year of uncertainty, during which various factions contested for power, a former government official, Yoweri Museveni, assumed control of the country in 1986 as head of the National Resistance Party (NPR). Museveni introduced democratic and economic reforms that have brought Uganda relative stability and some degree of prosperity. Museveni has received high marks from international agencies for an aggressive campaign to halt the spread of HIV infection which has devastated many parts of Africa. He was elected to the presidency in 1996 in Uganda's first direct presidential election and reelected in 2001. Nonetheless, he has come in for criticism for maintaining what amounts to one-party rule and suppressing political opposition. He promulgated a form of one-party rule called the Movement, a system of government in which individual candidates could run for office on their own credentials but which effectively banned competing political parties. More recently he has announced a referendum in which voters will decide whether to support a multiparty system.

Museveni has also drawn the ire of the international community for intervening in neighboring Democratic Republic of the Congo in the late 1990s. Ugandan forces in the Congo were alleged to have stirred up ethnic strife between the Hema and Lendu peoples, whose bitter rivalry has led to the loss of over 7,000 lives and displaced 200,000. Ugandan security agencies in the Ituri region in eastern Congo have been implicated in TORTURE, illegal detention, and EXTRAJUDICIAL KILLINGS. Most of the Ugandan troops were later withdrawn under terms of a peace accord intended to bring a halt to fighting that at one time had involved nine African states and countless factions and armies within the Congo.

But the gravest threat to security and human rights within Uganda itself is posed by a cultlike insurgency in the north of the country—centered mainly in Acholiland—spearheaded by the Lord's Resistance Army (LRA). The rebellion by the shadowy group under Joseph KONY, which extends back to Museveni's rise to power in the mid-1980s, has accounted for the killings, kidnappings, and displacement of tens of thousands of people. The conflict is further complicated by tensions between Uganda and Sudan. The government in Kampala has supported rebels in Sudan, which in retaliation has supplied financing to the LRA in its campaign against Ugandan forces.

Considered the most brutal and effective guerrilla organization in Africa, the LRA claims that it is waging a war to overthrow Museveni's government and replace it with one based on the Ten Commandments. Although it purports to be a Christian fundamentalist group, Christian evangelicals have strongly denounced the LRA. The U.S. State Department has branded it a terrorist group that seeks to impose "a regime that will implement the group's brand of Christianity." The LRA is certainly well armed; it is said to have a formidable arsenal that includes shoulder-fired rocket launchers, making it, as one observer put it, "better equipped than many African armies." LRA guerrillas frequently conduct raids at night on villages, abducting children who then are either conscripted into their ranks or turned into sex slaves or forced laborers. Children who fail to obey orders are often executed—by other children. According to UNICEF, about 30 children are abducted every day, often from boarding schools or their homes. Some 34,000 children have been abducted since 1994.

Aid agencies estimate that 23,000 people have been killed by both LRA and Ugandan forces in 18 years of civil war. The refugee population has swollen to over 1.2 million who have found temporary shelter in makeshift camps where health conditions are grim and children often suffer from malnutrition. In addition to the Ugandan refugee population, there are at least 24,000 Sudanese REFUGEES in the country who have been forcibly displaced by the conflict and several thousand more—the number is not known—who have been displaced inside the Sudan. In 2002 the LRA threatened to attack international aid agencies working with DISPLACED PERSON CAMPS. While relief agencies did scale back their staff and diminished their role, they did not close operations altogether. According to Médecins sans Frontières (DOCTORS WITHOUT BORDERS), "civilians are forced to choose between staying in insecure villages and towns, thereby risking another attack that could cost them their lives, or fleeing to urban areas that cannot offer them even the minimum conditions necessary to survive."

In March 2002 Kampala mounted a massive operation code-named Iron Fist to eliminate the LRA once and for all, sending 10,000 soldiers to the north. But the rebels put up stiff resistance, and the violence only escalated. "The rebels are all over," reported a local missionary. "I would say practically the whole countryside is in their hands." Just weeks after Musveni announced that they had "nearly defeated the LRA," guerrillas attacked a refugee camp in an unusual show of force, killing more than 50. "They don't usually attack in such a large group and they rarely use these big machine guns and mortar bombs," one witness said. "They must have amassed new supplies from somewhere." A government spokesman dismissed the strategic significance of the attack as "just a desperate attempt at getting publicity, because they know they are being crushed by our forces on the ground." But there is little evidence that the LRA has suffered a crippling blow in spite of Kampala's efforts. If anything, the number of kidnappings actually increased. In the two years since Operation Iron Fist, more than 10,000 children were abducted. As a result, families in the beleaguered region are sending their children into nearby towns in what amounts to a nightly exodus.

In February 2004 LRA insurgents raided a refugee camp, killing more than 200 before vanishing into the night. Just a month previously, the United Nations had decided to act. Luis Moreno-Ocampo, chief prosecutor of the INTERNATIONAL CRIMINAL COURT, announced that the court was considering an inquiry into rights abuses by the LRA in response to a request from Museveni, who appeared at a joint news conference with Moreno-Ocampo at the time. The court charged the LRA with child abductions, summary executions, torture, rape and sexual assault, FORCED LABOR, and mutilation. Uganda thus became the first government to refer a case to the ICC since the court began its work. (The Ugandan parliament ratified the ICC treaty on June 14, 2002.) By referring the complaint to the ICC, the Ugandan government is committing itself to cooperating with the ICC "to investigate crimes, provide evidence, arrest and surrender persons sought by the court, and protect witnesses and victims. Such cooperation must extend to investigation by the prosecutor into UPDF [Ugandan People's Defense Forces] crimes."

In fact, many human rights groups, including HUMAN RIGHTS WATCH and AMNESTY INTERNATIONAL, expressed concern that any investigation by the court would concentrate wholly on crimes committed by the guerilla group and ignore those carried out by Kampala. According to these groups, the UPDF, a government paramilitary force, is guilty of "extrajudicial killings, rape and sexual assault, forcible displacement of over one million civilians, and the recruitment of children under the age of 15 into government militias." "Human Rights Watch has documented many shocking abuses by the LRA in Uganda," said Richard Dicker, director of the International Justice program at Human Rights Watch. "But the ICC prosecutor cannot ignore the crimes that Ugandan government troops allegedly have committed."

The Ugandan government announced that it was removing one possible obstacle to an ICC investigation by exempting leaders of the LRA from an AMNESTY law that the parliament had passed that would have immunized individuals responsible for war crimes in the conflict. Some international organizations, however, objected on the grounds that removing a blanket amnesty would only fuel the conflict because the guerrilla leaders in effect had nothing left to lose. For instance, the Refugee Law Project, a Kampala-based advocacy group, asserted that LRA leader Joseph Kony would rebuff any effort to bring him to the negotiating table because he was "fighting for survival" and probably assumed that he would be killed if he tried to surrender or negotiate. In addition, many experts believe that without the cooperation of neighboring Sudan, which has backed the LRA, the ICC will make little progress. Sudanese cooperation, however, is likely only if Kampala ends its own support for rebels operating against Khartoum. "Nobody is winning this war," observed one missionary priest, "we are all losers."

See also CHILDREN'S RIGHTS.

Further Reading:

Allen, Peter A. P. *Interesting Times: Life in Uganda under Idi Amin.* London: Book Guild, Limited, 2000.

Dodge, Cole P., and Magne Raundelen. *Reaching Children in War: Sudan, Uganda, and Mozambique.* London: Taylor & Francis, 1992.

Mutibwa, Phares. *Uganda since Independence: A Story of Unfulfilled Hopes.* London: Africa World Press, 1992.

Uighur, persecution of   *See* CHINA, HUMAN RIGHTS VIOLATIONS IN.

Ukraine, human rights violations in

The election of Viktor Yushchenko as Ukraine's president in December 2004 was hailed by human rights groups as a triumph of democracy that offered the prospect of political reform. The election that put Yushchenko into power only took place after an earlier disputed election in which his opponent, former prime minister Viktor Yanukovych, was declared the winner by the election commission. Until Yushchenko assumed the presidency in early 2005, Ukraine, the largest of the republics that formed the former Soviet Union, had been dominated by President Leonid Kuchma. Although Kuchma brought some measure of economic progress to Ukraine, he was dogged by allegations of corruption and human rights violations. During the first round of voting in October 2004, Kuchma's hand was seen in manipulating results to achieve Yanukovych's narrow win. According to the ORGANIZATION FOR SECURITY AND COOPERATION IN EUROPE (OSCE), state-owned media coverage was biased in favor of Kuchma's handpicked candidate. The national television channels from which most Ukrainians get their news were either state-owned or controlled by persons close to Kuchma. The International Election Observation Mission reported that "State executive authorities and the Central Election Commission (CEC) displayed a lack of will to conduct a genuine democratic election process."

Thousands of demonstrators gathered in central Kiev, the capital, to protest the results of the first election. Over the next several days the pro-Yuschenko demonstrators remained in place until the election was annulled and new—and fair—elections were held. Fears of violence, however, were not realized as the army and security forces stayed in their barracks. According to news reports, several high-ranking officers in the security police sided with the demonstrators and warned against the use of force to crush the protest. In a surprising ruling, the Ukrainian Supreme Court determined that the election had been flawed and called for new elections. Perhaps just as surprisingly, Kuchma accepted the outcome and withdrew his support from Yanukovych. The former prime minister did, however, retain considerable support in the east of the country, a manufacturing and mining region, while Yuschenko's base of support rested mostly in the west. Yuschenko had managed to mobilize such popular support because he promised a dramatic departure from authoritarian rule.

Throughout his contentious campaign, Yuschenko called for respect of basic rights and the need for political reform. Upon assuming office, he named as prime minister Yulia Tymoshenko, whose pro-Western stance has aggravated the Kremlin. (Russian president Vladimir Putin had opposed a second round of voting and made no secret of his preference for Yanukovych.) The need for reform is unquestionable. Under Kuchma, suspects were frequently tortured and mistreated by police, and there were reports of deaths in custody. According to AMNESTY INTERNATIONAL, alleged mistreatment included beatings, the use of electric shocks, pistol whippings, and asphyxiation. Freedom of expression was hampered and the media stifled. The government also put restrictions on freedom of assembly. The controversial presidential election in 2004 was not without precedent. In the past, parliamentary elections have been marred by incidents of violence, intimidation, and "inappropriate influencing" of voters. In some cases, opposition figures have been slain under mysterious circumstances.

Journalists who have written about political corruption were also at risk under Kuchma's rule. In a five-year period (1998–2003), 10 journalists were killed in the country, according to Paris-based Reporters Sans Frontières; most of the murders were never solved. Taped telephone conversations—smuggled to the West by a former presidential bodyguard—allegedly linked Kuchma himself to the 2000 kidnapping and beheading of 31-year-old Internet journalist Georgy Gongadze, who had been a frequent critic of the government. Claiming that they were unable to identify the voice on the tape—apparently sanctioning the murder—as Kuchma's, prosecutors dropped the case. The new government has promised to look into such cases, and there has been widespread speculation that Kuchma—who had stepped down voluntarily—might be indicted for the murder and for other charges, although the ex-president declared that he was innocent of any wrongdoing.

Within months of taking office, Yuschenko's government was rocked by scandal and allegations of corruption, forcing the president to fire his cabinet, including the popular but controversial Tymoshenko. Before he could win approval for a new government, though, he had to cut a deal with his old rival Yanukovych. One of the reported conditions was that any outstanding cases against partisans of Yanukovych would no longer go forward. Disappointed Yuschenko supporters viewed the agreement as an end to the reformist era ushered in by the Orange Revolution.

Further Reading:

Lieven, Anatol. *Ukraine and Russia: A Fraternal Rivalry.* Washington, D.C.: United States Institute of Peace Press, 1999.
Wilson, Andrew. *Ukraine: Unexpected Nation.* New Haven, Conn.: Yale University Press, 2002.

Ulemek, Milorad   *See* WAR CRIMINALS OF THE FORMER YUGOSLAVIA.

United Nations and the Geneva Conventions

The United Nations, which in 2004 had 191 members, is bound only by decisions of its Security Council and not necessarily by the GENEVA CONVENTIONS. This anomaly exists in spite of the fact that nearly all member states of the United Nations have also ratified the Geneva Conventions. The international body itself is not a party to the conventions. According to a representative of the UN Office of Legal Affairs (OLA) the role of the United Nations is "to carry out the will of the international community as expressed by it in the Security Council." In an essay for the CRIMES OF WAR PROJECT, Roy Gutman points out that citizens of a state bound by the conventions can "escape their legal obligations" by "donning the blue helmets"—that is, joining a UN peacekeeping force. That possibility arises because the force takes its orders directly from the Security Council, although in fact peacekeepers are equipped and supplied by their home countries. Resolutions by the Security Council responsible for deployment of UN peacekeepers do not invariably cite the applicability of provisions of the Geneva Conventions—for instance, the requirement of free passage for civilians through front lines even if they are citizens of the adversary.

The UN Charter defined the body's role as bringing peace to the world, and as a result the United Nations did not participate in the codification of rules of war that was the focus of the 1949 Geneva Conventions. "War having been outlawed, the regulation of its conduct has ceased to be relevant," stated the UN International Law Commission. In this view, the United Nations had no business becoming involved in drawing up an international accord to govern how conflict should be conducted. Instead, drafting of the conventions took place under the auspices of the INTERNATIONAL COMMITTEE OF THE RED CROSS (ICRC). Tensions between the two institutions periodically surfaces in conflict situations. In 1993, for example, UN forces involved in peacekeeping operations in Somalia detained hundreds of Somalis and then denied the ICRC access to the prisoners, causing the Red Cross to suspend its operations in protest.

The ICRC would prefer an explicit declaration "that UN troops are bound by INTERNATIONAL HUMANITARIAN LAW and that everyone under the UN flag will be informed, trained, and monitored," according to an ICRC representative quoted by Gutman. Discussions about drafting guidelines for UN deployments have in fact been ongoing between the ICRC and UN experts since 1993. The results of these negotiations did not satisfy the ICRC because the proposed drafts only held out the prospect of a UN soldier accused of a violation of the Geneva Conventions to be liable for trial in his own country. The concept of UNIVERSAL JURISDICTION—the right to try a human rights offender in any state with a competent and fair judiciary—was ruled out. Such a case is hardly theoretical; in late 2004 several UN peacekeepers in eastern Congo were implicated in rapes and other forms of sexual abuse of Congolese women and girls.

Further Reading:

Fasulo, Linda. *An Insider's Guide to the UN.* New Haven, Conn.: Yale University Press, 2003.

Gutman, Roy, ed. *Crimes of War: What the Public Should Know.* New York: W. W. Norton & Company, 1999.

Jinks, Derek. *The Rules of War: The Geneva Conventions in the Age of Terror.* Oxford: Oxford University Press, 2005.

Meisler, Stanley. *United Nations: The First Fifty Years.* New York: Atlantic Monthly Press, 1997.

Pilloud, Claude. *Commentary on the Additional Protocols of 8 June 1977 to the Geneva Conventions of 12 August 1949.* Boston: Brill Academic Publishers, 1987.

Roberts, Adam, and Richard Guelff. *Documents on the Laws of War.* Oxford: Oxford University Press, 2000.

Schlesigner, Stephen. *Act of Creation: The Founding of the United Nations: A Story of Superpowers, Secret Agents, Wartime Allies and Enemies, and Their Quest for a Peaceful World.* Westport, Conn.: Westview Press, 2003.

Trombly, Maria. *Journalist's Guide to the Geneva Conventions.* Indianapolis: Society of Professional Journalists, 2000.

Weiss, Thomas G., David P. Forsythe, and Roger A. Coate. *United Nations and Changing World Politics.* Westport, Conn.: Westview Press, 2004.

United Nations Commission on Human Rights

See UNITED NATIONS HUMAN RIGHTS COMMISSION.

United Nations Guiding Principles on Internal Displacement

The Guiding Principles on Internal Displacement were drafted by the United Nations to address the problems and needs of INTERNALLY DISPLACED PERSONS (IDPs) throughout the world. IDPs are defined by the United Nations as "persons or groups of persons who have been forced or obliged to flee or to leave their homes or places of habitual residence, in particular as a result of or in order to avoid the effects of armed conflict, situations of generalized violence, violations of human rights or natural or human-made disasters, and who have not crossed an internationally recognized State border." REFUGEES, by contrast, are people who are forced to flee across international borders. The Guiding Principles are designed to "identify rights and guarantees relevant to the protection of persons from forced displacement" and to ensure their protection and assistance while they remain displaced and when they are eventually returned to their home country or resettled in another country. Although the principles are not a binding legal instrument, they reflect and are consistent with international human rights and humanitarian law.

The creation of the Guiding Principles, which were issued in 1998, was impelled by a 1992 mandate by the UNITED NATIONS HUMAN RIGHTS COMMISSION (UNHRC) and reinforced by subsequent resolutions of both the UNHRC and the General Assembly. The United Nations was moved to act on the basis of a study that found that while existing law did provide for some needs of the internally displaced, there were significant gaps when it came to issues such as protecting and assisting displaced persons. The individual most responsible for laying the foundations for the Guiding Principles was the then Under-Secretary-General for Humanitarian Affairs Sérgio VIEIRA DE MELLO. He was tragically killed in a terrorist bombing of UN headquarters in Baghdad, Iraq, in 2003.

Further Reading:

Feller, Erika, Volker Turk, and Frances Nicholson, eds. *Refugee Protection in International Law: UNHCR's Global Consultations on International Protection.* Cambridge: Cambridge University Press, 2003.

Fritz, Mark. *Lost on Earth: Nomads of the New World.* New York: Routledge, 2000.

Groenewold, Julia, and Doctors Without Borders. *World in Crisis: The Politics of Survival at the End of the Twentieth Century.* London: Routledge, 1996.

Helton, Arthur C. *The Price of Indifference: Refugees and Humanitarian Action in the New Century.* A Council on Foreign Relations Book. Oxford: Oxford University Press, 2002.

Hyndman, Jennifer. *Managing Displacement: Refugees and the Politics of Humanitarianism.* Minneapolis: University of Minnesota Press, 2000.

Ingleby, David, ed. *Forced Migration and Mental Health: Rethinking the Care of Refugees and Displaced Persons.* New York: Plenum US, 2004.

Lischer, Sarah Kenyon. *Dangerous Sanctuaries: Refugee Camps, Civil War, and the Dilemmas of Humanitarian Aid.* Cornell Studies in Security Affairs. Ithaca, N.Y.: Cornell University Press, 2005.

Moorehead, Caroline. *Human Cargo: A Journey among Refugees.* New York: Henry Holt and Co., 2005.

United Nations High Commissioner for Human Rights

The United Nations High Commissioner for Human Rights, a post created in 1993, is the principal UN official with responsibility for human rights and is directly answerable to the secretary-general. The Office of the High Commissioner for Human Rights (OHCHR) is based in Geneva, Switzerland, with an office at United Nations Headquarters in New York.

Several human rights institutions and agencies exist within the United Nations, but they are all responsible for promoting and protecting human rights—civil, cultural, economic, political, and social—throughout the world based upon the principles affirmed by the UNIVERSAL DECLARATION OF HUMAN RIGHTS, adopted by the UN General Assembly in 1948. The High Commissioner is the public face of the UNITED NATIONS HUMAN RIGHTS COMMISSION and other human rights institutions; according to the UN job description, he or she serves as a "moral authority" and "voice for victims." The commissioner is also mandated to confer with governments, nongovernmental organizations (NGOs), academic institutions, and the private sector to ensure commitment to human rights. The commissioner has an educational role which he or she fulfills by promoting awareness of human rights issues and stimulating "thinking on prevention" of abuses. When new challenges arise—for example, TRAFFICKING IN PERSONS, HIV/AIDS, biotechnology, and the effects of globalization—it is the commissioner's role to address their human rights implications. The commissioner additionally supports other human rights agencies in the United Nations, providing expertise, research, advice, and administrative services.

Further Reading:

Brysk, Alison, ed. *Globalization and Human Rights.* Berkeley: University of California Press, 2002.

Fasulo, Linda. *An Insider's Guide to the UN.* New Haven, Conn.: Yale University Press, 2003.

Gutman, Roy, ed. *Crimes of War: What the Public Should Know.* New York: W. W. Norton & Company, 1999.

Trombly, Maria. *Journalist's Guide to the Geneva Conventions.* Indianapolis: Society of Professional Journalists, 2000.

Weiss, Thomas G., David P. Forsythe, Roger A. Coate. *United Nations and Changing World Politics.* Westport, Conn.: Westview Press, 2004.

United Nations High Commissioner for Refugees (UNHCR)

The position of the United Nations High Commissioner for Refugees (UNHCR) was established on December 14, 1950, by the UN General Assembly. The UNHCR was charged with leading and coordinating international action to protect refugees and resolve refugee problems worldwide. REFUGEES are legally defined "as people who are outside their countries because of a well-founded fear of persecution based on their race, religion, nationality, political opinion or membership in a particular social group, and who cannot or do not want to return home." The UNHCR has two primary purposes. The first is to protect the lives and rights of refugees, and the second is to ensure that refugees have the right to ASYLUM or are allowed to settle in the country where they have taken refuge or in third country if conditions at home make it impossible to return. The UNHCR also seeks to ensure that refugees are not repatriated against their will. In discharging its responsibility, the agency (the United Nations does not call it an "office") has assisted an estimated 50 million refugees over the last five decades; it is currently helping about 17 million people who meet the criteria of refugees. The agency has a staff of about 6,200 people based in more than 116 countries. The UNHCR's programs and policies are approved by an executive committee composed of 64 member states (which meets annually) and a "working group," or standing committee (which meets several times a year).

The office of High Commissioner for Refugees was one of the many attempts in the 20th century to provide protection and assistance to refugees. A similar position had been established by the LEAGUE OF NATIONS (the predecessor of the United Nations) in 1921. After World War II, two organizations—the United Nations Relief and Rehabilitation Administration and the International Refugee Organization—worked to address the refugee crisis created by the war. Initially the UNHCR was only supposed to exist for three years—sufficient time, it was thought, to resettle the 1.2 million European refugees that then remained from the war. But as continual conflicts around the world produced ever-greater populations of refugees, the mandate for the UNHCR was extended, and it is now a permanent institution within the United Nations. For its work the UNHCR has earned two Nobel Peace Prizes, in 1954 and 1981.

Further Reading:

Feller, Erika, Volker Turk, and Frances Nicholson, eds. *Refugee Protection in International Law: UNHCR's Global Consultations on International Protection.* Cambridge: Cambridge University Press, 2003.

Fritz, Mark. *Lost on Earth: Nomads of the New World.* New York: Routledge, 2000.

Groenewold, Julia, and Doctors Without Borders. *World in Crisis: The Politics of Survival at the End of the Twentieth Century.* London: Routledge, 1996.

Helton, Arthur C. *The Price of Indifference: Refugees and Humanitarian Action in the New Century.* A Council on Foreign Relations Book. Oxford: Oxford University Press, 2002.

Hyndman, Jennifer. *Managing Displacement: Refugees and the Politics of Humanitarianism.* Minneapolis: University of Minnesota Press, 2000.

Ingleby, David, ed. *Forced Migration and Mental Health: Rethinking the Care of Refugees and Displaced Persons.* New York: Plenum US, 2004.

Lischer, Sarah Kenyon. *Dangerous Sanctuaries: Refugee Camps, Civil War, and the Dilemmas of Humanitarian Aid.* Cornell Studies in Security Affairs. Ithaca, N.Y.: Cornell University Press, 2005.

Moorehead, Caroline. *Human Cargo: A Journey among Refugees.* New York: Henry Holt and Co., 2005.

United Nations Human Rights Commission (UNCHR)

Officially the United Nations Commission on Human Rights (UNCHR), the Human Rights Commission was established in 1946 to promote and protect human rights. It addresses such issues as arbitrary detention, the right to education, and INTERNALLY DISPLACED PERSONS and investigates reports of human rights abuses that may have occurred in any of the 53 states that are members of the UNCHR. (The representation is based on region; Western countries, for example, have three seats altogether.) The commission meets annually in the spring for six weeks in Geneva and may meet between sessions if the need arises. During its regular session, the UNCHR will adopt about 100 resolutions and decisions.

Founded after World War II, the UN was first chaired by Eleanor Roosevelt, the widow of U.S. president Franklin Delano Roosevelt. Under her leadership, in 1948 the Commission produced the UNIVERSAL DECLARATION OF HUMAN RIGHTS, a seminal document that called for the recognition of fundamental human rights for every man, woman, and child on the planet. For all its lofty goals, however, the UNHRC has repeatedly been mired in controversy over the half-century of its existence. It has condemned Israel for human rights violations by votes of 50-1, with the United States in lone opposition. In 2001 the commission actually expelled the United States even as Libya, Sudan, and Syria, none of them with good human rights records, were being offered seats on it. The ouster was regarded as a rebuke to policies of the Bush administration by delegates representing developing countries. (The United States rejoined a year later.) In another controversial move that called the body's credibility into question and sparked widespread criticism, Libya's representative was elected to chair the UNCHR in 2002. "Countries with dreadful rights records should never be in charge of chairing the Commission on Human Rights," Rory Mungoven, global advocacy director for HUMAN RIGHTS WATCH, said at the time. "Libya's long record of human rights abuses clearly does not merit such a reward."

Attempts to reform the Human Rights Commission or scrap it altogether and replace it with a new Human Rights Council with fewer—and more democratically responsive—members were still running into roadblocks in 2005. A document issued by the General Assembly after a summit in September attended by more than 150 world leaders said only that a Human Rights Council should be created. However, since the document left the details to the deeply divided General Assembly, it was uncertain whether any substantive change could be expected soon.

Further Reading:

Brysk, Alison, ed. *Globalization and Human Rights.* Berkeley: University of California Press, 2002.

Fasulo, Linda. *An Insider's Guide to the UN.* New Haven, Conn.: Yale University Press, 2003.

Gutman, Roy, ed. *Crimes of War: What the Public Should Know.* New York: W. W. Norton & Company, 1999.

Trombly, Maria. *Journalist's Guide to the Geneva Conventions.* Indianapolis: Society of Professional Journalists, 2000.

Weiss, Thomas G., David P. Forsythe, and Roger A. Coate. *United Nations and Changing World Politics.* Westport, Conn.: Westview Press, 2004.

United Nations Resolution 1368

United Nations Resolution 1368 was adopted by the UN Security Council on September 12, 2001, one day after the terrorist strikes on the World Trade Center and the Pentagon. In it the Security Council condemned "in the strongest possible terms" "the horrifying terrorist attacks which took place on 11 September 2001 in New York, Washington, D.C. and Pennsylvania and regards such acts, like any act of international terrorism, as a threat to international peace and security." The resolution called upon states to work together to bring to justice the "perpetrators, organizers and sponsors" of the attacks and warned that individuals or states who provided assistance or harbored those responsible would be held accountable. Two weeks later, on September 28, the Security Council adopted another resolution—1373—which invoked Chapter VII of the UN Charter, making the resolution binding upon UN member states, who were obliged to "ensure that any person who participates in the financing, planning, preparation or perpetration of terrorist acts or in supporting terrorist acts is brought to justice and ensure that, in addition to any other measures against them, such terrorist acts are established as serious criminal offences in domestic laws and regulations and that the punishment duly reflects the seriousness of such terrorist acts." The resolution also obliged member states to provide assistance to one another in connection with criminal investigations or legal proceedings

related to the "financing or support of terrorist acts." States were also urged to take all necessary measures to prevent the free movement of terrorist groups through their territory.

Further Reading:

Burke, Jason. *Al-Qaeda: Casting a Shadow of Terror.* London: I. B. Tauris, 2004.

———. *Al-Qaeda: The True Story of Radical Islam.* London: I. B. Tauris, 2004.

Gunaratna, Rohan. *Inside Al Qaeda: Global Network of Terror.* New York: Berkley Publishing Group, 2003.

Scheuer, Michael. *Imperial Hubris: Why the West Is Losing the War on Terror.* Washington, D.C.: Potomac Books, 2004.

Zayy-at, Montasser al-. *The Road to Al-Qaeda: The Story of Bin Laden's Right-Hand Man.* Critical Studies on Islam. Translated by Ahmed Fekry. Edited by Sara Nimis. Ann Arbor, Mich.: Pluto Press, 2004.

United Nations Working Group on Enforced or Involuntary Disappearances

The Declaration on the Protection of All Persons from Enforced Disappearance, proclaimed by the United Nations General Assembly, defined a *disappearance* as a situation when "persons are arrested, detained or abducted against their will or otherwise deprived of their liberty by officials of different branches or levels of Government, or by organized groups, or private individuals acting on behalf of, or with the support, direct or indirect, consent or acquiescence of the Government, followed by a refusal to disclose the fate or whereabouts of the persons concerned or a refusal to acknowledge the deprivation of their liberty, which places such persons outside the protection of the law." The practice of DISAPPEARANCES has become increasingly frequent in recent years, especially in internal conflicts such as the Algerian civil war and the so-called dirty wars in Latin American countries during the 1970s.

In February 1980 the UNITED NATIONS HUMAN RIGHTS COMMISSION decided to "establish for a period of one year a working group consisting of five of its members, to serve as experts in their individual capacities, to examine questions relevant to enforced or involuntary disappearances of persons." The mandate for the working group has been renewed ever since. The Working Group on Enforced or Involuntary Disappearances deals with specific violations anywhere in the world. (Similar groups established previously were only mandated to address disappearances in a particular country.) The Working Group is charged with assisting the relatives of disappeared persons to ascertain the fate and whereabouts of their missing family members. The group then communicates reports of disappearances to the governments of the relevant countries (regardless of whether the government has ratified the Declaration on the Protection of All Persons from Enforced Disappearance).

The group "acts essentially as a channel of communication." Since its inception, some 50,000 individual cases in more than 70 countries have come to the attention of the group. Only a fraction of those cases have been "clarified" by the group, however, because the facts in many cases are still in doubt. The Working Group is credited with preventing further disappearances "through its patient and persistent contacts with the Governments concerned," according to the United Nations. The group has also been mandated by the Human Rights Commission to "take action in connection with acts of intimidation or reprisals against relatives of missing persons and private individuals or groups who seek to cooperate or have cooperated with United Nations." The group meets three times a year in New York and Geneva, although it has a mechanism to respond to urgent cases between sessions. The group then informs governments about the decisions it takes regarding cases in their countries. It also prods governments to take action about cases requiring additional clarification.

Further Reading:

Arditti, Rita. *Searching for Life: The Grandmothers of the Plaza De Mayo and the Disappeared Children of Argentina.* University of California Press, 1999.

Davis, William Columbus. *Warnings from the Far South: Democracy versus Dictatorship in Uruguay, Argentina, and Chile.* New York: Praeger Publishers, 1995.

Guest, Iain. *Behind the Disappearances: Argentina's Dirty War against Human Rights and the United Nations.* Pennsylvania Studies in Human Rights. Philadelphia: University of Pennsylvania Press, 2000.

Gutman, Roy, ed. *Crimes of War: What the Public Should Know.* New York: W. W. Norton & Company, 1999.

Kornbluh, Peter. *The Pinochet File: A Declassified Dossier on Atrocity and Accountability.* A National Security Archive Book. New York: New Press, 2003.

Politzer, Patricia, and Diane, Wachtel. *Fear in Chile: Lives under Pinochet.* New York: New Press, 2001.

Unit 731   *See* MANCHURIA, JAPANESE WAR CRIMES IN.

Universal Declaration of Human Rights

The Universal Declaration of Human Rights, adopted by the United Nations on December 10, 1948, is an affirmation of the dignity and rights of all human beings based on principles expressed in the UN Charter. Adopted in 1945,

the UN Charter set the goal of "promoting and encouraging respect for human rights and for fundamental freedoms of all without distinction as to race, sex, language, and religion." Article 1 of the Universal Declaration echoes these sentiments: "All human beings are born free and equal in dignity and human rights. They are endowed with reason and conscience and should act towards one another in a spirit of brotherhood."

The UN Charter, while giving new emphasis to human rights, was considered insufficient by many human rights advocates. What was needed, they believed, was an international equivalent of the United States Bill of Rights, which affirmed such liberties as freedom of the press, freedom of worship, and the right to DUE PROCESS. The declaration of 1948 is considered the first of a three-part international covenant addressing human rights. (The second part deals with civil and political rights and the third with economic, social, and cultural rights.) The Universal Declaration consists of 30 articles that set out such rights as life, liberty, and security of person; freedom of conscience, religion, opinion, expression, association, and assembly; freedom from arbitrary arrest; the right to a fair and impartial trial; the presumption of innocence; the right to privacy; the right to an adequate standard of living; the right to education; the right to marry and raise a family; the right to participate in government and in the social life of society; and the right to rest and leisure. In addition, all human beings are entitled to own property and enjoy the right to leave and return to their home country; they also have the right to work under acceptable conditions, receive equal pay for equal work, and join labor unions.

All signatories to the Universal Declaration were urged to publish—and publicize—it in their own countries. Provisions of some 90 national constitutions drafted since 1948 can be traced to the declaration, according to the Franklin and Eleanor Roosevelt Institute in New York. The actual work was carried out by the UNITED NATIONS HUMAN RIGHTS COMMISSION, which held its first session in January 1947 in New York; its first chair was Eleanor Roosevelt, the widow of President Franklin Roosevelt. What the commission intended to do was unprecedented: set forth a number of inalienable rights applicable to every man, woman, and child on the planet. In spite of the differences in cultures, ideologies, religions, and ethnicity, the commission delegates were all united by the wish never to see a recurrence of the horrors of World War II, which had concluded only two years previously. The delegates had some historical models to draw upon, including the 1941 Atlantic Charter, a joint U.S.-British accord establishing principles for implementing postwar policies, and Roosevelt's famous Four Freedoms speech, delivered earlier the same year to Congress, in which the president declared that all people were guaranteed freedom of speech and expression, freedom of worship, freedom from want, and freedom from fear. The delegates also took guidance from the principles set forth at the NUREMBERG TRIALS and TOKYO TRIALS, which the Allies conducted to try Nazi and Japanese war criminals, respectively. Both tribunals had made it clear that human rights violators should be punished for their individual actions and could not justify their abuses by claiming that they were only obeying orders. The delegates also realized that there was a need to forge treaties containing mechanisms to uphold human rights and punish offenders.

Governments were not the only players at the UN sessions; nongovernmental organizations (NGOs), especially human rights organizations, also had a significant input. In large measure, though, the groundwork for the Universal Declaration was laid by Eleanor Roosevelt, who, after her husband's death, became a leading exponent of human rights throughout the world. She was chosen as the U.S. representative to the commission, and because of her stature she was named chairperson. The drafting of the Universal Declaration did not proceed smoothly, however, since there was considerable disagreement about the nature and extent of the rights that should be accorded women, racial minorities, and religious liberty. There were disputes over the protections necessary for a free speech, the right to dissent, and what role social and economic rights should have. The most strident opposition came from the Soviet bloc, which held a conception of freedom totally at odds with that of the West. "The cult of individualism" so cherished by the West, declared the Soviet delegate, only led to economic exploitation. The communist regimes believed that economic rights should have priority over political rights. In one of the most famous exchanges, the British delegate countered, "This declaration must uphold as a model for all humanity the figure of free men, not well-fed slaves."

In an attempt to hamper the process of drafting the Universal Declaration, delegates from the communist countries would sometimes deliver speeches that went on as long as eight hours. Roosevelt was not about to allow Soviet tactics to impede the process forever, setting a deadline of Christmas 1948. "I drive hard, and when I get home I will be tired. The men on the commission will be also," she said. There was another rift, one between mostly smaller states, which wanted the declaration to include legally binding restraints, and larger states, including the United States, which preferred that the legal mechanisms wait for future treaties. Just to put together the declaration itself was difficult enough, the latter group argued; to try to add legally binding provisions would probably delay agreement for years. Their view prevailed, and the Universal Declaration of Human Rights, adopted as a resolution, has no force of law. The Human Rights Commission was,

however, able to complete its work in time for the General Assembly to adopt the declaration on December 10, 1948, meeting Roosevelt's deadline. Of the 58 members represented at the General Assembly session, 48 voted in favor, none voted against, eight abstained, and two were absent. Most of the abstentions came from Soviet bloc delegates, but Saudi Arabia also abstained on the grounds that the declaration was too "Western-oriented," and South Africa did the same because it believed that the declaration had taken too expansive a view of liberties. (South Africa's misgivings were understandable in light of APARTHEID, the white supremacist regime's suppression of black rights.)

After the vote, Roosevelt declared, "We stand today at the threshold of a great event both in the life of the United Nations and in the life of mankind. This Declaration may well become the international Magna Carta of all men everywhere. We hope its proclamation by the General Assembly will be an event comparable to the proclamation of the Rights of Man by the French people in 1789, the adoption of the Bill of Rights by the people of the United States, and the adoption of comparable declarations at different times in other countries." The UN Human Rights Commission meets annually in Geneva to assess how member states are complying with the declaration's provisions and determine how violators should be punished, although critics contend that enforcement mechanisms remain inadequate.

See also RELIGIOUS PERSECUTION.

Further Reading:

Brysk, Alison, ed. *Globalization and Human Rights*. Berkeley: University of California Press, 2002.

Fasulo, Linda. *An Insider's Guide to the UN*. New Haven, Conn.: Yale University Press, 2003.

Gutman, Roy, ed. *Crimes of War: What the Public Should Know*. New York: W. W. Norton, 1999.

Trombly, Maria. *Journalist's Guide to the Geneva Conventions*. Indianapolis: Society of Professional Journalists, 2000.

Weiss, Thomas G., David P. Forsythe, and Roger A. Coate. *United Nations and Changing World Politics*. Westport, Conn.: Westview Press, 2004.

universal jurisdiction

Universal jurisdiction is the principle holding that national courts have a right—and even the obligation—to prosecute crimes of GENOCIDE, CRIMES AGAINST HUMANITY, war crimes, TORTURE, EXTRAJUDICIAL KILLINGS, and DISAPPEARANCES regardless of where the crime took place or the country of the perpetrator's or victim's origin. Traditionally, national courts have only heard cases involving crimes committed in their territory. However, ever since the Second

World War, national courts have begun to extend their jurisdiction to cover war crimes and human rights abuses that occurred elsewhere. More than a dozen states have conducted investigations or trials or at the very least arrested suspected war criminals wanted in other countries, including Australia, Austria, Belgium, Canada, Denmark, France, Germany, Israel, Mexico, Netherlands, Senegal, Spain, Switzerland, the United Kingdom, and the United States. A recent worldwide study of national laws by AMNESTY INTERNATIONAL found that more than 125 states had enacted laws that to one degree or another provided for universal jurisdiction over certain types of criminal conduct, though many of these laws are flawed. No state, however, has universal jurisdiction for all crimes involving human rights violations.

In one form of universal jurisdiction, national courts apply procedures ordinarily followed in domestic criminal cases to violations of human rights and war crimes, based on standards set out in United Nations conventions. This approach allows prosecutors in one country to seek offenders beyond their borders by means of demanding their extradition from third countries. This was the strategy that was taken to secure the arrest of Ricardo Miguel CAVALLO, an Argentine naval officer who was accused of state-sponsored murder and torture while Argentina was under the grip of military rule. Even though he was immune from prosecution in his native land because of AMNESTY laws and his residence in Mexico, he was ultimately extradited to Spain to answer an indictment issued by a Spanish judge.

The second approach to enforcing universal jurisdiction is by bringing offenders before the INTERNATIONAL CRIMINAL COURT (ICC), which is based on a treaty created by a conference in Rome in July 1998 and signed by 95 states, including most European countries. Presumably the ICC intends to follow the precedent established by special UN courts such as the INTERNATIONAL CRIMINAL TRIBUNAL FOR THE FORMER YUGOSLAVIA (ICTY), where former Yugoslav president Slobodan MILOŠEVIĆ was tried.

More far-reaching efforts to define the concept of universal jurisdiction have occurred in Belgium, where the government authorized its courts to prosecute perpetrators of crimes against humanity committed in any part of the world. Within a short time the Belgian courts were flooded with lawsuits alleging human rights violations against various U.S. officials and military leaders, including the American military commander in Iraq, General Tommy Franks; former president George H. W. Bush; former secretary of state Colin Powell; and Norman Schwarzkopf, who had led coalition forces in the 1991 Gulf War. These cases were either dismissed or transferred to U.S. courts. Belgium later backed down under pressure from the United States. "By passing this law, Belgium has turned its legal system into a platform for divisive politicized lawsuits against her NATO allies," argued U.S. secretary of defense Donald Rumsfeld. The law was subsequently modified to make it more difficult to bring lawsuits before Belgian courts without first filing them in the defendant's own country, so long as that country's legal system is considered fair and functioning.

The very concept of universal jurisdiction is fairly recent, even if the philosophy underlying it dates back centuries. The sixth edition of *Black's Law Dictionary,* published in 1990, contains no entry for the term. Where universal justice was applied in practice, if not in name, was in cases where the crimes were committed outside any sovereignty—by pirates, hijackers, and terrorists, for instance. To critics of the concept, the idea that universal jurisdiction could cover high officials for crimes committed in other countries is both novel and alarming. One of the most ardent critics is former secretary of state and national security adviser Henry Kissinger. He traces the origin of universal jurisdiction to principles enshrined in the UNIVERSAL DECLARATION OF HUMAN RIGHTS of 1948, the GENOCIDE CONVENTION of 1948, and the CONVENTION AGAINST TORTURE of 1988. He also cites The Final Act of the Conference on Security and Cooperation in Europe, signed in Helsinki in 1975 by President Gerald Ford on behalf of the United States, which obligated the 35 signatory nations to observe certain stated human rights; violators would face international pressure to change their ways.

At the time the Helsinki agreement was signed, the Soviet Union was considered the principal offender, and the U.S. Congress passed several important pieces of legislation to punish the USSR for flouting the standards agreed upon in Helsinki. But in Kissinger's view, these accords were never intended to give individual nations the right to prosecute political leaders who might be in violation of these standards, even if their actions occurred in another country. In 1998, however, a Spanish court indicted Augusto PINOCHET, the former Chilean president, for crimes against humanity; at the time Pinochet was in the United Kingdom on an unofficial visit. He was placed under house arrest until a British court refused to extradite him to Spain and he was freed to return to Chile. The danger in this approach, Kissinger warned in an article written for *Foreign Affairs,* "lies in pushing the effort to extremes that risk substituting the tyranny of judges for that of governments; historically, the dictatorship of the virtuous has often led to inquisitions and even witch-hunts. To be sure, human rights violations, war crimes, genocide, and torture have so disgraced the modern age and in such a variety of places that the effort to interpose legal norms to prevent or punish such outrages does credit to its advocates."

Kissinger and other critics of the concept of universal jurisdiction contend that these prosecutions, because they may be initiated in practically any country, are liable to be arbitrary and capricious. Kissinger pointed out some of the difficulties: "What legal norms are being applied? What are the rules of evidence? What safeguards exist for the defendant?" It is important to bring war criminals to account, say these critics, but it cannot be done without a system of checks and balances. Too much power is placed in the hands of individual magistrates who might act more from political or personal motives rather than in the interest of justice. In addition, a defendant might be forced to deal with a legal system with which he is unfamiliar. For that matter, what safeguards will be available to ensure the defendant's rights? Moreover, unlike domestic criminal cases, cases involving war criminals and human rights abusers are likely to have implications for the conduct of foreign policy and international relations. The arrest of Pinochet, for instance, heightened tensions between the United Kingdom and Chile. Kissinger also points out that such prosecutions may hamper reconciliation in countries where the crimes were committed; he goes on to assert that in many instances, coming to terms with the past is better left to the people in the country involved; in this view, a third country that seeks to redress historical grievances is butting in where it does not belong. Bringing charges against a suspect in a national court is quite different from prosecuting war criminals in international courts, Kissinger argues: "Such a system goes far beyond the explicit and limited mandates established by the UN Security Council for the tribunals covering war crimes in the former Yugoslavia and Rwanda as well as the one being negotiated for Cambodia."

But Kissinger is no more sanguine about the existence of the International Criminal Court, either. The goal of those who support the court, he says, "is to criminalize certain types of military and political actions and thereby bring about a more humane conduct of international relations." This is better than allowing individual states and magistrates to apply universal jurisdiction, but he contends that even so, "in its present form of assigning the ultimate dilemmas of international politics to unelected jurists—and to an international judiciary at that—it represents such a fundamental change in U.S. constitutional practice that a full national debate and the full participation of Congress are imperative." Many cases are fraught with ambiguity, and it is unclear as to what standards of law their actions are being held to by justices appointed to the ICC who may be operating under different guidelines than those followed by judges and juries in U.S. courts. As an example Kissinger worries that U.S. leaders could be put in the dock in a tribunal that might have been established for another purpose entirely, pointing to the ICTY, where judges briefly flirted with the idea of prosecuting NATO for crimes against humanity for its bombing campaign during the war in Kosovo.

Not surprisingly, advocates of the concept of universal jurisdiction take a distinctly different view of its validity and applicability. Far from being a relatively new idea, they say,

universal jurisdiction has been exercised by U.S. courts (among others) for a considerable period of time. Hijackers and terrorists have often been extradited to face charges in the United States. Manuel NORIEGA was toppled from power in Panama by U.S. forces and then forced to stand trial on drug-smuggling charges. Israeli agents were in effect operating under the principle of universal jurisdiction when they abducted Adolf EICHMANN in 1961 from Buenos Aires and brought him to Israel to be tried for presiding over the extermination of 6 million Jews in Nazi-occupied Europe. Kenneth Roth, director of HUMAN RIGHTS WATCH, argued in a rebuttal to Kissinger (which also appeared in *Foreign Affairs*) that international agreements on human rights were fully intended by the signatories to have more teeth than he will acknowledge. "To the contrary," Roth writes, "the Torture Convention of 1984, ratified by 124 governments including the United States, requires states either to prosecute any suspected torturer found on their territory, regardless of where the torture took place, or to extradite the suspect to a country that will do so." He also points out that the Geneva convention of 1949 on the conduct of war, which was ratified by 189 countries including the United States, "require each participating state to 'search for' persons who have committed grave breaches of the conventions and to 'bring such persons, regardless of nationality, before its own courts' "—as succinct a definition of universal jurisdiction as it is possible to get. It is not the concept of extraterritorial jurisdiction that is so new, says Roth, but rather "the willingness of some governments to fulfill this duty against those in high places."

Increasingly, national courts are becoming more aggressive in pursuing war criminals and human rights abusers. In some cases, magistrates in third countries have launched prosecutions because the courts in countries where the crimes have been committed will not or cannot bring the criminals to justice themselves. That is what happened in Cavallo's case. Because of amnesty laws in place at the time in his own country, he would have escaped prosecution. It took a Spanish court to indict him and a Mexican court to extradite him to Madrid. This case, while important, is hardly unique. Were it not for the actions of national courts, it is likely that many Bosnian war criminals, Rwandan killers, and other Argentine torturers like Cavallo would still be at large and not be held to account for their crimes. In 2004 the U.S. Supreme Court affirmed the doctrine of universal jurisdiction—at least in civil cases—when it ruled that the ALIEN TORT CLAIMS ACT, an 18th-century statute, had broad application. Under the statute, for example, an individual can bring a civil suit in the United States against someone who tortured him in a third country.

Similarly, Roth challenges Kissinger's attack on the ICC because the crimes detailed in its establishing treaty are "vague and highly susceptible to politicized application." This is not the case at all, Roth asserts, pointing out that the treaty's definition of war crimes echoes that found in the Pentagon's own manuals. The definition is derived from the Genocide Convention of 1948 as well as the GENEVA CONVENTIONS and their ADDITIONAL PROTOCOLS TO THE GENEVA CONVENTIONS adopted in 1977. The United States itself is a signatory to all of these treaties. Moreover, the ICC borrowed the definition of crimes against humanity from the NUREMBERG CHARTER, which proscribes conduct that even Kissinger states is "self-evident[ly]" wrong. Nor does Roth envision much danger of an out-of-control prosecutor bringing capricious indictments since a simple majority of governments that ratified the treaty setting up the court can remove a prosecutor. A two-thirds vote of signatories can remove a judge. The absence of a jury system in the ICC is no reason to dispute its authority, Roth argues, citing martial-law courts in the United States that also do not use juries.

While it can be argued that the Belgian courts had overstepped their bounds by allowing lawsuits to be filed against high-profile political leaders and military officials in other countries, defenders of universal jurisdiction contend that there is little reason to fear courts routinely extraditing suspects simply out of political motives or a desire for retribution. Governments routinely deny extradition to courts, as British judges did in Pinochet's case. Foreign requests for extradition are also regularly denied by governments, especially when political concerns trump the prospect of prosecuting an individual.

See also BELGIAN WAR CRIMES TRIBUNAL; HELSINKI ACCORDS; ORGANIZATION FOR SECURITY AND COOPERATION IN EUROPE; ROME STATUTE OF THE INTERNATIONAL CRIMINAL COURT; WAR CRIMES, CATEGORIZATION OF.

Further Reading:

Ball, Howard. *Prosecuting War Crimes and Genocide: The Twentieth-Century Experience.* Lawrence: University Press of Kansas, 1999.

Beigbeder, Yves, and Theo van Boven. *Judging War Criminals: The Politics of International Justice.* Sidney, Australia: Palgrave Macmillan, 1999.

Bloxham, Donald. *Genocide on Trial: War Crimes Trials and the Formation of Holocaust History and Memory.* Oxford: Oxford University Press, 2003.

Brysk, Alison, ed. *Globalization and Human Rights.* Berkeley: University of California Press, 2002.

Cooper, Belinda, and Richard Goldstone. *War Crimes: The Legacy of Nuremberg.* New York: TV Books Inc., 1999.

Dormann, Knut, and Louise Doswald-Beck. *Elements of War Crimes under the Rome Statute of the International Criminal Court: Sources and Commentary.* Cambridge: Cambridge University Press, 2003.

Jinks, Derek. *The Rules of War: The Geneva Conventions in the Age of Terror.* Oxford: Oxford University Press, 2005.

Kissinger, Henry. *Does America Need a Foreign Policy?: Toward a Diplomacy for the 21st Century.* New York: Simon & Schuster; Touchstone edition, 2002.

Pilloud, Claude. *Commentary on the Additional Protocols of 8 June 1977 to the Geneva Conventions of 12 August 1949.* Boston: Brill Academic Publishers, 1987.

Roberts, Adam, and Richard Guelff. *Documents on the Laws of War.* Oxford: Oxford University Press, 2000.

Roth, Kenneth, ed. *Torture: A Human Rights Perspective.* New York: New Press, 2005.

Shelton, Dinah. *International Crimes, Peace, and Human Rights: The Role of the International Criminal Court.* Ardsley, N.Y.: Transnational Publishers, Inc., 2000.

Trombly, Maria. *Journalist's Guide to the Geneva Conventions.* Indianapolis: Society of Professional Journalists, 2000.

unlawful imprisonment

Unlawful imprisonment refers to the confinement of civilians during a conflict. INTERNATIONAL HUMANITARIAN LAW covers unlawful imprisonment in both international and internal conflicts. However, the law is much more explicit and extensive in its application to the former than it is to the latter. In general, the use of imprisonment as a form of persecution because of a person's nationality, religion, or ethnic group is banned. Under the Fourth Geneva Convention of 1949 unlawful confinement in an international conflict is considered a grave breach of the law. The INTERNATIONAL CRIMINAL TRIBUNAL FOR THE FORMER YUGOSLAVIA (ICTY), hearing cases involving the Balkan conflict of the 1990s, has ruled that unlawful confinement—which it defined as "seizure, collection, segregation, and forced transfer of civilians to camps"—is a crime against humanity. There is an exception under Article 42 of the Fourth Convention, which does allow a "detaining power" to intern people who pose a threat to its security—espionage, for instance, would constitute such a threat—if "absolutely necessary" or if the person has committed certain acts—such as sabotage or belonging to "organizations whose object is to cause disturbances"—against the detaining power. In addition, civilians may be temporarily relocated from their homes if it is required for security reasons or for their own safety, but the detaining power is obliged to treat them humanely; ensure that they have adequate food, medicine, and shelter in their new home; and make certain that they are returned home as soon as circumstances permit. Civilians may also be interned if "necessary, for imperative reasons of security, to take safety measures concerning protected persons." However, an individual cannot be interned simply because he or she is an enemy national. Detainees are permitted to keep personal possessions; seizure of personal articles or valuables by the detaining power is banned. A detaining power can arrest and intern a person for a criminal act but must guarantee that the suspect receives a fair trial.

The law is less explicit about when civilians may be interned during an internal armed conflict. ARTICLE 3 COMMON TO THE GENEVA CONVENTIONS, which applies to internal conflicts, states that "persons taking no active part in the hostilities . . . shall in all circumstances be treated humanely, without any adverse distinction founded on race, color, religion or faith, sex, birth or wealth, or any other similar criteria." Article 3 also prohibits "violence to life . . . in particular murder of all kinds, mutilation, cruel treatment and torture" and "the passing of sentences and the carrying out of executions without previous judgment pronounced by a regularly constituted court." Additional Protocol II of 1977 requires that any civilians who are confined in a conflict must be humanely treated. Prisoners must be protected from attack and provided with adequate resources including medicines and health care if required. Detainees cannot be held in close, unhealthy quarters unless it is necessary to "safeguard their health." In addition, they must be allowed to practice their faith without interference. The INTERNATIONAL COMMITTEE OF THE RED CROSS (ICRC) has a mandate to monitor conditions in any internment camps established by a detaining power during a conflict although the ICRC has been barred from making inspections in some conflicts, notably the Bosnian War when Serbs prevented any ICRC monitors from visiting internment camps where Muslims were being held.

See also ADDITIONAL PROTOCOLS TO THE GENEVA CONVENTIONS; GENEVA CONVENTIONS.

Further Reading:

Berry, Nicholas O. *War and the Red Cross: The Unspoken Mission.* New York: St. Martin's Press, 1997
Gutman, Roy, ed. *Crimes of War: What the Public Should Know.* New York: W. W. Norton & Company, 1999.
International Committee of the Red Cross. *International Law Concerning the Conduct of Hostilities: Collection of Hague Conventions and Some Other Treaties.* Geneva: International Committee of the Red Cross, 1989.

Uruguay, human rights violations in

A modern democracy today, Uruguay has yet to undertake a full investigation of grave human rights abuses that occurred in the "dirty war" of 1975–85, a period during which the country was run by a military dictatorship. As of 2004 the government had failed to investigate or prosecute any active or retired military official for TORTURE or murder committed while the military held power. Like other dirty wars in Latin America (which also took place in Argentina, Bolivia, Chile, Brazil, and Paraguay), the one in Uruguay involved a confrontation between an authoritarian regime and leftist insurgents and their supporters. Legal action involving suspects was halted in 1986 under an AMNESTY law, which even its sponsors say was passed under pressure from the military. Nonetheless, Uruguayan voters approved the law in a national referendum.

One loophole remained in the law that allowed investigations into the fate of the estimated 160 people who were "disappeared" and whose cases have never been resolved; this loophole has been employed in Chile. Even so, neither the government of Uruguayan presidents Julio Sanguinetti (1985–90 and 1995–2000) and Luis Lacalle (1990–95) took any steps to initiate investigations. (Most of the disappeared were detained in Argentina, presumably in collaboration with the military regime in that country.) A peace commission was established in 2000 by President Jorge Batlle to fulfill Article 4 of the amnesty law, which covers DISAPPEARANCES. The commission did little more than state that 26 people had been tortured and killed in Uruguay and that their bodies were cremated and dumped into the sea. Not surprisingly, families of the victims were not satisfied. "We believe that now it is Uruguay's turn. We have high expectations and hopes, because of the new government," said a representative of Mothers and Relatives of Detained-Disappeared Uruguayans. The situation might change if Tabaré Vázquez, who was elected president in October 2004, fulfills his promise to emphasize human rights issues during his term, which ends in 2009.

Many of the officers responsible for the abuses have not shied away from public attention. They regularly gather on national holidays and commemorate comrades who were killed in what they call "the war on sedition," referring to the suppression of the Tupamaro National Liberation Movement (MLN), a leftist guerrilla movement that they blame for any human rights abuses. Founded in 1963, the guerrilla group emerged at a time when Uruguay's democratic welfare state was collapsing and a political stalemate had developed between the two major political parties. The Tupamaros took their name (as did a later Peruvian insurgency) from the legendary 18th-century Inca chief Tupac Amaru, who had resisted the Spanish invaders. Intent on transforming Uruguay into a Marxist state, the Tupamaros became the forerunner of and model for several similar Marxist guerrilla groups in Latin America. They initiated their insurgency with a series of bank robberies to fund their terrorist operations. In 1968 they launched their insurgency in earnest, carrying out a string of terrorist attacks, including assassinations, bombings, and spectacular kidnappings, taking hostage several British and United

States citizens to gain international attention. In the late 1970s the Tupamaros briefly threatened to overrun the capital of Montevideo. In response the military cracked down, and over the next few years the army assassinated 300 guerrillas and locked up another 3,000. When democracy was restored in 1985, imprisoned Tupamoros were freed, and the former insurgent group became a legal political party.

Nevertheless, the majority of the human rights violations that took place in Uruguay occurred after the Tupamaros were defeated in 1972. The military crackdown occurred at a turbulent time characterized by labor strikes, student demonstrations, and militant street violence. The Tupamaros had attracted public attention by kidnapping prominent figures and trying them before special "People's Courts." "Unlike other Latin-American guerrilla groups," the *New York Times* stated in 1970, "the Tupamaros normally avoid bloodshed when possible. They try instead to create embarrassment for the Government and general disorder." As the government cracked down, the Tupamaros responded with increasing violence. The military had significant support from outside its borders—specifically from other states in Latin America and from the United States. Concerns about the spread of communist influence in Latin America had prompted Washington to provide assistance to several military regimes in the Southern Cone of South America. One of the men responsible for the secret U.S. effort in Montevideo was Dan Mitrione, nominally head of the Office of Public Safety (OPS), a division of the U.S. Agency for International Development (USAID). In an interview given to a leading Brazilian newspaper in 1970, the former Uruguayan chief of police intelligence, Alejandro Otero, credited Mitrione and other U.S. advisers for refining the practice of TORTURE in Uruguay by introducing psychological methods. For example, the police would play a tape of women and children screaming in a room adjacent to the prisoner's cell and tell the prisoner that he was hearing his family being tortured. "The violent methods which were beginning to be employed," said Otero, "caused an escalation in Tupamaro activity. Before then their attitude showed that they would use violence only as a last resort." Mitrione was later killed, and in 1977 a Tupamoro adherent was sentenced to 30 years in prison for the assassination.

Torture by security forces became so common that the Uruguayan Senate launched an investigation. After a five-month study, the senate commission concluded unanimously that torture in Uruguay had become a "normal, frequent and habitual occurrence," which was not limited to the Tupamaros. The commission cited such methods as the use of electric shocks to the genitals, electric needles under the fingernails, burning with cigarettes, and use of psychological torture. Even pregnant women were brutal-ized. A death squad, composed largely of police officers, began to conduct operations marked by assassinations, kidnappings, and bombing of homes of suspected Tupamaro sympathizers. The restoration of democracy in the mid-1980s has fostered a spirit of reconciliation. Several former insurgents who have been released from prison now sit in the national legislature.

See also OPERATION CONDOR.

Further Reading:

Davis, William Columbus. *Warnings from the Far South: Democracy versus Dictatorship in Uruguay, Argentina, and Chile.* New York: Praeger Publishers, 1995.

Gonzalez, Luis E. *Political Structures and Democracy in Uruguay.* Notre Dame, Ind.: University of Notre Dame Press, 1992.

Hampstein, Elizabeth. *Uruguay Nunca Mas: Human Rights Violations, 1972–1985.* Philadelphia: Temple University Press, 1993.

Ustache (Ustaše, Ustasha)

The Ustache was an extremist Croatian movement that began as a terrorist organization and later turned into a powerful fascist political party. Literally, *Ustache* means "rebellion." When World War II broke out and the Germans and Italians took over what was then the Kingdom of Yugoslavia, the Ustache aligned itself with the occupation forces and was installed as head of a puppet state. In their four years in power, they carried out a campaign of terror against Serbs, Muslims, Jews, Rom (Gypsies), and other minorities in Croatia and Bosnia and Herzegovina. It is estimated that the Ustache might have killed as many as 500,000 Serbs alone in what amounted to GENOCIDE. Executions were carried out by any means possible, including bullets, axes, knives, and chainsaws. In addition to the killings, the Ustache were responsible for uprooting and expelling hundreds of thousands of minorities from their homes and the forcible conversion of Eastern Orthodox Serbs to Catholicism, the dominant faith of Croatia.

The reign of the Ustache was arguably the most barbaric of any regime collaborating with the Nazis. The group was founded in 1929 as a nationalist political movement. Its cofounder, Ante PAVELIĆ, would later become the head of the Independent State of Croatia (which included parts of Bosnia and Herzegovina). To assert its authority, the Ustache also relied on military units—the Ustasha Army (Ustaška Vojnica)—which eventually could muster up to 76,000 men. In September 1944 Josef Broz (Tito), the leader of Yugoslav partisans fighting the German occupation, made a secret deal with Joseph STALIN that allowed the Red Army to enter Yugoslavia on the condition that the Soviet force help to eliminate the remnants of the German army and their Ustache allies. Seeing that the end was near, Ustache leaders, including Pavelić, fled the country, many taking refuge in Austria and later in South America. A number of Ustache members, however, were extradited and tried by the the postwar Yugoslav Communist government under Tito's rule.

See also CROATIA, HUMAN RIGHTS VIOLATIONS IN; TUDJMAN, FRANJO; YUGOSLAVIA, WAR CRIMES IN.

Further Reading:

Goldstein, Ivo. *Croatia: A History.* Montreal: McGill-Queen's University Press, 2000.

Muñoz, Antonio J. *For Croatia and Christ: The Croatian Army in World War II, 1941–1945.* Bayside, N.Y.: Europa Books Inc., 2004.

Tanner, Marcus. *Croatia: A Nation Forged in War.* New Haven, Conn.: Yale University Press, 2001.

Uzbekistan, human rights violations in

Uzbekistan gained its independence in the wake of the collapse of the former Soviet Union in 1991. With 25 million people, it is the most populous nation in the region. Uzbekistan also boasts the largest armed forces in central Asia, and in the aftermath of the terrorist attacks on September 11, 2001, has become an important strategic ally of the United States. It also has one of the worst human rights records of any of the former Soviet republics. Political opposition cannot freely function, the media are under state control, and religious and political dissension is dealt with severely by security forces. Poverty is endemic, and economic progress halting at best. A 2003 World Bank report observed that living standards were among the lowest in the former Soviet Union. Uzbekistan remains stubbornly independent as well, resisting cooperation with other central Asian republics even at the risk of heightened interregional tensions.

Since independence, Uzbekistan has been steered by the one-man rule of Islam Karimov, a onetime Communist Party leader. In 2000 he won the presidency in an election in which he ran unopposed; two years later he staged a referendum that extended his term two years beyond the initial five-year term. In 2003 the parliament granted him immunity from prosecution in the unlikely event that he leaves office voluntarily. The growth of militant Islamic groups has provided a pretext for Karimov to crack down on the opposition, with security forces targeting nonviolent Islamic movements in particular. There is some debate among political analysts as to just how serious a threat the Islamic terrorist groups actually pose to Uzbekistan's security. In 1999 more than a dozen people died in a series of bomb blasts in the capital of Tashkent that were blamed on "religious extremists." Karimov declared that these fundamentalists intended to destabilize the country and kill him.

Several thousand people have been thrown in jail because of their religious affiliation. Those Muslims who practice their faith outside state-approved mosques or other religious institutions are especially at risk of arrest. In the past year alone, HUMAN RIGHTS WATCH gathered materials on the trials of hundreds of individuals facing charges based on their religious practices and affiliations. In March 2004 Tashkent was again gripped by several days of bombings and gun battles between suspected Islamic militants and police. Scores were killed in the ensuing chaos, prompting human rights groups to fear that the government would use the incident to become even more repressive. Already an estimated 4,000 members of Hizb ut-Tahrir (Party of Liberation), which advocates the peaceful establishment of an Islamic state in Uzbekistan, have been detained on charges stemming from their affiliation with the group. Human rights groups and independent analysts estimate that Uzbek prisons hold as many as 7,000 political prisoners altogether.

Islamic groups are not the only ones to suffer from the crackdown. Political opposition groups and parties are also banned, and any expression of political dissent is ruthlessly suppressed. Members of outlawed political parties—Erk ("Freedom") Democratic Party and Birlik ("Unity")—are persecuted and harassed by police. Human rights advocates are also are routinely imprisoned or persecuted. The law requires that all independent political, religious, or human rights organizations register with the government. But the government makes it almost impossible for organizations it opposes to do so. The government has begun to impose onerous restrictions on the registration of international human rights groups, including Human Rights Watch, so as to minimize the possibility that abuses by the regime will be reported. The country's own media are hardly in a position to press for change. Although officially government censorship has been lifted, journalists practice self-censorship, saying nothing to criticize the government or its leader. Topics such as political opposition, corruption, or civil liberties are considered too sensitive to be raised. Those journalists who break the silence often find themselves in prison for their presumption.

According to both the United Nations and the U.S. State Department, the use of TORTURE in Uzbekistan is "systemic." In May 2003 alone, Human Rights Watch documented four new deaths in custody apparently due to torture. Judges regularly discount numerous allegations of torture by defendants charged with nonviolent crimes and convict them anyway. Few police officers or security agents have had to face trial for torture or killing prisoners. Even in the face of international pressure to investigate these abuses, the government has done little to investigate any allegations of torture.

Uzbekistan occupies a strategic position in the region because it shares a border with Afghanistan. Since the 9/11 terrorist attacks, the government has allowed the United States to establish a military presence on its territory. As a result, Washington has treated the Karimov regime with unusual delicacy. To placate the United States and ensure annual State Department certification—a necessary step if it is to receive continual assistance—Tashkent has responded with small gestures. The government, for instance, insisted that it had changed its legal definition of torture to bring it in line with the CONVENTION AGAINST TORTURE. Nonetheless, few concrete steps have been taken to actually do anything about putting a stop to it.

In another step aimed at defusing international criticism, the government stages well-publicized amnesties, releasing religious and political prisoners at regular intervals, although the releases are often provisional—the freed prisoners must abide by certain conditions—and the number of people released minimal. The government has also opened up the country for inspections of prison facilities by a UN special rapporteur and human rights groups, but these gestures have yet to result in any dramatic changes in policy, according to human rights advocates. The State Department formally acknowledged the lack of progress in correcting human rights abuses, and in January 2004 it decertified Uzbekistan for aid under a U.S. nonproliferation-assistance program, which is intended to help former Soviet republics get rid of nuclear, chemical, and BIOLOGICAL WEAPONS. Even though it received a waiver, allowing such assistance

to continue, the decertification, it was hoped, would send a powerful message to the Karimov regime about the need to take concerted action.

The effectiveness of such diplomatic action was called into question after violence erupted in the southern city of Andijan in May 2005. Protests were triggered by the arrests of 23 businessmen, supposedly for supporting fundamentalist Islamic causes. Gunmen freed them and several other prisoners as well. In the crackdown that followed, security forces fired on thousands of protesters gathered in the main square, killing several. Reports of the dead varied from ten to two or three hundred, many of them reportedly civilians. The harsh response of the regime indicated how seriously the Karimov regime considered the uprising, which it blamed on Islamic militants. After the fall of the government in neighboring Kyrgyzstan only a couple of months previously, it was clear that unrest was spreading through the former Soviet republics of central Asia. No one was willing to predict where it would end.

Further Reading:

Akbarzadeh, Shahram. *Uzbekistan and the United States: Authoritarianism, Islamism and Washington's New Security Agenda.* London: Zed Books, 2005.

Rashid, Ahmed. *Taliban: Militant Islam, Oil, and Fundamentalism in Central Asia.* New Haven, Conn.: Yale University Press, 2001.

Velpke Baby Farm

The Velpke Baby Farm—a home established in Velpke, Germany, for infant children of Polish female workers—achieved notoriety after the end of World War II when it was revealed that most of the children had sickened or died because of deliberate neglect on account of actions by Nazi officials. Several individuals associated with the baby farms—principally Heinrich Gerike—were tried for war crimes as a result, charged with "killing by willful neglect of a number of children."

The children had been compulsorily separated from their parents so that their parents—deported Poles—would not be distracted from their work on nearby farms to maintain the supply of food. In May 1944 Gerike, a high-ranking official (*Kreisleiter*) in nearby Helmstedt, was ordered to build a home to house the children. Gerike settled for a corrugated iron hut without running water, light, telephone, or a separate clinic. As a matron to run the home, he chose a former German teacher named Valentina Bilien, who had no experience caring for infants or children. Gerike ordered her not to return the children to their mothers or send any to the hospital if they took sick, although she was allowed to "call in a doctor if necessary." Bilien was assigned four helpers. At no time during the six months that the baby farm was in operation did Gerike express any interest in the deaths or trouble to visit the home to inspect conditions there. When Bilien realized that some children were dying because they needed their mothers' milk she relented and sent some back to their mothers, but once her action was discovered, she was admonished not to do so again in the future.

More than 80 Polish infants died from what was described in the indictment as "general weakness, dysentery, and what they called catarrh of the intestines." What made this case so unusual was that in contrast to most crimes of which Nazi war criminals were accused, this was a crime not of commission but rather of omission—that is, the children were mistreated and died because of neglect rather than because of violence done to them. Nonetheless, the prosecutor contended that the accused were in breach of Article 46 of the Regulations Annexed to the Hague Convention of 1907, which states: "Family honor and rights, individual life, and private property, as well as religious convictions and worship, must be respected. Private property may not be confiscated." In addition, he pointed out that international law forbids the killing of innocent or defenseless people in any conquered area "either in their own country or in the country of the occupying power." The prosecutor also made a novel case in which he maintained that the accused had also violated laws forbidding an OCCU-PYING POWER to deport slave labor from the occupied country to its own territory in the first place. The Polish parents forced to work on the farms, he pointed out, fell into this category. Their status, he argued, should also apply to their children, who were born to them in captivity. Four of the defendants, including Gerike and Bilien, were found guilty while two others were acquitted. Bilien was sentenced to 15 years' imprisonment, and Gerike and another defendant were sentenced to death and hanged.

Vergès, Jacques (1925–) *French lawyer*

The French lawyer Jacques Vergès, known as "the Devil's Advocate," has courted more than his share of controversy defending such notorious figures as Nazi war criminal Klaus BARBIE and Carlos the Jackal, the Venezuelan-born terrorist. More recently Vergès announced that he was representing former Yugoslav dictator Slobodan MILOŠEVIĆ (although Milošević begged to differ), and he has long claimed friendships with former Khmer Rouge leaders, including the late POL POT, who were responsible for the deaths of nearly a million Cambodians while they were in power. Even before trial dates had been set, Vergès declared that he had agreed to represent Saddam HUSSEIN and Saddam's foreign minister, Tariq Aziz.

Born in Thailand and raised on Reunion Island, Vergès fought with the Free French Army under General Charles de Gaulle during World War II, but he later became a dedicated communist. He identified in particular with anti-colonialist insurgents, and he took on several cases of Algerians charged with sabotage against French colonial rule. One of his clients was a woman named Djamila Bouhired, who was convicted and sentenced to death for planting bombs in cafés in Algiers. Vergès succeeded in getting her sentence commuted and later married her.

In spite of his communist leanings, Vergès was equally prepared to lend his legal expertise to radical rightists and fascists as well. It did not appear to matter what his defendants' politics were as long as they were sufficiently radical or militant in expressing them. He has defended Palestinians charged with attacks against Israeli civilians as well as neo-Nazi bombers. In 1987 he enthusiastically seized the opportunity to defend Klaus Barbie, the former GESTAPO chief known as "the Butcher of Lyon," who was implicated in the TORTURE and killing of hundreds of Jews. Barbie, Vergès told the court, was no worse than French soldiers who had committed atrocities in French colonial wars. In spite of his lawyer's spirited representation, Barbie was sentenced to life in prison on 341 charges.

Vergès had no better luck defending Illich Ramirez Sanchez, also known as Carlos the Jackal, who was convicted in 1997 of killing two French secret agents and a Lebanese revolutionary, though the crimes attributed to him include a slew of bombings, kidnappings, and hijackings. "He is a fascist," one of Vergès's detractors told CBS, and went on to describe the lawyer as "anti-democrat, anti-liberal (and) anti-Jew. . . . But he's a clever man. You can be a fascist and be a clever man."

Further Reading:
Bower, Tom. *Klaus Barbie, the Butcher of Lyons.* New York: Pantheon Books, 1984.
Dabringhaus, Erhard. *Klaus Barbie: The Shocking Story of How the U.S. Used This Nazi War Criminal as an Intelligence Agent.* New York: Acropolis Books, 1984.

victims, rights of

International law, as first spelled out in the Hague Convention of 1907, makes states liable for paying compensation to victims of violations of the convention on the grounds that the state is "responsible for all acts committed by persons forming part of its armed forces." In practice, however, victims seldom turn to the very state whose military abused them for restitution. It is more likely that in times of conflict victims will seek help from the INTERNATIONAL COMMITTEE OF THE RED CROSS (ICRC), which has the mandate under the GENEVA CONVENTIONS of ensuring the protection of civilians caught up in a conflict as well as PRISONERS OF WAR. The ICRC has the responsibility of monitoring the treatment of civilians and prisoners of war under an OCCUPYING POWER to ascertain their well-being; the ICRC is also charged with reuniting victims with their families as soon as circumstances permit.

The UNITED NATIONS HIGH COMMISSIONER FOR REFUGEES (UNHCR) assumes responsibility for both REFUGEES—civilians who are forced to seek refuge across international borders—and INTERNALLY DISPLACED PERSONS (IDPs) who are uprooted from their homes and are relocated within their own country. The problem of settling—or resettling—refugees and IDPs has grown exponentially in recent years because of the proliferation of internal conflicts throughout the world. Nongovernmental organizations (NGOs) such as the ICRC, DOCTORS WITHOUT BORDERS, OXFAM, Care, and so on, are coming under increasing pressure from belligerents in many conflicts who frequently ignore their neutrality and attack aid workers. In many cases NGOs have simply pulled out of a beleaguered country, as Doctors Without Borders did in Afghanistan following attacks on its volunteers, further imperiling the conflicts victims. In the Bosnian War, the ICRC temporarily withdrew its workers after the head of the mission was deliberately killed in June 1992. In Burundi, three Red Cross workers were killed in 1996.

Even when international organizations such as the United Nations take an active role in the protection of civilians in conflicts, there is no guarantee that the victims will enjoy the safeguards to which they are entitled. This problem was vividly demonstrated in the Bosnian War when the United Nations declared certain parts of Bosnia and Herzegovina as SAFE HAVENS where Muslim civilians could seek sanctuary from Serb forces and enjoy UN protection. However, Serb forces overran one of these safe havens at Srebrinica without encountering any resistance from UN peacekeepers; they then proceeded to massacre some 7,000 Muslim men and boys.

Although in principle states have the obligation to prevent violations of international law or, failing that, to punish the offenders if violations do occur, in practice judicial institutions often refuse to address these cases. After the Bosnian War, for instance, Serbia and Croatia both resisted demands to try war criminals or hand them over to the INTERNATIONAL CRIMINAL TRIBUNAL FOR THE FORMER YUGOSLAVIA (ICTY) in The Hague. To many nationalists in both countries, the suspects were not regarded as criminals at all but rather as war heroes. Further, the law itself sometimes makes it difficult to determine whether a serious violation is occurring. The 1948 GENOCIDE CONVENTION, while requiring states to "prevent and to punish" GENOCIDE, provides no mechanism for assessing whether genocide is in fact taking place. Although tens of thousands of African Sudanese have been killed and driven from their homes in Darfur by Arab militias backed by the government, no consensus has emerged that the ethnic cleansing amounts to genocide. It should be noted that there is a provision in Additional Protocol I to the Geneva Conventions to establish a fact-finding commission to investigate charges of genocide. It also stipulates that both parties to a conflict agree before the commission can do anything at all, a situation that seldom arises, for obvious reasons.

The INTERNATIONAL CRIMINAL COURT (ICC) was established in 1998 under UN auspices in hope that it can rule on issues related to the rights of victims in the absence of action on the part of national governments. But because the United States and other countries have not recognized the authority of the court, it is unclear as to how much influence it will have. In the meantime the United Nations has set up other ad hoc courts to investigate war crimes committed in wars in the former Yugoslavia, Rwanda, and Sierra Leone while offering victims of those conflicts the satisfaction of seeing justice meted out to their oppressors. International law does allow victims to sue for violations of INTERNATIONAL HUMANITARIAN LAW, but they rarely have recourse to courts that could hear their cases. There are some exceptions. After the end of World War II, the West German government paid hundreds of millions of dollars in reparations to the survivors and families of victims of the Holocaust. In the United States, the ALIEN TORT CLAIMS ACT allows a victim of a human rights abuse to sue the perpetrator even if the parties are foreign nationals and the crime in question occurred in another country.

See also ADDITIONAL PROTOCOLS TO THE GENEVA CONVENTIONS; HAGUE CONVENTIONS.

Further Reading:
Dubber, Markus Dirk. *Victims in the War on Crime: The Use and Abuse of Victims' Rights.* New York: New York University Press, 2002.
Rieff, David. *A Bed for the Night: Humanitarianism in Crisis.* New York: Simon & Schuster, 2002.
Vaux, Anthony. *The Selfish Altruist: Relief Work in Famine and War.* London: Earthscan Publications, 2001.
Weissman, Fabrice. *In the Shadow of "Just Wars": Violence, Politics, and Humanitarian Action.* Ithaca, N.Y.: Cornell University Press, 2004.

Victims Trust Fund

The Victims Trust Fund was established by the INTERNATIONAL CRIMINAL COURT (ICC) to provide compensation or restitution to victims of the most serious crimes covered by its mandate. Victims include child soldiers, women who have been raped during conflicts, and civilians who have lost their homes as a result of fighting or atrocities. According to Article 75 of the Rome Statute, which established the court, the ICC has the right to order a defendant found guilty of crime to directly compensate the victim. Funds can be distributed either to individuals or to a collective group; by the same token, funds may be directed to individuals or channeled to aid organizations on behalf of several victims. Because the defendants may not have the resources to comply with the order to pay compensation, the fund also relies on additional funding from governments, international organizations, or individuals. The Victims Trust Fund is supervised by an independent board of directors.

See also ROME STATUTE OF THE INTERNATIONAL CRIMINAL COURT.

Further Reading:
Dormann, Knut, and Louise Doswald-Beck. *Elements of War Crimes under the Rome Statute of the International Criminal Court: Sources and Commentary.* Cambridge: Cambridge University Press, 2003.
Dubber, Markus Dirk. *Victims in the War on Crime: The Use and Abuse of Victims' Rights.* New York: New York University Press, 2002.
Gutman, Roy, ed. *Crimes of War: What the Public Should Know.* New York: W. W. Norton & Company, 1999.

Vieira de Mello, Sérgio (1948–2003) *UN envoy and human rights advocate*

A leading advocate of human rights, Sérgio Vieira de Mello served the UNITED NATIONS HIGH COMMISSIONER FOR REFUGEES (UNHCR) in several diplomatic posts over 33 years before his life was cut short by a bomb blast in Iraq. He was active in humanitarian and peace-keeping operations in BANGLADESH, SUDAN, CYPRUS, MOZAMBIQUE, AND PERU. In 2003 he was named by UN secretary general Kofi Annan to assume the post of UN representative in Iraq, which only a year before had been invaded by U.S.-backed coalition forces. He was killed in Baghdad during a terrorist bombing attack on August 19, 2003.

Known simply as Sérgio to his friends and colleagues, Vieira de Mello was born in Rio de Janeiro in 1948 and joined the United Nations in 1969 even as he continued to study philosophy and humanities at the University of Paris. His first major position was as senior political adviser to UN peacekeeping forces in Lebanon. Two years later he moved to UNHCR's headquarters in Geneva. From 1991 to 1996 he served in several top UN positions: as special envoy of the high commissioner for Cambodia, director of repatriation for the United Nations Transitional Authority in Cambodia (UNTAC), head of civil affairs of the United Nations Protection Force (UNPROFOR), and UN regional humanitarian coordinator for the Great Lakes Region of Africa. In 1996 Vieira de Mello was appointed UN assistant high commissioner for REFUGEES, and in January 1998 he became under secretary general for humanitarian affairs and emergency relief coordinator. He was instrumental in the creation of the UNITED NATIONS GUIDING PRINCIPLES ON INTERNAL DISPLACEMENT. Before assuming the post in Baghdad, he served as special representative of the UN secretary general in Kosovo and as UN transitional administrator in East timor.

In September 2002 Vieira de Mello was appointed UNITED NATIONS HIGH COMMISSIONER FOR HUMAN RIGHTS. In all of these many positions he proved himself a highly effective and pragmatic administrator and international civil servant. He is credited with instituting a program to protect and resettle Vietnamese refugees, overseeing the repatriation of 300,000 Cambodian refugees from Thailand, setting up a UN civil administration in Kosovo, and managing the political transition in East Timor.

Further Reading:

Feller, Erika, Volker Turk, and Frances Nicholson, eds. *Refugee Protection in International Law: UNHCR's Global Consultations on International Protection.* Cambridge: Cambridge University Press, 2003.

Groenewold, Julia and Doctors Without Borders. *World in Crisis: The Politics of Survival at the End of the Twentieth Century.* London: Routledge, 1996.

Helton, Arthur C. *The Price of Indifference: Refugees and Humanitarian Action in the New Century.* A Council on Foreign Relations Book. Oxford: Oxford University Press, 2002.

Hyndman, Jennifer. *Managing Displacement: Refugees and the Politics of Humanitarianism.* Minneapolis: University of Minnesota Press, 2000.

Ogata, Sadako, and Kofi Annan. *The Turbulent Decade: Confronting the Refugee Crises of the 1990s.* New York: W. W. Norton & Company, 2005.

Vienna Convention on Diplomatic Relations

The Vienna Convention on Diplomatic Relations, adopted on April 14, 1961, is intended to establish the basis for diplomatic relations and privileges as well as the immunities of a diplomatic mission. The Vienna Convention, however, has a direct bearing on citizens as well as diplomatic personnel based on a decision of the INTERNATIONAL COURT OF JUSTICE (better known as the World Court). In December 2004 the United States Supreme Court agreed to hear a case involving a Mexican national who was scheduled for execution in Texas. The question at issue was whether the execution of the convicted Mexican would constitute a violation of international law, which requires that a diplomatic representative from the country of the accused be present during the trial and sentencing. On March 31, 2004, the World Court ordered the United States to undertake "an effective review" of the convictions and sentences of the convicted man, José Ernesto Medellín, and 50 other Mexicans on death row in nine states. (Medellín had been convicted for a gang-related murder.) The World Court made its determination on the basis of the Vienna Convention. The convention, ratified by the United States in 1969, also calls upon a government that is detaining a foreign citizen to notify the prisoner "without delay" of his right to request help from a consul from his home country. This did not occur in Medellín's case. Mexico sued the United States in the World Court on behalf of Medellín and the other Mexican nationals sentenced to death by U.S. courts. The United States opposed Mexico's suit on the grounds as "an unjustified, unwise and ultimately unacceptable intrusion in the United States criminal justice system." Nonetheless, the World Court ruled in Mexico's favor. In 2005, after initially agreeing to accept the World Court's authority, the United States announced that it was withdrawing from the relevant protocol of the treaty on the grounds that the court was meddling in the U.S. legal system. The announcement, which seemed intended to placate foes of international institutions in the Bush White House and advocates of the death penalty, nonetheless represented a surprising about-face in view of the initial response from the White House. In its first response to the ruling, the Bush administration had acknowledged that the same provisions that guaranteed consular assistance to aliens on U.S. soil could apply to situations in foreign lands where American nationals were caught up in the legal system. Indeed, the United States had relied on the treaty when it took its case to the World Court demanding compensation for the Iranian authorities' taking of American diplomats as hostages in 1979–80.

Vietnam, human rights violations in

The Communist Vietnamese authorities have violated human rights on a frequent basis, although some improvements have taken place as the country has opened itself up to the outside world. And while the civilian authorities largely maintain control over the security forces, there are some elements that appear to act on their own initiative, which may account for a number of the serious human rights violations. But the larger problem remains the fact that the country is under one-party communist rule that denies the right of citizens to change their government. Freedoms of the press, assembly, association, and religion are all restricted. There are numerous incidents of arbitrary arrests and detention and beatings of suspects by police. Some prisoners reportedly died because of abuse while in police custody. According to the U.S. State Department *Country Report* of 2004, some DISAPPEARANCES have occurred as well. People are still being arrested because of their political opinions or for having participated in religious demonstrations and political protests. Arrests of political prisoners do not, however, occur on the same scale as they did in the immediate aftermath of the fall of South Vietnam in 1975 when the Communist North took over the whole country. The judiciary is not independent, and suspects have difficulty receiving fair and expeditious trials. The government infringes on privacy rights and has taken steps to limit citizens' access to the Internet.

In recent years, human rights groups have raised concerns about the actions of security forces in the Central Highlands, where political unrest among the indigenous Montagnards has led to a harsh crackdown. The turmoil began in February 2001 when many Montagnards staged demonstrations calling for religious freedom and return of ancestral lands. The military deployed special units that restrict the free movement of citizens in the troubled area. These units enforce a system of household registration and rely on block monitors to maintain watch over their neighbors. Many Montagnard Christians, a minority in a traditionally Buddhist-oriented nation, have been rounded up and arrested without warrants or formal charges and detained for unconscionable lengths of time. Apparently the authorities are convinced that religious gatherings—even when they are simple Christmas ceremonies—might develop into a forum for political dissent. Pledges by officials to respect religious freedom do not seem to be matched by actions.

See also FREE-FIRE ZONES; MY LAI MASSACRE; PHOENIX PROGRAM; TIGER FORCE.

Further Reading:
Karnow, Stanley. *Vietnam: A History.* New York: Penguin Books, 1997.
Lamb, David. *Vietnam, Now: A Reporter Returns.* New York: PublicAffairs, 2003.
Langguth, A. J. *Our Vietnam: The War 1954–1975.* New York: Simon & Schuster, 2002.

voluntary codes of conduct

Until recently, multinational corporations regarded human rights issues as of little or no concern, but revelations of corporate malfeasance and complicity in environmental and human rights abuses have led to a degree of soul-searching in corporate boardrooms. Corporations are beginning to realize that human rights issues should enjoy more recognition and that adherence to human rights enhances a company's reputation, making it more attractive for customers and clients while bolstering employee recruitment and morale. Several manufacturers of footwear and apparel in Southeast Asia and elsewhere, for instance, have tried to eliminate sweatshop conditions, improve the workplace, institute more equitable wages, and eliminate child labor. However, as human rights groups point out, these voluntary codes of conduct have built-in limitations. For one thing, they are voluntary—that is to say, there are no mechanisms for enforcement and no provision for monitoring by neutral bodies to ensure compliance. Nor are there any uniform standards for assessing compliance, which is now left up to local labor groups or nongovernmental organizations (NGOs) on an ad hoc basis. (Some initiatives have been undertaken by the Fair Labor Association and governments and NGOs to draw up industry standards for upholding human rights in the workplace.)

Voluntary codes, say human rights advocates, are generally drafted without consulting employees; indeed, workers may not even be aware that their employer has a code. Moreover, while the language in these codes may express lofty principles, it is often so ambiguous that it obliges the company to very little. There is the additional problem of reconciling the principles of a voluntary code with the laws or policies of a host country that may, for instance, forbid workers from organizing unions. In July 2004 the United Nations tried to jump into the breach by launching a Global Compact of business, labor, and civil society to promote social responsibility in the global economy. The compact includes some reporting requirements intended to make member corporations more accountable for their conduct. The compact has the support of companies in Europe, Africa, Asia, and South America, which to some extent belies the assertions by some U.S. corporations that a commitment to human rights—which might include higher pay for workers, for example—puts them at a competitive disadvantage. However, enforcement remains a problem. Human rights groups contend that for all the improvement that voluntary codes represent, the only real solution lies in instituting binding codes.

See also SULLIVAN PRINCIPLES.

Waldheim, Kurt (1918–) *UN secretary-general*

Until his reputation was irrevocably tarnished by revelations about his activities during World War II, Kurt Waldheim was a highly regarded Austrian diplomat who had attained the top post of the United Nations as secretary-general from 1971 to 1981. Waldheim's service in a German army unit in Yugoslavia during the war was not well known when he was elected to his first five-year term at the United Nations' helm. He had already earned a distinguished record of diplomatic service as Austria's permanent representative to the United Nations and later as its foreign minister. During his tenure as secretary-general, he tried to put an end to a number of conflicts—the Iraq-Iran war and the China-Vietnam war among them—without appreciable success. After serving two terms, he ran for an unprecedented third term but opposition from China forced his withdrawal.

Shortly after Waldheim stepped down as secretary-general stories, appeared in the press that he had been an officer in a German army unit that had committed atrocities in Yugoslavia during World War II. He adamantly denied that he knew anything about the crimes, and an international commission set up to investigate the matter found him innocent of any complicity in the atrocities. Waldheim ran for and won the presidency of Austria in spite of the scandal, but he was treated as an international pariah and denied a visa to travel to the United States based on the allegations. He did not run for a second term in 1992.

Further Reading:

Finger, Seymour Maxwell, and Arnold A. Saltzman. *Bending with the Winds: Kurt Waldheim and the United Nations.* New York: Praeger Publishers, 1990.

Ryan, James Daniel. *The United Nations under Kurt Waldheim, 1972–1981.* Lanham, Md.: Scarecrow Press, 2001.

Walleyn, Luc (1949–) *Belgian human rights advocate*

A Belgian judge, lawyer, and human rights advocate, Luc Walleyn has taken advantage of Belgium's former policy of bringing legal suits against accused human rights violators in cases involving other countries. (That policy has since been modified under U.S. pressure.) In recent years Walleyn has initiated lawsuits against Belgian soldiers participating in the peacekeeping operation in Somalia for racist behavior and has undertaken the defense of Belgian victims of the former military regime in Guatemala. Perhaps he is best known, though, for representing some 23 Palestinian survivors of massacres by Christian Phalange militias at the Sabra and Shatilla refugee camps in Lebanon in 1982. Approximately 2,000 Palestinians were killed after Israeli forces invaded Lebanon and briefly occupied the capital of Beirut. Israel was then aligned with Christian forces fighting Muslim factions in the Lebanese civil war. In 2001 Defense Minister Ariel Sharon (by then Israel's prime minister) was accused by the plaintiffs of being responsible for the massacres since Israeli forces were thought to be in control of the area of the camps and yet failed to intervene to stop the massacres. (A subsequent Israeli investigation did assign some of the blame for the events to Sharon.) When the complaint was announced, Israel's Foreign Ministry denounced the charges, saying, "Israel views with the utmost gravity the distorted, unfair, and intentionally hostile nature of the Panorama program. The timing of the program, 19 years after the events in question, shows a lack of good faith and an attempt to tarnish Israel and its leader [Sharon]." The case was later dropped.

As a former member of Avocats Sans Frontières (Lawyers Without Borders, ASF), Walleyn participated in ASF programs in Rwanda, Burundi, and Kosovo and represented the organization at the 1998 UN conference in Rome that established the INTERNATIONAL CRIMINAL COURT. Walleyn specializes in immigration law as well as in human rights and humanitarian law and serves as a lecturer in the chair for immigration law at the University of Antwerp and as a guest professor at the Institut des Hautes Etudes Politiques in Paris.

See also BELGIAN WAR CRIMES TRIBUNAL; SABRA AND SHATILLA, MASSACRES IN.

Wannsee Conference

On January 20, 1942, 15 top Nazi officials met in the Berlin suburb of Wannsee to decide the fate of the 11 million Jews living in Europe (including 330,000 in England). The conference, held at a villa on the shores of Lake Wannsee owned by the SS, was chaired by Reinhard HEYDRICH, the chief of the Reich Main Security Office and head of the German secret police apparatus. The objective of the conference was described in the minutes: "At the beginning of the discussion Chief of the Security Police and of the SD, SS-Obergruppenführer Heydrich, reported that the Reich Marshal [Hermann GÖRING] had appointed him delegate for the preparations for the FINAL SOLUTION of the Jewish question in Europe and pointed out that this discussion had been called for the purpose of clarifying fundamental questions. The wish of the Reich Marshal to have a draft sent to him concerning organizational, factual and material interests in relation to the final solution of the Jewish question in Europe makes necessary an initial common action of all central offices immediately concerned with these questions in order to bring their general activities into line."

By this point in the war, it was no longer thought feasible to eliminate so many people by the methods then in use—shooting and gassing using mobile vans. Although the EINSATZGRUPPEN—special death squads that operated behind advancing German forces—had killed over a million Jews and Slavs in conquered Soviet territory, they were not considered efficient or quick enough to meet the challenge.

Historians still debate when the Nazis determined on an official policy to annihilate European Jewry. Adolf HITLER had called for the execution of Jews in his book *Mein Kampf* (*My Struggle*), written in 1923, and in a speech delivered in Berlin the same year he had threatened the Jews with "total annihilation if a new world war should begin." Even if no explicit order was put in writing, there is general agreement that Hitler was responsible for putting the policy into effect. By late 1939 a special agency had been established under Adolf EICHMANN to organize the DEPORTATIONS of Jews from the occupied territories. The first gassing of Jews at a concentration camp (Auschwitz) took place on September 3, 1941, and the first test gassing by van a few months later. That same month the commander of one mobile unit known as extermination group A reported the execution of over 130,000 Jews. So the killings

of Jews were already well underway when the 15 SS officials gathered at the Wannsee villa.

The importance of the conference lay in the fact that it formalized as policy a systematic and massive extermination program. The participants also deliberated about how to distinguish the Jews subject to deportation to the death camps from those who were only partly Jewish. The minutes of the meeting were taken by Eichmann and edited by Heydrich, who carefully excised references to the intended extermination of Jews and substituted euphemisms in their place. Nonetheless, the document makes for chilling reading:

> The Reichsführer-SS and the Chief of the German Police [Chief of the Security Police and the SD] was entrusted with the official central handling of the final solution of the Jewish question without regard to geographic borders. The Chief of the Security Police and the SD then gave a short report of the struggle which has been carried on thus far against this enemy, the essential points being the following:
>
> a) the expulsion of the Jews from every sphere of life of the German people,
> b) the expulsion of the Jews from the living space of the German people.

The conferees weighed various "possible" solutions to the problem. Forced evacuations of Jews were considered only provisional, "but practical experience is already being collected which is of the greatest importance in relation to the future final solution of the Jewish question." Presumably, that "practical experience" referred to the experimentation with gassing Jews that was already occurring in Poland and the occupied parts of the Soviet Union. There were many impediments to putting the policy of extermination into effect, however: "The handling of the problem in the individual countries will meet with difficulties due to the attitude and outlook of the people there, especially in Hungary and Rumania. Thus, for example, even today the Jew can buy documents in Rumania that will officially prove his foreign citizenship." The issue of slave labor was discussed: "Under proper guidance, in the course of the final solution the Jews are to be allocated for appropriate labor in the East. Able-bodied Jews, separated according to sex, will be taken in large work columns to these areas for work on roads, in the course of which action doubtless a large portion will be eliminated by natural causes."

Wilhelm STUCKHART, the lawyer responsible for drafting the 1935 NUREMBERG LAWS banning Jews from Germany's public and economic life, asked how much "Jewish blood was enough to taint German purity" when determining how many people of "mixed blood" (partly Jewish) should be "sent east"—to the death camps of Poland. But there was no question that once taken into custody, no Jews could be liberated. "The possible final remnant will, since it will undoubtedly consist of the most resistant portion, have to be treated accordingly, because it is the product of natural selection and would, if released, act as the seed of a new Jewish revival (see the experience of history)."

See also CONCENTRATION CAMPS.

Further Reading:

Dawidowicz, Lucy. *A Holocaust Reader.* Library of Jewish Studies. Chicago: Behrman House Publishing, 1976.

Dwork, Deborah, and Robert Jan Van Pelt. *Holocaust: A History.* New York: W. W. Norton & Company, 2003.

Gilbert, Martin. *The Holocaust: A History of the Jews of Europe during the Second World War.* New York: Owl Books, 1987.

Lagnado, Lucette Matalon, and Sheila Cohn Dekel. *Children of the Flames: Dr. Josef Mengele and the Untold Story of the Twins of Auschwitz.* New York: Penguin Books, 1992.

Rees, Laurence. *Auschwitz: A New History.* New York: PublicAffairs, 2005.

Roseman, Mark. *The Wannsee Conference and the Final Solution: A Reconsideration.* New York: Metropolitan Books, 2002.

Wistrich, Robert S. *Hitler and the Holocaust.* Modern Library Chronicles. New York: Modern Library, 2001.

War Child Project

The War Child Project consists of a network of several independent organizations throughout the world working to help children affected by war. The War Child Project is based on the philosophy that it is morally impermissible to ignore the most helpless victims and that the protection and well-being of children is vital to the future of society. The project had its genesis in Britain when two filmmakers, Bill Leeson and David Wilson, returned from reporting on the plight of victims in the war in Bosnia in 1993. They were most appalled by the fact that civilians were at special risk of being made victims of the conflict. Even though they had no experience in philanthropy, they believed that they could be influential in gathering support for children using their contacts in media and entertainment. They received enough support to organize a convoy into the former Yugoslavia that was loaded with baking equipment to help feed REFUGEES in devastated parts of Bosnia and Herzegovina.

As the War Child Project grew, it received other sources of funding, including support from the UNITED NATIONS HIGH COMMISSIONER FOR REFUGEES and the European Union. It also had added support from celebrities such as the composer Brian Eno and the playwright Tom Stoppard. The War Child Project often works in partnership with local grassroots organizations, through both short-term emergency relief and long-term rehabilitation programs, to improve the living conditions of war-affected children. Branches of the War Child Project can be found in the United States, Italy, Canada, Ethiopia, Eritrea, and the Netherlands. Each organization is totally autonomous, with different trustees and financial structures.

See also CHILDREN'S RIGHTS.

Further Reading:

Apfel, Roberta, and Bennett Simon, eds. *Minefields in Their Hearts: The Mental Health of Children in War and Communal Violence.* New Haven, Conn.: Yale University Press, 1996.

Dodge, Cole P., and Magne Raundelen. *Reaching Children in War: Sudan Uganda and Mozambique.* London: Taylor & Francis, 1992.

Pran, Dith, comp. *Children of Cambodia's Killing Fields: Memoirs by Survivors.* Edited by Kim DePaul. New Haven, Conn.: Yale University Press, 1999.

Raymond, Alan. *Children in War.* New York: TV Books Inc, 2000.

Singer, P. W. *Children at War.* New York: Pantheon, 2005.

war crimes, categorization of

Efforts to impose restrictions on behavior in conflict are not new. The writings of the sixth-century Chinese scholar and soldier Sun Tzu refer to limitations on conduct in war. Both the ancient Greeks and the Hindus believed that certain practices in war should be prohibited. Generally speaking, war crimes are considered violations of war or INTERNATIONAL HUMANITARIAN LAW (IHL). One of the fundamental criteria, established by the trials of Nazi war criminals at the NUREMBERG TRIALS, is that criminal responsibility inheres in the individual. A suspect therefore cannot seek exoneration by claiming that he or she was acting under orders to commit a crime.

As far as is known, in 1474 Sir Peter von Hagenbach became the first person actually tried for war crimes. An emissary of Charles the Bold, duke of Burgundy (also known to his critics as Charles the Terrible), Hagenbach was instructed to impose order on the town of Breisach, on the Upper Rhine in present-day Germany. He carried out his instructions by means of murder, rape, illegal taxation, and confiscation of property. When he was finally ousted after a SIEGE, he was not put to death—at least not at once—but was rather tried by a special court set up by the archduke of Austria, who chose judges from among the ranks of each member of the coalition that had defeated his forces. (Similarly, judges on the Nuremberg Tribunal represented each of the Allies responsible for the defeat of Nazi Germany.) Hagenbach was charged with "trampling the laws of God and man," including murder, rape, perjury, and other *malefacta*—evil deeds. He was also accused of ordering mercenaries to invade private residences, where they would kill the male members of the family, leaving the women and children at their mercy. Hagenbach resorted to a line of defense that has become familiar. "Is it not known that soldiers owe absolute obedience to their superiors?" his counsel asked, contending that in any case the accused did not recognize any authority apart from the duke of Burgundy. Neither defense worked; Hagenbach was found guilty and put to death.

The 19th century saw several innovative attempts to codify the laws of war, among then the First Geneva convention (1864) in Europe and the LIEBER CODE (1863) in the United States. Further initiatives were taken to ban certain types of warfare in the HAGUE CONVENTIONS of 1899 and 1907—for example, the bombardment of undefended cities. In 1945 the Allies established a set of principles that would form the basis of prosecutions of Nazi war criminals at Nuremberg. War crimes were defined by the NUREMBERG CHARTER of the International Military Tribunal as "violations of the laws or customs of war," including murder, ill-treatment, or deportation of civilians in occupied territory; murder or ill-treatment of PRISONERS OF WAR; killing of HOSTAGES; plunder of public or private property; wanton destruction of municipalities; and devastation not militarily necessary." This document represented the first time that international humanitarian law had to be taken into account in judging culpability for war crimes. The four GENEVA CONVENTIONS of 1949 include as "grave breaches . . . any of the following acts, if committed against persons or property protected by the Convention: willful killing, torture or inhuman treatment, including biological experiments, willfully causing great suffering or serious injury to body or health, and extensive destruction and appropriation of property, not justified by military necessity and carried out unlawfully and wantonly." The conventions also consider as grave breaches (1) compelling a prisoner of war or civilian to serve in the forces of the hostile power, (2) willfully depriving a prisoner of war or protected civilian of the rights of a fair and regular trial, (3) unlawful deportation or transfer of a protected civilian, (4) unlawful confinement of a protected civilian, and (5) taking of hostages. These grave breaches would constitute war crimes. The 1977 ADDITIONAL PROTOCOLS TO THE GENEVA CONVENTIONS add to and elaborate on the grave breaches of international law as defined in the Geneva Conventions. Among other provisions, Additional Protocol 1 forbids certain types of MEDICAL EXPERIMENTS, targeting nondefended localities and civilian populations, the forced transfer of civilians by an OCCUPYING POWER, attacks on cultural property, and depriving individuals of a fair trial. Protocol I also calls on member states to try individuals accused of grave breaches or else hand the suspect over to a state willing to do so.

Because Protocol 1 only applies to international conflicts, PROTECTED PERSONS are defined as the wounded and sick, combatants, prisoners of war, and civilians captured by an occupying power. Additional Protocol II, which applies only to internal conflicts, carries no criminal liability for grave breaches of the law. As Steven R. Ratner points out in his essay on the subject for the CRIMES OF WAR PROJECT, nongrave breaches are not necessarily war crimes. Failure of a captive power to maintain a record of prisoners of war as required by law, for example, would be a violation of the Third Geneva Convention, but it would not necessarily be defined as a grave breach or rise to the level of a war crime. Violations could be considered illegal acts and thus become prosecutable by the state in which the violation occurred, but it would not be an indictable offense under the Geneva Convention or Additional Protocol I. Such a violation would not require a state to try or extradite the suspect to be tried elsewhere. "Distinguishing among nongrave breaches to determine which are crimes is not an exact science," Ratner admits, "though it would seem that the more serious nongrave breaches do incur individual responsibility. Even if an atrocity is not explicitly banned by international law, it may still be considered a crime as a violation 'of the laws and customs of war.' "

What would appear to be a theoretical distinction has crucial ramifications in light of the fact that such atrocities as those perpetrated by Joseph STALIN in the Soviet Union, the Khmer Rouge in Cambodia, Hutu militants in Rwanda, and Serb and Croatian forces in the Bosnian War are not considered war crimes. There have been several attempts to fill this gap by making violations not specifically covered by the Geneva Conventions or Additional Protocol I subject to prosecution in international courts. The ROME STATUTE OF THE INTERNATIONAL CRIMINAL COURT expands the number and types of crimes it covers by 26 beyond the grave breaches specified by the Geneva Conventions. Where international law is more ambiguous is in its application to civil conflicts. The Rome Statute of the INTERNATIONAL CRIMINAL COURT (ICC) lists as war crimes for internal conflicts four serious violations of ARTICLE 3 COMMON TO THE GENEVA CONVENTIONS—violence to life and person, attacks on personal dignity, hostage taking, and summary executions—as well as 12 serious violations of the laws and customs of war that include attacks on civilians, PILLAGE, rape, or mutilation. Article 3 forbids "violence to life and person," and "outrages upon personal dignity" against "persons taking no part in the hostilities." However, Article 3, which can be applied to civilians in internal conflicts, does not carry the same force of law as the provisions of the Geneva Conventions themselves. Under the tribunal's mandate, an individual can be prosecuted for such crimes as murder, ill-treatment, torture, mutilation, corporal punishment, rape, enforced prostitution, summary executions, hostage taking, COLLECTIVE PUNISHMENT, and PILLAGE. Similarly, the Statute of the INTERNATIONAL CRIMINAL TRIBUNAL FOR THE FORMER YUGOSLAVIA (ICTY) includes "serious violations of Common Article 3 of the Geneva Conventions."

Whatever the reach of the law, though, the problem of enforcement remains. As Ratner acknowledges, the "creation of a body of law criminalizing certain violations of the laws of war does not mean that war criminals will actually be prosecuted." States may prosecute nationals for war crimes committed on its own territory; in certain instances, states may rely on the principle of UNIVERSAL JURISDICTION to prosecute noncitizens who committed crimes in another country. Spanish judges, for instance, have initiated criminal prosecutions against Argentine and Chilean officials for torture and murder committed in their respective countries. Frequently, though, when states do prosecute citizens for crimes not specifically addressed by the Geneva Conventions or Additional Protocol I, they do not punish the offender severely or else allow him or her to escape prosecution altogether. In an attempt to find a solution to this problem, the United Nations has established ad hoc courts—such as the ICTY as well as the INTERNATIONAL CRIMINAL TRIBUNAL FOR RWANDA and the SPECIAL COURT FOR SIERRA LEONE—which can try suspected war criminals for both grave breaches of the Geneva Conventions and Additional Protocol I and crimes covered only by the law of the states where the crimes took place.

Further Reading:

Bassiouni, M. Cherif. *Crimes against Humanity in International Criminal Law.* Boston: Martinus Nijhoff, 1999.

Benson, Bruce. *The Enterprise of Law: Justice without the State.* San Francisco: Pacific Research Institute for Public Policy, 1990.

Dormann, Knut, and Louise Doswald-Beck. *Elements of War Crimes under the Rome Statute of the International Criminal Court: Sources and Commentary.* Cambridge: Cambridge University Press, 2003.

Gutman, Roy, ed. *Crimes of War: What the Public Should Know.* New York: W. W. Norton & Company, 1999.

Hagan, John. *Justice in the Balkans: Prosecuting War Crimes in the Hague Tribunal.* Chicago Series in Law and Society. Chicago: University of Chicago Press, 2003.

Hazan, Pierre, and James Thomas Snyder. *Justice in a Time of War: The True Story behind the International Criminal Tribunal for the Former Yugoslavia.* Eugenia and Hugh M. Stewart Series on Eastern Europe. Austin: Texas A&M University Press, 2004.

Ratner, Steven. "War Crimes, Categories of," *Crimes of War: What the Public Should Know.* Roy Guttman, editor. New York: W. W. Norton & Co., 1999.

Romano, Cesare, Andre Nollkaemper, and Jann K. Kleffner, eds. *Internationalized Criminal Courts and Tribunals: Sierra Leone, East Timor, Kosovo, and Cambodia.* International Courts and Tribunals Series. Oxford: Oxford University Press, 2004.

Shelton, Dinah. *International Crimes, Peace, and Human Rights: The Role of the International Criminal Court.* Ardsley, N.Y.: Transnational Publishers, Inc., 2000.

United Nations War Crimes Commission. *Law Reports of Trials of War Criminals: Four Genocide Trials.* Boulder, Colo.: Lynne Rienner Publishers, 1992.

war criminals of Japan

With few exceptions—Hideki TOJO for one—most of those Japanese war criminals found guilty of war crimes, crimes against peace, and CRIMES AGAINST HUMANITY by the International Military Tribunal for the Far East (the TOKYO TRIALS) and by other courts in China and the Philippines are not as well known as the Nazi officials brought before the NUREMBERG TRIALS. However, some individuals are worth noting both because of the nature of the crimes they committed and because of the legal precedent that their cases established in war crimes tribunals.

Abe Koso

Admiral Abe Koso was responsible for the execution of several American PRISONERS OF WAR during the Pacific campaign in World War II, a crime for which he was subsequently convicted and hanged. The incident stemmed from an audacious raid in summer 1942 by U.S. Marines on Japanese-held Butaritari Island in the Gilbert Islands. The raid, launched on the night of August 16, was intended to destroy enemy installations, gain as much intelligence as possible, and divert Japanese attention from U.S. operations on Guadalcanal and Tulagi, but the operation was hampered by terrible weather. During the fighting 18 marines were slain, and nine members of the force were left behind when the marines retreated. The stranded marines were captured by the Japanese, who transferred them to the island of Kwajalein. There the prisoners came under the authority of Vice Admiral Abe, commander of Japanese naval forces in the Marshall Islands. Early in October 1942, he was told that as a result of a new government policy he had no obligation to send the marines to Tokyo for detention and that he could dispose of them as he chose. Abe therefore ordered the prisoners beheaded. After the war he was convicted of war crimes largely on the basis of the testimony of an islander who had witnessed the executions. He was hanged on the island of Guam.

Isayama Harukei

Lieutenant General Isayama Harukei was one of many Japanese military defendants tried for war crimes after the end of World War II for mistreatment of American prisoners of war on the occupied island of Formosa (now Taiwan). He was accused of "willfully, unlawfully and wrongfully" committing "cruel, inhuman and brutal atrocities and other offences against certain American prisoners of war by permitting and participating in an illegal and false trial and unlawful killing of said prisoners of war, in violation of the laws and customs of war" in spring 1945. The trial, conducted before a Japanese military tribunal, was considered "false" because Isayama (and others) gave an unlawful order to the tribunal to sentence the American POWs to death. He was also charged with authorizing the executions themselves. The failure to afford a prisoner of war a fair trial is a violation of the 1929 Geneva Convention. During the war Japan had adopted a policy that called for the execution of enemy airmen who had participated in bombing raids against Japanese territory. The policy led to several trials such as the one that Isayama participated in, which resulted in the executions of several captured U.S. airmen. Isayama was found guilty and sentenced to life imprisonment.

Kimura Heitaro

General Kimura Heitaro was the Japanese army commander in occupied Burma between 1944 and 1945. He was tried by the Allies after World War II on charges that he had helped plan wars in China and in the Pacific, including surprise attacks on the Allies. He was also indicted for having brutalized civilian and POW slave labor working on the Siam-Burma Railway. He was convicted by the International Tribunal for the Far East on six counts and sentenced to death by hanging.

Minami Jiro

Minami Jiro served as governor-general of Korea between 1936 and 1942 and is best known for enforcing an assimilation campaign that, in the words of one commentator, remains "notorious for its unmatched scope and extremity." A former minister of war and a member of the inner circle of army officers that dominated Japan in the 1930s and 1940s, Minami was the last of eight governors-general to preside over Japanese-occupied Korea. Under the banner of *naisen ittai* (Japan and Korea as one body) and *kōminka* (imperialization), Minami instituted an assimilation campaign that enshrined Shintoism as the state religion and forced Koreans to use Japanese names instead of their Korean ones. Minami exploited the media, educational system, and police to promote this campaign. But rather than achieve its objective of making the Koreans more Japanese, the campaign provoked intense opposition and ended up solidifying Korean nationalism. After being convicted at the Tokyo War Crimes trial, Minami was paroled.

Nagano Osami

As commander in chief of the Japanese Combined Fleet and a member of Supreme War Council, Admiral Nagano Osami was among the military officials involved in planning and carrying out the surprise attack on Pearl Harbor. He was charged with war crimes by the International Military Tribunal for the Far East but died of a heart attack before he could be sentenced. Born in 1884, Nagano was a graduate of Japan's Naval Academy and later studied at Harvard Law School. He became a naval attaché to the United States in the early 1920s and represented the Japanese navy at the London Naval Conference, which was established to place limits on naval power; he withdrew in protest in 1935 when Japan was denied naval parity with the United States and Great Britain. Subsequently Nagano was among the hard-liners who pushed for expansion of the Japanese navy. In 1936 he was appointed minister of the navy and a year later commander in chief of the fleet. In 1941, now chief of the Naval General Staff, Nagano became responsible for implementing a plan to attack the U.S. Pacific Fleet at Pearl Harbor drawn up by Admiral Isoroku Yamamoto. In December 1941, when negotiations between the United States and Japan collapsed, he approved the attack. He remained chief of the Naval General Staff through 1944. After the navy had suffered serious reverses, Nagano lost the support of Emperor Hirohito and Prime Minister Tojo Hideki, and he was removed from his post. Captured by the Allies in 1945, he was brought before the International Military Tribunal for the Far East, where he assumed responsibility for the attack on Pearl Harbor. He died in 1947 while the trials were still continuing.

Tachibana Yoshio

Vice Admiral Tachibana Yoshio was executed by the Allies in Guam for war crimes committed under his command on the Bonin Islands in the Pacific. He was implicated in participating in murders and atrocities involving U.S. pilots captured in 1944 and 1945. Among the grisliest crimes was having taken part in a "sake-fuelled feast" in which the flesh of the executed prisoners was consumed by Japanese officers. The details of the deaths of the nine "flyboys" were sealed in top-secret files in Washington for many years to spare their families distress.

Tamenori Sato

Major General Tamenori Sato was among several high-ranking Japanese officers convicted for war crimes; he was charged with killing and mistreating Burmese civilians under Japanese occupation during World War II. In July

1945 Japanese forces were stationed on the Andaman Islands off the coast of Burma when they captured a number of Burmese civilians—18 men, nine women, and 34 children—attempting to escape in a large boat. This information was reported to Tamenori, who approved the decision to have the civilians executed. After the Japanese surrender to the Allies in August, Tamenori ordered the bodies exhumed so that they could be burned in hope of concealing the evidence of the crime. Brought before a British court in Singapore, he admitted the charges against him but maintained that he was under orders to administer "severe punishment" to anyone trying to escape the islands. The Burmese were aware of the possible penalties for their actions, Tamenori contended, and so in effect they brought about their deaths. At the same time he acknowledged that he might have done something wrong and said that he took full responsibility in an attempt to shield his subordinates. Tamenori and one other defendant, Lieutenant Colonel Tazawa Keizo, were found guilty and executed; the other three officers involved in the massacre received relatively light sentences.

See also MATSUOKA YOSUKE; MATSUI IWANE; OKAWA SHUMEI; SAKAI TAKASHI; SHIMADA SHIGETARO; YAMASHITA TOKOYUKI.

Further Reading:

Daws, Gavin. *Prisoners of the Japanese: POWs of World War II in the Pacific.* New York: Perennial, 1996.

Li, Peter, ed. *Japanese War Crimes: The Search for Justice.* New Brunswick, N.J.: Transaction Publishers, 2003.

Maga, Timothy P. *Judgment at Tokyo: The Japanese War Crimes Trials.* Lexington: University Press of Kentucky, 2001.

Mendelsohn, John. *The Preservation of Japanese War Crimes Trials Records in the National Archives.* Washington, D.C.: National Archives and Records Administration, 1982.

Minear, Richard R. *Victors' Justice: The Tokyo War Crimes Trial.* Michigan Classics in Japanese Studies. Ann Arbor: University of Michigan, Center for Japanese Studies, 2001.

Piccigallo, Philip R. *The Japanese on Trial: Allied War Crimes Operations in the East, 1945–1951.* Austin: Univ of Texas Press, 1980.

Rees, Laurence. *Horror in the East: Japan and the Atrocities of World War II.* New York: Da Capo Press, 2002.

Russell of Liverpool, Edward Frederick Langley Russell, Baron. *Knights of the Bushido: A Short History of Japanese War Crimes.* London: Greenhill Books, 2005.

Tanaka, Yuki. *Hidden Horrors: Japanese War Crimes in World War II.* Philadelphia: Westview Press, 1998.

war criminals of the former Yugoslavia

Even while the war in the former Yugoslavia was still raging in the early 1990s, the United Nations was already drawing up plans to bring to justice perpetrators of war crimes, CRIMES AGAINST HUMANITY, and other atrocities before a special court. This was eventually established as the INTERNATIONAL CRIMINAL TRIBUNAL FOR THE FORMER YUGOSLAVIA (ICTY), sitting in The Hague, Netherlands. Those individuals indicted for participation in the war in Bosnia, Croatia, and Kosovo have included nationals from all sides in the conflict, although the majority of the accused have been Serbs. The most famous defendant is the former Yugoslav strongman Slobodan MILOŠEVIĆ. Several others—notably Ratko MLADIĆ, the former Serbian army commander, and the Bosnian Serb militant Radovan KARADŽIĆ—were still at large in early 2005, a decade after the end of the Bosnian War. Nonetheless, several lower-ranking and less well-known officers implicated in various atrocities have been handed over to The Hague or, in a few cases, have turned themselves in. More recently, under pressure from the United States and the European Union, Croatia and Serbia have begun to try suspects in their own courts, although in some instances men considered war criminals in the eyes of the world still enjoy a reputation as war heroes for nationalists in their own countries. The individuals described below represent only a small number of those who have been indicted or convicted for crimes committed in Bosnia, Croatia, or Kosovo from 1992 to 1999, but their cases are worth noting both for the nature of their crimes and for the legal precedent that they have established.

Beara, Ljubisa

A former Serbian colonel, Ljubisa Beara was arrested and turned over to the ICTY in The Hague for war crimes committed in the Bosnian War. Beara was implicated in the slaying of more than 7,000 Muslim men and boys in the town of Srebrenica in July 1995, which had been considered a UN-protected zone. The indictment accused Beara of having overseen the beheading of 800–1000 men and boys in the town. In addition, as the commander of an engineering unit, he was alleged to have taken charge of the digging of MASS GRAVES and making floodlights available so that firing squads could continue their work at night. Beara's arrest and extradition to The Hague by Serbia in October 2004 came as something of a surprise since Serbia had balked at cooperating with the tribunal in the past. Belgrade's action was believed to have been motivated by a desire to gain favor with the European Union and the United States, which has made financial assistance contingent on bringing war criminals to justice. Nonetheless, it is believed that several suspects wanted in The Hague are still being harbored in Serbia.

Blagojević, Vidoje

Colonel Vidoje Blagojević became the second defendant convicted of GENOCIDE by the ICTY. The tribunal handed down its verdict for the Bosnian Serb officer on January 17, 2005, in connection with his role in the 1995 massacre of more than 7,000 Muslim boys and men near the Bosnian town of Srebrenica. The ICTY found him guilty because he was aware that the massacre was being planned and then went ahead and helped transfer the captive men and boys to the site where it was to take place. He was convicted of complicity in genocide, one step below a finding of outright genocide, and sentenced to 18 years in prison. A codefendant, Major Dragan Jokić, was convicted on charges of murder, extermination, and persecution for having sent men and equipment to dig mass graves for the victims. He was sentenced to nine years in prison.

Blaskić, Tihomir

Tihomir Blaskić, a former general in the Croatian army, had already served eight years of a 45-year sentence for war crimes in the former Yugoslavia when an appeals court found his conviction flawed and freed him. The unprecedented ruling by the ICTY cleared Blaskić of charges that he was responsible for the April 1993 killings of Muslim civilians in half a dozen western Bosnian villages, which had fallen under Croatian control. In one incident in the village of Ahmici, Croatian forces had killed over 100 civilians, many of them elderly people who were burned in their own homes. The objective was to spread terror among the Muslim population and uproot them from a region the Croatians sought to take over as a part of a program of ethnic cleansing.

General Blaskić's trial was complicated and unusually long, lasting two years. The appeals court found that the lower court had made numerous errors and misinterpreted the law. Although it determined that the general had committed lesser war crimes, the court ruled that he had been sufficiently punished. The legal turnaround was also due to the discovery of previously hidden documents that had not been available when Blaskić was initially tried. These documents, which were in the possession of the Croatian intelligence agency, revealed that Blaskić's role in the atrocities was relatively minor; then-president of Croatia Franjo TUDJMAN had refused to turn the material over to the ICTY. The new government, which took office after Tudjman's death in 1999, ordered the documents opened. Croatian attorneys examining the documents have concluded that they could have led to Tudjman's indictment for war crimes by the court.

Cesić, Rajko

Rajko Cesić, a Bosnian Serb officer, was convicted of war crimes in March 2004 by the ICTY in The Hague. In 1992, while the Balkan wars raged among Serbia, Croatia, and Bosnia, Cesić was stationed at the notorious Luka camp in Brcko, Bosnia, where Muslim prisoners were being held. A member of the Bosnian Serb reserve police corps, Cesić pleaded guilty to having personally committed 10 murders and two cases of sexual assault at the camp in May 1992. In one case he beat a Bosnian Muslim police officer to death, but not before first ordering him to shake the hands of his fellow inmates and say good-bye to them. He clubbed another to death and lined up eight other victims, whom he shot in two separate incidents. Cesić also admitted to holding a gun to two middle-aged Muslim brothers, both former neighbors, and forcing them to perform fellatio on each other while the other guards watched.

Cesić received an 18-year sentence even though he could have been sentenced to life. Defense lawyers asked the judges to take into account the fact that he was only 27 when he committed his crimes and that he was deprived as a child because he had been brought up by a single mother. In a novel defense, his lawyers also pointed out that since most of his victims had no idea that he would kill them, their executions were not quite as cruel as they would have been otherwise. His lawyers also claimed that Cesić had helped some inmates escape—those he had taken a liking to—and the judges agreed that the evidence supported this assertion. However, they were not terribly impressed. "These facts demonstrate that he was capable of some benevolence," said one judge, who observed that Cesić had demonstrated this characteristic only "on occasion" and that it should therefore not be given "undue weight." On the other hand, the judges did consider his cooperation a factor when determining his sentence and indicated that his expression of remorse appeared to be genuine.

Deronjić, Miroslav

Mirsoslav Deronjić is a former high Bosnian Serb official convicted for his actions in the Bosnian War; the ICTY sentenced him to 10 years in prison. Deronjić had pleaded guilty to a charge of ordering the burning and razing of a Bosnian Muslim village called Glogova in May 1992, which resulted in the deaths of at least 64 men, women, and children out of a population of almost 2,000. He admitted that the inhabitants had been assured that they would be safe if they handed over their weapons. Deronjić also cooperated with the tribunal as a prosecution witness in the trial of former Yugoslav strongman Slobodan Milošević. In that role he implicated the authorities in Belgrade for supplying arms and providing strategic advice to the Serbian forces in Bosnia, facilitating their ability to launch a war against the Muslim population. One of the judges sharply disagreed with Deronjić's sentence, saying that in view of the gravity of the offense it was much too light and violated the spirit and mandate of the tribunal. Some critics maintained that the verdict was part of a troubling pattern by the tribunal in its rush to render judgment on the suspects because of U.S. pressure to close down its investigations by the end of 2004 and conclude all trials by 2008. As a result, many cases involving low-ranking suspects may not be heard by the tribunal at all.

Galić, Stanislav

Stanislav Galić, commander of Serb forces besieging Sarajevo during the Bosnian War, was convicted by the ICTY in December 2003 for killing civilians. He was charged in the indictment with implementing a strategy of shelling and sniping intended to target civilians in the capital of Bosnia and Herzegovina. He was specifically cited for the killings of 66 and wounding of 140 in a mortar attack on a Sarajevo market in 1994. The indictment described his forces directing "shelling and sniping at civilians who were tending vegetable plots, queuing for bread, collecting water, attending funerals, shopping in markets, riding on trams, gathering wood or simply walking with their children and friends." One of the lead prosecutors described the siege of Sarajevo as "an episode of such notoriety that one must go back to World War II to find a parallel in European history." General Galić's superiors, General Ratko Mladić and the Bosnian Serb political leader, Radovan Karadźić, were also indicted but were still at large as of early 2005. Galić was sentenced to a prison term of 20 years.

Halilović, Sefer

Sefer Halilović was the highest-ranking Bosnian officer to be charged for criminal acts committed during the Bosnian War in the 1990s. As part of the command staff of the Bosnian military force in the region, Halilović was responsible for coordinating Operation Neretva aimed at lifting the siege of Mostar in 1993, according to the tribunal's indictment. He was charged with a single count of violating the laws or customs of war for the murder of 62 Bosnian Croats in the villages in September 1993. The indictment started then took no "effective measures to prevent killings of civilians" in both incidents nor take any action against the perpetrators. Halilović went on trial in January 2005. In November 2005 he was acquitted of all charges.

Haradinaj, Ramush

Just prior to his indictment by the ICTY in March 2005, Ramush Haradinaj had been prime minister of Kosovo, which, while officially still a part of Serbia, has gained a large measure of autonomy under the protection of UN peacekeepers. Before his ascension to the post, Haradinaj was a senior commander of the Kosovo Liberation Front (KLF), which had waged a long insurgency against Serbian forces, culminating in the war in Kosovo in 1998. The charges against Haradinaj stem from his involvement in the KLF; it is alleged that he took part in atrocities in which Serbian Kosovar civilians were targeted. Haradinaj denied culpability but resigned as prime minister and agreed to turn himself in to stand trial. He is the second KLF leader to have been indicted; the first, Fatmir Limaj, was indicted in 2003.

Janković, Gojko

A former Bosnian Serb police commander, Gojko Janković was indicted by the ICTY for crimes committed during the war in Bosnia between 1992 and 1995. In contrast to many other indicted individuals, he turned himself in after five years on the run. Janković was charged with torturing and raping Muslim women. What makes his case unusual was that according to reports (including an account by his own wife), Janković had sought refuge in Moscow and had enjoyed the protection of the Russian security services, although the government insists it had no knowledge of his whereabouts. (A Slavic country, Russia had been a political supporter of Serbia, another Slavic nation, during the conflict. Slobodan Milošević's wife, Mira Marković, also lives in Moscow.) Two other Serbian officers wanted in The Hague were also reportedly hiding out in Moscow under Russian protection.

Jelisić, Goran

As acting commander of Luka prison camp in the former Yugoslavia, Goran Jelisić reportedly used to introduce himself as "the Serb Adolf" before torturing and killing inmates, including children and the elderly. In 1995 the ICTY indicted him on seven charges, including genocide, crimes against humanity, and violations of CUSTOMARY LAW. The charges stem from acts committed by Jelisić during the Bosnian War. The Luka camp was established by Serb forces in 1992 in Bosnia and Herzegovina. The camp, also known as a collection center, was used to house Croat and Muslim REFUGEES who had been forced to flee their homes. Most of the detainees at Luka were men of military age, though there were also a number of women. According to the indictment, detainees were systematically killed at Luka over a period of two weeks in May 1992. Almost every day, guards entered the camp, singled out men for interrogation, then beat and killed them, usually by shooting them at close range. Victims were forced to place their heads on a metal grate that drained into a nearby river so that the guards would be spared the necessity of cleaning up after the executions. Before the camp was closed down in July 1992, hundreds of Muslims and Croats were killed.

The charge of genocide can only be brought if there is evidence that the accused intended to destroy a group based on its national origins, ethnic roots, or religious or political beliefs. Jelisić, the ICTY ruled, met this standard by announcing that he intended to kill Muslims and then systematically proceeded to do so. In October 1999 Jelisić was sentenced to 40 years' imprisonment, a sentence that was upheld on appeal. He was the 10th individual convicted by the ICTY to serve a sentence.

Krajisnik, Momcilo

Momcilo Krajisnik is one of the highest-ranking war criminals indicted for war crimes in the Bosnian War in 1991 and 1992. An aide to former Bosnian Serb leader Radovan Karadžić, Krajisnik was arrested by NATO peacekeepers in March 2004 and sent to The Hague to stand trial. Krajisnik was indicted by the ICTY in connection with his activities between July 1, 1991, and December 31, 1992, during which time Serbian forces under his command secured control of several municipalities that had been proclaimed part of the Serbian Republic of Bosnia and Herzegovina. He was accused by the tribunal of "genocide, crimes against humanity, violations of the laws and customs of war, and grave breaches of the GENEVA CONVENTIONS, including murder, WILLFUL KILLING, extermination, complicity in genocide, deportation, and inhumane acts." According to a court spokesperson, Krajisnik was one of "the individuals who ran illegal operations that resulted in the deaths of thousands of Bosnians." He took part in decisions "that resulted in DEPORTATIONS, illegal arrests, ethnic cleansing and the deaths of thousands of Bosnians." Amor Masović, head of the Muslim commission for missing persons, described Krajisnik as "one of the masterminds of the genocide and ethnic cleansing in Bosnia."

Krajisnik had earlier served as speaker of the separatist Serb parliament; in that capacity he had repeatedly hindered efforts by international mediators to end the conflict. He had also participated in the Serb siege of Sarajevo that had killed hundreds of people and was responsible for ethnic-cleansing campaigns to expel Bosnian Muslim and Croatian populations from Serb-occupied territory. In addition, he was implicated in the massacre of thousands of Muslim men killed by Serb security forces after they had seized control of the UN safe haven of Srebrenica. He also controlled the municipal authorities and police in Serb-held territory, giving him a power base which he reportedly used for war profiteering. After the end of the war, Krajisnik briefly served as a member of Bosnia's first multiethnic collective government, a position he used to undermine any effort at reconciliation between the ethnic groups. He lost his seat after being defeated at the polls. Even after his arrest, Krajisnik still had his defenders among Serb radicals who described him as "conservative and pious." A widower and father of three, Krajisnik clung to the belief that separation based on ethnicity and religion was "natural."

Krstić, Radislav

The Bosnian Serb general Radislav Krstić was the first major Bosnian Serb officer to be put on trial at the ICTY.

He was charged with eight counts of genocide, complicity to commit genocide, crimes against humanity, and violations of the laws and customs of war for actions he had taken in the Bosnian War. The most serious charges were based on Krstić's participation in the massacre of Muslim men and boys in the UN-protected enclave of Srebrenica in July 1995. At the time Krstić was a deputy commander of the Drina Corps. Known by his nickname "Krle," he became a valued ally of General Ratko Mladić, then the head of the Yugoslav forces who was also indicted by the ICTY for war crimes. Krstić maintained during his trial that he never discussed the fate of Bosnian Muslim civilians in Srebrenica with Mladić and insisted that he had nothing to do with organizing the deportation of women, children, or the elderly from the enclave. He further claimed that he had only heard about the executions of the Muslims a month or two after the fact. Nonetheless, the evidence indicated that Krstić was with Mladić in Srebrenica when Mladić announced that "the moment has finally come to take revenge on the Turks here"—a derogatory reference to the Muslims. Krstić was found guilty of genocide for the massacre at Srebrenica and was sentenced to 46 years' imprisonment, the longest sentence so far handed down by the ICTY. It was also the first time that the tribunal had found a defendant guilty of genocide. AMNESTY INTERNATIONAL hailed the verdict, saying that it represented "a significant contribution in achieving justice for the thousands of victims of summary executions in Srebrenica and their relatives."

Lazarević, Vladimir

Retired Serbian general Vladimir Lazarević possibly signaled a new spirit of cooperation by the Serbian government with the West when he agreed to surrender to the ICTY in January 2005. Lazarević was one of four generals indicted in absentia in connection with abuses committed by Serbian troops against ethnic Albanians in Kosovo. As commander of the Pristina Corps in the breakaway Yugoslav province, Lazarević was responsible for actions of all subordinates, according to charges brought by the ICTY. Among the actions of Serbian troops cited in the indictment were the forcible relocation of Albanian villagers; the shelling of villages; the killings of civilians, including, in one case, 17 men whose bodies were thrown into wells; the burning of houses; and destruction of cultural property and mosques.

For years Serbia had adamantly resisted sending accused war criminals to The Hague in marked contrast to Bosnia and Croatia. Under intense pressure from the United States (which threatened to cut off financial assistance) and the European Union, however, Serbia began to show tentative signs of cooperation with the ICTY, and Lazarević's decision to turn himself in was taken as a further indication of Belgrade's changing attitude. However, the government was not prepared to repudiate its native son in spite of the crimes with which he was charged. An official statement stated that the Serbian government and the prime minister "personally, all appreciate and respect this patriotic, highly moral and honorable decision made by General Lazarević."

Martić, Milan

A former Croatian Serb police officer, Milan Martić was indicted by the ICTY for war crimes committed during the Bosnian War. As of late 2004 he was still at large, although he managed to get word out that there would be "many deaths" if UN peacekeepers attempted to arrest him. In 1995 he ordered two rocket attacks on Zagreb, the capital of Croatia; seven people were killed and 40 wounded. The attack made him one of the most reviled figures in Croatia. "I feel responsible in that I was the leader," Martić said. "But I do not feel ethically guilty. The charges made against me are ridiculous. How can I sit on the [court] bench for firing a few dozen rockets at military targets when [President] Tudjman [of Croatia, now deceased] ordered the bombing of Serb women and children as they fled for their lives?" When Croatian forces successfully counterattacked and drove out Serb forces, he took refuge in Republika Srpska, the Serbian enclave in Bosnia. He reportedly lives openly in the capital of Banja Luka within walking distance of the UN's International Police Task Force headquarters. He is said to live in high style as well, riding around the city in a Rolls Royce. To avoid capture, he is protected by a contingent of security men posing as gardeners. "I move with good security, at night or day," he once boasted.

Meakić, Željko

A former commander of a Serbian concentration camp in northern Bosnia and Herzegovina, Željko Meakić was charged with genocide for participating in the ethnic cleansing of Bosnian territory seized by Serb forces during the Bosnian War. From May 25, 1992, to August 30, 1992, Serb forces detained more than 3,000 Bosnian Muslims and Bosnian Croats in a mining complex in Omarska in the former Yugoslavia. Under Meakić's direction, prisoners were allegedly beaten, tortured, and killed. In February 1995 the ICTY indicted Meakić and 19 other individuals under his supervision with violations of the laws and customs of war and crimes against humanity. The indictment alleged that Omarska and another camp called Keraterm were the scenes of "severe beatings, killings as well as other forms of physical and psychological abuse, including sexual assault." Meakić was transferred to a detention center operated by the court in July 2003. In 2005, the Bosnian authorities requested Meakić's transfer to Bosnia for trial.

Nikolić, Ivan

A Serbian army reservist, Ivan Nikolić was the first person convicted by a Yugoslav court for crimes committed in the 1999 Kosovo War. Nikolić was implicated in the killing of an ethnic Albanian man and woman in a Kosovo village. "This was a war crime against the civilian population," observed the presiding judge who heard the case in 2002. The case was initially heard by a military court, which failed to render judgment. After he was given a sentence of eight years in prison, Nikolić claimed that he was innocent and a victim of a "show trial." However, representatives of the ICTY were heartened by the verdict, which they said was "a very important event for the judiciary in Serbia." Until Nikolić's trial, the Yugoslavs had tried only one other officer for war crimes committed in the Balkan wars of the 1990s.

Perisić, Momcilo

Former Serbian general Momcilo Perisić is one of the highest-profile suspects to go on trial before the ICTY. According to the indictment, he is alleged to have directed proxy Serbian forces fighting in Croatia and Bosnia from Belgrade, ensuring that these forces were supplied with personnel, equipment, provisions, and funding. Born in 1944, he became commander of Yugoslavia's Third Army in April 1993, shortly after the war in Bosnia had broken out. It was hoped that his trial would reveal the extent of the clandestine support extended by the Milošević regime to the forces of the Serbian Bosnian Army of the Republika Srpska, known as the VRS, and the Army of the Serbian Krajina (Croatia), known by its initials FRY. As the highest-ranking officer in the Yugoslav army, Perisić had overall command and authority over the operations conducted by these proxy forces, answerable only to President Slobodan Milošević himself. His involvement also implicated him in atrocities committed by these armies. The indictment also charges him with establishing elaborate covers to disguise the source of the logistical and funding support. The indictment noted that those individuals who received their pay and benefits from the coffers of the Yugoslav army under Perisić's command "reads like a who's who of indicted war criminals" including General Ratko MLADIĆ and other generals who were responsible for the massacre of 7,000 Muslim men and boys at Srebrenica. In addition, Perisić is charged with providing personnel, weapons, and logistical support for the siege of Sarajevo and the shelling of the Croatian capital of Zagreb. The indictment specifically charges Perisić with "crimes against humanity for murder, inhumane acts, persecution and extermination and violations of the laws and customs of war for murder and attacks on civilians both the basis of his individual responsibility in aiding and abetting such crimes, and on the basis of command responsibility." Under pressure from the United

States and the European Union and with the acquiescence of the new government in Belgrade, Perisić turned himself over to the tribunal's jurisdiction in May 2005.

Strugar, Pavle

A Serbian officer, Pavle Strugar was sentenced by the ICTY to eight years in prison for the destruction of cultural property during the Bosnian War. Struger, who was convicted in 2005, was specifically charged with allowing the shelling of the historic Croatian coastal town of Dubrovnik in 1991. Dubrovnik's Old Town, which was dominated by several medieval buildings, had been a United Nations World Heritage site since 1979. According to the indictment, "in the course of an unlawful attack" by the Yugoslav army on the Old Town in December 1991, two people were killed, three were seriously wounded, and "many buildings of historic and cultural significance in the Old Town, including institutions dedicated to . . . religion, and the arts and sciences, were damaged." The violations caused the ICTY to file six counts of violations of the laws or customs of war against the officer. Although the tribunal agreed that Strugar had not ordered the shelling, he was in a position to stop it "when he could have done so."

Tadić, Dusan

Dusan Tadić was arrested in 1994 in Germany and charged with war crimes he was accused of committing as a member of Serb forces in the former Yugoslavia in June 1992. He was among the first defendants to be tried before the ICTY in The Hague, Netherlands. His conviction was considered a historical landmark in international law since it established the precedent that an individual can be found criminally responsible for serious violations of the laws or customs of war and crimes against humanity before an international criminal court. "International trials can work," declared former chief prosecutor Justice Richard GOLDSTONE when the guilty verdict was announced. The decision was also important because it marked the first judicial condemnation of ethnic cleansing by Serb forces. Tadić was charged for participating in the seizure, murder, and maltreatment of Bosnian Muslims and Croats in a region in Bosnia and Herzegovina taken by Serb forces. He was also indicted on 12 counts of grave breaches of the 1949 Geneva Conventions, torture or inhuman treatment, and abetting the commission of genocide. Some of the charges stemmed from his duties at the Omarska camp, one of several such camps set up to illegally detain thousands of Muslims and Croats. In his defense, Tadić argued that he had been elsewhere at the time the crimes attributed to him had occurred. The court found his defense implausible and pronounced him guilty on 11 counts, constituting both violations of the laws or customs of war and crimes against humanity.

Ulemek, Milorad

The *New York Times* dubbed Milorad Ulemek "Serbia's most infamous paramilitary soldier" who was responsible for innumerable atrocities during the Bosnian War of the 1990s. His nom de guerre Legija (which means "of the Legion") derives from the years he spent in the French foreign legion in the 1980s. In 1992, shortly after the outbreak of the war in his native country, he returned to Serbia and joined the Serb Volunteer Guard, a paramilitary group better known as ARKAN's Tigers. As a commander of the Tigers, Ulemek fought in both Croatia and Bosnia, which had declared their independence from Serb-dominated Yugoslavia. When the Tigers were disbanded, Ulemek then found employment with the Serb secret police, the Special Operations Unit, more popularly known as the Red Berets. In 1999, named as commander of the Red Berets, he fought in the war in the breakaway province of Kosovo. Ulemek is suspected in involvement in the killing of four political opposition figures (while President Slobodon Milošević was still in power) as well as an unsuccessful attempt on the life of Vuk Draskovic, head of the opposition Serbian Renewal Movement. Although the Red Berets were considered to be Milošević's "praetorian guard," it is believed that Ulemek took part in secret negotiations with opposition leaders to arrange for Milošević to step down peacefully in exchange for a guarantee that he would not be prosecuted for his crimes during the wars. He has since been arrested in Yugoslavia on charges of participating in the assassination of Prime Minister Zoran Djindjić, who was shot and killed in March 2003. In spite of Ulemek's notoriety, a novel attributed to Ulemek, entitled *Iron Trench*, about his experiences in the Balkan wars, became an instant best seller when it went on sale in Yugoslavia in 2004.

See also BOSNIA AND HERZEGOVINA, HUMAN RIGHTS VIOLATIONS IN; CROATIA, HUMAN RIGHTS VIOLATIONS IN; KOSOVO, WAR CRIMES IN; SARAJEVO, SIEGE OF; SERBIA, HUMAN RIGHTS VIOLATIONS IN; SREBRENICA, MASSACRE IN; YUGOSLAVIA, WAR CRIMES IN.

Further Reading:

Askin, Kelly Dawn. *War Crimes against Women: Prosecution in International War Crimes Tribunals.* Leiden, Netherlands: Brill Academic Publishers, 1997.

Clark, Wesley K. *Waging Modern War: Bosnia, Kosovo, and the Future of Combat.* New York: Public Affairs, 2001.

Hagan, John. *Justice in the Balkans: Prosecuting War Crimes in the Hague Tribunal.* Chicago Series in Law and Society. Chicago: University of Chicago Press, 2003.

Harris, Nathaniel. *The War in Former Yugoslavia.* London: Hodder & Stoughton, 1997.

Hazan, Pierre, and James Thomas Snyder. *Justice in a Time of War: The True Story behind the International Criminal Tribunal for the Former Yugoslavia.* Eugenia and Hugh M. Stewart Series on Eastern Europe. Austin: Texas A&M University Press, 2004.

Mertus, Julie. *Former Yugoslavia: War Crimes Trials in the Former Yugoslavia.* Helsinki: Human Rights Watch/Helsinki, 1995.

Naimark, Norman, and Holly Case. *Yugoslavia and Its Historians: Understanding the Balkan Wars of the 1990s.* Stanford, Calif.: Stanford University Press, 2003.

Rhode, David. *Endgame: The Betrayal and Fall of Srebrenica.* New York: Farrar, Straus & Giroux, 1997.

Rogel, Carole. *The Breakup of Yugoslavia and the War in Bosnia.* Westport, Conn.: Greenwood Press, 1998.

Scharf, Michael P. *Balkan Justice: The Story behind the First International War Crimes Trial since Nuremberg.* Durham, N.C.: Carolina Academic Press, 1997.

Whealey, Robert. *American Intervention in Yugoslavia: Civil War, 1991–1999.* Amherst, N.Y.: Humanity Books, 2005.

war dead, treatment of

The treatment of fatalities in war is rooted in religious tradition as much as it is in CUSTOMARY LAW. The inscription on the Tomb of the Unknown Soldier in Arlington Cemetery, Washington, D.C., underscores the respect in which the war dead are held: "Here Rests in Honored Glory an American Soldier Known But to God." Although the inscription refers to an unknown American soldier, it is a sentiment that is shared by people of almost every nationality, and indeed there are monuments to unknown soldiers in many countries of the world.

The proper disposal of the dead is considered an important responsibility of any party to a conflict, and this has been true since ancient times. Removing the dead from the battlefield and interring their bodies is not only a matter of showing respect but also serves a hygienic purpose. Allowing the corpses to decompose poses a grave risk of spreading disease to the living. Although the laws of war accept that death is an inherent part of war, they also recognize that the care of the living holds greater priority. The drafters of successive treaties dealing with conduct in war believed that the treatment of the war dead, however, could not depend on tradition alone but should be codified as well. Article 15 of the First Geneva Convention, adopted in 1864, provides that the parties must "at all times, and particularly after an engagement . . . search for the dead and prevent their being despoiled." The article also states that "whenever circumstances permit," an armistice should be concluded so as to facilitate the search for the wounded, which by implication means that in the process a search for the dead would also

be undertaken. In its Commentary to the Geneva Convention, the INTERNATIONAL COMMITTEE OF THE RED CROSS (ICRC) specifically states that the dead must be brought back along with the wounded. The Red Cross offers two compelling justifications for this position. On the one hand, in light of the chaotic situation on the battlefield, it is often difficult to distinguish between the gravely injured and the dead. For another, the rules of war oblige the belligerents to properly—and promptly—dispose of the dead.

In an essay for the CRIMES OF WAR PROJECT, H. Wayne Elliott writes that the treatment of the war dead consists of two aspects. The first is a prohibition against mistreatment of the body, whether through failure to treat it with respect because of neglect or deliberate mutilation. The second is a prohibition against pillaging the body. These restrictions, he says, are as much enshrined in customary law—the moral principles and values that are universally accepted—as they are in international law. While mutilation of the dead is relatively rare, as long as disciplined armies are involved in the conflict, PILLAGE of the dead poses a more serious problem. Soldiers are permitted to search bodies—there is always a possibility information of intelligence value will be found—and may succumb to the temptation to take personal property off the dead in spite of legal prohibitions.

Article 16 of the First Geneva Convention sets out additional rules as to how a body is to be disposed of. If a body of an enemy soldier is discovered, the body is to be returned to the adversary, generally through a neutral party or the ICRC. The body should be accompanied by written evidence of death along with one half of the double identity disk and any personal effects found on the body.

In Article 17 there are specific instructions regarding the burial of war dead. First, a body should be examined, preferably by a person with the requisite medical skill, to ensure that the combatant is, in fact, deceased. Where possible, the body should be interred in an individual grave both because of the need to honor the dead and because it will make subsequent identification much easier. However, the First Geneva Convention makes clear that these obligations can sometimes be waived depending on other factors including climate, sanitation, or the exigencies of conflict. Cremation is in general prohibited, except where sanitary conditions make it imperative or where the tradition or the religious background of the diseased dictates otherwise. (Cremation, for instance, is a time-honored way of disposing of bodies in the Hindu tradition.) By the same token, the Geneva Convention also calls for the burial (or cremation) to be performed in accordance with the religious practices of the deceased; remains are to be interred by nationality and cemeteries mapped so that future identification can be expedited. Graves are also to be protected.

The laws pertaining to the treatment of the dead, first codified in the middle of the 19th century, were reaffirmed by the Fourth Geneva Convention of 1949, which requires parties to the conflict to protect the dead against pillage and ill-treatment and obliges them to ensure that the dead are honorably interred, their graves respected, and information pertaining to their identity provided to the ICRC. In war, of course, ascertaining who exactly is dead may be a problem. Almost invariably some of those who are later found to be dead are first reported missing. To take that situation into account, Protocol I to the 1949 Geneva Conventions states that, as a general principle, each party to the conflict shall search for the missing and report all relevant information to their adversary as soon as circumstances permit—at the latest at the end of hostilities.

Determining when a body is being mistreated and can therefore be classified as a war crime is a difficult proposition. Failure on the part of a warring party to meet the obligations under international law may not always mean that a violation has been committed—if, for instance, bodies of an enemy force remain on the battlefield for a prolonged period because of military necessity. A breach of law would be more clearly established, however, if bodies still have not been collected after hostilities have ceased. Further, putting bodies on display for propaganda purposes or as a means of humiliating an opponent—as was done in Mogadishu, Somalia, where the corpses of UN peacekeepers were dragged through the streets—can never be justified. In a more recent incident, U.S. forces in Iraq were widely criticized for displaying the bodies of Saddam HUSSEIN's two sons after they were killed in a firefight, especially in the Islamic world, where bodies are supposed to be interred as quickly as possible. Presumably U.S. military authorities had intended to prove to a skeptical Iraqi public that the two men—who were both feared figures while their father was in power—were truly dead, but in doing so they might have crossed a line that put them at risk of violating international law.

See also ADDITIONAL PROTOCOLS TO THE GENEVA CONVENTIONS; GENEVA CONVENTIONS.

Further Reading:
Berry, Nicholas O. *War and the Red Cross: The Unspoken Mission.* New York: St. Martin's Press, 1997.
Gutman, Roy, ed. *Crimes of War: What the Public Should Know.* New York: W. W. Norton, 1999.
International Committee of the Red Cross. *International Law Concerning the Conduct of Hostilities: Collection of Hague Conventions and Some Other Treaties.* Geneva: International Committee of the Red Cross, 1989.

weapons in the conduct of war

According to international CUSTOMARY LAW, weapons should not cause "unnecessary suffering" or "superfluous injury." The foundation of law regarding the use of weapons in international conflicts was established at an international conference held in St. Petersburg, Russia, in 1868. The treaty that emerged from that conference—the St. Petersburg Declaration—stated that the only "legitimate object" of any war was "to weaken the military forces of the enemy"; while this necessitated incapacitating "the greatest possible number of men," using arms to "aggravate the sufferings of disabled men, or render their death inevitable" amounted to a disproportionate use of force and would be "contrary to the laws of humanity." As customary law, this principle was considered binding on all nations regardless of whether they signed or ratified the treaty.

The St. Petersburg Declaration was used as a basis for provisions regarding the use of arms in the 1897 and 1907 HAGUE CONVENTIONS. Explosive projectiles filled with glass or other fragments were outlawed on the grounds that they caused excessive injuries. The objective, after all, was to remove the soldier from combat, which could be done by means of a serious wound. Riddling a body full of fragments—which might be too small to be detectable by X-ray—was therefore superfluous aside from causing unnecessary suffering. Dumdum and poisoned bullets were outlawed for the same reasons. But some weapons whose use is banned in one context might be legitimate in another. In World War I, as Burrus Carnahan points out in an essay in the CRIMES OF WAR PROJECT, British warplanes used machine guns on planes that fired incendiary bullets, which were banned on the battlefield. Initially the Germans asserted that any downed pilot who had used such weapons was in violation of the St. Petersburg Declaration and, as a result, should be treated as a war criminal. Later the German government reversed its position. The weapon in question was not being used to "cause unnecessary suffering" to the enemy pilot but rather to bring the enemy warplane down, which was a legitimate military objective.

Customary law also forbids the use of indiscriminate weapons, which are difficult or impossible to target. That is to say, the attackers would have no way of ascertaining whether the use of the weapon would be justified by the destruction of a military objective. Under this definition, the German V-2 rockets that were launched against London in World War II were indiscriminate because their purpose was simply to cause widespread destruction and demoralize the civilian population, not to damage British military capacity. SCUD missiles directed at Israel by Iraq during the 1991 Gulf War were also considered indiscriminate by the U.S. Defense Department for much the same reason. This is not to say that a weapon is necessarily indiscriminate simply because it has the potential of causing a great deal of destruction. Some legal scholars, for instance, believe that under certain circumstances, nuclear weapons could be used if a state believes that its existence is in peril, although other international law experts have disputed this assessment.

See also MILITARY NECESSITY; NUCLEAR ARMS AND INTERNATIONAL LAW; WEAPONS OF MASS DESTRUCTION.

Further Reading:

Cornish, Paul. *Anti-personnel Mines: Controlling the Plague of "Butterflies."* London: Royal Institute of International Affairs, 1994.

Feaver, Peter. *Guarding the Guardians: Civilian Control of Nuclear Weapons in the United States.* Cornell Studies in Security Affairs. Ithaca, N.Y.: Cornell University Press, 1992.

Gutman, Roy, ed. *Crimes of War: What the Public Should Know.* New York: W. W. Norton & Company, 1999.

International Committee of the Red Cross. *International Law Concerning the Conduct of Hostilities: Collection of Hague Conventions and Some Other Treaties.* Geneva: International Committee of the Red Cross, 1989.

Langford, R. Everett. *Introduction to Weapons of Mass Destruction: Radiological, Chemical, and Biological.* New York: Wiley-Interscience, 2004.

Prokosch, Eric. *The Technology of Killing: A Military and Political History of Anti-personnel Weapons.* London: Zed Books, 1995.

Nichols, Gary W., and Milton L. Boykin, eds. *Arms Control and Nuclear Weapons: U.S. Policies and the National Interest.* Contributions in Military Studies. Westport, Conn.: Greenwood Press, 1987.

weapons of mass destruction

Weapons of mass destruction (WMD) is a term that generally refers to nuclear, biological, and chemical weapons, or NBC for short. There is, however, no authoritative definition of WMD in either treaty law or international CUSTOMARY LAW. Its absence is explained by the fact that nations have historically used international law to address each category of weapons that falls under the WMD classification,

Inspectors measuring the volume of nerve gas in a container *(United Nations)*

using three different sets of rules for each technology. General rules of international law also have applications to WMD, but no law specifically applies to WMD. The issue of WMD is governed by various arms control treaties, which have three objectives: the deterrence of the use of WMD by states, exemplified by the accords governing nuclear proliferation, testing, and production between the United States and the former Soviet Union; the banning of WMD from certain areas (treaties preventing their deployment in space and on the ocean floor); and disarmament (treaties that outlaw the development and use of BIOLOGICAL WEAPONS and CHEMICAL WEAPONS).

The term *weapons of mass destruction* gained popular currency in the run-up to the 2003 U.S.-backed invasion of Iraq. The Bush administration had warned that Saddam HUSSEIN was making every effort to acquire a nuclear capacity while retaining biological and chemical weapons. Indeed, precedent did argue in favor of this view since Iraq had used biological and chemical weapons in the past. An intensive search for such weapons after the occupation of Iraq turned up no WMD, however, leading many experts to believe that Saddam's stockpile of biological and chemical weapons had been destroyed or else had degraded significantly.

See also NUCLEAR ARMS AND INTERNATIONAL LAW.

Further Reading:

Alibek, Ken, and Stephen Handelman. *Biohazard: The Chilling True Story of the Largest Covert Biological Weapons Program in the World—Told from Inside by the Man Who Ran It.* New York: Delta, 2000.

Barnaby, Frank. *How to Build a Nuclear Bomb: And Other Weapons of Mass Destruction.* New York: Nation Books, 2004.

Feaver, Peter. *Guarding the Guardians: Civilian Control of Nuclear Weapons in the United States.* Cornell Studies in Security Affairs. Ithaca, N.Y.: Cornell University Press, 1992.

Guillemin, Jeanette. *Biological Weapons.* Columbia Contemporary Issues in National Security Policy. New York: Columbia University Press, 2005.

Krepon, Michael. *Strategic Stalemate: Nuclear Weapons and Arms Control in American Politics.* Sydney, Australia: Palgrave Macmillan, 1986.

Lederberg, Joshua, ed. *Biological Weapons: Limiting the Threat.* BCSIA Studies in International Security. Cambridge, Mass.: MIT Press, 1999.

Mangold, Tom, and Jeff Goldberg. *Plague Wars: The Terrifying Reality of Biological Warfare.* New York: St. Martin's Press, 2001.

Nichols, Gary W., and Milton L. Boykin, eds. *Arms Control and Nuclear Weapons: U.S. Policies and the National Interest.* Contributions in Military Studies. Westport, Conn.: Greenwood Press, 1987.

Price, Richard M. *The Chemical Weapons Taboo.* Ithaca, N.Y.: Cornell University Press, 1997.

Tucker, Jonathan B., ed. *Toxic Terror: Assessing Terrorist Use of Chemical and Biological Weapons.* BCSIA Studies in International Security. Cambridge, Mass.: The MIT Press, 2000.

Wei Jingsheng (Wei Ching-sheng) (1950–) *Chinese human rights activist*

Wei Jingsheng is a leading Chinese activist whose opposition to the Communist government resulted in years of imprisonment and exile. Wei, an electrician by profession, first came to prominence in the late 1970s during a period of political relaxation when the Communist Party under Deng Xiaoping was flirting with reform. Probably nothing embodied the spirit of reform more than Beijing's Democracy Wall, where, for a few months in the winter of 1978–79, people could express their political views. In effect, the Democracy Wall became the first public forum for an open political debate. In his first contribution to this discussion, Wei, 28 at the time, criticized Deng's economic reforms because there was no provision in his program called "The Four Modernizations" to open the country to democracy. The Chinese people had to take matters into their own hands, he wrote, rather than count on the guidance of enlightened leaders.

Wei's poster, called "The Fifth Modernization," caused a sensation; even fellow activists were stunned that he had dared to scold the government so directly. They feared that such attacks would impel the authorities to take down the Democracy Wall. Wei was not moved by their arguments. Democracy, he contended, could only be assured if human rights were also guaranteed. Five months after the Democracy Wall had gone up, Wei posted his last broadside, entitled "Do We Want Democracy or New Autocracy?" In it he questioned whether Deng was seriously committed to democracy and concluded that he was not: "History tells us that there must be a limit to the trust placed in any one person."

An attack on China's supreme ruler was not allowed to go unanswered. A week later, on March 29, 1979, Wei was arrested. In October he was convinced on charges of "slandering the socialist system" and "plotting to overthrow the people's democratic dictatorship" and sentenced to 15 years in prison. Even during his trial, Wei remained defiant. "Criticism may not be beautiful or pleasant to hear, nor can it always be completely accurate," he told the court. "If one insists on criticism being pleasant to hear and demands its absolute accuracy on pain of punishment, this is as good as forbidding criticism and banning reforms."

During his imprisonment, much of it spent in solitary confinement, Wei's health deteriorated—he lost at least a dozen teeth and developed a heart condition—but he showed no sign of remorse for having voiced his opinions so openly. In spite of his isolation, his words began to resonate with other Chinese reformists, never more so than when the government launched a brutal repression of demonstrators gathered in Tiananmen Square in June 1989. "The repression of the 1989 movement," Wei said after his release in 1993, "taught the Chinese people a very bitter lesson: . . . that relying on the dictators to gradually move towards democracy was a vain hope."

Six and a half months before his term was up, Wei was freed, probably because China was seeking to burnish its image to win the 2000 Olympic Games for Beijing. Although the authorities insisted that he refrain from engaging in political activities or speaking to foreign journalists, Wei showed no hesitancy about resuming his campaign for human rights. He called for the release of thousands of political prisoners and even supported Tibetan independence, a position vehemently opposed by Beijing. He helped poverty-stricken dissidents with money awarded from his international prizes. Even though he was kept under police surveillance, he insisted on giving interviews to foreign correspondents and writing articles for publications outside of China. In 1994 he met with John SHATTUCK, the U.S. assistant secretary of state for human rights and humanitarian affairs. He was again arrested and taken on what was said to be a "vacation"—which lasted for nearly five years. In November 1997, after spending cumulatively almost 18 years in prison, Wei was freed after an official visit to Washington by the Chinese president Jiang Zemin. He was forced to leave the country for the United States. Shortly after his arrival, he was received by President Bill Clinton, who acknowledged his long struggle for democracy and human rights.

See also CHINA, HUMAN RIGHTS VIOLATIONS IN.

Further Reading:

Foot, Rosemary. *Rights beyond Borders: The Global Community and the Struggle over Human Rights in China.* Oxford: Oxford University Press, 2001.

Kent, Ann. *Between Freedom and Subsistence: China and Human Rights.* Oxford: Oxford University Press, 1995.

Munro, R. *Punishment Season: Human Rights in China after Martial Law.* Asia Watch Report. New York: Human Rights Watch, 1990.

Santoro, Michael A. *Profits and Principles: Global Capitalism and Human Rights in China.* Ithaca, N.Y.: Cornell University Press, 2000.

Weatherley, Robert. *The Discourse of Human Rights in China: Historical and Ideological Perspectives.* Sydney, Australia: Palgrave Macmillan, 1999.

Wernich, Christián von (1939–) *Argentinean priest*

A Roman Catholic Argentine prelate, Father Christián von Wernich has been charged with 19 counts of murder and 33 of abduction and TORTURE in connection with his role as chaplain for the Buenos Aires police during Argentina's "dirty wars" in the 1970s. He was ordained a priest in 1976, the same year in which General Ramon Camps became head of the police of Buenos Aires. Camps chose Wernich as his personal confessor and made him police chaplain, allowing him access to secret prisons. He was also permitted to witness interrogations. It was in his capacity as police chaplain that Wernich was reported to have extorted money from the parents of seven left-wing youths who had been taken into custody. Once the money was paid, the prisoners, including a pregnant woman, were killed. According to an eyewitness, Wernich was present for three of the EXTRAJUDICIAL KILLINGS carried out by police. Afterward the priest attended a barbecue to celebrate. Although Wernich has admitted that he had frequently visited the secret police detention center, he refused to tell prosecutors what had ensued while he was there on the grounds that he would be violating "the secrecy of the confessional."

See also ARGENTINA, HUMAN RIGHTS VIOLATIONS IN.

Further Reading:

Arditti, Rita. *Searching for Life: The Grandmothers of the Plaza De Mayo and the Disappeared Children of Argentina.* Berkeley: University of California Press, 1999.

Davis, William Columbus. *Warnings from the Far South: Democracy versus Dictatorship in Uruguay, Argentina, and Chile.* New York: Praeger Publishers, 1995.

Lewis, Paul H. *Guerrillas and Generals: The Dirty War in Argentina.* New York: Praeger, 2001.

Moyano, Maria. *Argentina's Lost Patrol: Armed Struggle, 1969–1979.* New Haven, Conn.: Yale University Press, 1995.

White Brigades

The White Brigades, a clandestine Mexican paramilitary group, has been linked by human rights groups to operations conducted by the Mexican army. It is thought that the brigades collaborated with the army and security forces in 1968 in carrying out the massacre of hundreds of student protesters in Mexico City. During the late 1960s and much of the 1970s—the period of Mexico's "dirty war"—hundreds of suspected leftists and other political opponents were abducted by the White Brigades. About 600 people have been "disappeared" in this way and never accounted for, although it is assumed that most were executed at military bases or police detention centers. On July 21, 1978, members of the White Brigades and the Mexican police, disguised as civilians, arrested over 150 striking workers, many of whom were tortured during the next two days. In 2000 retired general Alberto Quintanar Alvarez gave an interview to the Mexico City daily *La Jornada* in which he denied that any "dirty war" had occurred, contending that it was "a cleansing operation of Maoists, Trotskyists . . . students supported by trade unions and political parties who were destabilizing the country." Quintanar did acknowledge, however, that the White Brigades and other paramilitary groups were in fact created by and under the direction of the interior ministry. More recently, the White Brigades have been implicated in such crimes as executions, rapes, kidnappings, and TORTURE, according to an investigation conducted by the government of Vincente Fox. There are nonetheless reports that the White Brigades and other paramilitaries continue operations in rural parts of Oaxaca and Guerrero, suppressing insurgent activity in those states on behalf of landowners and local political bosses.

See also MEXICO, HUMAN RIGHTS VIOLATIONS IN.

Further Reading:

Amnesty International. *Mexico: Human Rights in Rural Areas.* London: Amnesty International, 1986.

Brysk, Alison, ed. *Globalization and Human Rights.* Berkeley: University of California Press, 2002.

Cartwright, William, ed. *Mexico: Facing the Challenges of Human Rights and Crime.* Ardsley, N.Y.: Transnational Pub., 1999.

Human Rights Watch. *Unceasing Abuses: Human Rights in Mexico One Year after the Introduction of Reform.* Americas Watch Report. New York: Human Rights Watch, 1991.

Wiesenthal, Simon (1908–2005) *Nazi hunter and Holocaust chronicler*

An architectural engineer by training, Simon Wiesenthal has become best known for disseminating information about the Holocaust to bring to account Nazi war criminals who escaped justice after World War II. He was born on December 31, 1908, in Buczacz, then in Austria-Hungary (now part of Ukraine). When World War II broke out, Wiesenthal was living with his wife, the former Cyla Mueller, in Lvov, Poland, managing his own architectural firm. They resided in a part of Poland that was seized by the Soviet Union under the terms of the nonaggression pact with Germany. During a purge of Jewish intellectuals, Wiesenthal's stepfather was arrested by the NKVD, the Soviet secret police, and eventually died in prison; in addition, Wiesenthal's stepbrother was shot. Wiesenthal was forced to close his business, and it was only by bribing an NKVD commissar that he was able to save himself, his wife, and his mother from deportation to Siberia.

In 1941, after the Germans pushed the Red Army out and took all Polish territory, Wiesenthal and his wife were imprisoned in a FORCED LABOR camp where he worked in a repair shop for Lvov's Eastern Railroad. By September 1942, after the Germans had begun to implement the FINAL SOLUTION—the annihilation of all European Jewry—a total of 89 members of both his and his wife's families had been killed by the Nazis. Weisenthal survived by luck: His wife had blonde hair and as a result could pass for an Aryan (a non-Jew). Wiesenthal worked for the Polish underground, supplying strategic information about the Lvov Railroad that the resistance used to plan acts of sabotage. In exchange, his wife received false papers that allowed her to live in Warsaw for two years. She was later sent to the Rhineland as a forced laborer, but even then her true identity—and Jewish origins—remained a secret. Weisenthal himself escaped the work camp in 1943 just before the Germans began to exterminate its Jewish inmates. Recaptured in June 1944, he was interned in another concentration camp and would surely have been killed as well except for the fact that, with Germany's collapse inevitable, his SS guards decided to keep the remaining prisoners alive—34 out of an original 149,000—assuming that the Allies might give them lenient treatment.

Weisenthal was barely alive when he was rescued by American forces in 1945. Once he recovered his health, he went to work for the U.S. Army's Office of Strategic Services and Counter-Intelligence Corps, gathering documentation for impending war-crimes trials. He also headed the Jewish Central Committee of the United States Zone of Austria, a relief and welfare organization. In late 1945 he was reunited with his wife, whom he had believed dead. In 1947 he founded the Jewish Documentation Center in Linz, Austria, with several other survivors. He persisted in gathering information about war criminals even after it became apparent that the United States and Soviet Union had lost interest in pursuing many more prosecutions. When the Linz office was closed, its files were transferred to YAD VASHEM, the Holocaust memorial and museum in Israel.

Throughout the 1950s Weisenthal continued to hunt for the one war criminal he wanted to see brought to justice above all: Adolf EICHMANN, the Nazi official who had been in charge of the Final Solution. Israeli agents eventually tracked Eichmann down in Argentina, where he was living under an alias. He was then abducted to Israel, where he was tried, found guilty of GENOCIDE, and executed in May 1961. Weisenthal was also deeply involved in the apprehension of Karl Silberbauer, the GESTAPO officer responsible for the arrest of Anne Frank. His testimony helped debunk allegations that Frank's famous diary was a forgery. Her vivid account of life in hiding under the German occupation of Amsterdam gave a human face to the millions of Jewish victims of the Final Solution. Wiesenthal also helped find information responsible for tracking down nine of the 16 wanted SS officers who were put on trial in West Germany, including Franz Stangl, the commandant of the Treblinka and Sobibór extermination camps, and Hermine Braunsteiner, who had supervised the murder of hundreds of children during the war. (When she was discovered, Braunsteiner was living as a seemingly ordinary housewife in Queens, New York.)

Weisenthal operated out of the Jewish Documentation Center (JDC) in Vienna, which he had founded and is still in operation. Although it has only a small staff, it relies on a vast network of friends and sympathizers (and occasionally even former Nazis) for tips and documentation. Files have been gathered on 90,000 Nazi officials, most of whom have never been tried. The JDC is not only concerned with locating Nazi war criminals—whose numbers are shrinking because of old age—but also with monitoring right-wing extremist groups. In 1977 a Holocaust center opened in Los Angeles; it was named the Simon Wiesenthal Center in the Nazi hunter's honor. (There is a sister center in Jerusalem.)

Wiesenthal has received several honors for his work, including the French Legion of Honor, the United Nations League for the Help of Refugees Award, and the U.S. Congressional Gold Medal, which was presented to him by President Jimmy Carter in 1980. He has also been a consultant on documentaries about the Holocaust and the 1974 film thriller *The Odessa File*, and served as the model for the Laurence Olivier character, Herr Lieberman, in the 1977 movie *The Boys from Brazil*, based on the Ira Levin novel of the same name. Not surprisingly, Wiesenthal has received numerous death threats and once was the target of an abortive bomb attack by neo-Nazis in 1982. He announced his retirement in 2003 two years before his death. "I have survived them all. If there were any left, they'd be too old and weak to stand trial today," he said at the time. "My work is done."

Further Reading:

Levy, Alan. *Nazi Hunter: The Wiesenthal File*. New York: Carroll & Graf Publishers, 2002.

Wiesenthal, Simon. *Justice Not Vengeance: Recollections*. New York: Grove Press, 1990.

———. *The Sunflower: On the Possibilities and Limits of Forgiveness*. New York: Schocken, 1998.

willful killing

International law prohibits the intentional killing of civilians and considers it a war crime. This does not mean that all killings of civilians in a conflict are war crimes; according to Additional Protocol I to the GENEVA CONVENTIONS, civilian deaths that occur because of MILITARY NECESSITY are not crimes even if the belligerent knows in advance that civilian casualties will ensue before launching an attack. Bombing a military installation—permissible under international law—may kill civilians in the vicinity without the assailant being found culpable of a war crime. The killing of a civilian by a sniper is not necessarily a war crime, either. On the other hand, the execution of HOSTAGES or PRISONERS OF WAR would be classified as a war crime under the Geneva Conventions and Additional Protocol I. By the same token, the bombing of a town or city that has as its aim the terrorizing of its civilian inhabitants would be illegal. In addition to civilians, prisoners of war, the sick or wounded, and soldiers who have surrendered (HORS DE COMBAT) are protected from willful killing, as are medical and religious personnel unless they have taken up arms as combatants. The Fourth Geneva Convention of 1949 forbids "grave breaches" by an OCCUPYING POWER regarding its treatment of a civilian population, including "willful killing, TORTURE or inhuman treatment."

The Geneva Conventions only deal with international conflicts. ARTICLE 3 COMMON TO THE GENEVA CONVENTIONS, though legally weaker than the provisions in the conventions, has been applied to the protection of civilians in internal conflicts as well. Additional Protocol I, while covering only international conflicts, does set forth the principle that all parties to a conflict must "distinguish between the civilian population and combatants . . . and accordingly shall direct their operations only against military objectives." The protocol also requires that "the civilian population as such, as well as individual civilians, shall not be the object of attack." Additional Protocol II, which covers internal as well as international conflicts, emphasizes that "the civilian population . . . shall enjoy general protection against the dangers arising from military operations." This establishes the principle of civilian inviolability, although in most cases protections of civilians have traditionally applied only in interstate conflicts. But more recently, various ad hoc courts, established by the United Nations to try crimes in such internal conflicts as the war in the former Yugoslavia, Rwanda, and Sierra Leone, have expanded the protections of civilians. In 1996 the Trial Chamber of the INTERNATIONAL CRIMINAL TRIBUNAL FOR THE FORMER YUGOSLAVIA (ICTY) stated: "The rule that the civilian population as such as well as individual citizens, shall not be the object of attack is a fundamental rule of international law applicable to all armed conflicts . . . irrespective of their characterization as international or non-international." In its rulings, the ICTY has followed through on its words and made no distinction between international and internal armed conflict. "(A)ttacks on [civilians and] civilian objects are prohibited as a matter of CUSTOMARY LAW in all conflicts," declared the senior legal advisor in the ICTY Office of the Prosecutor. Several defendants in ICTY trials, which are conducted in The Hague in the Netherlands, have been charged with acts of willful killings in the Bosnian War.

See also ADDITIONAL PROTOCOLS TO THE GENEVA CONVENTIONS; PROTECTED PERSONS.

Further Reading:

Gutman, Roy, ed. *Crimes of War: What the Public Should Know.* New York: W. W. Norton & Company, 1999.

Mertus, Julie. *Former Yugoslavia: War Crimes Trials in the Former Yugoslavia.* Helsinki: Human Rights Watch/Helsinki, 1995.

Hagan, John. *Justice in the Balkans: Prosecuting War Crimes in the Hague Tribunal.* Chicago Series in Law and Society. Chicago: University of Chicago Press, 2003.

Hazan, Pierre, and James Thomas Snyder. *Justice in a Time of War: The True Story behind the International Criminal Tribunal for the Former Yugoslavia.* Eugenia and Hugh M. Stewart Series on Eastern Europe. Austin: Texas A&M University Press, 2004.

International Committee of the Red Cross. *International Law Concerning the Conduct of Hostilities: Collection of Hague Conventions and Some Other Treaties.* Geneva: International Committee of the Red Cross, 1989.

Wiranto (1947–) *Indonesian war criminal*

General Wiranto is one of Indonesia's most controversial military and political figures. Even as human rights advocates denounced him as a war criminal in connection with atrocities committed in East Timor, he was running for the presidency of his country. Specifically, he has been charged with the killings of more than 1,000 civilians in 1999 in East Timor while the province was in the process of obtaining its independence under UN supervision.

Until then Wiranto's career had proceeded on a fast track. Twenty years after graduating as a second lieutenant from the national military academy in 1968, he became an aide to former president SUHARTO, the undisputed ruler of Indonesia for decades. Wiranto (many Indonesians use only one name) became head of the military in 1998 as Suharto's regime was collapsing. (Wiranto is credited with prevailing on Suharto to relinquish his post voluntarily.) As commander of the Indonesian forces on East Timor, however, he was accused of failing to stop his soldiers or pro-Indonesian militias from committing serious human rights abuses and massacres. Although Wiranto initially suffered no consequences—on the contrary, he was appointed security minister—President Abdurrahman Wahid fired him in February 2000 when charges of human rights abuses failed to subside.

Wiranto has vigorously denied the charges and attributed the violence to long-simmering tensions between ethnic groups that had nothing to do with him. Indonesian security forces, he contended, "had an extraordinary difficult mission—I call it Mission Impossible." He maintained that his soldiers suffered from "psychological constraints" when faced with the prospect of acting against comrades who might have committed excesses. UN prosecutors were not swayed by his argument, and in February 2003 in East Timor they charged him in absentia for CRIMES AGAINST HUMANITY. The indictment named six other senior military officers and a former governor as well. Wiranto and his fellow officers, the UN prosecutors said, had "effective control" over the militia groups, which implicated them in 280 documented murders. Wiranto and the others charged were also held responsible for forcibly deporting 200,000 East Timorese to West Timor, which was under Indonesian control, after the vote in which the vast majority of the East Timorese opted for independence.

The Indonesian record of bringing alleged either political or military officials to justice for such crimes is very poor, and there is little likelihood of Wiranto ever being tried. When the indictments were issued, the Indonesian foreign minister defiantly declared that his government would "simply ignore" them; even the East Timor government has not tried to pursue the case, fearing a rupture in diplomatic relations with Indonesia. The accusations against Wiranto did not deter his supporters in the powerful Golkar Party from nominating him as their presidential candidate in 2003. His popularity was not so huge, however, as to convince Indonesian voters to put him into office. He came in third.

See also EAST TIMOR, WAR CRIMES IN; INDONESIA, HUMAN RIGHTS VIOLATIONS IN.

Further Reading:

Dunn, James, and Xanana Gusmao. *East Timor: A Rough Passage to Independence.* Seattle: University of Washington Press, 2004.

Jardine Matthew. *East Timor: Genocide in Paradise.* The Real Story Series. Monroe, Me.: Odonian Press, 2002.

Pinto, Constancio, and Jardine Matthew. *East Timor's Unfinished Struggle: Inside the Timorese Resistance.* Cambridge, Mass.: South End Press, 1996.

Romano, Cesare, Andre Nollkaemper, and Jann K. Kleffner, eds. *Internationalized Criminal Courts and Tribunals: Sierra Leone, East Timor, Kosovo, and Cambodia.* International Courts and Tribunals Series. Oxford: Oxford University Press, 2004.

women's rights, violations of

In principle, human rights have always been guaranteed to women in international law, but in practice women continue to be subjected to violence, rape, and other grave abuses as well as pervasive discrimination. Women and children are most likely to be victims of war; they are also more likely to be REFUGEES and INTERNALLY DISPLACED PERSONS. Women are not only discriminated against because of their sex; other factors such as race, ethnicity, caste, religion, class, and age may also play a role. In many regions of the world, violations of women's rights are defended as traditional or cultural practices, including honor killings, disenfranchisement, and genital mutilation. In North Africa, 6,000 women are genitally mutilated each day; each year more than 7,000 women in India are murdered by their families and in-laws in disputes over dowries. In countries such as Pakistan, South Africa, Peru, Russia, and Uzbekistan, women are beaten at home by their husbands at alarming rates. Annually it is estimated that 1,000 women are murdered in honor killings in Pakistan.

In recent conflicts in Sierra Leone, Kosovo, the Democratic Republic of the Congo, Afghanistan, and Rwanda, women have been raped as a deliberate tool of war. In Darfur in western Sudan, Arab militiamen known as *janjaweed* have raped black African women in order to stigmatize them, and women who bear children as a result are ostracized from their families and tribes. Governments often refuse to intervene, or else accuse the victim of being responsible. This phenomenon often occurs in cases where a rape victim is accused of infidelity or prostitution. According to a 2002 survey by the World Health Organization (WHO), nearly one in four women experiences sexual violence by an intimate partner during her life, and as many as one-third of all girls are forced into their first sexual experience. Abuses against women are hardly limited to the developing world. In the United States, for example, a woman is raped on the average of every six minutes, and a woman is battered every 15 seconds. In addition, millions of women throughout the world are forced to marry against their wishes. Women are also more vulnerable—socially and biologically—to infection from HIV/AIDS.

Women are also at higher risk of being trafficked for prostitution or enforced servitude because of inequalities in their native countries. Each year hundreds of thousands of women are trafficked from countries such as Nigeria, the Dominican Republic, Myanmar (Burma), Thailand, Ukraine, Moldova, Russia, Romania, and Poland. Probably more women are trafficked in and from Asia; about 15,000 women are sold into sexual SLAVERY in China alone every year.

Women in Arab countries frequently face discrimination that bars them from political, social, and cultural life. In Saudi Arabia, for instance, women cannot vote, take certain types of jobs, or even drive a car. In conservative Islamic countries they are required to wear chadors or burkas to conceal their faces and bodies. Legal restrictions

A woman wearing the traditional burka during the Taliban regime in Afghanistan *(Exile Images)*

in many countries prevent women from obtaining a divorce without their husband's consent, inheriting money or property, or retaining custody of children in the event of a divorce.

The first major international recognition of women's rights is found in the 1945 United Nations Charter, which afforded to women and men alike equal economic, social, cultural, political, and civil rights. The UNIVERSAL DECLARATION OF HUMAN RIGHTS of 1948 stipulates that human rights apply to all people equally, "without distinction of any kind such as race, color, sex, language . . . or any other status." In 1979 the UN General Assembly adopted the Convention on the Elimination of All Form of Discrimination Against Women (CEDAW), or the International Women's Human Rights Treaty, which was the first international accord to comprehensively address women's rights within political, cultural, economic, social, and family spheres. In 1993 the UN General Assembly adopted the Declaration on the Elimination of Violence Against Women (DEVAW), which sets forth the means by which states should protect and defend women's rights. The declaration directs member states to "exercise due diligence to prevent, investigate and, in accordance with national legislation, punish acts of violence against women, whether those acts are perpetrated by the state or by private persons."

In 1995 the Beijing Platform for Action—an initiative that grew out of the Fourth World Conference on Women—

called on governments to "condemn violence against women and refrain from invoking any custom, tradition or religious consideration to avoid their obligations with respect to its elimination as set out in the Declaration on the Elimination of Violence against Women. . . ." Further recognition of women's rights is found in the statutes establishing three special UN courts to try war crimes in the former Yugoslavia, Rwanda, and Sierra Leone as well as in the ROME STATUTE OF THE INTERNATIONAL CRIMINAL COURT, (1998). These statutes criminalize abuses of women's rights in times of conflict. Several states that have signed these accords have also enacted legislation providing for protection of women's rights in their own countries.

See also COMFORT WOMEN; RAPE AS A TACTIC OF WAR; TRAFFICKING IN PERSONS.

Further Reading:
Askin, Kelly Dawn. *War Crimes against Women: Prosecution in International War Crimes Tribunals.* Leiden, Netherlands: Brill Academic Publishers, 1997.

Bassiouni, M. Cherif. *Sexual Violence: An Invisible Weapon of War in the Former Yugoslavia.* Chicago: International Human Rights Law Institute, DePaul University, 1996.

Buergenthal, Thomas. *Religious Fundamentalisms and the Human Rights of Women.* Sydney, Australia: Palgrave Macmillan, 1999

Charrad, M. *States and Women's Rights: The Making of Postcolonial Tunisia, Algeria, and Morocco.* Berkeley: University of California Press, 2001.

Cook, Rebecca J. *Human Rights of Women: National and International Perspectives.* Pennsylvania Studies in Human Rights. Philadelphia: University of Pennsylvania Press, 1994.

Dormann, Knut, and Louise Doswald-Beck. *Elements of War Crimes under the Rome Statute of the International Criminal Court: Sources and Commentary.* Cambridge: Cambridge University Press, 2003.

Peters, Julie Stone, and Andrea Wolper. *Women's Rights, Human Rights: International Feminist Perspectives.* London: Routledge, 1995

Thomas, Dorothy Q., and Thomas Sidney Jones, eds. *A Modern Form of Slavery: Trafficking of Burmese Women and Girls into Brothels in Thailand.* New York: Human Rights Watch, 1994.

World Court   *See* INTERNATIONAL COURT OF JUSTICE.

Y

Yad Vashem

Yad Vashem was established in 1953 as a memorial to the 6 million Jews who perished in the Nazi campaign of extermination during World War II while also serving as an archive of material related to the Holocaust. Formally known as the Holocaust Martyrs' and Heroes' Remembrance Authority, Yad Vashem was founded by an act of the Israeli Knesset (parliament) and entrusted with the documenting of the life of Jews who were swept up in the FINAL SOLUTION, better known as the Holocaust. Yad Vashem, which is located on Har Hazikaron (the Mount of Remembrance) in Jerusalem, is composed of several elements: museums, archives, a library, a school, exhibits, sculptures, and a memorial for the Righteous Among the Nations, which is dedicated to non-Jews who risked their lives by sheltering and aiding the escape of Jews fleeing Nazi persecution. Its archival collection is the largest and most comprehensive repository of material on the Holocaust in the world, boasting 62 million pages of documents and nearly 267,500 photographs, along with thousands of films and videotaped testimonies of survivors. Its library contains more than 90,000 books, thousands of periodicals, and a number of rare items from the period. By 2005 Yad Vashem had computerized 3.2 million names of Holocaust victims and relevant biographical data. Its International School for Holocaust Studies is the only school of its kind in the world—both a resource and a teaching center with a staff of over 100 educators. Its staff classes are attended by more than 100,000 students, 50,000 Israeli soldiers, and thousands of educators from Israel and around the world every year.

Further Reading:

Abells, Chana Byers. *The Children We Remember: Photographs from the Archives of Yad Vashem, the Holocaust Martyrs' and Heroes' Remembrance Authority, Jerusalem, Israel*. New York: HarperTrophy, 2002.

Dafni, Reuven, and Yehudit Kleiman, eds. *Final Letters: From Victims of the Holocaust (From the Yad Vashem Archive)*. New York: Paragon House Publishers, 1991.

Yamashita Tomoyuki (1888–1946) *Japanese general*

Yamishita Tomoyuki commanded Japanese forces in the Far East during World War II and was subsequently tried and convicted for war crimes even though there was little evidence indicating that he was personally involved in any atrocities. Born in 1888, he began his long army career at the age of 20. He rose quickly in the ranks, earning a promotion from captain to lieutenant colonel in just three years. In 1936 members of a rightist military faction rebelled against moderates in the government. When the coup failed, Yamashita was asked to serve as a mediator between the military and the political opposition. Yamashita managed to avoid being implicated in the uprising. Nonetheless, Emperor Hirohito suspected that he was more sympathetic to the mutineers than he had let on and sent him into quasi exile in Korea, which was then under Japanese colonial rule.

Yamashita managed to regain his previous status in spite of an adversarial relationship with War Minister Hideki TOJO. In October 1941 Tojo was asked to form a government, and within weeks he initiated plans to go to war. Yamashita was invited to a cabinet meeting at the Imperial Headquarters in Tokyo to discuss the war, which, in his view, was justified for economic reasons. With Japan's population expanding, he believed, the country needed to import more of its resources. "In order to buy or import her commodities she [Japan] had to pay ultimately in commodities," he wrote. "This effort on her part was prevented for one reason or another by other countries. Japan made attempts to solve the misunderstandings through peaceful methods, but when all her efforts were thwarted or negated she felt it necessary to engage in open warfare."

Yamashita was given command of the Twenty-fifth Army, which was assigned the mission of conquering the

481

Malayan Peninsula, then part of the British Empire. Yamashita developed a strategy tailored for jungle fighting that ensured a quick and decisive victory within 10 weeks. In February 1943 he was promoted to general and given the command of Japanese ground troops in the Philippines who were coming under increasing pressure from American forces. Yamashita moved his headquarters repeatedly—from Manila to Mindro and then to Luzon and Bangbang—to escape advancing American troops. He was in the process of organizing guerrilla resistance to a U.S. takeover of the Philippines when Japan surrendered unconditionally in August 1945.

Captured in early September and charged with violating "the laws of war," Yamashita was put on trial in Manila. The charges against him were based on atrocities committed by Japanese troops under his command, including the murder, TORTURE, rape, and maltreatment of thousands of Filipinos and of hundreds of Americans. The prosecution contended that he should have known of the excesses committed by his troops. He was defended by U.S. military officers who objected to the use of hearsay evidence—not allowed in a U.S. court of law—and the admission of diary entries by Japanese soldiers that could not be corroborated. No evidence or eyewitness testimony was ever presented to show that Yamashita either knew about or ordered his troops to violate the rules of war. Nonetheless, he was found guilty and condemned to death. His attorneys petitioned the U.S. Supreme Court on the grounds that his trial did not rise to the same standards of DUE PROCESS guaranteed by the U.S. Constitution. The Supreme Court turned down the petition after determining that the commission hearing the case was "lawfully constituted." The ruling stated that "the petitioner was charged with violation of the law of war and that the Commission had authority to proceed with the trial and in doing so, did not violate any statutory or Constitutional command." The Supreme Court decision (with two justices dissenting) meant that the execution could go ahead as planned. "The Tiger of Malaya," as Yamashita was known for his wartime exploits, was hanged in February 1946.

Further Reading:

Li, Peter, ed. *Japanese War Crimes: The Search for Justice.* New Brunswick, N.J.: Transaction Publishers, 2003.

Piccigallo, Philip R. *The Japanese on Trial: Allied War Crimes Operations in the East, 1945–1951.* Austin: Univ of Texas Press, 1980.

Rees, Laurence. *Horror in the East: Japan and the Atrocities of World War II.* New York: Da Capo Press, 2002.

Russell of Liverpool, Edward Frederick Langley Russell, Baron. *Knights of the Bushido: A Short History of Japanese War Crimes.* London: Greenhill Books, 2005.

Yugoslavia, war crimes in

The most devastating conflict in Europe since World War II broke out in 1991. The immediate cause was the violent dissolution of the Yugoslavian Federation, which at one point had consisted of six constituent republics. However, the origins of the Balkan conflict that would take a decade to play itself out can be traced to the efforts of Slobodan MILOŠEVIĆ, first as president of the Serbian Nationalist Party and later president of Serbia, to centralize power.

Until 1980 the federation had been kept together by one man, Josip Broz, Marshal Tito (1892–1980), who had dominated Yugoslavia for 37 years. It was largely through his efforts that bitter ethnic tensions among Serbs, Croats, and Muslims did not explode into violence. Although Yugoslavia was communist, Tito steered a course independently of the Soviet Union. However, he had made little provision for an orderly transition after his passing. For several years the federation was governed by a collective presidency, representing the different nationalities that composed Yugoslavia. Milošević, however, advocated a federation that would be dominated by the Serbs. As Serbian president, Milošević stripped two provinces—Kosovo (with an Albanian majority) and Vojvodina (largely Hungarian)—of their autonomy. These and other actions intended to extend Serb power stirred fears that he would interfere in other republics.

In 1990 elections nationalist parties scored gains in every republic. Negotiations to keep the federation from splintering apart failed. On June 25, 1991, both Croatia and Slovenia declared independence. Less than a year later, in April 1992, so did Bosnia and Herzegovina. Serb forces fought a brief war against Slovenia, but ultimately Slovenia was allowed to go its own way because it was home to relatively few Serbs. That was not the case, however, in Bosnia or Croatia, both of which had significant Serbian populations. (At the start of the war Bosnia's population consisted of 4.4 million people, 44 percent of whom were Muslim, 31 percent Serb, 17 percent Croat, and 8 percent other nationalities.) As a result, the war in those republics would be anything but brief.

From the outset the Bosnian Serbs made it clear that they had no intention of supporting a fledgling republic under Muslim leadership, rejecting the notion of a multiethnic nation. Their leader, Radovan KARADŽIĆ, mobilized the Serb nationalists and organized paramilitary units—the Bosnian Serb armed militia (BSA)—which collaborated with the Serb-dominated Yugoslav national army. The BSA initiated a campaign of terror to seize large areas of Bosnia and Croatia with the intention of linking up to Serbia to create a Greater Serbia. In the interim Karadžić declared the establishment of the Republika Srpska, or Serb Republic, in eastern Bosnia. The BSO engaged in what became known as ethnic cleansing, driving out the Muslim populations from eastern and northern Bosnia, razing their villages, laying SIEGE to towns and cities, and imprisoning thousands of others in CONCENTRATION CAMPS. In spite of international pressure and the imposition of sanctions on Belgrade, the BSA continued its incursions, laying siege to Sarajevo, Bosnia's capital, in 1992, and undertaking ethnic-cleansing campaigns in Banja Luka, later the capital of the Bosnian Serb Republic, and Bijeljina. Sarajevo came under Serbian shelling and sniper fire for months on end, resulting in the killings of 10,000–12,000 civilians. In 1993 the Serbian paramilitary forces struck several other towns. Attacks were not exclusively directed against ordinary Muslim civilians; the BSA carried out targeted killings as well against political and religious figures in an effort to destabilize and eliminate the leadership of Muslim society.

Croatia had its own agenda in the war, which frequently put it at odds with both Bosnia and Serbia. Initially Croatian and Bosnian forces were allies against Serbia. Then clashes occurred between Bosnian government forces and Bosnian Croatian militias known as the Croatian Defense Council (HVO) under the leadership of Mate Boban. Following the example of the Bosnian Serbs, Boban advocated the creation of a separate Bosnian Croat Republic of Herceg-Bosna, with Mostar as its capital. When the Bosnian government objected to Boban's plan, the HVO attacked Mostar and, according to a U.S. State Department report, "brutalized, confined, and raped its Muslim residents in an assault containing some of the most extreme human rights abuses in Bosnia and Herzegovina in 1993." Croatian forces subsequently broke with the Bosnian Muslims and sided with Boban. In central Bosnia the HVO went on a rampage; in one hamlet they massacred as many as 100 civilians and then razed it to the ground. In some cases the HVO collaborated with the BSA, creating "conditions of extreme deprivation" in Bosnian enclaves. By summer 1993 the HVO was involved in herding an estimated 20,000 Bosnians into so-called collection centers in Mostar and other parts of Bosnia predominantly populated by ethnic Croatians. There is evidence that many of the detainees were tortured and murdered or died as a result of brutal conditions in the camps. Representatives of Helsinki Watch, the human rights group, were denied access to the camps to find out what was going on, but reports of atrocities still reached the international press, causing an uproar and embarrassment for the Croatian government, the principal sponsor of HVO.

The Bosnian government forces perpetrated their share of atrocities and abuses, killing Croat civilians and driving thousands of Croats from their homes. In October 1993 Bosnian government forces rounded up 1,000 Bosnian Croat refugees trying to flee the town of Konjic, then robbed and beat them. Boban claimed that 150,000–190,000 Bosnian Croats had been displaced by fighting in central Bosnia or driven out by the government that same year. In March 1994

a Washington-mediated accord between Muslims and Croatians was reached that established a Muslim-Croat federation in Bosnia. With Bosnian Muslims and Croats once again allied, the Serb forces no longer could count on a decisive military advantage.

By the end of 1992, the Bosnian Serb army already had control of about two-thirds of Bosnia and Herzegovina. Most of the Muslims and Croats had taken refuge in government-held territory. Their sanctuary was precarious; Serb forces surrounded many of the enclaves, preventing relief agencies from gaining access to them and shutting off their electrical and water supply. By this time more than a million people had been internally displaced and were in desperate need of emergency food and shelter. Hundreds of thousands of REFUGEES had fled the country altogether in search of asylum in western European countries. At one point in the conflict there may have been up to 2 million refugees and displaced persons. Those who were not able to escape were frequently imprisoned in concentration camps. It is believed that 260 of these camps were set up by the three sides during the war. In January 1993 the U.S. government estimated that there were 135 Serb-run detention centers alone in Bosnia. There were also Muslim and HVO camps, though many of these were closed by 1993. How many people were held is unknown; the three sides defined all males between 16 and 65 as combatants, a classification that included many civilians. Outside observers were only sporadically permitted to inspect the camps, and in some cases, because the camps were unregistered, no international monitors ever visited.

In an attempt to rein in the belligerents, if not to stop the fighting, the UN Security Council authorized a mission known as the United Nations Protection Force (UNPROFOR). But the mission was dangerous; by 1993 over 60 UNPROFOR soldiers had been killed in outright attacks or by sniper fire. In spring 1993 the United Nations designated six besieged Bosnian towns as SAFE HAVENS deserving of international protection. But providing relief to the besieged areas was a major challenge; if food and other provisions were allowed to reach the enclaves, it would hamper the Serb ability to overrun them, suggesting that force might be required to get the aid to the populations in need. The UN Security Council recognized the need and adopted Resolution 770, ordering states to take "all necessary measures" to facilitate aid deliveries in Bosnia. On the ground, though, the United Nations failed to exert force when it was most needed. In July 1995, rather than resist the Serb takeover of Srebrinica—one of the six safe areas—UN peacekeepers withdrew. Serb forces proceeded to expel the women and children and murder more than 7,000 Muslim men and boys. International aid workers were not spared in the fighting and suffered several losses; several journalists were killed as well—34 in the first two years of the war.

Even as fighting raged in Bosnia, Serbs were also attacking Croatia, even shelling the historic Croatian coastal city of Dubrovnik. In the initial phase of the war, the Serbs had taken nearly a third of Croatian territory. As in Bosnia, Serbs relied on Croatian Serbs as proxies who were responsible for atrocities and abuses against Croats. In November 1991, for instance, Serbs from the Croatian region of Krajina removed several hundred wounded Croatian soldiers from a hospital in the eastern Slavonian town of Vukovar, shot them in a field, and buried them in a mass grave. Four years later, though, the tide had turned against the Serbs, and Croatians launched a campaign of ethnic cleansing of their own, retaking Serb-occupied western Slavonia and the Krajina region and sending thousands of Serb civilians fleeing from their homes.

The war in Bosnia and Croatia was also notable for the systematic violence directed against women. Bosnian Muslim women were separated from their families and held in Serbian detention camps where they were raped, tortured and subject to other degrading treatment as part of a genocidal campaign. (Bosnian men were not spared, either; many were raped and forced to commit sexual acts with other male prisoners.) According to Kelly Dawn Askin, author of *War Crimes against Women*, Serbs targeted Bosnian Muslim women in particular because of the patriarchal nature of Muslim society; unmarried women who lost their virginity were stigmatized, and married women who were "tarnished" by having had sexual relations with other men suffered disgrace. Thus rape became a form of assault against the family and Bosnian Muslim community. In the Bosnian town of Foca, the Yugoslav army set up a detention center at the Partizan Sports Complex in 1992 in which both Bosnian Muslim and Bosnian Croat women were held. The detainees were often raped every night and denied medical care for any injuries they sustained. (Rape, committed as an act of war rather than as a consequence of conflict, is an indictable offense under international law.) Young girls and old women who were raped often died as a result. Videotapes were also made of some of these incidents and sold as pornography. The BSO, which used RAPE AS A TACTIC OF WAR beginning in 1992, were not alone. Members of HVO, the Croatian paramilitary units, also were implicated in rape. According to the UNITED NATIONS HIGH COMMISSIONER FOR REFUGEES (UNHCR), HVO soldiers may have raped as many as 100 women in one incident.

In summer 1995 the Serbs began to suffer reverses as Bosnian and Croatian troops retook areas that had fallen under Serb control. Finally, bowing to pressure from Washington and the United Nations, the leaders of the three belligerent states—Bosnian president Alija Izetbegović, Serbian president Slobodan Milošević, and Croatian president Franjo TUDJMAN—agreed to talks conducted under the auspices of the United States at an air force base near Dayton. Ohio. The three hammered out a comprehensive peace treaty known as the DAYTON ACCORDS, which was signed in Paris on December 1, 1995. Yet although the Bosnian war came to an end, the Balkans did not have much time to enjoy peace. In 1999 Milošević engineered another campaign of ethnic cleansing, this time against ethnic Albanians who made up the majority of the Yugoslav province of Kosovo. He launched his assault ostensibly to quell a separatist insurgency, but its real objective seemed to be a wholesale removal of Kosovo's Albanian population. That war was only halted because of an intensive bombing campaign carried out by NATO. A year later Milošević was forced to give up power.

Even while the Bosnian war was still going on, the United Nations recognized the need to address the atrocities and bring the perpetrators to account. In October 1992 the UN Security Council approved an impartial international investigation to identify persons responsible for human rights abuses. The Commission of Experts, as the panel was known, was able to document thousands of crimes. By spring 1993 the Security Council concluded that the atrocities that had taken place amounted to war crimes and had to be prosecuted. This determination led to the establishment of the INTERNATIONAL CRIMINAL TRIBUNAL FOR THE FORMER YUGOSLAVIA (ICTY). Three of the principal perpetrators were among the first to be indicted: Slobodan Milošević, Bosnian Serb leader Radovan Karadžić, and Bosnian Serb general Ratko MLADIĆ. Milošević was ousted from power in 2000 and handed over to the ICTY, which sits in The Hague, Netherlands. The former Serbian strongman was charged with 27 counts of war crimes and CRIMES AGAINST HUMANITY arising from the conflict in Bosnia and Herzegovina between 1992 and 1995. The charges were based on Milošević's "command responsibility" as president of Serbia and his alleged participation in a joint criminal enterprise. He was also charged in connection with the shelling of Sarajevo, the mass murder of thousands of Muslim men and boys at Srebrenica, and abuses committed at the Serbian-run Omarska detention camp. The indictment included one count of GENOCIDE and one count of complicity in genocide. He was also charged in connection with his role in organizing Serb attacks on Albanian civilians in the war in Kosovo in 1999.

As of early 2006 Karadžić and Mladić were still at large. The ICTY also undertook the investigation of allegations of atrocities committed by the Bosnian Muslim forces as well as the HVO and Croatian armed forces on Bosnian territory. At first Croatia resisted demands of the ICTY to arrest and transfer suspected war criminals to The Hague, where the court sits. In 1997, however, Zlatko Aleksovski, a former chief of an HVO army internment camp in Bosnia, was sent to The Hague, an action hailed as demonstrating a willingness on Croatia's part to cooperate with the court.

There is little question, however, that Croatia would not have acted if it were not for pressure from the West. The court later charged members of HVO with taking part in systematic attacks on Muslim villages and murdering civilians. In one case—the assault on the town of Ahmici—103 Muslims were killed by HVO militiamen. The court emphasized the link between the Croatian government and the HVO, charging the militia with committing grave breaches of the GENEVA CONVENTIONS of 1949: "[T]he Bosnian Croats can, for the purposes of these proceedings, be regarded as agents of Croatia in respect of discrete acts which are alleged to be violations of the grave breaches provisions of the Geneva Conventions. It appears that Croatia, in addition to assisting the Bosnian Croats . . . inserted its own armed forces into the conflict on the territory of Bosnia and exercised a high degree of control over both the military and political institutions of the Bosnian Croats." The ICTY found that then Croatian president Franjo Tudjman "was hoping to partition Bosnia and exercised such a degree of control over the Bosnian Croats and especially the HVO that it is justified to speak of overall control. [T]he close ties between Croatia and the Bosnian Croats did not cease with the establishment of the HVO."

See also BOSNIA AND HERZEGOVINA, HUMAN RIGHTS VIOLATIONS IN; CROATIA, HUMAN RIGHTS VIOLATIONS IN; KOSOVO, WAR CRIMES IN; ROM (ROMA, ROMANY, GYPSIES), PERSECUTION OF; SARAJEVO, SIEGE OF; SERBIA, HUMAN RIGHTS VIOLATIONS IN; SLOVENIA, HUMAN RIGHTS VIOLATIONS IN; SREBRENICA, MASSACRE IN; USTACHE; WOMEN'S RIGHTS, VIOLATIONS OF.

Further Reading:
Clark, Wesley K. *Waging Modern War: Bosnia, Kosovo, and the Future of Combat.* New York: Public Affairs.

Hagan, John. *Justice in the Balkans: Prosecuting War Crimes in the Hague Tribunal.* Chicago Series in Law and Society. Chicago: University of Chicago Press, 2003.

Harris, Nathaniel. *The War in Former Yugoslavia.* London: Hodder & Stoughton, 1997.

Hazan, Pierre, and James Thomas Snyder. *Justice in a Time of War: The True Story behind the International Criminal Tribunal for the Former Yugoslavia.* Eugenia and Hugh M. Stewart Series on Eastern Europe. Austin: Texas A&M University Press, 2004.

Kim, Julie. *War in the Former Yugoslavia: Chronology of Events August 16, 1992–May 30, 1993.* CRS Report for Congress. Washington, D.C.: Foreign Affairs and National Defense Division, Congressional Research Service, the Library of Congress, 1993.

Kipp, Jacob W. *International Ramifications of Yugoslavia's Serial Wars: The Challenge of Ethno-national Conflicts for a Post-Cold-War, European Order.* Fort Leavenworth, Ka.: European Military Studies Office, 1993.

Mertus, Julie. *Former Yugoslavia: War Crimes Trials in the Former Yugoslavia.* Helsinki: Human Rights Watch/Helsinki, 1995.

Naimark, Norman, and Holly Case. *Yugoslavia and Its Historians: Understanding the Balkan Wars of the 1990s.* Stanford, Calif.: Stanford University Press, 2003.

Rossanet, Bertrand de. *War and Peace in the Former Yugoslavia.* Boston: Martinus Nijhoff, 1997.

Scharf, Michael P. *Balkan Justice: The Story behind the First International War Crimes Trial since Nuremberg.* Durham, N.C.: Carolina Academic Press, 1997.

Whealey, Robert. *American Intervention in Yugoslavia: Civil War, 1991–1999.* Portland, Me.: Humanity Books, 2005.

Zimbabwe, human rights violations in

Since 1980, when majority rule came to Zimbabwe, President Robert Mugabe has kept a firm grip on the southern African nation. The mercurial former revolutionary has resorted to increasingly authoritarian methods to maintain control even though, in theory, Zimbabwe is a parliamentary democracy. Although the political opposition came close to winning power in parliamentary and presidential elections in 2000 and 2002, the governing Zimbabwe African National Union-Patriotic Front, or ZANU-PF, has managed to manipulate the law to forestall the prospect of losing at the ballot box a third time. Freedom of the press and freedom of assembly have been sharply curbed in recent years on the grounds of national security. The foreign media have been barred from the country. Email going in or out is censored, and the government has tried to ban cell-phone calls to anywhere outside Zimbabwe.

Licenses are required from the government for domestic journalists. A popular newspaper, the *Daily News,* was threatened when its directors were indicted on charges of illegal currency transactions. A law has been proposed to imprison anyone found guilty of writing "materially false" statements about the government. At the same time the government has moved to place nongovernmental organizations (NGOs)—including churches and charities—under government control. The government can shut down NGOs at its discretion. The largest trade union cannot call a meeting without first notifying the government, which has also established a vast network of security forces and informers whose ranks have swelled in recent years. According to the *New York Times,* one out of every 60 Zimbabweans is on the payroll of the security services. (The population is about 11.3 million.) Apparently there is plenty of work for them to do. The Solidarity Peace Trust, an NGO made up of clerics, estimated that between 2000 and November 2004, 300,000 Zimbabweans (or one out of every 40 people) had suffered from abuses by government agents that included beatings, torture, being uprooted from their land, and being denied food rations. The group also stated that another 300 people had died in politically motivated killings in the same period.

The political opposition is subject to systematic intimidation, beatings, and arrests. In some cases the price for political dissent is death. The main opposition party, the Movement for Democratic Change, continued to function, but under government restrictions it found it increasingly difficult to get out its message. Its leader, former presidential candidate Morgan Tsvangirai, was tried on charges of treason; while acquitted in 2004, he still faces the prospect of being hauled into court again on charges that he claims are trumped up.

To mobilize support among the country's most impoverished people, Mugabe has encouraged landless peasants to seize white-owned farms. The move to appropriate these farms—at a time of threatening famine due to drought, corruption, and misrule—is seen as a diversionary tactic: By directing the animosity of poverty-stricken Zimbabweans toward the relatively few wealthy whites, whose forbears had claimed the country (then called Rhodesia) for Great Britain, the government hopes to escape blame for the worsening economic conditions. Human rights groups say that Mugabe's government also rations food for political ends, distributing resources to its supporters while denying them to people who back the opposition. Even though half the citizens were going hungry by the end of 2004, Mugabe refused foreign aid and claimed in any case that there was no food shortage. All the same, polls conducted in 2004 showed that almost half the population voiced confidence in his leadership, double the level from 1999.

In 2005, after winning elections, seen by international observers as marred by rigging and intimidation, Mugabe launched an operation intended to uproot thousands of impoverished people from urban areas. In the past, the targeted population offered the opposition a reliable base

486

of support, especially the shantytowns of the capital Harare. Over the course of several weeks, security forces demolished the hovels and stalls belonging to poor families, often with little or no notice, forcing them to take refuge in rural areas. The humanitarian crisis this operation has triggered off has come on top of famine and a collapsing economy and has left hundreds of thousands of people homeless and without a means of making a living. According to Zimbabwe Doctors for Human Rights (ZDHR), between 1 and 2 million people have lost their homes. In addition, tens of thousands of children suddenly had no access to schools. Mugabe has ignored international condemnation and blocked humanitarian agencies from assisting the victims.

Further Reading:

Blair, David. *Degrees in Violence: Robert Mugabe and the Struggle for Power in Zimbabwe.* London: Continuum International Publishing Group, 2003.

Hill, Geoff. *The Battle for Zimbabwe.* Hendon, England: Struik Publishers, 2005.

Meredith, Martin. *Our Votes, Our Guns: Robert Mugabe and the Tragedy of Zimbabwe.* New York: Public Affairs, 2003.

List of Appendices

Primary Documents

Appendix 1: Geneva Convention relative to the Treatment of Prisoners of War (1949) URL: http://www.unhchr. ch/html/menu3/b/91.htm (UN Commission for Human Rights) Some of the ancillary material (addenda, etc.) has been deleted for the sake of space.   **490**

Appendix 2: Geneva Convention relative to the Protection of Civilian Persons in Time of War (1949) URL: http://www.unhchr.ch/html/menu3/b/92. htm   **520**

Appendix 3: Convention on the Prevention and Punishment of the Crime of Genocide (1948) URL: http://www.hrweb.org/ legal/genocide.html (Human Rights Web)   **525**

Appendix 4: Universal Declaration of Human Rights (1948) URL: http://www. un.org/Overview/rights.html   **527**

Appendix 5: United Nations Convention against Torture and Other Cruel, Inhuman or Degrading Treatment or Punishment (1985) URL: http://www.unhchr.ch/html/menu3/b/h_cat39.htm   **530**

Appendix 6: Charter of the Nuremberg International Military Tribunal URL: http:///www.derechos.org/nizkor/nuremberg/ ncharter.html   **537**

Appendix 7: Law for the Protection of Hereditary Health: The Attempt to Improve the German Aryan Breed (1933) URL: http://www. mtsu.edu/~baustin/nurmlaw1.html   **541**

Appendix 8: The Nuremberg Laws on Citizenship and Race (1935) Nuremberg Laws defining Aryans and Non-Aryans for citizenship rights: URL: http://www.mtsu.edu/~baustin/nurmlaw2.html   **542**

Primary Documents

Geneva Convention relative to the Treatment of Prisoners of War Adopted on 12 August 1949 by the Diplomatic Conference for the Establishment of International Conventions for the Protection of Victims of War, held in Geneva

from 21 April to 12 August, 1949
entry into force: 21 October 1950

PART I—General Provisions

Article 1

The High Contracting Parties undertake to respect and to ensure respect for the present Convention in all circumstances.

Article 2

In addition to the provisions which shall be implemented in peace time, the present Convention shall apply to all cases of declared war or of any other armed conflict which may arise between two or more of the High Contracting Parties, even if the state of war is not recognized by one of them.

The Convention shall also apply to all cases of partial or total occupation of the territory of a High Contracting Party, even if the said occupation meets with no armed resistance.

Although one of the Powers in conflict may not be a party to the present Convention, the Powers who are parties thereto shall remain bound by it in their mutual relations. They shall furthermore be bound by the Convention in relation to the said Power, if the latter accepts and applies the provisions thereof.

Article 3

In the case of armed conflict not of an international character occurring in the territory of one of the High Contracting Parties, each party to the conflict shall be bound to apply, as a minimum, the following provisions:

1. Persons taking no active part in the hostilities, including members of armed forces who have laid down their arms and those placed hors de combat by sickness, wounds, detention, or any other cause, shall in all circumstances be treated humanely, without any adverse distinction founded on race, colour, religion or faith, sex, birth or wealth, or any other similar criteria.

To this end the following acts are and shall remain prohibited at any time and in any place whatsoever with respect to the above-mentioned persons:

(a) Violence to life and person, in particular murder of all kinds, mutilation, cruel treatment and torture;

(b) Taking of hostages;

(c) Outrages upon personal dignity, in particular, humiliating and degrading treatment;

(d) The passing of sentences and the carrying out of executions without previous judgment pronounced by a regularly constituted court affording all the judicial guarantees which are recognized as indispensable by civilized peoples.

2. The wounded and sick shall be collected and cared for.

An impartial humanitarian body, such as the International Committee of the Red Cross, may offer its services to the Parties to the conflict.

The Parties to the conflict should further endeavour to bring into force, by means of special agreements, all or part of the other provisions of the present Convention.

The application of the preceding provisions shall not affect the legal status of the Parties to the conflict.

Article 4

A. Prisoners of war, in the sense of the present Convention, are persons belonging to one of the following categories, who have fallen into the power of the enemy:

1. Members of the armed forces of a Party to the conflict as well as members of militias or volunteer corps forming part of such armed forces.

2. Members of other militias and members of other volunteer corps, including those of organized resistance movements, belonging to a Party to the conflict and operating in or outside their own territory, even if this territory is occupied, provided that such militias or volunteer corps, including such organized resistance movements, fulfil the following conditions:

(a) That of being commanded by a person responsible for his subordinates;

(b) That of having a fixed distinctive sign recognizable at a distance;

(c) That of carrying arms openly;

(d) That of conducting their operations in accordance with the laws and customs of war.

3. Members of regular armed forces who profess allegiance to a government or an authority not recognized by the Detaining Power.

4. Persons who accompany the armed forces without actually being members thereof, such as civilian members of military aircraft crews, war correspondents, supply contractors, members of labour units or of services responsible for the welfare of the armed forces, provided that they have received authorization from the armed forces which they accompany, who shall provide them for that purpose with an identity card similar to the annexed model.

5. Members of crews, including masters, pilots and apprentices, of the merchant marine and the crews of civil aircraft of the Parties to the conflict, who do not benefit by more favourable treatment under any other provisions of international law.

6. Inhabitants of a non-occupied territory, who on the approach of the enemy spontaneously take up arms to resist the invading forces, without having had time to form themselves into regular armed units, provided they carry arms openly and respect the laws and customs of war.

B. The following shall likewise be treated as prisoners of war under the present Convention:

1. Persons belonging, or having belonged, to the armed forces of the occupied country, if the occupying Power considers it necessary by reason of such allegiance to intern them, even though it has originally liberated them while hostilities were going on outside the territory it occupies, in particular where such persons have made an unsuccessful attempt to rejoin the armed forces to which they belong and which are engaged in combat, or where they fail to comply with a summons made to them with a view to internment.

2. The persons belonging to one of the categories enumerated in the present Article, who have been received by neutral or non-belligerent Powers on their territory and whom these Powers are required to intern under international law, without prejudice to any more favourable treatment which these Powers may choose to give and with the exception of Articles 8, 10, 15, 30, fifth paragraph, 58–67, 92, 126 and, where diplomatic relations exist between the Parties to the conflict and the neutral or non-belligerent Power concerned, those Articles concerning the Protecting Power. Where such diplomatic relations exist, the Parties to a conflict on whom these persons depend shall be allowed to perform towards them the functions of a Protecting Power as provided in the present Convention, without prejudice to the functions which these Parties normally exercise in conformity with diplomatic and consular usage and treaties.

C. This Article shall in no way affect the status of medical personnel and chaplains as provided for in Article 33 of the present Convention.

Article 5

The present Convention shall apply to the persons referred to in Article 4 from the time they fall into the power of the enemy and until their final release and repatriation.

Should any doubt arise as to whether persons, having committed a belligerent act and having fallen into the hands of the enemy, belong to any of the categories enumerated in Article 4, such persons shall enjoy the protection of the present Convention until such time as their status has been determined by a competent tribunal.

Article 6

In addition to the agreements expressly provided for in Articles 10, 23, 28, 33, 60, 65, 66, 67, 72, 73, 75, 109, 110, 118, 119, 122 and 132, the High Contracting Parties may conclude other special agreements for all matters concerning which they may deem it suitable to make separate provision. No special agreement shall adversely affect the situation of prisoners of war, as defined by the present Convention, nor restrict the rights which it confers upon them.

Prisoners of war shall continue to have the benefit of such agreements as long as the Convention is applicable to them, except where express provisions to the contrary are contained in the aforesaid or in subsequent agreements, or where more favourable measures have been taken with regard to them by one or other of the Parties to the conflict.

Article 7

Prisoners of war may in no circumstances renounce in part or in entirety the rights secured to them by the present Convention, and by the special agreements referred to in the foregoing Article, if such there be.

Article 8

The present Convention shall be applied with the cooperation and under the scrutiny of the Protecting Powers whose duty it is to safeguard the interests of the Parties to the conflict. For this purpose, the Protecting Powers may appoint, apart from their diplomatic or consular staff, delegates from amongst their own nationals or the nationals of other neutral Powers. The said delegates shall be subject to the approval of the Power with which they are to carry out their duties.

The Parties to the conflict shall facilitate to the greatest extent possible the task of the representatives or delegates of the Protecting Powers.

The representatives or delegates of the Protecting Powers shall not in any case exceed their mission under the present Convention. They shall, in particular, take account of the imperative necessities of security of the State wherein they carry out their duties.

Article 9

The provisions of the present Convention constitute no obstacle to the humanitarian activities which the International Committee of the Red Cross or any other impartial humanitarian organization may, subject to the consent of the Parties to the conflict concerned, undertake for the protection of prisoners of war and for their relief.

Article 10

The High Contracting Parties may at any time agree to entrust to an organization which offers all guarantees of impartiality and efficacy the duties incumbent on the Protecting Powers by virtue of the present Convention.

When prisoners of war do not benefit or cease to benefit, no matter for what reason, by the activities of a Protecting Power or of an organization provided for in the first paragraph above, the Detaining Power shall request a neutral State, or such an organization, to undertake the functions performed under the present Convention by a Protecting Power designated by the Parties to a conflict.

If protection cannot be arranged accordingly, the Detaining Power shall request or shall accept, subject to the provisions of this Article, the offer of the services of a humanitarian organization, such as the International Committee of the Red Cross, to assume the humanitarian functions performed by Protecting Powers under the present Convention.

Any neutral Power or any organization invited by the Power concerned or offering itself for these purposes, shall be required to act with a sense of responsibility towards the Party to the conflict on which persons protected by the present Convention depend, and shall be required to furnish sufficient assurances that it is in a position to undertake the appropriate functions and to discharge them impartially.

No derogation from the preceding provisions shall be made by special agreements between Powers one of which is restricted, even temporarily, in its freedom to negotiate with the other Power or its allies by reason of military events, more particularly where the whole, or a substantial part, of the territory of the said Power is occupied.

Whenever in the present Convention mention is made of a Protecting Power, such mention applies to substitute organizations in the sense of the present Article.

Article 11

In cases where they deem it advisable in the interest of protected persons, particularly in cases of disagreement between the Parties to the conflict as to the application or interpretation of the provisions of the present Convention, the Protecting Powers shall lend their good offices with a view to settling the disagreement.

For this purpose, each of the Protecting Powers may, either at the invitation of one Party or on its own initiative, propose to the Parties to the conflict a meeting of their representatives, and in particular of the authorities responsible for prisoners of war, possibly on neutral territory suitably chosen. The Parties to the conflict shall be bound to give effect to the proposals made to them for this purpose. The Protecting Powers may, if necessary, propose for approval by the Parties to the conflict a person belonging to a neutral Power, or delegated by the International Committee of the Red Cross, who shall be invited to take part in such a meeting.

Part II—General Protection of Prisoners of War

Article 12

Prisoners of war are in the hands of the enemy Power, but not of the individuals or military units who have captured them. Irrespective of the individual responsibilities that may exist, the Detaining Power is responsible for the treatment given them.

Prisoners of war may only be transferred by the Detaining Power to a Power which is a party to the Convention and after the Detaining Power has satisfied itself of the willingness and ability of such transferee Power to apply the Convention. When prisoners of war are transferred under such circumstances, responsibility for the application of the Convention rests on the Power accepting them while they are in its custody.

Nevertheless if that Power fails to carry out the provisions of the Convention in any important respect, the Power by whom the prisoners of war were transferred shall, upon being notified by the Protecting Power, take effective measures to correct the situation or shall request the return of the prisoners of war. Such requests must be complied with.

Article 13

Prisoners of war must at all times be humanely treated. Any unlawful act or omission by the Detaining Power causing death or seriously endangering the health of a prisoner of war in its custody is prohibited, and will be regarded as a serious breach of the present Convention. In particular, no prisoner of war may be subjected to physical mutilation or to medical or scientific experiments of any kind which are not justified by the medical, dental or hospital treatment of the prisoner concerned and carried out in his interest.

Likewise, prisoners of war must at all times be protected, particularly against acts of violence or intimidation and against insults and public curiosity.

Measures of reprisal against prisoners of war are prohibited.

Article 14

Prisoners of war are entitled in all circumstances to respect for their persons and their honour. Women shall be treated with all the regard due to their sex and shall in all cases benefit by treatment as favourable as that granted to men. Prisoners of war shall retain the full civil capacity which they enjoyed at the time of their capture. The Detaining Power may not restrict the exercise, either within or without its own territory, of the rights such capacity confers except in so far as the captivity requires.

Article 15

The Power detaining prisoners of war shall be bound to provide free of charge for their maintenance and for the medical attention required by their state of health.

Article 16

Taking into consideration the provisions of the present Convention relating to rank and sex, and subject to any privileged treatment which may be accorded to them by reason of their state of health, age or professional qualifications, all prisoners of war shall be treated alike by the Detaining Power, without any adverse distinction based on race, nationality, religious belief or political opinions, or any other distinction founded on similar criteria.

Part III—Captivity

SECTION I: BEGINNING OF CAPTIVITY

Article 17

Every prisoner of war, when questioned on the subject, is bound to give only his surname, first names and rank, date of birth, and army, regimental, personal or serial number, or failing this, equivalent information. If he wilfully infringes this rule, he may render himself liable to a restriction of the privileges accorded to his rank or status.

Each Party to a conflict is required to furnish the persons under its jurisdiction who are liable to become prisoners of war, with an identity card showing the owner's surname, first names, rank, army, regimental, personal or serial number or equivalent information, and date of birth. The identity card may, furthermore, bear the signature or the fingerprints, or both, of the owner, and may bear, as well, any other information the Party to the conflict may wish to add concerning persons belonging to its armed forces. As far as possible the card shall measure 6.5 x 10 cm. and shall be issued in duplicate. The identity card shall be shown by the prisoner of war upon demand, but may in no case be taken away from him.

No physical or mental torture, nor any other form of coercion, may be inflicted on prisoners of war to secure from them information of any kind whatever. Prisoners of war who refuse to answer may not be threatened, insulted, or exposed to any unpleasant or disadvantageous treatment of any kind.

Prisoners of war who, owing to their physical or mental condition, are unable to state their identity, shall be handed over to the medical service. The identity of such prisoners shall be established by all possible means, subject to the provisions of the preceding paragraph.

The questioning of prisoners of war shall be carried out in a language which they understand.

Article 18

All effects and articles of personal use, except arms, horses, military equipment and military documents shall remain in the possession of prisoners of war, likewise their metal helmets and gas masks and like articles issued for personal protection. Effects and articles used for their clothing or feeding shall likewise remain in their possession, even if such effects and articles belong to their regulation military equipment.

At no time should prisoners of war be without identity documents. The Detaining Power shall supply such documents to prisoners of war who possess none.

Badges of rank and nationality, decorations and articles having above all a personal or sentimental value may not be taken from prisoners of war.

Sums of money carried by prisoners of war may not be taken away from them except by order of an officer, and after the amount and particulars of the owner have been recorded in a special register and an itemized receipt has been given, legibly inscribed with the name, rank and unit of the person issuing the said receipt. Sums in the currency of the Detaining Power, or which are changed into such currency at the prisoner's request, shall be placed to the credit of the prisoner's account as provided in Article 64.

The Detaining Power may withdraw articles of value from prisoners of war only for reasons of security; when such articles are withdrawn, the procedure laid down for sums of money impounded shall apply.

Such objects, likewise the sums taken away in any currency other than that of the Detaining Power and the conversion of which has not been asked for by the owners, shall be kept in the custody of the Detaining Power and shall be returned in their initial shape to prisoners of war at the end of their captivity.

Article 19

Prisoners of war shall be evacuated, as soon as possible after their capture, to camps situated in an area far enough from the combat zone for them to be out of danger.

Only those prisoners of war who, owing to wounds or sickness, would run greater risks by being evacuated than by remaining where they are, may be temporarily kept back in a danger zone.

Prisoners of war shall not be unnecessarily exposed to danger while awaiting evacuation from a fighting zone.

Article 20

The evacuation of prisoners of war shall always be effected humanely and in conditions similar to those for the forces of the Detaining Power in their changes of station.

The Detaining Power shall supply prisoners of war who are being evacuated with sufficient food and potable water, and with the necessary clothing and medical attention. The Detaining Power shall take all suitable precautions to ensure their safety during evacuation, and shall establish as soon as possible a list of the prisoners of war who are evacuated.

If prisoners of war must, during evacuation, pass through transit camps, their stay in such camps shall be as brief as possible.

SECTION II: INTERNMENT OF PRISONERS OF WAR

Chapter I—General Observations

Article 21

The Detaining Power may subject prisoners of war to internment. It may impose on them the obligation of not leaving, beyond certain limits, the camp where they are interned, or if the said camp is fenced in, of not going outside its perimeter. Subject to the provisions of the present Convention relative to penal and disciplinary sanctions, prisoners of war may not be held in close confinement except where necessary to safeguard their health and then only during the continuation of the circumstances which make such confinement necessary.

Prisoners of war may be partially or wholly released on parole or promise, in so far as is allowed by the laws of the Power on which they depend. Such measures shall be taken particularly in cases where this may contribute to the improvement of their state of health. No prisoner of war shall be compelled to accept liberty on parole or promise.

Upon the outbreak of hostilities, each Party to the conflict shall notify the adverse Party of the laws and regulations allowing or forbidding its own nationals to accept liberty on parole or promise. Prisoners of war who are paroled or who have given their promise in conformity with the laws and regulations so notified, are bound on their personal honour scrupulously to fulfil, both towards the Power on which they depend and towards the Power which has captured them, the engagements of their paroles or promises. In such cases, the Power on which they depend is bound neither to require nor to accept from them any service incompatible with the parole or promise given.

Article 22

Prisoners of war may be interned only in premises located on land and affording every guarantee of hygiene and healthfulness. Except in particular cases which are justified by the interest of the prisoners themselves, they shall not be interned in penitentiaries.

Prisoners of war interned in unhealthy areas, or where the climate is injurious for them, shall be removed as soon as possible to a more favourable climate.

The Detaining Power shall assemble prisoners of war in camps or camp compounds according to their nationality, language and customs, provided that such prisoners shall not be separated from prisoners of war belonging to the armed forces with which they were serving at the time of their capture, except with their consent.

Article 23

No prisoner of war may at any time be sent to or detained in areas where he may be exposed to the fire of the combat zone, nor may his presence be used to render certain points or areas immune from military operations.

Prisoners of war shall have shelters against air bombardment and other hazards of war, to the same extent as the local civilian population. With the exception of those engaged in the protection of their quarters against the aforesaid hazards, they may enter such shelters as soon as possible after the giving of the alarm. Any other protective measure taken in favour of the population shall also apply to them.

Detaining Powers shall give the Powers concerned, through the intermediary of the Protecting Powers, all useful information regarding the geographical location of prisoner of war camps.

Whenever military considerations permit, prisoner of war camps shall be indicated in the day-time by the letters PW or PG, placed so as to be clearly visible from the air. The Powers concerned may, however, agree upon any other system of marking. Only prisoner of war camps shall be marked as such.

Article 24

Transit or screening camps of a permanent kind shall be fitted out under conditions similar to those described in the present Section, and the prisoners therein shall have the same treatment as in other camps.

Chapter II—Quarters, Food and Clothing of Prisoners of War

Article 25

Prisoners of war shall be quartered under conditions as favourable as those for the forces of the Detaining Power who are billeted in the same area. The said conditions shall make allowance for the habits and customs of the prisoners and shall in no case be prejudicial to their health.

The foregoing provisions shall apply in particular to the dormitories of prisoners of war as regards both total surface and minimum cubic space, and the general installations, bedding and blankets.

The premises provided for the use of prisoners of war individually or collectively, shall be entirely protected from dampness and adequately heated and lighted, in particular between dusk and lights out. All precautions must be taken against the danger of fire.

In any camps in which women prisoners of war, as well as men, are accommodated, separate dormitories shall be provided for them.

Article 26

The basic daily food rations shall be sufficient in quantity, quality and variety to keep prisoners of war in good health and to prevent loss of weight or the development of nutri-

tional deficiencies. Account shall also be taken of the habitual diet of the prisoners.

The Detaining Power shall supply prisoners of war who work with such additional rations as are necessary for the labour on which they are employed.

Sufficient drinking water shall be supplied to prisoners of war. The use of tobacco shall be permitted.

Prisoners of war shall, as far as possible, be associated with the preparation of their meals; they may be employed for that purpose in the kitchens. Furthermore, they shall be given the means of preparing, themselves, the additional food in their possession.

Adequate premises shall be provided for messing.

Collective disciplinary measures affecting food are prohibited.

Article 27

Clothing, underwear and footwear shall be supplied to prisoners of war in sufficient quantities by the Detaining Power, which shall make allowance for the climate of the region where the prisoners are detained. Uniforms of enemy armed forces captured by the Detaining Power should, if suitable for the climate, be made available to clothe prisoners of war.

The regular replacement and repair of the above articles shall be assured by the Detaining Power. In addition, prisoners of war who work shall receive appropriate clothing, wherever the nature of the work demands.

Article 28

Canteens shall be installed in all camps, where prisoners of war may procure foodstuffs, soap and tobacco and ordinary articles in daily use. The tariff shall never be in excess of local market prices. The profits made by camp canteens shall be used for the benefit of the prisoners; a special fund shall be created for this purpose. The prisoners' representative shall have the right to collaborate in the management of the canteen and of this fund.

When a camp is closed down, the credit balance of the special fund shall be handed to an international welfare organization, to be employed for the benefit of prisoners of war of the same nationality as those who have contributed to the fund. In case of a general repatriation, such profits shall be kept by the Detaining Power, subject to any agreement to the contrary between the Powers concerned.

Chapter III— Hygiene and Medical Attention

Article 29

The Detaining Power shall be bound to take all sanitary measures necessary to ensure the cleanliness and healthfulness of camps and to prevent epidemics.

Prisoners of war shall have for their use, day and night, conveniences which conform to the rules of hygiene and are maintained in a constant state of cleanliness. In any camps in which women prisoners of war are accommodated, separate conveniences shall be provided for them.

Also, apart from the baths and showers with which the camps shall be furnished, prisoners of war shall be provided with sufficient water and soap for their personal toilet and for washing their personal laundry; the necessary installations, facilities and time shall be granted them for that purpose.

Article 30

Every camp shall have an adequate infirmary where prisoners of war may have the attention they require, as well as appropriate diet. Isolation wards shall, if necessary, be set aside for cases of contagious or mental disease.

Prisoners of war suffering from serious disease, or whose condition necessitates special treatment, a surgical operation or hospital care, must be admitted to any military or civilian medical unit where such treatment can be given, even if their repatriation is contemplated in the near future. Special facilities shall be afforded for the care to be given to the disabled, in particular to the blind, and for their rehabilitation, pending repatriation.

Prisoners of war shall have the attention, preferably, of medical personnel of the Power on which they depend and, if possible, of their nationality.

Prisoners of war may not be prevented from presenting themselves to the medical authorities for examination. The detaining authorities shall, upon request, issue to every prisoner who has undergone treatment, an official certificate indicating the nature of his illness or injury, and the duration and kind of treatment received. A duplicate of this certificate shall be forwarded to the Central Prisoners of War Agency.

The costs of treatment, including those of any apparatus necessary for the maintenance of prisoners of war in good health, particularly dentures and other artificial appliances, and spectacles, shall be borne by the Detaining Power.

Article 31

Medical inspections of prisoners of war shall be held at least once a month. They shall include the checking and the recording of the weight of each prisoner of war. Their purpose shall be, in particular, to supervise the general state of health, nutrition and cleanliness of prisoners and to detect contagious diseases, especially tuberculosis, malaria and venereal disease. For this purpose the most efficient methods available shall be employed, e.g. periodic mass miniature radiography for the early detection of tuberculosis.

Article 32

Prisoners of war who, though not attached to the medical service of their armed forces, are physicians, surgeons, dentists, nurses or medical orderlies, may be required by the Detaining Power to exercise their medical functions in the interests of prisoners of war dependent on the same Power. In that case they shall continue to be prisoners of war, but shall receive the same treatment as corresponding medical personnel retained by the Detaining Power. They shall be exempted from any other work under Article 49.

Chapter IV—Medical Personnel and Chaplains Retained to Assist Prisoners of War

Article 33

Members of the medical personnel and chaplains while retained by the Detaining Power with a view to assisting prisoners of war, shall not be considered as prisoners of war. They shall, however, receive as a minimum the benefits and protection of the present Convention, and shall also be granted all facilities necessary to provide for the medical care of, and religious ministration to, prisoners of war.

They shall continue to exercise their medical and spiritual functions for the benefit of prisoners of war, preferably those belonging to the armed forces upon which they depend, within the scope of the military laws and regulations of the Detaining Power and under the control of its competent services, in accordance with their professional etiquette. They shall also benefit by the following facilities in the exercise of their medical or spiritual functions:

(a) They shall be authorized to visit periodically prisoners of war situated in working detachments or in hospitals outside the camp. For this purpose, the Detaining Power shall place at their disposal the necessary means of transport.

(b) The senior medical officer in each camp shall be responsible to the camp military authorities for everything connected with the activities of retained medical personnel. For this purpose, Parties to the conflict shall agree at the outbreak of hostilities on the subject of the corresponding ranks of the medical personnel, including that of societies mentioned in Article 26 of the Geneva Convention for the Amelioration of the Condition of the Wounded and Sick in Armed Forces in the Field of August 12, 1949. This senior medical officer, as well as chaplains, shall have the right to deal with the competent authorities of the camp on all questions relating to their duties. Such authorities shall afford them all necessary facilities for correspondence relating to these questions.

(c) Although they shall be subject to the internal discipline of the camp in which they are retained, such personnel may not be compelled to carry out any work other than that concerned with their medical or religious duties.

During hostilities, the Parties to the conflict shall agree concerning the possible relief of retained personnel and shall settle the procedure to be followed.

None of the preceding provisions shall relieve the Detaining Power of its obligations with regard to prisoners of war from the medical or spiritual point of view.

Chapter V—Religious, Intellectual and Physical Activities

Article 34

Prisoners of war shall enjoy complete latitude in the exercise of their religious duties, including attendance at the service of their faith, on condition that they comply with the disciplinary routine prescribed by the military authorities.

Adequate premises shall be provided where religious services may be held.

Article 35

Chaplains who fall into the hands of the enemy Power and who remain or are retained with a view to assisting prisoners of war, shall be allowed to minister to them and to exercise freely their ministry amongst prisoners of war of the same religion, in accordance with their religious conscience. They shall be allocated among the various camps and labour detachments containing prisoners of war belonging to the same forces, speaking the same language or practising the same religion. They shall enjoy the necessary facilities, including the means of transport provided for in Article 33, for visiting the prisoners of war outside their camp. They shall be free to correspond, subject to censorship, on matters concerning their religious duties with the ecclesiastical authorities in the country of detention and with international religious organizations. Letters and cards which they may send for this purpose shall be in addition to the quota provided for in Article 71.

Article 36

Prisoners of war who are ministers of religion, without having officiated as chaplains to their own forces, shall be at liberty, whatever their denomination, to minister freely to the members of their community. For this purpose, they shall receive the same treatment as the chaplains retained by the Detaining Power. They shall not be obliged to do any other work.

Article 37

When prisoners of war have not the assistance of a retained chaplain or of a prisoner of war minister of their faith, a minister belonging to the prisoners' or a similar denomination, or in his absence a qualified layman, if such a course is feasible from a confessional point of view, shall be appointed, at the request of the prisoners concerned, to fill this office.

This appointment, subject to the approval of the Detaining Power, shall take place with the agreement of the community of prisoners concerned and, wherever necessary, with the approval of the local religious authorities of the same faith. The person thus appointed shall comply with all regulations established by the Detaining Power in the interests of discipline and military security.

Article 38

While respecting the individual preferences of every prisoner, the Detaining Power shall encourage the practice of intellectual, educational, and recreational pursuits, sports and games amongst prisoners, and shall take the measures necessary to ensure the exercise thereof by providing them with adequate premises and necessary equipment.

Prisoners shall have opportunities for taking physical exercise, including sports and games, and for being out of doors. Sufficient open spaces shall be provided for this purpose in all camps.

Chapter VI—Discipline

Article 39

Every prisoner of war camp shall be put under the immediate authority of a responsible commissioned officer belonging to the regular armed forces of the Detaining Power. Such officer shall have in his possession a copy of the present Convention; he shall ensure that its provisions are known to the camp staff and the guard and shall be responsible, under the direction of his government, for its application.

Prisoners of war, with the exception of officers, must salute and show to all officers of the Detaining Power the external marks of respect provided for by the regulations applying in their own forces.

Officer prisoners of war are bound to salute only officers of a higher rank of the Detaining Power; they must, however, salute the camp commander regardless of his rank.

Article 40

The wearing of badges of rank and nationality, as well as of decorations, shall be permitted.

Article 41

In every camp the text of the present Convention and its Annexes and the contents of any special agreement provided for in Article 6, shall be posted, in the prisoners' own language, at places where all may read them. Copies shall be supplied, on request, to the prisoners who cannot have access to the copy which has been posted.

Regulations, orders, notices and publications of every kind relating to the conduct of prisoners of war shall be issued to them in a language which they understand. Such regulations, orders and publications shall be posted in the manner described above and copies shall be handed to the prisoners' representative. Every order and command addressed to prisoners of war individually must likewise be given in a language which they understand.

Article 42

The use of weapons against prisoners of war, especially against those who are escaping or attempting to escape, shall constitute an extreme measure, which shall always be preceded by warnings appropriate to the circumstances.

Chapter VII—Rank of Prisoners of War

Article 43

Upon the outbreak of hostilities, the Parties to the conflict shall communicate to one another the titles and ranks of all the persons mentioned in Article 4 of the present Convention, in order to ensure equality of treatment between prisoners of equivalent rank. Titles and ranks which are subsequently created shall form the subject of similar communications.

The Detaining Power shall recognize promotions in rank which have been accorded to prisoners of war and which have been duly notified by the Power on which these prisoners depend.

Article 44

Officers and prisoners of equivalent status shall be treated with the regard due to their rank and age.

In order to ensure service in officers' camps, other ranks of the same armed forces who, as far as possible, speak the same language, shall be assigned in sufficient numbers, account being taken of the rank of officers and prisoners of equivalent status. Such orderlies shall not be required to perform any other work.

Supervision of the mess by the officers themselves shall be facilitated in every way.

Article 45

Prisoners of war other than officers and prisoners of equivalent status shall be treated with the regard due to their rank and age.

Supervision of the mess by the prisoners themselves shall be facilitated in every way.

Chapter VIII—Transfer of Prisoners of War after Their Arrival in Camp

Article 46

The Detaining Power, when deciding upon the transfer of prisoners of war, shall take into account the interests of the prisoners themselves, more especially so as not to increase the difficulty of their repatriation.

The transfer of prisoners of war shall always be effected humanely and in conditions not less favourable than those under which the forces of the Detaining Power are transferred. Account shall always be taken of the climatic conditions to which the prisoners of war are accustomed and the conditions of transfer shall in no case be prejudicial to their health.

The Detaining Power shall supply prisoners of war during transfer with sufficient food and drinking water to keep them in good health, likewise with the necessary clothing, shelter and medical attention. The Detaining Power shall take adequate precautions especially in case of transport by sea or by air, to ensure their safety during transfer, and shall draw up a complete list of all transferred prisoners before their departure.

Article 47

Sick or wounded prisoners of war shall not be transferred as long as their recovery may be endangered by the journey, unless their safety imperatively demands it.

If the combat zone draws closer to a camp, the prisoners of war in the said camp shall not be transferred unless their transfer can be carried out in adequate conditions of safety, or if they are exposed to greater risks by remaining on the spot than by being transferred.

Article 48

In the event of transfer, prisoners of war shall be officially advised of their departure and of their new postal address. Such notifications shall be given in time for them to pack their luggage and inform their next of kin.

They shall be allowed to take with them their personal effects, and the correspondence and parcels which have arrived for them. The weight of such baggage may be limited, if the conditions of transfer so require, to what each prisoner can reasonably carry, which shall in no case be more than twenty-five kilograms per head.

Mail and parcels addressed to their former camp shall be forwarded to them without delay. The camp commander shall take, in agreement with the prisoners' representative, any measures needed to ensure the transport of the prisoners' community property and of the luggage they are unable to take with them in consequence of restrictions imposed by virtue of the second paragraph of this Article.

The costs of transfers shall be borne by the Detaining Power.

Section III: Labour of Prisoners of War

Article 49

The Detaining Power may utilize the labour of prisoners of war who are physically fit, taking into account their age, sex, rank and physical aptitude, and with a view particularly to maintaining them in a good state of physical and mental health.

Non-commissioned officers who are prisoners of war shall only be required to do supervisory work. Those not so required may ask for other suitable work which shall, so far as possible, be found for them.

If officers or persons of equivalent status ask for suitable work, it shall be found for them, so far as possible, but they may in no circumstances be compelled to work.

Article 50

Besides work connected with camp administration, installation or maintenance, prisoners of war may be compelled to do only such work as is included in the following classes:

(a) Agriculture;

(b) Industries connected with the production or the extraction of raw materials, and manufacturing industries, with the exception of metallurgical, machinery and chemical industries; public works and building operations which have no military character or purpose;

(c) Transport and handling of stores which are not military in character or purpose;

(d) Commercial business, and arts and crafts;

(e) Domestic service;

(f) Public utility services having no military character or purpose.

Should the above provisions be infringed, prisoners of war shall be allowed to exercise their right of complaint, in conformity with Article 78.

Article 51

Prisoners of war must be granted suitable working conditions, especially as regards accommodation, food, clothing and equipment; such conditions shall not be inferior to those enjoyed by nationals of the Detaining Power employed in similar work; account shall also be taken of climatic conditions.

The Detaining Power, in utilizing the labour of prisoners of war, shall ensure that in areas in which prisoners are employed, the national legislation concerning the protection of labour, and, more particularly, the regulations for the safety of workers, are duly applied.

Prisoners of war shall receive training and be provided with the means of protection suitable to the work they will have to do and similar to those accorded to the nationals of the Detaining Power. Subject to the provisions of Article 52, prisoners may be submitted to the normal risks run by these civilian workers.

Conditions of labour shall in no case be rendered more arduous by disciplinary measures.

Article 52

Unless he be a volunteer, no prisoner of war may be employed on labour which is of an unhealthy or dangerous nature.

No prisoner of war shall be assigned to labour which would be looked upon as humiliating for a member of the Detaining Power's own forces.

The removal of mines or similar devices shall be considered as dangerous labour.

Article 53

The duration of the daily labour of prisoners of war, including the time of the journey to and fro, shall not be excessive, and must in no case exceed that permitted for civilian workers in the district, who are nationals of the Detaining Power and employed on the same work.

Prisoners of war must be allowed, in the middle of the day's work, a rest of not less than one hour. This rest will be the same as that to which workers of the Detaining Power are entitled, if the latter is of longer duration. They shall be allowed in addition a rest of twenty-four consecutive hours every week, preferably on Sunday or the day of rest in their country of origin. Furthermore, every prisoner who has worked for one year shall be granted a rest of eight consecutive days, during which his working pay shall be paid him.

If methods of labour such as piece-work are employed, the length of the working period shall not be rendered excessive thereby.

Article 54

The working pay due to prisoners of war shall be fixed in accordance with the provisions of Article 62 of the present Convention.

Prisoners of war who sustain accidents in connection with work, or who contract a disease in the course, or in consequence of their work, shall receive all the care their condition may require. The Detaining Power shall furthermore deliver to such prisoners of war a medical certificate enabling them to submit their claims to the Power on which they depend, and shall send a duplicate to the Central Prisoners of War Agency provided for in Article 123.

Article 55

The fitness of prisoners of war for work shall be periodically verified by medical examinations at least once a month. The examinations shall have particular regard to the nature of the work which prisoners of war are required to do.

If any prisoner of war considers himself incapable of working, he shall be permitted to appear before the medical authorities of his camp. Physicians or surgeons may recommend that the prisoners who are, in their opinion, unfit for work, be exempted therefrom.

Article 56

The organization and administration of labour detachments shall be similar to those of prisoner of war camps.

Every labour detachment shall remain under the control of and administratively part of a prisoner of war camp. The military authorities and the commander of the said camp shall be responsible, under the direction of their government, for the observance of the provisions of the present Convention in labour detachments.

The camp commander shall keep an up-to-date record of the labour detachments dependent on his camp, and shall communicate it to the delegates of the Protecting Power, of the International Committee of the Red Cross, or of other agencies giving relief to prisoners of war, who may visit the camp.

Article 57

The treatment of prisoners of war who work for private persons, even if the latter are responsible for guarding and protecting them, shall not be inferior to that which is provided for by the present Convention. The Detaining Power, the military authorities and the commander of the camp to which such prisoners belong shall be entirely responsible for the maintenance, care, treatment, and payment of the working pay of such prisoners of war.

Such prisoners of war shall have the right to remain in communication with the prisoners' representatives in the camps on which they depend.

Section IV: Financial Resources of Prisoners of War

Article 58

Upon the outbreak of hostilities, and pending an arrangement on this matter with the Protecting Power, the Detaining Power may determine the maximum amount of money in cash or in any similar form, that prisoners may have in their possession. Any amount in excess, which was properly in their possession and which has been taken or withheld from them, shall be placed to their account, together with any monies deposited by them, and shall not be converted into any other currency without their consent.

If prisoners of war are permitted to purchase services or commodities outside the camp against payment in cash, such payments shall be made by the prisoner himself or by the camp administration who will charge them to the accounts of the prisoners concerned. The Detaining Power will establish the necessary rules in this respect.

Article 59

Cash which was taken from prisoners of war, in accordance with Article 18, at the time of their capture, and which is in the currency of the Detaining Power, shall be placed to their separate accounts, in accordance with the provisions of Article 64 of the present Section.

The amounts, in the currency of the Detaining Power, due to the conversion of sums in other currencies that are taken from the prisoners of war at the same time, shall also be credited to their separate accounts.

Article 60

The Detaining Power shall grant all prisoners of war a monthly advance of pay, the amount of which shall be fixed by conversion, into the currency of the said Power, of the following amounts:

Category I: Prisoners ranking below sergeant: eight Swiss francs.

Category II: Sergeants and other non-commissioned officers, or prisoners of equivalent rank: twelve Swiss francs.

Category III: Warrant officers and commissioned officers below the rank of major or prisoners of equivalent rank: fifty Swiss francs.

Category IV: Majors, lieutenant-colonels, colonels or prisoners of equivalent rank: sixty Swiss francs.

Category V: General officers or prisoners of equivalent rank: seventy-five Swiss francs.

However, the Parties to the conflict concerned may by special agreement modify the amount of advances of pay due to prisoners of the preceding categories.

Furthermore, if the amounts indicated in the first paragraph above would be unduly high compared with the pay of the Detaining Power's armed forces or would, for any reason, seriously embarrass the Detaining Power, then, pending the conclusion of a special agreement with the Power on which the prisoners depend to vary the amounts indicated above, the Detaining Power:

(a) Shall continue to credit the accounts of the prisoners with the amounts indicated in the first paragraph above;

(b) May temporarily limit the amount made available from these advances of pay to prisoners of war for their own use, to sums which are reasonable, but which, for Category I, shall never be inferior to the amount that the Detaining Power gives to the members of its own armed forces.

The reasons for any limitations will be given without delay to the Protecting Power.

Article 61

The Detaining Power shall accept for distribution as supplementary pay to prisoners of war sums which the Power on which the prisoners depend may forward to them, on condition that the sums to be paid shall be the same for each prisoner of the same category, shall be payable to all prisoners of that category depending on that Power, and shall be placed in their separate accounts, at the earliest opportunity, in accordance with the provisions of Article 64.

Such supplementary pay shall not relieve the Detaining Power of any obligation under this Convention.

Article 62

Prisoners of war shall be paid a fair working rate of pay by the detaining authorities direct. The rate shall be fixed by the said authorities, but shall at no time be less than one-fourth of one Swiss franc for a full working day. The Detaining Power shall inform prisoners of war, as well as the Power on which they depend, through the intermediary of the Protecting Power, of the rate of daily working pay that it has fixed.

Working pay shall likewise be paid by the detaining authorities to prisoners of war permanently detailed to duties or to a skilled or semi-skilled occupation in connection with the administration, installation or maintenance of camps, and to the prisoners who are required to carry out spiritual or medical duties on behalf of their comrades.

The working pay of the prisoners' representative, of his advisers, if any, and of his assistants, shall be paid out of the fund maintained by canteen profits. The scale of this working pay shall be fixed by the prisoners' representative and approved by the camp commander. If there is no such fund, the detaining authorities shall pay these prisoners a fair working rate of pay.

Article 63

Prisoners of war shall be permitted to receive remittances of money addressed to them individually or collectively.

Every prisoner of war shall have at his disposal the credit balance of his account as provided for in the following Article, within the limits fixed by the Detaining Power, which shall make such payments as are requested. Subject to financial or monetary restrictions which the Detaining Power regards as essential, prisoners of war may also have payments made abroad. In this case payments addressed by prisoners of war to dependants shall be given priority.

In any event, and subject to the consent of the Power on which they depend, prisoners may have payments made in their own country, as follows: the Detaining Power shall send to the aforesaid Power through the Protecting Power a notification giving all the necessary particulars concerning the prisoners of war, the beneficiaries of the payments, and the amount of the sums to be paid, expressed in the Detaining Power's currency. The said notification shall be signed by the prisoners and countersigned by the camp commander. The Detaining Power shall debit the prisoners' account by a corresponding amount; the sums thus debited shall be placed by it to the credit of the Power on which the prisoners depend.

To apply the foregoing provisions, the Detaining Power may usefully consult the Model Regulations in Annex V of the present Convention.

Article 64

The Detaining Power shall hold an account for each prisoner of war, showing at least the following:

1. The amounts due to the prisoner or received by him as advances of pay, as working pay or derived from any other source; the sums in the currency of the Detaining Power which were taken from him; the sums taken from him and converted at his request into the currency of the said Power.

2. The payments made to the prisoner in cash, or in any other similar form; the payments made on his behalf and at his request; the sums transferred under Article 63, third paragraph.

Article 65

Every item entered in the account of a prisoner of war shall be countersigned or initialled by him, or by the prisoners' representative acting on his behalf.

Prisoners of war shall at all times be afforded reasonable facilities for consulting and obtaining copies of their accounts, which may likewise be inspected by the representatives of the Protecting Powers at the time of visits to the camp.

When prisoners of war are transferred from one camp to another, their personal accounts will follow them. In case of transfer from one Detaining Power to another, the monies which are their property and are not in the currency of the Detaining Power will follow them. They shall be given certificates for any other monies standing to the credit of their accounts.

The Parties to the conflict concerned may agree to notify to each other at specific intervals through the Protecting Power, the amount of the accounts of the prisoners of war.

Article 66

On the termination of captivity, through the release of a prisoner of war or his repatriation, the Detaining Power shall give him a statement, signed by an authorized officer of that Power, showing the credit balance then due to him. The Detaining Power shall also send through the Protecting Power to the government upon which the prisoner of war depends, lists giving all appropriate particulars of all prisoners of war whose captivity has been terminated by repatriation, release, escape, death or any other means, and showing the amount of their credit balances. Such lists shall be certified on each sheet by an authorized representative of the Detaining Power.

Any of the above provisions of this Article may be varied by mutual agreement between any two Parties to the conflict.

The Power on which the prisoner of war depends shall be responsible for settling with him any credit balance due to him from the Detaining Power on the termination of his captivity.

Article 67

Advances of pay, issued to prisoners of war in conformity with Article 60, shall be considered as made on behalf of the Power on which they depend. Such advances of pay, as well as all payments made by the said Power under Article 63, third paragraph, and Article 68, shall form the subject of arrangements between the Powers concerned, at the close of hostilities.

Article 68

Any claim by a prisoner of war for compensation in respect of any injury or other disability arising out of work shall be referred to the Power on which he depends, through the Protecting Power. In accordance with Article 54, the Detaining Power will, in all cases, provide the prisoner of war concerned with a statement showing the nature of the injury or disability, the circumstances in which it arose and particulars of medical or hospital treatment given for it. This statement will be signed by a responsible officer of the Detaining Power and the medical particulars certified by a medical officer.

Any claim by a prisoner of war for compensation in respect of personal effects, monies or valuables impounded by the Detaining Power under Article 18 and not forthcoming on his repatriation, or in respect of loss alleged to be due to the fault of the Detaining Power or any of its servants, shall likewise be referred to the Power on which he depends. Nevertheless, any such personal effects required for use by the prisoners of war whilst in captivity shall be replaced at the expense of the Detaining Power. The Detaining Power will, in all cases, provide the prisoner of war with a statement, signed by a responsible officer, showing all available information regarding the reasons why such effects, monies or valuables have not been restored to him. A copy of this statement will be forwarded to the Power on which he depends through the Central Prisoners of War Agency provided for in Article 123.

SECTION V: RELATIONS OF PRISONERS OF WAR WITH THE EXTERIOR

Article 69

Immediately upon prisoners of war falling into its power, the Detaining Power shall inform them and the Powers on which they depend, through the Protecting Power, of the measures taken to carry out the provisions of the present Section. They shall likewise inform the parties concerned of any subsequent modifications of such measures.

Article 70

Immediately upon capture, or not more than one week after arrival at a camp, even if it is a transit camp, likewise in case of sickness or transfer to hospital or another camp, every prisoner of war shall be enabled to write direct to his family, on the one hand, and to the Central Prisoners of War Agency provided for in Article 123, on the other hand, a card similar, if possible, to the model annexed to the present Convention, informing his relatives of his capture, address and state of health. The said cards shall be forwarded as rapidly as possible and may not be delayed in any manner.

Article 71

Prisoners of war shall be allowed to send and receive letters and cards. If the Detaining Power deems it necessary to limit the number of letters and cards sent by each prisoner of war, the said number shall not be less than two letters and four cards monthly, exclusive of the capture cards provided for in Article 70, and conforming as closely as possible to the models annexed to the present Convention. Further limitations may be imposed only if the Protecting Power is satisfied that it would be in the interests of the prisoners of war concerned to do so owing to difficulties of translation caused by the Detaining Power's inability to find sufficient qualified linguists to carry out the necessary censorship. If limitations must be placed on the correspondence addressed to prisoners of war, they may be ordered only by the Power on which the prisoners depend, possibly at the request of the Detaining Power. Such letters and cards must be conveyed by the most rapid method at the disposal of the Detaining Power; they may not be delayed or retained for disciplinary reasons.

Prisoners of war who have been without news for a long period, or who are unable to receive news from their next of kin or to give them news by the ordinary postal route, as well as those who are at a great distance from their homes, shall be permitted to send telegrams, the fees being charged against the prisoners of war's accounts with the Detaining Power or paid in the currency at their disposal. They shall likewise benefit by this measure in cases of urgency.

As a general rule, the correspondence of prisoners of war shall be written in their native language. The Parties to the conflict may allow correspondence in other languages.

Sacks containing prisoner of war mail must be securely sealed and labelled so as clearly to indicate their contents, and must be addressed to offices of destination.

Article 72

Prisoners of war shall be allowed to receive by post or by any other means individual parcels or collective shipments containing, in particular, foodstuffs, clothing, medical supplies and articles of a religious, educational or recreational character which may meet their needs, including books, devotional articles, scientific equipment, examination papers, musical instruments, sports outfits and materials allowing prisoners of war to pursue their studies or their cultural activities.

Such shipments shall in no way free the Detaining Power from the obligations imposed upon it by virtue of the present Convention.

The only limits which may be placed on these shipments shall be those proposed by the Protecting Power in the interest of the prisoners themselves, or by the International Committee of the Red Cross or any other organization giving assistance to the prisoners, in respect of their own shipments only, on account of exceptional strain on transport or communications.

The conditions for the sending of individual parcels and collective relief shall, if necessary, be the subject of special agreements between the Powers concerned, which may in no case delay the receipt by the prisoners of relief supplies. Books may not be included in parcels of clothing and foodstuffs. Medical supplies shall, as a rule, be sent in collective parcels.

Article 73

In the absence of special agreements between the Powers concerned on the conditions for the receipt and distribution of collective relief shipments, the rules and regulations concerning collective shipments, which are annexed to the present Convention, shall be applied.

The special agreements referred to above shall in no case restrict the right of prisoners' representatives to take possession of collective relief shipments intended for prisoners of war, to proceed to their distribution or to dispose of them in the interest of the prisoners.

Nor shall such agreements restrict the right of representatives of the Protecting Power, the International Committee of the Red Cross or any other organization giving assistance to prisoners of war and responsible for the forwarding of collective shipments, to supervise their distribution to the recipients.

Article 74

All relief shipments for prisoners of war shall be exempt from import, customs and other dues.

Correspondence, relief shipments and authorized remittances of money addressed to prisoners of war or despatched by them through the post office, either direct or through the Information Bureaux provided for in Article 122 and the Central Prisoners of War Agency provided for in Article 123, shall be exempt from any postal dues, both in the countries of origin and destination, and in intermediate countries.

If relief shipments intended for prisoners of war cannot be sent through the post office by reason of weight or for any other cause, the cost of transportation shall be borne by the Detaining Power in all the territories under its control. The other Powers party to the Convention shall bear the cost of transport in their respective territories.

In the absence of special agreements between the Parties concerned, the costs connected with transport of such shipments, other than costs covered by the above exemption, shall be charged to the senders.

The High Contracting Parties shall endeavour to reduce, so far as possible, the rates charged for telegrams sent by prisoners of war, or addressed to them.

Article 75

Should military operations prevent the Powers concerned from fulfilling their obligation to assure the transport of the shipments referred to in Articles 70, 71, 72 and 77, the Protecting Powers concerned, the International Committee of the Red Cross or any other organization duly approved by the Parties to the conflict may undertake to ensure the conveyance of such shipments by suitable means (railway wagons, motor vehicles, vessels or aircraft, etc.). For this purpose, the High Contracting Parties shall endeavour to supply them with such transport and to allow its circulation, especially by granting the necessary safe-conducts.

Such transport may also be used to convey:

(a) Correspondence, lists and reports exchanged between the Central Information Agency referred to in Article 123 and the National Bureaux referred to in Article 122;

(b) Correspondence and reports relating to prisoners of war which the Protecting Powers, the International Committee of the Red Cross or any other body assisting the prisoners, exchange either with their own delegates or with the Parties to the conflict.

These provisions in no way detract from the right of any Party to the conflict to arrange other means of transport, if it should so prefer, nor preclude the granting of safe-conducts, under mutually agreed conditions, to such means of transport.

In the absence of special agreements, the costs occasioned by the use of such means of transport shall be borne proportionally by the Parties to the conflict whose nationals are benefited thereby.

Article 76

The censoring of correspondence addressed to prisoners of war or despatched by them shall be done as quickly as possible. Mail shall be censored only by the despatching State and the receiving State, and once only by each.

The examination of consignments intended for prisoners of war shall not be carried out under conditions that will expose the goods contained in them to deterioration; except in the case of written or printed matter, it shall be done in the presence of the addressee, or of a fellow-prisoner duly delegated by him. The delivery to prisoners of individual or collective consignments shall not be delayed under the pretext of difficulties of censorship.

Any prohibition of correspondence ordered by Parties to the conflict, either for military or political reasons, shall be only temporary and its duration shall be as short as possible.

Article 77

The Detaining Powers shall provide all facilities for the transmission, through the Protecting Power or the Central Prisoners of War Agency provided for in Article 123, of instruments, papers or documents intended for prisoners of war or despatched by them, especially powers of attorney and wills.

In all cases they shall facilitate the preparation and execution of such documents on behalf of prisoners of war; in particular, they shall allow them to consult a lawyer and shall take what measures are necessary for the authentication of their signatures.

SECTION VI: RELATIONS BETWEEN PRISONERS OF WAR AND THE AUTHORITIES

Chapter I—Complaints of Prisoners of War Respecting the Conditions of Captivity

Article 78

Prisoners of war shall have the right to make known to the military authorities in whose power they are, their requests regarding the conditions of captivity to which they are subjected.

They shall also have the unrestricted right to apply to the representatives of the Protecting Powers either through their prisoners' representative or, if they consider it necessary, direct, in order to draw their attention to any points on which they may have complaints to make regarding their conditions of captivity.

These requests and complaints shall not be limited nor considered to be a part of the correspondence quota referred to in Article 71. They must be transmitted immediately. Even if they are recognized to be unfounded, they may not give rise to any punishment.

Prisoners' representatives may send periodic reports on the situation in the camps and the needs of the prisoners of war to the representatives of the Protecting Powers.

Chapter II—Prisoner of War Representatives

Article 79

In all places where there are prisoners of war, except in those where there are officers, the prisoners shall freely elect by secret ballot, every six months, and also in case of vacancies, prisoners' representatives entrusted with representing them before the military authorities, the Protecting Powers, the International Committee of the Red Cross and any other organization which may assist them. These prisoners' representatives shall be eligible for re-election.

In camps for officers and persons of equivalent status or in mixed camps, the senior officer among the prisoners of war shall be recognized as the camp prisoners' representative. In camps for officers, he shall be assisted by one or more advisers chosen by the officers; in mixed camps, his assistants shall be chosen from among the prisoners of war who are not officers and shall be elected by them.

Officer prisoners of war of the same nationality shall be stationed in labour camps for prisoners of war, for the purpose of carrying out the camp administration duties for which the prisoners of war are responsible. These officers may be elected as prisoners' representatives under the first paragraph of this Article. In such a case the assistants to the prisoners' representatives shall be chosen from among those prisoners of war who are not officers.

Every representative elected must be approved by the Detaining Power before he has the right to commence his duties. Where the Detaining Power refuses to approve a prisoner of war elected by his fellow prisoners of war, it must inform the Protecting Power of the reason for such refusal.

In all cases the prisoners' representative must have the same nationality, language and customs as the prisoners of war whom he represents. Thus, prisoners of war distributed in different sections of a camp, according to their nationality, language or customs, shall have for each section their own prisoners' representative, in accordance with the foregoing paragraphs.

Article 80

Prisoners' representatives shall further the physical, spiritual and intellectual well-being of prisoners of war.

In particular, where the prisoners decide to organize amongst themselves a system of mutual assistance, this organization will be within the province of the prisoners' representative, in addition to the special duties entrusted to him by other provisions of the present Convention.

Prisoners' representatives shall not be held responsible, simply by reason of their duties, for any offences committed by prisoners of war.

Article 81

Prisoners' representatives shall not be required to perform any other work, if the accomplishment of their duties is thereby made more difficult.

Prisoners' representatives may appoint from amongst the prisoners such assistants as they may require. All material facilities shall be granted them, particularly a certain freedom of movement necessary for the accomplishment of their duties (inspection of labour detachments, receipt of supplies, etc.).

Prisoners' representatives shall be permitted to visit premises where prisoners of war are detained, and every prisoner of war shall have the right to consult freely his prisoners' representative.

All facilities shall likewise be accorded to the prisoners' representatives for communication by post and telegraph with the detaining authorities, the Protecting Powers, the International Committee of the Red Cross and their delegates, the Mixed Medical Commissions and with the bodies which give assistance to prisoners of war. Prisoners' representatives of labour detachments shall enjoy the same facilities for communication with the prisoners' representatives of the principal camp. Such communications shall not be restricted, nor considered as forming a part of the quota mentioned in Article 71.

Prisoners' representatives who are transferred shall be allowed a reasonable time to acquaint their successors with current affairs.

In case of dismissal, the reasons therefore shall be communicated to the Protecting Power.

Chapter III—Penal and Disciplinary Sanctions

I. General provisions

Article 82

A prisoner of war shall be subject to the laws, regulations and orders in force in the armed forces of the Detaining Power; the Detaining Power shall be justified in taking judicial or disciplinary measures in respect of any offence committed by a prisoner of war against such laws, regulations or orders. However, no proceedings or punishments contrary to the provisions of this Chapter shall be allowed.

If any law, regulation or order of the Detaining Power shall declare acts committed by a prisoner of war to be punishable, whereas the same acts would not be punishable if committed by a member of the forces of the Detaining Power, such acts shall entail disciplinary punishments only.

Article 83

In deciding whether proceedings in respect of an offence alleged to have been committed by a prisoner of war shall be judicial or disciplinary, the Detaining Power shall ensure that the competent authorities exercise the greatest leniency and adopt, wherever possible, disciplinary rather than judicial measures.

Article 84

A prisoner of war shall be tried only by a military court, unless the existing laws of the Detaining Power expressly permit the civil courts to try a member of the armed forces of the Detaining Power in respect of the particular offence alleged to have been committed by the prisoner of war.

In no circumstances whatever shall a prisoner of war be tried by a court of any kind which does not offer the essential guarantees of independence and impartiality as generally recognized, and, in particular, the procedure of which does not afford the accused the rights and means of defence provided for in Article 105.

Article 85

Prisoners of war prosecuted under the laws of the Detaining Power for acts committed prior to capture shall retain, even if convicted, the benefits of the present Convention.

Article 86

No prisoner of war may be punished more than once for the same act, or on the same charge.

Article 87

Prisoners of war may not be sentenced by the military authorities and courts of the Detaining Power to any penalties except those provided for in respect of members of the armed forces of the said Power who have committed the same acts.

When fixing the penalty, the courts or authorities of the Detaining Power shall take into consideration, to the widest extent possible, the fact that the accused, not being a national of the Detaining Power, is not bound to it by any duty of allegiance, and that he is in its power as the result of circumstances independent of his own will. The said courts or authorities shall be at liberty to reduce the penalty provided for the violation of which the prisoner of war is accused, and shall therefore not be bound to apply the minimum penalty prescribed.

Collective punishment for individual acts, corporal punishments, imprisonment in premises without daylight and, in general, any form of torture or cruelty, are forbidden.

No prisoner of war may be deprived of his rank by the Detaining Power, or prevented from wearing his badges.

Article 88

Officers, non-commissioned officers and men who are prisoners of war undergoing a disciplinary or judicial punishment, shall not be subjected to more severe treatment than that applied in respect of the same punishment to members of the armed forces of the Detaining Power of equivalent rank.

A woman prisoner of war shall not be awarded or sentenced to a punishment more severe, or treated whilst undergoing punishment more severely, than a woman member of the armed forces of the Detaining Power dealt with for a similar offence.

In no case may a woman prisoner of war be awarded or sentenced to a punishment more severe, or treated whilst undergoing punishment more severely, than a male member of the armed forces of the Detaining Power dealt with for a similar offence.

Prisoners of war who have served disciplinary or judicial sentences may not be treated differently from other prisoners of war.

II. Disciplinary sanctions

Article 89

The disciplinary punishments applicable to prisoners of war are the following:

1. A fine which shall not exceed 50 per cent of the advances of pay and working pay which the prisoner of war would otherwise receive under the provisions of Articles 60 and 62 during a period of not more than thirty days.

2. Discontinuance of privileges granted over and above the treatment provided for by the present Convention.

3. Fatigue duties not exceeding two hours daily.

4. Confinement.

The punishment referred to under (3) shall not be applied to officers.

In no case shall disciplinary punishments be inhuman, brutal or dangerous to the health of prisoners of war.

Article 90

The duration of any single punishment shall in no case exceed thirty days. Any period of confinement awaiting the hearing of a disciplinary offence or the award of disciplinary punishment shall be deducted from an award pronounced against a prisoner of war.

The maximum of thirty days provided above may not be exceeded, even if the prisoner of war is answerable for several acts at the same time when he is awarded punishment, whether such acts are related or not.

The period between the pronouncing of an award of disciplinary punishment and its execution shall not exceed one month.

When a prisoner of war is awarded a further disciplinary punishment, a period of at least three days shall elapse between the execution of any two of the punishments, if the duration of one of these is ten days or more.

Article 91

The escape of a prisoner of war shall be deemed to have succeeded when:

1. He has joined the armed forces of the Power on which he depends, or those of an allied Power;

2. He has left the territory under the control of the Detaining Power, or of an ally of the said Power;

3. He has joined a ship flying the flag of the Power on which he depends, or of an allied Power, in the territorial waters of the Detaining Power, the said ship not being under the control of the last-named Power.

Prisoners of war who have made good their escape in the sense of this Article and who are recaptured, shall not be liable to any punishment in respect of their previous escape.

Article 92

A prisoner of war who attempts to escape and is recaptured before having made good his escape in the sense of Article 91 shall be liable only to a disciplinary punishment in respect of this act, even if it is a repeated offence.

A prisoner of war who is recaptured shall be handed over without delay to the competent military authority.

Article 88, fourth paragraph, notwithstanding, prisoners of war punished as a result of an unsuccessful escape may be subjected to special surveillance. Such surveillance must not affect the state of their health, must be undergone in a prisoner of war camp, and must not entail the suppression of any of the safeguards granted them by the present Convention.

Article 93

Escape or attempt to escape, even if it is a repeated offence, shall not be deemed an aggravating circumstance if the prisoner of war is subjected to trial by judicial proceedings in respect of an offence committed during his escape or attempt to escape.

In conformity with the principle stated in Article 83, offences committed by prisoners of war with the sole intention of facilitating their escape and which do not entail any violence against life or limb, such as offences against public property, theft without intention of self-enrichment, the drawing up or use of false papers, the wearing of civilian clothing, shall occasion disciplinary punishment only.

Prisoners of war who aid or abet an escape or an attempt to escape shall be liable on this count to disciplinary punishment only.

Article 94

If an escaped prisoner of war is recaptured, the Power on which he depends shall be notified thereof in the manner defined in Article 122, provided notification of his escape has been made.

Article 95

A prisoner of war accused of an offence against discipline shall not be kept in confinement pending the hearing unless a member of the armed forces of the Detaining Power would be so kept if he were accused of a similar offence, or if it is essential in the interests of camp order and discipline.

Any period spent by a prisoner of war in confinement awaiting the disposal of an offence against discipline shall be reduced to an absolute minimum and shall not exceed fourteen days.

The provisions of Articles 97 and 98 of this Chapter shall apply to prisoners of war who are in confinement awaiting the disposal of offences against discipline.

Article 96

Acts which constitute offences against discipline shall be investigated immediately.

Without prejudice to the competence of courts and superior military authorities, disciplinary punishment may be ordered only by an officer having disciplinary powers in his capacity as camp commander, or by a responsible officer who replaces him or to whom he has delegated his disciplinary powers.

In no case may such powers be delegated to a prisoner of war or be exercised by a prisoner of war.

Before any disciplinary award is pronounced, the accused shall be given precise information regarding the offences of which he is accused, and given an opportunity of explaining his conduct and of defending himself. He shall be permitted, in particular, to call witnesses and to have recourse, if necessary, to the services of a qualified interpreter. The decision shall be announced to the accused prisoner of war and to the prisoners' representative.

A record of disciplinary punishments shall be maintained by the camp commander and shall be open to inspection by representatives of the Protecting Power.

Article 97

Prisoners of war shall not in any case be transferred to penitentiary establishments (prisons, penitentiaries, convict prisons, etc.) to undergo disciplinary punishment therein.

All premises in which disciplinary punishments are undergone shall conform to the sanitary requirements set forth in Article 25. A prisoner of war undergoing punishment shall be enabled to keep himself in a state of cleanliness, in conformity with Article 29.

Officers and persons of equivalent status shall not be lodged in the same quarters as non-commissioned officers or men.

Women prisoners of war undergoing disciplinary punishment shall be confined in separate quarters from male prisoners of war and shall be under the immediate supervision of women

Article 98

A prisoner of war undergoing confinement as a disciplinary punishment, shall continue to enjoy the benefits of the provisions of this Convention except in so far as these are necessarily rendered inapplicable by the mere fact that he is confined. In no case may he be deprived of the benefits of the provisions of Articles 78 and 126.

A prisoner of war awarded disciplinary punishment may not be deprived of the prerogatives attached to his rank.

Prisoners of war awarded disciplinary punishment shall be allowed to exercise and to stay in the open air at least two hours daily.

They shall be allowed, on their request, to be present at the daily medical inspections. They shall receive the attention which their state of health requires and, if necessary, shall be removed to the camp infirmary or to a hospital.

They shall have permission to read and write, likewise to send and receive letters. Parcels and remittances of money, however, may be withheld from them until the completion of the punishment; they shall meanwhile be entrusted to the prisoners' representative, who will hand over to the infirmary the perishable goods contained in such parcels.

III. Judicial proceedings

Article 99

No prisoner of war may be tried or sentenced for an act which is not forbidden by the law of the Detaining Power or by international law, in force at the time the said act was committed.

No moral or physical coercion may be exerted on a prisoner of war in order to induce him to admit himself guilty of the act of which he is accused.

No prisoner of war may be convicted without having had an opportunity to present his defence and the assistance of a qualified advocate or counsel.

Article 100

Prisoners of war and the Protecting Powers shall be informed as soon as possible of the offences which are punishable by the death sentence under the laws of the Detaining Power.

Other offences shall not thereafter be made punishable by the death penalty without the concurrence of the Power upon which the prisoners of war depend.

The death sentence cannot be pronounced on a prisoner of war unless the attention of the court has, in accordance with Article 87, second paragraph, been particularly called to the fact that since the accused is not a national of the Detaining Power, he is not bound to it by any duty of allegiance, and that he is in its power as the result of circumstances independent of his own will.

Article 101

If the death penalty is pronounced on a prisoner of war, the sentence shall not be executed before the expiration of a period of at least six months from the date when the Protecting Power receives, at an indicated address, the detailed communication provided for in Article 107.

Article 102

A prisoner of war can be validly sentenced only if the sentence has been pronounced by the same courts according to the same procedure as in the case of members of the armed forces of the Detaining Power, and if, furthermore, the provisions of the present Chapter have been observed.

Article 103

Judicial investigations relating to a prisoner of war shall be conducted as rapidly as circumstances permit and so that his trial shall take place as soon as possible. A prisoner of war shall not be confined while awaiting trial unless a member of the armed forces of the Detaining Power would be so confined if he were accused of a similar offence, or if it is essential to do so in the interests of national security. In no circumstances shall this confinement exceed three months.

Any period spent by a prisoner of war in confinement awaiting trial shall be deducted from any sentence of imprisonment passed upon him and taken into account in fixing any penalty.

The provisions of Articles 97 and 98 of this Chapter shall apply to a prisoner of war whilst in confinement awaiting trial.

Article 104

In any case in which the Detaining Power has decided to institute judicial proceedings against a prisoner of war, it shall notify the Protecting Power as soon as possible and at least three weeks before the opening of the trial. This period of three weeks shall run as from the day on which such notification reaches the Protecting Power at the address previously indicated by the latter to the Detaining Power.

The said notification shall contain the following information:

1. Surname and first names of the prisoner of war, his rank, his army, regimental, personal or serial number, his date of birth, and his profession or trade, if any;

2. Place of internment or confinement;

3. Specification of the charge or charges on which the prisoner of war is to be arraigned, giving the legal provisions applicable;

4. Designation of the court which will try the case, likewise the date and place fixed for the opening of the trial.

The same communication shall be made by the Detaining Power to the prisoners' representative.

If no evidence is submitted, at the opening of a trial, that the notification referred to above was received by the Protecting Power, by the prisoner of war and by the prisoners' representative concerned, at least three weeks before the opening of the trial, then the latter cannot take place and must be adjourned.

Article 105

The prisoner of war shall be entitled to assistance by one of his prisoner comrades, to defence by a qualified advocate or counsel of his own choice, to the calling of witnesses and, if he deems necessary, to the services of a competent interpreter. He shall be advised of these rights by the Detaining Power in due time before the trial.

Failing a choice by the prisoner of war, the Protecting Power shall find him an advocate or counsel, and shall have at least one week at its disposal for the purpose. The Detaining Power shall deliver to the said Power, on request, a list of persons qualified to present the defence. Failing a choice of an advocate or counsel by the prisoner of war or the Protecting Power, the Detaining Power shall appoint a competent advocate or counsel to conduct the defence.

The advocate or counsel conducting the defence on behalf of the prisoner of war shall have at his disposal a period of two weeks at least before the opening of the trial, as well as the necessary facilities to prepare the defence of the accused. He may, in particular, freely visit the accused and interview him in private. He may also confer with any witnesses for the defence, including prisoners of war. He shall have the benefit of these facilities until the term of appeal or petition has expired.

Particulars of the charge or charges on which the prisoner of war is to be arraigned, as well as the documents which are generally communicated to the accused by virtue of the laws in force in the armed forces of the Detaining Power, shall be communicated to the accused prisoner of war in a language which he understands, and in good time before the opening of the trial. The same communication in the same circumstances shall be made to the advocate or counsel conducting the defence on behalf of the prisoner of war.

The representatives of the Protecting Power shall be entitled to attend the trial of the case, unless, exceptionally, this is held in camera in the interest of State security. In such a case the Detaining Power shall advise the Protecting Power accordingly.

Article 106

Every prisoner of war shall have, in the same manner as the members of the armed forces of the Detaining Power, the right of appeal or petition from any sentence pronounced upon him, with a view to the quashing or revising of the sentence or the reopening of the trial. He shall be fully informed of his right to appeal or petition and of the time limit within which he may do so.

Article 107

Any judgment and sentence pronounced upon a prisoner of war shall be immediately reported to the Protecting Power in the form of a summary communication, which shall also indicate whether he has the right of appeal with a view to the quashing of the sentence or the reopening of the trial. This communication shall likewise be sent to the prisoners' representative concerned. It shall also be sent to the accused prisoner of war in a language he understands, if the sentence was not pronounced in his presence. The Detaining Power shall also immediately communicate to the Protecting Power the decision of the prisoner of war to use or to waive his right of appeal.

Furthermore, if a prisoner of war is finally convicted or if a sentence pronounced on a prisoner of war in the first instance is a death sentence, the Detaining Power shall as soon as possible address to the Protecting Power a detailed communication containing:

1. The precise wording of the finding and sentence;

2. A summarized report of any preliminary investigation and of the trial, emphasizing in particular the elements of the prosecution and the defence;

3. Notification, where applicable, of the establishment where the sentence will be served.

The communications provided for in the foregoing subparagraphs shall be sent to the Protecting Power at the address previously made known to the Detaining Power.

Article 108

Sentences pronounced on prisoners of war after a conviction has become duly enforceable, shall be served in the same establishments and under the same conditions as in the case of members of the armed forces of the Detaining Power. These conditions shall in all cases conform to the requirements of health and humanity.

A woman prisoner of war on whom such a sentence has been pronounced shall be confined in separate quarters and shall be under the supervision of women.

In any case, prisoners of war sentenced to a penalty depriving them of their liberty shall retain the benefit of the provisions of Articles 78 and 126 of the present Convention. Furthermore, they shall be entitled to receive and despatch correspondence, to receive at least one relief parcel monthly, to take regular exercise in the open air, to have the medical care required by their state of health, and the spiritual assistance they may desire. Penalties to which they may be subjected shall be in accordance with the provisions of Article 87, third paragraph.

Part IV—Termination of Captivity

SECTION I: DIRECT REPATRIATION AND ACCOMMODATION IN NEUTRAL COUNTRIES

Article 109

Subject to the provisions of the third paragraph of this Article, Parties to the conflict are bound to send back to their own country, regardless of number or rank, seriously wounded and seriously sick prisoners of war, after having cared for them until they are fit to travel, in accordance with the first paragraph of the following Article.

Throughout the duration of hostilities, Parties to the conflict shall endeavour, with the cooperation of the neutral Powers concerned, to make arrangements for the accommodation in neutral countries of the sick and wounded prisoners of war referred to in the second paragraph of the following Article. They may, in addition, conclude agreements with a view to the direct repatriation or internment in a neutral country of able-bodied prisoners of war who have undergone a long period of captivity.

No sick or injured prisoner of war who is eligible for repatriation under the first paragraph of this Article, may be repatriated against his will during hostilities.

Article 110

The following shall be repatriated direct:

1. Incurably wounded and sick whose mental or physical fitness seems to have been gravely diminished.

2. Wounded and sick who, according to medical opinion, are not likely to recover within one year, whose condition requires treatment and whose mental or physical fitness seems to have been gravely diminished.

3. Wounded and sick who have recovered, but whose mental or physical fitness seems to have been gravely and permanently diminished.

The following may be accommodated in a neutral country:

1. Wounded and sick whose recovery may be expected within one year of the date of the wound or the beginning of the illness, if treatment in a neutral country might increase the prospects of a more certain and speedy recovery.

2. Prisoners of war whose mental or physical health, according to medical opinion, is seriously threatened by continued captivity, but whose accommodation in a neutral country might remove such a threat.

The conditions which prisoners of war accommodated in a neutral country must fulfil in order to permit their repatriation shall be fixed, as shall likewise their status, by agreement between the Powers concerned. In general, prisoners of war who have been accommodated in a neutral country, and who belong to the following categories, should be repatriated:

1. Those whose state of health has deteriorated so as to fulfil the conditions laid down for direct repatriation;

2. Those whose mental or physical powers remain, even after treatment, considerably impaired.

If no special agreements are concluded between the Parties to the conflict concerned, to determine the cases of disablement or sickness entailing direct repatriation or accommodation in a neutral country, such cases shall be settled in accordance with the principles laid down in the Model Agreement concerning direct repatriation and accommodation in neutral countries of wounded and sick prisoners of war and in the Regulations concerning Mixed Medical Commissions annexed to the present Convention.

Article 111
The Detaining Power, the Power on which the prisoners of war depend, and a neutral Power agreed upon by these two Powers, shall endeavour to conclude agreements which will enable prisoners of war to be interned in the territory of the said neutral Power until the close of hostilities.

Article 112
Upon the outbreak of hostilities, Mixed Medical Commissions shall be appointed to examine sick and wounded prisoners of war, and to make all appropriate decisions regarding them. The appointment, duties and functioning of these Commissions shall be in conformity with the provisions of the Regulations annexed to the present Convention.

However, prisoners of war who, in the opinion of the medical authorities of the Detaining Power, are manifestly seriously injured or seriously sick, may be repatriated without having to be examined by a Mixed Medical Commission.

Article 113
Besides those who are designated by the medical authorities of the Detaining Power, wounded or sick prisoners of war belonging to the categories listed below shall be entitled to present themselves for examination by the Mixed Medical Commissions provided for in the foregoing Article:

1. Wounded and sick proposed by a physician or surgeon who is of the same nationality, or a national of a Party to the conflict allied with the Power on which the said prisoners depend, and who exercises his functions in the camp.

2. Wounded and sick proposed by their prisoners' representative.

3. Wounded and sick proposed by the Power on which they depend, or by an organization duly recognized by the said Power and giving assistance to the prisoners.

Prisoners of war who do not belong to one of the three foregoing categories may nevertheless present themselves for examination by Mixed Medical Commissions, but shall be examined only after those belonging to the said categories.

The physician or surgeon of the same nationality as the prisoners who present themselves for examination by the Mixed Medical Commission, likewise the prisoners' representative of the said prisoners, shall have permission to be present at the examination.

Article 114
Prisoners of war who meet with accidents shall, unless the injury is self-inflicted, have the benefit of the provisions of this Convention as regards repatriation or accommodation in a neutral country.

Article 115
No prisoner of war on whom a disciplinary punishment has been imposed and who is eligible for repatriation or for accommodation in a neutral country, may be kept back on the plea that he has not undergone his punishment.

Prisoners of war detained in connection with a judicial prosecution or conviction and who are designated for repatriation or accommodation in a neutral country, may benefit by such measures before the end of the proceedings or the completion of the punishment, if the Detaining Power consents.

Parties to the conflict shall communicate to each other the names of those who will be detained until the end of the proceedings or the completion of the punishment.

Article 116
The costs of repatriating prisoners of war or of transporting them to a neutral country shall be borne, from the frontiers of the Detaining Power, by the Power on which the said prisoners depend.

Article 117
No repatriated person may be employed on active military service.

SECTION II: RELEASE AND REPATRIATION OF PRISONERS OF WAR AT THE CLOSE OF HOSTILITIES

Article 118
Prisoners of war shall be released and repatriated without delay after the cessation of active hostilities.

In the absence of stipulations to the above effect in any agreement concluded between the Parties to the conflict with a view to the cessation of hostilities, or failing any such agreement, each of the Detaining Powers shall itself establish and execute without delay a plan of repatriation in conformity with the principle laid down in the foregoing paragraph.

In either case, the measures adopted shall be brought to the knowledge of the prisoners of war.

The costs of repatriation of prisoners of war shall in all cases be equitably apportioned between the Detaining Power and the Power on which the prisoners depend. This apportionment shall be carried out on the following basis:

(a) If the two Powers are contiguous, the Power on which the prisoners of war depend shall bear the costs of repatriation from the frontiers of the Detaining Power.

(b) If the two Powers are not contiguous, the Detaining Power shall bear the costs of transport of prisoners of war over its own territory as far as its frontier or its port of embarkation nearest to the territory of the Power on which the prisoners of war depend. The Parties concerned shall agree between themselves as to the equitable apportionment of the remaining costs of the repatriation. The conclusion of this agreement shall in no circumstances justify any delay in the repatriation of the prisoners of war.

Article 119

Repatriation shall be effected in conditions similar to those laid down in Articles 46 to 48 inclusive of the present Convention for the transfer of prisoners of war, having regard to the provisions of Article 118 and to those of the following paragraphs.

On repatriation, any articles of value impounded from prisoners of war under Article 18, and any foreign currency which has not been converted into the currency of the Detaining Power, shall be restored to them. Articles of value and foreign currency which, for any reason whatever, are not restored to prisoners of war on repatriation, shall be despatched to the Information Bureau set up under Article 122.

Prisoners of war shall be allowed to take with them their personal effects, and any correspondence and parcels which have arrived for them. The weight of such baggage may be limited, if the conditions of repatriation so require, to what each prisoner can reasonably carry. Each prisoner shall in all cases be authorized to carry at least twenty-five kilograms.

The other personal effects of the repatriated prisoner shall be left in the charge of the Detaining Power which shall have them forwarded to him as soon as it has concluded an agreement to this effect, regulating the conditions of transport and the payment of the costs involved, with the Power on which the prisoner depends.

Prisoners of war against whom criminal proceedings for an indictable offence are pending may be detained until the end of such proceedings, and, if necessary, until the completion of the punishment. The same shall apply to prisoners of war already convicted for an indictable offence.

Parties to the conflict shall communicate to each other the names of any prisoners of war who are detained until the end of the proceedings or until punishment has been completed.

By agreement between the Parties to the conflict, commissions shall be established for the purpose of searching for dispersed prisoners of war and of assuring their repatriation with the least possible delay.

SECTION III: DEATH OF PRISONERS OF WAR

Article 120

Wills of prisoners of war shall be drawn up so as to satisfy the conditions of validity required by the legislation of their country of origin, which will take steps to inform the Detaining Power of its requirements in this respect. At the request of the prisoner of war and, in all cases, after death, the will shall be transmitted without delay to the Protecting Power; a certified copy shall be sent to the Central Agency.

Death certificates in the form annexed to the present Convention, or lists certified by a responsible officer, of all persons who die as prisoners of war shall be forwarded as rapidly as possible to the Prisoner of War Information Bureau established in accordance with Article 122. The death certificates or certified lists shall show particulars of identity as set out in the third paragraph of Article 17, and also the date and place of death, the cause of death, the date and place of burial and all particulars necessary to identify the graves.

The burial or cremation of a prisoner of war shall be preceded by a medical examination of the body with a view to confirming death and enabling a report to be made and, where necessary, establishing identity.

The detaining authorities shall ensure that prisoners of war who have died in captivity are honourably buried, if possible according to the rites of the religion to which they belonged, and that their graves are respected, suitably maintained and marked so as to be found at any time. Wherever possible, deceased prisoners of war who depended on the same Power shall be interred in the same place.

Deceased prisoners of war shall be buried in individual graves unless unavoidable circumstances require the use of collective graves. Bodies may be cremated only for imperative reasons of hygiene, on account of the religion of the deceased or in accordance with his express wish to this effect. In case of cremation, the fact shall be stated and the reasons given in the death certificate of the deceased.

In order that graves may always be found, all particulars of burials and graves shall be recorded with a Graves Registration Service established by the Detaining Power. Lists of graves and particulars of the prisoners of war interred in cemeteries and elsewhere shall be transmitted to the Power on which such prisoners of war depended. Responsibility for the care of these graves and for records of any subsequent moves of the bodies shall rest on the Power controlling the territory, if a Party to the present Convention. These provisions shall also apply to the ashes, which shall be kept by the Graves Registration Service until proper disposal thereof in accordance with the wishes of the home country.

Article 121

Every death or serious injury of a prisoner of war caused or suspected to have been caused by a sentry, another prisoner of war, or any other person, as well as any death the cause of which is unknown, shall be immediately followed by an official enquiry by the Detaining Power.

A communication on this subject shall be sent immediately to the Protecting Power. Statements shall be taken from witnesses, especially from those who are prisoners of war, and a report including such statements shall be forwarded to the Protecting Power.

If the enquiry indicates the guilt of one or more persons, the Detaining Power shall take all measures for the prosecution of the person or persons responsible.

Part V—Information Bureaux and Relief Societies for Prisoners of War

Article 122

Upon the outbreak of a conflict and in all cases of occupation, each of the Parties to the conflict shall institute an official Information Bureau for prisoners of war who are in its power. Neutral or non-belligerent Powers who may have received within their territory persons belonging to one of the categories referred to in Article 4, shall take the same action with respect to such persons. The Power concerned shall ensure that the Prisoners of War Information Bureau is provided with the necessary accommodation, equipment and staff to ensure its efficient working. It shall be at liberty to employ prisoners of war in such a Bureau under the conditions laid down in the Section of the present Convention dealing with work by prisoners of war.

Within the shortest possible period, each of the Parties to the conflict shall give its Bureau the information referred to in the fourth, fifth and sixth paragraphs of this Article regarding any enemy person belonging to one of the categories referred to in Article 4, who has fallen into its power. Neutral or non-belligerent Powers shall take the same action with regard to persons belonging to such categories whom they have received within their territory.

The Bureau shall immediately forward such information by the most rapid means to the Powers concerned, through the intermediary of the Protecting Powers and likewise of the Central Agency provided for in Article 123.

This information shall make it possible quickly to advise the next of kin concerned. Subject to the provisions of Article 17, the information shall include, in so far as available to the Information Bureau, in respect of each prisoner of war, his surname, first names, rank, army, regimental, personal or serial number, place and full date of birth, indication of the Power on which he depends, first name of the father and maiden name of the mother, name and address of the person to be informed and the address to which correspondence for the prisoner may be sent.

The Information Bureau shall receive from the various departments concerned information regarding transfers, releases, repatriations, escapes, admissions to hospital, and deaths, and shall transmit such information in the manner described in the third paragraph above.

Likewise, information regarding the state of health of prisoners of war who are seriously ill or seriously wounded shall be supplied regularly, every week if possible.

The Information Bureau shall also be responsible for replying to all enquiries sent to it concerning prisoners of war, including those who have died in captivity; it will make any enquiries necessary to obtain the information which is asked for if this is not in its possession.

All written communications made by the Bureau shall be authenticated by a signature or a seal.

The Information Bureau shall furthermore be charged with collecting all personal valuables, including sums in currencies other than that of the Detaining Power and documents of importance to the next of kin, left by prisoners of war who have been repatriated or released, or who have escaped or died, and shall forward the said valuables to the Powers concerned. Such articles shall be sent by the Bureau in sealed packets which shall be accompanied by statements giving clear and full particulars of the identity of the person to whom the articles belonged, and by a complete list of the contents of the parcel. Other personal effects of such prisoners of war shall be transmitted under arrangements agreed upon between the Parties to the conflict concerned.

Article 123

A Central Prisoners of War Information Agency shall be created in a neutral country. The International Committee of the Red Cross shall, if it deems necessary, propose to the Powers concerned the organization of such an Agency.

The function of the Agency shall be to collect all the information it may obtain through official or private channels respecting prisoners of war, and to transmit it as rapidly as possible to the country of origin of the prisoners of war or to the Power on which they depend. It shall receive from the Parties to the conflict all facilities for effecting such transmissions.

The High Contracting Parties, and in particular those whose nationals benefit by the services of the Central Agency, are requested to give the said Agency the financial aid it may require.

The foregoing provisions shall in no way be interpreted as restricting the humanitarian activities of the International Committee of the Red Cross, or of the relief Societies provided for in Article 125.

Article 124

The national Information Bureaux and the Central Information Agency shall enjoy free postage for mail, likewise all the exemptions provided for in Article 74, and further, so far as possible, exemption from telegraphic charges or, at least, greatly reduced rates.

Article 125

Subject to the measures which the Detaining Powers may consider essential to ensure their security or to meet any other reasonable need, the representatives of religious organizations, relief societies, or any other organization assisting prisoners of war, shall receive from the said Powers, for themselves and their duly accredited agents, all necessary facilities for visiting the prisoners, distributing relief supplies and material, from any source, intended for religious, educational or recreative purposes, and for assisting them in organizing their leisure time within the camps. Such societies or organizations may be constituted in the territory of the Detaining Power or in any other country, or they may have an international character.

The Detaining Power may limit the number of societies and organizations whose delegates are allowed to carry out their activities in its territory and under its supervision, on condition, however, that such limitation shall not hinder the effective operation of adequate relief to all prisoners of war.

The special position of the International Committee of the Red Cross in this field shall be recognized and respected at all times.

As soon as relief supplies or material intended for the above-mentioned purposes are handed over to prisoners of war, or very shortly afterwards, receipts for each consignment, signed by the prisoners' representative, shall be forwarded to the relief society or organization making the shipment. At the same time, receipts for these consignments shall be supplied by the administrative authorities responsible for guarding the prisoners.

Part VI—Execution of the Convention

SECTION I: GENERAL PROVISIONS

Article 126

Representatives or delegates of the Protecting Powers shall have permission to go to all places where prisoners of war may be, particularly to places of internment, imprisonment and labour, and shall have access to all premises occupied by prisoners of war; they shall also be allowed to go to the places of departure, passage and arrival of prisoners who are being transferred. They shall be able to interview the prisoners, and in particular the prisoners' representatives, without witnesses, either personally or through an interpreter.

Representatives and delegates of the Protecting Powers shall have full liberty to select the places they wish to visit. The duration and frequency of these visits shall not be restricted. Visits may not be prohibited except for reasons of imperative military necessity, and then only as an exceptional and temporary measure.

The Detaining Power and the Power on which the said prisoners of war depend may agree, if necessary, that compatriots of these prisoners of war be permitted to participate in the visits.

The delegates of the International Committee of the Red Cross shall enjoy the same prerogatives. The appointment of such delegates shall be submitted to the approval of the Power detaining the prisoners of war to be visited.

Article 127

The High Contracting Parties undertake, in time of peace as in time of war, to disseminate the text of the present Convention as widely as possible in their respective countries, and, in particular, to include the study thereof in their programmes of military and, if possible, civil instruction, so that the principles thereof may become known to all their armed forces and to the entire population.

Any military or other authorities, who in time of war assume responsibilities in respect of prisoners of war, must possess the text of the Convention and be specially instructed as to its provisions.

Article 128

The High Contracting Parties shall communicate to one another through the Swiss Federal Council and, during hostilities, through the Protecting Powers, the official translations of the present Convention, as well as the laws and regulations which they may adopt to ensure the application thereof.

Article 129

The High Contracting Parties undertake to enact any legislation necessary to provide effective penal sanctions for persons committing, or ordering to be committed, any of the grave breaches of the present Convention defined in the following Article.

Each High Contracting Party shall be under the obligation to search for persons alleged to have committed, or to have ordered to be committed, such grave breaches, and shall bring such persons, regardless of their nationality, before its own courts. It may also, if it prefers, and in accordance with the provisions of its own legislation, hand such persons over for trial to another High Contracting Party concerned, provided such High Contracting Party has made out a prima facie case.

Each High Contracting Party shall take measures necessary for the suppression of all acts contrary to the provisions of the present Convention other than the grave breaches defined in the following Article.

In all circumstances, the accused persons shall benefit by safeguards of proper trial and defence, which shall not be less favourable than those provided by Article 105 and those following of the present Convention.

Article 130

Grave breaches to which the preceding Article relates shall be those involving any of the following acts, if committed against persons or property protected by the Convention: wilful killing, torture or inhuman treatment, including biological experiments, wilfully causing great suffering or serious injury to body or health, compelling a prisoner of war to serve in the forces of the hostile Power, or wilfully depriving a prisoner of war of the rights of fair and regular trial prescribed in this Convention.

Article 131

No High Contracting Party shall be allowed to absolve itself or any other High Contracting Party of any liability incurred by itself or by another High Contracting Party in respect of breaches referred to in the preceding Article.

Article 132

At the request of a Party to the conflict, an enquiry shall be instituted, in a manner to be decided between the interested Parties, concerning any alleged violation of the Convention.

If agreement has not been reached concerning the procedure for the enquiry, the Parties should agree on the choice of an umpire who will decide upon the procedure to be followed.

Once the violation has been established, the Parties to the conflict shall put an end to it and shall repress it with the least possible delay.

Section 11: Final Provisions

Article 133

The present Convention is established in English and in French. Both texts are equally authentic. The Swiss Federal Council shall arrange for official translations of the Convention to be made in the Russian and Spanish languages.

Article 134

The present Convention replaces the Convention of 27 July 1929, in relations between the High Contracting Parties.

Article 135

In the relations between the Powers which are bound by The Hague Convention respecting the Laws and Customs of War on Land, whether that of July 29, 1899, or that of October 18, 1907, and which are parties to the present Convention, this last Convention shall be complementary to Chapter II of the Regulations annexed to the above-mentioned Conventions of The Hague.

Article 136

The present Convention, which bears the date of this day, is open to signature until February 12, 1950, in the name of the Powers represented at the Conference which opened at Geneva on April 21, 1949; furthermore, by Powers not represented at that Conference, but which are parties to the Convention of July 27, 1929.

Article 137

The present Convention shall be ratified as soon as possible and the ratifications shall be deposited at Berne.

A record shall be drawn up of the deposit of each instrument of ratification and certified copies of this record shall be transmitted by the Swiss Federal Council to all the Powers in whose name the Convention has been signed, or whose accession has been notified.

Article 138

The present Convention shall come into force six months after not less than two instruments of ratification have been deposited.

Thereafter, it shall come into force for each High Contracting Party six months after the deposit of the instrument of ratification.

Article 139

From the date of its coming into force, it shall be open to any Power in whose name the present Convention has not been signed, to accede to this Convention.

Article 140

Accessions shall be notified in writing to the Swiss Federal Council, and shall take effect six months after the date on which they are received.

The Swiss Federal Council shall communicate the accessions to all the Powers in whose name the Convention has been signed, or whose accession has been notified.

Article 141

The situations provided for in Articles 2 and 3 shall give immediate effect to ratifications deposited and accessions notified by the Parties to the conflict before or after the beginning of hostilities or occupation. The Swiss Federal Council shall communicate by the quickest method any ratifications or accessions received from Parties to the conflict.

Article 142

Each of the High Contracting Parties shall be at liberty to denounce the present Convention.

The denunciation shall be notified in writing to the Swiss Federal Council, which shall transmit it to the Governments of all the High Contracting Parties.

The denunciation shall take effect one year after the notification thereof has been made to the Swiss Federal Council. However, a denunciation of which notification has been made at a time when the denouncing Power is involved in a conflict shall not take effect until peace has been concluded, and until after operations connected with the release and repatriation of the persons protected by the present Convention have been terminated.

The denunciation shall have effect only in respect of the denouncing Power. It shall in no way impair the obligations which the Parties to the conflict shall remain bound to fulfil by virtue of the principles of the law of nations, as they result from the usages established among civilized peoples, from the laws of humanity and the dictates of the public conscience.

Article 143

The Swiss Federal Council shall register the present Convention with the Secretariat of the United Nations. The Swiss Federal Council shall also inform the Secretariat of the United Nations of all ratifications, accessions and denunciations received by it with respect to the present Convention.

IN WITNESS WHEREOF the undersigned, having deposited their respective full powers, have signed the present Convention.

DONE at Geneva this twelfth day of August 1949, in the English and French languages. The original shall be deposited in the Archives of the Swiss Confederation. The Swiss Federal Council shall transmit certified copies thereof to each of the signatory and acceding States.

Annex I

Model agreement concerning direct repatriation and accommodation in neutral countries of wounded and sick prisoners of war (see Article 110)

I. Principles for Direct Repatriation and Accommodation in Neutral Countries

A. Direct Repatriation

The following shall be repatriated direct:

1. All prisoners of war suffering from the following disabilities as the result of trauma: loss of limb, paralysis, articular or other disabilities, when this disability is at least the loss of a hand or a foot, or the equivalent of the loss of a hand or a foot.

Without prejudice to a more generous interpretation, the following shall be considered as equivalent to the loss of a hand or a foot:

(a) Loss of a hand or of all the fingers, or of the thumb and forefinger of one hand; loss of a foot, or of all the toes and metatarsals of one foot.

(b) Ankylosis, loss of osseous tissue, cicatricial contracture preventing the functioning of one of the large articulations or of all the digital joints of one hand.

(c) Pseudarthrosis of the long bones.

(d) Deformities due to fracture or other injury which seriously interfere with function and weight-bearing power.

2. All wounded prisoners of war whose condition has become chronic, to the extent that prognosis appears to exclude recovery-in spite of treatment-within one year from the date of the injury, as for example, in case of:

(a) Projectile in the heart, even if the Mixed Medical Commission should fail, at the time of their examination, to detect any serious disorders.

(b) Metallic splinter in the brain or the lungs, even if the Mixed Medical Commission cannot, at the time of examination, detect any local or general reaction.

(c) Osteomyelitis, when recovery cannot be foreseen in the course of the year following the injury, and which seems likely to result in ankylosis of a joint, or other impairments equivalent to the loss of a hand or a foot.

(d) Perforating and suppurating injury to the large joints.

(e) Injury to the skull, with loss or shifting of bony tissue.

(f) Injury or burning of the face with loss of tissue and functional lesions.

(g) Injury to the spinal cord.

(h) Lesion of the peripheral nerves, the sequelae of which are equivalent to the loss of a hand or foot, and the cure of which requires more than a year from the date of injury, for example: injury to the brachial or lumbosacral plexus, the median or sciatic nerves, likewise combined injury to the radial and cubital nerves or to the lateral popliteal nerve (*N. peroneus communes*) and medial popliteal nerve (*N. tibialis*); etc. The separate injury of the radial (musculo-spiral), cubital. lateral or medial popliteal nerves shall not, however, warrant repatriation except in case of contractures or of serious neurotrophic disturbance.

(i) Injury to the urinary system, with incapacitating results.

3. All sick prisoners of war whose condition has become chronic to the extent that prognosis seems to exclude recovery—in spite of treatment—within one year from the inception of the disease, as, for example, in case of:

(a) Progressive tuberculosis of any organ which, according to medical prognosis, cannot be cured, or at least considerably improved, by treatment in a neutral country.

(b) Exudate pleurisy.

(c) Serious diseases of the respiratory organs of non-tubercular etiology, presumed incurable, for example: serious pulmonary emphysema, with or without bronchitis, chronic asthma:° chronic bronchitis° lasting more than one year in captivity; bronchiectasis,° etc.

(d) Serious chronic affections of the circulatory system, for example: valvular lesions and myocarditis° which have shown signs of circulatory failure during captivity, even though the Mixed Medical Commission cannot detect any such signs at the time of examination; affections of the pericardium and the vessels (Buerger's disease, aneurism of the large vessels); etc.

(e) Serious chronic affections of the digestive organs, for example: gastric or duodenal ulcer-, sequelae of gastric operations performed in captivity; chronic gastritis, enteritis or colitis, having lasted more than one year and seriously affecting the general condition: cirrhosis of the liver, chronic cholecystopathy;° etc.

(f) Serious chronic affections of the genito-urinary organs, for example: chronic diseases of the kidney with consequent disorders; nephrectomy because of a tubercular kidney; chronic pyelitis or chronic cystitis: hydronephrosis or pyonephrosis; chronic grave gynaecological conditions, normal pregnancy, and obstetrical disorder, where it is impossible to accommodate in a neutral country; etc.

(g) Serious chronic diseases of the central and peripheral nervous system, for example: all obvious psychoses and psychoneuroses, such as serious hysteria, serious captivity psychoneurosis, etc., duly verified by a specialist;° any epilepsy duly verified by the camp physicians, cerebral arteriosclerosis, chronic neuritis lasting more than one year, etc.

(h) Serious chronic disease of the neuro-vegetative system, with considerable diminution of mental or physical fitness, noticeable loss of weight and general asthenia.

(i) Blindness of both eyes, or of one eye when the vision of the other is less than I in spite of the use of corrective glasses; diminution of visual acuity in cases where it is impossible to restore it by correction to an acuity of 1/2 in at least one eye;° other grave ocular affections, for example: glaucoma, iritis, choroiditis; trachoma, etc.

(k) Auditive disorders, such as total unilateral deafness, if the other ear does not discern the ordinary spoken word at a distance of one metre;° etc.

(l) Serious affections of metabolism, for example: diabetes mellitus requiring insulin treatment; etc.

(m) Serious disorders of the endocrine glands, for example: thyrotoxicosis; hypothyrosis; Addison's disease; Simmonds' cachexia; tetany; etc.

(n) Grave and chronic disorders of the blood-forming organs.

(o) Serious cases of chronic intoxication, for example: lead poisoning, mercury poisoning, morphinism, cocainism, alcoholism; gas or radiation poisoning; etc.

(p) Chronic affections of locomotion, with obvious functional disorders, for example: arthritis deformans, primary and secondary progressive chronic polyarthritis; rheumatism with serious clinical symptoms; etc.

(q) Serious chronic skin diseases, not amenable to treatment.

(r) Any malignant growth.

(s) Serious chronic infectious diseases, persisting for one year after their inception, for example: malaria with decided organic impairment, amoebic or bacillary dysentery with grave disorders; tertiary visceral syphilis resistant to treatment; leprosy; etc.

(t) Serious avitaminosis or serious inanition.

B. Accommodation in Neutral Countries

The following shall be eligible for accommodation in a neutral country:

1. All wounded prisoners of war who are not likely to recover in captivity, but who might be cured or whose condition might be considerably improved by accommodation in a neutral country.

2. Prisoners of war suffering from any form of tuberculosis, of whatever organ, and whose treatment in a neutral country would be likely to lead to recovery or at least to considerable improvement, with the exception of primary tuberculosis cured before captivity.

3. Prisoners of war suffering from affections requiring treatment of the respiratory, circulatory, digestive, nervous, sensory, genito-urinary, cutaneous locomotive organs, etc., if such treatment would clearly have better results in a neutral country than in captivity.

4. Prisoners of war who have undergone a nephrectomy in captivity for a nontubercular renal affection; cases of osteomyelitis, on the way to recovery or latent; diabetes mellitus not requiring insulin treatment; etc.

5. Prisoners of war suffering from war or captivity neuroses.

Cases of captivity neurosis which are not cured after three months of accommodation in a neutral country, or which after that length of time are not clearly on the way to complete cure, shall be repatriated.

6. All prisoners of war suffering from chronic intoxication (gases, metals, alkaloids, etc.), for whom the prospects of cure in a neutral country are especially favourable.

7. All women prisoners of war who are pregnant or mothers with infants and small children.

The following cases shall not be eligible for accommodation in a neutral country:

°The decision of the Mixed Medical Commission shall be based to a great extent on the records kept by camp physicians and surgeons of the same nationality as the prisoners of war, or on an examination by medical specialists of the Detaining Power.

1. All duly verified chronic psychoses.

2. All organic or functional nervous affections considered to be incurable.

3. All contagious diseases during the period in which they are transmissible, with the exception of tuberculosis.

II. General Observations

1. The conditions given shall, in a general way, be interpreted and applied in as broad a spirit as possible.

Neuropathic and psychopathic conditions caused by war or captivity, as well as cases of tuberculosis in all stages, shall above all benefit by such liberal interpretation. Prisoners of war who have sustained several wounds, none of which, considered by itself, justifies repatriation, shall be examined in the same spirit, with due regard for the psychic traumatism due to the number of their wounds.

2. All unquestionable cases giving the right to direct repatriation (amputation, total blindness or deafness. open pulmonary tuberculosis, mental disorder. malignant growth, etc.) shall be examined and repatriated as soon as possible by the camp physicians or by military medical commissions appointed by the Detaining Power.

3. Injuries and diseases which existed before the war and which have not become worse. as well as war injuries which have not prevented subsequent military service, shall not entitle to direct repatriation.

4. The provisions of this Annex shall be interpreted and applied in a similar manner in all countries party to the conflict. The Powers and authorities concerned shall grant to Mixed Medical Commissions all the facilities necessary for the accomplishment of their task.

5. The examples quoted under (1) above represent only typical cases. Cases which do not correspond exactly to these provisions shall be judged in the spirit of the provisions of Article I 10 of the present Convention, and of the principles embodied in the present Agreement.

Annex II

Regulations concerning Mixed Medical Commissions (see Article 112)

Article 1

The Mixed Medical Commissions provided for in Article 112 of the Convention shall be composed of three members, two of whom shall belong to a neutral country. the third being appointed by the Detaining Power. One of the neutral members shall take the chair.

Article 2

The two neutral members shall be appointed by the International Committee of the Red Cross, acting in agreement with the Protecting Power, at the request of the Detaining Power. They may be domiciled either in their country of origin, in any other neutral country, or in the territory of the Detaining Power.

Article 3

The neutral members shall be approved by the Parties to the conflict concerned, who notify their approval to the International Committee of the Red Cross and to the Protecting Power. Upon such notification, the neutral members shall be considered as effectively appointed.

Article 4

Deputy members shall also be appointed in sufficient number to replace the regular members in case of need. They shall be appointed at the same time as the regular members or, at least, as soon as possible.

Article 5

If for any reason the International Committee of the Red Cross cannot arrange for the appointment of the neutral members, this shall be done by the Power protecting the interests of the prisoners of war to be examined.

Article 6

So far as possible, one of the two neutral members shall be a surgeon and the other a physician.

Article 7

The neutral members shall be entirely independent of the Parties to the conflict, which shall grant them all facilities in the accomplishment of their duties.

Article 8

By agreement with the Detaining Power, the International Committee of the Red Cross, when making the appointments provided for in Articles 2 and 4 of the present Regulations, shall settle the terms of service of the nominees.

Article 9

The Mixed Medical Commissions shall begin their work as soon as possible after the neutral members have been approved, and in any case within a period of three months from the date of such approval.

Article 10

The Mixed Medical Commissions shall examine all the prisoners designated in Article 113 of the Convention. They shall propose repatriation, rejection, or reference to a later examination. Their decisions shall be made by a majority vote.

Article 11

The decisions made by the Mixed Medical Commissions in each specific case shall be communicated, during the month following their visit, to the Detaining Power, the Protecting Power and the International Committee of the Red Cross. The Mixed Medical Commissions shall also inform each prisoner of war examined of the decision made, and shall issue to those whose repatriation has been proposed, certificates similar to the model appended to the present Convention.

Article 12

The Detaining Power shall be required to carry out the decisions of the Mixed Medical Commissions within three months of the time when it receives due notification of such decisions.

Article 13

If there is no neutral physician in a country where the services of a Mixed Medical Commission seem to be required, and if it is for any reason impossible to appoint neutral doctors who are resident in another country, the Detaining Power, acting in agreement with the Protecting Power, shall set up a Medical Commission which shall undertake the same duties as a Mixed Medical Commission, subject to the provisions of Articles 1, 2, 3, 4, 5 and 8 of the Present Regulations.

Article 14

Mixed Medical Commissions shall function permanently and shall visit each camp at intervals of not more than six months.

Annex III

Regulations concerning collective relief (see Article 73)

Article 1

Prisoners' representatives shall be allowed to distribute collective relief shipments for which they are responsible, to all prisoners of war administered by their camp, including those who are in hospitals or in prisons or other penal establishments.

Article 2

The distribution of collective relief shipments shall be effected in accordance with the instructions of the donors and with a plan drawn up by the prisoners' representatives. The issue of medical stores shall, however, be made for preference in agreement with the senior medical officers, and the latter may. In hospitals and infirmaries, waive the said instructions, if the needs of their patients so demand. Within the limits thus defined, the distribution shall always be carried out equitably.

Article 3

The said prisoners' representatives or their assistants shall be allowed to go to the points of arrival of relief supplies near their camps. so as to enable the prisoners' representatives or their assistants to verify the quality as well as the quantity of the goods received, and to make out detailed reports thereon for the donors.

Article 4

Prisoners' representatives shall be given the facilities necessary for verifying whether the distribution of collective relief in all sub-divisions and annexes of their camps has been carried out in accordance with their instructions.

Article 5

Prisoners' representatives shall be allowed to fill up, and cause to be filled up by the prisoners' representatives of labour detachments or by the senior medical officers of infirmaries and hospitals, forms or questionnaires intended for the donors, relating to collective relief supplies (distribution, requirements, quantities, etc.). Such forms and questionnaires, duly completed, shall be forwarded to the donors without delay.

Article 6

In order to secure the regular issue of collective relief to the prisoners of war in their camp, and to meet any needs that may arise from the arrival of new contingents of prisoners, prisoners' representatives shall be allowed to build up and maintain adequate reserve stocks of collective relief. For this purpose, they shall have suitable warehouses at their disposal; each warehouse shall be provided with two locks, the prisoners' representative holding the keys of one lock and the camp commander the keys of the other.

Article 7

When collective consignments of clothing are available each prisoner of war shall retain in his possession at least one complete set of clothes. If a prisoner has more than one set of clothes, the prisoners' representative shall be permitted to withdraw excess clothing from those with the largest number of sets, or particular articles in excess of one, if this is necessary in order to supply prisoners who are less well provided. He shall not, however, withdraw second sets of underclothing, socks or footwear, unless this is the only means of providing for prisoners of war with none.

Article 8

The High Contracting Parties, and the Detaining Powers in particular, shall authorize, as far as possible and subject to the regulations governing the supply of the population, all purchases of goods made in their territories for the distribution of collective relief to prisoners of war. They shall similarly facilitate the transfer of funds and other financial measures of a technical or administrative nature taken for the purpose of making such purchases.

Article 9

The foregoing provisions shall not constitute an obstacle to the right of prisoners of war to receive collective relief before their arrival in a camp or in the course of transfer, nor to the possibility of representatives of the Protecting Power, the International Committee of the Red Cross, or any other body which may be responsible for the forwarding of such supplies, giving assistance to prisoners ensuring the distribution thereof to the addressees by any other means that they may deem useful.

Geneva Convention relative to the Protection of Civilian Persons in Time of War

Adopted on 12 August 1949 by the Diplomatic Conference for the Establishment of International Conventions for the Protection of Victims of War, held in Geneva from 21 April to 12 August, 1949 entry into force 21 October 1950.

Part I—General Provisions

Article 1

The High Contracting Parties undertake to respect and to ensure respect for the present Convention in all circumstances.

Article 2

In addition to the provisions which shall be implemented in peacetime, the present Convention shall apply to all cases of declared war or of any other armed conflict which may arise between two or more of the High Contracting Parties, even if the state of war is not recognized by one of them.

The Convention shall also apply to all cases of partial or total occupation of the territory of a High Contracting Party, even if the said occupation meets with no armed resistance.

Although one of the Powers in conflict may not be a party to the present Convention, the Powers who are parties thereto shall remain bound by it in their mutual relations. They shall furthermore be bound by the Convention in relation to the said Power, if the latter accepts and applies the provisions thereof.

Article 3

In the case of armed conflict not of an international character occurring in the territory of one of the High Contracting

Parties, each Party to the conflict shall be bound to apply, as a minimum, the following provisions:

1. Persons taking no active part in the hostilities, including members of armed forces who have laid down their arms and those placed hors de combat by sickness, wounds, detention, or any other cause, shall in all circumstances be treated humanely, without any adverse distinction founded on race, colour, religion or faith, sex, birth or wealth, or any other similar criteria.

To this end, the following acts are and shall remain prohibited at any time and in any place whatsoever with respect to the above-mentioned persons:

(a) Violence to life and person, in particular murder of all kinds, mutilation, cruel treatment and torture;

(b) Taking of hostages;

(c) Outrages upon personal dignity, in particular humiliating and degrading treatment;

(d) The passing of sentences and the carrying out of executions without previous judgment pronounced by a regularly constituted court, affording all the judicial guarantees which are recognized as indispensable by civilized peoples.

2. The wounded and sick shall be collected and cared for.

An impartial humanitarian body, such as the International Committee of the Red Cross, may offer its services to the Parties to the conflict.

The Parties to the conflict should further endeavour to bring into force, by means of special agreements, all or part of the other provisions of the present Convention.

The application of the preceding provisions shall not affect the legal status of the Parties to the conflict.

Article 4

Persons protected by the Convention are those who, at a given moment and in any manner whatsoever, find themselves, in case of a conflict or occupation, in the hands of a Party to the conflict or Occupying Power of which they are not nationals.

Nationals of a State which is not bound by the Convention are not protected by it. Nationals of a neutral State who find themselves in the territory of a belligerent State, and nationals of a co-belligerent State, shall not be regarded as protected persons while the State of which they are nationals has normal diplomatic representation in the State in whose hands they are.

The provisions of Part II are, however, wider in application, as defined in Article 13.

Persons protected by the Geneva Convention for the Amelioration of the Condition of the Wounded and Sick in Armed Forces in the Field of August 12, 1949, or by the Geneva Convention for the Amelioration of the Condition of Wounded, Sick and Shipwrecked Members of Armed Forces at Sea of August 12, 1949, or by the Geneva Convention relative to the Treatment of Prisoners of War of August 12, 1949, shall not be considered as protected persons within the meaning of the present Convention.

Article 5

Where, in the territory of a Party to the conflict, the latter is satisfied that an individual protected person is definitely suspected of or engaged in activities hostile to the security of the State, such individual person shall not be entitled to claim such rights and privileges under the present Convention as would, if exercised in the favour of such individual person, be prejudicial to the security of such State.

Where in occupied territory an individual protected person is detained as a spy or saboteur, or as a person under definite suspicion of activity hostile to the security of the Occupying Power, such person shall, in those cases where absolute military security so requires, be regarded as having forfeited rights of communication under the present Convention.

In each case, such persons shall nevertheless be treated with humanity, and in case of trial, shall not be deprived of the rights of fair and regular trial prescribed by the present Convention. They shall also be granted the full rights and privileges of a protected person under the present Convention at the earliest date consistent with the security of the State or Occupying Power, as the case may be.

Article 6

The present Convention shall apply from the outset of any conflict or occupation mentioned in Article 2.

In the territory of Parties to the conflict, the application of the present Convention shall cease on the general close of military operations.

In the case of occupied territory, the application of the present Convention shall cease one year after the general close of military operations; however, the Occupying Power shall be bound, for the duration of the occupation, to the extent that such Power exercises the functions of government in such territory, by the provisions of the following Articles of the present Convention: I to 12, 27, 29 to 34, 47, 49, 51, 52, 53, 59, 61 to 77, and 143.

Protected persons whose release, repatriation or re-establishment may take place after such dates shall meanwhile continue to benefit by the present Convention.

Article 7

In addition to the agreements expressly provided for in Articles 11, 14, 15, 17, 36, 108, 109, 132, 133 and 149, the High Contracting Parties may conclude other special agreements for all matters concerning which they may deem it suitable to make separate provision. No special agreement shall adversely affect the situation of protected persons, as defined by the present Convention, nor restrict the rights which it confers upon them.

Protected persons shall continue to have the benefit of such agreements as long as the Convention is applicable to them, except where express provisions to the contrary are contained in the aforesaid or in subsequent agreements, or where more favourable measures have been taken with regard to them by one or other of the Parties to the conflict.

Article 8

Protected persons may in no circumstances renounce in part or in entirety the rights secured to them by the present Convention, and by the special agreements referred to in the foregoing Article, if such there be.

Article 9

The present Convention shall be applied with the cooperation and under the scrutiny of the Protecting Powers whose duty it is to safeguard the interests of the Parties to the conflict. For this purpose, the Protecting Powers may appoint, apart from their diplomatic or consular staff, delegates from amongst their own nationals or the nationals of other neutral Powers. The said delegates shall be subject to the approval of the Power with which they are to carry out their duties.

The Parties to the conflict shall facilitate to the greatest extent possible the task of the representatives or delegates of the Protecting Powers.

The representatives or delegates of the Protecting Powers shall not in any case exceed their mission under the present Convention. They shall, in particular, take account of the imperative necessities of security of the State wherein they carry out their duties.

Article 10

The provisions of the present Convention constitute no obstacle to the humanitarian activities which the International Committee of the Red Cross or any other impartial humanitarian organization may, subject to the consent of the Parties to the conflict concerned, undertake for the protection of civilian persons and for their relief.

Article 11

The High Contracting Parties may at any time agree to entrust to an organization which offers all guarantees of impartiality and efficacy the duties incumbent on the Protecting Powers by virtue of the present Convention.

When persons protected by the present Convention do not benefit or cease to benefit, no matter for what reason, by the activities of a Protecting Power or of an organization provided for in the first paragraph above, the Detaining Power shall request a neutral State, or such an organization, to undertake the functions performed under the present Convention by a Protecting Power designated by the Parties to a conflict.

If protection cannot be arranged accordingly, the Detaining Power shall request or shall accept, subject to the provisions of this Article, the offer of the services of a humanitarian organization, such as the International Committee of the Red Cross, to assume the humanitarian functions performed by Protecting Powers under the present Convention.

Any neutral Power, or any organization invited by the Power concerned or offering itself for these purposes, shall be required to act with a sense of responsibility towards the Party to the conflict on which persons protected by the present Convention depend, and shall be required to furnish sufficient assurances that it is in a position to undertake the appropriate functions and to discharge them impartially.

No derogation from the preceding provisions shall be made by special agreements between Powers one of which is restricted, even temporarily, in its freedom to negotiate with the other Power or its allies by reason of military events, more particularly where the whole, or a substantial part, of the territory of the said Power is occupied.

Whenever in the present Convention mention is made of a Protecting Power, such mention applies to substitute organizations in the sense of the present Article.

The provisions of this Article shall extend and be adapted to cases of nationals of a neutral State who are in occupied territory or who find themselves in the territory of a belligerent State with which the State of which they are nationals has not normal diplomatic representation.

Article 12

In cases where they deem it advisable in the interest of protected persons, particularly in cases of disagreement between the Parties to the conflict as to the application or interpretation of the provisions of the present Convention, the Protecting Powers shall lend their good offices with a view to settling the disagreement. For this purpose, each of the Protecting Powers may, either at the invitation of one Party or on its own initiative, propose to the Parties to the conflict a meeting of their representatives, and in particular of the authorities responsible for protected person, possibly on neutral territory suitably chosen. The Parties to the conflict shall be bound to give effect to the proposals made to them for this purpose. The Protecting Powers may, if necessary, propose for approval by the Parties to the conflict, a person belonging to a neutral Power or delegated by the International Committee of the Red Cross who shall be invited to take part in such a meeting.

Part II—General Protection of Populations against Certain Consequences of War

Article 13

The provisions of Part II cover the whole of the populations of the countries in conflict, without any adverse distinction based, in particular, on race, nationality, religion or political opinion, and are intended to alleviate the sufferings caused by war.

Article 14

In time of peace, the High Contracting Parties and, after the outbreak of hostilities, the Parties thereto, may establish in their own territory and, if the need arises, in occupied areas, hospital and safety zones and localities so organized as to protect from the effects of war, wounded, sick and aged persons, children under fifteen, expectant mothers and mothers of children under seven.

Upon the outbreak and during the course of hostilities, the Parties concerned may conclude agreements on mutual recognition of the zones and localities they have created. They may for this purpose implement the provisions of the Draft Agreement annexed to the present Convention, with such amendments as they may consider necessary.

The Protecting Powers and the International Committee of the Red Cross are invited to lend their good offices in order to facilitate the institution and recognition of these hospital and safety zones and localities.

Article 15

Any Party to the conflict may, either directly or through a neutral State or some humanitarian organization, propose to the adverse Party to establish, in the regions where fighting is taking place, neutralized zones intended to shelter from the effects of war the following persons, without distinction:

(a) Wounded and sick combatants or non-combatants;

(b) Civilian persons who take no part in hostilities, and who, while they reside in the zones, perform no work of a military character.

When the Parties concerned have agreed upon the geographical position, administration, food supply and supervision of the proposed neutralized zone, a written agreement shall be concluded and signed by the representatives of the Parties to the conflict. The agreement shall fix the beginning and the duration of the neutralization of the zone.

Article 16

The wounded and sick, as well as the infirm, and expectant mothers, shall be the object of particular protection and respect.

As far as military considerations allow, each Party to the conflict shall facilitate the steps taken to search for the killed and wounded, to assist the shipwrecked and other persons exposed to grave danger, and to protect them against pillage and ill-treatment.

Article 17

The Parties to the conflict shall endeavour to conclude local agreements for the removal from besieged or encircled areas, of wounded, sick, infirm, and aged persons, children and maternity cases, and for the passage of ministers of all religions, medical personnel and medical equipment on their way to such areas.

Article 18

Civilian hospitals organized to give care to the wounded and sick, the infirm and maternity cases, may in no circumstances be the object of attack, but shall at all times be respected and protected by the Parties to the conflict.

States which are Parties to a conflict shall provide all civilian hospitals with certificates showing that they are civilian hospitals and that the buildings which they occupy are not used for any purpose which would deprive these hospitals of protection in accordance with Article 19.

Civilian hospitals shall be marked by means of the emblem provided for in Article 38 of the Geneva Convention for the Amelioration of the Condition of the Wounded and Sick in Armed Forces in the Field of August 12, 1949, but only if so authorized by the State.

The Parties to the conflict shall, in so far as military considerations permit, take the necessary steps to make the distinctive emblems indicating civilian hospitals clearly visible to the enemy land, air and naval forces in order to obviate the possibility of any hostile action.

In view of the dangers to which hospitals may be exposed by being close to military objectives, it is recommended that such hospitals be situated as far as possible from such objectives.

Article 19

The protection to which civilian hospitals are entitled shall not cease unless they are used to commit, outside their humanitarian duties, acts harmful to the enemy. Protection may, however, cease only after due warning has been given, naming, in all appropriate cases, a reasonable time limit, and after such warning has remained unheeded.

The fact that sick or wounded members of the armed forces are nursed in these hospitals, or the presence of small arms and ammunition taken from such combatants which have not yet been handed to the proper service, shall not be considered to be acts harmful to the enemy.

Article 20

Persons regularly and solely engaged in the operation and administration of civilian hospitals, including the personnel engaged in the search for, removal and transporting of and caring for wounded and sick civilians, the infirm and maternity cases, shall be respected and protected.

In occupied territory and in zones of military operations, the above personnel shall be recognizable by means of an identity card certifying their status, bearing the photograph of the holder and embossed with the stamp of the responsible authority, and also by means of a stamped, water-resistant armlet which they shall wear on the left arm while carrying out their duties. This armlet shall be issued by the State and shall bear the emblem provided for in Article 38 of the Geneva Convention for the Amelioration of the Condition of the Wounded and Sick in Armed Forces in the Field of August 12, 1949.

Other personnel who are engaged in the operation and administration of civilian hospitals shall be entitled to respect and protection and to wear the armlet, as provided in and under the conditions prescribed in this Article, while they are employed on such duties. The identity card shall state the duties on which they are employed.

The management of each hospital shall at all times hold at the disposal of the competent national or occupying authorities an up-to-date list of such personnel.

Article 21

Convoys of vehicles or hospital trains on land or specially provided vessels on sea, conveying wounded and sick civilians, the infirm and maternity cases, shall be respected and protected in the same manner as the hospitals provided for in Article 18, and shall be marked, with the consent of the State, by the display of the distinctive emblem provided for in Article 38 of the Geneva Convention for the Amelioration of the Condition of the Wounded and Sick in Armed Forces in the Field of August 12, 1949.

Article 22

Aircraft exclusively employed for the removal of wounded and sick civilians, the infirm and maternity cases, or for the transport of medical personnel and equipment, shall not be attacked, but shall be respected while flying at heights, times and on routes specifically agreed upon between all the Parties to the conflict concerned.

They may be marked with the distinctive emblem provided for in Article 38 of the Geneva Convention for the Amelioration of the Condition of the Wounded and Sick in Armed Forces in the Field of August 12, 1949.

Unless agreed otherwise, flights over enemy or enemy-occupied territory are prohibited.

Such aircraft shall obey every summons to land. In the event of a landing thus imposed, the aircraft with its occupants may continue its flight after examination, if any.

Article 23

Each High Contracting Party shall allow the free passage of all consignments of medical and hospital stores and objects necessary for religious worship intended only for civilians of another High Contracting Party, even if the latter is its adversary. It shall likewise permit the free passage of all consignments of essential foodstuffs, clothing and tonics intended for children under fifteen, expectant mothers and maternity cases.

The obligation of a High Contracting Party to allow the free passage of the consignments indicated in the preceding paragraph is subject to the condition that this Party is satisfied that there are no serious reasons for fearing:

(a) That the consignments may be diverted from their destination;

(b) That the control may not be effective; or

(c) That a definite advantage may accrue to the military efforts or economy of the enemy through the substitution of the above-mentioned consignments for goods which would otherwise be provided or produced by the enemy or through the release of such material, services or facilities as would otherwise be required for the production of such goods.

The Power which allows the passage of the consignments indicated in the first paragraph of this Article may make such permission conditional on the distribution to the persons benefited there by being made under the local supervision of the Protecting Powers.

Such consignments shall be forwarded as rapidly as possible, and the Power which permits their free passage shall have the right to prescribe the technical arrangements under which such passage is allowed.

Article 24

The Parties to the conflict shall take the necessary measures to ensure that children under fifteen, who are orphaned or are separated from their families as a result of the war, are not left to their own resources, and that their maintenance, the exercise of their religion and their education are facilitated in all circumstances. Their education shall, as far as possible, be entrusted to persons of a similar cultural tradition.

The Parties to the conflict shall facilitate the reception of such children in a neutral country for the duration of the conflict with the consent of the Protecting Power, if any, and under due safeguards for the observance of the principles stated in the first paragraph.

They shall, furthermore, endeavour to arrange for all children under twelve to be identified by the wearing of identity discs, or by some other means.

Article 25

All persons in the territory of a Party to the conflict, or in a territory occupied by it, shall be enabled to give news of a strictly personal nature to members of their families, wherever they may be, and to receive news from them. This correspondence shall be forwarded speedily and without undue delay.

If, as a result of circumstances, it becomes difficult or impossible to exchange family correspondence by the ordinary post, the Parties to the conflict concerned shall apply to a neutral intermediary, such as the Central Agency provided for in Article 140, and shall decide in consultation with it how to ensure the fulfilment of their obligations under the best possible conditions, in particular with the cooperation of the National Red Cross (Red Crescent, Red Lion and Sun) Societies.

If the Parties to the conflict deem it necessary to restrict family correspondence, such restrictions shall be confined to the compulsory use of standard forms containing twenty-five freely chosen words, and to the limitation of the number of these forms dispatched to one each month.

CONVENTION ON THE PREVENTION AND PUNISHMENT OF THE CRIME OF GENOCIDE

Adopted by Resolution 260 (III) A of the United Nations General Assembly on 9 December 1948.

Article 1

The Contracting Parties confirm that genocide, whether committed in time of peace or in time of war, is a crime under international law which they undertake to prevent and to punish.

Article 2

In the present Convention, genocide means any of the following acts committed with intent to destroy, in whole or in part, a national, ethnical, racial or religious group, as such:

(a) Killing members of the group;

(b) Causing serious bodily or mental harm to members of the group;

(c) Deliberately inflicting on the group conditions of life calculated to bring about its physical destruction in whole or in part;

(d) Imposing measures intended to prevent births within the group;

(e) Forcibly transferring children of the group to another group.

Article 3

The following acts shall be punishable:

(a) Genocide;

(b) Conspiracy to commit genocide;

(c) Direct and public incitement to commit genocide;

(d) Attempt to commit genocide;

(e) Complicity in genocide.

Article 4

Persons committing genocide or any of the other acts enumerated in Article 3 shall be punished, whether they are constitutionally responsible rulers, public officials or private individuals.

Article 5

The Contracting Parties undertake to enact, in accordance with their respective Constitutions, the necessary legislation to give effect to the provisions of the present Convention and, in particular, to provide effective penalties for persons guilty of genocide or any of the other acts enumerated in Article 3.

Article 6

Persons charged with genocide or any of the other acts enumerated in Article 3 shall be tried by a competent tribunal of the State in the territory of which the act was committed, or by such international penal tribunal as may have jurisdiction with respect to those Contracting Parties which shall have accepted its jurisdiction.

Article 7

Genocide and the other acts enumerated in Article 3 shall not be considered as political crimes for the purpose of extradition.

The Contracting Parties pledge themselves in such cases to grant extradition in accordance with their laws and treaties in force.

Article 8

Any Contracting Party may call upon the competent organs of the United Nations to take such action under the Charter of the United Nations as they consider appropriate for the prevention and suppression of acts of genocide or any of the other acts enumerated in Article 3.

Article 9

Disputes between the Contracting Parties relating to the interpretation, application or fulfilment of the present Convention, including those relating to the responsibility of a State for genocide or any of the other acts enumerated in Article 3, shall be submitted to the International Court of Justice at the request of any of the parties to the dispute.

Article 10

The present Convention, of which the Chinese, English, French, Russian and Spanish texts are equally authentic, shall bear the date of 9 December 1948.

Article 11

The present Convention shall be open until 31 December 1949 for signature on behalf of any Member of the United Nations and of any non-member State to which an invitation to sign has been addressed by the General Assembly.

The present Convention shall be ratified, and the instruments of ratification shall be deposited with the Secretary-General of the United Nations.

After 1 January 1950, the present Convention may be acceded to on behalf of any Member of the United Nations and of any non-member State which has received an invitation as aforesaid.

Instruments of accession shall be deposited with the Secretary-General of the United Nations.

Article 12

Any Contracting Party may at any time, by notification addressed to the Secretary-General of the United Nations, extend the application of the present Convention to all or any of the territories for the conduct of whose foreign relations that Contracting Party is responsible.

Article 13

On the day when the first twenty instruments of ratification or accession have been deposited, the Secretary-General shall draw up a proces-verbal and transmit a copy of it to each Member of the United Nations and to each of the non-member States contemplated in Article 11.

The present Convention shall come into force on the ninetieth day following the date of deposit of the twentieth instrument of ratification or accession.

Any ratification or accession effected subsequent to the latter date shall become effective on the ninetieth day following the deposit of the instrument of ratification or accession.

Article 14

The present Convention shall remain in effect for a period of ten years as from the date of its coming into force.

It shall thereafter remain in force for successive periods of five years for such Contracting Parties as have not denounced it at least six months before the expiration of the current period.

Denunciation shall be effected by a written notification addressed to the Secretary-General of the United Nations.

Article 15

If, as a result of denunciations, the number of Parties to the present Convention should become less than sixteen, the Convention shall cease to be in force as from the date on which the last of these denunciations shall become effective.

Article 16

A request for the revision of the present Convention may be made at any time by any Contracting Party by means of a notification in writing addressed to the Secretary-General.

The General Assembly shall decide upon the steps, if any, to be taken in respect of such request.

Article 17

The Secretary-General of the United Nations shall notify all Members of the United Nations and the non-member States contemplated in Article 11 of the following:

(a) Signatures, ratifications and accessions received in accordance with Article 11;

(b) Notifications received in accordance with Article 12;

(c) The date upon which the present Convention comes into force in accordance with Article 13;

(d) Denunciations received in accordance with Article 14;

(e) The abrogation of the Convention in accordance with Article 15;

(f) Notifications received in accordance with Article 16.

Article 18

The original of the present Convention shall be deposited in the archives of the United Nations.

A certified copy of the Convention shall be transmitted to all Members of the United Nations and to the non-member States contemplated in Article 11.

Article 19

The present Convention shall be registered by the Secretary-General of the United Nations on the date of its coming into force.

UNIVERSAL DECLARATION OF HUMAN RIGHTS

Adopted and proclaimed by General Assembly resolution 217 A (III)
of 10 December 1948

On December 10, 1948 the General Assembly of the United Nations adopted and proclaimed the Universal Declaration of Human Rights the full text of which appears in the following pages. Following this historic act the Assembly called upon all Member countries to publicize the text of the Declaration and "to cause it to be disseminated, displayed, read and expounded principally in schools and other educational institutions, without distinction based on the political status of countries or territories."

Preamble

Whereas recognition of the inherent dignity and of the equal and inalienable rights of all members of the human family is the foundation of freedom, justice and peace in the world,

Whereas disregard and contempt for human rights have resulted in barbarous acts which have outraged the conscience of mankind, and the advent of a world in which human beings shall enjoy freedom of speech and belief and freedom from fear and want has been proclaimed as the highest aspiration of the common people,

Whereas it is essential, if man is not to be compelled to have recourse, as a last resort, to rebellion against tyranny and oppression, that human rights should be protected by the rule of law,

Whereas it is essential to promote the development of friendly relations between nations,

Whereas the peoples of the United Nations have in the Charter reaffirmed their faith in fundamental human rights, in the dignity and worth of the human person and in the equal rights of men and women and have determined to promote social progress and better standards of life in larger freedom,

Whereas Member States have pledged themselves to achieve, in co-operation with the United Nations, the promotion of universal respect for and observance of human rights and fundamental freedoms,

Whereas a common understanding of these rights and freedoms is of the greatest importance for the full realization of this pledge,

Now, Therefore THE GENERAL ASSEMBLY proclaims THIS UNIVERSAL DECLARATION OF HUMAN RIGHTS as a common standard of achievement for all peoples and all nations, to the end that every individual and every organ of society, keeping this Declaration constantly in mind, shall strive by teaching and education to promote respect for these rights and freedoms and by progressive measures, national and international, to secure their universal and effective recognition and observance, both among the peoples of Member States themselves and among the peoples of territories under their jurisdiction.

Article 1.

All human beings are born free and equal in dignity and rights. They are endowed with reason and conscience and should act towards one another in a spirit of brotherhood.

Article 2.

Everyone is entitled to all the rights and freedoms set forth in this Declaration, without distinction of any kind, such as race, colour, sex, language, religion, political or other opinion, national or social origin, property, birth or other status. Furthermore, no distinction shall be made on the basis of the political, jurisdictional or international status of the country or territory to which a person belongs, whether it be independent, trust, non-self-governing or under any other limitation of sovereignty.

Article 3.

Everyone has the right to life, liberty and security of person.

Article 4.

No one shall be held in slavery or servitude; slavery and the slave trade shall be prohibited in all their forms.

Article 5.

No one shall be subjected to torture or to cruel, inhuman or degrading treatment or punishment.

Article 6.

Everyone has the right to recognition everywhere as a person before the law.

Article 7.

All are equal before the law and are entitled without any discrimination to equal protection of the law. All are entitled to equal protection against any discrimination in violation of this Declaration and against any incitement to such discrimination.

Article 8.

Everyone has the right to an effective remedy by the competent national tribunals for acts violating the fundamental rights granted him by the constitution or by law.

Article 9.

No one shall be subjected to arbitrary arrest, detention or exile.

Article 10.

Everyone is entitled in full equality to a fair and public hearing by an independent and impartial tribunal, in the determination of his rights and obligations and of any criminal charge against him.

Article 11.

(1) Everyone charged with a penal offence has the right to be presumed innocent until proved guilty according to law in a public trial at which he has had all the guarantees necessary for his defence.

(2) No one shall be held guilty of any penal offence on account of any act or omission which did not constitute a penal offence, under national or international law, at the time when it was committed. Nor shall a heavier penalty be imposed than the one that was applicable at the time the penal offence was committed.

Article 12.

No one shall be subjected to arbitrary interference with his privacy, family, home or correspondence, nor to attacks upon his honour and reputation. Everyone has the right to the protection of the law against such interference or attacks.

Article 13.

(1) Everyone has the right to freedom of movement and residence within the borders of each state.

(2) Everyone has the right to leave any country, including his own, and to return to his country.

Article 14.

(1) Everyone has the right to seek and to enjoy in other countries asylum from persecution.

(2) This right may not be invoked in the case of prosecutions genuinely arising from non-political crimes or from acts contrary to the purposes and principles of the United Nations.

Article 15.

(1) Everyone has the right to a nationality.

(2) No one shall be arbitrarily deprived of his nationality nor denied the right to change his nationality.

Article 16.

(1) Men and women of full age, without any limitation due to race, nationality or religion, have the right to marry and to found a family. They are entitled to equal rights as to marriage, during marriage and at its dissolution.

(2) Marriage shall be entered into only with the free and full consent of the intending spouses.

(3) The family is the natural and fundamental group unit of society and is entitled to protection by society and the State.

Article 17.

(1) Everyone has the right to own property alone as well as in association with others.

(2) No one shall be arbitrarily deprived of his property.

Article 18.

Everyone has the right to freedom of thought, conscience and religion; this right includes freedom to change his religion or belief, and freedom, either alone or in community with others and in public or private, to manifest his religion or belief in teaching, practice, worship and observance.

Article 19.

Everyone has the right to freedom of opinion and expression; this right includes freedom to hold opinions without interference and to seek, receive and impart information and ideas through any media and regardless of frontiers.

Article 20.

(1) Everyone has the right to freedom of peaceful assembly and association.

(2) No one may be compelled to belong to an association.

Article 21.

(1) Everyone has the right to take part in the government of his country, directly or through freely chosen representatives.

(2) Everyone has the right of equal access to public service in his country.

(3) The will of the people shall be the basis of the authority of government; this will shall be expressed in periodic and genuine elections which shall be by universal and equal suffrage and shall be held by secret vote or by equivalent free voting procedures.

Article 22.

Everyone, as a member of society, has the right to social security and is entitled to realization, through national effort and international co-operation and in accordance with the organization and resources of each State, of the economic, social and cultural rights indispensable for his dignity and the free development of his personality.

Article 23.

(1) Everyone has the right to work, to free choice of employment, to just and favourable conditions of work and to protection against unemployment.

(2) Everyone, without any discrimination, has the right to equal pay for equal work.

(3) Everyone who works has the right to just and favourable remuneration ensuring for himself and his family an existence worthy of human dignity, and supplemented, if necessary, by other means of social protection.

(4) Everyone has the right to form and to join trade unions for the protection of his interests.

Article 24.

Everyone has the right to rest and leisure, including reasonable limitation of working hours and periodic holidays with pay.

Article 25.

(1) Everyone has the right to a standard of living adequate for the health and well-being of himself and of his family, including food, clothing, housing and medical care and necessary social services, and the right to security in the event of unemployment, sickness, disability, widowhood, old age or other lack of livelihood in circumstances beyond his control.

(2) Motherhood and childhood are entitled to special care and assistance. All children, whether born in or out of wedlock, shall enjoy the same social protection.

Article 26.

(1) Everyone has the right to education. Education shall be free, at least in the elementary and fundamental stages. Elementary education shall be compulsory. Technical and professional education shall be made generally available and higher education shall be equally accessible to all on the basis of merit.

(2) Education shall be directed to the full development of the human personality and to the strengthening of respect for human rights and fundamental freedoms. It shall promote understanding, tolerance and friendship among all nations, racial or religious groups, and shall further the activities of the United Nations for the maintenance of peace.

(3) Parents have a prior right to choose the kind of education that shall be given to their children.

Article 27.

(1) Everyone has the right freely to participate in the cultural life of the community, to enjoy the arts and to share in scientific advancement and its benefits.

(2) Everyone has the right to the protection of the moral and material interests resulting from any scientific, literary or artistic production of which he is the author.

Article 28.

Everyone is entitled to a social and international order in which the rights and freedoms set forth in this Declaration can be fully realized.

Article 29.

(1) Everyone has duties to the community in which alone the free and full development of his personality is possible.

(2) In the exercise of his rights and freedoms, everyone shall be subject only to such limitations as are determined by law solely for the purpose of securing due recognition and respect for the rights and freedoms of others and of meeting the just requirements of morality, public order and the general welfare in a democratic society.

(3) These rights and freedoms may in no case be exercised contrary to the purposes and principles of the United Nations.

Article 30.

Nothing in this Declaration may be interpreted as implying for any State, group or person any right to engage in any activity or to perform any act aimed at the destruction of any of the rights and freedoms set forth herein.

United Nations Convention against Torture and Other Cruel, Inhuman or Degrading Treatment or Punishment

The States Parties to this Convention,

Considering that, in accordance with the principles proclaimed in the Charter of the United Nations, recognition of the equal and inalienable rights of all members of the human family is the foundation of freedom, justice and peace in the world,

Recognizing that those rights derive from the inherent dignity of the human person,

Considering the obligation of States under the Charter, in particular Article 55, to promote universal respect for, and observance of, human rights and fundamental freedoms,

Having regard to article 5 of the Universal Declaration of Human Rights and article 7 of the International Covenant on Civil and Political Rights, both of which provide that no one may be subjected to torture or to cruel, inhuman or degrading treatment or punishment,

Having regard also to the Declaration on the Protection of All Persons from Being Subjected to Torture and Other Cruel, Inhuman or Degrading Treatment or Punishment, adopted by the General Assembly on 9 December 1975 (resolution 3452 (XXX)),

Desiring to make more effective the struggle against torture and other cruel, inhuman or degrading treatment or punishment throughout the world,

Have agreed as follows:

Part I

Article 1

1. For the purposes of this Convention, torture means any act by which severe pain or suffering, whether physical or mental, is intentionally inflicted on a person for such purposes as obtaining from him or a third person information or a confession, punishing him for an act he or a third person has committed or is suspected of having committed, or intimidating or coercing him or a third person, or for any reason based on discrimination of any kind, when such pain or suffering is inflicted by or at the instigation of or with the consent or acquiescence of a public official or other person acting in an official capacity. It does not include pain or suffering arising only from, inherent in or incidental to lawful sanctions.

2. This article is without prejudice to any international instrument or national legislation which does or may contain provisions of wider application.

Article 2

1. Each State Party shall take effective legislative, administrative, judicial or other measures to prevent acts of torture in any territory under its jurisdiction.

2. No exceptional circumstances whatsoever, whether a state of war or a threat or war, internal political instability or any other public emergency, may be invoked as a justification of torture.

3. An order from a superior officer or a public authority may not be invoked as a justification of torture.

Article 3

1. No State Party shall expel, return ("refouler") or extradite a person to another State where there are substantial grounds for believing that he would be in danger of being subjected to torture.

2. For the purpose of determining whether there are such grounds, the competent authorities shall take into

account all relevant considerations including, where applicable, the existence in the State concerned of a consistent pattern of gross, flagrant or mass violations of human rights.

Article 4

1. Each State Party shall ensure that all acts of torture are offences under its criminal law. The same shall apply to an attempt to commit torture and to an act by any person which constitutes complicity or participation in torture.

2. Each State Party shall make these offences punishable by appropriate penalties which take into account their grave nature.

Article 5

1. Each State Party shall take such measures as may be necessary to establish its jurisdiction over the offences referred to in article 4 in the following cases:

   1. When the offences are committed in any territory under its jurisdiction or on board a ship or aircraft registered in that State;
   2. When the alleged offender is a national of that State;
   3. When the victim was a national of that State if that State considers it appropriate.

2. Each State Party shall likewise take such measures as may be necessary to establish its jurisdiction over such offences in cases where the alleged offender is present in any territory under its jurisdiction and it does not extradite him pursuant to article 8 to any of the States mentioned in Paragraph 1 of this article.

3. This Convention does not exclude any criminal jurisdiction exercised in accordance with internal law.

Article 6

1. Upon being satisfied, after an examination of information available to it, that the circumstances so warrant, any State Party in whose territory a person alleged to have committed any offence referred to in article 4 is present, shall take him into custody or take other legal measures to ensure his presence. The custody and other legal measures shall be as provided in the law of that State but may be continued only for such time as is necessary to enable any criminal or extradition proceedings to be instituted.

2. Such State shall immediately make a preliminary inquiry into the facts.

3. Any person in custody pursuant to paragraph 1 of this article shall be assisted in communicating immediately with the nearest appropriate representative of the State of which he is a national, or, if he is a stateless person, to the representative of the State where he usually resides.

4. When a State, pursuant to this article, has taken a person into custody, it shall immediately notify the States referred to in article 5, paragraph 1, of the fact that such person is in custody and of the circumstances which warrant his detention. The State which makes the preliminary inquiry contemplated in paragraph 2 of this article shall promptly report its findings to the said State and shall indicate whether it intends to exercise jurisdiction.

Article 7

1. The State Party in territory under whose jurisdiction a person alleged to have committed any offence referred to in article 4 is found, shall in the cases contemplated in article 5, if it does not extradite him, submit the case to its competent authorities for the purpose of prosecution.

2. These authorities shall take their decision in the same manner as in the case of any ordinary offence of a serious nature under the law of that State. In the cases referred to in article 5, paragraph 2, the standards of evidence required for prosecution and conviction shall in no way be less stringent than those which apply in the cases referred to in article 5, paragraph 1.

3. Any person regarding whom proceedings are brought in connection with any of the offences referred to in article 4 shall be guaranteed fair treatment at all stages of the proceedings.

Article 8

1. The offences referred to in article 4 shall be deemed to be included as extraditable offences in any extradition treaty existing between States Parties. States Parties undertake to include such offences as extraditable offences in every extradition treaty to be concluded between them.

2. If a State Party which makes extradition conditional on the existence of a treaty receives a request for extradition from another State Party with which it has no extradition treaty, it may consider this Convention as the legal basis for extradition in respect of such offenses. Extradition shall be subject to the other conditions provided by the law of the requested State.

3. States Parties which do not make extradition conditional on the existence of a treaty shall recognize such offences as extraditable offences between themselves subject to the conditions provided by the law of the requested state.

4. Such offences shall be treated, for the purpose of extradition between States Parties, as if they had been committed not only in the place in which they occurred but also in the territories of the States required to establish their jurisdiction in accordance with article 5, paragraph 1.

Article 9

1. States Parties shall afford one another the greatest measure of assistance in connection with civil proceedings brought in respect of any of the offences referred to in

article 4, including the supply of all evidence at their disposal necessary for the proceedings.

2. States Parties shall carry out their obligations under paragraph 1 of this article in conformity with any treaties on mutual judicial assistance that may exist between them.

Article 10

1. Each State Party shall ensure that education and information regarding the prohibition against torture are fully included in the training of law enforcement personnel, civil or military, medical personnel, public officials and other persons who may be involved in the custody, interrogation or treatment of any individual subjected to any form of arrest, detention or imprisonment.

2. Each State Party shall include this prohibition in the rules or instructions issued in regard to the duties and functions of any such persons.

Article 11

Each State Party shall keep under systematic review interrogation rules, instructions, methods and practices as well as arrangements for the custody and treatment of persons subjected to any form of arrest, detention or imprisonment in any territory under its jurisdiction, with a view to preventing any cases of torture.

Article 12

Each State Party shall ensure that its competent authorities proceed to a prompt and impartial investigation, wherever there is reasonable ground to believe that an act of torture has been committed in any territory under its jurisdiction.

Article 13

Each State Party shall ensure that any individual who alleges he has been subjected to torture in any territory under its jurisdiction has the right to complain to and to have his case promptly and impartially examined its competent authorities. Steps shall be taken to ensure that the complainant and witnesses are protected against all ill-treatment or intimidation as a consequence of his complaint or any evidence given.

Article 14

1. Each State Party shall ensure in its legal system that the victim of an act of torture obtains redress and has an enforceable right to fair and adequate compensation including the means for as full rehabilitation as possible. In the event of the death of the victim as a result of an act of torture, his dependents shall be entitled to compensation.

2. Nothing in this article shall affect any right of the victim or other person to compensation which may exist under national law.

Article 15

Each State Party shall ensure that any statement which is established to have been made as a result of torture shall not be invoked as evidence in any proceedings, except against a person accused of torture as evidence that the statement was made.

Article 16

1. Each State Party shall undertake to prevent in any territory under its jurisdiction other acts of cruel, inhuman or degrading treatment or punishment which do not amount to torture as defined in article 1, when such acts are committed by or at the instigation of or with the consent or acquiescence of a public official or other person acting in an official capacity. In particular, the obligations contained in articles 10, 11, 12 and 13 shall apply with the substitution for references to torture or references to other forms of cruel, inhuman or degrading treatment or punishment.

2. The provisions of this Convention are without prejudice to the provisions of any other international instrument or national law which prohibit cruel, inhuman or degrading treatment or punishment or which relate to extradition or expulsion.

Article 17

1. There shall be established a Committee against Torture (hereinafter referred to as the Committee) which shall carry out the functions hereinafter provided. The Committee shall consist of 10 experts of high moral standing and recognized competence in the field of human rights, who shall serve in their personal capacity. The experts shall be elected by the States Parties, consideration being given to equitable geographical distribution and to the usefulness of the participation of some persons having legal experience.

2. The members of the Committee shall be elected by secret ballot from a list of persons nominated by States Parties. Each State Party may nominate one person from among its own nationals. States Parties shall bear in mind the usefulness of nominating persons who are also members of the Human Rights Committee established under the International Covenant on Civil and Political Rights and are willing to serve on the Committee against Torture.

3. Elections of the members of the Committee shall be held at biennial meetings of States Parties convened by the Secretary-General of the United Nations. At those meetings, for which two thirds of the States Parties shall constitute a quorum, the persons elected to the Committee shall be those who obtain the largest number of votes and an absolute majority of the votes of the representatives of States Parties present and voting.

4. The initial election shall be held no later than six months after the date of the entry into force of this

Convention. At least four months before the date of each election, the Secretary-General of the United Nations shall address a letter to the States Parties inviting them to submit their nominations within three months. The Secretary-General shall prepare a list in alphabetical order of all persons thus nominated, indicating the States Parties which have nominated them, and shall submit it to the States Parties.

5. The members of the Committee shall be elected for a term of four years. They shall be eligible for re-election if renominated. However, the term of five of the members elected at the first election shall expire at the end of two years; immediately after the first election the names of these five members shall be chosen by lot by the chairman of the meeting referred to in paragraph 3.

6. If a member of the Committee dies or resigns or for any other cause can no longer perform his Committee duties, the State Party which nominated him shall appoint another expert from among its nationals to serve for the remainder of his term, subject to the approval of the majority of the States Parties. The approval shall be considered given unless half or more of the States Parties respond negatively within six weeks after having been informed by the Secretary-General of the United Nations of the proposed appointment.

7. States Parties shall be responsible for the expenses of the members of the Committee while they are in performance of Committee duties.

Article 18

1. The Committee shall elect its officers for a term of two years. They may be re-elected.

2. The Committee shall establish its own rules of procedure, but these rules shall provide, inter alia, that

    1. Six members shall constitute a quorum;

    2. Decisions of the Committee shall be made by a majority vote of the members present.

3. The Secretary-General of the United Nations shall provide the necessary staff and facilities for the effective performance of the functions of the Committee under this Convention.

4. The Secretary-General of the United Nations shall convene the initial meeting of the Committee. After its initial meeting, the Committee shall meet at such times as shall be provided in its rules of procedure.

5. The State Parties shall be responsible for expenses incurred in connection with the holding of meetings of the States Parties and of the Committee, including reimbursement of the United Nations for any expenses, such as the cost of staff and facilities, incurred by the United Nations pursuant to paragraph 3 above.

Article 19

1. The States Parties shall submit to the Committee, through the Secretary-General of the United Nations,

reports on the measures they have taken to give effect to their undertakings under this Convention, within one year after the entry into force of this Convention for the State Party concerned. Thereafter the States Parties shall submit supplementary reports every four years on any new measures taken, and such other reports as the Committee may request.

2. The Secretary-General shall transmit the reports to all States Parties.

3. [Each report shall be considered by the Committee which may make such comments or suggestions on the report as it considers appropriate, and shall forward these to the State Party concerned. That State Party may respond with any observations it chooses to the Committee.

4. The Committee may, at its discretion, decide to include any comments or suggestions made by it in accordance with paragraph 3, together with the observations thereon received from the State Party concerned, in its annual report made in accordance with article 24. If so requested by the State Party concerned, the Committee may also include a copy of the report submitted under paragraph 1.]

Article 20

1. If the Committee receives reliable information which appears to it to contain well-founded indications that torture is being systematically practised in the territory of a State Party, the Committee shall invite that State Party to co-operate in the examination of the information and to this end to submit observations with regard to the information concerned.

2. Taking into account any observations which may have been submitted by the State Party concerned as well as any other relevant information available to it, the Committee may, if it decides that this is warranted, designate one or more of its members to make a confidential inquiry and to report to the Committee urgently.

3. If an inquiry is made in accordance with paragraph 2, the Committee shall seek the co-operation of the State Party concerned. In agreement with that State Party, such an inquiry may include a visit to its territory.

4. After examining the findings of its member or members submitted in accordance with paragraph 2, the Committee shall transmit these findings to the State Party concerned together with any comments or suggestions which seem appropriate in view of the situation.

5. All the proceedings of the Committee referred to in paragraphs 1 to 4 of this article shall be confidential, and at all stages of the proceedings the co-operation of the State Party shall be sought. After such proceedings have been completed with regard to an inquiry made in accordance with paragraph 2, the Committee may, after consultations with the State Party concerned, decide to

include a summary account of the results of the proceedings in its annual report made in accordance with article 24.

Article 21

1. A State Party to this Convention may at any time declare under this article 3 that it recognizes the competence of the Committee to receive and consider communications to the effect that a State Party claims that another State Party is not fulfilling its obligations under this Convention. Such communications may be received and considered according to the procedures laid down in this article only if submitted by a State Party which has made a declaration recognizing in regard to itself the competence of the Committee. No communication shall be dealt with by the Committee under this article if it concerns a State Party which has not made such a declaration. Communications received under this article shall be dealt with in accordance with the following procedure:

1. If a State Party considers that another State Party is not giving effect to the provisions of this Convention, it may, by written communication, bring the matter to the attention of that State Party. Within three months after the receipt of the communication the receiving State shall afford the State which sent the communication an explanation or any other statement in writing clarifying the matter which should include, to the extent possible and pertinent, references to domestic procedures and remedies taken, pending, or available in the matter.

2. If the matter is not adjusted to the satisfaction of both States Parties concerned within six months after the receipt by the receiving State of the initial communication, either State shall have the right to refer the matter to the Committee by notice given to the Committee and to the other State.

3. The Committee shall deal with a matter referred to it under this article only after it has ascertained that all domestic remedies have been invoked and exhausted in the matter, in conformity with the generally recognized principles of international law. This shall not be the rule where the application of the remedies is unreasonably prolonged or is unlikely to bring effective relief to the person who is the victim of the violation of this Convention.

4. The Committee shall hold closed meetings when examining communications under this article.

5. Subject to the provisions of subparagraph (c), the Committee shall make available its good offices to the States Parties concerned with a view to a friendly solution of the matter on the basis of respect for the obligations provided for in the present Convention. For this purpose, the Committee may, when appropriate, set up an ad hoc conciliation commission.

6. In any matter referred to it under this article, the Committee may call upon the States Parties concerned, referred to in subparagraph (b), to supply any relevant information.

7. The States Parties concerned, referred to in subparagraph (b), shall have the right to be represented when the matter is being considered by the Committee and to make submissions orally and/or in writing.

8. The Committee shall, within 12 months after the date of receipt of notice under subparagraph (b), submit a report.

    1. If a solution within the terms of subparagraph (e) is reached, the Committee shall confine its report to a brief statement of the facts and of the solution reached.

    2. If a solution within the terms of subparagraph (e) is not reached, the Committee shall confine its report to a brief statement of the facts; the written submissions and record of the oral submissions made by the States Parties concerned shall be attached to the report.

In every matter, the report shall be communicated to the States Parties concerned.

2. The provisions of this article shall come into force when five States Parties to this Convention have made declarations under paragraph 1 of this article. Such declarations shall be deposited by the States Parties with the Secretary-General of the United Nations, who shall transmit copies thereof to the other States Parties. A declaration may be withdrawn at any time by notification to the Secretary-General. Such a withdrawal shall not prejudice the consideration of any matter which is the subject of a communication already transmitted under this article; no further communication by any State Party shall be received under this article after the notification of withdrawal of the declaration has been received by the Secretary-General, unless the State Party concerned has made a new declaration.

Article 22

1. A State Party to this Convention may at any time declare under this article that it recognizes the competence of the Committee to receive and consider communications from or on behalf of individuals subject to its jurisdiction who claim to be victims of a violation by a State Party of the provisions of the Convention. No communication shall be received by the Committee if it concerns a State Party to the Convention which has not made such a declaration.

2. The Committee shall consider inadmissible any communication under this article which is anonymous, or which it considers to be an abuse of the right of submission of such communications or to be incompatible with the provisions of this Convention.

3. Subject to the provisions of paragraph 2, the Committee shall bring any communication submitted to it under this article to the attention of the State Party to this Convention which has made a declaration under paragraph 1 and is alleged to be violating any provisions of the Convention. Within six months, the receiving State shall submit to the Committee written explanations or statements clarifying the matter and the remedy, if any, that may have been taken by that State.

4. The Committee shall consider communications received under this article in the light of all information made available to it by or on behalf of the individual and by the State Party concerned.

5. The Committee shall not consider any communication from an individual under this article unless it has ascertained that:

    1. The same matter has not been, and is not being examined under another procedure of international investigation or settlement;

    2. The individual has exhausted all available domestic remedies; this shall not be the rule where the application of the remedies is unreasonably prolonged or is unlikely to bring effective relief to the person who is the victim of the violation of this Convention.

6. The Committee shall hold closed meetings when examining communications under this article.

7. The Committee shall forward its views to the State Party concerned and to the individual.

8. The provisions of this article shall come into force when five States Parties to this Convention have made declarations under paragraph 1 of this article. Such declarations shall be deposited by the States Parties with the Secretary-General of the United Nations, who shall transmit parties thereof to the other States Parties. A declaration may be withdrawn at any time by notification to the Secretary-General. Such a withdrawal shall not prejudice the consideration of any matter which is the subject of a communication already transmitted under this article; no further communication by or on behalf of an individual shall be received under this article after the notification of withdrawal of the declaration has been received by the Secretary-General, unless the State Party concerned has made a new declaration.

Article 23

The members of the Committee, and of the ad hoc conciliation commissions which may be appointed under article 21, paragraph 1 (e), shall be entitled to the facilities, privileges and immunities of experts on missions for the United Nations as laid down in the relevant sections of the Convention on the Privileges and Immunities of the United Nations.

Article 24

The Committee shall submit an annual report on its activities under this Convention to the States Parties and to the General Assembly of the United Nations.

Part III

Article 25

1. This Convention is open for signature by all States.

    2. This Convention is subject to ratification. Instruments of ratification shall be deposited with the Secretary-General of the United Nations.

Article 26

This Convention is open to accession by all States. Accession shall be effected by the deposit of an instrument of accession with the Secretary-General of the United Nations.

Article 27

1. This Convention shall enter into force on the thirtieth day after the date of the deposit with the Secretary-General of the United Nations of the twentieth instrument of ratification or accession.

    2. For each State ratifying this Convention or acceding to it after the deposit of the twentieth instrument of ratification or accession, the Convention shall enter into force on the thirtieth day after the date of the deposit of its own instrument of ratification or accession.

Article 28

1. Each State may, at the time of signature or ratification of this Convention or accession thereto, declare that it does not recognize the competence of the Committee provided for in article 20.

    2. Any State Party having made a reservation in accordance with paragraph 1 of this article may, at any time, withdraw this reservation by notification to the Secretary-General of the United Nations.

Article 29

1. Any State Party to this Convention may propose an amendment and file it with the Secretary-General of the United Nations. The Secretary-General shall thereupon communicate the proposed amendment to the States Parties to this Convention with a request that they notify him whether they favour a conference of States Parties for

the purpose of considering and voting upon the proposal. In the event that within four months from the date of such communication at least one third of the State Parties favours such a conference, the Secretary-General shall convene the conference under the auspices of the United Nations. Any amendment adopted by a majority of the States Parties present and voting at the conference shall be submitted by the Secretary-General to all the States Parties for acceptance.

2. An amendment adopted in accordance with paragraph 1 shall enter into force when two thirds of the States Parties to this Convention have notified the Secretary-General of the United Nations that they have accepted it in accordance with their respective constitutional processes.

3. When amendments enter into force, they shall be binding on those States Parties which have accepted them, other States Parties still being bound by the provisions of this Convention and any earlier amendments which they have accepted.

Article 30

1. Any dispute between two or more States Parties concerning the interpretation or application of this Convention which cannot be settled through negotiation, shall, at the request of one of them, be submitted to arbitration. If within six months from the date of the request for arbitration the Parties are unable to agree on the organization of the arbitration, any one of those Parties may refer the dispute to the International Court of Justice by request in conformity with the Statute of the Court.

2. Each State may at the time of signature or ratification of this Convention or accession thereto, declare that it does not consider itself bound by the preceding paragraph. The other States Parties shall not be bound by the preceding paragraph with respect to any State Party having made such a reservation.

3. Any State Party having made a reservation in accordance with the preceding paragraph may at any time withdraw this reservation by notification to the Secretary-General of the United Nations.

Article 31

1. A State Party may denounce this Convention by written notification to the Secretary-General of the United Nations. Denunciation becomes effective one year after the date of receipt of the notification by the Secretary-General.

2. Such a denunciation shall not have the effect of releasing the State Party from its obligations under this Convention in regard to any act or omission which occurs prior to the date at which the denunciation becomes effective. Nor shall denunciation prejudice in any way the continued consideration of any matter which is already under consideration by the Committee prior to the date at which the denunciation becomes effective.

3. Following the date at which the denunciation of a State Party becomes effective, the Committee shall not commence consideration of any new matter regarding that State.

Article 32

The Secretary-General of the United Nations shall inform all members of the United Nations and all States which have signed this Convention or acceded to it, or the following particulars:

1. Signatures, ratifications and accessions under articles 25 and 26;

2. The date of entry into force of this Convention under article 27, and the date of the entry into force of any amendments under article 29;

3. Denunciations under article 31.

CHARTER OF THE NUREMBERG INTERNATIONAL MILITARY TRIBUNAL

★ ————————————————————————————————

Article 1.

In pursuance of the Agreement signed on the 8th day of August 1945 by the Government of the United States of America, the Provisional Government of the French Republic, the Government of the United Kingdom of Great Britain and Northern Ireland and the Government of the Union of Soviet Socialist Republics, there shall be established an International Military Tribunal (hereinafter called "the Tribunal") for the just and prompt trial and punishment of the major war criminals of the European Axis.

Article 2.

The Tribunal shall consist of four members, each with an alternate. One member and one alternate shall be appointed by each of the Signatories. The alternates shall, so far as they are able, be present at all sessions of the Tribunal. In case of illness of any member of the Tribunal or his incapacity for some other reason to fulfill his functions, his alternate shall take his place.

Article 3.

Neither the Tribunal, its members nor their alternates can be challenged by the prosecution, or by the Defendants or their Counsel. Each Signatory may replace its members of the Tribunal or his alternate for reasons of health or for other good reasons, except that no replacement may take place during a Trial, other than by an alternate.

Article 4

(a) The presence of all four members of the Tribunal or the alternate for any absent member shall be necessary to constitute the quorum.

(b) The members of the Tribunal shall, before any trial begins, agree among themselves upon the selection from their number of a President, and the President shall hold office during the trial, or as may otherwise be agreed by a vote of not less than three members. The principle of rotation of presidency for successive trials is agreed. If, however, a session of the Tribunal takes place on the territory of one of the four Signatories, the representative of that Signatory on the Tribunal shall preside.

(c) Save as aforesaid the Tribunal shall take decisions by a majority vote and in case the votes are evenly divided, the vote of the President shall be decisive: provided always that convictions and sentences shall only be imposed by affirmative votes of at least three members of the Tribunal.

Article 5.

In case of need and depending on the number of the matters to be tried, other Tribunals may be set up; and the establishment, functions, and procedure of each Tribunal shall be identical, and shall be governed by this Charter.

II. Jurisdiction and General Principles

Article 6.

The Tribunal established by the Agreement referred to Article 1 hereof for the trial and punishment of the major war criminals of the European Axis countries shall have the power to try and punish persons who, acting in the interests of the European Axis countries, whether as individuals or as members of organizations, committed any of the following crimes.

The following acts, or any of them, are crimes coming within the jurisdiction of the Tribunal for which there shall be individual responsibility:

(a) CRIMES AGAINST PEACE: namely, planning, preparation, initiation or waging of a war of aggression, or a war in violation of international treaties, agreements or assurances, or participation in a common plan or conspiracy for the accomplishment of any of the foregoing;

(b) WAR CRIMES: namely, violations of the laws or customs of war. Such violations shall include, but not be limited to, murder, ill-treatment or deportation to slave labor or for any other purpose of civilian population of or in occupied territory, murder or ill-treatment of prisoners of war or persons on the seas, killing of hostages, plunder of public or private property, wanton destruction of cities, towns or villages, or devastation not justified by military necessity;

(c) CRIMES AGAINST HUMANITY: namely, murder, extermination, enslavement, deportation, and other inhumane acts committed against any civilian population, before or during the war; or persecutions on political, racial or religious grounds in execution of or in connection with any crime within the jurisdiction of the Tribunal, whether or not in violation of the domestic law of the country where perpetrated.

Leaders, organizers, instigators and accomplices participating in the formulation or execution of a common plan or conspiracy to commit any of the foregoing crimes are responsible for all acts performed by any persons in execution of such plan.

Article 7.
The official position of defendants, whether as Heads of State or responsible officials in Government Departments, shall not be considered as freeing them from responsibility or mitigating punishment.

Article 8.
The fact that the Defendant acted pursuant to order of his Government or of a superior shall not free him from responsibility, but may be considered in mitigation of punishment if the Tribunal determines that justice so requires.

Article 9.
At the trial of any individual member of any group or organization the Tribunal may declare (in connection with any act of which the individual may be convicted) that the group or organization of which the individual was a member was a criminal organization.

After the receipt of the Indictment the Tribunal shall give such notice as it thinks fit that the prosecution intends to ask the Tribunal to make such declaration and any member of the organization will be entitled to apply to the Tribunal for leave to be heard by the Tribunal upon the question of the criminal character of the organization. The Tribunal shall have power to allow or reject the application. If the application is allowed, the Tribunal may direct in what manner the applicants shall be represented and heard.

Article 10.
In cases where a group or organization is declared criminal by the Tribunal, the competent national authority of any Signatory shall have the right to bring individual to trial for membership therein before national, military or occupation courts. In any such case the criminal nature of the group or organization is considered proved and shall not be questioned.

Article 11.
Any person convicted by the Tribunal may be charged before a national, military or occupation court, referred to in Article 10 of this Charter, with a crime other than of membership in a criminal group or organization and such court may, after convicting him, impose upon him punishment independent of and additional to the punishment imposed by the Tribunal for participation in the criminal activities of such group or organization.

Article 12.
The Tribunal shall have the right to take proceedings against a person charged with crimes set out in Article 6 of this Charter in his absence, if he has not been found or if the Tribunal, for any reason, finds it necessary, in the interests of justice, to conduct the hearing in his absence.

Article 13.
The Tribunal shall draw up rules for its procedure. These rules shall not be inconsistent with the provisions of this Charter.

III. Committee for the Investigation and Prosecution of Major War Criminals

Article 14.
Each Signatory shall appoint a Chief Prosecutor for the investigation of the charges against and the prosecution of major war criminals.

The Chief Prosecutors shall act as a committee for the following purposes:

(a) to agree upon a plan of the individual work of each of the Chief Prosecutors and his staff,

(b) to settle the final designation of major war criminals to be tried by the Tribunal,

(c) to approve the Indictment and the documents to be submitted therewith,

(d) to lodge the Indictment and the accompany documents with the Tribunal,

(e) to draw up and recommend to the Tribunal for its approval draft rules of procedure, contemplated by Article 13 of this Charter. The Tribunal shall have the power to accept, with or without amendments, or to reject, the rules so recommended.

The Committee shall act in all the above matters by a majority vote and shall appoint a Chairman as may be convenient and in accordance with the principle of rotation: provided that if there is an equal division of vote concerning the designation of a Defendant to be tried by the Tribunal, or the crimes with which he shall be charged, that proposal will be adopted which was made by the party which proposed that the particular Defendant be tried, or the particular charges be preferred against him.

Article 15.

The Chief Prosecutors shall individually, and acting in collaboration with one another, also undertake the following duties:

(a) investigation, collection and production before or at the Trial of all necessary evidence,

(b) the preparation of the Indictment for approval by the Committee in accordance with paragraph (c) of Article 14 hereof,

(c) the preliminary examination of all necessary witnesses and of all Defendants,

(d) to act as prosecutor at the Trial,

(e) to appoint representatives to carry out such duties as may be assigned them,

(f) to undertake such other matters as may appear necessary to them for the purposes of the preparation for and conduct of the Trial.

It is understood that no witness or Defendant detained by the Signatory shall be taken out of the possession of that Signatory without its assent.

IV. Fair Trial for Defendants

Article 16.

In order to ensure fair trial for the Defendants, the following procedure shall be followed:

(a) The Indictment shall include full particulars specifying in detail the charges against the Defendants. A copy of the Indictment and of all the documents lodged with the Indictment, translated into a language which he understands, shall be furnished to the Defendant at reasonable time before the Trial.

(b) During any preliminary examination or trial of a Defendant he will have the right to give any explanation relevant to the charges made against him.

(c) A preliminary examination of a Defendant and his Trial shall be conducted in, or translated into, a language which the Defendant understands.

(d) A Defendant shall have the right to conduct his own defense before the Tribunal or to have the assistance of Counsel.

(e) A Defendant shall have the right through himself or through his Counsel to present evidence at the Trial in support of his defense, and to cross-examine any witness called by the Prosecution.

V. Powers of the Tribunal and Conduct of the Trial

Article 17.

The Tribunal shall have the power

(a) to summon witnesses to the Trial and to require their attendance and testimony and to put questions to them

(b) to interrogate any Defendant,

(c) to require the production of documents and other evidentiary material,

(d) to administer oaths to witnesses,

(e) to appoint officers for the carrying out of any task designated by the Tribunal including the power to have evidence taken on commission.

Article 18.

The Tribunal shall

(a) confine the Trial strictly to an expeditious hearing of the cases raised by the charges,

(b) take strict measures to prevent any action which will cause reasonable delay, and rule out irrelevant issues and statements of any kind whatsoever,

(c) deal summarily with any contumacy, imposing appropriate punishment, including exclusion of any Defendant or his Counsel from some or all further proceedings, but without prejudice to the determination of the charges.

Article 19.

The Tribunal shall not be bound by technical rules of evidence. It shall adopt and apply to the greatest possible extent expeditious and nontechnical procedure, and shall admit any evidence which it deems to be of probative value.

Article 20.

The Tribunal may require to be informed of the nature of any evidence before it is entered so that it may rule upon the relevance thereof.

Article 21.

The Tribunal shall not require proof of facts of common knowledge but shall take judicial notice thereof. It shall also take judicial notice of official governmental documents and reports of the United Nations, including the acts and documents of the committees set up in the various allied countries for the investigation of war crimes, and of records and findings of military or other Tribunals of any of the United Nations.

Article 22.

The permanent seat of the Tribunal shall be in Berlin. The first meetings of the members of the Tribunal and of the Chief Prosecutors shall be held at Berlin in a place to be designated by the Control Council for Germany. The first trial shall be held at Nuremberg, and any subsequent trials shall be held at such places as the Tribunal may decide.

Article 23.

One or more of the Chief Prosecutors may take part in the prosecution at each Trial. The function of any Chief Prosecutor may be discharged by him personally, or by any person or persons authorized by him.

The function of Counsel for a Defendant may be discharged at the Defendant's request by any Counsel professionally qualified to conduct cases before the Courts of his own country, or by any other person who may be specially authorized thereto by the Tribunal.

Article 24.

The proceedings at the Trial shall take the following course:

(a) The Indictment shall be read in court.

(b) The Tribunal shall ask each Defendant whether he pleads "guilty" or "not guilty."

(c) The prosecution shall make an opening statement.

(d) The Tribunal shall ask the prosecution and the defense what evidence (if any) they wish to submit to the Tribunal, and the Tribunal shall rule upon the admissibility of any such evidence.

(e) The witnesses for the Prosecution shall be examined and after that the witnesses for the Defense. Thereafter such rebutting evidence as may be held by the Tribunal to be admissible shall be called by either the Prosecution or the Defense.

(f) The Tribunal may put any question to any witness and to any defendant, at any time.

(g) The Prosecution and the Defense shall interrogate and may crossexamine any witnesses and any Defendant who gives testimony.

(h) The Defense shall address the court.

(i) The Prosecution shall address the court.

(j) Each Defendant may make a statement to the Tribunal.

(k) The Tribunal shall deliver judgment and pronounce sentence.

Article 25.

All official documents shall be produced, and all court proceedings conducted, in English, French and Russian, and in the language of the Defendant. So much of the record and of the proceedings may also be translated into the language of any country in which the Tribunal is sitting, as the Tribunal is sitting, as the Tribunal considers desirable in the interests of the justice and public opinion.

VI. Judgment and Sentence

Article 26.

The judgment of the Tribunal as to the guilt or the innocence of any Defendant shall give the reasons on which it is based, and shall be final and not subject to review.

Article 27.

The Tribunal shall have the right to impose upon a Defendant, on conviction, death or such other punishment as shall be determined by it to be just.

Article 28.

In addition to any punishment imposed by it, the Tribunal shall have the right to deprive the convicted person of any stolen property and order its delivery to the Control Council for Germany.

Article 29.

In case of guilt, sentences shall be carried out in accordance with the orders of the Control Council for Germany, which may at any time reduce or otherwise alter the sentences, but may not increase the severity thereof. If the Control Council for Germany, after any Defendant has been convicted and sentenced, discovers fresh evidence which, in its opinion, would found a fresh charge against him, the Council shall report accordingly to the Committee established under Article 14 hereof, for such action as they may consider proper, having regard to the interests of justice.

VII. Expenses

Article 30.

The expenses of the Tribunal and of the Trials, shall be charged by the Signatories against the funds allotted for maintenance of the Control Council of Germany.

LAW FOR THE PROTECTION OF HEREDITARY HEALTH: THE ATTEMPT TO IMPROVE THE GERMAN ARYAN BREED, JULY 14, 1933

Article I.
(1.) Anyone who suffers from an inheritable disease may be surgically sterilized if, in the judgement of medical science, it could be expected that his decendants will suffer from serious inherited mental or physical defects. (2.) Anyone who suffers from one of the following is to be regarded as inheritably diseased within the meaning of this law:

    1. congenital feeble-mindedness
    2. schizophrenia
    3. manic-depression
    4. congenital epilepsy
    5. inheritable St. Vitus dance (Huntington's Chorea)
    6. hereditary blindness
    7. hereditary deafness
    8. serious inheritable malformations (3.) In addition, anyone suffering from chronic alcoholism may also be sterilized.

Article II.
(1.) Anyone who requests sterilization is entitled to it. If he be incapacitated or under a guardian because of low state of mental health or not yet 18 years of age, his legal guardian is empowered to make the request. In other cases of limited capacity the request must receive the approval of the legal representative. If a person be of age and has a nurse, the latter's consent is required. (2.) The request must be accompanied by a certificate from a citizen who is accredited by the German Reich stating that the person to be sterilized has been informed about the nature and consequence of sterilization. (3.) The request for sterilization can be recalled.

Article III.
Sterilization may also be recommended by: (1.) the official physician (2.) the official in charge of a hospital, sanitarium, or prison.

Article IV.
The request for sterilization must be presented in writing to, or placed in writing by the office of the Health Inheritance Court. The statement concerning the request must be certified by a medical document or authenticated in some other way. The business office of the court must notify the official physician.

Article VII.
The proceedings of the Health Inheritance Court are secret.

Article X.
The Supreme Health Insurance Court retains final jurisdiction.

THE NUREMBERG LAWS ON CITIZENSHIP AND RACE:
SEPTEMBER 15, 1935

THE REICH CITIZENSHIP LAW
OF SEPTEMBER 15, 1935

THE REICHSTAG HAS ADOPTED by unanimous vote the following law which is herewith promulgated.

Article 1.

(1) A subject of the state is one who belongs to the protective union of the German Reich, and who, therefore, has specific obligations to the Reich. (2) The status of subject is to be acquired in accordance with the provisions of the Reich and the state Citizenship Law.

Article 2.

(1) A citizen of the Reich may be only one who is of German or kindred blood, and who, through his behavior, shows that he is both desirous and personally fit to serve loyally the German people and the Reich. (2) The right to citizenship is obtained by the grant of Reich citizenship papers. (3) Only the citizen of the Reich may enjoy full political rights in consonance with the provisions of the laws.

Article 3.

The Reich Minister of the Interior, in conjunction with the Deputy to the *Fuehrer,* will issue the required legal and administrative decrees for the implementation and amplification of this law.
Promulgated: September 16, 1935. *In force:* September 30, 1935.

First Supplementary Decree of November 14, 1935

On the basis of Article III of the Reich Citizenship Law of September 15, 1935, the following is hereby decreed:

Article 1.

(1) Until further provisions concerning citizenship papers, all subjects of German or kindred blood who possessed the right to vote in the *Reichstag* elections when the Citizenship Law came into effect, shall, for the present, possess the rights of Reich citizens. The same shall be true of those upon whom the Reich Minister of the Interior, in conjunction with the Deputy to the *Fuehrer* shall confer citizenship. (2) The Reich Minister of the Interior, in conjunction with the Deputy to the *Fuehrer,* may revoke citizenship.

Article 2.

(1) The provisions of Article I shall apply also to subjects who are of mixed Jewish blood. (2) An individual of mixed Jewish blood is one who is descended from one or two grandparents who, racially, were full Jews, insofar that he is not a Jew according to Section 2 of Article 5. Full-blooded Jewish grandparents are those who belonged to the Jewish religious community.

Article 3.

Only citizens of the Reich, as bearers of full political rights, can exercise the right of voting in political matters, and have the right to hold public office. The Reich Minister of the Interior, or any agency he empowers, can make exceptions during the transition period on the matter of holding public office. The measures do not apply to matters concerning religious organizations.

Article 4.

(1) A Jew cannot be a citizen of the Reich. He cannot exercise the right to vote; he cannot hold public office. (2) Jewish

officials will be retired as of December 31, 1935. In the event that such officials served at the front in the World War either for Germany or her allies, they shall receive as pension, until they reach the age limit, the full salary last received, on the basis of which their pension would have been computed. They shall not, however, be promoted according to their seniority in rank. When they reach the age limit, their pension will be computed again, according to the salary last received on which their pension was to be calculated. (3) These provisions do not concern the affairs of religious organizations. (4) The conditions regarding service of teachers in public Jewish schools remains unchanged until the promulgation of new laws on the Jewish school system.

Article 5.

(1) A Jew is an individual who is descended from at least three grandparents who were, racially, full Jews . . . (2) A Jew is also an individual who is descended from two full-Jewish grandparents if: (a) he was a member of the Jewish religious community when this law was issued, or joined the community later; (b) when the law was issued, he was married to a person who was a Jew, or was subsequently married to a Jew; (c) he is the issue from a marriage with a Jew, in the sense of Section I, which was contracted after the coming into effect of the Law for the Protection of German Blood and Honor of September 15, 1935; (d) he is the issue of an extramarital relationship with a Jew, in the sense of Section I, and was born out of wedlock after July 31, 1936.

Article 6.

(1) Insofar as there are, in the laws of the Reich or in the decrees of the National Socialist German Workers' Party and its affiliates, certain requirements for the purity of German blood which extend beyond Article 5, the same remain untouched. . . .

Article 7.

The *Fuehrer* and Chancellor of the Reich is empowered to release anyone from the provisions of these administrative decrees.

LAW FOR THE PROTECTION OF GERMAN BLOOD AND GERMAN HONOR SEPTEMBER 15, 1935

Thoroughly convinced by the knowledge that the purity of German blood is essential for the further existence of the German people and animated by the inflexible will to safeguard the German nation for the entire future, the Reichstag has resolved upon the following law unanimously, which is promulgated herewith:

Section 1

1. Marriages between Jews and nationals of German or kindred blood are forbidden. Marriages concluded in defiance of this law are void, even if, for the purpose of evading this law, they are concluded abroad. 2. Proceedings for annulment may be initiated only by the Public Prosecutor.

Section 2

Relation outside marriage between Jews and nationals of German or kindred blood are forbidden.

Section 3

Jews will not be permitted to employ female nationals of German or kindred blood in their households.

Section 4

1. Jews are forbidden to hoist the Reich and national flag and to present the colors of the Reich. 2. On the other hand they are permitted to present the Jewish colors. The exercise of this authority is protected by the State.

Section 5

1. A person who acts contrary to the prohibition of section 1 will be punished with hard labor. 2. A person who acts contrary to the prohibition of section 2 will be punished with imprisonment or with hard labor. 3. A person who acts contrary to the provisions of section 3 or 4 will be punished with imprisonment up to a year and with a fine or with one of these penalties.

Section 6

The Reich Minister of the Interior in agreement with the Deputy of the Fuehrer will issue the legal and administrative regulations which are required from the implementation and supplementation of this law.

Section 7

The law will become effective on the day after the promulgation, section 3 however only on 1 January, 1936.
Nuremberg, the 15th day of September 1935 at the Reich Party Rally of Freedom.
The Fuehrer and Reich Chancellor Adolf Hitler
The Reich Minister of the Interior Frick
The Reich Minister of Justice Dr. Goertner
The Deputy of the Fuehrer R. Hess

Resources

Amnesty International

"A worldwide campaigning movement that works to promote all the human rights enshrined in the Universal Declaration of Human Rights and other international standards. In particular, Amnesty International campaigns to free all prisoners of conscience; ensure fair and prompt trials for political prisoners; abolish the death penalty, torture and other cruel treatment of prisoners; end political killings and 'disappearances'; and oppose human rights abuses by opposition groups."

5 Penn Plaza, 14th floor
New York, NY 10001
Tel: (212) 807-8400
Fax: (212) 463-9193 or (212) 627-1451
http://www.amnesty.org/

Carter Center

"Every day in countries all over the world, people live under difficult, life-threatening circumstances caused by war, disease, famine, and poverty. The non-profit Carter Center strives to relieve this suffering by advancing peace and health in neighborhoods and nations around the globe. The Center, in partnership with Emory University, is guided by a fundamental commitment to human rights, wages peace by bringing warring parties to the negotiating table, monitoring elections, safeguarding human rights, and building strong democracies through economic development."

One Copenhill
453 Freedom Parkway
Atlanta, GA 30307
Tel: (404) 420-5100
http://www.cartercenter.org/default.asp

Doctors Without Borders (Médecins Sans Frontières)

"Médecins Sans Frontières (also known as Doctors Without Borders or MSF) delivers emergency aid to victims of armed conflict, epidemics, and natural and man-made disasters, and to others who lack health care due to social or geographical isolation."

333 7th Avenue, 2nd Floor
New York, NY 10001-5004
Tel: (212) 679-6800
Fax: (212) 679-7016

2525 Main Street, Suite 110
Santa Monica, CA 90405
Tel: (310) 399-0049
Fax: (310) 399-8177
http://www.doctorswithoutborders.org/

Derechos Human Rights

"Derechos Human Rights, together with our sister organization Equipo Nizkor, work for the respect and promotion of human rights throughout the world. Our work includes the socialization of human rights related information and analysis through the internet and other media, the promotion of prosecutions of human rights violators and the support of local human rights NGOs and activists."

Equipo Nizkor
(Derechos Representative in Spain)
Apartado de Correo 156037
Madrid, Spain
Tel: (34) 91-526-7502
Fax: +34.91.526.7515
E-mail: nizkor@derechos.org
http://www.derechos.org

Health Rights Connection

"Comprised of four nongovernmental health and human rights organizations who joined together in 1997 to promote the link between health and human rights internationally by providing education, research, and advocacy for professionals working in health and human rights, students, educators, and the general public."

c/o Physicians for Human Rights
100 Boylston Street, Suite 702
Boston, MA 02116
Tel: (617) 695-0041
Fax: (617) 695-0307
http://www.phrusa.org/

François-Xavier Bagnoud Center for Health and Human Rights

"The François-Xavier Bagnoud Center for Health and Human Rights is the first academic center to focus exclusively on health and human rights. The Center combines the academic strengths of research and teaching with a strong commitment to service and policy development."

Harvard School of Public Health
651 Huntington Avenue, 7th floor
Boston, MA 02115
Tel: (617) 432-0656
Fax: (617) 432-4310
http://www.hsph.harvard.edu/fxbcenter/

Freedom House

"Freedom House, a nonprofit, nonpartisan organization, is a clear voice for democracy and freedom around the world. Through a vast array of international programs and publications, Freedom House is working to advance the remarkable worldwide expansion of political and economic freedom."

Washington, D.C. Office
1319 18th Street NW
Washington, DC 20036
Tel: (202) 296-5101
Fax: (202) 296-5078

New York, NY Office
120 Wall Street, Floor 26
New York, NY 10005
Tel: (212) 514-8040
Fax: (212) 514-8055
http://www.freedomhouse.org/

Gendercide Watch

"Gendercide Watch is working to raise awareness, conduct research, and produce educational resources on gendercide. In particular, we seek to dispel stereotypes that blame victims and survivors for their own suffering. Among our activities is the maintenance of this website, which represents our major means of outreach and public education. This site includes a constantly growing database of case-studies and other research materials on gendercide."

GIEF/Gendercide Watch
Ste. #501, 10011 - 116th St.
Edmonton, Alberta T5K 1V4
Canada
http://www.gendercide.org

Global Exchange

"A human rights organization dedicated to promoting environmental, political, and social justice around the world. Since our founding in 1988, we have been striving to increase global awareness among the US public while building international partnerships around the world."

2017 Mission Street, #303
San Francisco, CA 94110
Tel: (415) 255-7296
Fax: (415) 255-7498
http://www.globalexchange.org/

The Human Rights Internet

"Founded in 1976, Human Rights Internet (HRI) is a world leader in the exchange of information within the worldwide human rights community. Launched in the U.S., HRI has its headquarters in Ottawa, Canada. From Ottawa, HRI communicates by phone, fax, mail and the information highway with more than 5,000 organizations and individuals around the world working for the advancement of human rights. A key objective of the organization is to support the work of the global non-governmental community in its struggle to obtain human rights for all. To this end, HRI promotes human rights education, stimulates research, encourages the sharing of information, and builds international solidarity among those committed to the principles enshrined in the International Bill of Human Rights."

One Nicholas Street, Suite 300
Ottawa, Ontario K1N 7B7
Canada

Tel: (1-613) 789-7407
Fax: (1-613) 789-7414
E-mail: hri@hri.ca
http://www.hri.ca

Human Rights Library

"Located at the University of Minnesota, this comprehensive web-site offers access to documents, reports, legislation, and reports from national and international organizations."

Human Rights Center
University of Minnesota
Mondale Hall, N-120
229 19th Avenue South
Minneapolis, MN 55455
Tel: (612) 626-0041
   1-888-HREDUC8
Fax: (612) 625-2011
http://www1.umn.edu/humanrts/

Human Rights Watch

"Dedicated to protecting the human rights of people around the world. We stand with victims and activists to prevent discrimination, to uphold political freedom, to protect people from inhumane conduct in wartime, and to bring offenders to justice. We investigate and expose human rights violations and hold abusers accountable. We challenge governments and those who hold power to end abusive practices and respect international human rights law. We enlist the public and the international community to support the cause of human rights for all."

http://www.hrw.org/

New York Office
350 Fifth Avenue, 34th floor
New York, NY 10118-3299
Tel: (212) 290-4700
Fax: (212) 736-1300
E-mail: hrwnyc@hrw.org

Washington, DC Office
1630 Connecticut Avenue NW, Suite 500
Washington, DC 20009
Tel: (202) 612-4321
Fax: (202) 612-4333
E-mail: hrwdc@hrw.org

Los Angeles Office
11500 W. Olympic Blvd., Suite 441
Los Angeles, CA 90064
Tel: (310) 477-5540
Fax: (310) 477-4622
E-mail: hrwla@hrw.org

San Francisco Office
100 Bush Street, Suite 1812
San Francisco, CA 94104
Tel: (415) 362-3250
Fax: (415) 362-3255
E-mail: hrw-sf@hrw.org

Toronto Office
2300 Yonge Street
Suite 803, Box 2376
Toronto, Ontario M4P 1E4
Canada
E-mail: toronto@hrw.org

International Criminal Court

"The International Criminal Court (ICC) is the first ever permanent, treaty based, international criminal court established to promote the rule of law and ensure that the gravest international crimes do not go unpunished."

P.O. Box 19519
2500 CM, The Hague
The Netherlands
Tel: + 31 (0)70 515-8515
Fax: +31 (0)70 515-8555
http://www.icc-cpi.int/

International Criminal Tribunal for the Former Yugoslavia

"Spearheading the shift from impunity to accountability, establishing the facts, bringing justice to thousands of victims and giving them a voice, the accomplishments in international law, strengthening the Rule of Law."

P.O. BOX 13888
2501 EW The Hague
The Netherlands
Press Tel: +31 (70) 512-5343 or 512-5356 or 512-8752
Fax: +31 (70) 512-5355
http://www.un.org/icty/

International Commission on Missing Persons

"As a political transition unfolds after a period of armed conflict, violence or repression, a society is confronted with a difficult legacy of human rights abuses that often include large numbers disappearances of persons never to be heard from again. Resolving their fate is important."

ICMP Headquarters
Alipašina 45 A
71000 Sarajevo
Bosnia and Herzegovina

Tel: + 387 33 218 660
Fax: + 387 33 203 297
http://www.ic-mp.org

International Committee of the Red Cross

"Whether through formal dissemination sessions or sponta-neously at military checkpoints, reminding actual and potential warring parties of their rights and obligations under international humanitarian law is one of the ICRC's major activities worldwide."
2025 E Street NW
Washington, DC 20006
Tel: (202) 303-5279 (General)
    (202) 303-5211 (International Policy and Relations)
Fax: (202) 303-0054 (General)
Telex: ARC TLX WSH 892636
Telegram: AMCROSS WASHINGTON DC
E-mail: postmaster@usa.redcross.org
Web: http://www.redcross.org

International Humanitarian Fact-Finding Commission

"A major objective of the two Additional Protocols to the 1949 Geneva Conventions, which were drafted at the Diplomatic Conference held from 1974 to 1977, is to improve implementation of the Conventions and Protocols. The first of the Protocols addresses international armed conflicts, the second non-international armed conflicts. To help ensure the protection afforded to the victims of armed conflicts, Article 90 of the First Protocol provides for the establishment of a permanent International Fact-Finding Commission. The Commission is empowered to enquire into allegations of breaches of international humanitarian law and to restore compliance with it by providing good offices."

Federal Palace (West)
CH - 3003 Berne
Switzerland
Tel: + 41 31 32 50768
Fax: + 41 31 32 50767
http://www.ihffc.org/

International Labor Organization (ILO)

"The International Labour Organization is the UN special-ized agency which seeks the promotion of social justice and internationally recognized human and labour rights. It was founded in 1919 and is the only surviving major creation of the Treaty of Versailles which brought the League of Nations into being and it became the first specialized agen-cy of the UN in 1946."

International Labour Office
4, route des Morillons
CH-1211 Geneva 22
Switzerland
Tel: 212.697.01.50
http://www.ilo.org/

International Physicians for the Prevention of Nuclear War (IPPNW)

"A non-partisan global federation of medical organizations dedicated to research, education, and advocacy relevant to the prevention of nuclear war. To this end, IPPNW seeks to prevent all wars, to promote non-violent conflict resolution, and to minimize the effects of war and preparations for war on health, development, and the environment."

727 Massachusetts Ave.
Cambridge, MA 02139
Tel: (617) 868-5050
Fax: (617) 868-2560
http://www.ippnw.org/

Lawyers Without Borders

"Lawyers Without Borders is a US-based non-profit orga-nization whose goal is to engage the legal profession, on a global basis supporting capacity building of NGOs world-wide, advancing Rule of Law, protecting the integrity of legal process through neutral observation, offering support to lawyers in the field and serving as a law oriented clear-inghouse linking needs with the legal resources to meet them."

330 Main Street
Hartford, CT 06106 USA
Tel: (860) 541-2288
Fax: (860) 525-0287
http://www.lawyerswithoutborders.org/

National Center for Human Rights Education (USA)

"Founded in 1996, the National Order is the first human rights education organization in the United States that focuses primarily on domestic human rights violations. CHRE works to build a domestic human rights movement by training community leaders and student activists to apply human rights standards to issues of injustice in the United States. As an information clearinghouse and tech-nical assistance provider, CHRE seeks to increase human rights understanding, improve cooperation among progres-sive social change movements, and use human rights edu-cation as a catalyst for social transformation."

P.O. Box 311020
Atlanta, GA 31131
Tel: (404) 344-9629
Fax: (404) 346-7517
http://www.nchre.org/

Office of Special Investigations

"The Office of Special Investigations detects and investigates individuals who took part in Nazi-sponsored acts of persecution abroad before and during World War II, and who subsequently entered, or seek to enter, the United States illegally and/or fraudulently. It then takes appropriate legal action seeking their exclusion, denaturalization and/or deportation. The unit also detects, investigates and takes legal action to denaturalize persons who participated abroad in acts of genocide or in acts of torture or extrajudicial killings committed under color of foreign law. OSI also handles emerging war crimes issues."

Department of Justice
Criminal Division
950 Pennsylvania Avenue
Washington, DC 20530-0001
http://www.usdoj.gov/criminal/osi.html

Organization for Security and Co-operation in Europe

"The Organization for Security and Co-operation in Europe (OSCE) is the largest regional security organization in the world with 55 participating States from Europe, Central Asia and North America. It is active in early warning, conflict prevention, crisis management and post-conflict rehabilitation."

OSCE Secretariat • Press and Public Information Section
Kärntner Ring 5-7, 4th floor, 1010
Vienna, Austria
Tel: +43-1 514 36 180
Fax: +43-1 514 36 105
http://www.osce.org/

Organization of American States

"The Organization of American States (OAS) brings together the countries of the Western Hemisphere to strengthen cooperation and advance common interests. It is the region's premier forum for multilateral dialogue and concerted action."

Headquarters:
17th Street & Constitution Avenue NW
Washington, DC 20006
Tel: (202) 458-3000
http://www.oas.org/

Oxfam

"Oxfam believes that in a world rich in resources, poverty isn't a fact of life but an injustice which must be overcome. We believe that everyone is entitled to a life of dignity and opportunity; and we work with poor communities, local partner organisations, volunteers, and supporters to make this a reality."

Oxfam House
274 Banbury Road
Oxford
OX2 7DZ
England
Tel: 0870 333 2700
http://www.oxfam.org.uk/

Peoples' Decade of Human Rights Education

"Founded in 1988, the People's Decade of Human Rights Education (PDHRE-International) is a non-profit, international service organization that works directly and indirectly with its network of affiliates primarily women's and social justice organizations to develop and advance pedagogies for human rights education relevant to people's daily lives in the context of their struggles for social and economic justice and democracy."

The People's Movement for Human Rights Learning (PDHRE)
New York Office
526 West 111th Street
New York, NY 10025
Tel: (212) 749-3156
Fax: (212) 666-6325
http://www.pdhre.org/

Physicians for Human Rights

"An organization of health professionals, scientists, and concerned citizens that uses the knowledge and skills of the medical and forensic sciences to investigate and prevent violations of international human rights and humanitarian law."

Two Arrow Street, Suite 301
Cambridge, MA 02138
Tel: (617) 301-4200
Fax: (617) 301-4250
http://www.phrusa.org/

Physicians for Social Responsibility

"Physicians for Social Responsibility combines the power of an active and concerned citizenry with the credibility of physicians and other health professionals to promote public policies that protect human health from the threats of

nuclear war and other weapons of mass destruction, global environmental degradation, and the epidemic of gun violence in our society today."

1875 Connecticut Avenue NW, Suite 1012
Washington, DC 20009
Tel: (202) 667-4260
Fax: (202) 667-4201
http://www.psr.org/

Refugees International

"Refugees International generates lifesaving humanitarian assistance and protection for displaced people around the world and works to end the conditions that create displacement."

1705 N Street NW
Washington, DC 20036
Tel: (202) 828-0110
   800-REFUGEE
   (800-733-8433)
Fax: (202) 828-0819
http://www.refugeesinternational.org/

Reporters Without Borders

"Reporters Without Borders works constantly to restore their right to be informed. Forty-two media professionals lost their lives in 2003 for doing what they were paid to do—keeping us informed. Today, more than 130 journalists around the world are in prison simply for doing their job. In Nepal, Eritrea and China, they can spend years in jail just for using the "wrong" word or photo. Reporters Without Borders believes imprisoning or killing a journalist is like eliminating a key witness and threatens everyone's right to be informed. It has been fighting such practices for more than 18 years."

5, rue Geoffrey-Marie
75009 Paris, France
Tel: (33) 44838484
E-mail: rsf@rsf.org

Simon Wiesenthal Center

"The Simon Wiesenthal Center is an international Jewish human rights organization dedicated to preserving the memory of the Holocaust by fostering tolerance and understanding through community involvement, educational outreach and social action. The Center confronts important contemporary issues including racism, antisemitism, terrorism and genocide and is accredited as an NGO both at the United Nations and UNESCO. With a membership of over 400,000 families, the Center is headquartered in Los Angeles and maintains offices in New York, Toronto, Miami, Jerusalem, Paris and Buenos Aires."

International Headquarters
1399 South Roxbury Drive
Los Angeles, CA 90035
Tel: (310) 553-9036
Tel: (800) 900-9036 (toll-free from within the U.S.)
Fax: (310) 553-4521
http://www.wiesenthal.com

Union of Concerned Scientists

"UCS is an independent nonprofit alliance of more than 100,000 concerned citizens and scientists. We augment rigorous scientific analysis with innovative thinking and committed citizen advocacy to build a cleaner, healthier environment and a safer world."

National Headquarters
2 Brattle Square
Cambridge, MA 02238-9105
Tel: (617) 547-5552
Fax: (617) 864-9405

Washington Office
1707 H St NW, Suite 600
Washington, DC 20006-3962
Tel: (202) 223-6133
Fax: (202) 223-6162

West Coast Office
2397 Shattuck Avenue, Suite 203
Berkeley, CA 94704-1567
Tel: (510) 843-1872
Fax: (510) 843-3785
http://www.ucsusa.org/

United Nations High Commissioner for Human Rights

"The United Nations vision is of a world in which the human rights of all are fully respected and enjoyed in conditions of global peace. The High Commissioner works to keep that vision to the forefront through constant encouragement of the international community and its member States to uphold universally agreed human rights standards."

Case Postale 2500
CH-1211 Genève 2 Dépôt
Switzerland
Tel: +41 22 739 8111
http://www.unhcr.ch

United States Department of State

"The protection of fundamental human rights was a foundation stone in the establishment of the United States over 200 years ago. Since then, a central goal of U.S. foreign policy has been the promotion of respect for human rights, as embodied in the Universal Declaration of Human Rights. The United States understands that the existence of human rights helps secure the peace, deter aggression, promote the rule of law, combat crime and corruption, strengthen democracies, and prevent humanitarian crises."

2201 C Street NW
Washington, DC 20520
Tel: (202) 647-4000
   (800) 877-8339 (Federal Relay Service)
http://contact-us.state.gov/

Universal Rights Network

"A meeting place for the peoples of the world to share their stories of the importance of universal human rights and fundamental freedom to us all."

http://www.universalrights.net/

WITNESS

"A pioneer in the use of video and technology to fight for human rights. WITNESS gives human rights activists video cameras and help them to expose the crimes, right the wrongs, and end impunity for human rights violators. WITNESS partners with human rights organizations throughout the world, and trains grassroots activists in video and investigative techniques. WITNESS equips them with the latest technology, provides assistance in field video productions, and ensures that the evidence generated gets an international audience."

80 Hanson Place, 5th Floor
Brooklyn, NY 11217
Tel: (718) 783-2000
Fax: (718) 783-1593
http://www.witness.org/

Selected Bibliography

Aall, Pamela R., Daniel Miltenberger, and George Weiss. *IGOs, NGOs, and the Military in Peace and Relief Operations.* Washington, D.C.: United States Institute of Peace Press, 2000.

Aburish, Saïd K. *Saddam Hussein: The Politics of Revenge.* London: Bloomsbury Publishing, 2000.

Adebajo, Adekeye. *Building Peace in West Africa: Liberia, Sierra Leone, and Guinea-Bissau.* International Peace Academy Occasional Paper Series. Boulder, Colo.: Lynne Rienner Publishers, 2002.

———. *Liberia's Civil War: Nigeria, ECOMOG, and Regional Security in West Africa.* Boulder, Colo.: Lynne Rienner Publishers, 2002.

AkCam, Taner. *From Empire to Republic: Turkish Nationalism and the Armenian Genocide.* London: Zed Books, 2004.

Alibek, Ken, and Stephen Handelman. *Biohazard: The Chilling True Story of the Largest Covert Biological Weapons Program in the World—Told from Inside by the Man Who Ran It.* New York: Delta, 2000.

Allen, John. *Idi Amin. History's Villains.* San Diego: Blackbirch Press, 2003.

Allen, Peter A. P. *Interesting Times: Life in Uganda under Idi Amin.* London: Book Guild, Limited, 2000.

Andreopoulous, George J., and Richard Pierre Claude, eds. *Human Rights Education for the Twenty-First Century.* Pennsylvania Studies in Human Rights. Philadelphia: University of Pennsylvania Press, 1997.

Applebaum, Anne. *Gulag: A History.* New York: Anchor, 2004.

Arditti, Rita. *Searching for Life: The Grandmothers of the Plaza De Mayo and the Disappeared Children of Argentina.* Berkeley: University of California Press, 1999.

Armstrong, Robert. *El Salvador: The Face of Revolution.* Boston: South End Press, 1982.

Arthur, Charles. *Haiti: A Guide to the People, Politics, and Culture.* New York: Interlink Publishing Group, 2002.

Aspinall, Edward. *The Aceh Peace Process: Why It Failed.* Washington, D.C.: East-West Center, 2003.

Balakian, Peter. *The Burning Tigris: The Armenian Genocide and America's Response.* New York: HarperCollins, 2003.

Ball, Howard. *Prosecuting War Crimes and Genocide: The Twentieth-Century Experience.* Lawrence: University Press of Kansas, 1999.

Barnaby, Frank. *How to Build a Nuclear Bomb: And Other Weapons of Mass Destruction.* New York: Nation Books, 2004.

Barnett, Michael. *Eyewitness to a Genocide: The United Nations and Rwanda.* Ithaca, N.Y.: Cornell University Press, 2003.

Bass, Gary Jonathan. *Stay the Hand of Vengeance: The Politics of War Crimes Tribunals.* Princeton, N.J.: Princeton University Press, 2001.

Bassiouni, M. Cherif. *Crimes against Humanity in International Criminal Law.* Boston: Martinus Nijhoff, 1999.

———. *Sexual Violence: An Invisible Weapon of War in the Former Yugoslavia.* Chicago: International Human Rights Law Institute, DePaul University, 1996.

Beigbeder, Yves, and Theo van Boven. *Judging War Criminals: The Politics of International Justice.* Sidney, Australia: Palgrave Macmillan, 1999.

Benenson, Peter. *Persecution.* London: Penguin Books, 1961.

Benson, Bruce. *The Enterprise of Law: Justice without the State.* San Francisco: Pacific Research Institute for Public Policy, 1990.

Bergquist, Charles, Ricardo Penaranda, and Gonzalo Sanchez, eds. *Violence in Colombia 1990–2000:*

Waging War and Negotiating Peace. Wilmington, Del.: Scholarly Resources Inc., 2001.

Berkhoff, Karel C. *Harvest of Despair: Life and Death in Ukraine under Nazi Rule.* Cambridge, Mass.: Belknap Press, 2004.

Berry, Nicholas O. *War and the Red Cross: The Unspoken Mission.* New York: St. Martin's Press, 1997.

Bertrand, Jacques, and John Ravenhill. *Nationalism and Ethnic Conflict in Indonesia.* Cambridge: Cambridge University Press, 2003.

Bilton, Michael, and Kevin Sim. *Four Hours in My Lai.* New York: Penguin Books, 1993.

Bloxham, Donald. *Genocide on Trial: War Crimes Trials and the Formation of Holocaust History and Memory.* Oxford: Oxford University Press, 2003.

Bodansky, Yossef. *The Secret History of the Iraq War.* New York: Regan Books, 2004.

Bortolotti, Dan. *Hope in Hell: Inside the World of Doctors Without Borders.* Richmond Hill, Ontario: Firefly Books Ltd., 2004.

Bose, Sumanira. *Kashmir: Roots of Conflict, Paths to Peace.* Cambridge, Mass.: Harvard University Press, 2003.

Bower, Tom. *Klaus Barbie, the Butcher of Lyons.* New York: Pantheon Books, 1984.

Broome, Richard. *Aboriginal Australians.* London: Allen & Unwin, 2002.

Browder, George C. *Hitler's Enforcers: The Gestapo and the Ss Security Service in the Nazi Revolution.* Oxford: Oxford University Press, 1996.

Brysk, Alison, ed. *Globalization and Human Rights.* Berkeley: University of California Press, 2002.

Buergenthal, Thomas. *Religious Fundamentalisms and the Human Rights of Women.* Sidney, Australia: Palgrave Macmillan, 1999.

Burke, Jason. *Al-Qaeda: Casting a Shadow of Terror.* London: I. B. Tauris, 2004.

———. *Al-Qaeda: The True Story of Radical Islam.* London: I. B.Tauris, 2004.

Buscher, Frank. M. *The U.S. War Crimes Trial Program in Germany, 1946–1955.* Contributions in Military Studies. Westport, Conn.: Greenwood Press, 1989.

Butler, Rupert. *The Gestapo: A History of Hitler's Secret Police 1933–45.* Havertown, Pa.: Casemate Publishers and Book Distributors, 2004.

Byman, Daniel, Ian Lesser, Bruce Pirnie, Cheryl Benard, and Matthew Waxman. *Strengthening the Partnership: Improving Military Coordination with Relief Agencies and Allies in Humanitarian Operations.* Santa Monica, Calif.: Rand Corporation (NBN), 2000.

Campbell, Greg. *Blood Diamonds: Tracing the Deadly Path of the World's Most Precious Stones.* New York: Perseus Books Group, 2002.

Carter, Jimmy. *The Personal Beliefs of Jimmy Carter: Winner of the 2002 Nobel Peace Prize.* New York: Three Rivers Press, 2002.

Chandler, David. *A History of Cambodia.* Philadelphia: Westview Press, 2000.

———. *The Tragedy of Cambodian History: Politics, War, and Revolution since 1945.* New Haven, Conn.: Yale University Press, 1993.

Charrad, M. *States and Women's Rights: The Making of Postcolonial Tunisia, Algeria, and Morocco.* Berkeley: University of California Press, 2001.

Chinnery, Philip D. *Korean Atrocity!: Forgotten War Crimes, 1950–1953.* Annapolis, Md.: United States Naval Institute, 2001.

Clark, Wesley K. *Waging Modern War: Bosnia, Kosovo, and the Future of Combat.* New York: Public Affairs, 2001.

Clarke, Walter, and Jeffrey Herbst, eds. *Learning from Somalia: The Lessons of Armed Humanitarian Intervention.* Boulder, Colo.: Westview Press, 1997.

Claude, Richard Pierre, and Burns H. Weston. *Human Rights in the World Community: Issues and Action.* Philadelphia: University of Pennsylvania Press, 1992.

Coates, Karen J. *Cambodia Now: Life in the Wake of War.* Jefferson, N.C.: McFarland & Company, 2005.

Cockburn, Andrew, and Patrick Cockburn. *Out of the Ashes: The Resurrection of Saddam Hussein.* New York: Perennial.

Coll, Steve. *Ghost Wars: The Secret History of the CIA, Afghanistan, and Bin Laden, from the Soviet Invasion to September 10, 2001.* New York: Penguin, 2004.

Conquest, Robert. *Stalin: Breaker of Nations.* New York: Penguin Books, 1992.

Constable, Pamela. *A Nation of Enemies: Chile under Pinochet.* New York: W. W. Norton & Company, 1993.

Cook, Rebecca J. *Human Rights of Women: National and International Perspectives.* Pennsylvania Studies in Human Rights. Philadelphia: University of Pennsylvania Press, 1994.

Cooper, Belinda, and Richard Goldstone. *War Crimes: The Legacy of Nuremberg.* New York: TV Books Inc., 1999.

Cornish, Paul. *Anti-personnel Mines: Controlling the Plague of "Butterflies."* London: Royal Institute of International Affairs, 1994.

Coughlin, Con. *Saddam: King of Terror.* New York: Ecco, 2002.

Cox, Margaret, and Jon Sterenberg. *Forensic Archaeology, Anthropology and the Investigation of Mass Graves.* London: CRC Press, 2006.

Dabringhaus, Erhard. *Klaus Barbie: The Shocking Story of How the U.S. Used This Nazi War Criminal as an Intelligence Agent.* New York: Acropolis Books, 1984.

Dalacoura, Katerina. *Engagement or Coercion?: Weighing Western Human Rights Policies towards Turkey, Iran, and Egypt*. London: Royal Institute of International Affairs, 2004

Dallaire, Romeo, and Brent Beardsley. *Shake Hands with the Devil: The Failure of Humanity in Rwanda*. New York: Carroll & Graf, 2004.

Danner, Mark. *The Massacre at El Mozote*. New York: Vintage, 1994.

———. *Torture and Truth: America, Abu Ghraib, and the War on Terror*. New York: New York Review of Books, 2004.

Davis, William Columbus. *Warnings from the Far South: Democracy versus Dictatorship in Uruguay, Argentina, and Chile*. New York: Praeger Publishers, 1995.

Dawidowicz, Lucy. *A Holocaust Reader*. Library of Jewish Studies. Chicago: Behrman House Publishing, 1976.

Daws, Gavin. *Prisoners of the Japanese: POWs of World War II in the Pacific*. New York: Perennial, 1996.

De Waal, Alexander. *Famine That Kills: Darfur, Sudan*. Oxford Studies in African Affairs. Oxford: Oxford University Press, 2004.

Dinges, John. *The Condor Years: How Pinochet and His Allies Brought Terrorism to Three Continents*. New York: New Press, 2004.

Dodge, Cole P., and Magne Raundelen. *Reaching Children in War: Sudan, Uganda and Mozambique*. London: Taylor & Francis, 1992.

Dodge, Toby. *Inventing Iraq: The Failure of Nation-Building and a History Denied*. New York: Columbia University Press, 2003.

Dorfman, Ariel. *Exorcising Terror: The Incredible Unending Trial of Augusto Pinochet*. New York: Seven Stories Press, 2002.

Dormann, Knut, and Louise Doswald-Beck. *Elements of War Crimes under the Rome Statute of the International Criminal Court: Sources and Commentary*. Cambridge: Cambridge University Press, 2003.

Dubber, Markus Dirk. *Victims in the War on Crime: The Use and Abuse of Victims' Rights*. New York: New York University Press, 2002.

Dunn, James, and Xanana Gusmão. *East Timor: A Rough Passage to Independence*. Seattle: University of Washington Press, 2004.

Dwork, Deborah, and Robert Jan Van Pelt. *Holocaust: A History*. New York: W. W. Norton & Company, 2003.

Edgerton, Robert. *The Troubled Heart of Africa: A History of the Congo*. New York: St. Martin's Press, 2002.

Ekwe-Ekwe, Herbert. *The Biafra War: Nigeria and the Aftermath*. African Studies, vol. 17. Philadelphia: Edwin Mellen Press, 1990.

El-Kikhia, Mansour O. *Libya's Qaddafi: The Politics of Contradiction*. Gainsville: University Press of Florida, 1998.

Ellils, Stephen. *The Mask of Anarchy: The Destruction of Liberia and the Religious Dimension of an African Civil War*. New York: New York University Press, 2001.

Erskins, Toni. *Can Institutions Have Responsibilities: Collective Moral Agency and International Relations*. Global Issues Series. Sydney, Australia: Palgrave Macmillan, 2004.

Ewans, Martin. *Afghanistan: A Short History of Its People and Politics*. New York: Perennial, 2002.

Falk, Richard A. *Human Rights Horizons: The Pursuit of Justice in a Globalizing World*. London: Routledge, 2000.

Farmer, Paul. *The Uses of Haiti*. 2d ed. Monroe, Me.: Common Courage Press, 2003.

Fasulo, Linda. *An Insider's Guide to the UN*. New Haven, Conn.: Yale University Press, 2003.

Feaver, Peter. *Guarding the Guardians: Civilian Control of Nuclear Weapons in the United States*. Cornell Studies in Security Affairs. Ithaca, N.Y.: Cornell University Press, 1992.

Feller, Erika, Volker Turk, and Frances Nicholson, eds. *Refugee Protection in International Law: UNHCR's Global Consultations on International Protection*. Cambridge: Cambridge University Press, 2003.

Ferme, Mariane C. *The Underneath of Things: Violence, History, and the Everyday in Sierra Leone*. Berkeley: University of California Press, 2001.

Foot, Rosemary. *Rights beyond Borders: The Global Community and the Struggle over Human Rights in China*. Oxford: Oxford University Press, 2001.

Forsythe, David P. *Human Rights in International Relations*. Themes in International Relations. Cambridge: Cambridge University Press, 2000.

Fritz, Mark. *Lost on Earth: Nomads of the New World*. New York: Routledge, 2000.

Ganguly, Sumit. *Conflict Unending*. New York: Columbia University Press, 2002.

Gerlach, Allen. *Indians, Oil, and Politics: A Recent History of Ecuador*. Wilmington, Del.: Scholarly Resources, 2003.

Giblin, James Cross. *The Life and Death of Adolf Hitler*. New York: Clarion Books, 2002.

Gilbert, Martin. *The Holocaust: A History of the Jews of Europe during the Second World War*. New York: Owl Books, 1987.

Glenny, Misha. *The Fall of Yugoslavia: The Third Balkan War*. New York: Penguin Books, 1996.

Goldstone, Richard. *For Humanity: Reflections of a War Crimes Investigator*. Castle Lectures Series. New Haven, Conn.: Yale University Press, 2000.

Goni, Uki. *The Real Odessa: How Peron Brought the Nazi War Criminals to Argentina*. London: Granta Books, 2003.

Gottesman, Evan. *Cambodia after the Khmer Rouge: Inside the Politics of Nation Building.* New Haven, Conn.: Yale University Press, 2004.

Gourevich, Philip. *We Wish to Inform You That Tomorrow We Will Be Killed with Our Families: Stories from Rwanda.* New York, Picador, 1999.

Groenewold, Julia, and Doctors Without Borders. *World in Crisis: The Politics of Survival at the End of the Twentieth Century.* London: Routledge, 1996.

Grotius, Hugo. *On the Law of War and Peace.* Kila: Kessinger Publishing, 2004.

Guillemin, Jeanette. *Biological Weapons.* Columbia Contemporary Issues in National Security Policy. New York: Columbia University Press, 2005.

Guimaraes, Fernando Andresen. *The Origins of the Angolan Civil War: Foreign Intervention and Domestic Political Conflict.* Sydney, Australia: Palgrave Macmillan, 2001.

Gunaratna, Rohan. *Inside Al Qaeda: Global Network of Terror.* New York: Berkley Publishing Group, 2003.

Gutierrez, Alberto Ostria. *The Tragedy of Bolivia: A People Crucified.* Westport, Conn.: Greenwood Press, 1981.

Gutman, Roy, ed. *Crimes of War: What the Public Should Know.* New York: W. W. Norton & Company, 1999.

Hagan, John. *Justice in the Balkans: Prosecuting War Crimes in the Hague Tribunal. Chicago Series in Law and Society.* Chicago: University of Chicago Press, 2003.

Hampstein, Elizabeth. *Uruguay Nunca Mas: Human Rights Violations, 1972–1985.* Philadelphia: Temple University Press, 1993.

Harpviken, Kristian Berg, ed. *The Future of Humanitarian Mine Action (Third Worlds).* Sydney, Australia: Palgrave Macmillan, 2004.

Harris, Nathaniel. *The War in Former Yugoslavia.* London: Hodder & Stoughton, 1997.

Harris, Sheldon. *Factories of Death: Japanese Biological Warfare 1932–45 and the American Cover-Up.* London: Routledge, 1995.

Hazan, Pierre, and James Thomas Snyder. *Justice in a Time of War: The True Story behind the International Criminal Tribunal for the Former Yugoslavia.* Eugenia and Hugh M. Stewart Series on Eastern Europe. Austin: Texas A&M University Press, 2004.

Helton, Arthur C. *The Price of Indifference: Refugees and Humanitarian Action in the New Century.* Oxford: Oxford University Press, 2002.

Hersh, Seymour M. *Chain of Command: The Road from 9/11 to Abu Ghraib.* New York: HarperCollins, 2004.

———. *My Lai 4: A Report on the Massacre and Its Aftermath.* New York: Random House Trade, 1970.

Hicks, Neil. *Escalating Attacks on Human Rights Protection in Egypt: A Report of the Lawyers Committee for Human Rights.* New York: Lawyers Committee for Human Rights, 1995.

Hinton, Alexander Laban, and Robert Jay Lifton. *Why Did They Kill?: Cambodia in the Shadow of Genocide.* California Series in Public Anthropology, vol. 11. Berkeley: University of California Press, 2004.

Hitler, Adolf. *Mein Kampf.* New York: Mariner Books, 1998.

Hochschild, Adam. *King Leopold's Ghost.* Boston: Mariner Books, 1999.

Hodges, Tony. *Angola from Afro-Stalinism to Petro-Diamond Capitalism.* Bloomington: Indiana University Press, 2001.

Hohne, Heinz Zollen. *The Order of the Death's Head: The Story of Hitler's SS.* Classic Military History. New York: Penguin, 2001.

Holzgrefe, J. L., and Robert O. Keohane, eds. *Humanitarian Intervention: Ethical, Legal and Political Dilemmas.* Cambridge: Cambridge University Press, 2003.

Honda, Katsuichi, and Frank Gibney, eds. *The Nanjing Massacre: A Japanese Journalist Confronts Japan's National Shame. Studies of the Pacific Basin Institute.* Armonk, N.Y.: East Gate Book, 1999.

Honig, Jan Willem, and Norbert Both. *Srebrenica: Record of a War Crime.* New York: Penguin Books, 1997.

Hufbauer, Gary Clyde, and Nicholas K. Mitrokostas. *Awakening Monster: The Alien Tort Statute of 1789.* Policy Analyses in International Economics. Washington, D.C.: Institute for International Economics, 2003.

Hyndman, Jennifer. *Managing Displacement: Refugees and the Politics of Humanitarianism.* Minneapolis: University of Minnesota Press, 2000.

Ignatieff, Michael. *Virtual War: Kosovo and Beyond.* New York: Picador, 2001.

Ingleby, David, ed. *Forced Migration and Mental Health: Rethinking the Care of Refugees and Displaced Persons.* New York: Plenum US, 2004.

International Committee of the Red Cross. *International Law Concerning the Conduct of Hostilities: Collection of Hague Conventions and Some Other Treaties.* Geneva, Switzerland: International Committee of the Red Cross, 1989.

Ishay, Micheline R., ed. *The Human Rights Reader: Major Political Writings, Essays, Speeches, and Documents from the Bible to the Present.* London: Routledge, 1997.

Jackson, Michael. *In Sierra Leone.* Durham, N.C.: Duke University Press, 2004.

Jackson, Nyamuya Maogoto. *War Crimes and Realpolitik: International Justice from World War I to the 21st Century.* Boulder, Colo.: Lynne Rienner Publishers, 2004.

Jacquin-Berdal, Dominique. *Unfinished Business: Ethiopia and Eritrea at War.* London: Red Sea Press, 2004.

Jardine, Matthew. *East Timor: Genocide in Paradise. The Real Story Series.* Monroe, Me.: Odonian Press, 2002.

Jaskof, Paul B. *The Architecture of Oppression: The SS, Forced Labor and the Nazi Monumental Building Economy.* London: Routledge, 2000.

Jinks, Derek. *The Rules of War: The Geneva Conventions in the Age of Terror.* Oxford: Oxford University Press, 2005.

Johnson, Douglas Hamilton. *The Root Causes of Sudan's Civil Wars.* Bloomington: Indiana University Press, 2003.

Jok, Madut Jok. *War and Slavery in Sudan.* Philadelphia: University of Pennsylvania Press, 2001.

Jokie, Aleksandar, ed. *War Crimes and Collective Wrongdoing: A Reader.* London: Blackwell Publishers, 2001.

Jones, Adam, ed. *Genocide, War Crimes and the West: History and Complicity.* London: Zed Books, 2004.

Judah, Tim. *Kosovo: War and Revenge.* New Haven, Conn.: Yale University Press, 2002.

Karsh, Efraim. *The Iran-Iraq War 1980–1988.* London: Osprey Publishing, 2002.

Karsh, Efraim, and Inari Rautsi. *Saddam Hussein: A Political Biography.* New York: Grove Press, 2003.

Kavass, Igor I., ed. *Human Rights, European Politics, and the Helsinki Accord: The Documentary Evolution of the Conference on Security and Co-operation in Europe 1973–1975.* Buffalo, N.Y.: William S. Hein & Co., 1981.

Keddie, Nikki R. *Modern Iran: Roots and Results of Revolution.* New Haven, Conn.: Yale University Press, 2003.

Keegan, John. *The Iraq War.* New York: Knopf, 2004.

Kennedy, David. *The Dark Sides of Virtue: Reassessing International Humanitarianism.* Princeton, N.J.: Princeton University Press, 2004.

Kenney, Charles D. *Fujimori's Coup and the Breakdown of Democracy in Latin America.* Notre Dame, Ind.: University of Notre Dame Press, 2004.

Kent, Ann. *Between Freedom and Subsistence: China and Human Rights.* Oxford: Oxford University Press, 1995.

Khlevnink, Oleg. *The History of the Gulag: From Collectivization to the Great Terror.* Translated by Vadim A. Staklo. *Annals of Communism Series.* New Haven, Conn.: Yale University Press, 2004.

Kiernan, Ben. *How Pol Pot Came to Power: Colonialism, Nationalism, and Communism in Cambodia, 1930–1975.* New Haven, Conn.: Yale University Press, 2004.

———. *The Pol Pot Regime: Race, Power, and Genocide in Cambodia under the Khmer Rouge, 1975–79.* New Haven, Conn.: Yale University Press, 2002.

Kim, Julie. *War in the Former Yugoslavia: Chronology of Events August 16, 1992–May 30, 1993.* CRS report for Congress. Washington, D.C.: Foreign Affairs and National Defense Division, Congressional Research Service, the Library of Congress, 1993.

Kimura, Rei. *Alberto Fujimori of Peru: The President Who Dared to Dream.* Woodstock, N.Y.: Beekman Books Inc., 1998.

King, Peter. *West Papua and Indonesia since Suharto: Independence, Autonomy or Chaos?* Sydney, Australia: University of New South Wales Press, 2004.

Kipp, Jacob W. *International Ramifications of Yugoslavia's Serial Wars: The Challenge of Ethno-national Conflicts for a post-Cold-War, European Order.* Fort Leavenworth, Kans.: European Military Studies Office, 1993.

Kissinger, Henry. *Does America Need a Foreign Policy?: Toward a Diplomacy for the 21st Century.* New York: Simon & Schuster; Touchstone edition, 2002.

Kizny, Tomasz. *Gulag: Life and Death Inside the Soviet Concentration Camps 1917–1990.* London: Firefly Books Ltd, 2004.

Knock, Thomas J. *To End All Wars: Woodrow Wilson and the Quest for a New World Order.* Princeton, N.J.: Princeton University Press, 1995.

Korey, William. *Human Rights and the Helsinki Accord: Focus on U.S. Policy.* New York: Foreign Policy Assn., 1983.

Kornbluh, Peter. *The Pinochet File: A Declassified Dossier on Atrocity and Accountability. A National Security Archive Book.* New York: New Press, 2003.

Krepon, Michael. *Strategic Stalemate: Nuclear Weapons and Arms Control in American Politics.* Sydney, Australia: Palgrave Macmillan, 1986.

Kulah, Arthur F. *Liberia Will Rise Again: Reflections on the Liberian Civil Crisis.* Nashville, Tenn.: Abingdon Press, 1999.

Lagnado, Lucette Matalon, and Sheila Cohn Dekel. *Children of the Flames: Dr. Josef Mengele and the Untold Story of the Twins of Auschwitz.* New York: Penguin Books, 1992.

Lamont-Brown, Raymond. *Ships from Hell: Japanese War Crimes on the High Seas.* Phoenix Mill, U.K.: Sutton Publishing, 2002.

Lang, Anthony F., Jr., ed. *Just Intervention.* Washington, D.C.: Georgetown University Press, 2003.

Langford, R. Everett. *Introduction to Weapons of Mass Destruction: Radiological, Chemical, and Biological.* New York: Wiley-Interscience, 2004.

Lauren, Paul Gordon. *The Evolution of International Human Rights: Visions Seen. Pennsylvania Studies in Human Rights.* Philadelphia: University of Pennsylvania Press, 2003.

Lederberg, Joshua, ed. *Biological Weapons: Limiting the Threat. BCSIA Studies in International Security.* Cambridge, Mass.: MIT Press, 1999.

Legge, John D. *Sukarno: A Political Biography.* Burlington, Vt.: Butterworth-Heinemann, 2003.

Leith, Denise. *The Politics of Power: Freeport in Suharto's Indonesia.* Honolulu: University of Hawaii Press, 2002.

Lemarchand, Reni, and Lee H. Hamilton. *Burundi: Ethnic Conflict and Genocide.* Cambridge: Cambridge University Press, 1996.

Lewis, Paul H. *Guerrillas and Generals: The Dirty War in Argentina.* New York: Praeger, 2001.

Leyton, Elliot. *Touched by Fire: Doctors Without Borders in a Third World Crisis.* Toronto: McClelland & Stewart, 1998.

Li, Peter, ed. *Japanese War Crimes: The Search for Justice.* New Brunswick, N.J.: Transaction Publishers, 2003.

Lifton, Robert. *The Nazi Doctors: Medical Killing and the Psychology of Genocide.* New York: Basic Books, 2000.

Lischer, Sarah Kenyon. *Dangerous Sanctuaries: Refugee Camps, Civil War, and the Dilemmas of Humanitarian Aid. Cornell Studies in Security Affairs.* Ithaca, N.Y.: Cornell University Press, 2005.

MacDonald, C. A. *The Killing of Reinhard Heydrich: The SS "Butcher of Prague."* New York: Da Capo Press, 1998.

MacKey, Sandra. *The Reckoning: Iraq and the Legacy of Saddam Hussein.* New York: W. W. Norton & Company, 2003.

Maga, Timothy P. *Judgment at Tokyo: The Japanese War Crimes Trials.* Lexington: University Press of Kentucky, 2001.

Malcolm, Noel. *Kosovo: A Short History.* New York: HarperPerennial, 1999.

Mamdani, Mahmood. *When Victims Become Killers: Colonialism, Nativism, and the Genocide in Rwanda.* Princeton, N.J.: Princeton University Press, 2002.

Mangold, Tom, and Jeff Goldberg. *Plague Wars: The Terrifying Reality of Biological Warfare.* New York: St. Martin's Press, 2001.

Marrus, Michael R. *The Nuremberg War Crimes Trial of 1945–46: A Documentary History. Bedford Series in History and Culture.* Sydney, Australia: Palgrave Macmillan, 1997.

Matar, Khalil I., and Robert W. Thabit. *Lockerbie and Libya: A Study in International Relations.* Jefferson, N.C.: McFarland & Company, 2003.

May, Larry, and Gerald Postema. *Crimes against Humanity: A Normative Account. Cambridge Studies in Philosophy and Law.* Cambridge: Cambridge University Press, 2004.

Mayer, Ann Elizabeth. *Islam and Human Rights: Tradition and Politics.* Philadelphia: Westview Press, 1998.

McNamara, Ronald J. *Democracy and Human Rights in the Mediterranean Partner States of the Osce: Algeria, Egypt, Israel, Jordan, Morocco and Tunisia: Briefing of the Committee on Security and Cooperation in Europe.* Chicago: Diane Pub Co., 2004.

Meisler, Stanley. *United Nations: The First Fifty Years.* New York: Atlantic Monthly Press, 1997.

Melvern, Linda. *A People Betrayed: The Role of the West in Rwanda's Genocide.* London: Zed Books, 2000.

Mendelsohn, John. *The Preservation of Japanese War Crimes Trials Records in the National Archives.* Washington, D.C.: National Archives and Records Administration, 1982.

Menkhaus, Ken. *Somalia: State Collapse and the Threat of Terrorism.* London: International Institute for Strategic Studies, 2004.

Meron, Theodor. *War Crimes Law Comes of Age: Essays.* Oxford: Oxford University Press, 1999.

Mertus, Julie. *Former Yugoslavia: War Crimes Trials in the Former Yugoslavia.* Helsinki: Human Rights Watch/ Helsinki, 1995.

———. *Kosovo: How Myths and Truths Started a War.* Berkeley: University of California Press, 1999.

Micheletti, Eric. *Special Forces in Afghanistan 2001–2003: War against Terrorism.* Translated by Cyril Lombardini. Paris: Historie & Collections, 2003.

Miller, Donald E., and Lorna Touryan Miller. *Survivors: An Oral History of the Armenian Genocide.* Berkeley: University of California Press, 1999.

Miller, John, and Aaron Kenedi. *Inside Iraq: The History, the People, and the Modern Conflicts of the World's Least Understood Land.* New York: Marlowe & Company, 2003.

Minear, Richard R. *Victors' Justice: The Tokyo War Crimes Trial. Michigan Classics in Japanese Studies.* Ann Arbor: University of Michigan, Center for Japanese Studies, 2001.

Montefiore, Simon Sebag. *Stalin: The Court of the Red Tsar.* New York: Knopf, 2004.

Moorehead, Caroline. *Dunant's Dream: War, Switzerland, and the History of the Red Cross.* New York: Carroll & Graf Publishers, 1999.

———. *Human Cargo: A Journey among Refugees.* New York: Henry Holt and Co., 2005.

Mosley, Leonard. *The Reich Marshal: A Biography of Hermann Göring.* London: Weidenfeld and Nicolson, 1974.

Moyano, Maria. *Argentina's Lost Patrol: Armed Struggle, 1969–1979.* New Haven, Conn.: Yale University Press, 1995.

Munro, R. *Punishment Season: Human Rights in China After Martial Law. Asia Watch Report.* New York: Human Rights Watch, 1990.

Naimark, Norman, and Holly Case. *Yugoslavia and Its Historians: Understanding the Balkan Wars of the 1990s.* Stanford, Calif.: Stanford University Press, 2003.

Neier, Aryeh. *War Crimes: Brutality, Genocide, Terror, and the Struggle for Justice.* New York: Crown, 1998.

Nichols, Gary W., and Milton L. Boykin, eds. *Arms Control and Nuclear Weapons: U.S. Policies and the National Interest.* Contributions in Military Studies. Westport, Conn.: Greenwood Press, 1987.

Njoku, H. *Tragedy without Heroes: The Nigeria-Biafra War.* Chicago: Fourth Dimension Publications Ltd., 1987.

Ogata, Sadako, and Kofi Annan. *The Turbulent Decade: Confronting the Refugee Crises of the 1990s.* New York: W. W. Norton & Company, 2005.

Olson, James S., and Randy Roberts, eds. *My Lai: A Brief History with Documents. The Bedford Series in History and Culture.* Sydney, Australia: Palgrave Macmillan, 1998.

Orford, Anne, James Crawford, and John Bell, eds. *Reading Humanitarian Intervention: Human Rights and the Use of Force in International Law.* Cambridge Studies in International and Comparative Law. Cambridge: Cambridge University Press, 2003.

Overbey, Fern. *The Dachau Defendants: Life Stories from Testimony and Documents of the War Crimes Prosecutions.* Jefferson, N.C.: McFarland & Company, 2004.

Paul, Wolfgang. *Hermann Göring: Hitler Paladin or Puppet?* Translated by Helmet Bogler. New York: Arms & Armour, 1998.

Pausewang, Siegfried, Kjetil Tronvoll, and Lovise Aaeln, eds. *Ethiopia since the Derg: A Decade of Democratic Pretension and Performance.* London: Zed Books, 2003.

Pearce, Jenny. *Inside Colombia: Drugs, Democracy, and War.* New Brunswick, N.J.: Rutgers University Press, 2004.

Peterson, Merrill D. *Starving Armenians: America and the Armenian Genocide, 1915–1930 and After.* Charlottesville: University Press of Virginia, 2004.

Peterson, Scott. *Me against My Brother: At War in Somalia, Sudan and Rwanda.* London: Routledge, 2001.

Pham, John-Peter. *Liberia: Portrait of a Failed State.* London: Reed Press, 2004.

Piccigallo, Philip R. *The Japanese on Trial: Allied War Crimes Operations in the East, 1945–1951.* Austin: University of Texas Press, 1980.

Pilloud, Claude. *Commentary on the Additional Protocols of 8 June 1977 to the Geneva Conventions of 12 August 1949.* Boston: Brill Academic Publishers, 1987.

Pinto, Constancio, and Jardine Matthew. *East Timor's Unfinished Struggle: Inside the Timorese Resistance.* Boston: South End Press, 1996.

Politzer, Patricia, and Diane Wachtel. *Fear in Chile: Lives under Pinochet.* New York: New Press, 2001.

Power, Samantha. *A Problem from Hell.* New York: Perennial, 2003.

Pran, Dith, comp. *Children of Cambodia's Killing Fields: Memoirs by Survivors.* Edited by Kim DePaul. New Haven, Conn.: Yale University Press, 1999.

Price, Monroe, and Mark Thompson, eds. *Forging Peace: Intervention, Human Rights, and the Management of Media Space.* Bloomington: Indiana University Press, 2002.

Price, Richard M. *The Chemical Weapons Taboo.* Ithaca, N.Y.: Cornell University Press, 1997.

Prokosch, Eric. *The Technology of Killing: A Military and Political History of Anti-personnel Weapons.* London: Zed Books, 1995.

Rabasa, Angel, and Peter Chalk. *Colombian Labyrinth: The Synergy of Drugs and Insurgency and Its Implications for Regional Stability.* Santa Monica, Calif.: Rand Corporation (NBN), 2001.

Radzinsky, Edvard. *Stalin: The First In-Depth Biography Based on Explosive New Documents from Russia's Secret Archives.* New York: Anchor, 1997.

Rashid, Ahmed. *Taliban: Militant Islam, Oil and Fundamentalism in Central Asia.* New Haven, Conn.: Yale University Press, 2001.

Razack, Sherene H. *Dark Threats and White Knights: The Somalia Affair, Peacekeeping, and the New Imperialism.* Toronto: University of Toronto Press, 2004.

Read, Anthony. *The Devil's Disciples: Hitler's Inner Circle.* New York: W. W. Norton & Company, 2004.

Rees, Laurence. *Horror in the East: Japan and the Atrocities of World War II.* New York: Da Capo Press, 2002.

Rhode, David. *Endgame: The Betrayal and Fall of Srebrenica.* New York: Farrar, Straus & Giroux, 1997.

Rieff, David. *A Bed for the Night: Humanitarianism in Crisis.* New York: Simon & Schuster, 2002.

Roberts, Adam, and Richard Guelff. *Documents on the Laws of War.* Oxford: Oxford University Press, 2000.

Roberts, Jeremy. *Joseph Goebbels: Nazi Propaganda Minister.* Holocaust Biographies. New York: Rosen Publishing Group, 2000.

Robertson, Geoffrey. *Crimes against Humanity: The Struggle for Global Justice.* New York: New Press, 2003.

Rogel, Carole. *The Breakup of Yugoslavia and the War in Bosnia.* Westport, Conn.: Greenwood Press, 1998.

Romano, Cesare, Andre Nollkaemper, and Jann K. Kleffner, eds. *Internationalized Criminal Courts and Tribunals: Sierra Leone, East Timor, Kosovo, and Cambodia.* International Courts and Tribunals Series. Oxford: Oxford University Press, 2004.

Rone, Jemera. *Famine in Sudan, 1998: The Human Rights Causes.* New York:Human Rights Watch, 1999.

Roseman, Mark. *The Wannsee Conference and the Final Solution: A Reconsideration.* New York: Metropolitan Books, 2002.

Ross, James D. *Human Rights in Burma (Myanmar) since the May 1990 National Election.* New York: Lawyers Committee for Human Rights, 1991.

Rossanet, Bertrand de. *War and Peace in the Former Yugoslavia.* Boston: Martinus Nijhoff, 1997.

Roth, Kenneth, ed. *Torture: A Human Rights Perspective.* New York: New Press, 2005.

Russell of Liverpool, Edward Frederick Langley Russell, Baron. *Knights of the Bushido: A Short History of Japanese War Crimes.* London: Greenhill Books, 2005.

———. *The Scourge of the Swastika: A Short History of Nazi War Crimes.* London: Greenhill Books/Lionel Leventhal, 2002.

Sammakia, Nejla. *Algeria, Elections in the Shadow of Violence and Repression.* New York: Human Rights Watch/ Middle East, 1997.

Santoro, Michael A. *Profits and Principles: Global Capitalism and Human Rights in China.* Ithaca, N.Y.: Cornell University Press, 2000.

Saracin, Philip. *Blood Diamonds.* Victoria, Canada: BookSurge Publishing, 2002.

Scharf, Michael P. *Balkan Justice: The Story behind the First International War Crimes Trial since Nuremberg.* Durham, N.C.: Carolina Academic Press, 1997.

Scheuer, Michael. *Imperial Hubris: Why the West Is Losing the War on Terror.* Washington, D.C.: Potomac Books, 2004.

Schlesigner, Stephen. *Act of Creation: The Founding of the United Nations: A Story of Superpowers, Secret Agents, Wartime Allies and Enemies, and Their Quest for a Peaceful World.* Boulder, Colo.: Westview Press, 2003.

Schofield, Victoria. *Kashmir in Conflict: India, Pakistan and the Unending War.* London: I. B. Tauris, 2002.

Schultz, William. *Tainted Legacy: 9/11 and the Ruin of Human Rights.* New York: Nation Books, 2003.

Schulze, Kirsten E. *The Free Aceh Movement (GAM): Anatomy of a Separatist Organization.* Washington, D.C.: East-West Center, 2004.

Schwarz, Adam. *A Nation in Waiting: Indonesia's Search for Stability.* Philadelphia: Westview Press, 1999.

Sciolino, Elaine. *Persian Mirrors: The Elusive Face of Iran.* New York: Free Press, 2001.

Shelton, Dinah. *International Crimes, Peace, and Human Rights: The Role of the International Criminal Court.* Ardsley, N.Y.: Transnational Publishers, Inc., 2000.

———. *Remedies in International Human Rights Law.* Oxford: Oxford University Press, 2001.

Sherry, Virginia N. *Cleaning the Face of Morocco: Human Rights Abuses and Recent Developments/North Africa.* New York: Human Rights First, 1990.

Short, Philip. *Pol Pot: Anatomy of a Nightmare.* New York: Holt Rinehart, 2005.

Siegel, James T. *The Rope of God.* Ann Arbor: University of Michigan Press, 2000.

Simons, Geoff. *Libya and the West: From Independence to Lockerbie.* London: I. B. Tauris, 2004.

Sjamsuddin, Nazaruddin. *The Republican Revolt: A Study of the Acehnese Rebellion.* Singapore: Institute of Southeast Asian Studies, 1988.

Slyomovics, Susan. *The Performance of Human Rights in Morocco.* Pennsylvania Studies in Human Rights. Philadelphia: University of Pennsylvania Press, 2005.

Solzhenitsyn, Aleksandr. *The Gulag Archipelago.* New York: Harpercollins, 1978.

Southall, Roger, and Kristina Bentley. *African Peace Process: Mandela, South Africa, and Burundi.* Pretoria, South Africa: Human Sciences Research Council, 2005.

Steiner, Henry J., and Philip Alston. *International Human Rights in Context: Law, Politics, Morals.* Oxford: Oxford University Press, 2000.

Steinhardt, Ralph G., and Anthony A. D'Amato. *The Alien Tort Claims Act: An Analytical Anthology.* Ardsley, N.Y.: Transnational Publishers, 1999.

Sukma, Rizal. *Security Operations in Aceh: Goals, Consequences, and Lessons.* Washington: East-West Center, 2004.

Talbott, Strobe. *Engaging India: Diplomacy, Democracy, and the Bomb.* Washington, D.C.: Brookings Institution Press, 2004.

Tamm, Ingrid J. *Diamonds in Peace and War: Severing the Conflict Diamond Connection.* WPF Report #30. Cambridge, Mass.: World Peace Foundation, 2002.

Tanaka, Toshiyuki. *Hidden Horrors: Japanese War Crimes in World War II.* Boulder, Colo.: Westview Press, 1998.

Taylor, David. *The Wars of Former Yugoslavia.* Austin, Tex.: Bloomington: Raintree, 2003.

Taylor, Telford. *Nuremberg and Vietnam: An American Tragedy.* New York: Times Books, 1970.

Temple-Rason, Dina. *Justice on the Grass: Three Rwandan Journalists, Their Trial for War Crimes and a Nation's Quest for Redemption.* New York: Free Press, 2005.

Thompson, Joseph E. *American Policy and African Famine: The Nigeria-Biafra War, 1966–1970.*

Contributions in Afro-American and African Studies. Westport, Conn.: Greenwood Press, 1990.

Toland, John. *Adolf Hitler: The Definitive Biography.* New York: Anchor, 1991.

Trombly, Maria. *Journalist's Guide to the Geneva Conventions.* Indianapolis: Society of Professional Journalists, 2000.

Tuck, Richard. *The Rights of War and Peace: Political Thought and the International Order from Grotius to Kant.* Oxford: Oxford University Press, 2001.

Tucker, Jonathan B., ed. *Toxic Terror: Assessing Terrorist Use of Chemical and Biological Weapons.* BCSIA Studies in International Security. Cambridge, Mass.: MIT Press, 2000

Tutorow, Norman E. *War Crimes, War Criminals, and War Crimes Trials: An Annotated Bibliography and Source Book. Bibliographies and Indexes in World History.* Westport, Conn.: Greenwood Publishing Group, 1986.

Ulam, Adam B. *Stalin: The Man and His Era.* Boston: Beacon Press, 1987.

United Nations War Crimes Commission. *Law Reports of Trials of War Criminals: Four Genocide Trials.* Boulder, Colo.: Lynne Rienner Publishers, 1992.

Vargas, Llosa, Alvaro. *The Madness of Things Peruvian: Democracy under Siege.* New Brunswick, N.J.: Transaction Publishers, 1994.

Vatikiotis, Michael R. *Indonesian Politics under Suharto: The Rise and Fall of the New Order.* London: Routledge, 1999.

Vaux, Anthony. *The Selfish Altruist: Relief Work in Famine and War.* London: Earthscan Publications, 2001.

Veloso, Caetano. *Tropical Truth: A Story of Music and Revolution in Brazil.* New York: Knopf, 2002.

Vietnam Veterans against the War. *The Winter Soldier Investigation: An Inquiry into American War Crimes.* Boston: Beacon Press, 1972.

Vyver, Johan D. van der, and John Witte, Jr., eds. *Religious Human Rights in Global Perspective: Legal Perspectives.* 2d ed. Grand Rapids: Wm. B. Eerdmans Publishing Company, 2000.

Waltz, Susan Eileen. *Human Rights and Reform: Changing the Face of North African Politics.* Berkeley: University of California Press, 1995.

Weatherley, Robert. *The Discourse of Human Rights in China: Historical and Ideological Perspectives.* Sydney, Australia: Palgrave Macmillan, 1999.

Weiss, Thomas G., David P. Forsythe, and Roger A. Coate. *United Nations and Changing World Politics.* Westport, Conn.: Westview Press, 2004.

Weissman, Fabrice. *In the Shadow of "Just Wars": Violence, Politics, and Humanitarian Action.* Ithaca, N.Y.: Cornell University Press, 2004.

Welch, Claude E., Jr. *Ngos and Human Rights: Promise and Performance.* Pennsylvania Studies in Human Rights. Philadelphia: University of Pennsylvania Press, 2000.

Welsh, Jennifer M. *Humanitarian Intervention and International Relations.* Oxford: Oxford University Press, 2004.

Whealey, Robert. *American Intervention in the Yugoslavia: Civil War, 1991–1999.* Amherst, N.Y.: Humanity Books, 2005.

Wheeler, Nicholas J. *Saving Strangers: Humanitarian Intervention in International Society.* Oxford: Oxford University Press, 2003.

Whitley, Andrew. *Human Rights Abuses in Algeria: No One Is Spared.* New York: Human Rights Watch, 1994.

Wiendling, Paul Julian. *Nazi Medicine and the Nuremberg Trials: From Medical War Crimes to Informed Consent.* Sydney, Australia: Palgrave Macmillan, 2005.

Wilkinson, Daniel. *Silence on the Mountain: Stories of Terror, Betrayal, and Forgetting in Guatemala.* Boston: Houghton Mifflin, 2002.

Winner, David. *Peter Benenson: Taking a Stand against Injustice—Amnesty International (People Who Have Helped the World).* Milwaukee: Gareth Stevens Pub., 1992.

Winslow, Philip C. *Sowing the Dragon's Teeth: Land Mines and the Global Legacy of War.* Boston: Beacon Press, 1998.

Wistrich, Robert S. *Hitler and the Holocaust. Modern Library Chronicles.* New York: Modern Library, 2001.

Wood, Elisabeth Jean, Peter Lange, et al., eds. *Insurgent Collective Action and Civil War in El Salvador. Cambridge Studies in Comparative Politics.* Cambridge: Cambridge University Press, 2003,

Wrong, Michela. *In the Footsteps of Mr. Kurtz: Living on the Brink of Disaster in Mobutu's Congo.* New York: HarperCollins Publishers, 2001.

Zayy-at, Montasser al-. *The Road to Al-Qaeda: The Story of Bin Laden's Right-Hand Man.* Critical Studies on Islam. Translated by Ahmed Fekry. Edited by Sara Nimis. Ann Arbor, Mich.: Pluto Press, 2004.

Encyclopedias, Guides, and Handbooks

Encyclopedia of Human Rights. 2nd ed. E. Lawson. Comprehensive compendium including texts of 200 instruments, descriptions of human rights organizations, status of human rights in countries, etc.

Encyclopedia of Human Rights Issues since 1945. W. Langley.

Encyclopedia of the United Nations. 3rd ed. 4 vols. Useful background information on human rights and the relevant conventions, including texts of the major instruments.

Great Events from History II: Human Rights Series. 5 vols. Articles covering over 460 topics in the history of human rights arranged chronologically from 1900 to 1991. Each essay provides a summary of the event and its impact along with a bibliography and cross-references.

Historical Dictionary of Human Rights and Humanitarian Organizations. R. Gorman.

Human Rights Encyclopedia. J. Lewis, ed. 3 vols.

Human Rights: The Essential Reference. C. Devine, et al.

International Encyclopedia of Human Rights: Freedoms, Abuses, and Remedies. R. Maddex.

United Nations and Human Rights, 1945–1995. UN Blue Book series, vol. 7.

United Nations Reference Guide in the Field of Human Rights.

Guides to Research

Guide to Human Rights Research. J. Tobin. Comprehensive guide to the literature

Guide to International Human Rights Practice. 2nd ed., 1992. H. Hannum.

Human Rights: A Reference Handbook. 2nd ed. N. Redman and L. Whalen.

Document Sources

Basic Documents on Human Rights. 3rd ed. I. Brownlie.

Human Rights: A Compilation of International Instruments. 7th ed. United Nations.

Human Rights Documents: Compilation of Documents Pertaining to Human Rights: US Laws on Human Rights; Basic UN Human Rights.

Annuals

Amnesty International Report.

Country Reports on Human Rights Practices. Dept. of State. (also on Dept. of State web page)

European Union Annual Report on Human Rights.

For the Record: The UN Human Rights System 1997–.

Freedom in the World: Political Rights and Civil Liberties. Freedom House.

Human Rights in Developing Countries.

Human Rights Watch World Report.

Nations in Transit: Civil Society, Democracy and Markets in East Central Europe and the Newly Independent States. 1997–.

World Refugee Survey.

Yearbook of the United Nations.

Periodicals Indexes/Databases

Bibliographic Databases and Online Catalogs

Human rights law and related commentaries are growing at an amazing rate. The two major bibliographic databases in the United States are RLG and OCLC.

A guide is available about how to research human rights on the Internet. The Concise Guide to Human Rights on the Internet can be found at http://www.derechos.org/humanrights/manual.htm.

Alternative Press Index
http://www.altpress.org/
Index to more than 380 alternative, radical, and left publications from 1991 to present

CLC (the Online Computer Library Center)
http://www.oclc.org/home
This data bank includes the records of many academic institutions, law firm libraries, and smaller libraries in the U.S. Some large libraries have their holdings on both systems. Most bibliographic databases and online catalogs use standard Library of Congress Subject Headings (LCSH).

CIAO (Columbia International Affairs Online).
http://www.ciaonet.org/
Provides full text of working papers, conferences, abstracts of journal articles, web links, etc.

EUREKA (Eureka Guide to UN Information)
http://www.library.yale.edu:80/un/un2a5.htm
The Dag Hammarskjöld Library (United Nations Library) has allowed their records to be included.

Expanded Academic ASAP
http://www.galegroup.com/tlist/sb5019.html
Indexes 1,600 popular and scholarly journals from 1988 to present.

Human Rights and Humanitarian Affairs: Information Resources
http://www.columbia.edu/cu/lweb/indiv/lehman/guides/human.html
This is a selective guide to resources at Columbia University Libraries and on the Internet, for conducting research on international human rights issues.

PAIS International
http://www.pais.org/
Indexes books, articles, government documents and working papers from around the world.

ProQuest
http://www.proquestk12.com/
Index to general interest and academic periodicals with full text for most, 1986 to present.

RLG Union Catalog (the Research Libraries Group)
http://www.rlg.org/
The RLGU contains the holdings of some of the major academic institutions such as University of California at Berkeley, Columbia University, Harvard University, and Yale University. This is a database from 1979 to the present with quarterly updates.

Worldwide Political Science Abstracts
http://www.asu.edu/lib/resources/db/polscbib.htm
Indexes and abstracts journals from political science and related fields.

Periodicals

Columbia Human Rights Law Review
CSCE Digest (Commission on Security and Cooperation
   in Europe)
   http://www.law.columbia.edu/current_student/
   student_service/Law_Journals/human_rights
Harvard Human Rights Journal
   http://www.law.harvard.edu/students/orgs/hrj/
*Human Rights: A Quarterly Review of the Office of
   UNHCHR*
Human Rights Internet Reporter
   http://www.osa.ceu.hu/lpe?id=1380
Human Rights Law Journal
*Human Rights Quarterly: A Comparative and International
   Journal of the Social Sciences, Philosophy, and Law*
Human Rights Tribune [Human Rights Internet]
   http://www.hrtribune.com/
Human Rights Watch [reports] (also available on HRW
   website: http://www.hrw.org/)
Brief reports documenting current human rights abuses in
   countries/regions around the world
Index on Censorship [Writers and Scholars International]
   Presents issues on censorship of writers worldwide
International Human Rights Reports
International Journal of Human Rights
Netherlands Quarterly of Human Rights
South African Journal on Human Rights
Yale Human Rights and Development Law Journal
   http://islandia.law.yale.edu/yhrdlj/

News Sources

Lexis/Nexis Academic
http://www.lexisnexis.com/
Full-text database of news, legal, and business sources.

America's Newspapers
Full text of over 200 U.S. newspapers on political, economic, and social events at the local, state, national and international levels.

Global NewsBank 1996–
Full-text international news from 1,500 newspapers, wire services, radio, and TV broadcasts and periodicals. All sources translated to English.
http://www.newsbank.com/academic/global.html

Indexes

Lexis/Nexis Legislative
http://www.lexisnexis.com/academic/3cis/cisl/

LegislativePublications.asp
Indexes congressional publications from 1970 to present and provides full text of bills, laws, regulations, testimony, and other congressional sources.

Lexis/Nexis Statistical
Indexes federal, state, and international statistical sources and provides links to online text where available.
http://www.lexisnexis.com/academic/1univ/stat/default.asp

UNBISnet
http://www.un.org.pk/library/biblo-ref-data.htm
Compilation of 10 databases providing bibliographic access to UN and non-UN publications. Includes full text of resolutions, voting records, and citations to speeches and agendas.

Access UN
http://www.newsbank.com/un/
1948–
Indexes United Nations documents with links to online text where available; documents also available on fiche, 1983 to present as well as in paper. Check for periodic reports by states parties to various international human rights agreements and reports of the special rapporteurs on the status of human rights in particular countries.

UN Documents Sources

UN High Commissioner for Human Rights
http://www.ohchr.org/english/

UN Human Rights Reports
For a guide to the documents issued by the various human rights committees see http://www.un.org/Depts/dhl/resguide/spechr.htm.

The most comprehensive source for UN human rights documentation is the home page of the United Nations. This site provides electronic text of the human rights treaty and charter-based bodies and periodic reports by states, press releases, etc.

Additionally, UN-I-QUE, a reference database of the Dag Hammarskjöld (UN) Library, indexes selected UN documents from 1946 to present.

Internet Sources

Council of Europe Human Rights
http://www.hri.org/docs/ECHR50.html
Provides access to the European Court of Human Rights and other relevant human rights instruments for Europe.

Derechos Human Rights
http://www.derechos.org
The first Internet-based human rights organization. It works with human rights situations in countries.

Human Rights Internet
http://www.hri.ca/index.aspx
International NGO, documentation center, and publishing house in Canada. See section: UN Processes and Documentation and click on "For the Record: The UN Human Rights System" which provides an annual country-by-country overview of human rights issues with links to relevant UN documents. Reports are available from 1997 to present.

University of Minnesota Human Rights Library
http://www1.umn.edu/humanrts/
A joint project of Yale Law School, University of Toronto Law School and the University of Minnesota. Each site has different information—Yale focuses on human rights legal cases and documents, and Toronto on women's human rights resources.

Index

★ ───

Note: *Italic* page numbers refer to illustrations. **Bold** page numbers indicate main discussions.

A

Abacha, Sani 318, 399
Abbas, Mahmoud 340–342
Abdullah (crown prince of Saudi Arabia) 383
Abdullah II (king of Jordan) 254
Abdullah Ahmad Badawi 286–287
Aboriginals (Australia), mistreatment of **1–2**, 33, 148, 366
abortion 67, 77–78
Abu Ghraib prison 173, 181, 236, 245–246, 427
Abu Sayyaf Group (ASG) 345, 359
Aceh, war crimes in **2–3**, 229
Acosta, Jorge Eduardo **3**
acquired immunodeficiency syndrome/human immunodeficiency virus. *See* AIDS/HIV
act of war **3–4**
Additional Protocols to the Geneva Conventions **4–5**
  belligerent status 42
  carpet bombing 65
  civilian immunity 85–86
  collateral damage 87–88
  collective punishment 89, 90
  Colombia 92
  combatants, rights of 95
  crimes against humanity 111
  cultural property, protection of 114, 115
  customary law 116
  Geneva Conventions 165
  hostages 208
  humanitarian aid, barring of 209
  IHL 240, 241
  illegal acts 223
  immunity from attack 223
  indiscriminate attacks 227
  internally displaced persons 231–232
  International Humanitarian Fact-Finding Commission 240
  irregulars 247
  journalists, protection of 254
  legitimate military targets 276
  Martens Clause 289
  mass graves 289
  mercenaries 296
  POWs 353
  protected persons 354–355
  Protocol to the Hague Convention of 1954 for the Protection of Cultural Property 356
  public property, protection of 356
  reprisal 367
  safe havens 377
  siege 391–392
  slavery 394
  starvation as a tactic of war 406–407
  terrorism and international humanitarian law 420
  transfer of civilians 430
  universal jurisdiction 449
  unlawful imprisonment 450
  victims, rights of 456
  war crimes, categorization of 462, 463
  willful killing 477
Adly, Magda 138
Afghanistan. *See also* Mullah Omar; Taliban
  arms, trafficking in and control mechanisms 28
  Australia 33
  Global Rights 173–174
  Mullah Omar 309–310
  Jose Padilla 338
  al-Qaeda 358
  refoulement 362
  refugees 364
  Uzbekistan 452
Afghanistan, human rights violations in **5–9**, 196, 209, 415
Afghanistan, U.S. invasion of 195–196, 309, 310, 420, 421
Africa. *See also specific headings, e.g.:* Nigeria
  arms, trafficking in and control mechanisms 29

The Carter Center 66
children's rights 77, 78
Equatorial Guinea 145
Ethiopia 146–147
Ivory Coast 247–249
Mau Mau uprising 291
North Africa 42–43, 360, 479
refugees 363
Russia 372
Togo 423–424
Uganda 438–439
women's rights, violations of 479
African Americans 55–56, 366
African National Congress (ANC) 121, 432
Africans (black) ix, 15, 16, 118, 479
African Union (AU) 119, 281, 423
Afwerki, Issayas 146
Agent Orange 73, 88
aggression **9**
Agreement for the Prosecution and Punishment of the Major War Criminals of the European Axis and Charter of the International Military Tribunal; London Charter. *See* Nuremberg Charter
Aguiyi-Ironsi, Johnson 44
Ahmadinejad, Mahmoud 244–245
Ahmed, Iajuddin 36
AIDS/HIV
  Bangladesh 36
  Burundi 58
  Nicolae Ceauşescu 68
  children's rights 74, 76, 78
  China 83
  Congo, Democratic Republic of the 102
  Haiti 191
  India 226
  Kazakhstan 261
  Rwanda, genocide in 373
  Thailand 422
  Uganda 438
  women's rights, violations of 479

Akayesu, Jean-Paul 237, 375
Akayev, Askar 274
Al Aksa Brigades 341
Albania, human rights violations in **10**
Albanians 270, 271, 285, 286, 303, 388, 468, 484
Albright, Madeleine 4, 24, 266
Aleksovski, Zlatko 484
Alexander II (czar of Russia) 349
Alfonsín, Raúl 22
Algeria, human rights violations in **10–11**, 42–43, 89, 359, 399
Ali, Ahmed Abu 200–201
Alien Tort Claims Act **11–13**, 383, 448, 456
Aliyev, Heydar 34
Allawi, Ayad 245
Allende, Salvador 78–80, 347, *347*, 348
Altmann, Klaus 38
American Convention on Human Rights **13–14**, 230
American embassy bombings, Nairobi and Tanzania 359
Amherst, Jeffrey Amherst, first baron **14**
Amin, Bakhtiar 219, 245
Amin, Idi **14–17**, 331, 438
amnesty **17–18**
Amnesty International **18–19**, 544
  Aboriginals (Australia), mistreatment of 1
  Aceh 2
  Algeria 10, 11
  Louise Arbour 21
  Aung San Suu Kyi 32
  Australia 33
  Azerbaijan 34
  Bangladesh 36
  Peter Benenson 42
  Brazil 53
  Cameroon 65
  China 81
  collective punishment 90
  conflict diamonds 101
  Congo (Brazzaville) 102

Amnesty International (*continued*)
  Cuba 113, 114
  Ecuador 137
  Egypt 138
  Georgia (Republic of) 171
  Guyana 187
  Iran 244
  Ivory Coast 249
  Kashmir and Jammu 260
  Sean Macbride 285
  Mexico 298
  Morocco 308
  Myanmar 311
  Nepal 316
  Nigeria 318
  North Korea 321
  Philippines 345
  prisoners of conscience 352–353
  Sudan 411
  Syria 414
  Ta Mok 416
  Togo 424
  Tunisia 434
  Ukraine 440
  universal jurisdiction 447
  war criminals of the former
    Yugoslavia 468
ANC. *See* African National
  Congress
Anderson, David 423
Angola 100, 364
Angola, war crimes in **19–20**
Annan, Kofi
  arms, trafficking in and control
    mechanisms 29
  Burundi 58
  Cyprus 116
  Darfur 119
  Carla Del Ponte 122
  humanitarian intervention 210,
    211
  Ivory Coast 248
  Sierra Leone 393
Ansar al Islam 359
ANSESAL 119
anthrax 45, 172
Anti-Personnel (AP) Mine Ban
  Convention 355
antipersonnel mines (APMs) 108,
  355
anti-Semitism 205, 407–409. *See
  also* Jews, persecution of
Anti-Terrorism, Crime and Security
  Act (2001) **20**
Anwar Ibrahim 287
apartheid **20–21**
  Wouter Basson 39
  Biafra 44
  Congo, Democratic Republic of
    the 103
  Eugene de Kock 121
  Freedom House 158
  Richard J. Goldstone 176
  slavery 393
  Sudan 411
  Sullivan Principles 412
  Truth and Reconciliation
    Commission 432
  Desmond Tutu 437
  Universal Declaration of Human
    Rights 446

APMs. *See* antipersonnel mines
Arafat, Yasser 41, 340, 341, 377
Aramburu, Pedro 22
Arar, Maher 107
Arbenz, Jacob 368
Arbour, Louise **21**, 118
Ardeatine caves massacre 352
Ardito Barletta, Nicolás 321
ARENA. *See* Nationalist
  Republican Alliance
Arendt, Hannah 141
Argentina 66–67, 295, 344, 352
Argentina, human rights violations
  in **21–23**
  Jorge Eduardo Acosta 3
  amnesty 17
  dirty war 123, 124
  Adolf Eichmann 140
  forensic medicine and human
    rights 156
  José López Rega 284
  Mothers of the Plaza de Mayo
    309
  universal jurisdiction 447
  war crimes, categorization of
    463
  Christián von Wernich 475
Argentine Anticommunist Alliance
  (the Triple A) 22, **23**
Aristide, Jean-Bertrand 191–194
Arkan (Željko Ražnatović) **23–24**
Arkan's Tigers 470
armed conflict 29, 46, 74
Armenia, human rights violations in
  24–25, 436
Armenian genocide **25–27**, 110,
  153, 169
arms, trafficking in and control
  mechanisms **27–29**, 160, 233
Army, U.S. 345, 423
Article 3 Common to the Geneva
  Conventions **29–30**
  belligerent status 42
  Colombia 91
  crimes against humanity 111
  disappearances 124–125
  due process 130
  forced labor 155
  Geneva Conventions 165
  hors de combat 208
  hostages 208
  incitement to genocide 224
  irregulars 247
  rape as a tactic of war 361
  Rwandan human rights violators
    375
  terrorism and international
    humanitarian law 421
  torture 427
  unlawful imprisonment 450
  war crimes, categorization of
    462
  willful killing 477
Artuković, Andrija 333
Arusha Accords 373
Aryans 152, 153, 176, 476
ASF. *See* Lawyers Without Borders
ASG. *See* Abu Sayyaf Group
Asia 363, 372. *See also* Southeast
  Asia; *specific headings, e.g.:* China
Asians, explusions of 15, 16

Askin, Kelly Dawn 484
Assad, Bashar al- 413
Assad, Hafiz al- 195, 413
assembly, freedom of 55, 81, 457
association, freedom of 40, 82
Astiz, Alfredo 22
asylum, political **30–31**, 33, 109,
  364, 443
Atlacal Battalion 142, 143
AUC (United Defense Units of
  Colombia) 91, 95
Aum Shinrikyo 74
Aung San, Daw 32
Aung San Suu Kyi 18, **31–33**, 311
Auschwitz concentration camp
  Adolf Eichmann 140
  Final Solution 154
  Imre Finta 154
  forced labor 155
  Izieu, children of 249
  Josef Kramer 271
  Gustav von Bohlen Krupp 272
  Josef Mengele 294–295
  Maurice Papon 343
  Erich Priebke 352
  Rom, persecution of 369
  Arthur Seyss-Inquart 389
Australia 31, 39, 362. *See also*
  Howard, John
Australia, human rights violations in
  33. *See also* Aboriginals
  (Australia), mistreatment of
Austria 139, 369, 459
Azerbaijan, human rights violations
  in 24, **34**
Azzam, Abdullah 358

B
Baath Party 195, 216, 219, 245,
  286, 413
Babi Yar 35, **35**, 141
Bachelet, Michelle 80
Bagram (U.S. air base, Afghanistan)
  8, 9
Bahrain, human rights situation in
  35
Bakr, Hassan al- 216
Bali nightclub bombing 39, 252,
  359
Balkan Archives 243
Balkan wars (1912 and 1913) 25
Balkan wars (1990s). *See also*
  Bosnian wars
  Louise Arbour 21
  Bosnia and Herzegovina 49
  crimes against humanity 111
  Dayton accords 49, 112,
    120–121, 258, 303, 305, 433, 484
  ethnic cleansing 147
  Ante Gotovina 178
  humanitarian aid, barring of 209
  ICC 236, 237
  IMI 243
  International Commission on
    Missing Persons 233
  Macedonia 285
  Serbia 387
  Vojislav Seselj 388
  Telford Taylor 419
  Franjo Tudjman 432–433
  Yugoslavia 482

Bangladesh 360, 365, 456
Bangladesh, human rights
  violations in **35–36**
Bantustans 20–21
Baptiste, Jean Pierre. *See* Tatoune,
  Jean
Barak, Aharon 215
Barayagwiza, Jean-Bosco 225
Barbie, Klaus **36–38**, 37
  amnesty 18
  Izieu, children of 249
  Serge Klarsfeld 267, 268
  Office of Special Investigations
    333
  Paul Touvier 428
  Jacques Vergès 454, 455
Barnes de Carlotto, Estela 309
Barreda Moreno, Luis de la
  314–315
Bashir, Abu Bakar **38–39**, 229,
  252
Bashir, Omar Hassan al- 410
Bassiouni, Cherif 110
Basson, Wouter **39–40**
Batista, Fulgencio 132
Batlle, Jorge 450
Bavaria 371
Beara, Ljubisa 465
Bédié, Henri Konan 247–248
Bedjaoui, Mohammed 323
Begin, Menachem 377
Beirut, Lebanon 377, 414
Belarus, human rights violations in
  40–41, 385
Belgian Congo 148, 278
Belgian war crimes tribunal **41**
Belgium 189, 278, 372, 373, 447,
  459–460
belligerent status **41–42**
Belo, Carlos Filipe Ximenes 134
Ben Ali, Zine El Abidine 434
Benenson, Peter 18, **42**
Benson, Bruce 115
Berbers, human rights abuses of
  42–43
Beria, Lavrenti 406
Bernays, Murray 328
Beslan school terrorist siege (North
  Ossetsia) 72
Betancourt, Romulo 431
Bhutan, human rights violations in
  43–44
Biafra, war crimes in **44–45**
Biamby, Philippe 193
Bilien, Valentina 454
Bingham, Lord 348, 349
Bin Laden, Osama 309, 310, 358,
  359, 383, 415
biological weapons **45–46**
  Jeffrey Amherst Amherst 14
  Wouter Basson 40
  customary law 116
  Geneva Conventions 165
  germ warfare 172
  Hague Conventions 190
  Manchuria, Japanese war crimes
    in 287, 288
  weapons of mass destruction
    474
Birkenau 154
black market 27, 59

"Black October" riots 43
black state 15, 16
Blagojević, Vidoje 466
Blair, Tony 20
Blaškić, Tihomir 466
blood diamonds. *See* conflict diamonds
Boban, Mate 483
Boer War of 1902 41, 97, 98
Bokassa, Jean-Bédel **47**
Bolívar, Simón 336
Bolivia 38
Bolivia, human rights violations in **47–48**
Bolton, John 28
bonded labor 77, 78
Bonner, Raymond 142–143, 197–198
booby traps 108, 355
Bormann, Martin **48–49**, 202, 272, 326, 386
Boskovski, Ljube 239
Bosnia and Herzegovina, human rights violations in **49–51**, *50*
 Dayton accords 120
 Carla Del Ponte 122
 forced labor 155
 genocide 167
 hostages 208
 International Commission on Missing Persons 233
 Radovan Karadić 257–259
 Theodor Meron 297
 Slobodan Milošević 302, 303
 rape as a tactic of war 361
 refugees 364
 Sarajevo, siege of 223, 258, 304, 382–383, 392, 467, 468, 483
 Vojislav Seselj 388
 Srebrenca, massacre in 402
 Franjo Tudjman 433
Bosnian Muslims 147, 239, 305, 382, 402
Bosnian wars (1990s)
 Arkan (Želiko Raźnatović) 22–23
 collateral damage 88
 Croatia 112
 Ratko Mladić 304–305
 pillage 347
 al-Qaeda 359
 rape as a tactic of war 361
 religious persecution 365
 safe havens 378
 Franjo Tudjman 432–433
 unlawful imprisonment 450
 victims, rights of 455
 war criminals of the former Yugoslavia 465–470
 Yugoslavia 484, 485
Bouhired, Djamila 455
Bourguiba, Habib 434
Bousquet, René **51–52**, 267
Bouteflika, Abdelaziz 11, 43
Bracker, Milton 99
Brandt, Karl **52–53**, 126, 149
Brandt, Karl, et al., United States v. *See* Doctors' Trial
Brauman, Rony 127
Braun, Eva 49, 205
Braunsteiner, Hermine 477

Brazil, human rights violations in **53–54**
Breitman, Richard 205
Britain. *See* Great Britain
Brody, Reed 21
Brossolette, Pierre 37
Brown Shirts 408
Brunner, Alois **55**, 267
Bryant, Charles Gyude 281
Brzezinski, Zbigniew 63
Buchenwald concentration camp *98, 99,* 369, 389
Buddhism 43–44, 83, 350, 351, 458
Buha, Bosko 387–388
Bulgaria, human rights violations in **55**
Bunche, Ralph Johnson **55–56**
Burkina Faso, human rights violations in **56–57**
Burma. *See* Myanmar, human rights violations in
burqas (burkas) 6, 7, 479, *479*
Burundi 364, 374
Burundi, war crimes in **57–58**
Bush, George H. W., and administration 217, 321, 396, 447
Bush, George W., and administration
 act of war 4
 Alien Tort Claims Act 13
 arms, trafficking in and control mechanisms 28
 Colombia 93–94
 combatants, rights of 95
 Darfur 119
 Carla Del Ponte 122
 extraordinary rendition 151
 Guantánamo detainees 179–182
 Saddam al-Tikriti Hussein 218
 ICC 236
 Nepal 316
 OSI 333
 Jose Padilla 338, 339
 Syria 413
 terrorism and international humanitarian law 420, 421
 UNCCR 443
 Vienna Convention on Diplomatic Relations 457
 weapons of mass destruction 474
Butler, Smedley 398

C

Cairo Conference 425
Calley, William 312, 419
Cambodia 174, 365
Cambodia, human rights violations in **59–60**
Cambodia, war crimes in *60,* **60–64**. *See also* Khmer Rouge
 genocide 166
 Ieng Sary 222
 Khieu Samphan 264
 Kiang Kek Iev 264–265
 Nuon Chea 323–324
 Pol Pot 350–352, *351*
 Ta Mok 416
Cambodian Genocide Program (CGP) **64**
Cameroon, human rights violations in **64–65**

Camp Mercury 246
Canaris, Wilhelm 386
capital punishment. *See* death penalty
Carlino, Michael A. 223
Carlos the Jackal 455
Carmi, Israel 320
carpet bombing 65, 85, 88, 178, 240
Carrillo, Ignacio 300
Carter, Jimmy, and administration
 Idi Amin 16
 Cambodia, war crimes in 62–63
 The Carter Center 65, 66
 El Salvador 144
 Haitian human rights violators 193
 Kim Il Sung 266
 Mexico 298
 Refugees International 365
Carter, Rosalynn 65
Carter Center, The **65–66**, 544
Casa Alianza 207
Casalis, Georges 401
Castaño, Carlos 91, 94
Castro, Fidel 19, 132
CAT. *See* Convention against Torture
Catholics 25
Cavallo, Ricardo Miguel **66–67**, 164, 447, 448
CCW. *See* Convention on Prohibitions or Restrictions on the Use of Certain Conventional Weapons
Ceauşescu, Nicolae **67–68**
Cédras, Raoul 191, 193
CEHES. *See* Commission on Human Rights of El Salvador
Central Intelligence Agency (CIA)
 Afghanistan 9
 Chile 78
 CIA war crimes archive 84–85
 extraordinary rendition 151
 ghost prisoners 173
 Guantánamo detainees 180, 182
 Hmong, persecution of 206
 Mobutu Sese Seko 305
 Miguel Nazar Haro 314
 Manuel Noriega 320, 321
 Operation Condor 334
 Phoenix program 345–346
 Augusto Pinochet 348
 al-Qaeda 358
 José Efraín Ríos Montt 368
 Rafael Molino Trujillo 431
Česić, Rajko 466
CGP (Cambodian Genocide Program) **64**
Chad, human rights violations in **68–69**, 189
Chamberlain, Neville 204
Chamblain, Louis Jodel 191, 193–194
Chamorro Cardenal, Pedro Joaquín 397
Chandler, David 62
Chapare region (Bolivia) 48
Chapultepec Peace Accords 143, 144
Charles the Bold (duke of Burgundy) 361, 461

Charter of the Nuremberg International Military Tribunal. *See* Nuremberg Charter
Chechnya 358, 359
Chechnya, war crimes in **69–72**, *70,* 209, 211, 371, 372
chemical weapons *73,* **73–74**
 arms, trafficking in and control mechanisms 27
 Wouter Basson 39
 biological weapons 45, 46
 customary law 116
 Geneva Conventions 165
 Hague Conventions 190
 Halabajah 195
 Saddam al-Tikriti Hussein 217
 IHL 242
 IMI 243
 Kurdistan (Iraq), suppression of 273
 Ali Hassan al-Majid 286
 weapons of mass destruction 474
Chemical Weapons Convention (CWC) 73, 74
Cheney, Dick 182
Chertoff, Michael 181
Chiang Kai-shek 117, 313
child labor 76–78, 77, 155, 243
children
 Albania 10
 Angola 19
 Argentina 22
 Bangladesh 36
 Klaus Barbie 37, 38
 Jean-Bédel Bokassa 47
 Bolivia 48
 René Bousquet 51, 52
 Karl Brandt 52
 Brazil 53, 54
 Alois Brunner 55
 Bulgaria 55
 Ricardo Miguel Cavallo 66
 Nicolae Ceauşescu 67
 Chechnya 72
 civilian immunity 85
 Colombia 92
 Congo, Democratic Republic of the 103
 Jamaica 251
 Jedwabne, massacre in 252
 Joseph Kony 269
 Kosovo 270
 Palestine 341
 Velpke Baby Farm 454
 War Child Project 461
 Simon Wiesenthal 477
children's rights **74–78**, *75, 76*
 Convention on the Rights of the Child 109
 disappearances 125
 Ecuador 137
 India 226
 Mauritania 292
 Sri Lanka 403
 Togo 424
 Uganda 438–439
child soldiers
 Angola 19
 children's rights 75, *75*
 Colombia 92

child soldiers (continued)
Congo, Democratic Republic of the 105
Joseph Kony 269
Myanmar 311–312
Special Court for Sierra Leone 400
Chile, human rights violations in 17, **78–80**, 105–106, 187–188, 313–314, *347*, 347–349. *See also specific headings, e.g.:* Pinochet, Augusto
China
arms, trafficking in and control mechanisms 28
dams and dikes, protection of 117
Deng Xiaoping 222, 474
Jiang Yanyong 253
Kim Il Sung 266
Nanjing (Nanking), massacre in 313
North Korea 322
Pol Pot 351
refugees 364
Sakai Takashi 378–379
China, human rights violations in **80–84**
children's rights 77–78
Doihara Kenji 127–128
germ warfare 172
ICC 236
Ieng Sary 222
Wei Jingsheng 474–475
women's rights, violations of 479
Chittagong Hill Tracts 36
Christians
Armenia 24
Berbers, human rights abuses of 42
Biafra 44
Martin Bormann 49
China 81, 82
Ivory Coast 248
Nigeria 319
Sudan, human rights violations 410
Uganda 438
Vietnam 458
Christmas Island 33
Churchill, Winston 199, 329, 405, 418
CIA. *See* Central Intelligence Agency
CIA war crimes archive **84–85**
Cicek, Cemil 436
civilian immunity **85–86,** 223, 227–228, 240
civilians, death of
Aceh 2
Idi Amin 15
arms, trafficking in and control mechanisms 27, 28
Biafra 45
Bolivia 47–48
Burundi 57
carpet bombing 65
collateral damage 87–88
Colombia 92
Congo (Brazzaville) 102

Convention on the Prohibition of the Use, Stockpiling, Production and Transfer of Anti-Personnel Mines and their Destruction 108
free-fire zones 158
Guatemala 183, 184
Guyana 187
Alfred Jodl 253
Kashmir and Jammu 260
Erich Priebke 352
willful killing 477
Wiranto 478
Yugoslavia 483
civilians, protection of 4, 165, 166, 332, 354–356, 462, 477
civil war
Angola 19
Biafra 44–45
Burundi 57, 58
Cambodia, war crimes in 61
Colombia 90, 93
Congo (Brazzaville) 102
Congo, Democratic Republic of the 102
Guatemala 183
Rwandan human rights violators 375
Civil War (U.S.) 242, 283, 361, 387, 393
Clark, Ramsay **86–87**
Clauberg, Carl **87**
Clinton, Bill, and administration
Stuart Eizenstat 142
extraordinary rendition 151
Guatemala 184
Haitian human rights violators 193
International Commission on Missing Persons 233
Slobodan Milošević 303
No Gun Ri (Korea), massacre in 320
Rwanda, genocide in 374
John Shattuck 390
Wei Jingsheng 475
coca eradication 46, 48, 94
Colby, William 345–346
Cold War 19, 62, 196–197, 213, 305, 405–406
Cole, USS (ship) 359
collateral damage **87–89,** 114, 169, 223, 241, 301, 356
collective punishment **89–90,** 279, 282–283, 341, 380, 420, 463
Colombia, human rights violations in 75–76, **90–95**
Colombian civil war 247
combatants, rights of **95–96,** 115–116, 165–166, 354, 355
Combatant Status Review Tribunals 180, 182
comfort women **96–97,** 360
Commission for Investigation of Violations of Human Rights in East Timor (KPP-HAM) 135–136
Commission of Truth and Friendship (East Timor) 136
Commission on Human Rights of El Salvador (CEHES) 144

Committee to Protect Journalists (CPJ) **97,** 225, 254
Communist Party of Kampuchea (CPK) 60, 61, 222
Comoros, human rights violations in **97**
concentration camps **97–100,** *98.* *See also specific headings, e.g.:* Auschwitz concentration camp
Klaus Barbie 37
Martin Bormann 49
Karl Brandt 52
Alois Brunner 55
collective punishment 89
Doctors' Trial 125–126
Adolf Eichmann 140
ethnic cleansing 148
euthanasia program (Nazi) 150
Final Solution 153, 154
forced labor 155
Hans Frank 157
Wilhelm Frick 159
Walther Funk 162
Gestapo 173
Joseph Goebbels 175
Hermann Göring 177
Reinhard Tristan Heydrich 200
Heinrich Himmler 201–202
Adolf Hitler 204
imprisonment of civilians 224
Izieu, children of 249
Ernst Kaltenbrunner 257
Serge Klarsfeld 267
Erich Koch 268
Josef Kramer 271
Gustav von Bohlen Krupp 272
medical experiments 292
Josef Mengele 294–295
Nokmin (Avengers) 320
Nuremberg Trials 328
Herta Oberheuser 331
OSI 333
Maurice Papon 343
Ante Pavelić 344
pillage 347
Oswald Pohl 350
reparations 366
Joachim von Ribbentrop 368
Rom, persecution of 369
Fritz Sauckel 383
Hjalmar Horace Greeley Schacht 385
Baldur von Schirach 386
Arthur Seyss-Inquart 389
Albert Speer 401
SS 403
Wannsee Conference 460
Yugoslavia 483
Conference on Security and Cooperation in Europe (CSCE) 196, 197
conflict diamonds 18, **100–101,** 105, 174, 392
Congo, Democratic Republic of the, war crimes in **102–105,** *103*
Belgian war crimes tribunal 41
humanitarian aid, barring of 209
humanitarian intervention 211
Leopold II 278
Mobutu Sese Seko 305–307

Sebastian Nzapali 330
Uganda 438
Congo (Brazzaville), human rights violations in **101–102**
Congress, U.S. 276, 297, 306, 366
Conquest, Robert 406
Constant, Emmanuel "Toto" 191, 194
Constitution of the United States of America 129, 420
Conte, Lansana 186
Contreras, Manuel 79, 80, **105–106,** 313, 334, 348, 349
Convention against Torture (CAT) **106–107,** 530–536
Afghanistan 7
Ethiopia 147
extraordinary rendition 151
Geneva Conventions 165
Guantánamo detainees 181
high-value detainees 201
Iran 244
Sebastian Nzapali 330
Augusto Pinochet 348
Rwandan human rights violators 375
torture 426
Uzbekistan 453
Convention against Transnational Organized Crime 28
Convention for the Protection of Human Rights and Fundamental Freedoms **212**
Convention of the Prohibition of the Development, Production, Stockpiling and Use of Chemical Weapons and on Their Destruction. *See* Chemical Weapons Convention
Convention on Prohibitions or Restrictions on the Use of Certain Conventional Weapons (CCW) **107–108,** 355
Convention on the Prevention and Punishment of the Crime of Genocide 278, 525–526
Convention on the Prohibition of the Use, Stockpiling, Production and Transfer of Anti-Personnel Mines and their Destruction **108–109**
Convention on the Rights of the Child 74, 92, **109,** 125, 394, 427
Convention Relating to the Status of Refugees **109–110**
Cook, Robin 24
corporal punishment 77, 463
corporations 12, 13, 458
Council of Europe 212
courts, national 29, 30
CPJ. *See* Committee to Protect Journalists
CPK. *See* Communist Party of Kampuchea
crimes against humanity **110–111**
amnesty 17
Article 3 Common to the Geneva Conventions 29
Belgian war crimes tribunal 41
René Bousquet 51
Alois Brunner 55

Cambodian Genocide Program 64
Chile 78
China 84
Colombia 91
Congo, Democratic Republic of the 104
Convention Relating to the Status of Refugees 109
Darfur 119
deportations 122
Jean-Claude "Baby Doc" Duvalier 133
Adolf Eichmann 140
Hans Frank 157
Wilhelm Frick 159
Hans Fritzsche 159
Walther Funk 161
Balthasar Garzón 163
Gestapo 173
Hermann Göring 178
Guatemala 184
humanitarian intervention 210
Saddam al-Tikriti Hussein 216
ICC 236
ICTY 239
IHL 242
imprisonment of civilians 224
incitement to genocide 225
Indonesia 229
Robert Houghwout Jackson 250
Alfred Jodl 253
Radovan Karadžić 257
Wilhelm Keitel 263
Josef Mengele 295
Mengistu Haile Mariam 296
Theodor Meron 297
Ratko Mladić 305
Nazi Party, Leadership Corps of 315
Konstantin von Neurath 317
Nuon Chea 324
Nuremberg Charter 324
Nuremberg Trials 328
Sebastian Nzapali 330
Maurice Papon 343
rape as a tactic of war 361
Joachim von Ribbentrop 368
José Efaín Ríos Montt 368
Alfred Rosenberg 371
Rwandan human rights violators 375
Sakai Takashi 378
Alvaro Sarvia 383
Hjalmar Horace Greeley Schacht 386
Arthur Seyss-Inquart 390
Special Court for Sierra Leone 399
Julius Streicher 407
Charles Ghankay Taylor 417
Paul Touvier 428
unlawful imprisonment 449
war criminals of Japan 463
war criminals of the former Yugoslavia 465, 469, 470
Wiranto 478
Yugoslavia 484
crimes against peace 9, 110
Crimes of War Project (CWP) 111–112

civilian immunity 85
crimes against humanity 110
forced labor 155
free-fire zones 158
hostages 208
ICC 236
military necessity 301
reprisal 367
United Nations and the Geneva Conventions 441
war crimes, categorization of 462
war dead, treatment of 471
weapons in the conduct of war 472
Cristiani, Alfredo 120
Croatia, human rights violations in 112–113
Arkan (Željko Ražnatović) 24
Bosnia and Herzegovina 49, 50
Dayton accords 120
Carla Del Ponte 122
Ante Gotovina 178–179
Theodor Meron 297
Slobodan Milošević 302, 303
Ante Pavelić 343–334
Vojislav Seselj 388
Franjo Tudjman 112, 120, 121, 303, 432–434, 466, 469, 484, 485
Ustache 451–452
war criminals of the former Yugoslavia 465, 466, 469, 470
Yugoslavia 483–485
Croatian Defense Council (HVO) 483–485
Croatian Democratic Union (HDZ) 433
Croatian Spring 433
CSCE. See Conference on Security and Cooperation in Europe
Cuba 31, 132, 364, 380
Cuba, human rights violations in 113–114, 334
cultural property, protection of 4–5, 114–115, 355–356, 462
customary law 115–116
carpet bombing 65
crimes against humanity 110
deportations 123
IHL 241
reprisal 367
Rwandan human rights violators 375
slavery 394
terrorism and international humanitarian law 420
torture 427
war criminals of the former Yugoslavia 467
war dead, treatment of 471
weapons in the conduct of war 472
weapons of mass destruction 473
willful killing 477–478
CWC. See Chemical Weapons Convention
CWP. See Crimes of War Project
Cyprus 456
Cyprus, human rights violations in 116

Czechoslovakia 200, 204, 282–283, 368, 369

D

Dachau concentration camp 154, 369, 386
Dacko, David 47
Dalai Lama 83
dams and dikes, protection of 117–118
Darfur, war crimes in 118, 118–119
Chad 69
deportations 123
ethnic cleansing ix, 148
genocide 167
humanitarian intervention 210
ICC 236
scorched earth 387
Sudan, human rights violations 410
victims, rights of 455–456
women's rights, violations of 479
D'Aubuisson, Roberto 119–120, 143, 144, 383
Davaks 229
Dayton accords 49, 112, 120–121, 258, 303, 305, 433, 484
death camps 183. See also concentration camps
death penalty 14, 81, 212, 267
Death's Head units 350
death squads
Idi Amin 16
Argentine Anticommunist Alliance 22
Brazil 53
Chile 79
Manuel Contreras 105–106
Roberto D'Aubuisson 119–120
El Salvador 143
extrajudicial killings 150
Final Solution 153
Vladimiro Ilyich Montesinos 307
Déby, Idriss 68, 69, 189
Declaration on the Elimination of Violence Against Women (DEVAW) 479, 480
de Klerk, F. W. 21
de Kock, Eugene 121
Delestraint, Charles 37
Del Ponte, Carla 112, 121–122, 239, 305
del Río, Rita Alejo 94–95
Demajanjuk, John Iwan 333
Democratic Republic of the Congo 75, 75, 364
Deng, Francis 232
Deng Xiaoping 222, 474
Denmark 360
Department of Justice, U.S. 182, 333
deportations 122–123
Armenian genocide 26, 27
Alois Brunner 55
Chechnya 72
Adolf Eichmann 139
Final Solution 152
Imre Finta 154
Hans Frank 157

Indonesia 229
Serge Klarsfeld 267
Erich Koch 268
Nuremberg Trials 329
Maurice Papon 343
Arthur Seyss-Inquart 389
transfer of civilians 430
Wannsee Conference 460
war criminals of the former Yugoslavia 468
Deringil, Selim 26
Deronjić, Miroslav 466–467
desaparecidos 22. See also disappearances
detentions 36, 81, 105, 253, 457
DEVAW. See Declaration on the Elimination of Violence Against Women
Díaz Ordaz, Gustavo 299–300
Dicker, Richard 439
Dieselsstrasse 369
DINA. See National Intelligence Directorate
dirty war(s) 123–124
amnesty 17
Argentina 21–22
Argentine Anticommunist Alliance 22
disappearances 124
extrajudicial killings 150
forensic medicine and human rights 156
IHL 241
mass graves 289
Mexico 298, 300
Mothers of the Plaza de Mayo 309
torture 427
Uruguay 450
Christián von Wernich 475
White Brigades 475, 476
disappearances 124, 124–125
Jorge Eduardo Acosta 3
Algeria 10
amnesty 17
Amnesty International 18
Argentina 22
Belarus 40
Brazil 54
Burundi 58
Cambodia, human rights violations in 59
Ricardo Miguel Cavallo 66
Chechnya 69, 71
Chile 78–80
Colombia 91
Comoros 97
Congo (Brazzaville) 101, 102
Congo, Democratic Republic of the 105
Manuel Contreras 106
Cyprus 116
Ethiopia 147
forensic medicine and human rights 156
Balthasar Garzón 163
Ante Gotovina 179
Guatemala 183
Honduras 207
human rights reports (U.S. State Department) 213

disappearances *(continued)*
Indonesia 228
International Commission on
Missing Persons 233
Iran 244
Ivory Coast 248
Kashmir and Jammu 260
Kim Jong Il 267
Morocco 308
Nepal 315
Nigeria 318
Operation Condor 334
Philippines 344, 345
Physicians for Human Rights
346
José Efaín Ríos Montt 368
Russia 371
Sri Lanka 402–403
Turkey 435
United Nations Working Group
on Enforced or Involuntary
Disappearances 444–445
Uruguay 450
Vietnam 457–458
discrimination 1, 20–21, 54, 77,
479
displaced person camps **125,** 439
Djindjić, Zoran 387, 470
DNA evidence 156
Doctors' Trial 52, **125–126,** 156,
292, 331
Doctors Without Borders
126–127, 209, 234, 439, 455, 544
Doe, Samuel 280, 417
Doihara Kenji **127–128**
domestic abuse 30, 479
Dominican Republic, human rights
violations in **128,** 132, 430–431
Donaldson, Sam 352
Dönitz, Karl 52, **129,** 205, 360
Dostum, Abdul Rashid 7, 8
"Douala 9" 64
Drašković, Vuk 388, 470
Dresden, Germany 65, 88
drugs, war on. *See* war on drugs
drug trafficking (trade)
Albania 10
Colombia 90, 92, 93, 95
Alberto Fujimori 160, 161
Georgia (Republic of) 171
Mexico 299
Manuel Noriega 321
Tokyo Trials 426
dual-use 46, 73
Duarte, José Napoléon 120, 144
Dubrovnik, Croatia 470
Due Obedience Laws 22
due process **129–130**
China 81
Cuba 113
Ethiopia 147
European Convention for the
Protection of Human Rights
149
extrajudicial killings 150
Yaser Esam Hambi 196
Iran 244
Laos 275
Pakistan 339
terrorism and international
humanitarian law 420

Universal Declaration of Human
Rights 445
Yamashita Tomoyuki 482
Dunant, Jean-Henri **130–131,**
165, 234, 242
Duvalier, François "Papa Doc"
131–132, 132, *132,* 191, 192
Duvalier, Jean-Claude "Baby Doc"
132, **132–133,** 192
Dwarkin, Anthony 236, 237

E

Eastern Orthodox Church 382
East Germany 366
East Timor, human rights violations
in **134–136,** *135*
Alien Tort Claims Act 12
genocide 166–167
Indonesia 229–230
religious persecution 366
Suharto 412
Wiranto 478
Ebadi, Shirin 244
Echeverría, Luis 298–300
ECHO. *See* European Community
Humanitarian Organization
Economic Community of West
African States 28
Economic Community of West
African States (ECOWAS)
Monitoring Group. *See* ECOWAS
Monitoring Group
ECOWAS Monitoring Group
(ECOMOG) **136–137,** 280, 392,
400
Ecuador, human rights violations in
137–138
Edward VIII (king of England)
386
Egan, John Patrick 22
Egypt 28, 255, 358, 359, 373
Egypt, human rights violations in
77, **138–139,** 221
Eichmann, Adolf *139,* **139–141**
Martin Bormann 49
Alois Brunner 55
Final Solution 153
Heinrich Müller 310
universal jurisdiction 448
Wannsee Conference 460
Simon Wiesenthal 476
Eicke, Theodor 403
Einsatzgruppen 35, 139, **141,** 153,
199, 204–205, 403, 460
Eisenhower, Dwight D. 99
Eizenstat, Stuart **142**
elections
Afghanistan 6
Armenia 24
Azerbaijan 34
Bahrain, human rights situation
in 35
Bangladesh 36
Belarus 41
Jean-Bédel Bokassa 47
Cambodia, human rights
violations in 59
The Carter Center 66
Alberto Fujimori 160
Georgia (Republic of) 171
Kazakhstan 261, 262

Philippines 344
Ukraine 440
Elkins, Caroline 291
Elliott, H. Wayne 471
El Mozote, massacre in **142–143**
ELN (National Liberation Army)
90, 92
El Salvador, war crimes in 31,
119–120, 142–143, **143–145,**
197–198, 383
embargo 28, 44, 63, 113–114
Emergency Law (Egypt) 138
Enders, Thomas 142
enemy combatants 95, 338–339
England. *See* Great Britain
Entebbe Airport 9, 16
environment 4, 5, 12
Equatorial Guinea, human rights
violations in **145**
Erdogan, Recep Tayyip 436
Eritrea, human rights violations in
145–146, *146,* 147
Escobar, Pablo 307
Estonia 368
Ethiopia 358, 365
Ethiopia, human rights violations in
145, **146–147,** 295–296, 361
ethnic cleansing **147–148**
Arkan (Željko Ražnatović) 24
in Darfur region ix
Dayton accords 120
humanitarian intervention 211
Kosovo 270
rape as a tactic of war 361
Alfredo Strössner 409
Tamil Tigers 423
war criminals of the former
Yugoslavia 468
Yugoslavia 482
ethnic tensions 8, 50
Europe 363
European Community
Humanitarian Organization
(ECHO) **148–149**
European Convention for the
Protection of Human Rights **149,**
165, 285
European Union (EU) 28–29, 116,
148, 424, 433, 435, 436
euthanasia program (Nazi) 52,
149–150
extrajudicial killings **150**
Algeria 11
Alien Tort Claims Act 12
Amnesty International 18
Armenia 24
Bahrain, human rights situation
in 35
Bangladesh 35, 36
Brazil 53, 54
Burkina Faso 56, 57
Burundi 58
Cambodia, human rights
violations in 59
Chad 69
Chechnya 69, 71
Chile 78
Colombia 91
Comoros 97
Congo (Brazzaville) 102
Manuel Contreras 106

Egypt 138
Equatorial Guinea 145
Ethiopia 147
Balthasar Garzón 163
Guatemala 184
Guyana 187
Haiti 192
Honduras 207
human rights reports (U.S. State
Department) 213
Saddam al-Tikriti Hussein 217
India 226, 227
Indonesia 228
Iran 244
Ivory Coast 248
Kashmir and Jammu 260
Kenya 263
Kim Jong Il 267
mass graves 289
Nepal 315
Nigeria 318
Philippines 344
Phoenix program 346
Physicians for Human Rights
346
Alvaro Sarvia 383
Somalia 396
Habib Souaidia 399
Sri Lanka 402
Thailand 421
Truth and Reconciliation
Commission 432
Turkey 435
Uganda 438
Christián von Wernich 475
extraordinary rendition **150–151**
Eyadéma, Gnassingbé 423, 424

F

Falklands War 4, 22, 124, 284
Fallujah, Iraq 90
Falun Gong 82, 83
Farabundo Martí National
Liberation Front (FMLN) 142,
143
FARC. *See* Revolutionary Armed
Forces of Colombia
Fay, George R. 246
FDD. *See* Forces for the Defense
of Democracy
Federenko, Feodor 333
Feldblum, Lea 249
Filartiga, Joel 12
Final Solution (Holocaust)
152–154
Alois Brunner 55
concentration camps *98,* 99–100
Adolf Eichmann 139, 140
ethnic cleansing 148
euthanasia program (Nazi) 150
Wilhelm Frick 158
Genocide Convention 168
Joseph Goebbels 175
Reinhard Tristan Heydrich
199–200
Heinrich Himmler 201–202
Adolf Hitler 204–206
Heinrich Müller 310
Nuremberg Laws 325–326
Rom, persecution of 369
Alfred Rosenberg 371

Stockholm Declaration on Genocide 407
Wilhelm Stuckart 410
Wannsee Conference 460
Simon Wiesenthal 476, 477
Yad Vashem 481
Finta, Imre **154–155**
first use 4, 9, 46
Floyd, Henry 339
Floyd, John 225
FMLN. *See* Farabundo Martí National Liberation Front
Foley, Laurence 359
forced labor **155–156**. *See also* slavery/slave labor
  Cambodia, war crimes in 61, 62
  Human Rights Convention 212
  Erich Koch 268
  Joseph Kony 269
  Robert Ley 279
  Liberia 281
  Libya 282
  Mauritania 292
  Myanmar 312
  Fritz Sauckel 383
  Arthur Seyss-Inquart 389
  slavery 393
  Albert Speer 401
  Telford Taylor 419
  Trafficking Protocol 429
  Uganda 439
  Simon Wiesenthal 476
forced relocation 1, 486–487
Forces for the Defense of Democracy (FDD) (Burundi) 57, 58
Ford, Gerald, and administration 298, 423, 447
Foreign Assistance Act 213
forensic medicine and human rights **156–157**, 233, 289
Fourteenth Amendment 129, 130
Fox, Vicente, and administration 298–300, 314, 476
France. *See also* Vichy France
  amnesty 18
  Armenian genocide 27
  Klaus Barbie 37, 38
  Jean-Bédel Bokassa 47
  René Bousquet 51–52
  Hissene Habré 189
  Ieng Sary 222
  Ivory Coast 247–249
  Izieu, children of 249
  levée en masse 279
  Oradour, massacre in 335
  al-Qaeda 359
  reparations 366
  Joachim von Ribbentrop 368
  Rom, persecution of 369
  Paul Touvier 428
  Jacques Vergès 454–455
Frank, Anne 476
Frank, Hans 99, **157**, 389
Franks, Tommy 41, 447
FRAPH. *See* Revolutionary Front for Haitian Advancement and Progress
Free Aceh Movement (GAM) 2, 3
Freedom House **157–158**, 213, 545

free-fire zones **158**
Frei, Eduardo 79
French and Indian War 14, 45
Fretilin 134
Frick, Wilhelm **158–159**
Fritzsche, Hans **159**, 326
FSLN. *See* Sandinista National Liberation Front
Fujimori, Alberto **159–161**, 307, 391
Funk, Walther **161–162**
Furundzija, Anto 361

G
Gabcik, Josef 200
Gacumbitsi, Sylvestre 375
Gadhafi, Muammar al- 16, 189, 281–282, 381, 417
Galić, Stanislav 382, 467
Galindez, Jesus de 431
Galtieri, Leopoldo 22
GAM. *See* Free Aceh Movement
Garang, John 410
García, Romeo Lucas 184
García-Castellon, Manuel 348
Garzón, Balthasar 66, **163–164**, 169, 188, 348
gas chambers 99, 154, 257, 460
Gaulle, Charles de 335, 343
Gbagbo, Laurent 248, 249
Gehlen, Reinhard 55, 84
Geisel, Ernesto 54
Gemayel, Bashir 377
Gendercide Watch 545
General Framework Agreement for Peace. *See* Dayton accords
Geneva Conventions **164–166**, 361. *See also* Additional Protocols to the Geneva Conventions
  act of war 4
  Additional Protocols to the Geneva Conventions 4
  Afghanistan 8
  Article 3 Common to the Geneva Conventions 29–30
  carpet bombing 65
  civilian immunity 85
  collateral damage 88
  collective punishment 89, 90
  Colombia 91
  combatants, rights of 95
  cultural property, protection of 114
  CWP 111
  dams and dikes, protection of 117
  deportations 122
  disappearances 124
  due process 130
  extrajudicial killings 150
  extraordinary rendition 151
  forced labor 155
  free-fire zones 158
  Geneva Conventions 164–166
  genocide 167
  Genocide Convention 169
  ghost prisoners 173
  Hugo Grotius 179
  Guantánamo detainees 179–182
  humanitarian aid, barring of 209

human shields 215
identification of combatants 221, 222
IHL 240–242
illegal acts 223
immunity from attack 223
indiscriminate attacks 227, 228
internally displaced persons 231
International Humanitarian Fact-Finding Commission 240
Robert Houghwout Jackson 251
journalists, protection of 254
legitimate military targets 276
Lieber Code 283
Martens Clause 289
medical experiments 292
medical personnel, protection of 293
mercenaries 296
military necessity 301
Ratko Mladić 305
nondefended localities 320
Nuremberg Trials 328
occupying power 332
Jose Padilla 338
Phoenix program 346
pillage 346, 347
POWs 353
protected persons 354
Protocol to the Hague Convention of 1954 for the Protection of Cultural Property 356
public property, protection of 356
relative to the protection of civilian persons in time of war 520–524
relative to the treatment of prisoners of war 490–519
reprisal 367
Rwandan human rights violators 375
safe havens 377
scorched earth 387
siege 391
Sierra Leone 393
starvation as a tactic of war 406
terrorism and international humanitarian law 420, 421
torture 427
United Nations and the Geneva Conventions 441
universal jurisdiction 448, 449
victims, rights of 455
war crimes, categorization of 462, 463
war criminals of Japan 464
war criminals of the former Yugoslavia 468
war dead, treatment of 471, 472
Yugoslavia 485
Geneva Protocol to the Hague Convention (1925) 45, 46, 190
Genghis Khan 166
genocide **166–168**. *See also* incitement to genocide
  Jorge Eduardo Acosta 3
  Arkan (Željko Ražnatović) 24
  Article 3 Common to the Geneva Conventions 30

Wouter Basson 39
Belgian war crimes tribunal 41
Karl Brandt 52
Burundi 57, 58
Cambodia, war crimes in 60
Cambodian Genocide Program 64
Ricardo Miguel Cavallo 66, 67
Nicolae Ceaușescu 68
Ramsay Clark 87
Colombia 91
concentration camps 100
Congo, Democratic Republic of the 104
crimes against humanity 110
Darfur 118, 119
Dayton accords 120
deportations 122–123
Final Solution 152, 154
forensic medicine and human rights 156
Freedom House 158
Genocide Convention 168–170
Genocide Watch 170
Guatemala 184
humanitarian intervention 210, 211
ICTY 239
IHL 241, 242
illegal acts 223
International Criminal Tribunal for Rwanda 237, 238
Alfred Jodl 253
Radovan Karadžić 257, 258
Khieu Samphan 264
Raphael Lemkin 277, 278
mass graves 289
Mexico 300
Slobodan Milošević 302
Nuon Chea 324
Nuremberg Trials 326
Ante Pavelić 343
rape as a tactic of war 361
Rwanda, genocide in 373
Rwandan human rights violators 375
John Shattuck 390
Stockholm Declaration on Genocide 407
Ustache 451
war criminals of the former Yugoslavia 466–468, 470
Simon Wiesenthal 476
Yugoslavia 484
Genocide Convention **168–170**
  Darfur 119
  Geneva Conventions 165
  Genocide Watch 170
  incitement to genocide 224
  Rwandan human rights violators 375
  Stockholm Declaration on Genocide 407
  victims, rights of 455
Genocide Watch **170**
George VI (king of Great Britain) 368
Georgia (Republic of), human rights violations in **170–172**
Gerike, Heinrich 454
Gerlach, Christian 205

Germany. *See also* Nazi Germany
Martin Bormann 48–49
Karl Brandt 52–53
carpet bombing 65
Final Solution 152–154
genocide 166
Erich Koch 268
Gustav von Bohlen Krupp 272
League of Nations 276
Raphael Lemkin 277
Nazi Party, Leadership Corps of 315
Oradour, massacre in 335
Franz von Papen 342
Erich Priebke 352
al-Qaeda 359
reparations 366
Joachim von Ribbentrop 368
Rom, persecution of 369
Sant'Anna di Stazzema, massacre in 382
Telford Taylor 418–419
Velpke Baby Farm 454
Kurt Waldheim 459
weapons in the conduct of war 472
germ warfare **172**
Gestapo **172–173**
Klaus Barbie 37
Martin Bormann 49
René Bousquet 51
Karl Brandt 52
concentration camps 99
Adolf Eichmann 139
Final Solution 153
Wilhelm Frick 158
Hermann Göring 177
Reinhard Tristan Heydrich 199
Heinrich Himmler 201–202
Izieu, children of 249
Ernst Kaltenbrunner 257
Wilhelm Keitel 262
Serge Klarsfeld 267, 268
Heinrich Müller 310–311
Nuremberg Trials 327, 329
Erich Priebke 352
SS 403
Paul Touvier 428
Jacques Vergès 455
Simon Wiesenthal 476
Gheorghiu-Dej, Gheorghe 67
ghost prisoners **173**
Glenny, Misha 433
Global IDP Project. *See* Internal Displacement Project
Global Rights **173–174**
Global Sullivan Principles for Corporate Social Responsibility. *See* Sullivan Principles
Global Witness 101, **174**
Glogova, Bosnia 466
Gnassingbé, Faure 423
Goebbels, Joseph 159, **174–176**, *175*, 203, 205, 400
Goldhagen, Daniel J. 205
Goldstone, Richard J. *176*, **176–177**, 219, 470
Gongadze, Georgy 440
Gonzales, Alberto 181
Gorbachev, Mikhail 395
Gordon, Joy 169

Göring, Hermann **177–178**
cultural property, protection of 114
Adolf Eichmann 140
Gestapo 172, 173
Reinhard Tristan Heydrich 199, 200
Adolf Hitler 203
Robert Houghwout Jackson 250, 251
Nuremberg Trials 326, 329
Erich Raeder 360
Alfred Rosenberg 371
Hjalmar Horace Greeley Schacht 385
Julius Streicher 409
Wannsee Conference 460
Gotovina, Ante **178–179**, 297
Gowon, Yakubu "Jack" 44, 45
Grandmothers of the Plaza de Mayo. *See* Mothers of the Plaza de Mayo
Grant, Thomas D. 332
Great Britain 359, 368. *See also* United Kingdom
act of war 4
Idi Amin 15, 16
Anti-Terrorism, Crime and Security Act 20
Armenian genocide 27
Biafra 44
carpet bombing 65
concentration camps 97, 98, 100
displaced person camps 125
Rudolf Hess 198–199
Adolf Hitler 204
Mau Mau uprising 291
Augusto Pinochet 348–349
Erich Raeder 360
reparations 366
weapons in the conduct of war 472
Zimbabwe 486
Great Terror 405
Green, Joyce Hens 180, 182
Gross, Jan 251, 252
Grotius, Hugo **179**, 242, 255
Grozny, Chechnya 69–71, *70*
Guangdong and Hainan, massacre in 379
Guantánamo detainees 20, 95, 173, **179–183**, *180*, 196, 246, 421
Guatemala, human rights violations in *183*, **183–185**
Gueï, Robert 248
Guillermoprieto, Alma 142, 143
Guinea, human rights violations in 76, **185–186**
Gujarat, massacres in **186,** 227
Gul, Abdullah 436
gulag 98–100, **186–187,** 293, 405
The Gulag Archipelago (Solzhenitsyn) 395
Gulf War. *See* Persian Gulf War (1991)
Gusmão, José Alexandre 134
Guterres, Eurico 136
Gutic, Viktor 147
Gutman, Roy 441
Guyana, human rights violations in **187**

Guzmán, Juan 22, 160, **187–188**
Guzmán Reynoso, Abimael 391
Gyanendra (king of Nepal) 316–317
Gypsies. *See* Rom, persecution of

H
Habib, Mamdouh 181
Habibie, Bucharuddin Jusuf 134
Habré, Hissene **189**
Habyariman, Juvenal 373
Hagenbach, Sir Peter von 361, 461–462
Hague, Netherlands, The. *See* International Criminal Court
Hague Conventions **189–190**
crimes against humanity 110
customary law 115
dams and dikes, protection of 117
deportations 123
Hague Conventions 189–190
IHL 241, 242
illegal acts 223
Martens Clause 288–289
nuclear arms and international law 323
Nuremberg Trials 328
Protocol to the Hague Convention of 1954 for the Protection of Cultural Property 356
rape as a tactic of war 361
war crimes, categorization of 462
weapons in the conduct of war 472
Haile Selassie 295
Haiti, human rights violations in 131–133, **190–192,** *191*
Haiti and Haitians 31, 128, 131–133, 364, 365, 431
Haitian human rights violators 131–133, **192–195**
Halabajah (Iraqi Kurdistan) **195,** 217, 273
Halilović, Sefer 467
Hama, massacre in **195**
Hamas 341–342
Hamdi, Yaser Esam **195–196,** 338
Hampson, Françoise 301
Haradinaj, Ramush 467
Hariri, Rafik 413, 414
Hassan II (king of Morocco) 308
Havel, Václav 18
Hazara, persecution of 8, **196**
Health Rights Connection 545
Heder, Stephen 351
Helsinki accords **196–197,** 214, 336
herbicides 73, 88, 94
Hernández Martínez, Maximiliano **197–198**
Hersh, Seymour 312
Herzegovina 361, 364
Hesb' I Islami 359
Hess, Rudolf 48–49, 149, **198–199,** 315, 326, 419
Heydrich, Reinhard Tristan **199–200**
collective punishment 89

Adolf Eichmann 140
Final Solution 153
Hermann Göring 177
Ernst Kaltenbrunner 257
Lidice, massacre in 282
Heinrich Müller 310
Konstantin von Neurath 317
Walter Schellenberg 386
SS 403
Wannsee Conference 460
Hezbollah 100, 101, 359
high-value detainees **200–201**
Hills, Dennis 16
Himmler, Heinrich **201–202**
Adolf Eichmann 139, 140
Hans Frank 157
Wilhelm Frick 159
Walther Funk 162
Gestapo 173
Hermann Göring 177
Reinhard Tristan Heydrich 199
Adolf Hitler 205
Wilhelm Keitel 262
Erich Koch 269
Heinrich Müller 310
Oswald Pohl 350
Alfred Rosenberg 371
Walter Schellenberg 386
Albert Speer 400
SS 403
Hindenburg, Paul von 204, 385
Hindus 186, 260
Hirohito (emperor of Japan) 425, 426
Hiroshima 88, 323
Hitler, Adolf **202–206,** *203*
Armenian genocide 25–27
Martin Bormann 48, 49
Karl Brandt 52
cultural property, protection of 114
Karl Dönitz 129
euthanasia program (Nazi) 149
Final Solution 152, 153
Hans Frank 157
Wilhelm Frick 158, 159
Walther Funk 161
Gestapo 172
Joseph Goebbels 174–176
Hermann Göring 177, 178
Rudolf Hess 198, 199
Reinhard Tristan Heydrich 200
Heinrich Himmler 201, 202
Alfred Jodl 253
Ernst Kaltenbrunner 257
Wilhelm Keitel 262, 263
Erich Koch 268
Gustav von Bohlen Krupp 272
League of Nations 276
Robert Ley 279
Josef Mengele 294
Heinrich Müller 310, 311
Nazi Party, Leadership Corps of 315
Konstantin von Neurath 317
Nuremberg Trials 326
Franz von Papen 342
Erich Raeder 360
Joachim von Ribbentrop 368
Rom, persecution of 369
Alfred Rosenberg 370

Hjalmar Horace Greeley Schacht 385
Walter Schellenberg 386
Baldur von Schirach 386
Arthur Seyss-Inquart 389
Albert Speer 400, 401
SS 403
Joseph Stalin 405
Julius Streicher 407
Wannsee Conference 460
Hitler Youth 386
HIV. *See* AIDS/HIV
Hmong, persecution of **206–207**, 275
Hoffman, Leonard 20
Hoffman, Paul 13
Holbrooke, Richard 120
Holocaust. *See* Final Solution
homosexuality 37, 99, 138, 153
Honduras, human rights violations in **207**
Hong Kong 81, 83
honor killings 254, 339, 479
Horman, Charles 349
hors de combat 5, **208**, 223, 276, 354, 477
hospitals 85, 86, 88, 356
hostages 29, **208–209**, 241, 253, 285, 354, 462, 477
Houphouët-Boigny, Félix 247, 417
house arrest 32, 33
Howard, John 1, 33
humanitarian aid, barring of **209–210**
humanitarian intervention **210–211**
human rights
American Convention on Human Rights 13–14
Peter Benenson 42
Bosnia and Herzegovina 50
Ralph Johnson Bunche 55–56
Burundi 58
The Carter Center 65–66
Chad 69
Chechnya 69, 71, 72
investigation/prosecution of abuses viii
voluntary codes of conduct 458
Luc Walleyn 459–460
Wei Jingsheng 474–475
women's rights, violations of 479
Human Rights Convention (European Union) 20, **212**
Human Rights Internet, The 545–546
Human Rights Library 546
human rights reports (U.S. State Department) **212–214**
Human Rights Watch **214–215**, 215, 546
Afghanistan 7
Ali Hassan al-Majid 286
Angola 19
Louise Arbour 21
Armenia 24
Aung San Suu Kyi 33
Australia 33
Azerbaijan 34
Bangladesh 36
Belarus 40

Bolivia 48
Burundi 57
Cambodia, human rights violations in 59
Ricardo Miguel Cavallo 66
Chechnya 71
children's rights 74, 76
Colombia 91, 94
Croatia 112
Cuba 113
East Timor 136
ECOMOG 137
Egypt 138
Guatemala 184
Guinea 185
Gujarat, massacres in 186
Haiti 192
human shields 215
Saddam al-Tikriti Hussein 218
India 226
Iraq, post-Saddam 245, 246
Jamaica 251
Kazakhstan 262
Kosovo 270
Kyrgyzstan 274
Libya 281
Macedonia 286
Malaysia 287
Mauritania 291–292
Mexico 299
Morocco 308
Myanmar 312
Nepal 316
Nigeria 318, 319
North Korea 321
Pakistan 339
Somalia 396
Sri Lanka 403
Thailand 422
Togo 424
Turkey 435
Uganda 439
UNCCR 443
Uzbekistan 452
human shields 208, **215–216**, 227, 258, 354
human trafficking. *See* trafficking in persons
Hungary 369
Hun Sen 59, 62, 63, 324, 351, 416
Hussein (king of Jordan) 253, 254
Hussein, Qusay 218
Hussein, Saddam al-Tikriti **216–220**, 217
Ramsay Clark 86
Genocide Convention 169
Halabajah 195
humanitarian intervention 211
human shields 215, 216
Iraq, post-Saddam 245
Kurdistan (Iraq), suppression of 273
legitimate military targets 277
Ali Hassan al-Majid 286
occupying power 332
safe havens 378
sanctions 379
Syria 413
Jacques Vergès 454
war dead, treatment of 472
weapons of mass destruction 474

Hussein, Uday 218
Huto 362
Hutus
arms, trafficking in and control mechanisms 28
Burundi 57, 58
Congo, Democratic Republic of the 104
ethnic cleansing 148
Genocide Convention 169
identification of combatants 222
incitement to genocide 225
International Criminal Tribunal for Rwanda 237, 238
Rwanda, genocide in 372, 373
war crimes, categorization of 462
HVO. *See* Croatian Defense Council

I

IACHR. *See* Inter-American Court of Human Rights
IANSA (International Action Network on Small Arms) **233**
Ibrahim, Ashraf **221**
Ibrahim, Saad Eddin 138
ICC. *See* International Criminal Court
ICCPR. *See* International Covenant on Civil and Political Rights
ICJ. *See* International Court of Justice
ICRC. *See* International Committee of the Red Cross
ICTR. *See* International Criminal Tribunal for Rwanda
ICTY. *See* International Criminal Tribunal for the former Yugoslavia
identification of combatants **221–222**
IDF. *See* Israeli Defense Force
Ieng Sary 63, **222–223**, 351
IHL. *See* international humanitarian law
illegal acts **223**
ILO. *See* International Labor Organization
Immigration and Naturalization Service (INS) 194
immunity 58, 79, 80, 85–86, 111
immunity from attack **223–224**
imprisonment of civilians **224**
impunity 17, 26, 36, 53, 102
IMTFE. *See* Tokyo Trials
incitement to genocide **224–225**, 238
India 259–261, 358
India, human rights violations in 77, 78, 186, **225–227**, 365–366, 479
indiscriminate attacks 85, 87, 88, **227–228**, 241, 354
Indonesia 38–39, 359
Indonesia, human rights violations in 2–3, 134–136, **228–230**, 366, 412, 478. *See also* Aceh, war crimes in; Suharto
Indonesian Commission for Disappearances and Victims of Violence (KONTRAS) 228

INS. *See* Immigration and Naturalization Service
Instructions for the Government of the Armies of the United States in the Field. *See* Lieber Code
insurgency 41, 269, 345
Inter-American Court of Human Rights (IACHR) 14, **230**, 336
internal conflict 29, 30, 42, 46, 165, 477
Internal Displacement Project **230–231**
internally displaced persons 231, **231–233**
Internal Displacement Project 230–231
refugees 364
safe havens 378
Somalia 396
transfer of civilians 430
UNCCR 443
United Nations Guiding Principles on Internal Displacement 441–442
victims, rights of 455
women's rights, violations of 479
International Action Network on Small Arms (IANSA) **233**
International Commission on Missing Persons **233**, 546–547
International Committee of the Red Cross (ICRC) **234**, 547
Afghanistan 8
Angola 19
arms, trafficking in and control mechanisms 27
Article 3 Common to the Geneva Conventions 29
China 82
civilian immunity 85
collective punishment 89
combatants, rights of 95
Doctors Without Borders 127
Jean-Henri Dunant 130, 131
Eritrea 146
Geneva Conventions 165
ghost prisoners 173
Guantánamo detainees 180
hors de combat 208
hostages 208
humanitarian aid, barring of 209
identification of combatants 221
IHL 241, 242
internally displaced persons 232
Iraq, post-Saddam 246
mass graves 289
POWs 353
public property, protection of 356
refoulement 362
Sabra and Shatilla, massacre in 377
starvation as a tactic of war 406
terrorism and international humanitarian law 420–421
Turkmenistan 436
United Nations and the Geneva Conventions 441
unlawful imprisonment 450
victims, rights of 455
war dead, treatment of 471, 472

International Convention on the Prevention and Punishment of the Crime of Genocide. *See* Genocide Convention
International Court of Justice (ICJ) **234–235**
  amnesty 17
  Amnesty International 18
  Belgian war crimes tribunal 41
  Ramsay Clark 87
  military necessity 301
  nuclear arms and international law 323
  Palestine 341
  Vienna Convention on Diplomatic Relations 457
International Covenant on Civil and Political Rights (ICCPR) 130, 155, **235**, 394, 426
International Criminal Court (ICC) **235–237**, 546. *See also* Rome Statute of the International Criminal Court
  Afghanistan 7
  Belgian war crimes tribunal 41
  Congo, Democratic Republic of the 105
  Darfur 119
  Genocide Convention 170
  Juan Guzmán 188
  Saddam al-Tikriti Hussein 219
  IHL 242
  imprisonment of civilians 224
  Ivory Coast 248
  Nuremberg Charter 325
  protected persons 354
  public property, protection of 356
  rape as a tactic of war 361
  Rome Statute of the International Criminal Court 370
  Uganda 439
  universal jurisdiction 447–449
  victims, rights of 456
  Victims Trust Fund 456
  Luc Walleyn 459
  war crimes, categorization of 462
International Criminal Tribunal for Rwanda (ICTR) **237–238**
  Carla Del Ponte 122
  forensic medicine and human rights 156
  Genocide Convention 170
  Richard J. Goldstone 176
  IHL 242
  incitement to genocide 225
  Nuremberg Charter 325
  Rome Statute of the International Criminal Court 370
  Rwandan human rights violators 375
  war crimes, categorization of 463
International Criminal Tribunal for the former Yugoslavia (ICTY) **238–240**, 546
  Louise Arbour 21
  Arkan (Želiko Ražnatović) 24

Bosnia and Herzegovina 51
Croatia 112
cultural property 114–115
customary law 116
Carla Del Ponte 121, 122
due process 130
extrajudicial killings 150
forensic medicine and human rights 156
Genocide Convention 170
Richard J. Goldstone 176
Ante Gotovina 178, 179
hostages 208
IHL 242
IMI 243
Radovan Karadžić 259
Kosovo 271
Theodor Meron 297
Slobodan Milošević 303
Ratko Mladić 305
Nuremberg Charter 325
rape as a tactic of war 361
Rome Statute of the International Criminal Court 370
Serbia 387
Vojislav Seselj 388
siege 392
Srebrenica, massacre in 402
universal jurisdiction 447
unlawful imprisonment 449
victims, rights of 455
war crimes, categorization of 463
war criminals of the former Yugoslavia 465–470
willful killing 477–478
Yugoslavia 484, 485
International Humanitarian Fact-Finding Commission **240**, 547
international humanitarian law (IHL) viii, **240–242**
  customary law 115
  CWP 111
  dams and dikes, protection of 117
  deportations 122
  disappearances 124
  Ethiopia 147
  Final Solution 154
  forced labor 155
  free-fire zones 158
  Geneva Conventions 165
  Guantánamo detainees 181
  ICRC 234
  ICTY 238
  identification of combatants 221
  immunity from attack 223
  internally displaced persons 231
  International Criminal Tribunal for Rwanda 237
  International Humanitarian Fact-Finding Commission 240
  Robert Houghwout Jackson 250
  journalists, protection of 254
  Kosovo 270
  legitimate military targets 276
  limited war 283
  mass graves 289
  medical personnel, protection of 293

mercenaries 296
military necessity 300–301
nuclear arms and international law 323
Nuremberg Trials 326
Palestine 341
POWs 353
protected persons 354
public property, protection of 356
religious persecution 365
reprisal 367
siege 391
starvation as a tactic of war 406
Stockholm Declaration on Genocide 407
Charles Ghankay Taylor 417
terrorism and international humanitarian law 420, 421
torture 426
total war 427–428
transfer of civilians 430
United Nations and the Geneva Conventions 441
unlawful imprisonment 449
victims, rights of 456
war crimes, categorization of 461, 462
International Labor Organization (ILO) 77, 155, **242–243**, 276, 393, 547
international law. *See also* international humanitarian law
  act of war 3
  Additional Protocols to the Geneva Conventions 4
  Alien Tort Claims Act 13
  arms, trafficking in and control mechanisms 27
  belligerent status 41, 42
  carpet bombing 65
  civilian immunity 85–86
  collateral damage 87–88
  collective punishment 89
  Colombia 92
  crimes against humanity 110
  Genocide Convention 168
  Hugo Grotius 179
  pillage 346, 347
  reprisal 367
  victims, rights of 455
  war dead, treatment of 472
International Military Tribunal at Nuremberg. *See* Nuremberg Trials
International Military Tribunal for the Far East. *See* Tokyo Trials
International Monitor Institute **243**
International Physicians for the Prevention of Nuclear War (IPPNW) 547
interrogation techniques 8, 181, 182
IPPNW (International Physicians for the Prevention of Nuclear War) 547
IRA (Irish Republican Army) 285
Iran 217
Iran, human rights violations in **243–245**, 273

Iranian hostage crisis 285
Iranian Revolution (1979) 243
Iran-Iraq war 73, 195, 217, 243
Iraq, human rights violations in post-Saddam **245–247**, 297. *See also* Abu Ghraib prison
Iraq and Iraqis. *See also specific headings, e.g.:* Hussein, Saddam al-Tikriti
  arms, trafficking in and control mechanisms 28
  asylum, political 31
  Australia 33
  biological weapons 46
  carpet bombing 65
  civilian immunity 85
  Ramsay Clark 86, 87
  Halabajah 195
  immunity from attack 223
  Kurdistan (Iraq), suppression of 273
  Ali Hassan al-Majid 286
  mass graves 289
  occupying power 332
  al-Qaeda 359
  refugees 364
  sanctions 379, 380
  Sérgio Vieira de Mello 456, 457
  war dead, treatment of 472
Iraq War (1991). *See* Persian Gulf War (1991)
Iraq War (2003)
  collateral damage 88
  collective punishment 90
  cultural property, protection of 114, 115
  humanitarian intervention 211
  human shields 215–216
  Saddam al-Tikriti Hussein 218
  Iraq, post-Saddam 245
  journalists, protection of 254, 255
  Kurdistan (Iraq), suppression of 273
  legitimate military targets 276
  Ali Hassan al-Majid 286
  mercenaries 297
  weapons of mass destruction 474
Irish Republican Army (IRA) 285
irregulars **247**
Irving, David 205
Isayama Harukei 464
Ishii, Chujo Shiro 287–288
Islam 39, 70, 358. *See also* Muslims
Islamic fundamentalists and militants
  Bangladesh 36
  Abu Bakar Bashir 39
  Berbers, human rights abuses of 43
  Iran 243, 244
  Jemaah Islamiyah 252
  Malaysia 286–287
  Mullah Omar 309, 310
  Nigeria 318–319
  Saudi Arabia 383
  Uzbekistan 452
Islamic insurgency 10, 11, 345
Islamic Jihad 341, 359

Islamic law. *See* sharia
Israel
   aggression 9
   Idi Amin 15
   Belgian war crimes tribunal 41
   Ralph Johnson Bunche 56
   civilian immunity 85
   collective punishment 89
   displaced person camps 125
   human shields 215
   Saddam al-Tikriti Hussein 217
   just and unjust wars 255
   Palestine 340–342
   al-Qaeda 359
   UNCCR 443
   Luc Walleyn 459
   Yad Vashem 481
Israeli Defense Force (IDF) 89,
   90, 215, 340, 341, 377
Israeli War of Independence (1948)
   123
Istanbul synagogue bombing 359
Italy 204, 352, 368, 369, 381–382
Ivory Coast, human rights violations
   in **247–249**
Izetbegovic, Alija 120, 121, 303,
   484
Izieu, children of 55, **249**
Izméry, Antoine 193–194

J
Jackson, Jesse 393
Jackson, Robert Houghwout *250,*
   250–251, 278, 418
Jamaica, human rights violations in
   251
Janjaweed 118, 119, 148
Janković, Gojko 467
Japan
   China 83–84
   comfort women 96–97
   Doihara Kenji 127–128
   germ warfare 172
   Adolf Hitler 204
   Manchuria, Japanese war crimes
      in 287–288
   Matsui Iwane 290
   Matsuoka Yosuke 290
   medical experiments 292–293
   Nanjing (Nanking), massacre in
      313
   Okawa Shumei 333–334
   reparations 366
   Joachim von Ribbentrop 368
   Sakai Takashi 378–379
   Shimada Shigetaro 390–391
   Tojo Hideki 424–425
   Tokyo Trials 425–426
   war criminals of Japan
      463–465
   Yamashita Tomoyuki 481–482
JDC. *See* Jewish Documentation
   Center
Jedwabne, massacre in **251–252**
Jehovah's Witnesses 171, 372
Jelisić, Goran 467–468
Jemaah Islamiyah (JI) 39, 229,
   252, 359
Jewish Documentation Center
   (JDC) 476, 477
Jewish Question 371

Jews, persecution of
   Babi Yar 35
   Klaus Barbie 37, 38
   Martin Bormann 49
   René Bousquet 52
   Alois Brunner 55
   concentration camps 99–100
   displaced person camps 125
   Adolf Eichmann 139, 140
   Einsatzgruppen 141
   Stuart Eizenstat 142
   ethnic cleansing 148
   euthanasia program (Nazi) 150
   Final Solution 152–154
   Imre Finta 154
   Hans Frank 157
   Walther Funk 162
   genocide 166
   Genocide Convention 168
   Gestapo 173
   Joseph Goebbels 175
   Hermann Göring 177–176
   Reinhard Tristan Heydrich
      199–200
   Heinrich Himmler 201–202
   Adolf Hitler 203, 204
   Izieu, children of 249
   Jedwabne, massacre in 251–252
   Serge Klarsfeld 267, 268
   Nokmin 320
   Nuremberg Laws 325–326
   Maurice Papon 343
   Ante Pavelić 343, 344
   pillage 347
   pogrom 349–350
   Oswald Pohl 350
   Erich Priebke 352
   Anthony Sawoniuk 385
   Hjalmar Horace Greeley Schacht
      385
   Arthur Seyss-Inquart 389–390
   Julius Streicher 407–409
   Wilhelm Stuckart 410
   Wannsee Conference 460, 461
   Simon Wiesenthal 476–447
   Yad Vashem 481
Jiang Yanyong **253**
Jiang Zemin 475
Jodl, Alfred **253**
Johnson, Lyndon 86
Johnson, Prince 280
Jokić, Dragan 466
Jones, Anthony R. 246
Jones, Sidney 229
Jordan, human rights violations in
   253–254, *254,* 359
Jordan, Steven L. 246
journalists 262, 345, 349, 486
journalists, protection of **254–255.**
   See also Committee to Protect
   Journalists
just and unjust wars **255–256**
Justice Department, U.S. 179, 180,
   338, 420, 429

K
Kabbah, Ahmed Tejan 381, 392
Kabila, Joseph 103, 104
Kabila, Laurent 306
Kabul, Afghanistan 6
Kadyrov, Akmad 71, 72

Kagame, Paul 374
Kahn, Irene 21
Kalimantan 229
Kalshoven, Frits 367
Kaltenbrunner, Ernst **257,** 389
Kambanda, Jean 238, 375
Kappler, Herbert 352
Karadžić, Radovan **257–259**
   Bosnia and Herzegovina 51
   Ramsay Clark 86, 87
   hostages 208
   Theodor Meron 297
   Ratko Mladić 304
   war criminals of the former
      Yugoslavia 465, 467, 468
   Yugoslavia 482, 484
Karimov, Islam 452, 453
Karpinski, Janis L. 246
Karzai, Hamid 6, 296, 415
Kashmir and Jammu, human rights
   violations in 226, **259–261**
Katyn Forest, massacre in **261**
Kazakhstan, human rights violations
   in **261–262**
Keenan, Joseph 425
Keitel, Wilhelm 253, **262–263,**
   326
Keith, Sir Kenneth 240
Keller, Allen 31
Kemal, Mustafa 26
Kemal, Yasar 435–436
Kenya, human rights violations in
   263–264, 291, 317–318, 359
Kenyatta, Jomo 317
KGB 395, 405
Khalid, Shazia 340
Khamenei, Ayatollah Seyyed Ali
   243
Khatami, Mohammed 244
Khieu Samphan 60, 222, **264,** 416
Khmer Rouge
   Cambodia, human rights
      violations in 59
   Cambodia, war crimes in 60–63
   Cambodian Genocide Program
      64
   Global Witness 174
   Ieng Sary 222
   Khieu Samphan 264
   Kiang Kek Iev 264–265
   Nuon Chea 323–324
   Pol Pot 350–352, *351*
   Ta Mok 416
   war crimes, categorization of
      462
Khobar Towers bombing (Saudi
   Arabia) 359
Khomeini, Ayatollah Ruholla
   Mussaui 217
Khrushchev, Nikita 406
Kiang Kek Iev **264–265**
kidnapping 66, 92, 94
Kiernan, Ben 64
Kiev, Ukraine 35
"killing fields" 351
Kimberly Process 101, 174
Kim Dae-jung 18
Kim Il Sung 67, 68, **265–266,** 266,
   321
Kim Jong Il 266, **266–267,** 321
Kimura Heitaro 464

Kirchner, Nestor 22
Kirov, Sergey *404*
Kirsch, Philippe 236
Kissinger, Henry 164, 213,
   447–449
KLA (Kosovo Liberation Army)
   303
Klarsfeld, Beate 38, *267*
Klarsfeld, Serge 38, 51–52, *267,*
   267–268
Koch, Erich **268–269,** 371
Kocharian, Robert 24
Köchler, Hans 380
Kodoha movement 333
KONTRAS (Indonesian
   Commission for Disappearances
   and Victims of Violence) 228
Kony, Joseph 237, **269–270,** 438,
   439
Korea 96–97, 360, 464
Korea, North. *See* North Korea,
   human rights violations in
Korea, South. *See* South Korea
Korean War 4, 284, 319–320
Kosovo
   Arkan (Željko Ražnatović) 24
   dams and dikes, protection of
      117
   humanitarian intervention 211
   International Commission on
      Missing Persons 233
   Macedonia 285
   Slobodan Milošević 301–303
   al-Qaeda 358
   Rom, persecution of 369
Kosovo, war crimes in **270–271**
   Arkan (Željko Ražnatović) 24
   Carla Del Ponte 122
   ethnic cleansing 147
   International Commission on
      Missing Persons 233
   Slobodan Milošević 301–302
   pillage 347
   religious persecution 365
   Vojislav Seselj 388
   war criminals of the former
      Yugoslavia 465, 467, 468, 470
   Yugoslavia 482, 484
Kosovo Liberation Army (KLA)
   303
Koštunica, Vojislav 303
Kovner, Abba 320
KPP-HAM. *See* Commission for
   Investigation of Violations of
   Human Rights in East Timor
Krajisnik, Momcilo 468
Kramer, Josef **271–272**
Kristallnacht (Night of Broken
   Glass) 153, 162, 204, 350, 360
Krstic, Radislav 468
Krupp, Alfried 385
Krupp, Gustav von Bohlen **272,**
   326, 342, 385, 419
Kubis, Jan 200
Kuchma, Leonid 440
Kurdish Workers Party (PKK) 435
Kurdistan (Iraq), suppression of
   272–273
   chemical weapons 73
   civilian immunity 85
   Halabajah 195

Kurdistan (Iraq), suppression of (*continued*)
　Saddam al-Tikriti Hussein 217, 218
　Iran 243, 244
　limited war 283
　Ali Hassan al-Majid 286
　safe havens 378
Kurds 413, 435–436
Kuwait 9, 123, 217, 286, 347, 359
Kwasniewski, Aleksander 252
Kyrgyzstan, human rights violations in 273–274

L

labor, bonded. *See* bonded labor
labor, child. *See* child labor
labor, forced. *See* forced labor
labor, slave. *See* slavery/slave labor
labor rights 82, 242–243, 279
Lacalle, Luis 450
Lakwena, Alice 269
land mines 51, 59, 108, 355. *See also* Anti-Personnel Mine Ban Convention
language (Berber) 42, 43
Laos, human rights violations in 206, **275**
Las Dos Erres massacre 184, 185
Laskov, Chaim 320
Latin America. *See also* Organization of American States; *specific headings, e.g.:* Argentina, human rights violations in
　arms, trafficking in and control mechanisms 29
　children's rights 77
　dirty war 123–124
　forensic medicine and human rights 156
　Inter-American Court of Human Rights 230
　OAS 336
　Operation Condor 334–335
　Shining Path 391
　Alfredo Strössner 409
Latortue, Gérard 192
Latvia 368
Lavalas Party 192
Lawal, Amina 173, 319
Law for the Protection of Hereditary Health: The Attempt to Improve the German Aryan Breed, July 14, 1933 541
Lawyers Without Borders (ASF) **275**, 459, 547
Lazarevic, Vladimir 468–469
League of Nations **275–276**, 277, 290, 394, 443
Lebanon 377, 413–414
lebensraum 370, 371
Leeson, Bill 461
Lefebvre, Marcel 428
Legija. *See* Ulemek, Milorad
legitimate military targets **276–277**
Leighton, Bernardo 334
Lemkin, Raphael **277–278**
Lenin, Vladimir 404
Leopold II (king of the Belgians) 278, **278–279**

Letelier, Orlando 334, 348, 349
letter-writing campaigns 18, 19
levée en masse **279**
Lewis, Bernard 26
Ley, Robert **279**, 326
Liberation of Angola (FNLA) 19
Liberation Tigers of Tamil Eelam (LTTE). *See* Tigers, Tamil
Liberia 185, 365
Liberia, human rights violations in 137, **279–281**, 361, 381, 417–418. *See also* Taylor, Charles Ghankay
Liberians United for Reconciliation and Democracy (LURD) 185, 280–281, 417
Libya 16, 189, 364, 381, 443. *See also* Gadhafi, Muammar al-
Libya, human rights violations in **281–282**
Lidice, massacre in 89, **282–283**
Lie, Trygve 56
Lieber, Francis 283, 361
Lieber Code 114, 242, **283**, 361, 393, 462
limited war **283–284**, 427
Lincoln, Abraham 283, 361, 393
Li Peng 12
Lithuania 368
Lome Peace Accords 393
Lona Reyes, Arturo 298–299
London Charter viii
Lon Nol 61
López Rega, José **284**
Lord's Resistance Army (LRA) 75, 237, 269, 438, 439
Lozada, Sánchez de 47
LRA. *See* Lord's Resistance Army
LTTE. *See* Tigers, Tamil
Lucas Garcia, Romeo 369
Ludendorff, Erich 203
Luftwaffe 177, 178, 360
Luka camp 467
Lukashenko, Alexander 39–41
Lula da Silva, Luiz Inácio 53, 54
Lumumba, Patrice 305
LURD. *See* Liberians United for Reconciliation and Democracy
Lyon, France 37, 38

M

MacArthur, Douglas 426
Macbride, Sean 18, **285**
Macedonia, human rights violations in 239, **285–286**
Mackay, Hugh 2
Madrid, Miguel de la 299
Madrid commuter train bombings 359
Madurese 229
Maguire, Sean 208
Mahathir bin Mohamad 286
Mahrzan 369
Mai, Mukhtar 340
Majid, Ali Hassan al- 195, **286**
Malaysia, human rights violations in **286–287**
Mali 29
Manchuria, Japanese war crimes in 128, **287–288**, 290, 293
Mandela, Nelson 21, 40, 413, 432, 437

Manipur 226–227
Mant, Keith 156
Maoists 315–317, 323, 391
Marcos, Ferdinand 12
Marines, U.S. 398, 463
Mars, Jean Price 131
Martens, Friedrich von 288
Martens Clause 115–116, **288–289**
Martić, Milan 469
Mašović, Amor 468
massacres. *See also* genocide; *specific headings, e.g.:* Srebrenica, massacre in
　Aceh 2, 3
　Algeria 10
　Armenian genocide 25–27, 110, 153, 169
　arms, trafficking in and control mechanisms 28
　Babi Yar 35, 141
　Biafra 44
　Jean-Bédel Bokassa 47
　Burundi 57, 58
　Chechnya 72
　Colombia 92, 95
　Congo, Democratic Republic of the 104
　Darfur 119
　Guatemala 184, 185
　Radovan Karadžić 258
　Erich Priebke 352
　Luc Walleyn 459
　war criminals of the former Yugoslavia 466, 468, 469
　Yugoslavia 483, 484
Massera, Emilio 22
mass graves 7–8, 261, **289–290**, 346, 465, 484
Matamoros, Víctor 94
Matsui Iwane **290**, 313
Matsuoka Yosuke **290–291**
Mau Mau uprising **291**
Mauritania, human rights violations in **291–292**
Mauthausen 389
Maya 183, 368
Mazar-i-Sharif 196
McCarthy, Joseph 419
McClellan, George 283
McKay, Fiona 219
Meakić, Željko 469
Médecins Sans Frontières (MSF). *See* Doctors Without Borders
Medellín, José Ernesto 457
media 36, 40, 44, 50–51, 262. *See also* journalists; radio; television
medical experiments **292–293**
　Karl Brandt 52
　Carl Clauberg 87
　Doctors' Trial 126
　Manchuria, Japanese war crimes in 287–288
　Josef Mengele 126, 294, *294*, **294–295**, 333, 409
　Nuremberg Trials 329
　Herta Oberheuser 331
　Office of Special Investigations 333
　protected persons 354
　Telford Taylor 418, 419

Tojo Hideki 424
　war crimes, categorization of 462
medical personnel, protection of 85, 165, **293**, 356
Medina, Ernest 312
Megawati Sukarnoputri 228, 229
Mein Kampf (Hitler) 149, 152, 198, 203, 371, 460
Memorial 71, 72, **293–294**
Menem, Carlos 22
Mengele, Josef 126, 294, **294–295**, 333, 409
Mengistu Haile Mariam 145, 146, **295–296**
mercenaries 247, **296–297**, 306
"mercy deaths" 52
Meron, Theodor 116, **297–298**
Mesa, Carlos 47, 48
Mesić, Stepjan 112
Mexico, human rights violations in **298–300**
　Alien Tort Claims Act 12–13
　Ricardo Miguel Cavallo 66, 67
　children's rights 77
　Chile 79
　Miguel Nazar Haro 314–315
　Vienna Convention on Diplomatic Relations 457
　White Brigades 475–476
Milford, Canon T. R. 337
military necessity **300–301**, 356
militias 102, 105
Milošević, Slobodan **301–304**, *302*
　Louise Arbour 21
　Bosnia and Herzegovina 51
　Ramsay Clark 87
　crimes against humanity 111
　Dayton accords 120, 121
　Carla Del Ponte 122
　due process 130
　Genocide Convention 169
　ICTY 238, 239
　Radovan Karadžić 258
　Kosovo 270
　Ratko Mladić 305
　Serbia 387
　Vojislav Seselj 388
　Franjo Tudjman 433
　universal jurisdiction 447
　Jacques Vergès 454
　war criminals of the former Yugoslavia 465, 466, 469, 470
　Yugoslavia 482, 484
Milutinović, Milan 21
Minami Jiro 464
Mindanao, Philippines 345
mines (land). *See* land mines
MINUSTAH (United Nations Stabilization Mission in Haiti) 192
Mirabel, Minerva and Maria Teresa 431
Mitrione, Dan 451
Mitterrand, François 52
Mladić, Ratko **304–305**
　Bosnia and Herzegovina 51
　hostages 208
　Radovan Karadžić 258, 259
　Theodor Meron 297
　Serbia 387

war criminals of the former
Yugoslavia 465, 467–469
Yugoslavia 484
MLN. *See* Tupamaro National
Liberation Movement
Mobutu Sese Seko 103, 104,
305–307, *306*, 330
Modagishu, Somalia 472
Mohamed VI (king of Morocco)
43, 308
Moi, Daniel arap 318
Molotov, Vyacheslav 368, 406
Moluccas 229
Mommsen, Hans 205
Montagnards 458
Monteneros 22–23
Montesinos, Vladimiro Ilyich 160,
161, **307**
Morales, Evo 48
Moreno-Ocampo, Luis 439
Morocco, human rights violations in
42, 43, **308–309**, 359
Morris, Christopher 4
Mortan, Sue 365
Moscow 371
Moscow Conference 425
Mossad 140
Mothers of the Plaza de Mayo 125,
309
Moulin, Jean 37
Movement for Democratic Change
486
Mozambique 75, 76, 456
MPLA (Popular Movement for the
Liberation of Angola) 19
MSF. *See* Doctors Without Borders
Mubarak, Hosni 138, 358
Mueller, Cyla 476
Mugabe, Robert 12, 486
mujahideen 358, 415
Mukden Incident 128
Mullah Omar **309–310**, 358, 359,
415
Müller, Heinrich 173, **310–311**
Mungoven, Roy 443
Munich Beer Hall Putsch 203,
370–371
Murray, Gilbert 337
museums 114, 347, 356, 481
Museveni, Yoweri 331, 332, 438,
439
Musharraf, Pervez 339, 340
Muslims
Aceh 2
Algeria 10
Arkan (Željko Ražnatović) 24
Armenia 24
Armenian genocide 25
Bahrain, human rights situation
in 35
Bangladesh 36
Berbers, human rights abuses of
42
Biafra 44
Bosnia and Herzegovina 49, 50
Bosnian Muslims 147, 239, 305,
382, 402
Chechnya 69
China 83
ethnic cleansing 147
Guantánamo detainees 181

Gujarat, massacres in 186
Hama, massacre in 195
ICTY 239
India 227
Ivory Coast 248
Radovan Karadžić 258, 259
Kashmir and Jammu 260
Macedonia 285, 286
Slobodan Milošević 303
Ratko Mladić 305
Morocco 308
Nigeria 318–319
Pakistan 339
Philippines 344
Sarajevo, siege of 382
Shiite 35, 196, 218, 244, 339,
383
Srebrenca, massacre in 402
Sudan, human rights violations
410
Sunni 35, 195, 273, 339, 415,
436
Taliban 415
Thailand 421, 422
Turkey 435
war criminals of the former
Yugoslavia 465–470
Yugoslavia 482–485
Myanmar, human rights violations
in 31–33, 75, 215, **311–312**, 361,
464–465
My Lai massacre **312**, 422

N

Nablus 89
Nagano Osami 464
Nagasaki 88, 323
Nagorno-Karabakh 24, 34
Nahimana, Ferdinand 225
Nanjing (Nanking), massacre in
290, **313**, 360, 426
Napoleon Bonaparte 279
Napoleonic Wars 366, 387
National Center for Human Rights
Education 547–548
National Human Rights
Commission (NHRC) 226
National Intelligence Directorate
(DINA) 79, 80, 105–106,
313–314, 334, 348
National Intelligence Service (SIN)
160, 161
Nationalist Republican Alliance
(ARENA) 120, 143, 144
National League for Democracy
(NLD) (Myamar) 32, 33
National Socialist German Workers
Party (NSDAP) 368, 370
National Union for the Total
Independence of Angola (UNITA)
19, 100
Native Americans 14, 147
NATO. *See* North Atlantic Treaty
Organization
Nauru 33, 362
Navy Mechanics School (Argentina)
3, 22, 66
Naxalites 226
Nazarbayev, Nursultan Abish-uly
261
Nazar Haro, Miguel 300, **314–315**

Nazi Germany. *See also* Final
Solution; Gestapo; *specific
headings, e.g.:* Hitler, Adolf
Babi Yar 35
Klaus Barbie 36–38
Martin Bormann 48–49
Karl Brandt 52
Alois Brunner 55
CIA war crimes archive 84
Carl Clauberg 87
collective punishment 89
concentration camps 98–100
deportations 123
Doctors' Trial 125–126
Karl Dönitz 129
Adolf Eichmann 139–141
Einsatzgruppen 141
Stuart Eizenstat 142
ethnic cleansing 148
euthanasia program (Nazi)
149–150
Final Solution 153
forced labor 155
Hans Frank 157
Wilhelm Frick 158–159
Hans Fritzsche 159
Walther Funk 161–162
genocide 166
Genocide Convention 169
Gestapo 172–173
Joseph Goebbels 174–176, *175*
Hermann Göring 177–178
Rudolf Hess 198–199
Reinhard Tristan Heydrich
199–200
Heinrich Himmler 201–202
hostages 208
imprisonment of civilians 224
incitement to genocide 225
Robert Houghwout Jackson 250
Jedwabne, massacre in 252
Alfred Jodl 253
Wilhelm Keitel 262–263
Raphael Lemkin 277
Robert Ley 279
Lidice, massacre in 282–283
Matsuoka Yosuke 290
medical experiments 292
Josef Mengele 294–295
Heinrich Müller 310–311
Nazi Party, Leadership Corps of
315
Konstantin von Neurath 317
Nokmin 320
Nuremberg Laws 325–326
OSI 333
Franz von Papen 342
Maurice Papon 343
Ante Pavelić 343–344
pillage 346–347
pogrom 350
Oswald Pohl 350
Erich Priebke 352
Erich Raeder 360
Alfred Rosenberg 370–371
Sant'Anna di Stazzema, massacre
in 381–382
Fritz Sauckel 383
Anthony Sawoniuk 385
Hjalmar Horace Greeley Schacht
385–386

Walter Schellenberg 386
Baldur von Schirach 386
Arthur Seyss-Inquart 389–390
Albert Speer 400–401
SS 403–404
Joseph Stalin 405
Julius Streicher 407–409
Alfredo Strössner 409
Wilhelm Stuckart 410
Paul Touvier 428
transfer of civilians 430
Ustache 451
Nazi hunters 267, 267–268, 272,
333, 454, 460, 476–477
Nazi Party, Leadership Corps of
198–199, 201–202, **315**, 329
Ndombasi, Yerodia 41
Nebuchadnezzar 117
Neelapajit, Somchai 422
Nepal, human rights violations in
30, 44, **315–317**
Neptune, Yvon 192
Netherlands 359, 370, 389, 390
Neto, Agostinho 19
Neuffer, Elizabeth 289
Neurath, Konstantin von **317**, 368
New People's Army (NPA)
(Philippines) 345
Ngeze, Hassan 225
NGOs. *See* nongovernmental
organizations
Nguema, Teodoro Obiang 145
Ngugi wa Thiong'o **317–318**
NHRC (National Human Rights
Commission) 226
Niblock, John 12
Nicaragua 321, 397–399
Nigeria 137, 392, 418
Nigeria, human rights violations in
44–45, **318–319**, 399. *See also*
Biafra, war crimes in
Nikolić, Dragan 239
Nikolić, Ivan 469
Nimeiry, Jaafar 410
Nixon, Richard M., and
administration 46, 78, 298, 312,
345, 397, 409, 423
Niyazov, Saparmurat 436
NLD. *See* National League for
Democracy
Nobel Peace Prize
Aung San Suu Kyi 32
Ralph Johnson Bunche 56
Nicolae Ceauşescu 68
Doctors Without Borders 127
Jean-Henri Dunant 130
ICRC 234
Raphael Lemkin 278
Sean Macbride 285
Physicians for Human Rights 346
Desmond Tutu 437
Nobel Prize in Literature 395, 399
No Gun Ri (Korea), massacre in
319–320
Nokmin (Avengers) **320**
noncombatants 29, 354
nondefended localities **320**
nongovernmental organizations
(NGOs). *See also* specific NGOs
Afghanistan 6
Bangladesh 36

nongovernmental organizations (*continued*)
China 82
forensic medicine and human rights 156
humanitarian aid, barring of 209
humanitarian intervention 210
human rights reports (U.S. State Department) 213
Kazakhstan 262
Universal Declaration of Human Rights 446
voluntary codes of conduct 458
Noriega, Manuel **320–321**, 448
North Africa 42–43, 360, 479. *See also specific headings, e.g.:* Morocco
North Atlantic Treaty Organization (NATO) 120, 122, 211, 270, 271, 302–303, 433
Northern Alliance 196, 310, 415
Northern Ireland 285
North Korea, human rights violations in 82–83, 100, *265,* 265–267, **321–322**, 364
North Vietnam 60, 61
Norway 360
Norwegian Refugee Council 231
NPA. *See* New People's Army
NSDAP. *See* National Socialist German Workers Party
nuclear arms and international law 266, **322–323**, 472–473
Nunn, Sam 193
Nuon Chea 60, **323–324**, 416
Nuremberg Charter 110, 323, **324–325**, 327, 449, 462, 537–540
Nuremberg Laws 158, 204, **325–326**, 460
Nuremberg Laws on Citizenship and Race, The: September 15, 1935 542–543
Nuremberg Medical Trial. *See* Doctors' Trial
Nuremberg Trials **326–330**, *327*
Additional Protocols to the Geneva Conventions 4
aggression 9
Martin Bormann 49
Karl Brandt 52
carpet bombing 65
concentration camps 100
cultural property, protection of 114
customary law 116
deportations 122, 123
Doctors' Trial 125–126
Karl Dönitz 129
Einsatzgruppen 141
Final Solution 154
Imre Finta 155
Hans Frank 157
Wilhelm Frick 159
Hans Fritzsche 159
Walther Funk 161
Genocide Convention 170
Gestapo 173
Hermann Göring 178
Rudolf Hess 199
IHL 241, 242
imprisonment of civilians 224

incitement to genocide 225
Robert Houghwout Jackson *250,* 250–251
Alfred Jodl 253
Ernst Kaltenbrunner 257
Wilhelm Keitel 263
Josef Kramer 271
Gustav von Bohlen Krupp 272
Raphael Lemkin 277–278
London Charter viii
Nazi Party, Leadership Corps of 315
Konstantin von Neurath 317
Nuremberg Charter 324–325
Herta Oberheuser 331
Franz von Papen 342
Oswald Pohl 350
Erich Raeder 360
rape as a tactic of war 361
Joachim von Ribbentrop 368
Rom, persecution of 369
Alfred Rosenberg 370, 371
Fritz Sauckel 383
Hjalmar Horace Greeley Schacht 385
Walter Schellenberg 386
Baldur von Schirach 386
Arthur Seyss-Inquart 389, 390
Albert Speer 400, 401
SS 403
Julius Streicher 407
Wilhelm Stuckart 410
Telford Taylor 418–419
Tokyo Trials 425
transfer of civilians 430
Universal Declaration of Human Rights 446
war crimes, categorization of 461
war criminals of Japan 463
Nzapali, Sebastian **330**

O

OAS. *See* Organization of American States
OAU. *See* Organization for African Unity
Obasanjo, Olusegun 318
Oberhauser, Herta **331**
Obote, Milton 15, **331–332**, 438
Ocampo, Luis Moreno 105
occupying power **332–333**
Additional Protocols to the Geneva Conventions 4
collective punishment 89
forced labor 155
humanitarian aid, barring of 209
IHL 240
levée en masse 279
Martens Clause 288
medical experiments 292
transfer of civilians 430
Velpke Baby Farm 454
victims, rights of 455
war crimes, categorization of 462
willful killing 477
Office of Special Investigations (OSI) **333**, 548
Ohrid agreement 286
oil 145, 216, 319, 410, 411

Ojdanić, Dragoljub 21
Ojukwu, Odemegwu 44, 45
Okawa Shumei **333–334**
Olivera Castillo, Jorge **334**
Olympic Games (1936) 326
Olympic Games (1980) 67
Olympic Games (2000) 475
Olympio, Gilchrist 424
Omarska camp 361
Ong Thong Hoeung 62
Operasi Sadar Rencong II/III 2–3
Operation Barbarossa 141, 360, 371, 405
Operation Condor 187, **334–335**, 348
Optional Protocol 235
Oradour, massacre in **335**
Orbinski, James 127
Organization for African Unity (OAU) 28, 296
Organization for Security and Cooperation in Europe (OSCE) **336**, 548
arms, trafficking in and control mechanisms 28
Azerbaijan 34
Belarus 40
Chechnya 71
Georgia (Republic of) 171
Helsinki accords 197
Kosovo 270
Turkmenistan 436
Ukraine 440
Organization of American States (OAS) 13–14, 29, 160, 230, **336–337**, 398, 431, 548
OSCE. *See* Organization for Security and Cooperation in Europe
OSI. *See* Office of Special Investigations
Osinde, Jorge 284
Otero, Alejandro 451
Ottawa Convention. *See* Anti-Personnel Mine Ban Convention
Ottoman Empire 25, 110
Ouattara, Alassane 247–248
Oxfam 102, **337**, 455, 548

P

Pact of San Jose, Costa Rica. *See* American Convention on Human Rights
Padilla, Jose **338–339**
Padilla v. Rumsfeld 338
Pakistan, human rights violations in **339–340**
collective punishment 90
Hazara, persecution of 196
Kashmir and Jammu 259, 260
al-Qaeda 358
refugees 364
religious persecution 366
Taliban 415
Palestine, human rights violations in **340–342**
Palestine and Palestinians. *See also specific headings, e.g.:* Arafat, Yasser
and Idi Amin 15, 16
Belgian war crimes tribunal 41

Ralph Johnson Bunche 56
collective punishment 89–90
humanitarian aid, barring of 209
Jordan 254
Nokmin 320
Hjalmar Horace Greeley Schacht 385
Luc Walleyn 459
Palestine Liberation Organization (PLO) 87, 377
Pamuk, Orhan 436
Panama 193, 320–321
Papen, Franz von 204, 317, 329, **342**
Papon, Maurice 267, **343**
Pappas, Thomas M. 246
Papua New Guinea 33
Paraguay 12, 334, 335, 409
paramilitary 90, 91, 93–95, 260, 475–476
Pashtuns 8, 310, 415
Pass Laws 20
Pastrana, Andres 93
Paulus, Friedrich von 205
Pavelić, Ante **343–344**, 451, 452
peacekeeping operations 6, 49, 456, 459
Pearl Harbor 128, 426, 464
Peninsular War 387
Pentagon attack (2001). *See* September 11, 2001 terrorist attacks
Peoples' Decade of Human Rights Education 548
Perišić, Momcilo 469–470
Perón, Evita 284
Perón, Juan 284, 344
Persian Gulf War (1991)
Belgian war crimes tribunal 41
carpet bombing 65
chemical weapons 74
collateral damage 88
deportations 123
human shields 215
Saddam al-Tikriti Hussein 217–218
immunity from attack 223
indiscriminate attacks 228
al-Qaeda 358
universal jurisdiction 447
Peru 159–161, 307, 391, 456
Petrescu, Elena 67
Phalangist Party 377
Philippines, human rights violations in **344–345**, 358, 482
Phillips, Carter 13
Phnom Penh, Cambodia 61, 62
Phoenix program **345–346**
PHR. *See* Physicians for Human Rights
Physicians for Human Rights (PHR) 31, 73, 156, **346**, 548
Physicians for Social Responsibility 548–549
Piedra Ibarra, Jesús 314
pillage **346–347**
Chechnya 69
collective punishment 89
cultural property, protection of 115
IHL 241

illegal acts 223
rape as a tactic of war 361
Shimada Shigetaro 391
war crimes, categorization of
462, 463
war dead, treatment of 471
Pinochet, Augusto 347, **347–349**
amnesty 17
Chile 78–80
Manuel Contreras 105, 106
DINA 313
Balthasar Garzón 163–164
Genocide Convention 169
Juan Guzmán 187, 188
Hissene Habré 189
ICC 236
Operation Condor 334
universal jurisdiction 447–449
Pius XII (pope) 344
PKK (Kurdish Workers Party)
435
plague 45, 172
Plan Colombia 93–94
PLO. *See* Palestine Liberation
Organization
Pobzeb, Vang 206
pogrom 153, 162, 199, 252,
349–350
Pohl, Oswald **350,** 403, 404
Poland
Armenian genocide 27
Adolf Eichmann 139
Final Solution 153, 154
forced labor 155
Hans Frank 157
Reinhard Tristan Heydrich 200
Heinrich Himmler 202
Adolf Hitler 204
Jedwabne, massacre in
251–252
Katyn Forest, massacre in 261
Erich Koch 269
Heinrich Müller 310–311
Joachim von Ribbentrop 368
Rom, persecution of 369
Arthur Seyss-Inquart 389
Joseph Stalin 405
Polo Uscanga, Abraham 298
Pol Pot 60, 61, 63, 64, 222, 264,
350–352, *351,* 416, 454
Pompidou, Georges 428
Popular Movement for the
Liberation of Angola (MPLA) 19
Portillo, José López 298
POTA (Prevention of Terrorism
Act) 226
Potsdam Declaration 425
Powell, Colin
Colombia 94
Darfur 118, 119
Georgia (Republic of) 172
Guantánamo detainees 182
Haiti 192
Haitian human rights violators
193
Tunisia 434
universal jurisdiction 447
Powell, John W., Jr. 288
POWs. *See* prisoners of war
Prabhakaran, Velupillai 423
Prats, Carlos 79, 80, 106, 334, 349

press, freedom of
Armenia 25
Azerbaijan 34
Bosnia and Herzegovina 50
Bulgaria 55
Burkina Faso 56–57
Cambodia, human rights
violations in 59
Chad 69
China 82
Comoros 97
CPJ 97
Kyrgyzstan 274
Vietnam 457
Préval, René 192
Prevention of Terrorism Act
(POTA) 226
Priebke, Erich **352**
prisoners
Afghanistan 8–9
Algeria 11
asylum, political 31
Azerbaijan 34
Bulgaria 55
Cambodia, war crimes in 62
Chile 79
China 81–82
Cuba 113
gulag 186–187
Jamaica 251
Palestine 341
Vietnam 458
prisoners of conscience 18,
352–353
prisoners of war (POWs) 353,
353–354
Additional Protocols to the
Geneva Conventions 5
amnesty 18
Article 3 Common to the Geneva
Conventions 29
combatants, rights of 95
concentration camps 97–99
Croatia 112
Jean-Henri Dunant 130
Eritrea 145
Ethiopia 147
Final Solution 153
forced labor 155
Walther Funk 161
genocide 166
ghost prisoners 173
Hugo Grotius 179
Guantánamo detainees 179, 181,
182
gulag 187
hostages 208
human shields 215
ICRC 234
IHL 240
immunity from attack 223
irregulars 247
journalists, protection of 254
Ernst Kaltenbrunner 257
legitimate military targets 276
levée en masse 279
Lieber Code 283
Martens Clause 288
medical experiments 292–293
Heinrich Müller 311
Nuremberg Trials 326

Sakai Takashi 379
Shimada Shigetaro 390
terrorism and international
humanitarian law 420, 421
terrorists treatment as viii
Tojo Hideki 424
victims, rights of 455
war crimes, categorization of
462
war criminals of Japan 463, 464
willful killing 477
prisons 53, 56, 64
Prosper, Pierre-Richard 236
prostitution (forced) 10, 37, 77,
96–97, 354, 479
protected persons **354–355,** 462
Protection of Roma (Gypsies) 370
Protocol on Prohibitions or
Restrictions on the Use of Mines,
Booby-Traps and Other Devices
108, **355**
Protocol to the Hague Convention
of 1954 for the Protection of
Cultural Property in the Event of
Armed Conflict, Second
355–356
public property, protection of
356–357
Punjab region (Pakistan) 227, 340
Putin, Vladimir 71, 72, 371, 440

Q
Qaeda, al- **358–359**
Afghanistan 6, 8
aggression 9
Alien Tort Claims Act 12
Amnesty International 19
Abu Bakar Bashir 39
biological weapons 45
Chechnya 71
collective punishment 90
conflict diamonds 100, 101
Balthasar Garzón 164
Geneva Conventions 165
Guantánamo detainees 180–182
Yaser Esam Hambi 195–196
Jemaah Islamiyah 252
Morocco 308
Mullah Omar 310
Jose Padilla 338–339
Pakistan 340
Philippines 345
Saudi Arabia 383
Taliban 415
terrorism and international
humanitarian law 421
Qaeda-al-Jihad 358
Qassem, Abdel Karim 216
Quintanar Alvarez, Alberto 476

R
Rabbani, Burhanuddin 415
racial discrimination 1, 20–21, 54
radio 34, 59, 334
Radio Martí 334
Raeder, Erich 129, 326, **360**
Ramos-Hora, José 134, 136
Ranariddh, Norodom 59
rape as a tactic of war **360–362**
Afghanistan 6
Angola 19

Burundi 57, 58
children's rights 77
comfort women 96
crimes against humanity 110
Darfur 118, 119
Georgia (Republic of) 171
International Criminal Tribunal
for Rwanda 237
Kosovo 270
Pakistan 339
protected persons 354
Rwanda, genocide in 373
Rwandan human rights violators
375
war crimes, categorization of
462, 463
war criminals of the former
Yugoslavia 467
women's rights, violations of 479
Yamashita Tomoyuki 482
Yugoslavia 483, 484
Ratner, Steven R. 462, 463
Reagan, Ronald, and administration
142, 369
rebel groups 41, 42
Red Cross. *See* International
Committee of the Red Cross
reeducation-through-labor camps
81, 82
refoulement **362–363**
Refugee Act of 1980 30
refugees 363, **363–364.** *See also*
United Nations High
Commissioner for Refugees
Afghanistan 8
Albania 10
Angola 19
asylum, political 30–31
Australia 33
Bhutan 44
Biafra 44, 45
Bosnia and Herzegovina 51
Burundi 57
CAT 107
Chad 69
Chechnya 72
children's rights 76
China 82–83
Congo, Democratic Republic of
the 104
Convention Relating to the
Status of Refugees 109
Croatia 112
Cyprus 116
Darfur 118
displaced person camps 125
Stuart Eizenstat 142
Eritrea 146
Guinea 185
Gujarat, massacres in 186
Human Rights Watch 214
identification of combatants 222
Indonesia 229
internally displaced persons
231–232
Kosovo 270, 271
Kurdistan (Iraq), suppression of
273
military necessity 301
Ratko Mladić 304
No Gun Ri (Korea) 319

refugees *(continued)*
North Korea 321
Office of Special Investigations
333
Pakistan 339, 340
refoulement 362
Refugees International 365
Rwanda, genocide in 373
safe havens 378
Uganda 439
United Nations Guiding
Principles on Internal
Displacement 441
victims, rights of 455
Ségio Vieira de Mello 456, 457
War Child Project 461
war criminals of the former
Yugoslavia 467
women's rights, violations of 479
Yugoslavia 483
Refugees International **364–365,**
549
Rega, Jose Lopez 22
religion, freedom of 40, 55, 83,
113, 457, 458
religious persecution **365–366**
Azerbaijan 34
Bhutan 43–44
Cambodia, war crimes in 61
China 82
Eritrea 146
Georgia (Republic of) 171
Turkmenistan 436
religious violence 186, 339
reparations 82–83, 142, 354,
366–367, 385
Reporters Without Borders 549
reprisal 208, **367,** 371, 428
resettlement 25, 33
Revolutionary Armed Forces of
Colombia (FARC) 90–94, 307
Revolutionary Front for Haitian
Advancement and Progress
(FRAPH) 191–194
Revolutionary United Front (RUF)
100, 101, 381, 392, 393, 400
Rhodesia 89. *See also* Zimbabwe,
human rights violations in
Ribbentrop, Joachim von 200, 317,
326, **368,** 371
Ridenhour, Ron 312
Ríos Montt, José Efraín 185,
368–369
riots 43, 186
Rodriguez, Andres 409
Rohm, Ernst 203
Rom, persecution of **369–370**
genocide 166
Genocide Convention 168
Gestapo 173
Joseph Goebbels 175
Josef Mengele 294
Ante Pavelić 343, 344
Russia 372
Romania 67–68
Romero, Oscar 120, 144, 383
Rome Statute of the International
Criminal Court **370**
disappearances 125
Genocide Convention 168, 170
ICC 235–237

medical experiments 292
rape as a tactic of war 361
slavery 394
Victims Trust Fund 456
war crimes, categorization of
462
women's rights, violations of
480
Roosevelt, Eleanor 157, 443, 445,
446
Roosevelt, Franklin D. 45, 250,
276, 385, 398, 405
Roosevelt, Theodore 190
Rosenberg, Alfred 205, **370–371**
Rossi, Luiz Basilio 18
Roth, Kenneth 448–449
Rudolph, Arthur 333
RUF. *See* Revolutionary United
Front
Rumsfeld, Donald 41, 182, 338,
447
Russia. *See also specific headings,
e.g.:* Yeltsin, Boris
arms, trafficking in and control
mechanisms 28
Chechnya 69–72
children's rights 78
Georgia (Republic of) 171–172
Hague Conventions 189
Memorial 293
pogrom 349–350
refugees 364
religious persecution 366
Aleksandr Isayevich Solzhenitsyn
395
Russia, human rights violations in
371–372
Russian Civil War 370
Russian Federation 371
Russian Orthodox Church 372
Rwanda, genocide in **372–374,**
373. *See also* Hutus; International
Criminal Tribunal for Rwanda;
Tutsis
arms, trafficking in and control
mechanisms 27–28
Belgian war crimes tribunal 41
Burundi 57
Congo, Democratic Republic of
the 103, 104
ethnic cleansing 148
genocide 167
Genocide Convention 169
humanitarian intervention 211
Human Rights Watch 214
ICC 236, 237
IHL 241
incitement to genocide 225
rape as a tactic of war 361
refoulement 362
safe havens 378
John Shattuck 390
Rwandan human rights violators
374–376
Ryle, John 155–156

S

Saakashvili, Mikhail 171, 172
Sabra and Shatilla, massacre in
377, 459
Saca, Antonio 144

Sachsenhausen 369
safe havens **377–378,** 382, 402,
455, 483
Šainović, Nikola 21
St. Petersburg Declaration 472
Sakai Takashi **378–379**
Salinas de Gortari, Carlos 298
Saloth Sar. *See* Pol Pot
Sanchez, Illich Ramirez 455
sanctions **379–380**
Sandinista National Liberation
Front (FSLN) 397, 398
Sandino, Augusto César 398
Sanguinetti, Julio 450
Sankoh, Foday 100, 280, 281,
380–381, 392, 393, 399, 400, 417
Sant'Anna di Stazzema, massacre in
381–382
Santos, Jose dos 19
Sapién, Norma Corona 298
Sarajevo, siege of 223, 258, 304,
382–383, 392, 467, 468, 483
Saravia, Alvaro 144, **383**
SARS. *See* Severe Acute
Respiratory Syndrome
Sauckel, Fritz **383**
Saudi Arabia, human rights
violations in 16, 200–201, 358,
359, **383–384,** 446, 479
Savimbi, Joseph 19
Sawoniuk, Anthony **385**
Scalia, Anthony 13
Schabas, William 169, 170
Schacht, Hjalmar Horace Greeley
329, 342, **385–386**
Schakowsky, Jan 297
Schellenberg, Walter 199, **386**
Schirach, Baldur von **386**
Schlesinger, James 246
Schwarzkopf, Norman 447
scorched earth 148, **386–387,** 390,
411
SD (Sicherheitsdienst) 199–201
security forces 64, 65
Security Wall 341
Sejested, Francis 32
self-defense 9, 255
Sendero Luminoso. *See* Shining
Path
September 11, 2001, terrorist
attacks
act of war 4
Alien Tort Claims Act 12
arms, trafficking in and control
mechanisms 28
asylum, political 30
Iran 244
Libya 282
Malaysia 287
Mullah Omar 309
al-Qaeda 358
Taliban 415
terrorism and international
humanitarian law 420
United Nations Resolution 1368
444
Uzbekistan 452
Serbia, human rights violations in
387–388
Arkan (Želiko Ražnatović) 22–24
Dayton accords 120

ethnic cleansing 147
Radovan Karadžić 258–259
Theodor Meron 297
Ratko Mladić 51, 208, 258, 259,
297, 304–305, 387, 465,
467–469, 484
Franjo Tudjman 433
war criminals of the former
Yugoslavia 465, 466, 468
Yugoslavia 482
Serbs
Bosnia and Herzegovina 50, 51
Croatia 112
Ante Gotovina 178
ICTY 239
Radovan Karadžić 258
Kosovo 270, 271
Slobodan Milošević 301–304
Ratko Mladić 304–305
Ante Pavelić 343, 344
Sarajevo, siege of 382
Srebrenca, massacre in 402
Ustache 451
Yugoslavia 484
Serb Volunteer Guard (SDG/SSJ).
See the Tigers
Service, Robert 406
Seselj, Vojislav **388–389**
Severe Acute Respiratory
Syndrome (SARS) 83, 253
sexual slavery 10, 19, 75, 96–97,
269
Seyss-Inquart, Arthur **389–390**
Shah, Adbullah 7
Shahroudi, Ayatollah Mahmoud
244
Shalikashvili, John 74
sharia 39, 318–319, 383, 415
Sharon, Ariel 41, 340–342, 377,
459
Shattuck, John **390,** 475
Shevardnadze, Eduard 171
Shignori Togo 425
Shiite Muslims 35, 196, 218, 244,
339, 383
Shimada Shigetaro **390–391**
Shinawatra, Thaksin 421, 422
Shining Path 160, **391**
Shintoism 464
Siberia 187
sick persons 95, 164, 165, 462, 477
siege 93, 117, 382, **391–392,** 461,
483. *See also* Sarajevo, siege of
Sierra Leone, human rights
violations in **392–393**
children's rights 75, 76
conflict diamonds 100, 101
ECOMOG 137
Guinea 185
Liberia 280, 281
Foday Sankoh 380–381
Special Court for Sierra Leone
399–400
Charles Ghankay Taylor 417
Sihanouk, Norodom 61, 63, 222,
351
Sikhs 227
Simon, Joel 225
Simon Wiesenthal Center 549
SIN. *See* National Intelligence
Service

Singapore massacre 426
Singh, Manmohan 226
Sinhalese 423
Sino-Japanese War 387
Six-Day War of 1967 340, 341
SLA. *See* Sudan Liberation Army
Slavery Convention of 1926
    393–394
slavery/slave labor 393, **393–394**.
    See also forced labor
    children's rights 77
    concentration camps 99
    forced labor 155
    Walther Funk 161
    Human Rights Convention 212
    Erich Koch 268
    Gustav von Bohlen Krupp 272
    Fritz Sauckel 383
    Albert Speer 401
    Alfredo Strössner 409
    Telford Taylor 419
    trafficking in persons 429
    Trafficking Protocol 429
    Wannsee Conference 460
    war criminals of Japan 464
    women's rights, violations of 479
Slavs 49, 153
sleep deprivation 8, 81
Slovenia, human rights violations in
    388, **394–395**
smallpox 14, 45, 172
Smith, Ian 89
Smits, Jan 20
Soares, Abilio 229–230
soldiers 347, 472, 477
soldiers, child. *See* child soldiers
Solidarity Peace Trust 486
Solzhenitsyn, Aleksandr Isayevich
    186, **395–396**
Somalia, human rights violations in
    211, 232, 358, **396–397**
Somoza Debayle, Anastasio 397,
    397–398, 399
Somoza García, Anastasio 397,
    398–399
Souaidia, Habib **399**
Souter, David H. 13
South Africa
    amnesty 17
    Wouter Basson 39–40
    children's rights 77
    concentration camps 97, 98
    Eugene de Kock 121
    Rwanda, genocide in 373
    Sullivan Principles 412–413
    Truth and Reconciliation
        Commission 432
    Desmond Tutu 437
    Universal Declaration of Human
        Rights 446
Southal, Jarrell 245
Southeast Asia 77, 206, 252, 458
South Korea 266, 322, 364
South Vietnam 345, 346, 458
Soviet Union (USSR). *See also*
    specific headings, e.g.: Stalin,
    Joseph
    Biafra 44
    biological weapons 46
    Nicolae Ceauşescu 67
    concentration camps 98–99

deportations 123
Einsatzgruppen 141
forced labor 155
Walther Funk 161
germ warfare 172
gulag 186–187
Helsinki accords 196, 197
Adolf Hitler 204, 205
Katyn Forest, massacre in 261
Kazakhstan 261
Kim Il Sung 265, 266
Kyrgyzstan 273
League of Nations 276
Matsuoka Yosuke 290
Memorial 293
Mengistu Haile Mariam 295
pogrom 350
POWs 354
Erich Raeder 360
Joachim von Ribbentrop 368
Alfred Rosenberg 371
Aleksandr Isayevich Solzhenitsyn
    395
Joseph Stalin 404–406
Taliban 415
Turkmenistan 436
Universal Declaration of Human
    Rights 446
Ustache 451–452
Uzbekistan 452
weapons of mass destruction
    474
Soyinka, Wole **399**
Spadafora, Hugo 321
Spain
    Argentina 22
    Ricardo Miguel Cavallo 66, 67
    Chile 79
    Balthasar Garzón 163–164
    Ante Pavelić 344
    Augusto Pinochet 348
    al-Qaeda 359
    war crimes, categorization of
        463
Spanish Flu 172
Special Court for Sierra Leone
    170, 242, 281, 381, 393, **399–400**,
    417–418, 463
Special Powers Act (India) 260
speech, freedom of 34, 50, 97, 113
Speer, Albert 279, **400–402**
SPLA. *See* Sudanese People's
    Liberation Army
Srebrenica, massacre in **402**
    ICTY 239
    Ratko Mladić 304, 305
    nondefended localities 320
    safe havens 378
    war criminals of the former
        Yugoslavia 466, 468, 469
    Yugoslavia 483, 484
Sri Lanka, human rights violations
    in **402–403**, 423
SS (Schutzstaffel) **403–404**
    Klaus Barbie 37
    Reinhard Tristan Heydrich 199
    Heinrich Himmler 201, 202
    Adolf Hitler 203
    Lidice, massacre in 282, 283
    Konstantin von Neurath 317
    Nuremberg Trials 329

Sant'Anna di Stazzema, massacre
    in 381–382
    Walter Schellenberg 386
SSI (State Security Intelligence)
    138
Stalin, Joseph *404*, **404–406**
    concentration camps 98
    deportations 123
    forced labor 155
    gulag 186, 187
    Memorial 293
    Nuremberg Trials 329
    pogrom 350
    Aleksandr Isayevich Solzhenitsyn
        395
    Telford Taylor 418
    Ustache 451
    war crimes, categorization of
        462
Stangl, Franz 477
Stanley, Henry Morton 278
Stanton, Gregory 167
starvation as a tactic of war 45, 267,
    406–407
State Department, U.S. 138,
    212–214, 226, 229, 453
State Security Intelligence (SSI)
    138
Stockholm Declaratiion on
    Genocide **407**
Stojiljković, Vlajko 21
Stoppard, Tom 461
Strasser, Valentine 381
Streicher, Julius 205, 225, 385,
    407–409, 408
Strössner, Alfredo **409**
Strugar, Pavle 470
Stuckart, Wilhelm **410**, 460
Sudan, human rights violations in
    ix, **410–412**. *See also* Darfur, war
    crimes in
    Chad 69
    al-Qaeda 358
    refugees 364
    Refugees International 365
    religious persecution 366
    scorched earth 387
    Uganda 439
    victims, rights of 455–456
    Ségio Vieira de Mello 456
    women's rights, violations of 479
Sudanese People's Liberation Army
    (SPLA) 410, 411
Sudan Liberation Army (SLA) 118
Suharto 39, 134, 228, **412**, 478
suicide bombings 71, 341, 423
Sukarno 412
Sukarnoputri, Megawati 3
Sukma Darmawan 287
Sullivan, Leon 413
Sullivan Principles **412–413**
Sungkar, Abdullah 252
Sunni Muslims 35, 195, 273, 339,
    415, 436
Sun Tzu 241, 461
Suny, Grigor 26
Supreme Court, U.S.
    Alien Tort Claims Act 12–13
    combatants, rights of 95
    due process 129
    Guantánamo detainees 180

Yaser Esam Hambi 196
Padilla v. Rumsfeld 338
Sosa v. Alvarez-Machain 12–13
Yamashita Tomoyuki 482
Syria, human rights violations in
    195, 359, **413–414**

T

Tachinbana Yoshio 464
Tadić, Duško 361, 470
Taguba, Antonio 246
Tajikistan 359
Tajiks 8
Taliban **415–416**
    Afghanistan 5–8
    Amnesty International 19
    Chechnya 71
    collective punishment 90
    combatants, rights of 95
    Guantánamo detainees 182
    Yaser Esam Hambi 195–196
    Hazara, persecution of 196
    Mullah Omar 309
    Pakistan 339
    al-Qaeda 358
    refugees 364
    Saudi Arabia 384
    terrorism and international
        humanitarian law 421
Tamazight language 42, 43
Tamenori Sato 464–465
Tamil Tigers. *See* Tigers, Tamil
Ta Mok 60, 63, **416**
Tanzania 16, 57, 76, 359, 374
Tarculovski, Johan 239
Tatoune, Jean 192, 194
Taya, Ould 292
Taylor, Charles Ghankay 87, 100,
    185, 280, 381, **417–418**
Taylor, Telford 126, **418–420**, *419*
Tazawa Keizo 465
television 34, 55, 59
Tenant, George 150–151
terrorism and international
    humanitarian law viii, **420–421**.
    See also specific headings, e.g.:
    Qaeda, al-
    Algeria 10–11
    Anti-Terrorism, Crime and
        Security Act (2001) 20
    Argentina 21, 22
    Bali nightclub bombing 39, 252,
        359
    Abu Bakar Bashir 39
    CAT 107
    Ricardo Miguel Cavallo 66, 67
    Chechnya 70–72
    chemical weapons 74
    China 81
    collective punishment 90
    Colombia 92
    conflict diamonds 100, 101
    extraordinary rendition
        150–151
    Balthasar Garzón 163, 164
    germ warfare 172
    ghost prisoners 173
    Guantánamo detainees 181
    Guyana 187
    high-value detainees 200–201
    Indonesia 228

terrorism and international
humanitarian law *(continued)*
Jemaah Islamiyah 252
Kim Il Sung 266
Libya 281–282
Malaysia 287
Morocco 308
Jose Padilla 338–339
Pakistan 339
Palestine 341
Philippines 345
Erich Priebke 352
Shining Path 391
United Nations Resolution 1368
444
Ustache 451
Thailand, human rights violations in
421–422
Thatcher, Margaret 164, 348
Thayer, Nate 324
Theresienstadt 389
Theron, Joahn 39, 40
Third Reich 129, 204, 205, 368,
383, 386. *See also* Nazi Germany
Thirty Years' War 366
Tiananmen Square 475
Tibet 83
Tiger Force **422–423**
Tigers, the 23, 24, 470
Tigers, Tamil 402, 403, **423**
Tito, Josip Broz 301, 302, 451, 452,
482
Togo, human rights violations in
423–424
Tojo Hideki 128, 334, *424,*
424–425, 426, 464, 481
Tokyo subway attacks 74
Tokyo Trials **425–426**
aggression 9
China 84
Doihara Kenji 127, 128
Genocide Convention 170
IHL 242
Manchuria, Japanese war crimes
in 288
Matsui Iwane 290
Nanjing (Nanking), massacre in
313
Nuremberg Trials 329
Okawa Shumei 333
rape as a tactic of war 361
Shimada Shigetaro 390
Tojo Hideki 424
Universal Declaration of Human
Rights 446
war criminals of Japan 463
Tolbert, William 280
Tontons Macoutes 132
Torres, Juan Jose 334
Torrijos Herrera, Omar 320–321
torture **426–427**
Aceh 2
Jorge Eduardo Acosta 3
Afghanistan 6–9
Albania 10
Algeria 10
Alien Tort Claims Act 12–13
Idi Amin 15
Amnesty International 18
Article 3 Common to the Geneva
Conventions 29, 30

Bahrain, human rights situation
in 35
Bangladesh 36
Klaus Barbie 37, 38
Belarus 40
Jean-Bédel Bokassa 47
Bolivia 48
Brazil 53, 54
Burundi 58
Cambodia, human rights
violations in 59
Cambodia, war crimes in 62
CAT 106–107
Ricardo Miguel Cavallo 66
Chad 68, 69
Chechnya 69, 71
children's rights 74
Chile 78, 80
China 81, 82
Carl Clauberg 87
Colombia 91, 92
combatants, rights of 95
Comoros 97
Congo (Brazzaville) 101
Congo, Democratic Republic of
the 104
Manuel Contreras 106
crimes against humanity 110
Croatia 112
disappearances 124
Ecuador 137
Egypt 138
Equatorial Guinea 145
Eritrea 146
Ethiopia 147
extraordinary rendition 151
forensic medicine and human
rights 156
Wilhelm Frick 159
Balthasar Garzón 163, 164
Geneva Conventions 165
Georgia (Republic of) 171
Guantánamo detainees 181, 182
Guatemala 183
Guyana 187
Hissene Habré 189
Haiti 192
high-value detainees 201
Human Rights Convention 212
Saddam al-Tikriti Hussein 217
IHL 241
Indonesia 228
Iran 243, 244
Iraq, post-Saddam 245
Jamaica 251
Radovan Karadžić 259
Kashmir and Jammu 260
Kenya 263
Kiang Kek Iev 264, 265
Laos 275
Libya 282
Macedonia 286
Malaysia 287
mass graves 289
Mau Mau uprising 291
Mexico 298
Morocco 308
Myanmar 311
Nigeria 318
Nuon Chea 324
Sebastian Nzapali 330

occupying power 332
Operation Condor 334
Pakistan 340
Palestine 340
Philippines 344
Physicians for Human Rights
346
Augusto Pinochet 347–349
protected persons 354
José Efaín Ríos Montt 368
Russia 371
Rwandan human rights violators
375
Serbia 387
Shimada Shigetaro 391
Habib Souaidia 399
Sri Lanka 402
Alfredo Strössner 409
Paul Touvier 428
Rafael Molino Trujillo 431
Truth and Reconciliation
Commission 432
Tunisia 434
Turkey 435
Turkmenistan 436
Uganda 438
Ukraine 440
Uruguay 450, 451
Uzbekistan 452, 453
Jacques Vergès 455
war criminals of the former
Yugoslavia 467, 469, 470
Christián von Wernich 475
White Brigades 476
Yamashita Tomoyuki 482
Yugoslavia 484
total war 284, **427–428**
Touvier, Paul 267, **428**
Townley, Michael 348
toxins 46, 88
trafficking in persons 77, 171, 394,
428–429, 479
Trafficking Protocol 429, **429–430**
transfer of civilians **430**
treaties viii, 73, 336, 474. *See also
specific treaty*
Trinidad and Tobago 236
Trotsky, Leon 404–405
Trujillo, Rafael Molino 132,
430–432
Trujillo, Ramfi 431
Truman, Harry S. 250, 419
Truth and Reconciliation
Commission 121, 176, 236, **432,**
437
Truth Commission (El Salvador)
144
Tshombe, Moise 305
Tsvangirai, Morgan 486
Tudjman, Franjo 112, 120, 121,
303, **432–434,** 466, 469, 484, 485
Tunisia, human rights violations in
42, **434–435**
Tupamaro National Liberation
Movement (MLN) 160, 450–451
Turkana Massacre 15
Turkey, human rights violations in
25, 110, 116, 169, 273, 359,
435–436
Turkmenistan, human rights
violations in **436–437**

Turns, David 4
Tutsis
arms, trafficking in and control
mechanisms 28
Burundi 57, 58
Congo, Democratic Republic of
the 103–104
ethnic cleansing 148
incitement to genocide 225
International Criminal Tribunal
for Rwanda 237, 238
refoulement 362
Rwanda, genocide in 372, 373
Tutu, Desmond 432, **437**
Tymoshenko, Yulia 440

U
U-boats 129, 360
Uganda 75, 269–270, 331–332,
361, 365, 373
Uganda, human rights violations in
14–17, 237, **438–439**
Ukraine, human rights violations in
268–269, **440**
Ulemek, Milorad 470
UNCHR. *See* United Nations
Human Rights Commission
UNHCR. *See* United Nations High
Commissioner for Refugees
Union of Concerned Scientists 549
Union of Soviet Socialist Republics.
See Soviet Union
UNITA. *See* National Union for the
Total Independence of Angola
United Kingdom 31, 46, 358, 367
United Nations (UN)
act of war 4
and ad hoc courts ix
aggression 9
Ralph Johnson Bunche 56
Cambodia, war crimes in 63
dams and dikes, protection of
118
Darfur 118, 119
Dayton accords 120, 121
East Timor 134, 135
El Salvador 144
ethnic cleansing 148
humanitarian intervention 210,
211
Saddam al-Tikriti Hussein 218
ICC 235–236
ICJ 234–235
ILO 242–243
imprisonment of civilians 224
International Criminal Tribunal
for Rwanda 238
Ivory Coast 248, 249
League of Nations 276
Raphael Lemkin 278
Foday Sankoh 381
Sarajevo, siege of 382
Sierra Leone 393
slavery 394
Somalia 396
Anastasio Somoza Debayle 398
Special Court for Sierra Leone
399–400
Stockholm Declaration on
Genocide 407
Syria 414

trafficking in persons 429
Trafficking Protocol 429
Universal Declaration of Human
  Rights 445–446
Sérgio Vieira de Mello 456–457
voluntary codes of conduct 458
Kurt Waldheim 459
women's rights, violations of 479
United Nations and the Geneva
  Conventions **441**
United Nations Assistance Mission
  in Rwanda UNAMIR II 373
United Nations Charter 379, 380
United Nations Commission of
  Experts 243
United Nations Convention Against
  Torture and Other Cruel,
  Inhuman or Degrading Treatment
  or Punishment 530–536. *See also*
  Convention against Torture
United Nations Convention
  Relating to the Status of Refugees
  362
United Nations Diplomatic
  Conference of Plenipotentiaries
  on the Establishment of an
  International Criminal Court 370
United Nations General Assembly
  235, 296, 365
United Nations Guiding Principles
  on Internal Displacement 231,
  441–442, 457
United Nations High
  Commissioner for Human Rights
  21, 118, 248, **442,** 457, 549
United Nations High
  Commissioner for Refugees
  (UNHCR) **442–443**
  Afghanistan 8
  Convention Relating to the
    Status of Refugees 109
  Croatia 112
  Cyprus 116
  rape as a tactic of war 360
  refoulement 362
  refugees 363, 364
  Rom (Roma, Romany, Gypsies),
    persecution of 370
  victims, rights of 455
  War Child Project 461
  Yugoslavia 484
United Nations Human Rights
  Commission (UNCHR)
  443–444
  Algeria 11
  amnesty 17
  Libya 281
  mercenaries 296
  rape as a tactic of war 361
  reparations 367
  United Nations Guiding
    Principles on Internal
    Displacement 442
  United Nations High
    Commissioner for Human
    Rights 442
  United Nations Working Group
    on Enforced or Involuntary
    Disappearances 444
  Universal Declaration of Human
    Rights 445

United Nations Military Observer
  Group (UNMOGIP) 365
United Nations peacekeeping force
  373
United Nations Protection Force
  (UNPROFOR) 483
United Nations Refugee
  Convention 378
United Nations Resolution 1368
  444
United Nations Security Council 9,
  236–238, 241, 374, 379, 380
United Nations Small Arms
  Conference 233
United Nations Stabilization
  Mission in Haiti (MINUSTAH)
  192
United Nations Truce Supervision
  Organization in Jerusalem
  (UNTSO) 365
United Nations Working Group on
  Enforced or Involuntary
  Disappearances **444–445**
United States. *See also* Iraq,
  human rights violations in post-
  Saddam; *specific headings, e.g.:*
  Bush, George W., and
  administration
  Afghanistan 7–9
  Alien Tort Claims Act 11–13
  Armenian genocide 27
  arms, trafficking in and control
    mechanisms 28
  Article 3 Common to the Geneva
    Conventions 29
  asylum, political 30–31
  Abu Bakar Bashir 39
  Biafra 44
  biological weapons 46
  Cambodia 61
  Cambodia, war crimes in 62
  carpet bombing 65
  CAT 107
  children's rights 77
  China 81, 82
  collateral damage 87, 88
  collective punishment 90
  Colombia 93–95
  Cuba 113–114
  Roberto D'Aubuisson 119
  free-fire zones 158
  Georgia (Republic of) 171–172
  germ warfare 172
  ghost prisoners 173
  Guantánamo detainees 20, 95,
    173, 179–183, *180,* 196, 246,
    421
  Hissene Habré 189
  Haitian human rights violators
    193, 194
  Maximiliano Hernández
    Martínez 198
  Hmong, persecution of 206
  ICC 236
  Kurdistan (Iraq), suppression of
    273
  Libya 282
  Lieber Code 283
  mercenaries 296–297
  Mexico 298
  Morocco 308

No Gun Ri (Korea), massacre in
  319–320
Manuel Noriega 320, 321
occupying power 332
Jose Padilla 338–339
Pakistan 339
pillage 347
al-Qaeda 358
refugees 364
sanctions 380
Sierra Leone 393
Somalia 396
Anastasio Somoza Debayle 397
Anastasio Somoza García 398
Alfredo Strössner 409
Taliban 415
Charles Ghankay Taylor 417
Rafael Molino Trujillo 431
Tunisia 434
UNCCR 443
universal jurisdiction 447
Uzbekistan 453
victims, rights of 456
Vienna Convention on
  Diplomatic Relations 457
war dead, treatment of 472
weapons of mass destruction 474
Yamashita Tomoyuki 482
United States Department of State
  550
*United States of America v. Karl
  Brandt et al. See* Doctors' Trial
Universal Declaration of Human
  Rights 445–446, 527–529
  Amnesty International 18
  Ramsay Clark 86–87
  combatants, rights of 96
  Convention Relating to the
    Status of Refugees 109
  disappearances 125
  European Convention for the
    Protection of Human Rights
    149
  Geneva Conventions 165
  ICCPR 235
  internally displaced persons 232
  religious persecution 365
  slavery 394
  UNCCR 443
  United Nations High
    Commissioner for Human
    Rights 442
  women's rights, violations of 479
universal jurisdiction **446–449**
  Afghanistan 7
  Alien Tort Claims Act 11–12
  Belgian war crimes tribunal 41
  Ricardo Miguel Cavallo 66
  Hissene Habré 189
  illegal acts 223
  terrorism and international
    humanitarian law 420
  war crimes, categorization of
    463
unlawful combatants 8, 182, 421
unlawful imprisonment 69, 241,
  449–450
UNMOGIP (United Nations
  Military Observer Group) 365
UNPROFOR (United Nations
  Protection Force) 483

UNTAET. *See* UN Transitional
  Administration in East Timor
UN Transitional Administration in
  East Timor (UNTAET) 134–136
UNTSO (United Nations Truce
  Supervision Organization in
  Jerusalem) 365
Uribe, Alvaro 92–95
Uruguay, human rights violations in
  17, **450–451**
USA PATRIOT Act of 2001 20
"useless eaters" 159
U.S. Holocaust Memorial Council
  369
USSR. *See* Soviet Union
Ustache 284, 343, 344, 432, 433,
  451–452
Uzbekistan, human rights violations
  in 358, 359, **452–453**
Uzbeks 8, 273

V

V-2 rockets 472
Vázquez, Tabaré 450
Velpke Baby Farm **454**
Venezuela 66
Vennhausen 369
Vergès, Jacques 38, **454–455**
Versailles, Treaty of 204, 243, 276,
  370
Vichy France 51–52, 255, 343, 428
victims, rights of **455–456**
Victims Trust Fund **456**
Videla, Jorge Rafael 22
Vieira de Mello, Sérgio 248, 442,
  456–457
Vienna Convention on Diplomatic
  Relations **456–457**
Vietcong 345, 346
Vietnam 62, 74, 351
Vietnam, human rights violations
  in 206, 312, 419, 422–423,
  457–458
Vietnam, North. *See* North
  Vietnam
Vietnam, South. *See* South
  Vietnam
Vietnam War
  Cambodia, war crimes in 61
  carpet bombing 65
  collateral damage 88
  dams and dikes, protection of
    117
  free-fire zones 158
  journalists, protection of 254
  limited war 284
  Phoenix program 345–346
  rape as a tactic of war 360
Villaflor de Vicenti, Azucena 309
Viola, Roberto 22
Vivanco, José Miguel 66
Vlakplaas 121
Voelkischer Beobachter 370
voluntary codes of conduct
  412–413, **458**
VX nerve agents 73

W

Wahhabi Islam 383
Waldheim, Kurt **459**
Walleyn, Luc **459–460**

Wannsee Conference 200, 204, 371, 410, **460–461**
War Child Project **461**
war crimes, categorization of 30, **461–463**
war criminals of Germany. *See* Nazi Germany; Nuremberg Trials
war criminals of Japan **463–465**
war criminals of the former Yugoslavia **465–471**
war dead, treatment of **471–472**
warlords 6, 7–8, 22–24
war on drugs 299, 422
war on terrorism 4, 12, 83, 107, 274, 344, 359. *See also* Afghanistan, U.S. invasion of; Iraq War (2003)
weapons in the conduct of war 233, **472–473**
weapons of mass destruction 27, 473, **473–474**
Wechsler, Lawrence 241
Wedgwood, Ruth 219
Wei Jingsheng **474–475**
Weimar Republic 203
Wernich, Christián von **475**
West Bank 89, 90, 340, 341
Western Europe 359
West Germany (Federal Republic of Germany) 366
White, Robert 119
White Brigades 298, **475–476**
Wiesel, Elie 369
Wiesenthal, Simon **476–477**
willful killing 468, **477–478**
Wilson, David 461
Wilson, Heather A. 41
Wilson, Woodrow 276, 366
Wiranto 135–136, 229, **478**
WITNESS 550
women's rights, violations of **478–480,** 479
   Afghanistan 6
   Albania 10
   Amnesty International 18
   Armenian genocide 26
   asylum, political 30
   Bangladesh 36
   Brazil 54

Burundi 58
children's rights 77
Georgia (Republic of) 171
Global Rights 173–174
Guantánamo detainees 181
Iran 243, 244
Pakistan 339, 340
protected persons 354
Saudi Arabia 383
Taliban 415
trafficking in persons 429
war criminals of the former Yugoslavia 467
Yugoslavia 484
Worker's Party 53, 54
workers' rights. *See* labor rights
World Court. *See* International Court of Justice
World Trade Center attack (1993) 359
World Trade Center attack (2001). *See* September 11, 2001 terrorist attacks
World War I
   Armenian genocide 25
   biological weapons 45
   Martin Bormann 48
   chemical weapons 73
   germ warfare 172
   Adolf Hitler 203
   IHL 242
   reparations 366
   Joachim von Ribbentrop 368
   weapons in the conduct of war 472
World War II
   biological weapons 45
   Martin Bormann 48
   China 83–84
   collateral damage 88
   collective punishment 89
   comfort women 96
   concentration camps 97–100
   crimes against humanity 110
   dams and dikes, protection of 117
   displaced person camps 125
   Karl Dönitz 129
   Adolf Eichmann 139

Stuart Eizenstat 142
ethnic cleansing 148
Final Solution 152
genocide 166
germ warfare 172
gulag 187
Helsinki accords 196, 197
hostages 208
IHL 242
imprisonment of civilians 224
Izieu, children of 249
Erich Koch 268
League of Nations 276
Raphael Lemkin 277
Lidice, massacre in 282–283
limited war 284
Matsuoka Yosuke 290
medical experiments 292
Heinrich Müller 310–311
Konstantin von Neurath 317
Franz von Papen 342
pillage 346–347
POWs 354
Erich Raeder 360
rape as a tactic of war 360
religious persecution 365
reparations 366
Joachim von Ribbentrop 368
Rom, persecution of 369
Sant'Anna di Stazzema, massacre in 381–382
Fritz Sauckel 383
Anthony Sawoniuk 385
scorched earth 387
Arthur Seyss-Inquart 389–390
Shimada Shigetaro 390–391
Anastasio Somoza García 398
Albert Speer 401
Joseph Stalin 405
Telford Taylor 418–419
Tojo Hideki 424–425
Tokyo Trials 425–426
total war 427
Paul Touvier 428
Ustache 451–452
Kurt Waldheim 459
war criminals of Japan 463–465
Simon Wiesenthal 476
Yamashita Tomoyuki 481

wounded persons 5, 29, 30, 95, 164, 165, 462, 477, 484

Y

Yad Vashem 476, **481**
Yamamoto, Isoroku 425
Yamashita Tomoyuki **481–482**
Yanukovych, Viktor 440
Yeltsin, Boris 46, 69, 395
Yemen 358
Yoo, John C. 181
Yoruba 44
Young Turks 25, 26
Yudhoyono, Susilo Bambang 229
Yugoslavia 49, 155, 162
Yugoslavia, war crimes in **482–485**. *See also* Balkan wars (1990s); International Criminal Tribunal for the former Yugoslavia; *specific headings, e.g.:* Milošević, Slobodan
   ICC 236, 237
   IHL 241
   Theodor Meron 297
   Ratko Mladić 304–305
   rape as a tactic of war 361
   Sarajevo, siege of 382
   Slovenia 394
   Srebrenca, massacre in 402
   Franjo Tudjman 433
   Ustache 451–452
   war criminals of the former Yugoslavia 465–470
Yushchenko, Viktor 440

Z

Zaire 362, 374. *See also* Congo, Democratic Republic of the, war crimes in
Zambia 375
Zapatistas 299
Zawahiri, Ayman 310
Zedillo, Ernesto 299
Zenawi, Meles 147
Zimbabwe, human rights violations in **486–487**
Zlatin, Miron 249
Zlatin, Sabina 249
Zongo, Norbert 57